A PEOPLE AND A NATION

A PEOPLE AND A NATION

A History of the United States

VOLUME TWO
SINCE 1865

SIXTH EDITION

Mary Beth Norton
Cornell University

David M. Katzman
University of Kansas

David W. Blight
Amherst College

Howard P. Chudacoff
Brown University

Thomas G. Paterson
University of Connecticut

William M. Tuttle, Jr.
University of Kansas

Paul D. Escott
Wake Forest University

Houghton Mifflin Company   Boston   New York

The icons used throughout Chapters 1–16 are details from "Sampler Block Quilt" by Evelyn Derr. National Museum of American Art, Smithsonian Institution, Washington, D.C./Art Resource, N.Y.

Sponsoring Editor: Colleen S. Kyle
Development Editor: Ann Hofstra Grogg
Editorial Assistant: Michael Kerns
Senior Project Editor: Christina M. Horn
Senior Production/Design Coordinator: Carol Merrigan
Senior Designer: Henry Rachlin
Senior Manufacturing Coordinator: Sally Culler
Senior Marketing Manager: Sandra McGuire

Picture research by Pembroke Herbert and Sandi Rygiel, Picture Research Consultants & Archives.

Cover design: Diana Coe / ko Design Studio
Cover image: *Florence Davey*, 1914, by George Bellows. National Gallery of Art, Washington, D.C.

Text credits:

Pages 787–788: Adapted from *The Greatest Generation*, by Tom Brokaw. Copyright © 1998 by Tom Brokaw. Used by permission of Random House, Inc.

Page 798: Robert Thomas, "Self-Analysis," from *Senior Scholastic*, October 6, 1947. Copyright © 1947 by Scholastic, Inc. Reprinted by permission of Scholastic, Inc.

Printed in the U.S.A.

Library of Congress Catalog Card Number: 00-103884

ISBN: 0-618-00552-8

4 5 6 7 8 9-VH-04 03

BRIEF CONTENTS

Contents

33 PROSPERITY, POWER, AND PERIL: AMERICA IN THE 1990S   947

APPENDIX

MAPS

CHARTS

PREFACE

"What? Another edition?" asked one of our friends. "History hasn't changed that much in the last few years!" Wrong. "History" *has* changed, in several ways. More of "history's" story has been told in new books and articles and revealed in newly released documents. Our interpretation of "history" has changed because new perspectives on familiar topics have continued to emerge from the prolific writings of historians, anthropologists, and other scholars. And, last, our understanding of "history" has changed as our engagement with current events reshapes how we remember the past.

Like other teachers and students, we are always recreating our past, restructuring our memory, rediscovering the personalities and events that have influenced us, inspired us, and bedeviled us. This book represents our rediscovery of America's history—its diverse people and the nation they created and have nurtured. As this book demonstrates, there are many different Americans and many different memories. We have sought to present all of them, in both triumph and tragedy, in both division and unity.

Although much is new in this Sixth Edition in coverage, interpretation, and organization, we have sustained the qualities that have marked *A People and a Nation* from the beginning: our approach of telling the story of all the people; our study of the interaction of the private sphere of everyday life with the public sphere of politics and government; our integration of political and social history; our spirited narrative based on diaries, letters, oral histories, and other sources; and our effort to challenge readers to think about the meaning of American history, not just to memorize facts. Students and instructors have commented on how enjoyable the book is to read. Scholars have commended the book for its up-to-date scholarship.

About *A People and a Nation*

Readers have also told us that we have demonstrated, in section after section and in the "How Do Historians Know?" feature, how the historian's mind works asking questions and teasing conclusions out of vast and often conflicting evidence. Each chapter's highlighted "How Do Historians Know?" explains how historians go about using sources—such as artifacts, cartoons, census data, medical records, and popular art—to arrive at conclusions. This feature also helps students understand how scholars can claim knowledge about historical events and trends. Chapter-opening vignettes, dramatically recounting stories of people contending with their times, continue to define the key questions of each chapter. Succinct introductions and summaries still frame each chapter. As before, myriad illustrations, maps, tables, and graphs tied closely to the text encourage visual and statistical explorations. Readability, scholarship, critical thinking, clear structure, instructive illustrative material—these strengths have been sustained in this edition.

What's New in This Edition

Guided by Houghton Mifflin's excellent editorial and design staffs, by instructors' thorough reviews, by the authors' ongoing research, and by our frank and friendly planning sessions and critical reading of one another's chapters, we worked to improve every aspect of the book. We added a distinguished new author, David W. Blight, whose expertise on the antebellum period, slavery, the Civil War, and historical memory has strengthened these topics in the book. To reflect new scholarship and to satisfy instructors' needs for improved chronological flow, we substantially reorganized the chapters that cover the antebellum and post-1945 periods. We have expanded our treatment of slavery, women, religion in America's social and political life, race theory and the social construction of racial identity, the West, the South's relationship to the nation, cultural expansion as a dimension of foreign relations, and the globalization of the U.S. economy. Throughout the book, we reexamined every sentence, interpretation, map, chart, illustration, and caption, refining the narrative, presenting new examples, and rethinking and labeling the Summary section for each chapter. More than half of the chapter-opening vignettes are new to this edition, as are more than one-third of the "How Do Historians Know?" entries. The "Important Events" tables have been trimmed for easier reference. The "Suggestions for Further Reading" have been revised to include new literature and conveniently consolidated at the end of the book.

Eager to help students link the past to the present, to identify the origins of issues of current interest, we have introduced in each chapter a new feature: "Legacy for a People and a Nation." Appearing after each chapter's Summary, the Legacy feature spotlights a specific contemporary topic; examples include Columbus Day, women's education, Bible Belt, revolutionary violence, Fourteenth Amendment, ethnic food, intercollegiate athletics, Peace Corps, atomic waste, and the Internet. After exploring the subject's beginnings, a few tightly focused paragraphs trace its important history to the present, inviting students to think about the historical roots of their world today and to understand the complexity of issues that on the surface seem so simple. For students who ask what history has to do with the immediate events and trends that swirl around them—or who wonder why we study history at all—these timely legacies provide telling answers.

New "Legacy for a People and a Nation"

As in previous editions, several themes and questions stand out in our concerted effort to incorporate the most recent scholarship that integrates political, social, and cultural history. We study the many ways Americans have defined themselves—gender, race, class, region, ethnicity, religion, sexual orientation—and the many subjects that have reflected their multidimensional experiences: social, political, economic, diplomatic, military, environmental, intellectual, cultural, technological, and more. We highlight the remarkably diverse everyday life of the American people—in cities and on farms and ranches, in factories and in corporate headquarters, in neighborhood meetings and in powerful political chambers, in love relationships and in hate groups, in recreation and in work, in the classroom and in military uniform, in secret national security conferences and in public foreign relations debates, in church and in prison, in polluted environments and in conservation areas. We pay particular attention to lifestyles, diet and dress, family life and structure, labor conditions, gender roles, and childbearing and child rearing. We explore how Americans have entertained and informed themselves by discussing their music, sports, theater, print media, film, radio, television, graphic arts, and literature, in both "high" culture and "low" culture. We study how technology has influenced Americans' lives, such as through the internal combustion engine and the computer.

Themes in This Book

The private sphere of everyday life always interacts with the public sphere of politics and government. To understand how Americans have sought to protect their different ways of life and to work out solutions to thorny problems, we emphasize their expectations of governments at the local, state, and federal levels; governments' role in providing answers; the lobbying of interest groups; the campaigns and outcomes of elections; and the hierarchy of power in any period. Because the United States has long been a major participant in world affairs, we explore America's descent into wars, interventions in other nations, empire-building, immigration patterns, images of foreign peoples, cross-national cultural ties, and international economic trends.

Mary Beth Norton, who had primary responsibility for Chapters 1–8, expanded and revised her coverage of the peopling of the Americas and early settlements, the Salem witchcraft crisis, and masculinity and public rituals in the colonial period. She reorganized Chapter 3 to highlight new scholarship identifying the 1670s as a crucial turning point in the relationships of Europeans and Indians in several regions of North America, and to emphasize the key role of the slave trade in the economy of all the colonies. In Chapter 4, she added a discussion of regional differences in African American family life. Chapters 3, 4, and 8, moreover, all incorporate recent scholarship on the complex relationship between the development of the slave system and the creation of racial categories.

Section-by-Section Changes in This Edition

David M. Katzman, who had primary responsibility for Chapters 9–12, substantially reorganized the early-nineteenth-century chapters. Chapters 9–11 now have a more focused chronological narrative, integrating political events with related social, economic, and cultural developments. The antebellum chapters give added emphasis to regional interconnections in the emerging market economy, Indian–white relations and Native American adaptations to the market economy, demographic changes, internal migration, popular culture, and the formation of racial ideas. Katzman also gives new attention to the Barbary captives, the Lewis and Clark expedition, early Texas settlement, and population movements. He also explores anew immigration, ethnicity and race, frontier communities in the West, and the links between reform politics and religion.

David W. Blight, who had primary responsibility for Chapters 13–16, brought fresh perspectives to the antebellum South and its relation to the nation's cultural life and market revolution. He added new material on slave culture and resistance, slavery's intersection with westward expansion, the War with Mexico, and the Underground Railroad. In his discussion of the South, he increased coverage of free blacks and social reform movements. In the Civil War and Reconstruction chapters, Blight has revised the history of military battles, women and nursing, emancipation, wartime reconstruction, the meanings of freedom for former slaves, and the Fourteenth Amendment. He has introduced the problem of memory—especially Americans' difficulty in confronting the Reconstruction period of their history. Replacing Paul D. Escott, who brought distinction to *A People and a Nation* for five editions and whose fine writing and scholarship remain evident throughout, Blight has worked with co-author Katzman to reorganize all the antebellum period chapters.

Howard P. Chudacoff, who had primary responsibility for Chapters 17–21 and 24, reconfigured material throughout these chapters. Chapter 17 now focuses solely on the West, with additions on Indian economic and cultural life, women in frontier communities, mining, irrigation, and transportation. In his other chapters, he has increased the coverage of southern industrialization, immigrants and migrants in southern cities, and southern Progressivism. He also presents new discussion of the characteristics of the industrial revolution, race and ethnicity in urban borderlands, Mexican American farmers, religion and science, technology, the clash between modernism and fundamentalism, women's political activities, and the causes of the Great Depression.

Thomas G. Paterson, who had primary responsibility for Chapters 22–23, 26, 29, and 31, and shared responsibility for 33, and who served as the book's co-ordinating author, offers new material throughout on cultural expansion and on the influence of ideology and images of foreign peoples on foreign policy decisions. He has augmented coverage of religious missionaries, Anglo-American cooperation, and navalism. Labor issues, Indian soldiers, weapons technology, and gas warfare receive new treatment for World War I. As part of the restructuring of the post-1945 chapters, Chapters 29 and 31 are newly designed to parallel chapters on domestic history. Paterson reexamines the Korean War, U.S. Information Agency activities, and popular fears of nuclear war. For the Vietnam War, he has revisited presidential leadership, the war's impact on domestic reform, and military experiences. The last chapter newly explores environmental diplomacy, the globalization of U.S. culture, intrastate wars, and humanitarian intervention.

William M. Tuttle, Jr., had primary responsibility for Chapters 25, 27–28, 30, and 32, and shared responsibility for 33. In Chapter 25, he expanded treatment of New Deal cultural programs, unionism, and the question of "whiteness." For World War II, he added new material on the cultural history of the home front, the wartime economy, technological research, and homosexuals in the armed forces. In his post-1945 chapters, Tuttle has revised his coverage of McCarthyism, race relations, the New Left and counterculture, Indian protest, immigration legislation, the Reagan presidency, AIDS, and the anti-abortion movement. In the last chapter, Tuttle has expanded his discussion of political violence and public dissatisfaction with government, and he has included new material on school shootings and the presidential impeachment crisis.

The multidimensional Appendix, prepared by Thomas G. Paterson, has been brought up to date. Once again, the Appendix includes a guide to reference works on key subjects in American history. Students may wish to use this updated and enlarged list of encyclopedias, atlases, chronologies, and other books, for example, when they start to explore topics for research papers, when they seek precise definitions or dates, when they need biographical profiles, or when they chart territorial or demographic changes. The tables of statistics on key features of the American people and nation also have been updated, as have the tables on the states (and the District of Columbia and Puerto Rico), presidential elections, presidents and vice presidents, party strength in Congress, and the justices of the Supreme Court. Other information, including the Articles of Confederation and a complete table of the cabinets by administration, is available on the *A People and a Nation* web site.

A People and a Nation continues to be supported by an extensive supplements package. For this edition, many more resources will be available to students and instructors online and on CD-ROM. We have also revised and updated all elements of our existing package.

Study and Teaching Aids

A new version of *@history*, Houghton Mifflin's CD-ROM featuring nearly one thousand primary source materials, including video, audio, visual, and textual resources, has been keyed to the organization of the Sixth Edition of *A People and a Nation*. Available in both instructor's and student's versions, *@history* is an interactive multimedia tool that can improve the analytical skills of students and introduce them to historical sources.

American History GeoQuest is a CD-ROM designed to improve students' geographical literacy. The program consists of thirty interactive historical maps, each of which provides background information and a series of self-correcting quizzes so that students can master the information on their own.

The *A People and a Nation* web site has been redesigned, updated, and augmented for users of the Sixth Edition. An *Instructor's Web Site* includes the *Online Instructor's Resource Manual* (see below), downloadable PowerPoint lecture outline slides, interactive Legacy activities, online primary sources with teaching instructions, and annotated links to other sites. The *Student's Web Site* includes ACE reading self-quizzes; online primary sources, including text, photo, and audio resources; an annotated guide of the top historical research Web sites; and interactive Legacy activities.

The *Study Guide*, prepared by George Warren of Central Piedmont Community College, includes an introductory chapter on studying history that focuses on interpreting historical facts, test-taking hints, and critical analysis. The guide also includes learning objectives, a thematic guide, lists of terms, multiple choice and essay questions with answer keys, and map exercises.

A new *Online Instructor's Resource Manual*, also created by George Warren, will now be downloadable from Houghton Mifflin's web site. For each chapter, the manual includes a content overview, a brief list of learning objectives, a comprehensive chapter outline, ideas for classroom activities, discussion questions, and ideas for paper topics.

A *Test Bank*, also prepared by George Warren, provides approximately 1,700 new multiple choice questions, more than 1,000 identification questions, and approximately 500 essay questions. This content is also available in a *Computerized Test Bank* for both Windows and Macintosh platforms.

A set of *American History Map Transparencies* is also available to instructors upon adoption.

At each stage of this revision, a sizable panel of historian reviewers read drafts of our chapters. Their suggestions, corrections, and pleas helped guide us through this momentous revision. We could not include all of their recommendations, but the book is better for our having heeded most of their advice. We heartily thank

Acknowledgments

Patrick Allitt, *Emory University*

Cara Anzilotti, *Loyola Marymount University*

Felix Armfield, *Western Illinois University*

Robert Becker, *Louisiana State University*

Jules Benjamin, *Ithaca College*

Roger Bromert, *Southwestern Oklahoma State University*

Jonathan Chu, *University of Massachusetts at Boston*

Nathaniel Comfort, *George Washington University*

Mary DeCredico, *U.S. Naval Academy*

Judy DeMark, *Northern Michigan University*

Jonathan Earle, *University of Kansas*

Alice Fahs, *University of California, Irvine*

Neil Foley, *University of Texas*

Colin Gordon, *University of Iowa*

Robert Gough, *University of Wisconsin at Eau Claire*

Brian Greenberg, *Monmouth University*

Harland Hagler, *University of North Texas*

Elizabeth Haiken, *University of British Columbia*

Benjamin Harrison, *University of Louisville*

Elizabeth Cobbs Hoffman, *San Diego State University*

Marianne Holdzkom, *Ohio State University*

John Inscoe, *University of Georgia*

Frank Lambert, *Purdue University*

David Rich Lewis, *Utah State University*

Nancy Mitchell, *North Carolina State University*

Patricia Moore, *University of Utah*

John Neff, *University of Mississippi*

James Reed, *Rutgers University*

Joseph Rowe, *Sam Houston State University*

Sharon Salinger, *University of California, Riverside*

Richard Stott, *George Washington University*

Daniel B. Thorp, *Virginia Polytechnic Institute and State University*

Marilyn Westerkamp, *University of California, Santa Cruz*

John Wigger, *University of Missouri, Columbia*

John Scott Wilson, *University of South Carolina*

The authors once again thank the extraordinary Houghton Mifflin people who designed, edited, produced, and nourished this book. Their high standards and acute attention to both general structure and fine detail are cherished in the publishing industry. Many thanks, then, to Colleen Shanley Kyle, sponsoring editor; Ann Hofstra Grogg, freelance development editor; Christina Horn, senior project editor; Jean Woy, editor-in-chief; Sandra McGuire, senior marketing manager; Pembroke Herbert, photo researcher; Charlotte Miller, art editor; and Michael Kerns, editorial assistant.

The authors also extend their thanks to the following for helping us: Sandra Greene, Karin Beckett, Nancy Board, Frank Couvares, Jan D. Emerson, Alice Fahs, Jeffrey Ferguson, Irwin Hyatt, Steven Jacobson, Andrea Katzman, Eric Katzman, Henry W. Katzman, Julie Stephens Katzman, Sharyn Katzman, Ariela Katzman-Jacobson, Elizabeth Mahan, Terri Rockhold, Martha Sandweiss, Martha Saxton, Barry Shank, John David Smith, Kathryn Nemeth Tuttle, and Samuel Watkins Tuttle.

We welcome comments from instructors and students about this new edition of *A People and a Nation*, which can be communicated through its accompanying web site, found at **http://college.hmco.com.**

For the authors, THOMAS G. PATERSON

THE AUTHORS

Mary Beth Norton

Born in Ann Arbor, Michigan, Mary Beth Norton received her B.A. from the University of Michigan (1964) and her Ph.D. from Harvard University (1969). She is now Mary Donlon Alger Professor of American History at Cornell University. Her dissertation won the Allan Nevins Prize. She has written *The British-Americans* (1972), *Liberty's Daughters* (1980), and *Founding Mothers and Fathers* (1996), which was one of three finalists for the Pulitzer Prize in 1997. She has coedited *To Toil the Livelong Day* (1987), *Women of America* (1979), and *Major Problems in American Women's History* (1995). Her articles have appeared in such journals as the *William and Mary Quarterly*, *Signs*, and the *American Historical Review*. Mary Beth has served on the National Council on the Humanities, as president of the Berkshire Conference of Women Historians, as vice president for research of the American Historical Association, and as general editor of the *AHA Guide to Historical Literature* (1995). In 1999 she was elected a fellow of the American Academy of Arts and Sciences. The National Endowment for the Humanities, Guggenheim Foundation, and Rockefeller Foundation have assisted her scholarship.

David M. Katzman

Born in New York City and a graduate of Queens College (B.A., 1963) and the University of Michigan (Ph.D., 1969), David M. Katzman is professor of American studies and courtesy professor of history and African American studies at the University of Kansas. He has written *Before the Ghetto* (1973) and *Seven Days a Week* (1978), which won the Philip Taft Labor History Prize. He has coedited *Plain Folk* (1982) and *Technical Knowledge in American Culture* (1996). He has also coauthored *Three Generations in Twentieth-Century America* (1982). David has been a visiting professor at University College, Dublin, Ireland, the University of Birmingham, England, Hong Kong University, and the University of Tokushima, Japan. He has also directed National Endowment for the Humanities Summer Seminars for College Teachers. He has sat on the Board of Directors of the National Commission on Social Studies and is coeditor of *American Studies*. At the University of Kansas, he is a former director of the College Honors Program. The Guggenheim Foundation, National Endowment for the Humanities, Ford Foundation, and Rockefeller Foundation have supported his research.

David W. Blight

Born in Flint, Michigan, David W. Blight received his B.A. from Michigan State University (1971) and his Ph.D. from the University of Wisconsin (1985). He is now Class of 1959 Professor of History and Black Studies at Amherst College. For the first seven years of his career, David was a public high school teacher in Flint. He has written *Frederick Douglass's Civil War* (1989) and *Race and Reunion: The Civil War in American Memory, 1863–1915* (2000). His edited works include *When This Cruel War Is Over: The Civil War Letters of Charles Harvey Brewster* (1992), *Narrative of the Life of Frederick Douglass* (1993), W. E. B. Du Bois, *The Souls of Black Folk* (with Robert Gooding Williams, 1997), *Union and Emancipation* (with Brooks Simpson, 1997), and *Caleb Bingham, The Columbian Orator* (1997). David's essays have appeared in the *Journal of American History*, *Civil War History*, and Gabor Boritt, ed., *Why the Civil War Came* (1996), among others. In 1992–1993 he was senior Fulbright Professor in American Studies at the University of Munich, Germany. A consultant to several documentary films, David appeared in the 1998 PBS series, *Africans in America*. In 1999 he was elected to the Council of the American Historical Association. David also teaches summer seminars for secondary school teachers, as well as for park rangers and historians of the National Park Service.

Howard P. Chudacoff

A University Professor and professor of history at Brown University, Howard P. Chudacoff was born in Omaha, Nebraska. He earned his A.B. (1965) and Ph.D. (1969) from the University of Chicago. He has written *Mobile Americans* (1972), *The Evolution of American Urban Society* (with Judith Smith, 1999), *How Old Are You?* (1989), and *The Age of the Bachelor* (1999). He has also edited *Major Problems in American Urban History* (1993). His articles have appeared in such journals as the *Journal of Family History, Reviews in American History,* and *Journal of American History.* At Brown University, Howard has cochaired the American Civilization Program, chaired the Department of History, and since 1990 has been faculty adviser to the women's basketball team. He has also served on the board of directors of the Urban History Association. The National Endowment for the Humanities, Ford Foundation, and Rockefeller Foundation have given him awards to advance his scholarship.

Thomas G. Paterson

Born in Oregon City, Oregon, and graduated from the University of New Hampshire (B.A., 1963) and the University of California, Berkeley (Ph.D., 1968), Thomas G. Paterson is professor emeritus of history at the University of Connecticut. He has written *Soviet-American Confrontation* (1973), *Meeting the Communist Threat* (1988), *On Every Front* (1992), *Contesting Castro* (1994), *American Foreign Relations* (with J. Garry Clifford and Kenneth J. Hagan, 2000), and *America Ascendant* (with Clifford, 1995). Tom has also edited *Kennedy's Quest for Victory* (1989), *Explaining the History of American Foreign Relations* (with Michael J. Hogan, 1991), and *Major Problems in American Foreign Relations* (with Dennis Merrill, 2000). With Bruce Jentleson he was senior editor for the four-volume *Encyclopedia of U.S. Foreign Relations* (1997). He has served on the ed-

itorial boards of the *Journal of American History* and *Diplomatic History.* He has been president of the Society for Historians of American Foreign Relations and has directed National Endowment for the Humanities Summer Seminars for College Teachers. He has won fellowships from the Guggenheim Foundation, among others. In 2000 the New England History Teachers Association awarded him the Kidger Award for excellence in teaching and mentoring.

William M. Tuttle, Jr.

A native of Detroit, Michigan, William M. Tuttle, Jr., received his B.A. from Denison University (1959) and his Ph.D. from the University of Wisconsin (1967). A professor of history and American studies at the University of Kansas, Bill has written *Race Riot* (1996) and *"Daddy's Gone to War"* (1993). He has also edited *W. E. B. Du Bois* (1973) and coedited *Plain Folk* (1982). His articles have appeared in such journals as the *Journal of American History, American Studies,* and *Child Welfare.* He has been a research associate at the Institute of Human Development at the University of California, Berkeley. As a historical consultant, Bill has helped prepare several public television documentaries and docudramas, including *The Killing Floor,* which appeared on PBS's *American Playhouse.* Bill's scholarly work has been assisted by the American Council of Learned Societies, Institute of Southern History at Johns Hopkins University, Charles Warren Center, Guggenheim Foundation, Stanford Humanities Center, Radcliffe College, and National Endowment for the Humanities. In 1998 Bill was awarded the William T. Kemper Fellowship for Teaching Excellence.

In 1861 Robert Smalls was a slave in South Carolina, while Wade Hampton was a South Carolina legislator and one of the richest planters in the South. The events of the next fifteen years turned each man's world upside down more than once.

Robert Smalls became a Union hero in 1862 when he escaped from slavery by stealing a Confederate ship from Charleston harbor and piloting it to the blockading federal fleet. Thereafter, Smalls guided Union gunboats and toured the North recruiting black troops. Though he enjoyed celebrity status, Smalls encountered racial discrimination in the North and found in 1865 that neither his heroism nor his freedom entitled him to vote. But by 1868 that, too, had changed, and he began a career in politics. Smalls helped write his state's constitution, served in the legislature, and won election to Congress. There he denounced white violence and worked for educational and economic opportunity for his people. But Smalls was helpless to prevent the return of white control in South Carolina in 1877.

Wade Hampton joined the Confederate Army in 1861 and soon became a general. The South's defeat profoundly shocked him; and as Union forces closed in, he spoke wildly of "forc[ing] my way across the Mississippi" with "a devoted band of Cavalry" and continuing to fight. The postwar years brought further painful changes, including forced bankruptcy. In 1867 Hampton surprised other privileged whites by supporting suffrage for a few educated and propertied former slaves. By 1876, though, Hampton's fortunes were again on the rise: Democrats nominated him for governor, promising that he would "redeem" South Carolina from Republican misrule. Among Hampton's white supporters were the paramilitary Red Shirts who pledged to "control the vote of at least one Negro, by intimidation, purchase," or other means. Hampton won the governor's chair, then a seat in the U.S. Senate, and eventually an honored place as a distinguished Confederate veteran.

As the careers of Smalls and Hampton suggest, Reconstruction was revolutionary, but revolutions can

On January 6, 1874, Congressman Robert B. Elliott of South Carolina made an eloquent defense of the proposed civil rights bill. After a review of legal issues, he called on Congress to ignore the opposition of southerners, who he said had tried to destroy the nation, and deal justly with the Negro race, which had faithfully defended the Union.   (Chicago Historical Society)

RECONSTRUCTION: AN UNFINISHED REVOLUTION 1865–1877

427

go backward. Robert Smalls rose from bondage to experience glory, emancipation, political power, and, ultimately, disappointment. Wade Hampton fell from privilege to endure defeat, failure, bankruptcy, and, eventually, a return to leadership in his state. Unprecedented changes took place in American society, but the underlying realities of economic power, racial prejudice, and judicial conservatism limited Reconstruction's revolutionary potential.

Nowhere was the turmoil of Reconstruction more evident than in national politics. Lincoln's successor, Andrew Johnson, fought bitterly with Congress over the shaping of a plan for Reconstruction. Though a southerner, Johnson had always been a foe of the South's wealthy planters, and his first acts as president suggested that he would be tough on "traitors." Before the end of 1865, however, Johnson's policies changed direction, and he became the friend and protector of southern interests. Jefferson Davis stayed in prison for two years, but Johnson quickly pardoned other rebel leaders and allowed them to occupy high offices. He also ordered the return of plantations to their original owners, including abandoned coastal lands on which forty thousand freed men and women had settled by order of General William Tecumseh Sherman early in 1865. Burdened by a train of thousands of black refugees following his army on the march to the sea, Sherman issued special Field Order Number 15 in February 1865. The order set aside 400,000 acres of land in the Georgia and South Carolina Sea Islands region for the exclusive settlement of the freedpeople. Hope swelled among ex-slaves as 40-acre plots, mules, and "possessary titles" were promised to them. But President Johnson ordered them removed in October and returned the land to its original owners under army protection.

Johnson imagined a lenient and rapid "restoration" of the South to the Union rather than the fundamental "reconstruction" that Republican congressmen favored. Between 1866 and 1868, the president and the Republican leadership in Congress engaged in a bitterly antagonistic power struggle over how to put the United States back together again.

Before these struggles were over, Congress had impeached the president, enfranchised the freed men, and given them a role in reconstructing the South. The nation also adopted the Fourteenth and Fifteenth Amendments, ushering equal protection of the law, a definition of citizenship, and universal manhood suffrage into the Constitution. Yet some underlying realities never changed. Little was done to open the doors of economic opportunity to black southerners, and throughout this period of upheaval, the cause of equal rights for African Americans as the central aim of Reconstruction rose and fell.

By 1869 the Ku Klux Klan employed extensive violence and terror to thwart Reconstruction and undermine black freedom. As white Democrats in the South recaptured state governments, undoing the political revolution, they encountered little opposition from the North. Voters had grown weary and suspicious of the use of federal power to prop up failing Republican governments. Moreover, as the 1870s advanced, industrial growth accelerated, creating new opportunities and raising new priorities. A new economic depression after 1873 refocused northerners' attention. Political corruption became a nationwide scandal, bribery a way of doing business. "Money has become the God of this country," wrote one disgusted observer, "and men, otherwise good men, are almost compelled to worship at her shrine."

Thus Reconstruction became a revolution eclipsed. The white South's desire to take back control of their states and of race relations overwhelmed the national interest in stopping them. But Reconstruction left enduring legacies the nation has struggled with ever since. ◼

Wartime Reconstruction

 Civil wars leave immense challenges of healing, justice, and physical rebuilding. Anticipating that process, Reconstruction of the Union was an issue as early as 1863, well before the war ended. Many key questions loomed on the horizon when and if the North succeeded on the battlefield. How would the nation be restored? How would southern states and leaders be treated? As errant brothers, or as traitors? What was the constitutional basis for readmission of states to the Union and where, if anywhere, could American statesmen look for precedence or guidance? More specifically, four vexing problems compelled early thinking and would haunt the Reconstruction era throughout. One, *who* would rule in the South once it was defeated? Two, *who* would rule in the federal government, Congress or the president? Three, what were the dimensions of *black freedom*, and what rights under law would the freedmen enjoy? And four, would Reconstruction be a preservation of the *old* republic, or a second revolution, a re-invention of a *new* republic?

IMPORTANT EVENTS

1865 Johnson begins rapid and lenient
Reconstruction
Confederate leaders regain power
White southern governments pass
restrictive black codes
Congress refuses to seat southern
representatives
Thirteenth Amendment ratified

1866 Congress passes Civil Rights Act and
renewal of Freedmen's Bureau over
Johnson's veto
Congress approves Fourteenth Amendment
Most southern states reject Fourteenth
Amendment
In *Ex parte Milligan* the Supreme Court
reasserts its influence
In congressional elections, Republicans
win more than two-thirds majority, a
renunciation of Johnson's plan of
Reconstruction

1867 Congress passes Reconstruction Act and
Tenure of Office Act
Secretary of State William Seward arranges
purchase of Alaska
Constitutional conventions called in
southern states

1868 House impeaches Johnson; Senate
acquits him
Most southern states gain readmission to
the Union under Radical plan
Fourteenth Amendment ratified
Grant elected president

1869 Congress approves Fifteenth Amendment
(ratified in 1870)

1870 Congress passes first Enforcement Act

1871 Congress passes second Enforcement Act
and Ku Klux Klan Act
Treaty with England settles *Alabama* claims

1872 Amnesty Act frees almost all remaining
Confederates from restrictions on holding
office
Liberal Republicans organize and oppose
Grant
Debtors urge government to keep greenbacks
in circulation
Grant reelected

1873 *Slaughter-House* cases limit power of
Fourteenth Amendment
Panic of 1873 sends economy into extended
depression, leading to widespread
unemployment and labor strife

1874 Grant vetoes increase in supply of paper
money
Democrats win majority in House of
Representatives

1875 Several Grant appointees indicted for
corruption
Congress passes weak Civil Rights Act
Congress requires that after 1878 greenbacks
be convertible into gold
Democratic Party continues to "redeem"
control of southern states with white
supremacy campaigns

1876 *U.S. v. Cruikshank* and *U.S. v. Reese* further
weaken Fourteenth Amendment
Presidential election disputed

1877 Congress elects Hayes president
Exodusters migrate to Kansas
"Home rule" returns to three remaining
southern states not yet controlled by
Democrats; Reconstruction considered
over

Abraham Lincoln had never been antisouthern,
though he had grown to become the leader of an
antislavery war. He lost three broth-
ers-in-law killed in the war on the
Confederate side. His worst fear was
that the war would collapse at the
end into guerrilla warfare across the
South, with surviving bands of Confederates carrying

**Lincoln's
10 Percent Plan**

on resistance. Lincoln insisted that his generals give
lenient terms to southern soldiers once they surrendered. He planned early for a swift and moderate
Reconstruction process. In his Second Inaugural Address, delivered only a month before his assassination,
Lincoln promised "malice toward none; with charity
for all," as Americans strove to "bind up the nation's
wounds."

In his "Proclamation of Amnesty and Reconstruction," issued in December 1863, Lincoln proposed to replace majority rule with "loyal rule" as a means of reconstructing southern state governments before hostilities ended. He envisioned Reconstruction as a process of experimentation. He proposed pardons to all ex-Confederates except the highest ranking military and civilian officers. Then, as soon as 10 percent of the voting population in the 1860 election had taken an oath and established a government, it would be recognized. Lincoln did not consult Congress in these plans, and "loyal" assemblies (known as "Lincoln governments") were created in Louisiana, Tennessee, and Arkansas in 1864, states largely occupied by Union troops. These governments were weak and dependent on northern armies for survival.

Congress responded with great hostility to Lincoln's moves to readmit southern states in what seemed such a premature manner. Many Radical Republicans, strong proponents of emancipation and aggressive prosecution of the war against the South, considered the 10 percent plan a "mere mockery" of democracy. Led by Thaddeus Stevens of Pennsylvania in the House and Charles Sumner of Massachusetts in the Senate, congressional Republicans locked horns with Lincoln and proposed a longer and harsher approach to Reconstruction. Stevens advocated a "conquered provinces" theory, and Sumner, recovered from his beating at the hands of Preston Brooks (see page 375), employed an argument of "state suicide." Both contended that southerners had organized as a foreign nation to make war on the United States and, by secession, had destroyed their status as states. They therefore must be treated as "conquered foreign lands" and reverted to the status of "unorganized territories" before any process of readmission could be entertained (by Congress).

Congress and the Wade-Davis Bill

In July 1864, the Wade-Davis bill, named for its sponsors, Senator Benjamin Wade of Ohio and Congressman Henry W. Davis of Maryland, emerged from Congress with three specific conditions for southern readmission: one, it demanded a "majority" of white male citizens participating in the creation of a new government; two, to vote or be a delegate to constitutional conventions, men had to take an "iron-clad" oath (declaring they had never aided the Confederate war effort); and three, all officers above the rank of lieutenant, and all civil officials in the Confederacy,

would be disfranchised and deemed "not a citizen of the United States." The Confederate states were to be defined as "conquered enemies," said Davis, and the process of readmission was to be harsh and slow. Lincoln, ever the adroit politician, pocket-vetoed the bill and issued a conciliatory proclamation of his own announcing that he would not be inflexibly committed to any "one plan" of Reconstruction.

The timing of this exchange came during Grant's bloody campaign in Virginia against Lee. The outcome of the war and Lincoln's reelection were still in doubt. Radical members of his own party, indeed, were organizing a dump-Lincoln campaign for the 1864 election. On August 5, Radical Republicans issued the "Wade-Davis Manifesto" to newspapers, which contained an unprecedented attack on a sitting president by members of his own party. They accused Lincoln of usurpation of presidential powers and disgraceful leniency toward an eventually conquered South. What emerged in 1864–1865 was a clear-cut debate and a potential constitutional crisis. Lincoln saw Reconstruction as a means of weakening the Confederacy and winning the war; the Radicals saw it as a longer-term transformation of the political and racial order of the country.

Thirteenth Amendment and the Freedmen's Bureau

In early 1865, Congress and Lincoln joined in passing two important measures that recognized slavery's centrality to the war. On January 31, with strong administration backing, Congress passed the Thirteenth Amendment, which had two provisions. It abolished involuntary servitude everywhere in the United States and declared that Congress shall have power to enforce this outcome by "appropriate legislation." When the measure passed by 119 to 56, a mere two votes more than the necessary two-thirds, unprecedented rejoicing broke out in Congress. A Republican recorded in his diary: "Members joined in the shouting and kept it up for some minutes. Some embraced one another, others wept like children. I have felt ever since the vote, as if I were in a new country."

Potentially as significant, on March 3, 1865, Congress created the Bureau of Refugees, Freedmen, and Abandoned Lands—the Freedmen's Bureau, an unprecedented agency of social uplift, necessitated by the ravages of the war. Americans had never engaged in federal aid to citizens on such a scale. With thousands of refugees, white and black, displaced in the South, the government continued what private freedmen's aid societies had started as early as 1862. In the mere four years of its existence, the Freedmen's Bureau supplied food and medical services, built several thousand schools and some colleges, negotiated several hundred thousand employment contracts between freedmen and their former masters, and tried to manage confiscated land.

The Bureau would be a controversial aspect of Reconstruction, within the South where whites generally hated it, and within the federal government where politicians divided over its constitutionality. Some Bureau agents were devoted to freedmen's rights, while others were opportunists who exploited the chaos of the postwar South. The war had forced into the open an eternal question of republics: What are the social welfare obligations of the state toward its people, and what do people owe their governments in return? Apart from their conquest and displacement of the eastern Indians, Americans were relatively inexperienced at the Freedmen's Bureau's task—social reform through military occupation.

The Meanings of Freedom

 Black southerners entered into life after slavery with hope and circumspection. A Texas man recalled his father telling him, even before the war was over, "Our forever was going to be spent living among the Southerners, after they got licked." Expecting hostility, freed men and women tried to gain as much as they could from their new circumstances. Often the changes they valued the most were personal—alterations in location, employer, or living arrangements.

For America's former slaves, Reconstruction had one paramount meaning: a chance to explore freedom.

The Feel of Freedom

A southern white woman admitted in her diary that the black people "showed a natural and exultant joy at being free." Former slaves remembered singing far into the night after federal troops, who confirmed rumors of their emancipation, reached their plantations. The slaves on a Texas plantation shouted for joy, their leader proclaiming,

Post-emancipation society in the South brought about the renegotiation of old relationships, as in the scene depicted in Winslow Homer's *A Visit From the Old Mistress* (1876).   (National Gallery of American Art/Art Resource)

"We is free—no more whippings and beatings." A few people gave in to the natural desire to do what had been impossible before. One angry grandmother dropped her hoe and ran to confront her mistress. "I'm free!" she yelled. "Yes, I'm free! Ain't got to work for you no more! You can't put me in your pocket [sell me] now!" Another man recalled that he and others "started on the move," either to search for family members or just to exercise the human right of mobility.

Many freed men and women reacted more cautiously and shrewdly, taking care to test the boundaries of their new condition. "After the war was over," explained one man, "we was afraid to move. Just like terrapins or turtles after emancipation. Just stick our heads out to see how the land lay." As slaves they had learned to expect hostility from white people, and they did not presume it would instantly disappear. Life in freedom might still be a matter of what was allowed, not what was right. "You got to say master?" asked a freedman in Georgia. "Naw," answered his fellows, but "they said it all the same." One sign of this shrewd caution was the way freed people evaluated potential employers. "Most all the Negroes that had good owners stayed with 'em, but the others left. Some of 'em come back and some didn't," explained one man. After considerable wandering in search of better circumstances, a majority of blacks eventually settled as agricultural workers back on their former farms or plantations. But they relocated their houses and did their utmost to control the conditions of their labor.

Former slaves concentrated on improving their daily lives. Throughout the South they devoted themselves to reuniting their families, separated during slavery by sale or hardship, and during the war by dislocation and the emancipation process. The search for family members who had been sold away during slavery was awe inspiring. With only shreds of information to guide them, thousands of freed people embarked on odysseys in search of a husband, wife, child, or parent. By relying on the black community for help and information, and placing ads in black newspapers that continued to appear well into the 1880s, some succeeded in their quest, sometimes almost miraculously. Others trudged through several states and never found loved ones.

Reunion of African American Families

Husbands and wives who had belonged to different masters established homes together for the first time, and parents asserted the right to raise their own children. A mother bristled when her old master claimed a right to whip her children. She informed him that "he warn't goin' to brush none of her chilluns no more." The freed men and women were too much at risk to act recklessly, but, as one man put it, they were tired of punishment and "sure didn't take no more foolishness off of white folks."

Many black people wanted to minimize contact with whites because, as Reverend Garrison Frazier told General Sherman in January 1865, "There is a prejudice against us . . . that will take years to get over." To avoid contact with overbearing whites who were used to supervising them, blacks abandoned the slave quarters and fanned out to distant corners of the land they worked. "After the war my stepfather come," recalled Annie Young, "and got my mother and we moved out in the piney woods." Others described moving "across the creek to [themselves]" or building a "saplin house . . . back in the woods." Some rural dwellers established small all-black settlements that still exist today along the back roads of the South.

Blacks' Search for Independence

Even once-privileged slaves desired such independence and social separation. One man turned down the master's offer of the overseer's house and moved instead to a shack in "Freetown." He also declined to let the former owner grind his grain for free because it "make him feel like a free man to pay for things just like anyone else." One couple, a carriage driver and trusted house servant during slavery, passed up the fine cooking of the "big house" to move "in the colored settlement."

In addition to a fair employer, what freed men and women most wanted was the ownership of land. Land represented their chance to farm for themselves, to enjoy the independence that self-sufficient farmers value. It represented compensation for generations of travail in bondage. A northern observer noted that slaves freed in the Sea Islands of South Carolina and Georgia made "plain, straight-forward" inquiries as they settled the land set aside for them by Sherman. They wanted to be sure the land "would be theirs after they had improved it." Everywhere, blacks young and old thirsted for homes of their own.

African Americans' Desire for Land

But how much of a chance would whites give to blacks? Most members of both political parties opposed genuine land redistribution to the freedmen. Even northern reformers who with Lincoln's encouragement had administered the Sea Islands during the war showed little sympathy for black aspirations. The former Sea Island slaves wanted to establish small, self-sufficient farms. Northern soldiers, officials, and missionaries of both races brought education and aid to the freedmen but also insisted that they grow cotton. They emphasized profit, cash crops, and the values of competitive capitalism.

"The Yankees preach nothing but cotton, cotton!" complained one Sea Island black. "We wants land," wrote another, but tax officials "make the lots too big, and cut we out." Indeed, the U.S. government sold thousands of acres in the Sea Islands for nonpayment of taxes, but 90 percent of the land went to wealthy investors from the North. At a protest against evictions from a contraband camp in Virginia in 1866, freedman Bayley Wyatt made black desires and claims clear: "We has a right to the land where we are located. For why? I tell you. Our wives, our children, our husbands, has been sold over and over again to purchase the lands we now locates upon; for that reason we have a divine right to the land."

Ex-slaves reached out for valuable things in life that had been denied them. One of these was education. Blacks of all ages hungered for the knowledge in books that had been permitted only to whites. With freedom, they started schools and filled classrooms both day and night. On log seats and dirt floors, freed men and women studied their letters in old almanacs and discarded dictionaries. Young children brought infants to school with them, and adults attended at night or after "the crops were laid by." Many a teacher had "to make herself heard over three other classes reciting in concert" in a small room. The desire to escape slavery's ignorance was so great that, despite their poverty, many blacks paid tuition, typically $1 or $1.50 a month. These small amounts constituted major portions of a person's agricultural wages and added up to more than $1 million by 1870.

The federal government and northern reformers of both races assisted this pursuit of education. In its brief life the Freedmen's Bureau founded over four thousand schools, and idealistic men and women from the North established and staffed others founded by private northern philanthropy. The Yankee school-marm—dedicated, selfless, and religious—became an agent of progress in many southern communities. Thus did African Americans seek a break from their pasts through learning. The results included the beginnings of a public school system in each southern

The Black Embrace of Education

African Americans of all ages eagerly pursued the opportunity in freedom to gain an education. This young woman in Mt. Meigs, Alabama, is helping her mother learn to read.   (Smithsonian Institute, photo by Rudolf Eickemeyer)

state and the enrollment of over six hundred thousand African Americans in elementary school by 1877.

Blacks and their white allies also saw the need for colleges and universities to train teachers, ministers, and professionals for leadership. The American Missionary Association founded seven colleges, including Fisk and Atlanta Universities, between 1866 and 1869. The Freedmen's Bureau helped to establish Howard University in Washington, D.C., and northern religious groups such as the Methodists, Baptists, and Congregationalists supported dozens of seminaries and teachers' colleges. By the late 1870s black churches had joined in the effort, founding numerous colleges despite limited resources.

During Reconstruction, African American leaders often were highly educated individuals; many of them came from the prewar elite of free people of color. This group had benefited from its association with wealthy whites, many of whom were blood relatives; some planters had given their mulatto children an outstanding education. Francis Cardozo, who held various offices in South Carolina, had attended universities in Scotland and England. P. B. S. Pinchback, who became lieutenant governor of Louisiana, was the son of a planter who had sent him to school in Cincinnati. Both of the two black senators from Mississippi, Blanche K. Bruce and Hiram Revels, possessed privileged educations. Bruce was the son of a planter who had provided tutoring at home; Revels was the son of free North Carolina mulattos who had sent him to Knox College in Illinois. These men and many self-educated former slaves brought to political office their experience as artisans, businessmen, lawyers, teachers, and preachers.

Freed from the restrictions and regulations of slavery, blacks could build their own institutions as they saw fit. The secret churches of slavery came into the open; in countless communities throughout the South, ex-slaves "started a brush arbor." A brush arbor was merely "a sort of . . . shelter with leaves for a roof," but the freed men and women worshiped in it enthusiastically. "Preachin' and

Growth of Black Churches

shouting sometimes lasted all day," they recalled, for the opportunity to worship together freely meant "glorious times."

Within a few years independent branches of the Methodist and Baptist denominations had attracted the great majority of black Christians in the South. By 1877, in South Carolina alone, the African Methodist Episcopal Church had 1,000 ministers, 44,000 members, and its own school of theology, while the A.M.E. Zion Church had 45,000 members. In the rapid growth of churches, some of which became the wealthiest and the most autonomous institutions in black life, the freedpeople demonstrated their most secure claim on freedom as they created enduring communities.

The desire to gain as much independence as possible also shaped the former slaves' economic arrangements. Since most of them lacked money to buy land, they preferred the next best thing: renting the land they worked. But the South had a cash-poor economy with few sources of credit, and few whites would consider renting land to blacks. Most blacks had no means to get cash before the harvest, and thus other alternatives had to be tried.

Rise of the Sharecropping System

Churches became a center of African American life, for social and political purposes as well as for worship. This engraving, which appeared in *Harper's Weekly* in 1874, shows the minister of the First African Baptist Church of Richmond, Virginia, preaching to the congregation from an elevated pulpit.   (The Valentine Museum, Richmond, Virginia)

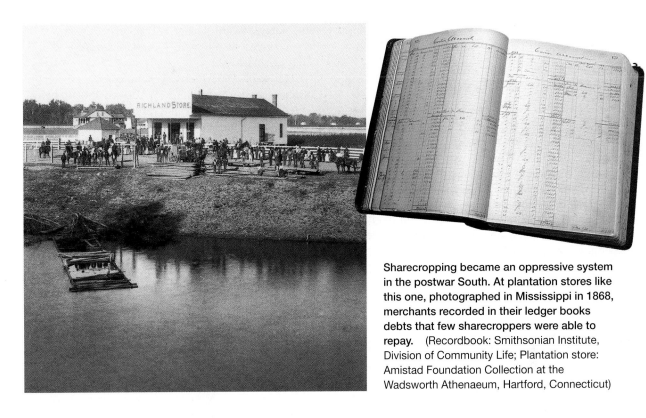

Sharecropping became an oppressive system in the postwar South. At plantation stores like this one, photographed in Mississippi in 1868, merchants recorded in their ledger books debts that few sharecroppers were able to repay. (Recordbook: Smithsonian Institute, Division of Community Life; Plantation store: Amistad Foundation Collection at the Wadsworth Athenaeum, Hartford, Connecticut)

Black farmers and white landowners therefore turned to sharecropping, a system in which farmers kept part of their crop and gave the rest to the landowner while living on his property. The landlord or a merchant "furnished" food and supplies needed before the harvest, and he received payment from the crop. Republican laws gave laborers the first lien, or legal claim, on the crop, enhancing their sense of ownership. Although landowners tried to set the laborers' share at a low level, black farmers had some bargaining power, at least at first. Sharecroppers would hold out, or move and try to switch employers from one year to another.

The sharecropping system, which materialized as early as 1868 in parts of the South, originated as a desirable compromise. It eased landowners' problems with cash and credit, and provided them a permanent, dependent labor force; blacks accepted it because it gave them more freedom from daily supervision. Instead of working under a white overseer, as in slavery, they farmed a plot of land on their own in family groups. But sharecropping later proved to be a disaster. Owners and merchants developed a monopoly of control over the agricultural economy, as sharecroppers found themselves riveted into ever-increasing debt (see pages 563–564).

The fundamental problem, however, was that southern farmers as a whole still concentrated on cotton, a crop with a bright past and a dim future. During the Civil War, India, Brazil, and Egypt had begun to supply cotton to Britain, and the South lost markets as well as income. In freedom, black women, like their white counterparts, often stayed away from the fields. Black families placed greater value on human dignity than on reaching higher levels of production. By 1878 the South had recovered its prewar share of British cotton purchases. But even as southerners grew more cotton, their reward diminished. Cotton prices began a long decline, as world demand fell off.

Overdependence on Cotton

In these circumstances overspecialization in cotton was a mistake, but for most southern farmers there was no alternative. Landowners required sharecroppers to grow the salable cash crop. Thus southern agriculture slipped deeper and deeper into depression. Black sharecroppers struggled under a growing burden of debt that reduced their independence and bound them to landowners and to furnishing merchants almost as oppressively as slavery had bound them to their masters. Many white farmers became debtors, too, and gradually lost their land. This economic transformation took place as the nation struggled to put its political house back in order.

Johnson's Reconstruction Plan

 When Reconstruction began under President Andrew Johnson, many expected his policies to be harsh. Throughout his career in Tennessee he had criticized the wealthy planters and championed the small farmers. When an assassin's bullet thrust Johnson into the presidency, many former slaveowners shared the dismay of a North Carolina woman who wrote, "Think of Andy Johnson [as] the president! What will become of us— 'the aristocrats of the South' as we are termed?" Northern Radicals also had reason to believe that Johnson would deal sternly with the South. When one of them suggested the exile or execution of ten or twelve leading rebels to set an example, Johnson replied, "How are you going to pick out so small a number? . . . Treason is a crime; and crime must be punished."

Like his martyred predecessor, Johnson followed a path in antebellum politics from obscurity to power.

Who Was Andrew Johnson?

With no formal education, he became a tailor's apprentice. But from 1829, while in his early twenties, he held nearly every office in Tennessee politics: alderman, state representative, congressman, two terms as governor, and U.S. senator by 1857. Although elected as a southern Democrat, Johnson was the only senator from a seceded state who refused to follow his state out of the Union. Lincoln appointed him war governor of Tennessee in 1862, and hence, his symbolic place on the ticket in the president's bid for reelection in 1864.

Johnson's political beliefs made him look a little like a Republican, but at heart he was an old Jacksonian Democrat. And as they said in the mountainous region of east Tennessee, where Johnson established a reputation as a stump speaker, "Old Andy never went back on his 'raisin.'" Although a staunch Unionist, he was also an ardent states' rightist. Before the war, Johnson had supported tax-funded public schools and homestead legislation, fashioning himself as a champion of the common man. Although he vehemently opposed secession, Johnson advocated limited government. Above all, when it came to race, Johnson was a thoroughgoing white supremacist. He shared none of the Radicals' expansive conception of federal power. Johnson accepted emancipation as a result of the war, but he did not favor black civil and political rights. His philosophy toward Reconstruction may be summed up in the slogan he adopted: "The Constitution as it is, and the Union as it was."

Through 1865 Johnson alone controlled Reconstruction policy, for Congress recessed shortly before he became president and did not reconvene until December. In the following eight months, Johnson put into operation his own plan, forming new state governments in the South by using his power to grant pardons.

Johnson's Leniency and Racial Views

Johnson followed Lincoln's leniency by extending even easier terms to southerners. But which southerners would be allowed to vote?

Johnson held that black suffrage could never be imposed on a southern state by the federal government. His racism put him on a collision course with the Radicals. Johnson held what one politician called "unconquerable prejudices against the African race." In perhaps the most blatantly racist official statement ever delivered by an American president, Johnson declared in his annual message of 1867 that blacks possessed less "capacity for government than any other race of people. No independent government of any form has ever been successful in their hands; . . . wherever they have been left to their own devices they have shown a constant tendency to relapse into barbarism."

This racial conservatism had an enduring effect on Johnson's policies. Where whites were concerned, however, Johnson seemed to be pursuing changes in class relations. He proposed rules that would keep the wealthy planter class at least temporarily out of power. White southerners were required to swear an oath of loyalty as a condition of gaining amnesty or pardon, but Johnson barred several categories of people from taking the oath: former federal officials, high-ranking Confederate officers, and political leaders or graduates of West Point or Annapolis who had violated their oaths to support the United States by aiding the Confederacy. To this list Johnson added another important group: all southerners who aided the rebellion and whose taxable property was worth more than $20,000. These individuals had to apply personally to the president for pardon and restoration of their political rights.

Thus it appeared that the leadership class of the Old South would be removed from power, for virtually all the rich and powerful whites of prewar days needed Johnson's special pardon. The president, it seemed, meant to take revenge on the haughty

Johnson's Pardon Policy

aristocrats and thereby promote a new leadership of deserving yeomen.

Johnson appointed provisional governors who began the Reconstruction process by calling constitutional conventions. The delegates chosen for these conventions had to draft new constitutions that eliminated slavery and invalidated secession. After ratification of these constitutions, new governments could be elected, and the states would be restored to the Union with full congressional representation. But only those southerners who had taken the oath of amnesty and been eligible to vote on the day the state seceded could participate in this process. Thus unpardoned whites and former slaves were not eligible.

If Johnson intended to strip the old elite of its power, he did not hold to his plan. The old white leadership proved resilient and influential; prominent Confederates (a few with pardons but many without) won elections and turned up in various appointive offices. Then, surprisingly, Johnson helped to subvert his own plan: he started pardoning aristocrats and leading rebels who should not have been in office. He hired additional clerks to write out the necessary documents and then began to issue pardons to large categories of people. By September 1865 hundreds were being issued in a single day. These pardons, plus the rapid return of planters' abandoned lands, restored the old elite to power and quickly gave Johnson the image as the South's champion. He further gained southern loyalty with his hostility to the Freedmen's Bureau.

Why did Johnson allow the planters to regain power? Perhaps vanity betrayed his judgment. Too long an isolated outsider, Johnson may have succumbed to the attention and flattery of the pardon seekers. He was also determined upon a rapid Reconstruction in order to deny the Radicals the opportunity for the more thorough racial and political changes they desired in the South. And, given Johnson's need for southern support in the 1866 elections, he decided to endorse the new governments and declare Reconstruction complete only eight months after Appomattox. Thus in December 1865 many Confederate congressmen traveled to Washington to claim seats in the U.S. Congress. Even Alexander Stephens, vice president of the Confederacy, returned to Capitol Hill as a senator-elect.

The election of such prominent rebels troubled many northerners. So did other results of Johnson's program. Some of the state conventions were slow to repudiate secession; others admitted only grudgingly that slavery was dead. Two refused to take any action

Combative and inflexible, President Andrew Johnson contributed greatly to the failure of his own Reconstruction program.   (Library of Congress)

to repudiate the large Confederate debt, which northerners felt should not be paid. Even Johnson admitted that these acts showed "something like defiance, which is all out of place at this time."

Furthermore, to define the status of freed men and women and control their labor, some legislatures merely revised large sections of the slave codes by substituting the word **Black Codes** *freedmen* for *slaves.* The new black codes compelled the former slaves, now supposedly free, to carry passes, observe a curfew, live in housing provided by a landowner, and give up hope of entering many desirable occupations. Stiff vagrancy laws and restrictive labor contracts bound supposedly free laborers to plantations, and "anti-enticement" laws punished anyone who tried to lure these workers to other employment. State-supported schools and orphanages excluded blacks entirely.

It seemed to northerners that the South was intent on returning African Americans to servility and that

Johnson's Reconstruction policy held no one responsible for the terrible war. But memories of the war—not yet a year over—were still raw, and would dominate political behavior for several elections to come. Thus the Republican majority in Congress decided to call a halt to the results of Johnson's plan. On reconvening, the House and Senate considered the credentials of the newly elected southern representatives and decided not to admit them. Instead, they bluntly challenged the president's authority and established a joint committee to study and investigate a new direction for Reconstruction.

The Congressional Reconstruction Plan

 Northern congressmen were hardly unified, but they did not doubt their right to shape Reconstruction policy. The Constitution mentioned neither secession nor reunion, but it gave Congress the primary role in the admission of states. Moreover, the Constitution declared that the United States shall guarantee to each state a republican form of government. This provision, legislators believed, gave them the authority to devise policies for Reconstruction.

They soon found that other constitutional questions affected their policies. What, for example, had rebellion done to the relationship between southern states and the Union? Lincoln had always insisted that states could not secede—they had engaged in an "insurrection"—and that the Union remained intact. Not even Andrew Johnson, however, accepted the southern position that state governments of the Confederacy could simply reenter the nation. Johnson argued that the Union had endured, though individuals had erred—thus the use of his power to grant or withhold pardons. Congressmen who favored vigorous Reconstruction measures argued that the war had broken the Union, and that the South was subject to the victor's will. Moderate congressmen held that the states had forfeited their rights through rebellion and thus had come under congressional supervision.

These theories mirrored the diversity of Congress itself. Northern Democrats, weakened by the war

The Radicals most of them had opposed in its final year, denounced any idea of racial equality and supported Johnson's policies. Conservative Republicans, despite their party loyalty, favored a limited federal role in Reconstruction. The Radical Republicans, led by

Thaddeus Stevens, Charles Sumner, and George Julian, wanted to transform the South. Although they were a minority within their party, they had the advantage of a clearly defined goal. They believed it was essential to democratize the South, establish public education, and ensure the rights of freed people. They favored black suffrage, often supported land confiscation and redistribution, and were willing to exclude the South from the Union for several years if necessary to achieve their goals. Born of the war and its outcome, the Radicals brought a new civic vision to American life; they wanted to create an activist federal government and the beginnings of racial equality. A large group of moderate Republicans did not want to go as far as the Radicals but believed some reworking of Johnson's policies was necessary.

One overwhelming political reality faced all four groups: the 1866 elections were approaching in the fall. Having questioned Johnson's program, Congress needed to develop an alternative plan and avoid going before the voters empty-handed. Ironically, Johnson and the Democrats sabotaged the possibility of a conservative coalition. They refused to cooperate with conservative or moderate Republicans and insisted that Reconstruction was over, that the new state governments were legitimate, and that southern representatives should be admitted to Congress. To devise a Republican program, conservative and moderate elements in the party had to work with the Radicals, whose influence grew in proportion to Johnson's intransigence.

Trying to work with Johnson, Republicans believed a compromise had been reached in the spring of

Congress Wrests Control from Johnson 1866. Under its terms Johnson would agree to two modifications of his program: extension of the life of the Freedmen's Bureau for another year and passage of a civil rights bill to counteract the black codes. This bill would force southern courts to practice equality before the law by allowing federal judges to remove from state courts cases in which blacks were treated unfairly. Its provisions applied to public, not private, acts of discrimination. The civil rights bill of 1866 was the first statutory definition of the rights of American citizens.

Johnson destroyed the compromise, however, by vetoing both bills (they later became law when Congress overrode the president's veto). Denouncing any change in his program, the president condemned Congress's action and revealed his own racism. Because the civil rights bill defined U.S. citizens as native-born

How do historians know...

that the Radical Republican vision of Reconstruction had a popular base and was not solely the creation of a few ambitious politicians? How do we understand and evaluate the contending wills and bitterness that existed in North and South as Reconstruction policies developed? Moreover, why did the Republicans take back control of the Reconstruction process from President Andrew Johnson in late 1865 and throughout 1866? This excerpt from a letter by Brigadier General James S. Brisbin on December 29, 1865, to Congressman Thaddeus Stevens (the principal architect of Radical Reconstruction) indicates both practical and philosophical reasons why many northerners supported a harsher plan for bringing the South back into the Union than Johnson had put in place. Brisbin had just read Stevens's speech on Reconstruction in Congress, in which the congressman had called for a halt to the seating of any representatives elected by the "Johnson governments" and proposed a lengthy investigation of southern conditions. Brisbin speaks as soldier and citizen, fearing that "the fruits of our toils and battles and sieges were to be bartered away and treason made as honorable as loyalty." Brisbin, who was commanding occupation troops in Arkansas, encouraged Stevens in his effort to slow down Reconstruction. "These people are not loyal," he writes; "they are only conquered." The letter anticipates much of what soon occurred in the bitter struggle to bind up sectional hatreds and respond to the profound challenges of emancipation and reunion. If Stevens needed any encouragement or justification in leading Congress in taking control of Reconstruction, he received it in this letter. This photograph of Congressman Thaddeus Stevens was taken during the early years of Reconstruction. (Photo: National Archives)

After four years of war during which we suffered all that men could suffer and after finally beating the rebles in battle we began to fear that the fruits of our toils our battles and seiges were to be bartered away and treason made as honorable as loyalty. For the assurance that rebles whose hands red with the blood of our brothers, are not just yet to be allowed to set themselves up to rule over us, thousands of loyal soldiers will thank you. . . .

These people are not loyal; they are only conquered, I tell you there is not as much loyalty in the South to day as there was the day Lee surrendered to Grant. The moment they lost their cause in the field they set about to gain by politics what they had failed to obtain by force of arms. . . .

My God can any sane man look at the men who fill their so called state Legislatures and then say the states are loyal. . . .

The bones of our dead brothers, falling in the great struggle lie buried in the soil of every Southern state and at least until they have returned to dust and their graves grown green we should not shake the bloody hands of the men who robbed them of life. The immodest haste (and it should be called brazen impudence) of the Southern people in attempting to get their delegations into Congress should be sufficient to arouse the suspicions of every Northern man that they were not sincere. . . .

These people are most anxious to renew their practical relations with the Federal Govt because . . . then they can go to work in earnest in their state Legislatures to pass vagrant laws and reduce the blacks to a slavery worse than that from which they have just escaped. Loyal men will not be elected to office in the South until the blacks are allowed to vote and I hope you will not allow any Southern member of his seat until he comes there elected by a majority _of all the people of his District_. I am no politician but what I see I know and I tell you you are right in what you said on re-construction. . . .

In 1866, as Congress reviewed the progress of Reconstruction, news from the South had a considerable impact. Violence against black people, like the riot in Memphis depicted here, helped convince northern legislators that they had to modify President Johnson's policies. (Library of Congress)

persons who were taxed, Johnson claimed it discriminated against "large numbers of intelligent, worthy, and patriotic foreigners . . . in favor of the negro." The bill, he said, operated "in favor of the colored and against the white race."

All hope of presidential-congressional cooperation was now dead. In 1866 newspapers reported daily violations of blacks' rights in the South and carried alarming accounts of antiblack violence—notably in Memphis and New Orleans, where police aided brutal mobs in their attacks. In Memphis forty blacks were killed and twelve schools burned by white mobs, and in New Orleans the toll was thirty-four African Americans dead and two hundred wounded. Such violence convinced Republicans, and the northern public, that more needed to be done. A new Republican plan took the form of a proposed amendment to the Constitution, forged out of a compromise between radical and conservative elements of the party. The Fourteenth Amendment, passed and sent to the states in June 1866, was Congress's alternative to Johnson's program of Reconstruction.

Of the four parts of the Fourteenth Amendment, the first would have the greatest legal significance in later years. It conferred citizenship on the freedmen

The Fourteenth Amendment

and prohibited states from abridging their constitutional "privileges and immunities" (see the Constitution in this book's Appendix). It also barred any state from taking a person's life, liberty, or property "without due process of law" and from denying "equal protection of the laws." These resounding phrases became powerful guarantees of African Americans' civil rights—indeed, of the rights of all citizens—in the twentieth century.

Nearly universal agreement emerged among Republicans on the amendment's second and third provisions. The second declared the Confederate debt null and void and guaranteed the war debt of the United States. Northerners rejected the notion of paying taxes to reimburse those who had financed a rebellion, and business groups agreed on the necessity of upholding the credit of the U.S. government. The third provision barred Confederate leaders from holding state and federal office. Only Congress, by a two-thirds vote of each house, could remove the penalty. The amendment thus guaranteed a degree of punishment for the leaders of the Confederacy.

The fourth part of the amendment dealt with representation and embodied the compromises that produced the document. Northerners disagreed about whether black citizens should have the right to vote. As a citizen of Indiana wrote to a southern relative, there was strong feeling in favor of "humane and liberal laws for the government and protection of the colored population." But there was prejudice, too. "Although there is a great deal [of] profession among us for the relief of the darkey yet I think much of it is far from being sincere. I guess we want to compel you to do right by them while we are not willing ourselves to do so." Those arched words are indicative of not only how revolutionary Reconstruction had become, but also how far the public will lagged behind the enactments that became new constitutional cornerstones.

Republican congressmen shied away from confronting this ambivalence, but political reality required them to do something. Emancipation made every former slave a full rather than three-fifths of a person, which would increase southern representation. Thus the postwar South stood to gain power in Congress, and if white southerners did not allow blacks to vote, former secessionists would derive the political benefit from emancipation. That was more irony than most northerners could bear. So Republicans determined that if a southern state did not grant black men the vote, their representation would be reduced proportionally. If they did enfranchise black men, their representation would be increased proportionally. This compromise avoided a direct enactment of black suffrage, but would deliver future black voters to the Republican Party.

The Fourteenth Amendment paved the way for black male suffrage but ignored female citizens, black and white. For this reason it provoked a strong reaction from the women's rights movement. Advocates of women's equality had worked with abolitionists for decades, often subordinating their cause to that of the slaves. During the drafting of the Fourteenth Amendment, however, female activists demanded to be heard. When legislators defined women as nonvoting citizens, prominent leaders such as Elizabeth Cady Stanton and Susan B. Anthony decided that it was time to end their alliance with abolitionists and fight more determinedly for themselves. Thus the amendment infused new life into the women's rights movement and caused considerable strife among old allies. Many male former abolitionists, white and black, were willing to delay the day of woman suffrage in favor of securing freed men the right to vote in the South.

In 1866, however, the major question in Reconstruction politics was how the public would respond to the congressional initiative. Johnson did his best to

The South's and Johnson's Defiance, 1866

block the Fourteenth Amendment in both North and South. Condemning Congress for its refusal to seat southern representatives, the president urged state legislatures in the South to vote against ratification. Every southern legislature except Tennessee's rejected the amendment by a wide margin. In three other states the amendment received no support at all.

To present his case to northerners, Johnson organized a National Union Convention and took to the stump himself. In an age when active personal campaigning was rare for a president, Johnson boarded a special train for a "swing around the circle" that carried his message deep into the Northeast, the Midwest, and then back to Washington. In city after city, he criticized the Republicans in a ranting, undignified style. Increasingly, audiences rejected his views and hooted and jeered at him. In this whistle-stop tour, Johnson began to hand out American flags with thirty-six rather than twenty-five stars, declaring that the Union was already restored. At many towns he likened himself to a "persecuted" Jesus who might now be martyred "upon the cross" for his magnanimity toward the South. And, repeatedly, he labeled the Radicals "traitors" for their efforts to take over Reconstruction. Johnson was shouted down and forced from the stage in Pittsburgh.

The elections of 1866 were a resounding victory for Republicans in Congress. Radicals and moderates whom Johnson had denounced won reelection by large margins, and the Republican majority grew to two-thirds of both houses of Congress. The North had spoken clearly: Johnson's policies were prematurely giving the advantage to rebels and traitors. Although the Radicals may have been out ahead of public opinion, most northerners feared for "the future peace and safety of the Union" if Johnson's approach to Reconstruction prevailed. Thus Republican congressional leaders won a mandate to pursue their Reconstruction plan.

But, thanks to Johnson and southern intransigence, that plan had reached an impasse. Nothing could be accomplished as long as the "Johnson governments" existed and the southern electorate remained exclusively white. Republicans resolved to form new state governments in the South and enfranchise the freedmen. The unavoidable logic of the situation forced the majority to accept the Radical plan. (See Table 16.1.)

After some embittered debate in which Republicans and the remaining Democrats in Congress argued

Table 16.1   Plans for Reconstruction Compared

	Johnson's Plan	Radicals' Plan	Fourteenth Amendment	Reconstruction Act of 1867
Voting	Whites only; high-ranking Confederate leaders must seek pardons	Give vote to black males	Southern whites may decide but can lose representation if they deny black suffrage	Black men gain vote; whites barred from office by Fourteenth Amendment cannot vote while new state governments are being formed
Officeholding	Many prominent Confederates regain power	Only loyal white and black males eligible	Confederate leaders barred until Congress votes amnesty	Fourteenth Amendment in effect
Time out of Union	Brief	Several years; until South is thoroughly democratized	Brief	3–5 years after war
Other change in southern society	Little; gain of power by yeomen not realized; emancipation grudgingly accepted, but no black civil or political rights	Expand public education; confiscate land and provide farms for freedmen; expansion of activist federal government	Probably slight, depending on enforcement	Considerable, depending on action of new state governments

The Reconstruction Acts of 1867–1868

over the meaning and memory of the Civil War itself, the First Reconstruction Act passed in March 1867. This plan, under which the southern states were actually readmitted to the Union, incorporated only a part of the Radical program. Union generals, commanding small garrisons of troops and charged with supervising all elections, assumed control in five military districts in the South (see Map 16.1). Confederate leaders designated in the Fourteenth Amendment were barred from voting until new state constitutions were ratified. The act guaranteed freedmen the right to vote in elections for state constitutional conventions and in subsequent elections. In addition, each southern state was required to ratify the Fourteenth Amendment, to ratify its new constitution by majority vote, and to submit it to Congress for approval.

Thus African Americans gained an opportunity to fight for a better life through the political process, and ex-Confederates were given what they interpreted as a bitter pill to swallow in order to return to the Union. The Second, Third, and Fourth Reconstruction Acts, passed between March 1867 and March 1868, provided for the details of operation for voter registration boards, the adoption of constitutions, and the admin-

istration of "good faith" oaths on the part of white southerners.

In the words of one historian, the Radicals succeeded in "clipping Johnson's wings." But they had hoped Congress could do much more. Thaddeus Stevens, for example, argued that economic opportunity was essential to the freedmen. "If we do not furnish them with homesteads from forfeited and rebel property," Stevens declared, "and hedge them around with protective laws . . . we had better left them in bondage." Stevens therefore drew up a plan for extensive confiscation and redistribution of land. Only one-tenth of the land affected by his plan was earmarked for freedmen, in 40-acre plots. The rest was to be sold to generate money for Union veterans' pensions, compensation to loyal southerners for damaged property, and payment of the federal debt.

The Failure of Land Redistribution

By these means Stevens hoped to win support for a basically unpopular measure. But he failed, and in general the Radicals were not able to generate public support. Northerners were accustomed to a limited role for government, and the business community staunchly opposed any interference with private property rights, even for former Confederates. Thus black

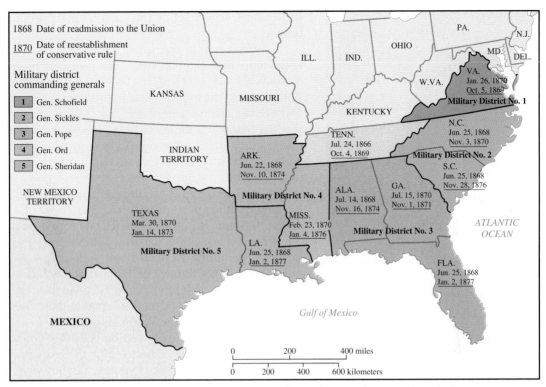

Map 16.1 The Reconstruction This map shows the five military districts established when Congress passed the Reconstruction Act of 1867. As the dates within each state indicate, conservative Democratic forces quickly regained control of government in four southern states. So-called Radical Reconstruction was curtailed in most of the others as factions within the weakened Republican Party began to cooperate with conservative Democrats.

farmers were forced to seek work in a hostile environment in which landowners opposed their acquisition of land, even as renters.

Congress's role as the architect of Reconstruction was not quite over, for its quarrels with Andrew Johnson were growing more bitter. To restrict Johnson's influence and safeguard its plan, Congress passed a number of controversial laws. First, it set the date for its own reconvening—an unprecedented act, for the president traditionally summoned legislators to Washington. Then it limited Johnson's power over the army by requiring the president to issue military orders through the General of the Army, Ulysses S. Grant, who could not be dismissed without the Senate's consent. Finally, Congress passed the Tenure of Office Act, which gave the Senate power to approve changes in the president's cabinet. Designed to protect Secretary of War Stanton, who sympathized with the Radicals, this law violated the tradition that a president controlled appointments to his own cabinet.

Constitutional Crisis

All of these measures, as well as each of the Reconstruction Acts, were passed by a two-thirds override of presidential vetoes. The situation led some to believe that the federal government had reached a stage of "congressional tyranny," and others to conclude that Johnson had become an obstacle to the legitimate will of the people in reconstructing the nation on a just and permanent basis.

Johnson took several belligerent steps of his own. He issued orders to military commanders in the South limiting their powers and increasing the powers of the civil governments he had created in 1865. Then he removed military officers who were conscientiously enforcing Congress's new law, preferring commanders who allowed disqualified Confederates to vote. Finally, he tried to remove Secretary of War Stanton. With that attempt the confrontation reached its climax.

Impeachment is a political procedure provided for in the Constitution. It is a remedy for crimes or serious abuses of power by presidents, federal judges, and other high officials in the government. Those who are impeached (judged or politically indicted) in the

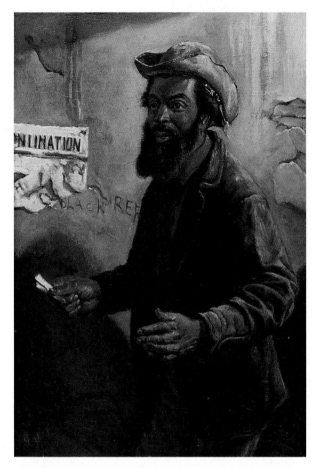

Thomas Waterman Wood, who had painted portraits of society figures in Nashville before the war, sensed the importance of Congress's decision in 1867 to enfranchise the freedmen. This oil painting, one of a series on suffrage, emphasizes the significance of the ballot for the black voter. (Cheekwood Museum of Art, Nashville, Tennessee)

Impeachment of President Johnson

House are then tried in the Senate. Historically, this power has generally not been used as a means to investigate and judge the private lives of presidents, although in recent times it was used in this manner in the case of President Bill Clinton.

Twice in 1867, the House Judiciary Committee had considered impeachment of Johnson, rejecting the idea once and then recommending it by only a 5-to-4 vote. That recommendation was decisively defeated by the House. After Johnson tried to remove Stanton, however, a third attempt to impeach the president carried easily. The indictment concentrated on his violation of the Tenure of Office Act, though modern scholars regard his efforts to impede enforcement of the Reconstruction Act of 1867 as a far more serious offense.

Johnson's trial in the Senate began promptly and lasted more than three months. The prosecution, led by Radicals such as Thaddeus Stevens and Benjamin Butler, attempted to prove that Johnson was guilty of "high crimes and misdemeanors." But they also argued that the trial was a means to judge Johnson's performance, not a judicial determination of guilt or innocence. The Senate ultimately rejected such reasoning, which could have made removal from office a political weapon against any chief executive who disagreed with Congress. Although a majority of senators voted to convict Johnson, the prosecution fell one vote short of the necessary two-thirds majority. Johnson remained in office, politically weakened and with only a few months left in his term. The Republicans, in effect, managed the vote in Johnson's trial; they had their eyes on the 1868 election and did not want to hurt their prospects of regaining the White House.

Election of 1868

In the 1868 presidential election Ulysses S. Grant, running as a Republican, defeated Horatio Seymour, a New York Democrat. Grant was not a Radical, but his platform supported congressional Reconstruction and endorsed black suffrage in the South. (Significantly, Republicans stopped short of endorsing it in the North.) The Democrats, meanwhile, vigorously denounced Reconstruction and thus renewed the sectional conflict. Indeed, in the 1868 election, the Democrats conducted the most openly white supremacist campaign to that time in American history. Both sides waved the "bloody shirt," accusing each other as the villains of the war's sacrifices. By associating themselves with rebellion and with Johnson's repudiated program, the Democrats went down to defeat in all but eight states, though the popular vote was fairly close. Participating in their first presidential election ever on a wide scale, blacks decisively voted en masse for General Grant.

In office Grant acted as an administrator of Reconstruction but not as its enthusiastic advocate. He vacillated in his dealings with the southern states, sometimes defending Republican regimes and sometimes currying favor with Democrats. On occasion Grant called out federal troops to stop violence or enforce acts of Congress. But he never imposed a true military occupation on the South. Rapid demobilization had reduced a federal army of more than 1 million to 57,000 within a year of the surrender at Appomattox. Thereafter the number of troops in the South continued to fall, until in 1874 there were only 4,000

A Republican Party brass band in action during the 1868 election campaign in Baton Rouge, Louisiana. The Union regimental colors and soldier caps demonstrate the strong federal presence in the South at this pivotal moment in radical Reconstruction. (Andrew D. Lytle Collection, Louisiana and Lower Mississippi Valley Collections, LSU Libraries, Louisiana State University, Baton Rouge, La.)

in the southern states outside Texas. Throughout Reconstruction, the strongest federal units were in Texas and the West, fighting Indians, not white southerners. The later legend of "military rule," so important to southern claims of victimization during Reconstruction, was steeped in myth.

In 1869, in an effort to write democratic principles into the Constitution, the Radicals passed the Fifteenth

Fifteenth Amendment

Amendment. This measure forbade states to deny the right to vote "on account of race, color, or previous condition of servitude." Such wording did not guarantee the right to vote. It deliberately left states free to restrict suffrage on other grounds so that northern states could continue to deny suffrage to women and certain groups of men—Chinese immigrants, illiterates, and those too poor to pay poll taxes.

Ironically, the votes of four uncooperative southern states—compelled by Congress to approve the amendment as an added condition to rejoining the Union—proved necessary to impose even this language on parts of the North. Although several states outside the South refused to ratify, three-fourths of the states approved the measure, and the Fifteenth Amendment became law in 1870. It too had been a political compromise, and though African Americans rejoiced all across the land at its enactment, it left open the possibility for states to create countless qualification tests to obstruct voting in the future.

With passage of the Fifteenth Amendment, many Americans, especially supportive northerners, considered Reconstruction essentially completed. "Let us have done with Reconstruction," pleaded the *New York Tribune* in April 1870. "The country is tired and sick of it. . . . Let us have Peace!" But some northerners, like radical abolitionist Wendell Phillips, worried. "Our day," he warned, "is fast slipping away. Once let public thought float off from the great issue of the war, and it will take . . . more than a generation to bring it back again."

Reconstruction Politics in the South

 From the start, Reconstruction encountered the resistance of white southerners. In the black codes and in private attitudes, many whites stubbornly opposed emancipation, and the former planter class proved especially unbending. In 1866 a Georgia newspaper frankly observed that "most of the white citizens believe that the institution of slavery was right, and . . . they will believe that the condition, which comes nearest to slavery, that can now be established will be the best."

Thomas Nast, in this 1868 cartoon, pictured the combination of forces that threatened the success of Reconstruction: southern opposition and the greed, partisanship, and racism of northern interests. (Library of Congress)

Fearing loss of control over their slaves, some planters attempted to postpone freedom by denying or misrepresenting events. Former slaves reported that their owners "didn't tell them it was freedom" or "wouldn't let [them] go." Agents of the Freedmen's Bureau reported that "the old system of slavery [is] working with even more rigor than formerly at a few miles distant from any point where U.S. troops are stationed." To hold onto their workers, some landowners claimed control over black children and used guardianship and apprentice laws to bind black families to the plantation.

White Resistance

Whites also blocked blacks from acquiring land. A few planters divided up plots among their slaves, but most condemned the idea of making blacks landowners. A Georgia woman whose family was known for its support of religious education for slaves was outraged that two property owners planned to "rent their lands

to the Negroes!" Such action was, she declared, "injurious to the best interest of the community."

Adamant resistance by propertied whites soon manifested itself in other ways, including violence. In one North Carolina town a local magistrate clubbed a black man on a public street, and bands of "Regulators" terrorized blacks in parts of that state and in Kentucky. Such incidents were predictable in a defeated society in which many planters believed, as a South Carolinian put it, that blacks "can't be governed except with the whip."

After President Johnson encouraged the South to resist congressional Reconstruction, white conservatives worked hard to capture the new state governments. Many whites also boycotted the polls in an attempt to defeat Congress's plans; by sitting out the elections, whites might block the new constitutions, which had to be approved by a majority of registered voters. This tactic was tried in North Carolina and succeeded in Alabama, forcing Congress to base ratification of the Fourteenth Amendment and of new state constitutions on a majority of "votes cast" (the provision of the Fourth Reconstruction Act).

Very few black men stayed away from the polls. Enthusiastically and hopefully, they voted Republican.

Black Voters and Emergence of a Southern Republican Party

Most agreed with one man who felt he should "stick to the end with the party that freed me." Illiteracy did not prohibit blacks (or uneducated whites) from making intelligent choices. Although Mississippi's William Henry could read only "a little," he testified that he and his friends had no difficulty selecting the Republican ballot. "We stood around and watched," he explained. "We saw D. Sledge vote; he owned half the county. We knowed he voted Democratic so we voted the other ticket so it would be Republican." Women, who could not vote, encouraged their husbands and sons, and preachers exhorted their congregations to use the franchise. With such group spirit, zeal for voting spread through the entire black community.

Thanks to a large black turnout and the restrictions on prominent Confederates, a new southern Republican Party came to power in the constitutional conventions of 1868–1870. Republican delegates consisted of a sizable contingent of blacks (265 out of the total of just over 1,000 delegates throughout the South), some northerners who had moved to the South, and native southern whites who favored change. Together these Republicans brought the South into line with progressive reforms adopted earlier in the rest of the nation. The new constitutions were more democratic. They eliminated property qualifications for voting and holding office, and they turned many appointed offices into elective posts. They provided for public schools and institutions to care for the mentally ill, the blind, the deaf, the destitute, and the orphaned.

The conventions broadened women's rights in property holding and divorce. Usually, the goal was not to make women equal with men but to provide relief to thousands of suffering debtors. In families left poverty-stricken by the war and weighed down by debt, it was usually the husband who had contracted the debts. Thus giving women legal control over their own property provided some protection to their families. The goal of some delegates, however, was to elevate women. Blacks in particular called for laws to provide for woman suffrage, but they were ignored by their white colleagues.

Under these new constitutions the southern states elected Republican-controlled governments. For the

Triumph of Republican Governments

first time, the ranks of state legislators in 1868 included some black southerners. It remained to be seen now how much social change these new governments would bring about. Contrary to what white southerners would later claim, the Republican state governments did not disfranchise ex-Confederates as a group. The vexing questions of land reform and the assurance of racial equality all but overwhelmed the "radical" governments.

These new biracial regimes appreciated the realities of power and the depth of racial enmity. In most states, whites were in the majority and former slave-owners controlled the best land and other sources of economic power. James Lynch, a leading black politician from Mississippi, explained why African Americans shunned the "folly" of disfranchisement. Unlike northerners who "can leave when it becomes too uncomfortable," landless former slaves "must be in friendly relations with the great body of the whites in the state. Otherwise . . . peace can be maintained only by a standing army." Despised and lacking economic or social power, southern Republicans strove for acceptance and legitimacy.

Blacks also believed in the principle of universal suffrage and the Christian goal of reconciliation. Far from being vindictive toward the race that had enslaved them, they treated leading rebels with generosity and appealed to white southerners to adopt a spirit of fairness and cooperation. In this way the South's Republican Party condemned itself to defeat if white voters would not cooperate. Within a few years Republicans were reduced to the embarrassment of making futile appeals to whites while ignoring the claims of their strongest supporters, blacks. But for a time both Republicans and their opponents, who called themselves Conservatives or Democrats, moved to the center and appealed for support from a broad range of groups. Some propertied whites accepted congressional Reconstruction as a reality and declared themselves willing to compete under the new rules. All sides found an area of agreement in economic policies.

Reflecting northern ideals and southern necessity, the Reconstruction governments enthusiastically promoted industry. Confederates had

Industrialization

seen how industry aided the North during the war. Accordingly, Reconstruction legislatures encouraged investment with loans, subsidies, and exemptions from taxation for periods up to ten years. The southern railroad system was rebuilt and expanded, and coal and iron mining made possible Birmingham's steel plants. Between 1860 and 1880, the number of manufacturing establishments in the South nearly doubled.

This emphasis on big business, however, produced higher state debts and taxes, drew money away from schools and other programs, and multiplied possibilities for corruption. It also locked Republicans into a conservative strategy. In courting elite whites who never joined the Republican Party, Republicans lost the opportunity of building support among poorer whites.

Policies appealing to African American voters never went beyond equality before the law. In fact, the

Republican Policies on Racial Equality

whites who controlled the southern Republican Party were reluctant to allow blacks a share of offices proportionate to their electoral strength. Aware of their weakness, black leaders did not push very far for revolutionary economic or social change. In every southern state, they led efforts to establish public schools, although they did not press for integrated facilities. In 1870 South Carolina passed the first comprehensive school law in the South. By 1875, 50 percent of black school-age children in that state were enrolled in school, and approximately one-third of the three thousand teachers were black.

Some African American politicians did fight for civil rights and integration. Most were mulattos from cities such as New Orleans or Mobile, where large populations of light-skinned free blacks had existed before the war. Their experience in such communities

One notable success in Reconstruction efforts to stimulate industry was Birmingham, Alabama. Here workers cast molten iron into blocks called pigs.   (Birmingham Public Library)

had made them sensitive to issues of status, and they spoke out for open and equal public accommodations. Laws requiring equal accommodations won passage throughout the Deep South, but they often went unenforced or required an injured party to bring expensive legal action for enforcement.

Economic progress was uppermost in the minds of most freed people and black representatives from rural districts. Black southerners needed land, but only a few promoted confiscation. In fact, much land did fall into state hands for nonpayment of taxes and was offered for sale in small lots. But most freedmen had too little cash to bid against investors or speculators, and few acquired land in this way. South Carolina established a land commission, but it could help only those with money to buy. Any widespread redistribution of land had to arise from Congress, which never supported such action. The lack of genuine land redistribution remained the significant lost opportunity of Reconstruction.

Within a few years, as centrists in both parties met with failure, white hostility to congressional Reconstruction began to dominate. Some conservatives had always desired to fight Reconstruction through pressure and racist propaganda. They put

The Myth of "Negro Rule"

economic and social pressure on blacks: one black Republican reported that "my neighbors will not employ me, nor sell me a farthing's worth of anything." Charging that the South had been turned over to ignorant blacks, conservatives deplored "black domination," which became a rallying cry for a return to white supremacy.

Such attacks were inflammatory propaganda, and part of the growing myth of "Negro rule," which would serve as a central theme in battles over the memory of Reconstruction. African Americans participated in politics but hardly dominated or controlled events. They were a majority in only two out of ten state constitutional writing conventions (transplanted northerners were a majority in one). In the state legislatures, only in the lower house in South Carolina did blacks ever constitute a majority; among officeholders, their numbers generally were far fewer than their proportion in the population. Sixteen blacks won seats in Congress before Reconstruction was over, but none was ever elected governor. Only eighteen served in a high state office such as lieutenant governor, treasurer, superintendent of education, or secretary of state. In all, some four hundred blacks served in political office during the Reconstruction era. Although they never dominated the process, they established a rich tradition of government service and civic activism. Elected officials, such as Robert Smalls in South Carolina, labored tirelessly for cheaper land prices, better healthcare, access to schools, and the enforcement of civil rights for their people. The black politicians of Reconstruction are lost in the mists, the forgotten heroes of this seedtime of America's long civil rights movement.

Conservatives also assailed the allies of black Republicans. Their propaganda denounced whites from the North as "carpetbaggers," greedy

Carpetbaggers and Scalawags

crooks planning to pour stolen tax revenues into their sturdy luggage made of carpet material. Immigrants from the North, who held the largest share of Republican offices, were all tarred with this brush.

In fact, most northerners who settled in the South had come seeking business opportunities or a warmer climate and never entered politics. Those who did enter politics generally wanted to democratize the South and to introduce northern ways, such as industry, public education, and the spirit of enterprise. Carpetbaggers' ideals were tested by hard times and ostracism by white southerners.

In addition to tagging northern interlopers as carpetbaggers, Conservatives invented the term *scalawag* to discredit any native white southerner who cooperated with the Republicans. A substantial number of southerners did so, including some wealthy and prominent men. Most scalawags, however, were yeoman farmers, men from mountain areas and nonslaveholding districts who had been restive under the Confederacy. They saw that they could benefit from the education and opportunities promoted by Republicans. Banding together with freedmen, they pursued common class interests and hoped to make headway against the power of long-dominant planters. Cooperation even convinced a few scalawags that "there is but little if any difference in the talents of the two races," as one observed, and that all should have "an equal start." Yet this black-white coalition was vulnerable to the race issue, and most scalawags did not support racial equality. Republican tax policies also cut into upcountry yeoman support because reliance on the property tax hit many small landholders hard.

Taxation was a major problem for the Reconstruction governments. Republicans wanted to maintain prewar services, repair the war's destruction, stimulate industry, and support important new ventures such as public schools. But the Civil War had destroyed much of the South's tax base. One category of valuable property—slaves—had disappeared entirely. And hundreds

Albion Winegar Tourgee, a former Union soldier severely wounded at the Battle of Bull Run in 1861, became a carpetbagger and was elected a district judge in North Carolina during Reconstruction. In 1879 he published a best-selling novel, *A Fool's Errand,* which told his own story of travail as a Yankee immigrant in the South confronting the Ku Klux Klan and implementing freedmen's rights. (Chautauqua County Historical Society, Westfield, N.Y.)

Tax Policy and Corruption as Political Wedges

of thousands of citizens had lost much of the rest of their property—money, livestock, fences, and buildings—to the war. Thus an increase in taxes was necessary even to maintain traditional services, and new ventures required still higher taxes. Inevitably, Republican tax policies aroused strong opposition, especially among the yeomen.

Corruption was another serious charge levied against the Republicans. Unfortunately, it often was true. Many carpetbaggers and black politicians engaged in fraudulent schemes, sold their votes, or padded expenses, taking part in what scholars recognize was a nationwide surge of corruption in an age ruled by "spoilsmen" (see pages 554–556). Corruption carried no party label, but the Democrats successfully pinned the blame on unqualified blacks and greedy carpetbaggers among southern Republicans.

All these problems hurt the Republicans, whose leaders also allowed factionalism along racial and class lines to undermine party unity. But in many southern states the deathblow came through violence. The Ku Klux Klan, a secret veterans' club that began in

Ku Klux Klan

Tennessee in 1866, spread through the South and rapidly evolved into a terrorist organization. Violence against African Americans occurred from the first days of Reconstruction but became far more organized and purposeful after 1867. Klansmen rode to frustrate Reconstruction and keep the freedmen in subjection. Nighttime harassment, whippings, beatings, and murder became common, and terrorism dominated some counties and regions.

Although the Klan persecuted blacks who stood up for their rights as laborers or individuals, its main purpose was political. Lawless nightriders made active Republicans the target of their attacks. Leading white and black Republicans were killed in several states. After freedmen who worked for a South Carolina scalawag started voting, terrorists visited the planta-

Members of the Ku Klux Klan devised ghoulish costumes to heighten the terror inspired by their acts. This photograph shows the costume of a Mississippi Klansman from 1871. (Courtesy of Mr. Herbert Peck, Jr.)

tion and, in the words of one victim, "whipped every nigger man they could lay their hands on." Klansmen also attacked Union League clubs—Republican organizations that mobilized the black vote—and schoolteachers who were aiding the freedmen.

Klan violence was not a spontaneous outburst of racism; very specific social forces shaped and directed it. In North Carolina, for example, Alamance and Caswell Counties were the sites of the worst Klan violence. Slim Republican majorities there rested on co-operation between black voters and white yeomen, particularly those whose Unionism or discontent with the Confederacy had turned them against local Democratic officials. Together, these black and white Republicans had ousted officials long entrenched in power. The wealthy and powerful men in Alamance and Caswell who had lost their accustomed political control were the Klan's county officers and local chieftains. They organized a deliberate campaign of terror, recruiting members and planning atrocities. By whipping up racism or intimidating enough Republicans, the Ku Klux Klan weakened the Republican coalition and restored a Democratic majority.

Klan violence injured Republicans across the South. No fewer than one-tenth of the black leaders who had been delegates to the 1867–1868 state constitutional conventions were attacked, seven fatally. In one judicial district of North Carolina the Ku Klux Klan was responsible for twelve murders, over seven hundred beatings, and other acts of violence, including rape and arson. A single attack on Alabama Republicans in the town of Eutaw left four blacks dead and fifty-four wounded. In South Carolina five hundred masked Klansmen lynched eight black prisoners at the Union County jail, and in nearby York County the Klan committed at least eleven murders and hundreds of whippings. According to historian Eric Foner, the Klan "made it virtually impossible for Republicans to campaign or vote in large parts of Georgia."

Thus a combination of difficult fiscal problems, Republican mistakes, racial hostility, and terror brought down the Republican regimes. In

Failure of Reconstruction

most southern states, "Radical Reconstruction" lasted only a few years (see Map 16.1). The most enduring failure of Reconstruction, however, was not political; it was social and economic. Reconstruction failed to alter the South's social structure or its distribution of wealth and power. Without land of their own, freed men and women were dependent on white landowners who could and did use their economic power to compromise blacks' political freedom.

Armed only with the ballot, freed men in the South had little chance to effect major changes.

To reform the southern social order, Congress would have had to redistribute land, but most lawmakers opposed an attack on private property. Radical Republicans like Albion Tourgée, a former Union soldier who moved to North Carolina and was elected a judge, condemned Congress's timidity. Turning the freedman out on his own without protection, said Tourgée, constituted "cheap philanthropy." Indeed, African Americans who had to live with the consequences of Reconstruction considered it a failure, for the North "threw all the Negroes on the world without any way of getting along." Moreover, without careful supervision by Congress, the situation of the freed men and women deteriorated. Whenever the North lost interest, Reconstruction would collapse.

Reconstruction Reversed

 Northerners had always been more interested in suppressing rebellion than in aiding southern blacks, and by the early 1870s the North's commitment to bringing about change in the South was weakening. Criticism of the southern governments grew, new issues captured public attention, and sentiment for national reconciliation gained popularity in politics. In one southern state after another, Democrats regained control, and they threatened to defeat Republicans in the North as well. Whites in the old Confederacy referred to this decline of Reconstruction as "southern redemption," and by the 1870s, "redeemer" Democrats claimed to be the saviors of the South from alleged "black domination" and "carpetbag rule." And for one of only a few times in American history, violence and terror emerged as a tactic in normal politics.

In 1870 and 1871 the violent campaigns of the Ku Klux Klan forced Congress to pass two Enforcement Acts and an anti-Klan law. These laws made actions by individuals against the civil and political rights of others a federal criminal offense for the first time. They also provided for election supervisors and permitted martial law and suspension of the writ of habeas corpus to combat murders, beatings, and threats by the Klan. Federal prosecutors used the laws rather selectively. In 1872 and 1873 Mississippi and the Carolinas saw many prosecutions; but in other states where violence flourished, the laws were virtually ignored. Southern juries sometimes refused to convict Klansmen; out of a total

Political Implications of Klan Terrorism

of 3,310 cases, only 1,143 ended in convictions. Though many Klansmen (roughly two thousand in South Carolina alone) fled their states to avoid prosecution, and the Klan officially disbanded, the threat of violence did not end. Paramilitary organizations known as Rifle clubs and Red Shirts often took the Klan's place.

Klan terrorism openly defied Congress, yet even on this issue there were ominous signs that the North's commitment to racial justice was fading. Some conservative but influential Republicans opposed the anti-Klan laws. Rejecting other Republicans' arguments that the Thirteenth, Fourteenth, and Fifteenth Amendments had made the federal government the protector of the rights of citizens, these dissenters echoed an old Democratic charge that Congress was infringing on states' rights. Senator Lyman Trumbull of Illinois declared that the states remained "the depositories of the rights of the individual." If Congress could punish crimes like assault or murder, he asked, "what is the need of the State governments?" For years Democrats had complained of "centralization and consolidation"; now some Republicans seemed to agree with them. This opposition foreshadowed a more general revolt within Republican ranks in 1872.

Disenchanted with Reconstruction, a group calling itself the Liberal Republicans bolted the party in 1872 and nominated Horace Greeley, the well-known editor of the *New York Tribune*, for president. The Liberal Republicans were a varied group, including civil service reformers, foes of corruption, and advocates of a lower tariff. Normally such disparate elements would not cooperate with one another, but two popular and widespread attitudes united them: distaste for federal intervention in the South and an elitist desire to let market forces and the "best men" determine events, both in the South and in Washington.

The Liberal Republican Revolt

The Democrats also gave their nomination to Greeley in 1872. The combination was not enough to defeat Grant, who won reelection, but it reinforced Grant's desire to avoid confrontation with white southerners. Greeley's campaign for North-South reunion, for "clasping hands across the bloody chasm," was a bit premature to win at the polls, but a harbinger of the future of American politics. Organized Blue-Gray fraternalism (gatherings of Union and Confederate veterans) began as early as 1874 in some states. Grant continued to use military force sparingly and in 1875 refused a desperate request for troops from the governor of Mississippi to quell racial and political terrorism in that state.

Dissatisfaction with Grant's administration grew during his second term. Strong-willed but politically naive, Grant made a series of poor appointments. His secretary of war, his private secretary, and officials in the Treasury and Navy Departments were involved in bribery or tax-cheating scandals. Instead of exposing the corruption, Grant defended some of the culprits. In 1874, as Grant's popularity and his party's prestige declined, the Democrats recaptured the House of Representatives. This stunning turnabout signaled the beginning of the end of the old Radical Republican vision of Reconstruction. The Republican Party faced more unfavorable publicity in 1875, when several of Grant's appointees were indicted for corruption.

The effect of Democratic gains in Congress was to weaken legislative resolve on southern issues. Congress had already lifted the political disabilities of the Fourteenth Amendment from many former Confederates. In 1872 it had adopted a sweeping Amnesty Act, which pardoned most of the remaining rebels and left only five hundred barred from political officeholding. In 1875 Congress passed a Civil Rights Act, partly as a tribute to the recently deceased Charles Sumner, purporting to guarantee black people equal accommodations in public places, such as inns and theaters, but the bill was watered down and contained no effective provisions for enforcement. (The Supreme Court later struck down this law; see page 562.)

A General Amnesty

Democrats regained power in the South rather quickly, redeeming control of state governments in four states before 1872 and in a total of eight by January 1876 (see Map 16.1). In the North Democrats successfully stressed the failure and scandals of Reconstruction governments. As opinion shifted, historian Brooks Adams, the grandson and great-grandson of presidents, published an article condemning the enfranchisement of blacks as "a wholesale creation of the most ignorant mass of voters to be found in the civilized world." Many Republicans sensed that their constituents were tiring of southern issues and the legacies of the war. Despite the consequences for the freedpeople, sectional reconciliation now seemed crucial for commerce. The nation was expanding westward rapidly, and the South was a new frontier for investment.

Both industrialization and immigration were surging, hastening the pace of change in national life. Within only eight years, postwar industrial production increased by an impressive 75 percent. For the first time, nonagricultural workers outnumbered farmers, and only Britain's industrial output was greater than that of the United States. Government financial policies did much to bring about this rapid growth. Soon after the war Congress used a portion of tax revenues to pay off the interest-bearing war debt: the debt fell from $2.33 billion in 1866 to only $587 million in 1893, and every dollar repaid was a dollar injected into the economy for potential reinvestment. Low taxes on investment and high tariffs on manufactured goods also aided industrialists. With such help, the northern economy quickly recovered its prewar rate of growth.

Reconciliation and Industrial Expansion

Between 1865 and 1873, 3 million new immigrants entered the country, most of them joining the labor force of industrial cities in the North and West. As the number of immigrants rose, a corresponding revival of suspicion and hostility among native-born Americans took place. Also prominent was the question of how Utah's growing Mormon community, which practiced polygamy, could be reconciled to American law.

Then the Panic of 1873 ushered in over five years of economic contraction. Three million people lost their jobs, and the clash between labor and capital became the major issue of the day (see Chapter 18). Class attitudes diverged, especially in the large cities. Debtors and the unemployed sought easy money policies to spur economic expansion (workers and farmers desperately needed cash). Businessmen, disturbed by the widespread strikes and industrial violence that accompanied the panic, became increasingly concerned about the defense of property.

Class conflict fueled a monetary issue: whether paper money—the Civil War greenbacks—should be kept in circulation. In 1872 Democratic farmers and debtors urged this policy to expand the money supply and raise prices, but businessmen, bankers, and creditors overruled them. Now hard times swelled the ranks of the "greenbackers"—voters who favored easy money.

Greenbacks Versus Sound Money

Congress voted in 1874 to increase the number of greenbacks in circulation, but Grant vetoed the bill in deference to the opinions of financial leaders. The next year, "sound money" interests prevailed in Congress, winning passage of a law requiring that greenbacks be convertible into gold after 1878. The chasm between farmers and workers and wealthy industrialists grew even wider.

In international affairs, there was renewed pressure for, and controversy about, expansion (see Chapter 22).

Foreign Expansion

In 1867 Secretary of State William H. Seward arranged a vast addition of territory to the national domain through the purchase of Alaska from the Russian government for $7.2 million. Opponents ridiculed Seward's venture, calling Alaska Frigidia, the Polar Bear Garden, and Walrussia. But Seward convinced important congressmen of Alaska's economic potential, and other lawmakers favored the dawning of friendship with Russia.

Also in 1867 the United States took control of the Midway Islands, a thousand miles from Hawai'i. And in 1870 President Grant tried unsuccessfully to annex the Dominican Republic. Seward and his successor, Hamilton Fish, also resolved troubling Civil War grievances against Great Britain. Through diplomacy they arranged a financial settlement of claims on Britain for damage done by the *Alabama* and other cruisers built in England and sold to the Confederacy (see page 616).

Meanwhile, the Supreme Court played its part in the northern retreat from Reconstruction. During the

Judicial Retreat from Reconstruction

Civil War the Court had been cautious and inactive. Reaction to the *Dred Scott* decision (1857) had been so violent, and the Union's wartime emergency so great, that the Court avoided interference with government actions. The justices breathed a collective sigh of relief, for example, when legal technicalities prevented them from reviewing the case of Clement Vallandigham, a Democratic opponent of Lincoln's war effort, who had been convicted by a military tribunal of aiding the enemy. But in 1866 a similar case, *Ex parte Milligan*, reached the Court through proper channels.

Lambdin P. Milligan of Indiana had plotted to free Confederate prisoners of war and overthrow state governments. For these acts a military court sentenced Milligan, a civilian, to death. Milligan challenged the authority of the military tribunal, claiming that he had a right to a civil trial. The Supreme Court declared that military trials were illegal when civil courts were open and functioning, and its language indicated that the Court intended to reassert its authority.

In the 1870s the Court successfully renewed its challenge to Congress's actions when it narrowed the meaning and effectiveness of the Fourteenth Amendment. The *Slaughter-House* cases (1873) began in 1869, when the Louisiana legislature granted one company a monopoly on the slaughtering of livestock in New Orleans. Rival butchers in the city promptly sued. Their attorney, former Supreme Court justice John A. Campbell, argued that Louisiana had violated the rights of some of its citizens in favor of others. The Fourteenth Amendment, Campbell contended, had revolutionized the constitutional system by bringing individual rights under federal protection. Campbell thus articulated an original goal of the Republican Party: to nationalize civil rights and guard them from state interference.

But in the *Slaughter-House* decision, the Supreme Court dealt a stunning blow to the scope and vitality of the Fourteenth Amendment. Refusing to accept Campbell's argument, it interpreted the "privileges and immunities" of citizens so narrowly that it reduced them almost to trivialities. State citizenship and national citizenship were separate, the Court declared. National citizenship involved only matters such as the right to travel freely from state to state and to use the navigable waters of the nation, and only these narrow rights were protected by the Fourteenth Amendment.

The Supreme Court also concluded that the butchers who sued had not been deprived of their rights or property in violation of the due-process clause of the amendment. Shrinking from a role as "perpetual censor upon all legislation of the States, on the civil rights of their own citizens," the Court's majority declared that the framers of the recent amendments had not intended to "destroy" the federal system, in which the states exercised "powers for domestic and local government, including the regulation of civil rights." Thus the justices severely limited the amendment's potential for securing and protecting the rights of black citizens—its original intent.

The next day the Court decided *Bradwell v. Illinois*, a case in which Myra Bradwell, a female attorney, had been denied the right to practice law in Illinois on account of her gender. Pointing to the Fourteenth Amendment, Bradwell's attorneys contended that the state had unconstitutionally abridged her "privileges and immunities" as a citizen. The Supreme Court rejected her claim, alluding to women's traditional role in the home.

In 1876 the Court weakened the Reconstruction era amendments even further by emasculating the enforcement clause of the Fourteenth Amendment and revealing deficiencies inherent in the Fifteenth Amendment. In *U.S. v. Cruikshank* the Court overruled the conviction under the 1870 Enforcement Act of Louisiana whites who had attacked a meeting of blacks and conspired to deprive them of their rights. The justices ruled that the Fourteenth Amendment did not give the federal government power to act against these whites. The duty of protecting citizens' equal rights, the Court said, "rests alone with the States." Such judicial conservatism had profound impact down through the next century, as the revolutionary potential in the Civil War amendments was blunted, if not destroyed.

As the 1876 elections approached, most political observers saw that the North was no longer willing to pursue the goals of Reconstruction.

Disputed Election of 1876 and the Compromise of 1877

The results of a disputed presidential election confirmed this fact. Samuel J. Tilden, the Democratic governor of New York, ran strongly in the South and needed only one more electoral vote to triumph over Rutherford B. Hayes, the Republican nominee. Nineteen electoral votes from Louisiana, South Carolina, and Florida (the only southern states yet "unredeemed" by Democratic rule) were disputed; both Democrats and Republicans claimed to have won

in those states despite fraud committed by their opponents. One vote from Oregon was undecided because of a technicality (see Map 16.2).

To resolve this unprecedented situation, on which the Constitution gave little guidance, Congress established a fifteen-member electoral commission. In the interest of impartiality, membership on the commission was to be balanced between Democrats and Republicans. But one independent Republican, Supreme Court Justice David Davis, refused appointment in order to accept his election as a senator. A regular Republican took his place, and the Republican Party prevailed 8 to 7 on every attempt to count the returns, along strict party lines. Hayes would become president if Congress accepted the commission's findings.

Congressional acceptance was not certain. Democrats controlled the House and could filibuster to block action on the vote. Many citizens worried that the nation had entered a major constitutional crisis and would slip once again into civil war, as some southerners vowed "Tilden or Fight." The crisis was resolved when Democrats acquiesced in the election of Hayes based on a "deal" cut in a Washington hotel. Negotiations took place between Hayes's supporters and southerners who wanted federal aid to railroads, internal improvements, federal patronage, and removal of troops from southern states. Neither party was well enough organized to implement and enforce the various parts of this bargain between the sections. Northern and southern Democrats simply decided they could not win and did not contest the election of a Republican who was not going to continue Reconstruction. Thus Hayes became president, inaugurated privately inside the White House to avoid any threat of violence, southerners relished their promises of economic aid, and Reconstruction was unmistakably over.

Southern Democrats rejoiced, but African Americans grieved over the betrayal of their hopes for equality. Tens of thousands considered leaving the South, where real freedom was no longer a possibility. "[We asked] whether it was possible we could stay under a people who had held us in bondage," said Henry Adams, who led a migration to Kansas. In South Carolina, Louisiana, Mississippi, and other southern states, thousands gathered up their possessions and migrated to Kansas. They were known as Exodusters, disappointed people still searching for their share in the American dream. Even in Kansas they met disillusionment, as the welcome extended by

Map 16.2 Presidential Election of 1876 and the Compromise of 1877   In 1876 a combination of solid southern support and Democratic gains in the North gave Samuel Tilden the majority of popular votes, but Rutherford B. Hayes won the disputed election in the electoral college, after a deal satisfied Democratic wishes for an end to Reconstruction.

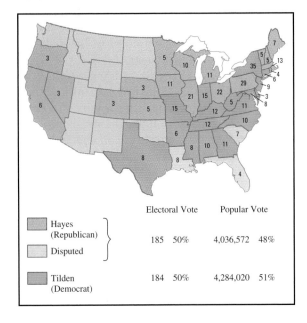

	Electoral Vote		Popular Vote	
Hayes (Republican)	185	50%	4,036,572	48%
Disputed				
Tilden (Democrat)	184	50%	4,284,020	51%

Betrayal of Black Rights and the Exodusters

These cartoons reveal the North's readiness to give up on a strong Reconstruction policy. According to the images on the left, only federal bayonets could support the "rule or ruin" carpetbag regimes that oppressed the South. What do the background and foreground of the cartoon on the right suggest will be the results of President Hayes's "Let 'Em Alone Policy"?   (Library of Congress)

the state's governor soon gave way to hostile public reactions.

Blacks now had to weigh their options, which were not much wider than they had ever been. The Civil War had brought emancipation, and Reconstruction had guaranteed their rights under law. But events and attitudes in larger white America were foreboding. In a Fourth of July speech in Washington, D.C., in 1875, Frederick Douglass anticipated this predicament. He reflected anxiously on the American centennial to be celebrated the following year. The nation, Douglass feared, would "lift to the sky its million voices in one grand Centennial hosanna of peace and good will to all the white race . . . from gulf to lakes and from sea to sea." Douglass looked back on fifteen years of unparalleled change for his people and worried about the hold of white supremacy on America's historical memory: "If war among the whites brought peace and liberty to the blacks, what will peace among the whites bring?" Douglass's question would echo down through American political culture for decades.

Summary

 Reconstruction left a contradictory record. It was an era of tragic aspirations and failures, but also of unprecedented legal, political, and social change. The Union victory brought about an increase in federal power, stronger nationalism, sweeping federal intervention in the southern states, and landmark amendments to the Constitution. But northern commitment to make these changes endure had eroded, and the revolution remained unfinished.

By 1876 in South Carolina, Wade Hampton ran successfully for governor, relying on a campaign of terror and intimidation carried out by his "Red Shirt" followers, crushing the black vote in many counties and ending Republican rule. Robert Smalls, however, managed to stay in office despite Democratic Party efforts to oust him. He won his final congressional election in 1884 against the viciously racist "Pitchfork" Ben Tillman. After leaving Congress, Smalls served from 1890 until 1913 as customs collector in his native Beaufort.

The North embraced emancipation, black suffrage, and constitutional alterations strengthening the central government. But it did so to defeat the rebellion and secure the peace. As the pressure of these crises declined, strong underlying continuities emerged and placed their mark on Reconstruction. The American people and the courts maintained a preference for state authority and a distrust of federal power. The ideology of free labor dictated that property should be respected and that individuals should be self-reliant. Racism endured and transformed into the even more virulent forms of Klan terror and theories that freedom would send blacks as a race back toward "barbarism." Concern for the human rights of African Americans was strongest when their plight threatened to undermine the interests of whites, and reform frequently had less appeal than moneymaking in an individualistic, enterprising society.

A host of other issues had arisen from industrialization. How would the country develop its immense resources in an increasingly interconnected national economy? How would farmers, industrial workers, immigrants, and capitalists fit into the new social system? Industrialization not only promised a higher standard of living but wrought increased exploitation of labor. Moreover, industry increased the nation's power and laid the foundation for an enlarged American role in international affairs. The American imagination again turned to the conquest of new frontiers.

In the wake of the Civil War Americans faced two profound tasks—the achievement of healing and the dispensing of justice. Both had to occur, but they never developed in historical balance. Making sectional reunion compatible with black freedom and equality overwhelmed the imagination in American political culture, and the nation still faced much of this dilemma more than a century later.

LEGACY FOR A PEOPLE AND A NATION
The Fourteenth Amendment

Before the Civil War, no definition of civil rights existed in America. Reconstruction legislation, especially the Fourteenth Amendment, changed that forever. Approved by Congress in 1866, the Fourteenth Amendment enshrined in the Constitution the ideas of birthright citizenship and equal rights. The Fourteenth Amendment was designed to secure and protect the rights of the freedpeople. But over time, the "equal protection of the law" clause became one of the most important and malleable provisions in the Constitution. It has been used at times to support the rights of states, cities, corporations, immigrants, women, religious organizations, gays and lesbians, students, and labor unions. It has advanced both tolerance and intolerance, affirmative action and anti-affirmative action programs. It provides the legal wellspring for the generations-old civil rights movement in the United States.

The amendment as originally written required individuals to pursue grievances through private litigation, alleging state denial of a claimed federal right. At first the Supreme Court interpreted it conservatively, especially on racial matters, and by 1900 the idea of color-blind liberty in America was devastated by Jim Crow laws, disfranchisement, and unpunished mob violence.

But Progressive reformers used the equal protection clause to advocate government support of health, union organizing, municipal housing, a progressive income tax, and the protection of woman and child laborers. In the 1920s and 1930s, a judicial defense of civil liberties and free speech took hold, especially from Justice Louis Brandeis. The Supreme Court expanded the amendment's guarantee of equality by a series of decisions upholding the rights of immigrant groups to resist "forced Americanization," especially Catholics in their creation of parochial schools. And, from its inception in 1910, the NAACP waged a long campaign to reveal the inequality of racial segregation in schooling and every other kind of public facility. Led by Charles Houston and Thurgood Marshall, this epic legal battle culminated in the *Brown v. Board of Education* desegregation decision of 1954. In the multilayered Civil Rights Act of 1964, the equal protection tradition was reenshrined into American law. Since 1964 Americans have lived in a society where the Fourteenth Amendment's legacy is the engine of expanded liberty for women and all minorities, as well as a political battleground for defining the nature and limits of human equality, and for redistributing justice long denied.

For Further Reading, see page A-20 of the Appendix. For Web resources, go to http://college.hmco.com.

THE DEVELOPMENT OF THE WEST 1877–1900

In 1893 a young historian named Frederick Jackson Turner delivered a stunning scholarly paper at the Columbian Exposition in Chicago. In it, Turner expounded a theory that would occupy the textbooks of high school and college students for several generations. Titled "The Significance of the Frontier in American History," the paper argued the "frontier thesis" that the existence of "free land, its continuous recession, and the advancement of American settlement westward" had created a distinctively American spirit of democracy and egalitarianism. The conquest of a succession of frontier Wests, in other words, explained American progress and character.

At a covered arena just across the street from this same world's fair, the folk character Buffalo Bill Cody staged two performances daily of an extravaganza he called the "Wild West." Though Cody also dramatized the conquest of frontiers, his perspective differed markedly from Turner's. While Turner described the relatively peaceful settlement of largely empty western land, Cody portrayed violent conquest of territory formerly occupied by savage Indians. Turner's heroes were persevering farmers who tamed the wilderness with axes and plows. Buffalo Bill's heroes were rugged scouts who braved danger and defeated Indians with rifles and bullets. Turner used images of log cabins, wagon trains, and wheat fields to argue that the western frontier fashioned a new, progressive race. Cody, who used a cast of actual Indians and soldiers (plus himself) to stage scenes of Indian attacks and clashes between native warriors and white cavalry, depicted the West as a place of brutal aggression and heroic victory.

In spite of their contradictions, exaggerations, and inaccuracies, both Turner and Cody were to some degree correct. The American West inspired material and cultural progress, and it also witnessed the forceful domination of one group of humans over another and over the environment. Both Turner and Cody believed that by the 1890s the era of the frontier had come to an end. In fact, Turner's essay had been sparked by an announcement from the superintendent of the 1890 cen-

This painting (1874) by Thomas Moran shows an American Indian dwarfed but not threatened by nature. The interaction of humans with the environment provided the major themes of western history in the nineteenth century. (Detail of *Cliffs of Green River,* Thomas Moran, oil on canvas, 1874, 1975.28. Copyright Amon Carter Museum, Fort Worth, Texas)

The Economic Activities of Native Peoples
The Transformation of Native Cultures
The Extraction of Natural Resources
Irrigation and Transportation
Farming the Plains
The Ranching Frontier
LEGACY FOR A PEOPLE AND A NATION
The West and Rugged Individualism

sus that "at present the unsettled area [of the West] has been so broken into by isolated bodies of settlement that there can be hardly said to be a frontier line." Over time, Turner's theory was abandoned (even by Turner himself) as too simplistic, and Buffalo Bill was relegated to the gallery of rogues and showmen (though he subsequently became an advocate of irrigated farming). Even so, both of the Wests that they depicted persist in the romance of American history, while the real story of western development in the late nineteenth century is much more complex than either myth.

One fact is certain. Much of the West was never empty, and those who inhabited it utilized its resources in quite different ways. Indians had managed the environment and sustained their needs for centuries before white settlers arrived on the scene. The Pawnees of the Plains, for example, planted crops in the spring, left their fields to hunt buffalo, then returned for harvesting. They sometimes battled with Cheyennes and Arapahos, who wanted hunting grounds and crops for their own purposes. Pawnee technology was simple. Though they sometimes splurged when feasting on buffalo, they survived by developing and using natural resources in limited ways. Concepts of private property and profit had little meaning for them.

For white Americans, however, expanses of land and water were assets to be utilized for economic gain. As whites settled the West in the late nineteenth century, they exploited the environment for profit far more extensively than did the Indians. They excavated deep into the earth to remove valuable minerals, cut down forests for lumber to construct homes and other buildings, built railroads to carry goods and link markets, and dammed the rivers and plowed the soil with machines to grow crops. Their goal was not survival; rather, it was buying and selling and opening markets nationally and internationally. As they transformed the landscape, the triumph of their market economies transformed the entire nation.

The West, which by 1870 referred to the vast area between the Mississippi River and the Pacific Ocean, actually consisted of several regions and a variety of economic potential. Abundant rainfall along the Pacific Coast fed huge forests. Farther south into California woodlands and grasslands existed, with fertile valleys capable of supporting vegetable fields and orange groves. Eastward, between the Cascade and Sierra Mountains and the Rocky Mountains where gold, silver, and other minerals lay buried, was an arid, desolate plateau that descended into the hot desert of

southeastern California and western Arizona. On the eastern side of the Rockies were the Great Plains, divided into a semiarid western side of few trees and tough buffalo grass and an eastern area of ample rainfall and tall grasses. The Plains could support grain crops and livestock.

Much of this territory had long been the scene of great migrations. Before contact with whites, thousands of Indian peoples had moved around and through the region. As they searched for food and shelter, they warred, traded, and sometimes negotiated with one another. In parts of the Southwest, Hispanics had built towns, farms, and ranches. But after the Civil War, white people flooded into the West overwhelming the native peoples. Between 1870 and 1890, the population living in the region swelled from 7 million to nearly 17 million.

The abundance of exploitable land, food, and raw materials in the West filled white Americans with faith that anyone eager and persistent enough could succeed. But this self-confidence rested on a belief that white people were somehow special, and individual advantage often asserted itself at the expense of people of color and the poor, as well as the environment. Americans rarely thought about conserving resources because there always seemed to be more territory to exploit and bring into the market economy.

By 1890 farms, ranches, mines, towns, and cities could be found in almost every corner of the present-day continental United States. Though of great symbolic importance, the fading of the frontier had little direct impact on people's behavior, for vast stretches of land remained unsettled. Pioneers who failed in one locale rarely starved to death; they moved on and tried again somewhere else. Although life in the West was less than comfortable, expanses of seemingly uninhabited land gave Americans the feeling that they would always have a second chance. It was this belief in an infinity of second chances, more than Turner's theory of frontier democracy or Cody's reenactments of western battles, that left a deep imprint on the American character. ∎

The Economic Activities of Native Peoples

 Historians once defined the American frontier as "the edge of the unused," implying, as Frederick Jackson Turner had, that the frontier disappeared once white men and women arrived to occupy supposedly open

IMPORTANT EVENTS

1862 Homestead Act grants free land to citizens who live on and improve the land

Morrill Land Grant Act gives states public lands to finance agricultural and industrial colleges

1864 Chivington's militia massacres Black Kettle's Cheyennes at Sand Creek

1872 Yellowstone becomes first national park

1873 Barbed wire invented, enabling western farmers to enclose and protect fields cheaply

1876 Sioux annihilate Custer's federal troops at Little Big Horn

1877 Nez Percé Indians under Young Joseph surrender to U.S. troops

1878 Timber and Stone Act allows citizens to buy timber land cheaply but also enables large companies to acquire huge tracts of forestland

1879 Utes surrender after resisting territorial concessions in western Colorado

Carlisle School for Indians established in Pennsylvania

Colorado creates water divisions to regulate water rights

1880–81 Manypenny's *Our Indian Wards* and Jackson's *A Century of Dishonor* influence public conscience about poor government treatment of Indians

1881 Shootout at OK Corral between Clantons and Earps

1881–82 Chinese Exclusion Acts prohibit Chinese immigration to the U.S.

1883 National time zones standardized

1884 U.S. Supreme Court first defines Indians as wards under government protection

1887 Dawes Severalty Act ends communal ownership of Indian lands and grants land allotments to individual Native American families.

Hatch Act provides for agricultural experiment stations in every state

California passes law permitting farmers to organize into districts that would sponsor the construction and operation of irrigation projects

1887–88 Devastating winter on Plains destroys countless livestock and forces farmers into economic hardship

1889 Statehood granted to North Dakota, South Dakota, Washington, and Montana

1890 Final suppression of Plains Indians by U.S. Army at Wounded Knee

Census Bureau announces closing of the frontier

Statehood granted to Wyoming and Idaho

Yosemite National Park established

Wyoming makes its rivers public property subject to state supervision

1892 Muir helps found Sierra Club

1893 Turner presents "frontier thesis" at Columbian Exposition

1896 Rural Free Delivery made available

Statehood granted to Utah

1902 Newlands Reclamation Act passed

land for farming or the building of cities. Scholars now acknowledge that Native Americans had settled and developed the West long before other Americans migrated there. Neither passive nor powerless in the face of nature, Indians had been shaping their environment—for better and for worse—for centuries. Nevertheless, almost all native economic systems weakened in the late nineteenth century. Why and how did these declines happen?

Western Indian cultures varied. Some Indians lived in permanent settlements; others moved their camps and villages. Seldom completely isolated, most Indians were participants and recipients in a large-scale flow of goods, culture, language, and disease carried by migrating bands who moved from one region to another. But regardless of their type of settlement, all Indians based their

Subsistence Cultures

The horses, sometimes numbering more than one hundred, and the women and children, usually twenty or thirty, were a liability as well as a help to a Plains Indian camp. The horses competed with buffalo for valuable pasturage, and the women and children made camps vulnerable when white soldiers attacked. (Denver Public Library, Western History Division)

economies to differing degrees on four activities: crop raising; livestock raising; hunting, fishing, and gathering; and trading and raiding. Corn was the most common crop; sheep and horses, acquired from Spanish colonizers, were the livestock; and buffalo (American bison) were the primary prey of hunts. Indians raided one another for food, tools, hides, and horses, which in turn they used in trading with other Indians and with whites. They also attacked one another to avenge wrongs and to displace competitors from hunting grounds. To achieve their standards of living, Indians tried to balance their economic systems. When a buffalo hunt failed, they could subsist on crops. When their crops failed, they could still hunt buffalo and steal food and horses in a raid or trade livestock and furs for necessities.

For Indians on the Great Plains, whether they were nomads such as the Lakotas or village dwellers such as the Pawnees, everyday life focused on the buffalo. They cooked and preserved buffalo meat; fashioned hides into clothing, shoes, and blankets; used sinew for thread and bowstrings; and carved tools from bones and horns. Buffalo were so valuable to them that the Pawnees and Lakotas often came into conflict over access to herds. The Plains Indians also depended on horses, which they used for transportation and hunt-

ing, and as symbols of wealth. To provide food for their herds, Pawnees and other Plains Indians altered the environment by periodically setting fire to tall-grass prairies. The fires burned away dead plants, facilitating the growth of new grass in the spring so horses could feed all summer.

In the Southwest, Indians were herders and placed great value on sheep, goats, and horses. Old Man Hat, a Navajo, explained, "The herd is money. . . . You know that you have some good clothing; the sheep gave you that. And you've just eaten different kinds of food; the sheep gave that food to you. Everything comes from the sheep." He was not speaking of money in a business sense, though. To the Navajos, the herds provided status and security. Like many Indians, the Navajos emphasized generosity and distrusted private property and wealth. Within the family, sharing was expected; outside the family, gifts and reciprocity governed personal relations. Southwestern Indians, too, altered the environment, building elaborate irrigation systems to maximize use of scarce water supplies.

What buffalo were to the Plains Indians and sheep were to Southwestern Indians, salmon were to Indians of the Northwest. Before the mid-nineteenth century, the Columbia River and its tributaries supported the densest population of native peoples in North America, all of whom fished the river for salmon in the summer and stored dried fish for the winter. The Clatsops, Klamathets, and S'Klallam applied their own technology of stream diversion, platform construction over the water, and special baskets to better harvest fish. Like natives of other regions, many of these Indians also traded for horses, buffalo robes, beads, cloth, and knives.

On the Plains and in parts of the Southwest, this native world began to dissolve after 1850 when whites entered the West and competed with Indians for access to and control over natural resources. Perceiving the buffalo and the Indians as hindrances to their ambitions, whites endeavored to eliminate both. Railroads sponsored hunts in which eastern sportsmen shot at the bulky targets from slow-moving trains. The army distributed ammunition to hunters and refused to enforce treaties that reserved hunting grounds for exclusive Indian use. Some hunters collected from $1 to $3 from tanneries for hides that were sent east to be used mainly as belts to drive industrial machinery; others did not even stop to pick up their kill.

Slaughter of Buffalo

Unbeknownst to both Indians and whites, however, a complex combination of circumstances had already doomed the buffalo before the slaughter of the late 1800s. Indians themselves were contributing to the depletion of the herds by increasing their kills, especially to obtain hides for trade with whites and other Indians. Also, a period of generally dry years in the 1840s and 1850s had forced Indians to set up camps in more fertile river basins, where they competed with buffalo for space and water. As a result, the bison were pushed out of important grazing territory and faced threats of starvation. When whites arrived on the Plains, they too sought to settle in the same river basin areas, thereby further forcing buffalo away from nutritious grasslands. At the same time, lethal animal diseases such as anthrax and brucellosis, brought in by white-owned livestock, were decimating buffalo, many of whom had been weakened by malnutrition and drought. The increased numbers of horses, oxen, and sheep owned by white newcomers, as well as by some Indians, also upset the grazing patterns of the bison by devouring grasses that buffalo depended on at certain times of the year. In sum, a convergence of human and environmental shocks created vulnerability among the buffalo to which the mass killing only struck the final blow. By the 1880s only a few hundred remained of the estimated 25 million bison that had existed in 1820.

In the Northwest, the basic wild source of Indian food supply, salmon, suffered a similar fate as the buffalo, but for different reasons. In the Lower Columbia and Willamette River valleys, diseases such as smallpox and malaria, caught from white explorers and fur traders, by the 1870s had decimated some two-thirds of northwestern Indian populations. As a result, fewer Indians were fishing for salmon. But as white commercial fishermen and canneries moved into the region, they greatly diminished the salmon runs on the Columbia by the 1880s. Increasing numbers of salmon running up the river to spawn were being caught before they laid their eggs so that the fish supply was not being replenished. By the twentieth century, the construction of dams on the river and its tributaries further impeded the salmon's ability to reproduce. The government protected Indian fishing rights on the river and hatcheries helped restore some of the fish supply, but the need for electrical power from dams, combined with depletion of the salmon from overfishing and pollution, ended the abundance of this resource in the Northwest.

Decline of Salmon

The Transformation of Native Cultures

Buffalo slaughter and salmon reduction undermined Indian subsistence, but a unique mix of human circumstances contributed as well. For most of the nineteenth century, the white population that migrated into western lands inhabited by Indians was overwhelmingly young and male. In 1870 white men outnumbered white women by three to two in California, two to one in Colorado, and two to one in Dakota Territory. By 1900, preponderances of men remained throughout these places. Most of these males were in their twenties and thirties, unmarried, and at the stage of life when they were most prone to violent behavior. In other words, the whites that Indians were most likely to come into contact with first were explorers, traders, trappers, soldiers, prospectors, and cowboys—almost all of whom possessed guns and had few qualms about using their weapons against animals and humans who got in their way.

Violence

Moreover, these men subscribed to prevailing attitudes that Indians were primitive, lazy, devious, and cruel. Such contempt made exploiting and killing natives all the easier, and violence was often "justified" by

Using buffalo hides to fashion garments, Indians often exhibited artistic skills in decorating their apparel. This Ute Indian hide dress shows symbolic as well as aesthetic representations.   (Denver Art Museum)

claims of preempting threats to life and property. When Indians raided white settlements, they sometimes did mutilate bodies, burn buildings, and kidnap women, acts that were embellished in campfire stories, pamphlets, and popular fiction—all with the result of reinforcing images of Indians as savages. Among the bachelor society of saloons and cabins, men boasted of their exploits in Indian fighting and showed off trophies of scalps and other body parts taken from victims.

Indian warriors also were young, armed, and prone to violence. Sensitive to values of bravery and vengeance, they boasted of fighting white interlopers. But Indian communities contrasted with those of whites in that they contained excesses of women and children, making native bands less mobile and therefore vulnerable to attack. They also were vulnerable to the bad habits of the bachelor white society. Indians copied white behavior of bingeing on cheap whiskey and indulging in prostitution. The syphilis and gonorrhea they contracted from Indian women infected by whites killed many and reduced the ability of natives to reproduce, a consequence that their already declining population could not afford. Thus the age and gender structure of the white frontier population combined with attitudes of racial contempt created a serious threat to Indian existence in the West.

Government policy reinforced individual efforts to remove Indians from the path of white ambitions.

Lack of Native Unity

North American natives were organized not so much into tribes, as whites believed, but rather into hundreds of bands and confederacies in the Plains and towns and villages in the Southwest and Northwest. Some two hundred distinct languages and dialects separated these groups and made it difficult for Indians to unite against white invaders. Although a language group could be defined as a tribe, separate bands and clans within each language group had their own leaders, and seldom did a tribal chief hold significant power. Moreover, bands usually spent more time quarreling among themselves than with white settlers, and sometimes bands from completely different peoples, such as Kiowas and Comanches in the southern Plains, lived together.

Nevertheless, the U.S. government needed some way of categorizing the natives so as to fashion a policy toward them. It did so by imputing more meaning to tribal organization than was warranted. After the Treaty of Greenville in 1795, American officials considered Indian tribes to be separate nations with which they could make treaties that ensured peace and defined boundaries between Indian and white lands. But a chief or chiefs who agreed to a treaty could not guarantee that all bands within the group would abide by it. Moreover, whites seldom accepted treaties as guarantees of the Indians' future land rights. In the Northwest, whites considered treaties protecting Indians' fishing rights at certain sites on the Columbia River to be nuisances and pushed Indians aside from the best locations so they could use their mechanical devices that harvested thousands of fish a day. On the Plains, whites assumed that they could settle wherever they wished, and they rarely hesitated to commandeer choice farmland along river basins. As white settlers pressed into Indian territories, treaties made one week were violated the next.

Territorial Treaties

From the 1860s to the 1880s, the federal government tried to force Indians onto reservations, where, it

Reservation Policy

was thought, they could be "civilized." Reservations usually consisted of those areas of a group's previous territory that were least desirable to whites. When assigning Indians to such parcels, the government promised protection from white encroachment and agreed to provide food, clothing, and other necessities.

The new post–Civil War reservation policy helped make way for the market economy. In the early years of contact in the West, trade had benefited both Indians and whites and had taken place on a nearly equal footing, much as it had between eastern Indians and whites in the years before the American Revolution. Indians had acquired clothing, guns, and horses in return for furs, jewelry, and, sometimes, military service. In the West, however, whites' needs and economic power grew disproportionate to the needs and power of Indians. Indians became more dependent, and whites increasingly dictated what was to be traded and on what terms. For example, white traders persuaded Navajo weavers in the Southwest to produce heavy rugs suitable for eastern customers and to adopt new designs and colors to boost sales. Meanwhile, Navajos raised fewer crops and were forced to buy food because the market economy lured them away from subsistence agriculture. Soon they were selling their land and labor to whites as well, which made it easier to force them onto reservations.

Reservation policy had degrading consequences. First, Indians had no say over their own affairs on reservations. Supreme Court decisions in 1884 and 1886 defined them as wards (falling, like helpless children, under government protection) and denied them the right to become U.S. citizens. Thus they were unprotected by the Fourteenth and Fifteenth Amendments,

Reformers established boarding schools to take Indian children off the reservations and teach them a new and allegedly better culture. As one white leader remarked, "They should be educated, not as Indians, but as Americans." At the Carlisle School in Pennsylvania, one of twenty-four such schools, Sioux youths *(left)* received new attire to make them look *(right)* as their teachers wanted them to look. (Smithsonian Institute, Washington, D.C.)

which had extended to African Americans the privileges and legal protections of citizenship. Second, pressure from white farmers, miners, and herders who continually sought Indian lands for their own purposes made it difficult for the government to preserve reservations intact. Third, the government ignored native history, even combining on the same reservation Indian bands that habitually had waged war against each other. Rather than serving as civilizing communities, reservations weakened every aspect of Indian life, except the resolve of some to survive.

Not all Indians succumbed to market forces and reservation restrictions. Pawnees in the Midwest, for

Native Resistance

example, resisted extensive trading and the disadvantageous deals that whites tried to impose on them. And some natives tried to preserve their cultures even as they became dependent on whites. Pawnees, for example, agreed to leave their Nebraska homelands for a reservation in the hope that they could hunt buffalo and grow corn as they once had done.

As they had done earlier in the East, whites responded to western Indian recalcitrance and revolt with organized military aggression.

Indian Wars

In 1864, for example, in order to eliminate Indians who blocked white ambitions in the Sand Creek region of Colorado, a militia force led by Methodist minister John Chivington attacked a Cheyenne band under Black Kettle, killing almost everyone. In 1877 four detachments of troops, aided by Crow and Cheyenne scouts, chased eight hundred Nez Percé Indians over rugged terrain in the Northwest, finally surrounding and killing many before one of their leaders, Young Joseph, surrendered. In 1879 four thousand U.S. soldiers mobilized and forced a surrender from Utes, who already had given up most of their ancestral territory in western Colorado but were resisting further concessions.

The most infamous of Indian battles occurred in June 1876 when 2,500 Lakotas led by Chiefs Rain-in-the-Face, Sitting Bull, and Crazy Horse surrounded and annihilated 256 government troops led by the rash Colonel George A. Custer near the Little Big Horn River in southern Montana. Though Indians consistently demonstrated military skill in such battles, shortages of supplies and relentless pursuit by U.S. soldiers, who often utilized Indian scouts from an enemy tribe, eventually overwhelmed armed Indian resistance. Native Americans were not so much conquered in battle as they were starved into submission.

By the 1870s and 1880s, government officials and reformers sought more peaceful means of dealing with western natives. Instead of being

Reform of Indian Policy

considered foreign nations, Indians would be "civilized" and "uplifted" through landholding and education. This meant changing their identities, community structures, and relationships to the federal government. With government encouragement, white missionaries and teachers would attempt to persuade Native Americans to adopt values of the new American work ethic: ambition, thrift, and materialism. To achieve this transformation, however, Indians would have to abandon their traditional cultures. Also, reform treaties—George Manypenny's *Our Indian Wards* (1880) and Helen Hunt Jackson's *A Century of Dishonor* (1881), for example—and unfavorable comparison with Canada's management of Indian affairs aroused the American conscience. Canada had granted native peoples the rights of British subjects, and the Royal Mounted Police defended them against whites. Canadian officials were more tolerant and proceeded more slowly than Americans in efforts to acculturate Indians. A high rate of intermarriage between Indians and Canadian whites also promoted smoother relations.

In the United States, the two most active Indian reform organizations were the Women's National Indian Association (WNIA) and the Indian Rights Association (IRA). The WNIA, composed mainly of white women who sought to use women's domestic skills to help people in need, urged gradual assimilation of Indians. The IRA, which was more influential but numbered few Native Americans among its members, supported citizenship and landholding by individual Indians. Most reformers believed Indians were culturally inferior to whites and assumed Indians could succeed economically only if they adopted middle-class values of diligence, monogamy, and education.

Reformers particularly deplored Indians' sexual division of labor. Women seemed to do all the work—tending crops, raising children, cooking, curing hides, making tools and clothes—and to be servile to men, who hunted but were otherwise idle. Ignoring the fact that white men were not always considerate of white women, groups such as the WNIA and IRA wanted Indian men to bear more responsibilities, to treat Indian women more respectfully, and to resemble male heads of white middle-class households. But because these groups often tried to coax Indian men and

How do historians know...

that Indians expressed values and messages in nonverbal ways? The Plains Indians did not write books or letters as whites did, but they did tell stories and spread news through art. Plains Indians painted scenes on buffalo hides and, later, in notebooks that they acquired from whites, a form of artwork called ledger drawings. These illustrations not only depict scenes but, together, also tell a story with motion, drama, and message almost as a motion picture might today. The drawings also conveyed important information such as directions to new campsites, the location of enemy bands, and messages of love. Look at the drawing reproduced here. It was painted in the 1870s by a Cheyenne named Howling Wolf, who signed his work not in letters but with a symbol of a wolf with its mouth open in a howl. Howling Wolf made himself the hero of the scene, identified by the line drawn from the wolf to the warrior on the left. The discharging pistol hanging in midair and the blood pouring from the enemy's chest and mouth show that Howling Wolf has earlier wounded his adversary, and the path of hoof prints shows the movement of the battle. With his gun back in his belt, Howling Wolf holds a long spear that has dislodged his opponent from his horse, and victory clearly is imminent. Within the limits of a small page, Howling Wolf has described his own heroic exploits with an active narrative. But he has also left an indication of how highly Cheyenne culture esteemed bravery and individual male conquest, how important guns and horses were to Indian combat, and how Indians dressed and prepared for battle.

Ledger drawings represent one of several ways that historians can discover cultural aspects of people who did not produce written records. Other forms of evidence include artwork such as the totems of Pacific Northwest Indians and oral testimonies from southwestern and Plains Indians. (Photo: Allen Memorial Art Museum, Oberlin College, Oberlin, Ohio)

women into adopting a model of white society, in which women were supposed to be submissive and private, Indian women lost much of the power over daily life as well as the economic independence that they once had.

In 1887 Congress reversed its reservation policy and passed the Dawes Severalty Act. The act, which achieved a goal long recommended by reformers, authorized dissolution of community-owned Indian property and granted land allotments to individual Native American families.

Dawes Severalty Act

The land was held in trust by the government for twenty-five years so the families could not sell their allotments. The act also awarded citizenship to all who accepted allotments (though an act of Congress in 1906 delayed citizenship for those Indians who had not taken their allotment). It also entitled the government to sell unallocated land to whites.

Indian policy, as carried out by the Interior Department, now took on two main features, both of which aimed at assimilating Indians into European and white American forms of culture. First and foremost, as required by the Dawes Act, the federal government

Attempts at Assimilation distributed reservation land to individual families in the belief that the American institution of private property would fashion good citizens and integrate Indians into the larger society. Second, officials believed that Indians would abandon their "barbaric" habits more quickly if their children were educated in boarding schools away from the reservations.

The Dawes Act reflected the Euro-American and Christian world-view, an earnest but narrow belief that a society of families headed by men was the most desired model. The reformers were deeply religious people who had long believed, as one expressed in 1887, that "civilization and the Gospel go hand in hand." They were joined by professional educators who viewed schools as tools to create a well-integrated, patriotic, industrial nation. Using the model of Hampton Institute, founded in Virginia in 1869 for the education of newly freed slaves, educators helped establish the Carlisle School in Pennsylvania in 1879, which served as the flagship of the government's Indian school system. In keeping with Euro-American custom, the boarding schools sought to impose white-defined sex roles: boys were taught farming and carpentry while girls learned sewing, cleaning, and cooking.

In 1890 the government made one last show of force—though such a demonstration was hardly necessary. With active resistance having **Ghost Dance** been suppressed, some Lakotas and other groups turned to the new religion of the Ghost Dance as a spiritual means of preserving native culture. Inspired by a Paiute prophet named Wovoka, the Ghost Dance involved movement in a circle until the dancers reached a trancelike state and envisioned dead ancestors. Some dancers believed these ancestral visitors heralded a day when buffalo would return to the plains and all elements of white civilization, including guns and whiskey, would be buried. The Ghost Dance expressed this messianic vision in a ritual involving several days of dancing and meditation.

Ghost Dancers forswore violence but appeared aggressive when they donned sacred shirts that they believed would repel the white man's bullets. As the religion spread, government agents became alarmed about the possibility of renewed Indian uprisings. Charging that the cult was anti-Christian, they began arresting Ghost Dancers. Late in 1890, the government sent the Seventh Cavalry, Custer's old regiment, to round up some Lakotas moving from the north toward Pine Ridge, South Dakota. Though the Indians were starving and seeking shelter, the army chose to assume they were armed for revolt. Overtaking the band at a creek called Wounded Knee, the troops massacred an estimated three hundred men, women, and children in the snow.

The Dawes Act effectively accomplished what whites wanted and Indians feared: it reduced native control over land. Eager speculators **The Losing of the West** induced Indians to sell their newly acquired property, in spite of federal safeguards against such practices. Between 1887 and the 1930s, Indian landholdings dwindled from 138 million acres to 52 million. Land-grabbing whites were particularly cruel to the Ojibwas of the northern plains. In 1906 Senator Moses E. Clapp of Minnesota attached to an Indian appropriations bill a rider declaring that mixed-blood adults on the White Earth reservation were "competent" (meaning educated in white ways) enough to sell their land without having to observe the twenty-five-year waiting period stipulated in the Dawes Act. When the bill became law, speculators duped many Ojibwas, whom white experts had declared mixed-bloods on the basis of fraudulent evidence, into signing away their land in return for counterfeit money and worthless merchandise. The Ojibwas lost more than half of their original holdings, and economic ruin overtook them.

The government's policy had other harmful effects on Indians' ways of life. The boarding-school program enrolled thousands of children and tried to teach them that their inherited customs were inferior, but most returned to their families demoralized and confused rather than ready to assimilate into white society. Polingaysi Qoyawayma, a Hopi woman forced to take the Christian name Elizabeth Q. White, recalled after four years spent at the Sherman Institute in Riverside, California, "As a Hopi, I was misunderstood by the white man; as a convert of the missionaries, I was looked upon with suspicion by the Hopi people."

Ultimately, political and ecological crises overwhelmed most western Indian groups. White violence and military superiority alone did not defeat them. Their economic systems had started to break down before the military campaigns occurred. Buffalo extinction, enemy raids, and disease, in addition to force, combined to hobble subsistence culture to the point that Native Americans had no alternative but to yield their lands to market-oriented whites. Believing their culture to be superior, whites determined to transform the Indians into virtuous farmers by teaching them the value of private property, educating them in American ideals, and forcefully eradicating their "backward" languages, lifestyles, and religions. Although Indians tried to retain their culture by both adapting and yielding to the various demands they faced, by the end of the century they had lost control of the land and were under increasing pressure to shed their group identity. The West was won at their expense, and to this day they remain casualties of an aggressive age.

The Extraction of Natural Resources

 In sharp contrast to the Indians, who used land and water mostly to meet subsistence needs, most whites who migrated to the West and the Great Plains, first in the 1850s and increasingly after the Civil War, were driven by the desire to get rich quick. To their eyes, the vast stretches of territory lay as untapped reservoirs of resources and wealth (see Map 17.1). Extraction of these resources advanced settlement and created new markets at home and abroad; it also fueled the revolutions

Map 17.1   The Development and Natural Resources of the West   By 1890 mining, lumbering, and cattle ranching had penetrated many areas west of the Mississippi River, and railroads had linked together the western economy. These characteristics, along with the spread of agriculture, contributed to the Census Bureau's observation that the frontier had disappeared; yet, as the map shows, large areas remained undeveloped.

in transportation, agriculture, and industry that swept the United States in the late nineteenth century. At the same time, extraction of nature's wealth gave rise to wasteful interaction with the environment and fed habits of racial and sexual oppression.

Mining and Lumbering

In the mid-1800s, eager prospectors began to comb western forests and mountains for gold, silver, timber, and copper. The mining frontier advanced rapidly, drawing thousands of people to Nevada, Idaho, Montana, Utah, and Colorado. California, already a thriving state with more than three hundred thousand people by 1860, furnished many of the miners, who traveled from west to east in search of riches. Others followed traditional routes, moving from the East and Midwest to western mining regions.

By the 1880s, large-scale operations had replaced solitary prospectors in the extraction of minerals from western territories. Here, powerful sprays of water are being used to wash silver from a deposit in Alma, Colorado.   (Colorado Historical Society)

Prospectors tended to be restless optimists, willing to climb mountains and trek across deserts in search of a telltale glint of precious metal. They shot game for food and financed their explorations by convincing merchants to advance credit for equipment in return for a share of the as-yet-undiscovered lode. Unlucky prospectors whose credit ran out took jobs and saved up for another search.

Digging for and transporting minerals was extremely expensive, so prospectors who did discover veins of metal seldom mined them. Instead, they sold their claims to large mining syndicates such as the Anaconda Copper Company. Financed by eastern capital, these companies could bring in engineers, heavy machinery, railroad lines, and work crews. Although discoveries of gold and silver first drew attention to the West and its resources, mining companies usually exploited less romantic but equally lucrative bonanzas of lead, zinc, tin, quartz, and copper.

Cutting fir and spruce trees for lumber to be used in construction, another large-scale extractive industry, needed vast tracks of forest land to be profitable. Lumber companies moving into the Northwest grabbed millions of acres under the Timber and Stone Act, passed by Congress in 1878 to stimulate settlement in California, Nevada, Oregon, and Washington. It allowed private citizens to buy, at a low price, 160-acre plots "unfit for cultivation" and "valuable chiefly for timber." Lumber companies hired seamen from waterfront boarding houses to register private claims to timberland and then transfer those claims to the companies. By 1900 private citizens had bought over 3.5 million acres, but most of that land belonged to corporations.

While lumber companies were acquiring timberlands in the Northwest, oil companies were beginning to drill for wells in the Southwest. In 1900 most of the nation's petroleum still came from the Appalachians and the Midwest, but rich oil reserves had been discovered in southern California and eastern Texas. Although oil and kerosene were still used mostly for lubrication and lighting, oil discovered in the Southwest later became a vital new source of fuel.

Women in Mining Regions

Though single white men numerically dominated the western natural-resource frontier, many communities did have substantial populations of white women who had come for the same reason as men: to find a fortune. But on the mining frontier as elsewhere, women's independence was limited; they usually accompanied a husband or father and seldom prospected themselves. Even so, many women used their labor as a resource and realized opportunities to earn money by cooking and laundering and in some cases providing sexual services for the miners in houses of prostitution. In the Northwest, they worked in the canneries, cleaning and salting the fish that their husbands caught.

Women also helped to bolster family and community life as members of the home mission movement. Protestant missions had long carried out benevolent activities in foreign areas, such as China, and had been crucial in the settlement of Oregon in the 1840s. But in the mid-nineteenth century a number of women broke away from male-dominated missionary organizations. Their efforts focused on aiding women in countries that supported "barbaric" practices such as polygamy and female infanticide. Soon, these women—middle-class and white—were establishing missionary societies in the United States to fulfill their slogan, "Woman's work for woman." In the West, they exercised moral authority by building homes to rescue women—unmarried mothers, Mormons, Indians, and Chinese immigrants—who they believed had fallen prey to men or who had not yet accepted the conventions of Christian virtue.

The West became a rich multiracial society, including not only Native Americans and native-born white migrants but also His-

A Complex Population

panics, African Americans, and Asians. A crescent of territory, a borderland stretching from western Texas through New Mexico and Arizona to northern California, supported Hispanic ranchers and sheepherders, descendants of the Spanish who originally had claimed the land. In New Mexico, Hispanics had mixed with Indians to form a *mestizo* population of small farmers and ranchers. All along the southwest border, Mexican immigrants moved into American territory to find work. Some returned to Mexico seasonally; others stayed. And, before federal law excluded them in 1881 and 1882, some two hundred thousand Chinese immigrants—most of them young, male, and single—came to the United States and constituted a sizable proportion of the work force in California, Oregon, and Washington. Japanese and eastern European immigrants also inhabited mining and agricultural communities. The region consequently developed its own migrant economy, with workers moving back and forth within a large geographical area as they took short-term jobs in mining, farming, and railroad construction. They periodically

Born in China, Polly Bemis, pictured here, came to America when her parents sold her as a slave. An Idaho saloon-keeper bought her, and she later married a man named Charlie Bemis, who won her in a card game. Her life story was common among the few Chinese women who immigrated to the United States in the 1860s and 1870s (most Chinese immigrants were men). Unlike many Chinese, however, she lived peacefully after her marriage until her death in 1933.   (Idaho Historical Society Library and Archives)

returned to their home villages where women preserved a domestic base.

To control labor and social relations within this complex population, white settlers made race an important distinguishing social charac-

Significance of Race

teristic in the West. They usually identified four nonwhite races: Indians, Mexicans (both Mexican Americans, who had originally inhabited western lands, and Mexican immigrants), "Mongolians" (a term applied to Chinese), and African Americans. In creating these categories, whites imposed racial distinctions on people who, with the possible exception of blacks, had never before considered themselves to be a "race." Whites using these categories ascribed demeaning characteristics to all non-

Dressed formally for the opening ceremony of the Mullan Tunnel in Montana in 1884, these Chinese railroad workers, who helped build the tunnel, have temporarily cast aside their traditional work clothes and are showing their embrace of a new culture. (Montana Historical Society)

whites, judging them to be not only inferior but permanently so.

Racial minorities in western communities occupied the bottom half of a two-tiered labor system. Whites dominated the top tier of managerial and skilled labor positions. Unskilled laborers, often Irish, Chinese, and Mexicans, worked in the mines, on railroad construction, and as agricultural laborers. Blacks also worked in railroad and mining camps, doing cooking and cleaning, while Indians barely participated in the white-controlled labor system at all. All nonwhite groups plus the Irish encountered prejudice, especially as whites tried to reserve for themselves whatever riches the West might yield. The few Chinese who went into commercial fishing or agriculture found their activities limited by federal laws and local persecution that resulted in loss of their property. Many became low-paid workers in California's laundry, tobacco, and domestic service establishments. Mexicans, many of whom had been the original owners of the land, saw their property claims ignored or stolen by white miners and farmers. In California, they too became an urban population, working at unskilled, low-paying jobs.

The multiracial quality of western society, however, also included a cross-racial quality. Because so many male migrants to these states, as well as to Texas and New Mexico, were single, intermarriage with Mexican and Indian women was common. Such intermarriage was acceptable for white men, but not for white women, especially where Asian immigrants were involved. Most miscegenation laws passed by western legislatures were intended to prevent Chinese and Japanese men from marrying white women.

As whites were wresting control of the land from the Indians and Spanish inhabitants of the Southwest and California, questions arose over control of the nation's oil, mineral, and timber resources. Much of the remaining undeveloped land west of the Mississippi was in the public domain, and some people believed that the federal government, as its owner, should limit its exploitation. Others, however, believed that their own and the na-

Conservation Movement

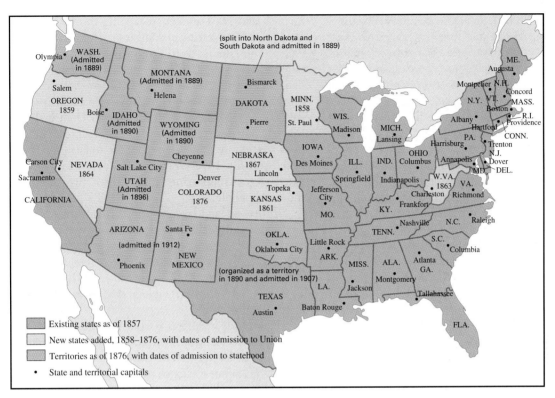

Map 17.2   The United States, 1876–1912   A wave of admissions between 1889 and 1912 brought remaining territories to statehood and marked the final creation of new states until Alaska and Hawai'i were admitted in the 1950s.

tion's prosperity depended on unlimited use of the land.

Questions about natural resources caught Americans between a desire for progress and a fear of spoiling the land. By the late 1870s, people eager to protect the natural landscape began to organize a conservation movement. They made Yellowstone Park in Wyoming the first national park in 1872. A prominent conservationist, naturalist John Muir, helped to establish Yosemite National Park in 1890. The next year, pressured by Muir and others, Congress authorized President Benjamin Harrison to create forest reserves—public lands protected from private-interest cutting. Such policies met with strong objections. Opposition came from lumber companies, lumber dealers, railroads, and householders accustomed to cutting timber freely for fuel and building material. Public opinion also split along sectional lines. Most supporters of conservation came from eastern states, where resources already had become less plentiful. Despite Muir's activism and efforts by the Sierra Club (which Muir helped found in 1892), opposition was loudest in the West, where people remained eager to take advantage of nature's bounty.

Development of the mining and forest regions, and of the farms and cities that followed, brought western territories to the threshold of statehood (see Map 17.2). In 1889 Republicans seeking to solidify their control of Congress passed an omnibus bill granting statehood to North Dakota, South Dakota, Washington, and Montana. Wyoming and Idaho were admitted the following year. Congress denied statehood to Utah until 1896, wanting assurances from the Mormons, who constituted a majority of the territory's population and controlled its government, that they would give up polygamy.

Admission of New States

Those states' mining towns and lumber camps spiced American folk culture and fostered a go-getter optimism that distinguished the American spirit. The lawlessness and hedonism of places such as Deadwood,

Legends of the West

in Dakota Territory, and Tombstone, in Arizona Territory, gave the West notoriety and romance. Legends grew up almost immediately about characters whose lives both typified and magnified western experience.

Arizona's mining towns, with their free-flowing cash and loose law enforcement, attracted gamblers, thieves, and opportunists whose names came to stand for the Wild West. Near Tombstone, the infamous Clanton family and their partner John Ringgold (known as Johnny Ringo) engaged in smuggling and cattle rustling. Inside the town, the Earp brothers—Wyatt, Jim, Morgan, Virgil, and Warren—and their friends William ("Bat") Masterson and John Henry ("Doc") Holliday operated on both sides of the law as gunmen, gamblers, and politicians. A feud between the Clanton and Earp clans climaxed on October 26, 1881, in a shootout at the OK Corral, where three Clantons were killed and Holliday and Morgan Earp were wounded. These characters and their exploits provided material for many movies and television programs in future years.

Mark Twain, Bret Harte, and other writers captured for posterity the flavor of mining life, and characters like Buffalo Bill, Annie Oakley, Wild Bill Hickok, Poker Alice, and Bedrock Tom became western folk heroes. But violence and eccentricity were far from common. Most miners and lumbermen worked long hours and had little time, energy, or money for gambling, carousing, or gunfights. Women worked as long or longer as teachers, cooks, laundresses, storekeepers, and housewives. Only a few were sharpshooters or dance-hall queens. For most, western life was a matter of adapting and surviving.

Irrigation and Transportation

Glittering gold, tall trees, and gushing oil shaped the popular image of the West, but water gave it life. If western territories and states promised wealth from mining, cutting, and drilling, their agricultural potential promised more—but only if settlers could find a way to bring water to the arid land. The economic development of the West is the story of how public and private interests used technology and organization to develop the region's river basins and make the land agriculturally productive. Just as control of land was central to western development, so too was control of water.

For centuries, Indians had irrigated southwestern lands to sustain their subsistence farming. When the Spanish arrived, they began tapping the Rio Grande River to irrigate farms in southwest Texas, New Mexico, and mission lands in California. Later they channeled water to the California mission communities of San Diego and Los Angeles. The first Americans of northern European ancestry to practice extensive irrigation were the Mormons. Arriving in Utah in 1847, they quickly diverted streams and rivers into networks of canals, whose water enabled them to farm the hard-baked soil. By 1890 Utah boasted over 263,000 irrigated acres supporting more than two hundred thousand people.

Efforts at land reclamation through irrigation in Colorado and California raised controversies over rights to the precious streams that flowed through the West. Americans had inherited the English common-law principle of riparian rights, which held that only those who owned land along the banks of a river could appropriate from the water's flow. The stream itself, according to riparianism, belonged to God; those who lived on its banks could take water for normal needs but were not to diminish the river. This principle, intended to protect nature, discouraged economic development because it prohibited each property owner from damming or diverting water at the expense of others who lived along the banks.

Rights to Water

Americans who settled the West rejected riparianism in favor of the doctrine of prior appropriation, which awarded a river's water to the first person who claimed it. Westerners, taking cues in part from eastern Americans who had diverted waterways to power mills and factories, asserted that water, like timber, minerals, and other natural resources, existed to serve human needs and advance profits. They argued that anyone intending a beneficial or "reasonable" (economically productive) use of river water should have the right to appropriation, and the courts ultimately agreed.

Under appropriation, those who dammed and diverted water often reduced the flow of water downstream. People disadvantaged by such action could protect their interests either by suing those who deprived them of water or by establishing a public authority to regulate water usage. Thus in 1879 Colorado created a number of water divisions, each with a commissioner to determine and regulate water rights. In 1890 Wyoming enlarged the concept of control with a constitutional provision declaring that the state's rivers were public property subject to state supervision of their use.

Destined to become the most productive agricultural state, California developed a dramatic solution to

Water, aided by human resolve, coaxed crops from the dry soil and helped make the West habitable for whites. On this Colorado farm, a windmill pumps water for irrigation.
(Longmont Museum, Longmont, Colorado)

California's Solution

the problem of water rights, sometimes called the "California Solution." In the 1860s a few individuals controlled huge tracts of land in the fertile Sacramento and San Joaquin River valleys, which they used for speculating in real estate, raising cattle, and growing wheat. But around the edges of the wheat fields lay unoccupied lands that could profitably support vegetable and fruit farming if irrigated properly.

Unlike western states that had opted for appropriation rights over riparian rights, California maintained a mixed legal system that upheld riparianism while allowing for some appropriation. This system put irrigators at a disadvantage and prompted them to seek a change in state law. In 1887 the state legislature passed a bill permitting farmers to organize into districts that would sponsor the construction and operation of irrigation projects. An irrigation district could use its public authority to purchase water rights, seize private property to build irrigation canals, and finance its projects through taxation or by issuing bonds. As a result of this legislation, California became the nation's leader in irrigated acreage, with more than 1 million irrigated acres by 1890, and the state's fruit and vegetable crops made its agriculture the most profitable in the country.

Though state irrigation provisions stimulated development, the federal government still owned most of western lands in the 1890s, ranging from 64 percent of California to 96 percent of Nevada. Prodded by land-hungry developers, the states wanted the federal government to transfer to them at least part of the public domain lands. States claimed that they could make these lands profitable through reclamation—providing them with irrigated water. For the most part, Congress refused such transfers because of the controversies they raised. If federal lands were transferred to state control for the purpose of water development, who would regulate waterways that flowed through more than one state or that potentially could provide water to a nearby state? If, for example, California received control of the Truckee River, which flowed westward out of Lake Tahoe on the California-Nevada border, how would Nevadans be assured that California would give them any water? Only the federal government, it seemed, had the power to regulate regional water development.

Newlands Reclamation Act

In 1902, after years of proposals and debates, Congress passed the Newlands Reclamation Act. Named for Nevada congressman Francis Newlands, the act allowed the federal government to sell western public lands to individuals in parcels not to exceed 160 acres, and to use the proceeds from such sales to finance irrigation projects. The Newlands Act provided for control but not conservation of water, because three-fourths of the water used in open-ditch irrigation, the most common form, was lost to evaporation. Thus the legislation fell squarely within the tradition of exploitation of nature for human profit. Often identified as an example of sensitivity to natural-resource conservation, the Newlands Reclamation Act in fact represented a decision by the federal government to aid the agricultural and general economic development of the West, just as state and federal subsidies to railroads during the 1850s and 1860s aided settlement of the West.

Post–Civil War Railroad Construction

Railroad construction boomed after the Civil War. Between 1865 and 1890, total track in the United States grew from 35,000 to 200,000 miles (see Map 17.1). By the turn of the century, the United States contained one-third of all the railroad track in the world. A diverse mix of workers made up construction crews. The Central Pacific, built eastward from San Francisco, imported seven thousand Chinese to build its tracks; the Union Pacific, extending westward from Omaha, Nebraska, used mainly Irish construction gangs. Workers lived in shacks and tents that could be dismantled, loaded on flatcars, and relocated at intervals of about 60 or 70 miles. After 1880, when steel rails began to replace iron rails, railroads helped to boost the nation's steel industry to international leadership. Railroad expansion also spawned a number of related industries, including coal production, passenger- and freight-car manufacture, and depot construction.

Rails and Markets

Influential and essential, railroads performed a uniquely American function. Europeans usually built railroads to link established market centers and to improve or replace existing routes for carrying raw materials, food, and manufactured goods. In the United States, railroads carried the same products, but they often created many of the very communities they were meant to serve and they carried traffic that had never before existed. With their ability to transport large loads of people and freight, lines such as the Union Pacific and Southern Pacific accelerated the growth of western regional centers such as Omaha, Kansas City, Cheyenne, Los Angeles, Portland, and Seattle.

Railroads accomplished these feats with the help of some of the largest government subsidies in Ameri-can history. Executives argued that because railroads benefited the public, the government should aid them by giving them land from the public domain. Congress, dominated by Republicans during and after the Civil War, was sympathetic, as it had been when it aided steamboat companies navigating on the Great Lakes and the Mississippi River earlier in the nineteenth century. To encourage rail construction, the federal government granted railroad companies over 180 million acres, mostly for interstate routes. These grants usually consisted of a right of way, plus alternate sections of land in a strip 20 to 80 miles wide along the right of way. Railroads funded construction by using the land as security for bonds or by selling it for cash. States and localities heaped on further subsidies. State legislators, many of whom had financial interests in a railroad's success, granted some 50 million acres. Counties, cities, and towns also assisted, usually by offering loans or by purchasing railroad bonds or stocks.

Government subsidies had mixed effects. Though capitalists often argued against government interference in economic affairs of private companies, privately owned railroads nevertheless accepted government aid and pressured governments into meeting their needs. The Southern Pacific, for example, threatened to bypass Los Angeles unless the city came up with a bonus and built a depot. Localities that could not or would not pay withered. Without public help, few railroads could have prospered sufficiently to attract private investment, yet public aid was not always salutary. During the 1880s, the policy of assistance haunted communities whose zeal had prompted them to commit too much to railroads that were never built or that defaulted on loans. Some laborers and farmers fought subsidies, arguing that companies like the Southern Pacific would become too powerful. Many communities boomed, however, because they had linked their fortunes to the iron horse. Moreover, railroads drew farmers into the market economy.

Standard Gauge; Standard Time

Railroad construction brought about important technological and organizational reforms. By the late 1880s, almost all lines had adopted standard-gauge rails so their tracks could connect with one another. Air brakes, automatic car couplers, standardized handholds on freight cars, and other devices made rail transportation safer and more efficient. The need for gradings, tunnels, and bridges spurred the growth of the American engineering profession. Organizational advances included systems for coordinating complex passenger and freight schedules and the adoption of uniform freight-classification systems.

Railroads also altered conceptions of time and space. First, by surmounting physical barriers to travel, railroads transformed space into time. Instead of expressing the distance between places in miles, people began to refer to the amount of time it took to travel from one place to another. Second, railroad scheduling required nationwide standardization of time. Before railroads, local church bells and clocks struck noon when the sun was directly overhead, and people set their clocks and watches accordingly. But because the sun was not overhead at exactly the same moment everywhere, time varied from place to place. Clocks in Boston, for instance, differed from those in New York by almost twelve minutes. To impose regularity, railroads created their own time zones. By 1880 there were nearly fifty different standards, but in 1883 the railroads finally agreed—without consulting anyone in government—to establish four standard time zones for the whole country. Most communities adjusted their clocks accordingly, and railroad time became national time.

Farming the Plains

"You are in a sea of wheat," rhapsodized the author of an 1880 magazine article about Oliver Dalrymple's farm in Dakota Territory's Red River valley. "The railroad train rolls through an ocean of grain. . . . We encounter a squadron of war chariots . . . doing the work of human hands. . . . There are 25 [machines] in this one brigade of the grand army of 115, under the marksmanship of this Dakota farmer." Dalrymple's farm exemplified two important achievements of the late nineteenth century: the transforming of arid, windswept prairies into arable land that would yield crops to benefit humankind, and the transformation of agriculture into big business by means of mechanization, long-distance transportation, and scientific cultivation.

These achievements did not come easily. The climate and terrain of the Great Plains presented formidable challenges, and overcoming them did not guarantee success. Technological innovation and the mechanization of agriculture enabled farmers to feed the nation's burgeoning population and turned the United States into the world's breadbasket, but it also scarred the lives of hundreds of thousands of men and women who made that development possible.

Settlement of the Plains

During the 1870s and 1880s, hundreds of thousands of hopeful farmers streamed into the Great Plains region. More acres were put under cultivation in states such as Kansas, Nebraska, and Texas during these two decades than in the entire country during the previous 250 years. The number of farms tripled from 2 million to over 6 million between 1860 and 1910. Several states opened offices in the East and in European ports to lure migrants westward. Land-rich railroads were especially aggressive, advertising cheap land, arranging credit terms, offering reduced fares, and promising instant success. Railroad agents—often former immigrants—traveled to Denmark, Sweden, Germany, and other European nations to recruit settlers and greeted newcomers at eastern ports. In California after the turn of the century, fruit and vegetable growers imported laborers from Japan and Mexico to work in the fields and canneries.

Most migrants went west because opportunities there seemed to promise a better life. Railroad expansion gave farmers in remote regions a way to ship produce to market, and the construction of grain elevators

Train schedules not only changed the American economy but also altered how Americans timed their daily lives. As people and businesses ordered their day according to the arrival and departure of trains, distances became less important than hours and minutes.   (Library of Congress)

eased problems of shipping and storage. As a result of worldwide as well as national population growth, the demand for farm products grew rapidly, and the prospects for commercial agriculture—growing crops for profit and for shipment to distant, including international, markets—became more favorable than ever.

Life on the farm, however, was much harder than the advertisements and railroad agents suggested. Migrants often encountered scarcities of essentials they had once taken for granted. The open prairies contained little lumber for housing and fuel. Pioneer families were forced to build houses of sod and to burn manure for heat. Water for cooking and cleaning was sometimes as scarce as timber. Few families were lucky or wealthy enough to buy land near a stream that did not dry up in summer and freeze in winter. Machinery for drilling wells was expensive, as were windmills for drawing the water to the surface.

Even more formidable than the terrain was the climate. The climate between the Missouri River and the Rocky Mountains divides along a line running from Minnesota southwest through Oklahoma, then south, bisecting Texas. West of this line, annual rainfall averages less than 28 inches, not enough for most crops or trees (see Map 17.3), and even that scant life-giving rain was never certain. Heartened by adequate water one year, farmers gagged on dust and broke plows on hardened limestone soil the next.

Weather seldom followed predictable cycles. In summer, weeks of torrid heat and parching winds suddenly gave way to violent storms that washed away crops and property. The wind and cold of winter blizzards piled up mountainous snowdrifts that halted all outdoor movement. During the Great Blizzard that struck Nebraska and the Dakota Territory in January 1888, the temperature plunged to 36 degrees below zero, and the wind blew at 56 miles per hour. The storm not only caused livestock to perish but also stranded schoolchildren and killed several parents who ventured out to rescue them. In springtime, melting

Hardship of Life on the Plains

Map 17.3 Agricultural Regions of the United States, 1890   In the Pacific Northwest and east of the 28-inch-rainfall line, farmers could grow a greater variety of crops. Territory west of the line was either too mountainous or too arid to support agriculture without irrigation. The grasslands that once fed buffalo herds now could feed beef cattle.

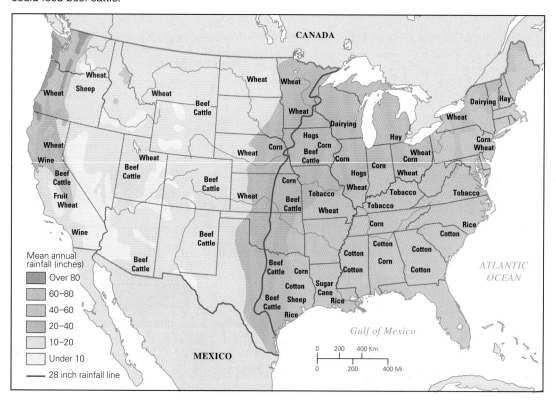

snow swelled streams, and floods threatened millions of acres. In the fall, a week without rain could turn dry grasslands into tinder, and the slightest spark could ignite a raging prairie fire.

Nature could be cruel even under good conditions. Weather that was favorable for crops was also good for breeding insects. Worms and flying pests ravaged corn and wheat. In the 1870s and 1880s swarms of grasshoppers virtually ate up entire farms. Heralded only by the din of buzzing wings, a mile-long cloud of insects would smother the land and devour everything: plants, tree bark, and clothes. As one farmer lamented, the "hoppers left behind nothing but the mortgage."

Settlers also had to contend with social isolation. Farmers in New England and in Europe lived in villages and traveled each day to nearby fields. This pattern was rare in the vast expanses of the Plains—and in the Far West and South as well—where peculiarities of land division compelled American rural dwellers to live apart from each other. The Homestead Act of 1862 and other measures to encourage western settlement offered cheap or free plots to people who would live on and improve their property. Because most plots acquired by small farmers were rectangular—usually encompassing 160 acres—at most

Social Isolation

four families could live near each other, but only if they congregated around the shared four-corner intersection. In practice, farm families usually lived back from their boundary lines, and at least a half-mile separated farmhouses.

Letters that Ed Donnell, a young Nebraska homesteader, wrote to his family in Missouri reveal how time and circumstances could dull optimism. In the fall of 1885, Donnell wrote to his mother: "I like Nebr first rate. . . . I have saw a pretty tuff time a part of the time since I have been out here, but I started out to get a home and I was determined to win or die in the attempt. . . . Have got a good crop of corn, a floor in my house and got it ceiled overhead." Already, though, Donnell was lonely. He went on: "There is lots of other bachelors here but I am the only one I know who doesn't have kinfolks living handy. . . . You wanted to know when I was going to get married. Just as quick as I can get money ahead to get a cow."

A year and a half later, Donnell's dreams were dissolving and, still a bachelor, he was beginning to look for a second chance elsewhere. As he explained to his brother, "The rats eat my sod stable down. . . . I may sell out this summer, land is going up so fast. . . . If I sell I am going west and grow up with the country." By fall things had worsened, and Donnell wrote, "We

Posing in front of their sod house, this proud Nebraska family displays the seriousness that derived from their hard lives on the Great Plains. Though bushes and other growth appear in the background, the absence of trees is notable.   (Nebraska State Historical Society, Solomon D. Butcher Collection)

have been having wet weather for 3 weeks. . . . My health has been so poor this summer and the wind and the sun hurts my head so. I think if I can sell I will . . . move to town for I can get $40 a month working in a grist mill and I would not be exposed to the weather." Donnell's doubts and hardships, shared by thousands of other people, fed the cityward migration of farm folk that fueled late-nineteenth-century urban growth (see Chapter 19).

Farm families survived by sheer resolve and by organizing churches and clubs where they could socialize a few times a month. By 1900 two developments had brought rural settlers into closer contact with modern consumer society (though people in sparsely settled regions west of the 28-inch rainfall line remained isolated for several more decades). First, mail-order companies—Montgomery Ward and Sears, Roebuck—made new products available to almost everyone by the 1870s and 1880s. Emphasizing personal attention to customers, Ward's and Sears were outlets for sociability as well as material goods. Letters

Mail-Order Companies and Rural Free Delivery

from customers to Mr. Ward often reported family news and sought advice on everything from gifts to childcare. A Washington State man wrote, "As you advertise everything for sale that a person wants, I thought I would write you, as I am in need of a wife, and see what you could do for me." Another wrote: "I suppose you wonder why we haven't ordered anything from you since the fall. The cow kicked my arm and broke it and besides my wife was sick, and there was the doctor bill. But now, thank God, that is paid, and we are all well again, and we have a fine new baby boy, and please send plush bonnet number 29d8077."

Second, rural communities petitioned Congress for extension of the postal service during the 1890s, and in 1896 the government made Rural Free Delivery (RFD), which had begun earlier in West Virginia, widely available. Farmers previously had to go to town to pick up their mail. Now, they could receive letters, newspapers, and catalogues in a mailbox on a road near their home nearly every day. In 1913 the postal service inaugurated parcel post, which enabled people to receive packages, such as orders from Ward's and Sears, more cheaply.

By the late nineteenth century, the industrial revolution was making a significant impact on farming. This scene from a Colorado wheat farm shows a harvest aided by a steam tractor and belt-driven thresher, equipment that made large-scale commercial crop production possible. (Colorado Historical Society)

The agricultural revolution that followed the Civil War would not have been possible without the expanded use of machinery. When the

Mechanization of Agriculture

Civil War drew men away from farms in the upper Mississippi River valley, the women and older men who remained behind began using reapers and other mechanical implements to satisfy demand for food and take advantage of high grain prices. After the war, continued demand and high prices encouraged farmers to depend more on machines, and inventors developed new implements for farm use. Seeders, combines, binders, mowers, and rotary plows, carried westward by railroads, were introduced on the Great Plains and in California in the 1870s and 1880s.

For centuries, the acreage of grain a farmer could plant had been limited by the amount that could be harvested by hand. Machines—driven first by animals, then by steam—increased productivity beyond farmers' imaginations. Before mechanization, a farmer working alone could harvest about 7.5 acres of wheat. Using an automatic binder that cut and bundled the grain, the same farmer could harvest 135 acres. Machines dramatically reduced the time and cost of farming other crops as well (see Table 17.1).

Meanwhile, Congress and scientists worked to improve existing crops and develop new ones. The 1862 Morrill Land Grant Act gave each

Legislative and Scientific Aids to Farming

state federal lands to sell in order to finance educational institutions that aided agricultural development. The act prompted establishment of state universities in Wisconsin, Illinois, Minnesota, California, and other states. (A second Morrill Act in 1890 aided more schools, including a number of black colleges.) The Hatch Act of 1887 provided for agricultural experiment stations in every state, further encouraging the advancement of farming science and technology.

Scientific advances enabled farmers to use the soil more efficiently. Researchers developed dry farming, a technique of plowing and harrowing that minimized evaporation of precious moisture. Botanists perfected varieties of "hard" wheat whose seeds could withstand northern winters, and millers invented a process for grinding the tougher wheat kernels into flour. Agriculturists also adapted new varieties of alfalfa from Mongolia, corn from North Africa, and rice from Asia. Californian Luther Burbank developed a multitude of new plants by crossbreeding. Chemist George Washington Carver of the Tuskegee Institute created hundreds of new products from peanuts, soybeans, sweet potatoes, and cotton wastes, and he introduced methods of soil improvement. Other scientists developed means of combating plant and animal diseases. These and other scientific and technological developments helped feed a burgeoning population and make America what one journalist called "the garden of the world."

The Ranching Frontier

While commercial farming was overspreading the West, it ran headlong into one of the region's most romantic industries—cattle ranching. Early in the nineteenth century herds of cattle, introduced by the Spanish and expanded by Mexican ranchers, roamed southern Texas and bred with cattle brought by Anglo settlers. The re-

Longhorns and the Long Drive

sulting longhorn breed multiplied and became valuable by the 1860s, when population growth boosted the

Table 17.1	**Time and Cost of Farming an Acre of Land by Hand and by Machine, 1890**			
	Hours Required		**Labor Cost**	
Crop	**Hand**	**Machine**	**Hand**	**Machine**
Wheat	61	3	$3.65	$.66
Corn	39	15	$3.62	$1.51
Oats	66	7	$3.73	$1.07
Loose hay	21	4	$1.75	$.42

Source: Ray Allan Billington, *Westward Expansion: A History of the American Frontier*, 2d ed. (New York: Macmillan, 1960), p. 697.

A group of cowboys prepare for a roundup. Note the presence of African Americans, who, along with Mexicans, made up one-fourth of all cowboys. Though they rarely became trail bosses or ranch owners, black cowboys enjoyed an independence on the trails that was unavailable to them on tenant farms and city streets.   (Nebraska State Historical Society)

demand for beef and railroads simplified the transportation of food. By 1870 drovers were herding thousands of Texas cattle northward to Kansas, Missouri, and Wyoming (see Map 17.1). On these long drives, mounted cowboys (as many as 25 percent of whom were African American) tended the herds, which fed on open grassland along the way. At the northern terminus—usually Abilene, Dodge City, or Cheyenne—the cattle were sold to northern ranches or loaded onto trains bound for Chicago and St. Louis for slaughter and distribution to national and international markets.

The long drive gave rise to romantic lore but was not very efficient. Trekking 1,000 miles or more for two to three months made cattle sinewy and tough. Herds traveling through Indian lands and farmers' fields were sometimes shot at and later prohibited from such trespass by state laws. Ranchers adjusted by raising herds nearer to railroad routes. When ranchers discovered that crossing Texas longhorns with heavier Hereford and Angus breeds produced animals better able to survive northern winters, cattle raising spread across the Great Plains. Between 1860 and 1880 the cattle population of Kansas, Nebraska, Colorado,

Wyoming, Montana, and the Dakotas increased from 130,000 to 4.5 million, crowding out already declining buffalo herds.

Cattle raisers needed vast pastures to graze their herds, and they wanted to incur as little expense as possible in using such land. Thus they often bought a few acres bordering a stream and turned their herds loose on adjacent public domain that no one wanted because it lacked water access. By this method, called open-range ranching, a cattle raiser could control thousands of acres by owning only a hundred or so. Neighboring ranchers often formed associations and allowed their herds to graze together. Owners identified their cattle by burning a brand into each animal's hide. Every ranch had its own brand—a shorthand method for labeling movable property. Cowboy crews rounded up the cattle twice each year, in the spring to brand new calves and in the fall to drive mature animals to market.

The Open Range

Roundups delighted easterners with colorful images of western life: bellowing cattle, rope-swinging cowboys, and smoky campfires. Opportunities for profit at first enriched ranchers in Texas and other

Bordered by the product it was promoting, this advertisement conveyed the message that railroads and farmers could protect their property from each other by utilizing a new type of fencing.   (Elwood House Museum, DeKalb, Illinois)

states. As one publication explained:

> A good sized steer when it is fit for the butcher market will bring from $45.00 to $60.00. The same animal at its birth was worth but $5.00. He has run on the plains and cropped the grass from the public domain for four or five years, and now, with scarcely any expense to its owner, is worth $40.00 more than when he started on his pilgrimage.

But as demand for beef kept rising and as ranchers and capital flowed into the Great Plains, cattle began to overrun the range.

Meanwhile, sheepherders from California and New Mexico also were using the public domain, spark-

Grazing Wars

ing conflict over land. Ranchers complained that sheep ruined grassland by eating down to the roots and that cattle refused to graze where sheep had been because the "woolly critters" left a repulsive odor. Armed conflict occasionally erupted when cowboys and sheepherders resorted to violence rather than settle disputes in court, where a judge might discover that both were using public land illegally.

More important, however, the farming frontier was advancing and generating new demands for land. Devising a way to organize the land resulted in an unheralded but highly significant invention. The problem was fencing. Lacking sufficient timber and stone for traditional fencing, western settlers faced a critical problem in defining and protecting their property. Tensions flared when farmers accused cattle raisers of allowing their herds to trespass on cropland and when herders in turn charged that farmers should fence their property against grazing animals. Ranchers and farmers alike may have wished to enclose their herds and fields, but they had no economical means of doing so.

The solution was barbed wire. Invented in 1873 by Joseph F. Glidden, a farmer in DeKalb, Illinois,

Barbed Wire

these fences consist of two wires held in place by sharp spurs twisted around them. Mass-produced by the Washburn and Moen Manufacturing Company of Worcester, Massachusetts—80.5 million pounds worth in 1880 alone—barbed wire provided a cheap and durable means of enclosure. It opened the Plains to homesteaders by enabling them to protect their farms from grazing cattle. It also ended open-range ranching not only because it removed grazing land that often had been used illegally but also because it enabled large-scale ranchers to isolate their herds within massive stretches of private property.

Open-range ranching made beef a staple of the American diet and created a few fortunes, but its features could not survive the spurs of barbed wire and the rush of history. Moreover, a devastating winter in 1887–1888 destroyed countless herds and drove small ranchers out of business. By 1890 big businesses were taking over the cattle industry and applying scientific methods of breeding and feeding. Most ranchers now owned or leased the land they used, though some illegal fencing persisted. The myth of the cowboy's freedom and individualism lived on, but most cowboys became ordinary wage earners.

Summary

Americans of all races developed the West with courage and creativity. Indians, the region's original inhabitants, had used, and sometimes abused, the land to support subsistence cultures that included trade and war as well as hunting and farming. Living mostly in small groups, they depended heavily on fragile resources such as buffalo herds and salmon runs. When they came into contact with aggressive, migratory Euro-Americans, their resistance to the market economy, the diseases, and the violence that the whites brought into the West failed.

White miners, timber cutters, farmers, and builders accomplished extraordinary feats. The extraction of raw minerals to supply eastern factories, the use of irrigation and mechanization to bring forth agricultural abundance from the land, the filling of pastures with cattle and sheep to expand food sources, and the construction of railroads to tie the nation together transformed half of the continent within a few decades. The new settlers, however, employed power, violence, and greed that sustained discrimination within a multiracial society, left many farmers feeling cheated and betrayed, kindled contests over use of water, and sacrificed environmental balance for market profits. The region's raw materials and agricultural products improved living standards and contributed to industrial progress, but not without human and environmental costs.

LEGACY FOR A PEOPLE AND A NATION
The West and Rugged Individualism

Though born in New York State, Theodore Roosevelt, twenty-sixth president of the United States, thought of himself as a westerner. In 1884, at the age of twenty-five, he moved to Dakota Territory to live on ranches he had bought there. He loved the uncharted world of what he called "vast silent spaces, a place of grim beauty," where he could mingle with cowboys, gamblers, and gunmen. In such a place, Roosevelt believed, he developed a character of "rugged individualism," an ability to conquer challenges through independent strength and fortitude. He once wrote of his experience that he "knew toil and hardship and hunger and thirst . . . but we felt the beat of hardy life in our veins, and ours was the glory of work and the joy of living."

Americans have long shared Roosevelt's fascination with the West and its reputation for rugged individualism. They have popularized western settings and characters in movies and on television. The film *Cimarron* (1930) was one of the first to win an Academy Award, and *Gunsmoke* held the record as one of the longest-running television series (1955–1975). Movie star John Wayne epitomized the rugged westerner in dozens of films. From *The Virginian*, first published in 1902, to the recent novels of Larry Mc-

Murtry, Americans have made stories about the West bestsellers. In each instance, a lone individual, usually male, overcomes danger and hardship with solitary effort. In their appreciation of this quality, Americans have not only infused political and moral rhetoric with references to rugged individualism; they also have tried to exhibit the quality in their attire. Over the years they have bought millions of dollars worth of Stetson cowboy hats, denim jeans, and buckskin jackets.

At the same time, however, the myth of rugged individualism that Roosevelt thought he could cultivate in the West had a different, ironic reality. In the late nineteenth century, migrants to the West traveled on railroads built with government subsidies, acquired land cheaply from the federal government under the Homestead and Timber and Stone Acts, depended on the army to remove Indians, and destroyed forests and diverted rivers with federal support. More recently, western politicians who oppose big government have received votes from constituents who depend on federal farm subsidies and price supports, free or subsidized water, and government-financed disaster relief from droughts, floods, and tornadoes.

Perhaps more important, the West could not have been settled and developed without both individualism *and* government assistance—what might be called "rugged cooperation." Here was the West's true legacy

Cliffs of Green River by Thomas Moran in 1874. A detail of this painting appears at the beginning of the chapter on page 458.   (Amon Carter Museum, Fort Worth, Texas)

to a people and a nation. The federal government, with state assistance, created opportunities that tenacious miners, ranchers, and farmers took advantage of. Those who populated the West had to be rugged. Like Roosevelt they had to have the vision and determination to endure "toil and hardship and hunger and thirst." They survived, but they had—and continue to need—help.

For Further Reading, see page A-21 of the Appendix. For Web resources, go to http://college.hmco.com.

The shoemaker known only as "S" appeared a beaten and bitter man. Interviewed by the Massachusetts Bureau of the Statistics of Labor in 1871, "S" reported that he was fifty years old and had been plying his trade for forty years. He and his three children each worked in a shoe factory ten hours a day, five days a week, and nine hours on Saturdays. His wife toiled in another factory, stitching the covering on baseballs from 5:30 A.M. to 10 A.M. every day.

"S" told the interviewer that ever since his factory had introduced machinery, he had lost control of his craft. He could no longer teach his sons the skill of shoemaking because they had been moved to another room to carry out just one task instead of assembling the whole shoe or boot. "S" hoped his sons would not be factory workers all their lives, but he also realized they had little other choice. The cost of living had risen, making it impossible for his family to sustain itself in any other way, especially when the shoe factory laid off its work force for four months every year because of slow business.

When asked his opinion about the economic system, "S" responded with frustration and anger. "It is hard to see why it is not better to make the consumer pay two or three cents more a pair for his shoes, than to cut down a man who cannot, by hard toil at the wages given, make a comfortable living."

"S" felt embittered by the homage being paid to supply and demand: "We have it constantly dinned in our ears that supply and demand govern prices, but we have found out to a certainty that this is not so. . . . [W]ithout the aid of machinery, six men will make a case of 60 pairs [of shoes] in a day, . . . which would give each man about $1.70 a day; on the other hand, with the machinery, three men will do the same amount of work in the same time, and get about the same pay [$1.70] each, as the men on hand work. . . . Who gets the difference in money saved by machinery? and how far does supply and demand govern in these things?"

The pessimistic testimony of "S" reflected one worker's reaction to the industrialization that was re-

THE MACHINE AGE 1877–1920

Steel became a vital component of American industrialization in the late nineteenth century, both as a product itself and as a material necessary for countless new machines. Steel mills—such as this one in Meadville, Pennsylvania—employed large work forces in ever more expansive, and dangerous, settings. (Library of Congress) lentlessly overtaking the nation's economy in the late 1800s. The new order was both exciting and daunting. Factories and machines divided production into minute, repetitive tasks and organized work according to the dictates of the clock. Workers like "S" who had long thought of themselves as valued producers found themselves struggling to avoid becoming slaves to machines. Meanwhile, in their quest for productivity, profits, and growth, corporations merged and amassed great power. Defenders of the new system devised theories to justify it, while critics tried to combat what they thought were abuses of power.

Industrialization is a complex process whose chief feature is production of goods by machine rather than by hand. In the early and mid-nineteenth century, an industrial revolution swept through parts of the United States, and the mechanization that characterized it set the stage for a second round in the latter half of the century. Three technological developments propelled this new stage: the rise of electric-powered machines; new applications in the use of chemicals; and expansion of engines powered by internal combustion. Earlier industrialization influenced the new technologies. Steam engines had reached their peak of utility, generating a need for a new power source—electricity. Chemical researchers experimented with dyes, bleaches, and cleaning agents in the textile industry. And the potential of railroad transportation spurred progress in automobile manufacture.

In 1860 only about one-fourth of the American labor force worked in manufacturing and transportation; by 1900 over half did so. As the twentieth century dawned, the United States was not only the world's largest producer of raw materials and food but also the most productive industrial nation (see Map 18.1). Between 1880 and 1920 migrants from farms and from abroad swelled the industrial work force (see Chapter 19); but machines, more than people, boosted American productivity. Innovations in business organization and marketing also fueled the drive for profits.

These developments had momentous effects on standards of living and everyday life. Between the end of Reconstruction and the end of the First World War, a new consumer society took shape. Farms and factories produced so much that growing numbers of Americans could afford to satisfy their material wants. What had once been accessible to a few was becoming available to many; what had formerly been luxuries were becoming necessities. Products such as canned foods and machine-made clothing that had hardly ex-

isted before the Civil War became common by the turn of the century. Yet the accomplishments of industrialism, like the natural resource extraction and agricultural expansion (see Chapter 17) that provided the raw materials on which the new industrialization was based, involved waste and greed. The vigor and creativity that marked the era gave rise to both constructive and destructive forces. ▮

Technology and the Triumph of Industrialism

In 1876 Thomas A. Edison and his associates set up a laboratory in a wooden shed in Menlo Park, New Jersey. There they intended to turn out "a minor invention every ten days and a big thing every six months or so." Edison envisioned this structure as an invention factory, where creative people would pool ideas and skills to fashion marketable products. Here he would blend brash enthusiasm with a systematic work ethic. If Americans wanted new products, Edison believed, they had to organize and work purposefully to bring about progress. Such efforts reflected the forward-looking spirit that enlivened American industrialization at the end of the nineteenth century.

In the closing years of the nineteenth century, mechanization fired American optimism. Like the image of second chances represented by the West, the machine symbolized opportunity. The patent system, created by the Constitution to "promote the Progress of science and useful Arts," testifies to an outburst of American mechanical inventiveness. Between 1790 and 1860 the U.S. Patent Office granted a total of 36,000 patents. In 1897 alone, however, it granted 22,000, and between 1860 and 1930 it registered 1.5 million. The inventions often sprang from a marriage between technology and business organization. The harnessing of electricity, internal combustion, and industrial chemistry illustrates how this marriage worked.

Most of Edison's more than one thousand inventions used electricity to transmit light, sound, and images. Perhaps his biggest "big thing" project began in 1878 when he formed the Edison Electric Light Company and embarked on a search for a cheap, efficient means of indoor lighting. After tedious trial-and-error

Birth of the Electrical Industry

IMPORTANT EVENTS

1859 Great Atlantic Tea Company (A&P), the nation's first grocery chain, founded

1860 Knights of Labor founded

1873–78 Economic decline results from overly rapid expansion

1876 Bonsack invents machine for rolling cigarettes

1877 Widespread railroad strikes protest wage cuts

1878 Edison Electric Light Company founded

1879 George's *Progress and Poverty* argues against economic inequality

1880s Chain-pull toilets spread across the United States

Doctors begin to accept germ theory of disease

Mass production of tin cans begins

1881 First federal trademark law begins spread of brand names

1882 Standard Oil Trust formed

1884–85 Economic decline results from numerous causes

1886 Haymarket riot in Chicago protests police brutality against labor demonstrators

American Federation of Labor (AFL) founded

1888 Bellamy's *Looking Backward* depicts utopian world free of monopoly, politicians, and class divisions

1890 Sherman Anti-Trust Act outlaws "combinations in restraint of trade"

1892 Homestead (Pennsylvania) steelworkers strike against Carnegie Steel Company

1893–97 Economic depression causes high unemployment and business failures

1894 Workers at Pullman Palace Car Company strike against exploitative policies

1895 *U.S. v. E. C. Knight Co.* limits Congress's power to regulate manufacturing

1896 *Holden v. Hardy* upholds law regulating miners' work hours

1898 Taylor promotes scientific management as efficiency measure in industry

1901–03 U.S. Steel Corporation founded

E. I. du Pont de Nemours and Company reorganized

Ford Motor Company founded

1903 Women's Trade Union League founded

1905 *Lochner v. New York* overturns law limiting bakery workers' work hours and limits labor protection laws

Industrial Workers of the World (IWW) founded

1908 *Muller v. Oregon* upholds law limiting women to ten-hour workday

First Ford Model T built

1911 Triangle Shirtwaist Company fire in New York City leaves 146 workers dead

1913 First moving assembly line begins operation at Ford Motor Company

1914 Ford offers Five-Dollar-Day plan to workers

1919 Telephone operator unions strike in New England

experiments, Edison perfected an incandescent bulb that used a vacuum to reduce oxidation of the filament, thereby extending the useful life of the bulb. At the same time, he devised a system of power generation and distribution—an improved dynamo and a parallel circuit of wires—to provide convenient power to a large number of customers.

To market his ideas, Edison acted as his own publicist. During the 1880 Christmas season he illuminated Menlo Park with forty incandescent bulbs, and in 1882 he built a power plant that could light eighty-five buildings in New York's Wall Street financial district. When this plant began service, a *New York Times* reporter marveled that working in his office at night "seemed almost like writing in daylight."

Edison's system of direct current could transmit electric power only a mile or two. George Westinghouse, a young inventor from Schenectady, New York,

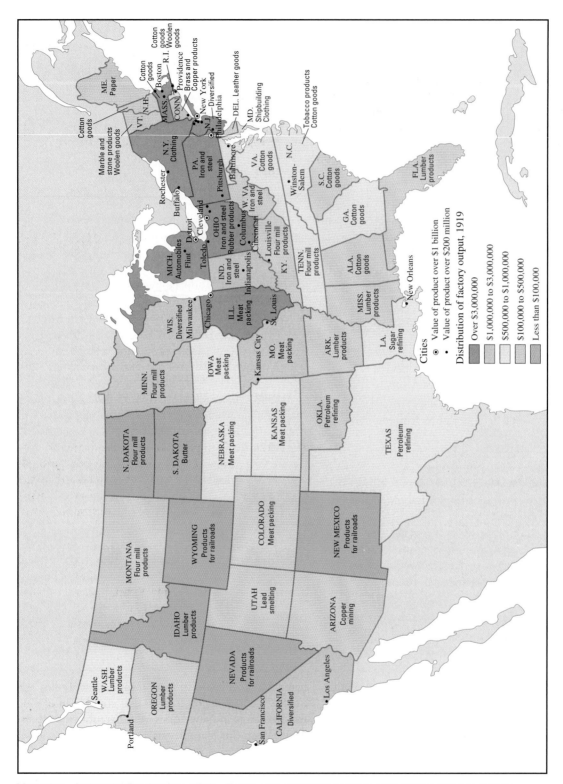

Map 18.1   Industrial Production, 1919   By the early twentieth century, each state could boast of at least one kind of industrial production. Although the value of goods produced was still highest in the Northeast, states like Minnesota and California had impressive dollar values of outputs.   (Source: Data from U.S. Bureau of the Census, *Fourteenth Census of the United States, 1920,* Vol. IX, *Manufacturing* [Washington, D.C.: U.S. Government Printing Office, 1921].)

George Westinghouse

who had become famous for devising an air brake for railroad cars, solved the problem. Westinghouse purchased patent rights to generators that used alternating current and transformers that reduced high-voltage power to lower voltage levels, thus making transmission over long distances cheaper.

Other entrepreneurs utilized new business practices to market Edison's and Westinghouse's technological breakthroughs. Samuel Insull, Edison's private secretary, attracted investors and organized Edison power plants across the country, amassing an electric-utility empire. In the late 1880s and early 1890s financiers Henry Villard and J. P. Morgan bought up patents in electric lighting and merged small equipment-manufacturing companies into the General Electric Company. Equally important, General Electric and Westinghouse Electric encouraged the practical application of electricity, formerly an experimental field for scientists, by establishing research laboratories that paid scientists to create electrical products for everyday use.

As corporations organized the process of invention in company labs, individual inventors continued to work independently and tried, sometimes successfully and sometimes not, to sell their handiwork and patents to manufacturing companies. One such inventor, Granville T. Woods, an engineer called by some the "black Edison," patented thirty-five devices vital to electronics and communications. Among his inventions, most of which he sold to companies such as General Electric, were an automatic circuit breaker, an electromagnetic brake, and various instruments to aid communications between railroad trains.

Development of the internal-combustion engine in France and Germany inspired the era's most visionary manufacturer, Henry Ford. In the 1890s Ford, an electrical engineer in Detroit's Edison Company, experimented in his spare time with a gasoline-burning engine to power a vehicle. George Selden, a lawyer from Rochester, New York, had already been tinkering with internal-combustion engines, but Ford applied organizational genius to this invention and spawned a massive industry.

Henry Ford and the Automobile Industry

Like Edison, Ford had a scheme as well as a product. In 1909 he declared, "I am going to democratize the automobile. When I'm through, everybody will be able to afford one, and about everyone will have one." Ford proposed to reach this goal by mass-producing thousands of identical cars in exactly the same way. Adapting methods of the meatpacking and metalworking industries, Ford engineers set up assembly lines that drastically reduced the time and cost of producing cars. Instead of performing numerous tasks, each worker was assigned only one task, performed repeatedly, using the same specialized machine. A conveyor belt moved past stationary workers who fashioned each component part, and progressively the entire car was assembled.

The Ford Motor Company began operation in 1903. In 1908, the first year it built the Model T, Ford sold 10,000 cars. In 1913 the company's first full assembly line began producing cars in Highland Park, outside Detroit, and the next year, 248,000 Fords were sold. Rising automobile production created more jobs, higher earnings, and greater profits in related industries such as oil, paint, rubber, and glass. As well, the internal-combustion engine helped give birth to the manufacture of trucks, buses, and, ultimately, airplanes.

By 1914 many Ford cars cost $490, only about one-fourth of their price a decade earlier. Yet even $490 was too much for many workers, who earned at best $2 a day. That year, however, Ford tried to spur productivity, prevent high labor turnover, head off unionization, and better enable his workers to buy the cars they produced by offering them the Five-Dollar-Day plan—combined wages and profit sharing equal to $5 a day.

Du Ponts and the Chemical Industry

During the same period, the du Pont family did for the chemical industry what Edison and Ford did for the electrical and automobile industries. Du Ponts had been manufacturing gunpowder since the early 1800s. In 1902 three cousins, Alfred, Coleman, and Pierre, took over E. I. du Pont de Nemours and Company and broadened production. In 1911 du Pont scientists and engineers working in the nation's first research laboratory adapted cellulose to the production of new materials such as photographic film, rubber, lacquer, textile fibers, and plastics; the innovation wrought a significant transformation in consumer products. The company also pioneered methods of efficient management, accounting, and reinvestment of earnings, all of which contributed to controlled production, better recordkeeping, and higher profits.

The assembly line broke the production process down into simple tasks that individual workers could efficiently repeat hour after hour. Here, assembly-line workers at the Ford plant in Highland Park, Michigan, outside Detroit, are installing pistons in engines of the Model T around 1914.   (Henry Ford Museum and Greenfield Village)

The South's two major staple crops, tobacco and cotton, propelled that region into the machine age.

Technology and Southern Industry

Before the 1870s, Americans used tobacco mainly for snuff, cigars, and chewing. But in 1876 a Virginian named James Bonsack, just eighteen years old, invented a machine for rolling cigarettes. Sales soared when James B. Duke of North Carolina, who popularized cigarettes just as Edison and Ford popularized their products, began marketing cigarettes in the North by enticing consumers with free samples, trading cards, and billboards. By 1900 his American Tobacco Company was a huge nationwide business, employing Jewish immigrant cigar makers who trained laborers in the mass production of cigarettes. Cigarette factories, located in southern cities, employed both black and white workers (including women), though in separate locations of the plant.

New technology also aided southern textile mills, which by 1900 numbered over four hundred and contained 4 million spindles. As the machinery of north-

Southern Textile Mills

ern mills became obsolete, the South, especially its small towns, had space for factory construction as well as a cheap labor force to tend new machines. Aided by electric motors, which could power individual machines rather than depend on a water-powered drive shaft with belts attached to numerous machines, southern mills could utilize automatic looms, which required fewer and less skilled workers. Moreover, southern mills could install electric lighting, which expanded the hours of production. The textile mills, financed mostly by local investors, paid women and children 50 cents a day for twelve or more hours of work—about half the wages northern workers received. Many companies built villages around their mills, where they controlled housing, stores, schools, and churches. Inside these towns, owners banned criticism of the company and squelched attempts at union organization.

Northern and European capitalists financed other southern industries. Between 1890 and 1900, northern lumber syndicates moved into pine forests

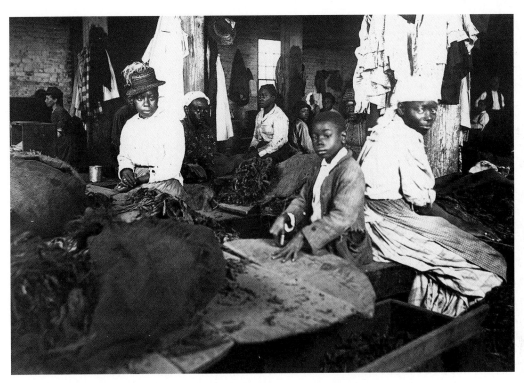

Tobacco production was one southern industry that traditionally hired African American laborers. This scene from a Richmond tobacco factory around 1880 shows women and children preparing leaves for curing by tearing off the stems.   (Valentine Museum)

of the Gulf states, boosting production 500 percent. During the 1880s, northern investors developed southern iron and steel manufacturing, much of it in the boom city of Birmingham. Except for some modernized plants, however, the South lacked the technological innovations, such as those in the machine-tool industry, that had enabled northern industries to compete with those of other industrializing nations.

Nevertheless, southern boosters heralded the emergence of a New South. Henry Grady, editor of the *Atlanta Constitution* and the most articulate voice of southern progress, proclaimed, "We have sowed towns and cities in the place of theories, and put business in place of politics. We have challenged your spinners in Massachusetts and your iron-makers in Pennsylvania. . . . We have fallen in love with work." Grady's optimism was premature. A New South would eventually emerge, but not until after the First World War.

In all regions of the country, the timing of technological innovation varied from one industry to another, but machines broadly altered the economy and everyday life. Telephones and typewriters revolutionized communications, making face-to-face conversations less important and facilitating correspondence and record-keeping in the growing insurance, banking, and advertising firms. Sewing machines made mass-produced clothing available to almost everyone. Refrigeration changed dietary habits by enabling the preservation and shipment of meat, fruit, vegetables, and dairy products. Cash registers and adding machines revamped accounting and created new clerical jobs.

Influence of New Machines

Profits resulted from higher production at lower costs. As technological innovations made large-scale production more economical, some owners replaced small factories with larger ones. Between 1850 and 1900 the average capital investment in a manufacturing firm increased from $700,000 to $1.9 million. Only large companies could afford to buy complex machines and operate them at full capacity. And large companies could best take advantage of discounts for shipping products in bulk and for buying raw materials in quantity. Economists call such advantages economies of scale.

Taken at the historic moment of liftoff, this photograph shows the first airplane flight at Kitty Hawk, North Carolina, December 17, 1903. With Orville Wright lying at the controls and brother Wilbur standing nearby, the plane was airborne only twelve seconds and traveled 120 feet. Even so, the flight marked the beginning of one of the twentieth century's most influential industries.   (Library of Congress)

Profitability depended as much on how production was arranged as on the machines in use. Where once shop-floor workers such as "S" had exercised control over how a product was made, by the 1890s engineers and managers with specialized knowledge acquired in specialized schools had assumed this responsibility and planned every task to increase output. Their efforts standardized production, which then required less skill and virtually no independent judgment from workers.

The most influential advocate of efficient production was Frederick W. Taylor. As foreman and engineer for the Midvale Steel Company in the 1880s, Taylor concluded that the best way a company could lessen fixed costs and increase profits was to apply scientific studies of "how quickly the various kinds of work . . . ought to be done." The "ought" in Taylor's formulation signified producing more for lower cost per unit, usually by eliminating unnecessary workers. Similarly, "how quickly" signified that time and money were equivalent. Above all, efficiency was a science.

Frederick W. Taylor and Efficiency

In 1898 Taylor took his stopwatch to the Bethlehem Steel Company to illustrate how his principles of scientific management worked. His experiments, he explained, required studying workers and devising "a series of motions which can be made quickest and best." Applying this technique to the shoveling of ore, Taylor designed fifteen kinds of shovels and prescribed the proper motions for using each one. He succeeded in reducing a crew of 600 men to 140.

As a result of Taylor's writings and experiments, time, as much as quality, became the measure of acceptable work, and science rather than experience determined the ways of doing things. As integral features of the assembly line, where work was divided into specific time-determined tasks, employees like "S" became another kind of interchangeable part.

Mechanization and the Changing Status of Labor

By 1880 the status of labor had undergone a dramatic shift in just a single generation. Technological innovation and assembly-line production created new jobs, but because most machines were labor-saving, fewer workers could produce more in less time. Moreover, as "S" knew firsthand, workers could no longer accurately be termed producers, as farmers and craftsmen had traditionally thought of themselves. The working class now consisted mainly of employees—men, women, and children who worked only when someone hired them. Producers had been paid by consumers in accordance with the quality of what they produced; now, employees received wages for time spent on the job.

As mass production subdivided manufacturing into small tasks, workers continually repeated the same specialized operation. One investigator found that the worker became "a mere machine. . . . Take the proposition of a man operating a machine to nail on 40 to 60 cases of heels in a day. That is 2,400 pairs, 4,800 shoes in a day. One not accustomed to it would wonder how a man could pick up and lay down 4,800 shoes in a day, to say nothing of putting them . . . into a machine. . . . That is the driving method of the manufacture of shoes under these minute subdivisions."

By reducing the manufacturing process to simplified tasks constantly repeated, and by coordinating production to the running of machinery, assembly lines also deprived employees of their independence. Workers could no longer decide when to begin and end the workday, when to rest, and what tools and techniques to use. As a Massachusetts factory operative testified in 1879, "During working hours the men are not allowed to speak to each other, though working close together, on pain of instant discharge. Men are hired to watch and patrol the shop." And workers were now surrounded by others who labored at the same rate for the same pay, regardless of the quality of their work.

Workers affected by these changes did not accept them passively. Employees struggled to retain independence and self-respect in the face of employers' ever-increasing power. As new groups encountered the industrial system, they resisted in various ways. Artisans such as cigar makers, glass workers, and coopers (barrel makers), caught in the transition from hand labor to machine production, fought to preserve their work pace and to retain shop customs such as appointing a fellow worker to read a newspaper aloud while they worked. When immigrants went to work in factories, they often persuaded foremen to hire their relatives and friends, thus preserving on-the-job family and village ties. Off the job, workers continued to gather for leisure-time activities such as social drinking and holiday celebrations, ignoring employers' attempts to control their social lives.

Employers established standards of behavior and work incentives that they thought would enhance efficiency and productivity. To make workers docile (like the machines they operated), employers supported temperance and moral-reform societies, dedicated to combating immoderate drinking and debauchery. Ford Motor Company required workers to meet the company's behavior code before they became eligible for the profit-sharing segment of the Five-Dollar-Day plan. Other employers established piecework rates, paying workers an amount per item produced, rather than an hourly wage, to increase productivity and maximize use of machines.

As machines and assembly lines reduced the need for skilled workers, employers cut labor costs by hiring women and children. Between 1880 and 1900, the numbers of employed women soared from 2.6 million to 8.6 million. At the same time their occupational patterns underwent striking changes (see Figure 18.1). The proportion of women in domestic-service jobs (maids, cooks, laundresses)—the most common and lowest-paid form of female employment—dropped dramatically as jobs opened in other sectors. In manufacturing, women usually held menial positions in textile mills and food-processing plants that paid as little as $1.56 a week for seventy hours of labor. (Unskilled men received $7 to $10 for a similar workweek.) Though the number of female factory hands tripled between 1880 and 1900, the proportion of women workers in these jobs remained about the same.

Employment of Women

General expansion of the industrial and retail sectors, however, caused the numbers and percentages of women in clerical jobs—typists, bookkeepers, sales clerks—to skyrocket. By 1920 nearly half of all clerical workers were women; in 1880 only 4 percent had been women. Previously, when sales and office positions had required accounting and letter-writing skills, men had dominated such jobs. Then, new inventions such as the typewriter, cash register, and adding machine simplified these tasks. Companies eagerly hired women who had taken trade-school courses in typing and shorthand and were looking for the better pay and conditions that clerical jobs offered compared to factory and domestic work. An official of a sugar company observed in 1919 that "all the bookkeeping of this company . . . is done by three girls and three bookkeeping machines . . . one operator takes the place of three men." Though paid low wages, women also were attracted to sales jobs because of the respectability, pleasant surroundings, and contact

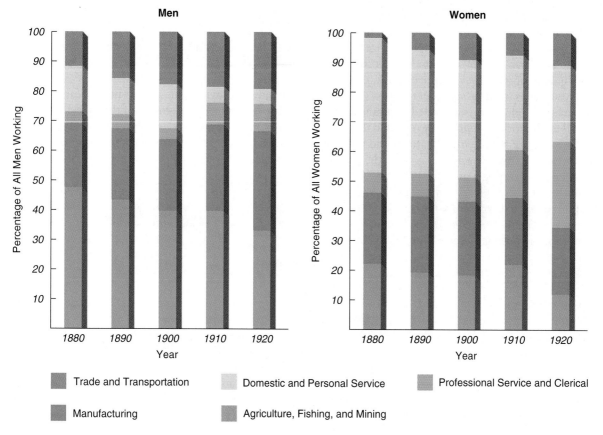

Figure 18.1 **Distribution of Occupational Categories Among Employed Men and Women, 1880–1920** The changing lengths of the bar segments of each part of this graph represent trends in male and female employment. Over the forty years covered by this graph, the agriculture, fishing, and mining segment for men and the domestic service segment for women declined the most, while notable increases occurred in manufacturing for men and services (especially store clerks and teachers) for women. (Source: U.S. Bureau of the Census, *Census of the United States, 1880, 1890, 1900, 1910, 1920* [Washington: U.S. Government Printing Office].)

with affluent customers that such positions offered. Nevertheless, sex discrimination pervaded the clerical sector. In department stores, male cashiers took in cash and made change; women were seldom given responsibility for billing or counting money. The new jobs offered women some opportunities for advancement to supervisory positions, but males dominated the managerial ranks.

Although most children who worked toiled on their parents' farms, the number in nonagricultural occupations tripled between 1870 and 1900. In 1890 over 18 percent of all children between ages ten and fifteen were gainfully employed (see Figure 18.2). Textile and shoe factories in particular employed many workers below age sixteen. Mecha-

Child Labor

nization created numerous light tasks, such as running errands and helping machine operators, that children could handle at a fraction of adult wages. Conditions were especially hard for child laborers in the South, where burgeoning textile mills needed unskilled hands. Mill owners induced white sharecroppers and tenant farm families, who otherwise might not have had any jobs or income, to bind their children over to factories at miserably low wages.

Several states, especially in the Northeast, passed laws specifying minimum ages and maximum workday hours for child labor. But most large companies could evade regulations because state statutes could regulate only firms operating within state borders, not those engaged in interstate commerce. Enforcing age requirements proved difficult because many parents,

Factories employed children from the early nineteenth century well into the twentieth. In textile mills like the one pictured here, girls operated machines, and boys ran messages and carried materials back and forth. Mill girls had to tie up their hair to keep it from getting caught in the machines. The girl posing here with a shawl over her head would not have worn that garment while she was working. (National Archives)

needing income from child labor, lied about their children's ages and employers rarely asked. One woman who had worked in the huge Amoskeag Mills of Manchester, New Hampshire, recalled how easy it was to get a job without proof of age. "I was twelve years old when I arrived here and started work," she recalled. "All we had to do was show them that we were fourteen years old. Tall or short, it didn't matter; they'd just ask, 'Are you fourteen years old?' OK. That's all. So that's how I went in to work." By 1900 state laws and automation had reduced the number of children employed in manufacturing, but many more worked at street trades—shining shoes and peddling newspapers and other merchandise—and as helpers in stores. Not until the Progressive era did reformers seek federal legislation to control child labor (see Chapter 21).

Although working conditions were often dangerous and unhealthy, low wages most often acted as the catalyst of worker unrest. Many employers believed in the "iron law of wages," which dictated that employees

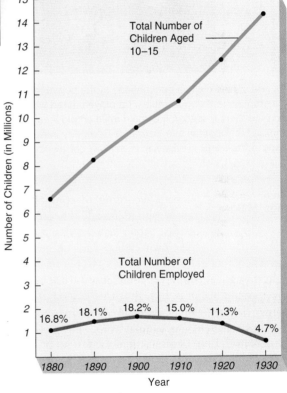

Figure 18.2 Children in the Labor Force, 1880–1930
The percentage of children in the labor force peaked around the turn of the century. Thereafter, the passage of state laws requiring children to attend school until age fourteen and limiting the ages at which children could be employed caused child labor to decline. (Source: Data from *The Statistical History of the United States from Colonial Times to the Present* [Stamford, Conn.: Fairfield Publishers, 1965].)

The rise of new clerical occupations at the beginning of the twentieth century gave women countless employment opportunities. Employers hired women to file company records and type letters and paid them less than they paid male employees. The floor-to-ceiling file cases in the records room of Metropolitan Life Insurance Company in New York was the largest outfit of steel file cases in the world.   (Museum of the City of New York, Gift of Donald Beggs)

Wage Work

be paid according to conditions of supply and demand. Theoretically, because laborers were free to make their own choices and because employers competed for labor, workers would receive the highest wages an employer could afford without being driven out of business. In reality, the "iron law" meant that employers could pay as little as possible, as long as there were workers willing to accept whatever wages were offered. Employers justified the system by invoking individual freedom: a worker who did not like the wages being paid was free to quit and find a job elsewhere.

Courts regularly denied workers the right to organize and bargain collectively on the grounds that wages should be individually negotiated between employee and employer. In contrast, wage earners believed the system trapped them. A factory worker told Congress in 1879, "The market is glutted, and we have seasons of dullness; advantage is taken of men's wants, and the pay is cut down; our tasks are increased, and if we remon-

strate, we are told our places can be filled. I work harder now than when my pay was twice as high."

Even steady employment proved insecure. Repetitive tasks using high-speed machinery dulled concentration, and the slightest mistake could cause serious injury. Industrial accidents rose steadily before 1920, killing or maiming hundreds of thousands of people each year. As late as 1913, after factory owners had installed safety devices, some 25,000 people died in industrial mishaps, and close to 1 million were injured. Each year sensational disasters, such as explosions and mine cave-ins, aroused public clamor for better safety regulations. The most notorious tragedy was a fire at New York City's Triangle Shirtwaist Company in 1911, which killed 146 workers, most of them teenage Jewish immigrant women who had been trapped in locked workrooms. Equally tragic, however, were the countless accidents that left workers with mangled limbs, infected cuts, chronic illness, and death. Because

Industrial Accidents

disability insurance and pensions were almost nonexistent, families stricken by such accidents suffered acutely.

Prevailing free-market views hampered the passage of legislation that would regulate hours and working conditions, and employers denied responsibility for employees' well-being. As one railroad manager declared, "The regular compensation of employees covers all risk or liability to accident. If an employee is disabled by sickness or any other cause, the right to claim compensation is not recognized." The only recourse for a stricken family was to sue and prove in court that the killed or injured worker had not realized the risks involved and had not caused the accident, an expensive route that very few ever took.

Reformers and union leaders lobbied Congress for laws to improve working conditions, but the Supreme Court limited the scope of such legislation by narrowly defining

Courts Restrict Labor Reform

what jobs were dangerous and which workers needed protection. In *Holden v. Hardy* (1896), the Court upheld a law regulating working hours of miners because overly long hours would increase the threat of injury. In *Lochner v. New York* (1905), however, the Court struck down a law limiting bakery workers to a sixty-hour week and a ten-hour day. Responding to the argument that states had the authority to protect workers' health and safety, the Court ruled that baking was not a dangerous enough occupation to justify restricting the right of workers to sell their labor freely. According to the Court, interference with the right of individuals to make contracts for their labor would violate the Fourteenth Amendment's guarantee that no state could "deprive any person of life, liberty, or property without due process of law."

In *Muller v. Oregon* (1908), the Court used a different rationale to uphold a law limiting women to a ten-hour workday in laundries. In this case, setting aside its *Lochner* argument, the Court asserted that women's health and reproductive functions required protection. According to the Court, a woman's well-being "becomes an object of public interest and care in order to preserve the strength and vigor of the race." Though the case represented a victory for those seeking government's right to regulate hours and working conditions, as a result of *Muller*'s success, later laws barred women from occupations such as printing and transportation, which required long hours or night work, and thus further confined women to menial, dead-end jobs.

Industrialization left numerous casualties from accidents involving machines and workers. Permanent disability and sometimes even death created dire hardship for working-class families living on the edge of subsistence.   (George Eastman House)

Throughout the nineteenth century, tensions rose and fell as workers confronted mechanization. Adjustments were made as different groups—rural migrants, foreign immigrants, women, and children—entered the industrial labor force. Some people submitted to the demands of the factory, machine, and time clock. Some tried to blend old ways of working into the new system. Some never adjusted and wandered from place to place, job to job. Others, however, turned to organized resistance.

The year 1877 marked a crisis for labor. In July a series of strikes broke out among unionized railroad workers who were protesting wage cuts. Violence spread from Pennsyl-

Railroad Strikes of 1877

vania and West Virginia to the Midwest, Texas, and California. Venting pent-up anger, rioters attacked railroad property, derailing trains and burning railroad yards. State militia companies, organized and commanded by employers, broke up picket lines and fired into threatening crowds. In several communities, factory workers, wives, and even merchants aided the strikers, while railroads enlisted strikebreakers to replace union men.

The worst violence occurred in Pittsburgh, where on July 21 militiamen bayoneted and fired on rock-throwing demonstrators, killing ten and wounding many more. Infuriated, the mob drove the soldiers into a railroad roundhouse and set fires that destroyed 39 buildings, 104 engines, and 1,245 freight and passenger cars. The next day, the troops shot their way out of the roundhouse and killed twenty more citizens before fleeing the city. After more than a month of unprecedented carnage, President Rutherford B. Hayes sent federal troops to end the strikes—the first significant use of soldiers to quell labor unrest.

The immediate cause of these strikes was the squeeze of hard times. In the economic slump that followed the Panic of 1873, railroad managers cut wages, increased workloads, and laid off workers, especially those who had joined unions. Such actions drove workers to strike and riot. Laborers in other industries sympathized with the strikers, as did residents of their communities. A Pittsburgh state militiaman, ordered out to break the 1877 strike, recalled, "I talked to all the strikers I could get my hands on, and I could find but one spirit and one purpose among them—that they were justified in resorting to any means to break down the power of the corporations."

The Union Movement

After 1877 anxiety over the loss of independence and a desire for better wages, hours, and working conditions pushed more workers into unions. Trade unions, which excluded everyone except skilled workers in particular crafts such as printing and iron molding, dated from the early nineteenth century, but the narrowness of their membership left them without broad power. The National Labor Union, founded in 1866, claimed 640,000 members in a variety of industries in 1868 but collapsed during the hard times of the 1870s. The only broad-based labor organization to survive that depression was the Knights of Labor.

Knights of Labor

Founded in 1869 by Philadelphia garment cutters, the Knights began recruiting other workers in the 1870s. In 1879 Terence V. Powderly, a machinist and mayor of Scranton, Pennsylvania, was elected grand master. Under his forceful guidance and, in contrast to most craft unions, will-

ingness to welcome women, African Americans, immigrants, and all unskilled and semiskilled workers, Knights membership mushroomed, peaking at 730,000 in 1886.

The Knights tried to avert the bleak future that they believed industrialism portended by building a workers' alliance that would offer an alternative to profit-oriented industrial capitalism. They believed they could eliminate conflict by establishing a cooperative society in which laborers worked for themselves, not for those who possessed capital. The goal, argued Powderly, was to "eventually make every man his own master—every man his own employer. . . . There is no good reason why labor cannot, through cooperation, own and operate mines, factories, and railroads." Like many farmers, the Knights saw producer and consumer cooperatives as preferable to capitalist control. This view simultaneously strengthened and weakened the organization. The cooperative idea, attractive in the abstract, gave laborers little bargaining power because employers held all the economic leverage. Strikes offered one means of achieving immediate goals, but Powderly and other Knights leaders opposed strikes, arguing that they tended to divert attention from the long-term goal of a cooperative society and that workers tended to lose more strikes than they won.

Some Knights, however, did support militant action. In 1886 the Knights demanded higher wages and union recognition from railroads in the Southwest. Railroad magnate Jay Gould refused to negotiate, and a strike began March 1 in Texas and spread to Kansas, Missouri, and Arkansas. As violence increased, Powderly met with Gould and called off the strike, hoping to settle the conflict. But Gould again rejected concessions, and the Knights had to give in. Militant craft unions began to desert the Knights, upset by Powderly's compromising position and confident that they could attain more on their own. Membership in the Knights dwindled, although the union survived in a few small towns, where it made a brief attempt to unite with Populists in the 1890s (see Chapter 20). The special interests of craft unions replaced the Knights' broad-based but often vague appeal, and dreams of labor unity faded.

Nevertheless, workers continued to strive to regain control of their work, and several groups rallied around the issue of an eight-hour workday. In Chicago on May 1, 1886, the campaign for the eight-hour day generated mass strikes and the largest spontaneous labor demonstration in the country's history. Some one hundred thousand workers

Haymarket Riot

The Haymarket Riot of 1886 was one of the most violent incidents of labor unrest in the late nineteenth century. This drawing, from *Frank Leslie's Illustrated Newspaper,* shows workers fleeing while police beat demonstrators with nightsticks. As this clash was occurring, a bomb, allegedly set off by anarchists, exploded, killing both police and workers.   (Library of Congress)

turned out, including not only craft unions but also radical anarchists who believed in using violence to replace all government with voluntary cooperation. In Europe, labor radicals had made May 1 a day of special demonstration, and Chicago police, fearing that European radicals were transplanting their tradition of violence to the United States, mobilized to prevent disorder, especially among striking workers at the huge McCormick reaper plant. The day passed calmly, but two days later police stormed an area near the factory and broke up a battle between striking unionists and nonunion strikebreakers. Police shot and killed two unionists and wounded several others.

The next evening, labor groups rallied at Haymarket Square, near downtown Chicago, to protest police brutality. As a police company approached, a bomb exploded, killing seven and injuring sixty-seven. In reaction against immigrant radicals, mass arrests of anarchists and unionists followed. Eventually a court convicted eight anarchists of the bombing, though the evidence of their guilt was questionable. Four were executed and one committed suicide in prison. The remaining three were pardoned in 1893 by Illinois governor John P. Altgeld, who believed they had been victims of the "malicious ferocity" of the courts. Altgeld's act of conscience ruined his political career when supporters of capitalism denounced him as a friend of anarchy.

The Haymarket bombing, like the 1877 railroad strikes, drew attention to the growing discontent of labor and revived fear of radicalism. The participation of anarchists and socialists, many of them foreign-born, created a feeling that forces of law and order had to act swiftly to prevent social turmoil. To protect their city, private Chicago donors helped to establish a military base at Fort Sheridan and the Great Lakes Naval Training Station. Elsewhere, governments strengthened police forces and armories. Employer associations, coalitions of manufacturers in the same industry, countered labor militancy by drawing up blacklists of union activists whom they would not employ, and by agreeing to resist strikes.

The American Federation of Labor (AFL) emerged from the 1886 upheavals as the major workers' organization. An alliance of national craft unions, the AFL had about 140,000 members, most of them skilled workers. Led by Samuel Gompers, a pragmatic and opportunistic immigrant who headed the Cigar Makers' Union, the AFL avoided the Knights' and anarchists' idealistic rhetoric of worker solidarity to press for concrete goals: higher wages, shorter hours, and the right to bargain collectively. As Gompers's associate Adolph Strasser explained, "We are fighting only for immediate objects . . . that can be realized in a few years." In contrast to the Knights of Labor, the AFL accepted the industrial system and worked to improve conditions within the wage-and-hours system. Member unions retained autonomy in their own areas of interest but tried to develop a general policy that would suit all members. Since these unions tried to protect skilled workers by organizing by craft rather than by workplace, they had little interest in recruiting unskilled workers.

The AFL grew to 1 million members by 1901 and 2.5 million by 1917, when it represented 111 national unions and 27,000 local unions. The national

American Federation of Labor

organization required constituent unions to hire organizers to expand membership, and it collected dues for a fund to aid members on strike. The AFL avoided party politics, adhering instead to Gompers's dictum to support labor's friends and oppose its enemies, regardless of party.

The AFL and the labor movement suffered a series of setbacks in the early 1890s, when once again labor violence stirred public fears. In July 1892 the AFL-affiliated Amalgamated Association of Iron and Steelworkers refused to accept pay cuts and went on strike in Homestead, Pennsylvania. Henry C. Frick, president of Carnegie Steel Company, then closed the plant. Shortly thereafter, Frick tried to protect the plant by hiring three hundred guards from the Pinkerton Detective Agency and floating them in by barge under cover of darkness. Lying in wait on the shore of the Monongahela River, angry workers attacked and routed the guards. State militiamen intervened, and after five months the strikers gave in. By then public opinion had turned against the union because of an attempt on Frick's life by a young anarchist who was not a striker.

In 1894 workers at the Pullman Palace Car Company walked out in protest over exploitative policies at the company town near Chicago.

Pullman Strike The paternalistic George Pullman provided everything for the twelve thousand residents of his so-called model town named after him. His company owned and controlled all land and buildings, the school, the bank, and the water and gas systems. It paid wages, fixed rents, and spied on disgruntled employees. As one laborer grumbled, "We are born in a Pullman house, fed from the Pullman shop, taught in the Pullman school, catechized in the Pullman church, and when we die we shall be buried in the Pullman cemetery and go to the Pullman hell."

One thing Pullman would not do was negotiate with workers. When the hard times that began in 1893 threatened his prosperity, Pullman protected profits and stock dividends by cutting wages 25 to 40 percent while holding firm on rents and prices in the town. Hard-pressed workers sent a committee to Pullman to protest his policies. He reacted by firing three members of the committee. Enraged workers, most of them from the American Railway Union, called a strike; Pullman retaliated by closing the factory. The union, led by the charismatic Eugene V. Debs, voted to aid the strikers by refusing to handle any Pullman cars attached to any trains. Pullman still rejected arbitration.

The railroad owners' association then enlisted aid from U.S. Attorney General Richard Olney, who obtained a court injunction to prevent the union from "obstructing the railways and holding up the mails." President Grover Cleveland ordered federal troops to Chicago, ostensibly to protect the rail-carried mails but in reality to crush the strike. Within a month strikers gave in, and Debs went to prison for defying the court injunction. The Supreme Court upheld Debs's six-month sentence on grounds that the federal government had the power to remove obstacles to interstate commerce.

In the West, radical labor activity arose among Colorado miners, who engaged in several bitter struggles and violent strikes. In 1905 these

IWW workers helped form a new labor organization, the Industrial Workers of the World (IWW). Unlike the AFL, the IWW strove like the Knights of Labor to unify all laborers, including the unskilled who were excluded from craft unions. Its motto was "An injury to one is an injury to all," and its goal was "One Big Union." But the "Wobblies," as IWW members were known, exceeded the goals of the Knights and espoused socialism and tactics of violence and sabotage.

Embracing the rhetoric of class conflict—"The final aim is revolution," according to IWW creed—and an ideology of socialism, Wobblies believed workers should seize and run the nation's industries. "Mother" Jones, an Illinois coalfield union organizer; Elizabeth Gurley Flynn, a fiery orator known as the "Joan of Arc of the labor movement"; and William D. (Big Bill) Haywood, the brawny, one-eyed founder of the Western Federation of Miners, led a series of strife-torn strikes. Demonstrations erupted in western lumber and mining camps, in the steel town of McKees Rocks, Pennsylvania (1907), and in the textile mills of Lawrence, Massachusetts (1912). Though the Wobblies' anticapitalist goals and aggressive tactics attracted considerable publicity, IWW membership probably never exceeded 150,000. The organization collapsed during the First World War when federal prosecution sent many of its leaders to jail and local police forces and mobs violently harassed IWW members.

Many unions, notably those of the AFL, openly rejected female members. Of 6.3 million employed women in 1910, fewer than 2 percent

Women and the Labor Movement belonged to unions. Male unionists often rationalized the exclusion of women by insisting that women should not be employed. According

In 1919, telephone operators, mostly female, went out on strike and shut down phone service throughout New England. These workers, who interrupted their picketing to pose for the photograph, showed that women could take forceful action in support of their labor interests. (Corbis-Bettmann)

to one labor leader, "Woman is not qualified for the conditions of wage labor. . . . The mental and physical makeup of woman is in revolt against wage service. She is competing with the man who is her father or husband or is to become her husband." Mostly, unionists feared competition. Because women were paid less than men, males worried that their own wages would be lowered or that they would lose their jobs if women invaded the workplace. Moreover, male workers, accustomed to sex segregation in employment, could not imagine working side by side with women.

Yet female employees could organize and fight employers as strenuously as men could. Since the early years of industrialization, women had formed their own unions. Some, such as the Collar Laundry Union of Troy, New York, organized in the 1860s, had successfully struck for higher wages. The "Uprising of the 20,000" in New York City, a 1909 strike by immigrant members—most of them women—of the International Ladies Garment Workers Union (ILGWU), was one of the country's largest strikes to that time. Women were also prominent in the 1912 Lawrence, Massachusetts, textile workers' "Bread and Roses" strike. Female trade-union membership swelled during the 1910s, but men monopolized national trade

union leadership, even in industries with large female work forces, such as garment manufacturing, textiles, and boots and shoes.

Women, however, did dominate one union: the Telephone Operators' Department of the International Brotherhood of Electrical Workers. Organized in Montana and San Francisco early in the twentieth century, the union spread throughout the Bell system, the nation's monopolistic telephone company and single largest employer of women. To promote solidarity among their mostly young members, union leaders organized dances, excursions, and bazaars. They also sponsored educational programs to enhance members' leadership skills. The union focused mainly on workplace issues. Intent on developing pride and independence among telephone operators, the union opposed scientific management techniques and tightening of supervision. In 1919 several militant union branches paralyzed the phone service of five New England states. The union collapsed after a failed strike, again in New England, in 1923, but not before women had proved to contemporaries that they could battle a powerful employer.

The first women's organization seeking to promote the interests of laboring women was the

Women's Trade Union League (WTUL), founded in 1903 and patterned after a similar organization in England. The WTUL sought protective legislation for female workers, sponsored educational activities, and campaigned for women's suffrage. It helped telephone operators organize their union, and in 1909 it supported the ILGWU's massive strike against New York City sweatshops. Initially the union's highest offices were held by middle-class women who sympathized with female wage laborers, but control shifted in the 1910s to forceful working-class leaders, notably Agnes Nestor, a glove maker; Rose Schneiderman, a cap maker; and Mary Anderson, a shoe worker. The WTUL advocated changes such as opening apprenticeship programs to women so they could enter skilled trades and training female workers to assume leadership roles. It served as a vital link between the labor and women's movements into the 1920s.

Immigrants, African Americans, and Labor Unions

Organized labor excluded most immigrant and African American workers, often fearing that such groups would depress wages. Some trade unions welcomed skilled immigrants—foreign-born craftsmen were prominent leaders of several unions—but only the Knights of Labor and the IWW had explicit policies of accepting immigrants and blacks. Blacks were prominent in the coal miners' union, and they were partially unionized in trades such as construction, barbering, and dock work, which had large numbers of African American workers. But they could belong only to segregated local unions in the South, and the majority of northern AFL unions had exclusion policies. Long-held prejudices were reinforced when blacks and immigrants, eager for any work they could get, worked as strikebreakers, hired to replace striking whites.

The dramatic labor struggles in the half-century following the Civil War make it easy to forget that only a small fraction of American wage workers belonged to unions. In 1900 about 1 million out of a total of 27.6 million workers were unionized. By 1920 total union membership had grown to 5 million, still only 13 percent of the work force. Unionization was strong in construction trades, transportation, communications, and, to a lesser extent, manufacturing. For many workers, getting and holding a job held priority over wages and hours. Job instability and the seasonal nature of work seriously hindered union-organizing efforts. Few companies employed a full work force all year round; most employers hired workers during peak seasons and laid them off during slack periods. Thus employment rates fluctuated wildly. The 1880 census showed that in some communities 30 percent of adult males had been jobless at some time during the previous year. Moreover, union organizers took no interest in large segments of the industrial labor force and intentionally barred others.

The millions of men, women, and children who were not unionized tried in their own ways to cope with pressures of the machine age.

Fraternal Societies

Increasing numbers, both native-born and immigrant, turned to fraternal societies such as the Polish Roman Catholic Union and the Jewish B'nai B'rith. For small monthly or yearly contributions these organizations provided members with life insurance, sickness benefits, and funeral expenses and became widespread by the early twentieth century.

For most American workers, then, the machine age had mixed results. Industrial wages rose between 1877 and 1914, boosting purchasing power and creating a mass market for standardized goods. Yet in 1900 most employees worked sixty hours a week at wages that averaged 20 cents an hour for skilled work and 10 cents an hour for unskilled. Moreover, as wages rose, living costs increased even faster.

Standards of Living

Some Americans, like "S," distrusted machines, but few could resist the changes that mechanization brought to everyday life. The expansion of railroad, postal, telephone, and electrical service drew even isolated communities into the orbit of a consumer-oriented society. American ingenuity combined with mass production and mass marketing to make available myriad goods that previously had not existed or had been the exclusive property of the wealthy. The new material well-being, heralded by products such as ready-made clothes, canned foods, and home appliances, had a dual effect. It blended Americans of differing status into consumer communities defined not by place or class but by possessions, and it accentuated differences between those who could afford goods and services and those who could not.

If a society's affluence can be measured by how it converts luxuries into commonplace articles, the United States was indeed becoming affluent in the years between 1880 and 1920. In 1880 smokers rolled their own cigarettes; only wealthy women could afford

New Availability of Products

silk stockings; only residents of Florida, Texas, and California could enjoy fresh oranges; and people made candy and soap at home. By 1899 manufactured goods and perishable foodstuffs had become increasingly available. That year Americans bought 2 billion machine-produced cigarettes and 151,000 pairs of silk stockings, consumed oranges at the rate of 100 crates for every 1,000 people, and spent an average of $1.08 per person on store-bought candy and 63 cents per person on soap. By 1921 the transformation had advanced even further. Americans smoked 43 billion cigarettes that year (403 per person), bought 217 million pairs of silk stockings, ate 248 crates of oranges per 1,000 people, and spent $1.66 per person on confectionery goods and $1.40 per person on soap.

What people can afford obviously depends on their resources and incomes. Data for the period show that incomes rose broadly. The expanding economy spawned massive fortunes and created a new industrial elite. An 1891 magazine article estimated that 120 Americans were worth at least $10 million. By 1920 the richest 5 percent of the population received almost one-fourth of all earned income. (The proportion received by the richest 5 percent declined over the next fifty years but has risen again to match the 1920 level.)

Incomes also rose among the middle class. For example, average pay for clerical workers rose 36 percent between 1890 and 1910 (see Table 18.1). At the turn of the century, employees of the federal executive branch averaged $1,072 a year, and college professors $1,100—not handsome sums, but much more than manual workers received. With such incomes, the middle class, whose numbers were increasing as a result of new job opportunities, could afford relatively comfortable housing. A six- or seven-room house cost around $3,000 to buy or build and from $15 to $20 per month to rent.

Though wages for industrial workers increased, their income figures were deceptive because jobs were not always stable and workers had to expend a disproportionate amount of income on necessities. On average, annual wages of factory workers rose from $486 in 1890 to $630 in 1910, about 30 percent. In industries with large female work forces, such as shoe and paper manufacturing, hourly rates remained lower than in male-dominated industries such as coal mining and iron production. Regional variations were also wide. Nevertheless, as Table 18.1 shows, most wages moved upward. Income for farm laborers followed the same

Table 18.1 American Living Standards, 1890–1910

	1890	1910
Income and earnings		
Annual income		
Clerical worker	$848	$1,156
Public school teacher	256	492
Industrial worker	486	630
Farm laborer	233	336
Hourly wage		
Soft-coal miner	0.18[a]	0.21
Iron worker	0.17[a]	0.23
Shoe worker	0.14[a]	0.19
Paper worker	0.12[a]	0.17
Labor statistics		
Number of people in labor force	28.5 million	41.7 million[b]
Average workweek in manufacturing	60 hours	51 hours

a. 1892
b. 1920

trend, though wages remained relatively low because farm workers generally received free room and board.

Wage increases mean little, however, if living costs rise as fast or faster. That is what happened. The weekly cost of living for a typical wage earner's family of four rose over 47 percent between 1889 and 1913. In other words, a combination of food and other goods that cost $6.78 in 1889 increased, after a slight dip in the mid-1890s, to $10 by 1913. In few working-class occupations did income rise as fast as the cost of living.

Cost of Living

How then could working-class Americans afford machine-age new goods and services? Many could not. The daughter of a textile worker, recalling her school days, described how "some of the kids would bring bars of chocolate, others an orange. . . . I suppose they were richer than a family like ours. My father used to buy a bag of candy and a bag of peanuts every payday. . . . And that's all we'd have until the next payday." Another woman explained how her family coped with high prices and low wages: "My mother made our clothes. People then wore old clothes. My mother would rip them out and make them over."

Still, a family could raise its income and partake modestly in consumer society by sending children and women into the labor market (see pages 495–497). In a household where the father made $600 a year, wages of other family members might lift total income, or the family wage, to $800 or $900. Many families also rented rooms to boarders and lodgers, a practice that could yield up to $200 a year. These means of increasing family income enabled people to spend more and save more. Between 1889 and 1901, working-class families markedly increased expenditures for life insurance, alcoholic beverages, and union dues as well as for new leisure activities (see Chapter 19). Workers were thus able to improve their living standards, but not without sacrifices.

Supplements to Family Income

More than ever, American working people engaged in a highly developed wage and money economy. Between 1890 and 1920, the labor force increased by 50 percent, from 28 million workers to 42 million. These figures, however, are somewhat misleading: in general, they represent a change in the nature of work as much as an increase in the number of available jobs. In the rural society that predominated in the nineteenth century, women and children per-

formed jobs crucial to the family's daily existence—cooking, cleaning, planting, and harvesting—but they seldom appeared in employment figures because they earned no wages. But as the nation industrialized, and the agricultural sector's share of national income and population declined, paid employment became more common. Jobs in industry and commerce were easier to define and easier to count. The proportion of Americans who worked—whether in fields, households, factories, or offices—probably did not increase markedly. Most Americans, male and female, had always worked. What was new was the increase in paid employment, making purchases of consumer goods and services more affordable.

Science and technology eased some of life's struggles, and their impact on living standards grew after 1900. Advances in medical care, better diets, and improved housing sharply reduced death rates and extended the life span. Between 1900 and 1920, life expectancy rose by fully six years and the death rate dropped by 24 percent. During this period notable declines occurred in deaths from typhoid, diphtheria, influenza (except for a harsh pandemic in 1918 and 1919), tuberculosis, and intestinal ailments—diseases that had been scourges of earlier generations. There were, however, significantly more deaths from cancer, diabetes, and heart disease, afflictions of an aging population and of new environmental factors such as smoke and chemical pollution. Americans also found more ways to kill one another: although the suicide rate remained stable, homicides and automobile-related deaths—effects of a fast-paced urban society—increased dramatically.

Higher Life Expectancy

Not only were amenities and luxuries more available than in the previous half-century, but the means to upward mobility seemed more accessible as well. Education increasingly became the key to success. Public education, aided by construction of new schools and passage of laws that required children to stay in school to age fourteen, equipped young people to achieve a standard of living higher than their parents'. Between 1890 and 1922, the number of students enrolled in public high schools rose dramatically. The creation of managerial and sales jobs in service industries helped to counter the downward mobility that resulted when mechanization pushed skilled workers out of their crafts. Yet inequities that had pervaded earlier eras remained in place. Race, gender, religion, and ethnicity still determined access to opportunity.

The Quest for Convenience

The toilet stood at the vanguard of a revolution in American lifestyles. The chain-pull washdown water closet, invented in England around 1870, reached the United States in the 1880s. Shortly after 1900 the flush toilet appeared; thanks to mass production of enamel-coated fixtures, it became standard in American homes and buildings. The toilet, cheap and easy to install, brought about a shift in habits and attitudes. Before 1880 only luxury hotels and estates had private indoor bathrooms. By the 1890s the germ theory of disease had raised fears about carelessly disposed human waste as a source of infection and water contamination. Much more rapidly than Europeans did, Americans combined a desire for cleanliness with an urge for convenience, and water closets became common, especially in middle-class urban houses. (Flush toilets were not prevalent in working-class homes until the 1920s.) Bodily functions took on an unpleasant image, and the home bathroom became a place of utmost privacy. Edward and Clarence Scott, who produced white tissue in perforated rolls, provided Americans a more convenient form of toilet paper than the rough paper they had previously used. At the same time, the toilet and the private bathtub gave Americans new ways to use—and waste—water. Plumbing advances belonged to a broader democratization of convenience that accompanied mass production and consumerism.

Flush Toilets

The tin can also altered lifestyles. Before the mid-nineteenth century, Americans typically ate only foods that were in season. Drying, smoking, and salting could preserve meat for a short time, but the availability of fresh meat and fresh milk was limited; there was no way to prevent spoilage. A French inventor developed the cooking-and-sealing process of canning around 1810, and in the 1850s an American man named Gail Borden devised a means of condensing and preserving milk. Canned goods and condensed milk became more common during the 1860s, but supplies remained low because cans had to be made by hand. By 1880, however, inventors had fashioned stamping and soldering machines to mass-produce cans from tin plate. Now, even people remote from markets, like sailors and cowboys, could readily con-

Processed and Preserved Foods

Industrialization enhanced the incomes of the middle classes, enabling them to purchase goods previously unavailable and to provide amenities to their families more conveniently. This advertisement for a portable stove shows a father heating up milk for a baby that the mother is coddling. Note the bottle, tube, and nipple that the father is holding as well as the rug, furniture, clothing, vases, clock, and other items of moderate affluence. (Private Collection)

sume tomatoes, milk, oysters, and other alternatives to previously monotonous diets. Housewives also preserved their own fruits and vegetables, "putting up" foods in sealed glass jars.

Other trends and inventions broadened Americans' diets. Growing urban populations created demands that encouraged fruit and vegetable farmers to raise more produce. Railroad refrigerator cars enabled growers and meatpackers to ship perishables greater distances and to preserve them for longer periods. By the 1890s northern city dwellers could enjoy southern and western strawberries, grapes, and tomatoes for up to six months of the year. Home iceboxes enabled middle-class families to store perishables. An easy means of producing ice commercially was invented in the 1870s, and by 1900 the nation had over two thousand commercial ice plants, most of which made home deliveries.

The availability of new foods also inspired health reformers to correct the American diet. In the 1870s John H. Kellogg, a nutritionist and manager of the Western Health Reform Institute in Battle Creek, Michigan, began serving patients healthy new foods, including peanut butter and wheat flakes. Several years later his brother, William K. Kellogg, invented corn flakes, and Charles W. Post introduced Grape-Nuts, revolutionizing breakfast by replacing eggs, potatoes, and meat with ready-to-eat cereal, which supposedly was healthier. Just before the First World War, scientists discovered the dietetic value of vitamins A and B (C and D were discovered after the war). Growing numbers of published cookbooks and the opening of cooking schools reflected heightened interest in food and its possibilities for health and enjoyment.

Dietary Reform

Even the working class enjoyed a more diversified diet. As in the past, the poorest people still ate cheap foods, heavy in starches and carbohydrates. Southern textile workers, for example, ate corn mush and fatback (the strip of meat from a hog's back) almost every day. Poor urban families seldom could afford meat. Now, though, many of them could purchase previously unavailable fruits, vegetables, and dairy products. Workers had to spend a high percentage of their income on food—almost half of the breadwinner's wages—but they never suffered the severe malnutrition that plagued other developing nations.

Just as tin cans and iceboxes made many foods widely available, the sewing machine brought about a revolution in clothing. Before 1850 nearly all the clothes Americans wore were made at home or by seamstresses and tailors, and a person's social status was apparent in what he or she wore. Then in the 1850s the sewing machine, invented in Europe but refined by Americans Elias Howe, Jr., and Isaac M. Singer, came into use in clothing and shoe manufacture. Demand for uniforms during the Civil War boosted the ready-made clothing industry, and by 1890 annual retail sales of mass-

Ready-made Clothing

produced garments reached $1.5 billion. Mass production enabled manufacturers to turn out good-quality apparel at relatively low cost and to standardize sizes to fit different body shapes. By 1900 only the poorest families could not afford "ready-to-wear" clothes. Tailors and seamstresses, once the originators of fashion, had been relegated to repair work. Some women continued to make clothing at home, to save money or as a hobby, but dress patterns intended for use with a sewing machine simplified the remaining home production of clothing and injected another form of standardization into everyday life.

Mass-produced clothing and dress patterns reinforced a concern for style. Restrictive Victorian fashions still dominated women's clothing, but women were abandoning the most burdensome features. As women's participation in work and leisure activities became more active, dress designers placed greater emphasis on comfort. In the 1890s long sleeves and skirt hemlines receded, and high-boned collars disappeared. Women began wearing tailored blouses called shirtwaists, mass-manufactured in factories such as the Triangle Shirtwaist Factory. Designers used less fabric; by the 1920s a dress required three yards of material instead of ten. Petite was still the ideal, however: the most desirable waist measurement was 18 to 20 inches, and corsets were big sellers. In the early 1900s, long hair tied behind the neck was the most popular style. By the First World War, when many women worked in hospitals and factories, shorter and less hindering hairstyles had become fashionable.

Men's clothes, too, became more lightweight and stylish. Before 1900 men in the middle and affluent working classes would have owned no more than two suits, one for Sundays and special occasions and one for everyday wear. After 1900, however, manufacturers began to produce garments from fabrics of different weights and for different seasons. Men replaced derbies with felt hats, and stiff collars and cuffs with soft ones; dark-blue serge gave way to lighter shades and more intricate weaves. Workingmen still needed the most durable, least expensive overalls, shirts, and shoes. But even for males of modest means, clothing was becoming something to be bought instead of made and remade at home.

Department stores and chain stores helped to create and serve this new consumerism. Between 1865 and 1900, Macy's in New York, Wanamaker's in Philadelphia, Marshall Field in Chicago, and Rich's in Atlanta became urban landmarks.

Department and Chain Stores

This photograph of the food counter at R. H. Macy's Department Store in 1902 indicates the large number of processed and preserved foods that became available to Americans at the end of the nineteenth century. The use of tin cans and glass bottles permitted food producers to sell products previously available only at limited times of the year.   (Museum of the City of New York, The Byron Collection)

Previously, working classes had bought their goods in stores with limited inventories, and wealthier people had patronized fancy shops; each was discouraged by price, quality of goods, and social custom from shopping at the other's establishments. Now department stores, with their open displays of clothing, housewares, and furniture—all available in large quantities to anyone with the purchase price—caused a merchandising revolution. They offered not only a wide variety but also home deliveries, exchange policies, and charge accounts.

Meanwhile, the Great Atlantic Tea Company, founded in 1859, became the first grocery chain. Renamed the Great Atlantic and Pacific Tea Company in 1869 (and known as A&P), the firm's stores bought in volume and sold to the public at low prices. By 1915 there were almost eighteen hundred A&P stores, and twelve thousand more were built in the next ten years. Other chains, such as Woolworth's, dime stores that sold inexpensive personal items and novelties, grew rapidly during the same period.

A society of scarcity does not need advertising: when demand exceeds supply, producers have no trouble selling what they market. But in a society of abundance such as industrial America, supply frequently outstrips demand, necessitating a means to increase and create demand. Thus advertising assumed a new scale and function. In 1865 retailers spent about $9.5 million on advertising; that sum reached $95 million by 1900 and nearly $500 million by 1919.

Advertising

A salesperson tries to convince an individual customer to buy a certain product—whether an insurance policy, an article of clothing, or a home appliance. Advertisers, by contrast, aim to invent needs and persuade large groups of people to buy a specific product—a brand of cigarettes, a particular cosmetic, a company's canned foods. In the late nineteenth century, large companies that mass-produced consumer goods charged advertisers to create "consumption communities," bodies of consumers loyal to a particular brand name.

How do historians know...

that traditional gender roles pervaded American consumer society in the late nineteenth century? Advertising, which developed into a powerful medium in the late nineteenth century, offers useful insights into prevailing social and cultural values, and advertisers, eager to sell new consumer products, helped shape those values with strong visual images. This 1882 advertisement for the W. J. Morgan Sewing Machine Company uses both explicit and implicit domestic images to reinforce a wife's role as homemaker. From the very onset of her family career, the ad implies, a woman assumes domestic tasks and obligations such as sewing and mending clothing, and her husband guides her into this role. The ad conveys other symbols and values as well, such as the devoted look on the woman's face and the strong and superior pose of the man. The clothing also implies a middle-class standard. Newspapers and magazine advertisements of the late nineteenth century are rich with clues about this period of flourishing consumerism.   (Photo: Library of Congress)

In 1881 Congress passed a trademark law enabling producers to register and protect brand names. Thousands of companies registered products as varied as Hires Root Beer, Uneeda Biscuits, and Carter's Little Liver Pills. Advertising agencies—a service industry pioneered by N. W. Ayer & Son of Philadelphia—in turn offered expert advice to companies that wished to cultivate brand loyalty. By the early 1900s, advertising techniques had been so perfected that French composer Jacques Offenbach observed, "Decidedly the American advertising men play upon the human mind as a musician plays on his piano."

Newspapers served as the prime vehicle for advertising. In the mid-nineteenth century, publishers began to pursue higher revenues by selling more ad space. Wanamaker's placed the first full-page ad in 1879, and advertisers began to print pictures of products. Such attention-getting techniques transformed advertising into news. More than ever before, people read newspapers to find out what was for sale as well as what was happening.

The Corporate Consolidation Movement

 Neither new products nor new marketing techniques could mask certain unsettling factors in the American economy. The huge capital investment in new technology meant that factories had to operate at near capacity to recover costs. But the more manufacturers produced, the more they had to sell. To sell more, they had to reduce prices. To increase profits and compensate for reduced prices, they further expanded production and often reduced wages. To expand, they borrowed money. And to repay loans, they had to produce and sell even more. This spiraling process strangled small firms that could not keep pace and thrust workers into constant uncertainty. The same cycle affected commerce, banking, and transportation as well as manufacturing.

In this environment, optimism could dissolve at the hint that debtors could not meet their obligations.

Indeed, financial panics afflicted the economy during every decade at the end of the nineteenth century, ruining businesses and destroying workers' security. Economic declines that began in 1873, 1884, and 1893 lingered for several years. Business leaders disagreed on what caused them. Some blamed overproduction; others pointed to underconsumption; still others blamed lax credit and investment practices. Whatever the explanation, businesspeople began seeking ways to combat the uncertainty of boom-and-bust business cycles. Many adopted centralized forms of business organization, notably corporations, pools, trusts, and holding companies.

Rise of Corporations

Unlike laborers, industrialists never questioned the capitalist system. They sought new ways to build on the base that had supported economic growth since the early 1800s, when states adopted incorporation laws to encourage commerce and industry. Under such laws, almost anyone could start a company and raise money by selling stock to investors. Stockholders could share in profits without personal risk because laws limited their liability for company debts to the amount of their own investment; the rest of their wealth was protected should the company fail. Nor did investors need to concern themselves with a firm's day-to-day operation; responsibility for company administration rested with its managers.

Corporations proved to be the best instruments to raise capital for industrial expansion, and by 1900 two-thirds of all goods manufactured in the United States were produced by corporate firms. Moreover, corporations won judicial protection in the 1880s and 1890s when the Supreme Court ruled that they, like individuals, are protected by the Fourteenth Amendment. That is, states could not deny corporations equal protection under the law and could not deprive them of rights or property without due process of law. Such rulings insulated corporations against government interference in their operations.

Pools

As downward swings of the business cycle threatened profits, corporation managers sought greater stability in new and larger forms of economic concentration. Between the late 1880s and early 1900s, an epidemic of business consolidation swept the United States, resulting in massive conglomerates that have since dominated the nation's economy. At first such alliances were tentative and informal, consisting mainly of cooperative agreements among firms that manufactured the same product or offered the same service. Through these arrangements, called pools, competing companies tried to control the market by agreeing how much each should produce and sharing profits. Employed by railroads (to divide up traffic), steel producers, and whiskey distillers, pools depended on their members' honesty. Such "gentlemen's agreements" worked during good times when there was enough business for all; but during slow periods, the desire for profits often tempted pool members to evade their commitments by secretly reducing prices or by selling more than the agreed quota. The Interstate Commerce Act of 1887 outlawed pools among railroads (see page 556), but by then the usefulness of the pooling strategy was already fading.

Trusts

John D. Rockefeller, boss of Standard Oil, disliked pools, calling them weak and undependable. In 1879 one of his lawyers, Samuel Dodd, devised a more stable means of dominating the market. Since state laws prohibited one corporation from holding stock in another corporation, Dodd adapted an old device called a trust, a legal arrangement whereby responsible individuals would manage the financial affairs of a person unwilling or unable to handle them alone. Dodd reasoned that one company could control an industry by luring or forcing stockholders of smaller companies in that industry to yield control of their stock "in trust" to the larger company's board of trustees. This device allowed Rockefeller to achieve horizontal integration of the profitable petroleum industry in 1882 by combining his Standard Oil Company of Ohio with other refineries he bought up.

Holding Companies

In 1888 New Jersey adopted new laws allowing corporations chartered there to own property in other states and to own stock in other corporations. (Trusts provided for trusteeship, not ownership.) This liberalization facilitated creation of the holding company, which owned a partial or complete interest in other companies. Holding companies could in turn merge their companies' assets (buildings, equipment, inventory, and cash) as well as their management. Under this arrangement, Rockefeller's holding company, Standard Oil of New Jersey, merged forty refining companies. By 1898 Standard Oil refined 84 percent of all oil produced in the nation, controlled most pipelines, and had moved into natural-gas production and ownership of oil-producing properties.

Believing that Rockefeller's Standard Oil monopoly was exercising dangerous power, this political cartoonist depicts the trust as a greedy octopus whose sprawling tentacles already ensnare Congress, state legislatures, and the taxpayer, and are reaching for the White House.   (Library of Congress)

Standard Oil's expansion into operations besides refining exemplified a new form of economic integration. To dominate their markets, many holding companies sought control over all aspects of their operations, including raw materials, production, and distribution. A model of such vertical integration, which fused related business activities into one entity under unified management, was Gustavus Swift's meat-processing operation. During the 1880s, Swift invested in livestock, slaughterhouses, refrigerator cars, and marketing to ensure profits from the sale of his beef at prices he could control.

Mergers provided an answer to industry's search for order and profits. Between 1889 and 1903, some three hundred combinations were formed, most of them trusts and holding companies. The most spectacular was U.S. Steel Corporation, financed by J. P. Morgan in 1901. This enterprise, made up of iron-ore properties, freight carriers, wire mills, plate and tubing companies, and other firms, was capitalized at over $1.4 billion. Other mammoth combinations included the Amalgamated Copper Company, American Sugar Refining Company, and U.S. Rubber Company. In 1896 fewer than a dozen corporations were worth over $10 million; by 1903 three hundred were worth that much and seventeen had assets exceeding $100 million. At the same time, these huge companies ruthlessly put thousands of smaller competitors out of business.

The merger movement created a new species of businessman, one whose vocation was financial organizing rather than producing a particular good or service. Shrewd operators sought opportunities for combination, formed a holding company, then persuaded producers to sell their firms to the new company. These financiers raised money by selling stock and borrowing from banks. Their attention ranged widely. W. H. Moore organized the American Tin Plate Company, Diamond Match Company, and National Biscuit Company, and he acquired control of the Rock Island Railroad. Elbert H. Gary similarly participated in consolidation of the barbed-wire industry and then of U.S. Steel. Investment bankers like J. P. Morgan and Jacob Schiff piloted the merger movement, inspiring awe with their financial power and organizational skills.

Financiers

The growth of corporations in the late nineteenth century turned financial stock and bond exchanges into hubs of activity. In 1886 trading on the New York Stock Exchange reached 1 million shares a day. By 1914 the number of industrial stocks traded reached 511, compared with 145 in 1869. Between 1870 and 1900, foreign investment in American companies rose from $1.5 billion to $3.5 billion. Personal savings and institutional investment also mushroomed: assets of savings banks, concentrated in the Northeast and West Coast, rose by 700 percent between 1875 and 1897 to a total of $2.2 billion. States loosened regulations to enable banks to invest in railroads and industrial enterprises. Commercial banks, insurance companies, and corporations also invested heavily. As one journal proclaimed, "Nearly the whole country (including the typical widow and orphan) is interested in the stock market." This exaggeration reflected what optimistic capitalists wanted to believe.

The Gospel of Wealth and Its Critics

Business leaders used corporate consolidation not to promote competition but to minimize it. To justify their tactics to a public committed to the free market, they called on the doctrine of Social Darwinism. Developed by British philosopher Herbert Spencer and preached in the United States by Yale professor William Graham Sumner, Social Darwinism loosely grafted Charles Darwin's theory of the survival of the fittest onto laissez faire, the doctrine that government should not interfere in private economic affairs. Social Darwinists reasoned that, in an unconstrained economy, power and wealth would flow naturally to the most capable people. Acquisition and possession of property were thus sacred and well-deserved rights. Civilization depended on this system, explained Sumner. "If we do not like the survival of the fittest," he wrote, "we have only one possible alternative, and that is survival of the unfittest." In this view, monopolies represented the natural accumulation of economic power by those best suited for wielding it.

Social Darwinism

Social Darwinists reasoned, too, that wealth carried moral responsibilities to provide for those less fortunate or less capable. Steel baron Andrew Carnegie asserted what he called "the Gospel of Wealth"—that he and other industrialists were guardians of society's wealth and that they had a duty to fulfill their obligation in humane ways. Over his lifetime, Carnegie donated more than $350 million to libraries, schools, peace initiatives, and the arts. Such philanthropy, however, also implied a right for benefactors like Rockefeller and Carnegie to define what was good and necessary for society; it did not translate into paying workers decent wages.

In contradiction, business leaders who extolled individual initiative and independence also pressed for government assistance. While denouncing efforts to legislate maximum working hours or regulate factory conditions as interference with natural economic laws, they lobbied forcefully and successfully for subsidies, loans, and tax relief to encourage business growth. Grants to railroads were one form of such assistance. Tariffs, which raised the prices of foreign products by placing an import tax on them, were another. When Congress imposed high tariffs on foreign goods such as kerosene, steel rails, woolen goods, and tin plate, American producers could raise prices on their own kerosene, rails, woolens, and tin to just under what comparable foreign goods would sell for with the tariff included. Since the inception of tariffs in the early nineteenth century, industrialists argued that tariff protection encouraged the development of new products and the founding of new enterprises. But tariffs also forced consumers to pay artificially high prices for many goods.

Government Assistance to Business

While defenders insisted that trusts and other forms of big business were a natural and efficient outcome of economic development, critics charged that these forms were unnatural because they stifled opportunity and originated from greed. Such charges emanating from farmers, workers, and intellectuals voiced an ardent fear of monopoly, the domination of an economic activity (such as oil refining) by one powerful company (such as Standard Oil). Those who feared monopoly believed—with considerable justification—that large corporations fixed prices, exploited workers by cutting wages, destroyed opportunity by crushing small businesses, and threatened democracy by corrupting politicians—all of which was not only unnatural but immoral. To critics, ethics eclipsed economics.

Dissenting Voices

Many believed in a better path to progress. By the mid-1880s, a number of intellectuals began to challenge Social Darwinism and laissez-faire economics. Sociologist Lester Ward attacked the application of evolutionary theory to social and economic relations. In *Dynamic Sociology* (1883), Ward argued that human control of nature, not natural law, accounted for the advance of civilization. A system that guaranteed survival only to the fittest was wasteful and brutal; instead, Ward reasoned, cooperative activity fostered by government intervention was more moral. Economists Richard Ely, John R. Commons, and Edward Bemis agreed that natural forces should be harnessed for the public good. They denounced the laissez-faire system for its "unsound morals" and praised the positive assistance that government could offer.

While academics endorsed intervention in the natural economic order, others more directly questioned why the United States had to have so many poor people while a few became fabulously wealthy. Henry George was a San Francisco printer and writer who had fallen into desperate poverty during the depression of the 1870s. Alarmed at the exploitative power of large enterprises, he came to believe that inequality stemmed from the ability of a few to profit from rising land values. George argued that such profits made speculators rich simply because of increased demand for living and working space, especially in cities. To prevent profiteering, George proposed to replace all taxes with a "single tax" on the "unearned increment"—the rise in property values caused by increased market demand rather than by owners' improvements. George's scheme, argued forcefully in *Progress and Poverty* (1879), had great popular appeal and almost won him the mayoralty of New York City in 1886.

Utopian Economic Schemes

Unlike George, who accepted private ownership, novelist Edward Bellamy believed competitive capitalism promoted waste. Instead, he proposed establishment of a state in which government owned the means of production. Bellamy outlined his dream in *Looking Backward* (1888). The novel, which sold over a million copies, depicted Boston in the year 2000 as a peaceful community where everyone had a job and a technological elite managed the economy according to scientific principles. Though a council of elders ruled and ordinary people could not vote in this utopia, Bellamy tried to convince readers that a "principle of fraternal cooperation" could replace vicious competition and wasteful monopoly. His vision, which he called "Nationalism," sparked formation of Nationalist clubs from Boston to Los Angeles and kindled popular appeals for civil service reform, social welfare measures, and government ownership of railroads and utilities.

Few people supported the universal government ownership envisioned by Bellamy, but several states took steps to prohibit monopolies and regulate business. By the end of the nineteenth century, fifteen states had constitutional provisions outlawing trusts, and twenty-seven had laws

Antitrust Legislation

forbidding pools. Most were agricultural states in the South and West that were responding to antimonopolistic pressure from farm organizations. But state authorities lacked the staff and judicial support for an effective attack on big business, and corporations always found ways to evade restrictions. Only national legislation, it seemed, could work.

Congress moved hesitantly toward such legislation and in 1890 finally passed the Sherman Anti-Trust Act. Introduced by Senator John Sherman of Ohio and rewritten by pro-business eastern senators, the law made illegal "every contract, combination in the form of trust or otherwise, or conspiracy in the restraint of trade." Those found guilty of violating the law faced fines and jail terms, and those wronged by illegal combinations could sue for triple damages. However, the law was left purposely vague so as to attract broad support. It did not clearly define "restraint of trade" and consigned interpretation of its provisions to the courts, which at the time were strong allies of business.

Judges used the law's vagueness to blur distinctions between reasonable and unreasonable restraints of trade. When in 1895 the federal government prosecuted the so-called Sugar Trust for owning 98 percent of the nation's sugar-refining capacity, eight of the nine Supreme Court justices ruled that control of manufacturing did not necessarily mean control of trade (*U.S. v. E. C. Knight Co.*). According to the Court, the Constitution empowered Congress to regulate interstate commerce, but manufacturing (which in the Knight case took place entirely within the state of Pennsylvania) did not fall under congressional control.

Between 1890 and 1900 the federal government prosecuted only eighteen cases under the Sherman Anti-Trust Act. The most successful involved railroads directly involved in interstate commerce. Ironically, the act equipped the government with a tool for breaking up labor unions: courts that did not consider monopolistic production a restraint on trade willingly applied antitrust provisions to boycotts encouraged by striking unions.

Summary

Mechanization and new inventions thrust the United States into the vanguard of industrial nations and immeasurably altered daily life between 1877 and 1920. But in industry, as in farming and mining, massive size and aggressive consolidation engulfed the individual, changing the nature of work from individual activity undertaken by producers to mass production undertaken by wage earners. Laborers fought to regain control of their work but struggled to develop well-organized unions that could meet their needs. The outpouring of products created a new mass society based on consumerism, but even the democratization of consumption did not benefit all social groups.

The problems of enforcing the Sherman Anti-Trust Act reflected the uneven distribution of power. Corporations consolidated to control resources, production, and politics. Farmers, laborers, and reformers had numbers and ideas but lacked influence. They benefited from the material gains that technology and mass production provided, but they charged that business was acquiring too much influence and profiting at their expense. In factories and farms, some people were celebrating the industrial transformation while others were struggling with the dilemma of industrialism: whether a system based on ever-greater profits was the best way for Americans to fulfill the nation's democratic destiny.

The march of industrial expansion proved almost impossible to stop, however, because so many powerful and ordinary people were benefiting from it. Moreover, the waves of people pouring into the nation's cities were increasingly providing both workers and consumers for America's expanding productive capacity. The dynamo of American vitality now rested in the cities.

LEGACY FOR A PEOPLE AND A NATION
Rockefeller and Standard Oil

For a generation after he founded his oil trust in 1882, John D. Rockefeller and Standard Oil evoked awe and fear of their power and wealth. Then, in 1911, the U.S. Supreme Court enforced anti-trust law and dissolved the company into thirty-four pieces. After the breakup, the Rockefeller family and the oil business drifted apart, but both left legacies to American society, though in different ways.

John D. Rockefeller personified the big-business "Robber Baron" for decades, even after he retired from managing his empire of oil, steel, and railroads. His wealth inspired dreams, with sayings and song lyrics expressing a person's hope of becoming "rich as Rockefeller." For years he regularly gave away millions

of dollars for educational and humanitarian purposes, and in 1913 he permanently endowed a philanthropic foundation "to promote the well-being of mankind throughout the world." Since then, the Rockefeller Foundation has disbursed some $100 million for education, the eradication of disease, food production, population research, and the arts and humanities. Rockefeller's only son, John, Jr., oversaw the foundation while he withdrew the family from the oil business in the 1920s and 1930s, and he sold oil stock to finance construction of the huge Rockefeller Center office complex in New York City. A grandson, John III, continued to give away money made by his grandfather.

Meanwhile, the business of oil refining became a critical element to everyday life, not just in the production of gasoline for cars, trucks, planes, and other machines driven by internal combustion, but also for the plastics industry that provides so many modern products that to list them would require volumes. In 1998, at the height of another era of corporate consolidation, the two largest segments of the former Standard Oil Trust—Exxon Corporation and Mobil Corporation (formerly Standard Oil of New Jersey and Standard Oil of New York)—negotiated an $83 billion merger that reunited them into the world's largest oil company with 123,000 employees and $200 billion in annual revenues. But the newly created Exxon Mobil did not presage the revival of a monopolistic trust. While in his day the senior Rockefeller controlled 90 percent of American refining capacity, the Exxon-Mobil combination would control 21 percent. Worldwide oil production has dispersed control of the industry, and competitive production has minimized the power of any one company.

The closest modern replica of Rockefeller might be William H. Gates, founder and chairman of Microsoft, the giant computer software firm. Also the target of anti-trust prosecution, Gates, like Rockefeller, drove rivals out of business through aggressive pricing and continually innovated to maintain a competitive edge. Gates also amassed a vast fortune, reputed to be the largest of any American, and gave away huge sums for humanitarian and educational purposes.

For Further Reading, see page A-21 of the Appendix. For Web resources, go to http://college.hmco.com.

It sounds like a movie story line. Rahel Gollop grew up in a village in western Russia. Her father, driven to desperation by persecution and poverty, left his family in 1890 to find a better life. Arrested by Russian soldiers, he escaped into Germany and found passage on a steamship bound for New York City. After two and a half years in the United States, he had saved enough to purchase tickets so Rahel and her aunt could join him in America. A year later, her mother, brothers, and sisters arrived.

Rahel's first impression of the American city was one of awe. "I was dazed by all there was to see," she recalled. "I looked with wonder at the tall houses, the paved streets, the street lamps. As I had never seen a large city and had had only a glimpse of a small one, I thought these things true only of America." But soon the Gollop's landlady, an immigrant who had been in the United States for several years, gave Rahel a dose of reality. Rahel wrote,

> When she asked us how we liked America, and we spoke of it with praise, she smiled a queer smile. "Life here is not all that it appears to the 'green horn' (new immigrant)," she said. She told us that her husband was a presser of coats and earned twelve dollars when he worked a full week. Aunt Masha thought twelve dollars a good deal. Again Mrs. Felesberg smiled. "No doubt it would be," she said, "where you used to live. You had your own house, and most of the food came from the garden. Here you will have to pay for everything; the rent!" she sighed, "for the light, for every potato, every grain of barley."

Like other immigrant families, the Gollops struggled and coped with this urban world where a family could not afford their own house and where they had to pay for everything. To help her parents and enable her brothers to attend school, Rahel, only twelve years old, went to work in a garment sweatshop. Before she was twenty, she held a variety of jobs, mostly doing

With hope and apprehension, millions of foreign immigrants poured into America's pulsing cities between 1880 and 1920. Bringing with them values, habits, and attire from the Old World, they faced a multitude of new experiences, expectations, and products in the New World and tried to negotiate their existence by combining the new with the old. (Albanian Woman, Ellis Island, 1905. © Collection for Creative Photography, The University of Arizona)

19

THE VITALITY AND TURMOIL OF URBAN LIFE 1877–1920

tailoring work. She witnessed—and went through—many of the travails suffered by other immigrants, including the beating of eastern European Jews on election night and the harassment of street vendors by drunken nativists. Like other immigrants, Rahel sought security by associating with her own kind, rarely mingling with strangers.

But gradually Rahel broke away. Health problems brought her into a Protestant hospital where she was exposed to another culture. She learned to read English and acquired an education. Rejecting the man whom her parents had selected for her husband, she married a grocer and became a writer. She published her autobiography in 1918 and died in 1925 at the age of forty-five, possibly of suicide.

The experiences of Rahel Gollop illustrate many themes characterizing urban life in America in the late nineteenth century and early twentieth. Where to live, where to work, how to support the family, the cash-based economy, ethnic consciousness and bigotry, the quest for individual independence and respectability—all these things and more made cities places of hope, frustration, satisfaction, and conflict. Their clanging trolleys, smoky air, crowded streets, and jumble of languages contrasted with the quiet pace of village and farm life.

Cities had exerted significant influence on the nation's history since its inception, but not until the 1880s did the United States begin to become a truly urban nation. The new industrialization and technological innovation of the late nineteenth century (see Chapter 18) fueled a tremendous social and geographical expansion that funneled millions of people into cities. By 1920 a milestone of urbanization was passed: that year's census showed that, for the first time, a majority of Americans (51.2 percent) lived in cities (settlements with more than 2,500 people). This new fact of national life was as symbolically significant as the disappearance of the frontier in 1890.

Cities served as marketplaces and forums, bringing together the people, resources, and ideas responsible for many of the changes in neighborhoods, politics, commerce, and leisure that American society was experiencing. By 1900 a network of small, medium, and large cities spanned every section of the country. Some people relished the opportunities and excitement cities offered; others found American cities disquieting and threatening. But whatever people's personal impressions, the city had become central to American life. The ways people built their cities and adjusted to the urban environment have shaped American society. ■

Electric trolley cars and other forms of mass transit enabled middle-class people like these women and men to reside on the urban outskirts and ride into the city center for work, shopping, and entertainment.   (Museum of the City of New York, The Byron Collection)

IMPORTANT EVENTS

1867 First law regulating tenements passes, in New York State

1870 One-fourth of Americans live in cities

1876 National League of Professional Baseball Clubs founded

1880s "New" immigrants from eastern and southern Europe begin to arrive in large numbers

1883 Brooklyn Bridge completed
Pulitzer buys *New York World* and creates a major vehicle for yellow journalism

1885 Safety bicycle invented

1886 First settlement house opens, in New York City

1889 Edison invents the motion picture and viewing device

1890s Electric trolleys replace horse-drawn mass transit

1893 Columbian Exposition opens in Chicago

1895 Hearst buys the *New York Journal*, another major popular yellow-journalism newspaper

1898 Race riot erupts in Wilmington, North Carolina

1900–10 Immigration reaches peak
Vaudeville rises in popularity

1903 Boston beats Pittsburgh in first baseball World Series

1905 Intercollegiate Athletic Association, forerunner of National College Athletic Association (NCAA), is formed and restructures rules of football

1906 Race riot erupts in Atlanta, Georgia

1915 Griffith directs *Birth of a Nation*, one of the first major technically sophisticated movies

1920 Majority (51.4 percent) of Americans live in cities

Industrial Growth and Transportation in the Modern City

Urban Industrial Development

Though their initial functions had been commercial, cities became the main arenas for industrial growth in the late nineteenth century. As centers of labor, transportation, and communication, cities provided everything factories needed. Capital accumulated by the cities' mercantile enterprises fed industrial investment. Urban populations also furnished consumers for myriad new products. Thus urban growth and industrialization wound together in a mutually advantageous spiral. The further industrialization advanced, the more opportunities it created for work and investment. Increased opportunity in turn drew more people to cities; as workers and as consumers, they fueled yet more industrialization.

Most cities housed a variety of industrial enterprises, but product specialization gradually became common. Mass production of clothing concentrated in New York; the shoe industry in Philadelphia; textiles in New England cities. Other cities processed products from surrounding agricultural regions: flour in Minneapolis; cottonseed oil in Memphis; beef and pork in Chicago and Omaha. Still others processed natural resources: gold and copper in Denver; fish and lumber in Seattle; coal and iron in Pittsburgh and Birmingham; oil in Houston and Los Angeles. Such activities increased cities' magnetic attraction for people in search of steady employment.

Urban and industrial growth transformed the national economy and freed the United States from dependence on European capital and manufactured goods. Imports and foreign investments still flowed into the United States. But by the early 1900s, cities and their factories, stores, and banks were converting America from a debtor agricultural nation into an industrial, financial, and exporting power.

Birth of the Modern City

Late in the nineteenth century, the compact city of the early nineteenth century, where residences mingled among shops, factories, and warehouses, burst open. From Boston to Los Angeles, the built environment sprawled several miles beyond the original central core. No longer did walking distance determine a city's size. No longer did different social groups live close together, poor near rich, immigrant near native-born, black near white. Instead, cities subdivided into distinct districts:

working-class and ethnic neighborhoods, downtown, a ring of suburbs. Two forces were responsible for this new arrangement. One, mass transportation, was centrifugal, propelling people and enterprises outward. The other, economic change, was centripetal, drawing human and economic resources inward.

Mass transportation moved people faster and farther. By the 1870s, horse-drawn vehicles were disappearing from city streets, replaced by motor-driven conveyances. Cable cars (carriages that moved by clamping onto a moving underground wire) came first. By the 1880s, cable-car lines operated in Chicago, San Francisco, and many other cities. Then in the 1890s, electric-powered streetcars began replacing horse cars and cable cars. Designed in Montgomery, Alabama, and Richmond, Virginia, electric trolleys spread to nearly every large American city. Between 1890 and 1902, total extent of electrified track grew from 1,300 to 22,000 miles. In a few cities, companies raised track onto trestles, enabling vehicles to travel without interference above jammed downtown streets. In Boston,

Mechanization of Mass Transportation

New York, and Philadelphia, transit firms dug underground passages for their cars, also to avoid traffic congestion. Because elevated railroads and subways were extremely expensive to construct, they appeared only in the few cities where companies could amass enough capital to lay track and buy equipment and where there were enough riders to ensure profits.

Another form of mass transit, the electric interurban railway, helped link nearby cities. Usually built over shorter distances than steam railroads, the interurbans operated between cities in areas with growing suburban populations and furthered urban development by making outer regions attractive for home buyers and businesses. The extensive network of the Pacific Electric Railway in southern California, for example, facilitated both travel and economic development in that region.

Mass-transit lines launched millions of urban dwellers into outlying neighborhoods and created a commuting public. Those who could afford the fare—usually a nickel a ride—could live beyond the crowded central city and commute there for

Beginnings of Urban Sprawl

Along with mass-produced consumer goods such as clothing and appliances, Sears, Roebuck and Company marketed architectural plans for middle-class suburban housing. This drawing, taken from the Sears catalogue for 1911, illustrates the kind of housing developed on the urban outskirts in the early twentieth century.   (Sears, Roebuck and Company)

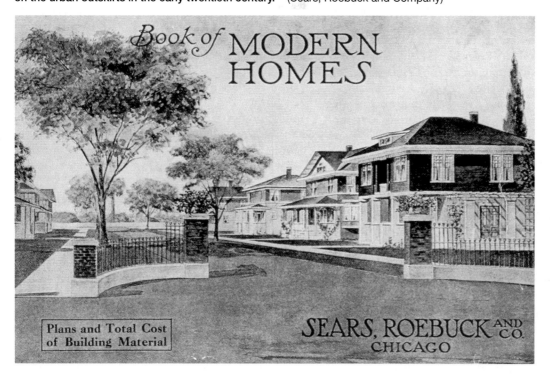

work, shopping, and entertainment. Working-class families, whose incomes rarely topped a dollar a day, found streetcar fares unaffordable. But the growing middle class could escape to quiet neighborhoods on the urban outskirts and live in bungalows with their own yards on tree-lined streets. Real-estate development boomed around the borders of cities. Between 1890 and 1920, for example, developers in the Chicago area opened 800,000 new lots—enough to house at least three times the city's 1890 population. A home several miles from downtown was inconvenient, but the benefits outweighed the costs. As one suburbanite wrote in 1902, "It may be a little more difficult for us to attend the opera, but the robin in my elm tree struck a higher note and a sweeter one yesterday than any prima donna ever reached."

Urban sprawl was essentially unplanned, but certain patterns did emerge. Eager to capitalize on commuting possibilities, thousands of small investors who bought land in anticipation of settlement paid little attention to the need for parks, traffic control, and public services. Construction of mass transit was guided by the profit motive and thus benefited the urban public unevenly. Streetcar lines serviced mainly those districts that promised the most riders—those whose fares would increase company profits.

Streetcars, elevateds, and subways altered commercial as well as residential patterns. When consumers moved outward, businesses followed. New commercial centers sprouted at trolley-line intersections and at elevated-railway stations. Branches of department stores and banks joined groceries, theaters, taverns, and shops to create neighborhood shopping centers, the forerunners of today's suburban malls. Meanwhile, the urban core became the work zone, where offices and stores loomed over streets clogged with people, horses, wagons, and trolleys. Districts such as Chicago's Loop and New Orleans's Canal Street employed thousands in commerce and finance.

Peopling the Cities: Migrants and Immigrants

Between 1870 and 1920, the number of Americans living in cities increased almost 550 percent, from 10 million to 54 million. During this period, the number of cities with more than 100,000 people grew from fifteen to sixty-eight; the number with more than 500,000 swelled from two to twelve (see Map 19.1).

These figures, dramatic in themselves, represent millions of stories of dreams and frustration, coping and confusion, success and failure.

A city can increase its population in three ways: by natural increase (an excess of births over deaths); by extending its borders to annex land and people; and by net migration (an excess of in-migrants over out-migrants). Between the 1870s and early 1900s, the number of people born in American cities was roughly equal to the number who died, so natural increase did not account for urban population growth in this period. Many cities, however, annexed nearby territory, thereby instantly increasing their populations. The most notable consolidation occurred in 1898 when New York City, which previously consisted of only Manhattan and the Bronx, merged with Brooklyn, Staten Island, and part of Queens and doubled overnight from 1.5 million to 3 million people. Suburbs often desired annexation for the schools, water, fire protection, and sewer systems that cities could provide. Sometimes annexation preceded settlement, adding vacant land where new city dwellers could live. In the 1880s, Chicago, Minneapolis, and Los Angeles incorporated hundreds of undeveloped square miles into their borders.

How Cities Grew

By far the greatest contribution to urban population growth was in-migration from the countryside and immigration from abroad. In fact, migration to cities nearly matched the massive migration to the West that was occurring at the same time. Urban newcomers arrived from two major sources: the American countryside and Europe. Asia, Canada, and Latin America also supplied immigrants, though in smaller numbers.

Despite land rushes in the West, rural populations declined as urban populations burgeoned. Low crop prices and high debts dashed white farmers' hopes and drove them off the land toward opportunities that cities seemed to offer. Such migration affected not only major cities such as Detroit, Chicago, and San Francisco but also secondary cities such as Indianapolis, Salt Lake City, Birmingham, Nashville, and San Diego. The thrill of city life beckoned especially to young people. A character in the play *The City* (1920) spoke for many youths when she exclaimed, "Who wants to smell new-mown hay, if he can breathe in gasoline on Fifth Avenue instead! Think of the theaters! The crowds! Think of being able to go out on the street and see someone you didn't know by sight!"

Migration from the Countryside

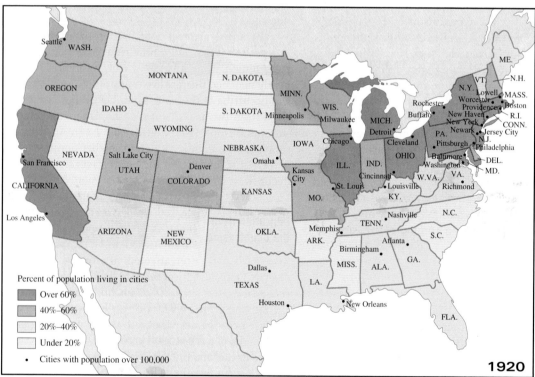

Map 19.1   Urbanization, 1880 and 1920   In 1880 the vast majority of states still were heavily rural. By 1920 only a few had less than 20 percent of their population living in cities.

The Caribbean as well as Europe sent immigrants to the United States. Proud and confident on arrival from their homeland of Guadeloupe, these women perhaps were unprepared for the double disadvantage they faced as both blacks and foreigners. (William Williams Papers, Manuscripts & Archives Division, The New York Public Library)

In the 1880s and 1890s, thousands of rural African Americans also moved cityward, seeking better employment and fleeing crop liens, ravages of the boll weevil on cotton crops, racial violence, and political oppression. Though black urban dwellers grew more numerous after 1915, thirty-two cities already had more than ten thousand black residents by 1900. Southern cities such as Baltimore, Atlanta, and Birmingham increased their black populations, but also northern and western places such as New York, Cleveland, and Chicago received thousands of African American migrants. These urban newcomers resembled other migrants in their rural backgrounds and economic motivations, but they

African American and Hispanic Migration to Cities

differed in several important ways. Because few factories would employ African Americans, most found jobs in the service sector—cleaning, cooking, and driving—rather than in industrial trades. Also, because most service openings were traditionally female jobs, black women outnumbered black men in cities such as New York, Baltimore, and New Orleans. In the South, an enlarged population of African Americans migrating from the countryside served as an important source of unskilled labor in the region's growing cities. By 1900 almost 40 percent of the total population of both Atlanta, Georgia, and Charlotte, North Carolina, were blacks.

In the West, many Hispanics, who once had been a predominantly rural population, moved into cities. They took over unskilled construction and grading jobs once held by Chinese laborers who were driven from southern California cities, and in some Texas cities native Mexicans (called *Tejanos*) held the majority of all unskilled jobs. In places such as Los Angeles, males often left for long periods of time to take temporary agricultural jobs, leaving behind many female heads of household.

Even more newcomers were immigrants from Europe who had fled foreign villages and cities for American shores. Smaller numbers from Asia, Canada, and

Those who wished to Americanize the immigrants believed the public schools could provide the best setting for assimilation. This 1917 poster from the Cleveland Board of Education and the Cleveland Americanization Committee used the languages most common to the new immigrants—Slovene, Italian, Polish, Hungarian, and Yiddish—as well as English to invite newcomers to free classes where they could learn "the language of America" and "citizenship."   (National Park Service Collection, Ellis Island Immigration Museum. Photo: Chermayeff & Geismar/MetaForm)

Immigration from Other Lands

Latin American came for the same reasons. The dream of many was not to stay but to make enough money to return home and live in greater comfort and security. For every hundred foreigners who entered the country, around thirty later left. Still, most of the 26 million immigrants who arrived between 1870 and 1920 and whose numbers peaked between 1900 and 1910 remained, and the great majority settled in cities, where they helped reshape American culture. Rahel Gollop, the Russian garment worker, fit this pattern of settlement and adaptation.

Immigrants to the United States were part of a worldwide movement pushing people away from traditional means of support and pulling them toward better opportunities. Population pressures, land redistribution, and industrialization induced millions of peasants, small farmers, and craftsmen to leave Europe and Asia for Canada, Australia, Brazil, and Argentina, as well as the United States. Religious persecution, too, particularly the violent pogroms and merciless military conscription that Jews suffered in eastern Europe, forced people to flee across the Atlantic. Migration always has been present in human history, but in the late nineteenth century technological developments in communications and transportation spread news of opportunities and made travel cheaper, quicker, and safer.

Immigrants from northern and western Europe had long made the United States their main destination, but after 1880 economic and demographic changes propelled a second wave of immigrants from other regions. Northern and western Europeans continued to arrive, but the new wave brought more people from eastern and southern Europe, plus smaller contingents from Canada, Mexico, and Japan (see Map 19.2 and Figure 19.1). Two-thirds of the newcomers who arrived in the 1880s came from Germany, England, Ireland, and Scandinavia; between 1900 and 1909, two-thirds came from Italy, Austria-Hungary, and Russia. By 1910 arrivals from Mexico were beginning to outnumber arrivals from Ireland, and large numbers of Japanese had moved to the West Coast and Hawai'i. Foreign-born blacks, chiefly from the West Indies, also increased in number. (See the Appendix for the nationalities of immigrants.)

The New Immigrants

Many Americans feared the customs, Catholic and Jewish faiths, and poverty of "new" immigrants, con-

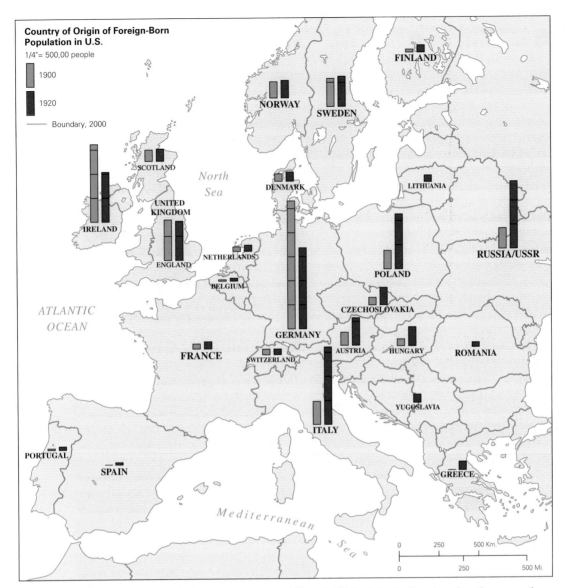

Map 19.2   Sources of European-born Population, 1900 and 1920   In just a few decades, the proportion of European immigrants to the United States who came from northern and western Europe decreased (Ireland and Germany) or remained relatively stable (England and Scandinavia), while the proportion from eastern and southern Europe dramatically increased.   (Data from U.S. Census Bureau, "Historical Census Statistics on the Foreign-born Population of the United States: 1850–1990," Feb. 1999. Retrieved Feb. 12, 2000, from the World Wide Web: http://www.census.gov/population.)

sidering them less desirable than "old" immigrants, whose languages and beliefs seemed less alien. Unlike earlier arrivals from Great Britain and Ireland, new immigrants did not speak English and more than half worked in the lowest skilled occupations. In reality, however, old and new immigrants closely resembled each other in their strategies for coping. The majority of both groups came from societies that made the family the focus of all undertakings. As Rahel Gollop's case

illustrates, whether and when to emigrate was decided in light of the family's needs, and family bonds continued to prevail after immigrants reached the New World. New arrivals usually knew where they wanted to go and how to get there because they received aid from relatives who had already immigrated. In many instances, workers helped kin obtain jobs, and family members pooled resources to maintain, if not improve, their standard of living.

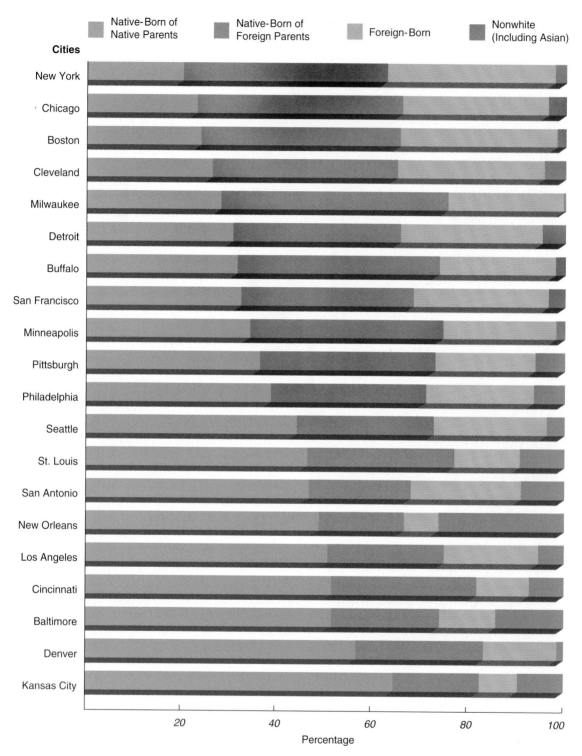

Figure 19.1   Composition of Population, Selected Cities, 1920   Immigration and migration made native-born whites of native-born parents minorities in almost every major city by the early twentieth century. Moreover, foreign-born residents and native-born whites of foreign parents (combining the green and purple segments of a line) constituted absolute majorities in numerous places.

The migration streams moving into American cities were only part of an extraordinary amount of movement because, once settled, immigrants and immigrants rarely stayed put. Each year millions of families packed up and moved elsewhere. As early as 1847, a foreign visitor, amazed by American transiency, wrote, "If God were suddenly to call the world to judgment He would surprise two-thirds of the American population on the road like ants." The urge to move affected every region, every city. From Boston to San Francisco, from Minneapolis to San Antonio, no more than half of the families residing in a city at any one time were still there ten years later.

Residential Mobility

Many who migrated, particularly unskilled workers, did not improve their status; they simply floated from one low-paying job to another. Others did find greener pastures. Studies of Boston, Omaha, Atlanta, and other cities show that most men who rose occupationally or acquired property had migrated from somewhere else. Thus while cities frustrated the hopes of some, they offered opportunities to others.

In addition to movement between cities, countless numbers of people moved within the same city. In American communities today, one in every five families changes residence in a given year. A hundred years ago, the proportion was closer to one in four or one in three. It was not uncommon for a family to live at three or more different addresses over a ten- or fifteen-year period. Population turnover affected almost every neighborhood, every ethnic and occupational group.

Thus the peopling of American cities was a very dynamic process. Americans of all groups, native and foreign, were always seeking a better life, and hope for improved conditions elsewhere acted as a safety valve, relieving some of the tensions and frustrations that simmered inside the city. Sometimes families moved a short distance to another home or another neighborhood; sometimes they simply picked up and left town. A railroad ticket to another city cost only a few dollars; there was little to lose by moving.

Urban Neighborhoods

Looking back from the 1920s, literary critic Randolph Bourne dubbed the United States "a cosmopolitan federation of national colonies." Such an observation, based on an image of the social organization of the inner city of New York and other metropolises, implies that immigrants huddled together in their own neighborhood enclaves, where they steadily preserved national cultures and customs. But the reality was more complicated. With so many people moving about and interacting on city streets and in workplaces and shops, cultural change was hard to avoid.

It is true that in their new surroundings—where the language was a struggle, the workday followed the clock rather than the sun, and housing and employment often were uncertain—immigrants first anchored their lives to the rock they knew best: their cultures. Old World customs persisted in immigrant enclaves of Italians from the same province, Japanese from the same island district, or Russian Jews from the same *shtetl* (village). Fraternal societies were re-created along village and provincial lines. For example, Japanese transferred their *ken* societies, which organized social celebrations and relief services, and Chinese from Canton brought *hui* institutions, which raised money to help members acquire businesses. People practiced religion as they always had, held traditional feasts and pageants, married within their group, and pursued old feuds with people from rival villages. Among Orthodox Jews from eastern Europe, men grew sidelocks, women wore wigs, and children attended afternoon religious training.

Immigrant Cultures

Southern Italians transplanted the system whereby a *padrone* (boss) found jobs for unskilled workers by negotiating with—and receiving a payoff from—an employer. Italians also re-created mutual benefit associations to provide families emergency aid as well as sickness and death benefits. Pasquale Cruci, an immigrant from Salerno, explained that he helped to found such an association in Bridgeport, Connecticut, because "I felt that the Italian people of this city should have some security from death and accidents. The Italian people of this time didn't trust the big insurance companies because they thought they would get cheated. They felt that if some organization was Italian that it was all right."

Yet, as Rahel Gollop discovered, the diversity of American cities forced immigrants to modify their attitudes and habits. Few newcomers could avoid contact with people different from themselves, and few could prevent such contacts from altering their traditional ways of life. Although many foreigners identified themselves by their village or region of birth, native-born Americans categorized them by nationality. People from County Cork and County Limerick were lumped together as Irish; those from Schleswig and Württemberg were Germans; those from Calabria and Campobasso became Italians. Immigrant institutions, such as newspapers and churches, found they had to appeal to the entire nationality in order to survive.

In most large cities, immigrants inhabited multiethnic neighborhoods, places one historian has called "urban borderlands" where a diversity of people, identities, and lifestyles coexisted. Even within districts identified with a certain group, such as Little Italy, Jewtown, Polonia, or Greektown, rapid mobility constantly undermined residential stability as over a period as short as a few years former inhabitants dispersed to other neighborhoods and new inhabitants

Ethnic and Racial Borderlands

moved in. But seldom did a single ethnic group predominate. Rather, an area's businesses and institutions, such as its bakeries, butcher shops, churches, and club headquarters, gave the neighborhood its identity.

Nevertheless, though different groups jointly inhabited these urban borderlands, various ethnic and racial groups insulated themselves culturally, or were isolated by outside forces, from other immigrants and from the majority population. Some groups, such as Italians, Jews, and Poles, deliberately tried to maintain their separate religious, linguistic, and cultural lifestyles. For such European immigrants, their neighborhoods acted as havens until individuals were ready to cross from the borderland into the majority society. For people of color, however—African Americans, Asians, and Mexicans—the borderlands had a more persistent character that, because of discrimination, became less multiethnic over time.

Though Chinese immigrants struggled, like other immigrants, to succeed in American society, they often faced severe discrimination because of their different lifestyles. As this photo of a San Francisco grocery shows, Chinese looked, dressed, and ate differently than did white Americans. Occasionally, they suffered from racist violence that caused them to fear not only for their personal safety but also for the safety of establishments like this one that might suffer damage from resentful mobs. (The Bancroft Library, University of California)

In industrial cities such as Chicago, Philadelphia, and Detroit, the availability of jobs and cheap housing prompted European immigrants initially to cluster together in inner-city neighborhoods. Though members of different ethnic groups lived nearby, members of the same group often tried to exclude outsiders from their neighborhoods and institutions. But these borderland experiences proved to be transitory. The expansion of mass transportation and outward movement of factories enabled many people to move to other neighborhoods, where they interspersed with families of their own socioeconomic class but not necessarily of their own ethnicity. European immigrants did encounter prejudice, such as the exclusion of Jews from certain professions and clubs or the inability of Italians to break into urban politics, but discrimination against them rarely was as systematic or complete as it was against blacks, Asians, and Mexicans.

Though African Americans originally may have lived in multiethnic, multiracial communities, by the early twentieth century institutionalized racial discrimination was forcing them into relatively permanent, highly segregated ghettos. By 1920 in Chicago, Detroit, Cleveland, and other cities outside the South, two-thirds or more of the total African American population lived in only 10 percent of the residential area. Circumscribed within color-line boundaries, blacks found it increasingly difficult to find jobs as well as housing outside the ghettos. The only way blacks could relieve the pressure resulting from increasing migration was to expand the ghetto borders into surrounding, previously white neighborhoods, a process often resulting in harassment and attacks on black families by white residents whose racist attitudes were intensified by fears that black neighbors would cause property values to decline.

Ghettos

Within the ghettos, African Americans, like other urban people, nurtured cultural institutions that helped them cope with urban life: shops, schools, clubs, theaters, dance halls, newspapers, and saloons. Churches, particularly those of the Baptist and African Methodist Episcopal (AME) branches of Protestantism, were especially influential. Pittsburgh blacks boasted twenty-eight such churches in the early 1900s. Membership in Cincinnati's black Baptist churches doubled between 1870 and 1900, from 1,027 to 2,011. In Louisville, blacks pooled their resources and built their own theological institute. In virtually all cities, black religious activity not only dominated ghetto life but also represented cooperation of blacks across class, cultural, and regional lines.

Asians encountered similar kinds of discrimination and ghetto experience. Although these immigrants often preferred to live in Chinatowns and Japanese sections, Anglos made every effort to keep them separated. In the 1880s, San Francisco's government, for example, prohibited Chinese laundries from locating in white neighborhoods, and its school board tried to isolate Japanese and Chinese children in Chinatown schools.

Mexicans in southwestern cities experienced somewhat more complex patterns. In some places, such as Los Angeles, Santa Barbara, and Tucson, Mexicans had been the original inhabitants and Anglos were migrants who overtook the city, pushing Mexicans into adjoining areas. Here, Mexicans became increasingly isolated in residential and commercial districts call *barrios*. Frequently, real-estate covenants, by which property owners pledge not to sell homes to Mexicans (or to African Americans, or to Jews), kept Mexican families confined in *barrios* of Los Angeles, Albuquerque, and San Antonio, though these areas tended to be located away from central city multiethnic borderlands housing European immigrants. To a considerable extent, then, race, more than any other factor, made the urban experiences of non-whites unique compared to those of whites.

Barrios

Everywhere, Old World culture mingled with New World realities. Immigrants struggled to maintain their native languages and to pass them down to younger generations. But English, taught in the schools and needed on the job, soon penetrated nearly every community. Foreigners fashioned homeland garments from American fabrics. Italians went to American doctors but still carried traditional amulets to ward off evil spirits. Chinese expanded their traditional gambling games to include poker. Music especially revealed adaptations. Polka bands entertained at Polish social gatherings, but their repertoires soon blended American and Polish folk music; once dominated by violins, the bands added accordions, clarinets, and trumpets so they could play louder. Mexican ballads acquired new themes that described the adventures of border crossing and the hardship of labor in the United States.

Americanization

The influx of so many immigrants between 1870 and 1920 transformed the United States from a basically Protestant nation into one composed of Protestants, Catholics, Orthodox Christians, and Jews. Newcomers from Italy, Hungary, Polish lands, and Slovakia joined Irish and Germans to boost the proportion

Accommodation of Religion of Catholics in many cities. In Buffalo, Cleveland, Chicago, and Milwaukee, Catholic immigrants and their offspring approached a majority of the population. Catholic Mexicans constituted over half of the population of El Paso. German and Russian immigrants gave New York one of the largest Jewish populations in the world.

Partly in response to Protestant charges that they could not retain Old World religious beliefs and still assimilate into American society, many Catholics and Jews tried to accommodate their faiths to the new environment. Catholic and Jewish leaders from more established immigrant groups supported liberalizing trends—the use of English in sermons, the phasing-out of Old World rituals such as saints' feasts, and a preference for public over religious schools. As long as new immigrants continued to arrive, however, these trends met stiff opposition.

Newcomers usually held on to familiar practices, whether the folk Catholicism of southern Italy or the Orthodox Judaism of eastern Europe. Because Catholic parishes served distinct geographical areas, immigrants who clustered in a particular area wanted clergy of their own kind in spite of church attempts to make American Catholicism more uniform. Bishops acceded to pressures from predominantly Polish congregations for Polish- rather than German-born priests. Eastern European Jews, convinced that Reform Judaism sacrificed too much to American ways, established the Conservative branch, which retained traditional ritual, though it abolished the segregation of women in synagogues and allowed English prayers.

Each of the three major migrant groups that peopled American cities—native-born whites, foreigners of various races, and native-born blacks—helped to mold modern American culture. The cities nurtured rich cultural variety: American folk music and literature, Italian and Mexican cuisine, Irish comedy, Yiddish theater, African American jazz and dance, and much more. Newcomers in the late nineteenth century changed their environment as much as they were changed by it.

Living Conditions in the Inner City

 Urban population growth created intense pressures on the public and private sectors. The masses of people who jammed inner-city districts were recognized more for their problems than for their cultural contributions. American cities seemed to harbor all the afflictions that plague modern society: poverty, disease, crime, and other unpleasant conditions that occur when large numbers of people live close together. City dwellers coped as best they could. Although technology, private enterprise, and public authority could not solve every problem, city officials and engineers achieved some remarkable successes. In the late nineteenth and early twentieth centuries, construction of buildings, homes, streets, sewers, and schools proceeded at a furious pace. American cities set world standards for fire protection and water purification. But even a century later, many problems still await solution.

One of the most persistent shortcomings—the failure to provide adequate housing for all who need it—has its origins in nineteenth-century urban development. In spite of massive construction in the 1880s and early 1900s, population growth outpaced housing supplies. Scarcity of inexpensive housing especially afflicted working-class families who, because of low wages, had to rent their living quarters. As cities grew, landlords took advantage of shortages in low-cost rental housing by splitting up existing buildings to house more people, constructing multiple-unit tenements, and hiking rents. Low-income families adapted to high costs and short supply by sharing space and expenses. Thus it became common in many big cities for a one-family apartment to be occupied by two or three families or by a single family plus several boarders.

Housing

The result was unprecedented crowding. In 1890 New York City's immigrant-packed Lower East Side averaged 702 people per acre, one of the highest population densities in the world. Low-rent districts had distinctive physical appearances in different cities: six- to eight-story barracks-like buildings in New York; dilapidated row houses in Baltimore and Philadelphia; converted slave quarters in Charleston and New Orleans; and crumbling two- and three-story frame houses in Seattle and San Francisco.

Inside these buildings, conditions were harsh. The largest rooms were barely ten feet wide, and interior rooms either lacked windows or opened onto narrow shafts that bred vermin and rotten odors. Describing such a shaft, one immigrant housekeeper said, "It's damp down there, and the families, they throw out garbage and dirty papers and the insides of chickens, and other unmentionable filth. . . . I just vomited when I first cleaned up the air shaft." Few buildings had indoor plumbing; the only source of heat was dangerous, polluting coal-burning stoves.

Housing problems aroused reform campaigns in several places. New York State took the lead by legis-

Housing Reform lating light, ventilation, and safety codes for new tenement buildings in 1867, 1879, and 1901. These and similar laws in other states could not remedy the ills of existing buildings, but they did impose minimal obligations on landlords. A few reformers, such as journalist Jacob Riis and humanitarian Lawrence Veiller, advocated housing low-income families in "model tenements," with more spacious rooms and better facilities. Model tenements, however, required landlords to accept lower profits—a sacrifice few were willing to make. Both reformers and public officials opposed government financing of better hous-

ing, fearing that such a step would undermine private enterprise. Still, the new housing codes and regulatory commissions strengthened the power of local government to oversee construction.

Eventually, new technology brought about unheralded but momentous changes in home life. As histo-

Changes in Household Technology rian Thomas Schlereth has pointed out, new systems of central heating (furnaces), artificial lighting, and modern indoor plumbing created a new kind of consumption, first for middle-class households and later for most others. Whereas formerly families chopped wood for cooking and heating, made candles for light, and hauled water for bathing, they increasingly were connected to outside utilities for gas, electricity, and water. Moreover, these utilities helped foment new attitudes about privacy. Bedrooms and bathrooms enabled

Inner-city dwellers used not only indoor space as efficiently as possible but also what little outdoor space was available to them. Scores of families living in this cramped block of six-story tenements in New York strung clotheslines behind the buildings. Notice that there is virtually no space between buildings, so only rooms at the front and back received daylight and fresh air.   (Library of Congress)

How do historians know...

that urban reformers tried to manipulate public opinion? Journalist Jacob Riis wrote a landmark investigation of slum life in New York City, *How the Other Half Lives* (1890). Riis was one of the first to use the camera as a reform tool, supplementing his accounts of poverty and crowding with moving photographs of poor people (mostly immigrants) and their surroundings. For many readers, these photographs provided what one reformer called "added realism" and "an inherent attraction not found in other forms of illustration." But is a photograph always completely "real"? This Riis photo shows three "street arabs," homeless boys living and sleeping outdoors away from adult care. They are dressed in rags, and their look of innocence evokes the viewer's pathos. Because the shutter speed of his camera was slow (high-speed shutters of today did not exist in early cameras) and because he wanted to maximize the emotional effect of his images, Riis staged his photographs. Here, he has carefully selected his subjects and focused on them in his own way to stir up sympathy and, he hoped, action. Though the picture contains a large portion of reality, it also serves notice that the historian must be aware that a photographer—any photographer—does more than record a scene. Even if not posed, every photograph in its selection of subjects, framing of the scene, and focus (long shot or close-up, for example) reveals as much about the photographer as it does about the subject. Thus, though photographs like this one may be valuable historical documents, historians must look beyond the image to consider what biases it might represent.   (Photo: Museum of the City of New York, the Jacob Riis Collection)

middle-class family members to withdraw into private spaces where they still could have the comfort of light, heat, and water. Instead of doubling or tripling up in one room or even one bed, children could have their own bedrooms, complete with individualized decoration. Finally, these utilities erased the inconveniences of nature. Though not affordable for the poor, central heat and artificial light made it possible for the middle class to enjoy a steady, comfortable temperature and turn night into day, while indoor plumbing removed the unpleasant experiences of the outhouse.

Housing reforms for the poor had only limited success, but scientific and technological advances eventually enabled city dwellers and the entire nation to live in greater comfort and safety. By the 1880s, some doctors had begun to accept the theory that microorganisms (germs) cause disease. In response, cities established more efficient systems of water purification and sewage disposal. Although disease and death rates remained higher in cities than in the countryside, and tuberculosis and other respiratory ills continued to plague inner-city districts, public health regulations as applied to water purity, sewage disposal, and food quality helped to control dread diseases such as cholera, typhoid fever, and diphtheria.

Sanitation and Construction Technology

Meanwhile, street paving, modernized firefighting equipment, and electric street lighting spread rapidly across urban America. Steel-frame construction, which supports a building with a metal skeleton rather than with masonry walls, made possible the erection of skyscrapers—and thus more efficient use of scarce and costly urban land. Electric elevators and steam-heating systems serviced these buildings. Steel-cable suspension bridges, developed by John A. Roebling and epitomized by his great Brooklyn Bridge (completed in 1883), linked metropolitan sections more closely.

None of these improvements, however, lightened the burden of poverty. The urban economy, though generally expanding, advanced erratically. Employment, especially for unskilled workers in manufacturing and construction, rose and fell with business cycles and changing seasons. An ever-increasing number of families lived on the margins of survival.

Urban Poverty

Since colonial days, Americans have disagreed about how much responsibility the public should assume for poor relief. According to traditional beliefs, still widespread at the turn of the century, anyone could escape poverty through hard work and clean living; indigence existed only because some people were morally weaker than others. Such reasoning bred fear that aid to poor people would encourage paupers to rely on public support rather than their own efforts. As the business cycle fluctuated and poverty increased, this attitude hardened, and city governments discontinued direct grants of food, fuel, and clothing to needy families. Instead, cities provided relief in return for work on public projects and sent special cases to state-run almshouses, orphanages, and homes for the blind, deaf, and mentally ill.

Efforts to rationalize relief fostered some change in attitude. Between 1877 and 1892, philanthropists in ninety-two cities formed Charity Organization Societies, an attempt to put social welfare on a systematic basis by merging disparate charity groups into coordinated units. Believing poverty to be caused by personal defects such as alcoholism and laziness, members of these organizations spent most of their time visiting poor families and encouraging them to be thriftier and more virtuous.

Close observation of the poor, however, prompted some humanitarians to conclude that people's environments, not their personal shortcomings, caused poverty. In turn, they had faith that poverty could be prevented and eliminated by improving housing, education, sanitation, and job opportunities rather than admonishing the poor to be more moral. This attitude, which had been gaining ground since the mid-nineteenth century, fueled drives for building codes, factory regulations, and public health measures in the Progressive era of the early twentieth century (see Chapter 20). Still, most middle- and upper-class Americans continued to endorse the creed that in a society of abundance only the unfit were poor and that poverty relief should be tolerated but never encouraged. As one charity worker put it, relief "should be surrounded by circumstances that shall . . . repel every one . . . from accepting it."

More than crowding and pauperism, crime and disorder nurtured fears that urban growth, especially the slums, threatened the nation. The more cities grew, it seemed, the more they shook with violence. While homicide rates declined in industrialized nations such as England and Germany, those in America rose alarmingly: 25 murders per million people in 1881; 107 per million in 1898. Pickpockets, swindlers, and burglars roamed

Crime and Violence

every city. Some acquired as much notoriety as western desperadoes. One infamous urban outlaw was Rufus Minor, alias Rufus Pine. Short, stocky, and bald, Minor resembled a shy clerk, but one police chief labeled him "one of the smartest bank sneaks in America." A sometime associate of Billy "The Kid" Burke, Minor often grew a heavy beard before holding up a bank, then shaved afterward to avoid identification by eyewitnesses. Minor was implicated in bank heists in New York City, Cleveland, Detroit, Providence, Philadelphia, Albany, Boston, and Baltimore—all between 1878 and 1882.

Despite fears of robberies and violence, urban crime may simply have become more conspicuous and sensational, rather than more prevalent. To be sure, concentrations of wealth and the mingling of different peoples provided opportunities for larceny, vice, and assault. But urban lawlessness and brutality probably did not exceed that of backwoods mining camps and southern plantations. Nativists were quick to blame immigrants for urban crime and disorder, but there is little evidence that more foreigners than native-born Americans populated the rogues' gallery. One investigation of jails in 1900 concluded that "we have ourselves evolved as cruel and cunning criminals as any that Europe may have foisted upon us."

The cityward movement of African Americans especially roused white fears, and as the twentieth century dawned, a series of race riots spread across the nation. In 1898 white citizens of Wilmington, North Carolina, resenting the success of African Americans in local politics, rioted and killed dozens of blacks. In the wake of the fury, whites expelled all black officeholders and instituted restrictions to prevent blacks from voting. In Atlanta in 1906, a series of newspaper accounts alleging attacks by black men on white women provoked a wave of shooting and killing that left twelve blacks dead and over seventy injured. An influx of African American unskilled laborers and strikebreakers into the industrial city of East St. Louis, Illinois, heightened racial tensions that erupted in 1917 when blacks fired back at a car whose occupants they believed had shot into their homes. When whites discovered that the black shooters had mistakenly killed two policemen riding in the car, a full-scale riot erupted that ended only after nine whites and thirty-nine blacks had been killed and over three hundred buildings had been destroyed. In addition to such mass violence, innumerable disruptions ranging from domestic violence to muggings to gang fights made cities scenes of constant turbulence.

Promises of Mobility

 The persistence of poverty, crime, and violence undercut the image of cities as places of opportunity, yet as locales of economic progress, cities could provide avenues by which people might achieve some modicum of success. The story of urban social mobility is not one of rags to riches but rather of countless small triumphs mixed with dashed hopes, discrimination, and failure. Basically, there were two ways a person could get ahead: occupational advancement (and the higher income that accompanied it) through experience, education, and the expansion of new occupations; and acquisition of property (and the wealth it represented). These options were open chiefly to white men.

Many women held paying jobs, owned property, and migrated, but their economic standing was usually defined by the men in their lives—usually their husbands or fathers. Women could improve their status by marrying men with wealth or potential, but other avenues were mostly closed. Laws limited what women could inherit; educational institutions blocked their training in professions such as medicine and law; and prevailing assumptions attributed higher aptitude for manual skills and business to men than to women. For African Americans, American Indians, Mexican Americans, or Asian Americans opportunities were even fewer. Assigned to the lowest-paying occupations by prejudice, they could make few gains.

For white men, however, occupational mobility was a reality, thanks to urban and industrial expansion. Thousands of businesses were needed to supply goods and services to burgeoning urban populations. As corporations grew and centralized their operations, they required new managerial personnel. Capital for a large business was hard to amass, but aspiring merchants could open a saloon or small shop for a few hundred dollars. Knowledge of accounting could qualify one for white-collar jobs that sometimes paid better than manual labor. Thus nonmanual work and the higher social status and income that tended to accompany it were attainable.

Occupational Mobility

Such advancement occurred often. To be sure, only a very few traveled the rags-to-riches path that Andrew Carnegie and Henry Ford discovered. The vast majority of the era's wealthiest businessmen began their careers with distinct advantages: American birth, Protestant religion, superior education, and relatively affluent parents. Yet considerable movement occurred along the road from poverty to moderate success, as men climbed from manual to nonmanual jobs. Personal successes like that of Meyer Grossman, a Russian immigrant to Omaha, Nebraska, who worked as a teamster before saving enough to open a successful furniture store, were common.

Rates of occupational mobility were slow but steady between 1870 and 1920. In fast-growing cities such as Atlanta, Los Angeles, and Omaha, approximately one in five white manual workers rose to white-collar or owner's positions within ten years—provided they stayed in the city that long. In older cities such as Boston and Philadelphia, upward mobility averaged closer to one in six workers in ten years. Some men slipped from a higher to a lower rung on the occupational ladder, but rates of upward movement usually doubled those of downward movement. Though patterns were not consistent, immigrants generally experienced less upward and more downward mobility than the native-born did. Still, regardless of birthplace, the chances for a white male to rise occupationally over the course of his career or to hold a higher-status job than his father had were relatively good.

What constitutes a better job, however, depends on one's definition of improvement. Many an immigrant artisan, such as a German carpenter or Italian shoemaker, would have considered an accountant's job demeaning. People with traditions of pride in manual skills neither desired nonmanual jobs nor encouraged their children to seek them. As one Italian tailor explained, "I learned the tailoring business in the old country. Over here, in America, I never have trouble finding a job because I know my business from the other side [Italy]. . . . I want that my oldest boy learn my trade because I tell him that you could always make at least enough for the family."

Business ownership, moreover, entailed risks. Failure rates were high among shopkeepers, saloon owners, and other small proprietors in working-class neighborhoods because the low incomes of their customers made business uncertain. Many manual workers sought security rather than mobility, preferring a steady wage to the risks of ownership. A Sicilian who lived in Bridgeport, Connecticut, observed that "the people that come here they afraid to get in business because they don't know how that business goes. In Italy these people don't know much about these things because most of them work on farms or in [their] trade."

In addition to advancing occupationally, a person might achieve social mobility by acquiring property

Acquisition of Property

such as a building or a house. But property was not easy to acquire. Banks and savings-and-loan institutions had far stricter lending practices than they did after the 1930s, when the federal government began to insure real-estate financing. Before then, mortgage loans carried high interest rates and short repayment periods. Thus renting, even of single-family houses, was common, especially in big cities. A general rise in wage rates nevertheless enabled many families to amass savings, which they could use as down payments on property. Ownership rates varied regionally—higher in western cities, lower in eastern cities—but 36 percent of all urban American families owned their homes in 1900, the highest homeownership rate of any Western nation except for Denmark, Norway, and Sweden.

The possibilities of upward mobility seemed to temper people's dissatisfaction. Although the gap between the very rich and the very poor widened, the expanding economies of American cities created room in the middle of the socioeconomic scale. Few could become another Rockefeller, but many did become respectable shopkeepers, foremen, clerks, and agents. Some also used politics and management of the city as routes to status and success.

Managing the City

Those concerned with managing cities faced daunting challenges in the late nineteenth century. Burgeoning populations, business expansion, and technological change created urgent needs for sewers, police and fire protection, schools, parks, and other services. Such needs strained municipal resources beyond their capacities. Furthermore, city governments approached these needs in a disorganized fashion. Legislative and administrative functions were typically scattered among a mayor, city council, and independent boards that administered health regulations, public works, and poverty relief. Philadelphia at one time had thirty different boards, plus a mayor and council. Also, state governments often interfered in local matters, appointing board members and limiting cities' abilities to levy taxes and borrow money.

Since the mid-nineteenth century, city dwellers had gradually overcome their resistance to professional law enforcement and increasingly depended on the police to protect life and property. By the early 1900s, however, law enforcement had become compli-

Role of the Police

cated and controversial because various groups differed in their views of the law and how it should be enforced. Disadvantaged groups—notably ethnic and racial minorities—could not escape arrest as easily as those with economic or political influence. And police officers applied the law less harshly to members of their own ethnic groups and to people who bought exemptions with bribes.

As chief urban law enforcers, police forces, who often were poorly trained and prone to corruption, were caught between pressures for swift and severe action on one hand and leniency on the other. Some people clamored for crackdowns on drunkenness, gambling, and prostitution at the same time that others favored loose law enforcement so they could indulge in these customer-oriented crimes. As urban society diversified, different groups tried to protect their particular interests—such as keeping saloons open late at night, indulging in social gambling, or even applying their own notions of law and order. Achieving a balance between the idealistic intentions of criminal law and people's desire for individual freedom grew increasingly difficult, and it has remained so to this day.

Out of the apparent confusion surrounding urban management arose political machines, organizations whose main goals were the rewards—money, influence, and prestige—of getting and keeping political power.

The Machine

Machine politicians routinely used bribery and graft to further their ends. But machines needed popular support, and they could not have succeeded if they had not provided relief, security, and services to large numbers of people, especially to the hordes of newcomers who crowded into cities. By meeting those needs, machine politicians accomplished things that other agencies had been unable or unwilling to attempt.

Machines bred leaders—bosses—who were adept at satisfying special-interest groups while simultaneously catering to the urban working classes. Bosses and machines established power bases among new immigrant voters and used politics to solve important urban problems. Most bosses had immigrant backgrounds and had grown up in the inner city, so they knew their constituents' needs firsthand. Machines made politics a full-time profession. According to George Washington Plunkitt, a small-time boss in New York City who published his memoirs in 1905, "As a rule [the boss] has no business or occupation other than politics. He plays politics every day and night in the year and his headquarters bears the inscription, 'Never closed.'"

Machines were rarely as dictatorial or corrupt as critics charged. To be sure, fraud, bribery, and thievery tainted the system. Bosses such as Philadelphia's "Duke" Vare, Kansas City's Tom Pendergast, and New York's Richard Croker lived like kings, though their official incomes were slim. A few bosses had no permanent organization; they were freelance opportunists who bargained for power, sometimes winning and sometimes losing. But from the 1880s onward, most machines evolved into highly organized political structures, such as New York's Tammany Hall, that wedded public accomplishments with personal gain.

The system rested on a popular base and was held together by loyalty and service. Machines usually were coalitions of smaller organizations that derived power directly from inner-city working-class neighborhoods. In return for votes, bosses provided jobs, built parks and bathhouses, distributed food and clothing to the needy, and helped when someone ran afoul of the law. Such personalized service cultivated mass attachment to the boss; never before had public leaders assumed such responsibility for people in need. Bosses, moreover, were genuinely public people. They attended weddings and wakes, joined clubs, and held open houses in saloons where neighborhood folk could talk to them personally.

To finance their activities and campaigns, bosses exchanged favors for votes or money. Power over local government enabled machines to control the awarding of public contracts, the granting of utility or streetcar franchises, and the distribution of city jobs. Recipients of city business and jobs were expected to repay the machine with a portion of their profits or salaries and to cast supporting votes on election day. Critics called this process graft; bosses called it gratitude.

The Boss

Machine-led city governments constructed public buildings, sewer systems, and mass-transit lines that otherwise might not have been built; but bribes and kickbacks made such projects costly to taxpayers. In the late nineteenth century, cities financed their expansion projects with loans from the public in the form of municipal bonds. Critics of bosses charged that these loans were inflated or unnecessary. Whether necessary or not, municipal bonds caused public debts to soar, and taxes had to be raised to repay their interest and principal. In addition, machines dispensed favors to legal and illegal businesses. Payoffs from

"Big Tim" Sullivan, a New York City ward boss, rewarded "repeat voters" with a new pair of shoes. Sullivan once explained, "When you've voted 'em with their whiskers on, you take 'em to a barber and scrape off the chin fringe. Then you vote 'em again. . . . Then to a barber again, off comes the sides and you vote 'em a third time with the mustache. . . . [Then] clean off the mustache and vote 'em plain face. That makes every one of 'em for four votes."   (Library of Congress)

gambling, prostitution, and illicit liquor traffic became important sources of machine revenue.

Bosses held power because they tended to problems of everyday life. Martin Lomasney, boss of Boston's South End, explained, "There's got to be in every ward somebody that any bloke can come to—no matter what he's done—and get help. Help, you understand, none of your law and justice, but help." The boss system, however, was neither neutral nor fair. Racial minorities and new immigrant groups such as Italians and Poles received only token jobs and nominal favors, if any. But in an age of economic individualism, bosses were no more guilty of self-interest and discrimination than were business leaders who exploited workers, spoiled the landscape, and manipulated government in pursuit of profits. Sometimes humane and sometimes criminal, bosses acted as brokers between various sectors of urban society and an uncertain world.

While bosses were consolidating their power, others were attempting to destroy them. Many middle- and upper-class Americans feared that immigrant-

Urban Reform

based political machines menaced the republic and that unsavory alliances between bosses and businesses wastefully depleted municipal finances. Anxious over the poverty, crowding, and disorder that accompanied population expansion, and convinced that urban services were making taxes too high, civic reformers organized to install more responsible leaders at the helm of urban administrations.

Urban reform arose in part from the industrial system's emphasis on eliminating inefficiency. Business-minded reformers believed government should be run like a company. The way to achieve this goal, they believed, was to elect officials who would hold down expenses and prevent corruption. Thus they advocated reducing city budgets, making public employees work more efficiently, and cutting taxes.

To implement business principles in government, civic reformers supported structural changes such as the city-manager and commission forms of government, which would place administration in the hands

Structural Reform in Government

of experts rather than politicians, and nonpartisan, citywide election of officials. Armed with such strategies, reformers believed they could cleanse party politics and weaken bosses' power bases in the neighborhoods. They rarely realized, however, that bosses succeeded because they used government to meet people's needs. Reformers noticed only the waste and corruption that machines bred.

A few reform mayors moved beyond structural changes to address social problems. Hazen S. Pingree of Detroit, Samuel "Golden Rule" Jones of Toledo, and Tom Johnson of Cleveland worked to provide jobs for poor people, reduce charges by transit and utility companies, and promote governmental responsibility for the welfare of all citizens. They also supported public ownership of gas, electric, and telephone companies, a quasi-socialist reform that alienated their business allies. But Pingree, Jones, and Johnson were exceptions. Civic reformers achieved temporary successes but could not match the bosses' political savvy; they soon found themselves out of power.

Social Reform

A different type of reform arose outside politics. Driven by an urge to improve as well as manage society, social reformers—mostly young and middle class—embarked on campaigns to identify and solve urban problems. Housing reformers pressed local governments for building codes to ensure safety in tenements. Educational reformers sought to use public schools as a means of preparing immigrant children for citizenship by teaching them American values.

Perhaps the most ambitious and inspiring feature of urban reform movements was the settlement house. Located in slum neighborhoods and run mostly by women, settlements were buildings where middle-class young people went to live and work in order to bridge the gulf between social classes. The first American settlement, patterned after London's Toynbee Hall, opened in New York City in 1886, and others quickly appeared in cities across the country. Early settlement leaders such as Jane Addams, founder of Hull House in Chicago and one of the country's most influential women, and Florence Kelley, a brilliant political strategist who pioneered laws to protect consumers and working women, wanted to improve the lives of slum dwellers by helping them obtain education, appreciation of the arts, better jobs, and decent housing. Although working-class and immigrant neighborhood residents sometimes mistrusted them as outsiders, settlement workers achieved important successes with activities such as vocational classes, childcare, and ethnic pageants.

As they broadened their scope to fight for school nurses, building and factory safety codes, and public playgrounds, settlement workers became reform leaders in cities and in the nation. Their efforts to involve national and local governments in the solution of social problems later made them the vanguard of the Progressive era, when a reform spirit swept the nation (see Chapter 21). Moreover, activities of settlement houses created new professional opportunities for women in social work, public health, and child welfare. These professions enabled female reformers to build a dominion of influence over social policy independent of male-dominated professions and to make valuable contributions to national as well as inner-city life.

A contrast developed, however, between white female reformers and black female reformers. Middle-class white women lobbied for government programs to aid needy people, mostly white immigrant and native-born working classes. Black women, barred by their race from political institutions, raised funds from private donors and focused on helping members of their own race. African American women were especially active in founding schools, old-age homes, and hospitals, but they also worked for advancement of the race and protection of black women from sexual exploitation. Their ranks included women such as Jane Hunter, who founded a home for unmarried black working women in Cleveland in 1911 and influenced the establishment of similar homes in other cities, and Modjeska Simkins, who organized a program to address health problems among blacks in South Carolina.

Architects

While female reformers tried to revive neighborhoods, a group of male reformers organized the City Beautiful movement to improve cities' attractiveness. Inspired by the Columbian Exposition of 1893, a dazzling world's fair held in a "White City" built on Chicago's South Side, architects and planners worked to redesign the urban landscape. Led by architect Daniel Burnham, City Beautiful advocates built civic centers, parks, and boulevards that would make cities more economically efficient as well as beautiful. "Make no little plans," Burnham urged. "Make big plans; aim high in hope and work." This attitude spawned beautifying projects in Chicago, San Francisco, and Washington, D.C., in the early 1900s.

Yet most big plans turned out to be only big dreams. Neither government nor private businesses could finance large-scale projects, and planners disagreed among themselves and with social reformers over whether beautification would do anything to solve urban problems.

Regardless of their focus, urban reformers wanted to save cities, not abandon them. They believed they could improve urban life by restoring cooperation among all citizens. They often failed to realize, however, that cities were places of great diversity and that different people held very different views about what reform actually meant. To civic reformers, distributing city jobs on the basis of civil service exams rather than party loyalty meant progress, but to working-class men civil service signified reduced employment opportunities. Moral reformers believed that prohibiting the sale of alcoholic beverages would prevent working-class breadwinners from squandering their wages and ruining their health, but immigrants saw such crusades as interference in their private lives. Planners saw new streets and civic buildings as modern necessities, but such structures often displaced the poor. Well-meaning humanitarians criticized immigrant mothers for the way they shopped, dressed, did housework, and raised children, without regard for the inability of these mothers to afford the products that the consumer economy created. Thus urban reform merged idealism with naiveté and insensitivity.

At the same time, efforts of still a different sort were making cities more livable. Providing sanitation, street lighting, bridge and street construction, and other such needs required technological creativity, not political or humanitarian action. In addressing these critical urban issues, the American engineering profession developed new systems and standards of worldwide significance.

Engineers

Take, for example, the problem of refuse. Experts in 1900 estimated that every New Yorker generated annually some 160 pounds of garbage (food and bones), 1,200 pounds of ashes (from stoves and furnaces), and 100 pounds of rubbish (shoes, furniture, and other discarded items). Europeans of that era produced only about half as much trash. At the same time, there were as many as 3.5 million horses in American cities, each of which left behind about 20 pounds of manure and a gallon of urine daily. Overworked city horses died after only a few years, and each city had to dispose of thousands of carcasses every year. In past eras, trash, excrement, and dead animals could be dis-

missed as nuisances; by the twentieth century they became health and safety hazards, and citizens' groups protested against inadequate refuse collection and disposal.

The problem raised difficult questions. Who should be responsible for waste removal, city workers or a private contractor hired by the city? Previously, cities had dumped refuse on vacant land and in nearby rivers and lakes. What alternatives were there to these unsafe practices? How frequently should streets be cleaned, and by whom?

To solve such problems, cities increasingly depended on the technical expertise of engineers. By 1900 engineers were devising systems for incinerating refuse, dumping trash while safeguarding water supplies, constructing efficient sewers, and providing for regular street cleaning and snow removal. Engineers had similar influence in matters of street lighting, parks, and fire protection, and they also advised officials on budget and contracts. City officials, whether bosses or reformers, came to depend on the expertise of engineers, who seemed best qualified to supervise a city's expansion. Insulated within bureaucratic agencies from tumultuous party strife, engineers generally carried out their responsibilities efficiently and with little fanfare and made some of the most lasting contributions to urban management.

Family Life

Although the overwhelming majority of Americans continued to live within families, this basic social institution suffered strain during the era of urbanization and industrialization. New institutions—schools, social clubs, political organizations, and others—increasingly competed with the family to provide nurture, education, and security. Clergy and journalists warned that rising divorce rates, the growing separation between home and work, the entrance of numerous women into the work force, and loss of parental control over children spelled peril for home and family. Yet the family retained its fundamental role as a cushion in a hard, uncertain world.

Throughout modern Western history, most people have lived in two overlapping social units: household and family. A household is a group of people, related or unrelated, who share the same residence. A family is a group related by kinship, some members of which typically live

Family and Household Structures

The Hedlund family of St. Paul, Minnesota, celebrates the Fourth of July together in 1911 with flags and fireworks. Consisting of two parents and three children, the family represents the modern household of two generations and limited family size.   (Minnesota Historical Society)

together. In the late nineteenth and early twentieth centuries, different patterns characterized the two institutions.

Since colonial times, the vast majority of American households (75 to 80 percent) have consisted of nuclear families—usually a married couple, with or without children. About 15 to 20 percent of households consisted of extended families—usually a married couple, with or without children, plus one or more relatives such as parents, adult siblings, grandchildren, aunts, and uncles. About 5 percent of households consisted of people living alone or in boarding houses and hotels. Despite slight variations, this pattern held relatively constant among ethnic, racial, and socioeconomic groups.

Several factors explain this pattern. Because immigrants tended to be young, the U.S. population as a whole was young. In 1880 the median age was under twenty-one, and by 1920 it was still only twenty-five. (Median age at present is about thirty-six.) Moreover, in 1900 the death rate among people aged forty-five to sixty-four was double what it is today. As a result, there were relatively few older people: only 4 percent of the population was sixty-five or older, compared with about 15 percent today. Thus few families could form extended three-generation households, and fewer children than today had living grandparents. Migration separated many families, and the ideal of a home of one's own encouraged nuclear household organization.

The average size of nuclear families did change over time, though. Most of Europe and North America experienced falling birth rates in the nineteenth century. The decline in the United States began early in the 1800s and accelerated toward the end of the century. In 1880 the birth rate was 40 live births per 1,000 people; by 1900 it had dropped to 32; by 1920 to 28. Several factors explain this decline.

Declining Birth Rates

First, the United States was becoming an urban nation, and birth rates are historically lower in cities than in rural areas. On farms, where young children worked at home or in the fields, each child born represented a new set of hands for the family work force. In the wage-based urban economy, children could not contribute significantly to the family income for many years, and a new child represented another mouth to feed. Second, infant mortality fell as diet and medical care improved, and families did not have to bear many children just to ensure that some would survive. Third, awareness that smaller families meant improved quality of life seems to have stimulated decisions to limit family size—either by abstaining from sex during the wife's fertile period or by using contraception and abortion. Although fertility was higher among blacks, immigrants, and rural people than among white native-born city dwellers, birth rates of all groups fell. Families with six or eight children became rare; three or four became more usual. As a result, the nuclear family tended to reach its maximum size and then shrink faster than in earlier eras.

The household tended to expand and contract over the lifetime of a given family. Its size increased as children were born. Later, especially in working-class families, it shrank as children left home before they were twenty years old, usually to work.

Boarding

The process of leaving home altered household composition; huge numbers of young people—and some older people—lived as boarders and lodgers, especially in cities. Middle- and working-class families commonly took in boarders to occupy rooms vacated by grown children and to get additional income. Immigrants such as Rahel Gollop often lodged with relatives and fellow villagers until they could establish themselves. By the end of the nineteenth century, as many as 50 percent of city residents had lived either as, or with, boarders at some point during their lifetime. Housing reformers charged that boarding caused overcrowding and loss of privacy. Yet for those who boarded or took in boarders, the practice was highly useful. One immigrant woman recalled:

> We had four boarders and I had to cook for them. When I first came here I didn't want to do this because everybody want to have their own house. Well, I change my mind because everybody was doing this thing. That time some of the people that came from the other side didn't have no place to stay and we took some of the people in the house that we knew. . . . This is the way that everybody used to do it that time.

For people on the move, boarding was a transitional stage, providing them with a quasi-family environment until they set up their own households.

Some households took in extended-family members who lived as quasi-boarders. Especially in communities where economic hardship or rapid growth made housing expensive or scarce, newlyweds sometimes lived temporarily with one spouse's parents. Families also took in widowed parents or unmarried siblings who otherwise would have lived alone, and many young unmarried men and women continued to live at home although they had jobs and independent social lives.

Importance of Kinship

At a time when welfare agencies were rare, the family was the institution to which people could turn in times of need. Even when relatives did not live together, they often lived nearby and aided one another with childcare, meals, shopping, advice, and consolation. They also obtained jobs for each other. Factory foremen who had responsibility for hiring often recruited new workers recommended by their employees. According to one new arrival, "After two days my brother took me to the shop he was working in and his boss saw me and he gave me the job."

But obligations of kinship were not always welcome. Immigrant families often pressured last-born children to stay at home to care for aging parents, a practice that stifled opportunities for education, marriage, and economic independence. As an aging Italian-American father confessed, "One of our daughters is an old maid [and] causes plenty of troubles. . . . It may be my fault because I always wished her to remain at home and not to marry for she was of great financial help." Tensions also developed between generations, such as when immigrant parents and American-born children clashed over the abandonment of Old World ways or the amount of money employed children should contribute to the household. Nevertheless, for better or worse, kinship provided people a means of coping with the stresses caused by an urban-industrial society. Social and economic change did not sever family ties.

Large numbers of city dwellers lived beyond the haven of traditional family relationships, however. In 1890 almost 42 percent of adult American men and 37 percent of women were single, almost twice as high as the figures for 1960. (The proportions today have risen back to beyond the 1890 levels.) About half of them still lived in their parents' household, but many others inhabited boarding houses or rooms in the homes of strangers. Mostly young, these men and women constituted a separate subculture that helped support institutions

Unmarried People

like dance halls, saloons, cafés, and the YMCA and YWCA.

Some of these unmarried people numbered among the homosexual population that thrived especially in large cities like New York and Boston. Though their numbers are difficult to estimate, gay men had their own subculture complete with clubs, restaurants, coffeehouses, theaters, and support networks. A number of gay couples, especially women, formed lasting marriage-type relationships, sometimes called "Boston marriages." Some men cruised in the sexual underground of the streets and bars. People in the gay subculture were categorized more by how they acted—men acting like women, women acting like men—than by who their sexual partners were. Thus the term *homosexual* was not used. For example, men who dressed and acted like women were called "fairies," and men who displayed masculine traits could be termed "normal" even though they might have sexual relations with fairies. Gay women remained even more hidden, and a lesbian subculture of clubs and commercial establishments seldom existed until the 1920s. The gay world, then, was a complex one that included a variety of relationships and institutions.

Although the family remained resilient and adaptable, subtle but momentous changes began to occur in individual life patterns. Before the

Stages of Life

twentieth century, stages of life were less distinct than they are today, and generations blended together with relatively little differentiation. Childhood, for instance, had been regarded as a period during which young people prepared for adulthood by gradually assuming more adult roles and responsibilities. The subdivisions of youth—toddlers, schoolchildren, adolescents, and the like—were not recognized or defined. Because married couples had more children over a longer time span than is common today, active parenthood occupied most of their adult lives. Older children, who cared for younger sisters and brothers, might begin parenting even before reaching adulthood. And because relatively few people lived to advanced ages or left work voluntarily, and because old-age homes were rare, older people were not isolated from other age groups.

By the late nineteenth century, demographic and social changes had altered these patterns. Decreasing birth rates shortened the period of parental responsibility, so more middle-aged couples experienced an empty nest when all their children grew up and left

home. Longer life expectancy and a tendency by employers to force aged workers to retire separated the old from the young. At the same time, work became more specialized and education in grade schools more formalized, especially after states passed compulsory school-attendance laws in the 1870s and 1880s. Childhood and adolescence became more distinct from adulthood. As a result of these and other trends (including the lower birth rate, which gave people fewer sisters and brothers to relate to), Americans became more conscious of age and peer influence. People's roles in school, in the family, on the job, and in the community came to be determined by age more than by any other characteristic.

Thus by the early 1900s, family life and functions were both changing and holding firm. New institutions were assuming tasks formerly performed by the family. Schools were making education a community responsibility. Employment agencies, personnel offices, and labor unions were taking responsibility for employee recruitment and job security. Age-based peer groups were exerting greater influence over people's values and activities. In addition, migration and a soaring divorce rate seemed to be splitting families apart. Yet in the face of these pressures, the family adjusted by expanding and contracting to meet temporary needs, and kinship remained a dependable though not always appreciated institution. For the majority of people, family life was vital. "As I grew up, living conditions were a bit crowded," one woman reminisced, "but no one minded because we were a family . . . thankful we all lived together."

The New Leisure and Mass Culture

 On December 2, 1889, as hundreds of workers paraded through Worcester, Massachusetts, in support of shorter working hours, a group of carpenters hoisted a banner proclaiming "Eight Hours for Work, Eight Hours for Rest, Eight Hours for What We Will." That last phrase was significant, for it laid claim to a special segment of daily life that belonged to the individual. Increasingly, among all urban social classes, leisure activities filled this time segment.

American inventors had long tried to create labor-saving devices, but not until the late 1800s did technology become truly time-saving. Mechanization and assembly-line production helped to cut the average

Increase in Leisure Time

workweek in manufacturing from sixty-six hours in 1860 to sixty in 1890 and forty-seven in 1920. These reductions meant shorter workdays and freer weekends. White-collar workers spent from eight to ten hours a day on the job and often worked only half a day or not at all on weekends. To be sure, thousands of laborers still endured twelve- or fourteen-hour shifts in steel mills and sweatshops and had no time or energy for leisure. But as the nation's economy shifted from one of scarcity and production to one of surplus and consumption, more Americans began to engage in a variety of diversions, and a substantial segment of the economy began providing for—and profiting from—leisure. By the early 1900s, many Americans were enmeshed in the business of play.

After the Civil War, amusement became an organized, commercial activity. The production of games, toys, and musical instruments for indoor family entertainment expanded. Games such as checkers and backgammon had existed for decades, but improvements in printing and paper production and the rise of new manufacturers such as Milton Bradley and Parker Brothers increased the popularity of board games markedly. Significantly, the content of board games shifted from moral lessons to topics involving transportation, finance, and sports. Also, by the 1890s, middle-class families were buying mass-produced pianos and sheet music that made the singing of popular songs a favored form of home entertainment.

The vanguard of new leisure pursuits, however, was sports. Formerly a fashionable indulgence of elites, organized sports quickly became the most popular pastime of all classes, attracting huge numbers of participants and spectators. Even those who could not play or watch became involved by reading about sports in the newspapers.

The most popular organized sport was baseball. An outgrowth of older bat, ball, and base-circling games,

Baseball

baseball was formalized in 1845 by a group of wealthy New Yorkers—the Knickerbocker Club—who codified the rules of play. By 1860 at least fifty baseball clubs existed, and informal games were being played on city lots and rural fields across the nation. In 1869 a professional club, the Cincinnati Red Stockings, went on a national tour, and other clubs quickly followed suit. The National League of Professional Baseball Clubs, founded in 1876, gave the sport a stable, businesslike structure. Not all athletes could benefit; as

While baseball, football, boxing, and racing became popular sports for men, basketball became the most appealing sport for women, especially those in college. Special rules established in 1897 lessened the supposed dangers of rough, vigorous play by limiting the number of dribbles, confining players to particular zones on the court, and encouraging passing.   (Collection of Sally Fox)

early as 1867, a "color line" excluded black players from professional teams. Nevertheless, by the 1880s, professional baseball was a big business. In 1903 the National League and competing American League (formed in 1901) began a World Series between their championship teams, entrenching baseball as the national pastime. The Boston Red Socks beat the Pittsburgh Pirates in that first series.

Baseball appealed mostly to men. But croquet, which also swept the nation, attracted both sexes.

Croquet and Cycling

Middle- and upper-class people held croquet parties and outfitted wickets with candles for night contests. In an era when the departure of paid work from the home had separated men's from women's spheres, croquet increased opportunities for social contact between the sexes.

Meanwhile, cycling achieved a popularity rivaling that of baseball, especially after 1885, when the cumbersome velocipede, with huge front wheel and tall seat, gave way to the safety bicycle with pneumatic tires and wheels of identical size. By 1900 Americans owned over 10 million bicycles, and clubs like the League of American Wheelmen were pressing state governments to build more paved roads. One journal boasted that cycling cured dyspepsia, headaches, insomnia, and sciatica and gave "a vigorous tone to the whole system." Professional bicycle races brought success to riders such as Major Taylor, an African American who won fame in Europe and the United States. Like croquet, cycling brought men and women together, combining opportunities for courtship and exercise. Moreover, the bicycle played an influential role in freeing women from the constraints of Victorian fashions. In order to ride the dropped-frame female models, women had to wear divided skirts and simple undergarments. Gradually, cycling costumes influenced everyday fashions. As the 1900 census declared, "Few articles . . . have created so great a revolution in social conditions as the bicycle."

Other sports had their own patrons. Tennis and golf attracted both sexes but remained pastimes of the

Football

wealthy. Played mostly at private clubs, these sports lacked baseball's team competition and cycling's informality. American football also began as a sport for people of high social rank. As an intercollegiate competition, football attracted players and spectators wealthy enough to have access to higher education. By the end of the century, however, the game was appealing to a broader audience. The 1893 Princeton-Yale game drew fifty thousand spectators, and informal games were being played in yards and playgrounds throughout the country.

At the same time, college football became a national scandal because of its violence and use of "tramp athletes," nonstudents whom colleges hired to help their teams win. Critics charged that football mirrored the worst features of American society. An editor of *The Nation* charged in 1890 that "the spirit of the American Youth, as of the American man, is to win, to 'get there,' by fair means or foul; and the lack of moral scruple which pervades the struggles of the business world meets with temptations equally irresistible in the miniature contests of the football field."

The scandals climaxed in 1905, when 18 players died from game-related injuries and over 150 were seriously injured. President Theodore Roosevelt, a strong advocate of athletics, convened a White House conference to discuss ways to eliminate brutality and foul play. The conference founded the Intercollegiate Athletic Association (renamed the National College Athletic Association in 1910) to police college sports. In 1906 the association altered the games to make football less violent and more open. New rules outlawed "flying wedge" rushes, extended from five to ten yards the distance needed to earn a first down, legalized the forward pass, and tightened player eligibility requirements.

As more women enrolled in college, they began to pursue physical activities besides croquet and cycling. Believing that intellectual success required active and healthy bodies, college women participated in sports such as rowing, track, and swimming. Eventually women made basketball their most popular intercollegiate sport. Invented in 1891 as a winter sport for men, basketball was given women's rules (which limited dribbling and running and encouraged passing) by Senda Berenson of Smith College in the 1890s.

Paralleling the rise of sports, American show business also became a mode of leisure created by and for

Circuses

common people. Circuses—traveling shows of acrobats and animals—had existed since the 1820s. But after the Civil War, railroads enabled them to reach cities and towns across the country. Circuses offered two main attractions: so-called freaks of nature, both human and animal, and the temptation and conquest of death. At the heart of their appeal was the astonishment that trapeze artists, lion tamers, acrobats, and clowns aroused. Writer Hamlin Garland captured the circus's effect on a community:

> From the time the "advance man" flung his highly colored posters over the fence till the coming of the glorious day, we thought of little else. . . . It was our brief season of imaginative life. In one day—in a part of one day—we gained a thousand new conceptions of the world and of human nature. It was the embodiment of all that was skillful and beautiful in human action. . . . It gave us something to talk about.

Three branches of American show business—popular drama, musical comedy, and vaudeville—matured with the growth of cities. Theatrical performances offered audiences an escape from the harshness of urban-industrial life into melodrama, ad-

Popular Drama and Musical Comedy

venture, and comedy. Plots were simple, the heroes and villains recognizable. For urbanized people unfamiliar with the frontier, popular plays brought to life the mythical Wild West and Old South through stories of Davy Crockett, Buffalo Bill, and Civil War romances. Virtue, honor, and justice always triumphed in melodramas such as "Uncle Tom's Cabin" and "The Old Homestead," reinforcing faith that in an uncertain and disillusioning world, goodness would prevail.

Musical comedies entertained audiences with song, humor, and dance. American musical comedy grew out of lavishly costumed operettas common in Europe. By introducing American themes (often involving ethnic groups), folksy humor, and catchy tunes, these shows featured the nation's most popular songs and entertainers. George M. Cohan, a spirited singer, dancer, and songwriter born into an Irish family of entertainers, became the master of American musical comedy after the turn of the century. Drawing on urbanism, patriotism, and traditional values in songs like "Yankee Doodle Boy" and "You're a Grand Old Flag," Cohan helped bolster morale during the First World War. Comic opera, too, became popular. The first American comic operas imitated European musicals, but by the early 1900s composers like Victor Herbert were writing for American audiences. Shortly thereafter Jerome Kern began to compose more sophisticated musicals, and American musical comedy came into its own.

Vaudeville

Because of its variety, vaudeville was probably the most popular entertainment in early-twentieth-century America. Shows included, in rapid succession, acts of jugglers, dancing bears, pantomimists, storytellers, magicians, puppeteers, acrobats, comedians, singers, and dancers. Around 1900, the number of vaudeville theaters and troupes skyrocketed. Sharp entrepreneurs, who did for entertain-

Joe Weber and Lew Fields were one of the most popular comic teams in vaudeville. They and similar comedians used fast-paced dialogue to entertain audiences with routines such as this one: Doctor: Do you have insurance? Patient: I ain't got one nickel insurance. Doctor: If you die, what will your wife bury you with? Patient: With pleasure. (Corbis-Bettmann)

ment what Edison and Ford did for technology, made vaudeville big business. The famous promoter Florenz Ziegfeld brilliantly packaged shows in a stylish format—the Ziegfeld Follies—and gave the nation a new model of femininity, the Ziegfeld Girl, whose graceful dancing and alluring costumes suggested a haunting sensuality.

Show business provided new opportunities for female, African American, and immigrant performers, but it also encouraged stereotyping and exploitation. Comic opera diva Lillian Russell, vaudeville singer-comedienne Fanny Brice, and burlesque queen Eva Tanguay attracted intensely loyal fans, commanded handsome fees, and won respect for their talents. In contrast to the demure Victorian female, they conveyed pluck and creativity. There was something both shocking and refreshingly confident about Eva Tanguay when she sang earthy songs like "I Want Someone to Go Wild with Me," "It's All Been Done Before but Not the Way I Do It," and her theme song, "I Don't Care." But lesser female performers were often exploited by male promoters and theater owners, many of whom wanted only to titillate the public, for a price, with the sight of scantily clad women.

Before the 1890s, the chief form of commercial entertainment open to African American performers was the minstrel show, but vaudeville opened new opportunities to them. As stage settings shifted from the plantation to the city, music shifted from folk tunes to ragtime. Pandering to the prejudices of white audiences, composers and performers of both races ridiculed blacks. As songs like "He's Just a Little Nigger, but He's Mine All Mine" and "You May Be a Hawaiian on Old Broadway, but You're Just Another Nigger to Me" confirm, blacks on the stage suffered much as they did in society at large. Even Burt Williams, a talented and highly paid black comedian and dancer who achieved success by playing stereotypical roles of darky and dandy, was tormented by the humiliation he had to suffer.

An ethnic flavor gave much of American mass entertainment its uniqueness. Indeed, immigrants occupied the core of American show business. Vaudeville in particular utilized ethnic humor, exaggerating dialects and other national traits. Skits and songs reinforced ethnic stereotypes and made fun of ethnic groups, but such distortions were more self-conscious and sympathetic than those directed at blacks. Ethnic humor often focused on everyday difficulties that immigrants faced. A typical scene involving Italians, for example, revolved around a character's uncertain grasp of En-

glish, which caused him to confuse *mayor* with *mare*, *diploma* with the *plumber*, and *pallbearer* with *polar bear*. Such scenes allowed audiences to laugh with rather than at the foibles of the human condition. The conditions of African Americans, however, were subject to more vicious humor.

Shortly after 1900, live entertainment began to yield to a more accessible form of amusement: moving pictures. Perfected by Thomas Edison in the 1880s, movies began as slot-machine peepshows in penny arcades and billiard parlors. Eventually images were projected onto a screen so that large audiences could view them, and a new medium was born. At first, the subjects of films hardly mattered; scenes of speeding trains, acrobats, and writhing belly dancers were thrilling enough.

Movies

Producers soon discovered that a film could tell a story in exciting ways. Thanks to creative directors like D. W. Griffith, motion pictures became a distinct art form. Griffith's *Birth of a Nation* (1915), an epic film about the Civil War and Reconstruction, fanned racial prejudice by depicting African Americans as threats to white moral values. The National Association for the Advancement of Colored People (NAACP), formed in 1909, led an organized protest against it. But the film's innovative techniques—close-ups, fade-outs, and battle scenes—heightened the drama. By 1920, movies were popular among all classes (admission usually cost a nickel), and audiences idolized film stars such as Mary Pickford, Lillian Gish, and Charlie Chaplin.

The still camera, modernized by inventor George Eastman, enabled ordinary people to record their own visual images, especially useful for preserving family memories. The phonograph, another Edison invention, brought musical performances into the home. The spread of movies, photography, and phonograph records meant that access to live performances no longer limited people's exposure to art and entertainment. By making it possible to mass-produce sound and images, technology made entertainment a highly desirable consumer good.

News also became a consumer product. Using high-speed printing presses, cheap paper, and profits from growing advertisement revenues, a group of canny publishers created a medium that made people crave news just as they craved amusements. City life and increased leisure time seemed to nurture a fascination with the sensational, and from the 1880s onward popular urban newspapers increasingly whetted that appetite.

Joseph Pulitzer, a Hungarian immigrant who bought the *New York World* in 1883, pioneered journalism as a branch of mass culture.

Yellow Journalism

Believing that newspapers should be "dedicated to the cause of the people rather than to that of the purse potentates," Pulitzer filled the *World* with stories of disasters, crimes, and scandals. Sensational headlines, set in large bold type like that used for advertisements, screamed from every page. Pulitzer's journalists not only reported news but sought it out and even created it. *World* reporter Nellie Bly (real name, Elizabeth Cochrane) faked her way into an insane asylum and wrote a brazen exposé of the sordid conditions she found. Other reporters staged stunts and sought out heart-rending human-interest stories. Pulitzer also popularized comics, and the yellow ink they were printed in gave rise to the term *yellow journalism* as a synonym for sensationalism.

Pulitzer's strategy was immensely successful. In one year he increased the *World*'s daily circulation from 20,000 to 100,000, and by the late 1890s it reached 1 million. Soon other publishers, such as William Randolph Hearst, who bought the *New York Journal* in 1895 and started an empire of mass-circulation newspapers, adopted Pulitzer's techniques. Yellow journalism became a nationwide phenomenon, feeding interest in bizarre aspects of the human condition.

Pulitzer and his rivals boosted circulation further by emphasizing sports and women's news. Newspapers had previously reported sporting events, but yellow-journalism papers gave such stories far greater prominence by printing separate, expanded sports pages. Such sections promoted sports as a leisure-time attraction, as sports news re-created a game's drama through narrative and statistics. While increasing sports reporting, mostly for male readers, newspapers also added special sections devoted to household tips, fashion, decorum, and club news to capture female readers. Like crime and disaster stories, sports and women's sections helped to make news a mass commodity.

By the early twentieth century, mass-circulation magazines were overshadowing the expensive elitist journals of earlier eras. Publications

Magazines

such as *McClure's, Saturday Evening Post,* and *Ladies' Home Journal* offered human-interest stories, muckraking exposés (see page 581), titillating fiction, photographs, colorful covers, and eye-catching ads to a growing mass market. Meanwhile, the total number of books

Frank Merriwell, the fictional hero of hundreds of stories written by Burt Standish (the pen name used by Gilbert Patten), was a popular character in the early 1900s. In a series of adventures, most involving sports, Frank used his physical skills, valor, and moral virtue to lead by example, accomplish the impossible, and influence others to behave in an upstanding way.   (Collection of Picture Research Consultants)

published more than quadrupled between 1880 and 1917. This rising popular consumption of news and books reflected growing literacy. Between 1870 and 1920, the proportion of Americans aged ten and over who could not read or write fell from 20 percent to 6 percent.

Other forms of communication also expanded. In 1891 there was fewer than one telephone for every 100 people in the United States; by 1901 the number had grown to 2.1, and by 1921 it had swelled to 12.6. In 1900 Americans used 4 billion postage stamps; in 1922 they used 14.3 billion. The term *community* took on new dimensions, as people used the media, mail, and telephone to extend their horizons far beyond their immediate localities. More than ever before, people in different parts of the country knew about and discussed the same news event, whether it was a sensational murder, a sex scandal, or the fortunes of a particular entertainer or athlete. America was becoming a mass society.

To some extent, the cities' new amusements and pastimes had a homogenizing influence, bringing together ethnic and social groups to

Mass Culture and Americanization

share a common experience. Parks, ball fields, vaudeville shows, movies, and feature sections of newspapers and magazines were nonsectarian and apolitical, designed to appeal to everyone. Yet even though entrepreneurs were responsible for the spread of amusements, different groups of consumers often used them to reinforce their own cultural habits. In some cities, for example, working-class immigrants occupied parks and amusement areas as sites for family and ethnic gatherings. To the dismay of reformers who hoped that recreation would assimilate newcomers and teach them habits of restraint, immigrants used picnics and Fourth of July celebrations as occasions for boisterous drinking and sometimes violent behavior. Young working-class men and women resisted parents' and moralists' warnings and frequented urban dance halls, where they explored their own forms of courtship and sexual behavior. And children often used streets and rooftops to create their own entertainment rather than participate in adult-supervised games in parks and playgrounds. Thus as Americans learned to play, their leisure—like their work and their politics—expressed and was shaped by the pluralistic forces that thrived in the cities.

Summary

Much of what American society is today originated in the urbanization of the late nineteenth and early twentieth centuries. Though their governments and neighborhoods may have seemed chaotic, American cities experienced an "unheralded triumph" by the early 1900s. Amid corruption and political conflict, urban engineers modernized local infrastructures with new sewer, water, and lighting services, and urban governments made the environment safer by expanding professional police and fire departments. When native inventiveness met the traditions of European, African, and Asian cultures, a new kind of society emerged. This society seldom functioned smoothly; there really was no coherent urban community, only a collection of subcommunities. Yet the jumble of social classes, ethnic and racial groups, political organizations, and professional experts created a relatively stable though fragile harmony.

American cities exhibited bewildering diversity. Fearful and puzzled, native-born whites tried to Americanize and uplift immigrants, but newcomers stubbornly strained to protect their cultures. Optimists had envisioned the American nation as a melting pot, where various nationalities would blend to become a unified people. Instead, many ethnic groups proved unmeltable, and racial minorities got burned on the bottom of the pot. As a result of immigration and urbanization, the United States became a culturally pluralistic society—not so much a melting pot as a salad bowl, where ingredients retained their original flavor and occasionally blended. Often the results were hyphenated identifications: Irish-American, Italian-American, Polish-American, and the like.

Pluralism and interest-group loyalties enhanced the importance of politics. If America was not a melting pot, then different groups were competing for power, wealth, and status. Some people carried polarization to extremes and tried to suppress everything allegedly un-American. Efforts to enforce homogeneity generally failed, however, because the country's cultural diversity prevented domination by a single ethnic majority. By 1920, immigrants and their offspring outnumbered the native-born in many cities, and the national economy depended on these new workers and consumers. Migrants and immigrants transformed the United States into an urban nation. They gave American culture its rich and varied texture, and they laid the foundations for the liberalism that characterized American politics in the twentieth century.

LEGACY FOR A PEOPLE AND A NATION
Ethnic Food

Today, an ordinary American might eat a bagel for breakfast, a gyro sandwich for lunch, and wonton soup, shrimp creole, and rice pilaf for dinner, followed by chocolate mousse and espresso. An evening snack might consist of nachos and lager beer. These items, all identified with a different ethnic group, serve as tasty reminders that immigrants made important and lasting contributions to the nation's culinary culture. Yet also, the American diet represents one of the few genuine ways that the multicultural nation has served as a melting pot.

The American taste for ethnic food has a complicated history. Since the nineteenth century, the food business has offered immigrant entrepreneurs lucrative opportunities, many of which involved products unrelated to their own ethnic background. The industry is replete with success stories linked to names such as Hector Boiardi (Chef Boyardee), William Gebhardt (Eagle Brand chili and tamales), Jeno Paulucci (Chun-King), and Alphonse Biardot (Franco-American), all of whom immigrated to the United States in the late nineteenth or early twentieth century. But Americans have also supported unheralded immigrant merchants and restaurateurs who have offered special and regional fare—German, Chinese, Italian, Tex-Mex, "soul food," or Thai—in every era.

Unlike the strife that occurred over housing, jobs, schools, and politics when different nationalities collided, the evolution of American eating habits has been extremely peaceful. Occasionally, criticisms developed, such as when dietitians and reformers in the early twentieth century charged that Mexican immigrants were harming their digestion by overusing tomatoes and peppers and that the rich foods of eastern European Jews made them overly emotional and less capable of assimilating. But as historian Donna Gabaccia has observed, relatively conflict-free sharing and borrowing have characterized American foodways far more than "food fights" and intolerance. The sensory pleasure of eating has always overridden cultural loyalty, and mass marketers have been quick to capitalize.

As each wave of immigrants has entered the nation—and especially as these newcomers have occupied the cities, where cross-cultural contact has been inevitable—food has given them certain ways of becoming American, of finding some form of group acceptance, while also giving them a means of confirming their identity. At the same time, those who already thought of themselves as Americans have willingly made the cuisine of the newcomers a part of the existing culture and a part of themselves.

For Further Reading, see page A-22 of the Appendix. For Web resources, go to http://college.hmco.com.

He had one eye and a bad temper. Born in back-country South Carolina, Benjamin Tillman was only two when his father died. Of his five brothers, two were murdered, another killed a man in a gambling dispute, and another died in the Civil War. Benjamin enlisted in the Confederate Army but had to quit almost immediately because an abscess caused blindness in one eye. He began farming a small plot that he received from his mother, but drought, crop failures, and debt forced him to sell much of his land. Driven by a belief that the southern power structure was causing the "decay of that sturdy independence of character, which was once marked in our people," he entered politics.

Associates called him "Pitchfork Ben" because when he ran for the U.S. Senate in 1894, he promised to "stick a pitchfork" into Grover Cleveland to make the president more receptive to his ideas. A former slaveholder, he epitomized southern extremism. He never wavered in his belief that African Americans were inferior to whites, and he worked to exclude them from voting and advocated lynching in cases of rape. Yet Benjamin Tillman, two-term governor and four-term senator from South Carolina, also helped his state open new colleges, supported laws to regulate railroads, accused steelmakers of profiting at public expense, equalized state taxes, increased the education budget, helped secure direct primaries for nomination of state officers, and fought tirelessly on behalf of embattled farmers.

Tillman's turbulent career paralleled an eventful era, one that can be characterized by three themes: special interests, legislative accomplishment, and political exclusion. When he attacked railroads, the steel industry, and the merchants and lawyers whom he accused of exploiting farmers, Tillman expressed the growing dissatisfaction with the ways in which powerful private interests—manufacturers, railroad managers, bankers, and wealthy men in general—were exercising monumental greed in large corporations across the continent. The era's venality seemed so widespread that when, in 1874, Mark Twain and Charles Dudley Warner satirized America as a land of shallow money

GILDED AGE POLITICS 1877–1900

Politics in the late nineteenth century was a major community activity. In an age before movies, television, shopping malls, and widespread professional sports, forceful orators such as Socialist Party leader Eugene V. Debs, shown speaking in a railroad yard, attracted large audiences for speeches that sometimes lasted for hours. (Brown Brothers) grubbers in their novel, *The Gilded Age*, the name stuck. Historians have used the expression "Gilded Age" to characterize the late nineteenth century.

At the same time, Tillman's economic and political reforms reflected the era's accomplishments not just at the state level but also at the national level. Between 1877 and 1900, industrialization, urbanization, and the commercialization of agriculture altered national politics and government as much as they shaped everyday life. Congress achieved legislative landmarks in railroad regulation, tariffs, currency, civil service, and other important issues in spite of partisan and regional rivalries. Meanwhile, the judiciary actively supported big business by defending property rights against state and federal regulation. The presidency was occupied by honest, respectable men who, though not as exceptional as Washington, Jefferson, or Lincoln, prepared the office for its more activist character after the turn of the century.

Even so, exclusion—the third phenomenon—prevented the majority of Americans—including women, southern blacks, Indians, uneducated whites, and unnaturalized immigrants—from voting and from access to the tools of democracy. "Pitchfork Ben" Tillman represented an extreme example of individuals and groups who exacerbated a condition that plagued the nation in the years following Reconstruction.

Until the 1890s, those three phenomena of special interests, accomplishment, and exclusion existed within a delicate political equilibrium characterized by a stable party system and a balance of power among the country's geographical sections. Then in the 1890s rural discontent erupted in the West and South, and a deep economic depression bared flaws in the industrial system. Though he stood on the fringes of the mass agrarian reform movement, Tillman helped awaken the rural masses with his fiery rhetoric. Amid the economic and political disruption, a presidential campaign in 1896 stirred Americans as they had not been stirred for a generation. A new party arose, old parties split, sectional unity dissolved, and fundamental disputes about the nation's future climaxed. The nation emerged from the turbulent 1890s with new economic configurations and new political alignments. ■

The Nature of Party Politics

 At no other time in the nation's history was public interest in elections more avid than between 1870 and 1896. Consistently, 80 to 90 percent of eligible voters (white and black males in the North, mostly white males in the South) cast ballots in local and national elections. (Under 50 percent typically do so today.) Politics served as a form of recreation, more popular than baseball or circuses. Actual voting provided only the final stage in a process that included parades, picnics, and speeches. As one observer remarked, "What the theatre is to the French, or the bull fight . . . to the Spanish . . . [election campaigns] and the ballot box are to our people."

Party loyalty in part reflected American pluralism. As different groups competed for power, wealth, and status, they formed coalitions to achieve their goals. But such coalitions were fragile, and their memberships shifted according to the issue in question. With some exceptions, groups who opposed interference by government in matters of personal liberty identified with the Democratic Party, and those who believed government could be an agent of moral reform identified with the Republican Party. Democrats included immigrant Catholics and Jews, who believed that ritual and sacraments should guide personal behavior and prove one's faith in God. Republicans consisted mostly of native-born Protestants, who believed that religious salvation could best be achieved by purging the world of evil and that legislation could protect people from sin. Democrats would restrict government power. Republicans believed in direct government action.

Cultural-Political Alignments

At state and local levels, adherents of these two cultural traditions battled over how much control government should exercise over people's lives. The most contentious issues were use of leisure time and celebration of Sunday, the Lord's day. Protestant Republicans tried to keep the Sabbath holy through legislation that prohibited bars, stores, and commercial amusements from being open on Sundays. Immigrant Democrats, accustomed to feasting and playing after church, fought saloon closings and other restrictions on the only day they had free from work. Similar splits developed over public versus parochial schools and prohibition versus the free availability of liquor.

These issues made politics a personal as well as a community activity. In an era before movie stars and media heroes, people formed strong loyalties to individual politicians, loyalties that often overlooked crassness and corruption. James G. Blaine—Maine's flamboyant and powerful congressman, senator, presidential aspirant, and two-time secretary of state—typified this appeal. Followers called him the "Plumed Knight," composed songs and organized parades in his

IMPORTANT EVENTS

1873 Congress ends coinage of silver dollars

1874 Twain and Warner's *The Gilded Age* appears and gives a name to its era

1873–78 Economic hard times hit

1876 Hayes elected president

1877 Georgia passes poll tax and begins legislative movement to disfranchise African Americans in the South
Munn v. Illinois upholds principle of state regulation

1878 Bland-Allison Act requires Treasury to buy between $2 and $4 million in silver each month
Anthony-backed woman suffrage amendment defeated in Congress

1880 Garfield elected president

1881 Garfield assassinated; Arthur assumes the presidency

1883 Pendleton Civil Service Act creates Civil Service Commission to oversee competitive examinations for some government positions
Supreme Court strikes down 1875 Civil Rights Act

1884 Cleveland elected president

1886 *Wabash* case declares that only Congress can limit interstate commerce rates

1887 Farm prices collapse
Farmers' Alliances form
Interstate Commerce Act creates commission to regulate rates and practices of interstate shippers

1888 B. Harrison elected president

1890 McKinley Tariff raises tariff rates
Sherman Silver Purchase Act commits Treasury to buying 4.5 million ounces of silver each month
"Mississippi Plan" uses poll taxes and literacy tests to prevent African Americans from voting
National American Woman Suffrage Association formed

1892 Populist convention in Omaha draws up reform platform
Cleveland elected president

1893–97 Major economic depression hits U.S.

1893 Sherman Silver Purchase Act repealed

1894 Wilson-Gorman Tariff attempts to reduce rates; Senate Republicans restore House cuts
Eugene V. Debs arrested and turns to socialism
Coxey's army marches on Washington, D.C.

1895 Cleveland cuts deal with bankers to save gold reserves

1896 McKinley elected president
Plessy v. Ferguson establishes "separate-but-equal" doctrine, allowing segregation of African Americans in public accommodations

1897 Dingley Tariff raises duties

1898 Louisiana implements "grandfather clause" that keeps blacks from voting

1899 *Cummins v. County Board of Education* applies separate-but-equal doctrine to schools

1900 Gold Standard Act requires all paper money to be backed by gold
McKinley reelected president

honor, and sat mesmerized by his long speeches, while disregarding his corrupt alliances with businessmen and his animosity toward laborers and farmers.

Allegiances to national parties and candidates were so evenly divided that no faction gained control for any sustained period of time. Between 1877 and 1897, Republicans held the presidency for three terms, Democrats for two. Rarely did the same party control both the presidency and Congress simultaneously. From 1876 through 1892, presidential elections were extremely close. The outcome often hinged on the popular vote in a few populous states—Connecticut,

New York, New Jersey, Ohio, Indiana, and Illinois. Both parties tried to gain advantages by nominating presidential and vice-presidential candidates from these states (and also by committing vote fraud there on their candidates' behalf).

Moreover, internal quarrels split both the Republican and Democratic Parties. Among Republicans, a faction known as "Stalwarts" was led by New York's pompous Senator Roscoe Conkling. A physical-fitness devotee once labeled "the finest torso in public life," Conkling worked the spoils system to

Party Factions

President Rutherford B. Hayes (1822–1893) entered office amid numerous claims on him by special interests. This cartoon shows Hayes making the precarious journey from the Ohio State House, where he had served as governor, across a field of bayonets to his presidential chair, which is outfitted with a seat of spikes and propped up by the Republican Party.   (Library of Congress)

win government jobs for his supporters. The Stalwarts' rivals were the "Half Breeds," led by James G. Blaine, who pursued influence as blatantly as Conkling did. On the sidelines stood more idealistic Republicans, or "Mugwumps" (supposedly an Indian term meaning "mug on one side of the fence, wump on the other"). Mugwumps such as Senator Carl Schurz of Missouri disliked the political roguishness that tainted the Republican Party and believed that only righteous, educated men like themselves should govern. Meanwhile, Democrats tended to subdivide into white-supremacy southerners, immigrant-stock and working-class urban political machines, and business-oriented advocates of low tariffs. Like Republicans, Democrats eagerly pursued the spoils of office.

At the state level, one party usually dominated, and within that party a few men typically held dictatorial power. Often the state "boss" was a senator. Until the Seventeenth Amendment to the Constitution was ratified in 1913, state legislatures elected U.S. senators, and a senator could wield enormous influence

with his command of federal jobs. Many senators parlayed their state power into national influence. Besides Conkling and Blaine, their ranks included Thomas C. Platt of New York, Nelson W. Aldrich of Rhode Island, Mark A. Hanna of Ohio, Matthew S. Quay of Pennsylvania, and William Mahone of Virginia.

Politics in the Industrial Age

In Congress, issues of sectional controversies, patronage abuses, railroad regulation, tariffs, and currency provoked heated debates but also important legislation. Well into the 1880s, bitter hostilities left from the Civil War continued to divide Americans. Republicans capitalized on war memories by "waving the bloody shirt" at Democrats. As one Republican orator harangued in 1876, "Every man that tried to destroy this nation was a Democrat. . . . Soldiers, every scar you have on your heroic bodies was given you by a Democrat." In the South, Democratic candidates also waved the bloody shirt, calling Republicans traitors to white supremacy and states' rights.

Other Americans also sought advantages by invoking war memories. The Grand Army of the Republic, an organization of 400,000 Union Army veterans, allied with the Republican Party and cajoled Congress into providing generous pensions for former Union soldiers and their widows. Many pensions were deserved: Union troops had been poorly paid, and thousands of wives had been widowed. But for some veterans, the war's emotional memories furnished an opportunity to profit at public expense. Though the Union Army spent $2 billion to fight the Civil War, pensions to veterans ultimately cost taxpayers $8 billion, one of the largest welfare commitments the federal government has ever made. By 1900 soldiers' pensions accounted for roughly 40 percent of the federal budget. Confederate veterans received none of this money, though some southern states funded small pensions and built old-age homes for ex-soldiers.

Few politicians dared oppose Civil War pensions, but some attempted to dismantle the spoils system.

Civil Service Reform

The practice of awarding government jobs to party workers, regardless of their qualifications, had taken root before the Civil War and flourished after it. As the postal service, diplomatic corps, and other government agencies expanded, so did the public payroll. Between 1865 and 1891, the number of federal jobs tripled, from 53,000

How do historians know...

that Gilded Age politics evoked bitter criticism? Social commentary sometimes is expressed more effectively through art than with words. An artist can employ the tools of wit, caricature, and symbolism to make powerful statements from which historians can glean important insights into the past. Thomas Nast, whose political cartoons appeared in *Harper's Weekly* magazine between 1862 and 1885, expressed optimism after the Civil War and then disillusionment during the Gilded Age better than almost anyone else. A talented artist as well as a keen analyst, Nast used his skills to potent effect, influencing domestic policies as well as public attitudes. Thus his drawings, and the caricatures and cartoons of other artists, serve as important historical documents of American society and politics of the late nineteenth century.

This cartoon appeared in May 1881, at a time when Nast believed the federal government had little incentive to pass laws for national welfare and cared only about the spoils of office. Thus a sloth, a symbol of laziness, represents the lawmakers who occupy the Capitol and White House, in the background, and a beaver, the symbol of industriousness, represents the people busily toiling on behalf of workshops, banks, trade, and other economic institutions. While Citizen Beaver labors to achieve prosperity and good government, Statesman Sloth lies on its back contemplating laws to exploit the people and line its own pockets (spoils). Such images could exert powerful influence on public opinion, but because they exaggerate reality, they also reflect personal bias. (*Harper's Weekly*, May 21, 1881)

May 21, 1881

Our Stumbling-Block.

While the Citizen Beaver labors for prosperity and good government, the "Statesman" Sloth lies on his back and obstructs and destroys.

to 166,000. Elected officials scrambled to control these jobs as a means of cementing support for themselves and their parties. In return for comparatively short hours and high pay, appointees to federal positions pledged their votes and a portion of their earnings to their patrons.

Shocked by such corruption, especially after the revelation of scandals in the Grant administration, some reformers began advocating appointments and promotions based on merit rather than political connections. Civil service reform accelerated in 1881 with the formation of the National Civil Service Reform

Before the Pendleton Act of 1883, many government positions were filled by patronage; hat in hand, job seekers beseeched political leaders to find a place for them. Here a member of Congress presents office-seeking friends to President Hayes.   (Library of Congress)

League, led by editors E. L. Godkin and George W. Curtis. The same year, the assassination of President James Garfield by a demented job seeker hastened the drive for change. The Pendleton Civil Service Act, passed by Congress in 1882 and signed by President Chester Arthur in 1883, created the Civil Service Commission to oversee competitive examinations for government positions. The act gave the commission jurisdiction over only 10 percent of federal jobs, though the president could expand the list. Because the Constitution barred Congress from interfering in state affairs, civil service at the state and local levels developed in a more haphazard manner. Nevertheless, the Pendleton Act marked a beginning and provided impetus for wider changes.

Veterans' pensions and civil service reform were not representative issues of the Gilded Age, however. Rather, economic policymaking occupied congressional business more than ever before. Railroad expansion had become a particularly controversial issue. As the rail network spread, so did competition. In their quest for customers, railroad lines reduced rates to outmaneuver rivals, but rate wars cut into profits and

wildly fluctuating rates angered shippers and farmers. Ironically, as freight rates generally fell, complaints about high rates rose. On noncompetitive routes, railroads often boosted charges as high as possible to compensate for unprofitably low rates on competitive routes, making pricing disproportionate to distance. Charges on short-distance shipments served by only one line could exceed those on long-distance shipments served by competing lines. Railroads also played favorites, reducing rates to large shippers and offering free passenger passes to preferred customers and politicians.

Such favoritism stirred farmers, small merchants, and reform politicians to demand public regulation of railroad rates. Their efforts occurred first at the state level. By 1880 fourteen states had established commissions to limit freight and storage charges of state-chartered lines. Railroads fought these measures, arguing that the Constitution guaranteed them freedom to acquire and use property without government restraint. But in 1877, in *Munn v. Illinois*, the Supreme Court upheld the principle of state regulation, declaring that the grain warehouses owned by the railroads were acting in the public interest and therefore must submit to regulation for "the common good."

Railroad Regulation

State legislatures, however, could not regulate interstate lines, a limitation affirmed by the Supreme Court in the *Wabash* case of 1886, in which the Court declared that only Congress could limit rates involving interstate commerce. Reformers thereupon demanded federal action. Congress responded in 1887 by passing the Interstate Commerce Act. The law prohibited pools, rebates, and long-haul/short-haul rate discrimination, and it created the Interstate Commerce Commission (ICC) to investigate railroad rate-making methods, issue cease-and-desist orders against illegal practices, and seek court aid to enforce compliance. The legislation's lack of provisions for enforcement, however, left railroads room for evasion, and federal judges chipped away at ICC powers. In the *Maximum Freight Rate* case (1897), the Supreme Court ruled that the ICC did not have power to set rates; and in the *Alabama Midlands* case (1897), the Court overturned prohibitions against long-haul/short-haul discrimination. Even so, the principle of government regulation, though weakened, remained in force.

The economic issue of tariffs carried strong political implications. Congress initially had created tariffs

Tariff Policy

to protect American manufactured goods and agricultural products from European competition. But tariffs quickly became a tool by which special interests could protect and enhance their profits. By the 1880s these interests had succeeded in obtaining tariffs applied to more than four thousand items. A few economists and farmers argued for free trade, but most politicians still insisted that tariffs were a necessary form of government assistance to support industry and preserve jobs.

The Republican Party, claiming credit for economic growth, put protective tariffs at the core of its political agenda. Democrats complained that tariffs made prices artificially high by keeping out less expensive foreign goods, thereby benefiting manufacturers while hurting farmers whose crops were not protected and consumers who had to buy manufactured goods. For example, a yard of flannel produced abroad might cost 10 cents, but the imposition of an 8-cent tariff raised the price paid by American consumers to 18 cents. An American manufacturer of a similar yard of flannel, also costing 10 cents, could charge consumers 17 cents, underselling the foreign competition by 1 cent yet still pocketing a large profit because he did not have to pay the tariff.

During most of the Gilded Age, taxes, tariffs, and other levies created a surplus rather than a deficit in the federal budget. Most Republicans, being businessmen, liked the idea that the government was earning more than it spent and hoped to keep the extra money as a Treasury reserve or to spend it on projects like harbor improvement and federal buildings that would aid commerce. Democrats, however, pointed out that the federal government should not be a profit-making business. They insisted that the surplus should be reduced not by spending more but by reducing revenues—by cutting taxes and cutting tariffs. Democrats acknowledged a need for tariff protection of some manufactured goods and raw materials, but they favored lower rates to encourage foreign trade and to reduce the Treasury surplus.

Manufacturers and their congressional allies maintained control over tariff policy. The McKinley Tariff of 1890 boosted already-high rates by another 4 percent. When House Democrats supported by President Grover Cleveland passed a bill to reduce tariff rates in 1894, Senate Republicans, aided by southern Democrats eager to protect their region's infant industries, added six hundred amendments restoring most of the cuts (Wilson-Gorman Tariff). In 1897 the Dingley Tariff raised rates further. Attacks on the tariff, though unsuccessful, made tariffs the symbol of privileged business in the public mind and a target of reformers after 1900.

Monetary policy aroused even stronger emotions than tariffs did. When increased industrial and agricultural production caused prices to fall after the Civil War, debtors and creditors had opposing reactions.

Monetary Policy

Farmers suffered because the prices they received for their crops were dropping, but they had to pay high interest rates on money they borrowed to pay off their mortgages and other debts. They favored schemes like the coinage of silver to increase the amount of currency in circulation. An expanded money supply, they reasoned, would reduce interest rates, making their debts less burdensome, and their costs would be lower relative to the prices they received for their crops. Creditors believed that overproduction had caused prices to decline. They favored a more stable, limited money supply backed only by gold. They feared that the value of currency not backed by gold would fluctuate; the resulting uncertainty would threaten their wealth and undermine investors' confidence in the U.S. economy.

Arguments over the quantity and quality of money, however, transcended economics. Creditor-debtor tension translated into class divisions between haves and have-nots. The debate also represented sectional cleavages: western silver-mining areas and agricultural regions of the South and West against the more conservative industrial Northeast. And the issue carried moral, almost religious, overtones. Some Americans believed the beauty, rarity, and durability of gold gave it a magical potency. Others believed the gold standard for currency was too limiting; sustained prosperity, they insisted, demanded new attitudes.

By the 1870s, the currency controversy had boiled down to gold versus silver. Previously, the government had bought both gold and silver to back the national currency, setting a ratio that made a gold dollar worth sixteen times more than a silver dollar. Mining discoveries after 1848, however, increased the supply of gold and lowered its market price relative to that of silver. As a result, silver dollars disappeared from circulation—because of their inflated value relative to gold, owners hoarded them—and in 1873 Congress officially stopped coining silver dollars, an act that silver partisans later called the "Crime of '73." Europeans also stopped buying silver, and the United States and many of its trading partners unofficially adopted the gold standard, meaning that their currency was backed chiefly by gold.

Within a few years, new mines in the American West began to flood the market with silver, and its price dropped. Gold then became worth more than sixteen times the value of silver (the ratio reached twenty to one by 1890), and it became profitable to spend rather than hoard silver dollars. Silver producers wanted the government to resume buying silver at the old sixteen-to-one ratio, which amounted to a subsidy because they could sell silver to the government above market price. Debtors, hurt by falling prices and the economic hard times of 1873–1878, saw silver as a means of expanding the currency supply. They joined with silver producers to denounce the "Crime of '73" and to press for resumption of silver coinage at the old sixteen-to-one ratio.

With both parties split into silver and gold factions, Congress at first tried to compromise. The Bland-Allison Act of 1878 authorized the Treasury to buy between $2 million and $4 million worth of silver each month, and the Sherman Silver Purchase Act of 1890 increased the government's monthly purchase of silver by specifying weight (4.5 million ounces) rather than dollars. Neither act satisfied the different interest groups. The government paid for the silver with Treasury notes, not with gold dollars that silver interests wanted. Moreover, the acts failed to expand the money supply as substantially as debtors had hoped and failed to erase the impression that the government favored creditors' interests.

National politics was not a glamorous field of endeavor in the Gilded Age. For each constituent who received a patronage job, many more were disappointed. Senators and representatives received small salaries and usually had the financial burden of maintaining two homes: one in their home districts and one in Washington. Life in the nation's capital was oppressively hot in summer, muddy and icy in winter. Most members of Congress had no private office space, only a desk. They worked long hours responding to constituents' requests, wrote their own speeches, and had to pay for staff out of their own pockets. Yet, cynics to the contrary, most politicians were principled and dedicated. They managed to deal with important issues and pass significant legislation under difficult conditions.

Legislative Accomplishments

The Presidency Restrengthened

Operating under the cloud of Andrew Johnson's impeachment, Grant's scandals, and doubts about the legitimacy of the election of 1876 (see Chapter 16), American presidents between 1877 and 1900 moved gingerly to restore the authority of their office. Proper and honest, Presidents Rutherford Hayes (1877–1881), James Garfield (1881), Chester Arthur (1881–1885), Grover Cleveland (1885–1889 and 1893–1897), Benjamin Harrison (1889–1893), and William McKinley (1897–1901) tried to act as legislative as well as administrative leaders. Like other politicians, they used symbols. Hayes served lemonade at the White House to emphasize that he, unlike his predecessor Ulysses Grant, was no hard drinker. McKinley put aside his cigar in public so photographers would not catch him setting a bad example for youth. More important, each president initiated legislation and used the veto to guide national policy.

Rutherford B. Hayes had been a Union general and an Ohio congressman and governor before his disputed election to the presidency, an event that prompted opponents to label him "Rutherfraud." Though his party expected him to favor business interests, Hayes played a quiet role as reformer and conciliator. He emphasized national harmony over sectional rivalry and opposed violence of all kinds. He tried to overhaul the spoils system by appointing civil service reformer Carl Schurz to his cabinet and by battling New York's patronage king, Senator Conkling. (He fired Conkling's protégé, Chester Arthur, from the post of New York customs house collector.) Though he was too cautious to use government power to do so, Hayes believed society was obligated to help the oppressed, including American Chinese and Indians, and after retiring from the presidency he worked diligently to aid former slaves.

Hayes, Garfield, and Arthur

When Hayes declined to run for reelection in 1880, Republicans nominated another Ohio congressman and Civil War hero, James A. Garfield. A solemn and cautious man, Garfield defeated Democrat Winfield Scott Hancock, also a Civil War hero, by just forty thousand votes out of 9 million cast. By winning the pivotal states of New York and Indiana, however, Garfield carried the electoral college by a comfortable margin of 214 to 155.

Garfield spent most of his brief presidency trying to secure an independent position among party poten-

By the late nineteenth century, political parties merchandised their candidates in the same way manufacturers advertised consumer goods. Coins and ribbons, such as these showing the Republican and Democratic candidates for president and vice president in 1888, were designed to sell dignified images to the voting republic—similar to the way that some retailers tried to give their consumer products public appeal.   (Collection of David J. and Janice L. Frent)

tates. He hoped to reduce the tariff and develop economic relations with Latin America but had to spend most days dealing with hordes of men seeking government jobs. "Once or twice," Garfield admitted, "I felt like crying out against the greed for office and its consumption of my time." He pleased civil service reformers by rebuffing Conkling's patronage demands, but his chance to make lasting contributions ended in July 1881 when Charles Guiteau, a disappointed patronage seeker, shot him in a Washington railroad station. Gar-

field lingered for seventy-nine days while doctors tried vainly to remove a bullet lodged in his back, but he succumbed to infection and died September 19.

Garfield's successor was Vice President Chester A. Arthur, the New York spoilsman whom Hayes had fired in 1878. Republicans had nominated Arthur for vice president only to help Garfield carry New York State. Though his elevation to the presidency made reformers shudder, Arthur became a dignified and temperate executive. He signed the Pendleton Civil Service Act, urged Congress to modify outdated tariff rates, and supported federal regulation of railroads. He wielded the veto aggressively, killing several bills that excessively benefited railroads and corporations. But congressional partisans frustrated his plans for reducing the tariff and strengthening the navy. Arthur wanted to run for reelection in 1884 but lost the nomination to James G. Blaine at the Republican national convention.

To oppose Blaine, Democrats named New York's governor Grover Cleveland, a bachelor who had tainted his reputation when he fathered an illegitimate son—a fact he admitted during the campaign. Both parties focused on the sordid. (Alluding to Cleveland's bastard son, Republicans chided him with catcalls of "Ma! Ma! Where's my pa?" To which Democrats replied, "Gone to the White House, Ha! Ha! Ha!") Distaste for Blaine prompted some Mugwump Republicans to desert their party for Cleveland. On election day Cleveland beat Blaine by only 29,000 popular votes; his tiny margin of 1,149 votes in New York gave him that state's 36 electoral votes, enough for a 219-to-182 victory in the electoral college. Cleveland may have won New York thanks to last-minute remarks of a local Protestant minister, who equated Democrats with "rum, Romanism, and rebellion." Democrats eagerly publicized the slur among New York's large Irish-Catholic population, urging voters to protest by supporting Cleveland.

Cleveland, the first Democratic president since James Buchanan (1857–1861), echoed his Republican predecessors' complaints about the "cursed constant grind" of his office. He tried, however, to exert vigorous leadership. He expanded civil service, vetoed hundreds of private pension bills, and urged Congress to cut tariffs on raw materials and manufactured goods. When advisers warned that his stand might weaken his chances for reelection, the president retorted, "What is the use of being elected or reelected, unless you stand for something?" But the Mills tariff bill of 1888, passed by the House in

Cleveland and Harrison

response to Cleveland's wishes, died in the Senate. When Democrats renominated Cleveland for the presidency in 1888, protectionists in the party convinced him to temper his attacks on high tariffs.

Republicans in 1888 nominated Benjamin Harrison, former senator from Indiana and grandson of President William Henry Harrison (1841). During the campaign, some Republicans manipulated the British minister into stating that Cleveland's reelection would be good for England. Irish Democrats, who hated England's colonial rule over Ireland, took offense, as intended, and Cleveland's campaign was weakened. Perhaps more helpful to Harrison were the bribery and multiple voting that helped him win Indiana by 2,300 votes and New York by 14,000. (Democrats also indulged in bribery and vote fraud, but this time Republicans proved more successful at such deceits.) Those states ensured Harrison's victory. Though Cleveland outpolled Harrison by 90,000 popular votes, Harrison carried the electoral vote by 233 to 168.

Harrison was the first president since 1875 whose party had majorities in both houses of Congress. Using a variety of methods, ranging from threats of vetoes to informal dinners and consultations, Harrison influenced the course of legislation. The Congress of 1889–1891 passed 517 bills, two hundred more than the average passed by Congresses between 1875 and 1889. Harrison also showed support for civil service by appointing the reformer Theodore Roosevelt a civil service commissioner. But neither the president nor Congress could resist pressures from special interests, especially those waving the bloody shirt. Harrison signed the Dependents' Pension Act, which provided pensions for Union veterans who had suffered war-related disabilities and granted aid to their widows and minor children. The bill doubled the number of welfare recipients from 490,000 to 966,000.

The Pension Act and other appropriations pushed the federal budget past $1 billion in 1890 for the first time in the nation's history. Democrats blamed the "Billion-Dollar Congress" on spendthrift Republicans. Voters reacted by unseating seventy-eight Republicans in the congressional elections of 1890. Seeking to capitalize on voter unrest, Democrats nominated Cleveland to run against Harrison again in 1892. This time Cleveland attracted large contributions from business and beat Harrison by 370,000 popular votes (3 percent of the total) and by 277 to 145 electoral votes.

In office again, Cleveland moved boldly to address problems of currency, tariffs, and labor unrest. But his actions reflected a narrow orientation toward interests of business and bespoke political weakness. During his campaign Cleveland had promised sweeping tariff reform, but he made little effort to line up support in the Senate, where protectionists undercut all efforts to reduce rates. And when 120,000 boycotting railroad workers paralyzed commerce in the Pullman strike of 1894, Cleveland bowed to requests from railroad managers and Attorney General Richard Olney to send in troops (see page 502). Though he pursued an expansionist foreign policy (see Chapter 22), throughout Cleveland's second term, events at home—particularly economic downturn and agrarian ferment—seemed to overwhelm the president.

Limits of Gilded Age Politics

 Though the scope and size of government activity expanded during the Gilded Age, policies of discrimination and exclusion continued to haunt more than half of the nation's population. Just as before the Civil War, issues of race gave a peculiar quality to politics in the South. There, poor whites, facing economic losses, feared that newly enfranchised African Americans would challenge whatever political and social superiority (real and imagined) they enjoyed. Wealthy white landowners and merchants fanned these fears, using racism to divide whites and blacks and to distract poor whites from protesting their own economic subjugation.

The majority of the nation's African Americans lived in the South and worked in agriculture. Although the abolition of slavery had altered their legal status, it had not markedly improved their economic opportunities. In 1880, 90 percent of all southern blacks depended for a living on farming or personal and domestic service—the same occupations they had held as slaves. The New South, moreover, proved to be as violent for blacks as the Old South had been. Weapons, including a gun commonly known as a "nigger killer," were plentiful, and whites seldom hesitated to use them. More dramatically, between 1889 and 1909, more than seventeen hundred African Americans were lynched in the South. Most lynchings occurred in sparsely populated districts where whites felt threatened by an influx of migrant blacks who had no friends, black or white, to vouch for them. Most lynching victims were usually accused of an assault—rarely proved—on a white woman.

Violence Against African Americans

With slavery dead, white supremacists fashioned further ways to keep blacks in a position of inferiority. Southern leaders, embittered by northern interference in race relations during Reconstruction and eager to reassert authority over people whom they believed to be inferior, instituted measures to prevent blacks from voting and to segregate them legally from whites.

The end of Reconstruction had not stopped blacks from voting. Despite threats and intimidation, blacks still formed the backbone of the southern Republican Party and won elective offices. In North Carolina, for example, eleven African American men served in the state senate and forty-three in the house between 1877 and 1890. White politicians sought to discourage the "Negro vote" by imposing restrictions that appeared neutral but actually barred blacks from the polls. Beginning with Georgia in 1877, southern states levied taxes of $1 to $2 on all citizens wishing to vote. These poll taxes proved prohibitive to most black voters, who were so poor and deeply in debt that they rarely had cash for any purpose. Other schemes disfranchised blacks who could not read.

Disfranchise-ment Begins

Disfranchisement was accomplished in other devious ways. The Supreme Court affirmed in *U.S. v. Reese* (1876) that the Fifteenth Amendment prohibited states from denying the vote "on account of race, color, or previous condition of servitude." But, said the Court, Congress had no control over local and state elections other than the explicit provisions of the Fifteenth Amendment. State legislatures found ways to exclude black voters without mentioning race, color, or servitude. For instance, an 1890 state constitutional convention established the "Mississippi Plan," requiring all voters to pay a poll tax eight months before each election, to present the tax receipt at election time, and to prove that they could read and interpret the state constitution. Registration officials applied stiffer standards to blacks than to whites, even declaring college graduates ineligible on grounds of illiteracy. In 1898 Louisiana enacted the first "grandfather clause," which established literacy and property qualifications for voting but exempted sons and grandsons of those eligible to vote before 1867, the year the Fifteenth Amendment had gone into effect. Other southern states initiated similar measures.

Such restrictions proved highly effective. In South Carolina, for example, 70 percent of eligible blacks voted in the presidential election of 1880; by 1896 the rate had dropped to 11 percent. By the 1900s African

In the years after Reconstruction, lynchings of African American men occurred with increasing frequency, chiefly in sparsely populated areas where whites looked on strangers, especially black strangers, with fear and suspicion. (© R. P. Kingston/Index Stock Imagery, Picture Cube Division)

Americans had effectively lost political rights in every southern state except Tennessee. Disfranchisement also affected poor whites, few of whom could meet poll tax, property, and literacy requirements. Thus the total number of eligible voters in Mississippi shrank from 257,000 in 1876 to 77,000 in 1892.

Racial discrimination also stiffened in social affairs. After the Civil War, the existing customs of racial separation were expanded in law. In a series of cases during the 1870s, the Supreme Court opened the door to discrimination by ruling that the Fourteenth Amendment protected citizens' rights only against infringement by state governments. The federal government, according to the

Legal Segregation

Court, lacked authority over what individuals or organizations might do. If blacks wanted legal protection, the Court said, they must seek it from the states, which under the Tenth Amendment retained all powers not specifically assigned to Congress.

These rulings climaxed in 1883 when in the *Civil Rights* cases the Court struck down the 1875 Civil Rights Act, which had prohibited segregation in public facilities such as streetcars, hotels, theaters, and parks. Again the Court declared that the federal government could not regulate the behavior of private individuals in matters of race relations. Subsequent lower court rulings established the principle that blacks could be restricted to "separate but equal" facilities. The Supreme Court upheld the separate-but-equal doctrine in *Plessy v. Ferguson* (1896) and applied it to schools in *Cummins v. County Board of Education* (1899).

Thereafter, segregation laws—known as Jim Crow laws—multiplied throughout the South, confronting African Americans with daily reminders of their inferior status. State and local laws restricted them to the rear of streetcars, to separate public drinking fountains and toilets, and to separate sections of hospitals and cemeteries. A Birmingham, Alabama, ordinance required that the races be "distinctly separated . . . by well defined physical barriers" in "any room, hall, theatre, picture house, auditorium, yard, court, ballpark, or other indoor or outdoor place." Local laws defined neighborhoods as all-black or all-white. Mobile, Alabama, passed a curfew requiring blacks to be off the streets by 10 P.M., and Atlanta mandated separate Bibles for the swearing-in of black witnesses in court.

African American women and men coped with the political climate in the South in several ways. In the optimistic days following Reconstruction, a number of blacks used higher education as a means of elevating their status. In all-black teachers' colleges, most of which were coeducational, blacks sought opportunities for themselves and their race. Education also seemed to present a way to foster interracial cooperation. But the white supremacy campaigns that soon developed taught southern blacks that they would have to negotiate in a biracial, rather than interracial, society.

Political disfranchisement pushed African American men, who in contrast to women had previously been able to vote, out of public life. In their place,

Livingstone College in North Carolina was one of several institutions of higher learning established by and for African Americans in the late nineteenth century. With a curriculum that emphasized training for educational and religious work in the South and in Africa, these colleges were coeducational, operating on the belief that both men and women could have public roles. (Courtesy of Heritage Hall, Livingstone College, Salisbury, North Carolina)

African American women began using their traditional roles as mothers, educators, and moral guardians to seek services and reforms that reflected subtle yet important political activity. They participated in successful lobbying of local and state governments in the South for reforms such as cleaner city streets, better public health, expanded charity services, and vocational education. In less threatening means than casting ballots, black women found ways to join with white women for campaigns to improve the general community and to negotiate with the white male power structure to achieve their goals.

Women also contended head-on with male power structures. Their major goal was the vote; their successes in reaching this goal were limited. Prior to 1869, each state determined who was qualified to vote. The Fifteenth Amendment, adopted that year, forbade states to deny the vote "on account of race, color or previous condition" but omitted any reference to sex. For the next twenty years, two organizations—the National Woman Suffrage Association (NWSA) and the American Woman Suffrage Association (AWSA)—battled for female suffrage. The NWSA, led by militants Elizabeth Cady Stanton and Susan B. Anthony, advocated comprehensive women's rights in courts and workplaces as well as at the ballot box. The AWSA, led by former abolitionists Lucy Stone and Thomas Wentworth Higginson, focused more narrowly on suffrage.

Woman Suffrage

In 1878 Susan B. Anthony, who had lost in the courts when she tried to vote in 1872, persuaded Senator A. A. Sargent of California to introduce a constitutional amendment stating that "the right of citizens of the United States to vote shall not be denied or abridged by the United States or by any state on account of sex." A Senate committee killed the bill, but the NWSA had it reintroduced repeatedly over the next eighteen years. On the few occasions when the bill reached the Senate floor, it was voted down by senators who claimed that suffrage would interfere with women's family obligations.

While the NWSA fought for suffrage on the national level, the AWSA worked to amend state constitutions. (The groups merged in 1890 to form the National American Woman Suffrage Association.) Though these campaigns succeeded only slightly, they helped train a corps of female leaders in political organizing and public speaking. Women did win partial victories. Between 1870 and 1910, eleven states (mostly in the West) legalized woman suffrage. By 1890 nineteen states allowed women to vote on school issues, and three granted suffrage on tax and bond issues. But the right to vote in national elections awaited a later generation.

Agrarian Unrest and Populism

While voting concerned those suffering from political exclusion, inequities in the economic order sparked a mass movement that would shake American society. The agrarian revolt—a mixture of strident rhetoric, nostalgic dreams, and hard-headed egalitarianism—began in Grange organizations in the early 1870s. The revolt accelerated when Farmers' Alliances formed in Texas in the late 1870s and spread across the Cotton Belt and Great Plains in the 1880s. The Alliance movement had appeal chiefly in areas where tenancy, debt, railroads, weather, and insects threatened the well-being of hopeful farmers. Once under way, the agrarian rebellion inspired visions of a truly cooperative and democratic society.

Agricultural expansion in the West and Great Plains exposed millions of people to the hardships of rural life (see Chapter 17). Farmers who had moved into these areas knew life would be hard, but they had hoped that the rewards would be more promising than they turned out to be.

Whereas before the Civil War laborlords (slaveowners) dominated southern agriculture, now landlords who employed sharecroppers and tenants characterized the system. Sharecropping and tenant farming entangled millions of black and white southerners in a web of debt and humiliation, at whose center stood the crop lien. Most farmers, too poor to have cash on hand, borrowed in order to buy necessities. They could offer as collateral only what they could grow. A farmer in need of supplies dealt with a nearby "furnishing merchant," who would exchange supplies for a lien, or legal claim, on the farmer's forthcoming crop. After the crop was harvested and brought to market, the merchant collected his debt by claiming the portion of the crop that would satisfy the loan. All too often, however, the debt exceeded the crop's value. The farmer could pay off only part of the debt to the merchant but still needed food and supplies for the coming year. The only way he could get these supplies was to sink deeper into debt by reborrowing and giving the merchant a new lien on his next crop.

Sharecropping and Tenant Farming in the South

Merchants frequently took advantage of indebted farmers' powerlessness by inflating prices and charging them interest ranging from 33 to 200 percent on the advances they received. Suppose, for example, that a cash-poor farmer needed a 20-cent bag of seed or 20-cent piece of cloth. The furnishing merchant would sell him the goods on credit but would boost the price to 28 cents. At year's end that 28-cent loan would have accumulated interest, raising the farmer's debt to 42 cents—more than double the item's original cost. The farmer, having pledged more than his crop's worth against scores of such debts, fell behind in payments and never recovered. If he fell too far behind, he could be evicted.

The crop-lien system caused hardship in former plantation areas where tenants and sharecroppers grew cotton for the same markets that had existed before the Civil War. In the southern backcountry, which in the antebellum era had been characterized by small farms, few slaves, and diversified agriculture, the crop-lien problem was compounded by other economic changes. New spending habits of backcountry farmers illustrate these changes. In 1884 Jephta Dickson of the northern Georgia hills bought $55.90 worth of flour, potatoes, peas, meat, corn, and syrup from merchants. Such expenditures would have been rare in the upcountry before the Civil War, when farmers grew almost all the food they needed. But after the war, yeomen like Dickson shifted to commercial farming; in the South that meant raising cotton. This change came about for two reasons: debts incurred during the war and Reconstruction forced farmers to grow a crop that would bring in cash, and railroad expansion enabled them to transport cotton to markets more easily than before. As backcountry yeomen devoted more acres to cotton, they raised less of what they needed on a daily basis and found themselves more frequently at the mercy of merchants.

Hardship in the Midwest and West

In the Midwest, as growers cultivated more land, as mechanization boosted productivity, and as foreign competition increased, supplies exceeded national and worldwide demand for agricultural products. Consequently, prices for staple crops dropped steadily. A bushel of wheat that sold for $1.45 in 1866 brought only 80 cents in the mid-1880s and 49 cents by the mid-1890s. Meanwhile, transportation and storage fees remained high relative to other prices. Expenses for seed, fertilizer, manufactured goods, taxes, and mortgage interest trapped many farm families in troubling and sometimes desperate circumstances. In order to buy necessities and pay bills, farmers had to produce more. But the spiral wound ever more tightly: the more farmers produced, the lower prices for their crops dropped (see Figure 20.1).

The West suffered from special hardships. In Colorado absentee capitalists seized control of access to transportation and water, and concentration of technology in the hands of large mining companies pushed out small firms. Charges of monopolistic control by railroads echoed among farmers, miners, and stockmen in Wyoming and Montana. In California, Washington, and Oregon, wheat and fruit growers found their opportunities reduced by railroads' control of transportation and storage rates.

Even before they felt the full impact of these developments, farmers began to organize. With aid from

Grange Movement

Oliver H. Kelley, a clerk in the Department of Agriculture, farmers in almost every state during the 1860s and 1870s founded a network of local organizations called Granges. By 1875 the Grange had twenty thousand branches and a million members. Like other voluntary organizations throughout the country, Granges had constitutions, elected officers, and membership oaths. Strongest in the Midwest and South, Granges at first served a chiefly social function, sponsoring meetings and educational events to relieve the loneliness of farm life. Family-oriented and open to all, local Granges welcomed women's participation.

As membership flourished, Granges turned to economic and political action. Local branches formed cooperative associations to buy supplies and to market crops and livestock. In a few instances, Grangers operated farm-implement factories and insurance companies. Most of these enterprises failed, however, because farmers lacked capital for cooperative buying and because competition from large manufacturers and dealers undercut them. For example, the mail-order firm Montgomery Ward could furnish rural customers with cheaper products more conveniently than could Granges. Also, a requirement that Grange cooperatives run on a cash-only basis excluded large numbers of farmers who rarely had cash.

Despite their efforts, Granges declined in the late 1870s. Their promotion of thrift and hard work hardly helped families already practicing both virtues. Grangers had some political successes, convincing states to establish agricultural colleges, electing sympathetic legislators, and pressing for so-called Granger

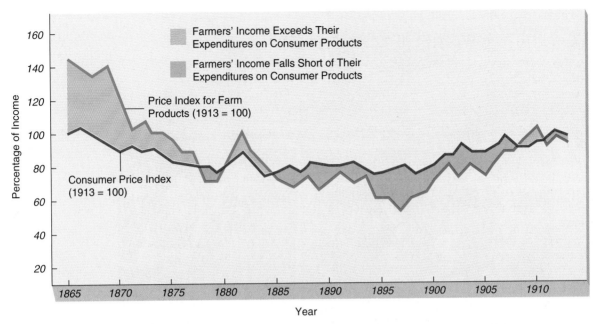

Figure 20.1   Consumer Prices and Farm Product Prices, 1865–1913   Until the late 1870s, in spite of falling farm prices, farmers were able to receive from their crops more income than they spent on consumer goods. But beginning in the mid-1880s, consumer prices leveled off and then rose while prices for farm products continued to drop. As a result, farmers found it increasingly difficult to afford consumer goods, a problem that plagued them well into the twentieth century.

laws to regulate transportation and storage rates. But these efforts faltered when corporations won court support to overturn Granger laws. Granges disavowed party politics but could not withstand the power of business interests within the two major parties. Thus after a brief assertion of economic and political influence, Granges again became farmers' social clubs.

In the Southwest, the movement of English-speaking ranchers into communal pastureland used by Mexican farmers and villagers sparked another kind of agrarian protest. In the late 1880s, a group calling itself *Las Gorras Blancas*, or White Hats, believed that they should have control of lands that their Mexican ancestors had once held. They harassed Anglo ranchers and destroyed the fences that they had erected on public land. Sounding like Grangers and Knights of Labor before them and Populists after them, the White Hats proclaimed in 1889, "Our purpose is to protect the rights and interest of the people in general and especially those of the helpless classes." Their cause, however, could not halt Anglos from legally buying and using public land, and by 1900 many Hispanics had given up farming on their

The White Hats

own to work as agricultural laborers or to migrate into the cities.

By 1890 rural activism shifted to the Farmers' Alliances, two networks of organizations—one in the Great Plains and one in the South—that constituted a new mass movement. (The West also had Alliance groups, but in that region they tended to be smaller and more closely linked to labor radicals, socialist clubs, and antimonopoly organizations.) The first Farmers' Alliances arose in Texas, where hard-pressed small farmers rallied against crop liens, merchants, and railroads in particular, and against money power in general. Using traveling lecturers to recruit members, Alliance leaders extended the movement into other southern states. By 1889 the southern Alliance boasted 2 million members, and a separate Colored Farmers' National Alliance claimed over 1 million black members. A similar movement flourished in the Plains, which by the late 1880s organized 2 million members in Kansas, Nebraska, and the Dakotas.

Like Granges, Farmers' Alliances fostered community loyalty through rallies, educational meetings,

Farmers' Alliances

Exhibited at the Chicago World's Fair of 1893, this cabin was the site of the first Farmers' Alliance meeting in Lampasas County, Texas. Using recruiters, rallies, and meetings replete with slogans such as "We Are All Mortgaged but Our Votes," the organization voiced the grievances of rural America and laid the groundwork for formation of the Populist party in the 1890s.   (Private Collection)

Subtreasury Plan

and cooperative buying and selling agreements. Also, women participated in all Alliance activities. Alliances also opened new paths. Beyond urging democratic cooperation, the Alliance movement proposed the subtreasury plan to relieve shortages of cash and credit, the most serious rural problems. The plan, originating in 1890, had two parts. One called for the federal government to construct warehouses where farmers could store nonperishable crops while awaiting higher prices; the government would then loan farmers Treasury notes amounting to 80 percent of the market price that the stored crops would bring. Farmers could use these notes as legal tender to pay debts and make purchases. Once the stored crops were sold, farmers would repay the loans plus small interest and storage fees. This provision would enable farmers to avoid the exploitative crop-lien system.

The second part of the subtreasury plan would have the government provide low-interest loans to farmers who wanted to buy land. These loans, along with the Treasury notes loaned to farmers who had temporarily stored crops in government warehouses, would inject cash into the economy and encourage the kind of inflation that advocates hoped would raise crop prices without raising other prices. If the government subsidized business through tariffs and land grants, reasoned Alliance members, why should it not help farmers earn a decent living, too?

If all Farmers' Alliances had been able to unite, they would have made a formidable political force; but sectional and racial differences and personality clashes thwarted early attempts at merging. At an 1889 meeting in St. Louis, white southerners, fearing reprisals from landowners and objecting to participation by blacks, rejected proposals that would have ended secret Alliance activities and whites-only membership rules. Northerners, too, renounced amalgamation, fearing domination by more experienced southern leaders. Differences on issues also prevented unity. Northern farmers, mostly Republicans, wanted protective tariffs to keep out foreign grain. White southerners, mostly Democrats, wanted low tariffs to hold down costs of foreign manufactured goods. Northern and southern Alliances both favored government regulation of transportation and communications, equitable taxation, currency reform, and prohibition of landownership by foreign investors.

Growing membership and rising confidence drew Alliances more deeply into politics. By 1890 farmers had elected several officeholders sympathetic to their programs, especially in the South, where Alliances controlled four governorships, eight state legislatures, and forty-seven seats in Congress (forty-four in the House, three in the Senate). In the Midwest, Alliance candidates often ran on third-party tickets and achieved some success in Kansas, Nebraska, and the Dakotas. Leaders crisscrossed the country organizing meetings to solidify support for a third party. During the summer of 1890, the Kansas Alliance held a "convention of the people" and nominated candidates who swept the state's fall elections. Formation of this People's Party, whose members were called Populists (from *populus*, the Latin word for "people"), gave a title to Alliance political activism.

Rise of Populism

Election results in 1890 energized efforts to unite Alliance groups into a single Populist party. A meeting in 1891 of northern and southern Alliances in Cincinnati failed when southerners chose to remain Democrats rather than risk joining a third party. But by 1892 southern Alliance members were ready for independent action. Meeting with northern counterparts in St. Louis, they summoned a People's Party convention in Omaha on July 4 to draft a platform and nominate a presidential candidate.

The new party's platform was an extraordinary reform document. Its preamble charged that the nation had been "brought to the verge of moral, political, and material ruin. Corruption dominates the ballot box, the legislatures, the Congress, and touches ... even the [courts]." More important, inequality threatened to splinter American society. "The fruits of the toil of millions," the platform declared, "are boldly stolen to build up colossal fortunes for a few." Claiming that "wealth belongs to him that creates it," the Omaha platform addressed three central sources of rural unrest: transportation, land, and money. Frustrated with weak state and federal regulation, Populists demanded government ownership of railroad and telegraph lines. They urged the federal government to reclaim all land owned for speculative purposes by railroads and foreigners. The monetary plank called on the govern-

Mary E. Lease (1850–1933) was one of the founders of the Populist party in Kansas. Tall and intense, she had a deep, almost hypnotic voice that made her an effective publicist for the farmers' cause. She gave a seconding speech to the presidential nomination of James B. Weaver in 1892.   (The Kansas State Historical Society, Topeka, Kansas)

ment to expand the currency by printing money to be made available for farm loans and by basing the money on free and unlimited coinage of silver. Other planks advocated a graduated income tax, postal savings banks, direct election of U.S. senators, and a shorter workday. As its presidential candidate, the People's Party nominated James B. Weaver of Iowa, a former Union general and supporter of an increased money supply.

The Populist campaign featured dynamic personalities and vivid rhetoric. The Kansas plains rumbled with speeches by "Sockless Jerry" Simpson, an unschooled but canny rural reformer, and by Mary Elizabeth Lease, a fiery orator who charged that "Wall Street owns the country. The great common people of the country are slaves, and monopoly is the master." The South produced equally forceful leaders, such as Texas's Charles

Election Rhetoric

W. Macune, Georgia's Tom Watson, and North Carolina's Leonidas Polk. Colorado's governor Davis "Bloody Bridles" Waite attacked mine owners with his prolabor and antimonopolist stance. Minnesota's Ignatius Donnelly, pseudoscientist and writer of apocalyptic novels, became chief ideologue of the northern plains and wrote the thunderous language in the Omaha platform. The campaign also attracted characters such as James Hogg, the 300-pound governor of Texas, and one-eyed Senator "Pitchfork Ben" Tillman of South Carolina, who were not genuine Populists but used the agrarian fervor for their own political ends.

Weaver garnered 8 percent of the popular vote in 1892, majorities in four states, and twenty-two electoral votes. Not since 1856 had a third party done so well in its first national effort. Nevertheless, disturbing factors had emerged. The party faced a dilemma of whether to uphold its principles at all costs or compromise in order to gain power. The election had been successful for Populists only in the West. The vote-rich Northeast had ignored Weaver, and Alabama was the only southern state that gave Populists as much as one-third of its votes. More ominously, by the end of 1892 Populist politics had diverted Alliance attention from social and economic reform, and defeat in all three areas caused the movement to wither.

Still, Populism gave rural dwellers in the South and West an emotional faith in the future. Although Populists were flawed egalitarians—they mistrusted blacks and foreigners—they sought change in order to fulfill their version of American ideals. Amid hardship and desperation, millions of people began to believe that a cooperative democracy in which government would ensure equal opportunity could overcome corporate power. A banner draped above the stage at the Omaha convention captured the movement's spirit: "We do not ask for sympathy or pity. We ask for justice."

The Depression of the 1890s

In 1893, shortly before Grover Cleveland's second presidency, the Philadelphia and Reading Railroad, once a thriving and profitable line, went bankrupt. Like other railroads, the Philadelphia and Reading had borrowed heavily to lay track and build stations and bridges. But overexpansion cut into profits, and ultimately the company was unable to pay its debts.

The same problem beset manufacturers. For example, output at McCormick farm machinery factories was nine times greater in 1893 than in 1879, but revenues had only tripled. To compensate, the company bought more factory equipment and squeezed more work out of fewer laborers. This strategy, however, only enlarged debt and unemployment. Jobless workers found themselves in the same plight as employers: they could not pay their creditors. Banks suffered, too, when their customers defaulted. The failure of the National Cordage Company in May 1893 accelerated a chain reaction of business and bank closings. By year's end, five hundred banks and sixteen hundred businesses had failed. A year later, an adviser warned President Cleveland, "We are on the eve of a very dark night." He was right. Between 1893 and 1897, the nation suffered a devastating economic depression.

Personal hardship followed business failures; nearly 20 percent of the labor force were jobless for a significant time during the depression. Falling demand caused prices to drop between 1892 and 1895, but layoffs and wage cuts more than offset declining living costs. Many people could not afford basic necessities. The New York police estimated that twenty thousand homeless and jobless people roamed the city's streets. Surveying the depression's impact on Boston, Henry Adams wrote, "Men died like flies under the strain, and Boston grew suddenly old, haggard, and thin."

As the depression deepened, the currency problem reached a crisis. The Sherman Silver Purchase Act of 1890 had committed the government to issue Treasury notes (silver certificates) to buy 4.5 million ounces of silver each month. These certificates could be redeemed in gold, at the ratio of one ounce of gold for every sixteen ounces of silver. But a western mining boom made silver more plentiful, causing its market value relative to gold to fall and prompting holders of Sherman silver notes and greenback currency issued during the Civil War to cash in their notes in exchange for gold whose worth remained fairly constant. As a result, the nation's gold reserve soon dwindled, falling below $100 million in early 1893.

Continuing Currency Problems

The $100 million level had psychological importance. If investors believed that the country's gold reserve was disappearing, they would lose confidence in America's economic stability and refrain from investing. British capitalists, for example, owned some $4 billion in American stocks and bonds. If the dollar were to depreciate too much, they would sell their holdings and stop investing in American economic growth. In fact, the lower the gold reserve dropped, the more people rushed to redeem their money and securities—to get gold before it disappeared. Panic spread, causing more bankruptcies and unemployment.

Vowing to protect the gold reserve from redeemers of silver certificates, President Cleveland called a special session of Congress to repeal the Sherman Silver Purchase Act. Repeal passed in late 1893, but the run on the Treasury continued through 1894. In early 1895 gold reserves fell to $41 million. In desperation, Cleveland accepted an offer of 3.5 million ounces of gold in return for $65 million worth of federal bonds from a banking syndicate led by financier J. P. Morgan. When the bankers resold the bonds to the public, they made about $2 million in profits. Cleveland claimed that he had saved the gold reserves, but discontented farmers, workers, silver miners, and even some of Cleveland's Democratic allies saw only humiliation in the president's deal with big businessmen. "When Judas betrayed Christ," charged Senator Tillman, "his heart was not blacker than this scoundrel, Cleveland, in betraying the [Democratic Party]."

Few people knew what the president was really enduring. At about the time Cleveland called Congress into special session, doctors discovered a malignant tumor on his palate that required immediate removal. Fearful that publicity of his illness would hasten the run on gold, and intent on preventing Vice President Adlai E. Stevenson, a silver supporter, from gaining influence, Cleveland kept his condition a secret. He announced that he was going sailing, and doctors removed his cancerous upper left jaw while the yacht floated outside New York City. Outfitted with a rubber jaw, Cleveland resumed a full schedule five days later, hiding terrible pain to dispel rumors that he was seriously ill. He eventually recovered, but those who knew of his surgery believed it had sapped his vitality.

The deal between Cleveland and Morgan did not end the depression. After improving slightly in 1895, the economy plunged again. Farm income, declining since 1887, continued to slide; factories closed; banks that remained open restricted withdrawals. The tight money supply depressed housing construction, drying up important jobs and reducing immigration. Cities such as Detroit allowed citizens to cultivate "potato patches" on vacant land to help alleviate food shortages. Each night urban police stations filled up with vagrants who had no place to stay.

Like previous hard times, the depression ultimately ran its course. In the final years of the century, gold discoveries in Alaska, good harvests, and industrial growth brought relief. But the downturn of the 1890s hastened the crumbling of the old economic

Effects of a New Economic System

system and the emergence of a new one. Since the 1850s, railroads had steered American economic development, opening new markets, boosting steel production, and invigorating banking. The central features of a new business system—consolidation and a trend toward bigness—were beginning to solidify just when the depression hit.

The American economy had become national rather than sectional; the fate of a large business in one part of the country had repercussions elsewhere. Before the depression many companies had expanded too rapidly. When contraction occurred, their reckless debts dragged them down, and they pulled other industries with them. In early 1893, for example, thirty-two steel companies, five hundred banks, and sixteen thousand other businesses filed for bankruptcy. European economies also slumped, and more than ever before the fortunes of one country affected the fortunes of other countries.

American farmers had to contend not only with discriminatory transportation rates and falling crop prices at home, but also with Canadian and Russian wheat growers, Argentine cattle ranchers, Indian and Egyptian cotton producers, and Australian wool producers. When farmers fell into debt and lost purchasing power, their depressed condition in turn affected the economic health of railroads, farm-implement manufacturers, banks, and other businesses. As well, the glutted domestic market persuaded businessmen to seek new markets abroad (see Chapter 22). The downward spiral ended late in 1897, but the depression exposed problems that demanded reform and set an agenda for future years.

Depression-Era Protests

The depression exposed fundamental tensions in the industrial system. Technological and organizational changes had been widening the gap between employees and employers for half a century. By the 1890s workers' protests against exploitation were threatening to spark an economic and political explosion. In 1894, the year the economy plunged into depression, there were over thirteen hundred strikes and countless riots. Contrary to accusations of business leaders, few protesters were anarchists or communists come from Europe to sabotage American democracy. Rather, the disaffected included thousands of men and women who believed that in a democracy their voices should be heard.

The era of protest began with the railroad strikes of 1877 (see page 499). The vehemence of those strikes, and the support they drew from working-class people, raised fears that the United States would experience a popular uprising like one in Paris six years earlier, which had briefly overturned the government and introduced communist principles. The Haymarket riot of 1886, a general strike in New Orleans in 1891, and a prolonged strike at the Carnegie Homestead Steel plant in 1892 (see page 502) heightened anxieties. In the West, embittered workers also took action. In 1892 violence erupted at a silver mine in Coeur d'Alene, Idaho. Angered by wage cuts and a lockout, striking miners seized the mine and battled federal troops sent to subdue them. Such defiance convinced some businessmen that only force could counter the radicalism allegedly promoted by socialists and anarchists.

Small numbers of socialists did participate in these and other confrontations. Furthermore, personal experience convinced many workers

Socialists

who never became socialists to agree with Karl Marx (1818–1883), the German philosopher and father of communism, that whoever controls the means of production holds the power to determine how well people live. Marx wrote that industrial capitalism generates profits by paying workers less than the value of their labor and that mechanization and mass production alienate workers from their labor. Thus, Marx contended, capitalists and laborers engage in an inescapable conflict over how much workers will benefit from their efforts. According to Marx, only by abolishing the return on capital—profits—could labor receive its true value, an outcome possible only if workers owned the means of production. Marx predicted that workers throughout the world would become so discontented that they would revolt and seize factories, farms, banks, and transportation lines. This revolution would establish a socialist order of justice and equality. Marx's vision appealed to some workers because it promised independence and abundance. It appealed to some intellectuals because it promised to end class conflict and crude materialism.

In America, socialism suffered from lack of strong leadership and disagreement over how to achieve Marx's vision. It splintered into small groups, such as the Socialist Labor Party, led by Daniel DeLeon, a fiery West Indian–born lawyer. DeLeon and other socialist leaders failed to attract the mass of unskilled laborers, even though many immigrant workers had been exposed to socialism in Europe. American social-

ists often focused on fine points of doctrine while ignoring workers' everyday needs; they could not rebut the clergy and business leaders who celebrated opportunity, self-improvement, and consumerism. Social mobility and the philosophy of individualism also undermined socialist aims. Workers hoped that they or their children would benefit through education and acquisition of property or by becoming their own bosses; thus most workers sought individual advancement rather than the betterment of all.

Events in 1894 triggered changes within the socialist movement. That year an inspiring new leader arose in response to the government's

Eugene V. Debs

quashing of the Pullman strike and of the newly formed American Railway Union. Eugene V. Debs, the union's intense and animated president, converted to socialism while serving a six-month prison term for defying an injunction against the strike (see page 502). Once released, Debs became the leading spokesman for American socialism, combining visionary Marxism with Jeffersonian and Populist antimonopolism. Though never good at organizing, Debs captivated audiences with passionate eloquence and indignant attacks on the free-enterprise system. "Many of you think you are competing," he would lecture. "Against whom? Against Rockefeller? About as I would if I had a wheelbarrow and competed with the Santa Fe [railroad] from here to Kansas City." By 1900 the group soon to be called the Socialist Party of America was uniting around Debs. It would make its presence felt more forcefully in the new century.

In 1894 Debs shared public attention with Jacob S. Coxey, a quiet businessman from Massillon, Ohio.

Coxey's Army

Like Debs, Coxey had a vision. He was convinced that, to aid debtors, the government should issue $500 million of "legal tender" paper money, make low-interest loans to local governments, and use the loans and money to pay the unemployed to build roads and other public works. He planned to publicize his scheme by leading a march from Massillon to Washington, D.C., gathering a "petition in boots" of unemployed workers along the way. Coxey even christened his newborn son Legal Tender and proposed that his teenage daughter lead the procession on a white horse.

Coxey's army, about two hundred strong, left in March 1894. Moving across Ohio into Pennsylvania, they received food and housing in depressed industrial towns and rural villages, and they won new recruits. Elsewhere, a dozen similar processions from places such as Seattle, San Francisco, and Los Angeles also began the trek eastward. Sore feet prompted some marchers to commandeer trains, but most processions were peaceful and law-abiding. One official called the marchers the "idle, useless dregs of humanity," but the troops kept themselves and their camps clean and well organized.

While other marchers were still on the road, Coxey's citizen army of five hundred, including women and children, entered Washington on April 30. The next day (May Day, a date traditionally associated with socialist demonstrations), the group, armed with "war clubs of peace," marched to the Capitol. When Coxey and a few others vaulted the wall surrounding the Capitol grounds, mounted police moved in and routed the crowd. Coxey tried to speak from the Capitol steps, but police dragged him away. As arrests and clubbings continued, Coxey's dream of a demonstration of 400,000 jobless workers dissolved. Like the strikes, the first people's march on Washington yielded to police muscle.

Unlike socialists, who wished to replace the capitalist system, Coxey's troops merely wanted more jobs and better living standards. Today, in an age of union contracts, regulation of business, and government-sponsored unemployment relief, their goals do not appear radical. The brutal reactions of officials, however, reveal how threatening dissenters such as Coxey and Debs seemed to defenders of the existing social order.

Populists, the Silver Crusade, and the Election of 1896

Populists did not suffer the suppression that unions and Coxey's army experienced, but they encountered roadblocks just when their political goals seemed attainable. As late as 1894, Populist candidates made good showings in elections in the West and South. Like earlier third parties, though, Populists were underfinanced and underorganized. They had strong and colorful candidates but not enough of them to effectively challenge the major parties. Voters remained reluctant to abandon old loyalties to the Republicans or Democrats.

Issues of race also permeated politics. The possibility of biracial political action posed by Farmers' Alliances in the early 1890s failed for two reasons. First, as noted above, southern white Democrats had succeeded in creating restrictions on voting rights that prevented African Americans from becoming a political force. Second, raw racism impeded the acceptance

Stifling of Biracial Dissent

of blacks by white Populists. Some Populists did seek to unite distressed black and white farmers. Tom Watson, Georgia's prominent Populist, noted that "the crushing burdens which now oppress both races in the South will cause each to . . . see a similarity of cause and a similarity of remedy." But poor white farmers could not forgo their racism. Many came from families that had supported the Ku Klux Klan during Reconstruction. Some had owned slaves, considered African Americans a permanently inferior people, and took comfort in the belief that there always would be people worse off than they were. Thus few Populists addressed the needs of black farmers, and many used white-supremacist rhetoric to guard against accusations that they encouraged race-mixing.

In the national arena, the Populist crusade against "money power" settled on the issue of silver. Many

Free Silver

people saw silver as a simple solution to the nation's complex ills. To them, free coinage of silver meant the end

Published in 1894, *Coin's Financial School* by William H. Harvey expressed the position of free silver in simple language and illustrations. Written in the form of lectures on the money question given by "Professor Coin," Harvey's book had enormous appeal to distressed farmers.

mercilessly scourges the money changers in the **Temple of the Republic.**
—*New York Recorder.*

This book tells its readers more about gold, silver and currency generally than any other publication we know of, and in a way that every man can fully comprehend.
—*Chicago Inter Ocean.*

Coin's Financial School

PUBLISHERS
COIN PUBLISHING COMPANY

During the 1896 presidential campaign, Republicans depicted their candidate, William McKinley, as holding the key to prosperity for both the working man and the white-collar laborer, shown here raising their hats to the candidate. Republicans successfully made this economic theme, rather than the silver crusade of McKinley's unsuccessful opponent, William Jennings Bryan, the difference in the election's outcome. (Collection of David J. and Janice L. Frent)

of special privileges for the rich and the return of government to the people. Populists agreed and made free coinage of silver their political battle cry.

As the election of 1896 approached, Populists had to decide how to translate their few previous electoral victories into larger success. Should they join with sympathetic factions of the major parties, thus risking a loss of identity, or should they remain an independent third party and settle for minor wins at best? Except in Rocky Mountain states, where free coinage of silver had strong support, Republicans were unlikely allies because their support for the gold standard and big-business orientation represented what Populists opposed.

In the North and West, alliance with Democrats was more plausible. There, the Democratic Party retained vestiges of antimonopoly ideology and some sympathy for a looser currency system, although "gold Democrats" such as President Cleveland and Senator David Hill of New York held powerful influence. Populists assumed they shared common interests with Democratic urban workers, who they believed suffered the same oppression that beset farmers. In the

South, fusion with Democrats seemed less likely, since there the party constituted the very power structure against which farmers had revolted in the late 1880s. Whichever option they chose, fusion or independence, Populists ensured that the political campaign of 1896 would be the most issue-oriented election since 1860.

The 1896 presidential election climaxed a generation of political turbulence. Each party was divided.

Republican Nomination of McKinley

Republicans, directed by Marcus A. Hanna, a prosperous Ohio industrialist, had only minor problems. For a year, Hanna had been maneuvering to win the nomination for Ohio's governor, William McKinley. By the time the party convened in St. Louis, Hanna had corralled enough delegates to succeed. "He had advertised McKinley," quipped Theodore Roosevelt, "as if he were a patent medicine." The Republicans' only distress occurred when they adopted a moderate platform supporting gold, rejecting a prosilver stance proposed by Colorado's Senator Henry M. Teller. Teller, who had been among the party's founders forty years earlier, walked out of the convention in tears, taking a small group of silver Republicans with him.

At the Democratic convention, prosilver delegates wearing silver badges and waving silver banners paraded through the Chicago Amphitheatre. Observing their tumultuous demonstrations, one delegate wrote, "For the first time I can understand the scenes of the French Revolution!" A *New York World* reporter remarked that "All the silverites need is a Moses." They soon found one in William Jennings Bryan.

Bryan, age thirty-six, arrived at the Democratic convention as a member of a contested Nebraska delegation. A former congressman

William Jennings Bryan

whose support for coinage of silver had annoyed President Cleveland, he was highly distressed by the depression's impact on midwestern farmers. The convention seated Bryan and his colleagues instead of a competing faction that supported the gold standard. Shortly afterward, as a member of the party's resolutions committee, Bryan helped write a platform calling for free coinage of silver. When the committee presented the platform to the full convention, Bryan rose to speak on its behalf. Bryan's now-famous closing words ignited the delegates:

> Having behind us the producing masses of this nation and the world, supported by the commercial interests, the laboring interests, and the toilers everywhere, we will answer [the wealthy classes'] demand for a gold standard by saying to them: You shall not press down upon the brow of labor this crown of thorns, you shall not crucify mankind upon a cross of gold.

The speech could not have been better timed. Delegates who backed Bryan for president now had no trouble enlisting support. It took five ballots to win the nomination, but the magnetic "Boy Orator" proved irresistible. In accepting the silverite goals of southerners and westerners and repudiating Cleveland's policies in its platform, the Democratic Party became more attractive to discontented farmers. But like the Republicans, it, too, alienated a dissenting minority wing. Some gold Democrats withdrew and nominated their own candidate.

Bryan's nomination presented the Populist party (as it was now called) with a dilemma. Should Populists join Democrats in support of Bryan, or should they nominate their own candidate? Tom Watson, expressing opposition to fusion with Democrats, warned that "the Democratic idea of fusion [is] that we play Jonah while they play whale." Others reasoned that supporting a different candidate would split the anti-

William Jennings Bryan (1860–1925) posed for this photograph in 1896, when he first ran for president at the age of thirty-six. Bryan's emotional speeches turned agrarian unrest and the issue of free silver into a moral crusade. (Library of Congress)

McKinley vote and guarantee a Republican victory. In the end the convention compromised, first naming Watson as its vice-presidential nominee to preserve party identity (Democrats had nominated Maine shipping magnate Arthur Sewall for vice president) and then nominating Bryan for president.

The campaign, as Kansas journalist William Allen White observed, "took the form of religious frenzy . . . as the crusaders of the revolution rode home, praising the people's will as though it were God's will and cursing wealth for its iniquity." The campaign rhetoric rang with emotionalism. Bryan preached that "every great economic question is in reality a great moral question." Republicans countered Bryan's evangelism and attacks on privilege by predicting chaos if he won. While Bryan raced around the country giving twenty speeches a day, Hanna invited thousands of people to

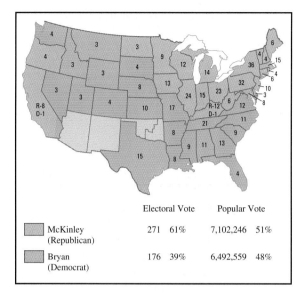

	Electoral Vote	Popular Vote
McKinley (Republican)	271 61%	7,102,246 51%
Bryan (Democrat)	176 39%	6,492,559 48%

Map 20.1   Presidential Election, 1896   William Jennings Bryan had strong voter support in the South and West, but the numerically superior industrial states, plus California, created majorities for William McKinley.

McKinley's home in Canton, Ohio, where the candidate plied them with homilies on moderation and prosperity, promising something for everyone. In an appeal to working-class voters, Republicans stressed the new jobs that a protective tariff would create.

Election Results   The election results revealed that the political standoff had finally ended. McKinley, symbol of Republican pragmatism and corporate ascendancy, beat Bryan by over 600,000 popular votes and won in the electoral college by 271 to 176 (see Map 20.1). It was the most lopsided presidential election since 1872.

Bryan worked hard to rally the nation, but obsession with silver undermined his effort and prevented Populists from building the urban-rural coalition that would have expanded their political appeal. The silver issue diverted voters from focusing on broader reforms deriving from the Alliance movement and the Omaha platform of 1892. Reformer Henry Demarest Lloyd summarized the matter succinctly: "Free silver," he wrote, "is the cowbird of the reform movement. It waited till the nest had been built by the sacrifices and labor of others, and then it laid its eggs in it, pushing out the others which it smashed to the ground." Urban workers, who might have benefited from Populist goals, shied away from the silver issue out of fear that free

coinage would reduce the value of their wages. Labor leaders such as the AFL's Samuel Gompers, though partly sympathetic, would not commit themselves fully because they viewed farmers as businessmen, not workers. And socialists such as Daniel DeLeon denounced Populists as "retrograde" because they, unlike socialists, believed in free enterprise. Thus the Populist crusade collapsed. Although Populists and fusion candidates won a few state and congressional elections in 1896, the Bryan-Watson ticket of the Populist party polled only 222,600 votes nationwide.

The McKinley Presidency   As president, McKinley signed the Gold Standard Act (1900), requiring that all paper money be backed by gold. A seasoned and personable politician, McKinley was best known for crafting protective tariffs; as a congressman from Ohio, he had guided passage of record-high tariff rates in 1890. He accordingly supported the Dingley Tariff of 1897, which raised duties even higher. Domestic tensions subsided during McKinley's presidency; an upward swing of the business cycle and a money supply enlarged by gold discoveries in Alaska, Australia, and South Africa helped restore prosperity. A believer in opening new markets abroad to sustain prosperity at home, McKinley encouraged imperialistic ventures in Latin America and the Pacific (see Chapter 22). Good times and victory in the Spanish-American-Cuban-Filipino War enabled him to beat Bryan again in 1900, using the slogan "The Full Dinner Pail."

Summary

Government during the Gilded Age succeeded in making many modest, and some major, accomplishments. Guided by well-meaning, generally competent people, much of what occurred in statehouses, the halls of Congress, and the White House prepared the nation for the twentieth century. Laws encouraging economic growth with some principles of regulation, measures expanding government agencies while reducing crass patronage, federal intervention in trade and currency issues, and a more active presidency all evolved during the 1870s and 1880s. Extremists such as "Pitchfork Ben" Tillman and those who supported disfranchisement of African Americans and continued discrimination against both blacks and women still polluted politics. Nor could the system tolerate radical views such as those expressed by socialists, Coxey, or Populists. But many politicians concerned themselves with more than patronage and influence; most genuinely wanted to create what they believed was a good society.

The 1896 election realigned national politics. The Republican Party, founded in the 1850s amid a crusade against slavery, became the majority party by emphasizing active government aid to business expansion, expanding its social base to include urban workers, and playing down its moralism. The Democratic Party miscalculated on the silver issue and held its traditional support only in the South. After 1896, however, party loyalties lacked the potency they once had. Suspicion of party politics increased, and voter participation rates declined. A new kind of politics was brewing, one in which technical experts and scientific organization would attempt to supplant the backroom deals and favoritism that had characterized the previous age.

In retrospect, it is easy to see that the Populists never had a chance. The political system lacked the ability to accept third parties. The structure of Congress was such that the two-party system had enormous power, making it difficult for the few Populist representatives even to speak, let alone serve on important committees and promote reform legislation.

Nevertheless, by 1920 many Populist goals were achieved, including regulation of railroads, banks, and utilities; shorter workdays; a variant of the subtreasury plan; a graduated income tax; direct election of senators; and the secret ballot. These reforms succeeded because a variety of groups united behind them. Immigration, urbanization, and industrialization had transformed the United States into a pluralistic society in which compromise among interest groups had become a political fact of life. As the Gilded Age ended, business was still in the ascendancy, and large segments of the population were still excluded from political and economic opportunity. But the winds of dissent and reform had begun to blow more strongly.

LEGACY FOR A PEOPLE AND A NATION
Politics and Popular Culture

The Wizard of Oz, one of the most popular movies of all time, began as a Populist fable penned by journalist L. Frank Baum in 1900. Originally titled "The Wonderful Wizard of Oz," the story used memorable characters to represent the conditions of overburdened farmers and laborers. Dorothy symbolized the well-intentioned common person; the Scarecrow, the struggling farmer; the Tin Man, the industrial worker.

Hoping for a better life, these new friends, along with the Cowardly Lion (William Jennings Bryan with a loud roar but little power), followed a yellow brick road (the gold standard) that led nowhere. Along their journey, they encountered the Wicked Witch of the East, who, Baum wrote, kept the little people (Munchkins) "in bondage, . . . making them slaves for her night and day." They also met the Wicked Witch of the West, who symbolized industrial corporations. The Emerald City they find is presided over by the Wizard of Oz (oz. is the abbreviation for ounces, the chief measurement of gold), who rules from behind a screen. A typical politician, the Wizard tries to be all things to all people, but Dorothy and her friends reveal him as a fraud, just "a little man, with a bald head and a wrinkled face." Dorothy is able to leave this muddled society and return to her simple Kansas farm family of Aunt Em and Uncle Henry by using her magical silver slippers (coinage of silver).

Baum used his tale to argue that powerful leaders were deceiving and manipulating ordinary people. He believed that if *Oz* exposed what really was going on, the people—no longer ignorant—would be outraged by the greed and deceit of politicians and industrialists, and would act. But this message disappeared when Metro Goldwyn Mayer (MGM) bought Baum's story and made it into a full-length motion picture to showcase their new child star, Judy Garland. The movie came out in 1939 and was an instant success. Broadcast on television since 1956, it is seen by millions each year.

The saga of *The Wizard of Oz* shows how modern popular culture can subsume politics. The adventures of four endearing characters came to have more appeal than their political symbolism. The rise of movies, television, and sports also altered the nature of fame. Whereas in the Gilded Age politicians held the spotlight as the nation's chief celebrities, by the twentieth century they had been bumped into the background. And instead of popular culture, such as Baum's fable, influencing politics, the legacy to a people and a nation has been the opportunity of some celebrities to use popular culture to become politicians. Thus the nation has seen movie stars and sports personalities become governors, senators, representatives, and even president.

For Further Reading, see page A-23 of the Appendix. For Web resources, go to http://college.hmco.com.

A coworker once described Florence Kelley as a "guerrilla warrior" in the "wilderness of industrial wrongs." A woman of sharp wit and commanding presence, Kelley accomplished as much as anyone in guiding the United States out of the tangled swamp of unregulated industrial capitalism into the uncharted seas of the twentieth-century welfare state.

Kelley's career traced a remarkable odyssey. Raised in middle-class comfort in Philadelphia, the daughter of a Republican congressman, Kelley graduated from Cornell in 1883. She prepared to study law, but the University of Pennsylvania denied her admission to its graduate school because of her gender. Instead, she traveled to Europe. In Zurich, Kelley joined a group of socialists who alerted her to the plight of the underprivileged. She married a socialist Russian medical student and returned to New York City in 1886. When the marriage collapsed from debts and physical abuse, Kelley took her three children to Chicago in 1891 to obtain a divorce. Later that year she moved into Hull House, a residence in the slums where middle-class reformers went to live in order to help and learn from working-class immigrants. There her transforming work truly began.

Until the 1890s, Kelley's life had been male-oriented, influenced first by her father, then by her husband. She had tried to enter public life by attending law school and participating in political organizations, but men had blocked her path at every turn. At Hull House, however, Kelley entered a female-dominated environment, where women sought to apply helping skills to the betterment of society. This environment encouraged Kelley to assert her powerful abilities.

Over the next decade, Kelley became the nation's most ardent advocate of improved conditions for working-class women and children. She investigated and publicized the exploitative sweatshop system in Chicago's garment industry, lobbied for laws to prohibit child labor and regulate women's working hours, and served as Illinois's first factory inspector. Her work

During the Progressive era, reformers advocated new ways of thinking and new techniques to achieve progress in a variety of fields. Progressive educators, for example, cast aside rigid methods of memorization and discipline in favor of encouraging children to use their minds and hands in ways that were relevant to their lives.   (Library of Congress)

21

THE PROGRESSIVE ERA 1895–1920

helped create new professions for women in social service, and her strategy of investigating, publicizing, and crusading for action became a model for reform. Perhaps most significant, she and fellow reformers like Jane Addams and Lillian Wald enlisted government to aid in the solution of social problems.

During the 1890s economic depression, labor violence, political upheaval, and foreign entanglements shook the nation. Technology had fulfilled many promises, but great numbers of Americans continued to suffer from poverty and disease. Some critics regarded industrialists as monsters who controlled markets, wages, and prices for the sole purpose of maximizing profits. Others believed government was corroded by bosses who enriched themselves through politics. Tensions created by urbanization and industrialization seemed to be fragmenting society into conflicting interest groups.

By 1900, however, the political tumult of the previous decade had died down, and the economic depression seemed to be over. The nation emerged victorious from a war (see Chapter 22), and a new era of dynamic political leaders such as Theodore Roosevelt and Woodrow Wilson was dawning. A sense of renewal served both to intensify anxiety over continuing social and political problems and to raise hopes that somehow such problems could be fixed and democracy could be reconciled with capitalism.

From these circumstances there emerged a complex, and many-sided, reform campaign. By the 1910s many reformers were calling themselves "Progressives"; in 1912 they formed a political party by that name to embody their principles. Historians have uniformly used the term *Progressivism* to refer to the era's reformist spirit while disagreeing over its meaning and over which groups and individuals actually were Progressive. Nonetheless, the era between 1895 and 1920 included a series of movements, each aiming in one way or another to renovate or restore American society, values, and institutions.

This painting (1904) by Everett Shinn depicts the disastrous consequences of poverty and the unkept promise of American life. Unable to pay the rent, thousands of families, along with their meager belongings, were forced into the streets. A painter of the so-called Ashcan School, Shinn captured the distress of poverty-stricken families forced to experience this humiliation.   (National Museum of American Art, Washington, D.C./Art Resource, N.Y.)

IMPORTANT EVENTS

1893 Anti-Saloon League founded

1895 Washington gives Atlanta Compromise speech
National Association of Colored Women founded

1896 *Holden v. Hardy* upholds limits on miners' working hours

1900 McKinley reelected

1901 McKinley assassinated; T. Roosevelt assumes the presidency

1904 T. Roosevelt elected president
Northern Securities case dissolves railroad trust

1905 Niagara Conference promotes African American rights
Lochner v. New York removes limits on bakers' working hours

1906 Hepburn Act tightens control over railroads
Sinclair's *The Jungle* exposes poor conditions in meatpacking plants
Meat Inspection Act passed
Pure Food and Drug Act passed

1907 Reckless speculation causes economic panic

1908 Taft elected president
Muller v. Oregon upholds limits on women's working hours

1909 NAACP founded
Payne-Aldrich Tariff passed

1910 Mann-Elkins Act reinforces ICC powers
White Slave Traffic Act prohibits transportation of women for "immoral purposes"
Ballinger-Pinchot controversy angers conservationists

1911 Society of American Indians founded

1912 T. Roosevelt runs for president on the Progressive (Bull Moose) ticket
Wilson elected president

1913 Sixteenth Amendment ratified, legalizing federal income tax
Seventeenth Amendment ratified, providing for direct election of U.S. senators
Underwood Tariff institutes income tax
Federal Reserve Act establishes central banking system

1914 Federal Trade Commission created to investigate unfair trade practices
Clayton Anti-Trust Act outlaws monopolistic business practices
Sanger indicted for sending articles on contraception through the mail

1916 Wilson reelected
Federal Farm Loan Act provides credit to farmers
Adamson Act mandates eight-hour workday for railroad workers

1919 Eighteenth Amendment ratified, establishing prohibition of alcoholic beverages

1920 Nineteenth Amendment ratified, giving women the vote in federal elections

1921 Sanger founds American Birth Control League

The reform impulse had many sources. Industrial capitalism had created awesome technology, unprecedented productivity, and a cornucopia of consumer goods. But it also brought harmful overproduction, domineering monopolies, labor strife, and the spoiling of natural resources. Burgeoning cities facilitated the amassing and distribution of goods, services, and cultural amenities; they also bred poverty, disease, and crime. Inflows of immigrants and the rise of a new class of managers and professionals reconfigured the social order. And the depression of the 1890s forced many leading citizens to realize what working people had known for some time: the central promise of American life was not being kept; equality of opportunity was a myth.

In addressing these problems, Progressives organized their ideas and actions around three goals. First, they sought to end abuses of power. Attacks on unfair privilege, monopoly, and corruption were not new; Jacksonian reformers of the 1830s and 1840s and Populists of the 1890s belonged to the same tradition. Progressives, however, intensified the attacks. Trust-busting, consumers' rights, and good government became compelling political issues.

Second, Progressives aimed to supplant corrupt power with humane institutions such as schools,

Judge Ben Lindsey (1869–1943) of Denver was a Progressive reformer who worked for children's legal protection. Like many reformers of his era, Lindsey had an earnest faith in the ability of humankind to build a better world.   (Library of Congress)

charities, and medical clinics. Though eager to protect individual rights, they abandoned individualistic notions that hard work and good character automatically ensured success and that the poor had only themselves to blame for their plight. Instead, Progressives acknowledged that society had responsibility and power to improve individual lives, and they believed that government, acting for society at large, must intervene in social and economic affairs to protect the common good and elevate public interest above self-interest. Their revolt against fixed categories of thought challenged entrenched views on women's roles, race relations, education, legal and scientific thought, and morality.

Third, Progressives wanted to apply scientific principles and efficient management to economic, social, and political institutions. Their aim was to establish bureaus of experts that would end wasteful competition and promote social and economic order. Science and the scientific method—planning, control, and predictability—were their central values. Just as corporations applied scientific management techniques to achieve economic efficiency, Progressives advocated expertise and planning to achieve social and political efficiency.

Befitting their name, Progressives had deep faith in the ability of humankind to create a better world. They used phrases such as "humanity's universal growth" and "the upward spiral of human development." Optimism arising from rising incomes, new educational opportunities, and increased availability of goods and services created an aura of confidence that social improvement would follow. Judge Ben Lindsey of Denver, who spearheaded reform in the treatment of juvenile delinquents, expressed the Progressive creed when he wrote, "In the end the people are bound to do the right thing, no matter how much they fail at times." ∎

The Varied Progressive Impulse

 Progressive reformers addressed vexing issues that had surfaced in the previous half-century, but they did so in a new political climate. As the twentieth century dawned, party loyalty eroded and voter turnout declined. In northern states, voter participation in presidential elections dropped from Gilded Age levels of over 80 percent of the eligible electorate to less than 60 percent. In southern states, where taxes and literacy tests excluded most African Americans and many poor whites from the polls, it fell below 30 percent. Parties and elections, it seemed, were losing influence over government policies. At the same time, the political system was opening to new interest groups, each of which championed its own cause.

Local voluntary associations had existed since the 1790s, but many organizations became nationwide in scope after the 1890s and tried to shape public policy to meet their needs and goals. These organizations included professional associations such as the American Bar Association; women's organizations such as the National American Woman Suffrage Association; issue-oriented groups such as the National Consumers League; civic clubs such as the National Municipal League; and minority-group associations, such as the National Negro Business League and the Society of American Indians. Because they usually acted independently of either of the established political parties, such groups made politics more fragmented and issue-focused than in earlier eras.

Also, American politics became receptive to foreign models and ideas for reorganizing society. A variety of programs and proposals traveled across the Atlantic; some were introduced by Americans such as Florence Kelley who had observed reforms in England, France, and Germany, others by foreigners traveling in the United States. (Europeans also learned of American reforms, but the balance of the idea flow tilted toward the United States.) Such reforms as old-age insurance, subsidized workers' housing, city planning, and rural reconstruction originated abroad and were adopted or modified in America.

Foreign Influences

Although goals of the rural-based Populist movement lingered—moral regeneration, political democracy, and antimonopolism—the Progressive quest for social justice, educational and legal reform, and government streamlining had a largely urban bent. Between 1890 and 1920 the proportion of the nation's population living in cities swelled from 35 percent to 51 percent; the number of cities with fifty thousand or more people rose from 58 to 144. By utilizing advances in mail, telephone, and telegraph communications, urban reformers exchanged information and coordinated efforts to alleviate the consequences of this change.

Organizations and individuals intent on achieving Progressive goals—ending the abuse of power, reforming social institutions, and promoting bureaucratic and scientific efficiency—existed in almost all

Urban Middle-Class Reformers and Muckrakers

levels of society. But the new middle class—men and women in professions of law, medicine, engineering, social work, religion, teaching, and business—formed the vanguard of reform. Offended by inefficiency and immorality in business, government, and human relations, these people set out to apply rational techniques they had learned in their professions to problems of the larger society.

Their indignation motivated many middle-class Progressive reformers to seek an end to abuses of power. Their views were voiced by journalists whom Theodore Roosevelt dubbed muckrakers (after a character in the Puritan allegory *Pilgrim's Progress* who, rather than looking heavenward at beauty, looked downward and raked the muck to find what was wrong with life). Muckrakers fed public taste for scandal and sensation by exposing social, economic, and political wrongs. Their investigative articles in *McClure's, Cosmopolitan*, and other popular magazines attacked adulterated foods, fraudulent insurance, prostitution, and other offenses. Lincoln Steffens's articles in *McClure's*, later published as *The Shame of the Cities* (1904), epitomized the muckraking style. Steffens hoped his exposés of bosses' misrule would inspire mass outrage and, ultimately, reform. Other well-known muckraking efforts included Upton Sinclair's *The Jungle* (1906), a novel that disclosed crimes of the meatpacking industry; Ida M. Tarbell's critical history of Standard Oil (1904); Burton J. Hendrick's *Story of Life Insurance* (1907); and David Graham Phillips's *Treason of the Senate* (1906).

To improve politics, Progressives advocated nominating candidates through direct primaries instead of party caucuses and holding nonpartisan elections to prevent the fraud and bribery bred by party loyalties. To make officeholders more responsible, Progressives pressed for three reforms: the initiative, which permitted voters to propose new laws; the referendum, which enabled voters to accept or reject a law; and the recall, which allowed voters to remove offending officials and judges from office before their terms expired. Their goal, like that of the business-consolidation movement, was efficiency: they would reclaim government by replacing the boss system with accountable managers chosen by a responsible electorate.

The Progressive spirit also stirred some elite business leaders. Executives like Alexander Cassatt of the Pennsylvania Railroad supported some government regulation and political reforms to protect their interests from more radical reformers. Others, like

Upper-Class Reformers

E. A. Filene, founder of a Boston department store, and Tom Johnson, a Cleveland streetcar magnate, were humanitarians who worked unselfishly for social justice. Business-dominated organizations like the Municipal Voters League and U.S. Chamber of Commerce thought that running schools, hospitals, and local government like efficient businesses would help stabilize society. Elite women often led organizations like the Young Women's Christian Association (YWCA), which aided growing numbers of unmarried working women, and the Women's Christian Temperance Union (WCTU), the largest women's organization of its time, which supported numerous causes besides abstinence from drinking.

Working-Class Reformers

Not all Progressives were middle- or upper-class. Vital elements of what became modern American liberalism derived from working-class urban experiences. By 1900 many urban workers were pressing for government intervention to ensure safety and security. They advocated "bread-and-butter reforms" such as safe factories, shorter workdays, workers' compensation, better housing, and health safeguards. Often these were the same people who supported political bosses, supposedly the enemies of reform. In fact, bossism was not necessarily at odds with humanitarianism. When "Big Tim" Sullivan, an influential boss in New York City's Tammany Hall political machine, was asked why he supported a shorter workday for women, he explained, "I had seen me sister go out to work when she was only fourteen and I know we ought to help these gals by giving 'em a law which will prevent 'em from being broken down while they're still young."

After 1900, voters from urban working-class districts elected several Progressive legislators who had trained in the trenches of machine politics. New York's Alfred E. Smith and Robert F. Wagner, Massachusetts's David I. Walsh, and Illinois's Edward F. Dunne—all from immigrant backgrounds—earnestly supported reform at the state and national levels. They wanted government to take responsibility for alleviating hardships that resulted from urban-industrial growth. They opposed reforms such as prohibition, Sunday closing laws, civil service, and nonpartisan elections, which conflicted with their constituents' interests. They were most successful when they joined with other reformers to pass laws aiding labor and promoting social welfare.

Some disillusioned people moved beyond Progressive reform; they wanted a different society altogether.

Socialists

A blend of immigrant intellectuals, industrial workers, disaffected Populists, miners, and women's rights activists—they turned to the socialist movement. The majority of socialists united behind Eugene V. Debs (see page 570), the American Railway Union organizer who drew nearly 100,000 votes in the 1900 presidential election. Although Debs failed to develop a consistent program beyond opposition to war and bourgeois materialism, he was a spellbinding spokesman for radical causes. As the Socialist Party's presidential candidate Debs won 400,000 votes in 1904, and in 1912, at the pinnacle of his and his party's career, he polled over 900,000.

With stinging rebukes of exploitation and unfair privilege, Debs and socialists like Milwaukee's Victor Berger and New York's Morris Hilquit made compelling overtures to reform-minded people. Some, such as Florence Kelley, joined the Socialist Party. But most Progressives had too much at stake in the capitalist system to want to overthrow it. Municipal ownership of public utilities represented their limit of drastic change. In Wisconsin, where Progressivism was most advanced, reformers refused to ally with Berger's more radical group. California Progressives temporarily allied with reactionaries to prevent socialists from gaining power in Los Angeles. And few Progressives objected when Debs was jailed in 1918 for giving an antiwar speech.

Opponents of Progressivism

It would be a mistake to assume that a Progressive spirit captured all of American society between 1895 and 1920. Large numbers of people, heavily represented in Congress, disliked government interference in economic affairs and found no fault with existing power structures. Defenders of free enterprise opposed many regulatory measures out of self-interest and fear that government programs would undermine the individual initiative and competition that they believed was basic to the free-market system. Government interference, they contended, contradicted the natural law of survival of the fittest. "Old-guard" Republicans like Senator Nelson W. Aldrich of Rhode Island and House Speaker Joseph Cannon of Illinois championed this ideology. Outside Washington, D.C., tycoons like J. P. Morgan and John D. Rockefeller insisted that progress would result only from maintaining the profit incentive and an economy unfettered by government regulation.

Though their objectives sometimes differed from those of middle-class Progressive reformers, socialists also became a more active force in the early twentieth century. Socialist parades on May Day, such as this one in 1910, were meant to express the solidarity of all working people.　(Library of Congress)

Progressive reformers occupied the center of the ideological spectrum. Moderate, socially aware, sometimes contradictory, they believed on one hand that the laissez-faire system was obsolete and on the other that a radical shift away from free enterprise was dangerous. Like Thomas Jefferson, they expressed faith in the conscience and will of the people; like Alexander Hamilton, they desired strong central government to act in the interests of conscience. Their goals were both idealistic and realistic. As minister-reformer Walter Rauschenbusch wrote, "We shall demand perfection and never expect to get it."

Governmental and Legislative Reform

A mistrust of tyranny had traditionally prompted American theorists and ordinary citizens to believe that democratic government should be small and unobtrusive, should interfere in private affairs only in unique circumstances, and should withdraw when balance had been restored. But in the late 1800s this point of view weakened when problems resulting from economic change seemed to overwhelm individual effort. Corporations pursued government aid and protection for their enterprises. Discontented farmers sought government regulation of railroads and other monopolistic businesses. And city dwellers, accustomed to favors performed by political machines, came to expect government to act on their behalf.

Progressive reformers supported the assumption that government should ensure justice and well-being. Increasingly aware that a simple, inflexible government was inadequate in a complex industrial age, they reasoned that public authority needed to counteract inefficiency and exploitation. But before activists could effectively use such power, they would have to reclaim government from politicians whose greed had soiled the democratic system. Thus eliminating corruption from government was a central thrust of Progressive activity.

Restructuring Government

Prior to the Progressive era, reformers had attacked corruption in cities (see Chapter 19). Between 1870 and 1900, opponents of boss politics tried to restructure government through reforms such as civil service, nonpartisan elections, and tighter scrutiny of public expenditures. A few reformers advocated poverty relief, housing improvement, and prolabor laws, but most worked for efficient—meaning economical—government. After 1900 reform campaigns installed city manager and commission forms of government (in which urban officials were chosen for professional expertise, rather than political connections) and public ownership of utilities (to prevent monopolistic gas, electric, and transit companies from profiting at public expense).

Reformers, however, found the city too small an arena for the changes they sought. Frustrated by limited victories, they theorized that state and federal governments offered better opportunities for enacting needed legislation. Their goals tended to vary regionally. In the Great Plains and Far West, they rallied behind railroad regulation and government control of natural resources. In the South reformers continued the Populist crusade against big business and autocratic politicians. In the Northeast and Midwest, they attacked corrupt politics and unsafe labor conditions.

Robert M. La Follette (1855–1925) was one of the most dynamic of Progressive politicians. As governor of Wisconsin, he sponsored a program of political reform and business regulation known as the Wisconsin Plan. In 1906 he entered the U.S. Senate and continued to champion Progressive reform. The National Progressive Republican League, which La Follette founded in 1911, became the core of the Progressive Party. (State Historical Society of Wisconsin)

Faith in a strong, fair-minded executive prompted Progressives to support a number of skillful and charismatic governors. The most forceful

Robert M. La Follette

Progressive governor was Wisconsin's Robert M. La Follette. A self-made small-town lawyer, La Follette rose through the state Republican Party and won the governorship in 1900. As governor he initiated a multipronged reform program including direct primaries, more equitable taxes, and regulation of railroad rates. He also appointed commissions staffed by experts, who supplied him with the facts and figures he used in fiery speeches to arouse public support for his policies. After three terms as governor, La Follette was elected to the U.S. Senate and carried his ideals into national politics. "Battling Bob" displayed a rare ability to approach reform scientifically while still exciting people with moving rhetoric. His goal, he asserted, "was not to 'smash' corporations, but to drive them out of politics, and then to treat them exactly the same as other people are treated."

The South experienced a brand of Progressive reform that in many ways resembled that of other regions. Essentially urban and middle

Southern Progressivism

class in nature, it included the same strategies of railroad and utility regulation, factory safety, pure food and drug legislation, and moral reform that existed in Wisconsin, California, and New York. The South led the way in political reform; the direct primary originated in North Carolina, the city commission plan arose in Galveston, Texas, and the city manager plan began in Staunton, Virginia. Progressive governors, such as Braxton Bragg Comer of Alabama and Hoke Smith of Georgia, introduced business regulation and other reforms that rivaled actions inspired by Robert La Follette.

But racial bitterness tainted southern Progressive politics, largely excluding former slaves from many benefits of reform. The exclusion of black men from voting through poll taxes, literacy requirements, and other means (see Chapter 20) meant that electoral reforms affected only whites—and then only white men with enough cash and education to satisfy voting prerequisites. Smith, Comer, and other Progressive governors such as Charles B. Aycock of North Carolina and James K. Vardamann of Mississippi rested their power on appeals to white supremacy. Racism was not unique to the South; Governor Hiram Johnson of California, a leading western Progressive, promoted discrimination against Japanese Americans, and New Jersey's Woodrow Wilson had no sympathy for African Americans. Yet discrimination did not lessen in the South just because reformers held office.

At the same time, however, southern women, white and black, made notable contributions to Progressive causes, just as they did in the North. Southern white women crusaded against child labor, ran social service organizations, and challenged unfair wage rates. African American women, using a nonpolitical guise as homemakers and religious leaders—roles that whites found more acceptable than political activism—attempted to serve their communities by acting as spokespersons for street cleaning, better education, and health reforms. Thus, though much of southern Progressivism was racist, it would have been even more so without the reformist efforts of women, especially black women.

In all regions, crusades against corrupt politics produced notable changes. By 1916 all but three states had direct primaries, and many had adopted the initiative, referendum, and recall. Political reformers achieved a major goal in 1913 with adoption of the Seventeenth Amendment, which provided for direct election of U.S. senators (they previously had been elected by state legislatures, many of which Progressives thought were corrupt). Such measures did not always help. Party bosses, better organized and more experienced than reformers, were still able to control elections. Efforts to use the initiative, referendum, and recall often failed because special-interest groups spent large sums to influence the voting. Moreover, courts usually aided rather than reined in entrenched power.

State laws to improve labor conditions had greater impact than did political reforms because both reformers and bosses could sometimes agree on issues affecting working people. Many states used their constitutional powers to protect public health and

Labor Reform

safety (police power) and to enact factory inspection laws, and by 1916 nearly two-thirds of the states required compensation for victims of industrial accidents. A coalition of labor and humanitarian groups even induced some legislatures to grant aid to mothers with dependent children. Under pressure from the National Child Labor Committee, nearly every state set a minimum age for employment (varying from twelve to sixteen) and prohibited employers from working children more than eight or ten hours a day. Such laws had limited effect, though, because they seldom provided for the close inspection of factories that full enforcement required. And families that needed extra income evaded the laws by encouraging their children to work and to lie about their ages.

Several groups united to achieve restricted working hours for women. After the Supreme Court, in *Muller v. Oregon*, upheld Oregon's ten-hour limit in 1908 (see page 499), more states passed laws protecting female workers. Meanwhile, in 1914 efforts of the American Association for Old Age Security showed signs of success when Arizona established old-age pensions. The courts struck down the law, but demand for pensions continued, and in the 1920s many states enacted laws to provide for needy elderly people.

Reformers themselves did not always agree about what was Progressive, especially in human behavior.

Moral Reform

The main question was whether state intervention was necessary to enforce purity, especially in drinking habits and sexual behavior. For example, the Anti-Saloon League, formed in 1893, intensified the long-standing campaign against drunkenness and its costs to society. This organization allied with the Women's Christian Temperance Union (founded in 1873) to publicize the role of alcoholism in liver disease and other health problems. The League was especially successful in shifting attention from the individual's responsibility for temperance to the alleged link between the drinking that saloons encouraged and the accidents, poverty, and poor productivity that were consequences of drinking.

The war on saloons prompted many states and localities to restrict consumption of liquor. By 1900 almost one-fourth of the nation's population lived in "dry" communities (which prohibited the sale of liquor). But consumption of alcohol, especially beer, increased after 1900, convincing prohibitionists that a nationwide ban was

The War on Alcohol

the best solution. By 1917 they had enlisted support from notables such as Supreme Court Justice Louis D. Brandeis and former president William Howard Taft. In 1918 Congress passed the Eighteenth Amendment (ratified in 1919 and implemented in 1920) outlawing the manufacture, sale, and transportation of intoxicating liquors. Not all prohibitionists were Progressive reformers, and not all Progressives were prohibitionists. Nevertheless, the Eighteenth Amendment can be seen as an expression of the Progressive goal to protect family and workplace through reform legislation.

Moral outrage erupted also when muckraking journalists charged that international gangs were kidnapping young women and forcing them into prostitution, a practice called white slavery. The charges were

In addition to crusading against drunkenness, moral reformers stirred up emotions over accusations that evil men were seducing innocent young women into prostitution—or white slavery, as it was called. In this posed photograph printed in a 1910 antivice publication, *The White Slave Hell: or, With Christ at Midnight in the Slums of Chicago,* the man supposedly has gotten the woman drunk and is about to lure her into a life of sin. (Collection of Perry R. Duis, from *The Saloon*)

Prostitution and White Slavery

more imagined than real, but they alarmed some moralists who falsely perceived a link between immigration and prostitution and feared that prostitutes were producing genetically inferior children. Nevertheless, those fearful about the social consequences of prostitution prodded governments to investigate the problem and pass corrective legislation. The Chicago Vice Commission, for example, undertook a "scientific" survey and published its findings, titled *The Social Evil in Chicago*, in 1911. The report underscored the poverty, ignorance, and desperation that drove women into prostitution.

Such investigations found rising numbers of prostitutes but failed to prove that criminal organizations deliberately lured women onto the streets. Reformers nonetheless believed they could attack prostitution by punishing those who promoted it. In 1910 Congress passed the White Slave Traffic Act, known as the Mann Act, prohibiting interstate and international transportation of a woman for immoral purposes. By 1915 nearly every state had outlawed brothels and solicitation of sex. Such laws ostensibly protected young women from exploitation, but in reality they failed to address the more serious problem of sexual violence that women suffered at the hands of family members and presumed friends and at the workplace.

Like prohibition, the Mann Act reflected growing sentiment that government could improve behavior by restricting it. Reformers believed that the source of evil was not original sin or human nature but the social environment. And if evil was created by human will, it followed that it could be eradicated by human effort. Intervention in the form of laws could help create a heaven on earth.

New Ideas in Education, Law, Religion, and the Sciences

In addition to legislative paths, reform impulses opened new vistas in ideas. Preoccupation with efficiency and scientific management infiltrated the realms of education, law, religion, and science. Darwin's theory of evolution had challenged traditional beliefs in a God-created world; immigration had created confusing social diversity; and technology had made old habits of production and consumption obsolete. Thoughtful people in a number of professions grappled with how to respond to the new era yet preserve what was best from the past.

In education, changing patterns of school attendance required new ways of thinking. As late as 1870, when families needed children at home to do farm work, Americans attended school for an average of only four years. By 1900, however, cities contained multitudes of children who had more time for school. Compulsory-attendance laws required children to be in school to age fourteen, and swelling populations of immigrant and migrant children jammed schoolrooms. Meanwhile, the number of public high schools grew from five hundred in 1870 to ten thousand in 1910. Before the Civil War, curricula had consisted chiefly of moralistic pieties from *McGuffey's Reader*. But in the late nineteenth century, psychologist G. Stanley Hall and philosopher John Dewey asserted that modern education ought to prepare children differently. They insisted that personal development, not subject matter, should be the focus of the curriculum. Education, argued Dewey, must relate directly to experience; children should be encouraged to discover knowledge for themselves. Learning relevant to students' lives should replace rote memorization and outdated subjects.

John Dewey and Progressive Education

Progressive education, based on Dewey's *The School and Society* (1899) and *Democracy and Education* (1916), was a uniquely American phenomenon. Dewey believed that learning should focus on real-life problems and that children should be taught to use their intelligence and ingenuity as instruments for controlling their environments. From kindergarten through high school, Dewey asserted, children should learn through direct experience. Dewey and his wife, Alice, put these ideas into practice in their own Laboratory School located at the University of Chicago.

A more practical curriculum became the driving principle behind reform in higher education as well. Previously, the purpose of American colleges and universities had resembled that of European counterparts: to train a select few for careers in law, medicine, teaching, and religion. But in the late 1800s, institutions of higher learning multiplied, aided by land grants and an increase in the number of people who could afford tuition. Between 1870 and 1910 the number of colleges and universities in the United States grew from 563 to nearly 1,000. Curricula expanded as educators sought

Growth of Colleges and Universities

to make learning more appealing and to keep up with technological and social changes. Harvard University, under President Charles W. Eliot, pioneered in substituting electives for required courses and experimenting with new teaching methods. The University of Wisconsin and other public universities achieved distinction in new areas of study such as political science and sociology. Many schools, private and public, considered athletics vital to a student's growth, and intercollegiate sports became a permanent feature of student life as well as a source of school pride.

Southern states, in keeping with separate-but-equal policies, set up segregated land-grant colleges for blacks in addition to the public institutions for whites. Separate was a more accurate description of these institutions than equal. African Americans continued to suffer from inferior educational opportunities in both state institutions and private all-black colleges. Nevertheless, African American men and women found intellectual stimulation in all-black colleges and hoped to use their educations to promote better race relations.

As higher education expanded, so did female enrollments. Between 1890 and 1910 the number of women in colleges and universities swelled from 56,000 to 140,000. Of these, 106,000 attended coeducational institutions (mostly state universities); the rest attended women's colleges. By 1920, 283,000 women were attending college, accounting for 47 percent of total enrollment. But discrimination lingered in admissions and curriculum policies. Women were encouraged (indeed, they usually sought) to take home economics and education courses rather than science and mathematics, and most medical schools, including Harvard and Yale, refused to admit women. Barred from such institutions, women continued to attend their own schools, most of which were founded in the late nineteenth century, places such as Women's Medical College of Philadelphia and women's colleges such as Smith, Mount Holyoke, and Wellesley.

American educators adopted the prevailing attitude of business: more is better. They justifiably congratulated themselves for increasing enrollments and making instruction more meaningful. By 1920, 78 percent of children between ages five and seventeen were enrolled in public elementary and high schools; another 8 percent attended private and parochial schools. These figures represented a huge increase over 1870 attendance rates. And there were 600,000 college and graduate students in 1920, compared with only 52,000

Poised and proud, these members of the University of Michigan's Class of 1892 represent the student body of a publicly funded college in the late nineteenth century. With their varied curricula, inclusion of women, and increasing enrollments, such schools transformed American higher education in the Progressive era. (University of Michigan)

in 1870. Yet few people looked beyond the numbers to assess how well schools were doing their jobs. Critical analysis seldom tested the faith that schools could promote equality and justice as well as personal growth and responsible citizenship.

The legal profession also embraced new emphases on experience and scientific principles. Harvard law professor Roscoe Pound, an influential proponent of the new outlook, urged that social reality should influence legal thinking. Oliver Wendell Holmes, Jr., associate justice of the Supreme Court between 1902 and 1932, led the attack on the traditional view of law as universal and unchanging. "The life of the law," said Holmes, sounding like Dewey, "has not been logic; it has been experience." The opinion that law should reflect society's needs challenged the practice of invoking inflexible legal precedents that often obstructed social legislation. Louis D. Brandeis, a lawyer who later joined Holmes on the Supreme Court, insisted that judges' opinions

Progressive Legal Thought

be based on factual, scientifically gathered information about social realities. Using the Progressive approach to problems, Brandeis collected extensive data on the harmful effects of long hours to convince the Supreme Court, in *Muller v. Oregon* (1908), to uphold Oregon's law limiting women's working hours.

The new legal thinking met with some resistance. Judges raised on laissez-faire economics and strict construction of the Constitution continued to overturn laws Progressives thought necessary for effective reform. Thus despite Holmes's forceful dissent, in 1905 the Supreme Court, in *Lochner v. New York*, revoked a New York law limiting bakers' working hours. As in similar cases, the Court's majority argued that the Fourteenth Amendment protected an individual's right to make contracts without government interference and that this protection superseded police power. Judges weakened other federal regulations by invoking the Tenth Amendment, which prohibited the federal government from interfering in matters reserved to the states.

Courts did uphold some regulatory measures, particularly those protecting public safety. A string of decisions beginning with *Holden v. Hardy* (1898), in which the Supreme Court sustained Utah's mining regulations, confirmed the use of state police power to protect health, safety, and morals. Judges also affirmed federal police power and Congress's authority over interstate commerce by supporting federal legislation such as the Pure Food and Drug Act, the Meat Inspection Law (see page 598), and the Mann Act. In these instances citizens' welfare took precedence over the Tenth Amendment.

But the concept of general welfare often conflicted with the concept of equal rights when the will of local majorities was imposed on minorities. Even if one agreed that laws should address society's needs, whose needs should prevail? The United States was a mixed nation; gender, race, religion, and ethnicity deeply influenced law. In many localities a native-born Protestant majority imposed Bible reading in public schools (offending Catholics and Jews), required businesses to close on Sundays, limited women's rights, restricted religious practices of Mormons and other groups, prohibited interracial marriage, and enforced racial segregation. Justice Holmes asserted that laws should be made for "people of fundamentally differing views," but were such laws possible in a nation of so many different interest groups? The debate continues to this day.

At the same time, social science—the study of society and its institutions—experienced changes similar to those engulfing law and education.

Social Science   In economics a group of young scholars used statistics to argue that laws governing economic relationships were not timeless. Instead, they claimed, theory should reflect prevailing social conditions. Richard T. Ely of Johns Hopkins University and the University of Wisconsin, reflecting this point of view, argued that poverty and impersonality resulting from industrialization required intervention by "the united efforts of Church, state, and science." A new breed of sociologists led by Lester Ward, Albion Small, and Edward A. Ross agreed, adding that citizens should actively plan to cure social ills rather than passively waiting for problems to solve themselves. In the field of psychology, female researchers challenged age-old beliefs that women's minds were different from, and inferior to, men's.

Meanwhile, Progressive historians Frederick Jackson Turner, Charles A. Beard, and Vernon L. Parring-

ton examined the past to explain present American society. Beard, like other Progressives, believed that the Constitution was a flexible document amenable to growth and change, not an inviolable code imposed by wise forefathers. His influential *Economic Interpretation of the Constitution* (1913) argued that a group of merchants and business-oriented lawyers created the Constitution to defend private property. If the Constitution had served special interests in one age, it could be changed to serve broader interests in another age. Meanwhile, political scientists like Woodrow Wilson emphasized the practical over the theoretical, advocating expansion of government power to ensure justice and progress.

In public health, organizations like the National Consumers League (NCL) joined physicians and social scientists to bring about some of the most far-reaching Progressive reforms. Founded by Florence Kelley in 1899, NCL activities included women's suffrage, protection of female and child laborers, and elimination of potential health hazards. After aiding in the success of *Muller v. Oregon* in 1908, the organization became active in sponsoring court cases on behalf of women workers and worked with reform lawyers Louis Brandeis and Felix Frankfurter in support of these cases. Local branches united with women's clubs to advance consumer protection measures such as the licensing of food vendors and inspection of dairies. They also urged city governments to fund neighborhood clinics that provided health education and medical care to the poor.

Much of Progressive reform rested on religious underpinnings. The distresses of modern society especially sparked new thoughts about fortifying social relations with moral principles. Particularly, a movement known as the Social Gospel, led by Protestant ministers Walter Rauschenbusch, Washington Gladden, and Charles Sheldon, would counter the brutality of competitive capitalism by interjecting Christian churches into practical, worldly matters such as arbitrating industrial harmony and improving the environment of the poor. Believing that service to fellow humans provided the way both to securing individual salvation and to creating God's kingdom on earth, Social Gospelers actively participated in social reform and governed their lives by asking, "What would Jesus do?"

The Social Gospel served as a reform response to Social Darwinism, the application of biological natural selection and survival of the fittest to human interac-

Eugenics

tions (see page 513). But another movement that flourished during the Progressive era, eugenics, sought to apply Darwinian principles to society in a more scientific way. The brainchild of Francis Galton, an English statistician and cousin of Charles Darwin, eugenics rested on the belief that human character and habits could be inherited. If good traits could be inherited so could bad traits, such as criminality, insanity, and feeblemindedness. Just as some Progressives believed that in order to create a better world, society had an obligation to intervene and erase poverty and injustice, eugenicists believed society had an obligation to prevent the reproduction of the mentally defective, the criminally inclined, and people generally deemed to be inferior. Inevitably such focus landed on immigrants and people of color.

There were two basic means by which followers of eugenics would eliminate people whose offspring might threaten American progress. One was to sterilize those identified as unfit to reproduce. Beginning around the turn of the century, several state legislatures began considering laws to legalize the sterilization (mostly involving vasectomies) of certain criminal and insane men. In 1907 Indiana enacted the country's first law permitting the involuntary sterilization of "confirmed criminals, idiots, imbeciles, and rapists" when a committee of experts considered such action advisable. By 1915 thirteen states had such laws, and by 1930 the number had reached thirty. The other method of protecting American society from reproduction by inferior people involved restricting immigration. Though not strictly a work of eugenics, the book *The Passing of the Great Race* (1916) by Madison Grant strongly bolstered theories that immigrants from southern and eastern Europe were threatening to weaken American society because they were inferior mentally and morally to earlier Nordic immigrants. Thus, many people, including some Progressives, concluded, new immigration laws should curtail the influx of Poles, Italians, Jews, and other eastern and southern Europeans. Such efforts reached fruition in the 1920s when restrictive legislation, often backed by eugenics theories, drastically closed the door to "new" immigrants (see page 682). Not all support for sterilization and immigration restriction came from eugenicists, but in the Progressive era, eugenics arose as an invidious way of applying science to social organization.

Thus a new breed of men and women pressed for institutional change as well as political reform in the two decades before the First World War. Largely middle class, trained in new professional standards, confident that new ways of thinking could bring about progress, these people helped broaden government's role to meet the needs of a mature industrial society. But their questioning of prevailing assumptions also unsettled conventional attitudes toward race and gender.

Challenges to Racial and Sexual Discrimination

The Progressive era, dominated as it was by white reformers, often ignored issues directly affecting former slaves, nonwhite immigrants, Indians, and women. Yet activists among these groups caught the Progressive spirit and strove for change in this time of challenge to entrenched ideas and customs. Their efforts, however, posed a dilemma. Should women and nonwhites aim to become just like white men, with white men's values as well as their rights? Or was there something unique about racial and sexual cultures that they should preserve at the risk of sacrificing some gains? Both groups fluctuated between attraction to and rejection of the culture that excluded them.

In 1900 nine-tenths of African Americans lived in the South, where repressive Jim Crow laws had multiplied in the 1880s and 1890s (see page 562). Denied legal and voting rights and officially segregated in almost all walks of life, southern blacks faced constant exclusion. In 1910 only 8,000 out of 970,000 high school–age blacks in the entire South were enrolled in high schools. And blacks met with constant violence. Between 1900 and 1914 white mobs, usually incensed over rumored sexual assaults or insults by black men on white women, lynched over a thousand blacks.

Disadvantages of African Americans

African Americans began to move northward in the 1880s, accelerating their migration after 1900. The conditions they found represented a relative improvement over the rural sharecropping existence, but job discrimination, inferior schools, and segregated housing existed in northern as well as southern cities. White authorities perpetuated segregation by maintaining separate and inferior institutions, such as hospitals and schools, for blacks. A half-century after slavery's abolition, most whites still agreed with historian James Ford Rhodes, who wrote that blacks were "innately inferior and incapable of citizenship."

African American leaders differed sharply over how—and whether—to pursue assimilation. In the wake of emancipation, ex-slave Frederick Douglass urged "ultimate assimilation through self-assertion, and on no other terms." Others favored separation from white society and supported migration to Africa or the establishment of all-black communities in Oklahoma Territory and Kansas. Others, as bitter as white racists, advocated militancy, believing, as one writer stated, "Our people must die to be saved and in dying must take as many along with them as it is possible to do with the aid of firearms and all other weapons."

Most blacks, however, could neither escape nor conquer white society. They sought other routes to economic and social improvement.

Booker T. Washington and Self-Help

Self-help, a strategy articulated by educator Booker T. Washington, offered one popular alternative. Born to slave parents in 1856, Washington obtained an education and in 1881 founded Tuskegee Institute in Alabama, a vocational school for blacks. There he developed a philosophy that blacks' best hopes for assimilation lay in at least temporarily accommodating to whites. Rather than fighting for political rights, Washington said, blacks should work hard, acquire property, and prove they were worthy of respect. Washington voiced his views in a speech at the Atlanta Exposition in 1895. "Dignify and glorify common labor," he urged in what became known as the Atlanta Compromise. "Agitation of questions of racial equality is the extremest folly." Envisioning a society where blacks and whites would remain apart but share similar goals, Washington observed that "in all things that are purely social we can be as separate as the fingers, yet one as the hand in all matters essential to mutual progress."

Whites welcomed Washington's accommodation policy because it urged patience and reminded black people to stay in their place. Because he said what they wanted to hear, white businesspeople, reformers, and politicians chose to regard Washington as representative of all African Americans. Yet though Washington endorsed a separate-but-equal policy, he projected a subtle racial pride that would find more direct expression in black nationalism later in the twentieth century, when some African Americans advocated control

Booker T. Washington's Tuskegee Institute helped train young African Americans in useful crafts such as shoemaking and shoe repair, as illustrated here. At the same time, however, Washington's intentions and the Tuskegee curriculum reinforced what many whites wanted to believe: that blacks were unfit for anything except manual labor. (Tuskegee University Library)

of their own businesses and schools. Washington never argued that blacks were inferior to whites; he asserted that they could enhance their dignity through self-improvement.

Some blacks thought that Washington favored a degrading second-class citizenship. His southern-based philosophy did not appeal to educated northern African Americans, such as William Monroe Trotter, the fiery editor of the *Boston Guardian*, or social scientist T. Thomas Fortune. In 1905 a group of "anti-Bookerites" convened near Niagara Falls and pledged militant pursuit of rights such as unrestricted voting, economic opportunity, integration, and equality before the law. Spokesperson for the Niagara movement was W. E. B. Du Bois, an outspoken critic of the Atlanta Compromise.

A New Englander and the first black to receive a Ph.D. from Harvard, Du Bois was both a Progressive and a member of the black elite. He held an undergraduate degree from all-black Fisk University and had studied in Germany, where he learned about scientific investigation. While a faculty member at Atlanta University, Du Bois compiled fact-filled sociological studies of black ghetto dwellers and wrote poetically in support of civil rights. He treated Washington politely but could not accept white domination. "The way for a people to gain their reasonable rights," Du Bois asserted, "is not by voluntarily throwing them away." Instead, blacks must agitate for what was rightfully theirs.

W. E. B. Du Bois and the Niagara Movement

Dissatisfied with Washington's strategy, Du Bois in 1905 organized a conference of blacks who favored more active opposition to racism. Meeting at Niagara Falls, the group took the name Niagara Conference and began meeting annually. Then, in 1909, Du Bois joined with a group of white liberals who also were discontented with Washington's accommodationism to form the National Association for the Advancement of Colored People (NAACP), which aimed to end racial discrimination and obtain voting rights by pursuing legal redress in the courts. By 1914 the NAACP had fifty branch offices and six thousand members.

Whatever their views, African Americans faced continued oppression. Those who managed to acquire property and education encountered white resentment, especially when they fought for equality. Black editor and reformer Ida B. Wells, who wrote *On Lynching* (1892) in support of antilynching legislation, suffered destruction of her property and threats against her life. The federal government only aggravated biases. During Woodrow Wilson's presidency, southern cabinet members supported racial separation in restrooms, restaurants, and government office buildings and balked at hiring black workers. Commenting on Wilson's racism in 1913, Booker T. Washington wrote, "I have never seen the colored people so discouraged and so bitter as they are at the present time."

African Americans still sought to fulfill the dream of success, but many wondered whether their goals should include membership in a corrupt white society. Du Bois voiced these doubts poignantly, observing that "one ever feels his twoness—an American, a Negro, two souls, two thoughts, two unreconciled strivings, two warring ideals in one dark body." Somehow blacks had to reconcile that "twoness" by combining racial pride with national identity. As Du Bois wrote in 1903, a black "would not Africanize America, for America has too much to teach the world and Africa. He would not bleach his Negro soul in a flood of white Americanism, for he knows that Negro blood has a message for the world. He simply wishes to make it possible for a man to be both a Negro and an American." That simple wish would haunt the nation for decades to come.

The dilemma of identity bedeviled Native Americans as well, but it had an added tribal dimension. Since the 1880s, Native American reformers had belonged to white-led Indian organizations. In 1911 educated, middle-class Indians formed their own association, the Society of American Indians (SAI), to work for better education, civil rights, and healthcare. It also sponsored "American Indian Days" to cultivate pride and offset images of savage peoples promulgated in Wild West shows.

Society of American Indians

The SAI's emphasis on racial pride, however, was squeezed between pressures for assimilation from one side and tribal allegiance on the other. Its small membership did not genuinely represent the diverse and unconnected Indian nations, and its attempt to establish a governing body fizzled. Some tribal governments no longer existed to select representatives, and most SAI members simply promoted their own self-interest. At the same time, the goal of achieving acceptance in white society proved elusive. Individual hard work was not enough to overcome white prejudice and condescension, and attempts to redress grievances through legal action faltered for lack of funds. Ultimately, SAI had to rely on rhetoric and moral exhortation, which had little effect on poor and powerless Indians who seldom knew that SAI even existed. Torn by internal disputes, the association folded in the early 1920s.

The challenges to established social assumptions also raised questions of identity among women. The

"The Woman Movement"

ensuing quandaries resembled those faced by racial minorities: What tactics should women use to achieve equality? What should be their role in society? Novelist Henry James expressed the dilemma from a male point of view when he complained that women who wanted to become just like men were disregarding their own uniqueness. Or, as some women put it, could women achieve equality with men and at the same time change male-dominated society?

The answers that women found involved a subtle but important shift in women's politics. Before about 1910, crusaders for women's rights referred to themselves as "the woman movement." This label applied to middle-class women striving to move beyond the household into social welfare activities, higher education, and paid labor. Like some African American and Indian leaders, women argued that legal and voting rights were indispensable to such moves. These women's rights advocates based their claims on the theory that women's special, even superior, traits as guardians of family and morality would humanize all of society. Settlement-house founder Jane Addams, for example, endorsed women's suffrage by asking, "If women have in any sense been responsible for the gentler side of life which softens and blurs some of its harsher conditions, may not they have a duty to perform in our American cities?"

Women's clubs represented a unique dimension of the woman movement. Originating as middle-class lit-

Women's Clubs

erary and educational organizations, women's clubs began taking stands on public affairs in the late nineteenth century. Because female activists were excluded from holding office, they were drawn less to government reform than to social betterment, an enterprise called social housekeeping. Rather than pressing for reforms such as trustbusting and direct primaries, these women worked for factory inspection, regulation of children's and women's labor, housing improvement, upgrading of education, and consumer protection.

Such efforts were not confined to white women. African American women had their own club move-

The rise of the settlement house movement and of the Visiting Nurse Association provided young middle-class women with opportunities to aid inner-city working-class neighborhoods and formed the basis of the social work profession. Here a group of visiting nurses prepare to apply their medical training to the disadvantaged.   (Corbis-Bettmann)

ment, including the Colored Women's Federation, which sought to establish a training school for "colored girls." Founded in 1895, the National Association of Colored Women was the nation's first African American social service organization; it concentrated on establishing nurseries, kindergartens, and retirement homes. Black women also developed their own reform organizations within Black Baptist and African Methodist Episcopal churches.

Around 1910 some of those concerned with women's place in society began using a new term, *feminism*, to refer to their ideas. Whereas

Feminism

the woman movement spoke generally of duty and moral purity, feminists—more explicitly conscious of

How do historians know...

that settlement houses structured their activities to satisfy middle-class objectives? Settlement houses were among the most influential agents of social reform during the Progressive era, attracting scores of young workers eager to help reform inner-city neighborhoods and residents. This document presents an actual listing of one week's activities at the Chicago Commons Settlement House in 1896. There are at least three ways to interpret these activities. First is the nature of the activities themselves: a blend of practical (savings bank, cooking, manual training) with intellectual (Shakespeare, French, elocution). Settlement workers were highly educated and believed that the people they served needed exposure to culture as well as life skills. Second is the age factor: note that the majority of entries are for children. As realists, settlement workers believed they had a greater chance of reaching the minds and hearts of the younger generation than the more suspicious parents. Third is the gender factor: though the settlement staff has scheduled a few activities for males, the selections are exclusively for boys, not adult men.

Moreover, the numerous activities for females reinforce prevailing stereotypes of women's role as housekeeper—though the daily kindergarten existed as a form of childcare for working mothers of young children. Even though many of the settlement workers were women, they still believed in maintaining women's traditional roles. (Photo: Library of Congress)

SCHEDULE OF OCCASIONS

LIST OF MEETINGS, CLASSES, CLUBS AND OTHER APPOINTMENTS OF THE WEEK AT CHICAGO COMMONS AND THE TABERNACLE DURING THE PAST WINTER.

AT THE COMMONS,
140 NORTH UNION STREET.

DAILY
All Day—House open for neighbors and friends.
9:00–12:00 a. m.—Free Kindergarten (except Saturday and Sunday). Mrs. Bertha Hofer Hegner, head kindergartner; Miss Alice B. Coggswell, assistant.
2:00–5:00 p. m.—Kindergarten Training Classes.
7:00 p. m.—Family Vespers (except Saturday).

SUNDAY
3:30 p. m.—Pleasant Sunday Afternoon.

MONDAY
4:00 p. m.—Manual Training (Girls.) Mr. N. H. Weeks.
7:30 p. m.—Penny Provident Bank.
8:00 p. m.—Girls' Clubs. Misses Coggswell, Taylor and Purnell.
Cooking Class (Girls). Miss Manning.
Girls' Progressive Club (Young Women). Classes in Art, Miss Cushman; Embroidery, Mrs. Gavit; Greek Mythology, Mrs. Follett; English History and Constitution, Miss Allen.
Shakespere Class. Mr. Gavit.

TUESDAY
2:00 p. m.—Woman's Club.
4:00 p. m.—Cooking Class (Girls). Miss Cookinham.
Manual Training. Mr. Weeks.
7:30 p. m.—Boys' Club. Mr. Weeks, Misses Alexander and Holdridge.
French. Miss Sayer.
Rhetoric. Mr. Wyatt.
Stenography. Mr. Fisher.
Cooking Class (Girls). Miss Thayer.
8:00 p. m.—Choral Club. Miss Hofer and Mr. C. E. Weeks.
8:15 p. m.—"The Tuesday Meeting," for Economic Discussion.

WEDNESDAY
4:00 p. m.—Kindergarten Clubs (children). Miss Purnell and Abbott.
Dressmaking Class (Girls). Miss Temple.
Piano. Miss Gavit.
7:00 p. m.—Piano. Miss Bemiss.
7:30 p. m.—Penny Provident Bank.
Girls' Clubs. Misses Coggswell, Gavit, Bosworth, Bemiss, Etheridge.
Boys' Club. Mr. Grant.
Cooking Class (Young Women). Miss Temple.

THURSDAY
4:00 p. m—Cooking Class (for Women). Miss Temple.
Elocution. Miss Ellis.
Manual Training (Girls). Mr. Weeks.
7:30 p. m.—Girls' Club. Miss Chandler.
Good Will ("Blue Ticket") Club. Mr. Weeks.
Elocution. Miss Ellis.
Grammar. Mr. Carr.
Cooking (for Girls). Miss Manning.
Mothers' Club (Fortnightly).
Seventeenth Ward Municipal Club (Monthly).

FRIDAY
4:00 p. m.—Manual Training (Boys'). Mr. Weeks.
7:30 p. m.—Penny Provident Bank.
Cooking Class (Girls). Miss Manning.
Boys' Clubs. Messrs. Burt, Carr, Crocker, Young, C. E. Weeks, N. H. Weeks.
Dressmaking. Mrs. Strawbridge.

SATURDAY
10:00 a. m.—Manual Training (Boys). Mr. Weeks.
2:00 p. m.—Manual Training (Boys). Mr. Weeks.
3:00 p. m.—Piano Lessons. Miss Bemiss.
6:30 p. m.—Residents' Meeting (for residents only).

Other Appointments, for Clubs, Study Classes, Social Gatherings, etc., are made from time to time and for special occasions.

their identity as women—emphasized rights and self-development. Feminism, however, contained an inherent contradiction. On one hand feminists argued that all women should unite in the struggle for rights because of their shared disadvantages as women. On the other, feminists insisted that sex-typing—treating women differently than men—must end because it resulted in discrimination. Thus feminists advocated the contradictory position that women should unite as a gender group for the purpose of abolishing all gender-based distinctions.

Feminism focused primarily on economic and sexual independence. Charlotte Perkins Gilman articulated feminist goals in *Women and Economics* (1898),

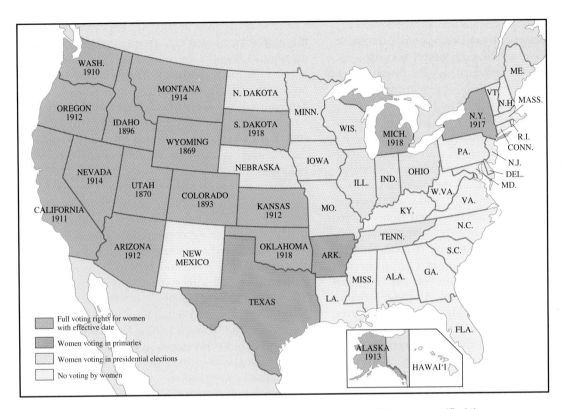

Map 21.1   Woman Suffrage Before 1920   Before Congress passed and the states ratified the Nineteenth Amendment, woman suffrage already existed, but mainly in the West. Several mid-western states allowed women to vote only in presidential elections, but legislatures in the South and Northeast generally refused such rights until forced to do so by constitutional amendment.

declaring that domesticity and female innocence were obsolete and attacking the male monopoly on economic opportunity. Gilman argued that modern women must take jobs in industry and the professions and that paid employees should handle domestic chores such as cooking, cleaning, and childcare.

Feminists also supported "sex rights"—a single standard of behavior for men and women—and several feminists joined the birth-control movement led by Margaret Sanger. As a visiting nurse in New York City's immigrant neighborhoods, Sanger attracted support from the Socialist Party in distributing information about contraception to help poor women prevent unwanted pregnancies. Though Sanger later gained acceptance among middle-class women, her actions initially aroused opposition from those who saw birth control as a threat to family and morality. In 1914 Sanger's opponents caused her to be indicted for defying an

Margaret Sanger's Crusade

1873 law that prohibited the sending of obscene literature (articles on contraception) through the mails, and she fled the country for a year. Sanger persevered and in 1921 formed the American Birth Control League, enlisting physicians and social workers to convince judges to allow distribution of birth-control information. Most states still prohibited the sale of contraceptives, but Sanger succeeded in introducing the issue into public debate and the American Birth Control League became Planned Parenthood, an organization currently at the forefront of birth-control issues.

During the Progressive era, a generation of feminists, represented by Harriot Stanton Blatch, who was the daughter of nineteenth-century suffragist Elizabeth Cady Stanton, carried on women's battle for the vote (see Map 21.1). Blatch made the improvement of working conditions for women a primary goal and agreed with those who saw the vote as the means by which women could effect

Woman Suffrage

such improvement. Declaring that all women worked, whether they performed paid labor or unpaid housework, Blatch believed that all women's efforts contributed to society's betterment. In Blatch's view, achievement rather than wealth and refinement was the best criterion for public influence. Thus women should exercise the vote not to enhance the power of elites but to promote and protect women's economic roles.

Despite internal differences, suffragists united behind their single goal and achieved some successes. Nine states, all in the West, allowed women to vote in state and local elections by 1912, and women continued to press for national suffrage. Their tactics ranged from moderate but persistent letter-writing and publications of the National American Woman Suffrage Association, led by Carrie Chapman Catt, to spirited meetings and militant marches of the National Woman's Party, led by Alice Paul. All these activities heightened public awareness. More decisive, however, were women's performances during the First World War as factory laborers, medical volunteers, and municipal workers (see pages 649–650). By convincing legislators that women could shoulder public responsibilities, women's wartime contributions gave final impetus to passage of the national suffrage amendment in 1920 (see Map 21.1).

The activities of women's clubs, feminists, and suffragists failed to create an interest group united or powerful enough to overcome men's political, economic, and social control. Like blacks, women knew that voting rights would mean little until society's attitudes changed. The Progressive era helped women to clarify issues that concerned them, but major reforms were not achieved until a later era. As feminist Crystal Eastman, echoing W. E. B. Du Bois, observed in the aftermath of the suffrage crusade: "Men are saying perhaps, 'Thank God, this everlasting women's fight is over!' But women, if I know them, are saying, 'Now at last we can begin.' . . . Now they can say what they are really after, in common with all the rest of the struggling world, is freedom."

Theodore Roosevelt and the Revival of the Presidency

 The Progressive era's theme of reform—in politics, institutions, and social relations—drew attention to government, especially the federal government, as the foremost agent of change. Though the federal government had made some notable accomplishments during the preceding Gilded Age (see Chapter 20), its role mainly had been to support rather than control economic expansion, as when it transferred western public lands and resources to private ownership. Then, in September 1901, the political climate suddenly shifted. The assassination of President William McKinley by anarchist Leon Czolgosz vaulted Theodore Roosevelt, the vigorous young vice president, into the White House.

Political manager Mark Hanna had warned fellow Republicans against running Roosevelt for vice president in 1900. "Don't any of you realize," Hanna asked after the nominating convention, "that there's only one life between that madman and the presidency?" As governor of New York, Roosevelt had angered Republican bosses by showing sympathy for regulatory legislation, so they rid themselves of their pariah by pushing him into national politics. Little did they anticipate that they were providing the steppingstone for the nation's most forceful president since Lincoln and a president who bestowed the office with much of its twentieth-century character.

As a youth Roosevelt had suffered from asthma and near-sightedness. He was driven throughout his

Theodore Roosevelt

life by an obsession to overcome his physical limitations and exert what he and his contemporaries called "manliness," meaning a zest for physical exertion and display of courage. In his teens he became an expert marksman and horseman and later competed on Harvard's boxing and wrestling teams. In the 1880s he went to live on a Dakota ranch, where he roped cattle and brawled with cowboys. Descended from a Dutch aristocratic family, Roosevelt had wealth to indulge in such pursuits. But he also inherited a sense of civic responsibility that guided him into a career in public service. He served three terms in the New York State Assembly, ran for mayor of New York City in 1886 (finishing third), sat on the federal Civil Service Commission, served as New York City's police commissioner, and was assistant secretary of the navy. In these offices Roosevelt earned a reputation as a combative, politically crafty leader. He also distinguished himself as a historian, writing *The Naval War of 1812* (1882) and *The Winning of the West* (1889). In 1898 Roosevelt thrust himself into the Spanish-American-Cuban-Filipino War by organizing a volunteer cavalry brigade, called the Rough Riders, to fight in Cuba (see page 622). Though his dramatic act had little impact on the war's outcome, it

Theodore Roosevelt (1858–1919) liked to think of himself as a great outdoorsman. He loved most the rugged countryside and believed that he and his country should serve as examples of "manliness." (California Museum of Photography, University of California)

excited the public's imagination. A publicity hound who craved the center of attention, Roosevelt returned a media hero.

As president, Roosevelt concurred with Progressives that a small, uninvolved government would not suffice in the industrial era. Instead, economic development necessitated a government powerful enough to guide national affairs broadly. "A simple and poor society," he observed, "can exist as a democracy on the basis of sheer individualism. But a rich and complex society cannot so exist." Especially in economic matters, he wanted the government to act as an umpire, deciding when big business was good and when it was bad. But his brash patriotism and dislike of weakness and indecisiveness, qualities he considered effeminate, also recalled earlier eras of unbridled expansion when raw power prevailed in social and economic affairs.

The federal regulation of the economy that characterized twentieth-century American history began with Roosevelt's presidency. Roosevelt turned his attention first to big business, where consolidation had

Regulation of Trusts

created massive, monopolistic trusts. Although Roosevelt was labeled a "trustbuster," he actually considered consolidation the most efficient means to achieve material progress. He believed in distinguishing between good and bad trusts and preventing bad ones from manipulating markets. Thus he instructed the Justice Department to use antitrust laws to prosecute railroad, meatpacking, and oil trusts, which he believed were unscrupulously exploiting the public. Roosevelt's policy triumphed in 1904 when the Supreme Court, convinced by the government's arguments, ordered the breakup of Northern Securities Company, the huge railroad combination created by J. P. Morgan and his business allies (*Northern Securities* case). Roosevelt chose, however, not to attack other gigantic trusts, such as U.S. Steel, another of Morgan's creations.

When prosecution of Northern Securities began, Morgan reportedly collared Roosevelt and offered, "If we have done anything wrong, send your man to my man and they can fix it up." The president refused but was more sympathetic to cooperation between business and government than his rebuff might suggest. Rather than prosecute at every turn, he urged the Bureau of Corporations (part of the newly created Department of Labor and Commerce) to assist companies on mergers and other forms of expansion. Through investigation and cooperation, the administration cajoled businesses to regulate themselves; corporations often accepted regulation because it helped them operate more efficiently and reduced overproduction.

Roosevelt also supported regulatory legislation, especially after his resounding electoral victory in 1904, in which he won votes from Progressives and businesspeople alike. After a year of wrangling, Roosevelt persuaded Congress to pass the Hepburn Act (1906), which gave the Interstate Commerce Commission (ICC) more authority to set railroad freight and storage rates, though it did allow the courts to overturn rate decisions. Progressive senator Robert La Follette complained that Roosevelt had compromised with congressional business allies to ensure the bill's passage. But Roosevelt chose to reaffirm the principle of regulation rather than risk defeat over unreachable, idealistic objectives.

Roosevelt showed similar willingness to compromise on legislation to ensure the purity of food and

Pure Food and Drug Laws

drugs. For decades reformers had been urging government regulation of processed meat and patent medicines. Public outrage at fraud and adulteration was heightened in 1906 when Upton Sinclair published *The Jungle*, a fictionalized exposé of Chicago meatpacking plants. Sinclair, a socialist whose prime objective was to improve working conditions, shocked public sensibilities with his vivid descriptions:

> There would be meat stored in great piles in rooms; and the water from the leaky roofs would drip over it, and thousands of rats would race about on it. It was too dark in these storage places to see well, but a man could run his hand over these piles of meat and sweep off handfulls of dried dung of rats. These rats were a nuisance, and the packers would put poisoned bread out for them; they would die, and then rats, bread, and meat would go into the hoppers together.

After reading the novel, Roosevelt ordered an investigation. Finding Sinclair's descriptions accurate,

he supported the Meat Inspection Act, which passed in 1906. Like the Hepburn Act, this law reinforced the principle of government regulation, requiring that government agents monitor the quality of processed meat. But as part of a compromise to pass the bill, the government, rather than the meatpackers, had to finance inspections, and meatpackers could appeal adverse decisions in court. Nor were companies required to provide date-of-processing information on canned meats. Most large meatpackers welcomed the legislation anyway, because it helped them force out smaller competitors and restored falling confidence in American meat products in foreign markets.

The Pure Food and Drug Act (1906) not only prohibited dangerously adulterated foods but also addressed abuses in the patent medicine industry. Makers of tonics and pills had long been making undue claims about their products' effects and liberally using alcohol and narcotics as ingredients. Ads in popular publications, such as one for a "Brain Stimulator and Nerve Tonic" in the Sears, Roebuck catalogue, had wildly exaggerated claims. Although the law did not ban such products, it did require that labels list the ingredients—a goal consistent with Progressive confidence that if people knew the truth they would make wiser purchases.

Roosevelt's approach to labor resembled his stance toward business. When the United Mine Workers struck against Pennsylvania coal mine owners in 1902 over an eight-hour workday and higher pay, the president employed Progressive tactics of investigation and arbitration. Owners, however, stubbornly refused to recognize the union or arbitrate grievances. As winter approached and fuel shortages threatened, Roosevelt roused public opinion. He threatened to use federal troops to reopen the mines, thus forcing management to accept arbitration of the dispute by a special commission. The commission decided in favor of higher wages and reduced hours and required management to deal with grievance committees elected by the miners, but it did not mandate recognition of the union. The decision, according to Roosevelt, provided a "square deal" for all. The settlement also embodied Roosevelt's belief that the president or his representatives should have a say in which labor demands were legitimate and which were not. In Roosevelt's mind there were good and bad labor organizations (socialists, for example, were bad), just as there were good and bad business combinations.

Makers of unregulated patent medicines advertised exorbitant results from using their products. This ad, while warning against "fraudulent claims," asserts that a wide belt can cure a variety of ailments. The Pure Food and Drug Act of 1906 did not ban such products but tried to prevent manufacturers from making such unsubstantiated statements. (Picture Research Consultants & Archives)

Roosevelt did not originate government involvement in modern resource conservation; important developments in this area, especially the establishment of national parks, had begun in the late nineteenth century (see pages 472–473). But he did combine the Progressive impulse for efficiency with his love for the great outdoors to advance conservation policy. Roosevelt warned Congress in 1907, "We are prone to think of the resources of this country as inexhaustible; this is not so." In this regard, he drastically revised federal policy toward the nation's resources, particularly in the West. Previously, the government had habitually transferred ownership and control of natural resources on federal land to the states and to private interests. Roosevelt, however, believed the most efficient way to use and conserve these resources would be for the government to retain public management over those lands that remained in the public domain.

Conservation

Roosevelt took steps to exert federal power over resources in several ways. He tried, though unsuccessfully, to revise an 1873 law under which the government sold western coal and oil lands at very cheap prices to private concerns. Roosevelt wanted to retain government ownership and charge producers lease fees (such a policy was instituted in 1920). He did succeed in protecting waterpower sites from sale and instead charged permit fees for users who wanted to produce hydroelectricity. He also supported the Newlands Reclamation Act of 1902, which controlled sale of irrigated federal land in the West (see page 475). He tripled the number and acreage of national forests and supported conservationist Gifford Pinchot in creating the U.S. Forest Service.

As chief forester, Pinchot advocated scientific management of the nation's woodlands to protect the land and water from overuse by timber cutters, farmers, and herders. Pinchot had management of the national forests transferred from the Interior Department to his bureau in the Agriculture Department by arguing that forests were crops grown on "tree farms." Under his guidance, the Forest Service charged fees for grazing livestock within the national forests, supervised bidding for the cutting of timber, and hired university-trained foresters as federal employees.

Gifford Pinchot

As historian Richard White has pointed out, Pinchot and Roosevelt did not seek to lock up resources permanently; rather they wanted to guarantee their efficient use. Although antifederal, anticonservation attitudes remained in the West, many of those involved in natural-resource exploitation welcomed such a policy because, like regulation of food and drugs, it enabled them to minimize overproduction and to restrict competition. They simply had to try to influence federal bureaucracies and Congress to act in their behalf while at the same time denouncing federal interference. As a result of new federal policies, the West and its resources fell under the Progressive spell of management.

In 1907 Roosevelt had to compromise his principles in the face of economic crisis. That year a financial panic caused by reckless speculation forced some New York banks to close to prevent frightened depositors from withdrawing money.

Panic of 1907

J. P. Morgan helped stem the panic by persuading financiers to stop dumping their stocks. In return for Morgan's aid, Roosevelt approved a deal allowing U.S. Steel to absorb the Tennessee Iron and Coal Company—a deal at odds with Roosevelt's trustbusting aims.

During his last year in office, Roosevelt retreated from the Republican Party's traditional friendliness to big business. He lashed out at the irresponsibility of "malefactors of great wealth" and supported stronger business regulation and heavier taxation of the rich. Having promised that he would not seek reelection, Roosevelt backed his friend Secretary of War William Howard Taft for the Republican nomination in 1908, hoping that Taft would continue his initiatives. Democrats nominated William Jennings Bryan for the third time, but the "Great Commoner" lost again. Aided by Roosevelt, who still enjoyed great popularity, Taft won by 1.25 million popular votes and a 2-to-1 margin in the electoral college.

Early in 1909 Roosevelt traveled to Africa to shoot game (his passion for the manly activity of hunting outweighed his support for conservation), leaving Taft to face political problems that his predecessor had managed to postpone. Foremost among them was the tariff; rates had risen to excessive levels. Honoring Taft's pledge to cut rates, the House passed a bill sponsored by Representative Sereno E. Payne that provided for numerous reductions. Protectionists in the Senate prepared, as in the past, to amend the House bill and revise rates upward. But Senate Progressives, led by La Follette, organized a stinging attack on the tariff for benefiting special interests, trapping Taft between reformers who claimed to be preserving Roosevelt's antitrust campaign and protectionists who still dominated the Republican Party. In the end, Senator Aldrich and other protectionists restored many of the cuts the Payne bill had made, and Taft—who believed the bill had some positive provisions and understood that more extreme cuts were not politically possible—signed what became known as the Payne-Aldrich Tariff (1909). In the eyes of Progressives, Taft had failed the test of filling Roosevelt's shoes.

Taft Administration

Progressive and conservative wings of the Republican Party were rapidly drifting apart. Soon after the tariff controversy, a group of insurgents in the House led by Nebraska's George Norris challenged Speaker "Uncle Joe" Cannon of Illinois, whose power over committee assignments and the scheduling of debates could make or break a piece of legislation. Taft first supported then abandoned the insurgents, who nevertheless managed to liberalize procedures by enlarging the influential Rules Committee and removing selection of its members from Cannon's control. In 1910 Taft also angered conservationists by firing Gifford Pinchot, who had protested Secretary of the Interior Richard A. Ballinger's plan to reduce federal supervision of western waterpower sites and his sale of coal lands in Alaska.

In reality Taft was as sympathetic to reform as Roosevelt was. He prosecuted more trusts than Roosevelt, expanded national forest reserves, signed the Mann-Elkins Act (1910), which bolstered the regulatory powers of the ICC, and supported labor reforms such as the eight-hour workday and mine safety legislation. The Sixteenth Amendment, which legalized the federal income tax, and the Seventeenth Amendment, which provided for direct election of U.S. senators, were initiated during Taft's presidency (and ratified in 1913). Like Roosevelt, Taft compromised with big business, but unlike Roosevelt he lacked the ability to manipulate the public with spirited rhetoric. Roosevelt had expanded presidential power and had infused the presidency with vitality. "I believe in a strong executive," he once asserted. "I believe in power." Taft, by contrast, believed in the strict restraint of law. He had been a successful lawyer and judge (and returned to the bench as chief justice of the United States between 1921 and 1930). His caution and unwillingness to offend disappointed those accustomed to Roosevelt's impetuosity.

In 1910, when Roosevelt returned from Africa boasting three thousand animal trophies, he found his party torn and tormented. Reformers, angered by Taft's apparent insensitivity to their causes, formed the National Progressive Republican League and rallied behind Robert La Follette for president in 1912, though many hoped Roosevelt would run. Another wing of the party remained loyal to Taft. Disappointed by Taft's performance (particularly his firing of Pinchot), Roosevelt began to speak out. He filled his speeches with references to "the welfare of the people" and stronger regulation of business. When La Follette became ill early in 1912, Roosevelt, proclaiming himself fit as a "bull moose," threw his hat into the ring for the Republican presidential nomination.

The Bull Moose Party

Taft's supporters controlled the Republican convention and nominated him for a second term. In protest, Roosevelt's supporters bolted the convention to form a third party—the Progressive, or Bull Moose, Party—and nominated the fifty-three-year-old former president. Meanwhile, Democrats took forty-six ballots to select their candidate, New Jersey's Progressive governor Woodrow Wilson. Socialists, by now an organized and growing party, again nominated Eugene V. Debs. The ensuing campaign exposed voters to the most thorough evaluation of the American system since 1896.

Woodrow Wilson and the Extension of Reform

In his acceptance speech before the Progressive Party, Theodore Roosevelt proclaimed, "We stand at Armageddon and we battle for the Lord." But on inauguration day in 1913, it was Woodrow Wilson who assumed command of the forces of good. "The Nation," he exhorted, "has been deeply stirred by a solemn passion. . . . The feelings with which we face this new age of right and opportunity sweep across our heartstrings like some air out of God's own presence, where justice and mercy are reconciled and the judge and the brother are one."

Election results illustrated the extent to which such moral pronouncements had swayed voter passions. Wilson won 42 percent of the popular vote. He was a minority president, though he did capture 435 out of 531 electoral votes (see Map 21.2). Roosevelt received

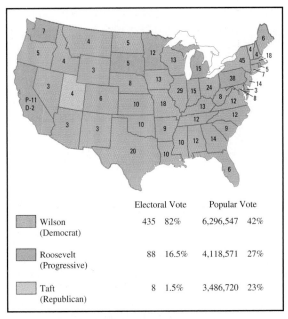

	Electoral Vote		Popular Vote	
Wilson (Democrat)	435	82%	6,296,547	42%
Roosevelt (Progressive)	88	16.5%	4,118,571	27%
Taft (Republican)	8	1.5%	3,486,720	23%

Map 21.2 Presidential Election, 1912 Though he won a minority of the popular votes, Woodrow Wilson captured so many states that he achieved an easy victory in the electoral college.

27 percent of the popular vote. Taft finished third, polling 23 percent of the popular vote and only 8 electoral votes. Debs won 901,000 votes, 6 percent of the total, but no electoral votes. Fully three-quarters of the electorate thus supported some alternative to the view of restrained government that Taft represented.

Sharp debate over Progressive fundamentals had characterized the campaign. Roosevelt offered voters the "New Nationalism," a term coined by reform editor Herbert Croly. Roosevelt foresaw an era of national unity in which government would coordinate and regulate economic activity. He would not destroy big business, which he viewed as an efficient organizer of production. Instead, he would establish regulatory commissions of experts who would protect citizens' interests and ensure wise use of economic power. "The effort at prohibiting all combinations has substantially failed," he claimed. "The way out lies . . . in completely controlling them."

New Nationalism and New Freedom

Wilson offered a more idealistic scheme, the "New Freedom," based on ideas of Progressive lawyer

Looking sober and stubborn, Woodrow Wilson (1856–1924) used a preacher's moralism and a professor's reasoning to raise expectations for the fulfillment of his idealistic promises.   (National Portrait Gallery, Smithsonian Institution/Art Resource, N.Y.)

Louis Brandeis. Wilson argued that concentrated economic power threatened individual liberty and that monopolies had to be broken up so the marketplace could become genuinely open. But he would not restore laissez faire. Like Roosevelt, Wilson would enhance government authority to protect and regulate. "Freedom today," he declared, "is something more than being let alone. Without the watchful . . . resolute interference of the government, there can be no fair play between individuals and such powerful institutions as the trust." Wilson stopped short, however, of advocating the cooperation between business and government inherent in Roosevelt's New Nationalism.

Roosevelt and Wilson stood closer together than their rhetoric implied. In spite of his faith in experts as regulators, Roosevelt harbored a belief in individual freedom as strong as Wilson's. And Wilson was not completely hostile to concentrated economic power.

Both men strongly supported equality of opportunity (chiefly for white males), conservation of natural resources, fair wages, and social betterment for all. Neither would hesitate to expand government activity through strong personal leadership and bureaucratic reform. Thus even though Wilson received a minority of the total vote in 1912, he could interpret the election results as a mandate to subdue trusts and broaden the federal government's role in social reform.

The public fondly called Roosevelt "Teddy" and "TR," but Thomas Woodrow Wilson was too aloof ever to be nicknamed "Woody" or "WW." Born in Virginia in 1856 and raised in the South, Wilson was the son of a Presbyterian minister. He earned a B.A. at Princeton University, studied law at the University of Virginia, received a Ph.D. from Johns Hopkins University, and became a professor of history, jurisprudence, and political economy. Between 1885 and 1908, he published several respected books on American history and government.

Woodrow Wilson

Wilson's manner and bearing reflected his background. He exuded none of Roosevelt's flamboyance, yet he was a charismatic leader. A superb orator, he could inspire intense loyalty with religious imagery and eloquent expressions of American ideals. Wilson's convictions led him early into reform. In 1902 he became president of Princeton, where he upset tradition with curricular reforms and battles against the university's aristocratic elements. In 1910 New Jersey's Democrats, eager for respectability, nominated Wilson for governor. After winning the election, Wilson repudiated the party bosses and promoted Progressive legislation. A poor administrator, he often lost his temper and stubbornly refused to compromise. His accomplishments nevertheless attracted national attention and won him the Democratic nomination for president in 1912.

As president, Wilson found it necessary to blend New Freedom competition with New Nationalism regulation; in so doing he set the direction of future federal economic policy. The corporate merger movement had proceeded so far that restoration of open competition proved impossible. Wilson could only try to prevent corporate abuses by expanding government's regulatory powers. His administration moved toward that end with passage in 1914 of the Clayton Anti-Trust Act and a bill creating the Federal Trade

Wilson's Policy on Business Regulation

Commission (FTC). The Clayton Act corrected deficiencies of the Sherman Anti-Trust Act of 1890 (see page 514) by outlawing monopolistic practices such as price discrimination (efforts to destroy competition by lowering prices in some regions but not in others) and interlocking directorates (management of two or more competing companies by the same executives). The FTC would investigate companies and issue cease-and-desist orders against unfair trade practices. Accused companies could appeal FTC orders in court; nevertheless, the FTC represented another step toward consumer protection.

Wilson expanded regulation of banking with the Federal Reserve Act (1913), which established the nation's first central banking system since 1836 when the Second Bank of the United States expired. The act was intended to break the power that powerful banking syndicates such as that of J. P. Morgan held over the money supply and credit. It created twelve district banks to hold reserves of member banks throughout the nation. The district banks, supervised by the Federal Reserve Board, would lend money to member banks at a low interest rate called the discount rate. By adjusting this rate (and thus the amount a bank could afford to borrow), district banks could increase or decrease the amount of money in circulation. In other words, in response to the nation's needs, the Federal Reserve Board could loosen or tighten credit. Monetary affairs no longer would depend on the gold supply, and interest rates would be fairer, especially for small borrowers.

Tariff and Tax Reform

Like his predecessors, Wilson attempted to restore competition in commerce with the Underwood Tariff, passed in 1913. By the 1910s, prices for some consumer goods had become unnaturally high because tariffs had discouraged the importation of cheaper foreign materials and manufactured goods. By reducing or eliminating certain tariff rates, the Underwood Tariff encouraged imports. To replace revenues lost because of tariff reductions, the act levied a graduated income tax on U.S. residents—an option made possible when the Sixteenth Amendment was ratified earlier that year. The income tax was tame by today's standards. Incomes under $4,000 were exempt; thus almost all factory workers and farmers escaped taxation. Individuals and corporations earning between $4,000 and $20,000 had to pay a 1 percent tax; thereafter rates rose gradually to a maximum of 6 percent on earnings over $500,000.

The outbreak of the First World War (see Chapter 23) and approaching presidential election campaign prompted Wilson to support stronger reforms in 1916. Concerned that farmers needed a better system of long-term mortgage credit, the president backed the Federal Farm Loan Act. This measure created twelve federally supported banks (not to be confused with the Federal Reserve banks) that would lend money at moderate interest to farmers who belonged to credit institutions—a watered-down version of the subtreasury plan that Populists had promoted a generation earlier (see page 566).

To forestall railroad strikes that might disrupt transportation at a time of national emergency, Wilson pushed passage of the Adamson Act, which mandated an eight-hour workday and time-and-a-half overtime pay for railroad laborers. He pleased Progressives by appointing Brandeis, the "people's advocate," to the Supreme Court, though an anti-Semitic backlash almost blocked Senate approval of the Court's first Jewish justice. Also, Wilson courted support from social reformers by backing laws that regulated child labor and provided workers' compensation for federal employees who suffered work-related injuries or illness.

Election of 1916

In selecting a candidate to oppose Wilson in 1916, Republicans snubbed Theodore Roosevelt in favor of Charles Evans Hughes, a Supreme Court justice and former reform governor of New York. Acutely aware of the First World War's impact on national affairs (Europe had been ablaze since 1914), Wilson ran for reelection on a platform of peace, Progressivism, and preparedness; his supporters used the campaign slogan "He Kept Us Out of War." Hughes and his fractured party could not muzzle Roosevelt, whose bellicose speeches suggested that Republicans would drag Americans into war. Wilson received 9.1 million votes to Hughes's 8.5 million, and the president barely won in the electoral college, 277 to 254. The Socialist candidate drew only 600,000 votes, down from 901,000 in 1912, largely because Wilson's reforms had won over some socialists and because the ailing Eugene Debs was no longer the party's standard-bearer.

During Wilson's second term, involvement in the First World War increased government regulation of the economy. In his first term Wilson had become convinced that regulatory commissions, which could easily fall under the influence of the very interests they were meant to regulate, should not govern social and economic behavior. Mobilization for the war effort, he came to believe, required coordination of production and cooperation between the public and private sectors. The War Industries Board (see pages 646–647) exemplified this cooperation: private businesses regulated by the board submitted to its control on condition that their own profit motives would continue to be satisfied. After the war the Wilson administration dropped most cooperative and regulatory measures, including farm price supports, guarantees of collective bargaining, and high taxes. This retreat from regulation, prompted in part by the election of a Republican Congress in 1918, stimulated a new era of business ascendancy in the 1920s.

Summary

By 1920 a quarter-century of reform had wrought momentous changes. Government, economy, and society as they had existed in the nineteenth century were gone forever. In their efforts to achieve their goals of ending abuses of power, reforming institutions, and applying scientific principles and efficient management, Progressives established the principle of public intervention to ensure fairness, health, and safety. Concern over poverty and injustice reached new heights. For every American who suffered some form of deprivation, three or four enjoyed unprecedented material comforts; and amid growing affluence, reformers could not sustain their efforts indefinitely. Although Progressive values lingered after the First World War, a mass consumer society began to refocus people's attention from reform to materialism.

The Progressive era was characterized by multiple and sometimes contradictory goals. By no means was there a single Progressive movement. Reform programs on the national level ranged from Roosevelt's faith in big government as a coordinator of big business to Wilson's promise to dissolve economic concentrations and legislate open competition. At state and local levels, reformers pursued causes as varied as neighborhood improvement, government reorganization, public ownership of utilities, betterment of working conditions, and control of morality. Local organizations and national associations coordinated efforts on specific issues, but reformers with different goals often worked at cross-purposes.

In spite of their remarkable successes, the outright failure of many Progressive initiatives indicates the strength of the opposition, as well as weaknesses within the reform movements themselves. Courts asserted constitutional and liberty-of-contract doctrines in striking down key Progressive legislation, notably the federal law prohibiting child labor. In states and cities, adoption of the initiative, referendum, and recall did not encourage greater participation in government as had been hoped; those mechanisms either were seldom used or became tools of special interests. On the federal level, regulatory agencies rarely had enough resources for thorough investigations; they had to depend on information from the very companies they policed. Progressives thus failed in many respects to redistribute power. In 1920 as in 1900, government remained under the influence of business and industry, a state of affairs that many people considered quite satisfactory.

Yet the reform movements that characterized the Progressive era reshaped the nation's future. Trust-busting, however faulty, forced industrialists to become more sensitive to public opinion, and insurgents in Congress partially diluted the power of dictatorial politicians. Progressive legislation equipped government with tools to protect consumers against price fixing and dangerous products. The income tax, created to redistribute wealth, also became a source of government revenue. Social reformers relieved some ills of urban life. And perhaps most important, Progressives challenged old ways of thinking. Although the questions they raised about the quality of American life remained unresolved, Progressives made the nation acutely aware of its principles and promises.

LEGACY FOR A PEOPLE AND A NATION
Women and Social Work

By the year 2000, human services—occupations catering to people's personal needs in the areas of health, education, housing, income, and justice and public safety—constituted the sixth-fastest-growing career field in the United States. Social workers dominated this profession, and over three-fourths of social workers were female, a legacy from the actions of concerned women during the Progressive era.

Jane Addams, the indomitable founder and leader of the Hull House settlement, laid the groundwork for the social work profession with her activities to understand and improve the lives of disadvantaged people. Almost all early social work pioneers who aided her were women, including Florence Kelley, Alice Hamilton, and Edith and Grace Abbott. These and other women used the field of social welfare to create occupations for other educated, ambitious, and service-minded women not only in social work but also in areas of child welfare, juvenile justice, and healthcare. Their early efforts focused on reforming existing institutions and lobbying for government aid and intervention, but by the end of the Progressive era social workers had made casework an important part of their professional activity. This shift reflected the particular interest and experience women had in attending to needs of individuals and families.

In 1898 formal organization of the profession began with the establishment of The New York School of Philanthropy, later named the Columbia University School of Social Work. Thereafter, programs for educating social workers appeared in other cities. Women continued to dominate the profession. Of 111 individuals listed as "social work pioneers" by the National Association of Social Workers over the past one hundred years, 77 are female. These leaders and the profession in general served critical functions in bringing public resources to people in need, especially during major periods of social action such as the New Deal of the 1930s, the Great Society of the 1960s, and today—especially in the area of assisting new immigrants.

Women's activities in social service have had drawbacks as well as successes. Throughout the twentieth century, men have held most of the top administrative positions in social work organizations and schools. Women in the profession still tend toward casework while men more frequently are involved in social welfare policymaking. And women social workers receive lower salaries than men and are less likely to be promoted. Moreover, psychological principles, which have become central to social work theory, carry a sexist tone in that they are likely to define "normal" social behavior in male-oriented terms, making it more likely for social workers to view female clients with social problems as having "abnormal" traits. Thus the pioneer efforts by women in social service dating from the Progressive era have still not erased gender-based biases in American culture.

For Further Reading, see page A-24 of the Appendix. For Web resources, go to http://college.hmco.com.

D evil!" they angrily shouted at Lottie Moon. "Foreign devil!" The Southern Baptist missionary braced herself against the antiforeign Chinese "rabble" she vowed to convert to Christianity. On a day in the 1880s, she walked "steadily and persistently" through the village hecklers, vowing to win their acceptance and then their souls. A daunting task.

Born in 1840 in Virginia and educated at what is now Hollins College, Charlotte Diggs Moon volunteered in 1873 for "woman's work" in northern China. There she taught and proselytized, largely among women and children because women seldom preached to men and men were forbidden to preach to women. This compassionate, pious, and courageous single woman, "putting love into action," worked in China until her death in 1912.

Lottie Moon (Mu Ladi or 幕拉第) made bold and sometimes dangerous evangelizing trips in the 1870s and 1880s to isolated Chinese hamlets. "O! The torture of human eyes upon you; scanning every feature, every look, every gesture!" Curious peasant women pinched her, pulling on her skirt, purring, "How white her hand is!" They peppered her with questions: "How old are you?" and "Where do you get money to live on?" Speaking in Chinese, she held high a picture book on Jesus Christ's birth and crucifixion, drawing the chattering crowd's attention to the "foreign doctrine" that she hoped would displace Confucianism, Buddhism, and Taoism.

In the 1890s a "storm of persecution" against foreigners swept China. Missionaries, because they were upending traditional ways and authority, became hated targets. One missionary conceded that in "believing Jesus," girls and women alarmed men who clamored that "disobedient wives and daughters" would no longer "worship the idols when told." In the village of Shaling in early 1890, Lottie Moon's Christian converts were beaten and the "foreign devils" ordered to move out. Fearing for her life, she had to flee. For several months in 1900, during the violent Boxer Rebellion, she had to leave China altogether as a multinational force (that included U.S. troops) intervened to save foreign missionaries, diplomats, and merchants.

The missionary Lottie Moon (1840–1912) is surrounded in 1901 by English-language students in Japan during her refuge from the Boxer Rebellion in China. (Virginia Baptist Historical Society & University Archives)

THE QUEST FOR EMPIRE 1865–1914

Imperial Promoters: The Foreign Policy Elite and Economic Expansion

Ideology, Culture, and Empire

Ambitions Abroad, 1860s–1880s

Crises in the 1890s: Hawai'i, Venezuela, and Cuba

The Spanish-American-Cuban-Filipino War and the Debate over Empire

Asian Encounters: Open Door in China, Philippine Insurrection, and Japan

Latin America, Europe, and International Rivalry

LEGACY FOR A PEOPLE AND A NATION

The Status of Puerto Rico

Lottie Moon and thousands of other missionaries managed to convert to Christianity only a very small minority of the Chinese people. Although she, like other missionaries, probably never shed the Western view that she represented a superior religion and culture, she seldom wavered from her affection for the Chinese people and from her devotion to the foreign missionary project—from her "rejoicing to suffer." In frequent letters and articles directed to a U.S. audience, she lobbied to recruit "a band of ardent, enthusiastic, and experienced Christian women," to stir up "a mighty wave of enthusiasm for Woman's Work for Woman." To this day, the Lottie Moon Christmas Offering in Southern Baptist churches raises millions of dollars for missions abroad.

Like so many other Americans who went overseas in the late nineteenth and early twentieth centuries, Lottie Moon helped spread American culture and implant U.S. influence abroad. In this complex process, other peoples sometimes adopted and sometimes rejected American ways. At the same time, American participants in this cultural expansion, and the cultural collisions it generated, became transformed. Lottie Moon, for example, strove to understand the Chinese people and learn their language. She abandoned the derogatory phrases "heathen Chinese" and "great unwashed" and even assumed their dress. She reminded other less sensitive missionaries that the Chinese rightfully took pride in their own ancient history and thus had no reason to "gape in astonishment at Western civilization."

Lottie Moon also changed—again, in her own words—from "a timid self-distrustful girl into a brave self-reliant woman." As she questioned the Chinese confinement of women, most conspicuous in arranged marriages, footbinding, and sexual segregation, she advanced women's rights. She understood that she could not convert Chinese women unless they had the freedom to listen to her appeals. Bucking the gender ideology of the times, she also uneasily rose to challenge the male domination of America's religious missions. When the Southern Baptist Foreign Mission Board, for example, denied women missionaries the right to vote in meetings, she resigned in protest. The board soon reversed itself.

Critics over the decades have labeled as "cultural imperialism" the activities of Lottie Moon and other missionaries, accusing the missionaries of seeking to subvert indigenous traditions and sparking destructive cultural clashes. Defenders of missionary work, on the other hand, have celebrated their efforts to break down cultural barriers and to bring the world's peoples closer together. Either way, Lottie Moon's story illustrates how Americans interacted with the world in diverse ways, how through their experiences the categories "domestic" and "foreign" intersected, and how they expanded abroad not only to seek land, trade, investments, and strategic bases but also to promote American culture, including the Christian faith.

Between the Civil War and the First World War, Americans ranked as unabashed expansionists and imperialists. Before the Civil War, Americans had repeatedly extended the frontier: they bought Louisiana; annexed Florida, Oregon, and Texas; pushed Indians out of the path of white migration westward; seized California and other western areas from Mexico; and acquired southern parts of present-day Arizona and New Mexico from Mexico (the Gadsden Purchase). Americans had also developed a lucrative foreign trade with most of the world and spread their culture wherever they traveled. They rekindled their expansionist course after the Civil War, building, managing, and protecting an overseas empire. In that imperialistic age of "living" and "dying" nations, as British prime minister Lord Salisbury observed, the international system witnessed an assertive Germany challenge an overextended Great Britain, an economic and military giant becoming, said one diplomat, the "weary titan" of the world. Japan expanded in Asia at the expense of both China and Russia. As for the "living" United States, it emerged as a great power with particular clout in Latin America, especially as the "dying" Spain declined and Britain disengaged from the hemisphere. "The old nations of the earth creep on at a snail's pace," the industrialist Andrew Carnegie bragged, but the United States "thunders past with the rush of the express [train]."

The United States's imperialist surge, however, sparked considerable opposition. Abroad, native nationalists, commercial competitors, and other imperial nations tried to block the spread of U.S. influence, while anti-imperialists at home stimulated a momentous debate over the fundamental course of American foreign policy. Most Americans applauded expansionism—the outward movement of goods, ships, dollars, people, and ideas—as a traditional feature of their nation's history. But many became uneasy whenever expansionism gave way to imperialism—the imposition of control over other peoples, undermining their sovereignty and usurping their freedom to make their own decisions. Imperial control could be imposed either formally (by military occupation, annexation, or

IMPORTANT EVENTS

1861–69 Seward sets expansionist course

1866 Transatlantic cable completed

1867 Alaska and Midway acquired

1868 Burlingame Treaty with China regulates immigration

1871 Anglo-American treaty sends *Alabama* claims issue to tribunal

1874 U.S. foreign trade shifts to favorable balance

1876 Pro-U.S. Díaz begins long rule in Mexico

1878 U.S. gains naval rights in Samoa

1880 Treaty limits Chinese immigration to the United States

1883 Congress votes funds for New Navy

1885 Strong's *Our Country* celebrates Anglo-Saxons

1887 U.S. gains naval rights to Pearl Harbor, Hawai'i

1889 First Pan-American Conference

1890 Mahan's *The Influence of Sea Power upon History* published

McKinley Tariff hurts Hawaiian sugar exports

1893 Severe economic depression begins

Turner sets forth frontier thesis

Hawaiian Queen Lili'uokalani overthrown

1894 Wilson-Gorham Tariff imposes duty on Cuban sugar

1895 Olney blasts Britain in Venezuelan crisis

Cuban revolution against Spain begins

Japan defeats China in war

1898 Publication of de Lôme letter

Sinking of the *Maine*

Spanish-American-Cuban-Filipino War

Hawai'i annexed by the United States

1899 Treaty of Paris enlarges U.S. empire

United Fruit Company forms and becomes influential in Central America

First Open Door note calls for equal trade opportunity in China

Philippine insurrection breaks out

Samoa partitioned

1900 Second Open Door note issued during Boxer Rebellion in China

U.S. exports total $1.5 billion

1901 Hay-Pauncefote Treaty allows U.S. canal

1903 Panama grants canal rights to U.S.

Platt Amendment subjugates Cuba

1904 Roosevelt Corollary declares U.S. a hemispheric "police power"

1905 Taft-Katsura Agreement gains Japanese pledge to respect Philippines

Portsmouth Conference ends Russo-Japanese War

U.S. financial supervision of Dominican Republic begins

1906 San Francisco school board segregates Asian schoolchildren

U.S. invades Cuba to quell revolt

1907 "Great White Fleet" makes world tour

"Gentleman's agreement" with Japan restricts immigration

1908 Root-Takahira Agreement with Japan reaffirms Open Door in China

1910 Mexican revolution threatens U.S. interests

1911 Treaty bans pelagic sealing in Bering Sea

1912 U.S. troops invade Cuba again

U.S. troops occupy Nicaragua

1914 U.S. troops invade Mexico

First World War begins

Panama Canal opens

colonialism) or informally (by economic domination, political manipulation, or the threat of intervention). As the informal methods indicate, imperialism meant far more than the taking of territory.

Critics in the late nineteenth century disparaged territorial imperialism as unbefitting the United States, and they opposed joining other great powers in the scramble for colonies in Asia and Africa. Would

not an overseas territorial empire, incorporating people of color living far from the United States, weaken institutions at home, threaten American culture, invite perpetual war, and violate honored principles? Although the United States preferred the "annexation of trade" to the annexation of territory, as Secretary of State James G. Blaine once declared, it became clear that economic expansionism sometimes led to the grabbing of colonies. Most Americans endorsed economic expansion as essential to the nation's prosperity and security, but anti-imperialists drew the line between expansionism and imperialism: profitable and fair trade relationships, yes; exploitation, no. And, some advised, American business activity abroad should not drag the United States into unwanted diplomatic crises and wars. But it did.

In the late nineteenth century the federal government sometimes failed to fund adequately the vehicles of expansion (such as the navy until the 1880s) and most businessmen ignored foreign commerce in favor of the domestic marketplace. Still, the direction of U.S. foreign policy after the Civil War became unmistakable: Americans intended to exert their influence beyond the continental United States, to reach for more space, more land, more markets, more cultural penetration, and more power. Republican Senator Henry Cabot Lodge of Massachusetts, claiming that the "great nations" were seizing "the waste areas of the world," advised that "the United States must not fall out of the line of march," because "civilization and the advancement of the [Anglo-Saxon] race" were at stake.

U.S. activity abroad heightened in the tumultuous decade of the 1890s, when doubters' voices were drowned out by calls for war and foreign territory, and when American power was sufficient to deliver both. U.S. entry into the Spanish-American-Cuban-Filipino War in 1898 and the subsequent subjugation of other peoples ignited a major political debate while lifting the United States to great-power status. ■

Imperial Promoters: The Foreign Policy Elite and Economic Expansion

 Foreign policy has always sprung from the domestic setting of a nation—its needs, wants, moods, ideology, and culture. The leaders who guided America's expansionist foreign relations were the same people who guided the economic development of the machine age, forged the transcontinental railroad, built America's bustling cities and giant corporations, and shaped a mass culture. They unabashedly espoused the idea that the United States was an exceptional nation, so different from and superior to others because of Americans' Anglo-Saxon heritage and their God-favored and prosperous history. The domestic and foreign spheres, as always, were inseparable.

"The people" may influence domestic policy, but they seldom shape foreign policy. Most Americans simply do not follow international relations or express themselves on foreign issues. The making of foreign policy, then, is usually dominated by what scholars have labeled the "foreign policy elite"—opinion leaders in politics, business, labor, agriculture, religion, journalism, education, and the military. In the post–Civil War era, this small group, whom Secretary of State Walter Q. Gresham called "the thoughtful men of the country," expressed the opinion that counted. Better read and better traveled than most Americans, more cosmopolitan in outlook, and politically active, they believed that U.S. prosperity and security depended on the exertion of U.S. influence abroad. Increasingly in the late nineteenth century, and especially in the 1890s, the expansionist-minded elite urged both formal and informal imperialism. These leaders created what the historian Emily Rosenberg has called "the promotional state"—a federal government committed to assisting American entrepreneurs who wished to trade and invest abroad and dedicated to making the United States a world power.

Foreign Policy Elite

Ambitious and clannish, the imperialists often met in Washington, D.C., at the homes of the historian Henry Adams and the writer and diplomat John Hay (who became secretary of state in 1898) or at the Metropolitan Club. They talked about building a bigger navy and digging a canal across Panama, Central America, or Mexico, establishing colonies, and selling surpluses abroad. Theodore Roosevelt, appointed assistant secretary of the navy in 1897, was among them; so were Senator Henry Cabot Lodge, who joined the Foreign Relations Committee in 1896, and the corporate lawyer Elihu Root, who later would serve as both secretary of war and secretary of state. Such well-positioned luminaries kept up the drumbeat for empire.

These American leaders believed that selling, buying, and investing in foreign marketplaces were important to the United States. Why? One reason was profits from foreign sales. "It is my dream," declared the governor of Georgia in 1878, to see "in every valley . . . a cotton factory to convert the raw material of the neighborhood into fabrics which shall warm the limbs of Japanese and Chinese." Fear helped make the case for foreign trade as well because the nation's farms and factories produced more than Americans could consume, all the more so during the 1890s depression. Foreign commerce might serve as a safety valve to re-

As one expression of the theme of economic expansion, this poster, advertising the Uncle Sam stove manufactured in New York by the Abendroth Bros. company, announces that food links the United States with the rest of the world. Although the foods on the long list are international—potatoes from Ireland and macaroni from Italy, for example—the message here is that the United States itself is "feeding the world." The turkey being removed from the oven seems to be the only unique American offering, but many of the items on the list were also produced in the United States. The poster was issued in 1876, which explains the image of the Centennial building in Philadelphia and the patriotic red, white, and blue colors. (© Collection of The New-York Historical Society)

lieve overproduction, unemployment, economic depression, and the social tension that arose from them. Surpluses had to be exported, the economist David A. Wells warned, or "we are certain to be smothered in our own grease." Economic ties also permitted political influence to be exerted abroad and helped spread the American way of life, creating a world more hospitable to Americans. In an era when the most powerful nations in the world were also the greatest traders, vigorous foreign economic expansion symbolized national stature.

Foreign trade figured prominently in the tremendous economic growth of the United States after the Civil War. Foreign commerce, in turn, stimulated the building of a larger protective navy, the professionalization of the foreign service, calls for more colonies, and a more interventionist foreign policy. In 1865 U.S. exports to-

Foreign Trade Expansion

taled $234 million; by 1900 they had climbed to $1.5 billion (see Figure 22.1). By 1914, at the outbreak of the First World War, exports had reached $2.5 billion, prompting some Europeans to protest an American "invasion" of goods. In 1874 the United States reversed its historically unfavorable balance of trade (importing more than it exported) and began to enjoy a long-term favorable balance (exporting more than it imported). Most of America's products went to Britain, continental Europe, and Canada, but increasing amounts flowed to new markets in Latin America and Asia. Meanwhile, direct American investments abroad reached $3.5 billion by 1914, placing the United States among the top four investor countries.

Agricultural goods accounted for about three-fourths of total exports in 1870 and about two-thirds in 1900, with grain, cotton, meat, and dairy products topping the export list that year. More than half of the annual cotton crop was exported each year. Midwestern

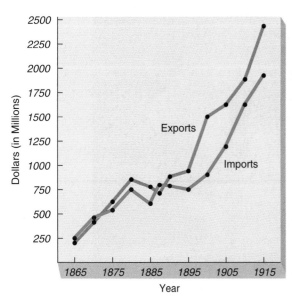

Figure 22.1 U.S. Trade Expansion, 1865–1914 This figure illustrates two key characteristics of U.S. foreign trade: first, that the United States began in the 1870s to enjoy a favorable balance of trade (exporting more than it imported); second, that U.S. exports expanded tremendously, making the United States one of the world's economic giants. (Source: Thomas G. Paterson, J. Garry Clifford, and Kenneth J. Hagan, *American Foreign Relations: A History,* 5th ed. Copyright © 2000 by Houghton Mifflin Company.)

farmers transported their crops by railroad to seaboard cities and then on to foreign markets. Farmers' livelihoods thus became tied to world-market conditions and the outcomes of foreign wars. Wisconsin cheesemakers shipped to Britain; the Swift and Armour meat companies exported refrigerated beef to Europe. To sell American grain abroad, James J. Hill of the Great Northern Railroad distributed wheat cookbooks translated into several Asian languages.

In 1913, when the United States outranked both Great Britain and Germany in manufacturing production (see Figure 22.2), manufactured goods led U.S. exports for the first time. Substantial proportions of America's steel, copper, and petroleum were sold abroad, making many workers in those industries dependent on American exports. George Westinghouse marketed his air brakes in Europe; almost as many Singer sewing machines were exported as were sold at home; and Cyrus McCormick's "reaper kings" harvested the wheat of Russian fields.

Ideology, Culture, and Empire

 In the American march toward empire, ideology and culture figured prominently. An intertwined set of ideas conditioned U.S. foreign relations. Nationalism, exceptionalism, capitalism, Social Darwinism, paternalism, and the categorization of foreigners in derogatory race-, age-, and gender-based terms—all influenced American leaders. Fear and prejudice infused many American ideas about the world and foreign peoples—fear of the social disorder stirred by revolution, fear of economic depression, fear of racial and ethnic mixing, fear of women's rights, fear of a closed frontier, fear of losing international stature. To calm their fears and promote their values, leaders exported American culture and sought to remake other societies in the image of the United States. "They are children and we are men in these deep matters of government," the future president Woodrow Wilson announced in 1898. The intersection of American and foreign cultures, however, bred not only adoption but rejection, not only imitation but clash, as Lottie Moon learned.

After the Civil War, leaders again put the United States on an expansionist course and championed a nationalism based on notions of American supremacy. The inflated rhetoric of American exceptionalism and manifest destiny revived, giving intensified voice to explanations for expansion based on race. Some Americans placed people with darker skin, such as blacks and Indians, at the bottom of a racial hierarchy, calling them "uncivilized." At the top sat "civilized" white Anglo-Saxon Americans. Near the top, but beneath Anglo-Saxons, came European peoples—"aggressive" Germans followed by "peasant" Slavs, "sentimental" French and Italians, and "Shylock" Jews. In the middle rank came Latinos, the Spanish-speaking people of Latin America. Theodore Roosevelt disparaged Latinos as "dagoes" and "darkeys" who lacked any ability to govern themselves. Americans debased Latin Americans as half-breeds needing close supervision, distressed damsels begging for manly rescue, or children requiring tutelage. Also midway in the hierarchy were East Asian peoples, the "Orientals" or "Mongolians" whom Americans thought inscrutable, crafty, and immoral, although, as in the case of the Japanese, sometimes capable of success.

Reverend Josiah Strong's popular and influential *Our Country* (1885) celebrated an Anglo-Saxon race

Race Thinking

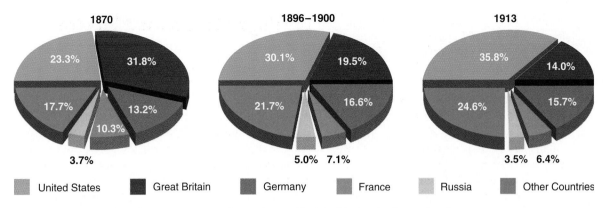

Figure 22.2   The Rise of U.S. Economic Power in the World   These pie charts showing percentage shares of world manufacturing production for the major nations of the world demonstrate that the United States came to surpass Great Britain in this significant economic measurement of power.   (Source: League of Nations data presented in Aaron L. Friedberg, *The Weary Titan: Britain and the Experience of Relative Decline, 1895–1905* [Princeton, N.J.: Princeton University Press, 1988], p. 26.)

destined to lead others. "As America goes, so goes the world," he declared. A few years later he wrote that "to be a Christian and an Anglo-Saxon and an American . . . is to stand at the very mountaintop of privilege." Social Darwinists saw Americans as a superior people certain to overcome all competition. Secretary of State Thomas F. Bayard (1885–1889) applauded the "overflow of our population and capital" into Mexico to "saturate those regions with Americanism," but, he added, "we do not want them" until "they are fit."

The magazine *National Geographic*, which published its first issue in 1888, chronicled with photographs America's new overseas possessions. The editors chose pictures that reflected prevailing American ethnocentric attitudes toward foreigners. Even when smiling faces predominated, the image portrayed was that of strange, exotic, premodern people who had not become "Western." Emphasizing this point, *National Geographic* regularly pictured women with naked breasts. Fairs, too, stereotyped other peoples as falling short of civilization. Fair managers not only celebrated the impressive technology of "Western civilization"; they also put people of color on display in the "freaks" or "midway" section. Alongside bearded women and the fattest man in the world were exhibits—as at the 1895 Atlanta and 1897 Nashville fairs—of Cubans and Mexicans in primitive village settings. Dog-eating Filipinos aroused particular comment at the 1904 St. Louis World's Fair.

Race thinking—popularized in world's fairs, magazine cartoons, postcards, school textbooks, and political orations—reinforced notions of American greatness, influenced the way U.S. leaders dealt with other peoples, and obviated the need to think about the subtle textures of other societies. Such racism downgraded diplomacy and justified domination and war because self-proclaimed superiors do not negotiate with people ranked as inferiors.

A masculine ethos also characterized American views of foreigners. The language of U.S. leaders was weighted with words such as *manliness* and *weakling*. Member of Congress, son-in-law of Senator Lodge, and 1898 war veteran Augustus P. Gardner extolled the "arena of lust and blood, where true men are to be found." The warrior and president Theodore Roosevelt prized the White House as the "bully pulpit" and celebrated the "strenuous life" against the "flapdoodle pacifists and mollycoddlers." But, more, he and his imperialist cohorts often described other nations (and the American peace movement) as effeminate—unable, in contrast to a masculine Uncle Sam, to cope with the demands of world politics. The gendered imagery prevalent in U.S.-foreign relations joined race thinking to place women, people of color, and nations weaker than the United States in the low ranks of the hierarchy of power and, hence, in a necessarily dependent status justifying U.S. hegemony. During and after the war of 1898, some activists in women's organizations bemoaned the "intoxication with the hashish of conquest" and "martial spirit" prevalent among male

Male Ethos

How do historians know...

that Americans in the imperial age disparaged people of other societies as "uncivilized," needing "civilization" from a superior United States? Historians interpret speeches, diaries, letters, tourist industry advertisements, fair exhibits, and cartoons to identify racist, age-biased, and gender-biased American ideas about foreigners. Especially revealing are the images on picture postcards of the era because they capture expressions of supremacy in their depictions of the "civilized" (modern) and the "wild" (premodern). As photographs, postcards provide historians with a detailed documentary record, a testimony of feelings, and a visual representation of the values and attitudes of the time.

Government-made postcards were first issued in Austria in 1869 as a way to reduce the expense of corresponding by mail (they cost just a penny to post). Privately or commercially printed picture postcards appeared elsewhere in Europe in the 1880s and in the United States in the 1890s. Collecting postcards immediately became popular as a hobby; the collection and study of postcards today is called deltiology. At the turn of the century, card subjects included humor, anniversaries, patriotic events, advertisements, street scenes, historic sites, romantic messages, famous leaders, art, and costumes. The images of foreign peoples on American postcards often communicated a message that denigrated indigenous life through contrast with "Western" ways. The Singer Manufacturing Company handed out the promotional postcard reproduced here as a souvenir from the firm's exhibit at the 1893 Columbian Exposition in Chicago. About three-quarters of all sewing machines sold in the world were Singers. The machine shown in this postcard was marketed in South Africa, where, the company advised, the "Zulus are a fine warlike people" who were moving toward "civilization," with Singer's help.   (Photo: State Historical Society of Wisconsin)

ZULULAND.

COPYRIGHT 1892, BY THE SINGER MANUFACTURING CO.

imperialists who denied voting rights to both Filipinos and American women.

Issues of race and gender also marked the experiences of religious missionaries, many of whom were single women (like Lottie Moon) or wives of clergymen. Missionaries dispatched to Asia and Africa helped spur the transfer of American culture

Missionaries

and power abroad—"the peaceful conquest of the world," as Reverend Frederick Gates put it. One organization, the Student Volunteers for Foreign Missions, began in the 1880s on college campuses and by 1914 had placed some six thousand missionaries abroad. In 1915 a total of 10,000 American missionaries worked overseas. In China by 1915 more than 2,500 American Protestant missionaries—most of them female—

labored to preach the gospel, to teach school, and to administer medical care. What motivated these women to endure such demanding work far from home and family? Many convictions led them to the mission field—deep piety, a theology of sacrificial service, the American tradition of volunteerism, a belief that a woman's mothering role made women especially suited to educate children, and a recognition that foreign missionary work empowered them as women at a time when men largely denied them a public life at home.

As they struggled to win converts, women missionaries also critiqued the Chinese gender system. When they judged non-Christian foreign societies as more exploitative of women than the United States was, in essence they perpetuated cultural stereotypes of Anglo-Saxon superiority that undergirded imperialism. *The Mother Goose Missionary Rhymes* betrayed traces of cultural imperialism: "Ten little heathen standing in a line; / One went to mission school, then there were but nine. . . . / Three little heathen didn't know what to do; / One learned our language, then there were two. . . . / One little heathen standing all alone; / He learned to love our flag, then there were none." At the same time, missionaries and Singer executives joined hands in promoting the "civilizing medium" of the sewing machine.

With a mixture of self-interest and idealism typical of American thinking on foreign policy, expansionists believed that empire benefited both Americans and those who came under their control. When the United States intervened in other lands or lectured weaker states, Americans claimed that in remaking foreign societies they were extending liberty and prosperity to less fortunate people. William Howard Taft, as civil governor of the Philippines (1901–1904), described the United States's mission in its new colony as lifting up Filipinos "to a point of civilization" that will make them "call the name of the United States blessed." Later, after becoming secretary of war (1904–1908), Taft said about the Chinese that "the more civilized they become . . . the wealthier they become, and the better market they become for us." "The world is to be Christianized and civilized," declared Reverend Josiah Strong. "And what is the process of civilizing but the creating of more and higher wants."

To critics at home and abroad, however, American paternalism appeared hypocritical—a violation of cherished principles. To impose on Filipinos an American-

The "Civilizing" Impulse

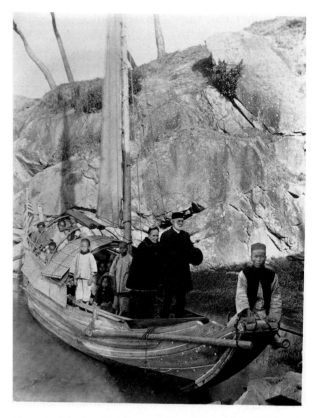

The missionaries Charles and Anna Hartwell, brother and sister, travel in 1901 on their "gospel boat," working out of the Fuzhou mission in China.   (ABCFM Pictures, courtesy of Houghton Library, Harvard University)

style political system, for example, U.S. officials censored the press, jailed critics, and picked candidates for public office. From this coercive experience, Filipinos may have learned more about how to fix elections than about how to make democracy work.

Ambitions Abroad, 1860s–1880s

The U.S. empire grew gradually, sometimes haltingly, as American leaders defined guiding principles and built institutions to support overseas ambitions. William H. Seward, one of its chief architects, argued relentlessly for extension of the American frontier as senator from New York (1849–1861) and secretary of state (1861–1869). "There is not in the history of the Roman Empire an ambition for aggrandizement so marked as that which characterizes the American people," he once said. Seward envisioned a large, coordinated U.S. empire encompassing Canada, the

Caribbean, Cuba, Central America, Mexico, Hawai'i, Iceland, Greenland, and Pacific islands. This empire would be built not by war but by a natural process of gravitation toward the United States. Commerce would hurry the process, as would a canal across Central America, a transcontinental American railroad to link up with Asian markets, and a telegraph system to speed communications.

Most of Seward's grandiose plans did not reach fruition in his own day. In 1867, for example, he signed a treaty with Denmark to buy the Danish West Indies (Virgin Islands), but his domestic political foes in the Senate and a hurricane that wrecked St. Thomas scuttled his effort. The Virgin Islanders, who had voted for annexation, had to wait until 1917 for official U.S. status. Also failing was Seward's scheme with unscrupulous Dominican Republic leaders to gain a Caribbean naval base at Samaná Bay. The stench of corruption rising over this unsavory deal-making wafted into the Ulysses S. Grant administration and foiled Grant's initiative in 1870 to buy the entire island nation. The Senate rejected annexation. Anti-imperialism, not just politics, blocked Seward. Anti-imperialists such as Senator Carl Schurz and E. L. Godkin, editor of the magazine *The Nation*, argued that the country already had enough unsettled land and that creating a showcase of democracy and prosperity at home would best persuade other peoples to adopt American institutions and principles. Some anti-imperialists, sharing the racism of the times, opposed the annexation of territory populated by dark-skinned people.

William H. Seward's Quest for Empire

Seward did enjoy some successes. In 1866, citing the Monroe Doctrine, he sent troops to the border with Mexico and demanded that France abandon its puppet regime there. Also facing angry Mexican nationalists, Napoleon III abandoned the Maximilian monarchy that he had installed by force three years earlier. In 1867 Seward paid Russia $7.2 million for the 591,000 square miles of Alaska—land twice the size of Texas. Some critics lampooned "Seward's Icebox," but the secretary of state extolled the Russian territory's rich natural resources, and the Senate voted overwhelmingly for the treaty. That same year, Seward laid claim to the Midway Islands in the Pacific Ocean.

Seward realized his dream of a world knit together into a giant communications system. In 1866, through the persevering efforts of the financier Cyrus Field, an underwater transatlantic cable linked European and American telegraph networks.

International Communications

Backed by J. P. Morgan's capital, the communications pioneer James A. Scrymser strung telegraph lines to Latin America, entering Chile in 1890. In 1903 a submarine cable reached across the Pacific to the Philippines; three years later it extended to Japan and China. Information about markets, crises, and war flowed steadily and quickly. Wire telegraphy—like radio (wireless telegraphy) later—shrank the globe. Nellie Bly, a reporter for the *New York World*, accented the impact of new technology in 1890 when she completed a well-publicized trip around the world in seventy-two days. Drawn closer to one another through improved communications and transportation, nations found that faraway events had more and more impact on their prosperity and security. Because of the communications revolution, "every nation elbows other nations to-day," observed Amherst College professor Edwin Grosvenor in 1898.

Gradually through the late nineteenth century, despite frequent squabbles over such issues as fishing rights along the North Atlantic coast, Britain and the United States worked to negotiate rather than fight over their differing interests. Seward's successor, Hamilton Fish (1869–1877), inherited the knotty problem of the *Alabama* claims. The *Alabama* and other vessels built in Great Britain for the Confederacy during the Civil War had preyed on Union shipping. Senator Charles Sumner demanded that Britain pay $2 billion in damages or cede Canada to the United States, but Fish favored negotiations. In 1871 Britain and America signed the Washington Treaty, whereby the British apologized and agreed to the creation of a tribunal, which later awarded the United States $15.5 million. Bitter controversy over sealing also ended in a peaceful settlement. Beginning in the late 1860s the United States sought to curb pelagic (open sea) sealing—especially the harvesting of fur seals as they swam in the Bering Sea. Pelagic poachers ignored the law as they slaughtered great numbers of breeding females. Despite U.S. seizures of ships, many of them Canadian, the seals faced extermination by the end of the century. Finally, in 1911, Great Britain, the United States, Russia, and Japan banned pelagic sealing altogether and limited land kills. The seal population gradually rejuvenated.

Anglo-Canadian-American Relations

The emerging Anglo-American rapprochement also figured in the outcome of a contest over Samoa, a group of South Pacific islands 4,000 miles from San Francisco on the trade route to Australia. In 1878 the United States gained exclusive right to a coaling station at Samoa's coveted port of Pago Pago. Also seek-

Contest over Samoa

ing imperial advantage, Britain and Germany began to cultivate ties with Samoan leaders. In the 1880s, responding to U.S. warnings to stay out, Berlin protested that Washington was treating the Pacific Ocean "as an American lake." Year by year tensions grew as the powers dispatched warships to Samoa and aggravated factionalism among Samoa's chiefs. Rather than go to war, Britain, Germany, and the United States met in Berlin in 1889 and, without consulting the Samoans, devised a three-part protectorate that limited Samoa's independence. Ten years later the three powers partitioned Samoa: the United States received Pago Pago through annexation of part of the islands (now called American Samoa and administered by the U.S. Department of the Interior); Germany took what is today independent Western Samoa; and Britain, for renouncing its claims to Samoa, obtained the Gilbert Islands and Solomon Islands. One result of the long-simmering Samoan crisis was an intensified U.S. Germanophobia, which also fed on testy German-American trade and naval rivalries and a growing perception that German autocracy and militarism threatened American democracy.

Americans realized far less gain in their relations with China. Missionaries became targets of Chinese nationalist anger, while American oil and textile companies sent their wares into a China market they dreamed was boundless but actually was limited. American religious leaders and business executives throughout the late nineteenth century appealed for official U.S. protection. At

Sino-American Troubles

Beginning in the late nineteenth century, Standard Oil (the forerunner of Exxon Corporation) sent agents to China to persuade the Chinese to use American-made kerosene in their lamps and cooking stoves. To promote sales, the American entrepreneurs gave away small lamps, which the Chinese called *Mei Foo* (Beautiful Companion). One agent who popularized the lamp was William P. Coltman, shown here with Chinese business associates. At right is one of the advertisements.   (EXXON Corporation)

home, although the Burlingame Treaty (1868) provided for free immigration between the United States and China and pledged Sino-American friendship, Sinophobia in the American West erupted again and again in riots against Chinese immigrants—in Los Angeles (1871), San Francisco (1877), Denver (1880), and Seattle (1886). A new treaty in 1880 permitted Congress to suspend Chinese immigration to the United States, and it did so two years later. A violent incident occurred in Rock Springs, Wyoming, in 1885, when white coal miners and railway workers rioted and massacred at least twenty-five Chinese. Weakened by internal strife and the imperial powers' encroachments, leaders in Beijing could do little but protest and remember, although a short-lived Chinese boycott of American products in 1905 revealed China's lingering anger over racist American practices.

In Latin America, meanwhile, the convening in 1889 of the first Pan-American Conference in Washington, D.C., demonstrated growing U.S. influence in the Western Hemisphere. Conferees from Latin America toured U.S. factories and then pledged support for reciprocity treaties to improve hemispheric trade. To encourage inter-American cooperation, they founded the Pan-American Union. In 1891 Latin Americans wondered what Pan-Americanism really stood for after the United States flexed its naval muscle and coerced Chile into a humiliating apology and indemnity after drunken sailors from the *Baltimore* battled Chileans outside a Valparaiso bar; two Americans lost their lives. "The American Republic will stand no more nonsense from any power, big or little," boomed Senator George Shoup of Iowa.

Pan-American Conference

With eyes on all parts of the world, even on Africa, where U.S. interests were minimal, ardent expansionists embraced navalism—the campaign to build an imperial navy. They argued for a bigger, modernized navy, adding the "blue water" command of the seas to its traditional role of "brown water" coastline defense and riverine operations. Captain Alfred T. Mahan became a major popularizer for this "New Navy." Because foreign trade was vital to the United States, he argued, the nation required an efficient navy to protect its shipping; in turn, a navy required colonies for bases. "Whether they will or no," Mahan wrote, "Americans must now begin to look outward. The growing production of the country demands it." Mahan's lectures

Alfred T. Mahan, Navalism, and the New Navy

at the Naval War College in Newport, Rhode Island, where he served as president, were published as *The Influence of Sea Power upon History* (1890). This widely read book sat on every serious expansionist's shelf, and foreign leaders turned its pages. Theodore Roosevelt and Henry Cabot Lodge eagerly consulted Mahan, sharing his belief in the links between trade, navy, and colonies, and his growing alarm over "the aggressive military spirit" of Germany.

Moving toward naval modernization, Congress in 1883 authorized construction of the first steel-hulled warships. American factories went to work to produce steam engines, high-velocity shells, powerful guns, and precision instruments. The navy shifted from sail power to steam and from wood construction to steel. Often named for states and cities to kindle patriotism and local support for naval expansion, New Navy ships such as the *Maine*, *Oregon*, and *Boston* thrust the United States into naval prominence, especially during crises in the 1890s.

Crises in the 1890s: Hawai'i, Venezuela, and Cuba

In the depression-plagued 1890s, crises in Hawai'i, Venezuela, and Cuba gave expansionist Americans opportunities to act on their zealous arguments for what Senator Lodge called a "large policy." Belief that the frontier at home had closed accentuated the expansionist case. In 1893 the historian Frederick Jackson Turner postulated that an ever-expanding continental frontier had shaped the American character. That "frontier has gone," Turner pronounced, "and with its going has closed the first period of American history." He did not explicitly say that a new frontier had to be found overseas in order to sustain the American way of life, but he did claim that "American energy will continually demand a wider field for its exercise."

Hawai'i, the Pacific Ocean archipelago of eight major islands located 2,000 miles from the West Coast of the United States, emerged as a new frontier for Americans. The Hawaiian Islands had long commanded American attention—commercial, religious missionary, naval, and diplomatic. Wide-eyed U.S. expansionists envisioned ships sailing from the eastern seaboard through a Central American canal to Hawai'i and then on to the fabled China market. Already by 1881 Secretary of

Annexation of Hawai'i

State James Blaine had declared the Hawaiian Islands "essentially a part of the American system." By 1890 Americans owned about three-quarters of Hawai'i's wealth and subordinated its economy to that of the United States through sugar exports that entered the U.S. marketplace duty-free. In Hawai'i's multiracial society Chinese and Japanese nationals far outnumbered Americans, who represented a mere 2.1 percent of the population. Prominent Americans on the islands—lawyers, businessmen, and sugar planters, many of them the sons of missionaries—organized secret clubs and military units to contest the royal government. In 1887 they forced the king to accept a constitution that granted foreigners the right to vote and shifted decision-making authority from the monarchy to the legislature. The same year, Hawai'i granted the United States naval rights to Pearl Harbor. Many native Hawaiians (53 percent of the population in 1890) believed that the *haole* (foreigners)—especially Americans—were taking their country from them.

The McKinley Tariff of 1890 created an economic crisis for Hawai'i that further undermined the native government. The tariff eliminated the duty-free status of Hawaiian sugar exports in the United States. Suffering declining sugar prices and profits, the American island elite pressed for annexation of the islands by the United States so that their sugar would be classified as domestic rather than foreign. When Princess Lili'uokalani assumed the throne in 1891, she sought to roll back the political power of the *haole*. The next year, the white oligarchy—questioning her moral rectitude, fearing Hawaiian nationalism, and reeling from the McKinley Tariff—formed the subversive Annexation Club.

The annexationists struck in January 1893 in collusion with John L. Stevens, the chief American diplomat in Hawai'i, who dispatched troops from the U.S.S. *Boston* to occupy Honolulu. The queen, arrested and confined, surrendered. However, rather than yield to the new provisional regime, headed by Sanford B. Dole, son of missionaries and a prominent attorney, she relinquished authority to the U.S. government. Up went the American flag. "The Hawaiian pear is now fully ripe and this is the golden hour to pluck it," a triumphant Stevens informed Washington. Against the queen's protests and those of Japan, President Benjamin Harrison hurriedly sent an annexation treaty to the Senate.

Sensing foul play, incoming President Grover Cleveland ordered an investigation, which confirmed a

Queen Lili'uokalani (1838–1917), ousted from her throne in 1893 by wealthy revolutionaries, vigorously protested in her autobiography and diary, as well as in interviews, the U.S. annexation of Hawai'i in 1898. For years she defended Hawaiian nationalism and emphasized that American officials in 1893 had conspired with Sanford B. Dole and others to overthrow the native monarchy. (Courtesy of the Lili'uokalani Trust)

conspiracy by the economic elite in league with Stevens and noted that most Hawaiians opposed annexation. Down came the American flag. But when Hawai'i gained renewed attention as a strategic and commercial way station to Asia and the Philippines during the Spanish-American-Cuban-Filipino War, President William McKinley maneuvered annexation through Congress on July 7, 1898, by means of a majority vote (the Newlands Resolution) rather than by a treaty, which would have required a two-thirds count. Under the organic act of June 1900, the people of Hawai'i became U.S. citizens with the right to vote in local elections and to send a nonvoting delegate to Congress. Statehood for Hawai'i came in 1959.

The Venezuelan crisis of 1895 also saw the United States in an expansive mood. For decades Venezuela and Great Britain had quarreled over the border between Venezuela and British Guiana. The disputed

Venezuelan Boundary Dispute

territory contained rich gold deposits and the mouth of the Orinoco River, a commercial gateway to northern South America. Venezuela asked for U.S. help. President Cleveland decided that the "mean and hoggish" British had to be warned away. In July 1895, Secretary of State Richard Olney brashly lectured the British that the Monroe Doctrine prohibited European powers from denying self-government to nations in the Western Hemisphere. He aimed his spread-eagle words at an international audience, proclaiming the United States "a civilized state" whose "fiat is law" in the Americas. The United States, he declared, is "master of the situation and practically invulnerable as against any or all other powers." The British, seeking international friends to counter intensifying competition from Germany, quietly retreated from the crisis. In 1896 an Anglo-American arbitration board divided the disputed territory between Britain and Venezuela. The Venezuelans were barely consulted. Thus the United States displayed a trait common to imperialists: disregard for the rights and sensibilities of small nations.

In 1895 came yet another crisis, this one in Cuba. From 1868 to 1878 the Cubans had battled Spain for their independence. Slavery was abolished but independence denied. While the Cuban economy suffered depression, repressive Spanish rule continued. Insurgents committed to *Cuba Libre* waited for another chance. José Martí, one of the heroes of Cuban history, collected money, arms, and men in the United States. This was but one of the many ways the lives of Americans and Cubans intersected. Their cultures, for example, melded. Cubans of all classes settled in Baltimore, New York, Boston, and Philadelphia. Prominent Cubans on the island sent their children to schools in the United States. When Cuban expatriates returned home, many came in American clothes, spoke English, had American names, played baseball, and jettisoned Catholicism for Protestant denominations. Struggling with competing identities, Cubans admired American culture but resented U.S. economic hegemony.

U.S. Interests and Revolution in Cuba

The Cuban and U.S. economies became integrated. American investments of $50 million, most in sugar plantations, dominated the Caribbean island. More than 90 percent of Cuba's sugar was exported to the United States, and most island imports came from the United States. The Florida and Cuban economies also fused. Havana's famed cigar factories relocated to Key West and Tampa to evade protectionist U.S. tariff laws. Martí feared that this "economic union means political union," for "the nation that buys, commands" and "the nation that sells, serves." Watch out, he warned, for a U.S. "conquering policy" that reduced Latin American countries to "dependencies." A change in American tariff policy hastened the Cuban revolution against Spain and the island's further incorporation into "the American system." The Wilson-Gorman Tariff (1894) imposed a duty on Cuban sugar, which had been entering the United States duty-free under the McKinley Tariff. The Cuban economy, highly dependent on exports, plunged into deep crisis.

From American soil, Martí launched a revolution in 1895 that mounted in human and material costs. Rebels burned sugar-cane fields and razed mills, conducting an economic war and using guerrilla tactics to avoid head-on clashes with Spanish soldiers. "It is necessary to burn the hive to disperse the swarm," explained the insurgent leader Máximo Gomez. U.S. investments went up in smoke and Cuban-American trade dwindled. To separate the insurgents from their supporters among the Cuban people, Spanish general Valeriano Weyler instituted a policy of "reconcentration." Some three hundred thousand Cubans were herded into fortified towns and camps, where hunger, starvation, and disease led to tens of thousands of deaths. As reports of atrocity and destruction became headline news in the American yellow press (see page 547), Americans sympathized increasingly with the insurrectionists. In late 1897 a new government in Madrid modified reconcentration and promised some autonomy for Cuba, but the insurgents continued to gain ground.

President William McKinley had come to office as an imperialist who advocated foreign bases for the New Navy, the export of surplus production, and U.S. supremacy in the Western Hemisphere. Vexed by the turmoil in Cuba, he came to believe that Spain should give up its colony. At one point he explored the purchase of Cuba by the United States for $300 million. Events in early 1898 caused McKinley to lose faith in Madrid's ability to bring peace to Cuba. In January, when antireform pro-Spanish loyalists and army personnel rioted in Havana, Washington ordered the battleship *Maine* to Havana harbor to demonstrate U.S. concern and to protect American citizens. On February 15 an explosion ripped the *Maine*, killing 266 of 354 American officers and crew. Just a week earlier, William Randolph Hearst's inflammatory *New York Journal* had published a stolen private letter written by the Spanish minister

Sinking of the *Maine*

in Washington, Enrique Dupuy de Lôme, who belittled McKinley as a "cheap politician" and suggested that Spain would fight on. Congress soon complied unanimously with McKinley's request for $50 million in defense funds. The naval board investigating the *Maine* disaster then reported that a mine had caused the explosion. Vengeful Americans blamed Spain. (Later, official and unofficial studies attributed the sinking to an accidental internal explosion.)

The impact of these events narrowed McKinley's diplomatic options. He decided to send Spain an ultimatum. In late March the United States insisted that Spain accept an armistice, end reconcentration altogether, and designate McKinley as arbiter. Madrid made concessions. It abolished reconcentration and rejected, then accepted, an armistice. The weary president hesitated, but he would no longer tolerate chronic disorder just 90 miles off the U.S. coast. On April 11 McKinley asked Congress for authorization to use force "to secure a full and final termination of

McKinley's Ultimatum and War Decision

hostilities between . . . Spain and . . . Cuba, and to secure in the island the establishment of a stable government, capable of maintaining order." American intervention, he said, meant "hostile constraint upon both the parties to the contest." McKinley listed the reasons for war: the "cause of humanity"; the protection of American life and property; the "very serious injury to the commerce, trade, and business of our people"; and, referring to the destruction of the *Maine*, the "constant menace to our peace." At the end of his message, McKinley mentioned Spain's recent concessions but made little of them. On April 19 Congress declared Cuba free and independent and directed the president to use force to remove Spanish authority from the island. The legislators also passed the Teller Amendment, which disclaimed any U.S. intention to annex Cuba or "control" the island "except for the pacification thereof." McKinley beat back a congressional amendment to recognize the rebel government. Believing that the Cubans were not ready for self-government, he argued that they needed a period of American tutoring.

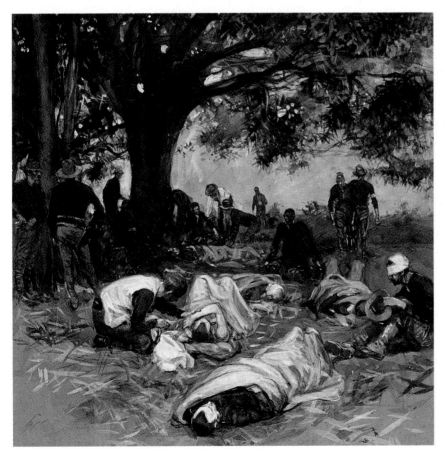

On July 1, 1898, U.S. troops stormed Spanish positions on San Juan Hill near Santiago, Cuba. Both sides suffered heavy casualties. A *Harper's* magazine correspondent reported a "ghastly" scene of hundreds killed and thousands wounded. The American painter William Glackens (1870–1938) put to canvas what he saw. Because Santiago surrendered on July 17, propelling the United States to victory in the war, and because Rough Rider Theodore Roosevelt fought at San Juan Hill and later gave a self-congratulatory account of the experience, the human toll has often gone unnoticed. (Wadsworth Atheneum, Hartford, Gift of Henry Schnakenberg)

The Spanish-American-Cuban-Filipino War and the Debate over Empire

 Diplomacy had failed. By the time the Spanish concessions were on the table, events had already pushed the antagonists to the brink. Washington might have been more patient, and Madrid might have faced the fact that its once-grand empire had disintegrated. Still, prospects for compromise appeared dim because the advancing Cuban insurgents would settle for nothing less than full independence, and no Spanish government could have given up and remained in office. Nor did the United States welcome a truly independent Cuban government that might attempt to reduce U.S. interests. As the historian Louis A. Pérez, Jr., has argued, McKinley's decision for war may have been "directed as much against Cuban independence as it was against Spanish sovereignty." Thus came a war best titled the "Spanish-American-Cuban-Filipino War" so as to represent all the major participants and to identify where the war was fought and whose interests were most at stake.

Motives for War

The motives of Americans who favored war were mixed and complex. McKinley's April message expressed a humanitarian impulse to stop the bloodletting, a concern for commerce and property, and the psychological need to end the nightmarish anxiety once and for all. Republican politicians advised McKinley that their party would lose the upcoming congressional elections unless he solved the Cuban question. Many businesspeople, who had been hesitant before the crisis of early 1898, joined many farmers in the belief that ejecting Spain from Cuba would open new markets for surplus production.

Inveterate imperialists saw war as an opportunity to fulfill expansionist dreams. Naval enthusiasts could prove the worth of the New Navy. Some religious leaders also saw merit in war. The Social Gospel advocate Washington Gladden remarked that "in saving others we may save ourselves." Conservatives, alarmed by Populism and violent labor strikes, welcomed war as a national unifier. One senator commented that "internal discord" was disappearing in the "fervent heat of patriotism." Sensationalism also figured in the march to war, with the yellow press exaggerating stories of Spanish misdeeds. Assistant Secretary of the Navy Theodore Roosevelt and others too young to remember the bloody Civil War looked on war as adventure and used masculine rhetoric to trumpet the call to arms. Anglo-Saxon supremacists such as the politician Albert Beveridge shouted, "God's hour has struck." Overarching all explanations for the 1898 war were expansionism and imperialism, whose momentum had been moving the nation ever outward in the last half of the nineteenth century.

The U.S. Military at War

More than 263,000 regulars and volunteers served in the army and another 25,000 in the navy during the war. Most of them never left the United States. The typical volunteer was young (early twenties), white, unmarried, native-born, and working-class. Deaths numbered 5,462—but only 379 in combat. The rest fell to yellow fever and typhoid, and most died in the United States, especially in camps in Tennessee, Virginia, and Florida, where in July and August a typhoid epidemic devastated the ranks. About 10,000 African American troops, assigned to segregated regiments, found no relief from racism and Jim Crow, even though black troops played a key role in the victorious battle for Santiago. For all, food, sanitary conditions, and medical care were bad. Still, Roosevelt could hardly contain himself. Although his Rough Riders, a motley unit of Ivy Leaguers and cowboys, proved undisciplined and often ineffective, they nonetheless received a good press largely because of Roosevelt's self-serving publicity efforts.

Dewey in the Philippines

To the surprise of most Americans, the first war news actually came from faraway Asia, from the Spanish colony of the Philippine Islands. On May 1, 1898, Commodore George Dewey's New Navy ship *Olympia* led an American squadron into Manila Bay and wrecked the outgunned Spanish fleet. Dewey and his sailors had been on alert in Hong Kong since February, when he received orders from imperial-minded Washington to attack the islands if war broke out. Manila ranked with Pearl Harbor and Pago Pago as a choice harbor, and the Philippines sat significantly on the way to China and its potentially huge market.

Facing rebels and Americans in both Cuba and the Philippines, Spanish resistance collapsed rapidly. U.S. ships blockaded Cuban ports to prevent Spain from resupplying its army, which suffered hunger and disease because Cuban insurgents had cut off supplies from the countryside. American troops saw their first ground-war action on June 22, the day several thousand of them landed near Santiago de Cuba and laid siege to the city. On July 3 U.S. warships sank the Spanish Caribbean squadron in Santiago harbor. American forces then assaulted the Spanish colony of Puerto Rico to obtain another Caribbean base for the navy and a strategic site to help protect a Central American canal. Losing on all fronts, Madrid sued for peace.

On August 12 Spain and the United States signed an armistice to end the war. In Paris, in December 1898, American and Spanish negotiators agreed on the peace terms: independence for Cuba from Spain; cession of the Philippines, Puerto Rico, and Guam (an island in the Pacific) to the United States; and American payment of $20 million to Spain for the territories. The U.S. empire now stretched deep into Asia; and the annexation of Wake Island (1898), Hawai'i (1898), and Samoa (1899) gave American traders, missionaries, and naval promoters other steppingstones to China.

Treaty of Paris

During the war with Spain, the *Washington Post* detected "a new appetite, a yearning to show our strength. . . . The taste of empire is in the mouth of the people." But as the nation debated the Treaty of Paris, anti-imperialists such as the author Mark Twain, the Nebraska politician William Jennings Bryan, the intellectual William Graham Sumner, the reformer Jane Addams, the industrialist Andrew Carnegie, and Senator George Hoar of Massachusetts argued vigorously against annexation of the Philippines. They were disturbed that a war to free Cuba had led to empire.

Some critics appealed to principle, citing the Declaration of Independence and the Constitution: the conquest of people against their wills violated the right of self-determination. The philosopher William James charged that the United States was throwing away its special place among nations; it was, he warned, about to "puke up its heritage." Other anti-imperialists argued that the United States could acquire markets without having to subjugate foreign peoples. To those who argued that the Filipinos were not yet fit for self-government, former senator Carl Schurz retorted that Manila's city council was probably less corrupt than Chicago's. Others claimed that to maintain empire, the president would repeatedly have to dispatch troops overseas. Because he could do so as commander-in-chief, he would not have to seek congressional approval, thus subverting the constitutional checks-and-balances system.

Anti-imperialist Arguments

Some anti-imperialists predicted that the very character of the American people was being corrupted by the imperialist zeal. Jane Addams, seeing children play war games in the streets of Chicago, pointed out that they were not freeing Cubans but were slaying Spaniards. Hoping to build a distinct foreign policy constituency out of networks of women's clubs and organizations, prominent women such as Addams endorsed peace and an end to imperial conquest. Some Americans protested that the United States was practicing a double standard—"offering liberty to the Cubans with one hand, cramming liberty down the throats of the Filipinos with the other, but with both feet planted upon the neck of the negro," as an African American politician from Massachusetts put it. Some white anti-imperialists, believing in a racial hierarchy, warned that annexing people of color would undermine Anglo-Saxon purity and supremacy at home.

Samuel Gompers and other anti-imperialist labor leaders worried about the possible undercutting of American labor by what Gompers called the "half-breeds and semi-barbaric people" of the new colonies. Might not the new colonials be imported as cheap contract labor to drive down the wages of American workers? Would not exploitation of the weak abroad become contagious and lead to further exploitation of the weak at home? Would not an overseas empire drain interest and resources from pressing domestic problems, delaying reform?

The anti-imperialists entered the debate with many handicaps and never launched an effective campaign. Although they organized the Anti-Imperialist League in November 1898, they differed so profoundly on domestic issues that they found it difficult to speak with one voice on a foreign question. They also appeared inconsistent: Gompers favored the war but not the postwar annexations; Carnegie would accept colonies if they were not acquired by force; Hoar voted for annexation of Hawai'i but not of the Philippines; Bryan backed the Treaty of Paris but only, he said, to hurry the process toward Philippine independence. Finally, possession of the Philippines was an established fact, very hard to undo.

The imperialists answered their critics with appeals to patriotism, destiny, and commerce. They sketched a scenario of American greatness: merchant ships plying the waters to boundless Asian markets; naval vessels cruising the Pacific to protect American interests; missionaries uplifting inferior peoples. It was America's duty,

Imperialist Arguments

they insisted, quoting a then-popular Rudyard Kipling poem, to "take up the white man's burden." Furthermore, insurgents were beginning to resist U.S. rule, and it seemed cowardly to pull out under fire. Germany and Japan, two powerful international competitors, were snooping around the Philippines, apparently ready to seize them if the United States's grip loosened. National honor dictated that Americans keep what they had shed blood to take. Senator Beveridge asked: "Shall [history] say that, called by events to captain and command the proudest, ablest, purest race of history in history's noblest work, we declined that great commission?"

In February 1899, by a 57-to-27 vote, the Senate passed the Treaty of Paris ending the war with Spain. Most Republicans voted "yes" and most Democrats "no." An amendment promising independence as soon as the Filipinos formed a stable government lost only by the tie-breaking ballot of the vice president. The Democratic presidential candidate Bryan carried the anti-imperialist case into the election of 1900, warning that repudiation of self-government in the Philippines would weaken the principle at home. But the victorious McKinley refused to apologize for American imperialism. "It is no longer a question of expansion with us," he asserted. "If there is any question at all it is a question of contraction; and who is going to contract?"

Asian Encounters: Open Door in China, Philippine Insurrection, and Japan

In 1895, the same year as the Venezuelan crisis and the outbreak of the Cuban revolution, Japan claimed victory over China in a short war. Outsiders had been pecking away at China since the 1840s, but the Japanese onslaught intensified the international scramble. Taking advantage of the Qing (Manchu) dynasty's weakness, the major powers carved out spheres of influence (regions over which the outside powers claimed political control and exclusive commercial privileges): Germany in Shandong; Russia in Manchuria; France in Yunnan and Hainan; Britain in Kowloon and Hong Kong. Japan controlled Formosa and Korea as well as parts of China proper (see Map 22.1). American religious and business leaders petitioned Washington to halt the dismemberment of China before they were closed out.

Secretary Hay knew that the United States could not force the imperial powers out of China, but he was determined to protect American commerce and missionaries such as Lottie Moon. In September 1899 Hay sent the imperial nations active in China a note asking them to respect the principle of equal trade opportunity—an Open Door. The recipients sent evasive replies, privately complaining that the United States was seeking for free in China the trade rights that they had gained at considerable military and administrative cost. The next year, a Chinese secret society called the Boxers incited riots that killed foreigners, including missionaries. The Boxers laid siege to the foreign legations in Beijing. The United States, applauded by American merchants and missionaries alike, joined the imperial powers in sending troops to lift the siege. Hay also sent a second Open Door note in July that instructed other nations to preserve China's territorial integrity and to honor "equal and impartial trade." Hay's protests notwithstanding, China continued for years to be fertile soil for foreign exploitation, especially by the Japanese.

Open Door Policy

Though Hay's foray into Asian politics settled little, the Open Door policy became a cornerstone of U.S. diplomacy. The "open door" had actually been a long-standing American principle, for as a trading nation the United States opposed barriers to international commerce and demanded equal access to foreign markets. After 1900, however, when the United States began to emerge as the premier world trader, the Open Door policy became an instrument first to pry open markets and then to dominate them, not just in China but throughout the world. The Open Door also developed as an ideology with several tenets: first, that America's domestic well-being required exports; second, that foreign trade would suffer interruption unless the United States intervened abroad to implant American principles and keep markets open; and third, that the closing of any area to American products, citizens, or ideas threatened the survival of the United States itself.

In the Philippines, meanwhile, U.S. occupation authorities soon antagonized their new "wards," as McKinley labeled them. The president intended to "uplift and civilize" the Filipinos, but they denied that they needed U.S. paternalism. Emilio Aguinaldo, the Philippine nationalist leader who had been battling the

Philippine Insurrection and Pacification

Map 22.1 Imperialism in Asia: Turn of the Century China and the Pacific region had become imperialist hunting grounds by the turn of the century. The European powers and Japan controlled more areas than the United States, which nonetheless participated in the imperial race by annexing the Philippines, Wake, Guam, Hawai'i, and Samoa, announcing the Open Door policy, and expanding trade. As the spheres of influence in China demonstrate, that besieged nation succumbed to outsiders despite the Open Door policy.

"Know Our Empire" reads the message on the box cover of a patriotic question-and-answer card game produced in 1899 by the New York company McLoughlin Bros. The outbreak of the Philippine insurrection and its suppression by U.S. military forces proved false the suggestion on one card that Filipinos welcomed their new imperial masters.
(© Collection of The New-York Historical Society)

Spanish for years, believed that American officials had promised independence for his country. But after the victory, U.S. officers ordered Aguinaldo out of Manila and isolated him from decisions affecting his nation. In January 1899, feeling betrayed by the Treaty of Paris, he proclaimed an independent Philippine Republic and took up arms. U.S. officials soon set their jaws against the rebellion.

In a war fought viciously by both sides, American soldiers burned villages, tortured captives, and introduced a variant of the reconcentration policy. Americans spoke of the "savage" Filipino; one soldier declared that the Philippines "won't be pacified until the niggers [Filipinos] are killed off like the Indians." In the province of Batangas, U.S. troops forced residents to live in designated zones in an effort to separate the insurgents from local supporters. Disaster

followed. Poor sanitation, starvation, and malaria and cholera killed several thousand people. Outside the secure areas, Americans destroyed food supplies to starve out the rebels. At least one-quarter of the population of Batangas died or fled. Before the Philippine insurrection was suppressed in 1902, more than 200,000 Filipinos and 5,000 Americans lay dead. Resistance to U.S. rule, however, did not abate. The fiercely independent, vehemently anti-Christian, and often violent Muslim Filipinos of Moro Province refused to knuckle under. The U.S. military ordered them to submit or be exterminated. In 1906 the Moros finally met defeat; six hundred of them, including many women and children, were slaughtered at the Battle of Bud Dajo. "Work of this kind," General Leonard Wood wrote Roosevelt, "has its disagreeable side."

U.S. officials, with a stern military hand, soon tried to Americanize the Philippines. The architect Daniel Burnham, leader of the City Beautiful movement (see page 538), planned modern Manila. Imported American teachers taught from the popular American primer *Baldwin Reader* (which included "A" for "apple," a fruit unknown to most Filipinos). Racial slurs—one teacher wrote home that he had been sent to Leyte "to teach these monkeys to talk"—insulted nationalistic Filipinos, as did the declaration of English as the official language. The University of the Philippines was founded in 1908 to train a pro-American elite. The Philippine economy grew as an American satellite, and a sedition act silenced critics of U.S. authority by sending them to prison. In 1916 the Jones Act vaguely promised independence once the Philippines established a "stable government." The United States finally ended its rule in 1946 during an intense period of decolonization after the Second World War (see page 829).

As the United States disciplined the Filipinos, Japan rose as the dominant power in Asia and as a U.S.

Japanese Expansion

rival. Many race-minded Japanese interpreted the U.S. advance into the Pacific as an attempt by whites to gain ascendancy over Asians. Japanese leaders nonetheless urged their citizens to go to America to study it as a model for industrializing and achieving world power. As the historian Walter LaFeber has put it: "The Japanese were determined to copy—not become subject to—the West." Although some Americans proudly proclaimed the Japanese the "Yankees of the East," gradually the United States had to make concessions to Japan to protect the vulnerable Philippines and to sustain the

Open Door policy. Japan continued to plant interests in China and then smashed the Russians in the Russo-Japanese War (1904–1905). President Roosevelt mediated the crisis at the Portsmouth Conference in New Hampshire and won the Nobel Peace Prize for this ultimately vain effort to preserve a balance of power in Asia and shrink Japan's "big head."

In 1905, in the Taft-Katsura Agreement, the United States conceded Japanese hegemony over Korea in return for Japan's pledge not to undermine the U.S. position in the Philippines. Three years later, in the Root-Takahira Agreement, the United States recognized Japan's interests in Manchuria, whereas Japan again pledged the security of the United States's Pacific possessions and endorsed the Open Door in China. Roosevelt also built up American naval power to deter the Japanese; in late 1907 he sent on a world tour the navy's "Great White Fleet" (so named because the ships were painted white for the voyage). Duly impressed, the Japanese began to build a bigger navy of their own.

President William Howard Taft thought he might counter Japanese advances in Asia through dollar diplomacy—the use of private funds to serve American diplomatic goals and at the same time to garner profits for American financiers. In this case, Taft induced American bankers to join an international consortium to build a railway in China. Taft's venture seemed only to embolden Japan to solidify and extend its holdings in China, where internal discord continued after the nationalistic revolution of 1911 overthrew the Qing dynasty.

Japanese-American relations also became tense over the treatment of Japanese citizens living in the

Anti-Japanese Bias in California

United States. In 1906 the San Francisco School Board, reflecting the anti-Asian bias of many West Coast Americans, ordered the segregation of all Chinese, Koreans, and Japanese in special schools. Tokyo protested the discrimination against its citizens. The following year, President Roosevelt quieted the crisis by striking a "gentleman's agreement" with Tokyo restricting the inflow of Japanese immigrants; San Francisco then rescinded its segregation order. Relations with Tokyo were jolted again in 1913 when the California legislature denied Japanese residents the right to own property in the state.

In 1914, when the First World War broke out in Europe, Japan seized Shandong and some Pacific islands from the Germans. In 1915 Japan issued its Twenty-One Demands, virtually insisting on hege-

mony over all of China. The Chinese door was being slammed shut, but the United States lacked adequate countervailing power in Asia to block Japan's imperial thrusts. President Woodrow Wilson worried about how the "white race" could blunt the rise of "the yellow race."

Latin America, Europe, and International Rivalry

Intense international rivalry also characterized U.S. relations with Latin America, where U.S. economic and strategic interests and power towered (see Map 22.2), and with Europe, where repeated political and military disputes persuaded Americans to develop friendlier relations with Great Britain while avoiding entrapment in the continent's troubles, many of which Americans blamed on Germany.

As U.S. economic interests expanded in Latin America, so did U.S. political influence. Exports to

Economic Hegemony in Latin America

Latin America, which exceeded $50 million in the 1870s, rose to more than $120 million in 1900 and then reached $300 million in 1914. Investments by U.S. citizens in Latin America climbed to a commanding $1.26 billion in 1914. In 1899 two large banana importers merged to form United Fruit Company. In Central America, United Fruit owned much of the land (more than a million acres in 1913) and the railroad and steamship lines, and the firm became an influential economic and political force in the region. The company also worked to eradicate yellow fever and malaria while it manipulated Central American politics.

After the destructive war in Cuba, U.S. citizens and corporations continued to dominate the island's

Cuba and the Platt Amendment

economy, controlling the sugar, mining, tobacco, and utilities industries and most of the rural lands. Private U.S. investments in Cuba grew from $50 million before the revolution to $220 million by 1913, and U.S. exports to the island rose from $26 million in 1900 to $196 million in 1917. The Teller Amendment outlawed the annexation of Cuba, but officials in Washington soon used the document's call for "pacification" to justify U.S. control. American troops remained there until 1902. Favoring the "better classes," U.S. authorities restricted voting rights largely to propertied Cuban males, excluding two-thirds of adult men and all women. American officials also forced the

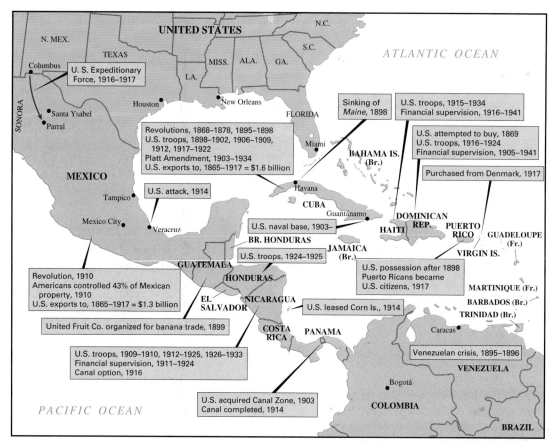

Map 22.2   U.S. Hegemony in the Caribbean and Latin America   Through many interventions, territorial acquisitions, and robust economic expansion, the United States became the predominant power in Latin America in the early twentieth century. The United States often backed up the Roosevelt Corollary's declaration of a "police power" by dispatching troops to Caribbean nations, where they met nationalist opposition.

Cubans to append to their constitution a frank avowal of U.S. hegemony known as the Platt Amendment. This statement prohibited Cuba from making a treaty with another nation that might impair its independence; in practice, this meant that all treaties had to have U.S. approval. Most important, another Platt Amendment provision granted the United States "the right to intervene" to preserve the island's independence and to maintain domestic order. Cuba also had to lease a naval base (at Guantánamo Bay, and still under U.S. jurisdiction today). Formalized in a 1903 treaty, the amendment governed Cuban-American relations until 1934. "There is, of course, little or no independence left Cuba under the Platt Amendment," General Wood noted.

The Cubans, like the Filipinos, chafed under U.S. mastery. Widespread demonstrations protested the Platt Amendment, and a rebellion against the Cuban government in 1906 prompted Roosevelt to order another invasion of Cuba. The marines stayed until 1909, returned briefly in 1912, and occupied the island again from 1917 to 1922. All the while, U.S. officials helped to develop a transportation system, expand the public school system, found a national army, and increase sugar production. When Dr. Walter Reed's experiments, based on the theory of the Cuban physician Carlos Finlay, proved that mosquitoes transmitted yellow fever, sanitary engineers controlled the insect and eradicated the disease.

Puerto Rico, the Caribbean island taken as a spoil of war in the Treaty of Paris, also developed under

U.S. Governance of Puerto Rico

U.S. tutelage. Although no Puerto Rican sat at the negotiating table for that treaty, the Puerto Rican elite at first welcomed the United States as an improvement over Spain. But disillusionment soon set in. The condescending U.S. military governor, General Guy V. Henry, regarded Puerto Ricans as naughty, ill-educated children who needed "kindergarten instruction in controlling themselves without allowing them too much liberty." Some residents warned against the "Yankee peril"; others applauded the "Yankee model" and futilely anticipated statehood (see page 631).

Panama, meanwhile, became the site of a bold U.S. expansionist venture. In 1869 the world had mar-

Panama Canal veled at the completion of the Suez Canal, a waterway that greatly facilitated travel between the Indian Ocean and Mediterranean Sea and enhanced the power of the British Empire. Surely that feat could be duplicated in the Western Hemisphere, possibly in Panama, a province of Colombia. One expansionist, U.S. navy captain Robert W. Shufeldt, predicted that a new canal would convert "the Gulf of Mexico into an American lake." Business interests joined politicians, diplomats, and navy officers in insisting that the United States control such an interoceanic canal. Daunting obstacles had to be overcome. The Clayton-Bulwer Treaty with Britain (1850) provided for joint control of a canal. The British, recognizing their diminishing influence in the region and cultivating friendship with the United States as a counterweight to Germany, stepped aside in the Hay-Pauncefote Treaty (1901) to permit a solely U.S.-run canal. When Colombia hesitated to meet Washington's terms, Roosevelt encouraged Panamanian rebels to declare independence and ordered American warships to the isthmus to back them. In 1903 the new Panama awarded the United States a canal zone and long-term rights to its control. The treaty also guaranteed Panama its independence. (In 1922 the United States paid Colombia $25 million in "conscience money" but did not apologize.) The completion of the Panama Canal in 1914 marked a major technological achievement. During the canal's first year of operation, more than one thousand merchant ships squeezed through its locks.

As for the rest of the Caribbean, Roosevelt resisted challenges to U.S. hegemony. Worried that Latin American nations' defaults on debts owed to European banks were provoking European intervention (England, Germany, and Italy sent warships to Venezuela in 1902), **Roosevelt Corollary** the president in 1904 issued the Roosevelt Corollary to the Monroe Doctrine. He warned Latin Americans to stabilize their politics and finances. "Chronic wrongdoing," the corollary lectured, might require "intervention by some civilized nation," and "in flagrant cases of such wrongdoing or impotence," the United States would have to assume the role of "an international police power." Laced with presumptions of superiority, Roosevelt's declaration provided the rationale for frequent U.S. interventions in Latin America.

From 1900 to 1917, the presidents ordered U.S. troops to Cuba, Panama, Nicaragua, the Dominican Republic, Mexico, and Haiti to quell civil wars, thwart

The Panama-Pacific Exposition in San Francisco in 1915 celebrated the opening of the Panama Canal with this official poster by Perham Nahl, "The Thirteenth Labor of Hercules." The artist commemorates the ten-year construction feat by using symbols that reflect the imperialism and male hegemony of that time: a gigantic, muscular Hercules (the powerful United States) forcibly opens the land (a yielding Panama) to make space for the canal. When President Theodore Roosevelt asked Secretary of War Elihu Root whether he had adequately defended himself against charges that the United States had acted imperialistically in helping to sever Panama from Colombia in 1903, Root replied: "You have shown that you were accused of seduction and you have conclusively proved that you were guilty of rape." (Courtesy of the Oakland Museum of California)

challenges to U.S. influence, gain ports and bases, and forestall European meddling (see Map 22.2). U.S. authorities ran elections, trained national guards that became politically powerful, and renegotiated foreign debts, shifting them to U.S. banks. They also took over customs houses to control tariff revenues and government budgets (as in the Dominican Republic, from 1905 to 1941).

A TRUE AMERICAN ROUGH RIDER.

This chauvinistic *Judge* magazine cartoon of 1904 appeared after President Theodore Roosevelt proclaimed the United States a "police power" in the Western Hemisphere (the Roosevelt Corollary to the Monroe Doctrine). "A True American Rough Rider," Roosevelt gallops across Central America and Panama into South America, all the while knocking down or chasing away European nations from the United States's sphere of influence. (Collection of Janice L. and David J. Frent)

In neighboring Mexico, the long-time (1876–1910) dictator Porfirio Díaz aggressively recruited foreign investors through tax incentives

U.S.-Mexico Relations Under Díaz

and land grants. American capitalists came to own Mexico's railroads and mines and invested heavily in petroleum and banking. By the early 1890s, the United States dominated Mexico's foreign trade. By 1910 Americans controlled 43 percent of Mexican property and produced more than half of the country's oil; in the state of Sonora 186 of 208 mining companies were American-owned. The Mexican revolutionaries who ousted Díaz in 1910, like

nationalists elsewhere in Latin America, set out to reclaim their nation's sovereignty by ending their economic dependency on the United States (see page 640).

As the United States reaffirmed the Monroe Doctrine against European expansion in the hemisphere and demonstrated the power to enforce it, European nations reluctantly honored U.S. hegemony in Latin America. In turn, the United States held to its tradition of standing outside European embroilments. The balance of power in Europe was precarious, and seldom did an American president involve the United States directly. Roosevelt did help settle a Franco-German clash over Morocco by mediating a settlement at Algeciras, Spain (1906). But the president drew American criticism for entangling the United States in a European problem. Americans endorsed the ultimately futile Hague peace conferences (1899 and 1907) and negotiated various arbitration treaties, but on the whole stayed outside the European arena, except to profit from extensive trade with it.

A special feature of American-European relations was the flowering of the Anglo-American cooperation that had been growing throughout

Anglo-American Rapprochement

the late nineteenth century. One outcome of the intense German-British rivalry and the rise of the United States to world power was London's quest for friendship with Washington. Already prepared by racial ideas of Anglo-Saxon kinship, a common language, and respect for representative government and private-property rights, Americans appreciated British support in the 1898 war and the Hay-Pauncefote Treaty, and London's virtual endorsement of the Roosevelt Corollary and withdrawal of British warships from the Caribbean. As Mark Twain said of the two imperialist powers: "We are kin in sin."

British-American trade and U.S. investment in Britain also secured ties. By 1914 more than 140 American companies operated in Britain, including H. J. Heinz's processed foods and F. W. Woolworth's "penny markets." Many Britons decried an Americanization of British culture. One journalist complained that a Briton "wakes in the morning at the sound of an American alarm clock; rises from his New England sheets, and shaves with . . . a Yankee safety razor. He . . . slips his Waterbury watch into his pocket [and] catches an electric train made in New York. . . . At his office . . . he sits on a Nebraskan swivel chair, before a Michigan roll-top desk." Such exaggerated fears and the always prickly character of the Anglo-American relationship, however, gave way to cooperation in world affairs, most evident in 1917 when the United States threw its weapons and soldiers into the First World War on the British side against Germany.

Summary

 In the years from the Civil War to the First World War, expansionism and imperialism elevated the United States to world power status. By 1914 Americans held extensive economic, strategic, and political interests in a world made smaller by modern technology. The victory over Spain in 1898 was but the most dramatic moment in the long process. The outward reach of U.S. foreign policy from Seward to Wilson sparked opposition from domestic critics, other imperial nations, and foreign nationalists, but expansionists prevailed and the trend toward empire endured.

From Asia to Latin America, economic and strategic needs and ideology motivated and justified expansion and empire. The belief that the United States needed foreign markets to absorb surplus production to save the domestic economy joined missionary zeal to reform other societies through the promotion of American products and culture. Notions of racial and male supremacy and appeals to national greatness also fed the appetite for foreign adventure and commitments. The greatly augmented navy became a primary means for satisfying American ideas and wants.

Revealing the great diversity of America's intersection with the world, missionaries such as Moon in China, generals such as Wood in Cuba, companies such as Singer in Africa and Heinz in Britain, and politicians such as Taft in the Philippines carried American ways, ideas, guns, and goods abroad to a mixed reception. The conspicuous declarations of Olney, Hay, Roosevelt, and other leaders became the guiding texts for U.S. principles and behavior in world affairs. A world power with far-flung interests to protect, the United States had to face a tough test of its self-proclaimed greatness and reconsider its political isolation from Europe when a world war broke out in August 1914.

LEGACY FOR A PEOPLE AND A NATION
The Status of Puerto Rico

Ever since the U.S. invasion of their island in July 1898 and their transfer under the Treaty of Paris from Spain to the United States, Puerto Ricans have debated their status, their very identity. Colony? territory? nation? state? or the "Commonwealth of Puerto Rico" that the U.S. Congress designated in 1952? A small Caribbean island with 3.8 million people (another 2.5 million Puerto Ricans live in the United States), Puerto Rico has held nonbinding plebiscites in 1967, 1993, and 1998, each time rejecting both statehood and independence in favor of commonwealth. In the 1998 referendum, 46.5 percent voted for statehood and 2.5 percent for independence. The U.S. Congress, which holds the constitutional authority to set the rules by which Puerto Ricans live, stands as sharply divided as the islanders, rejecting independent nationhood, unwilling to force statehood if Puerto Ricans do not want it, yet uneasy with the ambivalence that commonwealth status promotes.

Although a plurality of Puerto Ricans have narrowly endorsed commonwealth status, they remain troubled by their incomplete self-government. They are U.S. citizens (made so by the Jones Act of 1916) who can and do move freely between the island and the mainland and who are subject to the military draft, but they cannot vote in U.S. presidential elections. Although they send a delegate to the U.S. Congress, this representative cannot vote. Yet they have the attributes of a state, with a government modeled after the fifty states. Puerto Ricans pay Medicare and Social Security taxes, but not federal income taxes, and they receive benefits under federal programs. They also take pride in the symbols of nationalism, such as their own Olympic team, but the symbols do not signify independence.

The issue of cultural nationalism dominates the debate over Puerto Rico's political status. A majority of Puerto Ricans have rejected statehood because they fear it would mean giving up their Latin American culture and Spanish language. Most Puerto Ricans today, although bilingual, prefer Spanish over English, and many oppose the mandatory school courses in English. Commonwealthers warn that if Puerto Rico became a state, mainland conservatives might make English the official U.S. language. Puerto Rico's uncertain status persists as a legacy of turn-of-the-century empire building; then, as now, the issue centered on the rights of self-determination—in this case, the right to sustain a people's own culture.

For Further Reading, see page A-25 of the Appendix. For Web resources, go to http://college.hmco.com.

The medical case files listed him as "A.P.," an eighteen-year-old Marine Corps private who had volunteered to fight in the Great War. He thrived on the military life, and, like other young American soldiers, A.P. was ordered to the western front in France. During early 1918 the Germans relentlessly bombarded his position at Château-Thierry, where screeching shells and deafening explosions pounded the fresh American troops.

In June, A.P.'s company trudged forward to the battle lines, past the bodies of French soldiers dismembered by the big guns. His commanding officer detailed A.P. to bury the mangled corpses. For several nights thereafter the young man could not sleep. Artillery fire frightened him. During a bombardment on June 14, he began to tremble uncontrollably. Evacuated to a hospital, A.P. suffered horrifying dreams, and the slightest noise easily startled him.

Doctors who treated military casualties saw many such patients, whom they diagnosed as having a mental illness known as war neurosis or war psychosis—shell shock, for short. The symptoms: a fixed empty stare, violent tremors, paralyzed limbs, listlessness, jabbering, screaming, and haunting dreams. The illness could strike anyone; even those soldiers who appeared most manly and courageous cracked after days of incessant shelling and inescapable human carnage. "There was a limit to human endurance," one lieutenant explained.

Their nervous systems shattered, some one hundred thousand victims went to special military hospitals staffed by psychiatrists. A regimen of rest, military discipline, recreation, exercise, counseling, and reminders about patriotic duty restored many shell-shock victims to health. Some returned to the front lines, but others remained riven by anxiety and had to be assigned to noncombat duties. The very ill went home to the United States. Even cured shell-shocked soldiers had lingering mental problems—flashbacks, nightmares, and a persistent disorientation that made it difficult for them to make decisions or organize their lives. Thousands of the most severely afflicted remained in veterans' hospitals.

Harvey Dunn's 1918 painting (detail) of weary soldiers in the First World War captures the misery of frontline battle. (Smithsonian Institute, Division of Political History, Washington, D.C.)

23

AMERICANS IN THE GREAT WAR 1914–1920

Many Progressive era professionals and reformers found rewards and opportunities in the wrenching national emergency of World War I. The psychiatrists who treated the shell-shock victims, for example, wanted to apply their mental health expertise to help win the war. They also hoped to use their wartime medical experience later, at home, to improve care for the mentally ill. For them, the cataclysm of foreign crisis and the opportunity for domestic social betterment went hand in hand. That is what the philosopher and educator John Dewey meant when he said that the war presented "social possibilities." But the antiwar intellectual Randolph Bourne was not so sure that positive change could emerge from the war. "If the war is too strong for you to prevent," he lectured progressives, "how is it going to be weak enough for you to control and mold to your liberal purposes?"

The outbreak of the Great War in Europe in 1914 at first stunned Americans. For years their nation had participated in the international competition for colonies, markets, and weapons supremacy. But full-scale war seemed unthinkable. The new machine guns, howitzers, submarines, and dreadnoughts were such awesome death engines that leaders surely would not use them. When they did, moaned one social reformer, "civilization is all gone, and barbarism come." Progressives who had applauded Germany as a model of state welfare now wondered how it became so reactionary. Articulated by well-organized groups, peace sentiment in the United States strengthened with each grisly report from the European battlefield.

For almost three years President Woodrow Wilson kept America out of the war. During this time, he sought to protect U.S. trade interests and to improve the nation's military posture. He lectured the belligerents to rediscover their humanity and to respect international law. But American property, lives, and neutrality fell victim to British and German naval warfare. In April 1917, when the president finally asked Congress for a declaration of war, he did so with his characteristic crusading zeal. America entered the battle not just to win the war but to reform the postwar world—to "make the world safe for democracy," declared Wilson.

Even after more than a decade of Progressive reform, Americans remained a heterogeneous and fractious people at the start of the Great War. Headlines still trumpeted labor-capital confrontations such as the Ludlow Massacre in Colorado, in which two women and eleven children were killed when state militia fired on striking miners. Racial antagonisms were evident in Wilson's decision to segregate federal buildings in Washington and in continued lynchings of African Americans (fifty-one in 1914). Nativists protested the pace of immigration; 1.2 million immigrants entered the United States in 1914 alone. Ethnic groups eyed one another suspiciously. Activist women argued for equality between the sexes and at the ballot box, but many men preferred restrictive traditions.

The war experience accentuated and intensified the nation's social divisiveness. Whites who did not like the northward migration of southern blacks to work in defense plants incited race riots. War hawks harassed pacifists and German Americans. The federal government itself, eager to stimulate patriotism, trampled on civil liberties to silence critics. And as communism implanted itself in Russia, a postwar Red Scare repressed radicals and tarnished America's reputation as a democratic society. After the war, groups that sought to consolidate wartime gains vied with those who sought to restore the prewar status quo.

America's participation in the war wrought massive changes and accelerated ongoing trends. Wars are emergencies, and during such times normal ways of doing things surrender to the extraordinary and exaggerated. The U.S. government, more than ever before, became a manager—of people, prices, production, and minds. A compulsory draft pulled men into the armed services. The presidency assumed greater powers. Unprecedented centralization and integration of the economy, increased standardization of products, and unusual cooperation between government and business also characterized the times. Although reformers continued to devote themselves to issues such as prohibition and woman suffrage, the war experience helped splinter the Progressive movement. Jane Addams sadly remarked that "the spirit of fighting burns away all those impulses . . . which foster the will to justice."

The United States emerged from the war a major power in an economically hobbled world. Yet Americans who had marched to battle as if on a crusade grew disillusioned with the peace process. They recoiled from the spectacle of the victors squabbling over the spoils, and they chided Wilson for failing to deliver the "peace without victory" he promised. As in the 1790s, the 1840s, and the 1890s, Americans once again engaged in a searching national debate about the fundamentals of their foreign policy. After negotiating the Treaty of Versailles at Paris, the president urged U.S. membership in the new League of Nations, which he touted as a vehicle for reforming world politics. The

IMPORTANT EVENTS

1914 U.S. troops invade revolutionary Mexico
First World War begins in Europe

1915 *Lusitania* sinks
Secretary of State Bryan resigns

1916 Congress rejects Gore-McLemore resolution limiting travel on belligerent ships
U.S. troops invade Mexico again
After torpedoing *Sussex*, Germany pledges not to attack merchant ships without warning
National Defense Act expands military
Wilson reelected on platform of peace, progressivism, and preparedness

1917 Germany declares unrestricted submarine warfare
Zimmermann telegram aggravates U.S.-Mexico troubles
Russian Revolution ousts the czar
United States enters First World War
Selective Service Act creates the draft
Espionage Act limits First Amendment rights
Race riot in East St. Louis, Illinois
War Industries Board created to manage the economy
War Revenue Act raises taxes to control war profiteering
Fuel crisis during severe winter

1918 Wilson announces Fourteen Points for new world order
Sedition Act further limits free speech
Debs imprisoned for antiwar speech
U.S. troops at Château-Thierry help blunt German offensive
U.S. troops intervene in Russia against Bolsheviks
Flu pandemic
Republicans hand Wilson a setback by winning congressional elections
Armistice ends the First World War

1919 Paris Peace Conference punishes Germany and launches League of Nations
May Day bombings help instigate Red Scare
American Legion organizes for veterans' benefits and antiradicalism
Chicago race riot
Steelworkers strike
Communist Party of the United States of America founded
Wilson suffers stroke after speaking tour
Senate rejects Treaty of Versailles and U.S. membership in League
Schenck v. U.S. upholds Espionage Act

1920 Palmer Raids round up suspected radicals

Senate rejected his appeal (the League nonetheless organized without U.S. membership) because many Americans feared that the League might entangle Americans in Europe's problems, threaten the U.S. empire, and compromise the country's traditional unilateralism, or nonaligned course in foreign relations. On many fronts, then, Americans during the era of the First World War were at war with themselves. ■

Precarious Neutrality

The war that erupted in August 1914 grew from years of European competition over trade, colonies, allies, and armaments. Two powerful alliance systems had formed: the Triple Alliance of Germany, Austria-Hungary, and Italy, and the Triple Entente of Britain, France, and Russia. All had imperial holdings and ambitions for

more, but Germany seemed particularly bold as it rivaled Great Britain for world leadership. Many Americans saw Germany as a threat to U.S. interests in the Western Hemisphere and viewed Germans as an excessively militaristic people who embraced autocracy and spurned democracy.

Strategists said that Europe enjoyed a balance of power, but crises in the Balkan countries of southeastern Europe triggered a chain of events that shattered the "balance." Slavic nationalists sought to enlarge Serbia, an independent Slavic nation, by annexing regions such as Bosnia, then a province of the Austro-Hungarian Empire (see Map 23.1). On June 28, 1914, at Sarajevo, Bosnia, a member of the Black Hand, a Serbian terrorist group in collusion with Serbian officials, assassinated the heir to the Austro-Hungarian throne. Alarmed by the

Outbreak of the First World War

Map 23.1 Europe Goes to War, Summer 1914 Bound by alliances and stirred by turmoil in the Balkans, where Serbs repeatedly upended peace, the nations of Europe descended into war in the summer of 1914. Step by step a Balkan crisis escalated into the "Great War."

prospect of an engorged Serbia on its border, Austria-Hungary consulted its Triple Alliance partner Germany, which urged toughness. When Serbia called on its Slavic friend Russia for help, Russia in turn looked for backing from its ally France. In late July, Austria-Hungary declared war against Serbia. Russia then began to mobilize its armies.

Germany—having goaded Austria-Hungary toward war and believing war inevitable—struck first, declaring war against Russia on August 1 and against France two days later. Britain hesitated, but when German forces slashed into neutral Belgium to get at France, London declared war against Germany on August 4. Eventually Turkey (the Ottoman Empire) joined Germany and Austria-Hungary as the Central Powers, and Italy (switching sides) and Japan teamed up with Britain, France, and Russia as the Allies. Japan took advantage of the European war to seize Germany's sphere of influence in China, Shandong.

President Wilson at first sought to distance America from the conflagration by issuing a proclamation of neutrality—the traditional U.S. policy toward European wars. He also asked Americans to refrain from taking sides, to exhibit "the dignity of self-control." In private, the president said that "we definitely have to be neutral, since otherwise our mixed populations would wage war on each other." The United States, he fervently hoped, would stand apart as a sane, civilized nation in a deranged international system.

Wilson's lofty appeal for American neutrality and unity at home collided with several realities between August 1914 and April 1917. First, ethnic groups in the United States did take sides. Many German Americans and anti-British Irish Americans (Ireland was then trying to break free from British rule) cheered for the Central Powers. Americans of British and French ancestry and others with roots in Allied nations championed the Allied cause. Germany's attack on Belgium confirmed in many people's minds that Germany had become the archetype of unbridled militarism.

Taking Sides

The pro-Allied sympathies of Wilson's administration also weakened the U.S. neutrality proclamation. Honoring Anglo-American rapprochement (see page 630), Wilson shared the conviction with British leaders that a German victory would destroy free enterprise and government by law. If Germany won the war, he prophesied, "it would change the course of our civilization and make the United States a military nation." Wilson's chief advisers and diplomats—his assistant Edward House, Secretary of State Robert Lansing, and Ambassador to London Walter Hines Page—held similar anti-German views that often translated into pro-Allied policies.

U.S. economic links with the Allies also rendered neutrality difficult, if not impossible. England had long been one of the nation's best customers. Now the British flooded America with new orders, especially for arms. Sales to the Allies helped pull the American economy out of its recession. Between 1914 and 1916, American exports to England and France grew 365 percent, from $753 million to $2.75 billion. In the same period, however, largely because of Britain's naval blockade, exports to Germany dropped by more than 90 percent, from $345 million to only $29 million. Loans from private American banks—totaling $2.3 billion during the neutrality period—financed much of U.S. trade with the Allies. Germany received only $27 million in the same period. The Wilson administration, which at first frowned on these transactions, came to see them

Trade and Loans

as necessary to the economic health of the United States.

From Germany's perspective, the linkage between the American economy and the Allies meant that the United States had become the Allied arsenal and bank. Americans, however, faced a dilemma: cutting their economic ties with Britain would constitute an unneutral act in favor of Germany. Under international law, Britain—which controlled the seas—could buy both contraband (war-related goods) and noncontraband from neutrals. It was Germany's responsibility, not America's, to stop such trade in ways that international law prescribed—that is, by an effective blockade of the enemy's territory, by the seizure of contraband from neutral (American) ships, or by the confiscation of goods from belligerent (British) ships. Germans, of course, judged the huge U.S. trade with the Allies an act of unneutrality that had to be stopped.

The president and his aides believed, finally, that Wilsonian principles stood a better chance of international acceptance if Britain, rather than the Central Powers, sat astride the postwar world. "Wilsonianism," the cluster of ideas Wilson espoused, consisted of traditional American principles (such as democracy and the Open Door) and an ideology of internationalism and exceptionalism. The central tenet was that only the United States could lead the convulsed world into a new, peaceful era of unobstructed commerce, free-market capitalism, democratic politics, and open diplomacy. American Progressivism, it seemed, was to be projected onto the world. "America had the infinite privilege of fulfilling her destiny and saving the world," Wilson claimed. Empires had to be dismantled to honor the principle of self-determination. Armaments had to be reduced. Critics charged that Wilson often violated his own credos in his eagerness to force them on others—as his military interventions in Mexico in 1914, Haiti in 1915, and the Dominican Republic in 1916 testified. All agreed, though, that such ideals served the American national interest; in this way idealism and realism were married.

Wilsonianism

To say that American neutrality was never a real possibility given ethnic loyalties, economic ties, and Wilsonian preferences is not to say that Wilson sought to enter the war. He emphatically wanted to keep the United States out. Time and again, he tried to mediate the crisis to prevent one power from crushing another. In early 1917, the president remarked that "we are the only one of the great white nations that is free from war today, and it would be a crime against civilization for us to go in." But go in the United States finally did. Why?

Americans got caught in the Allied–Central Power crossfire. British naval policy aimed to sever neutral trade with Germany in order to crip-

British Violations of Neutral Rights

ple the German economy. The British, "ruling the waves and waiving the rules," declared a blockade of water entrances to Germany and mined the North Sea. They also harassed neutral shipping by seizing cargoes and defined a broad list of contraband (including foodstuffs) that they prohibited neutrals from shipping to Germany. American vessels bearing goods for Germany seldom reached their destination. Furthermore, to counter German submarines, the British flouted international law by arming their merchant ships and flying neutral (sometimes American) flags. Wilson frequently protested British violations of neutral rights, pointing out that neutrals had the right to sell and ship noncontraband goods to belligerents without interference. But London often deftly defused Washington's criticism by paying for confiscated cargoes, and German provocations made British behavior appear less offensive by comparison.

Unable to win the war on land and determined to lift the blockade and halt American-Allied commerce,

The German Submarine and International Law

Germany looked for victory at sea by using submarines. In February 1915 Berlin created a war zone around the British Isles, warned neutral vessels to stay out so as not to be attacked by mistake, and advised passengers from neutral nations to stay off Allied ships. President Wilson informed Germany that the United States was holding it to "strict accountability" for any losses of American life and property.

Wilson was interpreting international law in the strictest possible sense. The law that an attacker had to warn a passenger or merchant ship before attacking, so that passengers and crew could disembark safely into lifeboats, predated the emergence of the submarine as a major weapon. When Wilson refused to make adjustments, the Germans thought him unfair. As they saw the issue, the slender, frail, and sluggish *untersee-booten* (U-boats) should not be expected to surface to warn ships. Surfacing would nullify the U-boats' advantage of surprise and leave them vulnerable to British attack. Berlin protested that Wilson was denying it the one weapon that could break the British economic stranglehold, disrupt the Allies' substantial connection

with U.S. producers and bankers, and win the war. To all concerned—British, Germans, and Americans—this naval warfare became a matter of life and death.

Submarine Warfare and Wilson's Decision for War

 Over the next few months the U-boats sank ship after ship. In May 1915 the swift, luxurious British passenger liner *Lusitania* left New York City carrying more than twelve hundred passengers and a cargo of food and contraband, including 4.2 million rounds of ammunition for Remington rifles. Before "Lucy's" departure, the German embassy warned in a newspaper announcement that travelers on British vessels should know that Allied ships in war-zone waters "are liable to destruction." Few passengers paid attention or shifted to an American vessel for the transatlantic trip. On May 7, off the Irish coast, submarine U-20 torpedoed the four-stacked vessel. The *Lusitania* sank quickly, taking to their deaths 1,198 people, 128 of them Americans. Even if the ship was carrying armaments, argued Wilson, the sinking was a brutal assault on innocent people. But he ruled out a military response. Secretary of State William Jennings Bryan advised that Americans be prohibited from travel on belligerent ships and that passenger vessels be prohibited from carrying war goods. "Germany has a right to prevent contraband going to the Allies," wrote Bryan, "and a ship carrying contraband should not rely on passengers to protect her from attack—it would be like putting women and children in front of an army."

The president rejected Bryan's counsel, insisting on the right of Americans to sail on belligerent ships and demanding that Germany

Secretary Bryan's Resignation

cease its inhumane submarine warfare. When the Germans urged Wilson to rethink the relationship between international law and the submarine, the president fumed. After a stormy White House meeting marked by Bryan's charge that the cabinet was pro-Allied, Wilson reiterated his demand that submarines be kept in port. When the president refused to ban American travelers from belligerent ships, Bryan resigned in protest—an uncommon act for unhappy secretaries of state, who usually leave quietly. The pro-Allied Robert Lansing took Bryan's place. When criticized for pursuing a double standard in favor of the Allies, Wilson responded that the British were taking cargoes and violating property rights but the Germans were taking lives and violating human rights. Wilson's attitude toward Germany had noticeably hardened.

Seeking to avoid war with America, Germany ordered U-boat commanders to halt attacks on passenger liners. But in mid-August another British vessel, the *Arabic*, was sunk off Ireland and three Americans died. The Germans hastened to pledge that an unarmed passenger ship would never again be attacked without warning. But the sinking of the *Arabic* fueled debate over American passengers on belligerent vessels. Why not require Americans to sail on American craft? asked critics. From August 1914 to March 1917 only three Americans died on an American ship (the tanker *Gulflight* in May 1915), whereas about 190 were killed on belligerent ships.

In early 1916 Congress began to debate the Gore-McLemore resolution to prohibit Americans from traveling on armed merchant vessels or on ships carrying contraband. The resolution, its sponsors hoped, would prevent incidents such as the *Lusitania* sinking from hurtling the United States into war. But Wilson would tolerate no interference in the presidential making of foreign policy (he had just sent Edward House to Europe to mediate an end to the war) and no restrictions on American travel. The resolution, he argued, would destroy the "whole fine fabric of international law." After heavy politicking, Congress tabled the resolution, effectively killing it. Wilson's critics have pointed out that the Gore-McLemore resolution would have avoided or at least delayed a German-American confrontation over the submarine without undercutting U.S. interests or besmirching national honor.

Gore-McLemore Resolution

In March 1916 a U-boat attack on the *Sussex*, a French vessel crossing the English Channel, took the United States a step closer to war. Four Americans were injured on that ship, which the U-boat commander mistook for a minelayer. Stop the marauding submarines, Wilson lectured Berlin, or the United States will sever diplomatic relations. Again the Germans retreated, pledging not to attack merchant vessels without warning. At about the same time, relations with Britain soured. The British crushing of the Easter Rebellion in Ireland and further restriction of U.S. trade with the Central Powers aroused American anger.

As the United States became more entangled in the Great War, many Americans urged Wilson to keep the nation out. In early 1915, Jane Addams, Carrie Chapman Catt, and other suffragists helped found the

"Here's money for your Americans. I may drown some more," says Kaiser Wilhelm to President Wilson in this anti-German cartoon. It appeared in early 1916 after Germany finally expressed regret for having taken American lives almost a year earlier when a U-boat sank the *Lusitania*. The Germans offered an indemnity, but not until 1925 did a claims commission determine that Germany should pay $2.5 million to American claimants who had suffered losses because of the *Lusitania* tragedy.   (*Life* magazine, April 13, 1916. The Boston Athenaeum)

Peace Advocates

Woman's Peace Party, the U.S. section of the Women's International League for Peace and Freedom. "The mother half of humanity," claimed women peace advocates, had a special role as "the guardians of life." Later that same year, some pacifist Progressives—including Oswald Garrison Villard, Paul Kellogg, and Lillian Wald—organized an antiwar coalition, the American Union Against Militarism. The businessman Andrew Carnegie, who in 1910 had established the Carnegie Endowment for International Peace, helped finance peace groups. So did Henry Ford, who in late 1915 sent a "peace ship" to Europe to propagandize for a negotiated settlement. Socialists such as Eugene Debs added their voices to the peace movement.

Antiwar advocates emphasized several points: that war drained a nation of its youth, resources, and reform impulse; that it fostered repression at home; that it violated Christian morality; and that wartime business barons reaped huge profits at the expense of the people. Militarism and conscription, Addams pointed out, were what millions of immigrants had left behind in Europe. Were they now—in the United States—to be forced into the decadent system they had escaped? Although the peace movement was splintered—some of its followers endorsing peace but not pacifism—it carried political and intellectual weight that Wilson could not ignore, and it articulated several ideas that he shared. In fact, he campaigned on a peace platform in the 1916 presidential election. After his triumph, Wilson futilely labored once again to bring the belligerents to the conference table. In early 1917 he advised them to temper their acquisitive war aims, appealing for "peace without victory."

Unrestricted Submarine Warfare

Germany rejected Wilson's overture in early February 1917, when it launched unrestricted submarine warfare. All vessels—belligerent or neutral, warship or merchant—would be attacked if sighted in the declared war zone. This bold decision represented a calculated risk that submarines could impede American munitions shipments to England and permit Germany to defeat the Allies before U.S. troops could be ferried across the Atlantic. Wilson quickly broke diplomatic relations with Berlin.

This German challenge to American neutral rights and economic interests was soon followed by a German threat to U.S. security. In late February, British intelligence intercepted and passed to U.S. officials a telegram addressed to the German minister in Mexico from German Foreign Secretary Arthur Zimmermann. Its message: If Mexico joined a military alliance against the United States, Germany would help Mexico recover the territories it had lost in 1848, including several western states. Zimmermann hoped to "set new enemies on America's neck—enemies which give them plenty to take care of over there."

U.S. officials took the message seriously because Mexican-American relations had deteriorated recently.

Zimmermann Telegram and Mexican Revolution

The Mexican revolution, which began in 1910, had descended into a bloody civil war with strong anti-Yankee overtones, and the Mexican government intended to nationalize extensive American-owned properties (see Chapters 22 and 26). Wilson had twice ordered troops onto Mexican soil: in 1914, at Veracruz, to avenge a slight to the U.S. uniform and flag and to overthrow the nationalistic government of President Victoriano Huerta, who was also trying to import German weapons; and again in 1916, in northern Mexico, where General John J. "Black Jack" Pershing spent months pursuing Pancho Villa after the Mexican rebel had raided an American border town. Having failed to capture Villa and facing another nationalistic government led by Venustiano Carranza, U.S. forces departed in January 1917. Even though Mexico City rejected Germany's offer, the Wilson administration judged Zimmermann's telegram "a conspiracy against this country." Mexico still might let German agents use Mexican soil to propagandize against the United States if not sabotage American properties.

Soon after learning of Zimmermann's ploy, Wilson asked Congress for "armed neutrality" to defend American lives and commerce. He requested authority to arm American merchant ships and to "employ any other instrumentalities or methods that may be necessary." In the midst of the debate, Wilson released Zimmermann's telegram to the press. Americans expressed outrage. Still, antiwar senators Robert M. La Follette and George Norris, among others, saw the armed-ship bill as a blank check for the president to move the country to war, and they filibustered it to death. Wilson proceeded to arm America's commercial vessels anyway. The action came too late to prevent the sinking of several American ships. War cries echoed across the nation. In late March, an agonized Wilson called Congress into special session.

War Message and War Declaration

On April 2, 1917, the president stepped before a hushed Congress. Solemnly he accused the Germans of "warfare against mankind." Passionately and eloquently, Wilson enumerated U.S. grievances: Germany's violation of freedom of the seas, disruption of commerce, fomenting trouble with Mexico, and breach of human rights by killing innocent Americans. The "Prussian autocracy" had to be punished by "the democracies." Russia was now among the latter, he was pleased to report, because the Russian Revolution had ousted the czar just weeks before. Congress declared war against Germany on April 6 by a vote of 373 to 50 in the House and 82 to 6 in the Senate. The first woman ever to sit in Congress, Montana's Jeannette Rankin, cast a ringing "no" vote. "Peace is a woman's job," she declared, "because men have a natural fear of being classed as cowards if they oppose war" and because mothers should protect their children from death-dealing weapons.

For principle, for morality, for honor, for commerce, for security, for reform—for all of these reasons, Wilson took the United States into World War I. The submarine was certainly the culprit that drew a reluctant president and nation into the maelstrom. Yet critics such as Bryan, Gore, McLemore, and La Follette did not attribute the U.S. descent into war to the U-boat alone. They emphasized Wilson's rigid definition of international law, which did not take account of the submarine's tactics. They faulted his contention that Americans should be entitled to travel anywhere, even on a belligerent ship loaded with contraband. They criticized his policies as unneutral. But they lost the debate. Most Americans came to accept Wilson's view that the Germans had to be checked to ensure an open, orderly world in which U.S. principles and interests would be safe.

America went to war to reform world politics, not to destroy Germany. Wilson once claimed that the United States was "pure air blowing in world politics, destroying illusions and cleaning places of morbid miasmic gasses." By early 1917 the president concluded that America would not be able to claim a seat at the postwar peace conference unless it became a combatant. At the peace conference, Wilson intended to promote the principles he thought essential to a stable world order, to advance democracy and the Open Door, and to outlaw revolution and aggression. A heady mission.

Jeannette Rankin (1880–1973) of Montana was the first woman to sit in the House of Representatives (elected in 1916) and the only member of Congress to vote against U.S. entry into both world wars (in 1917 and 1941). A lifelong pacifist, she led a march in Washington, D.C.—at age eighty-seven—against U.S. participation in the Vietnam War.   (Brown Brothers)

Taking Up Arms and Winning the War

Even before the U.S. declaration of war, the Wilson administration—encouraged by groups such as the National Security League and the Navy League and by mounting public outrage against Germany's submarine warfare—had been beefing up the military under the banner of "preparedness." When the pacifist song "I Didn't Raise My Boy to Be a Soldier" became popular, preparedness proponents retorted: "I Didn't Raise My Boy to Be a Coward." Nonetheless, Senator La Follette and House Majority Leader Claude Kitchin, among others, worked to prevent passage of the National Defense Act of 1916. They failed. This legislation provided for increases in the army and National Guard and for summer training camps modeled on the one in Plattsburgh, New York, where a slice of America's social and economic elite had trained in 1915 as "citizen soldiers." The Navy Act of 1916 started the largest naval expansion in American history.

To raise an army after the declaration of war, Congress in May 1917 passed the Selective Service Act, requiring all males between the ages of twenty-one and thirty (later changed to eighteen and forty-five) to register. National service, proponents believed, would not only prepare the nation for battle but instill patriotism and respect for order, democracy, and personal sacrifice. One general claimed that compulsory national service would "heat up the melting pot." Critics feared that "Prussianism," not democratization, would be the likely outcome. On June 5, 1917, more than 9.5 million men signed up for

The Draft and the Soldier

the "great national lottery." By war's end, 24 million men had been registered by local draft boards. Of this number, 4.8 million had served in the armed forces, 2 million of that number in France. Among them were hundreds of thousands who had volunteered before December 1917, when the government prohibited enlistment because the military judged voluntarism too inefficient (many volunteers were more useful in civilian factories than in the army) and too competitive (enlistees got to choose the service they wanted, thus setting off recruiting wars). Millions of laborers received deferments from military duty because they worked in war industries or had dependents.

The typical soldier was a draftee in his early twenties, white, single, American-born, and poorly educated (most had not attended high school and perhaps 30 percent could not read or write). Tens of thousands of women enlisted in the Army Nurse Corps, served as "hello girls" in the Army Signal Corps, and became clerks in the Navy and Marine Corps. On college cam-

puses, 150,000 students joined the Student Army Training Corps or similar navy and marine units. At officer training camps, the army turned out "ninety-day wonders."

Some 400,000 African Americans also served in the military. Although some southern politicians feared arming African Americans, the army drafted them into segregated units and assigned them to menial labor. Draft boards frequently denied African Americans' legitimate requests for occupational or dependency deferments. Racist slang became common in the training camps. W. E. B. Du Bois, in July 1918, endorsed the NAACP's support for the war. He urged blacks to join the fight for "world liberty," in the hope that a war to make the world safe for democracy might also blur the color line at home. Sparking protest from some other black leaders who thought that wartime accommodationism would damage, not improve, race relations, Du Bois also accepted an army captaincy. A year earlier he had backed creation of a segregated, all-

Fast Fred Horse, a Rosebud Sioux, recuperates in a New York hospital after suffering injury and paralysis during the Meuse-Argonne campaign of fall 1918. Unlike African Americans, Native Americans were not assigned to segregated units during the war. Native Americans participated in all major battles against German forces and suffered a high casualty rate in large part because they served as scouts, messengers, and snipers. (William Hammond Mathers Museum, Indiana University)

black officers' training camp: "We must choose then between the insult of a separate camp and the irreparable injury of strengthening the present custom of putting no black men in positions of authority." Blacks, he insisted, had to "take advantage of the disadvantage." Black colleges such as Hampton Institute and Fisk University encouraged students to join the camp. Eventually fourteen hundred black officers served in the war.

Some 15,000 Native Americans served, too. Most of them were enlistees who sought escape from re-

Indian Enlistees

strictive Indian schools and lives of poverty, opportunities to develop new skills, and chances to prove their patriotism, which might later earn white respect. James McCarthy, a Papago from an Arizona reservation, volunteered because he wanted adventure; he got it: gas that blistered his body, a grenade wound, and German capture and imprisonment.

Approximately 3 million men evaded draft registration. Some were arrested and others fled to Mexico or Canada, but most stayed at home and were never discovered. Another 338,000 men who had registered and been summoned by their draft boards failed to show up for induction. According to arrest records, most of these "deserters" and the more numerous "evaders" were lower-income agricultural and industrial laborers. Some simply felt overwhelmed by the government bureaucracy and stayed away; others were members of minority or ethnic groups who felt alienated. Although nearly 65,000 draftees initially applied for conscientious-objector status (refusing to bear arms for religious or pacifistic reasons), some changed their minds or, like so many others, failed preinduction examinations. Quakers and Mennonites were numerous among the 4,000 inductees actually classified as conscientious objectors (COs). General Leonard Wood called COs "enemies of the Republic," and the military harassed them. COs who refused noncombat service, such as in the Medical Corps, faced imprisonment.

American leaders worried that the young soldiers, once away from home, would be tempted by vice—es-

Commission on Training Camp Activities

pecially by the saloons and houses of prostitution that quickly surrounded training camps. In the spirit of the Progressive era, to protect the supposed novices with "invisible armor," the government created the Commission on Training Camp Activities to coordinate

the work of the Young Men's Christian Association (YMCA) and other groups that dispensed food, showed movies, held athletic contests, and distributed books. Men in uniform were not permitted to drink. Alarmed by the spread of venereal disease, commission officials declared "sin-free" zones around military bases and exhorted soldiers to abstain from sex. American Federation of Labor President Samuel Gompers thought the moralizing ridiculous and the prohibitions unenforceable because "real men will be men." Navy Secretary Josephus Daniels replied that "men must live straight if they would shoot straight."

General John J. Pershing, head of the American Expeditionary Forces (AEF), insisted that his "sturdy rookies" remain a separate, indepen-

Trench Warfare

dent army. He was not about to turn over his "doughboys" to Allied commanders, who had become wedded to unimaginative and deadly trench warfare, producing a military stalemate and ghastly casualties on the western front. Zigzag trenches fronted by barbed wire and mines stretched across France. Between the muddy, stinking trenches lay "no man's land," denuded by artillery fire. When ordered out, soldiers would charge the enemy's trenches. Machine guns mowed them down; gas poisoned them. Little was gained. At the Battle of the Somme in 1916 the British and French suffered 600,000 dead or wounded to earn only 125 square miles; the Germans lost 500,000 men. Ambassador Page grew sickened by what Europe had become—"a bankrupt slaughter-house inhabited by unmated women."

The first American units landed in France on June 26, 1917, marched in a Fourth of July parade in Paris, and then moved by train toward the front. They soon learned about the horrors caused by advanced weaponry. An Army nurse probed one soldier's chest, finding his name tag deep in the "nasty" wound. "It probably saved his life." Poison gases (chlorine, phosgene, and mustard), first used by the Germans in spring 1915, blistered, incapacitated, and killed. Many men, like A.P., suffered shell shock. Providing some relief were Red Cross canteens, staffed by women volunteers, which gave soldiers way stations in a strange land and offered haircuts, food, and recreation. Some ten thousand Red Cross nurses also cared for the young warriors, while the American Library Association distributed 10 million books and magazines.

In Paris, where forty large houses of prostitution thrived, it became commonplace to hear that the

A U.S. soldier of Company K, 110th Infantry Regiment, receives aid during fighting at Verennes, France. (National Archives)

Problem of Venereal Disease

British were drunkards, the French were whoremongers, and the Americans were both. Venereal disease became a serious problem. French Prime Minister Georges Clemenceau offered licensed, inspected prostitutes in "special houses" to the American army. When the generous Gallic offer reached Washington, Secretary of War Newton Baker gasped, "For god's sake . . . don't show this to the President or he'll stop the war." By war's end, about 15 percent of America's soldiers had contracted venereal disease, costing the army $50 million and 7 million days of active duty. Periodic inspections, chemical prophylactic treatments, and the threat of court-martial for infected soldiers kept the problem from being even more disastrous.

The influx of American men and materiel—and the morale boost they gave to the Allies—decided the outcome of the First World War. With both sides virtually exhausted, the Americans tipped the balance toward the Allies. On the high seas, the U.S. Navy battled submarines and escorted troop carriers. Flying primarily French and British aircraft, pilots in the U.S. Air Service saw limited action, mostly against German ground troops and transport. But the aerial "dogfights" of such "aces" as Edward V. Rickenbacker helped advance the cause for military aviation. U.S. ground troops actually did not engage in much combat until after the lull in the fighting during the harsh winter of 1917–1918.

AEF Battles in France

The Germans launched a major offensive in March 1918, after Russia left the war, permitting the shift of German troops from the eastern front to France. By May, Kaiser Wilhelm's forces had stormed to within 50 miles of Paris. Late that month, troops of the U.S. First Division helped blunt the German advance at Cantigny

· PUBLIC · HEALTH · FILMS ·
Produced for
WAR DEPARTMENT
Commission on Training
Camp Activities.

" THE BOY WHO KEPT "
FIT TO WIN
with
SGT. RAY MᶜKEE
· *as* ·
"BILLY HALE"

THE FIRST MOTION PICTURE
TO TELL THE TRUTH ABOUT
THE CAUSE AND EFFECT OF
VENEREAL DISEASES.

Personally directed by Lieut. **E.H.GRIFFITH**

During the First World War, the War Department promoted a film to combat sexually transmitted diseases. After the war, the New York State Board of Censors declared the film obscene. (Social Welfare History Archives Center, University of Minnesota)

(see Map 23.2). In June the Third Division and French forces held positions along the Marne River at Château-Thierry, and the Second Division soon attacked the Germans in the Belleau Wood. American soldiers won the battle after three weeks of fighting, but thousands died or were wounded after they made almost sacrificial frontal assaults against German machine guns.

Allied victory in the Second Battle of the Marne in July 1918 seemed to turn the tide against the Germans. In September French and American forces took St. Mihiel, a ferocious battle in which American gunners fired 100,000 rounds of phosgene gas shells. Then the Allies began their massive Meuse-Argonne offensive. More than 1 million Americans joined British and French troops in weeks of fierce combat; some 26,000 Americans died before the Allies claimed the Argonne Forest on October 10. For Germany—its ground war stymied, its submarine warfare failed, its troops and cities mutinous, its allies Turkey and Austria dropping out, and its kaiser abdicated—peace became imperative. The Germans accepted an armistice on November 11, 1918.

The belligerents counted 10 million soldiers and 6.6 million civilians dead and 21.3 million people wounded. Fifty thousand American soldiers died in

Casualties battle, and another 62,000 died from disease—many from the influenza pandemic (see page 652). More than 200,000 Americans were wounded. Parents and widows pressed the War Department to return the remains of 70 percent of the American dead, but the others were buried in cemeteries in France, Belgium, and England.

Mobilizing and Managing the Home Front

"It is not an army that we must shape and train for war," declared President Wilson, "it is a nation." The United States was a belligerent for only nineteen months, but the war had a tremendous impact at home. The federal government quickly created a command economy to meet war needs and intervened in American life as never before. The vastly enlarged Washington bureaucracy managed the economy, labor force, military, public opinion, and more. Federal expenditures increased tremendously as the government spent more than $760 million a month from April 1917 to August 1919. War expenses ballooned to $33.5 billion (see

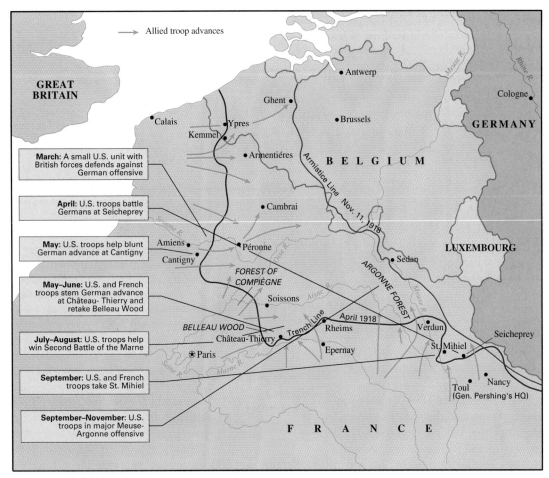

Allied troop advances

March: A small U.S. unit with British forces defends against German offensive

April: U.S. troops battle Germans at Seicheprey

May: U.S. troops help blunt German advance at Cantigny

May–June: U.S. and French troops stem German advance at Château- Thierry and retake Belleau Wood

July–August: U.S. troops help win Second Battle of the Marne

September: U.S. and French troops take St. Mihiel

September–November: U.S. troops in major Meuse-Argonne offensive

Map 23.2   American Troops at the Western Front, 1918   America's 2 million troops in France met German forces head-on, ensuring the defeat of the Central Powers in 1918.

Figure 23.1). The total cost of the war was probably triple that figure, since future generations would have to pay veterans' benefits and interest on loans. To Progressives of the New Nationalist persuasion, the wartime expansion and centralization of government power were welcome. To others, these changes seemed excessive, leading to concentrated, hence dangerous, federal power. "War is the health of the state," Randolph Bourne had warned.

The federal government and private business became partners during the war. Dollar-a-year executives flocked to the nation's capital from major companies; they retained their corporate salaries while serving in official administrative and consulting capacities. Early in the war, the government relied on several industrial committees for advice on purchases and prices. But ev-

Business-Government Cooperation

idence of self-interested businesspeople cashing in on the national interest aroused public protest. The head of the aluminum advisory committee, for example, was also president of the largest aluminum company. The assorted committees were disbanded in July 1917 in favor of a single manager, the War Industries Board. But the government continued to work closely with business through trade associations, which grew significantly to two thousand by 1920. The federal government suspended antitrust laws and signed cost-plus contracts, which guaranteed companies a healthy profit and a means to pay higher wages to head off labor strikes. Competitive bidding was virtually abandoned. Under these wartime practices, big business grew bigger.

Hundreds of new government agencies, staffed primarily by businesspeople, placed controls on the economy in order to shift the nation's resources to the

New Agencies for Economic Management

Allies, the AEF, and war-related production. The Food Administration, led by the engineer and investor Herbert Hoover, launched voluntary programs to increase production and conserve food—Americans were urged to grow "victory gardens" and to eat meatless and wheatless meals—but it also set prices and regulated distribution. The Railroad Administration took over the snarled railway industry. The Fuel Administration controlled coal supplies and rationed gasoline. When strikes threatened the telephone and telegraph companies, the federal government seized and ran them.

The largest of the superagencies was the War Industries Board (WIB), headed by the financier Bernard Baruch. At one point, this Wall Streeter frankly told Henry Ford that he would dispatch the military to seize his plants if the automaker did not accept WIB limits on car production. Ford relented. Although the WIB seemed all-powerful, in reality it had to conciliate competing interest groups and compromise with the business executives whose advice it so valued. Designed as a clearing-house to coordinate the national economy, the WIB made purchases, allocated supplies, and fixed prices at levels that business requested. The WIB also ordered the standardization of goods to save materials and streamline production. The varieties of automobile tires, for example, were reduced from 287 to 3.

The performance of the mobilized economy was mixed, but it delivered enough men and materiel to France to ensure the defeat of the Central Powers.

Economic Performance

About a quarter of all American production was diverted to war needs. As farmers enjoyed boom years of higher prices, they put more acreage into production and mechanized as never before. From 1915 to 1920 the number of tractors in American fields jumped tenfold. Gross farm income for the period from 1914 to 1919 increased more than 230 percent. Although manufacturing output leveled off in 1918, some industries realized substantial growth because of wartime demand. Steel reached a peak production of 45 million tons in 1917, twice the prewar figure. As U.S. soldiers popularized American brands in Europe, tobacconists profited from a huge increase in cigarette sales: from 26 billion cigarettes in 1916 to 48 billion in 1918. Overall, the gross national product in 1920 stood 237 percent higher than in 1914.

Because massive assignments had to be completed in a hurry, mistakes mounted. Weapons deliveries fell

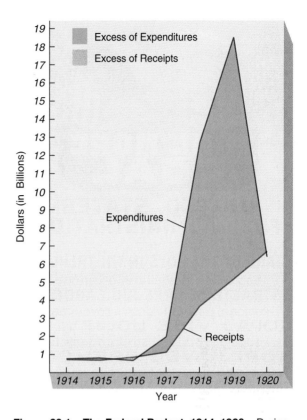

Figure 23.1 The Federal Budget, 1914–1920 During the First World War, the federal government spent more money than it received from increased taxes. It borrowed from banks or sold bonds through Liberty Loan drives. To meet the mounting costs of the war, in other words, the federal government had to resort to deficit spending. Expenditures topped receipts by more than $13 billion in 1919. Given this wartime fiscal pattern, moreover, the U.S. federal debt rose from $1 billion in 1914 to $25 billion in 1919. (Source: U.S. Department of Commerce, *Historical Statistics of the United States: Colonial Times to 1957* [Washington, D.C., Bureau of the Census, 1960], p. 711.)

short of demand; the bloated bureaucracy of the War Shipping Board failed to build enough ships. In the severe winter of 1917–1918, millions of Americans could not get coal. Coal companies held back on production to raise prices; railroads did not have enough coal cars; and harbors froze, closing out coal barges. In January, blizzards shut down midwestern railroads and factories, impeding the war effort. People died from pneumonia and freezing. A Brooklyn man went out in the morning to forage for coal and returned to find his two-month-old daughter frozen to death in her crib.

During the First World War, the United States Fuel Administration promoted economic mobilization at home in this poster printed in several languages. (National Park Service Collection, Ellis Island Immigration Museum. Photo Chermayeff and Geismar MetaForm)

Tax policies during the war sought to pull some of the profits reaped from high prices and defense contracts into the Treasury, reflecting the belief that wealth as well as labor should be conscripted. The Revenue Act in 1916 started the process by raising the surtax on high incomes and corporate profits, imposing a federal tax on large estates, and significantly increasing the tax on munitions manufacturers. Still, the government financed only one-third of the war through taxes. The other two-thirds came from loans, including Liberty bonds sold to the American people through aggressive campaigns. The War Revenue Act of 1917 provided for a more steeply graduated personal income tax, a corporate income tax, an excess-profits tax, and increased excise taxes on alcoholic beverages, tobacco, and luxury items. Although these taxes did curb excessive corporate profiteering, several loopholes tempted the unscrupulous. Sometimes companies inflated costs to conceal profits or paid high salaries and bonuses to their executives. Four officers of Bethlehem Steel, for example, divided bonuses of $2.3 million in 1917 and $2.1 million the next year. Corporate net earnings for 1913 totaled $4 billion; in 1917 they reached $7 billion; and in 1918, after the tax bite and the war's end, they still stood at $4.5 billion. Profits and patriotism went hand in hand in America's war experience. The abrupt cancellation of billions of dollars' worth of contracts at the end of the war, however, caused a brief economic downturn, a short boom, and then an intense depression (see Chapter 24).

Paying for the War

American workers benefited from the full-employment wartime economy, which increased their total earnings and gave many of them time-and-a-half pay for overtime work. Given the higher cost of living, however, workers saw minimal improvement in their economic standing. Turnover rates were high as workers switched jobs for higher pay and better conditions. Sometimes employers practiced "scamping": the pirating of laborers from other companies. Some employers sought to overcome labor shortages by expanding welfare and social programs and by establishing personnel departments—"specialized human nature engineers to keep its human machinery frictionless," as General Electric explained. To meet the labor crisis, the Department of Labor's U.S. Employment Service matched laborers with job vacancies, especially attracting workers from the South and Midwest to war industries in the East. The department also temporarily relaxed the literacy-test and head-tax

Labor Shortage

Government officials failed to stem inflation. The wholesale price index was 98 percent higher in 1918 than it had been in 1913. Though partly stimulated by demand exceeding supply because of increases in Allied buying, inflation also sprang from the government's liberal credit policies and high price levels. By fixing prices on raw materials rather than on finished products, moreover, the government lost control of inflation. By bowing to southern politicians who wanted cotton left unregulated, the government permitted runaway cotton prices. Clothing tripled in cost, and food prices more than doubled. A quart of milk that cost 9 cents in 1914 climbed to 17 cents in 1920. Fuel prices also skyrocketed: the price for a 100-pound sack of coal rose 100 percent. Inflation pinched household budgets.

Inflation

provisions of immigration law to attract farm labor, miners, and railroad workers from Mexico. Because the labor crisis also generated a housing crisis as workers crammed into cities, the U.S. Housing Corporation and Emergency Fleet Corporation, following British example, built row houses in Newport News, Virginia, and Eddystone, Pennsylvania.

In early 1918 Wilson instituted the National War Labor Board (NWLB), which discouraged strikes and lockouts and urged management to negotiate with existing unions. In July, after the Western Union Company fired eight hundred union members for trying to organize the firm's workers and then defied an NWLB request to reinstate the employees, the president nationalized the telegraph lines and put the laborers back to work. That month, too, the NWLB directed General Electric to raise wages and stop discriminating against metal trades union members in Schenectady, New York. On the other hand, in September the NWLB ordered striking Bridgeport, Connecticut, machinists back to munitions factories, threatening to revoke their draft exemptions (granted earlier because they worked in an "essential" industry).

National War Labor Board

For unions, the war seemed to offer opportunities for recognition and better pay through partnership with government. Samuel Gompers threw the AFL's loyalty to the Wilson administration, promising to deter strikes. Gompers and other moderate labor leaders accepted appointments to federal agencies. The antiwar Socialist Party blasted the AFL for becoming a "fifth wheel on [the] capitalist war chariot." But union membership climbed from roughly 2.5 million in 1916 to more than 4 million in 1919. The AFL, however, could not curb strikes by the radical Industrial Workers of the World (IWW) or rebellious AFL locals, especially those controlled by labor activists and socialists. In the nineteen war months, more than six thousand strikes expressed workers' demands for a "living wage" and improved working conditions (many called for an eight-hour workday). Exploiting Wilsonian wartime rhetoric, workers and their unions also sought to "de-Kaiser" American industry—that is, to create "industrial democracy," a more representative workplace with a role for labor in determining job categories and content and with workplace representation through shop committees. By 1920, in defiance of the national AFL, labor parties had sprung up in twenty-three states.

When immigration dropped off and some foreign nationals returned to Europe to fight for their home-

Women in the Work Force

lands, and when 16 percent of the male work force entered the military, business especially targeted women to fill vacancies. In Connecticut, a special motion picture, *Mr. and Mrs. Hines of Stamford Do Their Bit*, appealed to housewives' patriotism, urging them to take factory jobs. Although the total number of women in the work force increased slightly, the real story was that many changed jobs, sometimes moving into formerly male domains. Some white women left domestic service for factories, shifted from clerking in department stores to stenography and typing, or departed textile mills for employment in firearms plants. At least 20 percent of all workers in the wartime electrical-machinery, airplane, and food industries were women. Some one hundred

Using posters, many government agencies appealed to the American people to help win the war. This one, from the U.S. Employment Service, encouraged women to enter the work force.   (National Archives)

Stella Young (1896–1989), a Canadian-born woman from Chelsea, Massachusetts, became widely known as the "Doughnut Girl" because of her service during the First World War with the American branch of the Salvation Army, an international organization devoted to social work. She arrived in France in March 1918 and worked in emergency canteens near the battle front, providing U.S. troops with coffee, cocoa, sandwiches, doughnuts, pie, and fruit. Stella Young became famous when this picture of her wearing a khaki uniform and a "doughboy" steel helmet was widely circulated as a postcard. She served again in World War II. Chelsea named a city square in her honor in 1968.   (Collection of Colonel Stuart S. Corning, Jr.)

segregated occupations, serving as typists, nurses, teachers, and domestic servants.

Some male workers, unaccustomed to working beside women, complained that women destabilized the work environment with their higher productivity and acceptance of lower pay. Women pointed out that male-dominated companies discriminated against them and that unions largely denied them membership. Male employees also resented the spirit of independence evident among women. Other critics charged that working mothers neglected their children and their housework. Day nurseries were scarce and beyond the means of most working-class families, and few employers provided childcare facilities. The war experience barely changed the attitude that women's proper sphere was the home, and most women workers lost their jobs to the returning veterans.

Women participated in the war effort in other ways. As volunteers, they made clothing for refugees and soldiers, served at Red Cross facilities, and taught French to nurses assigned to the war zone. Many worked for the Women's Committee of the Council of National Defense, whose leaders included Ida Tarbell and Carrie Chapman Catt. A vast network of state, county, and town volunteer organizations, the council publicized government mobilization programs, encouraged home gardens, sponsored drives to sell Liberty bonds, and continued the push for social welfare reforms. This patriotic work won praise from men and improved the prospects for passage of the Nineteenth Amendment (see page 595–596)."We have made partners of women in this war," Wilson said as he endorsed woman suffrage in 1918. "Shall we admit them only to a partnership of suffering and sacrifice . . . and not to a partnership of privilege and right?"

War mobilization wrought significant change for the African American community as southern blacks

African American Migration North

undertook a great migration to northern cities to work in railroad yards, packing houses, steel mills, shipyards, and coal mines. Between 1910 and 1920, Cleveland's black population swelled by more than 300 percent, Detroit's by more than 600 percent, and Chicago's by 150 percent. Much of the increase occurred between 1916 and 1919. All told, about a half-million African Americans uprooted themselves to move to the North. Families sometimes pooled savings to send one member; others sold their household goods to pay for the journey. Most of the migrants were males—young (in their early twenties), unmarried, and skilled or semi-skilled. Wartime jobs in the North provided an escape

thousand women worked in the railroad industry. As white women took advantage of these new opportunities, black women took some of their places in domestic service and in textile factories. For the first time, department stores employed black women as elevator operators and cafeteria waitresses. Most working women were single and remained concentrated in sex-

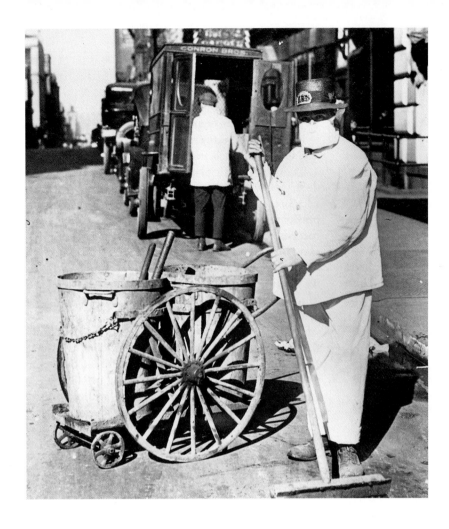

A New York City street cleaner, wearing a gauze mask, takes no chances during the influenza pandemic of 1918. Many of the people who wore the masks said it was better to look ridiculous than to be dead. (Corbis-Bettmann)

from low wages, sharecropping, tenancy, crop liens, debt peonage, lynchings, and political disfranchisement. To a friend back in Mississippi, one African American wrote: "I just begin to feel like a man. . . . I don't have to humble to no one. I have registered. Will vote the next election."

But African Americans continued to experience discrimination in both North and South. When the United States entered the First World War, there was not one black judge in the entire country. Segregation remained social custom. The Ku Klux Klan was reviving, and racist films such as D. W. Griffith's *The Birth of a Nation* (1915) fed prejudice. Lynching statistics exposed the wide gap between wartime declarations of humanity and the American practice of inhumanity at home: between 1914 and 1920, 382 blacks were lynched, some of them in military uniform.

Northern whites who resented "the Negro invasion" vented their anger in riots, as in East St. Louis, Illinois, in July 1917 (see page 534).

Race Riots

The next month, in Houston, where African American soldiers faced white harassment and refused to obey segregation laws, whites and blacks exchanged gunfire. Seventeen whites and two African Americans died, and the army sentenced thirteen black soldiers to death and forty-one to life imprisonment for mutiny. During the bloody "Red Summer" of 1919, race riots rocked two dozen cities and towns. The worst violence occurred in Chicago, a favorite destination for migrating blacks. In the very hot days of July 1919, a black youth swimming at a segregated white beach was hit by a thrown rock and drowned. Rumors spread, tempers flared, and soon blacks and whites were battling one another. Stabbings, burnings, and shootings went on for days until state police restored some calm. Thirty-eight people died, twenty-three African Americans and fifteen whites. By the time of this tragedy, a disillusioned W. E. B. Du Bois had already concluded that black support for the war had not diminished whites' adherence to inequality and segregation. That spring he vowed a struggle: "We return. We return from fighting. We return fighting."

Added to the nation's unsettling war experience was another home-front crisis that cut across race, gender, and class lines: the influenza pandemic that

Influenza Pandemic engulfed the world in 1918–1919. Before it abated, as many as 40 million people died worldwide, killing the young more than the elderly. The first case of the extremely contagious flu virus was reported at Camp Funston, in Kansas, on March 4, 1918. It quickly spread to most American cities and then to Europe, carried there by U.S. troops. High fevers, aching muscles, and headaches staggered people. To fend off the virus, people received flu vaccines of questionable value or wore gauze masks. But mostly they had to wait until the virus tailed off. In many cases, severe pneumonia set in, and victims' lungs filled with fluid. Seven hundred thousand people died from the killer disease in the United States.

Through its concerted propaganda effort, the Committee on Public Information helped sell to the American people U.S. participation in the First World War. In this 1917 poster, the committee also warned against German spies, perhaps even German American spies, who might pick up secrets from unsuspecting citizens. (Private Collection)

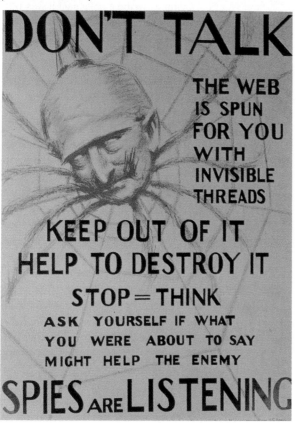

Emergence of the Civil Liberties Issue

"Woe be to the man that seeks to stand in our way in this day of high resolution," warned President Wilson. An official and unofficial campaign soon began to silence dissenters who questioned Wilson's decision for war or who protested the draft. In the end, the Wilson administration compiled one of the worst civil liberties records in American history. The targets of governmental and quasi-vigilante repression were the hundreds of thousands of Americans and aliens who refused to support the war: pacifists from all walks of life, conscientious objectors, socialists, radical labor groups, the debt-ridden tenant farmers of Oklahoma who staged the Green Corn Rebellion against the draft, the Non-Partisan League, reformers such as Robert La Follette and Jane Addams, and countless others. In the wartime process of debating the question of the right to speak freely in a democracy, the concept of "civil liberties" for the first time in American history emerged as a major public policy issue.

Shortly after the declaration of war in 1917, the president appointed George Creel, a Progressive journalist, to head the Committee on Public Information (CPI). Employing some of the nation's most talented writers and scholars, the CPI used propaganda to shape and mobilize public opinion. Pamphlets and films demonized the Germans, and CPI "Four-Minute Men" spoke at movie theaters, schools, and churches to pump up a patriotic mood. Encouraged by the CPI to promote American participation in the war, film companies and their trade association, the National Association of the Motion Picture Industry, produced documentaries, newsreels, and anti-German movies such as *The Kaiser, the Beast of Berlin* (1918) and *To Hell with the Kaiser* (1918). The committee also urged the press to practice "self-censorship" and encouraged people to spy on their neighbors. "Not a pin dropped in the home of any one with a foreign name," Creel claimed with satisfaction, "but that it rang like thunder on the inner ear of some listening sleuth." Exaggeration, fear-mongering, distortion, half-truths—such were the stuff of the CPI's "mind mobilization."

The Wilson administration also guided through an obliging Congress the Espionage Act (1917) and the Sedition Act (1918). The first statute forbade "false statements" designed to impede the draft or promote

Committee on Public Information

Espionage and Sedition Acts

military insubordination, and it banned from the mails materials considered treasonous. The Sedition Act made it unlawful to obstruct the sale of war bonds and to use "disloyal, profane, scurrilous, or abusive" language to describe the government, the Constitution, the flag, or the military uniform. These loosely worded laws gave the government wide latitude to crack down on critics. Fair-minded people could disagree over what constituted false or abusive language, but in the feverish home-front atmosphere of the First World War, the Justice Department's definition prevailed. More than two thousand people were prosecuted under the acts, and many others were intimidated into silence.

Stories of repression built up. The Woman's Peace Party's periodical *Four Lights* was denied use of the mails. When federal agents threatened to shut down the large-circulation black newspaper *Chicago Defender*, its editor reluctantly promised to refrain from criticizing the government. Put under surveillance by the Justice Department, Jane Addams also chose self-censorship, moderating her appeals for peace. Robert Goldstein, the producer of *The Spirit of '76* (1917), a film about the American Revolution complete with redcoats shooting minutemen, received a ten-year prison sentence for, said the judge, questioning the "good faith of our ally, Great Britain."

The war emergency gave Progressives and conservatives alike an opportunity to throttle the Industrial Workers of the World and the

Imprisonment of Eugene V. Debs

Socialist Party. Government agents raided IWW meetings, and the army marched into western mining and lumber regions to put down IWW strikes. By the end of the war most of the union's leaders were in jail. The Socialist Party fared little better. In summer 1918, with a government stenographer present, Socialist Party leader Eugene V. Debs delivered a spirited oration extolling socialism and freedom of speech—including the freedom to criticize the Wilson administration for taking America into the war. Federal agents arrested him. Debs told the court what many dissenters—and, later, many jurists and scholars—thought of the Espionage Act: it was "a despotic enactment in flagrant conflict with democratic principles and with the spirit of free institutions." Handed a ten-year sentence, Debs remained in prison until late 1921, when he received a pardon.

Intolerance knew few boundaries. Local school boards dismissed teachers who questioned the war. At Wellesley College, economics professor Emily Greene Balch was fired because of her pacifist views (she won the Nobel Peace Prize in 1946). Three Columbia University students were picked up in mid-1917 for circulating an antiwar petition. Columbia also fired Professor J. M. Cattell, a distinguished psychologist, for his antiwar stand. His colleague Charles Beard, a historian with a prowar perspective, resigned in protest: "If we have to suppress everything we don't like to hear, this country is resting on a pretty wobbly basis."

Encouraged by official behavior, ultrapatriotic groups such as the Sedition Slammers and the American Defense Society sought to cleanse the nation through vigilantism. A German American miner in Illinois was wrapped in a flag and lynched. In Hilger, Montana, citizens burned history texts that mentioned Germany. By the end of the war, sixteen states had banned the teaching of the German language. To avoid trouble, the Kaiser-Kuhn grocery in St. Louis changed its name to Pioneer Grocery. Because towns had Liberty Loan quotas to fill, they sometimes bullied "slackers" into purchasing bonds. Nativist advocates of "100% Americanism" exploited the emotional atmosphere to exhort immigrants to throw off their Old World cultures. Companies offered English-language and naturalization classes in their factories and refused jobs and promotions to those who did not make adequate strides toward learning English. Even labor's drive for compulsory health insurance, which before the war had gained advocates in several states, including New York and California, became victimized by the poisoned war atmosphere. Many physicians and insurance companies had for years denounced health insurance as "socialistic"; after the United States entered the war, they discredited it as "Made in Germany."

Prior to World War I, American citizens of good standing could freely express mainstream political views, whereas people more marginal

Roger Baldwin and Free Speech

to a community (such as recent immigrants) or local leaders with radical opinions sometimes met with harsh treatment for exercising what today would be termed their freedom of speech. Before the war, few formally questioned these informal restrictions on political dissent. Yet the Wilson administration's vigorous suppression of dissidents led some Americans, most notably a conscientious objector named Roger Baldwin, to reformulate the traditional definition of allowable speech. Baldwin founded the Civil Liberties Bureau (forerunner of the American Civil Liberties Union) to defend the rights of those people accused under the Espionage and Sedition Acts. He was the first to advance the ideas that the content of political speech could be separated from the identity of the speaker and that a patriotic American could—indeed should—defend the right of someone to express political beliefs abhorrent to his or her own.

In unanimously upholding the Espionage Act in *Schenck v. U.S.* (1919), the Supreme Court adhered to the traditional view rather than that developed by Baldwin. In time of war, Justice Oliver Wendell Holmes wrote, the First Amendment could be restricted: "Free speech would not protect a man falsely shouting fire in a theater and causing panic." If, according to Holmes, words "are of such a nature as to create a clear and present danger that they will bring about the substantial evils that Congress has a right to prevent," free speech could be limited. A few months later, however, Holmes and Louis Brandeis dissented when the Court similarly upheld the Sedition Act, in *Abrams v. U.S.* (1919). In the interim, pressed by friends to adopt Baldwin's approach to freedom of speech and of the press, Holmes had changed his mind and accepted the notion that active political dissent was essential to a democratic government.

The Bolshevik Revolution, Labor Strikes, and the Red Scare

The line between wartime suppression of dissent and the postwar Red Scare is not easily drawn. In the name of patriotism, both harassed suspected internal enemies and deprived them of their constitutional rights; both had government sanction. Together they stabbed at the Bill of Rights and wounded radicalism in America. In the last few months of the war, guardians of Americanism began to label dissenters not only pro-German but pro-Bolshevik. After the Bolshevik Revolution in fall 1917, American hatred for the Kaiser's Germany was readily transferred to communist Russia. When the new Russian government under V. I. Lenin made a separate peace with Germany in early 1918, Americans grew angry because the closing of the eastern front would permit the Germans to move troops west. Many lashed out at American radicals, casually applying the term "Red" (derived from the red flag used by communists) to discredit them.

The ordeal of Victor Berger illustrates the blending of the wartime and postwar suppression of civil lib-

Case of Victor Berger

erties. A socialist living in a heavily German district in Milwaukee, Wisconsin, and a former member of Congress, Berger was indicted under the Espionage Act for denouncing U.S. entry into the war. Voters nonetheless elected him once again to Congress in 1918. Early the next year Berger was convicted and sentenced to twenty years in federal prison. The House of Representatives thereupon refused to admit him, calling him a pro-German Bolshevik. While out on bail pending an appeal, Berger won the special election held to replace him. The House again blocked his admission. Berger's nightmare did not end until 1921, when the Supreme Court reversed his conviction. He was elected to Congress again in 1924. This time he took his seat.

The Wilson administration's ardent anti-Bolshevism became clear in mid-1918 when the president ordered five thousand American troops to northern Russia and ten thousand more soldiers to Siberia, where they joined other Allied contingents. Wilson did not consult Congress. He said the military expeditions would guard Allied supplies and Russian railroads from German seizure and would also rescue a group of Czechs who wished to return home to fight the Germans. Worried that the Japanese were building influence in Siberia and closing the Open Door, Wilson also hoped to deter Japan from further advances in Asia. Mostly he wanted to smash the infant Bolshevik government, a challenge to his new world order. So he waged an undeclared war against the new Russian regime, already engaged in a civil war with its opponents.

Intervention in Russia Against Bolsheviks

Despite his famed devotion to the principle of self-determination, Wilson backed an economic blockade of Russia, sent arms to anti-Bolshevik forces, and refused to recognize the Bolshevik government. The United States also clandestinely passed military information to anti-Bolshevik forces and used food relief to shore up anti-Bolsheviks in the Baltic region. Later, at the Paris Peace Conference, Russia was denied a seat. U.S. troops did not leave Siberia until spring 1920, after the Bolsheviks had demonstrated their staying power. These interventions in Russia embittered Washington-Moscow relations for many decades.

At home, too, the Wilson administration moved against radicals and others imprecisely defined as Bolsheviks or communists. By the war's close, Americans had become edgy. The war had exacerbated racial tensions. It had disrupted the workplace and the family.

Americans had suffered an increase in the cost of living, and postwar unemployment loomed. To add to their worries, Russians in 1919 created the Communist (Third) International (or Comintern) to promote world revolution. Already hardened by wartime violations of civil liberties, Americans found it easy to blame their postwar troubles on new scapegoats.

In 1919 a rash of labor strikes seeking to raise wages to meet rising prices and to retain wartime bargaining rights sparked the Red Scare.

Labor Strikes and the Red Scare

All told, more than thirty-three hundred strikes involving 4 million laborers jolted the nation that year, including the Seattle general strike in January. On May 1, a day of celebration for workers around the world, bombs were sent through the mails to prominent Americans. Most of the devices were intercepted and dismantled, but police never captured the conspirators. Most people assumed, not unreasonably, that anarchists and others bent on the destruction of the American way of life were responsible. Next came the Boston police strike in September. Some sniffed a Bolshevik conspiracy, but others thought it ridiculous to label Boston's Irish-American Catholic cops "radicals." The conservative governor of Massachusetts, Calvin Coolidge, gained national attention by proclaiming that nobody had the right to strike against the public safety. State guardsmen soon replaced the striking policemen.

Unrest in the steel industry in September stirred more ominous fears. Many steelworkers worked twelve hours a day, seven days a week, and lived in squalid housing. They looked to local steel unions, organized by the National Committee for Organizing Iron and Steel Workers, to help them improve their lives. When postwar unemployment in the industry climbed and the U.S. Steel Corporation refused to meet with committee representatives, some 350,000 workers walked off the job demanding the right to collective bargaining, a shorter workday, and a living wage. The steel barons hired strikebreakers and sent agents to club strikers. Worried about both the 1919 strikes and Bolshevism, President Wilson warned against "the poison of disorder" and the "poison of revolt." But in the case of steel, the companies won; the strike collapsed in early 1920.

One of the leaders of the steel strike was William Z. Foster, an IWW member and militant labor organizer who later joined the Communist Party. His presence in a labor movement seeking bread-and-butter goals permitted political and business leaders to

This anti-Bolshevik cartoon, titled "The Bull in the China Shop," represented the view of U.S. leaders during the Red Scare that Russia's radical Bolshevik revolution was threatening American principles and values.   (*San Francisco Chronicle*, February 27, 1919)

dismiss the steel strike as a foreign threat orchestrated by American radicals. There was in fact no conspiracy, and the American left was badly splintered. Two defectors from the Socialist Party, John Reed and Benjamin Gitlow, founded the Communist Labor Party in 1919. The rival Communist Party of the United States of America, composed largely of aliens, was launched the same year. Neither party commanded many followers—their combined membership probably did not exceed seventy thousand—and in 1919 the harassed Socialist Party could muster no more than thirty thousand members.

Although divisiveness among radicals actually signified weakness, both Progressives and conservatives interpreted the advent of the new parties as strengthening the radical menace. That is certainly how the American Legion saw the question. Organized in May 1919 to lobby for

American Legion

veterans' benefits, the Legion soon preached an anti-radicalism that fueled the Red Scare. By 1920, 843,000 Legion members, mostly middle and upper class, had become stalwarts of an impassioned Americanism that demanded conformity.

Wilson's attorney general, A. Mitchell Palmer, also insisted that Americans think alike. A Progressive reformer, Quaker, and ambitious politician, Palmer declared that "revolution" was "eating its way into the homes of the American workmen, licking the altars of the churches, leaping into the belfry of the school bell." Palmer appointed J. Edgar Hoover to head the Radical Division of the Department of Justice. The zealous Hoover compiled index cards bearing the names of allegedly radical individuals and organizations. During 1919 agents jailed IWW members; Palmer also saw to it that 249 alien radicals, including the anarchist Emma Goldman, were deported to Russia.

Again, state and local governments took their cue from the Wilson administration. States passed peacetime sedition acts under which hundreds of people were arrested. Vigilante groups and mobs flourished once again, their numbers swelled by returning veterans. In November 1919, in Centralia, Washington, American Legionnaires broke from a parade to storm the IWW hall. Several were wounded. A number of Wobblies were soon arrested, and one of them, an ex-soldier, was taken from jail by a mob, then beaten, castrated, and shot. The New York State legislature expelled five duly elected Socialist Party members in early 1920.

The Red Scare reached a climax in January 1920 in the Palmer Raids. Hoover planned and directed the operation; government agents in

Palmer Raids

thirty-three cities broke into meeting halls and homes without search warrants. More than four thousand people were jailed and denied counsel. In Boston some four hundred people were kept in detainment on bitterly cold Deer Island; two died of pneumonia, one leaped to his death, and another went insane. Because of court rulings and the courageous efforts of Assistant Secretary of Labor Louis Post, who deliberately held up paperwork, most of the arrestees were released, although in 1920–1921 nearly six hundred were deported.

Palmer's disregard for elementary civil liberties drew criticism. Civil libertarians and lawyers charged that his tactics violated the Constitution. Many of the arrested "Communists" had committed no crimes.

When Palmer called for a peacetime sedition act, he alarmed both liberal and conservative leaders. His dire prediction that serious violence would mar May Day 1920 proved mistaken. With the steel strike over, the threat of Bolshevism in Europe receding, and the nation returning to postwar "normalcy," Palmer could no longer count on stampeding the public.

The campaigns against free speech from 1917 through 1920 left casualties. Debate, so essential to democracy, was wounded. Reform suffered as reformers either joined in the antiradicalism or became victims of it. Radical groups were badly weakened: the IWW became virtually extinct, and the Socialist Party became paralyzed. Throughout, the president made it appear that his critics were attacking the nation itself when they were actually questioning the policies of his administration. Wilson's intolerance of those who disagreed with him seemed to bespeak a fundamental distrust of democracy. At the very least, it illustrated that some Progressives were willing to use coercion to achieve their goal of a reformed society.

The Peace Conference, League Fight, and Postwar World

 President Wilson seemed more focused on international relations than on the civil liberties issue at home. For the first time in its history, the United States offered a framework for world order, when, in January 1918, he announced his Fourteen Points. The first five points called for diplomacy "in the public view," freedom of the seas, lower tariffs, reductions in armaments, and the decolonization of empires. The next eight points specified the evacuation of foreign troops from Russia, Belgium, and France and appealed for self-determination for nationalities in Europe, such as the Poles. For Wilson, the fourteenth point was the most important—the mechanism for achieving all the others: "a general association of nations" or League of Nations. At the time of the armistice, the combatants reluctantly agreed that Wilson's principles should guide the peace negotiations.

When the president departed for the Paris Peace Conference in December 1918, he faced obstacles erected by his political enemies, by

Obstacles to a Wilsonian Peace

the Allies, and by himself. Some observers suggested that a cocky Wilson underestimated his task. During the 1918 congressional elections, Wilson had urged a vote for Democrats as a sign of support for his peace goals. But the American people did just the opposite. The Republicans gained control of both houses, signaling trouble for Wilson in two ways. First, a peace treaty would have to be submitted for approval to a potentially hostile Senate. Second, the election results at home diminished Wilson's stature in the eyes of foreign leaders. Wilson aggravated his political problems by not naming a senator to his advisory American Peace Commission. He also refused to take any prominent Republicans with him to Paris or to consult with the Senate Foreign Relations Committee before the conference. It did not help that the president denounced his critics as "blind and little provincial people."

Another obstacle in Wilson's way was the Allies' determination to impose a harsh, vengeful peace on the Germans. Georges Clemenceau of France, David Lloyd George of Britain, and Vittorio Orlando of Italy—with Wilson, the Big Four—became formidable adversaries. They had signed secret treaties in 1915 to grab German- and Turkish-controlled territories. When the Russian Bolsheviks published the treaties in early 1918, Wilson snarled that his European allies seemed to be waging a war "for some imperial or capitalist purpose." Allied leaders scoffed at the pious, headstrong, self-impressed president who wanted to deny them the spoils of war while he sought to expand U.S. power. "How can I talk to a fellow who thinks himself the first man for two thousand years who has known anything about peace on earth," Clemenceau growled. "Wilson imagines that he is a second Messiah."

At the conference, held at the ornate palace of Versailles, the Big Four met behind closed doors. Critics quickly pointed out that Wilson

Paris Peace Conference

had quickly abandoned the first of his Fourteen Points, diplomacy "in the public view." The victors demanded that Germany pay a huge reparations bill. Wilson instead called for a small indemnity, fearing that a resentful and economically hobbled Germany might turn to Bolshevism or disrupt the postwar community in some other way. Unable to moderate the Allied position, the president reluctantly gave way, agreeing to a clause blaming the war on the Germans and to the creation of a commission to determine the amount of reparations (later set at $33 billion). Wilson acknowledged that the peace terms were "hard," but he also came to believe that "the German people must be made to hate war."

As for the breaking up of empires and the principle of self-determination, Wilson could deliver on only some of his goals. Creating a League-administered "mandate" system, the conferees placed former German and Turkish colonies under the control of other imperial nations. France and Britain, for example, obtained parts of the Middle East, and Japan gained authority over Germany's colonies in the Pacific. In other arrangements, Japan replaced Germany as the imperial overlord of China's Shandong Peninsula, and France was permitted occupation rights in Germany's Rhineland. Elsewhere in Europe, Wilson's prescriptions fared better. Out of Austria-Hungary and Russia came the newly independent states of Austria, Hungary, Yugoslavia, Czechoslovakia, and Poland. Wilson and his colleagues also built a *cordon sanitaire* (buffer zone) of new westward-looking nations (Finland, Estonia, Latvia, and Lithuania) around Russia to quarantine the Bolshevik contagion (see Map 23.3).

Wilson worked hardest on the charter for the League of Nations. In the long run, he believed, such an organization would moderate the harshness of the Allied peace terms and temper imperial ambitions. The League reflected the power of large nations such as the United States: it consisted of an influential council of five permanent members and elected delegates from smaller states, an assembly of all members, and a World Court. Wilson identified Article 10 as the "kingpin" of the League covenant: "The Members of the League undertake to respect and preserve as against external aggression the territorial integrity and existing political independence of all Members of the League. In case of any such aggression or in case of any threat or danger of such aggression the Council shall advise upon the means by which this obligation shall be fulfilled." This collective-security provision, along with the entire League charter, became part of the peace treaty because Wilson insisted that there could be no future peace with Germany without a league to oversee it.

League of Nations and Article 10

German representatives at first refused to sign the punitive treaty but submitted in June 1919. They gave up 13 percent of Germany's territory, 10 percent of its population, all of its colonies, and a huge portion of its national wealth. Many people wondered how the League could function in the poisoned postwar atmosphere of revenge and humiliation. But Wilson waxed euphoric: "The stage is set, the destiny disclosed. It has come about by no plan of our conceiving, but by the hand of God."

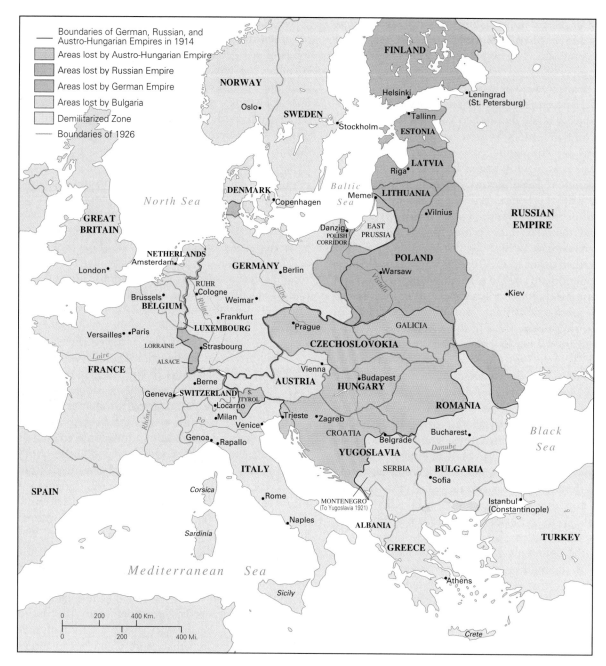

Map 23.3 Europe Transformed by War and Peace After President Wilson and the other conferees at the Paris Peace Conference negotiated the Treaty of Versailles, empires were broken up. In eastern Europe, in particular, new nations emerged.

In March 1919, thirty-nine senators (enough to deny the treaty the necessary two-thirds vote) had signed a petition stating that the League's structure did not adequately protect U.S. interests. Wilson denounced his critics as "pygmy" minds, but he persuaded the peace conference to exempt the Monroe Doctrine and domestic matters from League jurisdiction. Having made these concessions to senatorial advice, Wilson would budge no more. Compromises with other nations had been necessary to keep the conference going, he insisted, and the League would rectify wrongs. Could his critics not see that membership in the League would give the United States "leadership in the world"?

The president was not the only one posing questions. The journalist Walter Lippmann asked: "How in our consciences are we to square the results with the promises?" Criticism of the peace process and the treaty mounted: Wilson had bastardized his own principles. He had conceded Shandong to Japan. He personally had killed a provision affirming the racial equality of all peoples. The treaty did not mention freedom of the seas, and tariffs were not reduced. Reparations promised to be punishing. Senator La Follette protested that the League would perpetuate empire. Conservative critics feared that the League would limit American freedom of action in world affairs, stymie U.S. expansion, and intrude on domestic questions. And Article 10 raised serious questions: Would the United States be *obligated* to use armed force to ensure collective security? And what about colonial rebellions, such as in Ireland or India? Would the League feel compelled to crush them? "Were a League of Nations in existence in the days when George Washington fought and won," an Irish American editor wrote, "we would still be an English colony."

Critics of the Treaty

Senator Henry Cabot Lodge of Massachusetts boldly disputed Wilson. A Harvard-educated Ph.D. and partisan Republican, Lodge packed the Foreign Relations Committee with critics and prolonged public hearings. He introduced several reservations to the treaty: one stated that the nation's immigration acts could not be subject to League decision; another held that Congress had to approve any obligation under Article 10.

In September 1919 Wilson embarked on a speaking tour of the United States. Growing more exhausted every day, he dismissed his antagonists as "contemptible quitters." Provoked by Irish American and German American hecklers, he lashed out in Red-Scare terms: "Any man who carries a hyphen about him carries a dagger which he is ready to plunge into the vitals of the Republic." While doubts about Article 10 multiplied, Wilson tried to highlight neglected features of the League charter—such as the arbitration of disputes and an international conference to abolish child labor. In Colorado, a day after delivering another passionate speech, the president awoke to nausea and

In October 1919 President Woodrow Wilson (1856–1924) receives assistance after his massive stroke, which made it difficult for him to maintain his train of thought and manage government affairs. Historians continue to debate the influence of Wilson's poor health on the president's losing battle for U.S. membership in the League of Nations.   (Library of Congress)

that President Wilson suffered a disabling illness that seriously impaired his leadership during the League debate and that his severe incapacity was deliberately hidden from the public? Historians had long suspected the worst, but not until the private memoranda and medical records kept by Wilson's private physician, Dr. Cary T. Grayson, were published in 1990 and 1991 (as part of editor Arthur S. Link's *The Papers of Woodrow Wilson*) did they have a detailed account of the bedridden president's condition.

After a massive stroke had incapacitated the president on October 2, 1919, Edith Bolling Wilson insisted that Grayson issue only "general statements" about her husband's status. Although at first Grayson publicly described Woodrow Wilson as "a very sick man," thereafter he delivered upbeat statements about the clarity of the president's mind and his "comfortable" days. No mention was ever made publicly that Wilson had suffered a debilitating stroke that made it difficult for him to focus on the nation's business.

Instead, as the newspaper reports printed here indicate, Grayson's bulletins simply stated that the president was down with "nervous exhaustion." White House Head Usher Irwin Hood Hoover remembered the conspiratorial "deception" to hide Wilson's actual condition. When Grayson published a memoir in 1960, he still did not reveal the truth.

Long before the major stroke, Wilson had been ill. His medical history included hypertension, arteriosclerosis (hardening of the arteries), and several small strokes (the first in 1896) that caused impaired reasoning and memory loss. Wilson and his doctors had conspired to keep this information from the American people. During the Paris Peace Conference and the League fight, Wilson's health had deteriorated further. He suffered severe headaches and insomnia. After a speech in Colorado on September 25, 1919, he collapsed.

The devastating stroke of October 2 left Wilson partially paralyzed. The prostrate president could not lead because he could not concentrate on any subject for very long and he secluded himself from cabinet members. Wilson grew very angry when Secretary of State Robert Lansing quietly suggested that the president was so incapacitated that the vice president should take over. (The Constitution reads that in case of the president's "inability to discharge the powers and duties" of his office, the "same shall devolve on the Vice President.") Always stubborn, Wilson became more intransigent and more irascible, refusing to compromise with senators who said that they would vote for U.S. membership in the League of Nations if he would accept changes in the charter. Given the serious issues raised by the collective-security provision of the covenant, some historians wonder whether even a healthy Wilson could have reversed the negative Senate vote. But other scholars argue that Wilson's illness so impaired his rationality and that the cover-up so distorted the truth that the Senate's defeat of the treaty can be understood only in the context of the stricken president's medical history as documented in Dr. Grayson's private accounts. (Photos: Copyright © 1919 by The New York Times Company. Reprinted by permission.)

Text of Admiral Grayson's Official Bulletins Reporting President Wilson's Condition

Special to The New York Times.

WASHINGTON, Oct. 11.—The bulletin on the President's condition, issued at the White House tonight, was as follows:

WHITE HOUSE, Saturday, Oct. 11, 9:45 P. M.
The President has had a comfortable day.
GRAYSON.

The morning bulletin read:

WHITE HOUSE, Saturday, Oct. 11, 12:40 P. M.
The President shows signs of continued improvement, but his condition is such as to necessitate his remaining in bed for an extended period.
GRAYSON,
DERCUM,
RUFFIN,
STITT.

This d[...]
nounced aft[...]
come to W[...]
condition f[...]
week, and [...]
Cary T. Gr[...]
Ruffin and [...]

Physicians' Bulletins Say President Had a Good Night and Restful Day

Special to The New York Times.

WASHINGTON, Oct. 12.—The following bulletin on the President's condition was issued by his physician tonight:

WHITE HOUSE, Oct. 12, 10 P. M.
The President is in good spirits and has had a restful day.
GRAYSON.

The morning bulletin read:

WHITE HOUSE, Oct. 12, 11:30 A. M.
There is no notable change in the President's condition. He had a good night.
GRAYSON.
RUFFIN
STITT.

uncontrollable facial twitching. "I just feel as if I am going to pieces," he said. A few days later, back in Washington, he suffered a massive stroke that paralyzed his left side. He became peevish and even more stubborn, increasingly unable to conduct presidential business. Advised to placate senatorial critics so the treaty would have a chance of passing, Wilson rejected "dishonorable compromise." From Senate Democrats he demanded utter loyalty—a vote against all reservations.

Twice in November the Senate rejected the Treaty of Versailles and thus U.S. membership in the League.

Senate Rejection of the Treaty and League

In the first vote, Democrats joined sixteen "Irreconcilables," mostly Republicans who opposed any treaty whatsoever, to defeat the treaty with reservations (39 for and 55 against). In the second vote, Republicans and Irreconcilables turned down the treaty without reservations (38 for and 53 against). In March 1920 the Senate again voted; this time a majority (49 for and 35 against) favored the treaty with reservations, but the tally fell short of the two-thirds needed. Had Wilson permitted Democrats to compromise—to accept reservations—he could have achieved his fervent goal of membership in the League, which, despite the U.S. absence, came into being. "I would rather fail in a cause that will ultimately triumph than triumph in a cause that will ultimately fail," he once said.

Who or what was responsible for the defeat of the treaty? The stroke incapacitated the president, sapping his energy and his ability to lead effectively. The bitter personal feud between Wilson and Lodge accounts for some conflict but does not explain the determination of the Irreconcilables. Certainly Wilson's concessions to a harsh peace at Paris undercut his case in the United States, but even so, two-thirds of the senators seemed willing to forgive his errors at Versailles if he would only accept some reservations.

At the core of the debate lay a basic issue in American foreign policy: whether the United States would

Collective Security versus Unilateralism

endorse collective security or continue to travel the path of unilateralism articulated in George Washington's Farewell Address and in the Monroe Doctrine. In a world dominated by imperialist states unwilling to subordinate their selfish ambitions to an international organization, Americans preferred their traditional nonalignment and freedom of choice over binding commitments to collective action. That is why

so many of Wilson's critics targeted Article 10 and why the president was so adamant in defending it.

In the end, Woodrow Wilson failed to create a new world order through reform. He promised more than he could deliver. Still, the United States emerged from the First World War an even greater world power. By 1920 the United States had become the world's leading economic power, producing 40 percent of its coal, 70 percent of its petroleum, and half of its pig iron. It also rose to first rank in world trade. American companies took advantage of the war to nudge the Germans and British out of foreign markets, especially in Latin America. Goodyear went into the Dutch East Indies for rubber. Meanwhile, the United States shifted from being a debtor to a creditor nation, becoming the world's leading banker.

After the disappointment of Versailles, appeals for arms control accelerated and the peace movement revitalized. At the same time, the military became better armed and more professional. The Reserve Officers' Training Corps (ROTC) became permanent; military "colleges" provided upper-echelon training; and the Army Industrial College, founded in 1924, pursued business-military cooperation in the area of logistics and planning. The National Research Council, created in 1916 with government money and Carnegie and Rockefeller funds, continued after the war as an alliance of scientists and businesspeople engaged in research relating to national defense. Tanks, quick-firing guns, armor-piercing explosives, and oxygen masks for high-altitude flying pilots were just some of the technological advances that emerged from the First World War.

The international system born in these years was unstable and fragmented. Espousing decolonization and taking to heart the Wilsonian

Unstable International System

principle of self-determination, nationalist leaders active during the First World War, such as Ho Chi Minh of Indochina and Mohandas K. Gandhi of India, vowed to achieve independence for their peoples. Communism became a disruptive force in world politics, and the Soviets bore a grudge against those invaders who had tried to thwart their revolution. The new states in central and eastern Europe proved weak, dependent on outsiders for security. Germans bitterly resented the harsh peace settlement, and the war debts and reparations problems dogged international order for years. As it entered the 1920s, the international system that Woodrow Wilson had vowed to reform wobbled.

Summary

At the close of the First World War, the historian Albert Bushnell Hart observed that "it is easy to see that the United States is a new country." Actually, America came out of the war an unsettled mix of the old and the new. The war exposed deep divisions among Americans: white versus black, nativist versus immigrant, capital versus labor, men versus women, radical versus Progressive and conservative, pacifist versus interventionist, nationalist versus internationalist. It is little wonder that Americans—having experienced race riots, labor strikes, disputes over civil liberties, and the League fight—wanted to escape from what John Dewey called the "cult of irrationality" to what President Warren G. Harding called "normalcy."

During the war the federal government intervened in the economy and influenced people's everyday lives as never before. Centralization of control in Washington, D.C., and mobilization of the home front served as a model for the future. Although the Wilson administration shunned reconstruction or reconversion plans and quickly dismantled the many governmental agencies (war housing projects, for example, were sold to private investors), the World War I experience of the activist state served as guidance for 1930s reformers battling the Great Depression (see Chapter 25). The partnership of government and business in managing the wartime economy advanced the development of a mass society through the standardization of products and the promotion of efficiency. Wilsonian wartime policies also nourished the continued growth of oligopoly through the suspension of antitrust laws. Business power dominated the next decade. American labor, by contrast, entered lean years, although new labor management practices, including corporate welfare programs, survived.

Although the disillusionment evident after Versailles did not cause the United States to adopt a policy of isolationist withdrawal (see Chapter 26), skepticism about America's ability to right wrongs abroad marked the postwar American mood. The war was grimy and ugly, far less glorious than Wilson's lofty rhetoric suggested. People recoiled from photographs of shell-shocked faces and of bodies dangling from barbed wire. American soldiers, tired of idealism, craved the latest baseball scores and their regular jobs. Those Progressives who had believed that entry into the war would deliver the millennium, later marveled at their naiveté. Many lost their enthusiasm for crusades, and many others turned away in disgust from the bickering of the victors. Some felt betrayed. The journalist William Allen White angrily wrote to a friend that the Allies "have—those damned vultures—taken the heart out of the peace, taken the joy out of the great enterprise of the war, and have made it a sordid malicious miserable thing like all the other wars in the world."

Woodrow Wilson himself had remarked, soon after taking office in 1913 and before the Great War, that "there's no chance of progress and reform in an administration in which war plays the principal part." From the perspective of 1920, looking back on distempers at home and abroad, Wilson knew that progress and reform had taken a beating.

LEGACY FOR A PEOPLE AND A NATION

Remembering War at the Tomb of the Unknown Soldier

The much visited Tomb of the Unknown Soldier, or Tomb of the Unknowns, is a solemn place to remember the First World War and others in which Americans have died. At the marble plaza in Virginia's Arlington National Cemetery, overlooking Washington, D.C., stern-faced military guards stiffly march back and forth, twenty-four hours a day. Buried there are the remains of three (until mid-1998, four) unidentified American soldiers "known but to God."

After World War I, U.S. leaders declared that the ceremonial burial of an anonymous hero would remind Americans of the war and symbolize national unity while saluting diversity, for it could not be determined whether the "Unknown Soldier" was white or nonwhite, immigrant or native, rich or poor, young or old, Protestant, Catholic, or Jewish. Few in those days, however, could imagine the unknown as anyone other than a native-born, white Protestant. In fall 1921, four unknowns were exhumed from graves in France; one was selected. On Armistice Day, November 11, American dignitaries reburied the unidentified combatant. On Memorial Day, May 26, 1958, an unknown from World War II and an unknown from the Korean War were interred in crypts beside the World War I soldier.

On May 28, 1984, U.S. leaders buried a fourth unknown, this one from the Vietnam War. Controversy ensued. Military authorities had initially classified the remains as those of twenty-four-year-old Lieutenant Michael J. Blassie, a pilot shot down in South Vietnam.

But officials then changed their designation to unidentified. The Blassie family pressed for reconsideration. In 1998, five years after a CBS television program publicized the issue, a reluctant Department of Defense finally agreed to disinter the Vietnam War unknown. A DNA sample (deoxyribonucleic acid, the cellular material that determines individual heredity characteristics) was removed from the pelvis and successfully matched to blood from Blassie's mother, Jean. Blassie's remains were shipped to Missouri for reburial.

One crypt at Arlington now sits empty, and will remain so given the use of DNA testing by forensic scientists. Since 1994, moreover, the Pentagon has compiled DNA "prints" of all military personnel, making certain the identification of killed, badly mangled U.S. soldiers separated from their ID tags. Watching the changing of the guards at Arlington and musing about the role of science in changing how Americans remember war, a history teacher from Kentucky recently remarked that "we are losing our sense of meaning. I guess this memorial will have to stand for more than soldiers that are unknown. We are going to have to look deeper now." And perhaps look to new labels, such as "disappeared soldier" or "missing-in-action soldier," to sustain a legacy for a people and a nation.

For Further Reading, see page A-26 of the Appendix. For Web resources, go to http://college.hmco.com.

THE NEW ERA OF THE 1920S

Eager to win the $25,000 offered by a hotel owner to the first person to fly an airplane non-stop between New York and Paris, three different aircraft crews stood ready to go at Roosevelt Airfield in the spring of 1927. One man, Charles A. Lindbergh, the only one piloting his plane solo, decided to risk drizzly weather and start the trip May 20. For thirty-three hours, his craft, *The Spirit of St. Louis*, bounced across the Atlantic skies. The flight seized the attention of practically every American, as newspaper and telegraph reports followed Lindbergh's progress. He reached the Irish coast! He crossed over England! He entered France! And when he landed at Le Bourget Airfield, the nation rejoiced. The *New York Evening World* sold 114,000 extra newspapers on May 21; the *St. Louis Post-Dispatch* sold 40,000 extras. President Calvin Coolidge dispatched a warship to bring "Lucky Lindy" back home. Celebrants sent Lindbergh 55,000 telegrams and dropped 1,800 tons of shredded paper on him during a triumphant parade upon his return.

Charles Lindbergh was one of the most revered heroes in American history. Though he was not the first to fly across the ocean (in 1919 two men piloted a plane from Newfoundland to Ireland, and a crew of five reached Europe by way of the Azores) his feat temporarily united Americans and made a stunt pilot into an idol. During his flight, forty thousand spectators at New York's Yankee Stadium watching a boxing match stood in utter silence and prayed for Lindbergh's safety. One newspaper exclaimed that Lindbergh had accomplished "the greatest feat of a solitary man in the history of the human race." Among countless medals, Lindbergh received the Distinguished Flying Cross and the Congressional Medal of Honor. Promoters offered him millions of dollars to tour the world by air and $700,000 for a movie contract. Texas named a town after him.

Through it all, Lindbergh, nicknamed "The Lone Eagle," remained dignified, even aloof. His flight and its aftermath, however, open insights into his era. The burst of publicity and the thrill of celebration point to

Landing in France on May 21, 1927, Charles Lindbergh completed a flight across the Atlantic Ocean and instantly became one of the nation's most revered heroes. His accomplishment and the publicity surrounding it represented much of what made the 1920s a New Era. (Corbis/Bettmann)

the impact of commercialism, new technology, and mass entertainment. But Lindbergh himself epitomized individual achievement, high moral character, and patriotism—old-fashioned values that also vied for public allegiance in an era contemporaries themselves identified as "new."

During the 1920s, consumerism flourished. Although poverty beset small farmers, workers in declining industries, and nonwhites in inner cities, most other people enjoyed a high standard of living relative to previous generations. Spurred by advertising and installment buying, Americans eagerly acquired radios, automobiles, real estate, and stocks. As in the Gilded Age, government, as embodied in Congress, the presidency, and the Supreme Court, maintained a favorable climate for business. And in contrast to the Progressive era, few people worried about the abuse of private power. Yet state and local governments, extending the reach of public authority, undertook important reforms.

It was an era of contrast and complexity. Fads and frivolities coincided with new creativity in the arts and notable advances in science and technology. Changes in work habits, family responsibilities, and healthcare fostered new uses of time and new attitudes about behavior. While material bounty and leisure enticed Americans into new amusements, winds of change also stirred up waves of reaction. Liberal ideas repelled those who held tight to traditional beliefs.

An unseen storm lurked on the horizon, however. The glitter of consumer culture that dominated everyday life blinded Americans to rising debts and uneven prosperity. Just before the decade closed, a devastating depression brought the era to a brutal close. ■

Big Business Triumphant

 The 1920s began with a jolting economic decline. Shortly after the First World War ended, industrial output dropped and unemployment rose as wartime orders dried up, consumer spending dwindled, and demobilized soldiers poured into the work force. As European agriculture recovered from the war, American exports contracted and farm income plunged. Unemployment, around 2 percent in 1919, passed 12 percent in 1921. Railroads and mining industries suffered in the West. Layoffs spread through New England as textile companies abandoned outdated factories for the convenient raw materials and cheap labor of the South.

Aided by electric energy, a recovery began in 1922 and continued unevenly until 1929. By decade's end, factories using electric motors dominated American industry, increasing productivity and sending thousands of steam engines to the scrap heap. Electric power helped manufacturers produce new metal alloys such as aluminum and synthetic materials such as rayon. As well, most urban households now had electric lighting and could utilize new appliances such as refrigerators, toasters, and vacuum cleaners.

As Americans acquired spending money and leisure time, service industries such as restaurants, beauty salons and barbershops, and movie theaters boomed. Installment or time-payment plans ("A dollar down and a dollar forever," one critic quipped) drove the new consumerism. Of 3.5 million automobiles sold in 1923, some 80 percent were bought on credit.

The economic expansion brought a continuation of the corporate consolidation movement that had created trusts and holding companies in the late nineteenth century. Although Progressive era trustbusting had reined in big business, it had not eliminated control of an entire industry by a few large firms. By the 1920s such oligopolies dominated not only production but also marketing, distribution, and even finance. In basic industries such as steel production and electrical equipment, a few sprawling companies such as U.S. Steel and General Electric predominated.

Business Consolidation and Lobbying

Business and professional organizations that had come into being around 1900 also expanded in the 1920s. Retailers and manufacturers formed trade associations to swap information and coordinate planning. Farm bureaus promoted scientific agriculture and tried to stabilize markets. Lawyers, engineers, and social scientists expanded their professional societies. These special-interest groups participated in what has been called the "new lobbying." In a complex society in which government was playing an increasingly influential role, hundreds of organizations sought to convince federal and state legislators to support their interests. One Washington, D.C., observer contended that "lobbyists were so thick they were constantly falling over one another."

Government assistance helped business thrive, and legislators came to depend on the expertise of lobbyists in making decisions. Prodded by lobbyists, Congress reduced taxes on corporations and wealthy individuals in 1921 and the next year raised tariff rates in the Fordney-McCumber Tariff Act. Presidents

IMPORTANT EVENTS

1920 Nineteenth Amendment ratified, legalizing the vote for women in federal elections

Harding elected president

KDKA transmits first commercial radio broadcast

1920–21 Postwar deflation and depression occurs

1921 Federal Highway Act funds national highway system

Johnson Act establishes immigration quotas

Sacco and Vanzetti convicted

Sheppard-Towner Act allots funds to states to set up maternity and pediatric clinics

Fordney-McCumber Tariff raises rates on imports

1922 Economic recovery raises standard of living

Coronado Coal Company v. United Mine Workers rules that strikes may be illegal actions in restraint of trade

Bailey v. Drexel Furniture Company voids restrictions on child labor

Federal government ends strikes by railroad shop workers and miners

1923 Harding dies; Coolidge assumes the presidency

Adkins v. Children's Hospital overturns a minimum-wage law affecting women

Ku Klux Klan activity peaks

Aimee Semple McPherson opens Angelus Temple in Los Angeles

1923–24 Government scandals (Teapot Dome) exposed

1924 Johnson-Reid Act revises immigration quotas

Coolidge elected president

1925 Scopes trial highlights battle between religious fundamentalists and modernists

1927 Sacco and Vanzetti executed

Lindbergh pilots solo transatlantic flight

Ruth hits sixty home runs

The Jazz Singer, the first movie with sound, is released

1928 Stock market soars

Hoover elected president

1929 Stock market crashes; Great Depression begins

Warren G. Harding, Calvin Coolidge, and Herbert Hoover appointed cabinet officers who pursued policies favorable to business. Regulatory agencies such as the Federal Trade Commission and Interstate Commerce Commission monitored company activities but, under the influence of lobbyists, cooperated with corporations more than they regulated them.

The Supreme Court, led by Chief Justice William Howard Taft, the former president, protected business and private property as aggressively as in the Gilded Age and abandoned its antitrust action of the Progressive era. Its key decisions sheltered business from government regulation and hindered organized labor's ability to achieve its ends through strikes and legislation. In *Coronado Coal Company v. United Mine Workers* (1922), Taft ruled that a striking union, like a trust, could be prosecuted for illegal restraint of trade. Yet in *Maple Floor Association v. U.S.* (1929), the Court decided that trade associations that distributed antiunion information were not acting in restraint of trade. The Court also voided restrictions on child la-

bor (*Bailey v. Drexel Furniture Company*, 1922) and overturned a minimum-wage law affecting women because it infringed on liberty of contract (*Adkins v. Children's Hospital*, 1923).

Organized labor suffered other setbacks during the 1920s. Fearful of communism allegedly brought into the country by radical immigrants, public opinion turned against workers who disrupted everyday life with strikes. Perpetuating tactics used during the Red Scare (see pages 654–655), the Harding administration in 1922 obtained a sweeping court injunction to quash a strike by 400,000 railroad shop workers. The same year, the Justice Department helped put down a nationwide strike by 650,000 miners.

Fate of Organized Labor

Meanwhile, some large corporations countered the appeal of unions by offering pensions, profit sharing (which amounted to withholding wages for later distribution), and company-sponsored picnics and sporting events—a policy known as welfare capitalism.

State legislators aided employers by prohibiting closed shops (workplaces where union membership was mandatory) and permitting open shops (which could discriminate against nonunion workers). Concerned about job security, workers in turn shied away from unions; union membership fell from 5.1 million in 1920 to 3.6 million in 1929.

Agriculture was one sector of the national economy that languished during the 1920s. Pressed into competition with growers in other countries and trying hard to increase productivity by investing in new machines such as plows, harvesters, and tractors, American farmers found themselves further beset by debt. As in the 1880s and 1890s, overproduction and foreign competition depressed crop and livestock prices, in turn reducing incomes. Early in the decade, for example, the price that farmers could get for cotton dropped by two-thirds and that of hogs and cattle fell by half. As a result, farm income never recovered after the First World War, and the gap between a farmer's income and an urban worker's income widened. Many farmers became tenants because they lost their land; more quit farming altogether.

Farmers' Problems

Politics and Government

A series of Republican presidents in the 1920s extended Theodore Roosevelt's notion of government-business cooperation, but they made government a compliant coordinator rather than the active director Roosevelt had advocated. A symbol of government's goodwill toward business was President Warren G. Harding, elected in 1920 when the populace no longer desired national or international crusades. Democrats had nominated Ohio's Governor James M. Cox, who supported Woodrow Wilson's fading hopes for U.S. membership in the League of Nations. But Cox and his running mate, Franklin D. Roosevelt of New York, failed to excite voters. Harding, who kept his position on the League vague, captured 16 million popular votes to only 9 million for Cox. (The total vote in the 1920 presidential election was 36 percent higher than in 1916, reflecting the participation of women voters for the first time.)

A small-town newspaperman and senator from Ohio, Harding appointed some capable assistants, notably Secretary of State Charles Evans Hughes, Secretary of Commerce Herbert Hoover, Secretary of the Treasury Andrew Mellon, and Secretary of Agriculture Henry C. Wallace. Harding also backed some reforms. His administration helped streamline federal spending with the Budget and Accounting Act of 1921, supported antilynching legislation (rejected by Congress), and approved bills assisting farm cooperatives and liberalizing farm credit.

Harding Administration

Harding's problem was that he had some predatory friends. "Warren, it's a good thing you wasn't born a gal," his father reputedly remarked. "You'd be in the family way all the time—you can't say no." Harding said "yes" often, appointing cronies who saw officeholding as an invitation to personal gain. Charles Forbes of the Veterans Bureau went to federal prison, convicted of fraud and bribery in connection with government contracts. Attorney General Harry Daugherty was implicated in bribery and other fraudulent schemes; he escaped prosecution by refusing to testify against himself. Most notoriously, a congressional inquiry in 1923 and 1924 revealed that Secretary of the Interior Albert Fall had accepted bribes to lease oil-rich government property to private oil companies. For his role in the affair—called the Teapot Dome scandal after a Wyoming oil reserve that had been turned over to Mammoth Oil Company—Fall was fined $100,000 and spent a year in jail, the first cabinet officer ever to be so disgraced.

Teapot Dome

By mid-1923, Harding had become disillusioned. Amid rumors of mismanagement and crime, he told a journalist, "My God, this is a hell of a job. I have no trouble with my enemies. . . . But my friends, my God-damned friends . . . they're the ones that keep me walking the floor nights." On a speaking tour that summer, Harding became ill and died in San Francisco August 2. Though his death preceded revelation of the Teapot Dome scandal, some people speculated that to avoid the embarrassment of impeachment Harding had committed suicide or was poisoned by his wife. Most evidence, however, points to death from natural causes, probably a heart attack. At any rate, Harding was truly mourned. A warm, dignified-looking man who relished a good joke and an evening of poker, he seemed suited to a nation recovering from world war and domestic hard times.

Vice President Calvin Coolidge, Harding's successor, was far more dour. (Alice Roosevelt Longworth, Teddy's daughter, quipped that Coolidge looked as if he had been weaned on a pickle.) As governor of Massachusetts, Coolidge had attracted national attention in 1919 with his active stand against striking Boston policemen, a policy that won him business support and the vice-presidential nomination in 1920. Ordinarily, however, he was content to let events take their course, prompting columnist Walter Lippmann to remark on the "grim, determined, alert inactivity, which keeps Mr. Coolidge occupied constantly."

Coolidge Prosperity

Coolidge's presidency coincided with business prosperity. Respectful of private enterprise and aided by Andrew Mellon, whom he retained as secretary of the treasury, Coolidge's administration reduced government debt, lowered income-tax rates (especially for the rich), and began construction of a national highway system. Congress took little initiative during these years, with the exception of farm policy. Responding to farmers' complaints of falling prices, Congress twice passed bills to establish government-backed price supports for staple crops (the McNary-Haugen Bills of 1927 and 1928). Resembling the subtreasury scheme that farm alliances had advocated in the 1890s (see page 566), these bills would establish a complex system whereby the government would buy surplus farm products and either hold them until prices rose or sell them abroad. Farmers argued that they deserved as much government protection as manufacturers got. Coolidge, however, vetoed the measure both times as improper government interference in the market economy.

"Coolidge prosperity" was the decisive issue in the presidential election of 1924. Both major parties ran candidates who favored private initiative. Republicans nominated Coolidge with little dissent. At their national convention, Democrats first debated whether to condemn the newly aroused Ku Klux Klan (see page 681), voting 542 to 541 against condemnation. They then endured 103 ballots deadlocked between southern prohibitionists, who supported former secretary of the treasury William G. McAdoo, and antiprohibition easterners, who backed New York's governor Alfred E. Smith. They finally compromised on John W. Davis, a New York corporation lawyer. Remnants of the Progressive movement, along with various farm, labor, and socialist groups, formed a new Progressive Party and nominated Robert M. La Follette, the aging Wisconsin reformer. The new party revived issues of the previous decades: public ownership of utilities, aid to farmers, rights for organized labor, and regulation of business.

Basically shy and introverted, Calvin Coolidge was content to let business have free rein in the pursuit of profits. This ironic cartoon shows the president accompanying the lively performance of big business with a saxophone and a song of praise. (*Life,* December 10, 1925)

The election results ratified Coolidge prosperity. Coolidge beat Davis by 15.7 million to 8.4 million popular votes, 382 to 136 electoral votes. La Follette finished third, receiving a respectable but ineffective 4.8 million popular votes and only 13 electoral votes. The electorate showed no desire for change and voiced its expectation of extended prosperity in the new era.

Impressed by the triumph of business influence, political analysts claimed that Progressivism had died.

State and Local Reform

They were partly right. The urgency for political and economic reform that had moved the previous generation faded in the 1920s. Much reform, however, occurred at state and local levels. Following initiatives begun before the First World War, thirty-four states instituted or expanded workers' compensation laws in the 1920s. Many states established employee-funded old-age pensions and welfare programs for the indigent. In cities, social workers strived for better housing and poverty relief. By 1926 every major city and many smaller ones had planning and zoning commissions that aimed to harness physical growth to the common good. The nation's statehouses, city halls, and universities trained a new generation of reformers who later influenced national affairs.

The federal government's generally apathetic Indian policy disturbed some reformers. Organizations such as the Indian Rights Association, the Indian Defense Association, and the General Federation of Women's Clubs worked to obtain justice and social services, including better education and return of tribal lands. But Native Americans, no longer a threat to whites' ambitions, were treated by the general population like other minorities: as objects of discrimination who were expected to assimilate. Severalty, the policy created by the Dawes Act of 1887 (see page 467) of allotting land to individuals rather than to tribes, had failed to make Indians self-supporting. Indian farmers had to endure poor soil, lack of irrigation, scarce medical care, and cattle thieves. Deeply attached to their land, they showed little inclination to move to cities. Whites still hoped to convert native peoples into "productive" citizens, but in a way that ignored indigenous cultures. Reformers were especially critical of Indian women, who refused to adopt middle-class homemaking habits and balked at sending their children to boarding schools.

Indian Affairs

Meanwhile, the federal government struggled to clarify Indians' citizenship status. The Dawes Act had conferred citizenship on all Indians who accepted allotments of land but not on those who remained on reservations. Also, the government retained a measure of control over Indian citizens that it did not exercise over other citizens. For example, because of allegations of drunkenness on reservations, federal law prevented the sale of liquor to Indians even before ratification of prohibition. After several court challenges, Congress finally passed a law in 1924 granting full citizenship to all Indians who previously had not received it. Also, the administration of President Herbert Hoover reorganized the Bureau of Indian Affairs and increased expenditures for health, education, and welfare. Much of the money, however, went to enlarge the bureaucracy rather than into Indian hands.

Even after achieving suffrage in 1920 with final ratification of the Nineteenth Amendment, politically active women remained excluded from local and national power structures, but their voluntary organizations used tactics that contributed to modern pressure-group politics. Whether the issue was birth control, peace, education, Indian affairs, or opposition to lynching, women in these associations publicized their causes and lobbied legislators rather than trying to elect their own candidates. For example, the League of Women Voters, reorganized out of the National American Woman Suffrage Association, did encourage women to run for office but more extensively worked for laws that would improve conditions for working women, the mentally ill, and the urban poor.

Women and Politics

Action by women's groups persuaded Congress to pass the Sheppard-Towner Act (1921), which allotted funds to states to set up maternity and pediatric clinics. (The measure ended in 1929 when Congress, under pressure from private physicians, canceled funding.) The Cable Act of 1922 reversed the law under which an American woman who married a foreigner assumed her husband's citizenship; under the new law such a woman could retain U.S. citizenship. At the state level, women achieved other rights, such as the ability to serve on juries.

As new voters, however, women accomplished relatively little. The National Woman's Party remained the champion of feminism, but women pursued a variety of interests. African American women, for example, fought for the rights of minority women and men without support from either the National Woman's Party or the newly organized League of Women Voters. Some groups, such as the National Woman's Party, pressed for an equal rights amendment, to ensure women's equality with men under the law. But such activity alienated the National Consumers League, the Women's Trade Union League, the League of Women Voters, and other groups that supported protective legislation to limit the hours and improve conditions for employed women. And like men, women of all types seemed preoccupied by the new era's materialism.

Materialism Unbound

Between 1919 and 1929, the gross national product—the total value of all goods and services produced in the United States—swelled by 40 percent. Wages and salaries also grew (though not as drastically), while the cost of living remained relatively stable. People had more purchasing

Expansion of Consumer Society

power, and they spent as Americans had never spent. An article in *Survey* magazine contrasted one family's expenditures in 1900 with those of 1928:

1900

2 bicycles	$ 70*
wringer and washboard	5
brushes and brooms	5
sewing machine (mechanical)	25
Total	$ 105

1928

automobile	$ 700
radio	75
phonograph	50
washing machine	150
vacuum cleaner	50
sewing machine (electric)	60
other electrical equipment	25
telephone (per year)	35
Total	$1,145

The article's author cautioned that education and medical care had become costlier. Nevertheless, she regarded the change as worthwhile.

Technology's benefits were reaching more people than ever before. By 1929 two-thirds of all Americans lived in dwellings that had electricity, compared with one-sixth in 1912. In 1929 one-fourth of all families owned vacuum cleaners, and one-fifth had toasters. Many could afford goods such as radios, washing machines, and movie tickets only because more than one family member earned wages or because the breadwinner took a second job. Nevertheless, new products and services were available to more than just the rich.

The automobile stood as vanguard of all the era's material wonders. During the 1920s automobile registrations soared from 8 million to 23 million. Mass production and competition brought down prices, making cars affordable even to some working-class families. A Ford Model T cost less than $300 and a Chevrolet sold for $700 by 1926—when factory workers earned about $1,300 a year and clerical workers about $2,300. Used cars cost less. At those prices, people could consider the car a necessity rather than a luxury. "There is no such thing

Effects of the Automobile

---

* From *Another Part of the Twenties*, by Paul Carter. Copyright 1977 by Columbia University Press. Reprinted with permission of Paul A. Carter.

Electric appliances became commonplace in the 1920s and advanced the consumer economy. Note here the obvious link between a daughter and her mother, whose domestic tasks appear to be made easier and more appealing by an electric range, a vacuum cleaner, and an iron.   (Picture Research Consultants & Archives)

as a 'pleasure automobile,'" proclaimed one newspaper ad in 1925. "You might as well talk of 'pleasure fresh air,' or of 'pleasure beef steak.' . . . The automobile increases length of life, increases happiness, represents above all other achievements the progress and the civilization of our age."

The car altered American life as much as the railroad had seventy-five years earlier. City streets became much cleaner as autos replaced the numerous horses that had dumped tons of manure every day. Women who learned to drive achieved newfound independence, taking touring trips by themselves or with female friends, conquering muddy roads, and making

During the 1920s, the desire to own an automobile spread to members of all classes, races, and ethnic groups. Low prices and available credit enabled this family from Beaumont, Texas, to own a "touring car." (Tyrrell Historical Library)

repairs when their vehicles broke down. Families created "homes on wheels," packing up food and camping equipment to "get away from it all." By 1927 most autos were enclosed (they had previously been open), creating a new private space for courtship and sex. A vast choice of models (there were 108 automobile manufacturers in 1923) and colors allowed owners to express personal tastes. Some owners customized their cars, installing beds and mechanical gadgets such as special horns and starters. Most importantly, the car was the ultimate symbol of social equality. As one writer observed in 1924, "It is hard to convince Steve Popovich, or Antonio Branca, or plain John Smith that he is being ground into the dust by Capital when at will he may drive the same highways, view the same scenery, and get as much enjoyment from his trip as the modern Midas."

Americans' passion for driving necessitated extensive construction of roads and abundant supplies of fuel. Since the late 1800s farmers and bicyclists had been lobbying for improved roads. After the First World War motorists joined the campaign, and in the 1920s government aid made "automobility" truly feasible. In 1921 Congress passed the Federal Highway Act, providing money for state roads, and in 1923 the Bureau of Public Roads planned a national highway system. The oil industry, already vast and powerful, shifted emphasis from illumination and lubrication to propulsion. In 1920 the United States produced about 65 percent of the world's oil. The automobile also forced public officials to pay more attention to safety regulations and traffic control. General Electric Company produced the first timed stop-and-go traffic light in 1924.

Advertising whetted demand for automobiles and other goods and services. By 1929 more money was spent on advertising than on all types of formal education. Advertising became a new gospel for business-minded Americans. In his best-selling *The Man Nobody Knows* (1925), advertising executive Bruce Barton called Jesus "the founder of modern business" because he "picked up twelve men from the bottom ranks of business and forged them into an organization that conquered the world." About the same time, a pamphlet entitled *Moses, Persuader of*

Advertising

Men declared, "Moses was one of the greatest salesmen and real-estate promoters that ever lived." Cosmetics manufacturers such as Max Factor, Helena Rubenstein, and the African American entrepreneur Madame C. J. Walker used movie stars and beauty advice in magazine ads to induce women to buy their products. Blending psychological theory with practical cynicism, advertising theorists asserted confidently that any person's tastes could be manipulated.

As newspaper circulation declined, other media assumed vital advertising functions. Radio became one of the era's most influential agents.

Radio

By 1929 over 10 million families owned radios, which bombarded them with advertisements, and Americans were spending $850 million a year on radio equipment. In the early 1920s, Congress decided that radio should be a private enterprise, not a tax-supported public service as it was in Great Britain. As a result, American programming focused on entertainment rather than on educational content because entertainment attracted more audiences and therefore more profits from advertisers. Station KDKA in Pittsburgh, at first noncommercial, pioneered broadcasting in 1920. Soon stations began airing advertisements, and by 1922 there were 508 such stations. In 1929 the National Broadcasting Company began to assemble a network of stations and soon was charging advertisers $10,000 to sponsor an hour-long show. Highway billboards and commercials projected during intermissions at movie houses also reminded viewers to buy. Packaging and product display became sciences, all intended to entice consumers.

Although low-income people could not afford all modern products and services, some new trends benefited the working classes, especially those living in cities. Indoor plumbing and electricity became more common in private residences, and canned foods and ready-made clothes became more affordable. A little cash and a lot of credit enabled many wage earners to purchase an automobile. Spending became a national pastime. No wonder many Americans wanted Henry Ford to run for president in 1924.

Cities, Migrants, and Suburbs

Consumerism signified not merely an economically mature nation but an urbanized one. The 1920 federal census revealed that for the first time a majority of Americans lived in urban areas (defined as places with

America Acclaims the SUPERETTE
– the smallest *big* radio ever built

Full-size, 8-tube Super-Heterodyne . . . with new RCA Super-Control Tubes... tone color control...exquisite small-size cabinet...only $69.50 COMPLETE

RCA Victor Radio

Between 1922 and 1930, the number of families owning radios swelled from 60,000 to almost 14 million. Manufacturers such as RCA produced a variety of sizes and shapes and took out full-page advertisements in popular publications to inform the public about the latest developments in design and technology.   (Library of American Broadcasting, University of Maryland at College Park)

2,500 or more people); the city had become the focus of national experience. Growth in manufacturing and services helped propel urbanization. Industries such as steel, oil, and auto production energized cities like Birmingham, Houston, and Detroit; services and retail trades boosted expansion in Seattle, Atlanta, and Minneapolis. Explosive growth also occurred in warm-climate cities—notably Miami and San Diego—where promises of comfort and profit attracted thousands of speculators.

During the 1920s, 6 million Americans left their farms for the city. Midwestern migrants, particularly young single people, moved to regional centers like Kansas City and Indianapolis or to the West. Between 1920 and 1930, California's population increased 67 percent, and California became one of the nation's most urbanized

Farm-to-City Migration

states while retaining its status as a leading agricultural state. Meanwhile, streams of rural southerners moved to that region's burgeoning industrial cities or rode railroads northward to Chicago and Cleveland.

African Americans, involved in what has been called the Great Migration, made up a sizable portion of people on the move. Pushed from cotton farming by a boll weevil plague and lured by industrial jobs, 1.5 million blacks moved cityward during the 1920s, doubling the African American populations of New York, Chicago, Detroit, and Houston. Forced by low wages and discrimination to seek the cheapest housing, newcomers squeezed into low-rent ghettos. Unlike white migrants, who were free to move out from the inner-city when they could afford to, blacks found better housing closed to them. The only way they could expand their housing opportunities was to spill into nearby white neighborhoods, a process that sparked resistance and violence. Fears of such expansion prompted white neighborhood associations to adopt restrictive covenants, whereby homeowners pledged not to sell or rent property to blacks.

The Great Migration

In response to discrimination, threats, and violence, thousands of urban blacks joined movements that glorified racial independence. The most influential of these nationalist groups was the Universal Negro Improvement Association (UNIA), headed by Marcus Garvey, a Jamaican immigrant who believed blacks should separate themselves from corrupt white society. Proclaiming "I am the equal of any white man," Garvey cultivated racial pride with mass meetings and parades. He also promoted black-owned businesses. *Negro World*, Garvey's newspaper, refused to publish ads for hair straightening and skin-lightening cosmetics, and he set up the Black Star shipping line to help blacks emigrate to Africa.

Marcus Garvey

The UNIA declined in the mid-1920s after ten UNIA leaders were arrested on charges of anarchism, and Garvey was deported for mail fraud involving the bankrupt Black Star line—though the company's main problem was that unscrupulous dealers had sold it dilapidated ships. Middle-class black leaders like W. E. B. Du Bois and several ministers of black churches opposed the UNIA, fearing that its extremism would undermine their efforts and influence. Nevertheless, in New York, Chicago, Detroit, and other cities, the organization attracted a large following (contemporaries

estimated it at 500,000; Garvey claimed 6 million), and Garvey's speeches instilled many African Americans with a heightened sense of race pride.

The newest immigrants to American cities came from Mexico and Puerto Rico where, as in rural North America, declining fortunes pushed people off the land. Most Mexicans migrated to work as agricultural laborers in the Southwest, but many also were drawn to growing cities like Denver, San Antonio, Los Angeles, and Tucson. Like other immigrant groups, they generally lacked resources and skills, and men outnumbered women. Mexicans crowded into low-rent districts plagued by poor sanitation, poor police protection, and poor schools.

Mexican and Puerto Rican Immigrants

The 1920s also witnessed an influx of Puerto Ricans to the mainland. Puerto Rico had been a U.S. possession since 1898, and its natives were granted U.S. citizenship in 1917. A shift in the island's economy from sugar to coffee production created a surplus of workers. Attracted by contracts from employers seeking cheap labor, most Puerto Rican migrants moved to New York City, where they created *barrios* (communities) in Brooklyn and Manhattan and found jobs in manufacturing and in hotels, restaurants, and domestic service.

Within their communities, both Puerto Ricans and Mexicans maintained traditional customs and values and developed businesses—*bodegas* (grocery stores), cafés, boarding houses—and social organizations to help themselves adapt to American society. Educated elites—doctors, lawyers, business owners—tended to become community leaders.

As urban growth peaked, suburban growth accelerated. Although towns had clustered around cities since the nation's earliest years, prosperity and automobile transportation made the suburbs more accessible to those wishing to flee crowded urban neighborhoods in the 1920s. Between 1920 and 1930, suburbs of Chicago (such as Oak Park and Evanston), Cleveland (Shaker Heights), and Los Angeles (Burbank and Inglewood) grew five to ten times faster than did the central cities. Most suburbs were middle- and upper-class bedroom communities; some, like Highland Park (near Detroit) and East Chicago, were industrial satellites.

Growth of Suburbs

Increasingly, suburbs resisted annexation to core cities. Suburbanites wanted to escape big-city crime,

Cinco de Mayo Mogollon, N.M.

Mexican immigrants, like other immigrants, brought their homeland customs with them to the United States. Every year on May 5, Cinco de Mayo, with events such as this parade, held in 1914 in Mogollon, New Mexico, they commemorated the Mexican victory over French troops in the Battle of Puebla on May 5, 1862.   (Library of Congress)

dirt, and taxes, and they fought to preserve control over their own police, schools, and water and gas services. Particularly in the Northeast and Midwest, the suburbs' fierce independence choked off expansion by the central city and divided metropolitan areas in ways that would plague future generations. Moreover, automobiles and the dispersal of population spread the environmental problems of city life—trash, pollution, noise—across the entire metropolitan area.

Cities and suburbs fostered the mass culture that gave the decade its character. Most of the consumers who jammed shops, movie houses, and sporting arenas and who embraced fads like crossword puzzles, miniature golf, and marathon dancing lived in or around cities. These were the places where people defied law and morality by patronizing speakeasies (illegal saloons), wearing outlandish clothes, and listening to jazz. They were also the places where devout moralists strained to resist modernism. Yet the ideal of small-

town society survived. While millions thronged cityward, Americans reminisced about the innocence and simplicity of a world gone by. This was the dilemma the modern nation faced: how does one anchor oneself in a world of rampant materialism and rapid social change?

New Rhythms of Everyday Life

 Amid changes to modern society, Americans developed new ways of using time. People increasingly split their daily lives into distinct compartments: work, family, and leisure. Each type of time was altered in the 1920s. For many people, time on the job shrank. Though strikes following the First World War had failed to reduce working hours, increased mechanization and higher productivity enabled employers to shorten the workweek for many industrial laborers from six days to

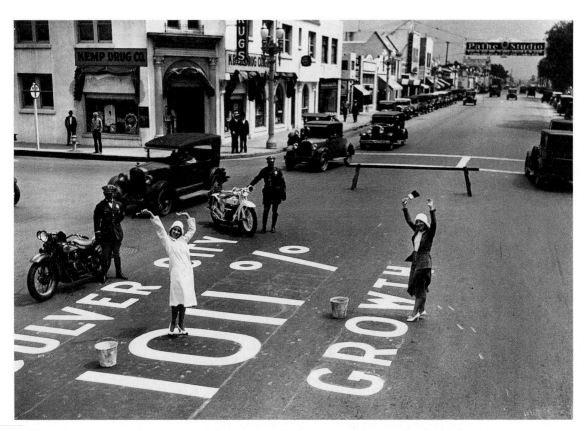

Wide highways, cheap land, and affordable housing allowed automobile commuters to move to the urban periphery. In this photo, young women wearing 1920s flapper-style outfits celebrate the phenomenal growth of Culver City, outside Los Angeles. Notice the strong presence of the motor car. (Security Pacific National Bank Collection, Los Angeles Public Library)

five and a half. White-collar employees often worked a forty-hour week and enjoyed a full weekend off. Annual vacations became a standard job benefit for white-collar workers.

Family time is harder to measure, but certain trends are clear. Family size decreased between 1920 and 1930 as birth control became more widely practiced. Among American women who married in the 1870s and 1880s, well over half who survived to age fifty had five or more children; of their counterparts who married in the 1920s, however, just 20 percent had five or more children. Meanwhile, the divorce rate rose. In 1920 there was 1 divorce for every 7.5 marriages; by 1929 the national ratio was 1 in 6, and in many cities it was 2 in 7. In conjunction with longer life expectancy, lower birth rates and more divorce meant that adults were devoting a smaller portion of their lives to raising children.

Family Time

Housewives still worked long hours cleaning, cooking, and raising children, but machines now lightened some of their tasks and enabled them to use their time differently than their forebears had. Especially in middle-class households, electric irons and washing machines simplified some chores. Gas- and oil-powered central heating and hot-water heaters eliminated the hauling of wood, coal, and water, the upkeep of a kitchen fire, and the removal of ashes.

Even as technology and economic change made life better and easier, they also created new demands on a woman's time. As daughters of working-class families stayed in school longer and as alternative forms of employment caused a shortage of servants in wealthier households, those who formerly had helped mothers and wives with cleaning, cooking, and childcare were less available. These factors, coupled with

Household Management

the spread of appliances such as washing machines, irons, and vacuum cleaners, shifted the entire task of household management to the wife. No longer a producer of food and clothing as her predecessors had been, a wife now became the chief shopper, responsible for making sure the family spent its money wisely. And the automobile made the wife a family's chief chauffeur. One survey found that urban housewives spent on average 13 percent of their work time, seven and a half hours per week, driving to shop and transport children.

A new emphasis on nutrition added a scientific dimension to housewives' responsibilities. With the discovery of vitamins between 1915 and 1930, nutritionists began advocating the consumption of certain foods to prevent illness. Giant food companies scrambled to advertise their products as filled with vitamins and minerals beneficial to growth and health. Not only did producers of milk and canned fruits and vegetables exploit the vitamin craze, but other companies made lofty claims that were hard to dispute because little was known about these invisible, tasteless ingredients. C. W. Post, for example, claimed that his Grape-Nuts contained "iron, calcium, phosphorus, and other mineral elements that are taken right up as vital food by the millions of cells in the body."

Nutrition

Better diets and improved sanitation made Americans generally healthier. Life expectancy at birth increased from fifty-four to sixty years between 1920 and 1930, and infant mortality decreased by two-thirds. Sanitation and research in bacteriology and immunology combined with better nutrition to reduce the risks of life-threatening diseases such as tuberculosis and diphtheria. But medical progress did not benefit all groups equally. Rates of infant mortality were 50 to 100 percent higher among nonwhites than among whites, and tuberculosis in inner-city slums remained alarmingly common. Moreover, fatalities from car accidents rose 150 percent, and deaths from heart disease and cancer—diseases of old age—increased 15 percent. Nevertheless, Americans in general were living longer: the total population over age sixty-five grew 35 percent between 1920 and 1930, while the rest of the population increased only 15 percent.

Longer life spans and the worsening economic status of the elderly stirred interest in government pensions and other forms of old-age assistance. Industrialism put a premium on youth and agility, pushing older people into poverty from forced retirement and reduced income. Recognizing the needs of aging citizens, most European countries established state-supported pension systems in the early 1900s. Many Americans, however, believed that individuals should prepare for old age by saving in their youth; pensions, they felt, smacked of socialism. As late as 1923 the Pennsylvania Chamber of Commerce labeled old-age assistance "un-American and socialistic . . . an entering wedge of communistic propaganda."

Older Americans and Retirement

Yet conditions were alarming. Most inmates in state poorhouses were older people, and almost one-third of Americans age sixty-five and older depended financially on someone else. Few employers offered pension plans; most, including the federal government, did not provide for retired employees. Noting that the government fed retired horses until they died, one postal worker complained, "For the purpose of drawing a pension, it would have been better had I been a horse than a human being." Resistance to pension plans finally broke at the state level in the 1920s. Led by Isaac Max Rubinow and Abraham Epstein, reformers persuaded voluntary associations, labor unions, and legislators to endorse the principle of old-age assistance through pensions, insurance, and retirement homes. By 1933 almost every state provided at least minimal assistance to needy elderly people, and a path had been opened for a national program of old-age insurance.

As people were exposed to new influences in their time away from work and family, new habits and values were inevitable. Aided by new fabrics and chemical dyes, clothes became a means of self-expression and personal freedom. Both men and women wore more casual and gaily colored styles than their parents would have considered. The line between acceptable and inappropriate behavior blurred as smoking, drinking, swearing, and frankness about sex became fashionable. Birth-control advocate Margaret Sanger, who a decade earlier had been accused of promoting race suicide, gained a large following in respectable circles. Newspapers, magazines, motion pictures, and popular songs (such as "Hot Lips" and "Burning Kisses") made certain that Americans did not suffer from "sex starvation." A typical movie ad promised "brilliant men, beautiful jazz babies, champagne baths, midnight revels, petting parties in the purple dawn, all ending in one terrific smashing climax that makes you gasp."

Social Values

How do historians know...

that individual and family life in the 1920s was hardly homogeneous but reflected many variations? The manuscript census schedules (the pages on which census takers actually recorded information) from the 1920 federal census contain extraordinarily rich information. By sampling, tabulating, and analyzing large numbers of census entries—after trying to decipher often illegible handwriting—historians raise and attempt to answer questions about everyday life and the environments in which ordinary people lived. The excerpt on this page reproduces the records from a few families living on Stamford Street in Boston and yields numerous insights into how these households were organized.

The Bradley household at 16 Stamford consisted of a middle-aged husband, who was born in Massachusetts and worked as a railroad baggage master; his wife, born in New Brunswick (Nova Scotia) and of British descent; and a middle-aged boarder, who worked as a painter. Given the ages of the household's residents, it is possible to assume that the Bradleys had extra space for a boarder because their children had grown up and moved away.

The Milkowski household at 10 Stamford was larger and more complex. It contained ten people, including three young children and five lodgers. Mr. and Mrs. Milkowski were from Russia, but their lodgers came from a variety of places, leaving the impression that the Milkowskis intentionally used their residence to earn extra income. A lone Chinese man lived at 8 Stamford. He worked in a laundry, and the schedule notes that he was married. He presumably had immigrated alone and hoped either to return to China or to earn enough to send for his wife.

Census data often must be combined with other sources in order to validate such speculations. Nevertheless, manuscript censuses provide important information, especially about people previously excluded from the historical record because they did not leave diaries or letters and were not famous enough to be the subjects of newspaper stories. (Photo: National Archives Records and Census Bureau)

DEPARTMENT OF COMMERCE-BUREAU OF THE CENSUS
FOURTEENTH CENSUS OF THE UNITED STATES: 1920-POPULATION

STATE Massachusetts ENUMERATOR Harry Hoffman
COUNTY Suffolk ENUMERATED BY ME AN THE 7 DAY OF Jan 1920

TOWNSHIP OR OTHER DIVISION OF COUNTY Tract 33 1413 NAME OF INCORPORATED PLACE Boston

STREET	HOUSE NUMBER	NAME		RELATION	SEX	COLOR OR RACE	AGE	SINGLE, MARRIED WIDOWED OR DIVORCED	YEAR OF IMMIGRATION	CITIZENSHIP	PERSON PLACE OF BIRTH	FATHER PLACE OF BIRTH	MOTHER PLACE OF BIRTH	ENGLISH SPEAKING	OCCUPATION
	22	Garrigan, James	step-son	M	W	20	S			Mass.	New York	Ireland	yes	chauffeur
		—, Ellen	step-dghtr	F	W	16	S			Mass.	New York	Ireland	yes	Laundry
	16	Bradley, George	Head	M	W	53	M			Mass.	Mass.	Mass.	yes	Railroad
		—, Carla A.	wife	F	W	52	M	1880		New Brunswick	New Brunswick	New Brunswick	yes	none
		Hart, Dennis	Lodger	M	W	49	wd.			Mass.	Ireland	Ireland	yes	Painter
Stamford Street	12	Sidlinger, Albert	Head	M	W	65	M			Maine	Maine	Maine	yes	none
		—, Catherine	wife	F	W	49	M	1886		Nova Scotia	Ireland	Nova Scotia	yes	none
		—, Albert K	son	M	W	29	S			Mass.	Maine	Nova Scotia	yes	Insurance Broker
	10	Milkowski, Stani	Head	M	W	34	M	1906		Russia	Russia	Russia	yes	cook
		—, Mary	wife	F	W	27	M	1908		Russia	Russia	Russia	yes	none
		—, Helen	dghtr	F	W	6½	S			Mass.	Russia	Russia		none
		—, Jennie	dghtr	F	W	5½	S			Mass.	Russia	Russia		none
		—, Peter	son	M	W	1½	S			Mass.	Russia	Russia		none
		McQuaid, Francis	Lodger	M	W	33	M			Mass.	Ireland	Ireland	yes	Reporter
		—, Frieda	wife	F	W	22	M	1899		Switzerland	Italy	Germany	yes	none
		White, Irwin	Lodger	M	W	37	M	1897		England	England	England	yes	Hospital handyman
		Blake, John	Lodger	M	W	38	M	1894		Ireland	Ireland	Ireland	yes	Laborer
		Miller, Harry	Lodger	M	W	44	S	1910		Norway	Norway	Norway	yes	waiters ship
	8	Ling, Chintung	Head	M	ch	60	M	1890		China	China	China	no	Laundry
	6	Ross, Frank	Head	M	W	45	M	1889		Italy	Italy	Italy	yes	Fish dealer
		—, Effie	wife	F	W	43	M			New Hampshire	New Hampshire	Maine	yes	none

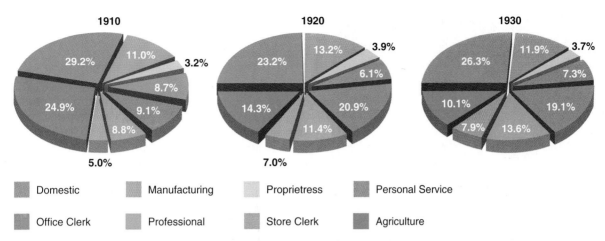

Figure 24.1   Changing Dimensions of Paid Female Labor, 1910–1930   These charts reveal the extraordinary growth in clerical and professional occupations among employed women and the accompanying decline in agricultural labor in the early twentieth century. Notice that manufacturing employment peaked in 1920 and that domestic service fluctuated as white immigrant women began to move out of these jobs and were replaced by women of color.

Other modern trends helped to weaken inherited customs. Because child-labor laws and compulsory-attendance rules kept children in school longer than ever before, peer groups played a more influential role in socializing children. In earlier eras, different age groups had shared the same activities: children had worked with older people in fields and kitchens, and young apprentices had toiled in workshops beside older journeymen and craftsmen. Now, graded school classes, sports, and clubs constantly brought together children of the same age, separating them from the company and influence of adults. Meanwhile, parents tended to rely less on family traditions of childcare and more on experts who wrote manuals on how best to raise children.

After the First World War, women continued to stream into the labor force. By 1930, 10.8 million women held paying jobs, an increase of over 2 million since the war's end (see Figure 24.1). The sex segregation that had long characterized workplaces persisted; most women took jobs that men seldom sought and vice versa. Over 1 million women were teachers and nurses. Some 2.2 million were typists, bookkeepers, and office clerks, a tenfold increase since 1920. Another 736,000 were store clerks, and growing numbers became waitresses and hairdressers. Though almost 2 million women worked in factories, their numbers grew very little over the decade. Wherever women

Employment for Women

were employed, their wages seldom exceeded half of those paid to men.

For many women, employment outside the home represented an extension of family roles. Although women worked for a variety of reasons, their families' economic needs were paramount. The consumerism of the 1920s tempted working-class and middle-class families to satisfy their wants by living beyond their means or by sending women into the labor force. In previous eras, most extra-wage earners had been young and single. Even though the vast majority of married women remained outside the work force (only 12 percent were employed in 1930), married women as a proportion of the work force rose by 30 percent, and the number of employed married women swelled from 1.9 million to 3.1 million. These figures omit countless widowed, divorced, and abandoned women who held jobs and who, like married women, often had children to support.

Women of racial minorities were the exception; the proportions of these women who worked for pay doubled that of white women. Often they entered the labor force because their husbands were unemployed or underemployed. The vast majority of African American women held domestic jobs doing cooking, cleaning, and laundry. The few who held factory jobs, such as in cigarette factories and meatpacking plants, performed the least desirable, lowest paying tasks. Some opportunities opened for

Jobs for Minority Women

The expansion of service-sector jobs and new technology opened new opportunities for women in the 1920s. This telephone operator handled scores of phone calls at the same time and monitored a huge switchboard. Her dress and jewelry contrasted with the simpler styles worn by factory women, who had to be more careful in working with dangerous machines.   (George Eastman House)

educated black women in social work, teaching, and nursing, but even these women faced harsh discrimination and pressures on their families. Grandmothers and aunts helped with childcare when mothers took outside employment, but such arrangements did not lessen the economic burdens on African American households beset by lack of skills, poverty and prejudice.

Economic necessity also drew thousands of Mexican women into wage labor, although their tradition resisted the employment of women. Exact figures are difficult to uncover, but it is certain that many Mexican women in the Southwest worked as field laborers, operatives in garment factories, and domestic servants. Next to black women, Japanese American women were the most likely to hold paying jobs. They too worked as field hands and domestics. And, like Mexican American and African American women, Japanese American women encountered racial bias and low pay.

Employed or not, some women were remaking the image of femininity. In contrast to the heavy, floor-length dresses and long hair of previous generations, the short skirts and bobbed hair of the 1920s "flapper" symbolized independence and sexual freedom. Though few women lived the flapper life, the new look became fashionable among office workers and store clerks as well as college coeds. As models of female behavior, chaste, modest heroines were eclipsed by movie temptresses like Clara Bow, known as the "It Girl," and Gloria Swanson, notorious for her torrid love affairs on and off the screen. Many women were asserting a new social equality with men. One observer described "the new woman" as intriguingly independent:

The New Woman

> She takes a man's point of view as her mother never could. . . . She will never make you a hatband or knit you a necktie, but she'll drive you from the station . . . in her own little sports car. She'll don knickers and go skiing with you, . . . she'll dive as well as you, perhaps better, she'll dance as long as you care to, and she'll take everything you say the way you mean it.

The era's openness regarding sexuality also enabled the underground homosexual culture to emerge a little more than in previous eras. In nontraditional city neighborhoods, such as New York's Greenwich Village and Harlem, cheap rents and an apparent tolerance of alternate lifestyles attracted gay men and lesbians who patronized dance halls, speakeasies, cafés, and other gathering places. Such establishments that catered to a gay clientele remained targets for police raids, however, demonstrating that homosexual men and women could not expect tolerance from the rest of society.

Gay and Lesbian Culture

These trends represented a break with the more restrained culture of the nineteenth century. But social change rarely proceeds smoothly. As the decade wore on, various groups mobilized to defend older values.

Lines of Defense

 Early in 1920 the leader of a newly formed organization hired two public relations experts to recruit members. The experts, Edward Clarke and Elizabeth Tyler, canvassed communities in the South, Southwest, and Midwest, where they found thousands of men eager to pay a $10 membership fee and another $6 for a white uniform. Clarke and Tyler pocketed $2.50 from each membership they sold. Their success helped build the organization to 5 million members by 1923.

No ordinary civic club like the Lions or Kiwanis, this was the Ku Klux Klan, a revived version of the

Ku Klux Klan

hooded order that had terrorized southern communities after the Civil War. Its appeal was based on fear, and it vowed to protect female purity as well as racial purity. As one pamphlet distributed by Clarke and Tyler declared, "Every criminal, every gambler, every thug, every libertine, every girl ruiner, every home wrecker, every wife beater, every dope peddler, every moonshiner, every white slaver, every Rome-controlled newspaper, every black spider—is fighting the Klan. Think it over, which side are you on?"

Reconstituted in 1915 by William J. Simmons, an Atlanta evangelist and insurance salesman, the Klan was the most sinister reactionary movement of the 1920s. It revived the hoods, intimidating tactics, and mystical terminology of its forerunner (its leader was the Imperial Wizard, its book of rituals the Kloran). But the new Klan had broader membership, including a female auxiliary group, and objectives than the old. It fanned outward from the Deep South and for a time wielded frightening power in places as diverse as Oregon, Oklahoma, and Indiana. Unlike the original Klan, which directed terrorist tactics at emancipated blacks (see pages 449–450), the new Klan targeted a variety of racial and religious groups.

One phrase summed up Klan goals: "Native, white, Protestant supremacy." Native meant no immigration, no "mongrelization" of American culture. According to Imperial Wizard Hiram Wesley Evans, white supremacy was a matter of survival. "The world," he warned, "has been so made so that each race must fight for its life, must conquer, accept slavery, or die. The Klansman believes the whites will not become slaves, and he does not intend to die before his time." Evans praised Protestantism for promoting "unhampered individual development," and he accused the Catholic Church of discouraging assimilation and enslaving people to priests and a foreign pope.

Using threatening assemblies, violence, and political pressure, the Klan menaced many communities in the early 1920s. Klansmen meted out vigilante justice to suspected bootleggers, wife beaters, and adulterers; forced schools to adopt Bible reading and to stop teaching the theory of evolution; campaigned against Catholic and Jewish political candidates; and fueled racial tensions against Mexicans in Texas border cities. By 1925, however, the Invisible Empire was on the wane, as scandal undermined its moral base. In 1925 Indiana Grand Dragon David Stephenson kidnapped and raped a woman who later died either from taking poison or from infection caused by bites on her body; Stephenson was convicted of second-degree murder on grounds that he caused her suicide. More generally, the Klan's negative, exclusive brand of patriotism and purity could not compete in a pluralistic society.

The Ku Klux Klan had no monopoly on bigotry in the 1920s; intolerance pervaded American society. Nativists had been urging an end to free immigration since the 1880s. They charged that Catholic and Jewish immigrants clogged city slums, flouted community norms, and stubbornly held to alien religious and political beliefs. As naturalist Madison Grant, whose study of zoology prompted him to believe that certain human races, mainly Nordics, were superior to others, wrote in *The Passing of the Great Race* (1916): "These immigrants adopt the language of the native American, they wear his clothes, they steal his name and they are beginning to take his women, but they seldom adopt his religion or understand his ideals."

Guided by such sentiments, the movement to restrict immigration gathered support. Labor leaders

Immigration Quotas

warned that floods of aliens would depress wages and raise unemployment. Business executives, who formerly had opposed restrictions because they desired cheap immigrant laborers, changed their minds, having realized that they could keep wages low by mechanizing and by hiring black workers. Drawing support from such groups, Congress drastically reversed previous policy and set yearly immigration quotas for each nationality. The limits favored northern and western Europeans, reflecting nativist prejudices against immigrants from southern and eastern Europe. By stipulating that annual immigration of a given nationality could not exceed 3 percent of the number of immigrants from that nation residing in the United States in 1910, the Quota (Johnson) Act of 1921 discriminated against immigrants from southern and eastern Europe, whose numbers were small in 1910 relative to those from northern Europe.

The Johnson Act did not satisfy restrictionists, so Congress replaced it with the Immigration Act (Johnson-Reid Act) of 1924. This law set quotas at 2 percent of each nationality residing in the United States in 1890. It limited total immigration to 165,000

Anti-immigrationists used songs, as well as speeches and posters, to promote their cause. This 1923 tune urges the government to "Close the Gates" lest foreigners betray the hard-won rights of Americans and "drag our Colors down." (National Park Service Collection, Ellis Island Immigration Museum)

people and further restricted southern and eastern Europeans, since fewer of those groups lived in the United States in 1890 than in 1910, though the law did allow wives and children of U.S. citizens to enter as nonquota immigrants. In 1929 the National Origins Act apportioned new quotas, totaling 150,000 possible immigrants, among European countries in proportion to the "national-origins" (country of birth or descent) of American people in 1920. People from Canada, Mexico, and Puerto Rico did not fall under the quotas (except for those whom the Labor Department might define as potential paupers), and soon they became the largest immigrant groups (see Figure 24.2).

Fear of immigrant radicalism, persisting from the Red Scare of 1919, fueled antiforeign flames. Heated debate occurred in 1921, when a court convicted Nicola Sacco and Bartolomeo Vanzetti, two immi-

Sacco and Vanzetti Case

grant anarchists, of murdering a guard and paymaster during a robbery in South Braintree, Massachusetts. Sacco and Vanzetti's main offenses seem to have been their political beliefs and Italian origins. Though the evidence failed to prove their guilt, Judge Webster Thayer openly sided with the prosecution and privately called the defendants "anarchist bastards." Appeals and protests failed to win a new trial, and the prisoners, who remained calm and dignified throughout their ordeal, were executed in 1927. Their deaths touched off rallies and riots in Europe, Asia, and South America, leaving doubts about the United States as the land that nurtured freedom of belief.

While nativists lobbied for racial purity, the pursuit of spiritual purity stirred religious fundamentalists. Millions of Americans sought

Fundamentalism

certainty and salvation against what they perceived as the skepticism and irreverence of a materialistic, hedonistic society by following evangelical denominations of Protestantism that accepted a literal interpretation of the Bible. Resolutely believing that God's miracles created life and the world, they were convinced that Darwin's theory of evolution was just that, a theory, and that if fundamentalists constituted a majority of a community, as they did throughout the South, they should be able to determine what would be taught in schools. Their enemies were "modernists," those who interpreted "truths" critically, using reasoning from psychology and anthropology. To modernists, the accuracy of the Bible did not matter; what was important was the historical relevance of God in culture and the role of science in advancing knowledge.

In 1925 Christian fundamentalism clashed with modernism in a celebrated case in Dayton, Tennessee.

Scopes Trial

Early that year the state legislature passed a law forbidding public school instructors to teach the theory that humans had evolved from lower forms of life rather than descended from Adam and Eve. Shortly thereafter, high school teacher John Thomas Scopes volunteered to serve in a test case and was arrested for violating the law. Scopes's trial that summer became a headline event. William Jennings Bryan, former secretary of state and three-time presidential candidate, argued for the prosecution, and a team of civil liberties lawyers headed by Clarence Darrow represented the defense. News correspondents

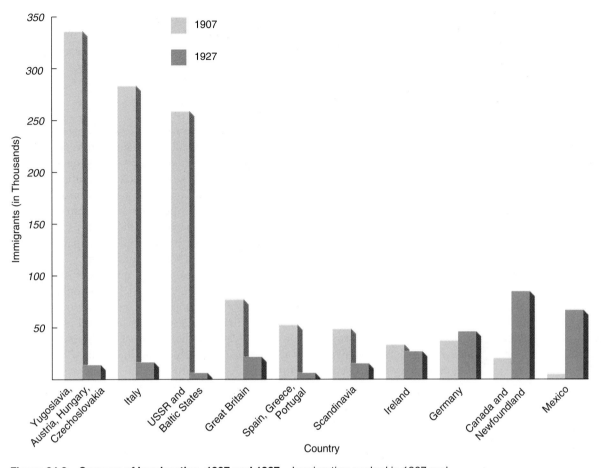

Figure 24.2 Sources of Immigration, 1907 and 1927 Immigration peaked in 1907 and 1908, when newcomers from southern and eastern Europe poured into the United States. After immigration restriction laws were passed in the 1920s, the greatest number of immigrants came from the Western Hemisphere (Canada and Mexico), which was exempted from the quotas, and the number coming from eastern and southern Europe shrank.

crowded into town, and radio stations broadcast the trial from coast to coast.

Although Scopes was convicted—clearly he had broken the law—modernists claimed victory. The testimony, they believed, showed fundamentalism to be illogical. The trial's climax occurred when Bryan himself took the witness stand as an expert on religion and science. Responding to Darrow's probing, Bryan asserted that Eve really had been created from Adam's rib, that the Tower of Babel was responsible for the diversity of languages, and that a big fish had swallowed Jonah. "One miracle is just as easy to believe as another," Bryan testified to cheering spectators. "I believe in creation [as told in the Bible], and if I am not able to explain it I will accept it."

After the contest between Bryan's blind faith and Darrow's bitter attack, one newspaper wrote, "Darrow succeeded in showing that Bryan knows little about the science of the world. Bryan succeeded in bearing witness bravely to the faith which he believes transcends all the learning of men." Most of the liberal press, however, mocked Bryan and his fundamentalist allies. Humorist Will Rogers quipped, "I see you can't say that man descended from the ape. At least that's the law in Tennessee. But do they have a law to keep a man from making a jackass of himself?" Nevertheless, fundamentalists were undeterred. They succeeded in getting many school boards to limit the teaching of evolution and influenced the content of high school biology books. As well, they created an independent subculture, with their own schools, camps, radio ministries, and missionary societies.

Klan rallies, immigration restriction, and fundamentalist literalism might appear as last gasps of a rural society yielding to modern urban-industrial values. Yet city dwellers swelled the ranks of all these movements. Nearly half the Klan's members lived in cities, especially in working-class neighborhoods where fear of invasion by racial minorities and foreigners was strong. Even urban reformers backed immigration restriction as a means of controlling poverty and quickening the assimilation of immigrants.

Cities also housed hundreds of Pentecostal churches, which attracted both blacks and whites struggling with economic insecurity

Revivalism

and swayed by the pageantry and closeness to God that such churches offered. Using modern advertising techniques and elaborately staged services broadcast live on radio, magnetic preachers such as flamboyant Aimee Semple McPherson of Los Angeles, former baseball player Billy Sunday, and Father Divine (George Baker, an African American who amassed a huge interracial following especially in eastern cities) stirred revivalist fervor. And many urban dwellers supported prohibition, believing that eliminating the temptation of drink would help win the battle against poverty, vice, and corruption.

These emotional responses represented an attempt to sustain old-fashioned values in a fast-moving and materialistic world. Some Americans lashed out at "different" cultures and hedonistic trends in behavior. Millions of Americans firmly believed that nonwhites and immigrants were inferior people who imperiled national welfare. Clergy and teachers of all faiths condemned drinking, dancing, new dress styles, and sex on the movie screen and in parked cars. Yet even while mourning a lost past, most Americans tried to adjust to the modern order in one way or another. Few refrained from listening to the radio and attending movies, activities that proved less corrupting than critics feared. Radio featured music, news, and drama, most of which did not threaten traditional values. Movie producers, bowing to pressure from legislators, instituted self-censorship in 1927, forbidding nudity, rough language, and plots that did not end with justice and morality triumphant. More than ever, Americans sought fellowship in civic organizations. Membership swelled in Rotary, Elks, and women's clubs, and the number of Community Chests—associations that coordinated lo-

cal welfare projects—grew from 12 in 1919 to 361 in 1930. Perhaps most important, more people were finding release in recreation and new uses of leisure.

The Age of Play

Americans in the 1920s engaged in commercial entertainment as never before. In 1919 they spent $2.5 billion on leisure activities; by 1929 such expenditures topped $4.3 billion, a figure not again equaled until after the Second World War. Spectator amusements—movies, music, and sports—accounted for about 21 percent of the 1929 total; the rest involved participatory recreation, such as games, hobbies, and travel.

Entrepreneurs responded quickly to an appetite for fads, fun, and "ballyhoo"—a blitz of publicity that lent exaggerated importance to some person or event. Games and fancies particularly attracted newly affluent middle-class families. Mahjong, a Chinese tile game, was the rage in the early 1920s. In the mid-1920s people popularized crossword puzzles, which mass-circulation newspapers and magazines had begun printing a decade earlier. Next, fun seekers adopted miniature golf as their new fad. By 1930 the nation boasted thirty thousand miniature golf courses featuring tiny castles, windmills, and waterfalls. Dance crazes like the Charleston riveted public attention throughout the country, aided by live and recorded music on radio and the growing popularity of jazz.

In addition to indulging actively, Americans were avid spectators, particularly of movies and sports. In total capital investment, motion pictures became one of the nation's

Movies

leading industries. Nearly every community had at least one theater, whether it was a hundred-seat Bijou on Main Street or a big-city "picture palace" with ornate lobbies and thousands of cushioned seats. In 1922 movies attracted 40 million viewers weekly; by 1930 the number reached 100 million—at a time when the nation's population was 120 million and total weekly church attendance was 60 million. The introduction of sound in *The Jazz Singer* in 1927, and of color a few years later, made movies even more exciting and realistic.

Responding to the tastes of mass audiences, the movie industry produced more escapist entertainment than art. The most popular films were spectacles such as Cecil B. DeMille's *The Ten Commandments* (1923)

Babe Ruth had widespread appeal as one of the country's first sports superstars. Here a photograph of his mighty home run swing appears on a school notebook, showing the new link between sports and consumerism. (Private collection)

and *The King of Kings* (1927); lurid dramas such as *Souls for Sale* (1923) and *A Woman Who Sinned* (1924); and slapstick comedies starring Fatty Arbuckle, Harold Lloyd, and Charlie Chaplin. Ironically, comedies, with their poignant satires of the human condition, carried the most thought-provoking messages.

Spectator sports also boomed. Each year millions packed stadiums and parks to watch athletic events. Gate receipts from college football surpassed $21 million by the late 1920s. In an age when technology and mass production had robbed experiences and objects of their uniqueness, sports provided an unpredictability and drama that people craved. Newspapers and radio magnified this drama, feeding news to an eager public and glorifying events with such unrestrained narrative that sports promoters did not need to buy advertising.

Baseball's drawn-out suspense, variety of plays, and potential for keeping statistics attracted a huge following. After the "Black Sox scandal" of 1919, when eight members of the Chicago White Sox were banned from the game for allegedly throwing the World Se-

ries to the Cincinnati Reds (even though a jury acquitted them), baseball regained its respectability by transforming itself. Discovering that home runs excited fans, the leagues redesigned the ball to make it livelier. Attendance at games skyrocketed. A record three hundred thousand people attended the six-game 1921 World Series between the New York Giants and New York Yankees. Millions more gathered regularly to watch local teams, and even more listened to professional games on the radio.

Sports, movies, and the news created a galaxy of heroes. As technology and mass society made the individual less significant, people clung to heroic personalities as a means of identifying with the unique. Names such as Bill Tilden in tennis, Gertrude Ederle in swimming (in 1926 she became the first woman to swim across the English Channel), and Bobby Jones in golf became household words. But the power and action of boxing, football, and baseball produced the most popular sports heroes. Heavyweight

Sports Heroes

Rudolph Valentino became the idol of men and women alike in *The Sheik,* his most famous movie. With flashing eyes and wanton smile, Valentino carries a swooning woman to his tent. This immensely popular movie earned $1 million for Paramount Pictures.   (Museum of Modern Art Film Still Archive)

champion Jack Dempsey, a brawler from Manassa, Colorado, attracted the first of several million-dollar gates in his fight with Georges Carpentier in 1921. Harold "Red" Grange, running back for the University of Illinois football team, thrilled thousands with his speed and power and became the idol of sportswriters.

Baseball's foremost hero was George Herman "Babe" Ruth, who began his career as a pitcher but found he could use his prodigious strength to better advantage hitting home runs. Ruth hit 29 in 1919, 54 in 1920 (the year the Boston Red Sox traded him to the New York Yankees), 59 in 1924, and 60 in 1927—each year a record. His prowess on the field, defiant lifestyle, and boyish grin endeared him to millions. Known for overindulgence in food, drink, and women, he charmed fans into forgiving his excesses by appearing at public events and visiting hospitalized children.

While admiring the physical exploits of sports stars, Americans fulfilled a yearning for romance and adventure through movie stars. The films and personal lives of Douglas Fairbanks, Gloria Swanson, and Charlie Chaplin were discussed in parlors and pool

Movie Stars

halls across the country. One of the decade's most ballyhooed personalities was Rudolph Valentino, whose smooth seductiveness made women swoon and men imitate his pomaded hairdo and slick sideburns. Valentino's image exploited the era's sexual liberalism and flirtation with wickedness. In his most famous film, Valentino played a passionate sheik who carried away beautiful women to his boudoir tent, combining the roles of seducer and abductor. When he died at thirty-one of complications from ulcers and appendicitis, the press turned his funeral into a public extravaganza. Mourners lined up for over a mile to file past his coffin.

In their quest for fun and self-expression, some Americans became lawbreakers by refusing to give up drinking. The Eighteenth Amendment (1919) and the federal law (1920) that prohibited the manufacture, sale, and transportation of alcoholic beverages worked well at first. Per capita consumption of liquor dropped, as did arrests for drunkenness, and the price of illegal booze rose higher

Prohibition

than average workers could afford. But aside from passing supportive laws, legislators refrained from enforcing prohibition. In 1922 Congress gave the Prohibition Bureau only three thousand employees and less than $7 million for nationwide enforcement.

If the Eighteenth Amendment had applied only to hard liquor and not to beer and wine, it might have succeeded. But after 1925 the so-called noble experiment broke down as thousands of people made their own wine and bathtub gin, and bootleg importers along the country's borders and shorelines easily evaded the few patrols that attempted to curb them. Moreover, drinking, like gambling and prostitution, was a business with willing customers, and criminal organizations quickly capitalized on public demand. The most notorious of such mobs belonged to Al Capone, a burly tough who seized control of illegal liquor and vice in Chicago and maintained his grip on both politicians and the vice business through intimidation, bribery, and violence. But Capone contended, in a statement revealing of the era, "Prohibition is a business. All I do is supply a public demand." Americans wanted their liquor, and until 1931 when a federal court convicted and imprisoned him for income-tax evasion (the only charge for which authorities could obtain hard evidence), Capone supplied it. Reflecting on the contradictions inherent in Prohibition, columnist Walter Lippmann wrote in 1931, "The high level of lawlessness is maintained by the fact that Americans desire to do so many things which they also desire to prohibit."

Al Capone

Cultural Currents

Intellectuals like Lippmann were quick to point to the era's hypocrisy. Serious writers and artists felt at odds with society, and their rejection of materialism and conformity was both biting and bitter.

Several writers of the so-called Lost Generation, including novelist Ernest Hemingway and poets Ezra Pound and T. S. Eliot, left the United States for Europe. Others, such as novelists William Faulkner and Sinclair Lewis, remained in America but, like the expatriates, expressed disillusionment with the materialism and hypocrisy that they witnessed. F. Scott Fitzgerald's *This Side of Paradise* (1920) and *The Great Gatsby* (1925); Lewis's *Babbitt*

Literature of Alienation

Florence Mills was a talented performer whose singing career received a major boost from her appearance in the musical comedy *Shuffle Along,* a show that heralded the beginning of the Harlem Renaissance.   (Howard Greenburg Galleries, © 1997 Donna VanDer Zee)

(1922), *Arrowsmith* (1925), and *Elmer Gantry* (1927); and Eugene O'Neill's plays exposed and derided Americans' preoccupation with money. Edith Wharton explored the clash of old and new moralities in novels such as *The Age of Innocence* (1921). Ellen Glasgow, one of the South's leading literary figures, lamented the trend toward impersonality in *Barren Ground* (1925). John Dos Passos's *Three Soldiers* (1921) and Hemingway's *A Farewell to Arms* (1929) interwove antiwar sentiment with critiques of the emptiness in modern relationships.

Spiritual discontent quite different from that of white writers inspired a new generation of African American artists. Middle class, well educated, and proud of their African heritage, these writers rejected white culture and exalted the militantly assertive "New Negro." Most of them lived in New York's Harlem; in this "Negro Mecca" black intellectuals and artists, aided by a few white patrons, celebrated black culture during what became known as the Harlem Renaissance.

Harlem Renaissance

This painting by the African American artist Archibald Motley represented the "Ash-Can" style, which considered no subject too undignified to paint, as well as the sensual relationship between jazz music and dancing within African American culture.   (Collection of Archie Motley and Valerie Gerrard Browne. Photo courtesy of The Art Institute of Chicago)

The popular 1921 musical comedy *Shuffle Along* is often credited with launching the Harlem Renaissance. The musical showcased talented African American artists such as lyricist Noble Sissle, composer Eubie Blake, and singers Florence Mills, Josephine Baker, and Mabel Mercer. Harlem in the 1920s also fostered a number of gifted writers, among them poets Langston Hughes, Countee Cullen, and Claude McKay; novelist Jean Toomer; and essayist Alain Locke. As well, the movement included visual artists such as Aaron Douglas, James A. Porter, and Augusta Savage.

Issues of identity troubled the Harlem Renaissance. Although intellectuals and artists cherished their African heritage, they realized that blacks had to come to terms with themselves as Americans. Thus Alain Locke urged that the New Negro should become "a collaborator and participant in American civilization." And Langston Hughes wrote, "We younger Negro artists who create now intend to express our individual dark-skinned selves without fear or shame. If white people are pleased, we are glad. If they are not, it doesn't matter. We know we are beautiful."

The Jazz Age, as the 1920s is sometimes called, owes its name to music that derived from black culture. Evolving from African and black American folk music, early jazz communicated an exuberance, humor, and authority that African Americans

Jazz

seldom expressed in their public and political lives. With emotional rhythms and emphasis on improvisation, jazz blurred the distinction between composer and performer and created intimacy between performer and audience. As African Americans moved northward, jazz traveled with them. Urban dance halls and bars often featured jazz, and gifted black performers like trumpeter Louis Armstrong, trombonist Kid Ory, and blues singer Bessie Smith enjoyed wide fame. Phonograph records and radio, better suited than sheet music to the spontaneity of jazz, helped to popularize it. Jazz greatly boosted the recording industry; music recorded by black artists and aimed at black consumers (sometimes called "race records") gave African Americans a place in the consumer culture. More important, jazz endowed America with its most distinctive art form.

In many ways the 1920s were the most creative years the nation had yet experienced. Painters such as Georgia O'Keeffe and John Marin

Experiments in Art and Music

tried to forge a uniquely American style of painting. European composers and performers still dominated classical music, but American composers such as Henry Cowell pioneered electronic music, and Aaron Copland built orchestral works around native folk motifs. George Gershwin blended jazz rhythms, classical forms, and folk melodies in his serious compositions (*Rhapsody in Blue*, 1924, and *Concerto in F*, 1925), musical dramas (*Funny Face*, 1927), and hit tunes such as "Summertime" and "Someone to Watch Over Me." In architecture the skyscraper boom drew worldwide attention, and Frank Lloyd Wright's "prairie-style" houses, churches, and schools celebrated the American landscape. At the beginning of the decade, essayist Harold Stearns had complained that "the most . . . pathetic fact in the social life of America today is emotional and aesthetic starvation." By 1929 that contention was hard to support.

The Election of 1928 and the End of the New Era

Intellectuals' uneasiness about materialism seldom affected the confident rhetoric of politics. Herbert Hoover voiced that confidence in his speech accepting the Republican nomination for president in 1928. "We in America today," Hoover boasted, "are nearer to the final triumph over poverty than ever before in the history of any land. . . . We have not yet reached the goal, but, given a chance to go forward with the policies of the last eight years, we shall soon, with the help of God, be in sight of the day when poverty will be banished from this nation."

Hoover was an apt Republican candidate in 1928 (Coolidge had chosen not to seek reelection) because

Herbert Hoover

he fused the traditional value of individual hard work with modern emphasis on collective action. A Quaker from Iowa, orphaned at age ten, Hoover worked his way through Stanford University and became a wealthy mining engineer. During and after the First World War, he distinguished himself as U.S. food administrator and head of food relief for Europe.

As secretary of commerce under Harding and Coolidge, Hoover had what has been called an "associational vision." Recognizing the extent to which nationwide associations had come to dominate commerce and industry, Hoover tried to stimulate cooperation between business and government. He took every opportunity to make the Department of Commerce a center for the promotion of business, encouraging the formation of trade associations, holding conferences, and issuing reports, all aimed at improving production, marketing, and profits. His active leadership prompted one observer to quip that Hoover was "Secretary of Commerce and assistant secretary of everything else."

As Hoover's opponent, Democrats chose New York's governor Alfred E. Smith, whose background contrasted sharply with Hoover's.

Al Smith

Hoover had rural, native-born, Protestant, business roots and had never run for public office. Smith was an urbane, gregarious politician of immigrant stock with a career rooted in New York City's Tammany Hall. His relish for the give-and-take of city streets is apparent in his response during the campaign to a heckler who taunted him by shouting, "Tell them all you know, Al. It won't take long!" Smith unflinchingly retorted, "I'll tell them all we both know, and it won't take any longer!"

Smith was the first Roman Catholic to run for president on a major party ticket. His religion enhanced his appeal among urban ethnics, who were voting in increasing numbers, but intense anti-Catholic sentiments lost him southern and rural votes. Smith had compiled a strong record of promoting Progressive reforms and civil rights during his governorship, but his campaign failed to build a coalition of farmers and city dwellers because he stressed issues unlikely to unite these groups, particularly his opposition to prohibition.

Smith waged a spirited campaign, directly confronting anti-Catholic critics, but Hoover, who stressed national prosperity under Republican administrations, won the popular vote by 21 million to 15 million, the electoral vote by 444 to 87. Smith's candidacy nevertheless had beneficial effects on the Democratic Party. He carried the nation's twelve largest cities, which formerly had given majorities to Republican candidates, and he lured millions of foreign-stock voters to the polls for the first time. From 1928 onward, the Democratic Party solidified this urban base, which in conjunction with its traditional strength in the South would make the party a formidable force in national elections.

At his inaugural, Hoover proclaimed a New Day, "bright with hope." His cabinet, composed mostly of businessmen committed to the existing order, included six millionaires. To the lower ranks of government Hoover appointed young professionals who agreed with him that scientific methods could solve national problems. If Hoover was optimistic, so were most Americans. The belief was widespread that individuals were responsible for their own success and that unemployment or poverty suggested personal failing. Prevailing opinion also held that the ups and downs of the business cycle were natural and therefore not to be tampered with by government.

Hoover's Administration

This confidence dissolved in the fall of 1929 when stock prices suddenly plunged after soaring in 1928. Analysts explained the drop as temporary, caused by a "lunatic fringe." But on October 24, "Black Thursday," panic selling set in. Prices of many stocks hit record lows; some sellers could find no buyers. Stunned crowds gathered outside the frantic New York Stock Exchange. At noon, leading bankers met at the headquarters of J. P. Morgan and Company. To restore faith, they put up $20 million and ceremoniously began buying stocks. The mood changed and some stocks rallied. The bankers, it seemed, had saved the day.

Stock Market Crash

But as news of Black Thursday spread, panicked investors decided to sell their stocks rather than risk

further losses. On "Black Tuesday," October 29, stock prices plummeted again. Hoover, who never had approved of what he called "the fever of speculation," assured Americans that the economy was sound. He shared the popular assumptions that the stock market's ills could be quarantined and that the economy was strong enough to endure until the market righted itself. Instead, the crash ultimately helped to unleash a devastating depression.

The economic weakness that underlay the Great Depression had several interrelated causes. One was declining demand. Since mid-1928, demand for new housing construction had faltered, leading to declining demand for building materials and unemployment among construction workers. Growth industries such as automobiles and electric appliances had been able to expand as long as consumers bought their products. Frenzied expansion, however, could not continue unabated. When demand leveled off, factory owners could not accumulate funds to build new plants and hire more workers. Instead, unsold inventories stacked up in warehouses, and laborers were laid off. Retailers also had amassed large inventories that crammed warehouses and store shelves, and in turn they were ordering less from manufacturers. Farm prices continued to sag, leaving farmers with less income to use in purchasing new machinery and goods. As wages and purchasing power stagnated, the workers who produced consumer products could not afford to buy them. Thus by 1929 a sizable population of underconsumers was causing serious repercussions.

Declining Demand

Underconsumption also resulted from the widening divisions in income distribution. As the rich grew richer, middle- and lower-income Americans made modest gains at best. Though average per capita disposable income (income after taxes) rose about 9 percent between 1920 and 1929, the income of the wealthiest 1 percent rose 75 percent, accounting for most of the increase. Much of this increase was put into stock market investments instead of being spent on consumer goods.

Furthermore, in their eagerness to expand and increase profits, many businesses overloaded themselves with debt. To obtain loans, they manipulated or misrepresented their assets in ways that weakened their ability to repay if forced to do so. Such practices, overlooked by lending agencies, put

Corporate Debt

As the stock market tumbled on October 24, 1929, a crowd of concerned investors gathered outside the New York Stock Exchange on Wall Street, unprepared for an unprecedented economic decline that would send the country into a tailspin for the next decade. (Corbis-Bettmann)

the nation's banking system also on precarious footing. When one part of the edifice collapsed, the entire structure crumbled.

The depression also derived from risky speculation on the stock market. Not only had corporations invested huge sums in stocks, but individuals also bought heavily on margin, meaning that they purchased stock by placing a down payment of only a fraction of the stock's actual price and then used stocks they had bought but not fully paid for as collateral for more stock purchases. When stock prices stopped rising, people tried to sell the holdings they had bought on margin to minimize their losses. But numerous investors selling at the same time caused prices to drop. As stock values collapsed, brokers demanded full payment for stocks bought on margin. Investors attempted to comply by withdrawing savings from banks

Speculation on the Stock Market

or selling stocks at a loss for whatever they could get. Bankers in turn needed cash and put pressure on brokers to pay back their loans, tightening the vise further. The more obligations went unmet, the more the system tottered. Inevitably, banks and investment companies collapsed.

International economic troubles also contributed to the crash and depression. During the First World War and postwar reconstruction, Americans had loaned billions of dollars to European nations. By the late 1920s, however, American investors were keeping their money at home, investing instead in the more lucrative U.S. stock market. Europeans, unable to borrow more funds and unable to sell their goods in the American market because of high tariffs, began to buy less from the United States. Moreover, the Allied nations depended on German war reparations to pay war debts

International Economic Troubles

to the United States. The German government depended on American bank loans to pay war reparations. When the depression choked off American loans, the Germans were unable to pay reparations debts, and in turn the Allies were unable to pay war debts. The world economy ground to a halt (see pages 735–736).

Government policies also contributed to the crash and depression. The federal government refrained from regulating wild speculation, con-

Drawbacks of Federal Policies

tenting itself with occasionally scolding bankers and businesspeople. In keeping with government support of business expansion, the Federal Reserve Board pursued easy credit policies before the crash, charging low discount rates (interest rates on its loans to member banks) even though easy money was financing the speculative mania.

Partly because of optimism and partly because of the relatively undeveloped state of economic analysis, neither the experts nor people on the street realized what really had happened in 1929. Conventional wisdom, based on experiences from previous depressions, held that little could be done to correct economic problems; they simply had to run their course. So in 1929 people waited for the tailspin to ease, never realizing that the era of expansion and frivolity had come to an end and that society and politics, as well as the economy, would have to be rebuilt.

Summary

Two disturbing events, the First World War and the Great Depression, marked the boundaries of the 1920s. In the war's aftermath, traditional customs weakened as women and men sought ways to balance new liberation with old-fashioned mores. A host of new effects from science and technology, the automobile revolution, new conveniences such as electric appliances, and broadened exposure from mass media, movies, and travel influenced the lives of rich and poor alike. Moreover, the decade's general prosperity and free-wheeling attitudes enabled countless Americans to emulate wealthier people not only by consuming more but also by trying to get rich through stock market speculation. The depression stifled some of these habits, but others were hard to break.

Beneath the "era of excess" lurked two important phenomena rooted in previous eras. One was the con-

tinued resurfacing of prejudice and intolerance that had long tainted the American dream. As prohibitionists, Klansmen, and immigration restrictionists made their voices heard, they encouraged discrimination against racial minorities and slurs against supposedly "inferior" ethnic groups. Meanwhile, the distinguishing forces of twentieth-century life—technological change, bureaucratization, and the growth of the middle class—accelerated, making the decade truly a "new era." Both phenomena would recur as major themes in the nation's history for the rest of the twentieth century.

Intercollegiate Athletics

In 1924 scandals of brutality, academic fraud, and illegal payments to recruits prompted the Carnegie Foundation for the Advancement of Higher Education to undertake a five-year investigation of college sports. Its 1929 report condemned coaches and alumni supporters for violating the amateur code. The report had minimal effect, however. As the career of Red Grange illustrated, football had become big-time during the 1920s, and other sports followed suit as scores of colleges and universities built stadiums and arenas to attract spectators, bolster alumni allegiance, and promote school spirit.

For most of the twentieth century, intercollegiate athletics ranked as one of the nation's major commercial entertainments. Highly paid coaches and highly recruited student-athletes have been common ever since the 1920s. At the same time, American colleges and universities have struggled to reconcile conflicts between the commercialism of athletic competition on one hand and the restraints of educational objectives and athletic amateurism on the other. Supposedly, cultivation of the mind is the main objective of higher education. But the economic potential of college sports coupled with rise in the 1920s of athletic departments, complete with athletic directors, staffs, and tutors as well as coaches and trainers, has created programs that compete with and sometimes overshadow the academic operations of the institutions that sponsor intercollegiate athletics.

Since the 1920s, recruiting scandals, cheating incidents, and accusations of academic fraud in college sports have sparked continual controversy and criticism. In 1952, after revelations of point-shaving (fixing the outcome) of college basketball games, the American Council on Education undertook a study of all college sports similar to that of the Carnegie Foundation a generation earlier. Its recommendations, including the abolition of bowl games, went largely unheeded. Then, in 1991, further abuses, especially in academics, prompted the Knight Foundation Commission on Intercollegiate Athletics to conduct a study that ultimately urged college presidents to take the lead in reforming intercollegiate athletics. Again, few significant changes resulted.

The most sweeping reforms followed court rulings in the 1990s that mandated expenditures for women's sports in proportion to women's share of a school's total enrollment (mandated under Title IX of the Educational Amendments Act of 1972). But as long as millions of dollars were involved and sports remained such a vital component of college as well as national culture, the system established in the 1920s has withstood most pressures for change.

For Further Reading, see page A-28 of the Appendix. For Web resources, go to http://college.hmco.com.

In late 1937 on a farm near Stigler, Oklahoma, Marvin Montgomery counted up his assets: $53 and a car—a 1929 Hudson that he had just bought to take himself, his wife, and their four children to California. Times in Oklahoma had been tough for Montgomery's family. Like other farm families on the Plains, Marvin explained, they had suffered from "the drought and such as that, it just got so hard, . . . I decided it would help me to change countries." The combined disasters of soil exhaustion, drought, and dust storms were driving farm families from their homes. In addition, machines, such as mechanical cotton pickers, were replacing the labor of men, women, and children in the cotton fields. Finally, farm policies under the New Deal of President Franklin D. Roosevelt often benefited landowners at the expense of tenant farmers and sharecroppers, tens of thousands of whom were evicted during the 1930s.

Marvin Montgomery believed that he could have held out. "I might have drug by like some of the rest of them," he said, "and sort of lived." But he wanted more than that. Above all, he wanted work. At the same time, circulars and newspaper advertisements held out the promise of jobs aplenty in the fields of California; and as many as four hundred thousand people decided to make the westward trek. Some of the migrants were from Arkansas, Texas, Missouri, and Kansas, but more came from Oklahoma than from any other state. Among them were Montgomery and his wife and children, who, on December 29, squeezed into the Hudson, along with their furniture, bedding, and pots and pans. "I had that old car loaded to the full capacity," Marvin acknowledged, "on top, the sides, and everywhere else." Traveling west on Route 66, the Montgomerys left Oklahoma for California.

There was never any doubt that the Montgomery family's destination would be California, where their married daughter and oldest son had already moved. "Yes, sir. I knew right where I was coming to," Marvin Montgomery told a congressional committee that in 1940 held hearings in a migratory labor camp in California's San Joaquin valley. But the trip had not been

Sharecropper, an oil painting by Jerry Bywaters, shows one of the major problems facing farmers on the southern plains in the 1930s: grasshoppers, which along with drought and dust storms ravaged crops in Oklahoma, Kansas, and other states. (Dallas Museum of Art, Allied Arts Civic Prize, Eighth Annual Dallas Arts Exhibition)

The Great Depression and the New Deal 1929–1941

easy, largely because the Hudson proved to be an expensive gas-guzzler. "On the way, you know my car," he explained. "I got to where I had to blindfold it to get it past a filling station. It was taking on lots of gas and oil." The car also broke down twice. While they were crossing Arizona, their money ran out, and the family had to stop to work in the cotton fields for five weeks before they could afford to resume the trip. And once in California, Marvin said, there was little work: "Well, I hoed beets some; hoed some cotton, and I picked some spuds."

Their dream was one day to have a home and some land of their own in California, but they knew that low-paid farm work would never make the dream come true. In the meantime, though, the Montgomerys were relieved to be able to live in the housing provided for farm workers by the federal government through the Farm Security Administration (FSA). The FSA camp at Shafter in Kern County had 240 tents and forty small houses. For nine months the Montgomery family of six lived in a tent 14 by 16 feet, which rented for 10 cents a day plus four hours of volunteer labor a month. Then they proudly moved into an FSA house, "with water, lights, and everything, yes sir; and a little garden spot furnished."

What did the future hold for the Montgomerys? Marvin conceded that he became homesick for Oklahoma and "would rather be back on the farm, if you want to know." But his seventeen-year-old son Harvey saw a future for himself in California. When asked whether he wanted to return to Oklahoma, he replied: "I like California. . . . No. I would rather stay out here." And soon there were bountiful employment opportunities in California not only for the Montgomery family but for many other newcomers, in aircraft factories and shipyards mobilizing for the Second World War.

Statistics suggest the magnitude of the Great Depression's human tragedy. Between 1929 and 1933, a hundred thousand businesses failed, corporate profits fell from $10 billion to $1 billion, and the gross national product was cut in half. Banks failed by the thousands. Americans who believed that saving was a virtue discovered that their deposits had disappeared with the banks. Americans lost jobs as well. Thousands of men and women received severance slips every day. At the beginning of 1930 the number of jobless reached at least 4 million; by November it had jumped to 6 million. When President Herbert Hoover left office in 1933, about one-fourth of the labor force was idle—13 million workers—and millions more were underemployed, working only part-time. Unemployment strained relations within families. African Americans and other minorities sank deeper into destitution. Overall, the economic catastrophe aggravated old tensions: labor versus capital, white versus black, male versus female.

Elected amid prosperity and optimism, Herbert Hoover spent the years from late 1929 to his departure from office in March 1933 presiding over a gloomy and sometimes angry nation. Although he activated more of the federal government's resources than had any of his predecessors in an economic crisis, he opposed direct relief payments for the unemployed, and voters turned him out of office in 1932. His successor was Franklin D. Roosevelt, who promised vigorous action and projected hope in a time of despair.

From the first days of his presidency, Roosevelt displayed a buoyancy and willingness to experiment that helped to restore public confidence in the government and the economy. He acted not only to reform the banks and stock markets but also to provide central planning for industry and agriculture and direct government relief for the jobless. This sweeping emergency legislation was based on the concept of "pump priming," or pouring billions of federal dollars into the economy to generate business and industrial activity, thereby stimulating employment and consumer spending. Although Roosevelt's New Deal was opposed from both the left and the right, ultimately he prevailed, vastly expanding the scope of the federal government and the popularity of the Democratic Party, and in the process establishing America's welfare system.

During these years several million workers seized the chance to organize for better wages and working conditions. New Deal legislation made union organizing and collective bargaining legal. The new Congress of Industrial Organizations (CIO) established unions in the automobile, steel, meatpacking, and other major industries. Blacks registered political and economic gains, too, though they benefited less from the New Deal than did whites. Two and a half million additional women workers joined the labor force during the 1930s, but mostly in low-paying jobs that were not covered by New Deal legislation. Thus many women lacked Social Security coverage and minimum-wage protection.

The New Deal was not a revolution, but it transformed the United States. The elderly and disabled still collect Social Security payments. The Federal Deposit Insurance Corporation still insures bank deposits. The Securities and Exchange Commission still

IMPORTANT EVENTS

1929 Stock market crash (Oct.); Great Depression begins

Agricultural Marketing Act establishes Federal Farm Board to support crop prices

1930 Hawley-Smoot Tariff raises rates on imports

1931 Nine African American men arrested in Scottsboro affair

Hoover declares moratorium on First World War debts and reparations

1932 Reconstruction Finance Corporation established to make loans to banks, insurance companies, and railroads

Bonus Expeditionary Force marches on Washington

Roosevelt elected president

Revenue Act raises corporate, excise, and personal income taxes

1933 13 million Americans unemployed

National bank holiday suspends banking activities

Agricultural Adjustment Act (AAA) encourages decreased farm production

Civilian Conservation Corps provides jobs to young men

Tennessee Valley Authority established

Banking Act creates Federal Deposit Insurance Corporation

National Industrial Recovery Act (NIRA) attempts to spur industrial growth

Twentieth (Lame Duck) Amendment sets presidential inaugurations at January 20

Twenty-first Amendment repeals Eighteenth (Prohibition) Amendment

1934 Townsend devises Old Age Revolving Pensions plan

Long starts Share Our Wealth Society

Indian Reorganization (Wheeler-Howard) Act restores lands to tribal ownership

Taylor Grazing Act closes grasslands to further settlement

Democrats win victories in congressional elections

1935 Emergency Relief Appropriation Act authorizes establishment of public works programs

Works Progress Administration creates jobs in public works projects

Schechter v. U.S. invalidates NIRA

National Labor Relations (Wagner) Act grants workers the right to unionize

Social Security Act establishes insurance for the aged, the unemployed, and needy children

Committee for Industrial Organization established

Congress passes Public Utility Holding Company Act

Revenue (Wealth Tax) Act raises taxes on business and the wealthy

1936 9 million Americans unemployed

U.S. v. Butler invalidates AAA

Roosevelt defeats Landon

United Auto Workers hold sit-down strike against General Motors

1937 Roosevelt's court-packing plan fails

NLRB v. Jones & Laughlin upholds Wagner Act

Memorial Day Massacre of striking steelworkers

Farm Security Administration established to aid farm workers

National Housing Act establishes United States Housing Authority

1937–39 Business recession

1938 10.4 million Americans unemployed

AFL expels CIO unions

Fair Labor Standards Act establishes minimum wage

Missouri ex rel. Gaines v. Canada orders law school established for African Americans

1939 Marian Anderson performs at Lincoln Memorial

Social Security amendments add benefits for spouses and widows

1940 Roosevelt defeats Willkie

1941 African Americans threaten to march on Washington to protest unequal access to defense jobs

Fair Employment Practices Committee prohibits discrimination in war industries and government monitors the stock exchanges. But the New Deal did not accomplish one of its goals—putting back to work all the people who wanted jobs. That would await the nation's entry into the Second World War in 1941. ■

Hoover and Hard Times: 1929–1933

 As the Great Depression deepened in the early 1930s, its underlying causes—principally overproduction and underconsumption—grew in severity (see Chapter 24). So too did instability in the banking industry. What happened to America's banks illustrates the cascading nature of the depression. Banks that had invested depositors' money in the stock market or foreign investments were badly weakened. When nervous Americans made runs on banks to salvage their threatened savings, a powerful momentum—panic—set in. In 1929, 659 banks folded; in 1930 the number of failures more than doubled to 1,350. The Federal Reserve Board blundered after the crash, drastically raising interest rates and thus tightening the money supply when just the opposite was needed: lowering interest rates to spur borrowing and spending. In 1931, 2,293 banks shut their doors, and another 1,453 ceased to do business in 1932. When banks failed, depositors lost everything.

Without jobs and without money, even necessities became luxuries. In the cities, some people quietly

No Food, No Home

lined up at soup kitchens or in bread lines. Others ate only potatoes, crackers, or dandelions or scratched through garbage cans for bits of food. As diets deteriorated, malnutrition became common, and the undernourished frequently fell victim to disease. Millions of Americans were not only hungry and ill; they were cold. Unable to afford fuel, they huddled in unheated tenements and shacks. Families doubled up in crowded apartments, and those unable to pay the rent were evicted. The homeless created shantytowns, called "Hoovervilles," where they lived in shacks made of everything from egg crates to discarded boards and bricks.

In the countryside, economic hardship deepened. Between 1929 and 1933 farm prices dropped 60 percent. At the same time, production decreased only 6 percent as individual farmers tried to make up for lower prices by producing more, thus adding to the surplus and depressing prices even further. The surplus could not be exported because foreign demand

had shrunk. Drought, foreclosure, clouds of hungry grasshoppers, and bank failures also plagued American farmers. Entire families, like the Montgomerys, left their homes in search of jobs or food; some men and women, including thousands of teenagers, jumped aboard freight trains as hoboes to seek salvation elsewhere.

Hard times also affected marriage patterns and family life. People postponed marriage, and married couples postponed having children. Out-of-work fathers felt frustrated and ashamed. "A child who was playing irritated him," recalled the son of an unemployed tool-and-die maker. "It wasn't just my own father. They all got shook up." Divorces declined, but desertions rose as husbands unable to provide for their families simply took off.

Most Americans met the crisis not with protest or violence but with bewilderment. Who was responsible? Hard-pressed citizens

Farmers' Holiday Association

blamed businesspeople and bankers, of course, but often faulted themselves as well. Some people were angry, though, and scattered protests raised the specter of popular revolt. Farmers in the Midwest prevented evictions and slowed foreclosures on farm properties by harassing sheriffs, judges, and lawyers. They also tried to stop farm produce from reaching the market. In Nebraska, Iowa, and Minnesota, farmers protesting low prices put up barricades of spiked logs and telegraph poles. They stopped trucks, smashed headlights, and dumped milk and vegetables in roadside ditches. Some of these demonstrations were organized by the Farmers' Holiday Association, which encouraged farmers to take a "holiday"—a strike that would keep farm products off the market until they commanded better prices.

Isolated protests also broke out in cities and in mining regions. In Chicago, Los Angeles, and Philadelphia, the unemployed marched on city halls. In Harlan County, Kentucky, when miners struck against wage reductions, mine owners responded with strikebreakers, bombs, the National Guard, the closing of relief kitchens, and evictions from company-owned housing.

The most spectacular confrontation shook Washington, D.C., in the summer of 1932. Congress was

Bonus Expeditionary Force

considering a bill to authorize immediate issuance of $2.4 billion in bonuses promised to First World War veterans by Congress in 1924, but not due for payment for twenty

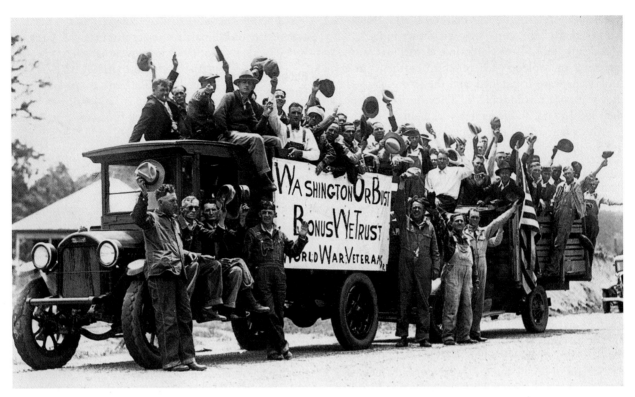

In June 1932 unemployed veterans of the First World War board a truck in Girard, Alabama, and Columbus, Georgia, and travel to Washington, D.C., to join the "Bonus Army" and demand payment of their soldiers' bonuses.   (Wide World Photos, Inc.)

years, or until 1945. To lobby for the bill, fifteen thousand unemployed veterans and their families converged on the tense nation's capital, calling themselves the Bonus Expeditionary Force (BEF), or "Bonus Army," and camping on vacant lots and in empty government buildings. President Hoover threw his weight against the bonus bill, and after much debate the Senate voted it down. One bonus marcher shouted: "We were heroes in 1917, but we're bums today."

Much of the BEF left Washington, but several thousand stayed on during the summer. Hoover carelessly labeled them "insurrectionists" and refused to meet with them. Then, in July, General Douglas MacArthur, assisted by Major Dwight D. Eisenhower and Major George S. Patton, confronted the veterans and their families with cavalry, tanks, and bayonet-wielding soldiers. The BEF hurled back stones and bricks. What followed shocked the nation. Men and women were chased down by horsemen; children were tear-gassed; shacks were set afire. When presidential hopeful Franklin D. Roosevelt heard about the attack on the Bonus Army, he turned to his friend Felix Frankfurter and remarked, "Well, Felix, this will elect me."

With capitalism on its knees, American Communists in various parts of the nation encouraged the jobless to join "unemployment councils," which led urban demonstrations, agitated for jobs and food, and sought to raise class consciousness. On March 6, 1930, which the Communists labeled International Unemployment Day, hundreds of thousands of jobless Americans marched in the streets of New York, Chicago, and other cities. And in 1931 the Communists led a hunger march on Washington, D.C. In resisting efforts to evict jobless people, the unemployment councils often clashed with local police. The Communists' tangles with authority publicized the human tragedy of the depression. Still, total party membership in 1932 remained small at twelve thousand. The Socialist Party, which took issue with both capitalists and Communists, fared better. In 1932 the Socialist presidential candidate attracted 880,000 votes. More reformist than radical, the Social-

Communists and Socialists

ists also ran well in municipal elections after the stock market crash but scored few victories. Indeed, few Americans looked to left-wing doctrines, protest marches, or violence for relief from their misery. Americans were frightened, and they were angry, but they were not revolutionaries. They turned instead to their local, state, and federal governments.

But when urgent daily appeals for government relief for the jobless reached the White House, Hoover at first became defensive, if not hostile, rejecting direct relief in the belief that it would undermine character and individualism. To a growing number of Americans, Hoover seemed heartless and inflexible. True to his beliefs, the president urged people to help themselves and their neighbors. He applauded the work of private voluntary relief through charities, but as the need increased, donations declined. State and urban officials found their treasuries drying up, too. Meanwhile, those calling for federal aid got no sympathy from Secretary of the Treasury Andrew Mellon, who believed that business cycles of boom and bust were not only inevitable but desirable. He advised Hoover to "let the slump liquidate itself. Liquidate labor, liquidate stocks, liquidate the farmers, liquidate real estate. . . . It will purge the rottenness out of the system."

Hoover's Response

As the depression intensified, Hoover's opposition to federal action gradually diminished. He rejected Mellon's insensitive counsel, hesitantly energizing the White House and federal agencies to take action— more action than the government had taken before. He won pledges from business and labor leaders to maintain wages and production and to avoid strikes. He urged state governors to increase their expenditures on public works. And he created the President's Organization on Unemployment Relief (POUR) to generate private contributions for relief of the destitute.

Though POUR proved ineffective, Hoover's spurring of federal public works projects (including Hoover and Grand Coulee Dams) did provide some jobs. Help also came from the Federal Farm Board, created under the Agricultural Marketing Act of 1929, which supported crop prices by lending money to cooperatives to buy crops and keep them off the market. But the board soon found itself short of money, and unsold surpluses jammed warehouses. To retard the collapse of the international monetary system, Hoover in 1931 announced a moratorium on the payment of First World War debts and reparations.

The president also asked Congress to charter the Reconstruction Finance Corporation (RFC). Created in 1932 and eventually empowered with $2 billion, the RFC was designed to make loans to banks, insurance companies, and railroads and later to state and local governments. In theory, the RFC would lend money to large entities at the top of the economic system, and benefits would filter down to people at the bottom. It did not work; banks continued to collapse and small companies went into bankruptcy.

Reconstruction Finance Corporation

Despite warnings from prominent economists, Hoover also signed into law the Hawley-Smoot Tariff (1930). The tariff raised duties by about one-third and further weakened the economy by making it even more difficult for foreign nations to sell their products and thus to earn dollars to pay back their debts to the United States and to buy American products.

Hawley-Smoot Tariff

Like most of his contemporaries, Hoover believed that a balanced budget was sacred and deficit spending sinful. In 1931 he therefore appealed for a decrease in federal expenditures and an increase in taxes. The following year he supported a sales tax on manufactured goods. The sales tax was defeated, but the Revenue Act of 1932 raised corporate, excise, and personal income taxes. Hoover seemed tangled in a contradiction: he urged people to spend to spur recovery, but his tax policies deprived them of spending money. Nor did he ever balance the budget.

Although Hoover expanded public works projects and approved loans to some institutions, he vetoed a variety of relief bills presented to him by Congress. In rejecting a public power project for the Tennessee River, he argued that its inexpensive electricity would compete with power from private companies. Hoover's traditionalism also was well demonstrated by his handling of prohibition. Despite the Eighteenth Amendment, Americans were producing and drinking liquor with grand illegality and hypocrisy. Although the law was not and could not be enforced, Hoover resisted mounting public pressure for repeal. Opponents of prohibition argued not only that it encouraged crime but also that its repeal would stimulate economic recovery by reviving the nation's breweries and distilleries. But the president refused to tamper with the Constitution; he declared that the liquor industry, hav-

Hoover's Traditionalism

ing no socially redemptive value, was best left depressed. After Hoover left office in 1933, prohibition was repealed through ratification of the Twenty-first Amendment.

Still, President Hoover stretched governmental activism as far as he thought he could without violating his cherished principles. On the eve of Hoover's departure from the presidency in 1933, the journalist William Allen White pondered "whether Herbert Hoover . . . by pointing the way to social recovery . . . is the first of the new Presidents . . . or whether . . . he is the last of the old." Perhaps he was both. Because Hoover mobilized the resources of the federal government as never before, some historians have depicted him as a bridge to the New Deal of the 1930s. If nothing else, he prepared the way for massive federal activity by giving private enterprise the opportunity to solve the depression—and to fail in the attempt.

Franklin D. Roosevelt and the Election of 1932

Herbert Hoover and the Republican Party faced dreary prospects in 1932. The president kept blaming international events for the economic crisis, but Americans were less concerned with abstract explanations than with tomorrow's meal. He grumbled and grew impatient with his critics. But what soured public opinion most was that Hoover did not offer leadership when the times required it. So unpopular had he become by 1932 that Republicans who did not want to be associated with a loser ran independent campaigns.

Franklin D. Roosevelt enjoyed quite a different reputation. Though born into the upper class of old money and privilege, the smiling, ingratiating governor of New York appealed to people of all classes, races, and regions, and he shared the American penchant for optimism. After serving as assistant secretary of the navy under Woodrow Wilson and running as the Democratic Party's vice-presidential candidate in 1920, Roosevelt was stricken with polio and left totally paralyzed in both legs. What should Roosevelt do next? Should he retire from public life, a rich invalid? His answer and his wife Eleanor's was "no." Throughout the 1920s the Roosevelts contended with his handicap. Rejecting self-pity, Franklin Roosevelt worked to rebuild his body. Friends commented that his fight against polio

Franklin D. Roosevelt

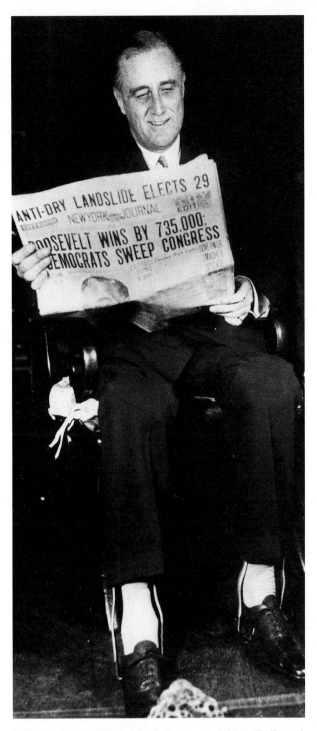

In November 1930 Franklin D. Roosevelt (1882–1945) read the good news. Reelected governor of New York by 735,000 votes, he immediately became a leading contender for the Democratic presidential nomination. Notice Roosevelt's leg braces, rarely shown in photographs because of an unwritten agreement by photographers to shoot him from the waist up. (Corbis-Bettmann)

had given him new moral and physical strength. As Roosevelt explained it, "If you had spent two years in bed trying to wiggle your big toe, after that anything would seem easy."

For her part, Eleanor Roosevelt—who had grown up shy and sheltered—launched her own career in public life. In her memoirs, she described having changed in the 1920s from a depressed, isolated person into an independent woman with significant political commitments and personal relationships. Eleanor Roosevelt worked hard to become an effective public speaker and participated in the activities of the League of Women Voters, the Women's Trade Union League, and the Democratic Party. In a short time, she became a leading figure in a network of women activists. She became deeply committed to equal opportunity for women and for African Americans and wanted to alleviate the suffering of the poor. On these issues, she served as her husband's conscience.

Eleanor Roosevelt

Roosevelt was elected governor of New York in 1928 and reelected in 1930; his terms coincided with Hoover's presidency. But whereas Hoover appeared hardhearted and unwilling to help the jobless, Roosevelt seemed quite the opposite. He supported direct relief payments for the unemployed, declaring that

Roosevelt as Governor of New York

such aid "must be extended by Government, not as a matter of charity, but as a matter of social duty." As governor of New York, Roosevelt created jobs in publicly funded reforestation, land reclamation, and hydroelectric power projects, and he endorsed old-age pensions and protective legislation for labor unions. With his record, Roosevelt became an obvious prospect for the 1932 Democratic presidential nomination.

To prepare a national political platform, Roosevelt surrounded himself with a "Brain Trust" of lawyers and university professors. These experts reasoned that bigness was unavoidable in the modern American economy. It thus followed that the cure for the nation's ills was not to go on a rampage of trustbusting but to place large corporations, monopolies, and oligopolies under effective government regulation.

Roosevelt's "Brain Trust"

Roosevelt and his Brain Trust also agreed that it was essential to restore purchasing power to farmers, blue-collar workers, and the middle classes, and that the way to do so was to cut production. If demand for a product remained constant and the supply were cut, they reasoned, the price would rise. Producers would make higher profits, and workers would earn more. This method of combating a depression has been called "the economics of scarcity," which the Brain Trust at the time saw as the preferred alternative to pump priming through deficit spending, in which the government borrowed money to prime the economic pump and thereby revive purchasing power.

Roosevelt and Hoover both campaigned as fiscal conservatives committed to a balanced budget. But Roosevelt, unlike Hoover, also advocated immediate and direct relief to the unemployed. And Roosevelt demanded that the federal government engage in centralized economic planning and experimentation to bring about recovery.

Upon accepting the Democratic nomination, Roosevelt called for a "new deal for the American people." To that end, the Democrats were willing to abandon prohibition and to launch federal relief. More people went to the polls in 1932 than in any election since the First World War. In a crisis-ridden moment, Americans followed their traditional pattern and exchanged one government for another. The presidential election of 1932

1932 Election Results

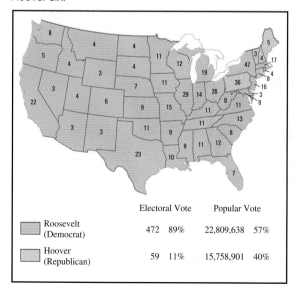

Map 25.1 Presidential Election, 1932 One factor above all decided the 1932 presidential election: the Great Depression. Roosevelt won forty-two states, Hoover six.

	Electoral Vote		Popular Vote	
Roosevelt (Democrat)	472	89%	22,809,638	57%
Hoover (Republican)	59	11%	15,758,901	40%

was never much of a contest: Roosevelt's 22.8 million popular votes far outdistanced Hoover's 15.8 million; Roosevelt won forty-two states to Hoover's six (see Map 25.1). Cities continued the trend, begun in 1928, of voting Democratic. Democrats also won overwhelming control of the Senate and the House.

Once elected, Roosevelt had to wait until his inauguration on March 4, 1933, to act. (To eliminate similar losses of time, the Twentieth Amendment to the Constitution—the so-called Lame Duck Amendment, ratified in 1933—shifted all future inaugurations to January 20.) It was a troubled four months. Millions of jobless Americans walked the streets; prices for agricultural and manufactured goods continued to plummet; industrial production sank to new depths. And throughout the United States, depositors lined up in front of banks to withdraw their savings. Banks with insufficient funds on hand to pay depositors had to close their doors and declare themselves insolvent. In February, Michigan and Maryland suspended banking operations, and by early March thirty-six other states, including New York, had declared bank holidays.

On March 2, 1933, President-elect Roosevelt and his family and friends boarded a train for Washington, D.C., and the inauguration ceremony. Roosevelt was carrying with him rough drafts of two presidential proclamations, one summoning a special session of Congress, the other declaring a national bank holiday, suspending banking transactions throughout the nation.

A gloomy Hoover and a buoyant Roosevelt ride to the inauguration in 1933. This magazine cover was never published, apparently because the editors of *The New Yorker* thought it inappropriate after an assassination attempt on the president-elect just three weeks before.   (Franklin D. Roosevelt Library)

Launching the New Deal and Restoring Confidence

"First of all," declared the newly inaugurated president, "let me assert my firm belief that the only thing we have to fear is fear itself—nameless, unreasoning, unjustified terror." In his inaugural address Roosevelt scored his first triumph as president, instilling hope and courage in the American people. He invoked "the analogue of war," asserting that, if need be, "I shall ask the Congress for the one remaining instrument to meet the crisis—broad Executive power to wage a war against the emergency, as great as the power that would be given to me if we were in fact invaded by a foreign foe."

The next day, Roosevelt declared a four-day national bank holiday and summoned Congress to an emergency session, beginning March 9, that would

Launching the New Deal

launch the New Deal. Roosevelt's first measure, the Emergency Banking Relief Bill, was introduced that very day, passed sight unseen by unanimous House vote, approved 73 to 7 in the Senate, and signed into law by the president that evening. The new law provided for the reopening, under Treasury Department license, of banks that were solvent and for the reorganization and management of those that were not. It also prohibited the hoarding and export of gold. It was, however, a fundamentally conservative law that upheld the status quo and left the same bankers in charge.

On the next day, March 10, the second bill of the New Deal was introduced in Congress. It too was conservative, and ten days later it became law. Called the Economy Act, its purpose was to balance the budget by reducing veterans' pensions and federal employees' pay. Under Roosevelt, the budget balancers had won a battle that could not have been won under Hoover.

On March 12, a Sunday evening, the president broadcast the first of his "fireside chats," and 60 million people heard his reassuring words on their radios.

Under the Agricultural Adjustment Act, farmers received government payments for not planting crops or for destroying crops they already had planted. Some farmers, however, needed help of a different kind. The Resettlement Administration, established by executive order in 1935, was authorized to resettle destitute farm families from areas of soil erosion, flooding, and stream pollution to homestead communities. This poster was done by Ben Shahn. (Library of Congress)

First Fireside Chat

His message: banks were once again safe places for depositors' savings. On Monday morning the banks opened their doors, but instead of queuing up to withdraw their savings, people were waiting outside to deposit their money. The bank runs were over; Roosevelt had reestablished people's confidence in their political leadership, their banks, even their economic system.

Roosevelt next pursued a measure, the Beer-Wine Revenue Act, that was deflationary because it actually took money out of people's pockets by imposing new taxes. The act, which legalized the sale of low-alcohol wines and beers, levied taxes on these products. (Congress had proposed repeal of prohibition in February 1933 in the Twenty-first Amendment, and the states ratified it by December 1933.) To many, levying new taxes seemed a strange way to restore purchasing power to people who could not afford to buy what they needed. Roosevelt knew that, but he predicted the situation would change. "It is simply inevitable," he wrote a friend, "that we must inflate." He added that his "banker friends may be horrified" by the large-scale federal spending that was to come.

Beer-Wine Revenue Act

In mid-March Roosevelt sent to Congress the Agricultural Adjustment Bill to restore farmers' purchasing power. If overproduction was the cause of farmers' problems, then the government had to encourage farmers to grow less. Under the domestic allotment plan, the government would pay farmers to reduce their acreage or plow under crops already in the fields. Farmers would receive payments based on *parity*, a system of regulated prices for corn, cotton, wheat, rice, hogs, and dairy products that would provide them the same purchasing power they had had during the prosperous period of 1909 to 1914. In paying price supports, the government was making up the difference between the current prices for farm products and the income that farmers needed to survive. The subsidies would be funded by taxes levied on the processors of agricultural commodities.

Agricultural Adjustment Act

Roosevelt's farm plan immediately encountered vehement opposition. How could there be crop surpluses when some Americans were hungry and even starving? Underconsumption, critics argued, was the result of a maldistribution of incomes and wealth.

Some politicians wanted to put more money into circulation by coining silver or printing greenbacks. Cheap money, they contended, not price supports, would make it easier for farmers to repay their debts. On May 12, Congress finally overcame opposition to the domestic allotment plan and passed the Agricultural Adjustment Act (AAA). A month later the Farm Credit Act was passed, providing short- and medium-term loans that enabled many farmers to refinance their mortgages and hang onto their homes and land. Another New Deal measure assisted homeowners in the towns and cities; the Home Owners Refinancing Act provided $2 billion in bonds to refinance nonfarm home mortgages.

Meanwhile, other relief measures became law. On March 21 the president requested direct cash grants to

Other Relief Measures

the states for relief payments to needy citizens and two federal programs that would create jobs. Ten days later Congress approved the Civilian Conservation Corps (CCC), a job agency that ultimately put 2.5 million young men aged eighteen to twenty-five to work planting trees, clearing camping areas and beaches, and building bridges, dams, reservoirs, fish ponds, and fire towers. Then on May 12 Congress passed the Federal Emergency Relief Act, which authorized $500 million in aid to state and local governments. Finally, on June 16 Title II of the National Industrial Recovery Act established the Public Works Administration (PWA) and appropriated $3.3 billion for hiring the unemployed to build roads, sewage and water systems, public buildings, and a host of other projects. These were worthwhile in themselves, but the key purpose of the PWA was to pump federal money into the economy.

If the AAA was the agricultural cornerstone of the New Deal, the National Industrial Recovery Act was

National Recovery Administration

the industrial cornerstone. The act, which established the National Recovery Administration (NRA), was a testimony to the New Deal belief in national economic planning as opposed to an intensely competitive, laissez-faire economy. It was essential, planners argued, for businesses to cooperate in ending cutthroat competition and to raise prices by limiting production. Under NRA auspices, competing businesses met with each other, as well as with representatives of workers and consumers, to draft codes of fair competition, which limited production and established prices. With

businesses enjoying new benefits from cooperation, workers wanted a share of the pie, too. Congress responded with Section 7(a) of the National Industrial Recovery Act, which guaranteed their right to unionize and to bargain collectively.

The New Deal also strengthened public confidence in the stock exchanges and banks. Roosevelt signed the Federal Securities Act, which compelled brokers to tell the truth about new securities issues, and the Banking Act of 1933, which set up the Federal Deposit Insurance Corporation (FDIC) for insuring bank deposits. In June Roosevelt also took the United States off the gold standard, no longer guaranteeing the gold value of the dollar abroad. Freed from the requirement that all paper money be backed by gold, the Federal Reserve Board could expand the supply of currency in circulation, thus enabling monetary policy to become another weapon for economic recovery.

One of the boldest programs enacted by Congress addressed the badly depressed Tennessee River valley,

TVA

which runs through Virginia, North Carolina, Tennessee, Georgia, Alabama, Mississippi, and Kentucky (see Map 25.2). For years Progressives had advocated government operation of the Muscle Shoals electric power and nitrogen facilities on the Tennessee River. Roosevelt's Tennessee Valley Authority (TVA), established in May, was a much broader program. Its dams would not only control floods but generate hydroelectric power as well. In constructing public power facilities, the TVA would provide a yardstick for determining fair rates for privately produced electric power. Most important, the goal of the TVA was nothing less than enhancement of the economic well-being of the entire Tennessee River valley.

The TVA achieved its goals but, in the process, it became a major polluter. TVA strip mining caused soil

TVA's Environmental Legacy

erosion. Its coal-burning generators released sulfur oxides, which combined with water vapor to produce acid rain. Above all, the TVA degraded the water by dumping untreated sewage, toxic chemicals, and metal pollutants from strip mining into streams and rivers. Though an economic miracle, the TVA proved to be a monumental disaster in America's environmental history.

The special session of Congress adjourned on June 16, 1933. In just over three months, Roosevelt had delivered fifteen messages to Congress proposing

Map 25.2 The Tennessee Valley Authority To control flooding and to generate electricity, the Tennessee Valley Authority constructed dams along the Tennessee River and its tributaries from Paducah, Kentucky, to Knoxville, Tennessee.

End of the First Hundred Days

major legislation, and Congress had passed fifteen significant laws (see Table 25.1). The United States had rebounded from hysteria and near collapse. As columnist Walter Lippmann wrote, at the time of Roosevelt's inauguration the country was a collection of "disorderly panic-stricken mobs and factions. In the hundred days from March to June we became again an organized nation confident of our power to provide for our own security and to control our own destiny." Journalists called this period of remarkable achievement the Hundred Days.

Throughout the remainder of 1933 and the spring and summer of 1934, more New Deal bills became law, benefiting farmers, the unemployed, investors, homeowners, workers, and the environment. The Commodity Credit Corporation, organized in 1933, bolstered crop prices by lending farmers money secured by their underpriced crops, thereby allowing them to withhold

Other Legislation

their crops from the market until prices rose. In 1934 additional hundreds of millions of federal dollars were appropriated for unemployment relief and public works. Legislation that year also established the Securities and Exchange Commission, the National Labor Relations Board, and the Federal Housing Administration. In 1934, too, the Taylor Grazing Act was passed. For years, use of the public lands had been largely unregulated, and overgrazing of cattle had caused severe soil erosion. The Taylor Act, which created the Grazing Service (later to become the Bureau of Land Management), established federal supervision of most of the remaining public domain, and it closed 80 million acres of grasslands to further settlement and use.

New Deal legislation seemed to promise something for every group: industrial workers, urban dwellers, landowning farmers, and the jobless, not to mention industrialists, bankers, stockbrokers, educators, and social workers. This was interest-group democracy at work. In

Interest-Group Democracy

Table 25.1   New Deal Achievements

Year	Labor	Agriculture and Environment	Business and Industrial Recovery	Relief	Reform
1933	Section 7(a) of NIRA	Agricultural Adjustment Act Farm Credit Act	Emergency Banking Relief Act Economy Act Beer-Wine Revenue Act Banking Act of 1933 (guaranteed deposits) National Industrial Recovery Act	Civilian Conservation Corps Federal Emergency Relief Act Home Owners Refinancing Act Public Works Administration Civil Works Administration	TVA Federal Securities Act
1934	National Labor Relations Board	Taylor Grazing Act			Securities Exchange Act
1935	National Labor Relations (Wagner) Act	Resettlement Administration Rural Electrification Administration		Works Progress Administration National Youth Administration	Social Security Act Public Utility Holding Company Act Revenue Act (wealth tax)
1937		Farm Security Administration		National Housing Act	
1938	Fair Labor Standards Act	Agricultural Adjustment Act of 1938			

Source: Adapted from Charles Sellers, Henry May, and Neil R. McMillen, *A Synopsis of American History*, 6th ed. Copyright © 1985 by Houghton Mifflin Company. Reprinted by permission.

the midst of this coalition of special interests was President Roosevelt, the artful broker, who pointed to the economy as proof that this approach was working (see Figure 25.1). As the New Deal became law, unemployment fell steadily from 13 million in 1933 to 9 million in 1936. Net farm income rose from just over $3 billion in 1933 to $5.85 billion in 1935. Manufacturing salaries and wages also increased, from $6.25 billion in 1933 to almost $13 billion in 1937.

During the early years of Roosevelt's presidency, there was no question about the popularity of either the New Deal or the president. In the 1934 congressional elections, the Democrats gained nine seats in the House and nine in the Senate. The New Deal, according to Arthur Krock of the *New York Times*, had won "the most overwhelming victory in the history of American politics."

Opposition to the New Deal

There was, however, more than one way to read employment and income statistics and election returns. Although unemployment had dropped from a high of 25 percent in 1933 to 16.9 percent in 1936, it was still much higher than in 1929, when unemployment had been only 3.2 percent. And although manufacturing wages and salaries had reached almost $13 billion in

Figure 25.1 The Economy Before and After the New Deal, 1929–1941 The New Deal reduced bank closings, business failures, and unemployment, and it increased farm prices, wages, and salaries. Some of the nation's most persistent economic problems, however, did not disappear until the advent of the Second World War.

Plagued by dust storms and evictions, thousands of tenant farmers and sharecroppers were forced to leave their land during the Great Depression. Known as "Okies" and "Arkies," they took off for California with their few belongings. These refugees from drought-stricken Oklahoma experienced car trouble and were stalled on a New Mexico highway.   (Library of Congress)

1937, that figure was less than the total for 1929. In other words, the New Deal had a long way to go before reaching predepression standards.

With the arrival of partial economic recovery, many businesspeople and conservatives became vo-

Conservative Critics of the New Deal

cal critics of the New Deal. Some charged that there was too much taxation and government regulation. Others condemned the deficit financing of relief and public works. In 1934 the leaders of several major corporations joined with Al Smith, John W. Davis, and disaffected conservative Democrats to establish the American Liberty League. Members of the Liberty League contended that the New Deal welfare payments were subverting individual initiative and self-reliance.

While businesspeople considered the government their enemy, others thought the government favored business too much. Critics argued that NRA codes fa-

Farmers and Laborers

vored industry's needs over those of workers and consumers. Farmers, labor unions, and individual entrepreneurs complained that the NRA set prices too high and favored large producers over small businesses. The federal courts also began to scrutinize the constitutionality of the legislation in cases brought by New Deal foes.

The AAA also came under attack for its encouragement of cutbacks in production. Farmers had plowed under 10.4 million acres of cotton and slaughtered 6 million pigs in 1933—a time when people were ill clothed and ill fed. Although for landowning farmers the program was successful, many others found such waste shocking. Tenant farmers and sharecroppers also were supposed to receive government payments for taking crops out of cultivation, but very few received what they were entitled to, especially if they were African American. Furthermore, the AAA's hopes that landlords would keep their tenants on the land even while cutting production were not fulfilled. In the South the number of sharecropper farms dropped by 30 percent between 1930 and 1940. The result was a homeless population, dispossessed Americans heading to cities and towns in all parts of the country.

Joining the migration to the West Coast were "Okies," such as Oklahoman Marvin Montgomery and his family traveling in their 1929 Hudson, and "Arkies" from Arkansas; many of them had been evicted from their tenant farms during the depression. Not all were driven by foreclosure; thousands took to the road to escape the drought that plagued the southern plains states of Kansas, Colorado, New Mexico, Oklahoma, Arkansas, and Texas—a region known in the mid-1930s as the Dust Bowl. The Dust Bowl was an ecological disaster. In the 1920s farmers on the southern plains had bought tens of thousands of tractors and plowed millions of acres. Then, in the 1930s, the rain stopped. Soil that had been plowed was particularly vulnerable to the

The Dust Bowl

drought that gripped the plains. Strong winds caused enormous dust storms; from 1935 through 1938, 241 dust storms suffocated the southern plains. Farmers shuttered their homes against the dust as tightly as possible, but, as a woman in western Kansas recounted in 1935, "those tiny particles seemed to seep through the very walls. It got into cupboards and clothes closets; our faces were as dirty as if we had rolled in the dirt; our hair was gray and stiff and we ground dirt between our teeth." Farm animals lacked protection. The photographer Margaret Bourke-White observed that "cattle quickly become blinded. They run around in circles until they fall and breathe so much dust that they die."

Some farmers blamed the government for their woes; others blamed themselves. As dissatisfaction mounted, so too did the appeal of various demagogues who presented an analysis of American society that people understood: the wealthy and powerful were ruling people's lives

Demagogic Attacks

In the 1930s, Senator Huey Long *(center)* had a mass following and presidential ambitions. But he was assassinated in 1935, the evening this photograph was taken. When Long was shot, he fell into the arms of James O'Connor *(left)*, a political crony. Louisiana Governor O. K. Allen *(right)* seized a pistol and dashed into the corridor in pursuit of the murderer shouting, "If there's shooting, I want to be in on it." (Wide World Photos, Inc.)

from distant cities, eroding community morale and ruining family farms and small businesses. One of the best-known demagogues was Father Charles Coughlin, a Roman Catholic priest whose weekly radio sermons offered a curious combination of anticommunism and anticapitalism. In addition to criticizing the New Deal, Coughlin became increasingly anti-Semitic, telling his listeners that the cause of their woes was an international conspiracy of Jewish bankers.

Another challenge to the New Deal came from Dr. Francis E. Townsend, a public health officer in Long Beach, California, who was thrown out of work at age sixty-seven with only $100 in savings. Disturbed by the plight of old people, Townsend devised the Old Age Revolving Pensions plan, under which the government would pay monthly pensions of $200 to all citizens older than sixty on condition that they spent the money in the same month they received it. Townsend claimed his plan not only would aid the aged but would cure the depression by pumping enormous purchasing power into the economy. The plan was fiscally impossible but recognized the real needs of elderly Americans.

Then there was Huey Long, perhaps the most successful demagogue in American history. Long was elected governor of Louisiana in 1928 with the slogan "Every Man a King, but No One Wears a Crown." As a U.S. senator, Long at first supported the New Deal, but he began to believe that Roosevelt had fallen captive to big business. Long countered in 1934 with the Share Our Wealth Society, which advocated the seizure by taxation of all incomes greater than $1 million and all inheritances of more than $5 million. With the resulting funds, the government would furnish each family a homestead allowance of $5,000 and an annual income of $2,000. By mid-1935 Long's movement claimed 7 million members, and few doubted that Long aspired to the presidency. An assassin's bullet extinguished his ambition in September 1935.

Some politicians, like Governor Floyd Olson of Minnesota, declared themselves socialists in the 1930s. In Wisconsin the left-wing Progressive Party reelected Robert La Follette, Jr. (son of "Battling Bob"), to the Senate in 1934, sent seven of the state's ten representatives to Washington, D.C., and placed La Follette's brother Philip in the governorship. And the old muckraker and socialist Upton Sinclair won the Democratic gubernatorial nomination in California in 1934 with the slogan "End Poverty in California."

Left-wing Critics

Perhaps the most controversial alternative to the New Deal was the Communist Party of the United States of America. In 1935 the party leadership changed its strategy. Proclaiming "Communism Is Twentieth Century Americanism," the Communists disclaimed any intention of overthrowing the U.S. government and began to cooperate with left-wing labor unions, student groups, and writers' organizations in a "Popular Front" against fascism abroad and racism at home. In 1938, at its high point for the decade, the party had fifty-five thousand members.

In addition to challenges from the right and the left, the New Deal was also subject to challenge by the Supreme Court. Many New Deal laws had been hastily drafted, and the majority of the justices feared that the legislation had vested too much power in the presidency. In 1935 the Court unanimously struck down the NIRA (*Schechter v. U.S.*), asserting that it granted the White House excessive legislative power and that the commerce clause of the Constitution did not give the federal government authority to regulate intrastate businesses. Roosevelt's industrial recovery program was dead. In early 1936 his farm program met a similar fate when the Court invalidated the AAA (*U.S. v. Butler*), deciding that agriculture was a local problem and thus, under the Tenth Amendment, subject to state, not federal, action.

Supreme Court Decisions Against the New Deal

The Second New Deal and Roosevelt's Second Term

As Roosevelt looked ahead to the presidential election of 1936, he foresaw the danger of losing his capacity to lead and to govern. His broad coalition of special interests was breaking up, radicals and demagogues were offering Americans alternative programs, and the Supreme Court was dismantling the New Deal. In early 1935 Roosevelt took the initiative once more. So impressive was the spate of new legislation that historians call it the Second New Deal.

The Second New Deal differed in important ways from the first. When the chief legislative goal had been economic recovery, Roosevelt had cooperated with business. Beginning in 1935, however, he denounced business leaders for placing their own selfish interests above the national welfare. The first triumph

Emergency Relief Appropriation Act

of the Second New Deal was an innocuous-sounding but momentous law called the Emergency Relief Appropriation Act, which authorized the president to establish massive public works programs for the jobless. Among the programs funded by the Emergency Relief Appropriation Act were the Resettlement Administration, which resettled destitute families and organized rural homestead communities and suburban greenbelt towns for low-income workers; the Rural Electrification Administration, which brought electricity to isolated rural areas; and the National Youth Administration, which sponsored work-relief programs for young adults and part-time jobs for students.

Perhaps the best-known program funded by the Emergency Relief Appropriation Act was the Works Progress Administration (WPA), later renamed the Work Projects Administration. The WPA ultimately employed more than 8.5 million people and built 650,000 miles of highways and roads, 125,000 public buildings, and 8,000 parks, as well as numerous bridges, reservoirs, irrigation systems, sewage treatment plants, and playgrounds and swimming pools. Among its construction projects, the WPA built or renovated 5,900 schools, 2,500 hospitals, and 1,000 airfields. The WPA also operated nurseries for preschool children, and it established schools in which 1.5 million adults were taught to read and write.

The WPA also sponsored a multitude of cultural programs, which not only provided employment for artists, musicians, writers, and actors,

The New Deal's Cultural Programs

but brought art in myriad forms to the people. The WPA's Federal Theater Project brought vaudeville, circuses, and theater, including African American and Yiddish plays, to cities and towns across the country; its Arts Project hired painters and sculptors to teach their crafts in rural schools, and it commissioned artists to decorate post office walls with murals depicting ordinary life in America past and present; and its Federal Music Project sponsored 225,000 concerts by symphony orchestras, jazz groups, and folk musicians. Perhaps the most ambitious of the New Deal's cultural programs was the WPA's Federal Writers Project, which hired talented authors such as John Steinbeck and Richard Wright to write local guidebooks and regional and folk histories. Many of these writers, like many of the artists, musicians, and actors, were politically sympathetic with the struggles of workers and farmers, and the WPA's arts

projects were as a result often controversial. Critics assailed them as left-wing propaganda, and in fact some of these artists were Marxists and a few were communists. However, as the historian Michael Denning has observed, the goal of this "Popular Front" culture was not to overthrow the government, but to recover a tradition of American radicalism through remembering, and celebrating artistically, the lives and labor of America's plain folk. Among the best-known writers' projects, for example, are the poignant "slave narratives," which were collected from formerly enslaved women and men, and the interviews with sharecroppers and textile workers published in *These Are Our Lives* (1939).

In 1935 Roosevelt also wanted new legislation aimed at controlling the activities of big business.

Control of Business

The Supreme Court had dissolved the government-business cooperation that had been the foundation of the First New Deal. In addition, businesspeople had become increasingly critical of Roosevelt and the New Deal, complaining that they were overtaxed and overregulated. If big business would not cooperate with government, Roosevelt decided, government should "cut the giants down to size" through antitrust suits and heavy corporate taxes. In 1935 he asked Congress to enact several major bills, including a labor bill sponsored by Senator Robert Wagner of New York, a Social Security bill, a measure to regulate public-utility holding companies, and a "soak-the-rich" tax bill.

When the summer of 1935, which constituted the Second Hundred Days, was over, the president had everything he had requested. First,

National Labor Relations Act

the National Labor Relations (Wagner) Act granted workers the right to unionize and bargain collectively with management. The act also created a new National Labor Relations Board empowered to guarantee democratic union elections and to penalize unfair labor practices by employers, such as firing workers for union membership.

The Social Security Act was a milestone that established old-age insurance under which workers who paid Social Security taxes out of their

Social Security Act

wages, matched by their employers, would receive retirement benefits beginning at age sixty-five. The act also created several welfare programs, including a cooperative federal-state system of unemployment compensation and Aid to Dependent Children (later renamed Aid to Families with Dependent Children, AFDC) for needy children in single-parent families.

Although a milestone, Social Security was in some ways a conservative measure. First, the government did not pay for old-age benefits; workers and their bosses did. Second, the tax was regressive in that the more workers earned, the less they were taxed proportionally. Third, it was deflationary because it took out of people's pockets money that it did not repay for years. Finally, the law had a disparate impact on Americans, as it excluded agricultural labor, domestic service, and "casual labor not in the course of the employer's trade or business." Thus a disproportionally high number of women and people of color, who worked as farm laborers, as domestic servants, and in service jobs in hospitals and restaurants, received no benefits. Nevertheless, the Social Security Act was a highly significant development. With its passage, the federal government took responsibility not only for the aged but also for the temporarily jobless, dependent children, and disabled people.

In the next two weeks Roosevelt gained the remainder of what he had asked for, including the Public Utility Holding Company (Wheeler-Rayburn) Act and the Wealth Tax Act, which some critics saw as the president's attempt to "steal Huey Long's thunder." The tax act helped achieve a slight redistribution of income by raising the income taxes of the wealthy. It also imposed a new tax on excess business profits and increased taxes on inheritances, large gifts, and profits from the sale of property.

The Second Hundred Days made it unmistakably clear that the president was once again in charge and preparing to run for reelection.

Election of 1936

Roosevelt won by a landslide, easily defeating the Republican nominee, Governor Alf Landon of Kansas, by a margin of 27.8 million votes to 16.7 million. The Democrats also won huge majorities in the House and Senate. Some observers even worried that the two-party system was about to collapse.

By 1936 Roosevelt and the Democrats had forged what observers have called the "New Deal coalition." This new alliance consisted of the urban masses—especially immigrants from southern and eastern Europe and their sons and daughters—organized labor, the eleven states of the

New Deal Coalition

Confederacy (the "Solid South"), and northern blacks (before the 1930s, most African Americans had voted Republican). With the New Deal coalition, the Democratic Party came to dominate the two-party system and would occupy the White House for most of the next thirty years.

But even Roosevelt's buoyant optimism and landslide victory could not sustain forward momentum in his second term. Some of Roosevelt's own actions, in fact, helped bring about the end of the New Deal.

Concerned that the Supreme Court would invalidate much of the Second Hundred Days legislation, as it had done to the First Hundred Days, Roosevelt concluded that what the federal judiciary needed was a more progressive world-view. His Judiciary Reorganization Bill of 1937 requested the authority to add a federal judge whenever an incumbent failed to retire within six months of reaching age seventy; the president also wanted the power to name up to fifty additional federal judges, including six to the Supreme Court. Roosevelt frankly envisioned using the reorganization as a mandate to create a Supreme Court sympathetic to the New Deal. Liberals joined Republicans and conservative Democrats in resisting the bill, and the president had to concede defeat. The bill he signed into law provided pensions to retiring judges but denied him the power to increase the number of federal judges.

Roosevelt's Court-packing Plan

The episode had a final, ironic twist. During the public debate over court packing, swing-vote justices on the Supreme Court began to vote in favor of liberal, pro–New Deal rulings. In short order the Court upheld both the Wagner Act (*NLRB v. Jones & Laughlin Steel Corp.*), ruling that Congress's power to regulate interstate commerce also involved the power to regulate the production of goods for interstate commerce, and the Social Security Act. Moreover, the new pensions encouraged judges older than seventy to retire, and the president was able to appoint seven new associate justices in the next four years, including notables such as Hugo Black, Felix Frankfurter, and William O. Douglas.

Another New Deal setback was the renewed economic recession of 1937–1939. Roosevelt had never abandoned his commitment to a balanced budget. In 1937, confident that the depression had largely been cured, he began to order drastic cut-

Recession of 1937–1939

backs in government spending. At the same time the Federal Reserve Board, concerned about a 3.6 percent inflation rate, tightened credit. The two actions sent the economy into a tailspin: unemployment climbed from 7.7 million in 1937 to 10.4 million in 1938. Soon Roosevelt resumed deficit financing.

The New Deal was in trouble in 1937 and 1938, and there ensued a wide-ranging ideological struggle to chart the future of liberal reform. Some New Dealers urged vigorous trustbusting; others advocated the resurrection of national economic planning as it had existed under the National Recovery Administration. But in the end Roosevelt rejected these alternatives and instead chose deficit financing as a quick fix to stimulate consumer demand and create jobs. And in 1939, with conflict over events in Europe commanding more and more of the nation's attention, the New Deal came to an end. Roosevelt sacrificed further domestic reforms in return for conservative support for his programs of military rearmament and preparedness. The last significant New Deal laws enacted were the National Housing Act (1937), which established the United States Housing Authority and built housing projects for low-income families; a new Agricultural Adjustment Act (1938); and the Fair Labor Standards Act (1938), which forbade labor by children younger than sixteen and established a minimum wage and forty-hour workweek for many, but by no means all, workers.

Industrial Workers and the Rise of the CIO

 New Deal legislation that gave workers the right to organize unions and bargain collectively invigorated the labor movement. Organizers in the coal fields told miners that "President Roosevelt wants you to join the union"; and join they did. In Woonsocket, Rhode Island, textile workers embraced the union as a right of American citizenship, and they compared it to the independence for which the American revolutionaries had fought. And in Flint, Michigan, a striking auto worker proudly compared his actions to those of Davy Crockett: "Yes sir, Chevy [Plant] No. 4 was my Alamo." Unions and "Americanism" went hand in hand, and workers in need responded. In 1929 union membership stood at 3.6 million; in mid-1938 it surpassed 7 million.

The gains, however, did not always come easily. Management resisted vigorously in the 1930s, relying on the police or hiring armed thugs to intimidate workers and break up strikes. Violence erupted in the steel, automobile, and textile industries and among lumber workers in the Pacific Northwest and teamsters in the Midwest. In 1934 a strike of longshoremen was met with violence by police on the docks of San Francisco; two union members were killed, and workers' anger spread to other industries. Eventually 130,000 workers joined the general strike.

Labor confronted yet another obstacle in the American Federation of Labor (AFL) craft unions' traditional hostility toward industrial unions. Craft unions typically consisted of skilled workers in a particular trade, such as carpentry or plumbing. Industrial unions represented all the workers, skilled and unskilled, in a given industry. The organizational gains of the 1930s were impressive in industrial unions, as hundreds of thousands of workers organized in industries such as autos, garments, rubber, and steel.

Rivalry Between Craft and Industrial Unions

Craft and industrial unions competed bitterly for control of the growing labor movement. Attempts to reconcile the craft and industrial union movements failed; and in 1935 John L. Lewis, a leading industrial unionist and head of the United Mine Workers, resigned as vice president of the AFL. He and other industrial unionists then formed the Committee for Industrial Organization (CIO). The AFL responded by suspending the CIO unions, and in 1938 the CIO held its first national convention, calling itself the Congress of Industrial Organizations. By that time CIO membership had reached 3.7 million, slightly more than the AFL's 3.4 million.

The CIO evolved during the 1930s into a pragmatic, bread-and-butter labor organization that brought together millions of workers, including numerous women and African Americans who never before had had an opportunity to join a union. One union, the United Auto Workers (UAW), scored a major victory in late 1936. The UAW demanded recognition from General Motors (GM), Chrysler, and Ford. When GM refused, workers at the Fisher Body plant in Flint, Michigan, launched a sit-down strike and refused to leave the building. To discourage the strikers, GM turned off

Sit-down Strikes

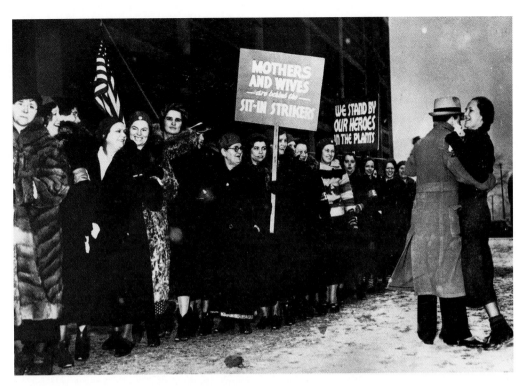

During the 1937 sit-down strike by automobile workers in Flint, Michigan, a women's "emergency brigade" of wives, mothers, daughters, sisters, and sweethearts conducted daily demonstrations at the plants. When the police sought to force the men out of Chevrolet Plant No. 9 by filling it with tear gas, the women armed themselves with clubs and smashed out the plant's windows to let in fresh air.   (Wide World Photos, Inc.)

the heat. When that tactic failed, GM called in the police, who were met by a barrage of steel bolts, coffee mugs, and bottles. The police then resorted to tear gas, and the strikers turned the plant's water hoses on them.

The strike lasted for weeks. General Motors obtained a court order to evacuate the plant, but the strikers stood firm, risking imprisonment and fines. With the support of their families and neighborhoods, and a women's "emergency brigade" that picketed and delivered food and supplies to the strikers, the UAW prevailed. GM agreed to recognize the union. Chrysler signed a similar agreement, but Ford held out for four more years. With these victories, the tactic of the sit-down strike spread dramatically; it was used by workers in the textile, glass, and rubber industries, as well as by dime-store clerks, janitors, dressmakers, and bakers. Most important, participation in the sit-downs gave the strikers self-respect.

In 1937 the Steel Workers Organizing Committee (SWOC) signed a contract with the nation's largest steelmaker, U.S. Steel, that guaranteed an eight-hour workday and a forty-hour workweek. Other steel companies, however, refused to go along. Confrontations between the so-called little steel companies and the SWOC soon led to violence. On Memorial Day, strikers and their families joined sympathizers on the picket line in front of the Republic Steel plant in Chicago. Violence erupted, the police opened fire, ten strikers were killed, and forty suffered gunshot wounds. The police explained that the marchers had attacked them with clubs and bricks and that they had responded with reasonable force to defend themselves and disperse the mob. Some newspapers agreed, among them the anti-labor *Chicago Tribune*, which described the attack as an invasion by "a trained military unit of a revolutionary

Memorial Day Massacre

body." The strikers saw it differently; the police, they argued, without provocation had brutally attacked citizens who were peacefully asserting their constitutional rights.

Though senseless, the Memorial Day Massacre was not surprising. During the 1930s industries had hired private police agents and accumulated large stores of arms and ammunition for use in deterring workers from organizing and joining unions. Meanwhile, the CIO continued to enroll new members. By 1938 industrial unions had enlisted 600,000 miners, 375,000 steelworkers, 400,000 auto workers, and

How do historians know...

that police officers were largely responsible for the 1937 Memorial Day Massacre in Chicago? There is both photographic and medical evidence of the police's culpability. Covering the story at the Republic Steel plant were a cameraman from Paramount News and photographers from *Life* magazine and the Wide World Photos syndicate. Paramount News suppressed its film footage, claiming that releasing it "might very well incite local riots," but an enterprising reporter alerted a congressional committee to its existence, and a private viewing was arranged. Spectators at this showing, the reporter noted, "were shocked and amazed by scenes showing scores of uniformed policemen firing their revolvers pointblank into a dense crowd of men, women, and children, and then pursuing the survivors unmercifully as they made frantic efforts to escape." Medical evidence also substantiated the picketers' version: none of the ten people killed by police had been shot from the front. Clearly, the demonstrators had been trying to flee the police when they were shot or clubbed to the ground.   (Photo: World Wide Photos, Inc.)

300,000 textile workers. By the end of the decade the CIO had succeeded in organizing most of the nation's mass-production industries.

Mixed Progress for People of Color

In 1930 about three-fourths of all African Americans lived in the South. Almost all southern blacks were prohibited from voting or serving on juries. They were routinely denied access to hospitals, universities, public parks, and swimming pools. And they were hired only for the least desirable, most menial jobs. Blacks living in rural areas in the South were propertyless sharecroppers, tenants, or wage hands. Caught in a cycle of poverty and disease, their life expectancy was ten years less than that of whites. The Great Depression plunged the vast majority of African Americans deeper into fear, political disfranchisement, Jim Crow segregation, and privation. And the specter of the lynch mob was a continuing threat in the South: in 1929, seven black men were lynched; in 1930, twenty; in 1933, twenty-four.

Racism also plagued African Americans living in the North. Southern blacks who migrated to northern cities found that employers discriminated against them. Black unemployment rates ran high; in Pittsburgh 48 percent of black workers were jobless in 1933, compared with 31 percent of white laborers. In northern industries in the 1930s, African Americans were the last hired and the first fired.

As African Americans were aware, President Herbert Hoover shared prevailing white racial attitudes.

Hoover and African Americans

Hoover sought a lily-white Republican Party and attempted to push blacks out of the party in order to attract white southern Democrats. He appointed few blacks to federal of-

Numerous African American families were evicted from their farms during the Great Depression. White planters who received government payments for taking land out of cultivation were supposed to share these payments with their tenants and sharecroppers. Instead, many kicked these families off the land and kept the money for themselves. This family in Putnam County, Georgia, loaded all its possessions into a rickety truck for the trip north. (National Archives)

fice, rejected appeals for a federal antilynching law, and perpetuated the segregation of the army and of facilities in federal buildings in the nation's capital. In 1930 the president demonstrated his racial insensitivity by nominating Judge John J. Parker of North Carolina to the Supreme Court. Ten years earlier Parker had endorsed the disfranchisement of blacks. The NAACP remembered and protested his nomination. The AFL joined the protest, and the joint opposition plus liberal votes in the Senate defeated Parker's nomination, 41 to 39.

Scottsboro Trials

Shortly thereafter, a celebrated trial revealed the ugliness of race relations in the depression era. In March 1931 nine African American teenagers who were riding a freight train near Scottsboro, Alabama, were arrested and charged with roughing up some white hoboes and throwing them off the train. Two white women removed from the same train claimed the nine men had raped them. Medical evidence later showed that the women were lying. But within two weeks, eight of the so-called Scottsboro boys were convicted of rape by all-white juries and sentenced to death. After the failure of several appeals, the first defendant, Haywood Patterson, was condemned to die. A Supreme Court ruling intervened, however, on the ground that African Americans were systematically excluded from juries in Alabama. Patterson was found guilty again in 1936 and was given a seventy-five-year jail sentence. Four of the other youths were sentenced to life imprisonment. Not until 1950 were all five out of jail—four by parole and Patterson by escaping from a work gang.

Organized Opposition

The Brotherhood of Sleeping Car Porters, under the astute leadership of A. Philip Randolph, fought for the rights of black workers. In Harlem the militant Harlem Tenants League fought rent increases and evictions, and African American consumers began to boycott white merchants who refused to hire blacks as clerks. Their slogan was "Don't Buy Where You Can't Work." But America's white leaders made few concessions. Only the Supreme Court provided a measure of protection for African Americans at this time. It declared unconstitutional the Texas law that barred blacks from voting in the Democratic primaries, and it attempted to correct the abuse in the Scottsboro trials.

African Americans coped with their white-circumscribed environment and fought racism in a va-

riety of ways. Lawyers for the NAACP, notably Charles Hamilton Houston and Thurgood Marshall, sued southern and border state universities for providing facilities for African American students that were separate, but decidedly unequal. The NAACP was victorious in 1938, when the Supreme Court ruled *(Missouri ex rel. Gaines v. Canada)* that Missouri, by offering a legal education only to qualified white law students, gave whites a "privilege" that was "denied to Negroes by reason of their race." Thus the Supreme Court ordered Missouri to establish a separate law school for its qualified African Americans.

With the election of Franklin D. Roosevelt, blacks' attitudes toward government changed, as did their political affiliation. For African Americans—an important component of the New Deal coalition— Franklin D. Roosevelt would become the most appealing president since Abraham Lincoln. For one thing, Roosevelt was a decided improvement over Hoover, and the personal magnetism and buoyancy he exhibited in his fireside chats seemed to speak directly to them. Blacks also were heartened by photographs of African American visitors at the White House, many of whom came to see Eleanor Roosevelt, and by news stories about Roosevelt's black advisers. Most important, through the WPA and other relief programs, the New Deal aided black people in their struggle for economic survival.

Black Cabinet

The "Black Cabinet," or black brain trust assembled by Roosevelt, was unique in U.S. history. Never before had there been so many African American advisers at the White House. Among the consultants were black lawyers, journalists, and Ph.D.'s and black experts on housing, labor, and social welfare. William H. Hastie and Robert C. Weaver, holders of advanced degrees from Harvard, served in the Department of the Interior. Mary McLeod Bethune, educator and president of the National Council of Negro Women, was director of the Division of Negro Affairs of the National Youth Administration. Also among the New Dealers were some whites who had committed themselves to first-class citizenship for African Americans. Foremost among these people was Eleanor Roosevelt. In 1939, when the acclaimed black contralto Marian Anderson was barred from performing in Washington's Constitution Hall by its owners, the Daughters of the American Revolution, Eleanor Roosevelt arranged for Anderson to sing at the Lincoln Memorial on Easter Sunday.

Mary McLeod Bethune, pictured here with her friend and supporter Eleanor Roosevelt, became the first African American woman to head a federal agency as director of the Division of Negro Affairs of the National Youth Administration.   (Corbis-Bettmann)

The president himself, however, remained uncommitted to African American civil rights. Fearful of alienating southern white Democrats, who controlled Congress and important committees such as the House Ways and Means Committee, he never endorsed two key goals of the civil rights struggle: a federal law against lynching and abolition of the poll tax. Moreover, many New Deal programs functioned in ways that were definitely damaging to African Americans. Rather than benefiting black tenant farmers and sharecroppers, the AAA had the effect of forcing many of them off the land. The Federal Housing Administration (FHA) refused to guarantee mortgages on houses purchased by blacks in white neighborhoods, the CCC was racially segregated, and the TVA followed local custom in handing out skilled jobs to whites first. Also, Social Security coverage and the minimum-wage provisions of the Fair Labor Standards Act of 1938 excluded menial occupations. This meant that janitors, farm workers, and domestics, many of whom were African Americans, received no benefits or protection.

Racism in the New Deal

Since its inception in the 1930s, America's welfare system has privileged white people over people of color, especially African Americans. With the New Deal's racial inequities in mind, the historian George Lipzitz has written that "the racialized nature of social democratic policies has . . . actually increased the possessive investment in whiteness among European Americans over the past half-century." Thus, while New Deal programs were generally inclusive of whites, they persistently excluded large numbers of blacks and other people of color from access to the things that American society defined as essential to first-class citizenship and human dignity, including decent housing and rewarding work.

"The Possessive Investment in Whiteness"

In short, although African Americans benefited from the New Deal, they did not get anything approaching their fair share. Even so, the large majorities they gave Roosevelt at election time demonstrated their appreciation for the aid they did receive. Not all African Americans, however, trusted the mixed message of the New Deal. Some concluded that they could depend only on themselves and organized self-help and direct-action movements. In 1934 black tenant farmers and sharecroppers joined with poor whites to form the Southern Tenant Farmers' Union. In the North, blacks organized tenants' unions, boycotted stores, and launched "Jobs for Negroes" campaigns. In 1935 when police in Harlem beat to death a black youth, a race riot erupted as mobs of poor and angry people smashed store windows and raided shelves. Working-class blacks criticized the NAACP for ignoring the economics of second-class citizenship and for being too middle class and legalistic in its war on racism. The NAACP was scoring notable victories in opening up graduate and professional schools to black students, but critics charged that these gains benefited only the middle class, not the masses who above all needed jobs.

Nowhere was the trend toward direct action more evident than in the March on Washington Movement in 1941. That year, billions of federal dollars flowed

March on Washington Movement

into American war industries as the nation rearmed for the possibility of another world war. Thousands of new jobs were created, but discrimination deprived blacks of a reasonable proportion of them. One executive notified black job applicants that "the Negro will be considered only as janitors and other similar capacities." Randolph, leader of the porters' union, proposed that blacks march on the nation's capital to demand equal access to jobs in defense industries.

By early summer thousands were ready to march. Fearing that the march might provoke riots and that communists might infiltrate the movement, Roosevelt announced that he would issue an executive order prohibiting discrimination in war industries and in the government if the march was canceled. The result was Executive Order No. 8802, which established the Fair Employment Practices Committee (FEPC). The March on Washington Movement anticipated future

In 1940 American Indians in Florida asked John Collier, U.S. commissioner of Indian affairs, to save their deer from slaughter in a government drive to eradicate cattle ticks. Collier (seated and wearing a white shirt) came to Miami to meet with Indians and hear their grievances.   (Wide World Photos, Inc.)

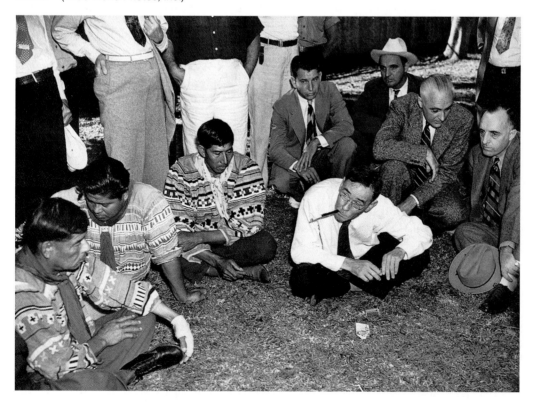

trends in the civil rights movement: it was all-black; its tactic was direct action, a threat by the masses to take to the streets; and its beneficiaries were the urban working class.

Another group, American Indians, sank further into malnutrition and disease during the Hoover administration. In the early 1930s in Oklahoma, where the Choctaws, Cherokees, Seminoles, and other tribes lived on infertile soil, three-fourths of all Native American children were undernourished. Tuberculosis swept through the reservations. At the heart of the problem was a 1929 ruling by the U.S. comptroller general that landless tribes were ineligible for federal aid. Not until 1931 did the Bureau of Indian Affairs take steps to relieve the suffering. A federal relief program was launched to provide aid, and Congress substantially increased the bureau's budget that year; yet much of the money went to hire more bureaucrats.

A New Deal for Native Americans

Beginning in 1933, the New Deal approach to Native Americans differed greatly from that of earlier administrations; as a result, Indians benefited more directly than blacks from the New Deal. As commissioner of Indian affairs, Roosevelt appointed John Collier, founder of the American Indian Defense Association, who sought an end to the allotment policy established by the Dawes Severalty Act of 1887 (see page 467). The Indian Reorganization (Wheeler-Howard) Act (1934) aimed to reverse the increasing landlessness of Native Americans by restoring lands to tribal ownership and forbidding future division of Indian lands into individual parcels. Other provisions of the act enabled tribes to obtain loans for economic development and to establish self-government. Under Collier, the Bureau of Indian Affairs also encouraged the perpetuation of Indian religions and cultures. In a remarkable about-face, one order stated, "The cultural history of Indians is in all respects to be considered equal to that of any non-Indian group."

Mexican Americans also suffered extreme hardship during the Great Depression, but no government programs benefited them. During these years many Mexicans and Mexican Americans packed up their belongings and moved south of the border; some did so willingly, but others were either deported by immigration officials or given one-way tickets to Mexico by California officials eager to purge

Depression Hardships of Mexican Americans

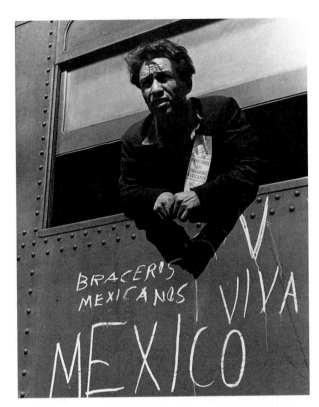

Many Mexican farm workers *(braceros)* were deported in the early 1930s, but by the end of the decade growers eager for the return of this source of cheap labor began to recruit trainloads of Mexicans as farm laborers in southwestern states. This photo, taken by Dorothea Lange in 1938, shows one of these workers.   (Dorothea Lange Collection, Oakland Museum of California, City of Oakland. Gift of Paul S. Taylor)

them from the relief rolls. According to the federal census, the Mexican-born population in the United States dropped from 617,000 in 1930 to 377,000 in 1940.

In addition, many employers changed their minds about the desirability of hiring Mexican American farm workers. Before the 1930s farmers had boasted that Mexican Americans were an inexpensive, docile labor supply and that they would not join unions. But in the 1930s Mexican Americans overturned the stereotype by engaging in prolonged and sometimes bloody strikes. In the San Joaquin valley, eighteen thousand cotton pickers walked off the fields in 1933 and set up a "strike city" after being evicted from the growers' camps. Shortly thereafter, their union hall was riddled with bullets, and two strikers died.

The New Deal offered Mexican Americans little help. The AAA was created to assist property-owning farmers, not migratory farm workers. The Wagner Act did not cover farm workers' unions, nor did the Social Security Act or the Fair Labor Standards Act cover farm laborers. One New Deal agency, the Farm Security Administration (FSA), was established in 1937 to help farm workers, in part by setting up migratory labor camps. But the FSA came too late to help Mexican Americans, most of whom by then had been replaced in the fields by dispossessed white farmers from the Dust Bowl states.

Women, Work, and the Great Depression

During the depression women had to work overtime to maintain themselves and their families. In *It's Up to the Women* (1933), Eleanor Roosevelt wrote that "women know that life must go on and that the needs of life must be met." Wives and mothers followed the maxim "Use it up, wear it out, make it do, or do without." Women bought day-old bread and cheap cuts of meat; they relined old coats with blankets, and they saved string, rags, and broken crockery for future use. Many families were able to maintain their standard of living only because of astute spending and because women substituted their own labor for goods and services they once purchased. Husbands shared these financial concerns, but it was usually women's responsibility to do the family budgeting; it was estimated that wives and mothers in the 1930s allocated over 80 percent of all family income.

While they were cutting corners to make ends meet, women were also seeking paid work outside the home. In 1930 approximately 10.5 million women were paid workers; ten years later, the female labor force exceeded 13 million. Many women were their families' sole providers and had to do it all, at home and on the job. Despite these social realities, most Americans believed that women should not take jobs outside the home, that they should strive instead to be good wives and mothers, and that women who worked were doing so for "pin money" to buy frivolous extras. When a 1936 Gallup poll asked whether wives should work if their husbands had jobs, 82 percent of the respondents (including 75 percent of the women) answered "no."

Women at Work Outside the Home

These attitudes resulted in severe job discrimination. For example, of the fifteen hundred urban school systems surveyed by the National Education Association in 1930 and 1931, 77 percent said that they refused to hire married women as teachers, and 63 percent said that they fired female teachers who married while employed. Most insurance companies, banks, railroads, and public utilities had similar policies against hiring married women. And from 1932 to 1937, federal law prohibited more than one family member from working for the civil service. Because wives usually earned less than their husbands, they were the ones who quit their government jobs.

Job Discrimination Against Married Women

In part, such thinking stemmed from the widely held belief that a woman who worked caused a man to be unemployed. That view missed the point, for three reasons. First, women were heavily concentrated in "women's jobs," including clerical positions, teaching, and nursing. Men rarely sought these jobs and probably would not have been hired to fill them had they applied. Second, most women workers (71 percent in 1930) were single and thus self-supporting. Third, the wages for "women's jobs" trailed far behind those for "men's jobs." Lagging further behind were women of color, some of whom lost their low-paying menial jobs to white women during the depression.

Although the preponderance of working women were single, married women too went to work during the depression. By 1940 married women constituted 35 percent of the female work force, up from 29 percent in 1930 and 15 percent in 1900. They worked to keep their families from slipping into poverty, but their assistance with family expenses did not improve their status. As the sociologists Robert and Helen Lynd observed at the time: "The men, cut adrift from their usual routine, lost most of their sense of time and dawdled helplessly and dully about the streets; while in the homes the women's world remained largely intact and the round of cooking, housecleaning, and mending became if anything more absorbing." And even though women were making greater contributions to the family, their husbands, including those without jobs, still expected to rule the roost and to remain exempt from childcare and housework.

Wives and Husbands Face Hard Times

The New Deal did take women's needs into account, but only when forcefully reminded to do so

**Women in
the New Deal**

by the activist women who advised the administration. These women, mainly government and Democratic Party officials, formed a network united by their commitment to social reform, to protective laws for women's health and safety on the job, and to the participation of women in politics and government. The network's most prominent member was Eleanor Roosevelt, who was her husband's valued adviser. Secretary of Labor Frances Perkins was the nation's first woman cabinet officer. Other historic New Deal appointments included the first woman federal appeals judge and the first women ambassadors. Molly Dewson, head of the Democratic Party's Women's Division, noted with pride: "The

change from women's status in government before Roosevelt is unbelievable."

Even with increased participation by women, however, New Deal provisions for women were mixed. The maximum-hour and minimum-wage provisions mandated by the NRA won women's support. Women workers in the lowest-paying jobs, many of whom labored under sweatshop conditions, had the most to gain from these standards. Some NRA codes mandated pay differentials based on gender, however, making women's minimum wages lower than men's. Federal relief agencies, such as the Civil Works Administration (1933) and the Federal Emergency Relief Administration, hired only one woman for every eight to ten men placed in relief jobs. A popular New Deal

Enacted in 1935, Social Security has been one of the most enduring of all New Deal programs. This poster urges eligible Americans to apply promptly for their Social Security cards.   (Library of Congress)

program, the Civilian Conservation Corps, was limited to young men. And women in agriculture and domestic service were not protected by the 1938 Fair Labor Standards Act.

Most important, the 1935 Social Security Act excluded not only agricultural labor and domestic service, as already noted, but also occupations in the public sector. That meant that many teachers, nurses, librarians, and social workers, the majority of whom were women, went uncovered. Although Social Security originally contained no retirement provisions for spouses or widows, in 1939 Congress added such benefits. But the Social Security amendments of 1939 were also far from inclusive. They were based on the government's unstated social policy of preserving the traditional family in which the husband was the breadwinner and the wife was the stay-at-home caregiver. Accordingly, the Social Security amendments of 1939 provided retirement benefits for women who had been supported by their husbands, including widows, but not for single women who were separated or divorced.

Nevertheless, significant changes in women's lives were imminent. The reason for the changes, however, was not that the government would suddenly decide to address women's equality with men, but that beginning in 1941 the country would be at war—a war it could not win without employing womanpower in the nation's aircraft factories, shipyards, and munitions works.

The Election of 1940 and the Legacy of the New Deal

No president had ever served more than two terms, and as the presidential election of 1940 approached, many Americans speculated about whether Franklin Roosevelt would run for a third term. Roosevelt seemed undecided until the spring of 1940, when Adolf Hitler's military advances in Europe apparently convinced him to stay on.

The Republican candidate was Wendell Willkie, an Indiana lawyer and utilities executive. A former Democrat, Willkie had become a prominent business opponent of Roosevelt's agenda and campaigned vigorously against the New Deal, contending that its meddling in business had failed to return the nation to prosperity. He also criticized the government's lack of military preparedness. But Roosevelt preempted the defense issue by expanding military and naval contracts. As workers streamed into the factories to fill new orders, unemployment figures dropped as well. When Willkie reversed his approach and accused Roosevelt of warmongering, the president promised Americans, "Your boys are not going to be sent into any foreign wars."

Wendell Willkie

Willkie never did come up with an effective campaign issue, and on election day Roosevelt received 27 million popular votes to Willkie's 22 million. In the electoral college Roosevelt buried Willkie 449 to 82 (see Map 25.3). Willkie did manage to win the farm and small-town vote in the Midwest, but the New Deal coalition was triumphant. As in 1936, Roosevelt won in the cities, primarily among blue-collar workers, ethnic Americans, and African Americans. He also carried every state in the South. Although the New Deal was over at home, Roosevelt was still riding a wave of public approval.

Any analysis of the New Deal must begin with Franklin Delano Roosevelt himself. Assessments of his career varied widely during his presidency. Most historians consider him a truly great president, citing his

Map 25.3 Presidential Election, 1940 Roosevelt won an unprecedented third term in the 1940 presidential election. He did not repeat his landslide 1936 victory, in which he won all but two states. But he did capture thirty-eight states in 1940 to Republican Wendell Willkie's ten.

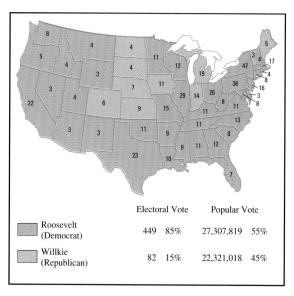

	Electoral Vote		Popular Vote	
Roosevelt (Democrat)	449	85%	27,307,819	55%
Willkie (Republican)	82	15%	22,321,018	45%

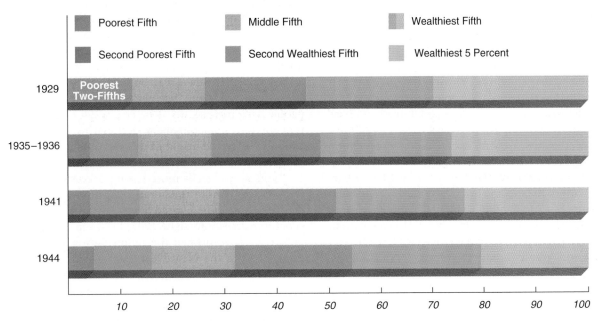

Figure 25.2   Distribution of Total Family Income Among the American People, 1929–1944 (Percentage)   Although the New Deal provided economic relief to the American people, it did not, as its critics so often charged, significantly redistribute income downward from the rich to the poor.   (Source: Adapted from U.S. Bureau of the Census, *Historical Statistics of the United States, Colonial Times to 1970,* 2 parts [Washington, D.C.: U.S. Government Printing Office, 1975], Part 1, p. 301.)

Roosevelt and the New Deal Assessed

courage and buoyant self-confidence, his willingness to experiment, and his capacity to inspire the nation during the most somber days of the depression. Those who criticize him charge that he lacked vision and failed to formulate a bold and coherent strategy of economic recovery and political and economic reform. He was not a socialist but a capitalist: he wanted to alleviate suffering but not at the expense of private property and the profit motive. Essentially he was a pragmatist whose goal was to preserve the system.

Even scholars who criticize Roosevelt's performance agree that he transformed the presidency. "Only Washington, who made the office, and Jackson, who remade it, did more than Roosevelt to raise it to its present condition of strength, dignity, and independence," according to political scientist Clinton Rossiter. Roosevelt personified the presidency, and with his fireside chats he became the first president to use the radio to appeal directly for the people's support. Other scholars, however, have charged that it was Roosevelt who initiated "the imperial presidency." Whether for good or ill, Roosevelt strengthened not only the presidency but the whole federal government. "For the first time for many Americans," the historian William Leuchtenburg has written, "the federal government became an institution that was directly experienced. More than state and local governments, it came to be the government."

In the past, the federal government had served primarily as an economic regulator and facilitator. During

Origins of America's Welfare System

the New Deal the government not only added to its regulatory responsibilities, including overseeing the nation's stock markets, but it became an economic guarantor and stimulator as well. For the first time the federal government assumed a responsibility to offer relief to the jobless and the needy, and for the first time it resorted to deficit spending to stimulate the economy. Millions of Americans benefited from government programs that are still operating today. The New Deal laid the foundation of the welfare system on which subsequent presidential administrations would build.

Although the government's role in the economy expanded under the New Deal, the economy itself continued to be capitalistic. The profit motive and private property remained fundamental to the system. Some redistribution of wealth did result from the New Deal, but the wealthy survived as a class. In 1929, for example, the most affluent 5 percent of the population received 30 percent of total family income. By 1941 their share had shrunk but was still a healthy 24 percent. Most of the income lost by the wealthy ended up in the pockets of the middle and upper-middle classes, not those of the poor (see Figure 25.2). Even the poor, however, would prosper in the years ahead, as the Second World War created jobs for all working Americans.

Summary

The New Deal brought about limited change in the nation's power structure. Beginning in the 1930s, business interests had to share their political clout with others. Labor gained influence in Washington, and farmers got more of what they wanted from Congress and the White House. If people wanted their voices to be heard, they had to organize into labor unions, trade associations, or other special-interest lobbies. Not everybody's voice was heard, however. Because of the persistence of racism, there was no real increase in the power of African Americans and other minorities.

The New Deal was a liberal, evolutionary reform program, not a revolutionary break with the past. Although the New Deal coalition emerged as a political force in the 1930s, New Deal ideas such as the TVA and Social Security had been around for decades. Moreover, prominent New Dealers had been active in reform movements since the Progressive era. Historians generally view the New Deal as a movement that benefited middle-class Americans. According to William Leuchtenburg, the New Deal "swelled the ranks of the bourgeoisie but left many Americans—sharecroppers, slum dwellers, most Negroes—outside of the new equilibrium."

The New Deal failed in one fundamental purpose: to put people back to work. As late as 1939, more than 10 million men and women were still jobless. That year, unemployment was 19 percent; over the next two years it fell no lower than 14 percent. What plagued the nation throughout the 1930s was underconsumption: people and businesses did not purchase enough goods to sustain high levels of employment. In the end it was not the New Deal but massive government spending during the Second World War that put people back to work. In 1941, as a result of mobilization for war, unemployment declined to 10 percent, and in 1944, at the height of the war, only 1 percent of the labor force was jobless.

The New Deal's most lasting accomplishments were its programs to ameliorate the suffering of unemployed people. The United States has suffered several economic recessions since 1945, but even Republican presidents have primed the pump during periods of slump. Before the New Deal, the United States had experienced a major depression every fifteen to twenty years. The Great Depression was the last of its kind. Since the New Deal, thanks to unemployment compensation, Social Security, and other measures, the United States has not experienced another such national nightmare.

LEGACY FOR A PEOPLE AND A NATION
Social Security for Retired Americans

In breaking with historical precedent by authorizing old-age insurance, as well as unemployment compensation and aid to dependent children, the Social Security Act of 1935 became the single most important piece of social welfare legislation in American history. Under Social Security, working Americans today still make monthly payments for old-age, survivors, and disability insurance (OASDI). Although Social Security initially excluded some of America's neediest citizens from participation in OASDI, such as people working in low-paying menial jobs, amendments to the law eased eligibility requirements. Twenty-four million Americans made monthly payments to the OASDI fund in 1939; ten years later, the figure had risen to 34 million. Legislation in the 1950s extended OASDI to self-employed workers, including farmers. By 1970, 69 million Americans were covered under OASDI; by 1980 that number had doubled; and by 1997 the figure had ballooned to 172 million. Prior to the enactment of Social Security, millions of elderly Americans had lived in poverty. But a 1999 study showed that Social Security benefits kept a third of the nation's elderly from slipping into poverty and helped significantly to narrow the income disparities between women and men in old age.

Today, Americans worry about the future of Social Security. They fear that the tens of millions of baby boomers born in the 1940s, 1950s, and early 1960s will bankrupt the system when they retire in the twenty-first century. Many also know that in the 1980s and 1990s the federal government raided the Social Security trust fund, diverting billions of dollars to pay for the skyrocketing national debt. Some reduction of the system's responsibilities has also occurred; in 1996, reflecting Americans' hostility to welfare, Congress passed and President Bill Clinton signed a law eliminating aid to families with dependent children and greatly tightening eligibility requirements for public assistance. The future of Social Security is hotly debated today, both in and out of government. Two of the most important proposals are, first, to allow Americans to invest their retirement contributions in the stock market and, second, to impose a federal "lock box" law that would safeguard Social Security's trust funds from future federal tampering.

For Further Reading, see page A-29 of the Appendix. For Web resources, go to http://college.hmco.com.

In 1921 the Rockefeller Foundation declared war on the mosquito in Latin America. As the carrier of yellow fever, the biting insect *Aedes aegypti* transmitted a deadly virus that caused severe headaches, vomiting, jaundice (yellow skin), and, for many, death. With clearance from the U.S. Department of State, the foundation dedicated several million dollars for projects to control yellow fever in Latin America, beginning with Mexico. Learning from the pioneering work of Carlos Juan Finlay of Cuba, Oswaldo Cruz of Brazil, and U.S. Army surgeon Walter Reed, scientists sought to destroy the mosquito in its larval stage, before it became an egg-laying adult.

Nothing less than U.S. hegemony in the hemisphere seemed at stake. U.S. diplomats, military officers, and business executives agreed with foundation officials that the disease threatened public health, which in turn disturbed political and economic order. When outbreaks occurred, ports were closed and quarantined, disrupting trade and immigration. The infection struck down American officials, merchants, investors, and soldiers stationed abroad. Workers became incapacitated, reducing productivity. Throughout Latin America, insufficient official attention to yellow-fever epidemics stirred public discontent against regimes the United States supported. When the Panama Canal opened its gates to ships from around the world in 1914, some leaders feared that the death-dealing disease would spread, even reinfecting the United States, which had suffered its last epidemic in 1905.

In Veracruz, a Mexican province of significant U.S. economic activity where American troops had invaded in 1914, a yellow-fever outbreak in 1920 killed 235 people. The next year, gradually overcoming strong local anti-U.S. feelings, Rockefeller personnel painstakingly inspected breeding places in houses and deposited larvae-eating fish in public waterworks. In 1924 La Fundación Rockefeller declared yellow fever eradicated in Mexico. In Latin America, the founda-

Officials of the Brazilian Federal Health Service, in cooperation with the Rockefeller Foundation, spray houses in Bahía to control mosquitoes during a campaign in the 1920s to battle yellow fever. (Courtesy of the Rockefeller Archive Center)

26

PEACESEEKERS AND WARMAKERS: AMERICANS IN THE WORLD 1920–1941

tion's antimosquito campaign proved successful in maritime and urban areas but less so in rural and jungle regions. Rockefeller Foundation efforts in the 1920s and 1930s also carried political effects: strengthening central governments by providing a national public health infrastructure and helping diminish anti-U.S. sentiment in a region known for virulent anti-Yankeeism.

The Rockefeller Foundation's drive to eradicate the mosquito exemplifies Americans' fervent but futile effort to build a stable international order between the First and Second World Wars. After World War I, Americans did not cut themselves off from international affairs, despite the tag "isolationist" that is sometimes still applied to U.S. foreign relations during the interwar decades. They remained very active in world affairs in the 1920s and 1930s—from gunboats on Chinese rivers, to negotiations in European financial centers, to marine occupations in Haiti and Nicaragua, to Hollywood films in Great Britain, to oil wells in the Middle East, to campaigns against diseases in Africa and Latin America. President Wilson had it right when he said after the First World War that the United States had "become a determining factor in the history of mankind, and after you have become a determining factor you cannot remain isolated, whether you want to or not."

"Internationalism has come," declared Senator Gilbert Hitchcock, "and we must choose what form the internationalism is to take." The most apt description of interwar U.S. foreign policy is "independent internationalism." That is, the United States was active on a global scale but retained its independence of action, its traditional unilateralism. American interests abroad were far-flung and vast—colonies, client states, naval bases, investments, trade, missionaries, humanitarian projects. Nevertheless, many Americans did think of themselves as isolationists, by which they meant that they wanted no part of Europe's political squabbles, military alliances and interventions, or the League of Nations, which might drag them unwillingly into war. Americans, then, were isolationists in their desire to avoid war but independent internationalists in their activities to shape the world to their liking.

In the aftermath of the First World War, Americans had grown disenchanted with military methods of achieving order and protecting American prosperity and security. "We can never herd the world into the paths of righteousness with the dogs of war," said Herbert Hoover. American diplomats thus increasingly sought to exercise the power of the United States

through conferences, humanitarian programs, cultural penetration ("Americanization"), moral lectures and calls for peace, nonrecognition of disapproved regimes, arms control, and economic and financial ties under the Open Door principle. In Latin America, for example, U.S. leaders downgraded military interventions to fashion a Good Neighbor policy.

But a stable world order proved elusive. Some nations schemed to disrupt it, and severe economic problems undercut it. Public health projects saved countless lives but could not address the low living standards and staggering poverty of dependent peoples across the globe. The debts and reparations bills left over from the First World War bedeviled the 1920s, and the Great Depression of the 1930s shattered world trade and finance. The depression threatened America's prominence in international markets; it also spawned revolutions in Latin America and political extremism, militarism, and war in Europe and Asia. As Nazi Germany marched toward world war, the United States tried to protect itself from the conflict by adopting a policy of neutrality. At the same time, the United States sought to defend its interests in Asia against Japanese aggression by invoking the Open Door policy.

In the late 1930s, and especially after the outbreak of European war in September 1939, many Americans came to agree with President Franklin D. Roosevelt that Germany and Japan imperiled the national interest because they were building exclusive, self-sufficient spheres of influence based on military power and economic domination. Roosevelt first pushed for American military preparedness and then for the abandonment of neutrality in favor of aiding Britain and France. A German victory in Europe, he reasoned, would undermine Western political principles, destroy traditional economic ties, threaten U.S. influence in the Western Hemisphere, and place at the pinnacle of European power a fanatical man—Adolf Hitler—whose ambitions and barbarities seemed limitless.

At the same time, Japan seemed determined to dismember America's Asian friend China, to emasculate the Open Door principle by creating a closed economic sphere in Asia, and to endanger a U.S. colony—the Philippines. To deter Japanese expansion in the Pacific, the United States ultimately cut off supplies of vital American products such as oil. But economic warfare only intensified antagonisms. Japan's surprise attack on Pearl Harbor, Hawai'i, in December 1941 finally brought the United States into the Second World War. ∎

IMPORTANT EVENTS

1921–22 Washington Conference limits naval arms
Rockefeller Foundation begins battle against yellow fever in Latin America

1922 Mussolini comes to power in Italy
Fordney-McCumber Tariff raises duties

1924 Dawes Plan eases German reparations
U.S. troops leave Dominican Republic

1926 U.S. troops occupy Nicaragua

1927 Jiang breaks with Communists in China

1928 Kellogg-Briand Pact outlaws war

1929 Great Depression begins
Young Plan reduces German reparations

1930 Hawley-Smoot Tariff raises duties

1931 Japan seizes Manchuria

1932 Stimson Doctrine protests Japanese control of Manchuria
Roosevelt elected president

1933 Hitler establishes Nazi regime in Germany
U.S. recognizes Soviet Union
Good Neighbor policy for Latin America

1934 Batista comes to power in Cuba
Export-Import Bank founded to expand trade
Johnson Act forbids loans to debt-defaulting countries
Reciprocal Trade Agreements Act lowers tariffs
U.S. troops withdraw from Haiti

1935 Italy invades Ethiopia
Neutrality Act stops U.S. arms shipments

1936 U.S. votes for nonintervention at Pan-American Conference
Germany reoccupies the Rhineland
Spanish Civil War breaks out between Loyalists and Franco's fascists

Neutrality Act forbids U.S. loans to belligerents
Rome-Berlin Axis created
Germany and Japan unite against Soviet Union in the Anti-Comintern Pact

1937 Neutrality Act creates cash-and-carry trade with warring nations
Sino-Japanese War breaks out
Quarantine speech against aggressors
Ponce Massacre in Puerto Rico

1938 Mexico nationalizes American-owned oil companies
Munich Conference grants part of Czechoslovakia to Germany

1939 Nazi-Soviet Pact carves up eastern Europe
Germany invades Poland
Second World War begins
U.S. repeals arms embargo to help Allies

1940 Soviet Union invades Finland
Germany invades Denmark, Belgium, the Netherlands, and France
Committee to Defend America by Aiding the Allies formed
Germany, Italy, and Japan join in Tripartite Pact
U.S. and Great Britain swap destroyers for military bases
Isolationists form America First Committee
Selective Training and Service Act starts first peacetime draft

1941 Lend-Lease Act gives aid to Allies
Germany attacks Soviet Union
U.S. freezes Japanese assets
Atlantic Charter produced at Roosevelt-Churchill meeting
Roosevelt exploits *Greer* incident
Japanese flotilla attacks Pearl Harbor, Hawai'i
U.S. enters Second World War

Searching for Peace and Order in the 1920s

 In the early 1920s Secretary of State Charles Evans Hughes predicted that "there will be no permanent peace unless economic satisfactions are enjoyed." Like the nation's business leaders, Hughes expected Ameri-can economic expansion to promote international stability—that is, out of economic prosperity would spring a world free from political extremes, revolution, arms races, aggression, and war.

The First World War left Europe in shambles. Between 1914 and 1921, Europe suffered 60 million casualties from world war, civil war, massacre, epidemic, and famine. Germany and France both lost 10

percent of their workers. Crops, livestock, factories, trains, forests, bridges—little was spared. The American Relief Administration and private charities delivered food to needy Europeans, including Russians wracked by famine in 1921 and 1922. Americans hoped not only to feed desperate Europeans but also to dampen any appeal political radicalism might have for them.

The Women's Peace Union (WPU) distributed this flier in the 1920s to remind Americans of the human costs of the First World War. One of many peace societies active in the interwar years, the WPU lobbied for a constitutional amendment requiring a national referendum on a declaration of war. In the 1930s Representative Louis Ludlow (Democrat of Indiana) worked to pass such a measure in Congress, but he failed.   (Schwimmer-Lloyd Collection, Freida Langer Lazarus Papers. The New York Public Library, Astor, Lenox, and Tilden Foundations)

War Is a Crime Against Humanity

Gassed; Near Dun-sur-Meuse, in the Woods, France

To you who are filled with horror at the sufferings of war-ridden mankind;

To you who remember that **ten million men** were slaughtered in the last war;

To you who have the courage to face the reality of **war, stripped of its sentimental "glory"**;

We make this appeal:—

Eight years since the signing of the Armistice! And peace is still hard beset by preparations for war. In another war men, women and children would be more wantonly, more cruelly massacred, by death rays, gas, disease germs, and machines more fiendish than those used in the last war. Those whom you love must share in its universal destruction.

Can You Afford Not To Give Your Utmost To Cleanse The World Of This Black Plague Of Needless Death and Suffering?

Send your contribution to an uncompromising Peace organization

THE WOMEN'S PEACE UNION
39 Pearl Street, New York

We Believe that Violence and Bloodshed Are Always Wrong in Principle and Disastrous in Practice. We Are working to Make War Illegal and to Ensure World Peace.

Senator Henry Cabot Lodge gloated in 1920 that "we have destroyed Mr. Wilson's League of Nations and . . . we have torn up Wilsonism by the roots." Not quite. The Geneva-headquartered League of Nations, envisioned as a peacemaker, did prove feeble, not just because the United States did not join but because members failed to utilize the new organization to settle important disputes. And, starting in the mid-1920s, American officials participated discreetly in League meetings on public health, prostitution, drug and arms trafficking, counterfeiting of currency, and other questions. American jurists served on the Permanent Court of International Justice (World Court), though the United States also refused to join that League body. The Rockefeller Foundation donated $100,000 a year to the League to support its work in public health.

American peace societies worked for international stability, many of them keeping alive the Wilsonian preference for a world body. During the interwar years, peace groups such as the Fellowship of Reconciliation and the National Council for Prevention of War drew widespread public support. Women peace advocates gravitated to several of their own organizations because they lacked influence in the male-dominated groups and because of the popular assumption that women—as life givers and nurturing mothers—had a unique aversion to violence and war. Carrie Chapman Catt's moderate National Conference on the Cure and Cause of War, formed in 1924, and the more radical U.S. Section of the Women's International League for Peace and Freedom (WILPF), organized in 1915 under the leadership of Jane Addams and Emily Greene Balch, became the largest women's peace groups (see page 639). When Addams won the Nobel Peace Prize in 1931, she transferred her award money to the League of Nations.

Peace Groups

Most peace groups pointed to the carnage of the First World War and the futility of war as a solution to international problems, but they differed over strategies to ensure world order. Some urged cooperation with the League and World Court. Others championed the arbitration of disputes, disarmament and arms reduction, the outlawing of war, and strict neutrality during wars. The WILPF called for an end to U.S. economic imperialism, which, the organization claimed, compelled the United States to intervene militarily in Latin America to protect U.S. business interests. The Women's Peace Union (organized in 1921) lobbied for a constitutional amendment to require a national referendum on a declaration of war. The Carnegie Endowment for International Peace (founded in 1910) promoted peace education through publications. Quakers, YMCA officials, and Social Gospel clergy in 1917 created the American Friends Service Committee to identify pacifist alternatives to warmaking. All in all, peaceseekers believed that their various reform activities could and must deliver a world without war.

The Washington Conference of November 1921– February 1922 seemed to mark a substantial step toward peace through arms control. At the invitation of the United States, delegates from Britain, Japan, France, Italy, China, Portugal, Belgium, and the Netherlands joined U.S. diplomats to discuss limits on naval armaments. Britain, the United States, and Japan were facing a naval arms race whose huge military spending endangered economic rehabilitation. American leaders also worried that an expansionist Japan, with the world's third largest navy, would overtake the United States, ranked second behind Britain.

Washington Conference on the Limitation of Armaments

The conference produced three treaties. The Five-Power Treaty set a ten-year moratorium on the construction of capital ships (battleships and aircraft carriers) and established total tonnage limits of 500,000 for Britain and the United States, 300,000 for Japan, and 175,000 for France and Italy. The first three nations actually agreed to dismantle some existing vessels to satisfy the 5:3:1.75 ratio. They also pledged not to build new fortifications in their Pacific possessions (such as the Philippines). In the Nine-Power Treaty, the conferees reaffirmed the Open Door in China, recognizing Chinese sovereignty. In the Four-Power Treaty, the United States, Britain, Japan, and France agreed to respect one another's Pacific possessions. The three treaties did not limit submarines, destroyers, or cruisers; nor did they provide enforcement powers for the Open Door declaration.

Peace advocates also welcomed the Locarno Pact of 1925, several agreements among European nations that sought to reduce tensions between Germany and France, and the Kellogg-Briand Pact of 1928. In the latter document, sixty-two nations agreed to "condemn recourse to war for the solution of international controversies, and renounce it as an instrument of national policy." The accord passed the Senate 85 to 1, but many senators

Kellogg-Briand Pact

French Foreign Minister Aristide Briand (1862–1932) *(left)* and U.S. Secretary of State Charles Evans Hughes (1862–1948) join other diplomats at the Washington Conference of 1921–1922, where they negotiated a naval arms control agreement. Years later Briand helped craft the Kellogg-Briand Pact outlawing war. A graduate of Brown University and Columbia Law School, Hughes also served on the Supreme Court at two different times: 1910–1916 (associate justice) and 1930–1941 (chief justice). Conservative and reserved (Theodore Roosevelt called him "the bearded iceberg"), Hughes argued that the United States must be internationalist, leading the world to respect law and order.   (National Archives)

considered it little more than a statement of moral preference because it lacked enforcement provisions. Although weak, the Kellogg-Briand Pact reflected popular opinion that war was barbaric and wasteful, and the agreement stimulated serious public discussion of peace and war. But arms limitations, peace pacts, and efforts by peace groups and international institutions all failed to muzzle the dogs of war, which fed on the economic troubles that upended world order.

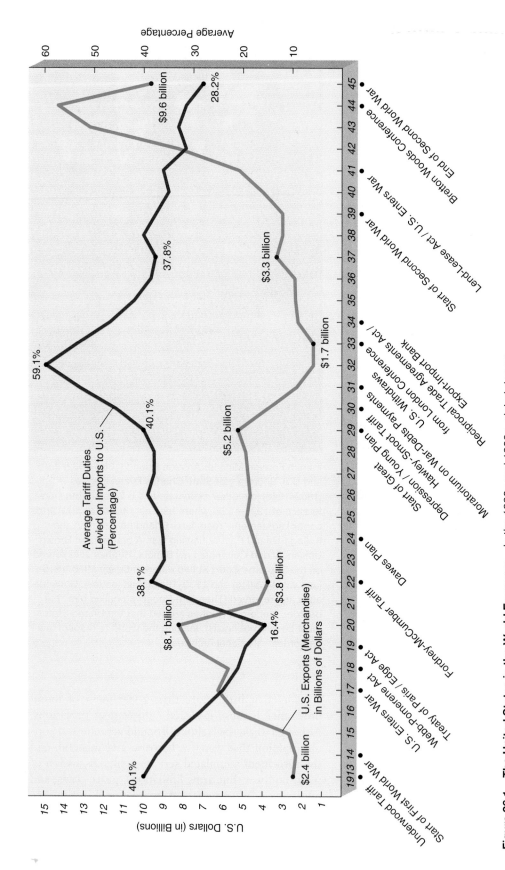

Figure 26.1 The United States in the World Economy In the 1920s and 1930s, global depression and war scuttled the United States's hope for a stable economic order. This graph suggests, moreover, that high American tariffs meant lower exports, further impeding world trade. The Reciprocal Trade Agreements program initiated in the early 1930s was designed to ease tariff wars with other nations. (Source: U.S. Bureau of the Census, *Historical Statistics of the United States, Colonial Times to 1970* [Washington, D.C., 1975].)

The World Economy, Cultural Expansion, and Great Depression

 While Europe struggled to recover from the ravages of the First World War, the international economy wobbled and then, in the early 1930s, collapsed. The Great Depression set off a political chain reaction that carried the world to war. Cordell Hull, secretary of state under President Franklin D. Roosevelt from 1933 to 1944, often pointed out that political extremism and militarism sprang from maimed economies. "We cannot have a peaceful world," he warned, "until we rebuild the international economic structure." Hull proved right.

For leaders such as Hughes and Hull, who believed that economic expansion by the United States would

U.S. Trade and Investment

stabilize world politics, America's prominent position in the international economy seemed opportune. Because of World War I, the United States became a creditor nation and the financial capital of the world (see Figure 26.1). From 1914 to 1930, private investments abroad grew fivefold to more than $17 billion. By the late 1920s the United States produced nearly half of the world's industrial goods and ranked first among exporters ($5.2 billion worth of shipments in 1929). For example, General Electric invested heavily in Germany, American companies began to exploit Venezuela's rich petroleum resources, and U.S. firms began to challenge British control of oil resources in the Middle East. Britain and Germany lost ground to American businesses in Latin America, where Standard Oil operated in eight nations and the United Fruit Company became a huge landowner.

America's economic prominence facilitated the export of American culture. Hollywood movies saturated the global market and stimulated interest in American ways and

Cultural Expansion

products. In Britain, where American silent and talkie films dominated, one woman from a mining town recalled seeing on the screen "all these marvelous [American] film stars. Everything was bright. I just wanted to go there and be like them." Although some foreigners warned against "Americanization," others aped American mass-production methods and emphasis on efficiency and modernization. Coca-Cola opened a bottling plant in Essen, Germany, and Ford built an automobile assembly plant in Cologne. The German writer Hans Joachim claimed that this cultural adop-

tion might help deliver a peaceful, democratic world because "our interest in elevators, radio towers, and jazz was . . . an attitude that wanted to convert the flame thrower into a vacuum cleaner." Germans marveled at Henry Ford's economic success and industrial techniques ("Fordismus"), buying out copies of his translated autobiography, *My Life and Work* (1922). In the 1930s, the Nazi leader Adolf Hitler sent German car designers to Detroit before he launched the Volkswagen. Further advertising the American capitalist model were the Phelps-Stokes Fund, exporting to black Africa Booker T. Washington's Tuskegee philosophy of education, and the Rockefeller Foundation, battling diseases in Latin America and Africa, supporting colleges to train doctors in Lebanon and China, and funding medical research and nurses' training in Europe.

The U.S. government assisted this cultural and economic expansion. The Webb-Pomerene Act (1918) excluded from antitrust prosecution those combinations set up for export trade; the Edge Act (1919) permitted American banks to open foreign branch banks; and the overseas offices of the Department of Commerce gathered and disseminated valuable market information. The federal government also stimulated foreign loans by American investors, discouraging those that might be used for military purposes. "In these days of competition," an American diplomat explained, "capital, trade, agriculture, labor, and statecraft all go hand in hand if a country is to profit." U.S. government support for the expansion of the telecommunications industry helped International Telephone and Telegraph (ITT), Radio Corporation of America (RCA), and the Associated Press (AP) become international giants by 1930. The U.S. Navy's cooperation with Juan T. Trippe's Pan American airline company helped its "flying boats" reach Asia.

Europeans watched American economic expansion with wariness and branded the United States stingy for its handling of World War

War Debts and German Reparations

I debts and reparations. Twenty-eight nations became entangled in the web of inter-Allied government debts, which totaled $26.5 billion ($9.6 billion of it owed to the U.S. government). Europeans owed private American creditors another $3 billion. Europeans urged Americans to erase the government debts as a magnanimous contribution to the war effort. During the war, they angrily charged, Europe had bled while America profited. "There is only one way we could be worse with the Europeans," remarked the humorist Will

John D. Rockefeller, Jr. (1874–1960), second from right, traveled to China in 1921 for the dedication of the Peking Union Medical College, a project of the Rockefeller Foundation, the philanthropic organization founded in 1913 by the oil industrialist John D. Rockefeller, Sr. At the center of this photograph is Xu Shi Chang (1855–1939), China's president.   (Courtesy of the Rockefeller Archive Center)

Rogers, "and that is to have helped them out in two wars instead of one." American leaders insisted on repayment, some pointing out that the victorious European nations had gained vast territory and resources as war spoils. Senator George Norris of Nebraska, emphasizing domestic priorities, declared that the United States could build highways in "every county seat" if only the Europeans would pay their debts.

The debts question became linked to Germany's $33 billion reparations bill—an amount some believed Germany had the capacity but not the willingness to pay. In any case, hobbled by inflation and economic disorder, Germany began to default on its payments. To keep the nation afloat and to forestall the radicalism that might thrive on economic troubles, American bankers loaned millions of dollars. A triangular relationship developed: American investors' money flowed to Germany, Germany paid reparations to the Allies, and the Allies then paid some of their debts to the United States. The American-crafted Dawes Plan of 1924 greased the financial tracks by reducing Germany's annual payments, extending the repayment period, and providing still more loans. The United States also gradually scaled down Allied obligations, cutting the debt by half during the 1920s.

But the triangular arrangement depended on continued German borrowing in the United States, and in

1928 and 1929 American lending abroad dropped sharply in the face of more lucrative opportunities in the stock market at home (see Chapters 24 and 25). The U.S.-negotiated Young Plan of 1929, which reduced Germany's reparations, salvaged little as the world economy sputtered and collapsed. That year Britain rejected an offer from President Herbert Hoover to trade its total debt for British Honduras (Belize), Bermuda, and Trinidad. By 1931, when Hoover declared a moratorium on payments, the Allies had paid back only $2.6 billion. Staggered by the Great Depression—an international catastrophe—they defaulted on the rest. Annoyed with Europe, Congress in 1934 passed the Johnson Act, which forbade U.S. government loans to foreign governments in default on debts owed to the United States.

As the depression accelerated, tariff wars revealed a reinvigorated economic nationalism. By 1932 some twenty-five nations had retaliated against rising American tariffs (created in the Fordney-McCumber Act of 1922 and the Hawley-Smoot Act of 1930) by imposing higher rates on foreign imports. From 1929 to 1933, world trade declined in value by some 40 percent. Exports of American merchandise slumped from $5.2 billion to $1.7 billion.

Tariffs and Economic Nationalism

Many nations contributed to the worldwide economic cataclysm. The United States might have lowered its tariffs so that Europeans could sell their goods in the American market and thus earn dollars to pay off their debts. Americans also might have worked for a comprehensive, multinational settlement. Instead, at the London Conference in 1933, President Roosevelt barred U.S. cooperation in international currency stabilization. Vengeful Europeans might have trimmed Germany's huge indemnity. The Germans might have borrowed less from abroad and taxed themselves more. The Soviets might have agreed to pay rather than repudiate Soviet Russia's $4 billion debt.

A revival of world trade, Secretary Hull insisted, not only would help the United States pull itself out of the economic doldrums but also would boost the chances for global peace. Calling the protective tariff the "king of evils," he successfully pressed Congress to pass the Reciprocal Trade Agreements Act in 1934. This important legislation empowered the president to reduce U.S. tariffs by as much as 50 percent through special agreements with foreign countries. The central feature of the act was the most-favored-nation principle, whereby the United States was entitled to the lowest tariff rate set by any nation with which it had an agreement. If, for example, Belgium and the United States granted each other most-favored-nation status, and Belgium then negotiated an agreement with Germany that reduced the Belgian tariff on German typewriters, American typewriters would receive the same low rate.

Reciprocal Trade Agreements Act

In 1934 Hull also helped create the Export-Import Bank, a government agency that provided loans to foreigners for the purchase of American goods. The bank stimulated trade and became a diplomatic weapon, allowing the United States to exact concessions through the approval or denial of loans. But in the short term, Hull's ambitious programs—examples of America's independent internationalism—brought only mixed results.

U.S. Hegemony in Latin America

Through the Platt Amendment, Roosevelt Corollary, Panama Canal, military intervention, and economic preeminence the United States had thrown an imperial net over Latin America in the early twentieth century (see Chapter 22). U.S. hegemony in the hemisphere

Cordell Hull (1871–1955) served as secretary of state from 1933 to 1944, concentrating on trade expansion, relations with Latin America, and negotiations with Japan. A Tennessean, Hull became known for his methodical style, hill-country drawl and lisp, and deep commitment to the premise that wars grow out of international economic competition. President Franklin Roosevelt, who relied on friends for advice and sent personal envoys on overseas diplomatic missions, often ignored Hull. (Brown Brothers)

grew apace after the First World War. A prominent State Department officer patronizingly remarked that Latins were incapable of political progress because of their "low racial quality." They were, however, "very easy people to deal with if properly managed." And managed they were. American-made schools, roads, telephones, and irrigation systems dotted Caribbean and Central American nations. American "money doctors" in Colombia and Peru helped reform tariff and tax laws and invited U.S. companies to build public works. Washington forced private high-interest loans on the Dominican Republic and Haiti as ways to wield influence there. In El Salvador, Honduras, and Costa Rica, the State Department pressed governments to silence anti-imperialist intellectuals. U.S. soldiers occupied Cuba, the Dominican Republic, Haiti, Panama,

Map 26.1 The United States and Latin America Between the Wars The United States often intervened in other nations to maintain its hegemonic power in Latin America, where nationalists resented outside meddling in their sovereign affairs. The Good Neighbor policy decreased U.S. military interventions, but U.S. economic interests remained strong in the hemisphere.

and Nicaragua. U.S. authorities maintained Puerto Rico as a colony (see Map 26.1).

By 1929 direct American investments in Latin America (excluding bonds and securities) totaled $3.5 billion, while U.S. exports dominated the trade of the area. Country after country experienced the repercussions of U.S. economic and political decisions. For example, the price that Americans set for Chilean copper determined the health of Chile's economy. North American oil executives bribed Venezuelan politicians for tax breaks. Latin American nationalists protested that their resources were being drained away as profits for U.S. companies, leaving too many nations in a status of dependency. A distinguished Argentine writer, Manuel Ugarte, asserted that the United States had become a new Rome that annexed wealth rather than territory, but unapologetic Americans believed that they were bringing not only material improvements to Latin American neighbors but also the blessings of liberty.

Criticisms of U.S. Interventionism

Criticism of U.S. imperialism in the region mounted in the interwar years. The president of Panama, a country dominated by the Canal Zone and, in 1925, occupied by U.S. military forces seeking to put down a popular revolt, told a diplomat that he was tired of being "treated" by Washington "like a child." Senator William Borah of Idaho urged that Latin Americans be granted the right of self-determination, letting them decide their own futures. Others charged that U.S. presidents were usurping constitutional power by ordering troops abroad without a congressional declaration of war. Businesspeople feared that Latin American nationalists would direct their anti-Yankee feelings against American-owned property. Some Americans also became troubled by the double standard that prevailed. Hoover's secretary of state, Henry L. Stimson, acknowledged the problem in 1932 when he was protesting Japanese incursions in China: "If we landed a single soldier among those South Americans now . . . it would put me absolutely in the wrong in China, where Japan has done all this monstrous work under the guise of protecting her nationals with a landing force."

Renouncing unpopular military intervention, the United States shifted to other methods to maintain its influence in Latin America: Pan-Americanism, support for strong local leaders, the training of national guards, economic and cultural penetration, Export-Import Bank loans, financial supervision, and political

Good Neighbor Policy

subversion. Although this general approach predated his presidency, Franklin D. Roosevelt gave it a name in 1933: the Good Neighbor policy. It meant that the United States would be less blatant in its domination—less willing to defend exploitative business practices, less eager to launch military expeditions, and less reluctant to consult with Latin Americans. "Give them a share," Roosevelt recommended. In 1936, for example, the United States restored some sovereignty to Panama and increased that nation's income from the canal. Such acts greatly enhanced Roosevelt's popularity in Latin America.

To avoid military interventions and occupations, the United States trained Latin American national guards and supported dictators. For example, before the United States withdrew its troops from the Dominican Republic in 1924, U.S. per-

National Guards and Dictators

This U.S. government recruiting poster captured the postwar American mood of independent internationalism by offering overseas duty to prospective marines.   (Library of Congress)

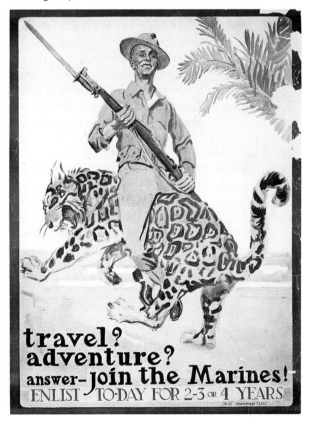

travel?
adventure?
answer- **join the Marines!**
ENLIST TO-DAY FOR 2-3 OR 4 YEARS

sonnel created a guard. One of its first officers was Rafael Leonidas Trujillo, who became head of the national army in 1928 and, through fraud and intimidation, became president two years later. Trujillo ruled the Dominican Republic with an iron fist until his assassination in 1961. "He may be an S.O.B.," Roosevelt supposedly remarked, "but he is our S.O.B."

Nicaraguans endured a similar experience. U.S. troops occupied Nicaragua from 1912 to 1925 and returned in late 1926 during a civil war. Nationalistic, anti-imperialist Nicaraguan opposition, led by César Augusto Sandino, who denounced the Monroe Doctrine as meaning "America for the Yankees," prompted Washington to end the occupation and move toward the Good Neighbor policy. In 1933 the marines departed, but they left behind a powerful national guard headed by General Anastasio Somoza, who "always played the game fairly with us," recalled a top U.S. officer. With backing from the United States, the Somoza family ruled Nicaragua from 1936 to 1979 through corruption, political suppression, and torture. The revolutionaries who overthrew the Somoza dictatorship in 1979 called themselves Sandinistas in honor of the patriot Sandino, who, more than three decades earlier, had battled the marines before he was assassinated by Somoza henchmen.

The marine occupation of black, French-speaking Haiti from 1915 to 1934 also left a negative legacy.

Marine Occupation of Haiti

U.S. officials censored the Haitian press, manipulated elections, wrote the constitution, jailed or killed protesters, managed government finances, and created a national guard. The National City Bank of New York became the owner of the Haitian Banque Nationale, and the United States became Haiti's largest trading partner. The American high commissioner, General John H. Russell of Georgia, boasted that the Haitian president "has never taken a step without first consulting me." In 1929 Haitians protested violently against foreign rule. U.S. soldiers withdrew, and Haiti continued to suffer Latin America's highest illiteracy rate, lowest per capita income, and poorest health, as well as dictatorship and police-state repression.

The Cubans, too, grew restless under North American domination. By 1929 North American investments in the Caribbean nation totaled $1.5 billion, including two-thirds ownership of the sugar industry. The U.S. military uniform remained conspicuous at the Guantá-

Backing Batista in Cuba

namo naval base. Especially among elites, American influences continued to permeate Cuban culture. In 1933 Cubans rebelled against the dictator and U.S. ally Gerardo Machado. In open defiance of U.S. warships cruising offshore, Professor Ramón Grau San Martín became president and declared the Platt Amendment null and void. His government also seized some North American–owned mills, refused to repay American bank loans, and debated land reform. Unsettled by this nationalistic "social revolution," U.S. officials plotted with army sergeant Fulgencio Batista to overthrow Grau in 1934.

During the Batista era, which lasted until Fidel Castro dethroned Batista in 1959 (see page 847), Cuba attracted and protected U.S. investments while it aligned itself with U.S. foreign policy goals. In return, the United States provided military aid and Export-Import Bank loans, abrogated the unpopular Platt Amendment, and gave Cuban sugar a favored position in the U.S. market. Cuba became further incorporated into the North American consumer culture, and American tourists flocked to Havana's night life of rum, rhumba, prostitution, and gambling. Nationalistic Cubans protested that their nation had become a mere extension—a dependency—of the United States.

In Puerto Rico throughout the 1920s and 1930s, incompetent and often tactless U.S. officials on the Caribbean island disparaged Puerto Ricans as people of color unfit to govern themselves. The Jones Act of 1916 had granted Puerto Ricans U.S. citizenship, but the United States rejected calls for the colony's independence or statehood. A few absentee American landowners and corporate barons made sugar the island's major economic activity. Under U.S. paternalism, schools and roads were improved, but 80 percent of the island's rural folk remained landless, and others crowded into urban slums. New Deal relief programs fell far short of need. Students, professors, and graduates of the Universidad de Puerto Rico formed the nucleus of islanders critical of U.S. tutelage. Some founded the Nationalist Party under the leadership of the Harvard-trained lawyer Pedro Albizo Campos, who eventually advocated the violent overthrow of U.S. rule. Police fired on a Nationalist Party march in 1937; nineteen people, including two policemen, died in the Ponce Massacre. Other Puerto Ricans followed the socialist Luis Muñoz Marín, whose Popular Democratic Party ultimately settled for the compromise of commonwealth status (officially conferred in 1952). To this day,

Control over Puerto Rico

Puerto Ricans remain divided into statehood, commonwealth, and independence factions (see page 631).

Mexico stood as a unique case in inter-American relations. Woodrow Wilson had sent troops there in 1914 and 1916 to tame the Mexican Revolution's anti-Americanism. But the opposite occurred. In 1917 the Mexicans openly threatened American-owned landholdings and oil interests by adopting a new constitution specifying that all "land and waters" and all subsoil raw materials (such as petroleum) belonged to the Mexican nation. U.S. officials worried that if Mexico succeeded in restricting the ownership of private property, other Latin Americans might also defy U.S. hegemony. For years, with some Americans claiming that Mexico had succumbed to Bolshevism, and Hollywood films disparagingly portraying Mexicans as villainous "greasers" and *bandidos*, Washington and Mexico City wrangled over the rights of U.S. economic interests. Still, the United States stood as Mexico's chief trading partner, accounting for 61 percent of Mexico's imports and taking 52 percent of its exports in 1934.

Clash with Mexican Nationalism

In 1938, during a petroleum workers' strike for higher wages and recognition, foreign oil companies, including Standard Oil, arrogantly rejected union appeals, hoping to send a message across the hemisphere that economic nationalism could never succeed. In a statement of economic independence, the Mexican government led by President Lázaro Cárdenas boldly expropriated the property of all foreign-owned petroleum companies, calculating that the approaching war in Europe would restrain the United States from attacking his country. The United States countered by reducing purchases of Mexican silver and promoting a multinational business boycott against the nation. But President Roosevelt decided to compromise because he feared that the Mexicans would increase oil sales to Germany and Japan. In a 1942 agreement the United States conceded that Mexico owned its raw materials and could treat them as it saw fit, and Mexico compensated the companies for their lost property. Although American investments in and trade with Mexico remained large, U.S. power there had been diminished. Nationalists across Latin America drew inspiration from Mexico's defiance of its giant neighbor.

Roosevelt's movement toward nonmilitary methods—the Good Neighbor policy—was also expressed in Pan-Americanism. Throughout the 1920s the United States had refused to renounce its self-declared

Ambassador Josephus Daniels (1862–1948) *(second from left)* and Mexican President Lázaro Cárdenas (1895–1970) *(second from right)* enjoy a cordial moment during the often stormy relations between the United States and Mexico in the 1930s. When Cárdenas attempted to regain control of his nation's oil resources from multinational corporations through expropriation, Daniels defended him as a "New Dealer" seeking to improve his country's living standards. Accepting Daniels's description and calling Cárdenas "one of the few Latin leaders who was actually preaching and trying to practice democracy," President Roosevelt compromised with Mexico in 1941.   (Library of Congress)

Pan-Americanism

right of intervention in the hemisphere. In 1936, however, at the Pan-American Conference in Buenos Aires, U.S. officials endorsed nonintervention. The new policy marked a distinct change from the Roosevelt Corollary and marine expeditions. One payoff was the Declaration of Panama (1939), in which Latin American governments drew a security line around the hemisphere and warned aggressors away. In exchange for more U.S. trade and foreign aid, Latin Americans also reduced their sales of raw materials to Germany, Japan, and Italy and increased shipments to the United States. On the eve of the Second World War, then, the U.S. sphere of influence in the hemisphere seemed intact, and most Latin American regimes backed U.S. diplomatic objectives. For a long time, however, memories of American strong-arm methods fueled nationalism throughout the region.

Nazi Germany, the Soviet Union, and War in Europe

In depression-wracked Germany, Adolf Hitler came to power in 1933. Like Benito Mussolini, who had gained control of Italy in 1922, Hitler was a fascist. Fascism (called Nazism, or National Socialism, in Germany) was a collection of ideas and prejudices that celebrated supremacy of the state over the individual; of dictatorship over democracy; of authoritarianism over freedom of speech; of a regulated, state-oriented economy over a free-market economy; and of militarism and war over peace. The Nazis vowed not only to revive German economic and military strength but also to cripple communism and "purify" the German "race" by destroying Jews and other people, such as homosexuals and Gypsies, whom Hitler disparaged as inferiors.

The German leader Adolf Hitler (1889–1945) is surrounded in this propagandistic painting by images that came to symbolize hate, genocide, and war: Nazi flags with emblems of the swastika, the iron cross on the dictator's pocket, Nazi troops in loyal salute. The anti-Semitic Hitler denounced the United States as a "Jewish rubbish heap" of "inferiority and decadence" that was "incapable of conducting war."   (U.S. Army Center of Military History)

Resentful of the punitive terms of the 1919 Treaty of Versailles, Hitler immediately withdrew Germany from the League of Nations, ended reparations payments, and began to rearm. While secretly laying plans for the conquest of neighboring states, he watched admiringly as Mussolini's troops invaded the African nation of Ethiopia in 1935. The next year Hitler ordered his own goose-stepping troopers into the Rhineland, an area that the Versailles treaty had demilitarized. When Germany's timid neighbor France did not resist this act, Hitler crowed: "The world belongs to the man with guts!"

German Aggression Under Hitler

Soon the aggressors joined hands. In 1936 Italy and Germany formed an alliance called the Rome-Berlin Axis. Shortly thereafter Germany and Japan united against the Soviet Union in the Anti-Comintern Pact. To these events Britain and France responded with a policy of appeasement, hoping to curb Hitler's expansionist appetite by permitting him a few territorial nibbles. The policy of appeasing Hitler proved disastrous, for the hate-filled German leader continually raised his demands.

In those hair-trigger times, a civil war in Spain soon turned into an international struggle. Beginning in 1936, the Loyalists defended Spain's elected republican government against Francisco Franco's fascist movement. About three thousand American volunteers, known as the Abraham Lincoln Battalion of the "International Brigades," joined the fight on the side of the Loyalist republicans, which also had the backing of the Soviet Union. Hitler and Mussolini sent military aid to Franco, who won in 1939, tightening the grip of fascism on the European continent.

Early in 1938 Hitler once again tested the limits of European tolerance when he sent soldiers into Austria to annex the nation of his birth. Then in September he seized the Sudeten region of Czechoslovakia. Appeasement reached its apex that month when France and Britain, without consulting the Czechs, agreed at Munich to allow Hitler this territorial bite. British Prime Minister Neville Chamberlain returned home to proclaim "peace in our time," confident that Hitler was satiated. In March 1939 Hitler swallowed the rest of Czechoslovakia (see Map 26.3 on page 749).

The Munich Conference

The Nazi leader next eyed another neighbor, Poland. Scuttling appeasement, London and Paris an-

Poland and the Outbreak of World War II

nounced that they would stand by their ally Poland. Undaunted, Berlin signed the Nazi-Soviet Pact with Moscow in August. Soviet leader Joseph Stalin believed that the West's appeasement of Hitler had left him no choice but to cut a deal with the Nazi ruler. But Stalin also coveted territory: a top-secret protocol attached to the pact carved eastern Europe into German and Soviet zones and permitted the Soviets to grab half of Poland and the three Baltic states of Lithuania, Estonia, and Latvia, formerly part of the Russian empire. On September 1 Hitler launched *blitzkrieg* (lightning war) attacks—highly mobile land forces and armor combined with tactical aircraft—against Poland. Britain and France declared war on Germany two days later. So started the Second World War.

As the world hurtled toward war, Soviet-American relations remained embittered. During the 1920s the United States refused to open diplomatic relations with the Soviet government, which had failed to pay $600 million for confiscated American-owned property and had repudiated preexisting Russian debts. To many Americans, the Communists ranked as godless, radical malcontents bent on destroying the American way of life through world revolution. American businesses such as General Electric and International Harvester nonetheless entered the Soviet marketplace. Henry Ford signed a contract in 1929 to build an automobile plant there. By 1930 the Soviet Union had become the largest buyer of American farm and industrial equipment.

In the early 1930s, when trade began to slump, some American business leaders lobbied for diplomatic recognition of the Soviet Union. "We

U.S. Recognition of the Soviet Union

would recognize the Devil with a false face if he would contract for some pitchforks," quipped the humorist Will Rogers. President Roosevelt himself concluded that nonrecognition had failed to alter the Soviet system, and he speculated that closer Soviet-American relations might deter Japanese expansion. In 1933 Roosevelt granted U.S. diplomatic recognition to the Soviet Union in return for Soviet agreement to discuss the debts question, to forgo subversive activities in the United States, and to grant Americans in the Soviet Union religious freedom and legal rights. The first U.S. embassy in Moscow opened in 1934, but relations soon deteriorated. Stalin's brutalities against his people and the

Nazi-Soviet Pact of August 1939 outraged many Americans—further evidence for them that Europe had gone mad once again.

Isolationism, Neutrality Acts, and Roosevelt's Cautious Foreign Policy

As authoritarianism, race hatred, and military expansion swept over Europe in the 1930s, Americans sought to distance themselves from the tumult by embracing isolationism, whose key elements were abhorrence of war, limited military intervention abroad, and freedom of action in international relations. Americans had learned powerful negative lessons from the First World War: war damages reform movements, undermines civil liberties, dangerously expands federal and presidential power, disrupts the economy, and accentuates racial and class tensions (see Chapter 23). A 1937 Gallup poll found that nearly two-thirds of the respondents thought U.S. participation in World War I had been a mistake.

Conservative isolationists feared higher taxes and increased executive power if the nation went to war again. Liberal isolationists worried

Variety of Isolationist Views

that domestic problems might go unresolved as the nation spent more on the military. Many isolationists predicted that in attempting to spread democracy abroad or to police the world, Americans would lose their freedoms at home. The vast majority of isolationists opposed fascism and condemned aggression, but they did not think the United States should have to do what Europeans themselves refused to do: block Hitler.

Isolationist sentiment was strongest in the Midwest and among anti-British ethnic groups, especially Americans of German or Irish descent, but it was a nationwide phenomenon that cut across socioeconomic, ethnic, party, and sectional lines and attracted a majority of the American people. Prominent isolationists in the 1930s included Republicans such as Representative Hamilton Fish of New York, Senator William Borah of Idaho, and former president Herbert Hoover; Democrats such as Representative Maury Maverick of Texas; Socialists such as Norman Thomas; Communists and Nazi sympathizers; and pacifists such as Representative Jeannette Rankin of Montana. They also included the publisher Robert R. McCormick of the *Chicago Tribune*, the historian Charles Beard, the physicist Albert Einstein, and the anti-Semitic radio priest Charles E. Coughlin. University students in 1936 organized the Veterans of Future Wars and asked for a bonus of $1,000 before going into battle because, they mockingly proclaimed, few would live through the next war. These dissimilar people united in the opinion that alternatives to American participation in another European war existed.

Nye Committee Hearings

Some isolationists charged that corporate "merchants of death" had promoted war and were assisting the aggressors. After Dorothy Detzer of the WILPF diligently lobbied Senator Gerald P. Nye to take up the issue, a congressional committee held hearings from 1934 to 1936 on the role of business and financiers in the U.S. decision to enter the First World War. The Nye committee did not prove that American munitions makers had dragged the nation into that war, but it did uncover evidence that corporations practicing "rotten commercialism" had bribed foreign politicians to bolster arms sales in the 1920s and 1930s and had lobbied against arms control.

Isolationists grew suspicious of American business ties with Nazi Germany and fascist Italy that might endanger U.S. neutrality. Twenty-six of the top one hundred American corporations, including Du Pont, Standard Oil, and General Motors, had contractual agreements in 1937 with German firms. And after Italy attacked Ethiopia in 1935, American petroleum, copper, and scrap iron and steel exports to Italy increased substantially, despite Roosevelt's call for a moral embargo on such commerce. A Dow Chemical official stated: "We do not inquire into the uses of the products. We are interested in selling them." Not all American executives thought this way. The Wall Street law firm of Sullivan and Cromwell, for example, severed lucrative ties with Germany to protest the Nazi persecution of Jews.

Neutrality Acts

Reflecting the popular desire for distance from Europe's disputes, President Roosevelt signed a series of neutrality acts. Congress sought to protect the nation by outlawing the kinds of contacts that had compromised U.S. neutrality during World War I. The Neutrality Act of 1935 prohibited arms shipments to either side in a war once the president had declared the existence of belligerency. Roosevelt had wanted the authority to name the aggressor and apply an arms embargo against it alone, but Congress would not grant the president such discretionary power. The Neutrality Act of 1936 forbade loans to belligerents. After a joint resolution in 1937 declared the United States neutral in the Spanish Civil War, Roosevelt embargoed arms shipments to both sides. The Neutrality Act of 1937 introduced the cash-and-carry principle: warring nations wishing to trade with the United States would have to pay cash for their nonmilitary purchases and carry the goods from U.S. ports in their own ships. The act also forbade Americans from traveling on the ships of belligerent nations.

Roosevelt's Evolving Views

President Roosevelt shared isolationist views in the early 1930s. Although prior to World War I he was an expansionist and interventionist like his older cousin Theodore, during the interwar period Roosevelt talked less about preparedness and more about disarmament and the horrors of war, less about policing the world and more about handling problems at home. In a passionate speech delivered in August 1936 at Chautauqua, New York, Roosevelt expressed prevailing isolationist opinion and made a pitch for the pacifist vote in the upcoming election: "I have seen war.... I have seen blood running from the wounded. I have seen men coughing out their gassed lungs.... I have seen the agony of mothers and wives. I hate war." The United States, he promised, would remain unentangled in the European conflict. During the crisis over Czechoslovakia in 1938 Roosevelt endorsed appeasement and greeted the Munich accord with a "universal sense of relief."

All the while, Roosevelt grew troubled by the arrogant behavior of Germany, Italy, and Japan—aggressors he tagged the "three bandit nations." He condemned the Nazi persecution of the Jews and the Japanese slaughter of Chinese civilians. Privately he chastised the British and French for failing to collar Hitler. Because he worried that the United States was ill prepared to confront the aggressors, his New Deal public works programs included millions for the construction of new warships. In 1935 the president requested the largest peacetime defense budget in American history. Three years later, in the wake of Munich, he asked Congress for funds to build up the air force, which he believed essential to deter aggression. Pressed hard by Roosevelt in early 1938, the House of Representatives defeated a constitutional amendment proposed by Indiana Democrat Louis Ludlow to require a majority vote in a national refer-

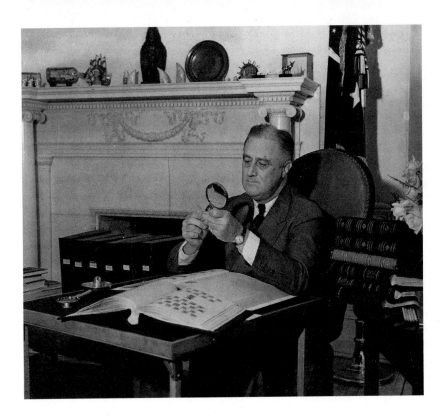

President Franklin D. Roosevelt relaxes with his favorite hobby, stamp collecting, from which he said he learned history and geography. During World War II he once showed British Prime Minister Winston Churchill a stamp from "one of your colonies." Churchill asked: "Which one?" Roosevelt replied: "One of your last. . . . You won't have them much longer, you know." (Franklin D. Roosevelt Library)

endum before a congressional declaration of war could go into effect (unless the United States were attacked). In January 1939 the president secretly decided to sell bombers to France, saying privately that "our frontier is on the Rhine." Although the more than five hundred combat planes delivered to France did not deter war, French orders spurred growth of the U.S. aircraft industry.

In early 1939 the president lashed out at the international lawbreakers and urged Congress to repeal the arms embargo and permit the sale of munitions to belligerents on a cash-and-carry basis. Roosevelt knew that repeal would aid Britain, which dominated the seas. When the Senate Foreign Relations Committee voted down repeal, Roosevelt raged: "I think we ought to introduce a bill for statues of [Senators] Austin, Vandenberg, Lodge and Taft . . . to be erected in Berlin and put the swastika on them." Feeling hampered by the isolationists, the president moved gradually toward a more interventionist posture, step by step, measuring public opinion while trying to change it. As a consummate politician, he developed a leadership style of caution, not wanting to get too far out front of popular isolationist sentiment. Roosevelt also liked to keep his options open. One scholar has likened him to a college professor who prefers to teach without a syllabus.

When Europe descended into the abyss of war in September 1939, Roosevelt declared neutrality and pressed again for repeal of the arms embargo. Isolationist senator Arthur Vandenberg of Michigan roared back that the United States could not be "an arsenal for one belligerent without becoming a target for the other." After much debate, however, Congress in November lifted the embargo on contraband and approved cash-and-carry exports of arms. Using "methods short of war," Roosevelt thus began to aid the Allies. Hitler sneered that a "half Judaized, half negrified" United States was "incapable of conducting war."

Repeal of the Arms Embargo

Japan, China, and a New Order in Asia

While Europe succumbed to political turmoil and war, Asia suffered the aggressive march of Japan. The United States had interests at stake in Asia: the Philippines and Pacific islands, religious missions, trade and investments, and the Open Door in China. In traditional missionary fashion, Americans also believed that they were China's special friend and protector. "With God's help," Senator Kenneth Wherry of Nebraska once proclaimed, "we will lift Shanghai up and up, ever up, until it is just like Kansas City." Pearl Buck's best-selling novel *The Good Earth* (1931), made into a widely distributed film six years later, countered prevailing images of the very different—and thus deviant—"heathen Chinee" by representing the Chinese as noble, persevering peasants. The daughter of Presbyterian missionaries, Buck helped shift negative American images of China to positive ones. By contrast, the aggressive Japan loomed as a threat to American attitudes and interests. The Tokyo government seemed bent on subjugating China and unhinging the Open Door doctrine of equal trade and investment opportunity.

The Chinese themselves were uneasy about the U.S. presence in Asia. Like the Japanese, they wished to reduce the influence of westerners. The Chinese Revolution of 1911 still rumbled in the 1920s as anti-foreign riots damaged American property and imper-

William E. Borah (1865–1940), chair of the Senate Foreign Relations Committee (*left*), and Henry L. Stimson (1867–1950), secretary of state (*right*), often clashed over foreign policy even though both were Republicans. The Idaho senator became a passionate anti-imperialist and isolationist who protested U.S. interventions abroad. Because of critics such as Borah, Stimson grew eager to find nonmilitary means to maintain U.S. hegemony in the Western Hemisphere.   (Corbis-Bettmann)

iled American missionaries. Chinese nationalists criticized Americans for the imperialist practice of extraterritoriality (the exemption of foreigners accused of crimes from Chinese legal jurisdiction), and they demanded an end to this affront to Chinese sovereignty.

In the late 1920s, civil war broke out in China when Jiang Jieshi (Chiang Kai-shek) ousted Mao Zedong and his Communist followers

Jiang Jieshi

from the ruling Guomindang Party. Americans applauded this display of anti-Bolshevism and Jiang's conversion to Christianity in 1930. Jiang's new wife, Soong Meiling, also won their hearts. American-educated, Madame Jiang spoke flawless English, dressed in Western fashion, and cultivated ties with prominent Americans. Warming to Jiang, U.S. officials abandoned one imperial vestige by signing a treaty in 1928 restoring control of tariffs to the Chinese. U.S. gunboats and marines still remained in China to protect American citizens and property.

The Japanese grew increasingly suspicious of U.S. ties with China. In the early twentieth century, Japanese-American relations steadily deteriorated as Japan gained influence in Manchuria, Shandong, and Korea. The Japanese sought not only to oust Western imperialists from Asia but also to dominate Asian territories that produced the raw materials that their import-dependent island nation required. The Japanese also resented the discriminatory immigration law of 1924, which excluded them from emigrating to the United States. Secretary Hughes urged Congress not to pass the act; when it rejected his counsel, he sadly called the law "a lasting injury" to Japanese-American relations. Despite the Washington Conference treaties, naval competition continued. Also, although the volume of Japanese-American trade was twice that of Chinese-American trade, commercial rivalry strained relations between Japan and the United States. The importation of inexpensive Japanese goods, especially textiles, spawned "Buy America" campaigns and boycotts.

Relations further soured in 1931 after the Japanese military seized Manchuria in China (see Map 26.2). Larger than Texas, Manchuria

Manchurian Crisis

served Japan both as a buffer against the Soviets and as a vital source of coal, iron, timber, and food. More than half of Japan's foreign investments rested in Manchuria. "We are seeking room that will let us breathe," said a Japanese politician, ar-

Map 26.2   Japanese Expansion Before Pearl Harbor   The Japanese quest for predominance began at the turn of the century and intensified in the 1930s. China suffered the most at the hands of Tokyo's military. Vulnerable U.S. possessions in Asia and the Pacific proved no obstacle to Japan's ambitions for a Greater East Asia Co-Prosperity Sphere.

guing that his heavily populated island nation (65 million people in an area slightly smaller than California) needed to expand in order to survive. Although the seizure of Manchuria violated the Nine-Power Treaty and the Kellogg-Briand Pact, the United States did not have the power to compel Japanese withdrawal, and the League of Nations did little but debate. The American response came as a moral lecture known as the Stimson Doctrine: the United States would not recognize any impairment of China's sovereignty or of the Open Door policy, Secretary Stimson declared in 1932. He himself later described his policy as largely "bluff."

Japan continued to harry China. In mid-1937 the Sino-Japanese War erupted. Japanese forces seized cities and bombed civilians. The gruesome bombing of Shanghai intensified anti-Japanese sentiment in the United States. Senator Norris, an isolationist who

moved further away from isolationism with each Japanese thrust, condemned the Japanese as "disgraceful, ignoble, barbarous, and cruel, even beyond the power of language to describe." In an effort to help China by permitting it to buy American arms, Roosevelt refused to declare the existence of war, thus avoiding activation of the Neutrality Acts.

In a speech denouncing the aggressors on October 5, 1937, the president called for a "quarantine" to curb the "epidemic of world lawlessness."

Roosevelt's Quarantine Speech

People who thought Washington had been too gentle with Japan cheered. Isolationists warned that the president was edging toward war. On December 12 Japanese aircraft sank the American gunboat *Panay*, an escort for Standard Oil Company tankers on the Yangtze River. Two American sailors died during the attack. Roosevelt was much relieved when Tokyo apologized and offered to pay for damages.

Japan's declaration of a "New Order" in Asia, in the words of one American official, "banged, barred, and bolted" the Open Door. Alarmed, the Roosevelt administration during the late 1930s gave loans and sold military equipment to the Chinese. Secretary Hull declared a moral embargo on the shipment of airplanes to Japan. Meanwhile, the U.S. Navy continued to grow, aided by a billion-dollar congressional appropriation in 1938. In mid-1939 the United States abrogated its trade treaty with Tokyo, yet Americans continued to ship oil, cotton, and machinery to Japan. The administration hesitated to initiate economic sanctions because such pressure might spark a Japanese-American war at a time when Germany posed a more serious threat and the United States was unprepared for war. When war broke out in Europe in fall 1939, Japanese-American relations were stalemated.

On a Collision Course with Japan and Germany, 1939–1941

President Roosevelt remarked in 1939 that the United States could not "draw a line of defense around this country and live completely and solely to ourselves." Thomas Jefferson had tried that with his 1807 embargo—"the damned thing didn't work" and "we got into the War of 1812." America, the president insisted, could not insulate itself from world war. Polls showed that Americans strongly favored the Allies and that most supported aid to Britain and France, but the great majority emphatically wanted the United States to remain at peace. Troubled by this conflicting advice—oppose Hitler, aid the Allies, but stay out of the war—the president gradually moved the nation from neutrality to undeclared war against Germany and then, after the Japanese attack on Pearl Harbor, to full-scale war itself.

Because the stakes were so high, Americans vigorously debated the direction of their foreign policy from 1939 through 1941. Unprecedented numbers of Americans spoke out on foreign affairs and joined organizations that addressed the issues. Spine-chilling events and the widespread use of radio, the nation's chief source of news, helped stimulate this high level of public interest. So did ethnic affiliations with the various belligerents and victims of aggression. The American Legion, the

Foreign Policy Debate

Stand Fast! America

William Randolph Hearst's newspaper, the *San Francisco Examiner,* reflected the publisher's isolationist views in 1939 at the outbreak of World War II. Here the United States is depicted as an island of peace and democracy in a mad, menacing world. (*San Francisco Examiner,* Oct. 8, 1939)

League of Women Voters, labor unions, and local chapters of the Committee to Defend America by Aiding the Allies and the isolationist America First Committee (both organized in 1940) provided outlets for citizen participation in the national debate. African American churches organized anti-Italian boycotts to protest Mussolini's pummeling of Ethiopia.

In March 1940 the Soviet Union invaded Finland. In April Germany invaded Denmark and Norway (see Map 26.3). "The small countries are smashed up, one by one, like matchwood," sighed Winston Churchill, who became Britain's prime minister on May 10, 1940, the day Germany attacked Belgium, the Netherlands, and France. German divisions ultimately pushed French and British forces back to the English Channel. At Dunkirk, France, between May 26 and June 6, more than three hundred thousand Allied soldiers frantically escaped to Britain on a flotilla of small boats. The Germans occupied Paris a week later. A new French government located in the town of Vichy decided to collaborate with the conquering Nazis and, on June 22, surrendered France to Berlin. With France knocked out of the war,

The Fall of France

Map 26.3   The German Advance, 1939–1942   Hitler's drive to dominate Europe pushed German troops deep into France and the Soviet Union. Great Britain took a beating but held on with the help of American economic and military aid before the United States itself entered the Second World War in late 1941.

the German Luftwaffe (air force) launched massive bombing raids against Great Britain in preparation for a full-scale invasion. Stunned Americans asked, Could Washington or New York be the Luftwaffe's next target?

Alarmed by the swift defeat of one European nation after another, Americans gradually shed their isolationist sentiment. Some liberals left the isolationist fold; it became more and more the province of conservatives. Emotions ran high. Roosevelt called the isolationists "ostriches" and charged that some were pro-Nazi subversives. The White House began to turn over to the Federal Bureau of Investigation letters criticizing Roosevelt's foreign policy.

After Roosevelt tried futilely to draw the belligerents to the peace table, he told his advisers that he was "not willing to fire the first shot" but was waiting for some incident to bring the United States into the war.

In the meantime, assuring Americans that New Deal reforms would not have to be sacrificed to achieve military preparedness, Roosevelt began to aid the beleaguered Allies to prevent the fall of Britain. In May 1940 he ordered the sale of old surplus military equipment to Britain and France. In July he cultivated bipartisan support by naming Republicans Henry L. Stimson and Frank Knox, ardent backers of aid to the Allies, secretaries of war and the navy respectively. In September, by executive agreement, the president traded fifty over-age American destroyers for leases to eight British military bases, including Newfoundland, Bermuda, and Jamaica.

Two weeks later Roosevelt signed into law the hotly debated and narrowly passed Selective Training and Service Act, the first peacetime military draft in American history. The act called for the registration of all men between the ages of twenty-one and thirty-

First Peacetime Military Draft

five. Soon more than 16 million men had signed up, and draft notices began to be delivered. Meanwhile, Roosevelt won reelection in November 1940 with promises of peace: "Your boys are not going to be sent into any foreign wars." Republican candidate Wendell Willkie, who in the emerging spirit of bipartisanship had not made an issue of foreign policy, snapped, "That hypocritical son of a bitch! This is going to beat me!" It did.

Roosevelt claimed that the United States could stay out of the war by enabling the British to win. The United States, he said, must become the "great arsenal of democracy." In January 1941 Congress debated the president's Lend-Lease bill. Because Britain was broke, the president explained, the United States should lend rather than sell weapons, much as a neighbor lends a garden hose to fight a fire. Roosevelt's analogy did not persuade strict isolationist Senator Burton K. Wheeler of Montana, who shouted out another comparison: Lend-Lease was "the New Deal's triple A foreign policy; it will plow under every fourth American boy." But in March 1941, with pro-British sentiment running high, the House passed the Lend-Lease Act by 317 votes to 71; the Senate followed with a 60-to-31 tally. The initial appropriation was $7 billion, but by the end of the war the amount had reached $50 billion, more than $31 billion of it for Britain.

Lend-Lease Act

To ensure the safe delivery of Lend-Lease goods, Roosevelt ordered the U.S. Navy to patrol halfway across the Atlantic, and he sent American troops to Greenland. In July, arguing that Iceland was also essential to the defense of the Western Hemisphere, the president dispatched marines there. He also sent Lend-Lease aid to the Soviet Union, which Hitler had attacked in June. If the Soviets could hold off two hundred German divisions in the east, Roosevelt calculated, Britain would gain some breathing time. Churchill, who had long thundered against Communists, now applauded aid to the Soviets: "If Hitler invaded Hell, I would make at least a favorable reference to the Devil in the House of Commons."

In August 1941 Churchill and Roosevelt met for four days on a British battleship off the coast of Newfoundland. They got along well, trading naval stories and enjoying the fact that Churchill was half American. The two leaders issued the Atlantic Charter, a set of war aims reminiscent of Wilsonianism (see page 637): collective security, disarmament, self-determination, economic cooperation, and freedom of the seas. Churchill later recalled that the president told him in Newfoundland that he could not ask Congress for a declaration of war against Germany but "he would wage war" and "become more and more provocative."

Atlantic Charter

On September 4, 1941, came an incident that Roosevelt could exploit. In the Atlantic, a German submarine launched torpedoes at (but did not hit) the American destroyer *Greer*, after it had cooperated with British patrol bombers that dropped depth charges on the submarine (see page 755). Roosevelt declared that the German vessel, without warning, had fired first. Henceforth, he said, the U.S. Navy would shoot on sight. He also announced a policy he already had promised Churchill in private: American warships would convoy British merchant ships across the ocean.

***Greer* Incident**

Thus the United States entered into an undeclared naval war with Germany. When in early October a German submarine torpedoed the U.S. destroyer

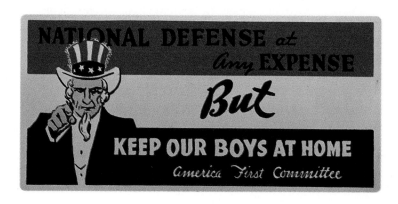

The isolationist America First Committee published this bumper sticker in 1941 in a vain attempt to halt the United States's descent into war. America Firsters organized in September 1940 and attracted many prominent members, including the famed aviator Charles Lindbergh. (Herbert Hoover Presidential Library)

President Franklin D. Roosevelt *(left)* and British Prime Minister Winston Churchill (1874–1965) confer on board a ship near Newfoundland during their summit meeting of August 1941. During the conference, they signed the Atlantic Charter. Upon his return to Great Britain, Churchill told his advisers that Roosevelt had promised to "wage war" against Germany and do "everything" to "force an incident."   (Franklin D. Roosevelt Library)

Kearny off the coast of Iceland, the president announced that "the shooting has started. And history has recorded who fired the first shot." Later that month, when the destroyer *Reuben James* went down with the loss of more than one hundred American lives, Congress scrapped the cash-and-carry policy and further revised the Neutrality Acts to permit transport of munitions to Britain on armed American merchant ships. The United States was edging very close to full-scale war in Europe.

Why War Came: Pearl Harbor and U.S. Entry into World War II

In retrospect, it seems ironic that the Second World War came to the United States by way of Asia. Roosevelt had wanted to avoid war with Japan in order to concentrate American resources on the defeat of Germany. In September 1940, after Germany, Italy, and Japan had signed the Tripartite Pact, Roosevelt slapped an embargo on shipments of aviation fuel and scrap metal to Japan. Because the president believed the Japanese would consider a cutoff of oil a life-or-death matter, he did not embargo that vital commodity. But after Japanese troops occupied French Indochina in July 1941, Washington froze Japanese assets in the United States, virtually ending trade (including oil) with Japan. "The oil gauge and the clock stood side by side" for Japan, wrote one observer.

Tokyo recommended a summit meeting between President Roosevelt and Prime Minister Prince Konoye, but the United States rejected the idea. American officials insisted that the Japanese first agree to respect China's sovereignty and territorial integrity and to honor the Open Door policy—in short, to get out of China. According to polls taken in fall 1941, the American people seemed willing to risk war with Japan to thwart further aggression. For Roosevelt, Europe still claimed first priority, but he supported Secretary Hull's hard-line policy against Japan's pursuit of the Greater East Asia Co-Prosperity Sphere—the name

U.S. Demands on Japan

Tokyo gave to the vast Asian region it intended to dominate.

Roosevelt told his advisers to string out ongoing Japanese-American talks to gain time—time to fortify the Philippines and check the fascists in Europe. By breaking the Japanese diplomatic code and deciphering intercepted messages through Operation MAGIC, American officials learned that Tokyo's patience with diplomacy was fast dissipating (see page 763). In late November the Japanese rejected American demands that they withdraw from Indochina. An intercepted message that American experts decoded on December 3 instructed the Japanese embassy in Washington to burn codes and destroy cipher machines—a step suggesting that war was coming. Secretary Stimson explained later that the United States let Japan fire the first shot so as "to have the full support of the Ameri-

can people" and "so that there should remain no doubt in anyone's mind as to who were the aggressors."

The Japanese plotted a daring raid on Pearl Harbor in Hawai'i. An armada of sixty Japanese ships, with a core of six carriers bearing 360 airplanes, crossed 3,000 miles of the Pacific Ocean. To avoid detection, every ship maintained radio silence.

Surprise Attack on Pearl Harbor

In the early morning of December 7, some 230 miles northwest of Honolulu, the carriers unleashed their planes, each stamped with a red sun representing the Japanese flag. They swept down on the unsuspecting American naval base and nearby airfields, dropping torpedoes and bombs and strafing buildings.

The battleship U.S.S. *Arizona* fell victim to a Japanese bomb that ignited explosives below deck,

The stricken U.S.S. *West Virginia* was one of eight battleships caught in the surprise Japanese attack at Pearl Harbor, Hawai'i, on December 7, 1941. In this photograph, sailors on a launch attempt to rescue a crew member from the water as oil burns around the sinking ship.   (U.S. Army)

killing more than one thousand sailors. The U.S.S. *Nevada* tried to escape the inferno by heading out to sea, but a second wave of aerial attackers struck the ship. Altogether the invaders sank or damaged eight battleships and many smaller vessels and smashed more than 160 aircraft on the ground. Huddled in an air-raid shelter, sixteen-year-old Mary Ann Ramsey watched the injured come in "with filthy black oil covering shredded flesh. With the first sailor, so horribly burned, personal fear left me; he brought me the full tragedy of the day." A total of 2,403 died; 1,178 were wounded. By chance, three aircraft carriers at sea escaped the disaster. The Pearl Harbor tragedy, from the perspective of the war's outcome, amounted to a military inconvenience more than a disaster.

How could the stunning attack on Pearl Harbor have happened? After all, American cryptanalysts had broken the Japanese diplomatic code.

Explaining Pearl Harbor

Although the intercepted Japanese messages told policymakers that war lay ahead, the intercepts never revealed naval or military plans and never specifically mentioned Pearl Harbor. Roosevelt did not, as some critics charged, conspire to leave the fleet vulnerable to attack so that the United States could enter the Second World War through the "back door" of Asia. The base at Pearl Harbor was not on red alert because a message sent from Washington warning of the imminence of war had been too casually transmitted by a slow method and had arrived too late. Base commanders were too relaxed, believing Hawai'i too far from Japan to be a target for all-out attack. Like Roosevelt's advisers, they expected an assault against British Malaya, Thailand, or the Philippines (see Map 26.2). The Pearl Harbor calamity stemmed from mistakes and insufficient information, not from conspiracy.

On December 8, referring to the previous day as "a date which will live in infamy," Roosevelt asked Congress for a declaration of war against Japan. He noted that the Japanese had also attacked Malaya, Hong Kong, Guam, the Philippines, Wake, and Midway, and he expressed the prevailing sense of revenge when he vowed that Americans would never forget "the character of the onslaught against us." A unanimous vote in the Senate and a 388-to-1 vote in the House thrust America into war. Representative Jeannette Rankin of Montana voted "no," repeating her vote against entry into the First World War.

Three days later, Germany and Italy, honoring the Tripartite Pact they had signed with Japan in September 1940, declared war against the United States. "Hitler's fate was sealed," Churchill later wrote. "Mussolini's fate was sealed. As for the Japanese, they would be ground to powder. . . . I went to bed and slept the sleep of the saved and thankful." On January 1, 1942, the United States was among the twenty-six nations that signed the Declaration of the United Nations, pledging allegiance to the Atlantic Charter.

A fundamental clash of systems explains why war came. Germany and Japan preferred a world divided into closed spheres of influence. The United States sought a liberal capitalist world order in which all nations enjoyed freedom of trade and investment. American principles manifested respect for human rights; fascists in Europe and militarists in Asia defiantly trampled such rights. The United States prided itself on its democratic system; Germany and Japan embraced authoritarian regimes backed by the military.

Clash of Systems

When the United States protested against German and Japanese expansion, Berlin and Tokyo reminded Washington of the United States's sphere in Latin America. German, Italian, and Japanese leaders also charged that Americans were applying a double standard, conveniently ignoring their own empire built through conquest, military occupation, and economic privilege. Americans rejected such comparisons and claimed that their expansionism had benefited not just themselves but the rest of the world. So many incompatible objectives and outlooks obstructed diplomacy and made war likely.

Summary

In the 1920s and 1930s, Americans proved unable to create a peaceful and prosperous world order. The Washington Conference treaties failed to curb a naval arms race or to protect China; the Dawes Plan collapsed; the Kellogg-Briand Pact proved ineffective; philanthropic activities fell short of need; the process of cultural "Americanization" provided no panacea; the aggressors Germany and Japan ignored repeated U.S. protests, from the Stimson Doctrine onward; recognition of the Soviet Union barely improved relations; U.S. trade policies, shifting from protectionist tariffs to reciprocal trade agreements, only minimally improved U.S. or international commerce in the era of the Great Depression; and the Neutrality Acts did not prevent U.S. entanglements in Europe. Even where

How do historians know...

that American leaders knew in December 1941, before the attack on Pearl Harbor, that Japan intended to go to war with the United States? In September 1940, U.S. cryptanalysts—code breakers—of the Signal Intelligence Service cracked the most secret diplomatic cipher used by the Japanese government, a machine they called PURPLE. The code breakers discovered patterns in the incoherent letters of telegraphed messages, produced texts, and even duplicated the complicated PURPLE machine (shown here). Thereafter, under Operation MAGIC, they decoded thousands of intercepted messages sent by Japanese officials around the world. Important intercepts such as the one shown below were delivered to a handful of top American leaders, including the president. These dispatches made increasingly clear through 1941 that Tokyo expected all-out war with the United States. An intercept on December 3, just a few days before the attack on Pearl Harbor, revealed that Tokyo had ordered the Japanese embassy in Washington to destroy all codes and cipher machines, a sure sign that war was imminent.

After the attack against Pearl Harbor, and after it became public knowledge that the United States had broken the Japanese diplomatic code, the cry sounded—especially from die-hard isolationists and Roosevelt-haters—that the president must have known what was coming yet failed to prepare the naval base for the assault. The many messages intercepted in the fall and winter of 1941, however, never revealed Japan's military plans. Not one intercepted message mentioned an attack on Pearl Harbor; indeed, even Japanese diplomats in Washington were never told that Pearl Harbor would be hit.   (Photos: National Archives)

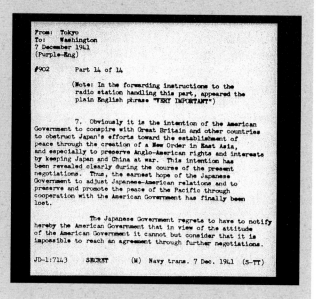

American power and policies seemed to work to satisfy Good Neighbor goals—in Latin America—nationalist resentments simmered and Mexico challenged U.S. hegemony.

During the late 1930s and early 1940s, President Roosevelt hesitantly but steadily moved the United States from neutrality to aid for the Allies, to belligerency, and finally to a declaration of war after the attack on Pearl Harbor. Congress gradually revised and retired the Neutrality Acts in the face of growing danger and receding isolationism. Independent internationalism and economic and nonmilitary means to peace gave way to alliance-building and war.

The Second World War offered yet another opportunity for Americans to set things right in the world. As the publisher Henry Luce wrote in *American*

Century (1941), the United States must "exert upon the world the full impact of our influence, for such purposes as we see fit and by such means as we see fit." As they had so many times before, Americans flocked to the colors. Isolationists joined the president in spirited calls for victory. "We are going to win the war, and we are going to win the peace that follows," Roosevelt predicted.

LEGACY FOR A PEOPLE AND A NATION
Presidential Deception of the Public

Before U-652 launched two torpedoes at the *Greer*, heading for Iceland on September 4, 1941, the U.S. destroyer had stalked the German submarine for hours. Twice the *Greer* signaled the U-boat's location to British patrol bombers, one of which dropped depth charges on the submarine. After the torpedo attack, the *Greer* also released depth charges. In a dramatic radio "fireside chat" on September 11, President Roosevelt protested German "piracy" as a violation of the principle of freedom of the seas.

Throughout the twentieth century, presidents have exaggerated, distorted, withheld, or even lied about the facts of foreign relations in order to shape a public opinion favorable to their policies. One result: the growth of the "imperial presidency"—the president's grabbing of power from and supremacy over Congress, and the president's use of questionable means to reach his objectives. Franklin D. Roosevelt provided a telling example in the *Greer* incident. The president deliberately misrepresented the encounter in order to whip up anti-German passions, to discredit isolationist critics who opposed his pro-British interventionism in World War II, to announce his policy to convoy commercial ships across the Atlantic, and to issue an order to the navy to shoot German ships on sight.

In the *Greer* case, Roosevelt did not tell everything about the events of September 4, and what he did tell was misleading. In his radio message a week later, he described the clash as an unprovoked German attack.

He never mentioned that the U.S. ship had been cooperating with British warplanes, and he failed to note that the *Greer* had been tracking the submarine for hours. Despite his pleading, the incident had little to do with freedom of the seas, which related to neutral merchant ships not to U.S. warships operating in a war zone. Roosevelt's words amounted to a call to arms, yet he never asked Congress for a declaration of war against Germany. The president believed that he had to deceive the public in order to move hesitant Americans toward noble positions that they would ultimately see as necessary. Public opinion polls soon demonstrated that the practice worked, as most Americans approved the shoot-on-sight policy.

Several years later, in his book *The Man in the Street* (1948), Thomas A. Bailey defended Roosevelt. The historian argued that "because the masses are notoriously shortsighted, and generally cannot see danger until it is at their throats, our statesmen are forced to deceive them into an awareness of their own long-term interests." Roosevelt's critics, on the other hand, even those who agreed with him that Nazi Germany had to be stopped, have seen in his methods a danger to the democratic process, which cannot work in an environment of dishonesty and usurped powers. In the 1960s, during America's descent into the Vietnam War, Senator J. William Fulbright of Arkansas recalled the *Greer* incident: "FDR's deviousness in a good cause made it easier for LBJ to practice the same kind of deviousness in a bad cause." Indeed, during the Tonkin Gulf crisis of 1964, President Lyndon B. Johnson shaded the truth in order to gain from Congress wide latitude in waging war. In the 1980s Reagan administration officials, in the Iran-contra affair, consciously and publicly lied about U.S. arms sales to Iran and about covert aid to Nicaraguan terrorists. Practicing deception of the public and Congress—advancing the imperial presidency—was one of Roosevelt's legacies for a people and a nation.

For Further Reading, see page A-30 of the Appendix. For Web resources, go to http://college.hmco.com.

In 1942, when recruiters from the U.S. Marine Corps came to the Navajo reservation in Shiprock, New Mexico, William Dean Wilson was only sixteen years old and a student at the Shiprock Boarding School. The marines came seeking young men who spoke both English and Navajo, which is an exceedingly complex language; fewer than thirty non-Navajos, none of them Japanese, could understand the language at the outbreak of the war. The Navajo recruits of 1942 would become not only U.S. Marines but also "code talkers" in the war against the Japanese.

Wilson volunteered. "I said I was eighteen," he recalled, too young to be drafted but eager to join up. His parents had opposed his decision, but he removed a note from his file that read "Parents will not consent" and was inducted. Wilson, eager to see the world, was among an initial group of thirty Navajos chosen for a project with an important goal: to prevent the Japanese from deciphering radio messages sent by American troops landing on the shores of Pacific islands.

Organized as the 382nd Platoon, Wilson and his fellow recruits went first to marine boot camp, then to Camp Pendleton in California, where they trained as radio operators. At Camp Pendleton, they also helped to devise a code based on the Navajo language; the code had the beauty of being unbreakable. In preparation for battle, the code talkers memorized a special Navajo-coded dictionary of 413 military terms. While in the marines and even under battle conditions, the code talkers maintained traditional beliefs and practices. To prepare the young men to fight the enemy, Navajo families had special "Blessing Way" ceremonies performed for them; and many of the men went to battle carrying bags of sacred corn pollen.

By the time Wilson's seventeenth birthday arrived, he was fighting in the Pacific. Beginning with the Battle of Guadalcanal, he and others from the corps of 420 Navajo code talkers took part in every assault the marines conducted in the Pacific from 1942

Navajo "code talkers," who were U.S. Marines, were among the first assault forces to land on Pacific beaches. Dodging enemy fire, they set up radio equipment and transmitted vital information to headquarters, including enemy sightings and targets for American shelling. The Japanese never broke the special Navajo code. The artist is Colonel C. H. Waterhouse, U.S. Marine Corps (retired). (U.S. Marine Corps Art Collection/Colonel C. H. Waterhouse)

27

THE SECOND WORLD WAR AT HOME AND ABROAD 1941–1945

to 1945. Usually, two code talkers were assigned to a battalion, one going ashore and the other remaining aboard ship. Those who went ashore led the assault forces landing on the beachheads. Often under hostile fire, they quickly set up their radio equipment and, using the special code, began transmitting, reporting sightings of enemy forces and directing shelling by American detachments.

Since the code talkers were responsible for the flow of vital battlefield information back to the ship and between advance units, they proved indispensable. Their work required great courage, and it paid off. "Were it not for the Navajos," declared Major Howard Conner, Fifth Marine Division signal officer, "the

Marines would never have taken Iwo Jima. The entire operation was directed by Navajo code. . . . I had six Navajo radio sets operating around the clock. In that period alone they sent and received over 800 messages without an error."

As it did for millions of other American fighting men and women, wartime service changed the Navajo code talkers' lives, broadening their horizons and often deepening their ambitions. Many became community leaders. William Dean Wilson, for example, became a tribal judge. From "the service," recalled Raymond Nakai, a navy veteran who became chairman of the Navajo nation, "the Navajo got a glimpse of what the rest of the world is doing." But in 1945 most Navajo war veterans were happy to return to their homes and traditional culture. And in accordance with Navajo ritual, the returning veterans participated in purification ceremonies to dispel the ghosts of the battlefield and invoke blessings for the future.

The Second World War marked a turning point in the lives of millions of Americans, as well as in the history of the United States. Most deeply affected were those who fought the war, on the beaches and battlefields, in the skies and at sea. For forty-five months Americans fought abroad to subdue the German, Italian, and Japanese aggressors. After military engagements against fascists in North Africa and Italy, American troops, together with Canadian, British, and Free French units, crossed the English Channel on D-Day in June 1944. The massive invasion forced the Germans to retreat through France to Germany. Battered by merciless bombing raids, leaderless after Adolf Hitler's suicide, and pressed by a Soviet advance from the east, the Nazis capitulated in May 1945. In the Pacific, Americans drove the Japanese back from one island to another before turning to the just-tested atomic bombs, which demolished Hiroshima and Nagasaki in August and helped spur a Japanese surrender.

Throughout the war the Allies—Britain, the Soviet Union, and the United States—stuck together to defeat Germany. But they squabbled over many issues: when to open a second front; how to structure a new international organization; how eastern Europe, liberated from the Germans, would be reconstructed; how Germany and Japan would be governed after defeat. At the end of the war, Allied leaders seemed more intent on retaining and expanding their own nations' spheres of influence than on building a community of mutual interest. Although the victors created the United Nations Organization, the prospects for postwar international cooperation seemed bleak, and the advent of the atomic age frightened everyone.

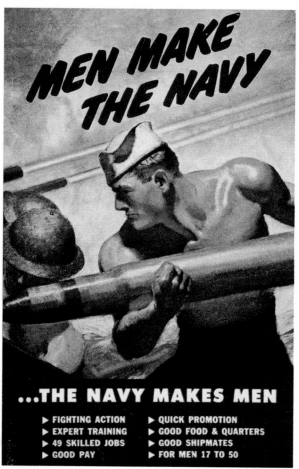

"MEN MAKE THE NAVY . . . ," proclaims this U.S. Navy recruiting booklet, which encourages men to enlist by highlighting the good pay, food, and shipmates, as well as the possibility of "fighting action." One hundred thousand women also responded to the navy's recruiting efforts by joining the WAVES.   (Private Collection)

IMPORTANT EVENTS

1941 Germany invades Russia

Roosevelt issues Executive Order No. 8802, forbidding racial discrimination by defense industry employers

Japan attacks Pearl Harbor

U.S. enters Second World War

1942 National War Labor Board created to deal with labor-management conflict

War Production Board begins to oversee conversion to military production

West Coast Japanese Americans interned in prison camps

Congress of Racial Equality established

War Manpower Commission created to manage labor supply

Office of Price Administration created to control inflation

U.S. defeats Japanese forces at Battles of the Coral Sea and Midway

Office of War Information created to maintain support for the war at home

Manhattan Project set up to produce atomic bomb

Synthetic-rubber program begins

Allies invade North Africa

Republicans gain in Congress

1943 Red Army defeats German troops at Stalingrad

Soft-coal and anthracite miners strike

Congress passes War Labor Disputes (Smith Connally) Act

Race riots break out in Detroit, Harlem, and forty-five other cities

Allies invade Italy

Hirabayashi v. U.S. upholds restrictions on personal liberties of Japanese Americans because of their race

Roosevelt, Churchill, and Stalin meet at Teheran Conference

1944 Roosevelt requests Economic Bill of Rights

War Refugee Board established to set up refugee camps in Europe

GI Bill of Rights provides educational benefits for veterans

Allied troops land at Normandy on D-Day

Dumbarton Oaks Conference approves charter for United Nations

Roosevelt reelected

U.S. retakes the Philippines

Korematsu v. U.S. upholds removal of Japanese Americans from the West Coast

1945 Roosevelt, Stalin, and Churchill meet at Yalta Conference

Battles of Iwo Jima and Okinawa result in heavy American and Japanese losses

Roosevelt dies; Truman becomes president

United Nations founded

Germany surrenders

First atomic bomb explodes in test at Alamogordo, New Mexico

Potsdam Conference calls for Japan's "unconditional surrender"

Atomic bombs devastate Hiroshima and Nagasaki

Japan surrenders

The war transformed America's soldiers and sailors. Horizons expanded for the more than 16 million men and women who ultimately served in the armed forces, seeing new parts of the world and acquiring new skills. But at war's end they were older than their years, both physically and emotionally; some were physically injured and psychologically scarred, and many felt they had sacrificed the best years of their lives.

During the war nearly one of every ten Americans moved permanently to another state (see Map 27.1). Most headed for war-production centers, especially cities in the North and on the West Coast. Japanese Americans moved, too, but involuntarily, as they were rounded up by the army and placed in internment camps. And while the war offered new economic and political opportunities for numerous African Americans, encouraging them to demand their full rights as citizens, competition for jobs and housing created the conditions for an epidemic of race riots. For women, the war offered new job opportunities in the armed forces and in war industries. For some, work was an economic necessity; for others, it was a patriotic obligation; for all, it brought financial independence and enhanced self-esteem.

The United States underwent profound changes during the war. The American people united behind the war effort, collecting scrap iron, rubber, and newspapers for recycling and planting "victory gardens." But more than national unity and enthusiasm were re-

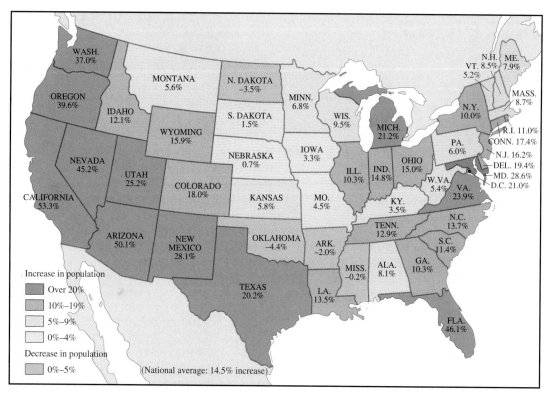

Map 27.1   A Nation on the Move, 1940–1950   American migration during the 1940s was the largest on record to that time. The farm population dropped dramatically as men, women, and children moved to war-production areas and to army and navy bases, particularly on the West Coast. Well over 30 million Americans migrated during the war. Many returned to their rural homes after the war, but 12 million migrants stayed in their new locations. Notice the population increases on the West Coast, as well as in the Southwest and Florida.

quired to win. Essential to victory was the mobilization of all sectors of the economy—industry, finance, agriculture, labor. America's big businesses got even bigger, as did its central government, labor unions, and farms. The federal government had the monumental task of coordinating activity in these spheres, as well as in two new ones: higher education and science. For this war was a scientific and technological war, supported by the development of new weapons such as radar and the atomic bomb. For all these reasons the Second World War transformed America. ■

Winning the Second World War

Two days after the surprise attack on Pearl Harbor, President Franklin D. Roosevelt spoke to the American people: "We are now in the midst of a war . . . for a world in which this Nation, and all that this Nation represents, will be safe for our children." Americans agreed with Roosevelt that they were defending their homes,

families, and way of life against aggressive, even satanic, Japanese and Nazis.

Immediately, the United States became an "Ally" in the war against Germany, Japan, and Italy. But wartime relations among the United States, Great Britain, and the Soviet Union ran hot and cold. Allied leaders knew that military decisions had political consequences. If one Ally became desperate, for instance, it might destroy the alliance by pursuing a separate peace. The positions of troops at the end of the war, moreover, might determine the politics of the regions they occupied. Thus an undercurrent of mutual suspicion ran just beneath the surface of Allied cooperation. The Allies, however, did reach one important agreement: recognizing that if Germany gained control over Europe's resources, the Nazis might directly threaten the Americas, and worrying that the Germans would develop an atomic bomb before the Japanese did, Allied strategists devised a "Europe first" formula—knock out Germany and then concentrate on an isolated Japan.

Roosevelt, British prime minister Winston Churchill, and Soviet premier Joseph Stalin differed vehemently over the opening of a second, or western, front in Europe. After Germany conquered France in 1940 and invaded the Soviet Union in 1941, the Soviets bore the brunt of the war until mid-1944, suffering millions of casualties. By late 1941, before the fierce Russian winter stalled their onslaught, German troops had nearly reached Moscow and Leningrad (present-day St. Petersburg) and had slashed deeply into the Ukraine, taking Kiev. Stalin pressed for a British-American landing on the western coast to draw German troops away from the eastern front, but Churchill would not agree. The Red Army therefore did most of the fighting and dying on land, while the British and Americans concentrated on getting Lend-Lease supplies across the

Second-front Controversy

Atlantic and harassing the Germans from the air with attacks on factories and civilians alike.

Roosevelt was both sensitive to the Soviets' burden and fearful that the Soviet Union might be knocked out of the war, leaving Hitler free to invade England. In 1942 he told the Soviets that they could expect the Allies to cross the English Channel and invade France later that year. This was exactly what Stalin sought to take pressure off his wracked country. But Churchill balked. His preference was a series of small jabs at the enemy's Mediterranean forces. Churchill feared heavy losses in a premature cross-Channel invasion, but some American officials suspected that Churchill's strategy derived from his desire to reassert British imperial power in the Mediterranean.

Churchill won the debate. Instead of attacking France, the British and Americans invaded North Africa in November 1942 (see Map 27.2). "We are

The first wave of U.S. troops hits Omaha Beach during the D-Day invasion on June 6, 1944. Steven Spielberg's film *Saving Private Ryan* (1998) reconstructed the horrors that greeted the landing forces, including land mines and enemy machine-gun fire. This photo—one of the first D-Day photos released—was taken by daring war photographer Robert Capa, who landed in Normandy with the first troops.   (Robert Capa/Magnum Photos, Inc.)

Map 27.2 The Allies on the Offensive in Europe, 1942–1945 The United States pursued a "Europe first" policy: first defeat Germany, then focus on Japan. American military efforts began in North Africa in late 1942 and ended in Germany in 1945 on May 8 (V-E Day).

striking back," Roosevelt declared. The news from the Soviet Union also buoyed Roosevelt. In the battle for Stalingrad (September 1942–January 1943)—probably the turning point of the European war—the Red Army defeated the Germans in bloody block-by-block fighting, forcing Hitler's divisions to retreat. But shortly thereafter, the president once again angered the Soviets by declaring another delay in launching the second front. Stalin was not mollified by the Allied invasion of Italy in the summer of 1943. Italy surrendered in September to American and British officers; Soviet officials were not invited to participate. Stalin grumbled that the arrangement smacked of a separate peace.

With the alliance badly strained, Roosevelt sought reconciliation through personal diplomacy. The three Allied leaders met in Teheran, Iran, in December 1943. Stalin dismissed Churchill's repetitious justifications for further delaying the second front. Roosevelt had had enough, too; he also rejected Churchill's proposal for another peripheral attack, this time through the Balkans to Vienna. The three finally agreed to launch Operation Overlord—the cross-Channel invasion of France—in early 1944. And the Soviet Union promised to aid the Allies against Japan once Germany was defeated.

Teheran Conference

The second front opened in the dark morning hours of June 6, 1944—D-Day. In the largest amphibious landing in history, two hundred thousand Allied troops under the command of American general Dwight D. Eisenhower scrambled ashore at Normandy, France. Thousands of ships ferried the men within a hundred yards of the sandy beaches. Landing craft and soldiers immediately encountered the enemy; they triggered mines and were pinned down by fire from cliffside pillboxes. Meanwhile, Allied airborne troops dropped behind German lines. Although heavy aerial and naval bombardment and the clandestine work of saboteurs had softened the German defenses, the fighting was ferocious.

D-Day

Allied troops soon spread across the countryside, liberating France and Belgium and entering Germany itself in September. In December, German armored divisions counterattacked in Belgium's Ardennes Forest, hoping to push on to Antwerp to halt the flow of Allied supplies through that Belgian port. After weeks of heavy fighting in what has come to be called the Battle of the Bulge—because of a noticeable bulge in the Allied line—the Allies pushed the enemy back

once again. Meanwhile, battle-hardened Soviet troops marched through Poland and cut a path to Berlin. American forces crossed the Rhine River in March 1945 and captured the heavily industrial Ruhr valley. Several units peeled off to enter Austria and Czechoslovakia, where they met up with Soviet soldiers. As the Americans marched east, a new president took office in Washington: Franklin D. Roosevelt died on April 12, and Harry S Truman became president and commander-in-chief. Eighteen days later, in bomb-ravaged Berlin, Adolf Hitler killed himself. On May 8 Germany surrendered.

The war in the Pacific was largely America's to fight, and at first, it did not go well. By mid-1942 Japan had seized the Philippines, Guam, Wake, Hong Kong, Singapore, Malaya, and the Dutch East Indies (Indonesia). In the Philippines in 1942, Japanese soldiers forced American and Filipino prisoners weakened by insufficient rations to walk 65 miles, clubbing, shooting, or starving to death about ten thousand of them. This so-called Bataan Death March intensified American hatred of the Japanese.

The War in the Pacific

In April 1942 Americans began to hit back, initially by bombing Tokyo. In May, in the momentous Battle of the Coral Sea, carrier-based American planes halted a Japanese advance toward Australia (see Map 27.3). The next month American forces defeated the Japanese at Midway, sinking four of the enemy's aircraft carriers. Thanks to the success of Operation MAGIC—the work of American experts who deciphered the secret code used by the Japanese to transmit messages—American naval officers knew ahead of time the approximate date and direction of the Japanese assault. The Battle of Midway was a turning point in the Pacific war, breaking the Japanese momentum and relieving the threat to Hawai'i. Thereafter, Japan was never able to match American fighting power or economic power.

Battle of Midway

American strategy was to "island-hop" toward Japan, skipping the most strongly fortified islands whenever possible and taking the weaker ones. In an effort to strand the Japanese armies on their island outposts and to cut off the supply of raw materials being shipped from Japan's home islands, Americans also set out to sink the Japanese merchant marine. The first U.S. offensive—at Guadalcanal in the Solomon Islands

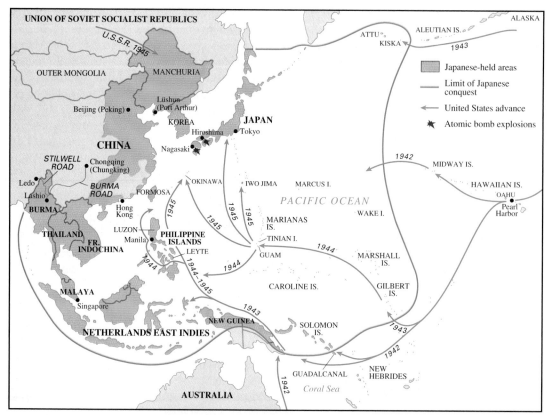

Map 27.3 The Pacific War The strategy of the United States was to "island-hop"—from Hawai'i in 1942 to Iwo Jima and Okinawa in 1945. Naval battles were also decisive, notably the Battles of the Coral Sea and Midway in 1942. The war in the Pacific ended with Japan's surrender on August 15, 1945 (V-J Day). (Source: Thomas G. Paterson, J. Garry Clifford, Kenneth J. Hagan, *American Foreign Policy: A History,* vol. 2, 3d ed. Copyright © 1991 by D. C. Heath Company. Used by permission of Houghton Mifflin Company.)

in mid-1942—gave American troops their first taste of jungle warfare: tropical heat, thick vegetation, savage mosquitoes. In 1943 and 1944 American troops attacked the enemy in the Gilbert, Marshall, and Mariana islands. And in October 1944, General Douglas MacArthur landed at Leyte to retake the Philippines for the United States.

Despite those victories, more tough fighting lay ahead in the Pacific. In February 1945 both sides took heavy losses at Iwo Jima, an island less than 5 miles long located 700 miles south of Tokyo. Stationed on the island were 21,000 Japanese troops living in pillboxes and miles of caves, trenches, and connecting tunnels. The American objective was Mount Suribachi, the highest point and most heavily fortified spot on Iwo Jima. From the outset, American casualties were heavy; the mountain had to be taken yard by yard.

Battles of Iwo Jima and Okinawa

After twenty days of fighting, victory finally came and marines planted the American flag atop Mount Suribachi. In this bitter battle, 6,821 Americans were killed along with all but 200 of the Japanese troops.

A month later, American troops landed on Okinawa, an island 350 miles from Japan. Fighting raged for two months; death was everywhere. Almost the entire Japanese garrison of 100,000 was killed, and there were 80,000 Okinawan civilian casualties. The American military lost 7,374 men. At sea, the supporting fleet reported almost 5,000 seamen killed or missing; most were the victims of *kamikaze* (suicide) attacks, in which Japanese pilots crashed their bomb-laden planes directly into American ships.

Still, Japanese leaders refused to admit defeat. Hoping to avoid a humiliating unconditional surrender (and to preserve the emperor's sovereignty), they hung on even while American bombers leveled their cities. In one staggering attack on Tokyo on May 23,

This scorched watch, found in the rubble at Hiroshima, stopped at the time of the blast—8:16. The shock waves and fires caused by the atomic bomb leveled great expanses of the city. Radiation released by the bomb caused lingering deaths for thousands who survived the explosion. The photo of Hiroshima shown above was taken eight months after the attack.   (Watch: John Launois/Black Star; Hiroshima: U.S. Air Force)

1945, American planes dropped bombs that engulfed the city in a firestorm, killing 83,000 people. Observers described the ghastly scene as a mass burning.

With victory in sight, American leaders began to plan a fall invasion of Japan's home islands, an expedition that was sure to incur high casualties. But the successful development of an atomic bomb by American scientists provided another route to victory. The secret atomic program, known as the Manhattan Project, had begun in August 1942, and the first bomb was exploded in the desert near Alamogordo, New Mexico, on July 16, 1945. Just three weeks later, on August 6, the Japanese city of Hiroshima was destroyed by a bomb dropped from an American B-29 plane called the *Enola Gay*, A

The Atomic Bomb

flash of dazzling light shot across the sky; then a huge purplish mushroom cloud boiled 40,000 feet into the atmosphere. Dense smoke, swirling fires, and suffocating dust soon engulfed the ground for miles. Much of the city was leveled almost instantly. Approximately 130,000 people were killed; tens of thousands more suffered severe burns and nuclear radiation poisoning.

American planes continued their devastating conventional bombing and also scattered leaflets over other Japanese cities, warning that they, too, would

How do historians know...

what motivated President Harry Truman to order the dropping of the atomic bomb? Truman explained that he did it for only one reason: to end the war as soon as possible and thus prevent the loss of 1 million American casualties in an invasion of Japan. An earlier generation of historians, writing in the aftermath of the war, echoed President Truman's explanation. But more recently historians have revised this interpretation: they argue that Japan might have surrendered even if the atomic bombs had not been dropped, and they dispute Truman's high estimate of casualties as being pure fiction and several times the likely figure. These revisionists have studied the Potsdam Conference of July 1945 attended by Truman, Joseph Stalin, and Winston Churchill. In their research, they have demonstrated the value of diaries as historical evidence by consulting those kept by certain participants, notably Secretary of War Henry Stimson and Truman himself.

Scholars cite Stimson's diary (excerpted here) as evidence that Truman's chief motivations included not only ending the war but also impressing the Soviet Union with America's military might and minimizing the USSR's military participation in the final defeat and postwar occupation of Japan. On July 21 Stimson reported to Truman that the army had successfully tested an atomic device in New Mexico. Clearly emboldened by the news, Truman said that possession of the bomb "gave him an entirely new feeling of confidence. . . ." The next day, Stimson discussed the news with British prime minister Churchill. "Now I know what happened to Truman," Churchill responded. "When he got to the meeting after having read this report he was a changed man. He told the Russians just where they got off and generally bossed the whole meeting." A few historians contend that the decision to drop the atomic bomb was partly racist. As evidence, they point to Truman's handwritten diary entry in which he discussed using the bomb against "the Japs," whom he denounced as "savages, ruthless, merciless and

fanatic." Others cite these words to claim that Truman desired to avenge the Japanese attack at Pearl Harbor. It is clear that while personal diaries can help to settle some historical disagreements, they can also generate new interpretive disputes.

The deeply emotional question about the necessity for dropping the atomic bomb has stirred debates among the public as well as among historians. In 1995, for example, the Smithsonian Institution provoked a furor with its plans for an exhibit prompted by the fiftieth anniversary of the decision to drop the bomb. Rather than incur the wrath of politicians, veterans' groups, and other Americans outraged by what they perceived to be an anti-American interpretation of events, the Smithsonian shelved most of the exhibit.   (Photo: Henry L. Stimson Papers, Yale University Library)

TOP SECRET

I also discussed with him Harrison's two messages. He was intensely pleased by the accelerated timetable. As to the matter of the special target which I had refused to permit, he strongly confirmed my view, and said he felt the same way.

At ten forty Bundy and I again went to the British headquarters and talked to the Prime Minister and Lord Cherwell for over an hour. Churchill read Groves' report in full. He told me that he had noticed at the meeting of the three yesterday, Truman was evidently much fortified by something that had happened, and that he stood up to the Russians in a most emphatic and decisive manner, telling them as to certain demands that they absolutely could not have, and that the United States was entirely against them. Churchill said he now understood how this pepping up had taken place and that he felt the same way. His own attitude confirmed this admission. He now not only was not worried about giving the Russians information of the matter, but was rather inclined to use it as an argument in our favor in the negotiations. The sentiment of the four of us was unanimous in thinking that it was advisable to tell the Russians at least that we were working on that subject, and intended to use it if and when it was successfully finished.

At twelve fifteen I called General Arnold over, showed him Harrison's two cables, showed him my answer to them and showed him Groves' report, which he read in its entirety. He told me that he agreed with me about the target which I had struck off the program. He said that it would take considerable hard work to organize the operations now that it was to move forward.

TOP SECRET

face atomic terror unless the Japanese Empire surrendered. On August 9 another atomic attack flattened Nagasaki, killing at least 60,000 people. Five days later the Japanese, who had been sending out peace feelers since June, surrendered. The victors promised that the Japanese emperor could remain as the nation's titular head. Formal surrender ceremonies were held September 2 aboard the battleship *Missouri*. The Second World War was over.

The Decision to Use the Atomic Bomb

Use of the bomb to achieve victory had been the primary goal of the Manhattan Project. Most Americans agreed with President Truman that the atomic bombing of Hiroshima and Nagasaki was necessary to end the war as quickly as possible and to save American lives. At the highest government levels and among atomic scientists, alternatives had been discussed: detonating the bomb on an unpopulated Pacific island, with international observers as witnesses; blockading and bombing Japan conventionally; following up on Tokyo's peace feelers; encouraging a Soviet declaration of war on Japan. Truman, however, had rejected these options because he believed they would take too long and would not convince the tenacious Japanese that they had been beaten. Then, too, memories of Pearl Harbor played a part. "When you have to deal with a beast, you have to treat him as a beast," Truman said.

Diplomatic considerations also influenced the decision to use the bomb. American leaders wanted to take advantage of the real and psychological power the bomb would bestow on the United States. It might serve as a deterrent against aggression; it might intimidate the Soviet Union into making concessions in eastern Europe; it might end the war in the Pacific before the Soviet Union could claim a role in the postwar management of Asia. "If it explodes, as I think it will," Truman remarked, "I'll certainly have a hammer on those boys [the Soviets]."

Mobilizing the American Home Front

In the aftermath of Pearl Harbor, the American people rushed to the defense not only of their country but also of what President Roosevelt had called the "four essential human freedoms"—freedom of speech, freedom of worship, freedom from want, and freedom from fear. Women in war-production work, as well as men on the battlefields, believed they were fighting for both democracy and the American family. Private advertisers as well as government agencies called on people to defend the "American Way of Life." For example, an advertisement for vacuum cleaners in the *Saturday Evening Post* urged women war workers to fight "for freedom and all that means to women everywhere. You're fighting for a little house of your own, and a husband to meet every night at the door. You're fighting for the right to bring up your children without the shadow of fear."

Why We Fight

Despite nearly unanimous support for the war effort, government leaders worried that, in a long war, public willingness to sacrifice might lag. To elicit the people's support, in 1942 President Roosevelt established the Office of War Information (OWI), which took charge of domestic propaganda and hired Hollywood filmmakers and New York copywriters to sell the war at home. The army responded by hiring movie director Frank Capra to produce a series of propaganda films called *Why We Fight*, which portrayed the Allies as heroic partners united in a common effort against evil.

Office of Price Administration

No wartime agency better exemplified Americans' willingness to sacrifice to win the war than the Office of Price Administration (OPA). Established by Congress in 1942 with the power to control inflation by fixing price ceilings on commodities, and by controlling rents in defense areas, the OPA instituted nationwide rationing for automobile tires and issued rationing books with coupons for sugar, coffee, and gasoline. Point rationing programs were introduced in 1943 with stamps for purchasing meats, butter and cheese, shoes, and other controlled commodities. Consumers became skilled at handling ration stamps, each worth ten points—red for meats and cheese, blue for canned goods. Most Americans abided by the rules, but some hoarded sugar and coffee or bought beef on the "black market"—under the counter or from the trunk of a car.

Women consumers were central to OPA's success. They enlisted in the "food fight for freedom" by signing "The Home Front Pledge" and promising to pay "no more than Ceiling Prices." The OPA was active in every community through its 5,525 local War Price and Rationing Boards, operated largely by women volunteers, which allocated coupons for each family. Some of the volunteers were veterans of labor unions and consumer groups, while others were ordinary shoppers determined to sacrifice for the war effort. But the

OPA's successes in enforcing price ceilings provoked opposition from businesses, large and small, which even in wartime wanted to charge whatever the market would bear. Ranging from local grocery stores to large trade associations, such as the National Association of Manufacturers, businesses blamed the OPA for the "scarcity" of consumer goods. The American Meat Institute attacked the OPA not only for the alleged shortages of meat, but also for alleged contamination of the meat supply. In fact, the packers' profits soared as war-working Americans with good jobs increased their annual consumption of meat from 127 to 150 pounds per capita.

While the guns boomed in Europe and Asia, the war was changing American lives and institutions.

War Production Board and War Manpower Commission

One month after Pearl Harbor, President Roosevelt established the War Production Board (WPB) and assigned to it the task of converting the economy from civilian to military production. Factories that had manufactured silk ribbons began to turn out silk parachutes; automobile companies switched to the production of tanks and airplanes; adding-machine companies started manufacturing automatic pistols. Factories had to be expanded and new ones built. Also established in 1942, the War Manpower Commission (WMC) recruited new workers for the nation's factories.

The war demanded sacrifices from Americans, but it also rewarded them with new highs in personal income (see Figure 27.1). Savings deposits jumped from $32.4 billion in 1942 to $51.4 billion in 1945. Corporations doubled their net profits between 1939 and 1943, and employees' wages and salaries rose more than 135 percent from 1940 to 1945. The government did not tax this extra income as heavily as it might have. Instead, it resorted to deficit financing and borrowed much of the cost of waging the war, about half of it in the form of war bonds sold to patriotic citizens. The national debt skyrocketed from $49 billion in 1941 to $259 billion in 1945.

The industrial mobilization was so successful that the production of durable goods more than tripled. Since this was the world's first massive air war, fighter planes and bombers were crucial, and America's factories responded to the need: the manufacture of military aircraft, which had totaled 6,000 in 1940, jumped to over 47,000 in 1942 and to 85,000 in 1943. Women workers made a major contribution to the rapidly expanding aircraft industry, whose female work force increased from 4,000 in December 1941 to 310,000 two years later.

The wartime emergency also spurred the establishment of totally new industries, most notably synthetic rubber. The Japanese, in their conquest of the South Pacific following Pearl Harbor, had captured 90 percent of the world's supply of crude rubber. The American government resorted to a national speed limit and gasoline rationing to save wear on tires, but the country still could not meet its wartime needs. So in 1942, with an investment of $700 million, the government underwrote the creation of a synthetic-rubber industry. By war's end the nation that had been the world's largest importer of rubber had become the world's largest exporter of rubber—all of it synthetic.

Government Incentives in Business

To gain the cooperation of business, the War Production Board and other government agencies met business more than halfway. The government guaranteed profits in the form of cost-plus-fixed-fee contracts, generous tax write-offs, and exemptions from antitrust prosecution. Such concessions made sense for a nation that wanted vast quantities of war goods manufactured in the shortest possible time. From mid-1940 through September 1944 the government awarded contracts totaling $175 billion, no less than two-thirds of which went to the top one hundred corporations. General Motors alone received 8 percent of the total; big awards also went to other automobile companies and to aircraft, steel, electrical, and chemical companies. Although the expression "military-industrial complex" had not yet been coined—President Dwight Eisenhower would do so in 1961 (see page 796)—the web of military-business interdependence had begun to be woven.

University Research and Weapons Development

In science and higher education, too, the big got bigger as federal contracts mobilized science and technology for the war effort. Massachusetts Institute of Technology was a major recipient for its development of radar. MIT received $117 million, followed by the California Institute of Technology, Harvard, and Columbia. Most federal research contracts with universities were for the development of devices for warfare, such as radar and the proximity fuse. The most spectacular result of such government contracts was the atomic bomb. The Manhattan Project, run by the army, financed research at the University of Chicago, which in 1942 was the site of the world's first

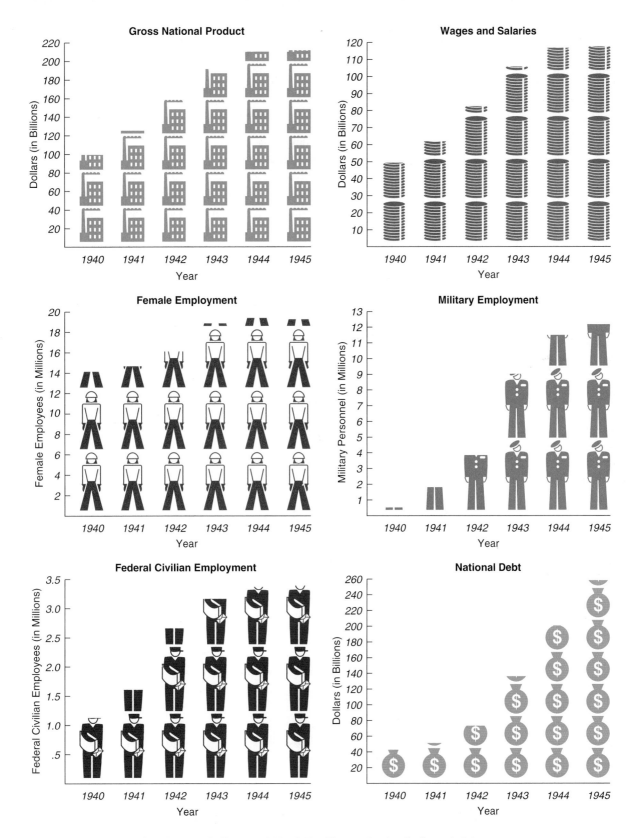

Figure 27.1   The Wartime Economic Boom, 1940–1945   War production finally ended the Great Depression. These graphs show the wartime increases in key economic indicators: gross national product; wages and salaries; female, military, and federal civilian employment; and national debt for financing the war.

sustained nuclear chain reaction. The University of California at Berkeley had a contract to operate the Los Alamos Scientific Laboratory in New Mexico, where the atomic bomb was tested. American universities became valued participants in the military-industrial complex.

Wartime contracts with universities also accelerated medical progress. Indeed, because of the development of antibiotics and sulfa drugs, which greatly reduced deaths from infected war wounds, the survival rate among injured soldiers was 90 percent, compared with 10 percent in the First World War. Penicillin made its debut in America in 1942, saving the life of a woman suffering from a once-fatal bacterial infection. The most dreaded home-front disease, especially by children, was polio. Although research for a polio vaccine advanced during the war, not until 1955 did the government approve a vaccine for public use (see Chapter 28).

Organized labor also grew during the war. Membership in unions ballooned from 8.5 million in 1940 to 14.75 million in 1945. Less than

Unions and Wartime Labor Strikes

a week after Pearl Harbor, a White House labor-management conference agreed to a no-strike/no-lockout pledge to guarantee uninterrupted war production. To minimize labor-management conflict, in 1942 President Roosevelt created the National War Labor Board (NWLB), sometimes referred to as the Supreme Court for labor disputes. Unions were permitted to enroll as many new members as possible, but workers could not be required to join a union. Thus the NWLB forged a temporary compromise between the unions' demand for a closed shop, in which only union members could be hired, and management's interest in open shops.

But when the NWLB attempted in 1943 to limit wage increases to cost-of-living pay hikes, workers responded with strikes that tripled the amount of lost production time over that of the previous year. The worst labor disruptions of 1943 occurred in the coal fields. To discourage further work stoppages, Congress passed the War Labor Disputes (Smith-Connally) Act in June 1943. The act gave the president authority to seize and operate any strike-bound plant deemed necessary to the national security, and it established a mandatory thirty-day cooling-off period before any new strike could be called. The Smith-Connally Act also gave the NWLB the legal authority to settle labor disputes for the duration of the war.

Agriculture also made an impressive contribution to the war effort, through hard work and the introduction of labor-saving machinery to re-

Wartime Changes in Agriculture

place men and women who had gone to the front or migrated to war-production centers. Before the war, farming had been in the midst of a transition from the family-owned and -operated farm to the large-scale, mechanized agribusiness dominated by banks, insurance companies, and farm co-ops. The Second World War accelerated the trend, for wealthy financial institutions were better able than family farmers to pay for expensive new machinery. From 1940 to 1945, while the value of farm machinery more than doubled, from $3.1 billion to $6.5 billion, the farm population fell from 30.5 million to 24.4 million people.

At the apex of the burgeoning national economy stood the federal government, the size and importance of which was mushrooming: from

Growth in the Federal Government

1940 to 1945 the federal bureaucracy expanded from 1.1 million workers to 3.4 million. The executive branch grew most dramatically. Besides raising the armed forces, mobilizing industrial production, and pacifying labor and management, the executive branch also had to manage the labor supply and control inflation. Although government-business-labor relations were sometimes bitter, and production was sometimes slowed as a result, Americans were generally ready to make personal sacrifices. They knew the war would be costly and long. In previous conflicts Americans had flocked to the colors with flags, wild rallies, and militaristic songs, but they fought the Second World War with a grim, realistic determination. They were in it "for the duration."

The Military Life

 America's men and women responded eagerly to their nation's call to arms. In 1941, only 1.8 million people were serving on active duty, although Selective Service had been functioning for a full year. By the end of the war, more than 16.3 million women and men had served in the army, navy, and marines. Fighting a world war on two fronts required a massive force. To American servicepeople in Asia and in Europe, the Second World War was a dirty job. Like cartoonist Bill Mauldin's popular GI characters Willy and Joe, who were more interested in tasty food and dry socks than

Lining the rails of their ship, African American army nurses arrive at the European theater of operations in August 1944. These nurses, like their white counterparts in America's segregated army, served in field and base hospitals, often right behind the fighting front.   (Library of Congress)

in abstractions, millions of GIs were simply eager to get it over with. American troops served overseas for an average of sixteen months. Some never returned: total deaths exceeded 405,000. In terms of lost American lives, the cost of the war was second only to that lost on both sides during the Civil War.

Military service demanded enormous personal adjustments. Soldiers and sailors who never had been more than a few miles from home became homesick; GIs joked, somewhat bitterly, about having found a new home in the army. But loneliness was inconsequential compared with the intense fear that soldiers admitted to feeling in battle. Combat veterans told a group of psychologists that a man who burst out weeping was "not regarded as a coward unless he made no apparent effort to stick to his job." Although the American Psychiatric Association did not identify the illness known as posttraumatic stress disorder until 1980, it is clear in retrospect that American veterans suffered from it after the war. The symptoms included nightmares and flashbacks to the battlefield, depression and anger, and widespread alcoholism.

The Ordeal of Combat

Among the millions of Americans who left home to join the armed forces were men and women who

Homosexuals on Active Duty

had experienced homosexual attraction in peacetime. Freed of their familial environments and serving in sex-segregated units, many acted on their feelings. "When I first got into the navy—in the recreation hall, for instance," recalled a chief petty officer, "there'd be eye contact. . . . All of a sudden you had a vast network of friends." The military court-martialed homosexuals, and nine thousand servicemen and -women were discharged because of their sexual orientation. Usually, however, gay relationships went unnoticed by the heterosexual world. For lesbians in the armed forces, the military environment offered friendships and a positive identity. "For many gay Americans," the historian John D'Emilio has written, "World War II created something of a nationwide coming out situation."

Wartime service not only broadened horizons but also fostered soldiers' ambitions. A soldier from the Midwest, who found himself "living among fellows from all over the country," observed that he had "picked up a lot of ideas from them . . . about how to live my own life and to get more out of it. I came out a lot more ambitious than I was before I went in." Many GIs returned to civilian

Postwar Ambitions

life with new skills they had learned in the military's technical schools. Still others took advantage of the educational benefits provided by the GI Bill of Rights (1944) to study for a college degree (see Chapter 28).

Still, after two or three years abroad, men and women in the service returned to the United States not knowing what to expect from civilian life. Some male war veterans expected that America's women, deeply appreciative of having been protected against a fearsome enemy, would repay their obligation with sexual favors. "We are not only fighting for the Four Freedoms," exclaimed one soldier, "we are also fighting for the priceless privilege of making love to American women." Many GIs, however, returned fearing that life at home had passed them by. They were much older in experience and exposure to brutality; many came back to the United States convinced that they had sacrificed their youth. And they found that home had changed as well. "Our friends are gone," one GI lamented. "The family and the town naturally had to go on even if we weren't there, and somehow it seems things have sort of closed in and filled that space we used to occupy."

Enemy Aliens, Conscientious Objectors, and Japanese American Internees

After the United States entered the war, American leaders had to consider whether enemy agents were operating within the nation's borders and threatening the war effort. It was clear that not all Americans were enthusiastic supporters of the nation's participation in the war. The Alien Registration (Smith) Act, passed in 1940, made it unlawful to advocate the overthrow of the U.S. government by force or violence or to join any organization that did so. After Pearl Harbor, the government drew upon this authority to take into custody thousands of Germans, Italians, and other Europeans as suspected spies and potential traitors. During the war, the government interned 14,426 Europeans in Enemy Alien Camps. Fearing subversion from aliens born in enemy countries, the government also prohibited ten thousand Italian Americans from living or working in restricted zones along the California coast, including San Francisco and Monterey Bay.

Some Americans had conscientious objections to war, particularly Quakers, Mennonites, and members of the Church of the Brethren. During the Second

World War conscientious objectors (COs) had to have a religious (as opposed to a moral or an ethical) reason for refusing military service. About 12,000 COs were sent to civilian public service camps, where they worked on conservation projects or as orderlies in hospitals. Approximately 5,500, three-fourths of whom were Jehovah's Witnesses, refused to participate in any way; they were imprisoned.

Compared with the First World War, the nation's wartime civil liberties record was generally creditable.

"An Enemy Race"

But there was one enormous exception: the internment in "relocation centers" of, ultimately, 120,000 Japanese Americans. Of these people, 77,000 were Nisei—native-born citizens of the United States. Their imprisonment was based not on suspicion or evidence of treason; their crime was solely that they were of Japanese descent. General John L. DeWitt, chief of the Western Defense Command, warned, "The Japanese race is an enemy race and while many second and third generation Japanese born on United States soil, possessed of United States citizenship, have become 'Americanized,' the racial strains are undiluted. . . . It, therefore, follows that along the vital Pacific Coast over 112,000 potential enemies, of Japanese extraction, are at large today." With strained logic DeWitt rationalized the internment: "The very fact that no sabotage [by Japanese Americans] has taken place to date is a disturbing and confirming indication that such action will be taken."

General DeWitt was not alone in his racist paranoia and hatred. Popular racial stereotypes held that Japanese people abroad and at home were sneaky and evil, and the American people, feeling that the Japanese had to be repaid for Pearl Harbor, generally regarded Japan as the United States's chief enemy. Several factors, however, should have disproved the accusation that Japanese Americans were members of "an enemy race." In Hawai'i, for example, where 160,000 people—one-third of the population—were of Japanese descent, fewer than a thousand people were taken into custody and sent to the mainland for internment. More to the point, Japanese American soldiers fought valiantly for the United States. The all–Japanese American 442nd Regimental Combat Team, drawn heavily from young men in internment camps, was the most decorated unit of its size in the armed forces. Suffering heavy casualties in Italy and France, members of the 442nd were awarded a Congressional Medal of Honor, 47 Distinguished Service

Crosses, 350 Silver Stars, and more than 3,600 Purple Hearts.

During the war, charges of criminal behavior were never brought against any Japanese Americans; none was ever indicted or tried for espionage, treason, or sedition. Nevertheless in 1942 all the 112,000 Japanese Americans living in California, Oregon, and the state of Washington were rounded up and imprisoned. "It was really cruel and harsh," recalled Joseph Y. Kurihara, a citizen and a veteran of the First World War. "To pack and evacuate in forty-eight hours was an impossibility. Seeing mothers completely bewildered with children crying from want and peddlers taking advantage and offering prices next to robbery made me feel like murdering those responsible."

The internees were sent to flood-damaged lands at Relocation, Arkansas; to the intermountain terrain

Life in the Internment Camps

of Wyoming and the desert of western Arizona; and to other arid and desolate spots in the West. The camps were bleak and demoralizing. Behind barbed wire stood tarpapered wooden barracks where entire families lived in a single room furnished only with cots, blankets, and a bare light bulb. Toilets and dining and bathing facilities were communal; privacy was almost nonexistent. Japanese Americans were forced to sell property valued at $500 million, and they lost their positions in the truck-garden, floral, and fishing industries. Indeed, their economic competitors were among the most vocal proponents of their relocation.

The Supreme Court upheld the government's policy of internment. In wartime, the Court ruled in *Hirabayashi v. U.S.* (1943), "residents having ethnic af-

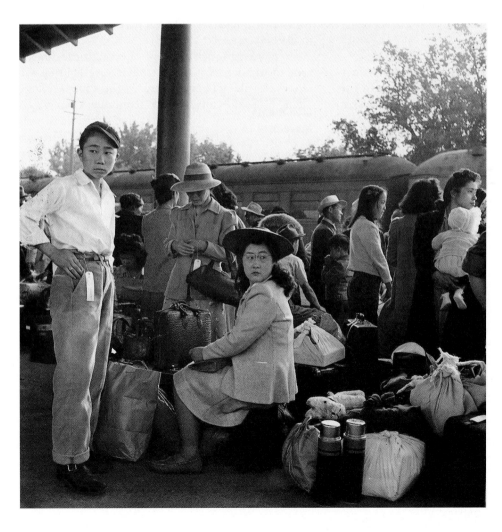

In February 1942 President Franklin D. Roosevelt ordered that all Japanese Americans living on the West Coast be rounded up and placed in prison camps. These families were awaiting a train to take them to an assembly center in Merced, California; from there, they would be sent to relocation camps in remote inland areas. (National Archives)

filiations with an invading enemy may be a greater source of danger than those of different ancestry." In *Korematsu v. U.S.* (1944), the Court, with three justices dissenting, approved the removal of the Nisei from the West Coast. One dissenter, Justice Frank Murphy, denounced the decision as the "legalization of racism."

In 1983, forty-one years after he had been sent to a government camp, Fred Korematsu had the satisfaction of hearing a federal judge rule that he—and by implication all detainees—had been the victim of "unsubstantiated facts, distortions and misrepresentations of at least one military commander whose views were affected by racism." A year earlier, the government's special Commission on Wartime Relocation and Internment of Civilians had recommended compensating the victims of this policy. Finally, in 1988, Congress voted to award $20,000 and a public apology to each of the surviving sixty thousand Japanese American internees.

Jobs and Racism on the Home Front

Even before Pearl Harbor, African Americans asserted their determination to participate in the war effort. In response to the March on Washington Movement of 1941 (see pages 720–721), the Selective Service System and the War Department agreed to increase the number of African Americans in uniform by drafting blacks in proportion to their presence in the population: about 10 percent. At the height of the war, the army had more than 700,000 African American troops. An additional 187,000 black men and women enlisted in the navy, the Coast Guard, and the once all-white Marine Corps.

Although they served in segregated units, African Americans fought on the front lines. For the first time the War Department sanctioned the training of blacks as pilots. After instruction at Tuskegee Institute in Alabama, pilots saw heroic service in all-black units such as the Ninety-ninth Pursuit Squadron, winner of eighty Distinguished Flying Crosses. In 1940 Colonel Benjamin O. Davis was the first African American to be promoted to brigadier general. More important, black people distinguished themselves on the battlefield. The performance of black marines in the Pacific theater was such that the corps commandant pro-

African Americans in Combat

claimed: "Negro Marines are no longer on trial. They are Marines, period."

Serious failures in race relations, however, undercut these accomplishments. Race riots instigated by whites broke out on military bases, and white civilians assaulted black soldiers and sailors throughout the South. In North Carolina a white bus driver who murdered an African American soldier in full view of the passengers was found not guilty. The worst racist outrage occurred at a munitions depot named Port Chicago in California. With a lack of training and a shocking disregard for safety by the navy, all-black squads of sailors were ordered to load explosives onto ships bound for the Pacific theater. On July 17, 1944, a tremendous ammunition explosion obliterated two vessels, shattered windows in San Francisco 35 miles away, and killed 320 people, including 202 African Americans. When the surviving black sailors were ordered to resume loading ammunition, fifty refused; the men were arrested, found guilty of mutiny by an all-white panel, dishonorably discharged, and sentenced to fifteen years at hard labor.

Experiences such as these caused African Americans to wonder what, in fact, they were fighting for. They rankled at the remark of the governor of Tennessee when blacks urged him to appoint African Americans to local draft boards: "This is a white man's country. . . . The Negro had nothing to do with the settling of America." They noted that the Red Cross separated blood according to the race of the donor, as if there were some difference. Although some African Americans even argued that the Second World War was a white man's war and that American racism was little different from German racism, there were persuasive reasons for blacks to participate in the war effort. Perhaps, as the NAACP believed, this was an opportunity "to persuade, embarrass, compel and shame our government and our nation . . . into a more enlightened attitude toward a tenth of its people." Proclaiming that in the Second World War they were waging a "Double V" campaign (for victory at home and abroad), blacks were more militant than before and readier than ever to protest. Membership in civil rights organizations soared. The NAACP, 50,000 strong in 1940, had 450,000 members by 1946. And in 1942 civil rights activists founded the Congress of Racial Equality (CORE), which stressed "nonviolent direct action" and staged sit-ins to desegregate restaurants and movie theaters in northern cities.

Civil Rights Movement

A leader of the Tuskegee airmen, Benjamin O. Davis, Jr., was the fourth African American to graduate from West Point. During the war, Colonel Davis commanded the 332d Fighter Group, which destroyed over two hundred enemy planes in southern Europe. (National Archives)

The war also created opportunities in industry. Roosevelt's Executive Order No. 8802, issued in 1941,

African American War Workers

required employers in defense industries to make jobs available "without discrimination because of race, creed, color or national origin." To secure defense jobs, 1.5 million black Americans migrated from the South to the industrial cities of the North and West in the 1940s. Almost three-fourths settled in the urban-industrial states of California, Illinois, Michigan, New York, Ohio, and Pennsylvania. More than half a million became active members of CIO unions like the United Auto Workers and United Steel Workers. African American voters in northern cities were beginning to constitute a vital swing vote, not only in local and state elections but also in presidential contests.

For African Americans, however, the benefits of urban life came with a high price tag. Migrants from the rural South had to adjust to life in big cities, and white hostility made the adjustment more difficult. Southern whites who had migrated north brought

Race Riots of 1943

with them the racial prejudices of the Deep South. Also hostile were the northern whites. In 1942 more than half of them believed that African Americans should be segregated in separate schools and neighborhoods. Such attitudes, and the competition between blacks and whites for jobs and housing, caused many people to fear that the summer of 1943 would be like 1919—another "Red Summer" (see page 651). Indeed, in 1943 almost 250 racial conflicts exploded in forty-seven cities. Outright racial warfare bloodied the streets of Detroit in June. At the end of thirty hours of rioting, twenty-five blacks and nine whites lay dead. White mobs, undeterred by police, had roamed the city attacking blacks and overturning cars. Blacks had hurled rocks at police and hauled white passengers off streetcars. Surveying the damage, an elderly black woman said, "There ain't no North any more. Everything now is South."

The federal government did practically nothing to prevent further racial violence. From President Roosevelt on down, most federal officials put the war first,

One hundred people were injured during the 1943 "zoot-suit riot" in Los Angeles, when white mobs attacked Mexican American men and tore off their zoot suits. During the riot, Los Angeles police arrested Mexican Americans for wearing such attire in violation of a city ordinance. These men in chains were headed to jail.   (Library of Congress)

domestic reform second. Unquestionably many government leaders held racist beliefs. Secretary of War Henry L. Stimson, for example, blamed the riots on "radical leaders of the colored race" who wanted to use the war to obtain "interracial marriages." But this time government neglect could not discourage African Americans and the century-old civil rights movement. By war's end they were ready—politically, economically, and emotionally—to wage a struggle for voting rights and for equal access to public accommodations and institutions.

Racial violence was not directed exclusively against blacks. Some whites judged people of Mexican origin as undesirable as those whose roots were African. In 1942 American farms and war industries needed workers, and the United States and Mexico had agreed to the *bracero* program, whereby Mexicans were admitted to the United States on short-term work contracts. Although the newcomers suffered racial discrimination and segregation, they seized the economic opportunities that had become available. In Los Angeles, seventeen thousand people of Mexican descent found shipyard jobs where before the war none had been available to them.

Ethnic and racial animosities intensified during the war. In 1943 Los Angeles witnessed the "zoot-suit riot," in which whites, most of them sailors and sol-

Bracero Program

diers, wantonly attacked Mexican Americans. Mexican American street gangs *(pachucos)* had adopted ducktail haircuts and zoot suits: long coats with wide padded shoulders, pegged pants, wide-brimmed hats, and dangling watch chains. White racist anger at the presumed arrogance of the zoot-suiters boiled over in June, and for four days mobs invaded Mexican American neighborhoods. According to one report, "Procedure was standard: grab a zooter. Take off his pants and frock coat and tear them up or burn them." Not only did white police officers look the other way during these assaults, but the city of Los Angeles passed an ordinance that made wearing a zoot suit within city limits a crime. Although the Second World War briefly provided economic opportunities for Mexican Americans, these years were not the transforming experience that they were for African Americans.

Women and Children in the War Effort

During the war large numbers of American women patriotically responded to their nation's call for help. The WACs (Women's Army Corps) enlisted 140,000 women, while 100,000 served in the navy's WAVES (Women Accepted for Volunteer Emergency Service)

and 39,000 in the Marine Corps and Coast Guard. Another 75,000 women served in the army and navy's Nursing Corps, where they saw duty during the invasions of North Africa, Italy, and France. Women also served as pilots in the WASP (Women Air Service Pilots), teaching basic flying, towing aerial targets for gunnery practice, ferrying planes across the country, and serving as test pilots. WASP flying duty was often hazardous; thirty-eight women lost their lives.

For economic as well as patriotic reasons, more than 6 million women entered the labor force during the war. During the Great Depression, when millions of men were unemployed, public opinion had been hostile to the hiring of women, but the war brought about a rapid increase in employment. Just when men were going off to war, industry had to recruit millions of new workers to supply the rapidly expanding need for military equipment. Filling these new jobs were African Americans, southern whites, Mexican Americans, and, above all, women.

No matter how impressive women's contributions were to the war effort, statistics tell only part of the story. Changes in people's attitudes were also important. Until early in the war, employers had insisted that women were not suited for industrial jobs. As labor shortages began to threaten the war effort, however, employers did an about-face. "Almost overnight," said Mary Anderson, head of the Women's Bureau of the Department of Labor, "women were reclassified by industrialists from a marginal to a basic labor supply for munitions making." Women became riveters, welders, crane operators, tool makers, shell loaders, lumberjacks ("lumberjills"), cowgirls, and police officers.

Women in War Production

During the war years, the number of working women increased by 57 percent. Two million women took clerical jobs; another 2.5 million worked in manufacturing. The significance of these figures lay not

Women workers mastered numerous job skills during the war. In 1942 crews of women cared for Long Island commuter trains like this one.   (Corbis-Bettmann)

just in the numbers themselves but also in the kinds of women who were entering the work force. The economist Claudia Goldin has observed that labor-force participation rates increased most for women over age forty-five, and that "married, rather than single women, were the primary means of bolstering the nation's labor force." Before the war the average female wage earner had been young, single, and largely self-supporting; by 1945 more working women were married than single, and more were over age thirty-five than under.

New employment opportunities also increased women's occupational mobility. Especially noteworthy were the gains made by African American women; over 400,000 quit work as domestic servants to enjoy the better working conditions, higher pay, and union benefits of industrial employment. To take advantage of the new employment opportunities, both black and white women willingly uprooted themselves. Over 7 million women moved to war-production areas, such as Willow Run, Michigan, site of a massive bomber plant, and southern California, home of both shipyards and aircraft factories.

As public opinion shifted to support women's war work, posters and billboards appeared urging women to "Do the Job HE Left Behind." Newspapers and magazines, radio, and movies proclaimed Rosie the Riveter a war hero. But few people asserted that women's war work should bring about a permanent shift in sex roles: it was merely a response to a national emergency. Once the victory was won, women should go back to nurturing their husbands and children, relinquishing their jobs to returning GIs. Wartime surveys, however, showed that many of the women wanted to remain in their jobs—80 percent of New York's women workers felt that way, as did 75 percent in Detroit. "War jobs have uncovered unsuspected abilities in American women," explained one woman. "Why lose all these abilities because of a belief that 'a woman's place is in the home'? For some it is," she added, "for others not."

Although women's wages rose when they acquired better jobs, they still received lower pay than men.

Discrimination Against Women

In 1945 women in manufacturing earned only 65 percent of what men were paid. An important reason for this inequality was the sex-segregated labor market. Although the wartime emergency caused some traditionally male jobs to be reclassified for women, most jobs were defined as either "women's work" or "men's work." Even in factories, most women worked in all-female shops. Working women, particularly working mothers, suffered in other ways as well. Early in the war, childcare centers were in short supply in war-boom areas. And even as mothers were being encouraged to work in the national defense, there was still opposition to their doing so. One form this campaign took was a series of exaggerated articles in mass-circulation magazines about the suffering of "eight-hour orphans" or "latchkey children," left alone or deposited in all-night movie theaters while their mothers worked eight-hour shifts in war plants.

By and large, however, the home-front children of working women were not neglected or abused during the war. Families made their own childcare arrangements, which often involved leaving children in the care of their grandmothers. Some families benefited from the Lanham Act of 1940, which provided federal aid to communities that had to absorb large war-related populations. Benefits included funds for childcare centers, hospitals, sewer systems, and additional police officers and firefighters. In late 1943, fewer than 60,000 children were enrolled in Lanham Act childcare centers; six months later, the number had more than doubled to 130,000. Another government program, Extended School Services, offered care for children before and after school; at the program's peak in 1943, it cared for 320,000 children. Although working mothers and their children received less of such help than they needed, the Second World War was a brief time of progress in the provision of childcare. Government support for these programs expired after the war.

Childcare in Wartime

America's children and youth made important contributions to the war effort. Children saved their nickels and dimes to buy war bonds, and they pulled wagons from house to house collecting old newspapers, rubber tires, and tin cans. "I became fiercely patriotic," recalled a Nebraska farm girl, "and participated in every war effort that I could." Thousands of young people also went to work during the war. In 1940, for example, 900,000 Americans between the ages of fourteen and eighteen were employed. By the spring of 1944 their number had climbed to 3 million—one-third of their age group. Teenagers were dropping out of high school in record numbers, and some observers believed that the most pressing social problem afflicting young people was not juvenile delinquency but failure to finish school. High-school enrollments hit new lows during the war, which prompted a back-to-school drive in 1944.

While millions of women were entering the work force, hundreds of thousands of women were also getting married. The number of marriages rose from 73 per 1,000 unmarried women in 1939 to 93 in 1942. Some couples scrambled to get married so they could live together before the man was sent overseas; others doubtless married and had children to qualify for military deferments. Many of these hasty marriages did not survive long military separations, and divorces soared, too—from 25,000 in 1939 to 359,000 in 1943 and 485,000 in 1945. As might be expected, the birth rate also climbed: total births rose from about 2.4 million in 1939 to 3.1 million in 1943. Many births were "goodbye babies," conceived as a guarantee that the family would be perpetuated if the father died in battle overseas.

Increase in Marriage, Divorce, and Birth Rates

Ironically, women's efforts to hold their families together during the war posed problems for returning fathers. Women war workers had brought home the wages; they had taken over the budgeting of expenses and the writing of checks. In countless ways they had proved they could hold the reins in their husbands' absence. Many husbands returned home to find that the lives of their wives and children seemed complete without them. And what of the women who wanted to remain in the labor market? In 1945 many such women were pushed out of the factories and shipyards to make way for returning veterans. Others chose to leave their jobs for a year or two before returning to work. But those who tried later to return to high-paying industrial work were discouraged, and many were forced into low-paying jobs in restaurants and laundries.

The Decline of Liberalism and the Election of 1944

Even before Pearl Harbor, political liberals had suffered major defeats. Some Democrats hoped to revive the reform movement during the war, but Republicans and conservative Democrats were on guard against such a move. In the 1942 elections, the Republicans, aided by a small voter turnout, scored impressive gains, winning forty-six new seats in the House and nine in the Senate and defeating Democratic governors in New York, California, and Michigan. Part of the Democrats' problem was that the war years, unlike the 1930s, were a time of full employment. Once people had acquired jobs and gained some economic security, they began to be more critical of New Deal policies. The New Deal coalition had always been a fragile alliance: southern white farmers had little in common with northern blacks or white factory workers. In northern cities, blacks and whites who had voted for Roosevelt in 1940 were competing for jobs and housing and soon would collide in race riots.

But though New Deal liberalism was enfeebled, it was far from dead. At its head still stood Franklin D. Roosevelt, and it had a program to present to the American people. The liberal agenda began with a pledge to secure full employment. Roosevelt emphasized the concept in his Economic Bill of Rights, delivered as part of his 1944 State of the Union address. Every American, the president declared, had a right to a decent job, to sufficient food, shelter, and clothing, and to financial security in unemployment, illness, and old age. If to accomplish those goals the government had to operate at a deficit, Roosevelt was willing to do so. But first he had to be reelected.

Wartime Liberalism

In 1944 Franklin D. Roosevelt looked like an exhausted old man. His eyes were tired and puffy, and the loose flesh that hung on his large frame made him appear emaciated. The president's personal physician pronounced "nothing organically wrong with him at all—he's perfectly O.K.," but rumors of his ill health persisted. Whether or not Roosevelt expected to survive his fourth term, he selected a running mate who was inexperienced in international affairs: Senator Harry S Truman of Missouri. Truman, who represented a border state and a big-city machine (the Pendergast machine in Kansas City), was acceptable both to southerners and to the party bosses. An ardent and loyal New Dealer, the senator also enjoyed the approval of liberals. There was little evidence, however, that he possessed the capacities for national and world leadership that he would need as president. Nor did Roosevelt take Truman into his confidence, failing even to inform his running mate about the atomic bomb project.

Roosevelt and Truman

Republicans were optimistic about their prospects for regaining the presidency. New York's Governor

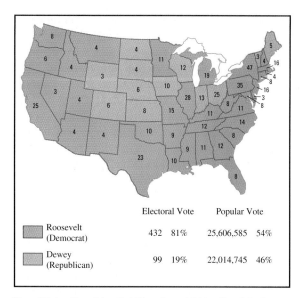

	Electoral Vote	Popular Vote
Roosevelt (Democrat)	432 81%	25,606,585 54%
Dewey (Republican)	99 19%	22,014,745 46%

Map 27.4   Presidential Election, 1944   Franklin D. Roosevelt's fourth—and last—presidential election was his closest yet, but he still carried thirty-six of the country's forty-eight states.

Thomas E. Dewey, who won the nomination on the first ballot, was moderate in his criticism of Roosevelt's foreign policy and did not advocate repeal of the essentials of the New Deal—Social Security, unemployment relief, collective bargaining, and parity payments for farmers. Dewey had one great liability—his public image. He was stiff in manner and bland in personality.

Roosevelt won a fourth term, but with his narrowest-ever margin of victory. Nevertheless, he won 53.5 percent of the popular vote **Roosevelt's Fourth-term Victory** and 432 electoral votes to Dewey's 99 (see Map 27.4). It was the urban vote that returned Roosevelt to the White House. Wartime population shifts had enhanced the Democrats' political clout: southern whites who had been lifelong Democrats, along with southern blacks who had never voted before, had migrated to the urban industrial centers and cast Democratic ballots.

Added to the Democrats' urban vote was a less obvious factor. Many voters seemed to be exhibiting what has been called "depression psychosis." Fearful that hard times would return once war contracts were terminated, they remembered New Deal relief programs and voted for Roosevelt. With victory within grasp, many Americans wanted Roosevelt's experienced hand to guide both the nation and the world to a lasting international peace. Roosevelt's death in April 1945, however, meant that Harry Truman would deal with the postwar world.

Planning for Peace

The aftermath of the First World War weighed heavily on the minds of American diplomats throughout the war. Americans vowed to make a peace that would ensure a postwar world free from economic depression, totalitarianism, and war. American goals included the Open Door policy and lower tariffs; self-determination for liberated peoples; avoidance of the debts-reparations fiasco that had plagued Europe after the First World War; expansion of the United States's sphere of influence; gradual and orderly decolonization; and management of world affairs by what Roosevelt once called the Four Policemen: the Soviet Union, China, Great Britain, and the United States.

Although the Allies concentrated on defeating the aggressors, their suspicions of one another undermined cooperation. Questions about **Allied Disagreement over Eastern Europe** eastern Europe proved the most difficult. The Soviet Union sought to fix its boundaries where they had stood before Hitler attacked in 1941. This meant that the part of Poland that the Soviets had invaded and captured in 1939 would become Soviet territory. The British and Americans hesitated, preferring to deal with eastern Europe at the end of the war. Yet in an October 1944 agreement, Churchill and Stalin struck a bargain: the Soviet Union would gain Romania and Bulgaria as a sphere of influence; Britain would have the upper hand in Greece; and the two countries would share authority in Yugoslavia and Hungary.

Poland stood as a special case. In 1943 Moscow had broken off diplomatic relations with the conservative Polish government-in-exile in London. The Poles had angered Moscow by asking the International Red Cross to investigate German charges, later substantiated, that the Soviets had massacred thousands of Polish army officers in the Katyn Forest in 1940. Then an uprising in Warsaw in 1944 complicated matters still further. Encouraged by approaching Soviet troops to expect assistance, the Warsaw underground rose against the occupying Germans. To the dismay of the world community, Soviet armies stood by as German troops slaughtered 166,000 people and devastated the city.

The Soviets then set up a pro-Communist government in Lublin. Thus near the end of the war Poland had two competing governments: one in London, recognized by America and Britain, and another in Lublin.

Early in the war the Allies had begun talking about a new international peacekeeping organization. At Teheran in 1943 Roosevelt called for an institution controlled by the Four Policemen. The next year, at a Washington, D.C., mansion called Dumbarton Oaks, American, British, Soviet, and Chinese representatives conferred on the details. The conferees approved a preliminary charter for a United Nations Organization, providing for a supreme Security Council dominated by the great powers and a weak General Assembly. The Security Council would have five permanent members, each with veto power (Britain had insisted that France be one of the permanent members). Meanwhile, the Soviet Union, hoping to counter pro-American and pro-British blocs in the General Assembly, asked for separate membership in the General Assembly for each of the sixteen Soviet republics. This issue was not resolved at Dumbarton Oaks, but the meeting proved a success nevertheless.

Creation of the United Nations

Diplomatic action on behalf of the European Jews, however, proved to be a tragic failure. By war's end, about 6 million Jews had been forced into concentration camps and systematically murdered, most by firing squads and in gas chambers. The Nazis also exterminated as many as 250,000 Gypsies and about 60,000 gay men. During the depression, the United States and other nations had refused to relax their immigration restrictions to save Jews fleeing persecution. Because of anti-Semitism and concern over competition for scarce jobs, American immigration officials applied the rules so strictly—requiring legal documents that fleeing Jews could not possibly provide—that otherwise-

Jewish Refugees

When the British liberated the Bergen-Belsen concentration camp near Hanover, Germany, in April 1945, they found this mass grave. It held the remains of thousands of Holocaust victims who had been starved, gassed, and machine-gunned by their Nazi jailers. This photograph and many others provide irrefutable proof of the Holocaust's savagery. (Imperial War Museum)

qualified refugees were kept out of the country. From 1933 to 1945, less than 40 percent of the German-Austrian immigration quota was filled.

Even the tragic voyage of the *St. Louis* did not change government policy. The vessel left Hamburg in mid-1939 carrying 930 desperate Jewish refugees who lacked proper immigration documents. Denied entry to Havana, the *St. Louis* headed for Miami, where Coast Guard cutters prevented it from docking. The ship was forced to return to Europe. Some of those refugees took shelter in countries that later were overrun by Hitler's legions. "The cruise of the *St. Louis*," wrote the *New York Times*, "cries to high heaven of man's inhumanity to man."

As evidence mounted that Hitler intended to ex-terminate the Jews, British and American representa-tives met in Bermuda in 1943 but

The Holocaust came up with no plans. Secretary of State Hull submitted a report to the president that emphasized "the un-known cost of moving an undetermined number of persons from an undisclosed place to an unknown des-tination." Appalled, Secretary of the Treasury Henry Morgenthau, Jr., charged that the State Department's foot-dragging made the United States an accessory to murder. "It takes months and months to grant the visa and then it usually applies to a corpse," he wrote bitterly. Early in 1944, stirred by Morgenthau's well-documented plea, Roosevelt created the War Refugee Board, which set up refugee camps in Europe and played a crucial role in saving 200,000 Jews from death. But, lamented one American official, "by that time it was too damned late to do too much."

With the war in Europe nearing an end, and a host of political questions—including what to do with Ger-many—yet to be settled, President

The Yalta Conference Roosevelt called for another summit meeting. The three Allied leaders met at Yalta, in the Russian Crimea, in early February 1945. Controversy has surrounded the conference ever since. Roosevelt was obviously ill, and critics of the Yalta agreements later charged that he was too weak to resist Stalin's cunning and that he struck a poor bargain. The evi-dence suggests, however, that Roosevelt was mentally alert and managed to sustain his strength during nego-tiations.

Each of the Allies arrived at Yalta with definite goals. Britain sought to make France a partner in the postwar occupation of Germany, to curb Soviet influ-ence in Poland, and to ensure protection for the vul-

nerable British Empire. The Soviet Union wanted reparations from Germany to assist in the massive task of rebuilding at home, possessions in Asia, continued influence in Poland, and a permanently weakened Germany so that the Soviet Union would never again suffer a German attack. The United States lobbied for the United Nations Organization, in which it believed it could exercise influence; for a Soviet declaration of war against Japan to aid in ending the war in the Pa-cific; for recognition of China as a major power; and for compromise between rival factions in Poland.

Military positions at the time of the conference helped to shape the final agreements. Soviet troops oc-cupied those countries in eastern Europe that they had liberated, including Poland, and Stalin repeatedly pointed out that twice in the century German armies had marched through Poland into Russian territory, killing millions. He insisted on a government friendly to Moscow—the Lublin regime—in order to pre-vent another German onslaught. He also demanded boundaries that would give Poland part of Germany in the west and the Soviet Union part of Poland in the east. Churchill boiled over in protest; he wanted the London government-in-exile to return to Poland.

With Roosevelt's help, a compromise was reached: a boundary favorable to the Soviet Union in the east; postponement of the western boundary issue; the cre-ation of a "more broadly based" coalition government that would include members of the London regime; and free elections to be held sometime in the future. The agreement was vague but, given Soviet occupa-tion of Poland, Roosevelt considered it "the best I can do."

As for Germany, the Big Three agreed that it would be divided into four zones, the fourth zone to be administered by France. Berlin, within the Soviet zone, also would be divided among the four victors. On the question of reparations, Stalin wanted a precise figure, but Churchill and Roosevelt insisted on determining Germany's ability to pay. With Britain abstaining, the Americans and Russians agreed that an Allied commit-tee would consider the sum of $20 billion as a basis for discussion in the future, with half of the amount to go to the Soviet Union.

Other issues led to tradeoffs. Stalin promised to declare war on Japan two or three months after Hitler's defeat. Since the Japanese were still resisting the American advance in Asia and since the atomic bomb was still on the drawing boards, American mili-tary leaders applauded the commitment. The Soviet premier also agreed to sign a treaty of friendship and

The three Allied leaders—Winston Churchill, Franklin D. Roosevelt, and Joseph Stalin—met at Yalta in February 1945. Having been president for twelve years, Roosevelt showed signs of age and fatigue. Two months later, he died of a massive cerebral hemorrhage.   (Franklin D. Roosevelt Library)

alliance with Jiang Jieshi (Chiang Kai-shek), America's ally in China, rather than with the Communist Mao Zedong (Mao Tse-tung). In return, the United States agreed to the Soviet Union's recovery of holdings Russia had lost to Japan after the Russo-Japanese War in 1905: the southern part of Sakhalin Island and the Kurile Islands. Regarding the new world organization, Roosevelt and Churchill granted the Soviets three votes in the General Assembly (fifty nations officially launched the United Nations Organization three months later). Finally, the conferees issued the Declaration of Liberated Europe, a pledge to establish order and to rebuild economies by democratic methods.

Yalta marked the high point of the Grand Alliance; in the tradition of diplomatic give-and-take,

Potsdam Conference

each of the Allies came away with something it wanted. But as the great powers jockeyed for influence at the close of the war, neither the spirit nor the letter of Yalta held firm. The crumbling of the alliance became evident almost immediately, at the Potsdam Conference, which began in mid-July. Roosevelt had died in April, and Truman—a novice at international diplomacy—was less patient with the Soviets. Truman also was emboldened by learning during the conference that the atomic test in New Mexico had been successful.

Despite major differences at Potsdam, the Big Three did agree on general policies toward Germany: complete disarmament, dismantling of industry used for military production, dissolution of Nazi institutions and laws, and war crimes trials. In a compromise over reparations, they decided that each occupying nation should extract reparations from its own zone; but they could not agree on a total figure. The Potsdam Conference also called for the "unconditional surrender" of Japan.

Potsdam left much undone. As the war drew to a close, there was little that bound the Allies together. Roosevelt's cooperative style was gone; the spirit of Yalta was evaporating; the common enemy, Hitler, was defeated. And the United States, with the awesome atomic bomb in the offing to force defeat on Japan, no longer needed or even wanted the Soviet Union in the Pacific war. Moreover, each of the victors was seeking to preserve and enlarge its sphere of influence. Britain claimed authority in Greece and parts of the Middle East; the Soviet Union already dominated much of eastern Europe; and the United States retained its hegemony in Latin America. The United States also seized several Pacific islands as strategic outposts and laid plans to dominate a defeated Japan. Let the Americans have their Pacific bases, responded Churchill, "but 'Hands off the British Empire' is our maxim."

Summary

Hitler once prophesied, "We may be destroyed, but if we are, we shall drag a world with us—a world in flames." Indeed, *rubble* was the word most often invoked to describe the European landscape at the end of the war. Hamburg, Stuttgart, and Dresden had been laid to waste; three-quarters of Berlin was in ruins; and in England, Coventry and London were bombed out. In Asia as well as in Europe, ghostlike people wandered about, searching desperately for food and mourning those who would never come home. The Soviet Union had suffered by far the greatest losses: more than 21 million military and civilian war dead—one-ninth of the total Soviet population. The Chinese calculated their war losses at 10 million, the Germans and Austrians at 6 million, and the Japanese at 2.5 million. And 6 million Jews had been killed during the Holocaust. In all, the Second World War caused the deaths of 55 million people.

Only one major combatant escaped such grisly statistics: the United States. Protected by ocean barriers, its cities were not burned and its fields were not trampled. American deaths from the war—405,399—

were few compared with the losses of other nations. In fact, the United States emerged from the Second World War more powerful than it had ever been. It alone had the atomic bomb. The U.S. Air Force and Navy were the largest anywhere. What is more, only the United States had the capital and economic resources to spur international recovery. In the coming struggle to fashion a new world out of the ashes of the old, soon to be called the Cold War (see Chapter 29), the United States held a commanding position.

On the home front, life for many Americans was fundamentally different in 1945 from what it had been before Pearl Harbor. For one thing, the war finally ended the Great Depression, reducing unemployment practically to zero. War jobs demanded workers, and women, people of color, and other Americans responded by moving to war-production centers. Among the migrants were African Americans, Mexican Americans, whites, and women of all races. Employers' negative attitudes toward women workers eased during the war, and millions of married middle-class women, many of them over forty-five, took jobs in shipyards and aircraft factories.

But life differed in other ways, too, especially for the American men and women who fought the war. The Academy Award for 1946 went to *The Best Years of Our Lives*, a painful film about the postwar readjustments of three veterans and their families and friends. Many men returned home suffering flashbacks, nightmares, and deep emotional distress. "Dad came home a different man," recalled one girl; "he didn't laugh as much and he drank a lot."

On another front, the Second World War stimulated the trend toward bigness, not only in business and labor but also in government, agriculture, higher education, and science. Over the next few years, government agencies that had been conceived as temporary became permanent and grew in size and influence, resulting in the Department of Defense (consolidating the War and Navy Departments), the Central Intelligence Agency (succeeding the Office of Strategic Services), and the Atomic Energy Commission. The seeds of the military-industrial complex were sown during these years. Moreover, with the advent of the Cold War, millions of young men would be inducted into the armed forces during the next thirty years. War and the expectation of war would become part of American life.

At the same time, the Second World War was a powerful engine of social change in the United States.

The gains made during the war by African Americans and women were overdue. And by blending New Deal ideology and wartime urgency, the government assumed the responsibility of ensuring prosperity and stepping in when capitalism faltered. Americans emerged from the war fully confident that theirs was the greatest country in the world. The United States, they boasted, had preserved democracy and freedom around the globe. For better or worse—and clearly there were elements of each—the Second World War was a turning point in the nation's history.

LEGACY FOR A PEOPLE AND A NATION
Atomic Waste

Although victory in the Second World War tasted sweet to the American people, the war's environmental legacy proved noxious, not to mention toxic and deadly. New industries brought with them hazardous pollutants. The production of synthetic rubber spewed forth sulfur dioxide, carbon monoxide, and other dangerous gases. War industries fouled the water and the soil with both solid and petrochemical wastes. Air pollution—smog—was first detected in Los Angeles in 1943, the result of that city's rapid wartime industrialization combined with widespread dependence on the automobile. Although these were ominous signs, few people at the time worried about human-made threats to America's seemingly endless supplies of fresh air, water, and soil.

No wartime, or postwar, weapons program became more threatening to the natural environment than the project to develop the atomic bomb. Many of the bomb's ingredients, notably plutonium, beryllium, and mercury, are highly toxic and contaminate the environment. The storing of radioactive waste began during the war at Oak Ridge, Tennessee, and Hanford, Washington, where plutonium was produced. During the postwar nuclear arms race with the Soviet Union, the United States opened other production facilities, for example, at Rocky Flats in Colorado and on the Savannah River in South Carolina. At these sites, radioactive waste seeped from leaky barrels into the soil and water, threatening human life and killing fish, birds, and other wildlife. Moreover, during 1945–1963, nuclear testing, which was done above ground, killed an estimated 800,000 Americans from cancer attributable to radioactive fallout.

As the United States enters the twenty-first century, the environmental legacy of the atomic bomb continues to threaten the American people. The biggest problem of the new millennium remains the oldest problem: how to dispose of radioactive materials. In 1999, when the federal government opened the nation's first nuclear dump in New Mexico, the initial shipment came from the Los Alamos National Laboratory, New Mexico, birthplace of the atomic bomb. Scientists, however, are skeptical that current technology is up to the task of cleaning soil and water at the nuclear weapons sites. "The technology . . . used to remediate contaminated sites," said the chairman of a National Research Council task force that studied the problem, "is simply ineffective and unable to accomplish the massive job that needs to be done."

For Further Reading, see page A-31 of the Appendix. For Web resources, go to http://www.college.hmco.com.

In 1945 Bob Bush was only eighteen years old, but he was already a veteran of the Second World War. And he was one of 440 Americans in the war to be awarded the Congressional Medal of Honor for valor on the battlefield. On May 2, 1945, Bush, a Navy medical corpsman, was attached to a marine rifle company fighting on the Japanese island of Okinawa. Firing from heavily fortified positions, the Japanese were inflicting heavy casualties on the Americans. Bush was constantly on the run, patching up one wounded marine after another. Lying in the open was a critically wounded officer; Bush rushed to the man's side and began giving him blood plasma just as the enemy opened fire again. Holding the bottle of plasma high in one hand, he drew his pistol with the other. According to the citation accompanying Bush's medal, he "fired into the enemy ranks until his ammunition was expended. Quickly seizing a discarded carbine, he trained his fire on the Japanese charging point blank over the hill," killing six men, "despite his own serious wounds and the loss of one eye. . . ."

Recovering from his wounds in a hospital in Hawai'i, Bob Bush thought about his future in postwar America. And in the navy plane carrying him back to the United States, he made a promise to himself: he was going to put the war behind him. "I was eighteen. I had to get back to school in the fall. I had the girlfriend back home in [the state of] Washington." Her name was Wonda Spooner, and she too was eighteen. Bob wanted to ask her to marry him, and he was pleased when she said yes; that summer they were married. For their honeymoon, the couple boarded a train for Washington, D.C., where President Harry S Truman awarded Bush the Medal of Honor.

Back home, Bush completed his high-school requirements and, under the GI Bill, enrolled in business courses at the University of Washington. Anticipating a postwar housing boom, Bush and another veteran

In postwar America, millions of families shopped for new houses in the country's burgeoning suburbs. In the first decade after the Second World War, 4.3 million veterans used GI Bill loan provisions to purchase single-family residences. Many of these men and women were members of what Tom Brokaw, NBC's news anchor, has called "the greatest generation." They survived the Great Depression, served in the war, and became parents of America's baby boomers. (H. Armstrong Roberts)

POSTWAR AMERICA: COLD WAR POLITICS, CIVIL RIGHTS, AND THE BABY BOOM 1945–1961

Cold War Politics: The Truman Presidency

Consensus and Conflict: The Eisenhower Presidency

McCarthyism

The Civil Rights Movement in the 1940s and 1950s

The Postwar Booms: Babies, Business, and Bigness

Conformity and Consumerism

The Other America

The Election of 1960 and the Dawning of a New Decade

LEGACY FOR A PEOPLE AND A NATION

The Eradication of Polio

then decided to buy a small lumberyard. As Tom Brokaw describes in his 1998 book *The Greatest Generation*, Bush was ambitious and hard working, putting in seven-day weeks and occasionally twenty-four-hour days. Like other veterans in postwar America, he felt he had to make up for lost time. "Everyone," Bush said, "should learn the meaning of that famous little four-letter word—*work*." In the 1940s and 1950s, his business boomed, and he acquired more lumberyards, eventually owning seven along with building supply stores, a ready-mix concrete business, and a mobile-home dealership.

Like so many veterans in postwar America, Bush had one overriding goal: to build a happy life for his family. While he was busy succeeding in business, Wonda was busy at home raising their baby-boom children, three boys and a girl. As in many families in the 1950s, Bob was often an absentee father. Wonda, on the other hand, was an indulgent mother who rose early to cook breakfast for the family, pack the school lunches, do laundry, and keep their comfortable house spotless. This division of gender roles and authority was the rule, not the exception, in postwar American homes.

The Bushes were not alone in having babies after the war. From 1946 until 1964, births hit record highs. During this period 76 million babies were born in the United States, compared with only 44 million during the period of depression and war from 1929 through 1945. The postwar baby boom was larger and in other ways different from increases in the birth rate that earlier generations had experienced. Parents who had grown up during the Great Depression were determined that their children's lives would be better than theirs had been. And many succeeded in making it so.

Material comfort was the hallmark for millions of middle-class families. In terms of both income level and lifestyle, more Americans were better off than ever before—and most expected their good fortune to continue. Often, however, both parents worked to pay for a new home and a second car. This meant that women had at least two jobs, for they still were expected to do the housework and cooking. In postwar America, "family togetherness" took on almost religious significance, including evenings watching television in the "family room" and family vacations to Disneyland.

Postwar America was not only prosperous, but also proud and boastful. From 1945 to the 1960s, the American people were in the grip of "victory culture"—that is, the belief that unending triumph was the nation's birthright and destiny. From the classroom, the pulpit, and the town hall, as well as from popular-culture avenues, came self-congratulatory rhetoric about America's invincibility. And the country had an enemy in a new conflict known as the Cold War: communism in both the Soviet Union and China (see Chapter 29). Americans believed that their nation was the greatest in the world, not only the most powerful but the most righteous. And, Americans agreed, it was getting better all the time.

As evidence of the nation's perfectibility, Americans pointed to the postwar economic boom. The cornerstones of the boom, which began in 1945 and lasted twenty-five years, were the automobile, construction, and defense industries. As the gross national product (GNP) grew, income levels rose and property ownership spread. Automobiles rolled off the assembly lines; new houses and schools sprang up throughout the country. More and more people bought homes in the suburbs.

Although the postwar years constituted an age of consensus, Cold War politics were often volatile. When Harry Truman became president in 1945, his initial response to the challenge was a deep feeling of inadequacy. As vice president, Truman had been kept ignorant by Franklin D. Roosevelt about crucial foreign and military initiatives; nevertheless, he would have to deal with the closing months of the war and with the onset of the Cold War. In domestic matters, too, the ill-prepared president would need a crash course in the intricacies of governing the United States. The nation's reconversion from war back to peace was not smooth, and Truman angered liberals, conservatives, farmers, consumers, and union members.

In 1948, Truman seemed politically vulnerable, but he confounded experts by winning the presidency in his own right. His victory demonstrated the volatility of politics. The key domestic issues of the postwar period—civil rights for African Americans and the anti-Communist crusade to be called McCarthyism—were both highly charged. Later, the outbreak of the Korean War in 1950 intensified discontent. The war, inflation, and corruption in the White House caused Truman's popularity to plummet. After twenty years of Democratic presidents, Americans in 1952 elected the Republican nominee, General Dwight D. Eisenhower.

Eisenhower was a decisive and decorated war hero, but as president he moved cautiously and hesitantly, particularly in dealing with civil rights and McCarthyism. His major goal was to promote economic growth, and he pursued staunchly Republican goals: a balanced budget, reduced taxes and government spending, low inflation, and a return of power to the

IMPORTANT EVENTS

1945 Roosevelt dies; Truman becomes president
12 million GIs demobilized
Truman's economic message to Congress

1946 Baby boom begins
Spock's *Baby and Child Care* changes child-rearing practices
More than 1 million GIs enroll in colleges
Coal miners strike
Inflation reaches 18.2 percent
Republicans win both houses of Congress

1947 Truman institutes employee loyalty program
Taft-Hartley Act limits power of unions
To Secure These Rights issued by the President's Committee on Civil Rights
Planned community begun in Levittown, N.Y.

1948 Truman appoints committee to oversee racial desegregation of the armed forces
Truman elected president
Kinsey's *Sexual Behavior in the Human Male* published

1949 Soviet Union explodes an atomic bomb
Communists win revolution in China
National Housing Act promises decent housing for all Americans

1950 Fuchs arrested as an atomic spy
Hiss convicted of perjury
McCarthy alleges Communists in government
Korean War begins
Rosenbergs charged with conspiracy to commit treason
Internal Security (McCarran) Act requires members of "Communist front" organizations to register with the government

1951 Supreme Court upholds the Alien Registration (Smith) Act in *Dennis et al. v. U.S.*

1952 Ellison's *Invisible Man* shows African Americans' exclusion from the American Dream
Eisenhower elected president
Republicans win both houses of Congress

1953 Korean War ends
Rosenbergs executed

Congress adopts termination policy for Native Americans
Kinsey causes further public uproar with *Sexual Behavior in the Human Female*

1954 *Brown* decision reverses "separate-but-equal" doctrine
Communist Control Act makes Communist Party membership illegal
Senate condemns McCarthy

1955 AFL and CIO merge
Rebel Without a Cause idealizes youth subculture
Disneyland opens in Anaheim, California
Montgomery bus boycott begins

1956 Highway Act launches interstate highway system
Eisenhower reelected
Ginsberg's poem *Howl*, anthem of the Beat generation, published
Presley releases his first single

1957 King elected first president of the Southern Christian Leadership Conference
Little Rock, Arkansas, desegregation crisis
Congress passes Civil Rights Act
Soviet Union launches *Sputnik*
Kerouac criticizes white middle-class conformity in *On the Road*

1958 Congress passes National Defense Education Act to improve education in mathematics, foreign languages, and science
Adams resigns over scandal
St. Lawrence Seaway opens

1960 Sit-in in Greensboro, North Carolina
Student Nonviolent Coordinating Committee formed
Kennedy elected president

1961 Eisenhower warns against "military-industrial complex"

1962 Harrington's *The Other America* creates awareness of America's poor
Carson's *Silent Spring* warns of dangers of DDT

states. During Eisenhower's eight-year presidency, the nation was generally quiescent politically. Americans celebrated the American Dream and their economic system for providing a high standard of living, and they liked the president's traditionalism, caution, and moderation.

It was the infant civil rights movement that challenged the national consensus. Most African Americans, still farm workers in the South, were at the bottom of the economic ladder and were being denied constitutional rights such as the right to vote. How would blacks be incorporated into the consensus? The president, Congress, southern whites, and black civil rights activists all gave different answers as they debated *Brown v. Board of Education of Topeka*, the Supreme Court's momentous decision of 1954 invalidating racial segregation in public schools.

Still, however fragile, the age of consensus remained basically intact. President Eisenhower was succeeded in 1961 by a much younger man, Democratic senator John F. Kennedy of Massachusetts. The 1960s would be a far different decade. For one thing, the exceptions to the American Dream, ignored by affluent Americans in the 1950s, got attention. By the early 1960s, it was clear that the American poor were much more numerous than many people had imagined. Meanwhile, throughout the country from 1945 to 1961, race relations and urban conditions continued to deteriorate. In the 1960s the nation would have to deal with problems it had postponed addressing for too long. ■

Cold War Politics: The Truman Presidency

After the initial joyous reaction to the end of the Second World War, Americans faced a number of important questions. What would be the effect of reconversion—the cancellation of war contracts, termination of wage and price controls, and expiration of wartime labor agreements? Would depression recur as the artificial stimulus of the war was withdrawn, throwing people out of work and sending prices downward? Or would Americans spend the money they had saved during the war years and go on a buying spree?

Even before the war's end, cutbacks in production had caused layoffs. At Ford Motor Company's massive Willow Run plant outside Detroit,

Postwar Job Layoffs

where nine thousand Liberator bombers had been produced, most workers were let go in the spring of 1945. Ten days after the victory over Japan, 1.8 million people nationwide received pink slips, and 640,000 filed for unemployment compensation. The employment picture was made more complex by the return of millions of discharged GIs in 1945 and 1946; 12 million GIs were demobilized in 1945 alone. At the peak of postwar unemployment in March 1946, 2.7 million people searched for work.

Fearing that an economic depression might result from the cancellation of war contracts, President Tru-

man declared his determination not only to combat unemployment but also to expand on New Deal programs begun in the 1930s. In September 1945 he delivered to Congress a twenty-one-point message urging extension of unemployment compensation, an increase in the minimum wage, adoption of permanent farm price supports, and new public works projects. Truman also revived Roosevelt's Economic Bill of Rights—its linchpin, the right of every able-bodied American to hold a job. If the economy failed to provide one, the government should create it.

Despite high unemployment immediately after the war, the United States was hardly on the brink of depression. In fact, after a brief period of readjustment, the economy embarked on a quarter-century of unprecedented boom. People had plenty of savings to spend in 1945 and 1946, and, in time, there were new houses and cars for them to buy. Easy credit also promoted the buying binge. As a result, despite the winding down of war production, the GNP continued to rise in 1945. The nation's most immediate postwar economic problem was not depression but inflation, fueled by maddening shortages of consumer goods like meat and housing. Throughout 1945 and 1946 prices skyrocketed; inflation exceeded 18 percent in 1946.

Beginnings of the Postwar Economic Boom

As prices spiraled upward, many people were earning less in real income (actual purchasing power) than they had earned during the war. Industrial workers had complained during the war that the National War Labor Board limited their pay increases to barely perceptible cost-of-living increments. In the immediate postwar period they protested that the end of war production had eliminated much of their overtime work. A primary reason for workers' discontent was that as their wages and salaries declined slightly in 1946, net profits reached all-time highs. Indignant that they were not sharing in the prosperity, unions forced nationwide shutdowns in the coal, automobile, steel, and electric industries and halted railroad and maritime transportation.

Upsurges in Labor Strikes

By 1946 there was no doubt about the growing unpopularity of labor unions and their leadership. Many Americans blamed the unions for strikes, which restricted the output of consumer goods and inflated prices. In May, when a nationwide railroad strike was threatened, Truman made a dramatic appearance before a joint session of Congress. If strikers in an industry deemed vital to the national security refused to honor a presidential order to return to work, he would "request the Congress immediately to authorize the President to draft into the Armed Forces of the United States all workers who are on strike against their government." Truman's speech alienated not just the railroad workers but union members in general. Many vowed to defeat him in the upcoming 1948 presidential election.

Truman fared little better in his direction of the Office of Price Administration (OPA). Now that the war was over, powerful interests wanted price controls lifted. Consumers grew impatient with shortages and black-market prices, and manufacturers and farmers wanted to raise prices legally. Yet when most controls expired in mid-1946 and inflation rose further, consumers grumbled. Truman's approval rating plunged from 87 percent in late 1945 to 32 percent in 1946. Republicans made the most of public discontent. "Got enough meat?" asked Republican congressman John M. Vorys of Ohio. "Got enough houses? Got enough OPA? . . . Got enough inflation? . . . Got enough debt? . . . Got enough strikes?" In 1946 the Republicans won a majority in both houses of the Eightieth Congress, and the White House in 1948 seemed within their grasp.

Consumer Discontent

But the politicians who dominated the Eightieth Congress, whether Republicans or southern Democrats, were committed conservatives, and if Truman had alienated labor and consumers, the Eightieth Congress made them livid. Particularly unpopular with workers was the Taft-Hartley Act, which Congress approved over Truman's veto in 1947. A revision of the Wagner Act of 1935, the bill prohibited the closed shop, a workplace where membership in a particular union was a prerequisite for being hired. It also permitted the states to enact right-to-work laws banning union-shop agreements, which required all workers to join if a majority voted in favor of a union shop. In addition, the law forbade union contributions to political candidates in federal elections, required union leaders to swear in affidavits that they were not Communists, and mandated an eighty-day cooling-off period before carrying out strikes that imperiled the national security. Truman's veto of the Taft-Hartley Act vindicated him in the eyes of labor.

Throughout 1947 and 1948, the conservative Eightieth Congress offended not only unions but numerous other interest groups, such as farm organizations, which in turn swung back to Truman. Indeed,

After the war, American Indians lost sacred land to both big corporations and the federal government. In 1948 George Gillette *(left),* chairman of the Fort Berthold, North Dakota, Indian Tribal Council, covers his face and weeps as Secretary of the Interior J. A. Krug signs a contract buying 155,000 acres of tribal land for a reservoir. (Wide World Photos, Inc.)

Republicans seemed oblivious to public opinion. Not since 1928 had they been so confident of capturing the presidency, and most political experts agreed. "Only a political miracle or extraordinary stupidity on the part of the Republicans," according to *Time,* "can save the Democratic party." At their national convention, Republicans strengthened their position by nominating the governors of two of the nation's most populous states: Thomas E. Dewey of New York for president and Earl Warren of California for vice president.

Democrats were up against more than Republicans in 1948. Two years before, Henry A. Wallace, the only remaining New Dealer in the cabinet, had been fired by Truman for publicly criticizing U.S. foreign policy. In 1948 Wallace ran for president on the Progressive Party ticket, which advocated friendly relations with the Soviet Union, racial desegregation, and nationalization of basic industries. A fourth party, the

Dixiecrats (States' Rights Democratic Party), was organized by southerners who walked out of the 1948 Democratic convention when it adopted a pro–civil rights plank; they nominated Governor Strom Thurmond of South Carolina. If Wallace's candidacy did not destroy Truman's chances, experts said, the Dixiecrats certainly would.

Truman's Upset Victory

But Truman had a few ideas of his own. He called the Eightieth Congress into special session and challenged it to enact all the planks in the Republican platform. If Republicans really wanted to transform their convictions into law, said Truman, this was the time to do it. After Congress had debated for two weeks and accomplished nothing of significance, Truman took to the road, delivering scores of speeches denouncing the "do-nothing" Eightieth Congress. Still, no amount of furious campaigning by Truman seemed likely to change the predicted outcome.

As the votes were counted, however, it was clear that Truman had confounded the experts. The final tally was 24 million popular votes and 303 electoral votes for Truman; 22 million popular votes and 189 electoral votes for Dewey (see Map 28.1). How and why did the upset occur? First, the United States was prosperous, at peace, and essentially united on foreign policy. Second, Roosevelt's legacy—the New Deal coalition—had endured: African Americans, union members, and voters in northern cities, along with most southern whites, had rallied to Truman's support. Many farmers also voted for Truman, fearful that the Republicans would drastically reduce price supports for agricultural goods. Finally, the extremist image of the Progressive and Dixiecrat Parties helped Truman by making the Democratic Party look moderate. Rather than receiving the predicted 5 million votes each, Wallace and Thurmond polled just over 1 million each.

Truman began his new term brimming with confidence. It was time, he believed, for government to fulfill its responsibility to provide economic security for the poor and the elderly. As he worked on his 1949 State of the Union message, he penciled in an expression of his intentions: "I expect to give every segment of our population a fair deal." Little of Truman's Fair Deal came to fruition, however, and he would leave office a highly unpopular president. One reason for the president's unpopularity was the Korean War, which broke out in 1950.

Korean War Discontent on the Home Front

In June 1950, following the invasion of South Korea by North Korea, President Truman ordered American troops to fight in Korea (see Chapter 29). There was much grumbling among Americans as the nation again mobilized for war. People remembered the shortages of the last war and flocked to their grocery stores for sugar, coffee, and canned goods. Fueled by panic buying, inflation began to rise again. Moreover, people disliked the draft, and many reservists and national guardsmen resented being among those called to active duty. Thanks to an unpopular war and charges of influence peddling by some of Truman's cronies, the president's public approval rating slumped to an all-time low of 23 percent in 1951 and stayed at that level for a year. Once again the Democratic Party appeared doomed along with its leader—and this time appearances proved correct.

Although Truman was highly unpopular when he left office in 1953, historians now rate him among the nation's ten best presidents. Truman was president at

Map 28.1   Presidential Election, 1948   In 1948 Harry S Truman won perhaps the biggest upset in a presidential election, defeating not only the Republican candidate but also challengers from the States' Rights Democratic (Dixiecrat) and Progressive Parties.

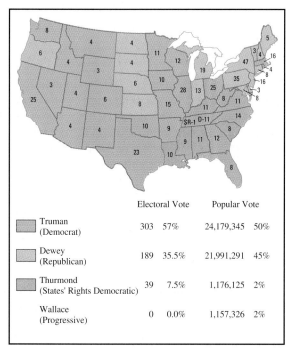

	Electoral Vote		Popular Vote	
Truman (Democrat)	303	57%	24,179,345	50%
Dewey (Republican)	189	35.5%	21,991,291	45%
Thurmond (States' Rights Democratic)	39	7.5%	1,176,125	2%
Wallace (Progressive)	0	0.0%	1,157,326	2%

Consensus and Conflict: The Eisenhower Presidency   **793**

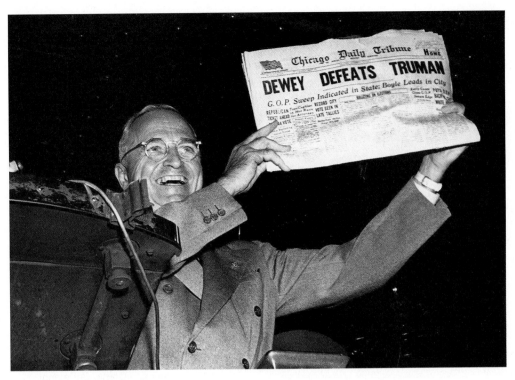

So few pollsters predicted that President Harry S Truman (1884–1972) would win in 1948 that the *Chicago Tribune* announced his defeat before all the returns were in. Here a victorious Truman pokes fun at the newspaper for its premature headline.   (Corbis-Bettmann)

Truman's Historical Standing

the beginning of the Cold War, and in eight years he strengthened the powers of the presidency. Agencies that had been set up for temporary duty during the Second World War were made permanent, among them the Atomic Energy Commission. And legislation in 1947 created a unified Department of Defense and a permanent intelligence service, the Central Intelligence Agency (CIA). On the domestic front, Truman was a New Dealer who fought for programs to benefit workers, African Americans, farmers, homeowners, retired persons, and people in need of healthcare. He showed his spunk and courage in 1948 when he pulled off the biggest upset in American political history. Although little of Truman's Fair Deal was enacted during his presidency, much of it became law as part of the Great Society in the 1960s, in such legislation as Medicare and the Civil Rights Acts of 1964 and 1965 (see Chapter 30).

Consensus and Conflict: The Eisenhower Presidency

In the 1952 presidential election, voters agreed with the Republican campaign slogan "It's Time for a Change." What sealed the fate of the Democratic Party was the Republican candidacy of General Dwight D. Eisenhower. A bona fide war hero who had come from humble origins in Kansas, "Ike" had a warm, friendly smile, and he seemed to embody the virtues Americans most admired: integrity, decency, and lack of pretense. Eisenhower's unlucky Democratic opponent was Adlai Stevenson, the thoughtful and witty governor of Illinois. It was never much of a contest, especially after Eisenhower promised to "go to Korea," implying he would end the war. The result was a landslide: Eisenhower and his running mate, Senator Richard M. Nixon of California, won almost 34 million popular votes and 442 electoral votes, to the Democrats' 27

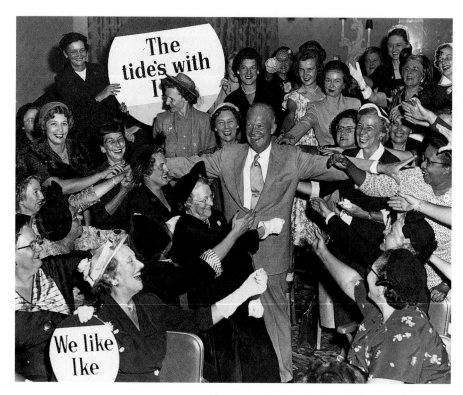

During the 1952 presidential campaign, Dwight D. Eisenhower (1890–1969) receives a delegation of Republican national committee women at his New York City headquarters. As the women chant "I Like Ike," the Republican candidate opens his arms to welcome them. (Corbis-Bettmann)

million popular and 89 electoral votes. The Republicans even lured to their fold four states in the once-solid Democratic South. Moreover, Eisenhower's coattails were long enough to carry other Republicans to victory; the party gained control of both houses of Congress, though with only a one-seat margin in the Senate.

Smiling Ike, with his folksy style, garbled syntax, and frequent escapes to the golf course, provoked Democrats to charge that he failed to lead. But Dwight D. Eisenhower was not that simple. He was no stranger to hard work. His low-key, "hidden-hand" style was a way of playing down his role as politician and highlighting his role as chief of state. Eisenhower relied heavily on staff work, delegating authority to cabinet members. Sometimes he was not well informed on details and gave the impression that he was out of touch with his own government. In fact, he was not, and he remained a very popular president.

During Eisenhower's presidency most Americans clung to the status quo. It was an era of both self-congratulation and constant anxiety.

The "Consensus Mood"

British journalist Godfrey Hodgson has described the "consensus mood," writing that Americans were "confident to the verge of complacency

about the perfectibility of American society, anxious to the point of paranoia about the threat of communism." Demand for reform at such a time seemed to most Americans unnecessary, if not unpatriotic. Historian Henry Steele Commager saw conformity everywhere in the 1950s, as evidenced by "the uncritical and unquestioning acceptance of America as it is." College students shunned passionate political convictions. A weak minority on the American left advocated checks on the political power of corporations, and a noisy minority on the right accused the government of a wishy-washy campaign against communism. But both liberal Democrats and moderate Republicans avoided extremism, satisfied to be occupying what the historian Arthur M. Schlesinger, Jr., called "the vital center."

In this age of consensus, President Eisenhower approached his duties with a philosophy he called "dynamic conservatism." He meant being "conservative when it comes to money and liberal when it comes to human beings." Eisenhower's was unabashedly "an Administration representing business and industry," as Interior Secretary Douglas McKay acknowledged. The president and his appointees gave priority to reducing the federal budget, but they did not always succeed; and they rec-

"Dynamic Conservatism"

ognized that dismantling New Deal and Fair Deal programs was politically impossible. The administration did try to remove the federal government from agriculture, but the effort failed because of the political power of the farm lobby. Despite several changes in federal farm price support policy, the government found itself spending more money and stockpiling increased amounts of surplus farm commodities.

Eisenhower made headway in other spheres. In 1954 Congress passed legislation to construct a canal, the St. Lawrence Seaway, between Montreal and Lake Erie. This inland waterway, which opened in 1958, was intended to spur the economic development of the Midwest by linking the Great Lakes to the Atlantic Ocean. Also in 1954 Eisenhower signed into law amendments to the Social Security Act that raised benefits and added 7.5 million workers, mostly self-employed farmers, to the program's coverage. Congress also obliged the president with tax reform that raised business depreciation allowances and with the Atomic Energy Act of 1954, which granted private companies the right to own reactors and nuclear materials for the production of electricity.

Eisenhower also presided over a dramatic change in the lives of Native Americans. After little consultation with Native Americans, the government embarked on a radical departure from policies established under the New Deal's Indian Reorganization Act of 1934 (see page 721). In 1953 Congress adopted a policy known as *termination*: the forced assimilation of Native Americans into the dominant culture by terminating the Indian reservations, as well as by ending tribal sovereignty and federal services to Indians. Another act of the same year made Indians subject to state laws. Eisenhower administration officials applauded the changes because they would reduce federal costs and serve states' rights. Critics—including most Indians—denounced termination as one more attempt to grab Indian lands and exploit Native Americans.

Termination Policy for Native Americans

Between 1954 and 1960, the federal government withdrew its benefits from sixty-one tribes. About one in eight Indians abandoned the reservations; many joined the ranks of the urban poor in low-paying jobs. The policy of termination and relocation was motivated largely by land greed. The Klamaths of Oregon, for example, lived on a reservation rich in ponderosa pine, which lumber interests coveted. Enticed by cash payments, almost four-fifths of the Klamaths accepted termination and voted to sell their shares of the forest-

land. With termination, their way of life collapsed. By the time termination was halted in the 1960s, so much human tragedy had struck Native Americans that observers compared the situation to the devastation their forebears had endured in the nineteenth century.

In the 1954 congressional elections, most Americans revealed that, though they still liked Eisenhower, they remained loyal to the Democratic Party. With a recession just winding down, the voters gave the Democrats control of both houses of Congress. Lyndon B. Johnson of Texas became the Senate's new majority leader. An energetic, pragmatic politician, Johnson worked with the Republican White House to pass legislation, including the Highway Act of 1956, which launched the largest public works program in American history, authorizing the construction over the next thirteen years of an interstate highway system. In 1955 Eisenhower suffered a heart attack but regained his strength and declared his intention to run again. The Democrats nominated Adlai E. Stevenson once more. Eisenhower, running again with Nixon, won a landslide victory in 1956: 36 million votes and 457 electoral votes to Stevenson's 26 million and 73. Americans decided to stick with an experienced military man and statesman at a time of world unrest. Still, the Democrats continued to dominate Congress.

Election of 1956

Eisenhower faced rising federal expenditures in his second term, in part because of the tremendous expense of America's global activities (see Chapter 29). In the first three years of his presidency he had managed to trim the budget, largely by controlling defense spending. But the president discovered that he had to tolerate deficit spending to achieve his goals. In 1959 federal expenditures climbed to $92 billion, about half of which went to the military. In fact, Eisenhower balanced only three of his eight budgets. The administration's resort to deficit spending also was fueled by the need to cushion the impact of three recessions—in 1953–1954, 1957–1958, and 1960–1961. A sluggish economy and unemployment also reduced the tax dollars collected by the federal government.

Setbacks in 1958 made that year a low point for the Eisenhower administration. Scandal unsettled the White House when the president's chief aide, Sherman Adams, resigned under suspicion of influencing government regulatory decisions in exchange for luxury gifts such as a fur coat. Then came large Republican losses in the 1958 congressional elections. The Democrats took the Senate by 64 seats to 34 and the

House by 283 seats to 153. In 1960 the economy was in a recession, and the Soviets downed a Central Intelligence Agency U-2 spy plane (see page 842). First, Eisenhower denied that it was a spy plane; and his credibility suffered when he later conceded that it was.

Eisenhower Presidency Assessed

Assessments of the Eisenhower administration used to emphasize its conservatism, passive style, limited achievements, and reluctance to confront difficult issues. In recent years, interpretations have been changing as scholars have begun examining the now-declassified documents of the consensus era. Current evaluations often stress Eisenhower's command of policymaking, sensibly moderate approach to most problems, political savvy, and great popularity. Eisenhower no longer appears to be just an aging bystander but a competent, pragmatic leader who gave most Americans what they wanted at the time—a grandfatherly figure in the White House, economic comfort, and unrelenting anticommunism.

The record of Eisenhower's presidency is nonetheless mixed. At home he failed to deal with poverty, urban decay, and blatant denials of civil rights—problems that would wrack the country in the next decade. But in comparison with his successors in the 1960s, Eisenhower was measured and cautious. He kept military budgets under control and managed crises adroitly so that the United States avoided major military ventures abroad. But he authorized CIA covert actions to overthrow elected governments in Iran and Guatemala. At home the Eisenhower administration curbed inflation, strengthened the infrastructure by building an interstate highway system, and expanded Social Security coverage. Eisenhower brought dignity to the presidency, and the American people respected him.

The "Military-Industrial Complex"

Just before leaving office in early 1961, Eisenhower went on national radio and television to deliver his farewell address to the nation. Because of the Cold War, he observed, the United States had been "compelled to create a permanent industry of vast proportions," as well as a standing army of 3.5 million. "This conjunction of an immense military establishment and a large arms industry is new in the American experience," Eisenhower noted. "The total influence—economic, political, even spiritual—is felt in every city, nomic, political, even spiritual—is felt in every city,

every statehouse, every office of the federal government." So powerful was this influence, the president declared, that it threatened the nation's democratic processes. Then Eisenhower issued a direct warning, urging Americans to "guard against . . . the military-industrial complex." They did not.

McCarthyism

One of the most volatile political issues in postwar America was the anti-Communist crusade known as McCarthyism. Both Truman and Eisenhower overreacted to the alleged threat of Communist subversion in government. Their alarmist rhetoric heightened public anxiety, and their loyalty programs ruined innocent people's lives and careers.

It is a misconception that anticommunism began in 1950 with the furious speeches of Senator Joseph R. McCarthy of Wisconsin. Actually, anticommunism had been a prominent strand in the American political fabric ever since the First World War and the Red Scare of 1919 and 1920. The Communist Party had never been strong in the United States, even during the hard times of the depression. But anticommunism persisted, and the Cold War heightened anti-Communist fears. In manipulating these fears to his own advantage, Joe McCarthy became the most successful and frightening redbaiter the country had ever seen.

Was there reason to fear Communist influence in the United States in the 1940s and 1950s? During the Second World War when the United States and the Soviet Union fought as allies, membership in the Communist Party of the United States of America (CPUSA) reached 80,000, up from 55,000 in 1938. In fact, as part of the war effort the United States voluntarily supplied valuable military intelligence to the Soviets, and 15,000 CPUSA members served in the American armed forces. In addition, however, documents selectively released in the 1990s from Russian archives suggest not only that Soviet spies had penetrated America's top-secret Manhattan Project to build the atomic bomb, but also that a handful of Americans working in sensitive government departments had provided classified documents to Soviet espionage agents. Was the CPUSA a tool of the Soviet Union? Its leaders were, but much of its membership was not. As the historian Ellen Schrecker has observed, the party "was both subservient to the Kremlin and genuinely dedicated to a wide range of social reforms," such as the elimination of racism in America.

In the postwar years, there was little hard evidence about Soviet espionage in the United States. Nevertheless, politicians of many stripes played on anti-Communist paranoia, and President Truman shared responsibility for initiating the postwar anti-Communist crusade. He was bothered by the revelation in 1945 that classified government documents had been found in a raid on the offices of *Amerasia*, a little-known magazine whose editors sympathized with the Communist revolution in China. Who had supplied the documents to the magazine, and why? Similar concerns greeted the release of a Canadian royal commission report in 1946, which asserted that Soviet spies were operating in Canada; among them, the report said, was a scientist who had transmitted atomic secrets to a Soviet agent.

Spurred by these revelations, Truman in 1947 ordered investigations into the loyalty of the more than 3 million employees of the U.S. government.

Truman's Loyalty Probe

In 1950 the government began discharging people deemed "security risks," among them alcoholics, homosexuals, and debtors thought to be susceptible to blackmail. In most cases there was no evidence of disloyalty. Others became victims of guilt by association. Their loyalty was considered questionable because they either knew or were related to people thought to be subversive or disloyal.

The wellspring of this fear of communism was the Cold War: fear of internal subversion was intertwined with fear of external attack. Truman was not alone in peddling fear; conservatives and liberal Democrats joined him in accusing their political enemies of being "soft on communism." Republicans used the same methods to attack the Democratic candidates for president in 1948 and 1952; liberal Democrats used them to discredit the far-left, pro-Wallace wing of their party. The anti-Communist crusade of the late 1940s, created by professional politicians, was embraced and promoted by labor union officials, religious leaders, media moguls, and other influential figures.

Americans began to point accusing fingers at one another. "Reds, phonies, and 'parlor pinks,'" in Truman's words, seemed to lurk everywhere. Hollywood film personalities who had been ardent left-wingers such as Will Geer and Zero Mostel were blacklisted and could not find

Victims of Anti-Communist Hysteria

work in the movies; and ten screenwriters and directors (the "Hollywood Ten") were sent to prison for contempt of Congress when they refused to provide names of alleged Communists. Schoolteachers and college professors were fired for expressing dissenting viewpoints. Anti-Communists also exploited the hysteria to drive homosexuals from their jobs. "Sexual perverts have infiltrated our government in recent years," warned the Republican national chairman in 1950, adding that homosexuals were "perhaps as dangerous as the actual Communists."

In labor union elections and even in local parent-teacher associations, redbaiting became a convenient tactic for discrediting the opposition. The hysteria was particularly damaging to the labor movement, which forsook its class-conscious militancy of the 1930s in favor of anticommunism. In 1949 the CIO expelled eleven unions, with a combined membership of over 900,000, for alleged Communist domination. All this occurred at a time when membership in the Communist Party of the United States of America was declining, from a high of about 83,000 in 1947 to 55,000 in 1950 and 25,000 in 1954.

Despite the rampant false accusations, there was cause for anxiety—especially in 1949. In that year the Soviets detonated their first atomic bomb, and the Chinese Communists, finally victorious in their civil war, proclaimed the People's Republic of China. Furthermore, a former State Department official, Alger Hiss, was on trial for perjury for swearing to a grand jury that he had never passed classified documents to his accuser, former American Communist spy Whittaker Chambers, and that he in fact had not seen Chambers since 1936. When Truman and Secretary of State Dean Acheson came to Hiss's defense, some people began to suspect that the Democrats had something to hide. In 1948 Congressman Richard M. Nixon of California, a Republican member of the House Committee on Un-American Activities (HUAC), appeared before a federal grand jury to urge that Hiss be indicted for espionage. Two days later, he was, and in early 1950 he was convicted of perjury.

Hiss Case

At the same time, a British court sentenced and sent to prison Klaus Fuchs, a nuclear scientist and Nazi refugee, for turning over to Soviet agents secrets from the atomic bomb project at Los Alamos, New Mexico. "Fuchs and Acheson and Hiss and hydrogen bombs threatening outside and New Dealism eating away at the vitals of the nation," exclaimed a Republican

How do historians know...

that the advent of atomic weapons shaped popular culture in postwar United States? Historians have examined the era's popular culture, including feature films, comic books, newsreels, and television shows, as well as photographs in popular magazines such as *Life*. Especially influenced by the popular culture of the atomic age were America's children, some of whom saw a newsreel in 1946 with footage of Hiroshima shot after the August 1945 bombing. The victims' skin was seared; a man missing an ear appeared, then staggered on, as did a woman whose body was imprinted with the design of the dress she had been wearing. Children reported being shocked by this newsreel.

After the Soviets exploded their first atomic bomb in 1949, the United States initiated air raid drills in its schools and issued metal identification tags to girls and boys. But nothing drove home the point about the atomic threat as well as popular culture, in this case, an animated cartoon featuring Bert the Turtle, who warned schoolchildren to "Duck and Cover" during an atomic attack.

In the 1950s public concern mounted over the medical consequences of radioactive fallout from atomic bomb tests, especially when traces of strontium 90, a radioactive isotope, began showing up in milk. Feature films heightened Americans' anxiety. Monsters—atomic mutants—began to rampage through America's movies. In the movie *Them!* (1954), ants on a nuclear test range mutated into giants and swarmed toward Los Angeles. Watching *Them!* in theaters, people squirmed as soldiers used flamethrowers to blast the gigantic ants choking the city's sewer system. Sometimes, atomic contamination made people smaller, even microscopic, as in *The Incredible Shrinking Man* (1957). The historian Paul Boyer has written that "nuclear fear," generated by newsreels and films, "was a shaping cultural force in these years."

Because research on children's nuclear fears did not begin until the 1960s, historians may never know exactly what impact the pop-

ular culture of the atomic age had on America's boys and girls in the 1940s and 1950s. Still, there is anecdotal and even literary evidence of the intensity of children's fears. Early in the atomic age, in 1947, *Senior Scholastic* published this poem, written by a schoolboy:

I am a child of the Atom
And I must make my roots in this age.
But I am afraid
And I would go back into my mother's
    womb where it is dark and quiet. . . .

(Photo: Collection of Hershenson-Allen Archives)

A HORROR HORDE OF CRAWL-AND-CRUSH GIANTS CLAWING OUT OF THE EARTH FROM MILE-DEEP CATACOMBS!

"THEM"

"This city is under martial law until we annihilate THEM!"

Kill one and two take its place!

THE AMAZING NEW WARNER BROS. SENSATION!

Congressman Richard M. Nixon (1913–1994) appears to take little satisfaction in the newspaper headline proclaiming Alger Hiss's perjury conviction in early 1950. As a member of the House Un-American Activities Committee, Nixon led the investigation into charges that Hiss had been a Communist Party member and a spy in the 1950s. (Corbis-Bettmann)

senator. "In the name of heaven, is this the best America can do?"

The circumstances were ripe for a demagogue. It was in this bedeviled atmosphere that Senator Joseph McCarthy mounted a rostrum in Wheeling, West Virginia, in February 1950 and gave a name to the hysteria: McCarthyism. "The State Department," he asserted, was "thoroughly infested with Communists," and the most dangerous person in the department was Dean Acheson. The senator claimed to have a list of 205 Communists working in the department; McCarthy later lowered the figure to "57 card-carrying members," then raised it to 81. But the number did not matter. What McCarthy needed was a winning campaign issue, and he had found it. Republicans, distraught over losing what had appeared to be a sure victory in the 1948 presidential election, were eager to support his attack in hopes of capturing the White House in 1952.

McCarthy's Attack on the State Department

McCarthy and McCarthyism gained momentum throughout 1950. McCarthy continued to display his unparalleled talent for demagoguery, implying guilt by association, interpreting writings out of context, and telling outright lies. Nothing seemed to slow the senator down, not even attacks by other Republicans. Seven Republican senators, led by Maine's Margaret Chase Smith, broke with their colleagues in 1950 and publicly condemned McCarthy for his "selfish political exploitation of fear, bigotry, ignorance, and intolerance"; a Senate committee reported that his charges against the State Department were "a fraud and a hoax." But McCarthy had much to sustain him, including Julius and Ethel Rosenberg's 1950 arrest for conspiracy to commit espionage. During the war, they allegedly had recruited and supervised a spy who worked at the Los Alamos atomic laboratory. Perhaps even more helpful to McCarthy than the Rosenberg case was the outbreak of the Korean War in June 1950, also believed to be Moscow driven.

Widespread support for anti-Communist measures was also apparent in the adoption, over Truman's veto, of the Internal Security (McCarran) Act of 1950, which required members of "Communist-front" organizations to register with the government and prohibited them from holding defense jobs or traveling abroad. In a telling decision in 1951 (*Dennis et al. v. U.S.*), the Supreme Court upheld the Smith Act of 1940, under which eleven Communist Party leaders had been convicted and imprisoned. These government attacks on the CPUSA decimated its ranks.

The conduct of Senator Joseph R. McCarthy was one of the most vexing problems facing Eisenhower's first administration. The Wisconsin senator's no-holds-barred search for subversives in government turned up none and was an affront to political fair play, decency, and civil liberties. Eisenhower avoided confronting McCarthy, saying privately that he would not "get into the gutter with that guy"; the president also feared that a showdown would splinter the Republican Party. Instead, he hoped the media and Congress would bring McCarthy down.

Eisenhower's Reluctance to Confront McCarthy

While Eisenhower pursued this indirect strategy to undermine the senator, his administration practiced its own brand of anticommunism. A new executive order in 1953 expanded the criteria under which federal workers could be dismissed as "security risks." In its first three years in office, the Eisenhower administration dismissed fifteen hundred people, more than Truman had fired in twice the time. One of Eisenhower's most controversial decisions was his denial of clemency to Julius and Ethel Rosenberg, who had two young sons. The Rosenbergs, having been sentenced to death, were executed in 1953.

In 1954 the Communist Control Act demonstrated that both liberals and conservatives shared in the consensus on anticommunism. The measure, which in effect made membership in the Communist Party illegal, passed in the Senate unanimously and in the House by 265 votes to 2. Its chief sponsor, liberal Democratic senator Hubert H. Humphrey of Minnesota, told his colleagues just before he cast his vote: "We have closed all of the doors. These rats will not get out of the trap."

As for Senator McCarthy, he finally transgressed the limits of what the Senate and the public would tolerate. His crucial mistake was taking on the U.S. Army in front of millions of television viewers. At issue was the senator's wild accusation that the army was shielding and promoting Communists; he cited the case of one army dentist. The so-called Army-McCarthy hearings, held by a Senate subcommittee in 1954, became a showcase for the senator's abusive treatment of witnesses. McCarthy, apparently drunk, alternately ranted and slurred his words. Finally, after he maligned a young lawyer who was not even involved in the hearings, army counsel Joseph Welch protested, "Have you no sense of decency, sir?" The gallery erupted in applause, and McCarthy's career as a witch-hunter was over. The Senate finally condemned McCarthy, in a 67-to-22 vote in December 1954, not for defiling the Bill of Rights, but for sullying the dignity of the Senate. He remained a senator, but exhaustion and alcohol took their toll. McCarthy died in 1957 at the age of forty-eight.

Army-McCarthy Hearings

President Eisenhower's reluctance to discredit McCarthy publicly had given the senator, other right-wing members of Congress, and some private and public institutions enough rein to divide the nation and destroy the careers of many innocent people. McCarthyism demoralized and frightened federal workers, some of whom were driven from public service. The anti-Communist campaigns of the 1950s also discouraged people from freely expressing themselves and hence from debating critical issues. Fear, in short, helped sustain the Cold War consensus.

In 1954 Senator Joseph R. McCarthy, surrounded by his own newspaper headlines, adorns the cover of *Time* magazine. His downfall came later that year, during the televised Army-McCarthy hearings. McCarthy's wild accusations and abusive treatment of witnesses disgusted millions of viewers.   (© 1954 Time Inc.)

The Civil Rights Movement in the 1940s and 1950s

 Ironically, Cold War pressures benefited the civil rights movement. As the Soviet Union was quick to point out, the United States could hardly pose as the leader of the free world or condemn the denial of human rights in eastern Europe and the Soviet Union if it practiced segregation at home. Nor could the United States convince new African and Asian nations of its dedication to human rights if African Americans were subjected to segregation, discrimination, disfranchisement, and racial violence. To win the support of nonaligned nations, the United States would have to live up to its own ideals. That the nation was not doing so was evident.

Americans had seen the Second World War as a struggle for democracy and against hatred. African

African Americans' Political "Balance of Power"

Americans who had helped win the war were determined that their lives in postwar America would be better because of their sacrifices. Moreover, politicians were beginning to pay attention to black aspirations. Drawn by opportunities in war industries, in the 1940s more than a million African Americans migrated from the South to the North and West (see Chapter 27). In some urban-industrial states, black voters began to control the political "balance of power." Harry Truman and other politicians knew they would have to compete for the growing African American vote in California, New York, Illinois, Michigan, Pennsylvania, and other large states. Many Republicans cultivated the black vote. Dewey, who as governor of New York had pushed successfully for a fair employment practices commission, was particularly popular with African Americans.

President Truman, in short, had compelling political reasons for supporting African American civil rights. But he also felt a moral obligation to do something, for he genuinely believed it was only fair that every American, regardless of race, should enjoy the full rights of citizenship. Truman also was disturbed by the resurgence of racial terrorism. To suppress black aspirations for civil rights unleashed by the war, a revived Ku Klux Klan was again burning crosses and murdering blacks who had had the audacity to vote. But what really horrified Truman was the report that police in Aiken, South Carolina, had gouged out the

eyes of a black sergeant just three hours after he had been discharged from the army. Several weeks later, in December 1946, Truman signed an executive order establishing the President's Committee on Civil Rights.

The committee's report, *To Secure These Rights* (1947), would become the agenda for the civil rights movement for the next twenty years.

President Truman's Committee on Civil Rights

Among its recommendations were the enactment of federal antilynching and antisegregation legislation. *To Secure These Rights* also called for laws guaranteeing voting rights and equal employment opportunity and for the establishment of a permanent commission on civil rights. Although Congress failed to act and some evidence suggests that Truman's real goal was the African American vote in 1948, his action was significant. For the first time since Reconstruction, a president had acknowledged the federal government's responsibility to protect blacks and strive for racial equality.

Truman took this responsibility seriously, and in 1948 he issued two executive orders declaring an end to racial discrimination in the federal government. One proclaimed a policy of "fair employment throughout the federal establishment" and created the Employment Board of the Civil Service Commission to hear charges of discrimination. The other ordered the racial desegregation of the armed forces and appointed the Committee on Equality of Treatment and Opportunity in the Armed Services to oversee this process. Despite strong, even fierce, opposition to desegregation within the military, segregated units were being phased out by the time the Korean War broke out.

African Americans also benefited from a series of Supreme Court decisions. The trend toward judicial support of civil rights had begun in

Supreme Court Decisions on Civil Rights

the late 1930s, when the NAACP established its Legal Defense Fund under Charles Hamilton Houston and Thurgood Marshall. In the 1940s and 1950s, Marshall (who in 1967 would become the first African American Supreme Court justice) and his colleagues set out to destroy the separate-but-equal doctrine established in *Plessy v. Ferguson* (1896) by insisting on its literal interpretation. In higher education, the NAACP calculated, the cost of true equality in racially separate schools would be prohibitive. "You can't build a cyclotron for one student," as the president of the University of Oklahoma acknowledged. As a result of NAACP lawsuits, African

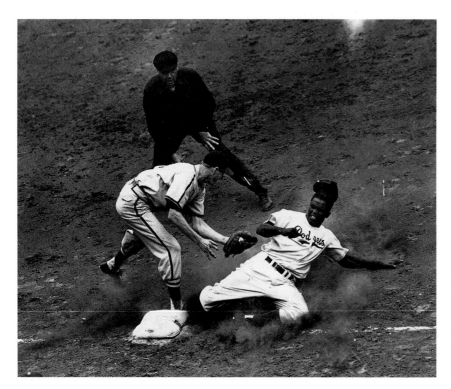

Jackie Robinson cracked the color line in major league baseball when he joined the Brooklyn Dodgers for the 1947 season. Sliding safely into third base, Robinson displays the aggressive style that won him rookie-of-the-year honors. He was later elected to the Baseball Hall of Fame.   (Hy Peskin, *Life* magazine © Time Inc.)

American students won admission to professional and graduate schools at a number of state universities. In *Smith v. Allwright* (1944), the Supreme Court also outlawed the whites-only primaries held by the Democratic Party in some southern states, branding them a violation of the Fifteenth Amendment's guarantee of the right to vote. Two years later the Court struck down segregation in interstate bus transportation (*Morgan v. Virginia*). And in *Shelley v. Kraemer* (1948), the Court held that racially restrictive covenants (private agreements among white homeowners not to sell to blacks) violated the equal protection clause of the Fourteenth Amendment.

A change in social attitudes accompanied these gains in black political and legal power. Books like Gunnar Myrdal's social science study *An American Dilemma* (1944) and Richard Wright's novels *Native Son* (1940) and *Black Boy* (1945) were increasing white awareness of the social injustices that plagued African Americans. A new black middle class was emerging, composed of college-educated activists, war veterans, and union workers. Blacks and whites also worked together in CIO unions and service organizations such as the National Council of Churches. In 1947 a black baseball player, Jackie Robinson, broke the major

league color barrier and electrified Brooklyn Dodgers fans with his spectacular hitting and base running.

Even so, segregation was still standard practice in the 1950s, and blacks continued to suffer disfranchisement, job discrimination, and violence, including the bombing murder in 1951 of the Florida state director of the NAACP and his wife. But in 1954 the NAACP won a historic victory that stunned the white South and energized African Americans to challenge segregation on several fronts. *Brown v. Board of Education of Topeka* incorporated cases from several states, all involving segregated schools. Written by Earl Warren, whom President Eisenhower had named chief justice in 1953, the Court's unanimous decision concluded that "in the field of public education the doctrine of 'separate but equal' has no place. Separate educational facilities are inherently unequal." Such facilities, Warren wrote, produced in black children "a feeling of inferiority" and deprived them of "the equal protection of the laws guaranteed by the Fourteenth Amendment." But the ruling did not demand immediate compliance. A year later the Court finally ordered school desegregation, but only "with all deliberate speed."

Brown v. Board of Education of Topeka

The lack of a timetable encouraged the southern states to resist.

Some communities in border states like Kansas and Maryland quietly implemented the order, and many southern moderates advocated a gradual rollback of segregation. But the forces of white resistance soon came to dominate, urging southern communities to defy the Court. The Klan experienced another resurgence, and business and professional people created White Citizens' Councils for the express purpose of resisting the order. Known familiarly as "uptown Ku Klux Klans," the councils brought their economic power to bear against black civil rights activists. One of the most effective resistance tactics was enactment of state laws that paid the private-school tuition of white children who had left public schools to avoid integration. In some cases, desegregated public schools were ordered closed.

White Resistance to Civil Rights

White resistance to civil rights also gained strength in large northern cities, such as Chicago and Detroit. Because of migration to Chicago in the 1940s and 1950s, for example, the city's African American population jumped from 275,000 in 1940 to 800,000 in 1960. The newcomers gained not only good jobs in industry, but also political power due to their increased numbers. At the same time, blacks continued to be segregated in housing and education. White mobs in Chicago and Detroit resorted to violence to frighten African Americans out of white neighborhoods. In 1951 in Cicero, Illinois, adjoining Chicago, several thousand whites eager to keep blacks out provoked a race riot. So racially divided was Chicago that the U.S. Commission on Civil Rights in 1959 described it as "the most residentially segregated city in the nation." Detroit and other northern cities were not far behind.

Unlike Truman, President Eisenhower wanted to avoid dealing with civil rights, preferring instead gradual and voluntary change in race relations. He came to regret his appointment of Earl Warren as "the biggest damn fool mistake I ever made." Although the president disapproved of racial segregation, he objected to "compulsory federal law" in the belief that race relations would improve "only if it starts locally." He also feared that the ugly public confrontations likely to follow rapid desegregation would jeopardize Republican inroads in the South. Thus Eisenhower did not state forthrightly that the federal government would enforce the Court's decision as the nation's law. In short, instead of leading, he spoke ambiguously and thereby tacitly encouraged white noncompliance.

Events in Little Rock, Arkansas, forced the president to stop sidestepping the issue. In September 1957 Governor Orval E. Faubus intervened to defy a court-ordered desegregation plan for Little Rock's Central High School. Faubus ordered the Arkansas National Guard to block the entry of black students. Eisenhower made no effort to impede Faubus's actions. Later that month, bowing to a federal judge's order, Faubus withdrew the guardsmen. As hundreds of jeering whites threatened to storm the school, eight black children entered Central High. The next day, fearing violence, Eisenhower dispatched army paratroopers to Little Rock to ensure the black students' safety. Troops patrolled the school for the rest of the year; in response, Little Rock officials closed all public high schools in 1958 and 1959 rather than desegregate them.

Crisis in Little Rock, Arkansas

Elsewhere, African Americans did not wait for Supreme Court or White House decisions to claim equal rights. In 1955 Rosa Parks, a department store seamstress and active member of the NAACP, was arrested for refusing to give up her seat to a white man on a public bus in Montgomery, Alabama. Local black women's organizations and civil rights groups decided to boycott the city's bus system, and they elected Martin Luther King, Jr., a recently ordained minister who had just arrived in Montgomery, as their leader. King launched the boycott with a moving speech in which he declared: "If we are wrong, the Constitution is wrong. If we are wrong, God Almighty is wrong. If we are wrong, Jesus of Nazareth was merely a utopian dreamer. . . . If we are wrong, justice is a lie."

Montgomery Bus Boycott

Martin Luther King, Jr., was a twenty-six-year-old Baptist minister who recently had earned a Ph.D. at Boston University. Disciplined and analytical, he was committed to nonviolent protest in the spirit of India's leader Mohandas K. Gandhi. Although he was jailed for refusing to comply with an unjust law and a bomb blew out the front of his house, King persisted. "Absence of fear," according to civil rights leader Bayard Rustin, was what King gave to black Americans. In 1957 King became the first president of the Southern Christian

Martin Luther King, Jr.

In 1957 white teenagers in Little Rock, Arkansas, angrily confront African American students who, under federal court order, are attempting to enter, and thus desegregate, Central High School. The Supreme Court's *Brown* decision of 1954 was resisted by whites throughout the South.   (Wide World Photos, Inc.)

Leadership Conference, organized to coordinate civil rights activities.

During the year-long Montgomery bus boycott, blacks young and old walked or carpooled. With the bus company near bankruptcy and downtown merchants hurt by declining sales, city officials adopted harassment tactics to frighten blacks into abandoning the boycott. King urged perseverance, and bolstered by a Supreme Court decision that declared Alabama's bus segregation laws unconstitutional, Montgomery blacks triumphed in 1956. They and others across the nation were further heartened when Congress passed the Civil Rights Act of 1957, which created the United States Commission on Civil Rights to investigate systematic discrimination, such as voting discrimination. But this measure, like a voting rights act passed three years later, proved ineffective. Critics charged that the Eisenhower administration was interested more in quelling the civil rights question than in addressing it.

African Americans responded by launching a campaign of sit-ins in the South. In February 1960 four black students from North Carolina Agricultural and

Sit-ins

Technical College in Greensboro ordered coffee at a dime-store lunch counter. Told they would not be served, the students refused to budge. "I felt as though I had gained my manhood," recalled one of the young men. Thus began the sit-in movement, which quickly spread throughout the South. And when whites brutally attacked the women and men sitting in at the lunch counters, the nightly news often featured the violence, provoking public sympathy for the civil rights movement. Inspired by the sit-ins, southern black college and high-school students met on Easter weekend in 1960 and organized the Student Nonviolent Coordinating Committee (SNCC). In the face of angry white mobs, SNCC members challenged the status quo, all the while singing the anthem of the civil rights movement, "We Shall Overcome," which includes the words "We are not afraid."

King personally joined the sit-in movement, and in October 1960 he was arrested at a sit-in to desegregate an Atlanta snack bar. Sent to a cold, cockroach-infested

For leading the movement to gain equality for blacks riding city buses in Montgomery, Alabama, Martin Luther King, Jr. (1929–1968), and other African Americans, including twenty-three other ministers, were indicted by an all-white jury for violating an old law banning boycotts. In late March 1956 King was convicted and fined $500. A crowd of well-wishers cheered a smiling King (here with his wife, Coretta) outside the courthouse, where King proudly declared, "The protest goes on!" King's arrest and conviction made the bus boycott front-page news across America.   (Corbis-Bettmann)

Civil Rights and the 1960 Election

state penitentiary where he faced four months at hard labor, he became ill. As an apathetic Eisenhower White House looked on, Senator John F. Kennedy, the Democratic presidential candidate, called King's wife, Coretta Scott King, to express support; and his brother, Robert F. Kennedy, persuaded the sentencing judge to release King on bond. In November grateful African Americans cast their ballots for Kennedy in the expectation that, as president, he would provide federal protection of their civil rights movement. Those committed to racial equality looked forward to great gains under Kennedy in the 1960s.

The Postwar Booms: Babies, Business, and Bigness

The postwar economic boom proved to be one of the longest periods of growth and prosperity the United States ever experienced. Its keys were increasing output and increasing demand. Despite occasional recessions

the gross national product more than doubled from $212 billion in 1945 to $520 billion in 1961 (see Figure 28.1).

The Harvard economist John Kenneth Galbraith gave a name to the United States during the postwar economic boom: the "affluent society." As U.S. productivity increased in the postwar years, so did Americans' appetite for goods and services. During the depression and the Second World War, many Americans had dreamed of buying a home or a car. In the flush postwar years they finally could satisfy those deferred desires. Some families bought two cars and equipped their new homes with the latest appliances and amusements, such as television. Easy credit was the economic basis of the consumer culture; when people lacked cash to buy what they wanted, they borrowed money. Consumer credit to support the nation's shopping spree grew from $5.7 billion in 1945 to $58 billion in 1961.

The Affluent Society

When the economy produced more, Americans generally brought home bigger paychecks and had more money to spend. Between the end of the war and

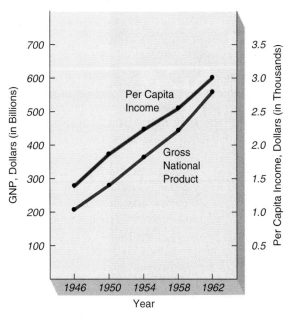

Figure 28.1   Gross National Product and Per Capita Income, 1946–1962   Both gross national product and per capita income soared during the economic boom from 1946 to 1962.   (Source: Adapted from U.S. Bureau of the Census, *Historical Statistics of the United States, Colonial Times to 1970,* Bicentennial Edition [Washington, D.C., U.S. Government Printing Office, 1975], p. 224.)

Figure 28.2   Birth Rate, 1945–1964   The birth rate began to rise in 1942 and 1943, but it skyrocketed during the postwar years beginning in 1946, reaching its peak in 1957. From 1954 to 1964, the United States recorded more than 4 million births every year. (Source: Adapted from U.S. Bureau of the Census, *Historical Statistics of the United States, Colonial Times to 1970,* Bicentennial Edition [Washington, D.C., U.S. Government Printing Office, 1975], p. 49.)

Increased Purchasing Power

1950, per capita real income (based on actual purchasing power) rose 6 percent—and that was only the beginning. In the 1950s it jumped another 15 percent; in the 1960s the increase was even greater—32 percent (see Figure 28.1). The result was a noticeable increase in the standard of living. To the vast majority of Americans, such prosperity was a vindication of the American system of free enterprise.

The baby boom was both a cause and an effect of prosperity. The birth rate, which had been very low during the 1930s, started to rise during the war. But the birth rate soared immediately after the war, and it continued to do so throughout the 1950s (see Figure 28.2). During the 1950s, the number of births exceeded 4 million per year, reversing the downward trend in birth rates that had prevailed for 150 years. Births began to decline after 1961 but con-

Baby Boom

tinued to exceed 4 million per year through 1964. The baby-boom generation was the largest by far in the nation's history. And as this vast age group grew older, it had successive impacts on housing, nursery schools, grade schools, and high schools, fads and popular music, colleges and universities, the job market, and retirement funds, including Social Security.

The baby boom meant business for builders, manufacturers, and school systems. "Take the 3,548,000 babies born in 1950," wrote Sylvia F. Porter in her syndicated newspaper column. "Bundle them into a batch, bounce them all over the bountiful land that is America. What do you get?" Porter's answer: "Boom. The biggest, boomiest boom ever known in history. Just imagine how much these extra people, these new markets, will absorb—in food, clothing, in gadgets, in housing, in services. Our factories must expand just to keep pace."

Of the three cornerstones of the postwar economic boom—construction, automobiles, and defense—two were directly related to the upsurge in births. Demand for housing and schools for all these children generated a building boom, furthered by construction of shopping centers, office buildings, and airports. Much of this construction took place in the suburbs. The postwar suburbanization of America in turn would have been impossible without automobile manufacturing, for the car provided access to the sprawling new communities. The number of registered automobiles climbed from 26 million in 1945 to 63 million in 1961.

Government funding helped new families to settle in the suburbs. Low-interest GI mortgages and Federal Housing Administration (FHA) mortgage insurance made the differ-

Housing Boom

ence for people who otherwise would have been unable to afford a home. This easy credit, combined with postwar prosperity, produced a construction boom. From 1945 to 1946, housing starts climbed from 326,000 to more than 1 million; they approached 2 million in 1950 and remained above 1.3 million in 1961. Never before had new starts exceeded 1 million.

To produce so much new, relatively inexpensive housing so fast, contractors had to operate on a massive scale. Arthur Levitt and Sons developed a system, adopted by other companies, of using interchangeable materials and designs to build nearly identical houses on uniform, treeless lots. In 1947 the construction of Levittown, New York, began; Levittowns also arose in New Jersey and Pennsylvania. To supply the new communities, shopping malls soon dotted the countryside.

As suburbia spread, pastures became neighborhoods with astounding rapidity. Highway construction was a central element in the transformation of rural land into suburbia.

Highway Construction

In 1947 Congress authorized construction of a 37,000-mile chain of highways, and in 1956 President Eisenhower signed the Highway Act, which approved funds for a 42,500-mile interstate highway system, intended to facilitate commerce and enable the military to move around the nation more easily. The interstate highways invigorated the tourist industry, further weakened the railroads to the advantage of the truck-

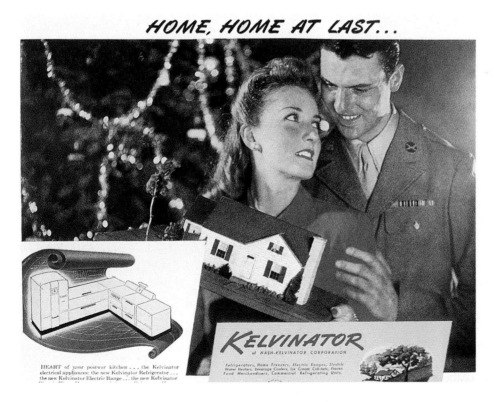

HOME, HOME AT LAST...

KELVINATOR
of NASH-KELVINATOR CORPORATION

Even during the Second World War, Americans dreamed about marriage, children, and a new house in the suburbs equipped with the latest kitchen appliances. This advertisement for Kelvinator appliances was published in *Life* magazine in December 1944.   (Ellen Kaiper Collection, Oakland, Calif.)

ing industry, and spurred the growth of suburbs farther and farther from the central cities.

Federal expenditures on highways swelled from $79 million in 1946 to $2.6 billion in 1961. State and local spending on highways also mushroomed. Highways both hastened suburbanization and homogenized the landscape. The high-speed trucking that highways made possible also accelerated the integration of the South into the national economy.

In the twenty-five years after the war, a mass movement was under way from the cities to the suburbs. In 1940, 19.5 percent of Americans lived in the suburbs. By 1970 that number had doubled, and for the first time in American history, more people lived in suburbs than in cities or in rural areas (see Table 28.1). A combination of motives drew people to the suburbs. Some wanted to leave behind the noise and smells of the city. Some white families moved out of urban neighborhoods because African American families were moving in. People living in row houses and apartments wanted to move into houses that had yards, family rooms, extra closets, and utility rooms. Many were also looking for a place where they could have a measure of political influence, particularly on the education their children received.

Growth of the Suburbs

Highway construction in combination with the growth of suburbia produced a new phenomenon, the *megalopolis*, a term coined by urban experts in the early 1960s to refer to the almost uninterrupted metropolitan complex stretching along the northeastern seaboard from Boston 600 miles south through New York, Philadelphia, and Baltimore all the way to Washington, D.C. "Boswash" encompassed parts of eleven states and a population of 49 million people, all linked by interstate highways. Another megalopolis that took shape was "Milipitts," a band of heavy industry and dense population stretching from Milwaukee to Pittsburgh.

Millions of Americans began their search for affluence by migrating to the Sunbelt—roughly, the southern third of the United States, running from southern California across the Southwest and South all the way to the Atlantic coast. Among the Sunbelt's booming cities were Houston, Phoenix, Los Angeles, San Diego, Dallas, and Miami. The population of Houston, which became a center not only of the aerospace industry but also of oil and petrochemical production, jumped from 385,000 in 1940 to 1,243,000 in 1960. California absorbed no less than one-fifth of the nation's entire population increase in the 1950s—enough by 1963 to make it the most populous state in the Union (see Map 28.2).

Growth of the Sunbelt

The mass migration to the Sunbelt had started during the war, when GIs and their families were ordered to new duty stations and war workers moved to defense plants in the West and South. The economic bases of the Sunbelt's spectacular growth were defense contractors, such as the aerospace industry, agribusiness, the oil industry, real-estate development, and recreation. Industry was drawn to the southern rim by right-to-work laws, which outlawed closed shops, and by low taxes and low heating bills. Government policies—generous tax breaks for oil companies, siting of military bases, and awarding of defense and aerospace contracts—were crucial to the Sunbelt's development. Crucial, too, was the air conditioning of houses, office buildings, and automobiles, which made bearable even the hottest Sunbelt days.

The third cornerstone of the postwar economic boom was military spending. When the Defense Department was established in 1947, its budget was just over $10 billion a year. In 1961 the total had risen to $98 billion. Many defense contracts went to industries and universities to develop weapons, and the government supported space research; funds spent on space research alone zoomed from $76 million in 1957 to almost $6 billion in 1966. Defense spending also helped stimulate rapid advances in the electronics industry. The ENIAC

Military Spending

Table 28.1	**Geographic Distribution of the U.S. Population, 1930–1970 (in Percentages)**		
Year	**Central Cities**	**Suburbs**	**Rural Areas and Small Towns**
1930	31.8%	18.0%	50.2%
1940	31.6	19.5	48.9
1950	32.3	23.8	43.9
1960	32.6	30.7	36.7
1970	31.4	37.6	31.0

Source: Adapted from U.S. Bureau of the Census, *Decennial Censuses, 1930–1970* (Washington, D.C., U.S. Government Printing Office).

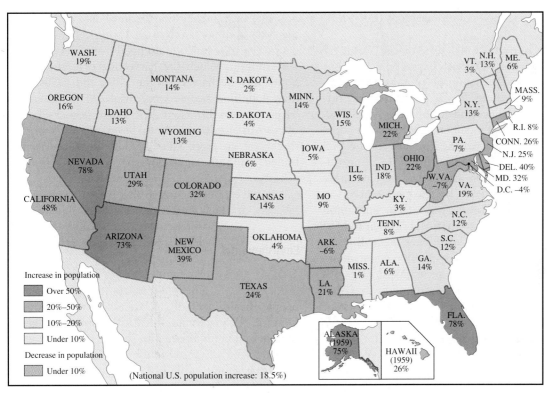

Map 28.2   Rise of the Sunbelt, 1950–1960   The years after the Second World War saw a continuation of the migration of Americans to the Sunbelt states of the Southwest and the West Coast.

computer, completed at the University of Pennsylvania in 1946, weighed fifty tons and required 18,000 vacuum tubes. Then, in the 1950s, introduction of the transistor accelerated the computer revolution; the silicon microchip in the 1960s inaugurated even more stunning advances in electronics. The microchip facilitated the shift from heavy manufacturing to high-technology industries in fiber optics, lasers, video equipment, robotics, and genetic engineering. Sales of office and business equipment reflected the growth in technology-based production.

The evolution of electronics meant a large-scale tradeoff for the American people. As industries automated, computerized processes replaced slower mechanical ones, increasing productivity but pushing people out of jobs. Electronic technology also promoted concentration of ownership in industry. Sophisticated technology was expensive, and small corporations were shut out of the market. Indeed, large corporations with capital and experience in high-tech fields expanded into related industries. General

Electric, which during the Second World War had manufactured electrical products, began producing computers, jet engines, and nuclear-powered generators.

Another kind of corporate expansion also marked the early 1950s. The third great wave of mergers swept across American business. The first

Conglomerate Mergers

two such movements, in the 1890s and 1920s, had tended toward vertical and horizontal integration, respectively (see pages 511 and 666). The postwar era was distinguished by conglomerate mergers. A *conglomerate* brings together companies in unrelated industries as a hedge against instability in a particular market. International Telephone and Telegraph (IT&T), for instance, bought up companies in several fields, including suburban development, insurance, and hotels. In keeping with the thrust of America's postwar boom, the country's ten largest corporations operated in core growth industries: automobiles (GM, Ford, Chrysler), oil (Exxon, Mobil, Texaco), and electronics and communications (GE, IBM, IT&T, AT&T).

The labor movement also experienced a postwar merger. In 1955 the American Federation of Labor and the Congress of Industrial Organizations finally put aside their differences and formed the AFL-CIO. Union membership grew slowly during the postwar years, increasing from just around 14.8 million in 1945 to 17.3 million in 1961. Some observers charged that union leaders had become smug and lost the zeal that had won over so many workers in the 1930s and 1940s; revelations of corrupt union practices, notably by the International Brotherhood of Teamsters, also tainted the labor movement. But the main reason for the slow growth of union membership was a shift in employment patterns. Most new jobs were being created not in the heavy industries that hired blue-collar workers but in the union-resistant white-collar service trades.

Labor Merger

The postwar economic boom was good for unionized blue-collar workers, many of whom won real increases in wages sufficient to enjoy a middle-class lifestyle that previously had been the exclusive province of white-collar workers and professionals. Union workers could qualify for mortgages for suburban homes, especially if their spouses also worked. Many enjoyed job security, paid vacations, and retirement plans. They also could aspire to college educations for their children. And they were more protected against inflation: in 1948 General Motors and the United Auto Workers agreed on automatic cost-of-living adjustments (COLAs) in workers' wages, a practice that spread to other industries.

The trend toward economic consolidation also changed agriculture. New machines, such as mechanical cotton-, tobacco-, and grape-pickers and crop-dusting planes revolutionized farming methods, and the increased use of fertilizers and pesticides raised the total value of farm output from $24.6 billion in 1945 to $38.4 billion in 1961. At the same time, farm labor productivity tripled. The resulting improvement in profitability drew large investors into agriculture, and average acreage per farm increased from 195 in 1945 to 306 in 1961. By the 1960s it took money—sometimes big money—to become a farmer. In many regions only banks, insurance companies, and large businesses could afford the necessary land, machinery, and fertilizer.

Agribusiness

The movement toward consolidation threatened the survival of the family farm. From 1945 to 1961 the nation's farm population declined from 24.4 million to 14.8 million. When the harvesting of cotton in the South was mechanized in the 1940s and 1950s, more than 4 million people were displaced. Southern tobacco growers dismissed their tenant farmers, bought tractors to plow the land, and hired migratory workers to harvest the crop. Many of these displaced farmers traded southern rural poverty for northern urban poverty.

Rapid economic growth also exacted environmental costs, to which most Americans were oblivious. Air, water, soil, and wildlife suffered degradation. Steel mills, coal-powered generators, and internal-combustion car engines burning lead-based gasoline polluted the air and imperiled people's health. In 1948, for example, twenty people in Donora, Pennsylvania, died of respiratory failure caused by air pollution; the smoke and sulfur gases pouring from a zinc smelter in Donora became so thick that people could not see or breathe. America's water supplies suffered as well. Human and industrial waste befouled many rivers and lakes, making them unfit for consumption or recreation. Vast quantities of water were diverted from lakes and rivers to meet the needs of America's burgeoning Sunbelt cities, including the swimming pools that dotted parched Arizona and southern California. The extraction of natural resources—strip mining of coal, for example—also scarred the landscape, and toxic waste from chemical plants seeped deep into the soil. America was becoming a dumping ground as never before.

Environmental Costs

Defense contractors and farmers were among the country's worst polluters. Refuse from nuclear weapons facilities at Hanford, Washington, and at Colorado's Rocky Flats arsenal polluted soil and water resources for years. Agriculture began employing massive amounts of pesticides and other chemicals. A chemical called DDT, for example, which had been used on Pacific islands during the war to kill mosquitoes and lice, was released for public use in 1945. During the next fifteen years, farmers eliminated chronic pests with DDT. In 1962, however, *Silent Spring* by Rachel Carson, a wildlife biologist, specifically indicted DDT for the deaths of mammals, birds, and fish. DDT accumulates in the fatty tissues of eagles, trout, and other wildlife, causing cancer in the animals. Because of Carson's book, many Americans finally re-

During the Second World War, DDT was used to protect American troops against bug-borne diseases and was hailed as a miracle insecticide. The use of DDT spread in postwar America, but little attention was paid to its often fatal consequences for birds, mammals, and fish. In 1945, even as children ran alongside, this truck sprayed DDT as part of a mosquito-control program at New York's Jones Beach State Park. (Corbis-Bettmann)

alized that there were costs to human conquest of the environment. The federal government finally banned the sale of DDT in 1972.

A "Throwaway" Society

Much of America's continued economic growth encouraged habits that would make the country a "throwaway" society. The auto industry intentionally made cars less durable ("planned obsolescence") and through advertising and revamping designs urged consumers to buy a new model every year or two. Increasing numbers of disposable products such as plastic cups and paper diapers were marketed as conveniences. Moreover, as Americans consumed goods and services, they were using up the world's resources. By the 1960s the United States, with only 5 percent of the world's population, produced and consumed more than one-third of the world's goods and services.

Conformity and Consumerism

For the generation of adults in postwar America—the women and men who had suffered economic deprivation during the depression and separation from loved ones during the war—the suburban home became a refuge, and family togetherness fulfilled a psychological need. But sociologists and other critics denounced the suburbs for breeding conformity and status seeking, and they scolded suburbanites for trying to keep up with the Joneses by buying new cars and appliances. William H. Whyte's *The Organization Man* (1956), a study of Park Forest, Illinois, pronounced these suburbanites mindless conservatives and extreme conformists. And the sociologist C. Wright Mills castigated white-collar suburbanites who "sell not only their time and energy but their personalities as well." Nonetheless, most residents of suburbia preferred their lifestyle to any other of which they were aware, and the vast majority of college students in the 1950s looked forward to settling in the suburbs.

Pressures in Education

Education at all levels, from preschool to graduate school, was a pressing concern for families in postwar America. Immediately after the Second World War, for example, many former GIs enrolled in college and set up housekeeping with their wives and babies in abandoned military barracks on college campuses. The legislation that made this possible was the Servicemen's Readjustment Act of 1944, popularly known as the GI Bill of Rights, which provided living allowances and tuition payments to college-bound veterans. Over 1 million veterans enrolled in 1946—accounting for one out of every two students. Despite pessimistic predictions, the veterans, who saw higher education as the key to upward mobility, succeeded as students. The downside of this success story was that colleges made places for male veterans by turning away qualified women.

As the baby boom became a grade-school boom in the 1950s, American families became preoccupied with the education of their children. Convinced that success in school was a prerequisite for success in adult life, parents joined parent-teacher associations so they would have a voice in the educational process. They worried that schools were overcrowded and that teachers were using obsolete methods. Then in 1957 education became a matter of national security. In that year the Soviet Union launched *Sputnik*, the first earth-orbiting satellite. The Soviet triumph threw into question American military and technological superiority, based ultimately on the nation's school system. Congress responded in 1958 with the National Defense Education Act (NDEA), which funded enrichment of elementary and high-school programs in mathematics, foreign languages, and the sciences, and offered fellowships and loans to college students.

As education became intertwined with national security, so religion became a matter of patriotism.

Growth of Religion

As President Eisenhower put it, "Recognition of the Supreme Being is the first, the most basic expression of Americanism." And in 1954 Eisenhower signed a law inserting the words "under God" after "one nation" in the Pledge of Allegiance to the flag. In America's Cold War with an atheistic enemy, religious leaders emphasized traditional values like family togetherness. The Bible topped the bestseller list, and a familiar refrain of the time was "The family that prays together stays together." Most impressive was the growth in membership in religious congregations; in the fifteen years after the Second World War, the total jumped 62 percent, from 71.7 million in 1945 to 116 million in 1961.

The postwar religious revival was also spurred by the introduction of a revolutionary influence in American life: television. The evangelist

Television Togetherness

Billy Graham, who preached in stadiums throughout the country, and Catholic Bishop Fulton J. Sheen could reach mass audiences on televi-

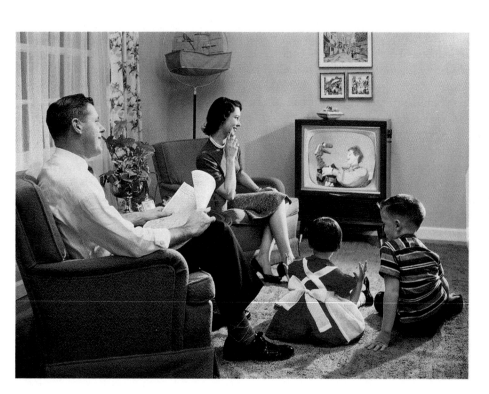

By the mid-1950s, the proliferation of television sets had transformed American family life. The number of households with television sets increased eightfold between 1950 and 1955. Rather than talking, listening to the radio, reading, or going to the movies, families stayed home to watch their favorite shows.   (Superstock)

sion. The growth of television was phenomenal. In 1946 only 8,000 households had TVs; that number skyrocketed to 3.9 million in 1950 and to more than 47 million in 1961. Most important, the introduction of television transformed family life in America. "And so the monumental change began in our lives and those of millions of other Americans," recalled a man whose parents bought their first television set in 1950. "More than a year passed before we again visited a movie theater. . . . Social evenings with friends became fewer and fewer still because we discovered we did not share the same television program interests." By 1950 television had loosened the grip of both radio and the movies on the American public.

Television was a crucial force in the evolution of both the consumer culture and family togetherness. "More appliances make mom's work easier," read a typical 1950s advertisement. TV told people what to buy; and as families strove to acquire the latest luxuries and conveniences, shopping became a form of recreation. TV's number-one product was entertainment, and situation comedies and action series were among the most popular shows. *Father Knows Best* and *Leave It to Beaver* celebrated family life. But as average TV-viewing time reached five hours a day in 1956 and continued to rise, critics worried that TV's distorted presentation of the world would significantly define people's sense of reality.

In 1946 the anthropologist Margaret Mead reflected on society's contradictory expectations of American women: "Choose any set of criteria you like, and the answer is the same: women—and men—are confused, uncertain, and discontented with the present definition of women's place in America." On the one hand, the home was premised on a full-time housewife who, with little regard for her own needs, provided her husband and children with a cozy haven from the outside world. On the other hand, women continued to enter the labor force for a variety of reasons. Many worked because they were their families' sole sources of income; they had to work. Others took jobs to supplement the family income. Indeed, the female labor force rose from 19.3 million in 1945 to 23.8 million in 1961 and to 31.6 million in 1970. Despite the cult of motherhood, most new entrants to the job market were married—a trend that had begun during the Second World War—and most were mothers (see Figure 28.3).

Women's Conflicting Roles and Dilemmas

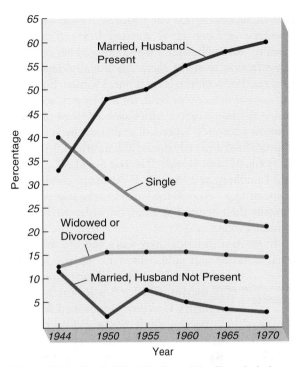

Figure 28.3   Marital Distribution of the Female Labor Force, 1944–1970   The composition of the female labor force changed dramatically from 1944 to 1970. In 1944, 41 percent of women in the labor force were single; in 1970, only 22 percent were single. During the same years, the percentage of the female labor force that had a husband in the home jumped from 34 to 59. The percentage who were widowed or divorced remained about the same from 1944 to 1970.   (Source: Adapted from U.S. Bureau of the Census, *Historical Statistics of the United States, Colonial Times to 1970*, Bicentennial Edition [Washington, D.C., U.S. Government Printing Office, 1975], p. 133.)

Women's responsibilities also increased at home after the war. Some of the change was due to the publication of Dr. Benjamin Spock's *Baby and Child Care* (1946). Unlike earlier manuals, *Baby and Child Care* urged mothers always to think of their children first (Spock assigned fathers little formal role in child rearing). Dr. Spock based his advice on new findings about the importance of responding to a baby's needs; and the millions of women who embraced his teachings tried to be mother, teacher, psychologist, and playmate to their children. If they "failed" in any of these roles, guilt frequently was the outcome.

On the other hand, the social critic Philip Wylie denounced such selfless behavior as "Momism." In the guise of sacrificing for her children, Wylie wrote in *Generation of Vipers* (1942, revised 1955), Mom was pursuing "love of herself." She smothered her children with affection to make them emotionally dependent on her and reluctant to leave home. Women, however, were caught in a double bind, for if they pursued a life outside the home, other critics accused them of being "feminist neurotics," contending that women could be happy and fulfilled only through domesticity. In a popular book, *Modern Woman: The Lost Sex* (1947), Ferdinand Lundberg and Marynia F. Farnham condemned feminism as a "deep illness" that encouraged women to reject their natural instincts in order to become "imitation men."

In postwar America, there was a wide gap between sexual behavior and public discourse on the subject.

Sexuality

When Dr. Alfred Kinsey, director of the Institute for Sex Research at Indiana University, published his pioneering study *Sexual Behavior in the Human Male* (1948), the American public was shocked. But five years later Kinsey caused an uproar with *Sexual Behavior in the Human Female*, which claimed that 62 percent of his subjects masturbated and 50 percent had had intercourse before marriage. Some angry Americans condemned the report as a slanderous attack on motherhood and the family, and a congressman charged Kinsey with "hurling the insult of the century against our mothers, wives, daughters and sisters."

Family, church, state, and media alike warned Americans that sex outside marriage was wrong and that premarital, extramarital, and homosexual behavior would bring "familial chaos and weaken the country's moral fiber." Women often were blamed for the impending disaster; despite any evidence of significant increases in women's sexual activity from the 1920s to the 1960s, female lust was perceived to pose a threat to the future of the family. In fact, increased interest in sex was coming from a different direction: in 1953 men began reading about the sexual joys of bachelorhood in a new magazine, *Playboy*. Nevertheless, from Momism to promiscuity, American women were the victims of male-inspired stereotypes.

There was confusion for girls, too, in postwar America. Motherhood was venerated in American society, but many daughters sensed that their own mothers were deeply disappointed with their lives. In fact, a 1962 Gallup poll revealed that only 10 percent of mothers wanted their daughters to emulate them.

Some urged their daughters to avoid the trap of early marriage and domesticity and to develop personally fulfilling and economically independent lives. It is clear that the seeds of feminist protest in the later 1960s and 1970s were planted during the postwar years. As the historian Ruth Rosen has observed, the "invisible ghost haunting" young women "wore an apron and lived vicariously through the lives of her husband and children. Against her, the women's liberation movement was forged."

During the postwar years, a distinctive youth subculture emerged. "Teenagers all have the same basic problems," wrote a young columnist in 1958; "it's only natural we create our own special brand of music." In the 1950s the music industry catered to teens with inexpensive 45-rpm records. Bored with the era's syrupy music, young Americans were electrified by the driving energy and hard beat of Bill Haley and the Comets, Chuck Berry, Little Richard, and Buddy Holly. Although few white musicians acknowledged the debt, the roots of rock 'n' roll lay in African American rhythm and blues. The release of Elvis Presley's first single, "Heartbreak Hotel," in 1956, and his appearance on Ed Sullivan's Sunday night TV show touched off a frenzy of adoration and hero worship. The fact that parents were scandalized by Presley's suggestive gyrations did not lessen his appeal to their children.

The Youth Subculture

The motion picture industry also catered to teenagers. From 1946 to 1948, Americans had attended movies at the rate of nearly 90 million a week, but by 1960 the number had dropped to 40 million. The postwar years saw the steady closing of movie theaters—with the notable exception of drive-ins, which appealed to teenagers as well as to car-oriented suburban families. In fact, teenagers were the one exception to the downturn in moviegoing. By the late 1950s the first wave of the postwar baby boom had reached adolescence, and teens and young adults were flocking to the theaters. No less than 72 percent of moviegoers during the 1950s were under age thirty. Hollywood catered to this new audience with films portraying young people as sensitive and insightful, adults as boorish and hostile. *Rebel Without a Cause* (1955), starring James Dean, was one such movie. The cult of youth had been born.

Consumerism, which was crucial to the cult of youth, was also strikingly evident in Americans' postwar play and in the era's fads. Slinky, selling for a dollar, began loping down people's stairs in 1947; Silly Putty was introduced in 1950; and 3-D movies and Hula-Hoops were all the rage. Although most crazes were short-lived, they created multi-million-dollar industries and promoted dozens of movies and TV shows. Another postwar activity was the family vacation. With more money and leisure time and a much-improved highway system, middle-class families took vacations that formerly had been restricted to the rich. The destination of many family vacations was Disneyland, which opened in Anaheim, California, in 1955.

The consumer society was unreceptive to social criticism. The filmgoing public preferred noncontroversial doses of Doris Day and Rock

Beat Generation

Hudson and Dean Martin and Jerry Lewis. Even serious artists tended to ignore the country's social problems. But there were exceptions. Ralph Ellison's *Invisible Man* (1952) gave white Americans a glimpse of the psychic costs to black Americans of exclusion from the American Dream. And one group of writers noisily repudiated the materialistic and self-congratulatory world of the middle class and the suburbs. Beat (for "beatific") writers rejected both social niceties and literary conventions and in the face of middle-class conformity flaunted their freewheeling sexuality and consumption of drugs. The Beats produced some memorable prose and poetry, including Allen Ginsberg's angry incantational poem *Howl* (1956) and Jack Kerouac's novel *On the Road* (1957). Although the Beats were largely ignored during the 1950s, millions of young Americans discovered their writings and imitated their lifestyle in the 1960s.

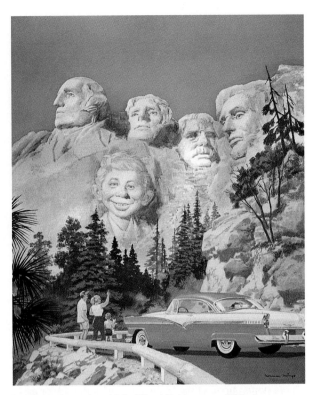

In this cartoon in which Alfred E. Neuman ("What, me worry?") joins the presidential pantheon on Mount Rushmore, *Mad* magazine parodied a venerable icon. Started in 1952, *Mad* was second in popularity only to *Life* magazine among teenagers by the early 1960s. *Mad* mocked suburbia, President Eisenhower, and the smugness of the American middle class.   (*Mad* magazine Mount Rushmore cover used with permission, © 1956, 1984 by E.C. Publications, Inc.)

The Other America

In an age of abundance and rampant consumerism, most Americans dismissed poverty, if they noticed it at all, as the fault of poor people themselves. But by 1961 about 42.5 million Americans (nearly one of every four) were poor—too large a group to ignore much longer. Age, race, gender, education, and marital status were all factors in their poverty. One-fourth of the poor were over age sixty-five. One-fifth were people of color, including almost half of the nation's African American population and more than half of all Native Americans. Two-thirds lived in households headed by a person with an eighth-grade education or less, one-fourth in households headed by a single woman. More

than one-third were under age eighteen. Few of these people had much reason for hope.

A disproportionate number of the poor in postwar America were women. Occupational segregation was

Women

pervasive. Men tended to receive the better-paying positions; thus many women were forced to take low-paying jobs as laundresses, short-order cooks, and janitors. Median annual earnings for full-time women workers stood at 60 percent of men's earnings in 1960. Moreover, many women's jobs were not covered by either the minimum wage or Social Security. And if divorce, desertion, or death did break up a family, the woman was usually left with responsibility for the children. Many divorced fathers evaded their regular child-support payments. Single mothers and

Three generations of the Moreira family gathered for an Easter celebration in Los Angeles in 1960. By the end of the 1950s many Mexican American families had established businesses, bought homes, and entered the middle class.   (Shades of L.A. Archives/Los Angeles Public Library)

their children, dependent on welfare or low wages, more often than not slipped into poverty.

While millions of Americans (most of them white) were settling in the suburbs, the poor were congregating in the inner cities, including African Americans who had migrated from the South. Joining African Americans in the exodus to the cities were poor whites from the southern Appalachians, many of whom moved to Cincinnati, Baltimore, and Detroit. Meanwhile, Latin Americans were arriving in growing numbers from Mexico, the Dominican Republic, Colombia, Ecuador, and Cuba. And New York City's Puerto Rican population exploded from 70,000 to over 600,000 in just twenty years.

Second only to African Americans in numbers of urban newcomers were Mexican Americans. Millions came as farm workers during and after the Second World War, and increasing numbers remained to make their lives in the United States. Despite the initiation in 1953 of Operation Wetback, a federal pro-

The Inner Cities

gram to find and deport illegal aliens, Mexicans continued to enter the country in large numbers, many of them illegally. Most settled in cities. According to the 1960 census, over a half-million Mexican Americans had migrated to the *barrios* of the Los Angeles–Long Beach area since 1940. Estimates of uncounted illegal aliens suggest that the actual total was far higher. The same was true in the *barrios* in southwestern and northern cities.

Native Americans, whose average annual income was barely half of the poverty level, were the country's poorest people. Many Native Americans moved to the cities in the 1950s and 1960s, particularly after Congress in 1953 adopted the termination policy (see page 795). Accustomed to semicommunal rural life on the reservation, many had difficulty adjusting to the urban environment. Like other groups who migrated to the cities in hope of finding a place to prosper, they found only a dumping ground for the poor.

Not all of the poor, however, lived in cities. In 1960, 30 percent of the poor still lived in small towns,

Rural Poverty

15 percent on farms. Tenant farmers and sharecroppers, both black and white, continued to suffer severe economic hardship. Migratory farm workers lived in abject poverty. In postwar America, elderly people tended to be poor regardless of where they lived.

Americans living in poverty were poor in part because federal legislation had shortchanged them. Government-sponsored housing and highways worked largely to improve life for middle-class whites; disadvantaged Americans did not share much in their benefits. For example, the National Housing Act of 1949, passed to make available "a decent home . . . for every American family," failed in several respects. A primary feature of the act was "urban redevelopment" (slum clearance). Unsightly structures were torn down; entire neighborhoods were leveled. They were replaced not with low-income housing but with luxury high-rise buildings, parking lots, and highways. Many poor people lost what little housing they had.

With the publication of Michael Harrington's *The Other America* in 1962, people became aware of the contradiction of poverty in their midst. America's poor, wrote Harrington, were "the strangest poor in the history of mankind," for they "exist within the most powerful and rich society the world has ever known. Their misery has continued while the majority of the nation talked of itself as being 'affluent.'" Whether living in urban obscurity or rural isolation, the poor had "dropped out of sight and out of mind"—particularly the minds of comfortable suburbanites.

The Election of 1960 and the Dawning of a New Decade

The election of 1960 was one of the closest and most hard-fought in the twentieth century. The forty-three-year-old Democratic candidate, Senator John F. Kennedy of Massachusetts, was handsome and intelligent; born to wealth, he injected new vigor and glamour into presidential politics. His running mate in 1960 was Senator Lyndon B. Johnson of Texas, added to the ticket to keep white southerners loyal to the Democratic Party as the civil rights issue heated up. The Republican candidate was Richard M. Nixon, the forty-seven-year-old two-term vice president from California. He and his running mate, Ambassador

Henry Cabot Lodge of Massachusetts, expected a rugged campaign.

Kennedy, exploiting the media to great advantage, ran a risky but ultimately brilliant race. Aware that his major liability with voters was his Roman Catholicism, he addressed the issue head-on: he went to the Bible belt to tell a group of Houston ministers that he respected the separation of church and state and would take his orders from the American people, not the pope. Seeing opportunity in the African American vote and calculating that Johnson could keep the white South loyal to the Democrats, Kennedy courted black voters. Foreign policy was another major issue. Nixon claimed that he alone knew how to deal with Communists, but Kennedy countered that Eisenhower and Nixon had let American prestige and power erode, and

John F. Kennedy is surrounded by supporters and the press as he arrives for the 1960 Democratic National Convention in Los Angeles. Young, handsome, and articulate, Kennedy introduced new vitality, and perhaps superficiality, into political campaigning. On television and in person, Kennedy was a popular politician; when he became president, he became a media star as well.   (Wide World Photos, Inc.)

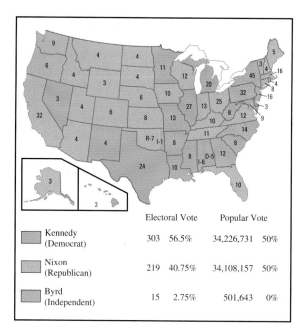

		Electoral Vote		Popular Vote	
	Kennedy (Democrat)	303	56.5%	34,226,731	50%
	Nixon (Republican)	219	40.75%	34,108,157	50%
	Byrd (Independent)	15	2.75%	501,643	0%

Map 28.3   Presidential Election, 1960   In 1960 John F. Kennedy won the closest presidential election in twentieth-century American history. In fact, Richard M. Nixon won the popular votes of twenty-six states to Kennedy's twenty-four. In the electoral college, fifteen southerners voted for neither Kennedy nor Nixon but cast protest votes for Harry F. Byrd, a conservative senator from Virginia.

he promised victory instead of stalemate in the Cold War. Kennedy subscribed to the two fundamental tenets of the postwar consensus—economic growth and anticommunism—and asserted that he could expand the benefits of economic progress and win foreign disputes through more vigorous leadership.

As Kennedy gained momentum, Nixon was saddled with the handicaps of incumbency: he had to answer for the recession of 1960 and the Soviet downing of a U-2 spy plane. Nixon also looked unsavory on TV; in televised debates with Kennedy, he came across as heavy-jowled and surly. Perhaps worse, Eisenhower gave him only a tepid endorsement. Asked to list Nixon's significant decisions as vice president, Eisenhower replied, "If you give me a week, I might think of one."

In an election characterized by the highest voter participation (63 percent) in a half-century, Kennedy defeated Nixon by the razor-slim margin of 118,000

votes. Kennedy's electoral college margin, 303 to 219, was much closer than the numbers suggest (see Map 28.3). Slight shifts in the popular vote in Illinois and Texas—two states where electoral fraud helped produce narrow Democratic majorities—would have made Nixon president. Although Kennedy's Catholicism lost him some votes, religious bigotry did not decide the election, and Kennedy became the first Roman Catholic U.S. president.

Summary

In the fifteen years after the Second World War, Americans focused on their private lives. Those who had served their country either on the battlefield or in defense factories believed they needed to make up for lost time. Millions of veterans used the GI Bill to attend college, buy homes, and start businesses. These Americans also wanted to have babies, and they worked hard to provide a comfortable standard of living for their growing families. And as their level of consumption rose in the 1940s and 1950s, American business boomed.

During the Cold War presidencies of Truman and Eisenhower, the country was engaged in a mortal struggle with communism; and during such a crusade, people believed, citizens should support, not criticize, the government. Much as they might bicker about how to wage the Cold War or how to manage the economy, they were one when it came to anticommunism and faith in economic progress. In the 1940s and 1950s the civil rights movement reminded the country that not all Americans were first-class citizens. But most white Americans believed that the United States was the greatest nation in the world and that its potential was boundless. For middle-class Americans who surrounded themselves with the trappings of economic success—automobiles, televisions, houses in suburbia—the American dream seemed a reality.

Only a few years later, however, comfortable middle-class Americans discovered that millions of poor people were living in their midst and that most of them had been deprived of the civil rights the rest of the nation took for granted. Ironically, it would be the privileged children of suburbia—the generation of the baby boom—who would energize the movement to eradicate not only racism and poverty but the whole value system of the postwar American middle class.

LEGACY FOR A PEOPLE AND A NATION
The Eradication of Polio

No disease was more dreaded by postwar Americans, especially the nation's families with children, than infantile paralysis, or poliomyelitis. Children of all ages knew that polio seemingly struck out of nowhere (it is a water-borne virus), caused intense pain, and could be a lifelong affliction, leaving paralysis. During the Second World War, newspapers and magazines carried alarming stories about polio epidemics and gave advice on how to reduce the risks to children. Although important medical advances occurred then, including the introduction of penicillin and antibiotics, research into polio failed to produce an effective vaccine to ward off the disease.

As frightening as the epidemics during the war had been, polio's most fearsome years came in 1949–1954, when the incidence of polio doubled the rate for the worst of the wartime epidemics. The year 1952 ranked as the worst ever, with 57,900 cases. The nation was in a panic in the early 1950s. Cities closed pools and beaches. Children were told not to jump in puddles or drink from water fountains, or even to make new friends. Polio was terrifying, recalled one girl; it was "a fear that gripped my life."

Year by year, tests for a polio vaccine showed success. Then, in April 1955, the federal government approved a vaccine developed by Dr. Jonas E. Salk at the University of Pittsburgh. In the preceding forty years polio had killed or crippled 357,000 people in the United States alone, not to mention millions of others worldwide. But in spring 1955, American children lined up in schools and clinics, even on street corners, to be injected by needle with the vaccine; and in 1962 an oral vaccine was licensed by the federal government. Between 1969 and 1979 the United States counted only 179 new polio cases. A terrible scourge, as well as a massive source of childhood fears, had been eradicated from the United States; in succeeding years, polio was also eliminated from most of the Western Hemisphere. Finally, in 1999, the World Health Organization announced that polio would be eradicated worldwide by the end of the year 2000—a triumphant legacy of medical research, government activism, and community cooperation.

For Further Reading, see page A-32 of the Appendix. For Web resources, go to http://college.hmco.com.

On July 16, 1945, the "Deer" Team leader parachuted into northern Vietnam, near Kimlung, a village nestled in a valley of rice paddies surrounded by mosquito-infested forests. Colonel Allison Thomas could not know that the end of the Second World War was just weeks away, but he and the other five members of his Office of Strategic Services (OSS) unit knew their mission: to work with the Vietminh, a nationalist Vietnamese organization, to sabotage Japanese forces that in March had seized Vietnam from France. After disentangling himself from the banyan tree into which his parachute had slammed him, Thomas spoke a "few flowery sentences" to two hundred Vietminh soldiers assembled near a banner proclaiming "Welcome to Our American Friends." Ho Chi Minh, head of the Vietminh, ill but speaking in good English, cordially greeted the OSS team and offered supper. The next day Ho denounced the French but remarked that "we welcome 10 million Americans." "Forget the Communist Bogy," Thomas radioed OSS headquarters in China.

A communist who had worked for decades to win his nation's independence from France, Ho helped supply information on Japanese military forces and rescue downed American pilots during the war. He also met in March 1945 with U.S. officials in Kunming, China. There he read the *Encyclopaedia Britannica* and *Time* magazine at an Office of War Information facility. Receiving no aid from his ideological allies in the Soviet Union, Ho hoped that the United States would favor his nation's long quest for liberation from colonialism.

Other OSS personnel soon parachuted into Kimlung, including a male nurse who diagnosed Ho's ailments as malaria and dysentery; quinine and sulfa drugs restored his health, but Ho remained frail. As a sign of friendship, the Americans in Vietnam named Ho "OSS Agent 19." Everywhere the Americans went, impoverished villagers thanked them with gifts of food and clothing, despite the devastating famine of 1944–1945 in which at least a million Vietnamese died. The villagers interpreted the foreigners' presence as a sign of U.S. anticolonial and anti-Japanese sentiments. In early August the "Deer" Team began to give Vietminh

The Vietnamese nationalist Ho Chi Minh (1890–1969) meets with OSS "Deer" team members in 1945. On the right is Colonel Allison Thomas. (Private Collection)

29

THE COLD WAR AND AMERICAN GLOBALISM 1945–1961

soldiers weapons training. During many conversations with the OSS members, Ho said that he hoped young Vietnamese could study in the United States and American technicians could help build an independent Vietnam. Citing history, Ho remarked that "your statesmen make eloquent speeches about . . . self-determination. We are self-determined. Why not help us? Am I any different from . . . your George Washington?"

A second OSS unit, the "Mercy" Team headed by Captain Archimedes Patti, arrived in the city of Hanoi on August 22. When Patti met Ho—"this wisp of a man"—the Vietminh leader applauded America's assistance and called for future "collaboration." But, unbeknownst to these OSS members, who believed that President Franklin D. Roosevelt's general sympathy for eventual Vietnamese independence remained U.S. policy, the new Truman administration in Washington had decided to let France, America's emerging Cold War ally, decide the fate of Vietnam. That change in policy explains why Ho never received answers to the several letters and telegrams he sent to Washington—the first dated August 30, 1945.

On September 2, 1945, amid great fanfare in Hanoi, with OSS personnel present, an emotional Ho Chi Minh read his declaration of independence for the Democratic Republic of Vietnam: "All men are created equal; they are endowed by their Creator with certain unalienable Rights; among these are Life, Liberty, and the pursuit of Happiness." Having borrowed from the internationally renowned 1776 American document, Ho then itemized Vietnamese grievances against France. At one point in the ceremonies, two American P-38 aircraft swooped down over the crowded square. The Vietnamese cheered, interpreting the flyby as U.S. endorsement of their independence. Actually, the pilots had no orders to make a political statement; they just wanted to see what was happening.

By late September both OSS teams had departed Vietnam. In a last meeting with Captain Patti, Ho expressed his sadness that the United States had armed the French to reestablish their colonial rule in Vietnam. Sure, Ho said, U.S. officials in Washington judged him a "Moscow puppet" because he was a communist. But Ho claimed that he drew inspiration from the American struggle for independence and that he was foremost "a free agent," a nationalist. If necessary, Ho insisted, the Vietnamese would go it alone, with or without American or Soviet help. And they did—first against the French and eventually against more than

half a million U.S. troops in what became America's longest war. How different world history would have been had President Harry S Truman responded favorably to Ho Chi Minh's last letter to Washington, dated February 16, 1946, which asked the United States "as guardians and champions of World Justice to take a decisive step in support of our independence."

Because Ho Chi Minh and many of his nationalist followers had declared themselves communists, U.S. leaders rejected their appeal. Endorsing the containment doctrine to draw the line against communism everywhere, American presidents from Truman to George Bush believed that a ruthless Soviet Union was directing a worldwide communist conspiracy against peace, free-market capitalism, and political democracy. Soviet leaders from Joseph Stalin to Mikhail Gorbachev protested that a militarized, economically aggressive United States sought nothing less than world domination. This protracted contest between the United States and the Soviet Union acquired the name Cold War.

The primary feature of world affairs for more than four decades, the Cold War was fundamentally a bipolar contest between the United States and the Soviet Union over spheres of influence, over world power. Decisions made in Moscow and Washington dominated world politics, as the capitalist "West" squared off with the communist "East." Like a glacier, the Cold War began in the 1940s to cut across the global terrain, changing the topography of international relations. The Cold War eventually took the lives of millions, cost trillions of dollars, spawned fears of doomsday, and destabilized one nation after another. On occasion the two superpowers negotiated at summit conferences and signed agreements to temper their dangerous arms race; at other times they went to the brink of war and armed allies to fight vicious wars in the Third World.

Vietnam was part of the Third World, a general term for those nations that during the Cold War era wore neither the "West" (the "First World") nor the "East" (the "Second World") label. Sometimes called developing countries, Third World nations on the whole were nonwhite, nonindustrialized, and located in the southern half of the globe—in Asia, Africa, the Middle East, and Latin America. Many of them had been colonies of European nations or Japan. The great-power Cold War rivalry intruded into the Third World. U.S. leaders often interpreted Third World anticolonialism, political instability, and restrictions on foreign-owned property as Soviet or communist in-

IMPORTANT EVENTS

1945 Yalta Conference charts postwar order
Roosevelt dies; Truman becomes president
OSS cooperates with Vietminh
Potsdam agreements on postwar Germany
Atomic bombings of Japan; Tokyo surrenders
Ho Chi Minh declares Vietnam independent
World Bank and IMF begin operations

1946 U.S. backs shah in contest over Iran
Kennan's "long telegram" criticizes USSR
Churchill's "iron curtain" speech
Philippines gain independence
Baruch Plan to control atomic weapons falters
Truman fires Wallace from cabinet
Vietnamese war against France erupts

1947 Truman Doctrine seeks aid for Greece
and Turkey
Communists take power in Hungary
Marshall offers Europe economic assistance
National Security Act reorganizes government
"X" article posits containment doctrine
Lippmann criticizes containment in *The
Cold War*

1948 Fulbright Program initiates academic
exchanges
Communists take power in Czechoslovakia
OAS founded as alliance in Latin America
Marshall Plan aids European economic
recovery
Truman recognizes Israel
U.S. organizes Berlin airlift

1949 Truman calls for Point Four technical
assistance
NATO founded as anti-Soviet alliance
Soviet Union explodes atomic bomb
Mao's Communists win power in China

1950 NSC-68 recommends major military buildup
U.S. aids France in Vietnam
Radio Free Europe begins broadcasts
Korean War starts in June; China enters
in fall

1951 Truman fires General MacArthur
Armistice talks open in Korea
U.S. signs security treaty with Japan

1952 U.S. explodes first H-bomb

1953 Eisenhower becomes president
Stalin dies
U.S. helps restore shah to power in Iran
USIA created as propaganda agency
Korean War ends

1954 Siege of Dienbienphu in Vietnam
Geneva accords partition Vietnam
CIA overthrows Arbenz in Guatemala
Crisis over islands of Jinmen and Mazu
SEATO alliance formed for Southeast Asia

1955 Formosa Resolution to defend Taiwan
Puerto Rico's Operation Bootstrap expands
U.S.-USSR summit meeting at Geneva
Occupation of Austria ends
Soviets create Warsaw Pact
U.S. backs Diem regime in Vietnam
Bandung Conference of nonaligned nations

1956 Soviets crush uprising in Hungary
Suez crisis sparks war in Middle East

1957 Eisenhower Doctrine for Middle East
Soviets fire first ICBM and launch *Sputnik*
SANE founded

1958 U.S.-USSR cultural exchanges begin
U.S. launches *Explorer I*
NASA created
U.S. troops land in Lebanon
Berlin crisis

1959 Castro ousts Batista in Cuba
Rostow's *Stages of Economic Growth*
Nixon-Khrushchev "kitchen debate" in
Moscow

1960 18 African colonies become independent
U.S. begins embargo against Cuba
Soviets shoot down U-2 spy plane
Vietcong organized in South Vietnam

1961 U.S. breaks relations with Cuba

spired or capable of being exploited by Moscow—in short, as Cold War matters rather than as expressions of profound indigenous nationalism. As an example, Vietnam became one among many sites where the Cold War and the Third World intersected, prompting U.S. intervention.

Critics in the United States challenged the architects of the Cold War, questioning their exaggerations of threats from abroad, meddlesome interventions in the Third World, and the expensive militarization of foreign policy. But when leaders such as Truman described the Cold War in extremist terms as a life-and-death struggle against a monstrous enemy, legitimate criticism became suspect and dissenters discredited. The critics' searching questions about America's global, interventionist foreign policy and reliance on nuclear weapons were drowned out by redbaiting charges that they were "soft on communism," if not un-American. Decision makers in the United States successfully cultivated a Cold War consensus that dampened debate (see Chapter 28). ■

Why the Cold War Began

After the Second World War, the international system was so unsettled that conflict became virtually inevitable. Throughout Europe and Asia, factories and transportation and communications links had been reduced to rubble. Agricultural production plummeted, and displaced persons wandered around in search of food and family. How would the devastated economic world be pieced back together? The United States and the Soviet Union offered very different answers and models. The collapse of Germany and Japan, moreover, had created power vacuums that drew the two major powers into collision as they sought influence in countries where the Axis aggressors once had held sway. And the political turmoil that many nations experienced after the war also spurred Soviet-American competition. For example, in Greece and China, where civil wars raged between leftists and conservative regimes, the two powers supported different sides.

The international system also became unstable because empires were disintegrating, creating the new Third World. Financial constraints and nationalist rebellions forced the European imperial states to set their colonies free. Britain exited India (and Pakistan) in 1947 and Burma and Sri Lanka (Ceylon) in 1948. After four years of battling nationalists in Indonesia, the Dutch left in 1949. In the Middle East, Lebanon (1943), Syria (1946), and Jordan (1946) gained independence. America and the Soviet Union vied to win new Third World states like these as allies that might provide military bases, resources, and markets. Some new nations chose nonalignment in the Cold War. "We do not intend to be the playthings of others," declared India's leader Jawaharlal Nehru.

Decolonization

Driven by different ideologies and different economic and strategic needs in this volatile international climate, the United States and the Soviet Union downgraded diplomacy to build what Secretary of State Dean Acheson called "situations of strength." Finding the Soviets rude and abusive, this conservative diplomat asserted that "it is a mistake to believe that you can, at any time, sit down with the Russians and solve problems." Both nations marched into the Cold War with convictions of righteousness that gave the contest an almost religious character. Each saw the other as the world's bully, itself as the world's savior. While Americans feared "communist aggression," Soviets feared "capitalist encirclement."

U.S. officials vowed never to repeat the experience of the 1930s: they would accept no more Munichs, no more appeasement, and no more depressions that might spawn political extremism and war. To growing numbers of Americans after the Second World War, it seemed that Soviet Russia had simply replaced Nazi Germany, that communism was simply the flip side of the totalitarian coin. The popular term "Red fascism" captured this sentiment.

U.S. leaders also knew that the nation's economic well-being depended on an activist foreign policy. An economic giant at a time when much of the world struggled to overcome the devastation of the Second World War, the United States stood as the largest supplier of goods to international markets. But that trade became jeopardized by the postwar economic paralysis of Europe—traditionally America's major customer— and by discriminatory trade practices that violated the Open Door doctrine (see page 624). Europe's economy was so prostrate that it could not earn dollars to buy American products (the "dollar gap"); if the gap were not closed, the United States might face a severe depression once again. U.S. automobile, steel, and machine-tool industries, as well as wheat, cotton, and tobacco farmers, relied heavily on foreign trade. Indeed, exports constituted about 10 percent of the gross national product. And the United States also needed to import essential minerals such as zinc, tin, and manganese. Thus economic expansionism, so much a part of pre–Cold War history, remained a central feature of postwar foreign relations.

U.S. Economic and Strategic Needs

New strategic theory also propelled the United States toward an expansionist, globalist diplomacy. The shrinkage of the globe with the advent of the "air age" made the world more compact. Faster travel brought nations closer at the same time that it made them more vulnerable to surprise attack from the air. "As top dog, America becomes target No. 1," warned air force general Carl Spaatz. The Americans and the Soviets collided as they strove to establish defensive positions, sometimes far from home. The United States sought overseas bases and air transit and landing rights to guard the approaches to the Western Hemisphere. These bases also would permit the United States to launch offensive attacks with might and speed. When asked where the U.S. Navy would float, Navy Secretary James Forrestal declared, "Wherever there is a sea."

President Truman, who shared these economic and strategic assumptions, had a personality ill suited for diplomacy. Whereas Franklin D.

Truman's Get-Tough Style

Roosevelt had been ingratiating, patient, and evasive, Truman was brash, impatient, and direct. He often glossed over nuances, ambiguities, and counterevidence; he preferred the simple answer stated in either-or terms. As Winston Churchill, who admired Truman's decisiveness, once observed, the president "takes no notice of delicate ground, he just plants his foot firmly on it." Truman constantly exaggerated, as when he declared in his undelivered farewell address that he had "knocked the socks off the communists" in Korea (see pages 834–838). Shortly after Roosevelt's death in early 1945, Truman met the Soviet commissar of foreign affairs, V. M. Molotov, at the White House. When the president sharply protested that the Soviets were not fulfilling the Yalta agreement on Poland, Molotov stormed out. Truman had self-consciously developed what he called his "tough method," and he bragged after the encounter that "I gave it to him straight 'one-two to the jaw.'" Although the Soviets acted heavy-handedly in Poland, whether they violated the vaguely written Yalta accord remains open to interpretation. Truman's display of toughness nonetheless became a trademark of American Cold War diplomacy.

The Soviets remembered that since the Bolshevik Revolution the hostile West had attempted to defeat and then ostracize them. Fearful of a revived Germany and a resurgent Japan, anticipating that capitalist nations once again would attempt to extinguish the communist flame, facing a monumental task of economic reconstruction in their devastated nation, and embracing Marxist-Leninist doctrine, the Soviets made territorial gains in eastern Poland, the Baltic states of Lithuania, Latvia, and Estonia, and parts of Finland

and Romania—some of these areas having once been part of the Russian Empire. In eastern Europe Soviet officials began to suppress noncommunists and install communist clients. The Americans, the steely premier Joseph Stalin protested, were surrounding the USSR with hostile bases and practicing atomic and dollar diplomacy. He nonetheless knew that the Soviets could not realize many of their goals without cooperation from the United States. That is why, the historian Melvyn Leffler has written, "Stalin's approach to international affairs" was "cautious" and "expedient," lacking a "distinct strategy."

Throughout the Cold War era, Americans debated Soviet intentions and capabilities. Many no doubt agreed with Churchill, who compared

Debate over Soviet Intentions and Behavior

dealing with the Soviet Union to "wooing a crocodile. You do not know whether to tickle it under the chin or to beat it over the head. When it opens its mouth you cannot tell whether it is trying to smile or . . . eat you up." Some diplomats believed that the Soviet Union—well armed, opportunistic, and aggressive—could never be trusted. On the other hand, critics of U.S. policies charged that American officials exaggerated the Soviet/communist threat, imagining a bigger-than-life, monolithic archenemy, finding it at work everywhere, blaming it for troubles it never started, attributing to it accomplishments it never achieved.

In the immediate postwar years, in fact, the Soviet Union suffered a hobbled economy and, like the United States, undertook a major postwar demobilization of its armed forces. The Soviet Union was a regional power in eastern Europe, not a global menace. American leaders feared that the ravaging postwar economic and social unrest abroad would leave American strategic and economic interests vulnerable to political disorders that the Soviets might exploit, perhaps through subversion. In other words, Americans feared Soviet seizure of opportunities to challenge U.S. interests more than they feared a direct Soviet attack on western Europe.

The United States took advantage of the postwar power vacuum and economic supremacy to expand its overseas interests and shape a peace on American terms. The U.S. pursuit of nuclear superiority, outlying bases, raw materials and markets, supremacy in Latin America, and control of the Atlantic and Pacific Oceans aroused many opponents, in particular the Soviet Union. To Americans who thought that vigorous U.S. globalism must and would save the world, Soviet opposition simply confirmed Moscow's wicked obstructionism.

Truman's Cold War: Europe and Global Containment

One of the first Soviet-American clashes came in Poland in 1945, when the Soviets refused to allow conservative Poles from London to join the communist government in Lublin. Truman officials argued that Stalin at the Yalta Conference had agreed to a democratic government for Poland, but the Soviet Union, fearing Western inroads into its sphere of influence, disputed that interpretation and sustained a procommunist regime. The Soviets also snuffed out civil liberties in the former Nazi satellite of Romania, justifying their actions by pointing to what they claimed was an equivalent U.S. manipulation of Italy. Moscow initially allowed free elections in Hungary and Czechoslovakia, but as the Cold War accelerated and U.S. influence in Europe expanded, the Soviets encouraged communist coups in Hungary (1947) and Czechoslovakia (1948). Yugoslavia stood as a unique case: its independent communist government, led by Josip Broz Tito, successfully broke with Stalin in 1948.

To defend their actions, the Soviets pointed out that the United States was reviving their traditional enemy, Germany. The Soviets also protested that the United States was meddling in eastern Europe. They cited clandestine American meetings with anti-Soviet groups, repeated calls for elections likely to produce anti-Soviet regimes, and the use of loans to gain political influence (dollar diplomacy). Moscow charged that the United States was pursuing a double standard—intervening in the affairs of eastern Europe but demanding that the Soviet Union stay out of Latin America and Asia. Americans called for free elections in the Soviet sphere, Moscow noted, but not in the U.S. sphere in Latin America, where several military dictatorships ruled.

The atomic bomb also divided the two major powers. The Soviets believed that the United States was practicing "atomic diplomacy"—maintaining a nuclear monopoly to scare the Soviets into diplomatic concessions. Secretary of State James F. Byrnes thought that the atomic bomb gave the United States bargaining power and could

Atomic Diplomacy

serve as a deterrent to Soviet expansion, but Secretary of War Henry L. Stimson thought otherwise in 1945. If Americans continued to have "this weapon rather ostentatiously on our hip," he warned Truman, the Soviets' "suspicions and their distrust of our purposes and motives will increase."

In this atmosphere of suspicion and distrust, Truman refused to turn over the weapon to an international control authority. In 1946 he backed the Baruch Plan, named after its author, financier Bernard Baruch. Largely a propaganda ploy, this proposal provided for U.S. abandonment of its atomic monopoly only after the world's fissionable materials were brought under the authority of an international agency. The Soviets retorted that this plan would require them to shut down their atomic-bomb development project while the United States continued its own. Washington and Moscow soon became locked into an expensive and frightening nuclear arms race.

Soviets and Americans clashed on every front in 1946. When the United States turned down a Soviet request for a reconstruction loan but gave a loan to Britain, Moscow upbraided Washington for using its dollars to manipulate foreign governments. The two Cold War powers also backed different groups in Iran, where the United States helped bring the pro-West shah to the throne. Unable to agree on the unification of Germany, the Cold War antagonists built up their zones independently.

The new World Bank and International Monetary Fund (IMF), created at the July 1944 Bretton Woods Conference by forty-four nations to stabilize trade and finance, also became tangled in the Cold War. The Soviets refused to join because the United States so dominated both institutions and because their purpose was to promote private investment and open and multilateral international commerce, which Moscow saw as capitalist tools of exploitation. With the United States as its largest donor, the World Bank opened its doors in 1945 and began to make loans to help members finance reconstruction projects; the IMF, also heavily backed by the United States, helped members meet their balance of payments problems through currency loans.

World Bank and International Monetary Fund

After Stalin gave a speech in February 1946 that depicted the world as threatened by capitalist acquisitiveness, the American chargé d'affaires in Moscow, George F. Kennan, sent a pessimistic "long telegram" to Washington. Kennan asserted that Soviet fanati-

Kennan and Churchill Warn Against Soviet Power

cism made even a temporary understanding impossible. His widely circulated report fed a growing belief among American officials that only toughness would work with the Soviets. The following month, Winston Churchill delivered a stirring speech in Fulton, Missouri. The former British prime minister warned that a Soviet-erected "iron curtain" had cut off eastern European countries from the West. With an approving Truman sitting on the stage, Churchill called for Anglo-American partnership to resist the new menace.

Secretary of Commerce Henry A. Wallace charged that Truman's get-tough policy was substituting atomic and economic coercion for diplomacy. Wallace told a Madison Square Garden audience in September 1946 that "'getting tough' never brought anything real and lasting—whether for schoolyard bullies or businessmen or world powers. The tougher we get, the tougher the Russians will get." Truman soon fired Wallace from the cabinet, blasting him privately as "a real Commy and a dangerous man" and boasting that he, Truman, had now "run the crackpots out of the Democratic Party." Such mistaken and extremist words helped kindle the exaggerations so common to the Cold War.

The Cold War escalated further in early 1947, when the British requested American help in Greece

Truman Doctrine

to defend their conservative client government against a leftist insurgency. In his March 12, 1947, speech to Congress, Truman requested $400 million in aid to Greece and Turkey. He had a selling job to do. The Republican Eightieth Congress wanted less, not more, spending, and many of its members had little respect for the Democratic president whose administration the voters had repudiated in the 1946 elections. Republican senator Arthur Vandenberg of Michigan, a bipartisan leader who backed Truman's request, bluntly told the president that he would have to "scare hell out of the American people" to gain congressional approval.

With that advice in mind, the president delivered a speech laced with alarmist language intended to stake out the United States's role in the postwar world. Truman claimed that communism, feeding on economic dislocations, imperiled the world. "If Greece should fall under the control of an armed minority," he gravely concluded in an early version of the domino theory (see page 839), "the effect upon its neighbor, Turkey, would be immediate and serious. Confusion and disor-

On March 5, 1946, former British prime minister Winston S. Churchill (1874–1965) delivered a speech, which he intended for a worldwide audience, at Westminster College in Fulton, Missouri. President Harry S Truman *(right)* had encouraged Churchill *(seated)* to speak on two themes: the need to block Soviet expansion and the need to form an Anglo-American partnership. Always eloquent and provocative, Churchill denounced the Soviets for drawing an "iron curtain" across eastern Europe. This speech became one of the landmark statements of the Cold War. (Harry S Truman Library)

der might well spread throughout the entire Middle East." At the time, civil war in which communists played a prominent role rocked Greece. Turkey bordered the Soviet Union, considered by American leaders to be masterminding global communist expansion. At issue, Truman insisted, was the very security of the United States.

Especially momentous in the dramatic speech were the words, later known as the Truman Doctrine, that would guide American policymakers for almost a half-century: "I believe that it must be the policy of the United States to support free peoples who are resisting attempted subjugation by armed minorities or by outside pressures." Secretary of State George C. Marshall privately questioned the "flamboyant anti-

Communism" of the speech, but two new and young members of the House of Representatives, John F. Kennedy and Richard M. Nixon, applauded Truman's message that day. When they assumed the presidency in the 1960s, the Truman Doctrine still guided their policies.

Critics correctly pointed out that the Soviet Union was little involved in the Greek civil war, that the communists in Greece were more pro-Tito than pro-Stalin, and that the resistance movement had noncommunist as well as communist members. Nor was the Soviet Union threatening Turkey at the time. Others suggested that such aid should be channeled through the United Nations. Truman countered that should communists gain control of Greece, they might open the door to Soviet power in the Mediterranean. After much debate, the Senate approved Truman's request by 67 to 23 votes. Using U.S. dollars and military advisers, the Greek government defeated the insurgents in 1949, and Turkey became a staunch U.S. ally on the Soviets' border.

Four months after Truman's speech, Kennan, having moved from the U.S. embassy in Moscow to the State Department in Washington,

The "X" Article published an influential statement of the containment doctrine. Writing as "Mr. X" in the magazine *Foreign Affairs*, Kennan advocated a "policy of firm containment, designed to confront the Russians with unalterable counterforce at every point where they show signs of encroaching upon the interests of a peaceful and stable world." Such counterforce, Kennan argued, would check Soviet expansion and eventually foster a "mellowing" of Soviet behavior. Along with the Truman Doctrine, Kennan's "X" article became a key manifesto of Cold War policy.

The veteran journalist Walter Lippmann took issue with the containment doctrine in his book *The Cold War* (1947), calling it a "strate-

The Containment Doctrine Debated gic monstrosity" that failed to distinguish between areas vital and peripheral to U.S. security. If American leaders defined every place on earth as strategically important, Lippmann reasoned, the nation's patience and resources soon would be drained. Nor did Lippmann share Truman's conviction that the Soviet Union was plotting to take over the world. The president, he asserted, put too little emphasis on diplomacy. Lippmann's critique, although prophetic, proved no match for the emerging Cold War mentality of 1947.

Invoking the containment doctrine, the United States in 1947 and 1948 began to build an international economic and defensive network to protect American prosperity and security and to advance U.S. hegemony. In western Europe, the region of primary concern, American diplomats pursued several objectives: partnership with Great Britain; economic reconstruction; ouster of communists from governments, as occurred in 1947 in France and Italy; blockage of "third force" or neutralist tendencies; keeping the decolonization of European empires orderly; creation of a military alliance; and unification of the western zones of Germany. At the same time, American culture—consumer goods, music, consumption ethic, and production techniques—permeated European societies. Some Europeans resisted Americanization, but transatlantic ties strengthened.

The first instrument designed to achieve U.S. goals in western Europe was the Marshall Plan. European nations, still reeling economically and

Marshall Plan unstable politically, lacked the dollars to buy vital American-made goods. Americans, who already had spent billions of dollars on European relief and recovery by 1947, remembered all too well the troubles of the 1930s: global depression, political extremism, and war born of economic discontent. Such cataclysms could not be allowed to happen again; communism must not replace fascism. Western Europe, said one State Department diplomat, was "the keystone in the arch which supports the kind of a world which we have to have in order to conduct our lives."

In June 1947 Secretary of State Marshall announced that the United States would finance a massive European recovery program. Launched in 1948, the Marshall Plan sent $12.4 billion to western Europe before the program ended in 1951 (see Map 29.1). To stimulate business at home, the legislation provided that the foreign-aid dollars must be spent in the United States on American-made products. The Marshall Plan proved a mixed success; some scholars today even argue that Europe could have revived without it. The program caused inflation, failed to solve a balance-of-payments problem, took only tentative steps toward economic integration, and further divided Europe between "East" and "West." But the program spurred impressive western European industrial production and investment and started the region toward self-sustaining economic growth. From the American perspective, moreover, the plan succeeded because it helped contain communism.

Under official postwar relief and recovery programs, including the Marshall Plan, the United States shipped billions of dollars' worth of food and equipment to western European nations struggling to overcome the destruction of the Second World War. Private efforts also succeeded, such as this one in 1950. The people of Jersey City, New Jersey, sent this snowplow to the mountainous village of Capracotta, Italy.   (Corbis-Bettman)

To streamline the administration of U.S. defense, Truman worked with Congress on the National Security Act of July 1947. The act created the Office of Secretary of Defense (which became the Department of Defense two years later), the National Security Council (NSC) of high-level officials to advise the president, and the Central Intelligence Agency (CIA) to conduct spy operations and information gathering. By the early 1950s the CIA had become a significant member of the national security state and had expanded its functions to include covert (secret) operations aimed at overthrowing unfriendly foreign leaders and, as a high-ranking American official put it, a "Department of Dirty Tricks" to stir up economic trouble in "the camp of the enemy."

National Security Act

In 1948 the United States implemented the Fulbright Program—a "cultural Marshall Plan for the intellectual reconstruction of the West," as the historian Richard Pells has written. The brainchild two years earlier of Democratic senator J. William Fulbright of Arkansas, a former Rhodes scholar and uni-

Fulbright Program and Cultural Expansion

versity president, this example of "public diplomacy" attempted to overcome cultural barriers to reach foreign peoples with a positive message about the United States. The Fulbright Program sponsored educational exchanges; professors and students from the United States went abroad to teach and study, and their counterparts from foreign countries came to the United States. By 1953 influential intellectual elites in twenty-eight nations were participating in the program in Europe, Asia, and the Middle East. In some countries, former Fulbrighters rose to political prominence, keeping their governments allied with the United States. Because considerable anti-Americanism still persisted, some American and European intellectuals in 1950 created a new organization, the Congress for Cultural Freedom, to blunt it; the CIA secretly subsidized this effort to promote America in Europe.

American officials also made military linkages around the world. The United States granted the Philippines independence in 1946 while retaining

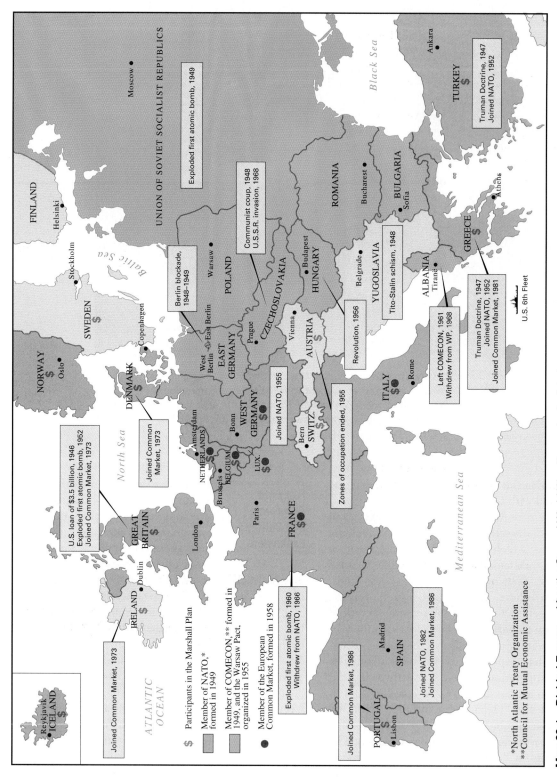

Map 29.1 Divided Europe   After the Second World War, Europe broke into two competing camps. When the United States launched the Marshall Plan in 1948, the Soviet Union countered with its own economic plan the following year. When the United States created NATO in 1949, the Soviet Union answered with the Warsaw Pact in 1955. On the whole, these two camps held firm until the late 1980s.

military and economic hegemony there. The following year, American diplomats created the Rio Pact in Latin America. To enforce this hemispheric military alliance, the United States helped found the Organization of American States (OAS) in 1948. Under this and other agreements the Truman administration sent several military missions to Latin America and to Greece, Turkey, Iran, China, and Saudi Arabia to improve the armed forces of those nations.

In May 1948 Truman quickly recognized the newly proclaimed state of Israel, which had been carved out of British-held Palestine after years of Arab-Jewish dispute. Despite State

Recognition of Israel

Department objection that recognition would alienate oil-rich Arab nations, Truman made the decision for three reasons: he believed that, after the Holocaust, Jews deserved a homeland; he desired Jewish-American votes in the upcoming election; and he sought another international ally, which Israel became.

In June 1948 the Americans, French, and British agreed to fuse their German zones, including their three sectors of Berlin. They sought

Berlin Blockade and Airlift

to integrate West Germany (the Federal Republic of Germany) into the western European economy, complete with a reformed German currency. Fearing a resurgent Germany tied to the American Cold War camp, the Soviets cut off Western land access to the jointly occupied city of Berlin, located well inside the Soviet zone. In response to this bold move, President Truman ordered a massive airlift of food, fuel, and other supplies to Berlin. Their spoiling effort blunted, the Soviets finally lifted the blockade in May 1949 and founded the German Democratic Republic, or East Germany.

In his inaugural address of January 20, 1949, President Truman announced "a bold new program" of technical assistance for "underdeveloped areas." Insisting on self-help by

Point Four Program

the participants, the Point Four Program began in 1950 with a comparatively meager $35 million to improve food supplies, public health, housing, and private investment in Third World countries that the United States sought to woo to its side in the Cold War. In 1953 fifteen hundred Point Four technicians visited thirty-five countries. They dug compost pits in India, combated a locust plague in Iran, and instructed teachers in Peru. Point Four lost its identity in 1953 when it became part of the Mutual Security Agency and

America's first ambassador to Israel, James G. MacDonald (1886–1964) *(left)* meets in 1948 with Israel's President Chaim Weizmann (1874–1952) *(center)* and Prime Minister David Ben-Gurion (1886–1973) *(right).* The historian Michelle Mart has written that "Jews in the postwar world first symbolized a complete lack of masculinity for their role as victims and then masculine resurgence in their survival and construction of a new state"—a change in image that conditioned American leaders to respect the new Israeli leaders.   (National Archives)

increasingly emphasized the flow of strategic raw materials to the United States. Still, the Truman administration championed Point Four as an inexpensive means to thwart communism—"less than the price of one battleship."

The administration gave far more attention to formation of a Western security pact. The United States, Canada, and many western European nations founded the North Atlantic

Founding of NATO

Treaty Organization (NATO) in April 1949 (see Map 29.1). The treaty aroused considerable domestic debate, for not since 1778 had the United States entered a formal European military alliance, and some critics, such as Senator Robert A. Taft, Republican of Ohio, claimed that NATO would provoke rather than deter war. Other critics argued that the Soviets did not pose a military threat. Administration officials themselves did not anticipate a Soviet military thrust against western Europe, but they responded that, should the Soviets ever probe westward, NATO would function as a "tripwire," bringing the full force of the United States to bear on the Soviet Union. Truman officials also hoped that NATO would keep western Europeans from embracing communism or even neutralism in the Cold War. The Senate ratified the treaty by 82 votes to 13, and the United States soon began to spend billions of dollars under the Mutual Defense Assistance Act.

In September 1949 an American reconnaissance aircraft detected unusually high radioactivity in the atmosphere. The news stunned U.S. officials: the Soviets had exploded an atomic bomb. With the American nuclear monopoly erased, western Europe seemed more vulnerable. At the same time, communists had won the civil war in China, and Moscow was scoring propaganda points by advocating "peaceful coexistence" with the West. American leaders did not respond to this changed state of affairs with a call for high-level negotiations but rather, in early 1950, with Truman's secret decision to start production of a hydrogen bomb, the "Super."

After Mao's victory in China and Moscow's acquisition of the atomic bomb, the National Security Council delivered to the president in April 1950 a significant top-secret document tagged NSC-68. Predicting continued tension with expansionistic communists and describing "a shrinking world of polarized power," the report appealed for a much enlarged military budget and the mobilization of public opinion to support such an increase. Officials worried about how to sell this prescription to voters and budget-conscious members of Congress. "We were sweating over it, and then—with regard to NSC-68—thank God Korea came along," recalled one U.S. official.

NSC-68

Asian Acrimony: Japan, China, and Vietnam

Asia, like Europe, became ensnared in the Cold War. The victors in the Second World War dismantled Japan's empire. The United States and the Soviet Union divided Korea into competing spheres of influence. Pacific islands (the Marshalls, Marianas, and Carolines) came under American control, and Formosa (Taiwan) was returned to China.

As for Japan itself, the United States monopolized its reconstruction through a military occupation directed by General Douglas MacArthur, who envisioned turning the Pacific Ocean into "an Anglo-Saxon lake." Truman did not like "Mr. Prima Donna,

Reconstruction of Japan

Brass Hat" MacArthur, but the general initiated "a democratic revolution from above," as the Japanese called it, that reflected Washington's wishes. MacArthur wrote a democratic constitution, gave women voting rights, revitalized the economy, and destroyed the nation's weapons. U.S. authorities also helped Americanize Japan through censorship; films that hinted at criticism of the United States (for the destruction of Hiroshima, for example) or that depicted traditional Japanese customs such as suicide, arranged marriages, and swordplay were banned. In 1951, against Soviet protests, the United States and Japan signed a separate peace that restored Japan's sovereignty and ended the occupation. A Mutual Security Treaty that year provided for the stationing of U.S. forces on Japanese soil, including a base on Okinawa.

Meanwhile, America's Chinese ally was faltering. The United States had long backed the Nationalists of Jiang Jieshi (Chiang Kai-shek) against Mao Zedong's communists. But after the Second World War, Generalissimo Jiang became an unreliable partner who rejected U.S. advice. His government had become corrupt, inefficient, and out of touch with discontented peasants, whom the communists enlisted with promises of land reform. Jiang also subverted American efforts to negotiate a cease-fire and a coalition government. "We picked a bad horse," Truman admitted, privately denouncing the Nationalists as "grafters and crooks." Still, seeing Jiang as the only alternative to Mao, Truman backed him to the end.

Communist Victory in Chinese Civil War

American officials divided on the question of whether Mao was a puppet of the Soviet Union. Some considered him an Asian Tito—communist but independent—but most believed him to be part of an international communist movement that might give the Soviets a springboard into Asia. Thus when the Chinese communists made secret overtures to the United States to begin diplomatic talks in 1945 and again in 1949, American officials rebuffed them. Mao decided to "lean" to the Soviet side in the Cold War. Because China always maintained a fierce independence that rankled the Soviets, before long a Sino-Soviet schism opened. Indeed, Mao deeply resented the Soviets' refusal to aid the communists during the civil war; Stalin offered no help, "not even a fart," Mao once growled.

In fall 1949 Jiang fled to the island of Formosa, and Mao proclaimed the People's Republic of China

U.S. Nonrecognition Policy

(PRC). Truman hesitated to extend diplomatic recognition to the new government. The British prime minister asked the president: "Are we to cut ourselves off from all contact with one-sixth of the inhabitants of the world?" Washington did precisely that. U.S. officials became alarmed by the 1950 Sino-Soviet treaty of friendship and by the harassment of Americans and their property in China. Truman also chose nonrecognition because a vocal group of Republican critics, the so-called China lobby, was winning headlines by charging that the United States had "lost" China. The publisher Henry Luce, Senator William Knowland of California, and Representative Walter Judd of Minnesota pinned Jiang's defeat on Truman. The president stoutly answered that the self-defeating Jiang, despite billions of dollars in American aid, had proven a poor instrument of the containment doctrine. The administration nonetheless took the politically safe route and rejected recognition. (Not until 1979 did official Sino-American relations resume; see page 903.)

Mao's victory in China drew urgent American attention to Indochina (Vietnam, Cambodia, and Laos).

Vietnam's Quest for Independence

Would the PRC attempt to exploit France's troubles with its rebellious colonies, converting them to communism, denying western Europe their raw materials, and closing them to the sale of Japanese goods, which Japan needed in order to reconstruct as a U.S. ally? For decades after the French takeover of Indochina in the late nineteenth century, France exploited Vietnam for its rice, rubber, tin, and tungsten. Although the French beat back recurrent rebellions, Vietnamese nationalists dedicated to independence grew in strength. Their leader Ho Chi Minh, born in 1890, lived in France before the First World War, and at the close of the war he joined the French Communist Party to use it as a vehicle for Vietnamese independence. For the next two decades, living in China, the Soviet Union, and elsewhere, Ho patiently planned and fought to free his nation from French colonialism. During World War II, as we have seen, Ho's Vietminh warriors harassed both French and Japanese forces—near the end of the war with OSS help.

Even though, as Secretary Marshall remarked, the French had a "dangerously outmoded colonial outlook and method," the Truman administration rejected Vietnam's independence in the 1940s in favor of the restoration of French rule. Why? First, Americans

CHILDREN'S CRUSADE AGAINST COMMUNISM

2. MacArthur Heads UN Forces

North Korean Reds attacked South Korea in what is believed to be part of a communist plan gradually to conquer the whole world. The United Nations pitched in to help the South Koreans, like your dad would help the folks next door if some bad men were beating them up. The troops sent to Korea for the UN were put under command of General Douglas MacArthur. "Mac" has a long military record. But you know him best as the general who led the Allied forces to victory in the Pacific during the second world war.

FIGHT THE RED MENACE

Intensely anticommunist groups thrived in the United States during the Cold War. The "Children's Crusade Against Communism" distributed its exaggerated message of a global communist conspiracy in the early 1950s through bubble-gum cards such as this one. (The Michael Barson Collection/Past Perfect)

wanted France's cooperation in the Cold War. Second, Southeast Asia was an economic asset: its rice could feed America's emerging ally Japan; it could provide markets for Japanese exports; and it was the world's largest producer of natural rubber. Third, the area seemed strategically vital to the defense of Japan and the Philippines. Finally, Ho Chi Minh, the State Department declared, was an "agent of international communism," who, it was assumed, would assist Soviet and Chinese expansionism. Overlooking the native roots of the nationalist rebellion against France, and the tenacious Vietnamese resistance to foreign intruders,

Washington officials took a globalist view of Vietnam, interpreting events through a Cold War lens.

In the 1940s Americans saw Vietnam as France's problem, even after the Vietminh and the French went to war in 1946. But when Jiang's regime collapsed in China three years later, the Truman administration made two crucial decisions—both in early 1950, before the Korean War. First, in February, Washington recognized the French puppet government of Bao Dai, a playboy and former emperor who had collaborated with the French and Japanese. In the eyes of the Vietnamese, the United States thus became in essence a colonial power, an ally of the hated French. Second, in May, the administration agreed to send weapons, and ultimately military advisers, to sustain the French in Indochina. From 1945 to 1954, the United States gave $2 billion of the $5 billion that France spent to keep Vietnam within its empire—to no avail, as we shall see (Chapter 31). How Vietnam ultimately became the site of America's longest war, and how the world's most powerful nation failed to subdue a peasant people who suffered enormous losses, is one of the most remarkable and tragic stories of modern history.

U.S. Aid to France in the War Against the Vietminh

The Korean War

In the early morning of June 25, 1950, a large military force of the Democratic People's Republic of Korea (North Korea) moved across the 38th parallel into the Republic of Korea (South Korea). Although the Soviets had armed the North and the Americans had armed the South (U.S. aid had reached $100 million a year), the Korean War began as a civil war. Since August 1945, when U.S. officials hastily cut Korea at the 38th parallel and then gained Soviet acceptance of the division, the two parts had been skirmishing along their supposedly temporary border while antigovernment (and anti-U.S.) guerrilla fighting flared in the South.

Both the North's communist leader Kim Il Sung and the South's president Syngman Rhee sought to reunify their nation. Kim's military especially gained strength when tens of thousands of battle-tested Koreans returned home in 1949 after serving in Mao's army. Displaying the Cold War mentality of the time, however, President Truman claimed that the Soviets had masterminded the North Korean attack. "Com-

munism was acting in Korea just as Hitler, Mussolini, and the Japanese had acted [in the 1930s]," he said.

Actually, Kim had to press a doubting Joseph Stalin, who only reluctantly approved the attack after Kim predicted an easy, early victory and after Mao backed Kim. The three communist leaders might have calculated that the United States would not come to South Korea's defense—indeed, that the United States was in the process of abandoning the Korean peninsula. In a public speech in early 1950, Secretary of State Acheson had drawn the American defense line in Asia through the Aleutians, Japan, and Okinawa to the Philippines. Formosa and Korea clearly lay beyond that line. Acheson did say, however, that those areas could expect U.N. (and hence U.S.) assistance if attacked. Kim, Stalin, and Mao must have missed that point. Two other thoughts probably convinced Stalin to support Kim: first, if he did not back North Korea, Mao might gain influence over Kim; second, if the United States rearmed Japan, South Korea might once again become a beachhead for Japanese (and American) expansion on the Asian continent.

Origins of the War

Whatever Stalin's reasoning, his support for Kim's venture remained lukewarm. When the United Nations Security Council voted to defend South Korea, the Soviet representative was not even present to veto the resolution because the Soviets were boycotting the United Nations to protest its refusal to grant membership to the People's Republic of China. During the war, Moscow gave limited aid to North Korea and China, which grew angry at Stalin for reneging on promised Soviet airpower. Stalin did not want to be dragged into a costly war.

The president first ordered General Douglas MacArthur to send arms and troops to South Korea. Worried that Mao might attempt to take Formosa, Truman also directed the Seventh Fleet to patrol the waters between the Chinese mainland and Jiang's sanctuary on Formosa, thus inserting the United States once again into Chinese politics. After the Security Council voted to assist South Korea, MacArthur became commander of U.N. forces in Korea (90 percent of them American). North Korean tanks and superior firepower sent the South Korean army into chaotic retreat. The first American soldiers, taking heavy casualties, could not stop the North Korean advance. Within weeks, the South Koreans and Americans had

Truman Commits U.S. Forces

How do historians know...

that the Korean War began as a civil war among Koreans, not as a Soviet-inspired thrust to advance an international communist conspiracy, and thus that U.S. officials misinterpreted the war's origins? After the Cold War ended in the late 1980s and early 1990s, especially after the collapse of the Soviet Union in 1991, politicians and records-keepers in the new noncommunist Russia opened previously classified documents to researchers. The Cold War International History Project, established in 1991 at the Woodrow Wilson Center for Scholars in Washington, D.C., has translated many released foreign documents and publishes them in its printed *Bulletin* (also available at http://cwihp.si.edu).

The opening of such documents invites historians to revisit key moments in the Cold War, such as the outbreak of the Korean War. In 1994 Russian President Boris Yeltsin presented to President Kim Young-Sam of South Korea 548 pages of high-level Soviet documents, including telegrams and letters between Moscow and Pyongyang (the capital of North Korea). The documents reveal that during 1949 Kim repeatedly asked Stalin for permission to launch a military attack against the South. Stalin repeatedly rebuffed Kim's requests. The initiative for the North Korean attack on South Korea was Kim's, not Stalin's, and stemmed from Kim's insistence on overthrowing the American-backed southern regime to achieve unification. As Stalin's telegram of January 30, 1950, to the Soviet ambassador in North Korea (reprinted here in its original Russian) indicates, not until early 1950 did Stalin give what might be construed an approval to invasion, and then coolly, noting that "large preparation" was needed first.

Historians use declassified documents—both American and foreign—with caution. The declassification process is often selective and incomplete (for national security reasons some materials remain classified as "Top-Secret" and some records have been lost or destroyed). Some documents are identified for release in the hope of making a political

point. Also, translations and word meanings can vary from interpreter to interpreter. Finally, historians need more than Soviet records; they also need greater access to the archives of South Korea, North Korea, the People's Republic of China, and the Republic of China (Taiwan) in order to understand fully how the Korean War started.

U.S. leaders claimed that the North Korean assault sprang from a Soviet-engineered plot to conquer the world. Scholars see the Korean War no longer as a simple Cold War contest, but rather as a chapter in *Korean* history that reveals how client states or local actors can foment crises that draw the great powers into confrontation. Declassified documents from foreign archives, then, help historians test the accuracy of American assumptions and weigh the terrible consequences of wrong assumptions—in this case, intensification of the Cold War.   (Photo: "The Cold War International History Project Bulletin," Spring 1995, Issue 5, p. 9. Courtesy of the Woodrow Wilson Center)

been pushed into the tiny Pusan perimeter at the base of South Korea (see Map 29.2).

General MacArthur planned a daring operation: an amphibious landing at heavily fortified Inchon, several hundred miles behind North Korean lines. After U.S. guns and bombs pounded Inchon, marines sprinted ashore on September 15, 1950. They soon liberated the South Korean capital of Seoul and pushed the North Koreans back to the 38th parallel. Even before Inchon, Truman had redefined the U.S. war goal, changing it from the containment of North Korea to the reunification of Korea by force. Communism not only would be stopped; it would be rolled back.

Map 29.2 The Korean War, 1950–1953   Beginning as a civil war between North and South, this war became international when the United States, under the auspices of the United Nations, and the People's Republic of China intervened with their military forces.   (Source: Adapted from Thomas G. Paterson, J. Garry Clifford, and Kenneth J. Hagan, *American Foreign Relations: A History,* vol. 2, 5th ed. Copyright © 2000 by Houghton Mifflin Company.)

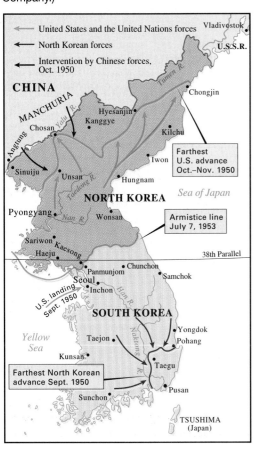

In September Truman authorized U.N. forces to cross the 38th parallel. These troops drove deep into North Korea, and American aircraft began strikes against bridges on the Yalu River, the border between North Korea and China. The Chinese watched warily, fearing that the Americans would next stab at the People's Republic. Mao publicly warned that China could not permit the bombing of its transportation links with Korea and would not accept the annihilation of North Korea itself. MacArthur shrugged off the warnings, and Washington officials agreed with the strong-willed general, drawing further confidence from the fact that the Soviets were not preparing for war.

Chinese Entry into the War

Concluding that the "Americans would run more rampant" unless stopped, Mao, on October 25, sent Chinese soldiers into the war near the Yalu. Perhaps to lure American forces into a trap or to signal willingness to begin negotiations, they pulled back after a brief and successful offensive against South Korean troops. Then, after MacArthur sent the U.S. Eighth Army northward, tens of thousands of Chinese troops counterattacked on November 26, surprising American forces and driving them pell-mell southward.

By early 1951 the front had stabilized around the 38th parallel. Both Washington and Moscow welcomed negotiations, but MacArthur had other ideas. The theatrical general recklessly called for an attack on China and for Jiang's return to the mainland. Now was the time, he insisted, to smash communism by destroying its Asian flank. Denouncing the concept of limited war (war without nuclear weapons, confined to one place), MacArthur hinted that the president was practicing appeasement. In April, backed by the Joint Chiefs of Staff (the heads of the various armed services), Truman fired MacArthur. The general, who had not set foot in the United States for more than a decade, returned home to ticker-tape parades and the lecture circuit but soon faded from the American political scene. Truman's popularity sagged, but he weathered demands for his impeachment.

Truman's Firing of General MacArthur

Armistice talks began in July 1951, but the fighting and dying went on for two more years. The most contentious point in the negotiations was the fate of prisoners of war (POWs). Defying the Geneva Prisoners of War Convention (1949), U.S. officials announced that only

Dispute over POWs

Chinese soldiers guard marching American prisoners of the Korean War during the cold winter of 1950.   (Xinhua, New China News Agency)

those North Korean and Chinese POWs who wished to go home would be returned. Responding to the American statement that there would be no forced repatriation, the North Koreans denounced forced retention. Both sides undertook "reeducation" or "brainwashing" programs to persuade POWs to resist repatriation. Tensions built up in prison camps in South Korea. In early 1952, at the Kobe camp, U.S. troops suppressed a Chinese/North Korean POW riot, killing more than one hundred. In North Korea's camps, murder and illness took the lives of hundreds of POWs.

As the POW issue stalled negotiations, U.S. officials made deliberately vague public statements about using atomic weapons in Korea. American bombers obliterated dams (whose rushing waters then destroyed rice fields), factories, airfields, and bridges in North Korea. Casualties on all sides mounted. Not until July 1953 was an armistice signed. Stalin's death in March and the coming to power of a more conciliatory Soviet government helped ease the way to a settlement that the Chinese especially welcomed. The combat-

Costs and Consequences of the War

ants agreed to hand over the POW question to a special panel of neutral nations, which later gave prisoners their choice of staying or leaving. (In the end, 70,000 of about 100,000 North Korean and 5,600 of 20,700 Chinese POWs elected to return home; 21 American and 325 South Korean POWs of some 11,000 decided to stay in North Korea.) The North Korean–South Korean borderline was set near the 38th parallel, the prewar boundary, and a demilitarized zone was created between the two Koreas.

American casualties totaled 54,246 dead and 103,284 wounded. Close to 5 million Asians died in the war: 2 million North Korean civilians and 500,000 soldiers; 1 million South Korean civilians and 100,000 soldiers; and at least 1 million Chinese soldiers—ranking Korea as one of the costliest wars of the twentieth century.

The Korean War carried major domestic political consequences. The failure to achieve victory and the public's impatience with a stalemated war undoubtedly helped to elect Eisenhower (see page 795). The powers of the presidency grew as Congress repeatedly deferred to Truman. The president had never asked Congress for a declaration of war, believing that as commander-in-chief he had the authority to send troops wherever he wished. A few dissenters such as Senator Taft disagreed, but Truman saw no need to consult Congress—except when he wanted the $69.5 billion Korean War bill paid.

The implementation of military containment worldwide became entrenched as U.S. policy. Increased American aid flowed to the French for their die-hard stand against nationalist insurgents in Vietnam. Because of heightened Sino-American hostility, South Korea and Formosa became major recipients of American foreign aid. The alliance with Japan strengthened as the island's economy boomed after filling large procurement orders from the United States. Australia and New Zealand joined the United States in a mutual defense agreement, the ANZUS Treaty (1951). The U.S. Army sent six divisions to Europe, and the administration initiated plans to rearm West Germany. The Korean War, Acheson cheerfully noted, removed "the recommendations of NSC-68 from the realm of theory and made them immediate budget issues." Indeed, the military budget shot up from $14 billion in 1949 to $44 billion in 1953; it remained between $35 billion and $44 billion a year throughout the 1950s. In sum, Truman's legacy was a highly militarized U.S. foreign policy active on a global scale.

Globalization of Containment

Eisenhower, Dulles, and Unrelenting Cold War

President Dwight D. Eisenhower largely sustained Truman's Cold War policies. Eisenhower brought considerable experience in foreign affairs to his presidency. He had lived and traveled in Europe, Asia, and Latin America and, as a general during the Second World War, had negotiated with world leaders. After the war, he served as army chief of staff and NATO supreme commander. Eisenhower accepted the Cold War consensus about the threat of communism and the need for global vigilance. Partisan Democrats promoted an image of Eisenhower as a bumbling, passive, aging hero. Granted, Eisenhower did not always stay abreast of issues because he chose to delegate authority to others, and he seemed stuck in tired views just when the international system was becoming more fluid. Without doubt, though, the president commanded the policymaking process and tamed the more hawkish

proposals of Vice President Richard Nixon and Secretary of State John Foster Dulles.

Eisenhower questioned Dulles's "practice of becoming a sort of international prosecuting attorney," but the president relied heavily on the strong-willed secretary of state. Few Cold Warriors rivaled Dulles's impassioned anticommunism, often expressed in biblical terms. A graduate of Princeton and George Washington Universities, Dulles had assisted Woodrow Wilson at Versailles, and later became a senior partner in a prestigious Wall Street law firm and an officer of the Federal Council of Churches. Though polished and articulate, Dulles impressed people as arrogant, stubborn, and hectoring—and averse to compromise, an essential ingredient in successful diplomacy.

John Foster Dulles

Like the president, Dulles conceded much to the anticommunist McCarthyites, who claimed that the State Department was infested with communists (see page 799). The State Department's chief security officer, a McCarthy follower, targeted homosexuals and other "incompatibles" and made few distinctions between New Dealers and Communists. Dulles thus forced many talented officers out of the Foreign Service with unsubstantiated charges that they were disloyal. Among them were Asia specialists whose expertise was thus denied to the American leaders who later plunged the United States into war in Vietnam. "The wrong done," the journalist Theodore A. White wrote, "was to poke out the eyes and ears of the State Department on Asian affairs, to blind American foreign policy."

Dulles considered containment too defensive a stance toward communism. He called instead for "liberation," although he never explained precisely how the countries of eastern Europe could be freed from Soviet control. "Massive retaliation" was the administration's phrase for the nuclear obliteration of the Soviet state or its assumed client, the People's Republic of China, if either one took aggressive actions. Eisenhower said it "simply means the ability to blow hell out of them in a hurry if they start anything." The ability of the United States to make such a threat was thought to provide "deterrence," the prevention of hostile Soviet behavior.

Eisenhower-Dulles Policies

In their "New Look" for the American military, Eisenhower and Dulles emphasized airpower and nuclear weaponry. The president's preference for heavy weapons stemmed in part from his desire to trim the

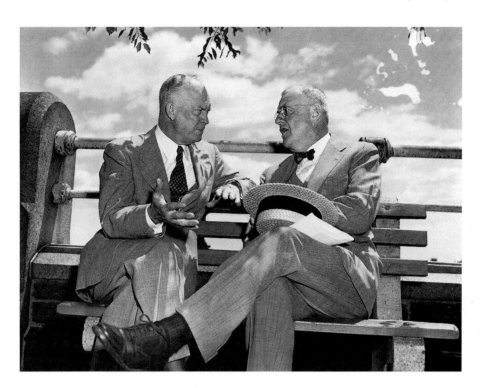

President Eisenhower *(left)* confers with Secretary of State John Foster Dulles (1888–1959), known for his strong anticommunism and his often self-righteous, lecturing style. Dulles once remarked that the United States "is almost the only country strong enough and powerful enough to be moral."   (Corbis-Bettmann)

federal budget ("More bang for the buck," as the saying went). The United States's stockpile of nuclear weapons grew during the Eisenhower presidency from 1,200 to 22,229. Backed by its huge military arsenal, the United States practiced "brinkmanship": not backing down in a crisis, even if it meant taking the nation to the brink of war. Eisenhower also popularized the "domino theory": that small, weak, neighboring nations would fall to communism like a row of dominoes if they were not propped up by the United States.

Eisenhower increasingly utilized the Central Intelligence Agency as an instrument of foreign policy.

CIA as Foreign Policy Instrument
Headed by Allen Dulles, brother of the secretary of state, the CIA put foreign leaders (such as King Hussein of Jordan) on its payroll; subsidized foreign labor unions, newspapers, and political parties (such as the conservative Liberal Democratic Party of Japan); planted false stories in newspapers through its "disinformation" projects; and trained foreign military officers in counterrevolutionary methods. The CIA hired American journalists and professors, secretly funded the National Student Association to spur contacts with foreign student leaders, used business executives as "fronts," and conducted experiments on unsuspecting Americans to determine the effects of "mind control" drugs (the MKULTRA program). The CIA also launched covert operations (including assassination schemes) to subvert or destroy governments in the Third World. The CIA helped overthrow the governments of Iran (1953) and Guatemala (1954) but failed in attempts to topple regimes in Indonesia (1958) and Cuba (1961).

The CIA and other components of the American intelligence community followed the principle of plausible deniability: covert operations should be conducted in such a way, and the decisions that launched them concealed so well, that the president could deny any knowledge of them. Thus President Eisenhower disavowed any U.S. role in Guatemala, even though he had ordered the operation. He and his successor Kennedy also denied that they had instructed the CIA to assassinate Cuba's Fidel Castro, whose regime after 1959 became stridently anti-American.

The Eisenhower administration also sought to interject American culture into the Soviet Union and its eastern European allies as a means to popularize democratic principles and to stimulate public discontent.

Propaganda and Cultural Infiltration
The primary propaganda tool was the United States Information Agency

On July 22, 1959, in Moscow, the Soviet capital, Vice President Richard M. Nixon (1913–1994) *(hands clasped)* and Premier Nikita Khrushchev *(finger pointing)* toured the American National Exhibition, sponsored by the U.S. Information Agency. When they stopped at this display of a modern American kitchen, Khrushchev doubted Nixon's claim that average American workers owned such appliances. In the "kitchen debate" that followed, the two leaders sparred over comparative national strengths and over whether capitalism or communism best served people's needs.   (Howard Sochurek, Time-Life Agency © Time Inc.)

(USIA), founded in 1953. One of the USIA's agencies, Voice of America, broadcast news, editorials, and music worldwide. The CIA secretly funded Radio Free Europe, operated since 1950 by anticommunist eastern European émigrés headquartered in Munich, West Germany. Radio Liberty, also CIA-subsidized, began in 1951 and beamed incendiary anti-Soviet messages into the USSR. The Soviets often jammed such broadcasts, but some got through. Did these broadcasts carry influence? Historians disagree. Some claim that they helped cultivate an anticommunism that eventually undermined pro-Soviet regimes. Others argue that they proved counterproductive because they raised hopes—ultimately false—that the United States would back its propaganda calls for liberation with power. In any case, throughout Europe, the popularity of American nonconformists, such as singer Elvis Presley and actors Marlon Brando and James Dean, attracted youth to American culture, including jazz, Coke, and blue jeans.

The United States and the Soviet Union attempted to regularize cultural relations in January 1958 through an agreement that provided for reciprocal exchange of radio and television broadcasts, films, students, professors, athletes, and civic groups. One result was Vice President Richard Nixon's trip in July 1959 to Moscow to open an American products fair, where, in the "kitchen debate," he extolled capitalist consumerism in a model six-room ranch-style house, while Soviet premier Nikita Khrushchev, Stalin's successor, touted the merits of communism. Khrushchev followed in September with an eye-opening tour of the United States.

Such expanded cultural relations did not calm the Cold War or temper the nuclear arms race. In November 1952 the United States detonated the first hydrogen bomb. Then, in early 1954, the largest bomb the United States has ever tested destroyed the Pacific island of Bikini. This H-bomb,

Hydrogen Bomb

packing the power of 15 million tons of TNT (750 times as powerful as the atomic bomb that leveled Hiroshima), produced a fallout of radioactive dust that showered a Japanese fishing boat in the area. The crew of the *Lucky Dragon* suffered severe nausea, fever, and blisters. When one of the sailors died, international protest bombarded the United States. Anti-American sentiment flared in Japan.

The Soviets tested their first H-bomb in 1953. Four years later, they shocked Americans by firing the world's first intercontinental ballistic missile (ICBM) and then propelling the satellite *Sputnik* into orbit in outer space. Americans felt more vulnerable to air attack and inferior in rocket technology, even though in 1957 the United States had 2,460 strategic weapons and a nuclear stockpile of 5,543, compared to the Soviet Union's 102 and 650. As President Eisenhower said, "If we were to release our nuclear stockpile on the Soviet Union, the main danger would arise not from retaliation but from fallout in the earth's atmosphere."

Sputnik and Missiles

The United States soon tested its own ICBMs, became embarrassed in late 1957 when the rocket for the *Vanguard* satellite caught fire and crashed on its launch pad, and then successfully launched the satellite *Explorer I* in early 1958. The administration also enlarged its fleet of long-range bombers (B-52s) and deployed intermediate-range missiles in Europe, targeted against the Soviet Union. At the end of 1960 the United States began adding Polaris missile–bearing submarines to its navy. To foster future technological advancement, the National Aeronautics and Space Administration (NASA) was created in 1958.

The CIA's U-2 spy planes collected information demonstrating that the Soviets had deployed very few ICBMs. Yet politically partisan critics charged that Eisenhower had allowed the United States to fall behind in the missile race. The much-publicized "missile gap" was actually not in the USSR's favor but rather America's. "Everyone knows," air force general Nathan Twining privately told the president, "we already have a [nuclear] stockpile large enough to obliterate the Soviet Union." As the 1950s closed, the United States enjoyed overwhelming strategic dominance because of its air-sea-land triad of long-range bombers, submarine-launched ballistic missiles (SLBMs), and ICBMs.

President Eisenhower grew uneasy about the arms race and the deterrence policy that became known as "mutual assured destruction," or MAD. He feared nuclear war, and the cost of the new weapons made it

Eisenhower's Critique of Nuclear Arms

difficult to balance the budget. In a 1953 speech, the president noted that "every gun that is made, every warship launched, every rocket fired signifies, in the final sense, a theft from those who hunger and are not fed. . . . The cost of one modern heavy bomber is this: a modern brick school in more than 30 cities." He also doubted the need for more and bigger nuclear weapons. How many times, he once asked, "could [you] kill the same man?" So devastating would be a nuclear war with the Soviet Union, he said, "you might as well go out and shoot everyone you see and then shoot yourself." Spurred by such thoughts, by citizens' groups such as the Committee for a Sane Nuclear Policy (SANE), founded in 1957, and by neutralist and Soviet appeals, the president cautiously initiated arms-control proposals.

Eisenhower's 1953 "atoms for peace" initiative recommended that fissionable materials be contributed to a U.N. agency for use in industrial projects. Two years later, to counter Soviet appeals for disarmament, the Eisenhower administration issued its own propaganda ploy—the "open skies" proposal: aerial surveillance of both Soviet and American military sites to reduce the chances of surprise attacks. In response to worldwide alarm over radioactive fallout, the two powers unilaterally suspended atmospheric testing from 1958 until 1961, when the Soviets resumed it. The United States also began testing again at the same time, but underground. Despite a series of disarmament talks in Geneva, Switzerland, and Eisenhower's meeting there in July 1955 with Khrushchev (the first summit meeting in ten years), neither side could agree on nuclear-testing bans or suitable inspection systems to ensure compliance should they sign arms-control treaties.

In May 1955, in a rare example of Cold War cooperation, the two great powers ended their ten-year occupation of Austria. But events in eastern Europe soon revived the customary acrimony of the Cold War. In 1956 Khrushchev called for "peaceful coexistence" between capitalists and communists, denounced Stalin, and suggested that Moscow would tolerate different brands of communism. Revolts against Soviet power erupted in Poland and Hungary, testing Khrushchev's new permissiveness. After a new Hungarian government in 1956 announced its withdrawal from the Warsaw Pact (the Soviet military alliance formed in 1955 with communist countries of eastern Europe), Soviet troops and

Rebellion in Hungary

tanks battled students and workers in the streets of Budapest and crushed the rebellion.

Although the Eisenhower administration's propaganda had been encouraging liberation efforts, U.S. officials found themselves unable to aid the rebels without igniting a world war. The United States could only welcome Hungarian immigrants in greater numbers than American quota laws allowed. The West could have reaped some propaganda advantage from this display of Soviet brute force had not British, French, and Israeli troops—U.S. allies—invaded Egypt during the Suez crisis just before the Soviets smashed the Hungarian uprising (see pages 848–849).

Hardly had the turmoil subsided in eastern Europe when the divided city of Berlin once again became a Cold War flash point. The Soviets railed against the placement in West Germany of American bombers capable of carrying nuclear warheads, and they complained that West Berlin had become an escape route for disaffected East Germans. In 1958 Khrushchev announced that the Soviet Union would recognize East German control of all of Berlin unless the United States and its allies began talks on German reunification and rearmament. The United States refused to give up its hold on West Berlin or to break West German ties with NATO. Khrushchev backed away from his ultimatum but promised to press the issue again.

Berlin and Germany were on the agenda of a summit meeting planned for Paris in mid-1960. On May 1, two weeks before the conference,

U-2 Incident

a U-2 spy plane carrying high-powered cameras crashed 1,200 miles inside the Soviet Union. Moscow claimed credit for shooting down the plane, which it put on display along with Francis Gary Powers, the captured CIA pilot, and the pictures he had been snapping of Soviet military sites. Khrushchev demanded an apology for the U.S. violation of Soviet airspace. When Washington refused, the Soviets walked out of the Paris summit—"a graveyard of lost opportunities," as a Soviet official put it. Eisenhower bemoaned "the stupid U-2 mess." U.S. reconnaissance continued, and with far greater sophistication than that provided by the U-2. In August 1960 the CIA's CORONA project saw its first successful mission when a spy satellite circling the globe ejected to earth a film capsule containing photographic coverage of the USSR. CORONA satellites provided data on Soviet missile bases for top-secret intelligence reports to the president.

While sparring over Europe, both sides kept a wary eye on the People's Republic of China, which denounced the Soviet call for peace-

Jinmen-Mazu Crisis

ful coexistence. Despite evidence of a widening Sino-Soviet split, most American officials still treated communism as a unified world movement. The isolation separating Beijing and Washington stymied communication and made continued conflict between China and the United States likely. In a dispute over Jinmen (Quemoy) and Mazu (Matsu), two tiny islands off the Chinese coast, the United States and the People's Republic of China lurched toward the brink. Jiang used these islands as bases from which to raid the mainland. Communist China's guns bombarded the islands in 1954. Thinking that U.S. credibility was at stake, Eisenhower decided to defend the outposts; he even hinted that he might use nuclear weapons. Why massive retaliation over such an insignificant issue? "Let's keep the Reds guessing," advised John Foster Dulles. But what if they guessed wrong? critics replied.

Congress passed the Formosa Resolution (1955), authorizing the president to deploy American forces to defend Formosa and adjoining islands, and two years later the United States installed tactical nuclear weapons on Taiwan. Although diplomats from the People's Republic of China and the United States held secret meetings in Geneva and Warsaw, war loomed again in 1958 over Jinmen and Mazu. But this time, after Washington strongly cautioned him not to use force against the mainland, Jiang withdrew some troops from the islands. China then relaxed its bombardments. One consequence accelerated the arms race: Eisenhower's nuclear threats persuaded the Chinese that they, too, needed nuclear arms. In 1964 China exploded its first nuclear bomb.

As the United States went to the brink with China, it went to the market with Japan, rebuilding the nation with foreign aid as an anti-

"Japanese Miracle"

communist military partner and trader, all the while worrying China, the Soviet Union, and other past victims of Japanese aggression. Huge U.S. purchases in Japan during the Korean War and American assistance in developing an export-oriented economy in the 1950s produced what many called the "Japanese miracle"—double-digit economic growth. Led by the powerful Ministry of International Trade and Industry (MITI), Japan copied American technology (Motorola, for example, helped start the electronics industry), practiced trade protectionism, and gained a reputation for industrial efficiency and quality control. Before long, Japan became a major economic competitor with the United States, stirring measures to curb Japanese goods—such as textiles—in the American marketplace. In Japan labor strikes and student riots against America's reliance on nuclear weapons and the substantial U.S. military presence forced Eisenhower to cancel a goodwill trip to Tokyo in 1960. Japan remained a Cold War ally, but uneasily.

Western Europeans also developed an uneasy relationship with Americans, raising doubts about the "family" the United States was trying to cultivate through NATO. McCarthyite extremism disturbed them. U.S. calls for German rearmament and for fighting in Vietnam alarmed them. They wondered about American credibility: would the United States really defend western Europe against a Soviet attack if such defense triggered a punishing Soviet nuclear assault against the United States itself? As well, NATO countries—especially France—thought that the United States, while championing an "Atlantic community," treated them like dependent clients, too seldom consulting with them.

At Odds with the Third World

A process of decolonization that began during the First World War accelerated after the Second World War, when the economically wracked imperial countries proved incapable of resisting their colonies' demands for freedom. A cavalcade of new nations cast off their colonial bonds (see Map 29.3). In 1960 alone, eighteen new African nations did so. From 1943 to 1994 a total of 125 countries became independent (the figure includes the former Soviet republics that departed the USSR in 1991). The emergence of so many new states in the 1940s and after, and the instability associated with the transfer of authority, shook the foundations of the international system. Power was redistributed, creating "near chaos," said one U.S. government report. In the United States's traditional sphere of influence, Latin America, nationalists once again challenged U.S. hegemony.

By the late 1940s, when Cold War lines were drawn fairly tightly in Europe, Soviet-American rivalry shifted increasingly to the Third World. Much was at stake. The new nations could buy American

Interests in the Third World

goods and technology, supply strategic raw materials, and invite investments (more than one-third of America's private foreign investments were in Third World countries in 1959). And they could build cultural ties with the United States. Both great powers, moreover, looked to these new states for votes in the United Nations and sought sites within their borders for military and intelligence bases. But, often poor and unstable, rife with tribal, ethnic, and class rivalries, many new nations sought to end the economic, military, and cultural hegemony of the West. Many of these new nations learned to play off the two superpowers against each other to garner more aid and arms. U.S. interventions—military and otherwise—in the Third World, American leaders believed, became necessary to impress Moscow with Washington's might and resolve and to counter nationalism and radical anticapitalist social change that threatened American strategic and economic interests.

To thwart nationalist, radical, and communist challenges, the United States directed massive resources—foreign aid, propaganda, development projects—toward the Third World. By 1961 more than 90 percent of U.S. foreign aid was going to developing nations. Washington also allied with native elites and with undemocratic but anticommunist regimes, meddled in civil wars, and unleashed CIA covert operations. Bitter resentments built up in the Third World, where millions of lives were lost in conflicts aggravated by U.S. intervention.

Many Third World states—notably India, Ghana, Egypt, and Indonesia—refused to take sides in the Cold War. To the dismay of both Washington and Moscow, they declared themselves nonaligned, or neutral. Nonalignment became an organized movement in 1955 when twenty-nine Asian and African nations met at the Bandung Conference in Indonesia. Secretary Dulles, alarmed that neutralist tendencies would deprive the United States of potential allies, denounced neutralism as a step on the road to communism. Both he and Eisenhower insisted that every nation should take a side in the life-and-death Cold War struggle. Neutralism had to be contained.

Nonaligned Movement

American leaders argued that technologically "backward" Third World peoples needed Western-induced capitalist development and modernization in

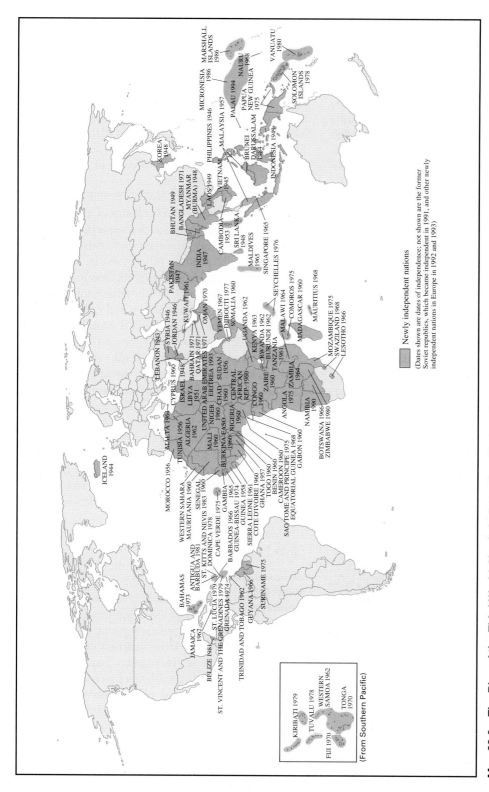

Map 29.3   The Rise of the Third World: Newly Independent Nations Since 1943   Accelerated by the Second World War, decolonization liberated many peoples from imperial rule. New
nations emerged in the postwar international system dominated by the Cold War rivalry of the
United States and the Soviet Union. Many newly independent states became targets of great-
power intrigue but chose nonalignment in the Cold War.

American Images of Third World Peoples

order to enjoy economic growth, social harmony, and political moderation. U.S. policymakers placed Third World peoples low in the hierarchy of power and claimed that they needed fatherly tutelage by the United States. American leaders ascribed stereotyped race-, age-, and gender-based characteristics to Third World peoples, seeing them as dependent, emotional, and irrational. Cubans, CIA director Allen Dulles told the National Security Council in early 1959, "had to be treated more or less like children. They had to be led rather than rebuffed. If they were rebuffed, like children, they were capable of almost anything." American officials also used gendered language, suggesting that Third World countries were weak women—passive and servile, unable to resist the menacing appeals of communists and neutralists. For example, such thinking conditioned U.S. relations with India, a neutralist nation that Americans deemed effeminate and submissive—a place where, said President Eisenhower, "emotion rather than reason seems to dictate policy." Changing images of Israel helped condition U.S. policy in the Middle East. From seeing Jews as pusillani-

mous and passive because of their role as victims to seeing them as masculine and tough in their fight to survive and construct a new state in the midst of violently hostile Arab neighbors, Americans moved toward alliance with a thus admirable Israel.

Racism and Segregation as U.S. Handicaps

Race attitudes and segregation practices in the United States especially influenced relations. In 1955 G. L. Mehta, the Indian ambassador to the United States, was refused service in the whites-only section of a restaurant at Houston International Airport. The insult stung deeply, as did many similar indignities experienced by other Third World diplomats. Fearing damaged relations with India, a large, neutralist nation whose allegiance the United States sought in the Cold War, John Foster Dulles apologized to Mehta. The secretary thought racial segregation in the United States a "major international hazard," spoiling American efforts to win friends in Third World countries and giving the Soviets a propaganda advantage. American practices and ideals did not align.

When the U.S. attorney general appealed to the Supreme Court to strike down segregation in public

In the 1950s, these specially outfitted jeeps (equipped with projectors, screens, and films) served America's overseas information program in what the State Department called "isolated areas." Believing that social modernization and economic progress would counter leftist and communist ideas, U.S. propaganda officials dispatched these "mobile motion picture units" to such places as rural Mexico, seeking to reach people with films on U.S. sports, music, health, and agriculture. (National Archives)

schools, he underlined that the humiliation of dark-skinned diplomats "furnished grist for the Communist propaganda mills." When the Court announced its *Brown* decision in 1954 (see page 802), Voice of America quickly broadcast news of the desegregation order around the world in thirty-five languages. But the problem did not go away. For example, after the 1957 Little Rock crisis (see page 803), Dulles remarked that racial bigotry was "ruining our foreign policy. The effect of this in Asia and Africa will be worse for us than Hungary was for the Russians." Still, when an office of the Department of State decided to counter Soviet propaganda by creating for the 1958 World's Fair in Brussels an exhibit titled "The Unfinished Business," on race relations in the United States and strides taken toward desegregation, southern conservatives kicked up such a furor that the Eisenhower administration closed the display.

The hostility of the United States toward revolution also obstructed its quest for influence in the Third World. In the twentieth century, the United States has openly opposed revolutions in Mexico, China, Russia, Cuba, Vietnam, Nicaragua, and Iran, among other nations. Americans celebrated the Spirit of '76 but grew intolerant of revolutionary disorder because many Third World revolutions arose against America's Cold War allies and threatened American investments, markets, and military bases. Indeed, by midcentury the United States stood as an established power in world affairs, eager for stability and order to protect American prosperity and security. During revolutionary crises, therefore, the United States usually supported its European allies or the conservative, propertied classes in the Third World. In 1960, for example, when forty-three African and Asian states sponsored a U.N. resolution endorsing decolonization, the United States abstained from the vote.

U.S. Hostility to Nationalist Revolution

Believing that Third World peoples craved modernization and that the American economic model of private enterprise and cooperation among business, labor, and government was best for them, American policymakers launched various "development" projects. Such projects held out the promise of sustained economic growth, prosperity, and stability, which the benefactors hoped would undermine radicalism. In the 1950s the Carnegie, Ford, and Rockefeller Foundations worked with the U.S. Agency for International

Development and Modernization

Development (AID) to sponsor a Green Revolution—a dramatic increase in agricultural production, for example, by the use of hybrid seeds. The Rockefeller Foundation supported foreign universities' efforts to train national leaders committed to nonradical development; in Nigeria from 1958 to 1969 the philanthropic agency spent $25 million. Before Dean Rusk became secretary of state in 1961, he served as president of the Rockefeller Foundation.

In the 1950s and 1960s the views of Massachusetts Institute of Technology professor Walt W. Rostow influenced U.S. leaders. Rostow wrote in his popular book, *Stages of Economic Growth: A Non-Communist Manifesto* (1959), that if the United States sponsored development projects in the Third World through capital investment and infusions of Western culture and technology, and U.S. foreign aid, then class conflict, civil war, and revolution would diminish if not disappear. They seldom did either, however.

To persuade Third World peoples to abandon radical doctrines and neutralism, American leaders, often in cooperation with the business-sponsored Advertising Council, directed propaganda at the Third World. The U.S. Information Agency used films, radio broadcasts, the magazine *Free World*, exhibitions, exchange programs, and libraries (in 162 cities worldwide by 1961) to trumpet the theme of "People's Capitalism." Citing America's economic success—contrasted with "slave-labor" conditions in the Soviet Union—the message showcased well-paid American workers, political democracy, and religious freedom. To counter ugly pictures of segregation and white attacks on African Americans and civil rights activists in the South, the USIA applauded success stories of individual African Americans such as the boxers Floyd Patterson and Sugar Ray Robinson. In 1960 alone some 13.8 million people visited U.S. pavilions abroad, including 1 million at the consumer-products exhibit "Tradeways to Peace and Prosperity" in Damascus, Syria. The Fulbright Program (see page 829) and trade fairs also brought America's message before the Third World.

Some Third World peoples did yearn to be like Americans—to enjoy their consumer goods, music, economic status, and educational opportunities. Hollywood movies offered enticing glimpses of middle-class materialism, and North American films dominated the Latin American market. Blue jeans, advertising billboards, and soft drinks flooded foreign societies.

Third World Views of the United States

If foreigners envied Americans, they also resented them for having so much and wasting so much while poorer peoples went without. The popular American novel *The Ugly American* (1958) spotlighted the "golden ghettoes" where American foreign diplomats lived in compounds separated from their poorer surroundings by high walls. The people of many countries, moreover, resented the ample profits that American corporations extracted from them. Americans often received blame for the persistent poverty of the Third World, even though the leaders of those nations made decisions that hindered their own progress, such as pouring millions of dollars into their militaries while their people craved food. Nonetheless, anti-American resentments could be measured in the late 1950s in attacks on USIA libraries in Calcutta (India), Beirut (Lebanon), and Bogotá (Colombia). The American film and television industries were so active abroad that some foreigners protested "cultural imperialism." Third World peoples also rejected unsavory aspects of American life, including racial segregation, political corruption, and drug abuse.

U.S. Interventions in the Third World

 Anti-Yankee feelings grew in Latin America, where poverty, class warfare, overpopulation, illiteracy, and foreign exploitation fed discontent, which U.S. leaders feared might be exploited by communists. Two examples spotlighted Latin American hostility toward the United States: in 1958 rioters in Venezuela and elsewhere interrupted Vice President Nixon's goodwill trip to South America and threatened his life; the following year Panamanians rioted after U.S. officials denied them permission to raise the Panamanian flag in the Canal Zone.

In 1951 the leftist Jacobo Arbenz Guzmán was elected president of Guatemala, a poor country whose largest landowner was the American-owned United Fruit Company (UF). United Fruit was an economic power throughout Latin America, where it owned 3 million acres of land and operated railroads, ports, ships, and telecommunications facilities. To fulfill his promise of land reform, Arbenz expropriated UF's uncultivated land and offered compensation. UF dismissed the offer and charged that Arbenz posed a communist threat—a charge that CIA officials had already floated because Arbenz employed

CIA in Guatemala

some communists in his government. The CIA began a secret plot to overthrow Arbenz. He turned to Moscow for military aid, thus reinforcing American suspicions. The CIA airlifted arms into Guatemala, dropping them at UF facilities, and in mid-1954 CIA-supported Guatemalans struck from Honduras. U.S. planes bombed the capital city, and the invaders drove Arbenz from power. The new pro-American regime returned United Fruit's land, but an ensuing civil war staggered the Central American nation into the 1990s.

The Cuban Revolution soon represented the greatest challenge to U.S. hegemony. In early 1959 Fidel Castro's rebels, or *barbudos* ("bearded ones"), driven by profound anti-American nationalism, had ousted Fulgencio Batista, a long-time U.S. ally who had welcomed North American investors, U.S. military advisers, and tourists to the Caribbean island. Batista's corrupt, dictatorial regime had helped turn Havana into a haven for gambling and prostitution run by organized crime. Cubans had resented U.S. domination ever since the early twentieth century, when the Platt Amendment was imposed on them (see page 627). Curbing U.S. influence became a rallying cry of the Cuban Revolution, all the more after the CIA conspired secretly but futilely to block Castro's rise to power in 1958. From the start Castro sought to roll back the influence of American business, which had invested some $1 billion on the island, and to break the U.S. grasp on Cuban trade.

The Cuban Revolution and Fidel Castro

Castro's increasing authoritarianism, anti-Yankee declarations, and growing popularity in the hemisphere alarmed Washington. In early 1960, after Cuba signed a trade treaty with the Soviet Union, Eisenhower ordered the CIA to organize an invasion force of Cuban exiles to overthrow the Castro government. The agency also began to plot an assassination of the Cuban leader. When the president drastically cut U.S. purchases of Cuban sugar, Castro seized all North American–owned companies that had not yet been nationalized. Threatened by U.S. decisions designed to bring him and his revolution down, Castro appealed to the Soviet Union, which offered loans and expanded trade. Just before leaving office in early 1961, Eisenhower broke diplomatic relations with Cuba and advised President-elect John F. Kennedy to advance plans for the invasion, which came in early 1961 (see page 888).

A different sort of U.S. intervention occurred in Puerto Rico—tourism and industrial development.

Operation Bootstrap in Puerto Rico

Under the leadership of Teodoro Moscoso, Operation Bootstrap attracted investments from U.S. corporations with tempting tax benefits. In 1955 a General Electric (GE) circuit-breaker facility became the four hundredth manufacturing plant to open under Bootstrap. A GE officer remembered that Puerto Rico "offered many of the advantages of the Third World, such as an abundant, relatively low-cost and eager-to-work labor force, but none of the disadvantages," such as political instability and hostility to foreign investment. Tourism

In 1960 Egypt's neutralist leader, Gamal Abdul Nasser (1918–1970), with raised hand, and revolutionary Cuba's Fidel Castro (b. 1926), center with beard, went together to New York City's Harlem area when both were attending a meeting of the United Nations. Often angering U.S. officials and thwarting U.S. foreign policy aims, the two strong-willed, nationalistic Third World leaders issued anti-American declarations and accepted Soviet military assistance.   (Corbis-Bettmann)

also expanded greatly in Puerto Rico; the opening of the Caribe Hilton hotel in late 1949 set off a resort-building boom along the island's beautiful beaches. In 1952, 37,000 tourists visited; by 1960 the number had leaped to 145,000. The lush hotels contrasted conspicuously with the squalor of the seaside slum La Perla, in the capital of San Juan, chronicled in the anthropologist Oscar Lewis's book *La Vida* (1966). Critics protested that Puerto Rico had spent millions on luxury hotels for North American tourists but little to combat poverty. At the same time, increasing numbers of Puerto Ricans journeyed to the United States, creating *barrios* in American cities, especially in New York.

In the Middle East, where the Arab-Israeli dispute particularly upended order, the Eisenhower administration confronted challenges to U.S.

U.S. Interests in the Middle East

influence from Arab nationalists (see Map 31.2 on page 904). American interests were conspicuous: survival of the Jewish state of Israel and extensive oil holdings (American companies produced about half of the region's petroleum in the 1950s). Oil-rich Iran had become a special friend. Its ruling shah had granted American oil companies a 40 percent interest in a new petroleum consortium in return for CIA help in the successful overthrow, in 1953, of his rival, Mohammed Mossadegh, who had attempted to nationalize foreign oil interests.

Egypt's Gamal Abdul Nasser became a towering figure in a pan-Arabic movement to reduce Western interests in the Middle East. Nasser vowed to expel the British from the Suez Canal and the Israelis from Palestine. The United States wished neither to anger the Arabs, for fear of losing valuable oil supplies, nor to alienate its ally Israel, which was supported at home by politically active American Jews. But when Nasser declared neutrality in the Cold War, Dulles lost patience.

In 1956 the United States abruptly reneged on its offer to Egypt to help finance the Aswan Dam, a project to provide inexpensive electricity

Suez Crisis

and water for thirsty Nile valley farmland. Secretary Dulles's blunt economic pressure backfired, for Nasser responded by nationalizing the British-owned Suez Canal, intending to use its profits to build the dam. At a mass rally in Alexandria, Nasser expressed the profound nationalism typical of Third World peoples shedding an imperial past: "Tonight our Egyptian canal will be run by Egyptians. Egyptians!" Fully 75 percent of western Europe's oil came from the Middle East, most of it transported through the Suez Canal. Fearing an interruption in this vital trade, the British and French conspired with Israel to bring down Nasser. On October 29, 1956, the Israelis invaded Suez, joined two days later by British and French forces.

Eisenhower fumed. America's allies had not consulted him and the attack had shifted attention from Soviet intervention in Hungary. The president also feared that the invasion would cause Nasser to seek help from the Soviets, inviting them into the Middle East. Eisenhower sternly demanded that London, Paris, and Tel Aviv pull their troops out, and they did. Egypt took possession of the canal, the Soviets built the Aswan Dam, and Nasser became a hero to Third World peoples. To counter Nasser, the United States determined to "build up" as an "Arab rival" the conservative King Ibn Saud of Saudi Arabia. Although the monarch renewed America's lease of an air base, few Arabs respected the notoriously corrupt Saud.

Washington officials worried that a "vacuum" existed in the Middle East—and that the Soviets might fill it. Nasserites insisted that there

Eisenhower Doctrine

was no vacuum but rather a growing Arab nationalism that provided the best defense against communism. In an effort to improve the deteriorating Western position in the Middle East and to protect American interests there, the president proclaimed the Eisenhower Doctrine in 1957. The United States would intervene in the Middle East, he declared, if any government threatened by a communist takeover asked for help. In 1958 fourteen thousand American troops scrambled ashore in Lebanon to quell an internal political dispute that Washington feared might be exploited by pro-Nasser groups or communists. By 1961, most analysts agreed, the Eisenhower administration had deepened Third World hostility toward the United States.

Such was especially true in Vietnam, where nationalists battled the French and Americans for independence. Despite substantial U.S.

Dienbienphu Crisis in Vietnam

aid, the French lost steadily to the Vietminh. Finally, in early 1954, Ho's forces surrounded the French fortress at Dienbienphu in northwest Vietnam (see Map 31.1 on page 892). Although some of Eisenhower's advisers recommended a massive American air strike against Vietminh positions, perhaps even using tactical atomic weapons, the president moved cautiously. The United States had been advising and bankrolling the French,

but it had not committed its own forces to the war. If American airpower did not save the French, would ground troops be required next, and in hostile terrain? As one high-level doubter remarked, "One cannot go over Niagara Falls in a barrel only slightly."

Worrying aloud about a communist victory, Eisenhower compared the weak nations of the world to a row of dominoes, all of which would topple if just one fell. He pressed the British to help form a coalition to address the Indochinese crisis, but they refused. At home, influential members of Congress told the president they wanted "no more Koreas" and warned him to avoid any U.S. military commitment, especially in the absence of cooperation from U.S. allies. Some felt very uneasy about supporting colonialism. The issue became moot on May 7, when the weary French defenders at Dienbienphu surrendered.

To compound the administration's problems, the French wanted out of the war. In April they had entered into peace talks at Geneva with

Geneva Accords

the United States, the Soviet Union, Britain, the People's Republic of China, Laos, Cambodia, and the competing Vietnamese regimes of Bao Dai and Ho Chi Minh. Asked at a press conference if he would meet with Chinese delegates, Dulles retorted, "Not unless our automobiles collide." The 1954 Geneva accords, signed by France and Ho's Democratic Republic of Vietnam, temporarily divided Vietnam at the 17th parallel; Ho's government was confined to the North, Bao Dai's to the South. Only after pressure from the Chinese, who feared U.S. intervention in Vietnam without an agreement, did Ho's government agree to this compromise. The 17th parallel was meant to serve as a military truce line, not a national boundary; the country was scheduled to be unified after national elections in 1956. In the meantime, neither North nor South was to join a military alliance or permit foreign military bases on its soil.

Certain that the Geneva agreements ultimately would mean communist victory, the United States and Bao Dai refused to accept the accords and set about to sabotage them. Soon after the conference, a CIA team entered Vietnam and undertook secret operations against the North, including commando raids across the 17th parallel. In fall 1954 the United States also joined Britain, France, Australia, New Zealand, the Philippines, Thailand, and Pakistan in the anticommunist Southeast Asia Treaty Organization (SEATO), one purpose of which was to protect the southern part of Vietnam.

In the South, the United States helped Ngo Dinh Diem push Bao Dai aside and inaugurate the Republic of Vietnam. A Catholic in a Buddhist

Backing the Diem Regime in South Vietnam

nation, Diem had many enemies and no mass support. But he was a nationalist and an anticommunist. With American aid he staged a fraudulent election that gave him 98 percent of the vote. When Ho called for national elections in keeping with the Geneva agreements, Diem and Eisenhower refused, fearing that the popular Vietminh leader would win. From 1955 to 1961, the Diem government received more than $1 billion in American aid, most of it military. American advisers organized and trained Diem's army, and American agriculturalists worked to improve crops. Diem's Saigon regime became dependent on the United States for its very existence, and the culture of southern Vietnam became increasingly Americanized.

Diem proved a difficult ally. He acted dictatorially, abolishing village elections and appointing to public office people beholden to him. He threw dissenters in jail and shut down newspapers that criticized his regime. Noncommunists and communists alike began to strike back at Diem's corrupt and repressive government. Not until early 1959 did Ho's regime in the northern capital of Hanoi begin to send aid to southern insurgents, who embarked on a program of terror, assassinating hundreds of Diem's village officials. In late 1960 southern communists organized the National Liberation Front (NLF), known as the Vietcong. The Vietcong in turn attracted other anti-Diem groups in the South. The war against imperialism had become a two-part civil war: Ho's North versus Diem's South, and NLF guerrillas versus the Diem government. And the United States, perceiving in Ho and the NLF the menace of a monolithic communism—a universal communist conspiracy to take over the world—marched into this multifaceted war certain that superior U.S. firepower and technology could succeed against inferior Asians.

Summary

The United States emerged from the Second World War preeminent in power but fearful that the unstable international system, an unfriendly Soviet Union, and the decolonizing Third World threatened American plans for the postwar world, American economic-strategic

interests, and principles such as the Open Door and political democracy. Locked with the Soviet Union in a "Cold War," U.S. leaders marshaled their nation's superior resources to influence and cajole other countries. Foreign economic aid, new international organizations, threats to use atomic weapons again, client states, reconstruction of former enemies Germany and Japan, development of new long-range missiles, military alliances, covert operations, interventions, propaganda, cultural infiltration—these and more became the instruments to wage the Cold War, a global war.

America's claim to international leadership sparked resistance. Communist countries condemned dollar and atomic diplomacy; Third World nations sought to undermine America's European allies and identified the United States as an imperial coconspirator; and even America's allies bristled at a United States that boldly proclaimed itself economic master and global policeman and haughtily touted its hegemonic status. Liberal and radical domestic critics protested that Presidents Truman and Eisenhower exaggerated the communist threat, wasting U.S. assets on immoral foreign ventures, crippled legitimate nationalist aspirations, and displayed racial bias. Still, these presidents and their successors held firm to the mission of creating a nonradical, capitalist, free-trade international order in the mold of domestic America. They seldom hesitated to flex American muscle to enlarge the American sphere of influence and shape the world in an age when the airplane shrank the globe, making the United States forever "de-isolated," as one foreign policy analyst remarked. In their years of nurturing allies and applying the containment doctrine worldwide, Truman and Eisenhower held the line—against the Soviet Union, the People's Republic of China, nonalignment, communism, nationalism, and revolution everywhere.

Putting itself at odds with the Third World, the United States usually stood with its European allies to slow decolonization and preach evolution rather than revolution. The globalist perspective of the United States prompted Americans to interpret many Third World troubles as Cold War conflicts, inspired if not directed by Soviet-backed communists. The intensity of the Cold War obscured for Americans the indigenous roots of most Third World troubles, as the wars in Korea and Vietnam attested. Nor could the United States abide Third World nations' drive for economic independence—for gaining control of their own raw materials and economies. Deeply intertwined in the global economy as importer, exporter, and investor, the

United States read Third World challenges as threats to the American standard of living and way of life characterized by private enterprise. The Third World, in short, challenged the United States's strategic power by forming a third force in the Cold War, and it challenged American economic power by demanding a new economic order of shared interests. Overall, the rise of the Third World introduced new actors to the world stage, challenging the bipolarity of the international system and diffusing power. So alarmed was the Democratic candidate for president in 1960, Senator John F. Kennedy of Massachusetts, that he charged that the United States under President Eisenhower's leadership was losing the Cold War, especially in the Third World.

All the while, the threat of nuclear war unsettled Americans and foreigners alike. In the film *Godzilla* (1956), a prehistoric monster, revived by atomic bomb tests, rampages through Tokyo. Stanley Kramer's popular but disturbing movie *On the Beach* (1959), based on Nevil Shute's bestselling 1957 novel, depicts a nuclear holocaust in which the last humans on earth choose to swallow government-issued poison tablets so that they could die before H-bomb radiation sickness kills them. Such doomsday or Armageddon attitudes contrasted sharply with official U.S. government assurances that Americans would survive a nuclear war. In *On the Beach*, a dying wife asks her husband, "Couldn't anyone have stopped it?" His answer: "Some kinds of silliness you just can't stop." Eisenhower did not halt it, even though he told Khrushchev in 1959 that "we really should come to some sort of agreement in order to stop this fruitless, really wasteful rivalry."

LEGACY FOR A PEOPLE AND A NATION
The National Security State

To build a cathedral, someone has observed, you first need a religion, and a religion needs inspiring texts that command authority. For decades, America's Cold War religion has been national security, its texts the Truman Doctrine, "X" article, and NSC-68, and its cathedral the national security state. The word *state* in this case means "civil government." During the Cold War, embracing preparedness for total war, the U.S. government essentially transformed itself into a huge military headquarters that interlocked with corporations and universities. Preaching the doctrine of national security, moreover, members of Congress strove to gain lucrative defense contracts for their districts.

Overseen by the president and his advisory body, the National Security Council, the national security state has had as its core what the National Security Act of 1947 called the National Military Establishment; in 1949 it became the Department of Defense. This department ranked as a leading employer; its payroll by 1990 included almost 5 million persons. It operated 1,265 major installations, 375 of them abroad. Spending for national defense and veterans topped $328 billion, a quarter of the federal budget. In 1998, years after the Cold War ended, with the closing of some military facilities and downsizing of staffs, the figure still stood at $300 billion (about 16 percent of the budget). Over time, critics railed against waste, cost overruns, and questionable military "toys," but the national security state continued to figure prominently in the U.S. economy, especially in California, Texas, Virginia, Colorado, and New York.

Joining the Department of Defense as instruments of national security policy were the Joint Chiefs of Staff, Central Intelligence Agency, National Security Agency, U.S. Information Agency, Agency for International Development, and dozens more government bodies. The national security state also built ties to corporations such as General Dynamics, General Electric, and Raytheon, which received much of their income from defense contracts and even shared executives through a revolving military-industrial door. Scientists and engineers also joined the partnership. In the early 1970s, at least 50 percent of America's aeronautical engineers and 30 percent of its physicists worked on military-related projects. MIT scientists and defense contractors turned Boston's Route 128 into a high-technology zone; California's Silicon Valley sprang from Stanford University's research links with defense industries.

In 1961 President Eisenhower warned against a "military-industrial complex," while others feared a "garrison state" or "warfare state." Despite the warnings, by the start of the twenty-first century, the national security state remained vigorous, a lasting legacy of the early Cold War period for a people and a nation.

For Further Reading, see page A-34 of the Appendix. For Web resources, go to http://college.hmco.com.

In 1964 politics and civil rights claimed front-page news, and they were inextricably tied together. When the Democrats convened in Atlantic City, New Jersey, to pick a presidential candidate in that election year, they discovered the volatility of the civil rights issue. Two delegations had arrived from Mississippi demanding to be seated. One was all white; the other was largely African American and called itself the Mississippi Freedom Democratic Party (MFDP). The MFDP asked the convention to honor its credentials instead of those of the state's vehemently segregationist regular Democratic organization.

In Mississippi, as a result of phony literacy tests, economic intimidation, and violence, less than 7 percent of the black population could vote. Civil rights activists had decided in 1963 to conduct their own "freedom vote"—a mock election to prove, as one worker put it, "that politics is not just white folks' business." And in 1964 the MFDP ran candidates for Congress. The same year, more than a thousand northern students traveled south to Mississippi to work for the Freedom Summer Project, registering voters and organizing protests against segregation. But these challenges to white supremacy did not go unanswered. White vigilantes bombed and burned two dozen black churches, and sheriff's deputies murdered three young civil rights workers—one black and two white—in Philadelphia, Mississippi.

The Democratic Party's credentials committee met on August 22, 1964, to hear the contesting delegations. The hearings were nationally televised. Speaking for the MFDP was an inspiring figure, Fannie Lou Hamer, a forty-six-year-old African American organizer for the Student Nonviolent Coordinating Committee (SNCC). Born in 1917, she was the twentieth child of sharecropper parents. At age six, she went to work chopping and picking in the cotton fields, and by the time she was thirteen, she was pick-

REFORM AND CONFLICT AT HOME: A TURBULENT ERA 1961–1974

Fannie Lou Hamer was an inspirational civil rights leader in Mississippi in the 1960s, and she spoke and sang gospel and freedom songs at numerous rallies for racial equality. In this photograph taken in 1966, Hamer sang at the campsite for a "march against fear" organized by James Meredith, another hero of the civil rights movement who earlier had desegregated the University of Mississippi. During the march Meredith was ambushed and shot in the back by a member of the Ku Klux Klan. (© Charmian Reading, NYC) ing from three to four hundred pounds a day on a plantation in Sunflower County.

In the early 1960s Fannie Lou Hamer began to envision a better future through the direct action of the civil rights movement. Paraphrasing John F. Kennedy's 1961 inaugural address, she explained, "I am determined to give my part not for what the movement can do for me, but what I can do for the movement to bring about a change in the State of Mississippi." In 1962 she lost her job on the plantation when she attempted to register to vote. Then, fearing violence, she fled to a neighbor's home, which was soon riddled with bullets intended for her. The next year, Hamer was arrested with five other SNCC volunteers in Winona, Mississippi, taken to jail, and brutally assaulted by police swinging blackjacks. By 1964 Hamer had become a field worker for SNCC, known for her courage and refusal to surrender as well as for her inspiring speeches and singing. She began her speeches with a spiritual; often it was her favorite, "This Little Light of Mine."

Sitting before the credentials committee and the television cameras in Atlantic City, Hamer told the country about her experience in the Winona jail. "I was beaten until I was exhausted," she recalled. "I began to scream, and one white man got up and began to beat me on the head and tell me to hush. . . . All of this on account we wanted to register, to become first class citizens." She insisted that the MFDP—those who had fought for freedom—be seated, not those who opposed it. If "the Freedom Party is not seated now, I question America," she said. Emotion filled her voice as she asked, "Is this America, the land of the free and the home of the brave, where we have to sleep with our telephones off the hooks because our lives be threatened daily, because we want to live as decent human beings, in America?"

The MFDP did not receive justice from President Johnson or the Democratic Party. Offered a consolation prize of two seats, the MFDP refused. "We didn't come all this way for no two seats," Hamer said, "when *all* of us is tired." In that election year, Johnson would not alienate powerful southern white politicians by seating the civil rights delegation, but his action threw into question the Democrats' commitment to racial equality. It was already too late, moreover, to placate white southerners who had begun to switch to the more conservative Republican Party. Despite Johnson's capitulation to Mississippi's regular Democrats, the state's whites voted for Senator Barry Goldwater, the Republican candidate, in 1964. Civil rights had become the most important political issue in the country, threatening to destroy the New Deal coalition in the South and the North.

The civil rights movement became a dynamic motive force in American society in the 1960s, helping to give birth in subsequent years to the antiwar movement, the New Left, a resurgent feminist movement, the environmental movement, and equality movements for other minorities. The civil rights movement also energized the presidential politics of John F. Kennedy and Lyndon B. Johnson. Kennedy's call for a New Frontier had inspired liberal Democrats, idealists, and brave young activists to work to eliminate poverty, segregation, and voting rights abuses. But Americans' dreams were shattered on November 22, 1963, when President Kennedy was assassinated in Dallas. For four days Americans wept, prayed, and gazed at their television sets, numbed by the unbelievable. "In retrospect," journalist Godfrey Hodgson has written, "people looked back to Friday, November 22, 1963, as the end of a time of hope, the beginning of a time of troubles."

Lyndon Johnson, who asked for national unity in the wake of the Kennedy assassination, was a strong political leader who knew what he wanted. Johnson presided over what he called the Great Society, a flood of legislation designed to eradicate poverty in the United States and guarantee equal rights to all its citizens. But even during these years of liberal triumph, anger and social tension intermittently flared into violence. Beginning with Kennedy's assassination in 1963, ten years of bloodshed—race riots, the murders of other political and civil rights leaders, and the war in Vietnam—shattered the optimism of the Kennedy and Johnson eras.

Urban blacks were angry that poverty and segregation persisted despite the passage of landmark civil rights laws, and their discontent exploded during the "long hot summers" of the 1960s. This social turbulence added to snowballing white opposition to the civil rights movement, prompting many Americans to shift to the right politically. In 1968 the Republican Richard M. Nixon was elected president, but his presidency polarized the nation still further. The presidencies of Nixon's two immediate predecessors had ended tragically: Dallas and Vietnam were the sites of their undoing. A third location, the Watergate apartment-office complex in Washington, D.C., marked Richard Nixon's downfall. In 1974, the corruption of his administration having been exposed, he resigned from office, the only American president to have done so.

IMPORTANT EVENTS

1960 Sit-ins begin in Greensboro
Birth-control pill approved for use
Kennedy elected president

1961 Freedom Rides protest segregation in transportation
President's Commission on the Status of Women established

1962 Glenn orbits globe in space capsule
Students for a Democratic Society issues Port Huron Statement
Meredith enters University of Mississippi
Baker v. Carr establishes "one person, one vote" principle

1963 Friedan's *The Feminine Mystique* published
Civil rights advocates march on Washington
Baptist church in Birmingham bombed
Kennedy assassinated; Johnson becomes president

1964 Economic Opportunity Act allocates funds to fight poverty
Civil Rights Act outlaws discrimination in jobs and public accommodations
Twenty-fourth Amendment outlaws the poll tax in federal elections
Riots break out in first of the "long hot summers"
Hamer speaks on behalf of Mississippi Freedom Democratic Party at Democratic convention
Free Speech movement begins at Berkeley
Johnson elected president

1965 Malcolm X assassinated
Voting Rights Act allows federal supervision of voting registration
Medicare and Medicaid programs begun
Elementary and Secondary Education Act provides federal aid to education
Watts race riot leaves thirty-four dead
Immigration and Nationality Act lowers barriers to certain ethnic and racial groups

1966 National Organization for Women founded
Miranda v. Arizona requires police to inform suspects of their rights

1967 Race riots erupt in Newark, Detroit, and other cities
Twenty-fifth Amendment establishes the order of presidential succession

1968 U.S.S. *Pueblo* captured by North Korea
Tet offensive causes fear of losing war
King assassinated
African Americans riot in 168 cities and towns
Civil Rights Act bans housing discrimination
Antiwar protests escalate
R. Kennedy assassinated
Violence erupts at Democratic convention
Nixon elected president

1969 Stonewall riot sparked by police harassment of homosexuals
Apollo 11 lands on moon
400,000 gather at Woodstock festival
Moratorium Day calls for end to war

1970 United States invades Cambodia
Students killed at Kent State and Jackson State Universities
First Earth Day celebrated
Environmental Protection Agency created

1971 *Pentagon Papers* published
Twenty-sixth Amendment extends vote to eighteen-year-olds
Inmates revolt at Attica prison
Swann v. Charlotte-Mecklenberg upholds North Carolina desegregation plan

1972 Nixon visits China and Soviet Union
Congress approves ERA
Wallace shot and paralyzed
"Plumbers" break into Watergate
Revenue sharing distributes funds to states
Nixon reelected

1973 Watergate burglars tried
Ervin chairs Watergate hearings
White House aides Ehrlichman and Haldeman resign
Roe v. Wade legalizes abortion
War Powers Act passed
Agnew resigns; Ford named vice president
Saturday Night Massacre provokes outcry

1974 Supreme Court orders Nixon to release White House tapes
House Judiciary Committee votes to impeach Nixon
Nixon resigns; Ford becomes president
Ford pardons Nixon
Freedom of Information Act passed over Ford's veto

Battered by more than a decade of turmoil, many Americans became cynical and ceased to believe in the American Dream. ■

Civil Rights and the New Frontier

President John F. Kennedy was, as the writer Norman Mailer observed, "our leading man." Young, handsome, and vigorous, the new chief executive was the first president born in the twentieth century. Kennedy had a genuinely inquiring mind, and as a patron of the arts he brought wit and sophistication to the White House. Kennedy was born to wealth and politics: his Irish American grandfather had been mayor of Boston, and his millionaire father, Joseph P. Kennedy, had served as ambassador to Great Britain. In 1946 the young Kennedy, having returned from the Second World War a naval hero, perpetuated the family tradition by campaigning to represent Boston in the House of Representatives. He won easily, served three terms in the House, and in 1952 was elected to the Senate.

President John F. Kennedy, his wife Jacqueline, and their two young children, John Jr. and Caroline, symbolized youthful energy and idealism. This photograph was taken at their vacation home at Hyannisport on Cape Cod in July 1963.   (John F. Kennedy Library)

As a Democrat, Kennedy inherited the New Deal commitment to America's social welfare system. He generally cast liberal votes in line with the prolabor sentiments of his low-income, blue-collar constituents. But he avoided controversial issues such as civil rights and the censure of Joseph McCarthy. Kennedy won a Pulitzer Prize for *Profiles in Courage* (1956), a study of politicians who had acted on principle, but he shaded the truth when he claimed sole authorship of the book, which had been written largely by his staff. As one critic put it, he himself showed "too much profile and not enough courage." Kennedy nevertheless enjoyed an enthusiastic following, especially after his landslide reelection to the Senate in 1958.

Kennedy's vitality and style captured the imagination of many Americans. In a departure from the Eisenhower administration's staid, conservative image, the new president surrounded himself with young men of intellectual verve who proclaimed that they had fresh ideas for invigorating the nation; the writer David Halberstam called them "the best and the brightest" (Kennedy appointed only one woman to a significant position). Secretary of Defense Robert McNamara (age forty-four) had been an assistant professor at Harvard at twenty-four and later the whiz-kid president of the Ford Motor Company. Kennedy's special assistant for national security affairs, McGeorge Bundy (age forty-one) had become a Harvard dean at thirty-four with only a bachelor's degree. Kennedy himself was only forty-three, and his brother Robert, the attorney general, was thirty-five.

"The Best and the Brightest"

Kennedy's ambitious program, the New Frontier, promised more than the president could deliver: an end to racial discrimination, federal aid to education, medical care for the elderly, and government action to halt the recession the country was suffering. Only eight months into his first year, it was evident that Kennedy lacked the ability to move Congress, which was dominated by a conservative coalition of Republicans and southern Democrats.

The New Frontier

Struggling to appease conservative southern members of Congress, the new president appointed five die-hard segregationists to the federal bench in the Deep South, and he pursued civil rights with a notable lack of vigor. Kennedy did establish the President's Committee on Equal Employment Opportunity to eliminate racial discrimination in government hiring. But he waited until late 1962 before honoring a 1960 campaign pledge to issue an executive order forbidding segregation in federally subsidized housing. The struggle for racial equality was the most important domestic issue of the time, and Kennedy's performance disheartened civil rights advocates.

Despite President Kennedy's lack of support, African American civil rights activists in the early 1960s continued their struggle through the tactic of nonviolent civil disobedience. Volunteers organized by SNCC and by the Southern Christian Leadership Conference (SCLC), headed by Reverend Martin Luther King, Jr., deliberately violated segregation laws by sitting in at whites-only lunch counters, libraries, and bus stations in the South. The Congress of Racial Equality (CORE) initiated the Freedom Rides in May 1961: an integrated group of thirteen people boarded a bus in Washington, D.C., and traveled into the South, where they braved attacks by white mobs for daring to desegregate interstate transportation.

In the South many black high-school and college students joined SNCC, established in 1960 soon after the sit-ins began in Greensboro, North Carolina (see page 804). These young people walked the dusty back roads of Mississippi and Georgia, encouraging African Americans to resist segregation and register to vote. Some SNCC volunteers were white, and some were from the North; but most were black southerners, and many were from low-income families. These volunteers understood from experience how racism, powerlessness, and poverty intersected in the lives of African Americans.

Student Nonviolent Coordinating Committee

As the civil rights movement gained momentum, President Kennedy gradually made a commitment to first-class citizenship for blacks. In 1962 he ordered U.S. marshals to protect James Meredith, the first African American student to attend the University of Mississippi. The

"I Have a Dream"

A historic moment for the civil rights movement was the March on Washington of August 28, 1963. The Reverend Martin Luther King, Jr. *(center),* joined a quarter of a million black people and white people in their march for racial equality. Addressing civil rights supporters, and the nation, from the steps of the Lincoln Memorial, King delivered his "I Have a Dream" speech.   (R. W. Kelley, LIFE magazine © Time, Inc.)

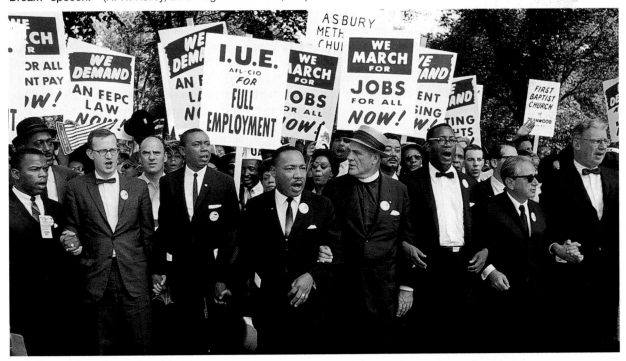

following spring, under court order, federal officials ignored the defiant governor of Alabama, George C. Wallace, and forced the desegregation of the University of Alabama. And in June 1963 Kennedy finally requested legislation to outlaw racial discrimination in employment and racial segregation in public accommodations. When more than 250,000 people, black and white, gathered at the Lincoln Memorial for a March on Washington that August, they did so with the knowledge that President Kennedy was at last on their side. They also heard a most memorable speech: "I have a dream," the civil rights movement's inspirational leader, Martin Luther King, Jr., told the crowd, "that my four little children will one day live in a nation where they will not be judged by the color of their skin but by the content of their character."

The television nightly news programs brought the civil rights struggles into Americans' homes. The story was sometimes grisly. In 1963 Medgar Evers, director of the NAACP in Mississippi, was gunned down in his own driveway. The same year police in Birmingham, Alabama, under the command of Sheriff "Bull" Connor attacked nonviolent civil rights demonstrators, including children, with snarling dogs, fire hoses, and cattle prods. Then two horrifying events helped to convince reluctant politicians that action on civil rights was long overdue. In September white terrorists exploded a bomb during Sunday morning services at Birmingham's Sixteenth Street Baptist Church. Sunday school was in session, and four black girls were killed. A little more than two months later, John Kennedy was assassinated in Dallas.

The first dreadful flash from Dallas clattered over newsroom Teletype machines across the country at

The Kennedy Assassination

1:34 p.m. Eastern Standard Time, November 22, 1963. Broadcast immediately on radio and television, the news was soon on the streets. Time stopped for Americans, and they experienced what psychologists call flashbulb memory, the freeze-framing of an exceptionally emotional event down to the most incidental detail. For an earlier generation, the indelible memory was of December 7, 1941. Now it was November 22, 1963, the day John Kennedy's promise was snuffed out.

In New York City a driver stopped in the middle of a busy intersection and ran over to a sidewalk luncheonette. "Is it true?" he shouted. Without looking up, the counterman replied, "Yes, he's dead." The man returned to his car and slumped over the wheel, obliv-

ious to the impatient honking around him. Ken Kesey's play *One Flew over the Cuckoo's Nest* had just opened on Broadway, and Kesey and a couple of friends were driving triumphantly back to the West Coast. They heard the news in Pennsylvania. As "we stopped in at service stations and Howard Johnson's and little fast-food places across the United States," Kesey later recalled, "a really profound thing happened to us. We felt like we were seeing the real soul of America with its shirt torn open in grief."

Kennedy's murder still baffles many Americans. Was the accused assassin, Lee Harvey Oswald, acting

Who Killed President Kennedy?

alone or as part of a conspiracy? What was his motive? Two days later, in full view of millions of TV viewers, Oswald himself was shot dead by a nightclub owner and small-time Mafia figure named Jack Ruby. The same questions were asked again: What was Ruby's motive? Was he silencing Oswald to prevent him from implicating others? Two years later, the seven-person Warren Commission, headed by Earl Warren, Chief Justice of the Supreme Court, issued a report that concluded Oswald had acted alone. But many Americans questioned this finding.

Historians have wondered what John Kennedy would have accomplished had he lived. Although his legislative achievements were meager, he inspired genuine idealism in Americans. When Kennedy exhorted Americans in his inaugural address to "Ask not what your country can do for you; ask what you can do for your country," tens of thousands volunteered to spend two years of their lives in the Peace Corps. "We had such faith in what Kennedy was doing," recalled one volunteer, "and we all wanted to be a part of it."

Kennedy also promoted a sense of national purpose through his vigorous support of the space program. America lagged behind the Soviet Union, which sent a missile carrying cosmonaut Yuri Gagarin into orbit around the earth in April 1961. But Americans celebrated a month later when Alan Shepard, one of the seven original astronauts, rode the Mercury 3 missile into space. After marine lieutenant colonel John Glenn orbited the globe in a space capsule in February 1962, the United States accelerated its Apollo program, which developed more powerful rocket boosters and lunar landing vehicles for the first astronauts on the moon. Americans embraced Kennedy's challenge to put a man on the moon before the Soviets did and by the end of the decade. And on July 20, 1969, that challenge was met when Apollo 11's lunar module, with two American astronauts aboard, landed on the moon.

In recent years, writers have drawn attention to Kennedy's recklessness in world events, such as authorizing the Bay of Pigs invasion of 1961 (see page 888) and CIA attempts to assassinate Cuba's leader Fidel Castro. They also have criticized his timidity in civil rights and have pointed to his extramarital sex life as evidence of a serious character flaw. It is clear, however, that Kennedy had begun to grow as president during his last few months in office. He made a moving appeal for racial equality and called for reductions in Cold War tensions. Partly because of the Kennedy aura of glamour and youth and hope, John Kennedy acquired an even loftier reputation in death than he had enjoyed in life. And in a peculiar way he accomplished more in death than in life. In the postassassination atmosphere of grief and remorse, Lyndon Johnson pushed through Congress practically the entire New Frontier agenda.

Kennedy in Retrospect

The Great Society and the Triumph of Liberalism

The new president was a big man and a passionate one. As Senate majority leader from 1954 to 1960, Lyndon Johnson had learned how to manipulate people and power to achieve his ends. "This ponderous . . . Texan knows more about the sources of power in the political world of Washington than any president in this century," wrote columnists Rowland Evans and Robert Novak. "He can be gentle and solicitous as a nurse, but as ruthless and deceptive as a riverboat gambler." In the aftermath of the assassination, Johnson resolved to unite the country behind the unfulfilled legislative program of the martyred president. More than that, he wanted to realize Roosevelt's and Truman's unmet goals. He called his new program the Great Society.

Johnson made civil rights his top legislative priority. "No memorial oration or eulogy," he told a joint session of Congress five days after the assassination, "could more eloquently honor President Kennedy's memory than the earliest passage of the civil rights bill." Within months Johnson had signed into law the Civil Rights Act of

Civil Rights Act of 1964

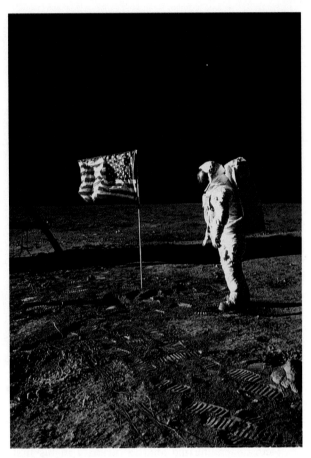

On July 20, 1969, American astronauts Neil A. Armstrong and Edwin E. (Buzz) Aldrin, Jr. *(shown above),* plant an American flag on the moon, thus fulfilling President John F. Kennedy's pledge to land a man on the moon by the end of the 1960s.   (NASA)

1964, which outlawed discrimination on the basis of race, color, religion, sex, or national origin, not only in public accommodations but also in employment. The act also authorized the government to withhold funds from public agencies that discriminated on the basis of race, and it empowered the attorney general to guarantee voting rights and end school segregation. In 1964 African Americans gained two additional victories. First, President Johnson appointed an Equal Employment Opportunity Commission to investigate and judge complaints of job discrimination. Second, the states ratified the Twenty-fourth Amendment to the Constitution, which outlawed the poll tax as a prerequisite for voting in federal elections.

Surrounded by an illustrious group of civil rights leaders and members of Congress, President Lyndon B. Johnson signs the Civil Rights Act of 1964. Standing behind the president is Reverend Martin Luther King, Jr. (Corbis-Bettmann)

Johnson enunciated another priority in his first State of the Union address: "The administration today, here and now, declares unconditional war on poverty." Eight months later, he signed into law the Economic Opportunity Act of 1964, which allocated almost $1 billion for programs to assist the poor. The act became the opening salvo in Johnson's War on Poverty.

In the year following Kennedy's death, Johnson sought to govern by appealing to the shared values and aspirations of the majority of the nation for continued economic growth and social justice. His lopsided victory over his conservative Republican opponent in 1964, Senator Barry Goldwater of Arizona, indicates that he succeeded. Johnson garnered 61 percent of the popular vote and the electoral votes of all but six states. Riding on Johnson's coattails, the Democrats won large majorities in both the House (295 to 140) and the Senate (68 to 32). Johnson recognized that the opportunity to push through further reform had arrived. Congress responded in 1965 and 1966 with the most sweeping reform legislation since 1935.

Election of 1964

Three bills enacted in 1965 were legislative milestones: the Medicare and Medicaid programs insured the elderly against medical and hospital bills and assisted the needy and disabled in paying for medical care; the Elementary and Secondary Education Act provided for general federal aid to education for the first time; and the Voting Rights Act of 1965 empowered the attorney general to supervise voter registration in areas where fewer than half of the minority residents of voting age were registered (see Map 30.1). In 1960 only 29 percent of the South's African American population was registered to vote; when Johnson left office in 1969, the proportion was approaching two-thirds. Even in Mississippi, one of the most resistant states, black registration figures grew from 7 percent in 1964 to 59 percent in 1968.

Voting Rights Act of 1965

The flurry of legislation enacted into law during Johnson's presidency was staggering: establishment of the Department of Housing and Urban Development, the Department of Transportation, and the National Endowments for the Arts and Humanities; water- and air-quality improvement acts; and appropriations for

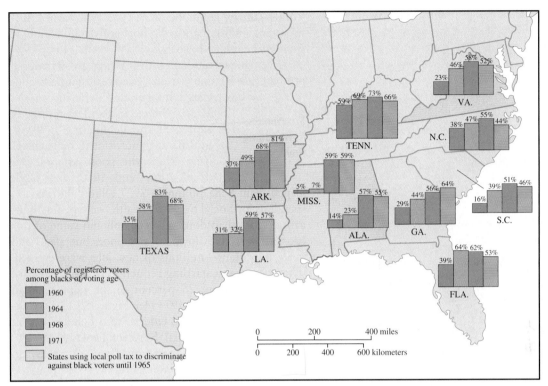

Map 30.1 African American Voting Rights, 1960–1971   After passage of the 1965 Voting Rights Act, African American registration skyrocketed in Mississippi and Alabama and rose substantially in other southern states.   (Source: Harold W. Stanley, *Voter Mobilization and the Politics of Race: The South and Universal Suffrage, 1952–1984* [Praeger Publishers, an imprint of Greenwood Publishing Group, Westport, CT, 1987], p. 97. Copyright © 1987 by Harold W. Stanley. Used with permission.)

the most ambitious federal housing program since 1949, including rent supplements to low-income families. The Immigration and Nationality Act of 1965, the first overhaul of immigration law in forty years, lowered the barriers erected by the national origins quota system, which had severely restricted, or excluded altogether, certain ethnic and racial groups (see page 681). In 1968 Johnson signed another Civil Rights Act—his third—banning racial and religious discrimination in the sale and rental of housing. Another provision of this legislation, known as the Indian Bill of Rights, extended those constitutional protections to Native Americans living under tribal self-government on reservations.

By far the most ambitious of Johnson's initiatives was the War on Poverty. Beginning with a $1 billion appropriation in 1964, the War on Poverty evolved in 1965 and 1966 to include the Job Corps, to provide

War on Poverty

marketable skills, work experience, and remedial education for young people; Project Head Start, to prepare preschoolers from low-income families for grade school; and Upward Bound, to help high-school students from low-income families to prepare for a college education. Other antipoverty programs were Legal Services for the Poor, Volunteers in Service to America (VISTA), and the Model Cities program, which channeled federal funds to upgrade employment, housing, education, and health in targeted urban neighborhoods.

The War on Poverty was a mixed success. For one thing, it was politically volatile because its "community-action programs" angered powerful mayors: it deliberately bypassed them and encouraged "maximum feasible participation" in decision making by the poor themselves, who served on antipoverty governing boards that allocated large sums of money. Furthermore, confusion abounded in the ambitious program.

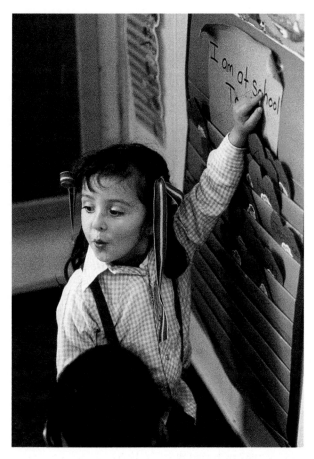

This three-year-old Hispanic girl learns to read in a Head Start program. One of several programs established by the 1964 Economic Opportunity Act, Head Start prepared preschoolers from low-income families for grade school. (E. Crews/The Image Works)

Not even R. Sargent Shriver, who administered the War on Poverty as head of the Office of Economic Opportunity (OEO), could deny this: "It's like we . . . launched a half-dozen rockets at once," he later conceded. Another failing was that the War on Poverty did little to reduce poverty in rural areas or to discourage the South-to-North migration that was worsening already overwhelming poverty in northern inner cities.

Another group that remained poor despite antipoverty initiatives consisted of women and children living in female-headed families; they constituted 40 percent of the poor in the United States. The economic boom that lasted from 1963 to 1969 lifted 12 million people in male-headed families out of poverty. Left behind were 11 million in families headed by women (the same number as in 1963) who earned pitiful wages and frequently did not receive child-support payments from ex-husbands.

Even so, in tandem with a rising gross national product (GNP), the War on Poverty substantially alleviated hunger and suffering in the United States. Its legislation directly addressed the debilitating housing, health, and nutritional deficiencies from which the poor suffered. Between 1965 and 1970, the GNP leaped from $685 billion to $977 billion, and federal spending for Social Security, health, welfare, and education more than doubled. Not only did some of this prosperity trickle down to the poor, but also—and more important—millions of new jobs were created. The result was a startling reduction in the number of poor people, from 25 percent of the population in 1962 to 11 percent in 1973 (see Figure 30.1). Particularly fortunate were the elderly, who benefited from large increases in Social Security benefits; poverty among the elderly dropped from about 40 percent in 1960 to 16 percent in 1974.

Successes in Reducing Poverty

The period of liberal ascendancy represented by the War on Poverty was short-lived; most of the Great Society's legislative achievements occurred in 1964, 1965, and 1966 (see Table 30.1). Disillusioned with America's deepening involvement in Vietnam (see Chapter 31) and upset by the violence of urban race riots (see page 865), many of Johnson's allies began to reject both him and his liberal consensus.

One branch of government, however, maintained the liberal tradition: the Supreme Court. Under the intellectual and moral leadership of Chief Justice Earl Warren, the Court in the 1960s was disposed by political conviction and a belief in judicial activism to play a central role in the resurgence of liberalism. In 1962 the Court began handing down a series of landmark decisions. *Baker v. Carr* (1962) and subsequent rulings established that the principle of "one person, one vote" must prevail at both the state and the national levels. This decision required the reapportionment of state legislatures by shifting seats from lightly populated rural areas to the burgeoning cities, so that each representative would serve the same number of constituents. The Court also outlawed required prayers and Bible reading in public schools, explaining that such practices imposed an "indirect coercive pressure upon religious minorities."

The Warren Court

The Court also attacked the legal underpinning of the anti-Communist crusade, ruling in 1965 that a person need not register with the government as a member of a subversive organization because doing so would violate constitutional safeguards against self-incrimination. In *Griswold v. Connecticut* (1965), the Court ruled that a state law prohibiting the use of contraceptives by married couples violated "a marital right of privacy" and was unconstitutional. The Court upheld the Civil Rights Act of 1964 and the Voting Rights Act of 1965. In other rulings that particularly upset conservatives, the Court decreed that books, magazines, and films could not be banned as obscene unless they were found to be "utterly without redeeming social value."

Civil Rights Rulings

Perhaps most controversial of all was the Court's transformation of the criminal justice system. Beginning with *Gideon v. Wainwright* (1963), the Court ruled that a poor person charged with a felony had the right to a state-appointed lawyer. In *Escobedo v. Illinois* (1964), it decreed that the accused had a right to counsel during interrogation and a right to remain silent. *Miranda v. Arizona* (1966) established that police had to inform criminal suspects that they had these rights and that any statements they made could be used against them. Critics denounced the decisions as victories for criminals, and the right-wing John Birch Society campaigned to impeach Earl Warren.

Despite conservatives' demands for Warren's removal, constitutional historians consider him one of the two most influential chief justices in the nation's history (the other was John Marshall). Whether or not one approved of the decisions of the Warren Court (which ended with Warren's retirement in 1969), its effect on the American people is undeniable.

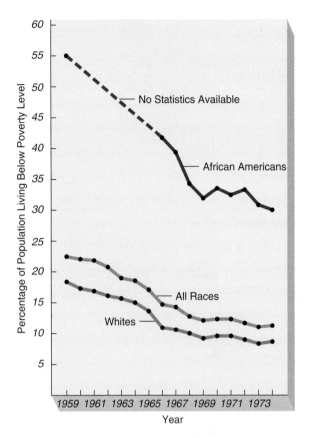

Figure 30.1 Poverty in America for Whites, African Americans, and All Races, 1959–1974 Because of rising levels of economic prosperity, combined with the impact of Great Society programs, the percentage of Americans living in poverty in 1974 was half as high as in 1959. African Americans still were far more likely than white Americans to be poor. In 1959 more than half of all blacks (55.1 percent) were poor; in 1974 the figure remained high (30.3 percent). The government did not record data on African American poverty for the years 1960 through 1965.

Civil Rights Disillusionment, Race Riots, and Black Power

Even while the civil rights movement was winning important victories in the mid-1960s, some activists began to grumble that the federal government was not to be trusted. Fannie Lou Hamer and the Mississippi Freedom Democratic Party felt betrayed by Lyndon Johnson and the Democrats at the 1964 Atlantic City convention, and evidence suggested that the Federal Bureau of Investigation was hostile to the civil rights

movement. Indeed, it turned out that at least one FBI informant not only was a member of the Ku Klux Klan but also was a terrorist who instigated violence against volunteers in the civil rights movement. FBI director J. Edgar Hoover was a racist, activists charged, and they were disturbed by rumors (later confirmed) that Hoover had wiretapped and bugged Martin Luther King, Jr.'s hotel rooms and planted allegations in the newspapers about his sexual improprieties.

The year 1964 witnessed the first of the "long hot summers" of race riots in northern cities. In Harlem

Table 30.1 Great Society Achievements, 1964–1966

	1964	1965	1966
Civil Rights	Civil Rights Act Equal Employment Opportunity Commission Twenty-fourth Amendment	Voting Rights Act	
War on Poverty	Economic Opportunity Act Office of Economic Opportunity Job Corps Legal Services for the Poor VISTA		Model Cities
Education		Elementary and Secondary Education Act Head Start Upward Bound	
Environment		Water Quality Act Air Quality Act	Clean Water Restoration Act
New Government Agencies		Department of Housing and Urban Development National Endowments for the Arts and Humanities	Department of Transportation
Miscellaneous		Medicare and Medicaid Immigration and Nationality Act	

The Great Society of the mid-1960s saw the biggest burst of reform legislation since the New Deal of the 1930s.

Explosion of Black Anger

and Rochester in New York, and in several cities in New Jersey, brutal actions by white police officers, including vicious, unprovoked beatings in police stations, sparked riots in black neighborhoods. African Americans deeply resented the unnecessary force that police sometimes used. As the black writer James Baldwin put it, the white officers patrolling black neighborhoods represented "the force of the white world."

Whites wondered why African Americans were venting their frustration violently at a time when they were making real progress in the civil rights struggle. The civil rights movement, however, had focused mostly on the South, aiming to abolish Jim Crow and black disfranchisement. In the North, African Americans could vote, but many were living in dire poverty. The median income of northern blacks was little more than half that of northern whites, and their unemployment rate was twice as high. Many African American families, particularly those headed by women, lived in

perpetual poverty. The primary assistance program, Aid to Families with Dependent Children (AFDC), failed to meet the needs of the poor. AFDC payments were inadequate to cover a family's rent, utilities, and household expenses, let alone its food.

Northern blacks, surveying the economic and civil rights gains of the 1960s, wondered when they, too, would benefit from the Great Society. Concentrated in the inner cities, they looked around the ghettos in which they lived and knew their circumstances were deteriorating. Their neighborhoods were more segregated than ever; in increasing numbers during the 1960s, whites had responded to the continuing black migration from the South by fleeing to the suburbs. And as inner-city neighborhoods became all black, so did the neighborhood schools. "It doesn't cost anything to move a few feet along a hamburger counter to make room for a Negro," one writer observed. "But the cost—economic, social, psychological—of abolishing forever a Negro ghetto of half a million souls is only now becoming apparent."

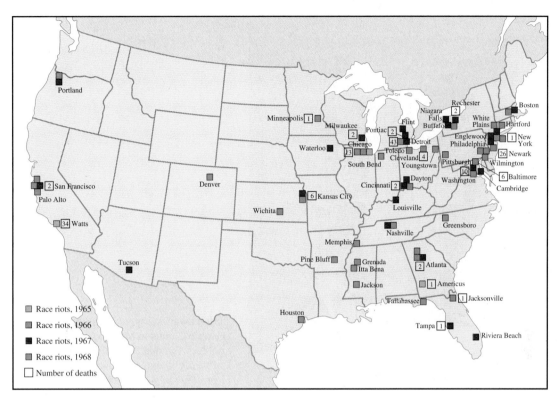

Map 30.2 Race Riots, 1965–1968 The first major race riot of the 1960s exploded in the Los Angeles neighborhood of Watts in 1965. The bloodiest riots of 1967 were in Newark, New Jersey, and Detroit. Scores of riots erupted in the aftermath of Martin Luther King, Jr.'s assassination in 1968.

If 1964 was fiery and violent, 1965 was even more so. In August an altercation between blacks and police sparked rioting in the Watts section of Los Angeles; thirty-four people were killed (see Map 30.2). White mobs did not initiate the violence (as they had done in Chicago in 1919 and Detroit in 1943); instead, blacks exploded in anger over their joblessness and lack of opportunity, as well as police brutality. They looted white-owned stores, set fires, and threw rocks at police and firefighters. The police retaliated, and twenty-eight blacks died in the Watts riot.

Race Riots

Other cities exploded in riots between 1966 and 1968. In July 1967 twenty-six people were killed in street battles between blacks and police and army troops in Newark, New Jersey. A week later a race riot in Detroit led to the deaths of forty-three people. In 1968 the National Advisory Commission on Civil Disorders, chaired by Governor Otto Kerner of Illinois, released a report blaming white racism for the riots: "The nation is rapidly moving toward two increasingly separate Americas . . . a white society principally located in suburbs . . . and a Negro society largely concentrated within large central cities."

Clearly, many blacks, especially in the North, were beginning to question whether the nonviolent civil rights movement was serving their needs. In 1963 Martin Luther King, Jr., had appealed to whites' humanitarian instincts in his "I Have a Dream" speech. Now another voice was beginning to be heard, one that urged blacks to seize their freedom "by any means necessary." It was the voice of Malcolm X, a one-time pimp and street hustler who had converted while in prison to the Nation of Islam faith, whose followers were commonly known as the Black Muslims.

A small sect that espoused black pride and separatism from white society, the Black Muslims condemned the "white devil" as the chief source of evil in the world, and they exhorted blacks to lead sober lives

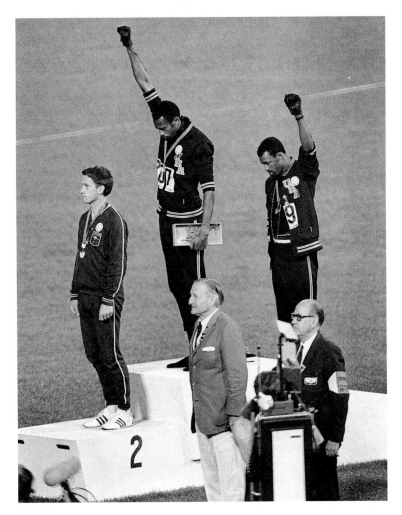

During award ceremonies at the 1968 Olympic Games in Mexico City, American sprinters Tommie Smith *(center)* and John Carlos *(right)* extend gloved hands skyward to protest racial inequality and express Black Power. In retaliation, Olympic officials suspended Smith and Carlos, but other African American athletes emulated them by repeating the clenched-fist salute on the victory stand. (Wide World Photos, Inc.)

Malcolm X

and practice thrift. By the early 1960s Malcolm X had become the Black Muslims' chief spokesperson, and his advice was straightforward: "If someone puts a hand on you, send him to the cemetery." But Malcolm X was murdered in early 1965. His assassins were Black Muslims who believed he had betrayed their cause because he said he had met whites who were not devils and had expressed cautious support for the nonviolent civil rights movement. Still, for both blacks and whites, Malcolm X symbolized black defiance and self-respect. A compelling figure in life, in death he would become a hero to increasing numbers of black nationalists and proponents of Black Power.

A year after Malcolm X's death, Stokely Carmichael, chairman of SNCC, denounced "the betrayal of black dreams by white America" and called on African Americans to assert "Black Power." To be truly free

Black Power

from white oppression, Carmichael proclaimed, blacks had to elect black candidates, organize their own schools, and control their own institutions. Several influential organizations that previously had been committed to racial integration and nonviolence embraced Black Power. SNCC in 1966 and CORE in 1967 expelled their white members and repudiated integration, arguing that black people needed power, not white friendship.

To many white Americans, one of the most fearsome of the new groups was the Black Panther Party. Blending black nationalism and revolutionary communism, the Panthers dedicated themselves to destroying both capitalism and "the military arm of our oppressors," the police in the ghettos. The Panthers defied authority and carried rifles, but they also instituted free breakfast and healthcare programs for ghetto children, taught courses in African American history, and demanded jobs and decent housing for the poor. What particularly worried white parents was that some of their own children agreed with the Panthers. Called the New Left, this vocal subset of the baby-boom generation set out to "change the system."

The New Left and the Counterculture

 "I'm tired of reading history," Mario Savio, a graduate student at the University of California, complained in a letter to a friend in 1964. "I want to make it." Within a few months Savio realized his ambition as a leader of the campus Free Speech movement. After teaching in SNCC's Mississippi Freedom Summer Project, Savio and others returned to Berkeley convinced that the power structure that dominated blacks' lives also controlled the bureaucratic machinery of the university.

In fact, the University of California was a model university in 1964, with a worldwide reputation for excellence and public service. Its chancellor, the economist Clark Kerr, had written approvingly that higher education had become "a component part of the 'military-industrial complex,'" and he likened the "multiversity" with its many separate colleges and research institutes to a big business. But its strength was also its weakness. The largest single campus in the country, with tens of thousands of students, Berkeley had become hopelessly impersonal by the 1960s. Some students complained that they felt like cogs in a machine.

The struggle at Berkeley began when the university administration yielded to pressure from political conservatives and banned recruit-

Free Speech Movement

ment by civil rights and antiwar organizations in Sproul Plaza, the students' traditional gathering place. Savio denounced the ban, saying that the time had come for students to "put [their] bodies against the gears . . . and make the machine stop until we are free." Militant students defied Kerr's ban; the administration suspended them or had them arrested. In December the Free Speech movement seized and occupied the main administration building. Governor Pat Brown dispatched state police to Berkeley, and more than eight hundred people were arrested. Angry students shut down classes for several days in protest.

The willingness of those in positions of authority to mobilize the police against unruly but not violent

students was shocking and radicalizing to many young people. Having grown up comfortable and even indulged, they soon found themselves treated like criminals for questioning authority. By the end of the decade, the activism born at Berkeley would spread to hundreds of other campuses as students actively opposed what they considered a criminal war in Vietnam and racial injustice in their own country.

Two years earlier, another group of students had founded Students for a Democratic Society (SDS).

Students for a Democratic Society and the New Left

Like their leaders Tom Hayden and Al Haber, most SDS members were white, middle-class college students. In 1962, meeting in Port Huron, Michigan, the SDS adopted a statement of principles. "We are people of this generation," the Port Huron Statement asserted, "bred in at least modest comfort, housed now in the universities, looking uncomfortably to the world we inherit." The statement condemned racism, poverty in the midst of plenty, and the Cold War. SDS sought nothing less than the revitalization of democracy by wresting power from the corporations, the military, and the politicians and returning it to the people.

Inspired by the Free Speech Movement and SDS, a minority of students identified themselves as members of the "New Left." The New Left was united in its hatred of racism and the Vietnam War, but it divided along philosophical and political lines. Some radicals were Marxists, others black nationalists, anarchists, or pacifists. Some believed in pursuing social change through negotiation; others were revolutionaries who regarded compromise as impossible.

As the slogan "Make Love, Not War" suggests, the New Left and the counterculture discovered a common cause as the war in Vietnam

Countercultural Revolution

escalated. Drugs and sexuality also were central to the "hippie" experience. Exhorted by Timothy Leary— a former Harvard instructor and advocate of expanded consciousness through use of LSD and other mind-altering drugs—to "turn on, tune in, drop out," millions of students experimented with marijuana and hallucinogenic drugs. Young people's drug experiences and experiments with communal living persuaded them that they lived in a new era unconnected to the past. In fact, in a list of twenty-one academic subjects, students in the sixties ranked history "the most irrelevant."

Inspired by Ken Kesey and his Merry Pranksters, who traveled in a 1939 International Harvester school bus, hippies seemed drawn to buses. This bus, named "The Road Hog," carries members of the New Buffalo Commune in the 1968 Fourth of July parade in El Rito, New Mexico.   (Lisa Law/Image Works)

Music more than anything else expressed the countercultural assault on the status quo. Bob Dylan promised revolutionary answers "blowin' in the wind," and young people cheered Janis Joplin, who brought African American blues to white Americans. Like sex and drugs, the music of the 1960s represented a quest to redefine reality and create a more just and joyful society. Rock festivals became cultural watersheds. In 1969 at Woodstock in upstate New York, more than four hundred thousand people ignored or reveled in rain and mud for days, without shelter and without violence. A number of them began to dream of a peaceful "Woodstock nation" based on love, drugs, and rock music.

Rock 'n' Roll

Some young people tried to construct alternative ways of life. In the Haight-Ashbury section of San Francisco, "flower children" created an urban subculture as distinctive as that of any Chinatown or Little Italy. "Hashbury" inspired numerous other communal

Gay Rights Movement

living experiments. The counterculture represented only a small proportion of American youth, but to middle-class parents, hippies seemed to be everywhere.

The so-called generation gap was yawning wide, but most disturbing to parents were the casual sexual mores that young people were adopting. In 1960 the government approved the birth-control pill, and use of the pill accelerated among young people. For many young people, living together no longer equaled living in sin; and as attitudes toward premarital sex changed, so did notions about homosexuality and sex roles.

Sexuality

The militancy of the 1960s helped inspire the gay rights movement. Homosexuals had long feared that disclosing their sexual orientation would mean losing not only their jobs but even their friends and families. That attitude began to change in June 1969. In New York's Greenwich

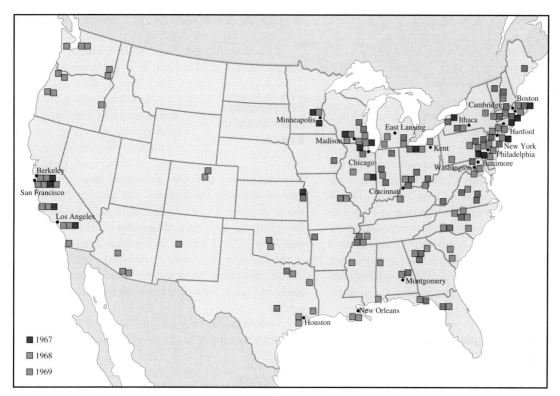

Map 30.3   Disturbances on College and University Campuses, 1967–1969   Students on campuses from coast to coast protested against the Vietnam War. Some protests were peaceful; others erupted into violent confrontations between protesters and police and army troops.

Village, a riot erupted when police raided the Stonewall Inn, a gay bar on Christopher Street, and were greeted with a volley of beer bottles hurled by patrons tired of police harassment. Rioting continued into the night, and graffiti calling for "Gay Power" appeared along Christopher Street. The Stonewall riot, as historian John D'Emilio has written, "marked a critical divide in the politics and consciousness of homosexuals and lesbians. A small, thinly spread reform effort suddenly grew into a large, grass-roots movement for liberation . . . as a furtive subculture moved aggressively into the open."

During Lyndon Johnson's presidency, antiwar marches and demonstrations became a widespread

Antiwar Protests

protest tactic (see Map 30.3), and students on campuses across the country held teach-ins—open forums for discussion of the war by students, professors, and guest speakers. Some young men fled the draft by moving abroad—mostly to Canada and Scandinavia—while others protested, violently and nonviolently, at local draft board offices.

The Johnson administration charged that such acts threatened the nation's war-making powers.

By this time, however, growing numbers of Americans, young and old, had quit believing their elected leaders. In 1965, having ordered combat troops to Vietnam, President Johnson claimed the United States was fighting for honorable reasons. But people wondered what goal could justify the murder of Vietnamese women and children. As troop levels increased, many recalled ruefully that in 1964 they had voted for Johnson as the "peace candidate." By 1968 almost a half-million American soldiers were stationed in Vietnam, and Johnson's credibility had evaporated.

1968: A Year of Protest, Violence, and Loss

 As stormy and violent as the years from 1963 through 1967 had been, many Americans still tried to downplay the nation's distress in the hope that it would go away. But in 1968 a series of shocks hit them harder than ever. The first jolt came in January 1968, when the U.S.S. *Pueblo*, a navy intelligence ship, was captured by North Korea. A week later came the Tet Offensive in Vietnam (see page 898). American casualties were climbing, and for the first time many Americans believed that they might lose the war.

Controversy over the war deepened within the Democratic Party, and two candidates rose to challenge Johnson for the 1968 presidential nomination. Senator Eugene McCarthy of Minnesota entered the New Hampshire primary on March 12 solely to contest the Vietnam War; when he won twenty of New Hampshire's twenty-four convention delegates, Johnson recognized that these voters had repudiated his war policies. Soon another Democrat, Senator Robert F. Kennedy of New York, brother of the late president, entered the race. Then, on March 31, President Johnson went on national television to announce a scaling-down of the bombing in North Vietnam and his decision not to run for reelection.

Less than a week later, Martin Luther King, Jr., was murdered in Memphis. It is still unclear whether

Assassination of Martin Luther King, Jr.

James Earl Ray, a white man convicted in the killing, was a deranged racist acting alone or a hireling in an organized conspiracy. As an outspoken critic of the Vietnam War and increasingly of American capitalism, King had many enemies. Whatever Ray's motive, the murder touched off massive grief and rage in the nation's ghettos. Riots erupted in 168 cities and towns, including the looting and burning of white businesses (see Map 30.2). Thirty-four blacks and five whites died in the violence. The terror provoked a white backlash. Tough talk was the response from Chicago mayor Richard Daley, who ordered police to shoot to kill arsonists.

Gallup polls in April and May reported Robert Kennedy to be the front-running Democratic presidential candidate, and in June he

Assassination of Robert Kennedy

won the California primary. After addressing his joyous supporters in a Los Angeles hotel, Kennedy took a shortcut through the kitchen to a press conference. A young man stepped forward with a .22-caliber revolver and fired. Sirhan Sirhan, the assassin, was an Arab nationalist who despised Kennedy for his unwavering support of Israel. Many antiwar liberals felt they had lost a friend in Robert Kennedy, who in the wake of his brother's assassination had developed deep empathy with the sufferings of the underprivileged and strong opposition to the Vietnam War.

Violence erupted again in August at the Democratic national convention in Chicago. The Democrats were divided over the war, and thou-

Violence at the Democratic Convention

sands of antiwar protesters and members of the zany and anarchic Youth International Party (Yippies) had traveled to Chicago. The Chicago police force was still in the psychological grip of Mayor Daley's shoot-to-kill directive. Twelve thousand police were assigned to twelve-hour shifts, and another twelve thousand army troops were on call with rifles, bazookas, and flamethrowers. They attacked in front of the Hilton Hotel, wading into the ranks of demonstrators, reporters, and TV camera operators. Throughout the nation, viewers watched as club-swinging police beat protesters to the ground.

To preserve law and order against protesters during the 1968 Democratic National Convention, Chicago Mayor Richard J. Daley *(center)* mobilized twelve thousand police officers. But in what a federal commission called a "police riot," the officers overreacted and used tear gas and clubs to stop protesters from marching to the convention hall.   (Collection of Philip J. and Suzanne Schiller)

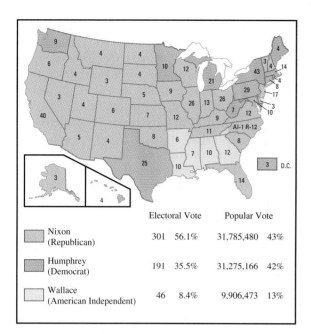

Map 30.4   Presidential Election, 1968   The popular vote was almost evenly split between Richard M. Nixon and Hubert Humphrey, but Nixon won 31 states to Humphrey's 14 and triumphed easily in electoral votes. George Wallace, the American Independent Party candidate, won 5 states in the Deep South.

The Democratic convention nominated Vice President Hubert Humphrey for president and Senator Edmund Muskie of Maine for vice president. Like Johnson and Kennedy before him, Humphrey was both an unstinting supporter of the Vietnam War and a political liberal supported throughout his career by big-city bosses, African Americans, and union members. The Republicans selected as their presidential nominee Richard M. Nixon; his running mate was the tough-talking Governor Spiro Agnew of Maryland. Another tough-talking governor, George C. Wallace of Alabama, ran as the nominee of the American Independent Party. Wallace was a segregationist, a proponent of reducing North Vietnam to rubble with nuclear weapons, and an advocate of "law and order."

When the votes were tabulated, Nixon emerged the winner by the slimmest of margins. Wallace collected nearly 10 million votes, or almost 14 percent of the total, the best performance by a third party since 1924. His strong showing made Nixon a minority president, elected with 43 percent of the popular vote (see Map 30.4). Moreover, the Dem-

Election of 1968

ocrats maintained control of the House (245 to 189) and the Senate (57 to 43).

Still, given that the combined vote for Nixon and Wallace was 57 percent, the 1968 election was a triumph for conservatism. The war had hurt the Democrats' appeal, but even more politically damaging was the party's identification with the cause of civil rights and welfare for the poor. In 1968 Humphrey received 97 percent of the black vote but only 35 percent of the white vote. Among the defectors from the New Deal coalition were not only southern whites but also northern blue-collar ethnic voters. "In city after city," one observer noted, "racial conflicts had destroyed the old alliance. The New Deal had unraveled block by block."

Unraveling of the New Deal Coalition

Rebirth of Feminism

Another liberation movement gained momentum during the turbulence of the 1960s, at first quietly and then on the picket line. The women's rights movement had languished after the adoption of the Nineteenth Amendment in 1920. But in the 1960s feminism was reborn. Many women were dissatisfied with their lives, and in 1963 they found a voice with the publication of Betty Friedan's *The Feminine Mystique.* According to Friedan, women across the country were deeply troubled by "the problem that has no name." Most women had grown up believing that "all they had to do was devote their lives from earliest girlhood to finding a husband and bearing children." The problem was that this "mystique of feminine fulfillment" left many wives and mothers feeling empty and incomplete.

President Kennedy appointed only one woman to a policymaking post in his administration, but she proved to be an effective advocate of women's rights. Esther Peterson served as assistant secretary of labor and director of the Women's Bureau. In 1961, at her urging, Kennedy established the first President's Commission on the Status of Women. Its report, *American Women* (1963), urged that every obstacle to women's full participation in society be removed. But little federal action resulted from the release of *American Women,* and the government was failing to enforce the gender-equality provisions of the Civil Rights Act of

National Organization for Women

1964. The need for action inspired the founding in 1966 of the National Organization for Women (NOW). In the reform tradition, NOW battled for "equal rights in partnership with men" by lobbying for legislation and testing laws in the courts.

Not long after NOW's formation, a new generation of radical feminists emerged. Most radical feminists were white and well educated; many were the daughters of working mothers. Most had been raised in the era of sexual liberation, taking for granted liberation from unwanted pregnancy. The intellectual ferment of their movement produced a new feminist literature. Radical feminists focused not only on legal barriers but also on cultural assumptions and traditions. In the process they introduced the term *sexism* to signify a phenomenon far more pervasive and demeaning than lack of legal equality, and they challenged everything from women's economic and political inequality to sexual double standards and sex-role stereotypes.

Radical feminists practiced what they called "personal politics." Charlotte Bunch, a feminist, explained,

"Personal Politics"

"There is no private domain of a person's life that is not political, and there is no political issue that is not ultimately personal." Unlike NOW, the radical feminists practiced direct action, such as picketing the 1968 Miss America contest in Atlantic City. One woman auctioned off an effigy of Miss America: "Gentlemen, I offer you the 1969 model. . . . She walks. She talks. She smiles on cue. *And she does the housework.*" Into the "freedom trash can" the pickets dumped false eyelashes, hair curlers, girdles, and *Playboy* magazine to protest the prevailing view of women as domestic servants and sex objects.

Many radical feminists were veterans of the struggles for black civil rights and against the Vietnam War. Even in movements dedicated to equality and peace, however, they often found that they were second-class citizens. Instead of making policy, they were expected to make coffee, take minutes, and even provide sexual favors. Many of these feminists organized consciousness-raising groups to discuss wide-ranging and sensitive matters such as homosexuality, abortion, and power relationships in romance and marriage. The issue of homosexuality caused a split in the women's movement. In 1969 and 1970 NOW forced lesbians to resign from membership and offices in the organization. The rift was healed in 1971, largely because lesbians as well as gay men had begun to fight back.

For working women in the 1960s, the most pressing problems were sex discrimination in employment, meager professional opportunities, low pay, lack of adequate daycare for children, and prohibitions against abortion. Although the Equal Pay Act of 1963 required equal pay for equal work in industries producing goods for commerce, such equality has been slow in coming. In 1963 the average woman earned 63 cents for every dollar a man earned. Ten years later the figure had fallen to 57 cents. The main cause of this pay disparity was "occupational segregation": throughout the labor force, women were concentrated in the low-paying positions. Because many women with college educations earned less than men with eighth-grade educations, it was natural that two of the most important women's goals of the 1960s were equal job opportunity and equal pay for equal work.

Working Women's Burdens

Another goal of working women was child daycare. In 1971 a bill passed Congress that would have set up a national system of daycare facilities for the children of working parents, but President Nixon vetoed it. The bill, Nixon asserted, would have committed government to "communal approaches to child-rearing over against the family-centered approach," thus imperiling the American family. In fact, there was a growing need for childcare: 11 million additional women joined the labor force between 1960 and 1972, and many were mothers of young children.

Despite opposition and setbacks, women were making impressive gains. They entered professional schools in record numbers: from 1969 to 1973, the number of women law students almost quadrupled, and the number of women medical students more than doubled. Under Title IX of the Educational Amendments of 1972, female college athletes gained the right to the same financial support as male athletes. The same year, Congress approved the Equal Rights Amendment (ERA)—"Equality of rights under the law shall not be denied or abridged by the United States or by any State on account of sex"—and sent it to the states for ratification. It fell three states shy of the three-fourths majority needed for adoption.

Women's Educational and Professional Gains

The Supreme Court also ruled on several issues particularly pertinent to women. In 1973, following the lead of some states, the Court struck down laws that made abortion a crime. Justice Harry A. Blackmun

Roe v. Wade

wrote the majority (7–2) opinion in *(Roe v. Wade):* The constitutional "right of privacy . . . is broad enough to encompass a woman's decision whether or not to terminate her pregnancy." Only in the last three months of pregnancy could a state bar abortion. The Court at this time also addressed sex discrimination. In a 1971 ruling *(Reed v. Reed)*, it held that legislation differentiating between the sexes "must be reasonable, not arbitrary," and in 1973 *(Frontiero v. Richardson)* the justices went a step further in declaring that job-related classifications based on sex, like those based on race, were "inherently suspect." These victories gave women new confidence in the 1970s.

Nixon and the Divided Nation

 Richard Nixon's presidency was born in chaos. Bloody confrontations occurred at Berkeley, Wisconsin, Cornell, Harvard, and scores of other colleges and universities in 1969. In October three hundred Weathermen (a splinter group of SDS) raced through Chicago's downtown district, smashing windows and attacking police officers in a deluded attempt to incite armed class struggle. Violence was absent a month later, however, when a half-million people assembled peacefully at the Washington Monument on Moratorium Day to call for an end to the Vietnam War.

If 1969 was bloody and turbulent, 1970 proved to be even more so. President Nixon appeared on television on April 30 to announce that the United States had launched an "incursion" into Cambodia (see page 899), a neutral country bordering Vietnam. Antiwar protest escalated. On May 4 national guardsmen in Ohio fired into a crowd of fleeing students at Kent State University, killing four young people. Ten days later, police and state highway patrolmen armed with automatic weapons blasted a women's dormitory at Jackson State, an all-black university in Mississippi, killing two students and wounding nine others. The police claimed they had been shot at, but no evidence of sniping could be found.

Kent State and Jackson State

Calling their movement "Red Power," these American Indian activists dance in 1969 while "reclaiming" Alcatraz Island in San Francisco Bay. Arguing that an 1868 Sioux treaty entitled them to possession of unused federal lands, the group occupied the island until mid-1971. (Ralph Crane, LIFE Magazine © Time, Inc.)

Many Americans, though disturbed by the increasing ferocity of campus confrontations, felt more personally endangered by street crime than student unrest. Sales of pistols, burglar alarms, and bulletproof vests soared, as did demand for private guards and special police. Conservatives accused liberals and the Supreme Court of causing the crime wave by coddling criminals.

Fear of Crime

Responding to public calls for crackdowns, government officials sometimes overreacted. Governor Nelson Rockefeller of New York did so in September 1971 when more than a thousand inmates of the state prison at Attica seized thirty-eight guards and took over a cellblock. Rather than agree to come to Attica to negotiate, Rockefeller ordered state troopers, sheriff's deputies, and guards to storm the prison. Under a pall of tear gas Rockefeller's army regained control, but at a horrifying cost: twenty-nine inmates and ten hostages were dead.

This new wave of riots, protests, and violent crime convinced Nixon that the nation was plunging into anarchy. Worried like Lyndon Johnson before him that the antiwar movement was communist inspired, he ordered the FBI, the CIA, the National Security Agency, and the Defense Intelligence Agency in mid-1970 to formulate a coordinated attack on "internal threats." Meanwhile, the administration also worked to put the Democratic Party on the defensive. The theme for the upcoming elections was enunciated in a memorandum by Jeb Stuart Magruder, a White House assistant: "The Democrats should be portrayed as being on the fringes: radical liberals who . . . excuse disorder, tolerate crime . . . and undercut the President's foreign policy." But Republican attempts in 1970 to discredit the Democrats failed. The Democrats gained seats in the House, and the Republicans lost eleven state governorships.

Politics of Divisiveness

Nixon's fortunes declined further in 1971. In June the *New York Times* began to publish the *Pentagon Papers*, a top-secret Defense Department study that revealed that the government had repeatedly lied to the American people about the Vietnam War (see page 899). Nixon also had to contend with inflation, a problem not entirely of his making. Lyndon Johnson's policy of "guns and butter"—massive deficit financing to support both the Vietnam War

Stagflation

and the Great Society—had fueled inflation. By early 1971 the United States was suffering from a 5.3 percent inflation rate and a 6 percent unemployment rate. The word *stagflation* soon would be coined to describe this coexistence of economic recession (stagnation) and inflation.

Nixon shocked both critics and allies by declaring in early 1971 that "I am now a Keynesian." (According to the British economist John Maynard Keynes, governments could stimulate economic growth in the private sector by means of "pump priming," even if it necessitated deficit financing.) Nixon's budget for fiscal 1971 would have a built-in deficit of $23 billion, just slightly less than the all-time high of $25 billion (1968 to 1969). Then in August, in an effort to correct the nation's balance-of-payments deficit, Nixon announced that he would devalue the dollar and allow it to "float" in international money markets. Finally, to curb inflation, the president froze prices, wages, and rents for ninety days. Wage and price controls exemplified what surprised observers called Nixon's "great turnabout" from outspoken conservative to pragmatic liberal.

One of Nixon's chief legislative aims was revenue sharing, a program that distributed federal funds to the states to use as they saw fit. In 1972 the president signed a revenue-sharing bill. Invoking the federalism of the nation's founders, he called this effort to shift responsibility back to state and local governments the New Federalism. The historian Stephen E. Ambrose has written that the program had special appeal to "the surburban, small-town, and rural homeowning Silent Majority," who expressed disgust that they had to pay "high taxes to support giveaway programs for the poor." They wanted to control their own tax dollars.

The environmental movement, which gained momentum in the 1960s, bore fruit during Nixon's first term. Alerted in 1962 to ecological hazards by Rachel Carson's *Silent Spring* (see page 810), growing numbers of Americans began to heed warnings of impending disaster due to rapid population growth and rampant development. Gradually, Congress responded, establishing the National Wilderness Preservation System (1964) and giving the federal government the power to set water-quality standards (1967).

Environmental Issues

Environmental tragedies such as a 1969 oil spill that fouled the beaches and killed wildlife in Santa Barbara, California, spurred citizen action. The En-

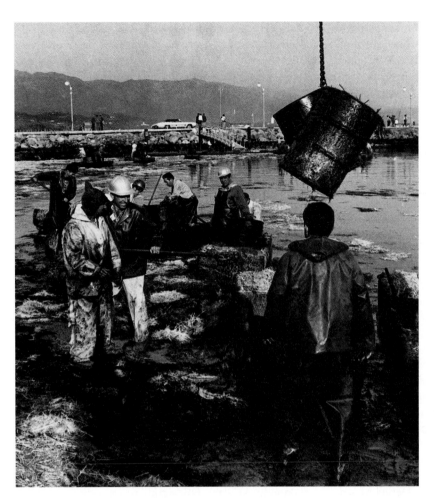

In 1969 a petroleum rig off the coast of Santa Barbara, California, ruptured, spilling millions of gallons of toxic oil. Fisheries were destroyed, and seabirds, seals, and other wildlife coated with viscous oil struggled to stay alive. The tragedy motivated environmental activists, who lobbied for laws that would protect nature. And in 1970, Americans concerned about pollution of the environment celebrated the first Earth Day.   (J. Eyerman/Black Star)

vironmental Defense Fund (founded in 1967) successfully fought the use of DDT, and Greenpeace (founded in 1969) protested radioactive poisoning from nuclear-bomb testing. In 1970 Americans celebrated the first Earth Day, convinced that the planet's fate hung in the balance. Barry Commoner's *The Closing Circle* (1971) put the issue squarely: "The environment got here first, and it's up to the economic system to adjust to the environment. Any economic system must be compatible with the environment, or it will not survive."

In the 1970s states took action; Oregon, for example, passed the first bottle-recycling act in 1972. And although President Nixon was personally unsympathetic to the environmental movement, some of his subordinates were not. Nixon acknowledged the movement's political appeal by reluctantly agreeing to the establishment of the Environmental Protection Agency in 1970 and by signing into law the Clean Air Act (1970), Clean Water Act (1972), and Pesticide Control Act (1972).

Nixon's Reelection and Resignation

Political observers believed that President Nixon would have a hard time running for reelection on his contrary first-term record. Having urged Americans to "lower our voices," he had ordered Vice President Agnew to denounce the press and student protesters. Having espoused unity, he had practiced the politics of polarization. Having campaigned as a fiscal conservative, he had authorized near-record budget deficits. And having promised peace, he had widened the war in Southeast Asia.

During Nixon's first term, the Democrats dominated both houses of Congress, and they continued to pursue a liberal agenda. Indeed, Congress's accomplishments were more despite Nixon than because of him. Congress increased Social Security payments and food-stamp funding and established the Occupational Safety and Health Administration to reduce hazards in the workplace. Moreover, in 1971 the states quickly ratified the Twenty-sixth Amendment, which extended the vote to eighteen-year-olds.

Liberal Legislative Victories

In his 1968 presidential campaign, Nixon had echoed George Wallace's appeal for the law and order vote. In his campaign for reelection, Nixon continued to employ a "southern strategy" of political conservatism. A product of the Sunbelt, he was acutely aware of the growing political power of that conservative region. He thus appealed to the Silent Majority. And as in the 1970 congressional elections, Nixon equated the Republican Party with law and order and the Democrats with permissiveness, crime, drugs, pornography, the hippie lifestyle, student radicalism, black militancy, feminism, homosexuality, and dissolution of the family.

Nixon's "Southern Strategy"

In some ways, Nixon had been pursuing a southern strategy all along. A furor had arisen in 1970 when the press published a memorandum by Daniel Moynihan, Nixon's adviser on urban affairs and social welfare, who had recommended that "the issue of race could benefit from a period of benign neglect." Incensed, blacks and white liberals responded that this was another example of how uncaring the Nixon administration was. Moreover, Attorney General John Mitchell had courted southern white voters by trying to delay school desegregation in Mississippi and to prevent extension of the 1965 Voting Rights Act.

The southern strategy also guided Nixon's nomination of Supreme Court justices. After appointing Warren Burger, a conservative federal judge, to succeed Earl Warren as chief justice, Nixon had selected two southerners to serve as associate justices, one of whom was a segregationist. When the Senate declined to confirm either nominee, Nixon protested angrily, "I understand the bitter feelings of millions of Americans who live in the South." By 1972, however, the president had

Nixon and the Supreme Court

managed to appoint three more conservatives to the Supreme Court. Ironically, the new appointees did not always vote as Nixon would have wished: the Court's decisions on abortion, publication of the *Pentagon Papers*, the death sentence, wiretapping, and busing for school desegregation all ran counter to Nixon's views.

The Court was at the center of one of the most emotional issues of the 1972 election: busing of schoolchildren for purposes of integration. In *Swann v. Charlotte-Mecklenberg* (1971), the justices had upheld a desegregation plan that required a school system in North Carolina to work toward racial integration through massive cross-town busing. The decision generated widespread protest. The next year Governor George Wallace of Alabama won the Democratic primary in Florida after taking a strong antibusing stand. Three days later Nixon proposed that Congress pass a busing moratorium, and he appeared on television to denounce busing as a reckless and extreme remedy for segregation. Nixon's opposition to busing was a well-planned aspect of his southern strategy, but it clearly appealed to many northern whites as well.

Besides Governor Wallace, the Democratic candidates for the 1972 presidential nomination were Senators Hubert Humphrey, George McGovern, Edmund Muskie, and Edward Kennedy, the younger brother of John and Robert Kennedy. Wallace fell victim to an assassination attempt: he was shot and paralyzed by a disturbed young man in Maryland and began a long convalescence. After his shooting, the right-wing law-and-order vote had no place to turn but to Nixon. Kennedy had ceased to be a serious contender in 1969; in that year, he left the scene of an accident in which a woman passenger in his car drowned, at Chappaquiddick, an island off the Massachusetts coast near Martha's Vineyard. The other Democratic candidates inspired little enthusiasm. Senator McGovern of South Dakota, who enjoyed the support of many followers of the late Robert F. Kennedy, won several primaries and arrived at the Democratic convention with enough votes to secure the nomination of his party.

Election of 1972

Nixon campaigned by assuming the elevated role of world statesman: in early 1972 he traveled to China and to the Soviet Union. Both trips were elaborately staged and televised for maximum political effect. But it was the inept campaign waged by George McGovern that handed victory to the Republicans. When

McGovern endorsed a $30 billion cut in the defense budget, people began to fear that he was a neo-isolationist who would reduce the United States to a second-rate power. McGovern's proposals split the Democrats between his supporters—antiwar activists, African Americans, feminists, young militants—and old-guard urban bosses, labor leaders, white southerners, and growing numbers of blue-collar workers.

Nixon benefited greatly from the rumor planted by his aides that the Vietnam War was near its end. Troops were being pulled out; by September 1972 the American death rate was almost zero. Then in late October, less than two weeks before the election, Henry Kissinger (then assistant to the president for national security affairs) announced a breakthrough in the peace negotiations. "Peace is at hand," he proclaimed. The announcement proved inaccurate but helped persuade some people to vote for Nixon.

Nixon's victory in November was overwhelming: he polled 47 million votes, more than 60 percent.

Nixon's Landslide Victory

McGovern received only 29 million and won just one state, Massachusetts, and the District of Columbia. Nixon's southern strategy had been supremely successful. He carried the entire Deep South, which once had been solidly Democratic. He also gained the suburbs and won over a majority of the urban vote, including long-time Democrats such as blue-collar workers, Catholics, and white ethnics. Only blacks, Jews, and low-income voters stuck by the Democratic candidate.

Yet the 1972 election had another significant result, one that would recur in subsequent elections. Despite Nixon's landslide victory, his coattails proved to be short, and the Democrats retained control of both houses of Congress. Democratic voters were becoming independent, resorting to ticket-splitting to reject an unacceptable Democratic presidential candidate but support the party's congressional candidates.

Little noticed during the campaign was a break-in at the Watergate apartment-office complex in Washington, D.C., on June 17, 1972. A

Watergate Break-in

watchman telephoned the police to report an illegal late-night entry into the building through an underground garage. At 2:30 A.M., police arrested five men who were attaching listening devices to telephones in the sixth-floor offices of the Democratic National Committee. The men had cameras and had been rifling through files.

One of those arrested was James W. McCord, a former CIA employee who had become security coordinator of the Committee to Re-Elect the President (CREEP). The other four were anti-Castro Cubans from Miami who had worked with the CIA before. Unknown to the police, two other men had been in the Watergate building at the time of the break-in. One was E. Howard Hunt, a one-time CIA agent who had become a White House consultant. The other was G. Gordon Liddy, a former FBI agent serving on CREEP's staff.

The Watergate fiasco actually began in 1971, when the White House established not only CREEP

White House Cover-up

but the Special Investigations Unit, known familiarly as the "Plumbers," to stop the leaking of secret government documents to the press. After publication of the *Pentagon Papers*, the Plumbers burglarized the office of Daniel Ellsberg's psychiatrist in an attempt to discredit Ellsberg, who had leaked the top-secret report to the press. It was the Plumbers who broke into the Democratic National Committee's headquarters to photograph documents and install wiretaps; money raised by CREEP was used to pay the Plumbers' expenses both before and after the break-ins. CREEP's official duty was to solicit campaign contributions, and the committee managed to collect $60 million, much of it donated illegally by corporations, including big oil companies like Gulf Oil and Phillips Petroleum, as well as defense contractors and airlines.

The arrest of the Watergate burglars generated furious activity in the White House. Incriminating documents were shredded; E. Howard Hunt's name was expunged from the White House telephone directory; and President Nixon ordered his chief of staff, H. R. Haldeman, to discourage the FBI's investigation into the burglary on the pretext that it might compromise national security. Nixon also authorized CREEP "hush money" payments in excess of $460,000 to keep Hunt and others from implicating the White House in the crime. And he assured the press that his White House counsel, John W. Dean III, had conducted a "complete investigation" and that no one in the administration "was involved in this very bizarre incident."

Because of successful White House efforts to cover up the scandal, the break-in was almost unnoticed by the electorate. Had it not been for the diligent efforts of reporters, government special prosecutors,

How do historians know...

that President Richard M. Nixon was guilty of obstructing justice in the Watergate affair? What was the evidence—the "smoking gun"—that established his guilt? The so-called smoking gun referred to the tape recording of a White House conversation on June 23, 1972, that proved Nixon had foreknowledge of the Watergate break-in, had instigated a cover-up, and had obstructed justice almost from the outset of the scandal. That day, Nixon ordered his top aide to stop the Federal Bureau of Investigation's inquiry into the Watergate break-in. Tell the Central Intelligence Agency, Nixon thundered, to call the FBI, claim that the break-in was a secret spy operation related to the 1961 Bay of Pigs invasion, and say ". . . that we wish for the country [that you] 'don't go further into this case,' period." In 1973 and 1974 special prosecutors and congressional committees sued for release of this and other tapes, but Nixon resisted. On August 5, 1974, the Supreme Court ruled that executive privilege did not protect the subpoenaed tapes; the next day, the White House turned over a number of tapes, including the smoking gun. Three days later, Richard Nixon resigned the presidency.

Afterward, historians sued for access to the thousands of hours of unreleased tapes; but for twenty-one years, Nixon and his family succeeded in keeping them private. In 1996, however, the Nixon estate, the National Archives and Records Administration, and Stanley I. Kutler, a history professor at the University of Wisconsin, reached an agreement that called for some 3,700 hours of tapes to be made public over the next several years. The first tapes released condemned President Nixon in his own words and shocked the American people. For example, on May 13, 1971, Nixon was recorded growling demands for a commissioner of the Internal Revenue Service, who "is a ruthless son of a bitch, that he will do what he is told, that every income tax return I want to see, I see. That he will go after our enemies and not go after our friends." A month later, Nixon ordered his aides to arrange a break-in at the Brookings Institution, a liberal think tank in Washington: "Goddammit," he swore, "get in and get those files. Blow the safe and get it." In January 2000 some of Watergate tapes became available to the public when the National Archives began to sell cassettes containing the 264 hours of so-called abuse of government power recordings. (Photo: Nixon Presidential Materials Project)

Watergate Hearings and Investigations

federal judges, and members of Congress, President Nixon might have succeeded in disguising his involvement in Watergate. Slowly, however, the tangle of lies and distortions began to unravel. In early 1973 U.S. District Judge John Sirica tried the burglars, one of whom implicated his superiors in CREEP and at the White House. From May until November, the Senate Select Committee on Campaign Practices, chaired by Senator Sam Ervin of North Carolina, heard testimony from White House aides. John W. Dean III acknowledged not only that there had been a cover-up but that the president had directed it. Another aide shocked the committee and the nation by disclosing that Nixon had had a voice-activated taping system installed in his White House office and that conversations about Watergate had been recorded.

Nixon feigned innocence. In April 1973 he tried to distance himself from the cover-up by announcing the resignations of his two chief White House aides, John Ehrlichman and H. R. Haldeman.

Saturday Night Massacre

The administration then appointed Archibald Cox, a Harvard law professor with a reputation for uncompromising integrity, to fill the new position of special Watergate prosecutor. But when Cox sought in October to obtain the White House tapes by means of a court order, Nixon decided to have him fired. Both Attorney General Elliot Richardson and his deputy resigned rather than carry out the dismissal order. It thus fell to the third-ranking person in the Department of Justice, Solicitor General Robert H. Bork, to fire Cox. The public outcry provoked by the so-called Saturday Night Massacre compelled the president to agree to the appointment of a new special prosecutor, Leon Jaworski. When Nixon still refused to surrender the tapes, Jaworski took him to court.

In the same month as the Saturday Night Massacre, the Nixon administration was stung by another scandal. Vice President Spiro Agnew resigned after pleading no contest to charges of income-tax evasion and acceptance of bribes when he was governor of Maryland. Under the provisions of the Twenty-fifth Amendment, ratified in 1967 after President Kennedy's assassination, Nixon nominated Gerald R. Ford, the House minority leader from Michigan, to replace Agnew. Ford's voting

Agnew's Resignation

record was conservative—he had opposed most of the 1960s reform legislation—but he was popular on Capitol Hill, and his nomination was promptly confirmed by Congress.

Throughout 1973 and 1974, enterprising reporters uncovered more details of the break-in, the hush money, and the various people from Nixon on down who had taken part in the cover-up. White House aides and CREEP subordinates began to go on trial, and Nixon was cited as an "unindicted co-conspirator." *Washington Post* reporters Carl Bernstein and Bob Woodward found an informant, known as Deep Throat, who provided damning information about Nixon and his aides. As Nixon's protestations of innocence became less credible, his hold on the tapes became more tenuous. In late April 1974 the president finally released an edited transcript of the recorded conversations.

The edited transcript, however, had a lot of gaps. It swayed neither the public nor the House Judiciary Committee, which had begun to draft articles of impeachment against the president. Nixon still was trying to hang onto the original tapes when the Supreme Court in July, in *U.S. v. Nixon*, unanimously ordered him to surrender the recordings to Judge Sirica. At about the same time, the Judiciary Committee conducted nationally televised hearings. After several days of testimony, the committee voted for impeachment on three of five counts: obstruction of justice through the payment of hush money to witnesses, lying, and withholding evidence; defiance of a congressional subpoena of the tapes; and use of the CIA, the FBI, and the Internal Revenue Service to deprive Americans of their constitutional rights of privacy and free speech.

On August 6 the president finally handed over the complete tapes, which he knew would condemn him.

Nixon's Resignation

Three days later he became the first president to resign from office. Nixon's successor was Gerald Ford. The first substantive act of the new president was to pardon Nixon. When the pardon was announced, some people concluded that Ford and Nixon had struck a deal.

The Watergate scandal prompted the reform of abuses that predated the Nixon administration. The executive's usurpation of legislative prerogatives, which historian Arthur M. Schlesinger, Jr., called "the imperial presidency," dated from Franklin D. Roosevelt's administration. Roosevelt had signed executive agreements that were in effect treaties with foreign nations, but he never sent them to the Senate for its advice and consent. Presidents Truman and Johnson had led the nation into the Korean and Vietnam Wars without securing a congressional declaration of war as required by the Constitution. And President Nixon had impounded—that is, refused to spend—federal funds appropriated for health, the environment, space exploration, and other programs.

To end the nation's participation in undeclared wars, Congress in 1973 overrode Nixon's veto and passed the War Powers Act, which

Post-Watergate Restrictions on Executive Power

mandated that "in every possible instance" the president must consult with Congress before sending American troops into foreign wars. Under this law the president could commit American troops abroad for no more than sixty days, after which he had to obtain congressional approval. (The act did not specify what Congress could do if the president refused to comply.) The next year Congress approved the Congressional Budget and Impoundment Control Act, which prohibited the impounding of federal money. Finally, to aid citizens who were victims of dirty-tricks campaigns, in 1974 Congress strengthened the Freedom of Information Act of 1966. The new legislation, which Congress passed over President Ford's veto, permitted access to government documents and provided penalties if the government "arbitrarily or capriciously" withheld such information.

Summary

The 1960s had begun with high hopes for a more democratic America. Starting with the first sit-ins in 1960, civil rights volunteers spread the quest for racial equality to all parts of the country. And activists in this movement were among the founders of other protest movements, including feminism, the New Left, Black Power, gay rights, and emerging civil rights movements for Native Americans and Mexican Americans. Although these movements achieved notable goals, including landmark civil rights legislation, another legacy was political disenchantment in the United States.

The thirteen years coinciding with the presidencies of John Kennedy, Lyndon Johnson, and Richard Nixon were a period of increasing disillusionment. As historian James T. Patterson observed, the period be-

gan with "grand expectations" about the attainability of "the Good Life." But riots in cities, violence on campus, diminished respect for government leaders, and growing economic uncertainty shattered Americans' illusions and supplanted earlier hopes for peaceful social change. "Americans had gone into the age of Kennedy and Nixon convinced that their government's action . . . could make over the world, at home and abroad," journalist Godfrey Hodgson explained, but "they had been burned." They had learned some hard lessons: how much harder it was to change the world than they thought it would be, and how there often was "little that political action could achieve, however idealistic its intentions, without evoking unforeseen and unwanted reaction."

When John F. Kennedy delivered his inaugural address in 1961, he challenged Americans to "pay any price, bear any burden, meet any hardship" to defend freedom and inspire the world. Twelve years later, Richard M. Nixon echoed that rhetoric: "Let us pledge to make these four years the best four years in America's history, so that on its 200th birthday America will be as young and vital as when it began, and as bright a beacon of hope for all the world." Largely because of his own actions, however, Nixon resigned the presidency before the nation could celebrate its bicentennial in 1976. Rather than young and vital, America seemed bruised and battered.

LEGACY FOR A PEOPLE AND A NATION
Watergate and Political Reforms

The legacy of Watergate has helped to undermine, if not destroy, many Americans' trust in their government. For the past twenty-five years, Watergate has contributed greatly to political cynicism, and it has cast a shadow over the presidencies of all of Nixon's successors, from Gerald Ford to Bill Clinton. Its legacy is evident in the proliferation of special prosecutors, independent counsels, and congressional investigating committees, not to mention TV and newspaper reporters, who have examined political and personal behavior in the White House as never before. Both John F. Kennedy and Lyndon B. Johnson were widely known to be philanderers, yet the press subscribed to an unwritten code that held that such behavior was off-limits to reporters. This hands-off decorum all changed with Watergate. After 1974 Washington became an increasingly paranoiac and cynical place where even the smallest presidential mistakes were scrutinized and vilified.

In 1978 Congress passed the Ethics in Government Act authorizing the appointment of special prosecutors to investigate criminal wrongdoing in the White House. Sometimes, the controversial decisions and behavior were substantive, such as Ronald Reagan's Iran-contra affair and Bill Clinton's host of scandals, including a sexual relationship with a White House intern. The last special prosecutor, known as an independent counsel, was Kenneth Starr, who in more than five years of investigating scandals in the Clinton White House spent $48 million for private investigators, office space, computers, travel, and other expenses. In 1999 the independent counsel law expired and was not extended.

Watergate's legacy, however, is not limited to scandal-mongering. Soon after Nixon's resignation, Congress made a modest attempt to reduce campaign fundraising abuses, setting ceilings on campaign contributions. However, instead of limiting such abuses, this legislation provided new loopholes for electioneers to exploit. To circumvent the ceilings on contributions, special-interest groups established political-action committees (PACs). In 1980 there were 2,765 PACs, more than four times as many as in 1974. Moreover, Capitol Hill was crawling as never before with lobbyists from trade associations, corporations, labor unions, and single-issue groups such as the National Rifle Association. As the influence of money in politics has grown in the aftermath of Watergate, so too has political disillusionment. In the 1998 congressional elections, spending on television advertising, largely negative "attack" ads, reached an all-time high, while voter turnout was the lowest in fifty-six years.

For Further Reading, see page A-36 of the Appendix. For Web resources, go to http://college.hmco.com.

South Vietnam was "crumbling fast," Secretary of Defense Robert McNamara remarked. So the Joint Chiefs of Staff boldly recommended that another hundred thousand American troops be added to the eighty thousand already in Vietnam. In a tense meeting on July 21, 1965, President Lyndon B. Johnson asked his advisers, "Is there anyone here of the opinion we should not do what the [JCS] memorandum says?" Only Undersecretary of State George Ball spoke up: "I can foresee a perilous voyage." Johnson responded, "What other road can I go?" Ball answered, "Take our losses, let their government fall apart, negotiate, discuss, knowing full well there will be a probable takeover by the Communists." The president, imbued with the Cold War mentality, recoiled from the conclusion that what he once called a "damn little pissant country" could deny victory to the United States.

At an afternoon session, Ball again forthrightly argued a case few of his colleagues endorsed. "The war will be long and protracted. The most we can hope for is a messy conclusion." Not only did dangers arise from possible Chinese intervention, negative world opinion, and domestic political dissent, but "the enemy cannot be seen in Vietnam. He is indigenous to the country." Ball doubted that "an army of Westerners can successfully fight Orientals in an Asian jungle." Remember what happened to France. In the long run, he insisted, "the war will disclose our weakness, not our strength." Worried about U.S. credibility, Johnson jumped in: "But, George, wouldn't all these countries say that Uncle Sam was a paper tiger?" "No sir," Ball retorted. "The worse blow would be that the mightiest power on earth is unable to defeat a handful of guerrillas."

The next day Johnson met with top military officials. They told him that more men, more bombings, and more money were needed to save America's ally South Vietnam from defeat at the hands of North Vietnamese and Vietcong forces. "But if we put in 100,000 men," the president asked, "won't they put in an equal number, and then where will we be?" And have the bombing raids hurt the enemy? Not really, the generals answered, but they would if more sites

In Chu Lai, Vietnam, U.S. soldiers of the 1st Cavalry Division (Airmobile) leap from a helicopter during Operation Oregon in 1967. (Sgt. Howard Breedlove, DASPO, U.S. Army)

DISASTER AND DÉTENTE: THE COLD WAR, VIETNAM, AND THE THIRD WORLD 1961–1989

were added to the target list. Johnson wondered: "Isn't this going off the diving board?" When McNamara argued that the United States had a commitment to South Vietnam and that America's credibility was on the line, Johnson shot back: "But, if you make a commitment to jump off a building and you find out how high it is, you may want to withdraw that commitment."

After asking searching questions and even revealing some doubts, Johnson nonetheless rejected a withdrawal strategy and gave the Joint Chiefs of Staff what they wanted. He thought that America could win the war. A turning point in the Vietnam War, this decision meant that the United States was for the first time assuming primary responsibility for fighting the war. Fearing that he might spark a national debate about the deepening U.S. role, Johnson practiced subterfuge, deliberately underplaying the decision's importance when he announced it. He chose to deceive the American people because if the public focused its attention on the war, he argued, his Great Society reform legislation might be derailed: his reform supporters might splinter and conservatives might cut his domestic budget in order to pay for the mounting costs of war.

By the end of 1965, nearly two hundred thousand American combat troops were at war in Vietnam. Yet Congress had not passed a declaration of war, and most of the American people remained ignorant of the venture. Ball later called Johnson's July decision "the greatest single error that America had made in its national history." McNamara, who vigorously challenged Ball's case in 1965, later wrote that he, McNamara, has been "wrong." Indeed, he conceded, "we were sinking into quicksand."

Vietnam bedeviled the United States from 1945, the year Vietnamese nationalists declared independence from France, to well beyond 1975, the year the last Americans withdrew in defeat. Presidents Truman and Eisenhower had taken the Cold War perspective and attempted to roll back the Vietnamese independence movement (see Chapter 29). President John F. Kennedy, sharing the Cold War faith and fearing that Communist China was expanding into Vietnam, greatly enlarged the U.S. presence there. Johnson "Americanized" the war, increasing U.S. troops to more than half a million. Presidents Richard Nixon and Gerald Ford pulled out American soldiers while further punishing the enemy in an attempt not to lose the war. Their successors had to deal with defeat and the anguished aftermath of America's longest war.

While the Vietnam War intensified, the Cold War that Truman and Eisenhower had waged became even more acrimonious, engulfing much of the world. Interventions and dangerous confrontations in the Third World, the nuclear arms race, propagandistic shouting matches, and brinkmanship unsettled people everywhere. The Cuban missile crisis of 1962 brought the Soviet Union and the United States close to nuclear disaster. In its drive to win the Cold War, deter neutralism, and defuse revolutionary nationalism, the United States employed a host of instruments—foreign aid, CIA covert actions, military assaults, cultural penetration, economic sanctions, and diplomacy, among them. But the world did not become a safer place, and the Vietnam War undermined the Cold War consensus in the United States. Other questions, long dwarfed by the superpower contest and global interventionism, began to crowd onto the international agenda, especially the deteriorating natural environment.

Ultimately the two great powers, the United States and the Soviet Union, weakened by the huge costs of their competition and challenged by other nations demanding that the Cold War end, faced an international system in which power became diffused. In an effort to stem their relative decline, the two adversaries began cautiously in the 1970s to embrace a process of détente, which soon sputtered. In the late 1980s, however, they took important steps toward ending the Cold War. ■

Kennedy's Nation Building, Arms Buildup, and the Cuban Missile Crisis

President John F. Kennedy's views owed much to the past. He criticized the appeasement policy of the 1930s for abetting aggressors (see page 742) and praised the containment doctrine of the 1940s for thwarting communists (see page 826). An eloquent speaker and fierce competitor known for his womanizing and cultivated image of manliness, he vowed to rout communism in the 1960s—to win the missile race, the arms race, the space race, and the race for influence in the Third World. "Everyone around him thought he had the Midas touch and could not lose," remarked an assistant, the historian Arthur M. Schlesinger, Jr. Kennedy's arrogant national security affairs adviser, McGeorge Bundy, asserted that "the United States is the engine of mankind, and the rest of the world is the

IMPORTANT EVENTS

1961 Kennedy becomes president
Peace Corps is initiated
Invasion at Cuba's Bay of Pigs fails
Alliance for Progress begins
Berlin Wall is built
Kennedy increases aid to South Vietnam

1962 Agreement on neutralizing Laos
Cuban missile crisis courts nuclear war

1963 Treaty bans atmospheric nuclear testing
U.S. cooperates in removal of Diem
Johnson becomes president

1964 Tonkin Gulf Resolution permits wider war

1965 Operation Rolling Thunder bombs North
Vietnam
Johnson increases troop strength in Vietnam
Antiwar teach-ins and demonstrations begin

1966 Fulbright's Senate hearings on Vietnam

1967 Six-Day War in the Middle East

1968 Tet Offensive sets back U.S. objectives
Dollar/gold crisis threatens U.S. economy
My Lai massacre leaves hundreds dead
U.S. invades Dominican Republic
Vietnam peace talks open in Paris

1969 Nixon becomes president; promotes détente
"Vietnamization" begins exit of U.S. troops
Nixon Doctrine calls for self-help by nations

1970 U.S. ratifies 1968 nuclear nonproliferation
treaty
Invasion of Cambodia sparks demonstrations
Senate repeals Tonkin Gulf Resolution

1971 *Pentagon Papers* reveal lies by U.S. leaders

1972 Nixon's trip to China thaws relations
SALT-I treaty limits nuclear weapons
"Christmas bombing" of North Vietnam

1973 Vietnam cease-fire agreement
Allende ousted in Chile
Arab-Israeli war and oil embargo
War Powers Act restricts president

1974 Ford becomes president
U.N. proposes "New International
Economic Order"

1975 Vietnam reunified under Communist rule
Helsinki accords endorse human rights

1977 Carter becomes president

1978 Senate approves Panama Canal treaties
Mideast peace accord made at Camp David

1979 SALT-II treaty recognizes nuclear parity
Hostages taken in Iran after shah falls
Soviets invade Afghanistan

1980 U.S. grain embargo and Olympics boycott
against USSR
Carter Doctrine for Persian Gulf

1981 Reagan becomes president
American hostages released in Iran
U.S. intervenes in Central America
Nuclear freeze movement grows worldwide

1982 U.S. troops intervene in Lebanon
START talks over nuclear forces begin
Law of the Sea Convention adopted, but not
by U.S.

1983 Reagan introduces SDI
Soviets shoot down Korean airliner
U.S. deploys Pershing missiles in Europe
Terrorists kill U.S. Marines in Lebanon
U.S. invasion of Grenada

1984 Reagan aids contras despite congressional ban

1985 Reagan Doctrine extols "freedom fighters"
Gorbachev promotes reforms in USSR
Geneva summit collapses over SDI

1986 Iran-contra scandal
U.S. economic sanctions against South Africa

1987 INF Treaty bans some missiles in Europe

1988 Negotiated settlement in Namibia

caboose." Kennedy's inaugural address suggested no halfway measures: "Let every nation know that we shall pay any price, bear any burden, meet any hardship, support any friend, oppose any foe to assure the survival and the success of liberty." A skeptical Adlai Stevenson, U.S. ambassador to the United Nations, told a friend that "they've got the damnedest bunch of boy commandos running around down there [in Washington] you ever saw."

After Khrushchev endorsed "wars of national liberation" such as the one in Vietnam, Kennedy called for "peaceful revolution" based on the concept of nation building. The administration set out to help developing nations through the early stages of nationhood

Seventy-year-old Lillian Carter, mother of future president Jimmy Carter, served as a Peace Corps volunteer in India in 1967–1968. Here she treats a tuberculosis patient. Most volunteers were young people better able to withstand difficult conditions, but Lillian Carter seldom shrunk from challenge, even when she became very homesick. "I've forgotten luxuries and most comforts," she wrote home. "I helped Dr. Bhatia today, and gave injections to three hundred and fifty children. I am so tired and REFRESHED!" As she prepared to leave India, she penned another letter: "I didn't dream that in this remote corner of the world . . . I would discover what Life is really all about. Sharing yourself with others, and accepting their love of you, is the most precious gift of all."   (National Archives)

Nation Building and Counterinsurgency

with aid programs aimed at improving agriculture, transportation, and communications. Kennedy thus initiated the multibillion-dollar Alliance for Progress in 1961 to spur economic development in Latin America. That year Kennedy also created the Peace Corps. This agency sent thousands of American teachers, agricultural specialists, and health workers into developing nations. The Peace Corps's humanitarian purpose, however, sometimes competed with the administration's political agenda. Conflicts arose between corps members in the field, many of whom identified with Third World peoples' desire for neutrality in the Cold War, and headquarters in Washington, where the goal was aligning those peoples with U.S. foreign policy. One group of corps volunteers—depicting themselves as "Marines in velvet gloves"—protested their role as instruments of policymakers.

Kennedy also relied on counterinsurgency to defeat revolutionaries who challenged Third World governments friendly with the United States. American military and technical advisers trained native troops and police forces to quell unrest. And American soldiers—especially the Special Forces (Green Berets)—provided a protective shield against insurgents while American civilian personnel worked on economic projects.

Nation building and counterinsurgency seldom worked. The Alliance for Progress stumbled; infant mortality rates improved, but Latin American economies registered unimpressive growth rates and class divisions continued to widen, exacerbating political unrest. Americans assumed that the U.S. model of capitalism and representative government could be transferred successfully to foreign cultures. But, although many foreign peoples welcomed U.S. economic assistance and craved U.S. material culture, they resented meddling by outsiders. And because aid was usually funneled through a self-interested elite, it often failed to reach the very poor. To people who preferred the relatively quick solutions of a managed economy, moreover, the American emphasis on private enterprise seemed inappropriate.

Under Kennedy, the CIA continued its covert operations, including training the Cuban exile brigade and Operation Mongoose against Cuba (see page 888). The agency also plotted in the Congo in 1960 and 1961 to poison Premier Patrice Lumumba with a lethal injection of a virus. A CIA-backed Congolese political faction finally murdered Lumumba, who had turned to the Soviet Union for help during a civil war. In Brazil the CIA spent $20 million to influence the 1962 elections against President João Goulart, who had expropriated the property of the U.S.-based firm International Telephone and Telegraph and had refused to vote to oust Cuba from the Organization of American States. When Goulart's supporters won, the CIA helped organize opposition groups. In 1964, with U.S. complicity, the Brazilian military overthrew Goulart.

In fall 1961 the Soviet Union ended its moratorium on above-ground nuclear testing by exploding a giant 50-megaton bomb. Khrushchev also bragged about Soviet ICBMs, raising American anxiety over Soviet capabilities. Intelligence

Military Expansion

data soon demonstrated that there was no "missile gap"—except the one in America's favor. Kennedy nonetheless sought to fulfill his campaign commitment to a military buildup based on the principle of flexible response: the capability to make any kind of war, from guerrilla combat to nuclear showdown. Thus the United States would be able to contain both the Soviet Union and revolutionary movements in the Third World. In 1961 the military budget shot up 15 percent; by mid-1964, U.S. nuclear weapons had increased by 150 percent. Government advice to citizens to build fallout shelters in their backyards intensified public fear of devastating war. Kennedy inaugurated the Arms Control and Disarmament Agency and signed the Limited Test Ban Treaty with the Soviet Union (1963), which banned nuclear testing in the atmosphere, in outer space, and under water, but his legacy was an accelerated arms race.

Once again, in 1961, the Soviets demanded negotiations to end Western occupation of West Berlin. Calling the city "the great testing place of Western courage and will," Kennedy rejected negotiations and asked Congress for an additional $3.2 billion for defense. In August the Soviets, at the urging of the East German regime, erected a concrete and barbed-wire barricade to halt the exodus of East Germans into the more prosperous and politically free West Berlin. The Berlin Wall inspired protests

Berlin Wall

When the East Germans first put up the Berlin Wall in 1961, they hastily constructed it of barbed wire. Later they added concrete blocks to the 28-mile barricade that divided East Berlin *(left)* and West Berlin *(right).* The large building with the chariot on top is the Brandenburg Gate. The ugly wall—symbol of the Cold War—came down in 1989, when the long Soviet-American conflict finally waned.   (Corbis-Bettmann)

throughout the noncommunist world, but Kennedy privately sighed that "a wall is a hell of a lot better than a war." The ugly barrier shut off the flow of refugees, and the crisis passed.

U.S. hostilities with Cuba provoked Kennedy's most serious confrontation with the Soviet Union. As in Vietnam, Cold War and Third World issues dramatically intersected in Cuba. Kennedy once acknowledged that most American allies thought the United States had a "fixation" with Cuba. The Eisenhower administration had contested the Cuban Revolution and bequeathed to the Kennedy administration a partially developed CIA plan to overthrow Fidel Castro (see page 847): Cuban exiles would land and secure a beachhead; the Cuban people would rise up against Castro and welcome a new government brought in from the United States. Because he felt uneasy over such a blatant attempt to topple a sovereign government, Kennedy ordered that the U.S. hand be kept hidden—wishful thinking at best given the size of the operation. The president never attempted to negotiate Cuban American troubles with Castro.

Bay of Pigs Invasion

On April 17, 1961, directed by the CIA and escorted by U.S. warships, some fourteen hundred commandos scrambled ashore at the Bay of Pigs (*Bahía de Cochinos*). A CIA scheme to assassinate Castro before the invasion had faltered. The Cuban people did not rise up against Castro. Within two days most of the invaders had been captured by Cubans loyal to Castro. Although Kennedy refused to order an air strike to aid the invaders when the landing was failing, the operation from the start never had much chance of success. Boats went aground on coral reefs that the CIA had identified as seaweed, and equipment malfunctioned. If the exiles had managed to move inland, they would have faced Castro's large armed militia. Before the operation was over, 4 Americans, 114 Cuban exile invaders, and 150 Cuban defenders had died. As for Castro, the Bay of Pigs invasion helped him remain popular as a nationalist hero, as did his land reform and improvements in healthcare and education. Concluding that the United States would not take defeat well and might launch another invasion, the Cuban leader looked even more toward the Soviet Union for a military and economic lifeline.

Kennedy vowed to bring Castro down. His brother, Attorney General Robert Kennedy, promised "to stir things up on the island with espionage, sabotage, [and] general disorder." The CIA soon hatched a project called Operation Mongoose to disrupt the is-

land's trade, support raids on Cuba from Miami, and plot with organized-crime bosses to assassinate Castro. The United States also tightened its economic blockade, engineered Cuba's eviction from the Organization of American States, and undertook military maneuvers in the Caribbean. The Joint Chiefs of Staff sketched plans to spark a rebellion in Cuba that would be followed by an invasion of U.S. troops. "If I had been in Moscow or Havana at that time," Defense Secretary Robert McNamara later remarked, "I would have believed the Americans were preparing for an invasion."

Had there been no Bay of Pigs invasion, no Operation Mongoose, no assassination plots, no program of diplomatic and economic isolation, and no military maneuvers and planning, there would have been no missile crisis. Cuba would have had no urgent need for Soviet military assistance. For Castro, relentless U.S. hostility represented a real threat to Cuba's independence. For the Soviets, American actions challenged the only procommunist regime in Latin America. Premier Khrushchev also saw an opportunity to improve the Soviet position in the nuclear arms race. Castro and Khrushchev devised a risky plan to deter any new U.S. intervention. In mid-1962 they agreed to install in Cuba nuclear armed missiles capable of hitting the United States. The world soon faced brinkmanship at its most frightening.

Cuban Missile Crisis

In mid-October 1962 a U-2 plane flying over Cuba photographed missile sites. The president immediately organized a special Executive Committee of advisers to find a way to force the missiles and their nuclear warheads out of Cuba. Some members advised a surprise air strike. The Joint Chiefs of Staff recommended a full-scale military invasion, an option that risked a prolonged war with Cuba, a Soviet attack against West Berlin, or even nuclear holocaust. The diplomat Charles Bohlen, a U.S. expert on Soviet affairs, unsuccessfully urged quiet, direct negotiations with Moscow. McNamara proposed the formula that the president accepted: a naval quarantine of Cuba.

Kennedy addressed the nation on television on October 22 to demand that the Soviets retreat. U.S. warships began crisscrossing the Caribbean, while B-52s with nuclear bombs took to the skies. Khrushchev replied that the missiles would be withdrawn if Washington pledged never to attack Cuba. And he added that American Jupiter missiles aimed at the Soviet Union must be removed from Turkey. Edgy advisers predicted war, but on October 28 came a Soviet-American compromise. The United States promised

How do historians know...

that, at the outset of the Cuban missile crisis, President John F. Kennedy preferred military action to diplomacy to force out the Soviet missiles? Months before that dangerous October 1962 crisis, Kennedy had ordered the Secret Service to install an audio-tape system to record White House meetings. The system recorded its first meeting on July 30, 1962. A Dictabelt system for recording telephone conversations was installed later, in early September. Besides Kennedy himself, only the president's personal secretary, two Secret Service agents, and possibly the president's brother Robert knew about the taping system. Microphones were concealed in light fixtures in the Cabinet Room and in the president's desk in the Oval Office. Kennedy could activate the system by flipping hidden switches. The recording quality proved poor, full of background noise, leaving some words unintelligible.

Whether Kennedy wanted the recordings as an accurate record for future memoirs or as protection against misrepresentations of private discussions, he left historians a rich source on high-level decision making in the White House: 127 audiotapes (248 hours) and 73 Dictabelts (12 hours) on wide-ranging topics. During the missile crisis, Kennedy regularly convened and taped meetings of an advisory Executive Committee. Shown below is an excerpt from the transcript of the committee's first meeting, 11:50 A.M. to 12:57 P.M., October 16, 1962, in which the president emphasizes "taking out" the missiles.

Some three decades after the event, the John F. Kennedy Library in Boston declassified the recordings, making them available to researchers. A Harvard University project headed by Ernest R. May and Philip D. Zelikow transcribed the recordings and published the results as *The Kennedy Tapes* (1997). Because of such tapes, historians can study the minute-by-minute, hour-by-hour handling of significant issues, in this case a crisis that brought the Soviet Union and the United States to the nuclear brink. (Photo: John F. Kennedy Library)

JFK?:	. . . is to figure out what are the minimum number of people that we really have to tell. ▓▓▓▓▓▓▓▓▓▓▓▓▓▓▓▓
Bundy:	Right. ▓▓▓▓▓▓▓▓▓▓▓▓▓▓▓▓ You've got to tell, it seems to me you're going to have to tell SACEUR*** . . .
JFK:	Umm.
Bundy:	. . . and, uh, and the commandant.
Dillon:	I would think this business about the Soviet reaction, that there, that might be helpful, uh, if we could maybe take some, uh, general war preparation type of action that would show them that we're ready if they want to start anything, without what you might, with starting anything.
Bundy:	One. . . .
Dillon:	You just don't know.
Bundy:	On this track, one obvious element on the political side is do we say something simultaneously or, uh, to the Cubans, to the Soviets, or do we let the action speak for itself?
Rusk:	This point whether we say something to the Cubans and the Soviets before any, before . . .
JFK:	I think we ought to, what we ought to do is, is, uh, after this meeting this afternoon, we ought to meet tonight again at six, consider these various, uh, proposals. In the meanwhile, we'll go ahead with this maximum, whatever is needed from the flights, and, in addition, we will. . . . I don't think we got much time on these missiles. They may be. . . . So it may be that we just have to, we can't wait two weeks while we're getting ready to, to roll. Maybe just have to just take them out, and continue our other preparations if we decide to do that. That may be where we end up. I think we ought to, beginning right now, be preparing to. . . . Because that's what we're going to do anyway. We're certainly going to do number one; we're going to take out these, uh, missiles. Uh, the questions will be whether, which, what I would describe as number two, which would be a general air strike. That we're not ready to say, but we should be in preparation for it. The third is the, is the, uh, the general invasion. At least we're going to do number one, so it seems to me that we don't have to wait very long. We, we ought to be making those preparations.
Bundy:	You want to be clear, Mr. President, whether we have definitely decided against a political track. I, myself, think we ought . . .

***Supreme Allied Commander, Europe.

not to invade Cuba and secretly pledged to withdraw the Jupiters from Turkey in exchange for the withdrawal of Soviet offensive forces from Cuba. Fearing accidents or some provocative action by Castro that might start a "real fire," Khrushchev decided to settle without consulting the Cubans. The missiles departed Cuba.

"I cut his balls off," Kennedy privately crowed to friends. Forcing Khrushchev to back down, many said, was his finest hour. But critics then and now hold Kennedy responsible in the first place for provoking the crisis through his anti-Cuban projects. These critics also reject the view that Kennedy practiced an exemplary model of crisis management. His handling of the crisis actually courted disaster. Accidents, near misses, and inadequate information caused events to come close to spinning out of control. On October 27, for example, a Soviet commander shot down a U-2 plane over Cuba. The Americans prepared to retaliate, not knowing that Soviet commanders had tactical nuclear weapons to use against an invasion. Robert Kennedy himself feared "a chain reaction will quickly start that will be very hard to stop." That same day, a U.S. military jet mistakenly crossed into Soviet territory, nearly setting off an air war. Finally, critics have argued that the strategic balance of power was not seriously altered by the missiles in Cuba; the United States still enjoyed a tremendous advantage over the Soviets in the nuclear arms race. Did Kennedy risk doomsday unnecessarily?

Kennedy's Handling of the Crisis

The Cuban missile crisis both calmed and accelerated the Cold War. In June 1963 Kennedy spoke at American University in conciliatory terms, urging cautious Soviet-American steps toward disarmament. In August the adversaries signed a treaty banning nuclear tests in the atmosphere. They also installed a coded wire-telegraph "hot line" staffed around the clock by translators and technicians. Both sides refrained from further confrontation in Berlin. Still, humiliated by the missile crisis, the Soviets determined to catch up in the nuclear arms race, sending the Cold War to a more dangerous stage. In mid-1963 Castro, seeking an accommodation with Washington because he was still angry with Moscow for failing to consult him during the missile crisis, directed "feelers" toward U.S. diplomats. Kennedy authorized contacts with Cuban intermediaries, but in June he also approved a new sabotage program against Cuba. The

Aftermath

CIA at the same time revitalized assassination plots, all of which failed. After Kennedy's death, Johnson decided to put the cautious diplomatic contacts "on ice," words that well describe the years of Cuban-U.S. antagonism that followed. Wondering why the United States did not simply overpower his small island nation, Castro later remarked that Cuba was "saved by Vietnam" because "the immense American drive that went into Vietnam" might very well "have been turned against Cuba."

Johnson and Americanization of the War in Vietnam

 Kennedy's successor, Lyndon B. Johnson, held firmly to ideas about U.S. superiority and the menace of communism. A supreme can-do politician from Texas—a "flawed giant" of a man, according to one biographer—Johnson saw the world in simple, bipolar terms: them against us, and he saw a lot of "them." A fierce competitor, Johnson once declared that he had sex with more women by accident than Kennedy had on purpose. Invoking macho images of a fight-to-the-last-man Alamo, Johnson often exaggerated, went into rages, and lied. He opened a credibility gap with the American people, many of whom came to wonder if he could tell the difference between truth and falsehood. An old New Dealer and ardent liberal reformer, the president talked about building Tennessee Valley Authorities around the world. "I want them to say, 'This is what Americans left—schools and hospitals and dams.'" The general problem, said Senator J. William Fulbright, chair of the Foreign Relations Committee, was that an "arrogance of power" made Americans such as Johnson believe that they could run the world.

Championing the global containment doctrine and holding a monolithic view of communism, Johnson drew the line not only in Southeast Asia but also in Latin America. In spring 1965, with the president fearing "another Cuba," twenty-three thousand U.S. troops landed in the Dominican Republic to prevent a leftist government from coming to power. Johnson growled, "What the hell can we do in Vietnam if we can't clean up the Dominican Republic?" His disparaging view of Dominicans (they needed "cleaning up") and continued worries about anti-Americanism led to U.S. backing of a dictatorship on the island that lasted some thirty years.

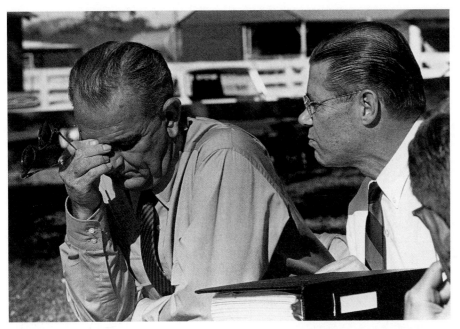

President Lyndon B. Johnson (1908–1973) *(left),* here meeting with Secretary of Defense Robert S. McNamara (b. 1919) at the president's Texas ranch in December 1964, agonized over the Vietnam War. That year, recorded telephone conversations reveal, the president remarked that the war was "just the biggest damn mess I ever saw." Johnson also lamented that "I don't think it's worth fighting for, and I don't think we can get out." Later, McNamara wrote in his memoir, *In Retrospect* (1995), that U.S. officials "acted according to what we thought were the principles and traditions of this nation. We made our [Vietnam] decisions in light of those values. Yet we were wrong, terribly wrong."   (Yoichi R. Okamoto/Lyndon B. Johnson Library)

As both the United States and the Soviet Union grew more alarmed by China's nuclear capability (the Chinese detonated their first atomic bomb in 1964), the Johnson administration in 1968 successfully completed negotiations for the Treaty on the Non-proliferation of Nuclear Weapons (which went into effect in 1970). But many nonnuclear states saw discrimination because they had to renounce nuclear weapons while the nuclear states (United States, Soviet Union, Britain, France, and China) could keep them. The treaty ran into other obstacles. Both France and China refused to sign the agreement and supplied nonnuclear countries with nuclear fuel, and other nations defied the treaty by eventually developing their own nuclear weapons—Israel, South Africa, India, and Pakistan, among them. The Soviet invasion of Czechoslovakia in 1968 to block a nationalist movement caused Johnson to shelve further arms-control talks. With the Soviet Union and

Nuclear Non-proliferation Treaty

the United States backing opposing forces in the Vietnam War, opportunities for relaxing the Cold War diminished even more.

Some observers called it "Johnson's War," but President Kennedy had significantly deepened U.S. engagement in Vietnam, where Ho Chi Minh's North assisted the Vietcong in the South to advance the reunification of his country under a Communist government. Kennedy stepped up aid dollars to the Diem regime in the South, increased the airdropping of raiding teams into North Vietnam, and launched crop destruction by herbicides to starve the Vietcong and expose their hiding places. Under Project Beef-up, he sent more U.S. military personnel to South Vietnam; by late 1963 some 16,000 of these American "advisers" operated in Vietnam, and, that year, 489 of them were killed.

Meanwhile, Diem's opponents grew in number. The U.S. Strategic Hamlet Program, which aimed to

Kennedy's Legacy in Vietnam

Map 31.1   Southeast Asia and the Vietnam War   To prevent communists from coming to power in Vietnam, Cambodia, and Laos in the 1960s, the United States intervened massively in Southeast Asia. The interventions failed, and the remaining American troops made a hasty exit from Vietnam in 1975, when the victorious Vietcong and North Vietnamese took Saigon and renamed it Ho Chi Minh City.

isolate peasants from the Vietcong by uprooting them into barbed-wire compounds, alienated villagers. Buddhist priests charged Diem with religious persecution. In the streets of Saigon, protesting monks poured gasoline over their robes and ignited themselves. Diem ran a corrupt government that handed out financial favors to family and friends. He jailed critics to silence them. U.S. officials, with Kennedy's approval, encouraged ambitious South Vietnamese generals to remove Diem. Working with a CIA agent, the generals struck on November 1, 1963, capturing and murdering Diem. Worried that the new military junta's reputation would be immediately sullied if the truth became known—that its leader had ordered the assassination of Diem—Kennedy engineered a cover-up. "It ought to be a true story," Kennedy told his aides, "if possible." Just a few weeks later Kennedy himself met death by an assassin's bullet.

With new governments in Saigon and in Washington, some analysts urged a reassessment. United Nations, Vietcong, and French leaders called for a coalition government in South Vietnam. But Lyndon Johnson vowed victory. On August 2, 1964, the U.S.S. *Maddox*, sailing in the Gulf of Tonkin off the coast of North Vietnam on an electronic intelligence–gathering patrol in an area where South Vietnamese commando raids recently had hit North Vietnam, came under attack from northern patrol boats (see Map 31.1). The unharmed *Maddox* inflicted heavy damage on the small craft. Two days later, the *Maddox*, joined by another destroyer, moved toward the North Vietnamese shore once again. In bad weather on a moonless night, sonar technicians reported torpedo attacks; the two destroyers began firing ferociously. Johnson quickly informed his advisers that the United States would retaliate. But then the *Maddox* sent a flash message: "Review of action makes many reported contacts and torpedoes fired appear doubtful." Indeed, no attack occurred on the pitch-black night of August 4; the *Maddox*'s sonar had probably picked up the noise of the destroyer itself. "Those dumb, stupid sailors," Johnson later said, "were just shooting at flying fish!"

President Johnson, aware at the time that the evidence was questionable, nonetheless pulled from his desk a resolution for Congress that he had had drafted months before. He announced on television that the United States would strike back against the "unprovoked" attack in the Tonkin Gulf by bombing North Vietnam. After this presidential deception and only brief debate, Congress passed the Tonkin Gulf Resolution, by 466 votes to 0 in the House and by 88 votes to 2 in the Senate. Only Wayne Morse of Oregon and Ernest Gruening of Alaska dissented from the resolution's sweeping language, which authorized the president to "take all necessary measures to repel any armed attack against the forces of the United States and to prevent further aggression." By passing the Tonkin Gulf Resolution—which Johnson considered nearly equivalent to a declaration of war—Congress essentially surrendered its powers in the foreign policy

Tonkin Gulf Incident

Senator J. William Fulbright (1905–1995), a Democrat from Arkansas who studied at Oxford as a Rhodes scholar and helped create the Fulbright scholarships, chaired the Foreign Relations Committee from 1959 to 1974. His committee held hearings and published reports to inform the public about the Vietnam War, which Fulbright increasingly saw as immoral and dangerous to U.S. interests. He opposed the bombing campaigns and the deepening U.S. intervention, arguing that the war undermined détente with the Soviet Union, threatened war with China, alienated the Third World, and corrupted American values. An intemperate President Lyndon B. Johnson, who Fulbright believed had misled him in order to gain his vote for the Tonkin Gulf Resolution, fumed against the senator, ridiculously suggesting that he was a communist dupe and tagging him "half-bright."   (Library of Congress)

process by giving the president wide latitude to conduct the war as he saw fit. The resolution, McNamara later noted, served "to open the floodgates."

Meanwhile, in Laos, Vietnam's neighbor, American bombers hit the "Ho Chi Minh Trail"—supply routes connecting the Vietcong with the North Vietnamese (see Map 31.1). The bombings were kept secret from Congress and the public. Despite a 1962 agreement among Laotian noncommunists and communists to create a neutralist government, "we ran Laos," Ambassador William H. Sullivan admitted. After winning the presidency in his own right in the fall of 1964, Johnson directed the military to plan stepped-up bombing of both Laos and North

Bombing Campaigns in Laos and Vietnam

Vietnam. Undersecretary Ball urged caution: "Once on the tiger's back we cannot be sure of picking the place to dismount."

In February 1965 the Vietcong, who controlled nearly half of South Vietnam, attacked the American airfield at Pleiku, killing nine Americans. In response, Johnson ordered Operation Rolling Thunder, a sustained bombing program by carrier-based jets that pounded the North (above the 17th parallel). Before the war was over, more bombs would fall on Vietnam than U.S. aircraft had dropped in the Second World War. The North Vietnamese, however, would not give up. They hid in shelters and rebuilt roads and bridges with a perseverance that frustrated and awed American decision makers. The war was not going well for the United States or its ally, the unstable and corrupt South Vietnamese government in Saigon, where hostility festered between Catholics and Buddhists and coups and countercoups by self-serving military leaders undermined U.S. efforts to win the war. "I don't think we ought to take this government seriously," Ambassador Henry Cabot Lodge told a White House meeting. "There is simply no one who can do anything."

Then came Johnson's July decision to increase significantly U.S. ground forces. Month by month the war became Americanized. In 1966 American troops climbed to 385,000. In 1967 alone U.S. warplanes flew 108,000 sorties and dropped 226,000 tons of bombs on North Vietnam. In 1968 U.S. troop strength reached 536,100; in 1969 it peaked at 543,400 before falling by the end of the year to 475,200 (see Figure 31.1). In 1967 the secret CIA-run Phoenix Program began to kill Vietcong leaders; probably 60,000 were assassinated. That year, too, the United States sent $625 million in foreign aid to South Vietnam—25 percent of America's total aid to the entire world. Undeterred, Ho increased the flow of arms and men to the rebels in the South.

Troop Strength

In this seemingly endless war of attrition, each American escalation begot a new Vietnamese escalation. "Vietnam is like being in a plane without a parachute when the engines go out," Johnson remarked. "If you jump, you'll probably be killed, and if you stay in you'll crash and probably burn." Rejecting the Joint Chiefs' view that U.S. reserve forces should be mobilized and a national emergency declared, the president kept thinking that the North Vietnamese and Vietcong, taking heavy casualties, had a breaking point. Johnson also worried that if he did not win that "bitch

Figure 31.1 U.S. Troops in Vietnam, 1960–1972
These numbers show the Americanization of the Vietnam War under President Johnson, who ordered vast increases in troop levels. President Nixon reversed the escalation, so that by the time of the cease-fire in early 1973 fewer than 25,000 American troops remained in Vietnam. Data are for December 31 of each year. (Source: U.S. Department of Defense)

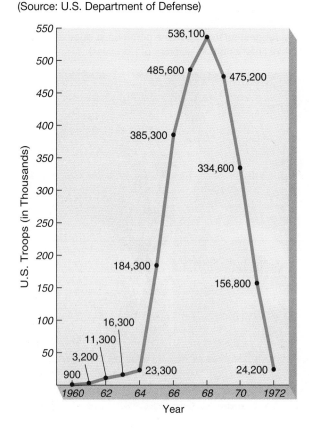

of a war" in Vietnam, members of Congress would cripple his Great Society reform program—"the woman I really loved" (see pages 859–862).

Vietnam: Escalation, Carnage, and Protest

The Americanization of the war under Johnson troubled growing numbers of Americans, especially as television coverage brought the war into their homes every night. Villages went up in flames, innocent civilians were maimed and died, and refugees straggled into "pacification" camps. U.S. planes sprayed chemicals such as Agent Orange to kill crops and forests. This ecological warfare meant that a once-rich agricultural nation became dependent on imports of food. The Vietcong and North Vietnamese contributed to the carnage and destruction, but American guns, bombs, and chemicals took by far the greater toll, and the Vietnamese people knew it. Indeed, America's search-and-destroy missions proved counterproductive; rather than winning the war, they were molding an ever-growing population of anti-American peasants who gave secret aid to the Vietcong. Even U.S. allies among the Vietnamese came to resent their nation's growing dependency. Their politics manipulated and their traditional culture challenged by rock-'n'-roll music, interracial marriages, honky-tonk bars, and prostitution, some anticommunist Vietnamese said that they feared becoming "a little America." One U.S. official later admitted, "It was as if we were trying to build a house with a bulldozer and wrecking crane."

Stories of atrocities made their way home. Most gruesome was the My Lai massacre of March 16, 1968.

My Lai Massacre

The freelance journalist Seymour Hersh broke the story after a military cover-up kept the tragedy out of the news for twenty months. A U.S. army unit led by Lieutenant William Calley entered the hamlet of My Lai and for four hours mutilated, raped, sodomized, and killed unarmed Vietnamese civilians, most of them women and children. Herding shrieking, pleading villagers near a ditch, Calley and his troops shot scores of them. When a two-year-old child, its mother dead, began to crawl out of the mass grave, Calley tossed the infant down the slope and shot it. The army awarded Calley's brigade a Special Commendation for 128 "enemy" killed even though there had been no combat and no

"There's Money Enough To Support Both Of You — Now, Doesn't That Make You Feel Better?"

President Johnson repeatedly claimed that the mounting costs of the war in Vietnam would not drain funds from his domestic reform programs. Others, such as Herblock in this August 1, 1967, cartoon, saw danger. So did Martin Luther King, Jr. He calculated that the United States was spending $500,000 to kill one enemy Vietnamese soldier but only $35 a year to assist one American in poverty. "The promises of the Great Society," King regretted, "have been shot down on the battlefield of Vietnam." (© 1967 by Herblock in *The Washington Post*)

battle at My Lai. The actual death toll numbered some 500.

An army photographer captured the horror in graphic pictures. Why did the massacre occur? Applying a "war is hell" theory, some soldiers explained that they had been trained to kill. Calley fingered anticommunism: "I looked at communism as a southerner looks at a Negro. . . . It's evil." Racism certainly played a role: dehumanizing Vietnamese as "gooks" and "slants," GIs murdered in cold blood people they ranked with animals. A culture of male supremacy, accentuated by the military environment, also influenced these infantrymen: girls and young women suffered gang rapes; some victims had their vaginas ripped

Aftermath of the My Lai massacre, March 16, 1968, photographed by U.S. Army photographer Ronald Haeberle of the 11th Infantry Brigade, Americal Division.   (Ron Haeberle/*Life Magazine* © Time Inc.)

open with knives and bayonets. Calley and the other rapists and killers had lost their moral bearings. But the aftermath reveals that U.S. officials had lost theirs too. In 1971 Calley was court-martialed, but President Nixon ordered him released from jail; three years later the mass murderer was paroled. Army juries acquitted and army officials dismissed murder and cover-up charges against all other personnel connected with the My Lai massacre. Today in Vietnam a museum and monument stand at the site of the massacre. In 1998 the U.S. government awarded the former pilot Hugh Thompson the prestigious Soldier's Medal for his heroism on March 16, 1968, at My Lai: he stopped some of the bloodletting by placing his helicopter between rampaging American GIs and villagers crowded in a hut.

Many incidents of deliberate shooting of civilians, torturing and killing of prisoners, taking of Vietnamese ears as trophies, and burning of villages have been recorded. Most American soldiers, however, were not committing atrocities. They were trying to save their own young lives (their average age was only nineteen)

American Soldiers in Vietnam

and to serve the U.S. mission of defeating enemy troops. Less than 15 percent actually served in combat units; most made up the important rear-echelon supply and medical services that supported the "grunts" in the field. But wherever they were, the environment was inhospitable, for no place in Vietnam was secure. Well-hidden booby traps blasted away body parts. And the enemy was everywhere yet nowhere, often burrowed into elaborate underground tunnels or melded into the population, where any Vietnamese might be a Vietcong.

Infantrymen on maneuvers carried heavy rucksacks into thick jungle growth, where every step was precarious. Insects swarmed, and leeches sucked at weary bodies. Boots and human skin rotted from the rains, which alternated with withering suns. "It was as if the sun and the land itself were in league with the Vietcong," recalled marine officer Philip Caputo in *A Rumor of War* (1977), "wearing us down, driving us mad, killing us." Wounded GIs shouted for a medic, who in turn might call in a "medevac" (medical evacuation helicopter). A medevac could carry the wounded within minutes to operating tables in MASH (Mobile Army Surgical Hospital) units or on hospital ships

Wounded American soldiers after a battle in Vietnam.   (Larry Burrows/*Life* Magazine © Time Warner, Inc.)

such as the U.S.S. *Sanctuary.* "What I saw were young men coming in, eighteen or nineteen years old . . . and they would be without a leg," remembered Gayle Smith, a nurse at the 3rd Surgical Hospital. She was one of 7,465 women who served in the military in Vietnam, most of them army nurses.

As the war ground on to no discernible conclusion and became increasingly unpopular at home, growing numbers of GIs became cynical, believing either that the administration in Washington restrained them from clobbering the enemy or that the United States had no business being in Vietnam. Leaders kept saying that the war was being won, but the GIs in the field knew better. The then Army captain and later chairman of the Joint Chiefs of Staff, Colin Powell, recalled that a "conspiracy of illusion" fed on "the secure-hamlet nonsense, the search-and-sweep nonsense, the body-count nonsense, all of which we knew was nonsense, even as we did it." Body counts of killed "enemy" forces became a false measure of success. Powell remembered the litany of each night: "'How many did your platoon get?' 'I don't

"Body-count Nonsense"

know. We saw two for sure.' 'Well, if you saw two, there were probably eight. So let's say ten.'" Powell later wrote that "counting bodies became a macabre statistical competition. Companies measured against companies, battalions against battalions, brigades against brigades. Good commanders scored high body counts. And good commanders got promotions."

Given these corrupting conditions and the war against what Powell called a "phantom enemy," morale in the U.S. armed forces sagged, and discipline sometimes lapsed. Disobedience, desertions, and absent-without-official-leave (AWOL) cases steadily increased. Racial tensions between whites and blacks intensified. Drug abuse became serious. Many soldiers smoked plentiful, cheap marijuana; 10 percent of the troops used heroin. "Fragging"—the murder of officers by enlisted men, usually using hand grenades— took at least a thousand lives between 1969 and 1972.

At home some young men were expressing their opposition to the war by fleeing the draft. By the end of 1972 more than thirty thousand draft resisters were living in Canada; thousands more had gone into exile in Sweden or Mexico or were living under false identities in the United States. During the war more than a half-million men committed draft violations, including a quarter-million who never registered and thousands who burned their draft cards. Others legally joined the National Guard to avoid the draft.

As American military engagement in Vietnam escalated, so did protest at home. Teach-ins at universities began in 1965, followed by years of campus and street demonstrations (see pages 867–869). In 1966 Senator Fulbright held televised public hearings on whether the national interest was being served by pursuing the war in Asia. What exactly was the threat? senators asked. To the surprise of some, George F. Kennan testified that his containment doctrine was meant for Europe, not the volatile environment of Southeast Asia. A year later, former Attorney General and then Senator Robert Kennedy pressed the president to try negotiations to end the war. In a White House meeting with Kennedy, an enraged Johnson warned, "I'll destroy you and every one of your dove friends." Not so; Kennedy went on to vie for the Democratic presidential nomination in 1968, but an assassin's bullet ended his life that year. In a direct rebuke of Johnson's policies, antiwar senator Eugene McCarthy of Minnesota announced his candidacy for the Democratic presidential nomination.

Growing Antiwar Sentiment

Disenchantment also rose in the administration itself. Defense Secretary Robert McNamara, once a vigorous advocate of prosecuting the war, became aghast over the Joint Chiefs' contemplating the use of nuclear weapons in Vietnam and came to believe that continued bombing would not win the war. "The picture of the world's greatest superpower killing or seriously injuring 1,000 noncombatants a week, while trying to pound a tiny backward nation into submission on an issue whose merits are hotly disputed, is not a pretty one," he told Johnson in mid-1967. But, publicly, McNamara endorsed the war until early 1968, when he left office to head the World Bank. Much later, in his 1995 autobiography, he lamented that the decisions of the Kennedy and Johnson administrations on Vietnam "were wrong, terribly wrong."

McNamara's Doubts

Cheered by opinion polls that showed Americans favored escalation over withdrawal, Johnson dug in, snapping at "those little shits on the campuses." Though on occasion he halted the bombing to encourage Ho Chi Minh to negotiate and to disarm critics, such pauses often were accompanied by increases in American troop strength. And the United States sometimes resumed or accelerated the bombing just when a diplomatic breakthrough seemed imminent—as in 1966, when a Polish diplomat's efforts were cut short by a resumption of bombing. The North demanded a complete suspension of bombing raids before sitting down at the conference table. And Ho could not accept American terms: nonrecognition of the Vietcong as a legitimate political organization, withdrawal of northern soldiers from the South, and an end to North Vietnamese military aid to the Vietcong—in short, abandonment of his lifelong dream of an independent, unified Vietnam.

In January 1968 a shocking event forced Johnson to reappraise his position. During Tet, the Vietnamese holiday of the lunar new year, Vietcong and North Vietnamese forces—intending to "deal" the United States "thundering blows"—struck all across South Vietnam, capturing provincial capitals (see Map 31.1). Vietcong raiders even penetrated the American embassy compound in Saigon. U.S. and South Vietnamese units eventually regained much of the ground they lost, including the cities, and inflicted heavy casualties on the enemy. In the process, numerous villages were devastated. As one sober-faced American officer explained about the leveling of Ben Tre to drive the Vietcong out: "It became necessary to destroy the town to save it."

Tet Offensive

The Tet Offensive jolted Americans. Although Tet ultimately counted as a U.S. military victory, it proved a psychological defeat for the U.S. war effort. Had not the Vietcong and North Vietnamese demonstrated that they could strike when and where they wished? Did they not have the advantage of fighting on home territory? Why did "their Vietnamese" fight harder than "our Vietnamese"? If all of America's airpower and dollars and half a million troops could not defeat the Vietcong once and for all, could anything do so? Had the American public been deceived? The highly respected CBS television anchorman Walter Cronkite went to Vietnam to find out. The military brass in Saigon assured him that "we had the enemy just where we wanted him." The newsman recalled, "Tell that to the Marines, I thought—the Marines in the body bags on that helicopter." When Cronkite somberly raised questions about the war on his evening telecasts, President Johnson sensed political trouble: "If I've lost Cronkite, I've lost middle America."

The new secretary of defense, Clark Clifford, told Johnson that the war—"a sinkhole"—could not be won, even if the 206,000 more soldiers requested by

Dollar/Gold Crisis

the army were sent to Vietnam. The ultimate Cold Warrior, Dean Acheson—one of the "wise men" Johnson brought in to advise him—bluntly told the surprised president that the generals did not know what they were talking about. The wise men were aware that the nation was suffering a financial crisis prompted by rampant deficit spending, largely due to heavy U.S. expenditures abroad to sustain the war and other global commitments. Nervous foreigners were exchanging their U.S. dollars for gold at an alarming rate. On March 14 alone, foreigners—especially Europeans—redeemed $372 million for gold. A post-Tet effort to take the initiative in Vietnam would surely cost billions more and thus further derail the budget, panic foreign owners of dollars, and wreck the economy. Clifford heard from his associates in the business community: "These men now feel we are in a hopeless bog," he told the president. To "maintain public support for the war without the support of these men" was impossible.

Johnson's Exit

Strained by exhausting sessions with skeptical advisers, troubled by the economic implications of escalation, sensing that more soldiers and firepower would not bring victory, meeting protesters wherever he went, and faced with serious opposition within his own party (McCarthy had just made a strong showing in the New Hampshire primary), Johnson changed course. On March 31 he announced that he had stopped the bombing of most of North Vietnam, and he asked Hanoi to begin negotiations. Then he stunned the television audience by dropping out of the presidential race. American leaders, having come reluctantly to the view that they could not win the war, at least would try not to lose it. Peace talks began in May in Paris, but the war ground on.

Nixon, Vietnamization, and the Impact of America's Longest War

"I'm not going to end up like LBJ," Richard Nixon vowed after winning the 1968 presidential election (see page 871). "I'm going to stop that war. Fast." He did not. In July 1969 the new president announced the Nixon Doctrine: the United States will help those nations that help themselves. Washington knew that it no longer could afford to sustain its many overseas commitments and that the United States would have to rely more on regional allies to maintain an anti-

communist world order. In Southeast Asia this doctrine translated into "Vietnamization" —building up South Vietnamese forces to replace U.S. forces. Nixon began to withdraw troops from Vietnam, decreasing their number to 156,800 by the end of 1971. But he also intensified the bombing of the North, hoping to pound Hanoi into concessions. As the death toll mounted in Southeast Asia, antiwar protest in the United States accelerated.

Nixon had been an ardent Cold Warrior before becoming president. Secretive, suspicious, and scowling, he spawned the Watergate political scandal and constitutional crisis that stemmed from his drive to "get" his enemies—especially critics of his Vietnam War policies. He resigned ignobly in 1974, and Gerald Ford succeeded him (see pages 879–880). Nixon believed that leaders earned greatness by acting decisively in "crisis situations" and by creating a "mystique," which "is more important than content." His self-professed "madman theory" was calculated to deter foreign adversaries by making them think that he was unpredictable and irrational—that "I might do *anything*," even use nuclear weapons in Vietnam. His chief foreign policy adviser, Henry A. Kissinger, once observed that Nixon liked the "jugular response" because "there was nothing he feared more than to be thought weak." In relations with China and the Soviet Union, Nixon shifted the Cold War from confrontation to negotiation (see pages 902–903). But in Vietnam, Nixon prolonged the war.

Telling his advisers that withdrawal was "a boy's job," Nixon decided to do a "man's job": in April 1970

Invasion of Cambodia

South Vietnamese and U.S. forces invaded Cambodia in search of arms depots and enemy forces using the neutral nation as a sanctuary. B-52 raids had been bombing Cambodia for more than a year, although Nixon never informed Congress or the American people. But the conspicuous venture into Cambodia could not be kept secret; it especially provoked angry demonstrations on college campuses (see page 873). In June the Senate joined the outcry against Nixon's broadening of the war by terminating the Tonkin Gulf Resolution of 1964.

Nixon's troubles at home mounted in June 1971 when the *New York Times* began to publish the *Pentagon Papers*, a top-secret official study of U.S. decisions in the Vietnam War. Secretary McNamara had initiated the study in 1967 to preserve the war's documentary record. Daniel Ellsberg, a former Defense Department official working at the RAND Corporation (a think tank for analyzing defense policy), leaked the report to the *Times*. Nixon secured an injunction to prevent publication, but the Supreme Court overturned the order. The *Pentagon Papers* revealed that leaders frequently had lied to the American people. President Johnson, for example, had claimed repeatedly in public that the United States increased its forces in South Vietnam only to respond to escalating North Vietnamese infiltration. The classified study, however, showed that after mid-1967 the United States itself escalated the war because American officials believed that more troops would deliver victory.

The Nixon administration continued to expand the war. Johnson had lacked the will to "go to the brink," Nixon told Kissinger. "I have the *will* in spades." In December 1972 the United States launched a massive air strike on the North—the "Christmas bombing." Kissinger called the saturation air terror of 20,000 tons of bombs "brutal unpredictability." At the same time, the United States lost fifteen B-52 bombers. "After B-52s, there doesn't seem to be anything more that they can do," claimed one North Vietnamese. "Apparently they have come to their technological limit."

In Paris, meanwhile, the peace talks begun in 1968 seemed to be going nowhere. The South Vietnamese delegate, who saw defeat coming, purposely stalled the negotiations. But Kissinger was also meeting privately with Le Duc Tho, North Vietnam's chief delegate. Nixon instructed Kissinger to make concessions because the president was eager to improve relations with the Soviet Union and China, to win back the allegiance of America's allies, and to restore stability at home. When President Nguyen Van Thieu of South Vietnam balked at compromise, Nixon decided to "let Thieu paddle his own canoe." On January 27, 1973, Kissinger and Le Duc Tho signed a cease-fire agreement, and Nixon compelled Thieu to accept it by threatening to cut off U.S. aid while at the same time promising to defend the South if the North violated the agreement. In the accord, the United States promised to withdraw all of its troops within sixty days. All Vietnamese troops would stay in place, and a coalition government that included the Vietcong eventually would be formed in the South.

Cease-fire Agreement

The United States pulled its troops out of Vietnam, leaving behind some advisers. Soon, both North and South violated the cease-fire, and full-scale war erupted once more. The feeble South Vietnamese government—for so long an American puppet—could not hold out. Just before its surrender, hundreds of

Americans and Vietnamese who had worked for them were hastily evacuated from Saigon. On April 29, 1975, the South Vietnamese government collapsed. Shortly thereafter Saigon was renamed Ho Chi Minh City for the persevering patriot, who had died in 1969.

The overall costs of the war were immense. More than 58,000 Americans and some 1.5 million Vietnamese had died. Civilian deaths in Cambodia and Laos numbered in the millions. The war cost the United States at least $170 billion, and billions more would be paid out in veterans' benefits. The vast sums spent on the war became unavailable for investment at home to improve the infrastructure and quality of life. Instead, the nation suffered inflation and retreat from reform programs (see Chapters 30 and 32), as well as political schism, violations of civil liberties, and abuses of executive power. The war also delayed accommodation with the Soviet Union and the People's Republic of China, fueled friction with allies, and alienated Third World nations.

Costs of the Vietnam War

In 1975 communists assumed control and instituted repressive governments in South Vietnam, Cambodia, and Laos, but the domino effect once predicted by U.S. officials never occurred. Acute hunger afflicted the people of those devastated lands. Soon refugees—"boat people"—crowded aboard unsafe vessels in an attempt to escape their battered homelands. Many emigrated to the United States, where they were received with mixed feelings by Americans reluctant to be reminded of defeat in Asia. But many Americans faced the fact that the United States, which had relentlessly bombed, burned, and defoliated once-rich agricultural lands, bore considerable responsibility for the plight of the Southeast Asian peoples.

This sad conclusion prompted an American ambassador to pose a central question about the U.S. defeat: How was it that "so many with so much could achieve so little for so long against so few"? General Maxwell Taylor, summarizing the reasons why Americans could not win the Vietnam War, answered that "we didn't know our ally. Secondly, we knew even less about the enemy. And, the last, most inexcusable of our mistakes, was not knowing our own people."

Debate over the Lessons of Vietnam

Americans seemed both angry and confused about the nation's war experience. For the first time in their history, the historian William Appleman Williams observed, Americans, having had their overseas sphere of influence violently pushed back, were suffering from a serious case of "empire shock." Hawkish leaders claimed that America's failure in Vietnam undermined the nation's credibility and tempted enemies to exploit opportunities at the expense of U.S. interests. They pointed to a "Vietnam syndrome"—a suspicion of foreign entanglements—that they feared would inhibit the exercise of U.S. power. Next time, they said, the military should be permitted to do its job—use nuclear weapons? invade the North? bomb more sites?—free from the constraints of whimsical public opinion, stab-in-the-back journalists, and meddlesome politicians. America lost in Vietnam, they asserted, because Americans lost their guts at home.

Dovish leaders drew different conclusions, denying that the military had suffered undue restrictions. Some blamed the war on an imperial presidency that had permitted strong-willed men to act without restraint, and on pusillanimous Congresses that had conceded too much power to the executive branch. Make the president adhere to the checks-and-balances system—make him go to Congress for a declaration of war—these critics counseled, and America would become less interventionist. This view found expression in the War Powers Act of 1973, which sought to limit the president's war-making freedom.

Other critics claimed that as long as the United States remained a major power with compelling ideological, strategic, economic, and political needs that could be satisfied only through activism abroad, the nation would continue to be interventionist, especially in the Third World. The United States was destined to intervene abroad, they argued, to sustain its hegemonic role as the world's policeman, teacher, social worker, banker, and merchant. Some critics blamed the containment doctrine—that "prison-house" for policymakers, according to the historian George C. Herring—for failing to make distinctions between areas vital and peripheral to the national security and for relying too heavily on military means. Containment could not work, they believed, if there were no political stability and no effective popular government in the country where it was being applied.

Public discussion of the lessons of the Vietnam War also was stimulated by veterans' calls for help in dealing with post-traumatic stress disorder, which afflicted thousands of the 2.8 million Vietnam veterans. Once home, they suffered nightmares and extreme nervousness. Doctors reported that the disorder stemmed primarily from the

Vietnam Veterans

Dedicated in 1993 in Washington, D.C., the Vietnam Women's Memorial honors the several thousand military women who served in Vietnam, many of them as nurses who volunteered for duty. One nurse, Judy Marron, remembered treating wounded soldiers round the clock: "There were days when the stress and strain and blood and guts almost had to equal the frontlines." This bronze sculpture, by Glenna Goodacre, stands near the long wall on which are etched the names of Americans who died in Vietnam. (Brad Markel/Liaison Agency)

soldiers' having seen so many children, women, and elderly people killed. Some GIs inadvertently killed these people; some killed them vengefully and later felt guilt. Other veterans heightened public awareness of the war by publicizing their deteriorating health from the effects of Agent Orange and other chemicals they had handled or were accidentally sprayed with in Vietnam. Feature films such as *Coming Home* (1978), *The Deer Hunter* (1978), and *Apocalypse Now* (1979), personal accounts such as Philip Caputo's *A Rumor of War* (1977), and novels such as James Webb's *Fields of Fire* (1978), all of which depicted the soldier's Vietnam, hinted that defeat had been inevitable, given the inhospitable environment and an elusive enemy fighting a guerrilla war. The Vietnam Veterans Memorial, erected in Washington, D.C., in 1982, has kept the question alive, as have many oral history projects of veterans conducted by school and college students in classes to this day.

Nixon, Kissinger, and Détente

Nixon's national security affairs adviser (1969–1973) and secretary of state (1973–1977), Henry Kissinger, often gets the credit (or blame) for the Nixon administration's grand strategy to promote a global balance of power. Actually, *Nixinger*—a term coined by the historian Joan Hoff—captures well the shared views of Nixon and Kissinger about the need boldly and repeatedly to demonstrate U.S. power. The first part of

Henry A. Kissinger (b. 1923) *(right)* walks with President Nixon. An ambitious, knowledgeable, and self-flattering German-born political scientist from Harvard University, Kissinger served as assistant for national security affairs and secretary of state. Although he and the president shared basic assumptions about U.S. foreign relations, especially the need to promote détente and curb revolution, Kissinger judged Nixon an "egomaniac." Critics on the left compared Kissinger to Dr. Strangelove, the fictional Germanic adviser—played by Peter Sellers in the movie of the same name—who was so deranged that he welcomed a nuclear holocaust. Critics on the right thought Kissinger too conciliatory to the communists. (Dennis Brack/Black Star)

the strategy was détente: measured cooperation with the Soviets through negotiations within a general environment of rivalry. Détente's primary purpose, like that of the containment doctrine it resembled, was to check Soviet expansion and limit the Soviet arms buildup. The second part of the strategy sought to curb revolution and radicalism in the Third World so as to quash threats to American interests.

The grand design seemed attractive to its architects: the Cold War and limited wars such as in Vietnam were costing too much; more trade with friendlier Soviets and Chinese might reduce the huge U.S. balance-of-payments deficit; and improving relations with both Communist giants, at a time when a Sino-Soviet split had opened wide, might exacerbate feuding between the two, weakening communism. Skeptics, however, soon faulted the Nixinger posture for its assumption that the United States had the right and the ability to manipulate a disorderly world. The travails of the Vietnam War—which Kissinger insensitively dismissed as a mere "footnote" in history—illustrated the point.

Pros and Cons of Détente

Nixon and Kissinger pursued détente with extraordinary energy and fanfare. They expanded trade with the Soviet Union; a 1972 deal sent $1 billion worth of American grain to the Soviets at bargain prices.

SALT

To slow the costly arms race, they initiated the Strategic Arms Limitations Talks (SALT). In May 1972 Soviet and American negotiators produced two SALT I agreements. The first treaty limited antiballistic missile (ABM) systems for each nation to just two sites. ABM systems had accelerated the arms race because both sides built more missiles to overcome the ABM protection. In essence, SALT I sustained the Mutual Assured Destruction (MAD) doctrine: by leaving cities and offensive missile bases in both countries vulnerable to nuclear attack by not protecting them with defensive ABMs, it was assumed that war would be deterred because neither Washington nor Moscow would want to trigger its own, assured destruction.

The other SALT I agreement imposed a five-year freeze on the number of offensive nuclear missiles each side could possess. At the time, the Soviets held an advantage in total strategic forces (ICBMs, SLBMs, and long-range bombers)—2,547 to 2,160. But the United States had more warheads per missile because it could outfit each missile with MIRVs (multiple independently targeted reentry vehicles) that could send warheads to several different targets. In short, the

United States had a two-to-one advantage in deliverable warheads (5,700 to 2,500). Because SALT did not restrict MIRVs, the nuclear arms buildup actually continued.

In 1975, at the Conference on Security and Cooperation in Helsinki, Finland, the United States,

Helsinki Accords

Canada, and most European nations signed several accords that accepted the permanence of existing European boundaries, including adjustments made in Germany and eastern Europe right after the Second World War. The conferees also applauded détente and endorsed human rights for all. Conservatives in the United States excoriated the Ford administration for a sellout to the Soviets, but dozens of "Helsinki groups," including Solidarity in Poland and Charter 77 in Czechoslovakia, sprang up to press Communist regimes to honor the human-rights pledge.

While cultivating détente with the Soviet Union, the United States took dramatic steps to end more than two decades of Sino-American

Opening to China

hostility. The Chinese welcomed the change because they wanted to spur trade and hoped that friendlier Sino-American relations would make their onetime ally and now enemy, the Soviet Union, more cautious. Nixon reasoned the same way: "We're using the Chinese thaw to get the Russians shook." In early 1972 Nixon made a historic trip to "Red China," where he and the venerable Chinese leaders Mao Zedong and Zhou Enlai agreed to disagree on a number of issues, except one: the Soviet Union should not be permitted to make gains in Asia. Nixon also hoped that China would press North Vietnam to make peace. Sino-American relations improved slightly, and official diplomatic recognition and the exchange of ambassadors came in 1979.

Events in the Third World—especially in the Middle East—revealed the fragility of the U.S. grand

War in the Middle East

strategy. Israel, using American weapons, had scored victories against Egypt and Syria in the Six-Day War (1967), seizing the West Bank and the ancient city of Jerusalem from Jordan, the Golan Heights from Syria, and the Sinai Peninsula from Egypt (see Map 31.2), and thereby creating the enduring problem of the "occupied territories." Israel's Arab adversaries had used Soviet weapons. Palestinians, many of them expelled from their homes in 1948 when the nation of Israel was created, had organized the Palestine Liberation Organization (PLO) and pledged to destroy Israel. PLO sympathizers made hit-and-run raids on Jewish settlements, hijacked jetliners, and murdered Israeli athletes at the 1972 Olympic Games in Munich, West Germany. The Israelis retaliated by assassinating PLO leaders.

In October 1973 Egypt and Syria attacked Israel. In spite of détente, Moscow (backing Egypt) and Washington (backing Israel) put their armed forces—including their nuclear forces—on alert. In an attempt to push Americans into a pro-Arab stance, the Organization of Petroleum Exporting Countries (OPEC) embargoed shipments of oil to the United States. An energy crisis and dramatically higher oil prices rocked the nation. Soon Kissinger arranged a cease-fire and undertook "shuttle diplomacy," flying repeatedly among Middle Eastern capitals in search of a settlement. In March 1974 OPEC lifted the oil embargo. The next year Kissinger persuaded Egypt and Israel to accept a U.N. peacekeeping force in the Sinai. But peace did not come to the region because Palestinian and other Arabs still vowed to destroy Israel, and Israelis insisted on building Jewish settlements in occupied lands.

In Latin America, meanwhile, the Nixon administration pursued the traditional antiradical course of the United States. In Chile, after vot-

Chile

ers in 1970 elected a Marxist president, Salvador Allende, the CIA began secret operations to disrupt Chile ("make the economy scream") and encouraged military officers to stage a coup. In 1973 a military junta ousted Allende and installed an authoritarian regime under General Augusto Pinochet. Washington publicly denied any role in the affair that implanted iron-fisted tyranny in Chile for two decades.

In Africa, from which Americans imported large quantities of oil, chromium, cobalt, and other strategic minerals, Washington preferred the status quo. Slurring black Africans as

Containing Radicalism in Africa

"jigs" and "niggers," Nixon backed the white-minority regime in Rhodesia (now Zimbabwe); activated the CIA in a failed effort to defeat a Soviet- and Cuban-backed faction in newly independent Angola's civil war; and in South Africa tolerated the white rulers who imposed the segregationist policy of apartheid on blacks (85 percent of the population), keeping them poor, disfranchised, and ghettoized in prison-like townships. After the leftist government came to power in Angola, however, Washington took a keener interest in the rest of Africa, building economic

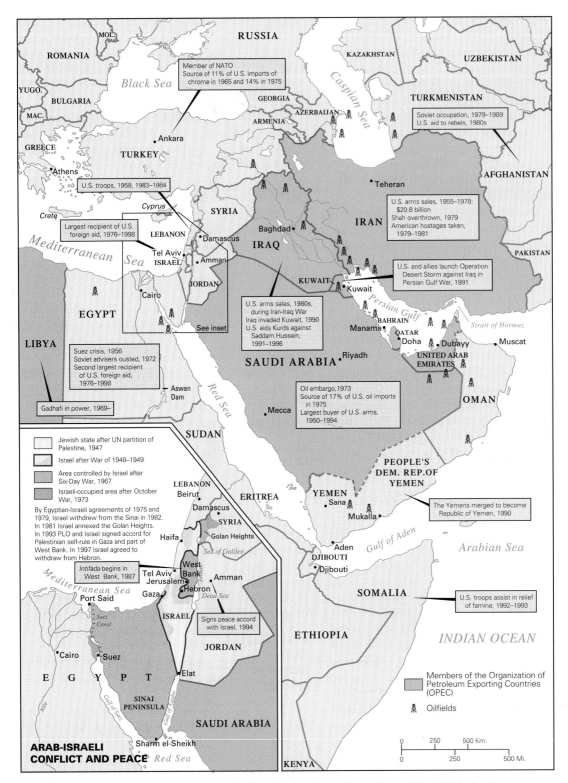

Map 31.2 The Middle East Extremely volatile and often at war, the nations of the Middle East maintained precarious relations with the United States. To protect its interests, the United States extended large amounts of economic and military aid and sold huge quantities of weapons to the area. At times, Washington ordered American troops to the region. The Arab-Israeli dispute particularly upended order, although the peace process moved forward.

ties and sending arms to friendly black nations such as Kenya and the Congo (then called Zaire). The administration also began to distance the United States from the white governments of Rhodesia and South Africa. America had to "prevent the radicalization of Africa," said Kissinger.

The United States was interventionist in the Third World in part because the American economy was so intertwined with the world economy. American investments abroad totaled more than $133 billion by the mid-1970s. Coca-Cola, Exxon, and many other American (or, more accurately, multinational) corporations earned at least half of their profits abroad. Furthermore, one-fourth of U.S. agricultural sales came from exports; one out of every nine manufacturing jobs depended on exports. The United States also depended on imports of strategic raw materials such as manganese (by 1980, 97 percent of America's consumption of this metal essential to steel production was imported from such countries as South Africa, Gabon, and Brazil). American leaders read threats to markets, investments, and raw materials as stabs at the high American standard of living, as when Venezuela nationalized American oil properties in 1976, India legislated that its nationals must own a majority of voting shares in industrial firms, and terrorists around the world destroyed American facilities and kidnapped American corporate executives. Particularly alarming was the United Nations' 1974 call for a "New International Economic Order" for the Third World: low-interest loans, lower prices for technology, and higher prices for raw materials. To counter such demands, some multinational corporations sought to influence foreign politics, as when International Telephone and Telegraph helped undermine Allende in Chile and Lockheed Aircraft bribed foreign leaders to promote sales. Multinationals also provided "cover" for CIA agents.

Global economic instability undercut the Nixon-Kissinger grand design. The worldwide economic downturn of the early 1970s was the worst since the 1930s. Inflation and high oil prices pinched rich and poor nations alike. Protectionist tendencies raised tariffs and impeded world trade. And debt-ridden Third World nations—sometimes called the "South"—insisted that countries of the industrial "North" share their wealth. In this turbulent setting, the United States began to suffer a trade deficit—importing more goods than it exported (see Figure 31.2). A "dollar glut" abroad threatened to drain the U.S. gold supply

United States in the World Economy

as foreigners exchanged their dollars for the precious metal. In 1971 Nixon shocked foreign capitals when he devalued the dollar, suspended its convertibility into gold, and imposed a surtax on imports, seeking thereby to reduce the influx of Japanese and European goods. All the while, Americans sensed a continued U.S. slippage in the international economy. "I think of what happened to Greece and Rome," Nixon said in reviewing statistics, "and, as you see, what is left? Only the pillars." He insisted that "it's terribly important that we be #1 economically because otherwise we can't be #1 diplomatically or militarily."

Economic relations with Japan soured. Kissinger's derogatory private comment about the Japanese as "little Sony salesmen" reflected American wariness of Japan's economic prowess. U.S. officials bristled that Japan sold plenty but did not buy enough in the world economy and discriminated against American autos in the Japanese marketplace. Nixon's 1971 decisions shocked Japan, which enjoyed a favorable balance of trade with the United States ($3.2 billion in 1971) derived from an increasing share of the American market in motor vehicles and electronics and from sales to U.S. forces in Vietnam and for maintaining the 169 U.S. military bases in Japan. Although the Japanese agreed to limit some exports to the United States (such as color televisions), the two nations were "getting bogged down in economic arm-wrestling," as Kissinger feared. By 1980 the trade balance had jumped even more in Japan's favor to $10.4 billion; by 1989 to $50 billion. Americans increasingly worried that in the contest between the two economic giants, Japan was winning. So it seemed in 1989 when the best-selling car in America was the Honda Accord and Sony bought Columbia Pictures. Still, by most measurements, Americans remained at the top of the economic hill.

Economic Competition with Japan

Changes in the natural environment also earned a place on America's foreign policy agenda. Public discussion of environmental degradation (the first Earth Day was celebrated in 1970) and of the imbalance between food supplies and burgeoning populations, along with the work of nongovernmental organizations (NGOs) such as Greenpeace, formed in 1969, pressed Washington to act. In 1972 the United States agreed to participate in a U.N.-sponsored environmental conference in Stockholm, Sweden. Attended by 113 nations and 400 NGOs, the conference created an en-

International Environmental Issues

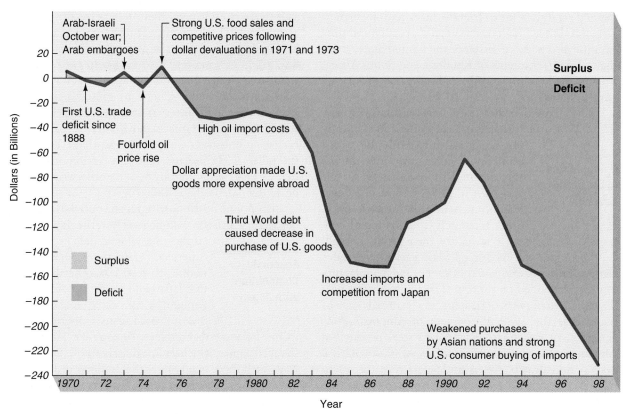

Figure 31.2 U.S. Trade Balance, 1970–1998 Importing more than it exports, the United States has suffered trade deficits for years. Foreign political and economic crises, growing competition from Japanese products in the American marketplace, and strong consumer buying have created large trade deficits, which must be financed by borrowing. One result has been a mounting U.S. external debt.   (Source: U.S. Department of State)

vironmental fund, a global monitoring system, and a new coordinating agency, the U.N. Environmental Program. The conferees especially spotlighted transborder pollution, the overkilling of whales to the point of endangerment, and goals for environmental protection that all nations should seek to meet.

Carter, Preventive Diplomacy, and a Reinvigorated Cold War

When President Jimmy Carter took office in 1977, he asked Americans to put their "inordinate fear of Communism" behind them. With reformist zeal, Carter vowed to reduce the U.S. military presence overseas (by persuading NATO countries to pay a greater share of their own defense), to cut back arms sales (which had reached the unprecedented height of $10 billion per year under Nixon), and to slow the nuclear arms race

(by spurring a new round of SALT talks). At the time, more than four hundred thousand American military personnel were stationed abroad, the United States had military links with ninety-two nations, and the CIA was active on every continent. Carter promised to avoid new Vietnams through an activist preventive diplomacy in the Third World and to give more attention to North-South and environmental issues. He especially determined to improve human rights abroad—the freedom to vote, worship, travel, speak out, and get a fair trial. Like his predecessors, however, Carter identified revolutionary nationalism as a threat to America's prominent global position.

Carter spoke and acted inconsistently, in part because in the post-Vietnam years no consensus existed in foreign policy and in part because **Carter's Divided Administration** his advisers squabbled among themselves. One source of the problem was the stern-faced Zbigniew Brzezinski, a Polish-born political scientist who became Carter's national security adviser. An old-fashioned Cold Warrior, Brzezinski viewed foreign crises in globalist terms—that is, he blamed them on the Soviet Union. Carter gradually listened more to Brzezinski than to Secretary of State Cyrus Vance, an experienced public servant who advocated quiet diplomacy. Vocal neoconservative intellectuals such as Norman Podhoretz, editor of *Commentary* magazine, and the Committee on the Present Danger, founded in 1976 by Cold War hawks such as Paul Nitze, who had composed NSC-68 in 1950, criticized Carter for any relaxation of the Cold War and demanded that he jettison détente.

Under Carter, détente deteriorated and the Cold War deepened. He at first angered Soviet leaders by insisting that their authoritarian regime respect human rights, including lifting restrictions on Jewish emigration from the USSR—an issue heated up in American politics by the 1974 Jackson-Vanik Amendment. This provision denied most-favored-nation trading status to the Soviet Union until it allowed free Jewish emigration. Moscow rejected Jackson-Vanik as U.S. interference in its domestic affairs and reproached the United States for dictating Soviet policy while playing its "China card"—building up China in order to threaten the Soviet Union.

Despite this rocky start, a new treaty, SALT II, codified Soviet-American nuclear parity in 1979. The agreement placed a ceiling of 2,250 delivery vehicles (long-range bombers, ICBMs, and SLBMs) on each side, capped MIRVed launchers at 1,200 for each, and limited the number of warheads per delivery vehicle. The Soviet Union had to dismantle more than 250 existing delivery vehicles, whereas the United States was permitted to expand from its existing 2,060 to the new ceiling. The treaty did not affect nuclear warheads, which stood at 9,200 for the United States and 5,000 for the Soviet Union. To win votes for the treaty from skeptical conservatives, Carter announced an expensive military expansion program and deployment of Pershing II missiles and cruise missiles in NATO countries.

SALT II

As Senate ratification of SALT II stalled and Moscow fumed over the Pershings, events in Afghanistan led to Soviet-American confrontation. In late 1979 the Red Army bludgeoned its way into Afghanistan to shore up a faltering Communist government under siege by Muslim rebels. Carter shelved SALT II (the two powers nonetheless unilaterally hon-

ored its terms later), suspended shipments of grain and high-technology equipment to the Soviet Union, and initiated an international boycott of the 1980 Summer Olympics in Moscow. The Soviets did not withdraw their forces from Afghanistan.

The president also announced the Carter Doctrine: the United States would intervene, unilaterally and militarily if necessary, should Soviet aggression threaten the petroleum-rich Persian Gulf. George F. Kennan called Carter's reaction exaggerated and wrongheaded in assuming that the Soviets would attack elsewhere in the Middle East. Kennan noted that in Afghanistan the Soviet Union was dealing with a local crisis in a strategically important client state on its southern border, not with the entire Gulf region. He faulted Carter for not trying diplomacy first.

Carter markedly improved the Mideast peace process. Through tenacious personal diplomacy at a Camp David, Maryland, meeting in September 1978 with Egyptian and Israeli leaders, the president persuaded Israel and Egypt to sign a peace treaty, gained Israel's promise to withdraw from the Sinai Peninsula, and forged an agreement that provided for continued negotiations on the future status of the Palestinian people living in the occupied territories of Jordan's West Bank and Egypt's Gaza Strip (see Map 31.2). Revealing a crack in Arab unity, other Arab states denounced the agreement for not requiring Israel to relinquish all occupied territories and for not guaranteeing a Palestinian homeland. But the treaty at least ended warfare along one frontier in that troubled area of the world.

Camp David Accords

Carter's toughest foreign policy test came in Iran. Many Iranians had not forgotten that the United States had meddled in Iranian affairs by backing the shah in the 1946 crisis and restoring him to his throne in 1953. Iranian revolutionaries led by Ayatollah Ruhollah Khomeini, a bitterly anti-American Muslim cleric, also resented the CIA's training of the shah's ruthless secret police and the huge infusion of U.S. arms into their country—$19 billion worth between 1973 and 1978 alone. When the shah was overthrown in 1979 and then admitted to the United States for medical treatment, mobs stormed the U.S. embassy in Teheran. They took American personnel as hostages, demanding the return of the shah to stand trial. The Iranians eventually released a few American prisoners, but fifty-two others languished more than a year under Iranian

Iranian Hostage Crisis

On March 26, 1979, Egypt's president Anwar el-Sadat (1918–1981) on the left, Israel's prime minister Menachem Begin (1913–1992) on the right, and U.S. president Jimmy Carter (b. 1924) signed a peace treaty known as the Camp David accords. Studiously negotiated by Carter, the Egyptian-Israeli peace has held to this day—despite conflict in much of the rest of the Middle East. (Jimmy Carter Presidential Library)

guard. They suffered solitary confinement, beatings, and terrifying mock executions.

Unable to gain the hostages' freedom through diplomatic intermediaries, Carter said that he felt "the same kind of impotence that a powerful person feels when his child is kidnapped." He took steps to isolate Iran economically, freezing Iranian assets in the United States. When the hostage takers paraded their blindfolded captives before television cameras to taunt the United States, Americans seethed in anger. In April 1980, frustrated and at low ebb in public opinion polls, Carter broke diplomatic relations with Iran and ordered a daring rescue mission. But the rescue effort miscarried after equipment failure in the sandy Iranian desert, and during the hasty withdrawal two aircraft collided, killing eight American soldiers. Critics chided Carter for undertaking a risky operation that surely would have cost the lives of many hostages. Secretary Vance, already troubled by the growing militancy of Carter's foreign policy and the president's acceptance of Brzezinski's "visceral anti-Sovietism," resigned in protest. The hostages were not freed until

January 1981, after Carter left office and the United States unfroze Iranian assets and promised not to intervene again in Iran's internal affairs.

In Latin America, Carter sought compromise with nationalists (see Map 31.3), even seeking to reduce tensions with Castro's Cuba by establishing limited diplomatic links. But a crisis in 1980, during which the island regime allowed a hundred thousand Cubans to sail to Florida from the port of Mariel, poisoned relations once again. When it was discovered that many of the migrants were mentally ill or prisoners freed from jail, the mayor of Miami charged that "Fidel has flushed his toilet on us."

In Panama, citizens longed for control over the Canal Zone, which they believed had been wrongfully taken from them in 1903 (see page 629). U.S. officials feared that Panamanians might try to seize the canal by force or damage the vulnerable waterway. Recognizing also that the canal's value had dwindled because of advances in air transportation and because many new, large ships

Panama Canal Treaties

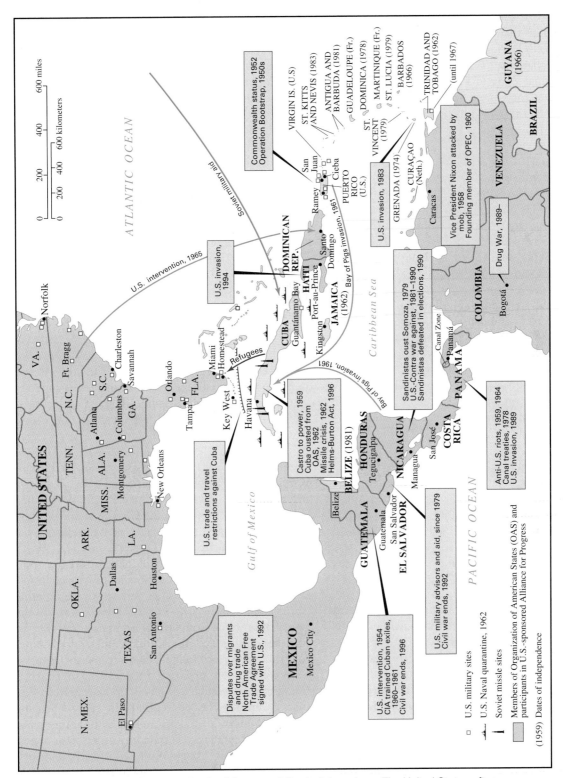

Map 31.3   The United States in the Caribbean and Central America   The United States often has intervened in the Caribbean and Central America. Geographical proximity, economic stakes, political disputes, security links, trade in illicit drugs, and Cuba's alliance with the Soviet Union and defiance of the United States have kept North American eyes fixed on events in the region.

could not squeeze through its locks, Carter reenergized negotiations that had begun after anti-American riots in Panama in 1964. The United States signed two treaties with Panama in 1977. One provided for the return of the Canal Zone to Panama in 2000, and the other guaranteed the United States the right to defend the canal after that time. With conservatives denouncing a retreat from greatness, the Senate narrowly endorsed both agreements in 1978.

Carter's record sparked considerable criticism from both left and right. Contrary to his goals, more American military personnel were stationed overseas in 1980 than in 1976; the defense budget climbed and sales of arms abroad grew to $15.3 billion in 1980. On human rights, the president proved inconsistent. He practiced a double standard by applying the human-rights test to some nations (the Soviet Union, Argentina, and Chile) but not to U.S. allies (South Korea, the shah's Iran, and the Philippines). Still, if inconsistent, Carter's human-rights policy was not unimportant: he gained the release and saved the lives of some political prisoners, and he popularized and institutionalized concern for human rights around the world. Carter did not satisfy Americans who wanted a post-Vietnam restoration of the economic hegemony and military edge the United States once enjoyed. He had earned some diplomatic successes in the Middle East, Africa, and Latin America, but the revived Cold War and the prolonged Iranian hostage crisis had politically hurt the administration. He lost the 1980 election to the hawkish Ronald Reagan, former Hollywood actor and governor of California.

The Ups and Downs of Reagan's World

Reagan did not have a firm grasp of world issues, history, or geography. After returning from his first trip to South America, he commented, "Well, I've learned a lot. . . . You'd be surprised. They're all individual countries." When Reagan told French president François Mitterand, a socialist, that communism and socialism were the same, Mitterand wondered, "What planet is that man living on?" Superficial and often mistaken about elementary facts, Reagan acted more on instinct than on analysis. Expressing the reformist message so common in U.S. foreign policy, he liked to quote Tom Paine of the American Revolution: "We have it in our power to begin the world over again."

Embracing traditional American bipolar thinking, Reagan endorsed a devil theory: a malevolent Soviet Union, the "evil empire," would "commit any crime," "lie," and "cheat" to achieve a communist world. Because he attributed Third World disorders to Soviet intrigue, the president in 1985 declared the Reagan Doctrine: the United States would openly support anticommunist movements—"freedom fighters"—wherever they were battling the Soviets or Soviet-backed governments. Under this doctrine, the CIA funneled aid to insurgents in Afghanistan, Nicaragua, Angola, and elsewhere. In open defiance of the sovereignty of those nations, Reagan worked to overthrow their governments.

Reagan officials also championed free-market capitalism, evident in their enthusiasm for the 1988 U.S.-Canada Free Trade Agreement, and in their rejection of the 1982 United Nations' Convention on the Law of the Sea, patiently crafted through compromise over a ten-year period. Third World nations argued that rich sea-bed resources of petroleum and minerals should be shared under international supervision among all nations as a "common heritage of mankind." The industrial states, which alone had the capital and equipment needed to conduct excavating and drilling operations, preferred private exploitation with minimal international management. The Reagan administration shelved the convention on the grounds that it did not adequately protect private American companies. (In 1994, when the treaty went into effect, the Clinton administration sent it to the Senate for approval; as of this writing the convention still languishes there.)

Law of the Sea Convention

Another Reagan tenet held that a substantial military buildup would thwart the Soviet threat and intimidate Moscow. Tainted CIA reports overestimating Soviet military strength—tainted because some of the information came from double agents working for the Soviet secret service (the KGB), as the Aldrich Ames spy scandal revealed in the 1990s—reassured the president that he was on the right track. Reagan launched the largest peacetime arms buildup in American history, driving up the federal debt. In 1985, when the military budget hit $294.7 billion (a doubling since 1980), the Pentagon was spending an average of $28 million an hour. Assigning low priority to arms-control talks, Reagan announced in 1983 development of an antimissile defense system in space: the Strategic Defense Initiative (SDI). His critics tagged it "Star Wars." As the veteran diplomat George Ball observed when U.S. forces overthrew a leftist, pro-Cuban government on the tiny Caribbean island of Grenada in 1983, once again "we shiver in the icy winds of the Cold War."

Reagan's first decision affecting the Soviets was actually friendly. Fulfilling a campaign pledge to help American farmers, in 1981 he lifted the grain embargo. The Soviet Union soon bought grain worth $3 billion. But bitter hostility soon followed when Poland's pro-Soviet leaders cracked down on the Solidarity labor movement in that nation bordering the USSR. In response, Washington placed restrictions on Soviet-American trade and hurled angry words at Moscow. In 1983 Reagan restricted commercial flights to the Soviet Union after a Soviet fighter pilot mistakenly shot down a South Korean commercial jet that had strayed some 300 miles off course into Soviet airspace. The world was shocked by the death of 269 passengers, and Reagan exploited the tragedy to score Cold War points.

When he came to office, Reagan believed that the Soviets and Castro's Cuba were fomenting disorder in Central America (see Map 31.3). In small, very poor El Salvador, revolutionaries challenged the government, which was dominated by the military and a landed elite. The regime used (or could not control) right-wing death squads, which by the end of the decade had killed forty thousand dissidents and other citizens as well as several American missionaries who had been working with landless peasants. Inheriting Carter's policy of backing the regime and looking the other way on human-rights abuses, Reagan officials hoped for reform but intended to prevent revolution in El Salvador. By 1989 the United States had spent $6 billion there in a counterinsurgency war.

Intervention in El Salvador

The U.S. intervention in the Salvadoran civil war sparked a debate much like the earlier one over Vietnam. Those who urged negotiations thought Reagan wrong to interpret the conflict as a Cold War contest; such civil wars stemmed not from Soviet meddling but from deep-seated economic instability, poverty, and class oppression. Resurrecting the discredited domino theory, Reagan retorted that the "Communists" would soon be at the Texas border if they were not stopped in El Salvador. Reagan also made a strategic argument: Central America hugs the Caribbean Sea, "our lifeline to the outside world." After intense debate, Congress repeatedly gave Reagan the funds he wanted for El Salvador, while the death squads murdered at will,

thwarting the radicals. "The less you know, the better," admitted a U.S. intelligence officer. In January 1992 the Salvadoran combatants finally negotiated a U.N.-sponsored peace.

The Reagan administration also meddled in the Nicaraguan civil war. In 1979 leftist insurgents in Nicaragua overthrew Anastasio Somoza, a long-time ally of the United States and member of the dictatorial family that had ruled the Central American nation since the mid-1930s. The revolutionaries called themselves Sandinistas in honor of the Nicaraguan who had fought U.S. Marines then (see page 740), and they denounced the tradition of U.S. imperialism in their country. When the Sandinistas aided rebels in El Salvador, bought Soviet weapons, and invited Cubans to work in Nicaragua's hospitals and schools and to help reorganize their army, Reagan officials charged that Nicaragua was becoming a Soviet client. In 1981 the CIA began to train, arm, and direct more than ten thousand counterrevolutionaries, called contras, to overthrow the Nicaraguan government. From CIA bases in Honduras and Costa Rica, the contras crossed into Nicaragua to kill officials and destroy oil refineries, transportation facilities, and medical clinics. As the contra attacks multiplied and the death toll mounted, the Nicaraguan government curbed civil liberties and shifted scarce money to its military.

Contra War in Nicaragua

In 1984 Congress voted to stop U.S. military aid to the contras ("humanitarian" aid was soon sent in its place). Secretly, the Reagan administration lined up other countries, including Saudi Arabia, Panama, and Korea, to funnel money and weapons to the contras, and in 1985 Reagan imposed an economic embargo against Nicaragua. The next year, Congress once again voted military aid for the contras after vigorous White House lobbying and apparent Sandinista intransigence. (The Sandinistas refused to accept a peace accord unless the United States halted support for the contras.) During the undeclared U.S. war against Nicaragua, Reagan rejected opportunities for diplomacy, especially the plan proposed by Costa Rica's president Oscar Arias Sánchez in 1987 to obtain a cease-fire in Central America through negotiations and cutbacks in military aid to all rebel forces. (Arias won the 1987 Nobel Peace Prize.) Three years later, under arrangements brokered by the Central American presidents, the Sandinistas lost a national election to a U.S.-funded party. After nearly a decade of civil war, thirty thousand Nicaraguans had died and the ravaged economy had dwindled to one of the poorest in the hemisphere.

Scandal tainted the North American crusade against the Sandinistas. It became known in 1986 that the president's national security ad-

Iran-Contra Scandal

viser, John M. Poindexter, and an aide, Marine Lieutenant Colonel Oliver North, in collusion with CIA director William J. Casey, had covertly sold weapons to Iran and then diverted the profits to the contras so that they could purchase arms. The diversion occurred after Congress had prohibited military assistance to the contras. During the same period, Washington had been condemning Iran as a terrorist nation and demanding that America's allies not trade with the radical Islamic state. North later admitted that he illegally had destroyed government documents and lied to Congress to keep the operation clandestine. President Reagan lied when he said that he knew nothing of these activities. In late 1992 outgoing president George Bush pardoned several former government officials who had been convicted of lying to Congress. Critics smelled a cover-up, for Bush himself, as vice president, had participated in high-level meetings on Iran-contra deals. As for North, his conviction was overturned on a technicality. The Iran-contra secret network, the scholar William LeoGrande has argued, "posed a greater threat to democracy in the United States than Nicaragua ever did."

Elsewhere in the Third World, the deeply divided Middle East continued to defy American solutions (see Map 31.2). The United States had

U.S. Interests in the Middle East

commitments (Israel, which in 1985 received more American foreign aid— $3 billion—than any other country), political friends (Saudi Arabia, to which the United States sold $8.5 billion worth of military equipment in 1981), and enemies (the Islamic states of Libya, which U.S. planes bombed, and Iran, against which the United States imposed an economic embargo). Mideast oil supplies fueled Western economies. An Iraqi-Iranian war, in which the United States aided Iraq, threatened Persian Gulf shipping. The Middle East was also a major source of the world's terrorism against U.S. citizens and property. In 1985 Shiite Muslim terrorists from Lebanon hijacked an American jetliner, killed one passenger, and held thirty-nine Americans hostage for seventeen days. Three years later, a Pan American passenger plane was destroyed over Scotland, probably by terrorists who concealed the bomb in a cassette player.

Even Israel gave the United States trouble. In retaliation for Palestinian shelling of Israel from Lebanon, the Israelis repeatedly

Crisis in Lebanon

bombed suspected Palestinian camps inside Lebanon, killing hundreds of civilians. And in 1981, without warning, Israel annexed the Syrian territory of the Golan Heights. Many American supporters of Israel, though well aware that the Jewish state faced hostile Arabs, became impatient with Israel's provocative acts toward its neighbors. The following year, Israeli troops invaded civil war–torn Lebanon, reaching the capital Beirut and inflicting massive damage. The beleaguered Palestine Liberation Organization and various Lebanese factions called on Syria to contain the Israelis. Thousands of civilians died in the multifaceted conflict, and a million people became refugees. Soon after Reagan sent U.S. Marines to Lebanon to join a peacekeeping force, the American troops became embroiled in a war between Lebanese factions. In October 1983 terrorist bombs demolished a barracks, killing 241 American servicemen. Four months later, Reagan recognized failure and pulled the remaining marines out.

Washington, which openly sided with Israel, continued to propose peace plans designed to persuade the Israelis to give back occupied territories and the Arabs to give up attempts to push the Jews out of the Middle East (the "land-for-peace" formula). As the peace process stalled in 1987, Palestinians living in the West Bank began an uprising called *intifada* against Israeli forces. Israel refused to negotiate, but the United States decided to reverse its policy and talk with PLO chief Yasir Arafat after he renounced terrorism and accepted Israel's right to live in peace and security.

In South Africa the Reagan administration at first followed a policy called "constructive engagement"—

South Africa

asking the white government to reform its repressive system. But many Americans demanded economic sanctions: cutting off imports from South Africa and pressing some 350 American companies—led by Texaco, General Motors, Ford, and Goodyear—to cease operations there. Some American cities and states passed divestment laws, withdrawing dollars (such as pension funds used to buy stock) from American companies active in South Africa. Public protest and congressional legislation forced the Reagan administration in 1986 to impose economic restrictions against South Africa. Within two years, about half of the American companies in South Africa had pulled out.

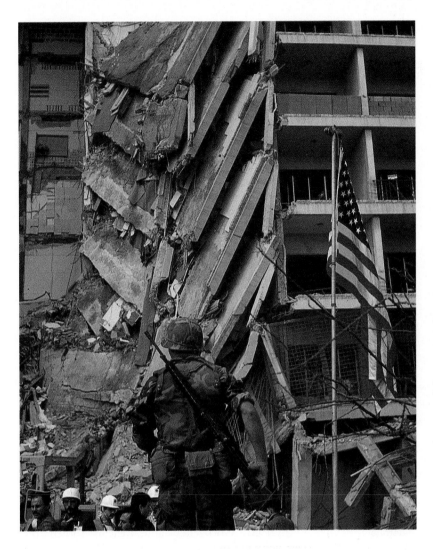

On April 18, 1983, a car bomb placed by terrorists demolished the U.S. embassy in Beirut, Lebanon, killing 63 people, 17 of them Americans. An American soldier stands guard near the destroyed building. Then in October of the same year, terrorist bombs leveled a military barracks, killing 241 American personnel. A few months later, President Reagan withdrew U.S. Marines from a multinational peace-keeping force that had been dispatched to Lebanon to calm a war waged there by Israel against PLO and Syrian forces.　(Bill Pierce/Sygma)

Elsewhere in Africa, hunger and famine exacerbated by drought and warfare took a ghastly human toll and contributed to political instability as governments failed to satisfy their people's basic needs. In the early 1980s experts estimated that annual hunger-related deaths numbered between 13 million and 18 million people—twenty-four people per minute, many of them in Africa. In Ethiopia and Sudan, both wracked by civil war, hundreds of thousands starved to death. Almost the only good news to come out of Africa was the 1988 agreement, engineered by U.S. negotiators, among Angola, Cuba, and South Africa: withdrawal of Cuban troops from Angola and black majority rule in Namibia, the former German colony that had come under South Africa's rule after the First World War.

Famine in Africa

The Third World also continued to suffer economic setbacks that endangered American prosperity. Third World nations had sunk into staggering debt. Having borrowed heavily in the 1970s, they were unable to repay the loans when world prices for sugar, coffee, and other commodities slumped. By 1989 they owed creditors, including American banks, more than $1.2 trillion. Many Third World nations burdened with such debt—Mexico alone owed more than $100 billion—had to cut back on imports of American goods. Hundreds of thousands of jobs in the United States were lost as a result, while economic instability spawned political unrest throughout the Third World. Reagan had intervened repeatedly in the Third World, but intervention served to aggravate not subdue economic crises, civil wars, and ethnic and class conflicts.

Reagan's expansion of the U.S. military, his careless utterances about winning a limited nuclear war, and his quest for nuclear supremacy provoked worldwide debate. In 1981 hundreds of thousands of marchers in London, Rome, Bonn, and other European cities demanded Soviet-

Debate over Nuclear Weapons

In one of several summit meetings, top Soviet leader Mikhail Gorbachev (b. 1932) and President Ronald Reagan (b. 1911) met in Moscow in May 1988 in hopes of signing a Strategic Arms Reduction Talks (START) agreement. The "chemistry" of warm friendship that Reagan later claimed characterized his personal relationship with Gorbachev fell short of producing cuts in dangerous strategic weapons. But their cordial interaction encouraged the diplomatic dialogue that helped end the Cold War.   (Ronald Reagan Presidential Library)

American negotiations to prevent a nuclear holocaust. The evangelist Billy Graham joined peace groups and politicians in appeals for a freeze in the nuclear arms race. In the largest peaceful protest in American history, a million people marched through New York City in June 1982 to support a freeze. Towns across the nation and the House of Representatives passed resolutions to freeze the development, production, and deployment of new weapons. Roman Catholic bishops in the United States issued a pastoral letter in 1983 condemning nuclear weapons as "immoral" and urging an end to the arms race, "which robs the poor and the vulnerable." Meanwhile, scientists described the "nuclear winter" that would follow a nuclear war: the earth, cut off from the sun's rays, would turn cold, and food sources would disappear.

In 1982 Reagan substituted the Strategic Arms Reduction Talks (START) for the inactive SALT talks. At the 1985 Geneva summit meeting, Reagan and the new Soviet leader Mikhail S. Gorbachev agreed in principle that strategic weapons should be substantially reduced, and at the 1986 Reykjavik, Iceland, meeting they came very close to a major reduction agreement. SDI, however, stood in the way: Gorbachev insisted that it be shelved, and Reagan refused to part with it despite widespread scientific opinion that it would cost billions of dollars and never work. But Reagan and Gorbachev warmed toward one another, and the American president, as his more hawkish advisers left the administration in the late 1980s, toned down his strident anti-Soviet rhetoric.

The turnaround in Soviet-American relations stemmed more from changes abroad than from Reagan's decisions. As Reagan said near the end of his presidency, he had been "dropped into a grand historical moment." Under Gorbachev, a younger generation of Soviet leaders came to power in 1985. They began to restructure and modernize the highly bureaucratized, decaying economy (a reform program called *perestroika*) and to liberalize the authoritarian political system (a reform program called *glasnost*). For these reforms to work, Soviet military expenditures had to be reduced and foreign aid decreased.

Gorbachev's Reforms

In 1987 Gorbachev and Reagan signed the Intermediate-range Nuclear Forces (INF) Treaty banning all land-based intermediate-range nuclear missiles in Europe. Soon began the destruction of 2,800 missiles, including Soviet SS-20s targeted at western Europe and NATO Pershing and cruise missiles aimed at the Soviet Union. Gorbachev also unilaterally reduced his nation's armed forces, helped settle regional conflicts, and began the withdrawal of Soviet troops from Afghanistan. After more than forty chilling years, the Cold War was waning.

Summary

Secretary of State Henry Kissinger once observed that the international order was coming apart "politically, economically, and morally." The world, he feared, was "tilting against us." Indeed, the emergence of the Third World in the 1950s and 1960s and growing independent decision making on the part of allies undermined the bipolar Cold War international system the

United States and the Soviet Union had constructed at the end of the Second World War. By the 1980s power had become more diffused: great-power management of world affairs had diminished, and international relations had become more fluid and less predictable as more and more nations demanded a voice and a vote. In this changed setting, the United States and the Soviet Union moved haltingly toward détente and a winding down of the Cold War, as the INF Treaty demonstrated.

But this superpower shift toward diplomacy and cooperation came only after dangerous crises, nuclear brinkmanship that courted doomsday, international economic instability, monumental expenditures, and interventionism in the Third World. Driven by Cold War calculations and fears that the Third World would undermine America's standard of living, Presidents Kennedy, Johnson, Nixon, Ford, Carter, and Reagan sought to sustain U.S. preeminence in the world through a variety of methods, from overt economic and military pressure and weapons programs to covert political manipulation. On the whole, they maintained U.S. supremacy, but at great costs.

For the United States, the Vietnam War proved the most damaging. Determined to contain communism, Washington threw its young armed services personnel and its national wealth into a war it could not and did not win in a country it did not understand. Steeped in the Cold War mentality, American officials wrongheadedly saw the Soviet Union and the People's Republic of China—leaders of a supposed international communist conspiracy—maliciously at work in Vietnam, where the issue was actually more one of independence than of communism. The Vietnam War, as did wars in the 1890s and 1930s, set off a major national debate about the fundamental purposes of American foreign policy—a debate that still resonates today when the United States engages in nation building and dispatches its military forces into foreign disputes.

LEGACY FOR A PEOPLE AND A NATION
The Peace Corps

"How many of you are willing to work in the foreign service and spend your lives traveling around the world?" Democratic presidential candidate John F. Kennedy asked University of Michigan students on October 14, 1960. He was trying out an idea he inherited from others: overseas service "working for freedom." The huge crowd cheered, many inspired to sign up for the "peace race." Some forty years later, a Peace Corps recruitment poster echoed the original challenge: "How far are you willing to go to make a difference?" Since the corps' founding in 1961 to promote world peace through cross-cultural understanding and economic development, more than 155,000 Americans have volunteered for service in 134 countries. Currently, 7,000 volunteers are active in 77 countries. Most volunteers are college educated, female, single, and white, and their average age is twenty-eight (2000 figures; for more recent data, see www.peacecorps.gov). Over the years, volunteers have built fish farms in Togo, water pumps in Kenya, sawmills in Peru, poultry cooperatives in India, and bridges in Sierra Leone. They have served as nurses in Tanganyika and as English teachers in country after country.

Today, many host nations instead want Peace Corps volunteers to run computer workshops, create management models, teach free-market business skills, launch small-business enterprises, and design web pages. In its first decades, volunteers largely went to the Third World, where they were sent not only as goodwill ambassadors but also as foreign policy instruments to win friends to the U.S. side of the Cold War. Today, in the post–Cold War era, increasing numbers serve in eastern Europe and in the former Soviet republics, helping them in the transition to market-oriented economies and political democracy.

From the beginning, not all Peace Corps projects have succeeded, and some volunteers proved ill-suited for corps work. Also, during the Vietnam War, after volunteers protested U.S. intervention, President Nixon demanded that the Peace Corps serve, not question, U.S. Cold War goals and sharply cut its budget. As the Vietnam War and Watergate scandal spawned public cynicism, and as the military-minded era of the Reagan eighties marginalized the volunteers' way of promoting peace, the number of volunteers dropped, hitting an all-time low of 5,219 in 1987.

Today, the Peace Corps is highly respected as an institution where American ideals of humanitarian service, cultural understanding, and self-determination repose, even when U.S. leaders sometimes trample on such principles. In 1999 Congress voted to increase the corps to 10,000 volunteers by 2003, allocating a generous budget of $241 million. With such assistance, a legacy from the 1960s has been secured for a people and a nation—and the world.

For Further Reading, see page A-38 of the Appendix. For Web resources, go to http://college.hmco.com.

THE END OF THE POSTWAR BOOM 1974–1989

Nguyet Thu Ha was twenty-two years old when South Vietnam capitulated to North Vietnamese and Vietcong forces in 1975. She had never before spent a night away from her parents; but North Vietnamese soldiers were fighting close to her home, so she fled, taking along her four younger brothers and sisters, all teenagers, and a six-year-old nephew whose distraught parents had entrusted him to Ha for safekeeping. The six found their way onto a fishing ship dangerously overcrowded with refugees. They stopped first at Guam, a Pacific island controlled by the United States; their second stop was a refugee camp in Arkansas; finally, Nguyet Ha and the children went to Kansas City, Missouri. Ha's immediate challenge was to earn enough money to support six people, but her dream was to reunite her family.

Nguyet Ha obtained a job working seven days a week as a hotel housekeeper, and at night she taught herself to sew, making shirts and dresses. She next worked as a waitress, saving her tips to buy a house. "I'm very tough about my budget," Ha explained, "even if I know something I really like to buy. I tell myself, 'Hold it, hold it until you can do it. For now, just forget it.'" Within eight months, she had saved enough for a down payment on a $16,000 house; she paid off the mortgage in three years. She married and had two daughters of her own, and in 1989 she bought a laundromat, five adjoining lots, and a vacant building to house her relatives, should they be allowed to emigrate to the United States. Ha also began to take college courses; she wanted to become a teacher. After earning two associate of arts degrees, she was hired as a paraprofessional at Kansas City's Northeast High School, a magnet school for law and public service.

What sustained Nguyet Thu Ha was her dream of bringing her entire family to Kansas City. Soon after she and the children fled Vietnam, Ha's father died, perhaps of sadness, she thought. Her mother and four older siblings and their families remained in Vietnam. Ha often dreamed about her mother, and sometimes her sobbing woke her daughters. "They wake me up and they wipe my tears and they say, 'Mommy, it's OK.'" For ten years, Ha filled out U.S. government forms and telephoned and visited the offices of the Im-

New immigrants were often eager to become new citizens. In 1996, in a naturalization ceremony held in San Jose, California, a woman from Southeast Asia proudly held an American flag as she took the oath to become a citizen of the United States. (© David Butow/Saba) migration and Naturalization Service (INS), but nothing happened. Then she received a call from the INS: Ha's mother, two brothers, a sister-in-law, and a niece would be arriving in a couple of days at Kansas City International Airport. Her mother, the last to leave the airplane, was engulfed by hugs. Ha was overjoyed: "I say, 'Is this real or I still dream?' You wish to have it for long time, and then one moment you have it, and you don't trust it." But it was real. (By 1997, not only Ha's mother but all eight of her siblings, most with their children, were living in the United States.)

Nguyet Thu Ha and her family were part of the "new immigration," which began in the early 1970s, when record numbers of immigrants came to the United States from Asia, Mexico, Central and South America, and the Caribbean. Many of the new immigrants came as families, though some—such as Nguyet Thu Ha's group—arrived a few family members at a time over a period of years. Unlike earlier immigrants, most of the new arrivals were people of color, and race proved to be both a barrier and a spur to success for the new immigrants. Established migration patterns tended to determine where the newcomers, such as Ha's family, went. "People immigrate to where they find connections and a measure of familiarity," explained Alejandro Portes, a sociologist at Johns Hopkins University. Almost 70 percent of the new immigrants settled in six states: California, Florida, Texas, New York, New Jersey, and Illinois. The newcomers redefined urban areas such as Los Angeles, Chicago, and Miami, where nearly three-quarters of city residents spoke a language other than English at home.

Although well-wishers often were on hand to greet the newcomers, the history of the nation's treatment of people of color did not augur well for them. Most found only low-paying jobs, and some suffered hostility and even violence from native-born Americans. Nevertheless, they persevered, pursuing their dreams in a country that was changing racially and ethnically. At Northeast High School, for example, where Nguyet Thu Ha found her first job as a teacher's aide, the student body was richly diverse: white, black, Hispanic, Asian, and American Indian. In their pursuit of both a magnet school and cultural diversity, these teenagers were bused to Northeast from all over Kansas City. Andrea Johnson, a junior and an African American, explained that it was "beneficial going to a school with different races because you learn about different cultures." Rebecca Hernandez, a senior, agreed, saying she believed it would get monotonous going to school "with the same people your whole life.

The world is not separate but equal. I don't want to crawl into my little Hispanic shell."

The American people experienced wrenching economic, political, and social change in the 1970s and 1980s. First, the new immigration touched millions of people's lives, immigrant and nonimmigrant alike. Second, in the 1970s, the twenty-five-year postwar economic boom ended. The rate of economic growth slowed and sometimes stalled, and disquieting signs of inflation materialized. Third, economic inequality and social polarization grew in the 1970s and 1980s, widening the gap between rich and poor, between whites and people of color, and between the suburbs and the inner cities. Fourth, a host of new social problems emerged in the 1980s, notably AIDS and crack cocaine. Finally, although women made significant gains in the 1970s and 1980s, especially in education, the professions, and the job market, they also suffered setbacks, including the emergence of an antifeminist movement that opposed women's aspirations for gender equality.

After Vietnam and Watergate, the American people were cynical about politics and skeptical of their leaders. The presidency of Gerald R. Ford was a time of healing, not activism. Ford's successor as president, Jimmy Carter, scored notable domestic successes, but he was unpopular with the public. Moreover, neither Ford nor Carter was able to restore economic or social health to the nation. But in response to their failures, there was a resurgence of conservatism, particularly among Americans who believed that the 1960s had been a period of immoral excesses, and who doubted that government had the capacity to serve the people, let alone solve major problems. Ronald Reagan became a hero to the conservatives, and after defeating Carter in 1980, he served as president for the next eight years. In 1988, when the voters went to the polls, the nation was at peace, both unemployment and inflation were at low levels, and Reagan was still a political hero to many Americans. ■

Economic Crisis and Ford's Response

 It was evident in the early 1970s that the United States was beginning to suffer economic decline. Recessions—which economists define as at least two consecutive quarters of no growth in the gross national product (GNP)—began to occur more frequently. An

IMPORTANT EVENTS

1974 OPEC increases oil prices
Nixon resigns; Ford becomes president
Ford creates WIN program to fight
inflation
Equal Credit Opportunity Act equalizes
loan and credit card terms for men and
women

1975 Nuclear accident occurs at Brown's Ferry
Antibusing agitation erupts in Louisville
and Boston
Economic recession hits nation

1976 Hyde Amendment cuts off Medicaid funds
for abortions
Carter elected president

1978 *Bakke v. University of California* outlaws
quotas but upholds affirmative action
California voters approve Proposition 13

1979 Three Mile Island nuclear accident raises
fears of meltdown
Moral Majority established
Federal Reserve Board tightens money
supply
American hostages seized in Iran

1980 Economic recession recurs
Race riots break out in Miami and
Chattanooga
Reagan elected president
Republicans gain control of Senate

1981 AIDS first observed in United States
Prime interest rate reaches 21.5 percent
Congress approves Reagan's budget and tax
cuts
Reagan breaks air traffic controllers strike
Economic recession; unemployment hits 8
percent

1982 Unemployment reaches 10 percent
Voting Rights Act of 1965 renewed

1983 More than half of adult women work outside
the home
ERA dies for lack of ratification

1984 Reagan reelected

1985 Gramm-Rudman bill calls for balanced
budget by 1991

1986 Tax Reform Act lowers personal income taxes
Immigration Reform and Control (Simpson-
Rodino) Act provides amnesty to undocu-
mented workers
Iran-contra scandal breaks
Republicans lose control of Senate

1987 Stock market prices drop 508 points in one
day

1988 *Understanding AIDS* mailed to 107 million
households
Bush elected president

eleven-month recession struck the country in 1969 and 1970, the first recession in almost a decade. Between 1973 and 1990, there were four more, and two (1973–1975, 1981–1982) were particularly long and harsh. Americans' economic insecurity, which was pronounced in the 1970s, persisted into the 1980s.

America's economic vulnerability was confirmed by the Arab oil embargo of 1973 (see page 903), which debunked the myth that the United States was a fortress that could stand alone. The country, which was importing one-third of its oil supplies, was dependent for its survival on imported oil. Even before the embargo, the United States had suffered occasional shortages of natural gas, heating oil, and gasoline. But the American people, who had grown up on inexpensive and abundant energy, made few efforts to conserve; they drove big cars and lived in poorly insulated homes.

In 1973 the American people also had to deal with the oil price increases ordered by the Organization of Petroleum Exporting Countries (OPEC). Oil prices rose 350 percent that year. As Americans grappled with the economic, social, and political costs of the price hikes, multinational oil companies prospered: their profits jumped 70 percent in 1973 and another 40 percent in 1974. Meanwhile, the steep rises in oil prices reverberated through the entire economy, tending to make everything that had to be shipped cost more. Inflation jumped from 3 percent in 1972 to a frightening 11 percent in 1974. Many Americans were suffering hard times.

OPEC Price Increases Fuel Inflation

In 1973 General Motors laid off 38,000 workers indefinitely—6 percent of its domestic work force—and put another 48,000 on leaves for up to ten days at

The Organization of Petroleum Exporting Countries (OPEC) raised oil prices several times in the 1970s. Each increase fueled the rise of inflation in the United States; and Americans, who had expected cheap energy to last forever, saw their expectations dashed. Long lines at the gas pumps were a reminder that an era of easy abundance had passed. (Don Wright in the *Miami News,* 1976, Tribune Media Services)

Auto Industry Recession

a time. Sales of gas-guzzling American autos plummeted as consumers rushed to purchase energy-efficient foreign subcompacts from Japan and Europe. Like Ford and Chrysler, GM was stuck with mostly large-car assembly plants. The recession that hit the auto industry in 1973 deepened in 1974. Moreover, there was an accelerator effect because the ailing American auto companies quit buying steel, glass, rubber, and tool-and-die products. And as the recession in the auto industry spread, other manufacturers began laying off experienced employees with seniority.

Unlike earlier postwar recessions, this one did not fade away in a year or two. Americans in the 1970s reeled under the one-two punch of *stagflation.* First, economic *stag*nation produced unemployment, particularly in heavy industry. Americans saw once-proud automobile and steel plants close. As a result of such "deindustrialization," many jobs were jeopardized while others disappeared forever. Second, in*flation* produced soaring prices, which eroded the purchasing power of workers' paychecks and forced them to raid their savings, sacrificing future security to current needs. The 1970s was the first decade since the Great Depression in which Americans' purchasing power declined, and the experience shook people's confidence that they could shape their personal destinies.

Stagflation also presented formidable problems to government policymakers. In earlier recessions, Republican as well as Democratic administrations had held to a policy of Keynesianism. To minimize the swings in the business cycle, they had manipulated federal policies—both fiscal policies (taxes and government spending) and monetary policies (interest rates and the money supply). They hoped by so doing to keep employment up and inflation down. Beginning in the 1970s, however, joblessness and prices both began to rise sharply. Policies designed to correct one problem seemed only to worsen the other.

Even in the best of times, the economy would have been hard-pressed to produce jobs for the millions of baby boomers who joined the labor market in the 1970s. As it was, economic activity created 27 million additional jobs during the decade, a remarkable increase of 32 percent.

The Shifting Occupational Structure

But deindustrialization was causing a shift in the occupational structure. As heavy industries collapsed, laid-off workers took jobs in the service sector, working in fast-food restaurants, all-night gas stations, and convenience stores—but at half of their former wages and without healthcare and other benefits. In 1979, 31 percent of households lived on incomes below $25,000; the comparable figure a decade later was 42 percent. Workers who once had held high-paying blue-collar jobs saw their middle-class standards of living slipping away from them.

A central economic problem was a slowing of growth in productivity—the average output of goods per hour of labor. Between 1947 and 1965, American industrial productivity had increased an average of 3.3 percent a year, raising manufacturers' profits and lowering the cost of products to consumers. From 1966 to 1970, annual productivity growth averaged only 1.5 percent; it fell further between 1971 and 1975 and reached a mere 0.2 percent between 1976 and 1980. Economists blamed lack of business investment in state-of-the-art technology, declining educational standards, and an alleged erosion of the work ethic. Whatever the causes, American goods cost more than those of foreign competitors; in the world's increasingly competitive markets, many American products fared poorly. The Joint Economic Committee of Congress warned, "The average American is likely to see his standard of living drastically decline in the 1980s unless the United States accelerates its rate of productivity growth."

Lagging Productivity

The lag in productivity was not matched by a decrease in workers' expectations. Wage increases regularly exceeded production increases, and some economists blamed the raises for inflation. Indeed, wages that went up seldom came down again. Managers of the nation's basic industries—steel, autos, rubber—complained that the automatic cost-of-living adjustments in their labor contracts left them little margin to restrain price hikes.

Another spur to inflation was easy credit. More people had credit cards; the number of MasterCard cardholders jumped from 32 million in 1974 to 57 million five years later. And with their credit cards in hand, Americans went on a buying spree; between 1975 and 1979, household and business borrowing more than tripled (from $94 billion to $328 billion). The credit explosion helped bid up the price of everything, from houses to gold. Farmers bought new farmland and expensive machinery and irrigation equipment. The nation's farm debt, $55 billion in 1971, had reached $166 billion by 1980. Overburdened with debts, many farmers faced bankruptcy in the 1980s.

Easy Credit and Inflation

Every expert had a scapegoat to blame for the nation's economic doldrums. Labor leaders cited foreign competition and called for protective tariffs. Some businesspeople and economists blamed the cost of obeying federal health and safety laws and pollution controls. They urged officials to abolish the Environmental Protection Agency and the Occupational Safety and Health Administration. They also pressed for deregulation of the oil, airline, and trucking industries on the theory that competition would drive prices down. Above all, critics attacked the federal government's massive spending programs; the mounting national debt, they said, was the sad result.

By the time Gerald Ford became president after Richard M. Nixon's resignation in 1974, OPEC price increases had pushed the inflation rate to 11 percent. Appalled, Ford created Whip Inflation Now (WIN), a voluntary program that encouraged businesses, consumers, and workers to save energy and organize grassroots anti-inflation efforts. In the 1974 congressional elections, voters responded to WIN, Watergate, and Ford's pardon of Nixon by giving the Democrats fifty-two additional seats in the House and four in the Senate. Ford showed political courage in 1974 when he offered clemency to Vietnam War draft evaders, but he received blistering criticism from veterans' groups and other conservatives.

President Ford's Response

Ford's response to inflation was to curb federal spending and encourage the Federal Reserve Board to raise its interest rates to banks, thus tightening credit. Ford was following the tenets of monetary theory, which held that the best way to reduce inflation was to keep the nation's money supply growing at a slow, consistent rate. With less money available to "chase" the supply of goods, monetarists contended, price increases would gently slow down. But these actions prompted yet another recession—only this time it was the worst in forty years. Unemployment jumped to 8.5 percent in 1975, and because the economy had stagnated, the federal deficit for fiscal year 1976–1977 hit a record $60 billion.

Ford devised no lasting solutions to the energy crisis, but the crisis seemed to pass when OPEC ended the embargo—and the incentive to prevent future shortages dissolved as well. The energy crisis, however, did intensify public debate over nuclear power. For the sake of energy independence, advocates asserted, the United States had to rely more on

Nuclear Power

nuclear energy. Environmental activists countered that the risk of nuclear accident was too great and that there was no safe way to store nuclear waste. Accidents in the nuclear power reactors at Brown's Ferry, Alabama (1975), and Three Mile Island, Pennsylvania (1979), gave credence to the activists' arguments. By 1979, however, ninety-six reactors were under construction throughout the nation, and thirty more were on order.

In the 1970s the combined effects of the energy crisis, stagflation, and the flight of industry and the middle class to the suburbs and the Sunbelt were producing fiscal disaster in the nation's cities (see Chapter 30). Not since 1933, when Detroit defaulted on its debts, had a major American city gone bankrupt. But New York City was near financial collapse by late 1975. President Ford vowed "to veto any bill that has as its purpose a federal bailout of New York City," but he relented after the Senate and House Banking Committees approved loan guarantees, and the city was saved. New York was not alone in its financial problems; other Frostbelt cities were in trouble, saddled with growing welfare rolls, deindustrialization, and a declining tax base. In 1978 Cleveland defaulted on its debts.

Throughout Ford's two-and-a-half-year presidential administration, relatively little was accomplished.

Gerald Ford's Presidency

After Vietnam and Watergate, Congress asserted itself and enjoyed new power. Ford almost routinely vetoed its bills, but Congress often overrode his vetoes. For the first time in the nation's history, furthermore, neither the president nor the vice president had been popularly elected. One of Ford's first acts as president had been to select Nelson Rockefeller, former governor of New York, as his vice president. But Republican prospects for retaining the presidency in the 1976 election seemed gloomy.

While Ford struggled with a Democratic Congress, the Democratic Party geared up for the presidential election of 1976. Against the

Election of 1976

background of Watergate secrecy and corruption, one candidate in particular promised honesty and openness. "I will never lie to you," pledged Jimmy Carter, an obscure former one-term governor of Georgia. Carter presented himself as both a fiscal conservative who would restrain government spending and a social liberal who would fight for the poor, the aged, people of color, workers, urban dwellers, and farmers. When

On inauguration day, President Jimmy Carter (b. 1924) and his wife Rosalyn caught the public's fancy by walking from the Capitol to the White House. Despite this symbolic beginning, Carter became increasingly isolated both from the American people and from Congress. (Jimmy Carter Library)

this born-again Christian promised voters efficiency and decency in government, they believed him. It helped, too, that Carter was a southerner, whose candidacy might block Republican electoral advances in the white South. Carter arrived at the convention with more than enough delegates to win the nomination. His choice of Senator Walter Mondale of Minnesota as his running mate served to cement relations with northern liberals, African Americans, union members, and political bosses.

Neither Carter nor President Ford, the Republican nominee, inspired much interest, and on election day only 54 percent of the electorate bestirred itself to vote. Nevertheless, an analysis of the turnout was instructive. Carter did carry ten of the eleven states in the Deep South. But as one political commentator observed, the vote nationwide was "fractured to a marked degree along the fault line separating the haves and have-nots." Although Carter won nearly 90 percent of the African American and Mexican American vote, he squeaked to victory by a slim 1.7 million votes out of 80 million cast. Ford's appeal was strongest among middle- and upper-middle-class white voters.

Continuing Economic Problems and the Carter Presidency

Economic troubles got worse, and by 1980 the economy was in a shambles. Inflation had jumped in 1979 to over 13 percent, and traders around the world had lost confidence in the dollar, causing unprecedented increases in the price of gold. To steady the dollar and curb inflation, the Federal Reserve Board took drastic measures. First, the board cut the money supply— partly by selling Treasury securities to take money out of circulation—thus forcing borrowers to bid up interest rates sufficiently to dampen the economy and reduce inflation. Second, it raised the rate at which the Federal Reserve loaned money to banks. As a result, mortgage-interest rates leaped beyond 15 percent, and the prime lending rate (the rate charged to businesses) hit an all-time high of 20 percent. Inflation fell, but only to 12 percent.

Worse still, by 1980 the nation was in a full-fledged recession. The 1980 unemployment rate of 7.5 percent, combined with the 12 percent inflation rate, had produced a staggeringly high "discomfort index" (the unemployment rate plus the inflation rate) of just

Economic Discomfort in 1980

under 20 percent (see Figure 32.1). Yet the government was unable to control the causes of the discomfort. In 1976 Carter had gibed at the incumbent president, Gerald Ford, by saying, "Anything you don't like about Washington, I suggest you blame on him." In 1980 Carter was the incumbent, and many Americans blamed *him* for the problems that beset the country.

Carter failed to inspire Americans, and he alienated Democratic Party members. Elected as an outsider, he remained one throughout his presidency. Moreover, Carter's conservative economic policies disenchanted Democrats who had grown up in the party's

Figure 32.1 "Discomfort Index" (Unemployment Plus Inflation), 1974–1989 Americans' economic discomfort directly determined their political behavior. When the "discomfort index" was high in 1976 and 1980, Americans voted for a change in presidents. When economic discomfort declined in 1984 and 1988, Ronald Reagan and George Bush were the political beneficiaries. (Source: Adapted from *Economic Report of the President, 1992* [Washington, D.C., 1992], pp. 340, 365.)

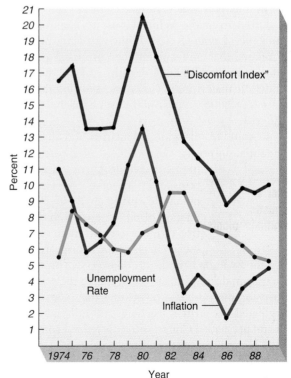

Carter's Flagging Popularity

New Deal liberal tradition. His support of deregulation and his opposition to wage and price controls and gasoline rationing ran counter to liberal Democratic principles. Seeing inflation as a greater threat to the nation's economy than either recession or unemployment, Carter announced that his top priority would be "to discipline the growth of government spending," even though doing so would add to the jobless rolls. But he was unable to gain Congress's cooperation, and both federal expenditures and inflation continued to rise.

Carter's problems were not entirely of his own making. In 1979 the shah of Iran's government fell to revolutionary forces. When Carter admitted the shah to the United States for medical treatment, mobs seized the American embassy in Teheran and held fifty-two Americans as hostages for 444 days (see page 907). The new Iranian government also cut off oil supplies to the United States. The same year OPEC raised its prices again, and the cost of crude oil nearly doubled. As Americans waited in long lines at gasoline pumps, and as they bridled at Carter's inability to free the hostages, public approval of the president reached a new low.

Carter also inherited political problems. In the wake of Vietnam and Watergate, power temporarily had shifted from the White House to Capitol Hill. Meanwhile, Congress was filling up with political newcomers, men and women unaccustomed to reflex obedience to established leadership. Despite the large Democratic majorities in Congress following the Watergate scandal, party discipline seemed to be a thing of the past.

Despite his flagging popularity and declining presidential authority, Carter scored noteworthy domestic accomplishments in energy, transportation, and conservation policy. To encourage domestic production of oil, he phased in decontrol of oil prices. To moderate the social effects of the energy crisis, he called for a windfall-profits tax on excessive profits resulting from decontrol, and for grants to the poor and elderly for the purchase of heating fuel. Carter also deregulated the airline, trucking, and railroad industries and persuaded Congress to ease federal control of banks. His administration established a $1.6 billion "superfund" to clean up abandoned chemical-waste sites and created two free-standing departments—the

Carter's Domestic Accomplishments

Departments of Energy and Education. Finally, he placed more than 100 million acres of Alaskan land under the federal government's protection as national parks, national forests, and wildlife refuges.

Conservative Resurgence and Reagan

Political and economic conservatives had long expressed doubt about whether big government programs can actually serve the people. Critics pointed to stagflation as evidence of the failure of New Deal and Great Society economics. Even some Democrats agreed. Senator Gary Hart, a Colorado Democrat, characterized this mood as "a nonideological skepticism about the old, Rooseveltian solutions to social problems."

In the 1970s conservatives at the state level worked to repeal the social welfare system. California voters approved a 1978 tax-cutting referendum called Proposition 13, which reduced property taxes and put stringent limits on state spending for social programs. Proposition 13 set off shock waves: nearly a score of other states imposed similar ceilings on taxes and expenditures. On the national level, conservatives lobbied for a constitutional amendment to prohibit federal budget deficits. Perhaps most significant, tax revolts became political vehicles for conservative candidates to win elections.

In the 1970s and 1980s political and economic conservatives joined forces with cultural and religious conservatives and thereby changed the political landscape. In 1979 Reverend Jerry Falwell, a minister from Virginia, helped to found the Moral Majority, which advocated what it called "family values," including opposition to abortion rights and homosexuality. Together with conservative think tanks like the Hoover Institution and the American Enterprise Institute and conservative magazines like *National Review*, the Moral Majority and various church groups formed a flourishing network of potential supporters for conservative candidates. By the late 1970s, conservatism was becoming a potent political force.

Resurgence of Conservatism

Ronald Reagan appealed mightily to both wings of the movement. A proponent of prayer in the public schools and an opponent of abortion, Reagan argued for a return to the morality that he believed had domi-

How do historians know...

that the political influence of Christian conservatives grew significantly in the 1970s and 1980s? Evidence can be found in the nation's media, including television, radio, and newspapers and magazines. References to numerous articles on the Christian right may be found in a number of indexes, including the *Reader's Guide to Periodical Literature* and the *New York Times Index*. The media reported extensively in 1979, for example, that the Reverend Jerry Falwell, a radio-TV preacher whose *Old Time Gospel Hour* reached 15 million Americans, had helped to establish the Moral Majority in support of "family values." The organization quickly registered between 2 and 3 million new voters, started a newspaper, and bought daily time on 140 radio stations. Increasingly, evangelical Christians believed they had a moral obligation to enter politics on the side of "a pro-life, pro-traditional family, pro-moral position." In 1980 the Republicans eagerly sought, and received, the political support of Falwell and his followers. During the 1980s Christian conservatives boosted Pat Robertson, another so-called televangelist, to national political influence. Robertson, a Baptist minister, was host of television's popular *700 Club*, as well as founder of the Christian Coalition, the nation's largest religious-political conservative organization, and, in 1988, a candidate for the Republican presidential nomination.

Evidence of Christian conservatives' growing political activism can also be found in local elections where the issues have frequently involved abortion, gay rights, prayer in the public schools, and the teaching of creationism. Evidence exists, too, in the published platforms of the Republican Party, particularly in 1992, when the party denounced any deviation from "family values." In 1994 the Christian Coalition reciprocated by endorsing the Republicans' Contract with America. With political success, however, have come divisions within the Christian conservative movement, as well as deep frustrations, especially over Congress's failure, in 1999, to remove Bill Clinton from the presidency. During that year's impeachment hearings, with Clinton enjoying widespread public support, some Christian conservatives withdrew from politics. Having concluded that the Moral Majority had become the moral minority, they vowed not to participate in the elections of 2000. (Photo: Dennis Brack/Black Star)

nated American culture before the 1960s. He promised a balanced budget, and he blamed government for fettering American economic creativity. Reagan's 1980 presidential victory revealed that conservatism had become the dominant mood of the nation.

The 1980 federal census provided additional insights into the reasons for conservatism's resurgence in

A Shifting Population

the United States. First, the 1980 census revealed significant growth in the more politically conservative elderly population—up 24 percent since 1970—and a two-year rise in the median age. In addition, the number of retired people increased by more than 50 percent in the

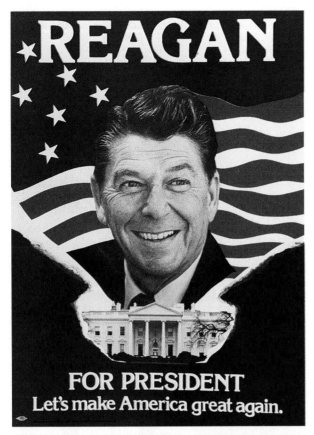

REAGAN

FOR PRESIDENT
Let's make America great again.

Ronald Reagan, the Republican presidential candidate in 1980, campaigned for "family values," an aggressive anti-Soviet foreign and military policy, and tax cuts. He also exuded optimism and appealed to Americans' patriotism. This poster issued by the Republican National Committee included Reagan's favorite campaign slogan, "Let's make America great again."   (Collection of David J. and Janice L. Frent)

1970s. Second, the census documented the continuing shift of large numbers of people from the politically liberal Frostbelt states of the Northeast and Midwest to the more conservative Sunbelt states of the South and West (see Map 32.1). The census findings also meant that seventeen seats in the House of Representatives would shift from the Frostbelt to the Sunbelt by the 1982 elections. Florida would gain four seats, Texas three, and California two; New York would lose five.

In 1980 several conservative Republican politicians ran for the White House. Foremost among them was Ronald Reagan, former movie star and two-term governor of California. When he was president of the Screen Actors Guild in Hollywood in the 1940s, his

Reagan's Early Career

politics were those of a New Deal Democrat. But touring the country in the 1950s as host of the television program *General Electric Theatre*, he became increasingly conservative. In 1964 he made a televised appeal for Senator Barry Goldwater, the Republican presidential candidate. Reagan's speech catapulted him to the forefront of conservative politics and became his personal platform for the presidency. America, Reagan said, had come to "a time for choosing" between free enterprise and big government, between individual liberty and "the ant heap of totalitarianism." Two years later he was elected governor of California.

During his two four-year terms as governor, Reagan maintained his conservative rhetoric but displayed a pragmatic approach to governing. While denouncing welfare, he presided over reform of the state's social welfare bureaucracy. While demanding that student radicals at the University of California either obey the rules or face the prospect of a "bloodbath," he endorsed most of the university's budget requests. And he signed one of the nation's most liberal abortion laws.

In the Republican primaries, Reagan triumphed easily over former CIA director George Bush and

Reagan as the Republican Candidate

Representative John Anderson, who ran as an independent. Reagan's appeal to the voters in the presidential campaign was much broader than experts had predicted. He promised economy in government and a balanced budget, and he committed himself to "supply-side" economics, or tax reductions to businesses to encourage capital investment. Although Reagan planned to slash federal spending, he also pledged to cut income taxes and boost the defense budget—a prescription that George Bush ridiculed as "voodoo economics." Reagan declared that he now opposed legalized abortion, and his stand against the Equal Rights Amendment (ERA) recommended him to social conservatives.

The strength of Reagan's candidacy was that it united the old right wing with the new. The old right had never been very interested in social or cultural issues, explained Richard Viguerie, a conservative fundraiser. "But when political conservative leaders began to . . . strike an alliance with social conservatives—the pro-life people, the anti-ERA people, the evangelical and born-again Christians, the people concerned about gay rights, prayer in the schools, sex in

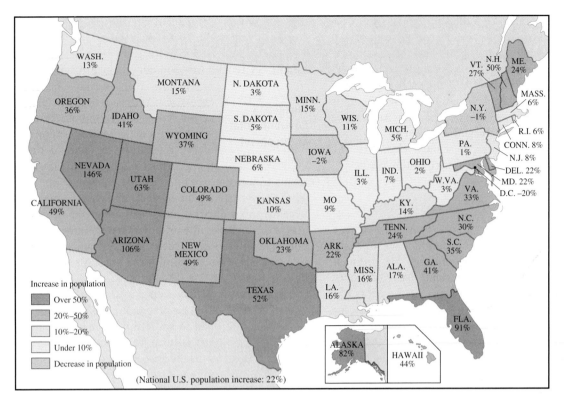

Map 32.1 The Continued Shift to the Sunbelt in the 1970s and 1980s Throughout the 1970s and 1980s, Americans continued to leave economically declining areas of the North and East in pursuit of opportunity in the Sunbelt. States in the Sunbelt and in the West had the largest population increases.

the movies or whatever—that's when this whole movement began to come alive."

In the 1980 election, President Carter faced formidable problems. American hostages were still held captive in Iran, and stagflation beset the economy. Carter's major problem was his abysmal approval rating of 21 percent, even lower than Richard Nixon's 24 percent during the Watergate crisis. And on election day, voters gave Reagan and his running mate George Bush 51 percent of the vote versus 41 percent for Carter and almost 7 percent for Anderson (see Map 32.2). Reagan's sweep was nationwide; Carter carried only six states and the District of Columbia. The vote was not only an affirmation of Reagan's conservatism but also a signal of the nation's deep dissatisfaction with Jimmy Carter's management of both the economy and foreign policy. As startling as Reagan's sweep was the capture of twelve Senate seats by Republican candidates, giving the Republicans a

Election of 1980

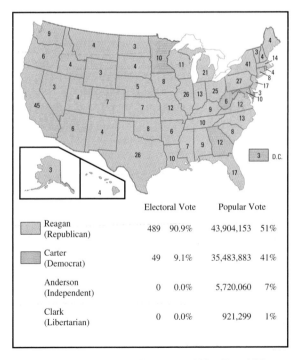

	Electoral Vote		Popular Vote	
Reagan (Republican)	489	90.9%	43,904,153	51%
Carter (Democrat)	49	9.1%	35,483,883	41%
Anderson (Independent)	0	0.0%	5,720,060	7%
Clark (Libertarian)	0	0.0%	921,299	1%

Map 32.2 Presidential Election, 1980 Ronald Reagan scored the first of two political landslides in 1980, when he won forty-four states to Jimmy Carter's six.

majority in that house. Republicans also gained thirty-five seats in the House and four state governorships.

The preceding fifteen years had been difficult ones for the Democratic Party. Fragmented by the issues of race and war, in the 1970s the party had lost the support of many whites, who viewed the Democrats as the party of welfare, taxes, and African Americans. With self-proclaimed "Reagan Democrats" supporting Republican candidates, it seemed clear that the Democrats would be running scared in the 1980s.

"Reaganomics"

 Upon taking office, President Reagan wasted little time announcing what he called "a new beginning." He immediately launched a double-barreled attack called "Reaganomics" on problems in the economy. First, he asked Congress to cut billions from domestic programs, including Medicare and Medicaid, food stamps, welfare subsidies for the working poor, and school meals. Congress endorsed most of Reagan's demands; joining the Republicans in support were conservative southern Democrats. Reagan soon initiated a second round of budget cuts, resulting among other things in the trimming of a million food-stamp recipients from government rolls.

Tax cuts were the second facet of Reagan's economic plan. A fervent believer in supply-side economics, he called for reductions in the income taxes of the affluent and of corporations in order to stimulate savings and investments. New capital would be invested, the argument went, and would produce new plants, new jobs, and new products. As prosperity returned, the profits at the top would "trickle down" to the middle classes and even to the poor. Congress responded with a five-year, $750 billion tax cut, the largest ever in American history, featuring a 25 percent reduction in personal income taxes over three years. Other provisions increased business investment tax credits and depreciation allowances and lowered the maximum tax on income from 70 to 50 percent.

Tax Cuts

The wealthy gained the most from these tax cuts. In the 1980s, the rich got richer, as poverty deepened for many others. Women and people of color were particularly hard hit, for they usually were the last hired and the first laid off. Even when they had jobs, they were paid less than white men, and experts pointed to the growing "feminization" and "blacken-ing" of poverty, which, after falling in the 1960s, climbed again in the 1970s and 1980s.

A third item occupied Reagan's agenda: a vigorous assault on federal environmental, health, and safety regulations that, Reagan believed, excessively reduced business profits and discouraged economic growth. The president appointed opponents of the regulations to enforce them. Some critics likened such appointments to hiring foxes to guard the chicken coop. Reagan officials explained that slackened enforcement was necessary to reduce business costs and make American goods competitive in world markets, but environmentalists countered that such policies invited disaster, such as toxic-waste poisoning and nuclear reactor accidents.

Weakened Environmental Enforcement

Hard times hit labor unions in the 1980s. Faced with recession and unemployment, union negotiators had to settle for less than they were accustomed to receiving. American workers who ratified contracts during the first three months of Reagan's term settled for pay increases averaging only 2.2 percent, the biggest drop in wage settlements since the government began collecting such data in 1954. Unions had suffered large membership losses when unemployment hit heavy industry, and their efforts to unionize the high-growth electronics and service sectors of the economy were failing.

Hard Times for Labor Unions

Reagan made the unions' hard times worse. He presided over the government's busting of the Professional Air Traffic Controllers Organization (PATCO) during the union's 1981 strike. His appointees to the National Labor Relations Board consistently voted against labor and for management. Although Reagan appeared to be an enemy of labor, an estimated 44 percent of union families had voted for him in 1980, and many still responded positively to his genial personality, espousal of old-fashioned values, and vigorous anticommunist rhetoric.

Reagan enjoyed two notable economic successes during his first two years in office. First, the inflation rate plummeted, falling from 12 percent in 1980 to less than 7 percent in 1982. Oil led the way in price declines; after eight years OPEC had at last increased its oil production, thus lowering prices. In 1981 the United States was awash with oil as world production exceeded demand by 2 million barrels a

Falling Inflation

day. Moreover, as inflation fell, so too did the cost of borrowing money. Interest rates for bank loans, which had stood at a record high of 21.5 percent in early 1981, dropped to 10.5 percent by 1983.

But there was a second, more sobering, explanation for the decline in inflation. By mid-1981 the nation was mired in a recession that not only persisted but deepened. During the last three months of the year, the GNP fell 5 percent, and sales of cars and houses dropped sharply. With declining economic activity, unemployment soared to 8 percent, the highest level in almost six years.

A year later, in late 1982, unemployment had reached 10.8 percent, the highest rate since 1940.

Rising Unemployment

Most of the jobless were adult men, particularly African Americans, who suffered an unemployment rate of 20 percent. Many of the unemployed were blue-collar workers in ailing "smokestack industries" such as autos, steel, and rubber. Reagan and his advisers had promised that supply-side economics would produce demand-side results and that consumers would lift the economy out of the recession by spending their tax cuts. But as late as April 1983, unemployment still stood at 10 percent and people were angry. Heavy industry was in a shambles. Jobless steelworkers paraded through McKeesport, Pennsylvania, carrying a coffin that bore the epitaph "American Dream." Agriculture, too, was faltering and near collapse. Farmers suffered not only from falling crop prices due to overproduction, but also from floods and droughts and from burdensome debts they had incurred at high interest rates. Many lost their property through mortgage foreclosures and farm auctions. Others filed for bankruptcy.

As the recession deepened in 1982, poverty rose to its highest level since 1965. The Bureau of the Census

Resurgence of Poverty

reported that the number of Americans living in poverty increased from 26 million in 1979 to 34 million in 1982. The largest single category of poor families consisted of households headed by women (36 percent). With one exception, poverty continued its rise in 1983, returning to the level that had prevailed before the enactment of President Johnson's Great Society. That exception was the elderly; politicians had begun paying attention to this vocal and rapidly growing population whose needs were ably articulated by the American Association of Retired Persons (AARP) and other groups.

President Reagan had announced that his administration would halt the expansion of social and health programs but would retain a "safety net" for the "truly needy." But he reneged on this promise, and Congress, unwilling to buck the popular president, sustained most of his decisions. Facing a budget deficit in excess of $200 billion in mid-1982, Reagan had three choices. First, he could cut back on his rearmament plans to spend $1.7 trillion over five years. This he refused to do; in fact, the budget he signed raised defense spending another 13 percent. Second, he could suspend or reduce the second installment of his tax cut. This choice, too, he found unacceptable. Third, he could—and did—cut welfare and social programs, pushing through Congress further cuts in Medicare and Medicaid, food stamps, federal pensions, and government-guaranteed home mortgages. Nevertheless, in the absence of budget cuts in other areas, or higher taxes, the federal debt continued to grow.

Democrats predicted victory for their party in the 1982 congressional elections. Just a week before the

1982 Elections

elections, however, a *New York Times*/CBS News poll reported that the American public was being tugged sharply in different directions: toward the Democrats by unemployment, toward the Republicans by declining inflation and the president's popularity. Nothing revealed Reagan's winning style better than his courageous response to an attempt on his life by a deranged young man in March 1981. John W. Hinckley, Jr., wounded the president, his press secretary, a Secret Service agent, and a police officer. Reagan's grace under fire caused his popularity ratings to soar. In the 1982 elections, 26 House seats swung to the Democrats, giving them a lead of 269 to 166. The Senate remained pro-Reagan, with a continued Republican majority of 54 to 46.

In another two years, there would be a presidential election. The president had to prove before then

The Election of 1984

that he could restore prosperity to the nation. As it turned out, Reagan's key reelection asset in 1984 was the economy, which was showing strong signs of recovery. In 1984 the GNP rose 7 percent, the sharpest increase since 1951, and midyear unemployment fell to a four-year low of 7 percent. The economy was heating up, but without sparking inflation. Indeed, inflation (4 percent in 1984) fell to its lowest level since 1967. A second factor in Reagan's favor was people's perception of him as

In 1984 Geraldine Ferraro, Democratic congresswoman from New York, made history by being the first woman nominated to run for the vice-presidency on a major party's ticket. (Collection of David J. and Janice L. Frent)

a strong leader in foreign as well as national affairs. Many Americans were proud that their nation was confronting the Soviets not only with firm words but with military interventions and a large military buildup (see Chapter 31). Third, Reagan was the enthusiastic choice of political conservatives of all kinds across the country. Patriotism was back in style, and Reagan won the approval of millions of other Americans who agreed with his television ads that it was "Morning in America" after two twilight decades of turmoil and self-doubt.

Aiding Reagan was the Democrats' failure to field a convincing alternative. The Democratic nominee—former vice president Walter Mondale—did not inspire Americans. Even the policies that Mondale espoused seemed timeworn and out of step with the nation's conservatism. Adding to Mondale's woes was the disarray of the Democratic Party; it had fragmented into separate caucuses of union members, African Americans, women, Jews, homosexuals, Hispanics, and other groups. Each caucus had its own agenda. The one bright spot for the Democrats was Mondale's historic selection of Representative Geraldine Ferraro of New York as the first woman vice-presidential candidate of a major political party. Ferraro showed herself to be an intelligent, indefatigable campaigner.

Mondale wanted to debate the federal deficit, but Reagan preferred to invoke the theme of leadership and rely on slogans. Mondale chastised Reagan for the mounting deficit, which had reached $175 billion in fiscal year 1984. But when Mondale announced that he would raise taxes to cut the deficit, he lost votes. Voters in 1984 had a clear choice, and in every state but Minnesota—Mondale's home state—they chose the Republican ticket. The election returns were the most convincing evidence yet that the nation had shifted to the right. The only groups still loyal to the Democratic ticket were African Americans, Hispanics, Jews, and the poor. Reagan scored solid victories with all other voting groups, including young people, whites in both North and South, high-school and college graduates, and Catholics as well as Protestants.

Fifty years earlier, the Democratic Party had gained the allegiance of millions of Americans, including blue-collar workers, who credited President Franklin Roosevelt's New Deal with having saved them during the Great Depression. The New Deal coalition controlled national politics for the next thirty years. But in the 1970s and 1980s, a deep reaction set in against the liberalized moral standards associated with the Democratic Party. Many Democrats held conservative views on welfare, abortion, homosexuality, and other social issues, and they switched their votes to Ronald Reagan and the Republican Party. Whether Reagan had forged a lasting conservative coalition—one that could repeal the New Deal—remained to be seen. What was not debatable was that, during his first term, he had succeeded in his principal aims.

People of Color and New Immigrants

Poverty was a growing problem in the 1970s and 1980s, particularly for people of color. Joblessness plagued blacks, Native Americans, and Hispanics, as well as many of the new immigrants. Most of America's poor were white, but African Americans made up a disproportionate share of the total. The overall poverty rate was 13 percent by 1980, but among blacks it was 33 percent and among Hispanics 26 percent, compared with 10 percent for whites. These figures had barely changed by the end of Ronald Reagan's presidency in 1989 (see Figure 32.2).

The weight of poverty fell most heavily on children, especially African American children, almost half of whom lived below the poverty line. A 1981 Children's Defense Fund survey reported that black children in the United States were four times more likely than whites to be born into poverty, twice as likely to drop out of school before twelfth grade, three times as likely to be unemployed, and five times as likely to be murdered. "Millions of black children lack self-confidence, feel discouragement, despair, numbness or rage as they try to grow up on islands of poverty, ill health, inadequate education . . . crime and rampant unemployment in a nation of boastful affluence," the report concluded. Many children lived in poor families headed by single women who earned meager incomes as domestic servants, laundresses, and kitchen helpers, supplemented by welfare assistance.

Some whites and even other blacks grumbled that poor blacks were responsible for their own poverty.

Declining Job Opportunities for African Americans

But the job market in the 1970s and 1980s was far different from that of twenty-five, fifty, or seventy-five years before. During periods of rapid industrialization, unskilled European immigrants and black migrants from the South had been able to find blue-collar jobs. Beginning in the 1970s, fewer such jobs were available; demand was greatest for skilled workers such as computer operators, bank tellers, secretaries, and bookkeepers. Most jobless people could not qualify. Moreover, blue-collar jobs in the inner cities were disappearing or moving to the suburbs. New York City alone had 234,000 fewer blue-collar workers in 1980 than it had at the beginning of the 1970s. For young African American men and women who lacked marketable skills, the situation was often tragic. The psychiatrist Alvin Poussaint observed, "A lot of black kids simply feel they don't count. . . . In terms of what makes this society run, they're expendable."

But a historical anomaly was at work. For even as the plight of the African American poor worsened, the

African American Middle Class

black middle class expanded. The number of black college students increased from 282,000 in 1966 to more than 1 million in 1980; by 1980 about one-third of all black high-school graduates were going on to college, the same proportion as among white youths. Some benefited from affirmative-action programs, which sought to compensate for decades of racial dis-

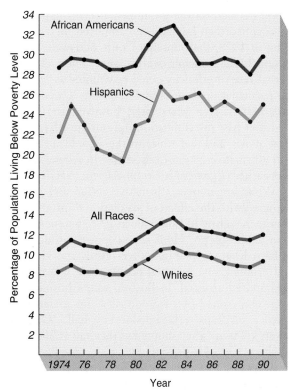

Figure 32.2   Poverty in America by Race, 1974–1990
Poverty in America rose in the early 1980s but subsided afterward. Many people of color, however, experienced little relief during the decade. Notice that the percentage of African Americans living below the poverty level was three times higher than that for whites. It also was much higher for Hispanics.   (Source: Adapted from U.S. Bureau of the Census, *Statistical Abstract of the United States* [Washington, D.C., 1992], p. 461.)

crimination by granting African American men and women educational (and employment) opportunities to advance themselves. By 1990 the number of black college students had increased further to 1.3 million. At least at the upper levels of black society, the dream of equality was being realized.

But as middle-class African Americans made gains, resentful whites complained that they were being victimized by "reverse discrim-ination." To meet federal affirmative-action requirements, some schools and companies had established quo-tas for minorities and women; in some cases the standards were lower than those for whites. When Allan Bakke, a white man, was denied admission to medical

White Backlash

school, he sued on the grounds that black applicants less qualified than he had been admitted. In a 5-to-4 ruling in 1978, the Supreme Court outlawed quotas but upheld the principle of affirmative action, explaining that race or ethnicity could be counted as "a 'plus' in a particular applicant's file" *(Bakke v. University of California)*. Eleven years later, however, the Court ruled that past discrimination did not "justify a rigid racial quota" and that white workers could sue to re-open affirmative-action cases settled in federal courts years earlier *(Richmond v. Croson, Martin v. Wilks)*.

White anger over affirmative action and busing combined with the effects of stagflation to produce an upsurge in racism. In Louisville in 1975, bumper stickers urged people to "Honk if you oppose busing," the Ku Klux Klan stepped up its recruiting, and violence soon erupted: one hundred people were injured and two hundred arrested. In Boston, where busing provoked numerous riots, a group of white students attacked a black passerby outside city hall. "Get the nigger; kill him!" they shouted as they ran at him with the sharp end of a flagstaff flying an American flag. Racial tension rose in cities across the nation.

African Americans were tense, and they showed their anger more openly than in the past. Charles Silberman wrote in *Criminal Violence,*

Black Anger

Criminal Justice (1978) that "black Americans have discovered that fear runs the other way, that whites are intimidated by their very presence. . . . The taboo against expression of antiwhite anger is breaking down, and 350 years of festering hatred has come spilling out." That hatred erupted several times in 1980, most notably in Miami and Chattanooga, after all-white juries acquitted whites in the killings of blacks. Miami's three days of rioting left eighteen dead and four hundred injured.

In the 1980s African American civil rights leaders denounced not only the judicial system but also the executive branch headed by President Ronald Reagan. Appointments were one issue: whereas 12 percent of President Jimmy Carter's high-level appointees had been black and 12 percent women, Reagan's were 4 percent black and 8 percent women. (Reagan did appoint four women to his cabinet and made history by appointing Sandra Day O'Connor the first woman associate justice of the Supreme Court.) Moreover, Reagan's civil rights chief in the Justice Department opposed busing and affirmative action, and he was criticized for lax enforcement of fair housing laws and laws banning sexual and racial discrimination in federal-

ly funded education programs. He also fought against renewing the Voting Rights Act of 1965, but Congress ignored his efforts and renewed the act in 1982.

"The Kerner report warning is coming true," asserted a group of scholars, politicians, and civil rights leaders who met in 1988 to assess race relations on the twentieth anniversary of the publication of the Kerner Commission report (see page 865). "America is again becoming two separate societies," with whites residing in the comfortable suburbs while African Americans in inner cities lived amid poverty, segregation, and crime. "Even the most pessimistic observers of the social scene in the later 1960s," observed a member of the group, "probably did not foresee or anticipate the sharp increases in the rates of social dislocation and massive breakdown of social institutions in ghetto areas."

Every bit as angry as African Americans were Native Americans. For one thing, in the 1970s and 1980s

Native Americans

they suffered the worst health of any group in the United States. American Indians suffered the highest incidence of tuberculosis, alcoholism, and suicide of any ethnic group in the country. Four in ten Native Americans were unemployed, and nine out of ten lived in substandard housing. The American Indian population did rise after the Second World War, reaching 1.7 million in 1990—more than half of whom lived in California, Oklahoma, Arizona, New Mexico, and North Carolina—but that was only a fraction of their population when the first Europeans arrived in North America. Faced with deplorable conditions in the 1970s, Native American militants were prepared to struggle to improve the quality of life on the reservations.

In 1973 members of the militant American Indian Movement (AIM) called for "Red Power." Demanding

"Red Power": Indian Self-Determination

the rights guaranteed Indians in treaties with the United States, they seized eleven hostages and a trading post on the Pine Ridge Reservation at Wounded Knee, South Dakota, where troops of the Seventh Cavalry had massacred three hundred Sioux in 1890 (see page 468). Their seventy-one-day confrontation with federal marshals ended with a government agreement to examine the treaty rights of the Oglala Sioux. Prosecution of AIM leaders for the Wounded Knee occupation was dismissed by a federal court in 1974. And for once, Congress listened to Native America, in 1974 passing

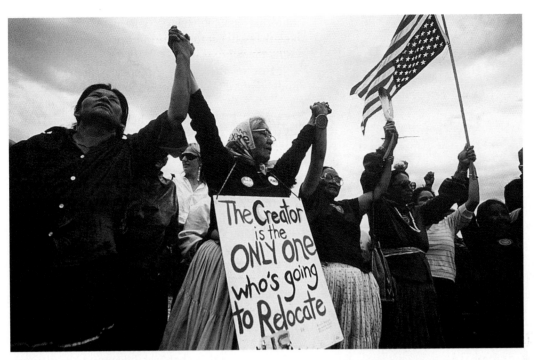

For nearly 115 years, an Arizona land dispute has divided the Hopi and Navajo tribes. A law passed by Congress in 1974 called for the division of 1.8 million acres between the tribes and ordered the relocation of tribal members living on land given to the other tribe. Hopi and Navajo traditionalists claimed that they had no dispute and that powerful economic interests were using the issue as a cover for seizing the area's rich coal and water rights. In 1986 these Hopis and Navajos joined forces to protest federal law directing the secretary of the interior to "expedite" relocation "without regard to any law or regulation."   (Lawrence Gus/Sygma)

the Indian Self-Determination Law, which provided Indians with greater control over federal programs, including schools, operating on reservations.

Native Americans also accused the federal government of breaking its treaty commitments—by seizing Indian lands, especially when they contained valuable minerals. In 1946 Congress established the Indian Claims Commission to compensate Indians for lands stolen from them. Under the legislation, lawyers for the Native American Rights Fund and other groups scored notable victories. In the 1970s the Chippewas in the upper Midwest, Indians on Washington's Puget Sound, and the Cheyenne-Arapaho tribes in Oklahoma won protection of their hunting and fishing rights and restitution of their land and water. And in 1980 the Supreme Court ordered the government to pay $106 million plus interest to the Sioux nation for the Black Hills of South Dakota, stolen when gold was found there in the 1870s. Nevertheless, corporations and govern-

Indian Suits for Lost Lands

ment agencies continued to covet Indian lands and disregard Indian religious beliefs: a coal company strip-mined a portion of the Hopi Sacred Circle, which according to tribal religion is the source of all life, and the sacred Black Hills of South Dakota are being mined again, this time for uranium.

As Indians fought to regain old rights, Hispanic Americans struggled to make a place for themselves. An inflow of immigrants unequaled since the turn of the century, coupled with a high birth rate, made Hispanic peoples America's fastest-growing minority by the 1970s. Of the more than 20 million Hispanics living in the United States in the 1970s, 8 million were Mexican Americans concentrated in California, Texas, Arizona, New Mexico, and Colorado. Several million Puerto Ricans, Cubans, Dominicans, and other immigrants from the Caribbean also lived in the United States, clustered principally on the East Coast in cities in Florida, New York, and other states.

Hispanic Americans

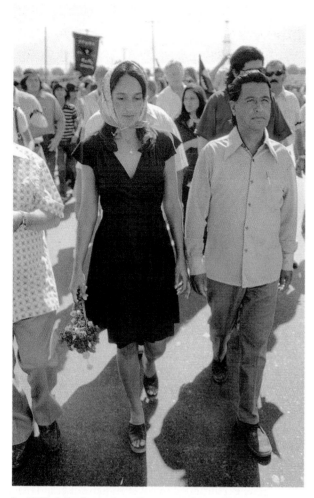

In 1976, folk singer Joan Baez and César Chávez, leader of the United Farm Workers (UFW), marched with other mourners through vineyards near Delano, California, at the funeral of Juan de la Cruz, a farm worker. De la Cruz had been murdered in a drive-by shotgun attack on a UFW picket line.   (Bob Fitch/Take Stock)

These officially acknowledged Hispanic Americans were joined by millions of undocumented workers, or illegal aliens. Beginning in the mid-1960s, large numbers of poverty-stricken Mexicans began to cross the poorly guarded 2,000-mile border. The movement north continued in the 1970s and 1980s. By 1990 one out of three Los Angelenos and Miamians were Hispanic, as were 48 percent of the population of San Antonio and 70 percent of El Paso. Discrimination awaited many of these new immigrants, as it had previous groups of newcomers. And the larger the Hispanic population has become, the more widespread has been the discrimination. "Anglos are afraid," said

California assemblyman Richard Alatorre. "They think they will get to be the minorities and we'll be opposing them."

Most of these new Americans preferred their family-centered culture to Anglo culture and, for that reason, resisted assimilation. "We want to be here," explained Daniel Villanueva, a TV executive in Los Angeles, "but without losing our language and our culture. They are a richness, a treasure that we don't care to lose."

Hispanic Cultural Pride

Like other minorities, Hispanics wanted political power—"brown power." In the 1960s César Chávez's United Farm Workers was the first Hispanic interest group to gain national attention. The militant Brown Berets attracted notice for their efforts to provide meals to preschoolers and courses in Chicano studies and consciousness raising to older students. And throughout the 1970s the Mexican American political party *La Raza Unida* was a potent force in the Southwest and in East Los Angeles.

Still, the group that was becoming the nation's largest minority exercised a disproportionately small share of political power. One reason was that Latin America is tremendously diverse. Although Mexican Americans, Puerto Ricans, Cubans, and other Hispanic groups shared a language and a religion, they differed in countless ways. And the differences were not only in country of origin: economic immigrants such as Mexican Americans crowded into West Coast *barrios* side by side with political refugees from Central American wars. Poverty was most severe where the population was most concentrated. "We need a Spanish Bobby Kennedy or Martin Luther King," observed Daniel Villanueva. "Right now he's just not there."

New Flux of Immigrants

During the 1970s and 1980s people of color immigrated to the United States in record numbers from Indochina, Mexico, Central and South America, and the Caribbean. Between 1970 and 1980 the United States absorbed more than 4 million immigrants and refugees and uncounted numbers of illegal aliens. High as these figures were, they doubled again during the next decade, with almost 9 million new arrivals. Many of the new immigrants came in family units, and women and children accounted for two-thirds of all legal immigrants. Although the new residents faced a long struggle, they were willing to work hard to succeed. Among the newcomers, Asian Americans seemed to be the most successful. There had been a burst of Asian immigration; the number of people whose origins were in Asia or the Pacific increased by 385 percent from 1971 to 1990.

The arrival of so many newcomers put pressure on Congress to curtail the flow and perhaps offer amnesty to aliens already living illegally in the United States. In 1978 Congress authorized a comprehensive reexamination of America's immigration policy. The immigration commission completed its study in 1981, but legislative solutions were delayed until 1986, when Congress passed the Immigration Reform and Control (Simpson-Rodino) Act, which provided amnesty to undocumented workers who had arrived before 1982. The act's purpose was to discourage illegal immigration by imposing sanctions on employers who hired undocumented workers, but it failed to stem the flow of people fleeing Mexico's economic woes. In 1988 the number of new immigrants from Mexico approached the record numbers reached before the reform law went into effect.

Immigration Reform

Feminism, Antifeminism, and Women's Lives

Women scored some impressive victories in the 1970s. In 1974 Congress passed the Equal Credit Opportunity Act, which enabled women to get bank loans and obtain credit cards on the same terms as men. In the field of criminal law, many states revised their statutes on rape, prohibiting defense lawyers from discrediting rape victims by revealing their previous sexual experience. Perhaps most significant were women's gains from affirmative action in hiring. As mandated by the Civil Rights Act of 1964 and the establishment of the Equal Employment Opportunity Commission, women and people of color applying for jobs had to receive the same consideration as white males. To take advantage of new opportunities, many women delayed having children until reaching their thirties and establishing themselves in their careers. The number of women enrolled in college rose 45 percent between 1970 and 1975, and numerous women were elected to political offices.

Still, women continued to encounter opposition in their struggle for gender equality. Particularly formidable was the antifeminist or "pro-family" movement, which contended that men should lead and

Antifeminist Movement

women should follow, especially within the family, and that women should stay home and raise children. In defense of the patriarchal, or father-led, family, antifeminists campaigned against the Equal Rights Amendment, the gay rights movement, and abortion on demand. The conservative backlash against feminism became an increasingly powerful political force in the United States, especially in the Republican Party.

Antifeminists blamed the women's movement for the country's spiraling divorce rate; they charged that feminists would jettison their husbands and even their children in their quest for job fulfillment and gender equality. The number of divorces jumped 56 percent from 1960 to 1970, 60 percent from 1970 to 1980, and remained near that level in the 1980s. Often, however, the decision to divorce was made not by the wives but by the husbands. According to Barbara Ehrenreich, a feminist scholar, men started walking out on their families in large numbers in the 1950s and 1960s, well before the rebirth of feminism. Tired of fulfilling the role of husband, father, and financial provider, men responded to the image of carefree bachelorhood presented in the pages of men's magazines such as *Playboy*, which attacked wives as parasites who gobbled up their husbands' salaries but were too sexually repressed to give much in return. Many men came to see their wives as the agents of their entrapment; in "flight from commitment," they chose divorce.

Antifeminists successfully stalled ratification of the Equal Rights Amendment, which after quickly passing thirty-five state legislatures fell three states short of success in the late 1970s. Phyllis Schlafly's "Stop ERA" campaign claimed that the ERA would abolish alimony, legalize homosexual marriages, and subject women to single-sex bathrooms and the draft. The debate was occasionally vicious. Refusing to acknowledge gender-based discrimination, Schlafly derided ERA advocates as "a bunch of bitter women seeking a constitutional cure for their personal problems." The ERA died in 1982 when an extended time limit expired for ratification by the states.

Equal Rights Amendment

Many conservative women also participated in the anti-abortion or "prolife" movement, which sprang up almost overnight in the wake of the Supreme Court's 1973 decision in *Roe v. Wade* (see page 872). People whose opposition to abortion was heartfelt and uncompromising denounced that ruling and called for an

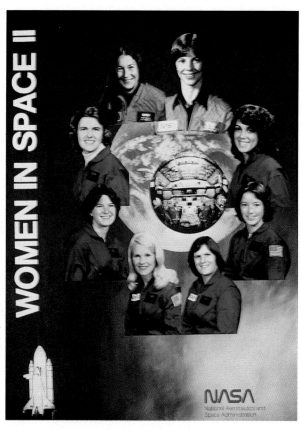

Women entered the space program as astronauts in the 1970s. Several members of the group shown in this poster from the National Aeronautics and Space Administration (NASA) achieved distinction. The two astronauts on the left side are *(above)* Shannon W. Lucid and *(below)* Sally K. Ride. Sally Ride was the first woman in space, spending six days in orbit in 1983. In 1996 Shannon Lucid set a longevity record for American astronauts, female or male: 188 days in orbit. Across from Lucid is Judith Resnik, who died in 1986 in the explosion of the space shuttle *Challenger.*   (Corbis-Bettmann)

amendment to the Constitution defining human life as beginning at conception. Along with Catholics, Mormons, and other religious opponents of abortion, including the Moral Majority, the anti-abortion movement supported the Hyde Amendment, the successful legislative effort of Representative Henry Hyde of Illinois in 1976 to cut off most Medicaid funds for abortions. At the state level, the anti-abortion movement lobbied for restrictions on access to the procedure, such as mandating parental notification. In 1989 the Supreme Court (in *Webster v. Reproductive Health Ser-*

vices) ruled that a Missouri law restricting the right to an abortion was constitutional, thus encouraging further assaults on *Roe v. Wade.*

Feminists fought back. Indeed, Ronald Reagan's most vocal critics were women who mobilized in opposition to the conservative agenda of the White House. The *New York Times* reported a "gender gap" between men's and women's opinions of Reagan's performance in 1983: far fewer women (38 percent) than men (53 percent) believed Reagan deserved reelection. What accounted most centrally for the gender gap were Reagan's social welfare, health, and education cuts. Many working mothers expressed shock at the Reagan administration's insensitivity to children's welfare. One feminist critic quipped that, for Reagan, "life begins at conception and ends at birth." Children's poverty continued its rise throughout the decade, and by 1989 children accounted for about 40 percent of America's poor people.

Women Opponents of Reagan's Conservatism

Reagan's critics assailed him for failing to reverse "the feminization of poverty" and for approving cuts in food stamps and school meals. The Reagan administration's opposition to federally subsidized childcare and the feminist goal of "comparable worth" also drew their ire. Because of persistent occupational segregation, 80 percent of all working women in 1985 were concentrated in low-paying "female" occupations such as clerking, selling, teaching, and waitressing. Recognizing this, feminists supplemented their earlier rallying cry of "equal pay for equal work" with a call for "equal pay for jobs of comparable worth." Why, women asked, should a grade-school teacher earn less than an electrician, if the two jobs require comparable training and skills and involve comparable responsibilities? In the 1970s female workers still took home only 60 cents to every male worker's dollar; by 1990 the figure had risen to 71 cents.

Activists in the women's struggle had to acknowledge certain harsh realities. One was the tight job market created by the economic recessions of the 1970s and 1980s. Other problems included a high teenage pregnancy rate and a rising divorce rate that left increasing numbers of women and their children with lower standards of living. The number of single mothers rose to 7.7 million in 1990, up from 5.8 million a decade earlier. The tandem of divorce and

Increased Burdens on Women

teenage pregnancy meant that a progressively smaller proportion of America's children lived with two parents. In 1990, about a quarter of all children, 16 million, lived with only one parent—double the percentage of 1970.

Many mothers thus had to find employment. Still others worked to preserve or improve the living standard of two-parent households that otherwise would have experienced substantial declines. Families were paying a higher percentage of their income to buy houses, and often two wage earners were required to pay the bills. In 1983, for the first time in the nation's history, more than half of all adult American women (51 percent) held jobs outside the home. Another milestone was recorded in 1987: the share of women returning to work or actively seeking jobs within a year after the arrival of a baby exceeded 50 percent for the first time. (By contrast, just ten years earlier, the figure had been 31 percent.) The working mother had become the norm in America.

Such women had to contend with what came to be called "the Superwoman Squeeze." According to a report by the Worldwatch Institute, most working wives and mothers, even those with full-time jobs, "retained an unwilling monopoly on unpaid labor at home." Combining housework and outside employment, wives

worked 71 hours a week; husbands worked 55 hours a week. Women traded stories of "couch-potato" husbands who watched television while their wives did chores. Soon only one in four wives would be a full-time housewife and mother. The remainder would be trying to balance the more-than-full-time demands of a family and a career without shortchanging either— or themselves—in the process.

A Polarized People: American Society in the 1980s

 The United States became an increasingly polarized society in the 1980s. The rich got richer, while the poor sank deeper into despair (see Figure 32.3). The incomes of the bottom fifth of American families fell by 13 percent, but the top fifth earned 27 percent more, and the top 1 percent saw their incomes double. Indeed, by 1989 the top 1 percent (834,000 households with $5.7 trillion in net worth) was worth more than the bottom 90 percent (84 million households with $4.8 trillion in net worth). The United States was polarizing not only economically but also socially, and societal divisions were exacerbated by new problems:

Figure 32.3   While the Rich Got Richer in the 1980s, the Poor Got Poorer   Between 1977 and 1989, the richest 1 percent of American families reaped most of the gains from economic growth. In fact, the average pretax income of families in the top percentage rose 77 percent. At the same time, the typical family saw its income edge up only 4 percent. And the bottom 40 percent of families had actual declines in income.   (Source: Data from the *New York Times*, March 5, 1992.)

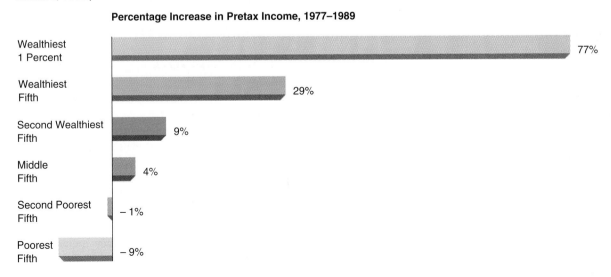

Percentage Increase in Pretax Income, 1977–1989

Wealthiest 1 Percent	77%
Wealthiest Fifth	29%
Second Wealthiest Fifth	9%
Middle Fifth	4%
Second Poorest Fifth	– 1%
Poorest Fifth	– 9%

A stunned nation watched in 1986 as the space shuttle *Challenger* exploded seventy-three seconds after lifting off. The *Challenger* explosion produces a flashbulb memory for many younger Americans who watched the tragedy on television at school (one of the *Challenger* crew, Christa McAuliffe, was an elementary school teacher). (Corbis-Bettmann)

AIDS (acquired immune deficiency syndrome) and the cocaine-derived drug known as crack.

By the end of the 1980s, as many Americans were living in poverty as had been in 1964, when 36 million were poor and President Johnson declared a War on Poverty. But the poor themselves were somewhat different. The poverty of the 1980s, explained the authors of a 1988 report of the Social Science Research Council, "is found less among the elderly and people living in nonurban areas and more among children living with one parent—in households headed principally by young women." In the 1970s the child poverty rate increased 6 percent; in the 1980s, it jumped 11 percent, with thirty-three states registering increases. As inequality grew, the gap widened between affluent whites and poor blacks, Indians, and Hispanics, and between the suburbs and the inner cities. And as inequality increased, so too did social pathology. Violent crime, particularly homicides and gang warfare, grew alarmingly, as did school dropout rates, crime rates, and child abuse.

Increasing Inequality

Poverty resulted not only from discrimination based on race and gender, but also from economic recessions and from the changing structure of the labor market. As deindustrialization took hold, the job market shifted from high-paying, unionized, blue-collar

Changing Job Market

jobs to low-paying service jobs. Minimum-wage employment burgeoned in fast-food restaurants, but such jobs meant a substantial drop in workers' standard of living. In 1974 blue-collar jobs accounted for half of the employment of African American males between the ages of twenty and twenty-four. Just ten years later, such jobs accounted for only one-fourth of their employment. North Lawndale, a black neighborhood on Chicago's West Side, exemplified the problem. In prosperous days, the community's economy had depended on the 43,000 jobs at the Hawthorne plant of Western Electric. But the Hawthorne plant closed in 1984. Soon, so did the banks and small stores that depended on the workers' wages.

According to sociologist William Julius Wilson, the issue of "the truly disadvantaged" was "one of the most important social issues of the remainder of the 20th century." Life was becoming precarious not only for the underclass but also for the working poor, whose numbers increased by more than one-third during the 1980s. By the end of the decade, 40 percent of the nation's poor were working, but few had full-time, year-round jobs. At the same time, social workers reported that more and more of the nation's homeless were families.

About a third of the homeless were former psychiatric patients who found themselves living on the streets after hospitals emptied their psychiatric wards in a burst of enthusiasm for "deinstitutionalization." By 1985, 80 percent of the total number of beds in state mental hospitals had been eliminated on the premise that small neighborhood programs would be more responsive than large state hospitals to people's needs. The truth was that such local programs failed to materialize, and former patients went to live in unsafe boarding houses and cheap hotels. Few provisions were made for medical treatment, and these troubled people increasingly found that they had nowhere to go except onto the streets.

Another cause of homelessness was drug use, which was the scourge of the urban underclass. Mired in hopelessness, poverty-stricken men and women tried to find forgetfulness in hard drugs, especially cocaine and its derivative crack, which first struck New York City's poorest neighborhoods in 1985. Crack's legacy included destroyed families, abused children, and drug dealers too young for a driver's license but with access to subma-

Drugs and Violence

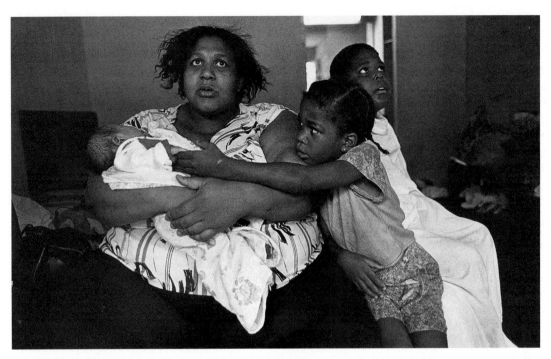

For this family, which includes a one-week-old baby, homelessness came suddenly. Home had been a squalid motor inn in North Bergen, New Jersey, but the board of health condemned the motel and the police put the family out on the street. In 1988 as many as a million people were homeless. (Eugene Richards/Magnum)

chine guns and other state-of-the-art firearms. Gang shootouts over drugs were deadly: the toll in Los Angeles in 1987 was 387 deaths; more than half of the victims were innocent bystanders. After a bloody drug murder in New York City's Spanish Harlem, a sixteen-year-old girl moaned, "It's frightening. . . . It's crazy. There's no answer to it. And there's no end to it."

Another lethal byproduct of the 1980s drug epidemic was the spread of AIDS. First observed in the

AIDS

United States in 1981, AIDS is a disease transmittable through the sharing of intravenous needles by drug users or through the exchange of infected body fluids, often during sexual contact. Caused by a virus that attacks cells in the immune system, AIDS makes its victims susceptible to deadly infections and cancers. In the United States, AIDS initially was confined to the sexual practices of male homosexuals, but the disease spread to heterosexuals and those receiving transfusions of tainted blood.

Between 1981 and 1988, of the 57,000 AIDS cases reported, nearly 32,000 resulted in death. Public health officials were slow to recognize the enormity of the epidemic, partly because the AIDS virus (HIV) can

In the 1980s there was an alarming spread of sexually transmitted diseases, especially acquired immune deficiency syndrome (AIDS). Campaigns for "Safe Sex," such as this New York City subway ad, urged people to use condoms. (Reprinted with permission of Saatchi & Saatchi)

lie dormant for several years before presenting symptoms. But the worst had not yet revealed itself. A 1988 study reported that half of the gay men in San Francisco would develop AIDS and another 25 percent would develop the AIDS-related complex within about nine years of infection. Some religious leaders and politicians heartlessly blamed the victims. "A man reaps what he sows," declared the Reverend Jerry Falwell of the Moral Majority. "If he sows seed in the field of his lower nature, he will reap from it a harvest of corruption."

AIDS divided American communities, and AIDS—along with other sexually transmitted diseases such as genital herpes and chlamydia—affected Americans' sexual behavior. In the 1980s caution replaced the sexual revolution. "Safe sex" campaigns urged the use of condoms. But conservative Protestant sects joined the Roman Catholic Church in warning that condom advertising implicitly sanctioned contraception and encouraged promiscuity. Sex education should not be offered in the schools, they contended, citing their deep belief that any sexual activity other than heterosexual matrimonial monogamy was wrong. The Supreme Court struck a blow against gay rights in 1986, when it upheld a Georgia felony statute that punished consensual anal or oral sex between men with up to twenty years in jail (*Bowers v. Hardwick*). Although gay men expected little assistance from the conservative executive branch, they were partly wrong. In 1988 the federal government mailed a booklet entitled *Understanding AIDS* to 107 million households. Nevertheless, AIDS continued to be one of several unsolved social problems dividing the nation in the late 1980s.

Economic Upturn and the Election of 1988

Despite Ronald Reagan's overwhelming reelection victory in 1984, for much of 1985 the president was on the defensive. One reason was the mounting fiscal deficit. A fiscal conservative long committed to balanced budgets, Ronald Reagan nonetheless oversaw the accumulation of more new debt than all previous American presidents put together.

Reagan had assailed President Carter's $74 billion deficit during the 1980 campaign, but the deficit exceeded $212 billion in fiscal 1985 and $221 billion in fiscal 1986. Although Republicans blamed the deficit

Mounting Fiscal Deficit

on the Democrats, almost half of the national debt derived from fiscal years 1982 through 1986, when Reagan occupied the White House and the Republicans controlled the Senate. Because of tax reductions, growing entitlement programs such as Social Security, and upwardly spiraling defense budgets, the national debt grew by $955 billion during this five-year period (see Figure 32.4).

In response, Reagan and Congress reluctantly agreed to the 1985 Gramm-Rudman bill, which called for a balanced federal budget by fiscal 1991 through a gradual reduction of the annual deficit. The deficit did drop, but for the three fiscal years from 1987 to 1989, it still totaled $457 billion. Another important bill, the Tax Reform Act of 1986, lowered personal income taxes while closing some flagrant loopholes and eliminating 6 million poor people from the tax rolls. The law represented a compromise between supply-side conservatives, who argued that lower tax rates would act as an incentive to savings, investment, and growth, and liberals whose focus was the unfairness of the tax codes.

During his second term, Reagan realized one of his most important goals: putting more conservative justices on the Supreme Court so as to overthrow liberal rulings made in the 1960s under Chief Justice Earl Warren (see page 862). After Warren Burger's decision to retire from the Supreme Court in 1986, Reagan nominated conservative William Rehnquist to serve as chief justice and conservative Antonin Scalia to fill Rehnquist's seat; the Senate confirmed both choices.

A Conservative Supreme Court

Until late 1986 Reagan's place in history was secure. But the Iran-contra disclosures caused his aura to fade, not only sullying his last two years in office but also endangering his historical reputation and raising the Democrats' hopes for a presidential victory in 1988. Reagan's political troubles began on election day 1986. First, the Republicans lost control of the Senate, stripping the president of a crucial power base. Second, from Lebanon came a bizarre story that the president's national security adviser had traveled to Iran with a Bible, a cake, and a planeload of weapons seeking the release of Americans held hostage in the Middle East. "No comment," Reagan told reporters, but details of the Iran-contra scandal soon began to surface (see page 912).

Iran-Contra Scandal

Figure 32.4   America's Rising National Debt, 1974–1989   America's national debt, which rose sporadically throughout the 1970s, soared to record heights during the 1980s. Under President Reagan, large defense expenditures and tax cuts caused the national debt to grow by $1.5 trillion.   (Source: Adapted from U.S. Bureau of the Census, *Statistical Abstract of the United States* [Washington, D.C., 1992], p. 315.)

"An irony of the Reagan era," wrote Senator Daniel Patrick Moynihan, Democrat of New York, "is

Reagan's Decline

that having at midpoint reached a crescendo of triumphalism—morning in America—it is closing amid talk of decline." On a personal level, President Reagan had lost his mastery; the Great Communicator had taken on the appearance of a tired, bumbling old man. "Who's in Charge Here?" asked a *Time* magazine headline. The Iran-contra hearings focused attention on President Reagan's hands-off management style. Some observers, both outsiders and insiders, argued that Reagan was unengaged and uninformed. Donald T. Regan described his experience: "In the four years that I served as Secretary of the Treasury I never saw President Reagan alone and never discussed economic philosophy or fiscal and monetary policy with him one-on-one."

Half of the people in the country believed that Reagan was lying about his lack of involvement in the Iran-contra scandal. Doubtless any lame-duck presi-

dent would have suffered a loss of power in his second term, but the scandal encouraged Reagan's opponents. "No one is afraid of him anymore," said one political observer. And the political satirists were in hot pursuit. The real question, went one gibe, was not "what did the President know and when did he know it?" but "what didn't the President know, and why didn't he know it?"

Reagan's problems continued in 1987 and 1988. Congress overrode his veto of a massive highway con-

Reagan's Ongoing Political Woes

struction bill, and twice his choices for the Supreme Court failed to win confirmation by the Senate. His first nominee, federal judge Robert Bork, who in 1973 had fired the special Watergate prosecutor during the Saturday Night Massacre (see page 879), failed to convince the Senate that he was not a right-wing ideologue. Reagan's second choice, another federal judge, withdrew his name from consideration after revelations that he had smoked marijuana while a professor at Harvard Law School. Then, on October 19, 1987,

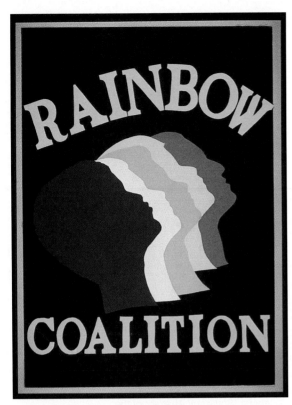

During the 1984 and 1988 campaigns, Reverend Jesse Jackson won a large following as the first African American to make a serious bid for the presidential nomination of a major party. His multiethnic political organization, the Rainbow Coalition, included people of all colors.   (Smithsonian Institution, Division of Political History, Washington, D.C.)

the stock market went into a nosedive and fell 508 points.

Still, as the 1988 elections approached, Republicans took heart over some excellent political and economic news for their party. First,

Continuing Economic Recovery

Reagan had moderated his anti-Soviet rhetoric and in 1988, to the applause of most Americans, had traveled to the Soviet Union—the first American president to visit Moscow since Richard Nixon in 1972. Second—and of greater importance to voters—after the economic recession of 1981 and 1982, the United States had embarked on a six-year business recovery. The discomfort index, which had risen alarmingly in the 1970s and early 1980s, dropped to more comfortable levels in the later 1980s. And although unemployment dropped to

a decade-low 5.4 percent in April 1988, it did so without refueling inflation (see Figure 32.1).

The Reagan administration pointed to the economy as proof of the success of supply-side economics. Critics retorted that Reagan's policy of pursuing massive tax cuts while greatly increasing the defense budget was just another form of Keynesianism—in this case, massive deficit financing to stimulate the economy. But the average American, caring little about this kind of debate, was content to enjoy the economic recovery. It was true that the poor had little to rejoice over and that Americans viewed the economic future with uncertainty. But it was also true that in the 1980s most Americans had jobs and were living very comfortably.

Ronald Reagan's reelection in 1984 was never in doubt, but his forty-nine-state sweep convinced some observers that he had transformed

Reagan's Presidency Assessed

American politics by forging a conservative coalition that could dominate for years. Still, as popular a president as Reagan was, his programs provoked severe criticism. Liberal opponents lambasted his economic policies as favoring the rich and penalizing the poor. Despite the criticism, Reagan seemed to escape personal blame. Representative Patricia Schroeder, a Colorado Democrat, gave this phenomenon a memorable label: Reagan, she said, was "perfecting a Teflon-coated presidency.... He sees to it that nothing sticks to him." Reagan's favorable image was tarnished by the Iran-contra scandal in late 1986 (see page 912), and his influence diminished during his final two years in office. But had Reagan been allowed by the Constitution to run for a third term, he probably would have ridden both his personal popularity and the economic boom to victory.

The 1988 election was for Reagan's successor, and the competition in both parties was intense. On the

George Bush

Republican side the candidates included Vice President George Bush, Senate minority leader Bob Dole, and Pat Robertson, a television evangelist. Bush emerged with the nomination after bitter Republican infighting in state primaries. A native of Connecticut and a Yale graduate whose father had been a U.S. senator, Bush had served heroically as a navy pilot during the Second World War. He had moved to Texas to enter the oil business and had become involved in politics. Bush possessed broad government experience, including service as a congressman, ambassador to China, and director of the Central Intelligence Agency. He had contested Reagan for the Republican nomination in 1980 and then served as Reagan's two-term vice president.

The Democratic side also saw a scramble for the presidential nomination. Beginning with a half-dozen campaigners, the race narrowed to a two-person contest between Michael Dukakis, under whose governorship Massachusetts had seemed a model of economic recovery and welfare reform, and Jesse Jackson, a former colleague of Reverend Martin Luther King, Jr., who had moved to Chicago to organize economic and educational programs for the poor. An eloquent preacher, Jackson campaigned on his dream of forming a "Rainbow Coalition" of the "rejected"—African Americans, women, Hispanics, the disabled. Jackson was the first African American to win mass support in seeking the presidential nomination of a major political party. But Dukakis won the Democratic nomination in 1988 by emerging victorious in key state presidential primary elections.

Both Bush and Dukakis avoided serious debate of the issues: drugs, environmental collapse, poverty, rising medical and educational costs, childcare, and the fiscal and trade deficits. Despite the gravity of the problems, the candidates relied on clichés and negative attack advertising. Television dominated the presidential election as never before. Bush aimed his appeals at the "Reagan Democrats" by pushing emotional "hot buttons" such as patriotism and the death penalty. A Republican advertisement for television appealed to racism and fear by accusing Dukakis of being soft on crime for furloughing Willie Horton, a black convicted murderer who while on weekend leave had stabbed a white man and raped a white woman. Voters expressed their disgust at the 1988 race. Former president Richard Nixon, no stranger to political combat, called the presidential campaign "trivial, superficial and inane."

But with America at peace and inflation and unemployment both low, Bush's victory was seldom in doubt. His margin over Dukakis was substantial: 53 percent of the popular vote to 46 percent (see Map 32.3). Significantly, Bush was the beneficiary of the Reagan political legacy. He retained 85 percent of Reagan's supporters by

Presidential Campaign of 1988

Bush's Victory in 1988

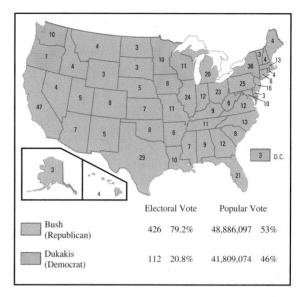

Map 32.3   Presidential Election, 1988   George Bush easily defeated Michael Dukakis in both popular and electoral votes. The key to Bush's victory was his ability to retain the political support that Ronald Reagan had enjoyed in 1980 and 1984.

promising to keep the nation on the course set by his predecessor, and Reagan Democrats again crossed over, this time voting for Bush in sufficient numbers for him to carry Michigan, Pennsylvania, and other key industrial states.

The 1988 election confirmed that the "Solid South," once a Democratic stronghold, had become solidly Republican. Bush won every state in the region. In both South and North, race was a key factor, as it had been in every presidential election since 1964: for twenty-five years, the Republican vote had been almost exclusively white, and almost all blacks had voted Democratic. Another political constant was low voter turnout. Only 50 percent of Americans who were eligible to vote in 1988 voted, compared with 63 percent in 1960. Voter turnout had declined markedly after the 1968 election, but after turning slightly upward in 1984 (53 percent), it fell again in 1988.

Many Americans seemed unconcerned as they confronted the new decade. College students in the 1980s, unlike many of their predecessors in the 1960s, aspired to join the system. Called Yuppies (young urban professionals), they yearned not to save the world but to scramble up the corporate ladder, and many educated young people worked long hours in pursuit of that goal. "If the 1970s were the Me Decade," *Newsweek* declared, "the 1980s have been the Work Decade." Baby boomers and their younger sisters and brothers reported frustration in their efforts to replicate their parents' standard of living, particularly because of high housing costs.

But polls in 1989 reported that Americans were generally happy with their lives. Many expressed pleasure with the new toys and amenities in their lives. Sales of videocassette recorders (VCRs), microwave ovens, camcorders, and compact disc players soared in the 1980s. At-home comfort was an important reason for buying a VCR. In just four years, from 1980 to 1984, the number of videotapes rented by Americans for viewing movies at home jumped from 26 million to 304 million.

Even more impressive was the phenomenal spread of computers, which revolutionized not only communications but also people's workplaces and lifestyles. In 1981 the number of personal computers in use in America numbered 2 million; in 1988 the figure was 45 million. Companies raced to market with ever-speedier technology. In 1985 a new computer was introduced to the public at the Lawrence Livermore Laboratory in California. "What took a year in 1952," explained a scientist, "we can now do in a second." But in the 1990s this, too, would be eclipsed by revolutionary advances in computer technology such as the phenomenal spread of the Internet.

Summary

The United States changed in fundamental ways between 1974 and 1989. The spread of technological developments was part of that change. So too was the new immigration, which in the 1970s and 1980s not only swelled tremendously but shifted in origin. People came from Mexico, Central and South America, and the Caribbean, as well as from the Philippines, Korea, Taiwan, and India. Refugees of the Vietnam War also arrived, and Cubans and Haitians risked their lives in flimsy boats to come to America. The totals of the new immigration exceeded those of the turn-of-the-century immigration of millions of people from southern and eastern Europe.

Another change was the country's shift to the right politically. The champion of this change was President Ronald Reagan, whose supporters included both economic and social conservatives and both Republicans and disillusioned Democrats. Moreover, after two presidents, Gerald Ford and Jimmy Carter, who were perceived to be weak or ineffective leaders, Reagan restored the presidency to its central role in politics and the government.

Despite Reagan's successes, when he left office in 1989, the country faced unsolved economic, social, and political issues of great importance. "Ronald Reagan leaves no Vietnam War, no Watergate, no hostage crisis," reported the *New York Times*. "But he leaves huge question marks—and much to do." First, inequality had escalated in the 1980s, as the poor got poorer and the rich got richer. The poorest Americans of all were children, and economics and racism had conspired to widen racial divisions. Second, the rise of the federal debt continued unabated. In 1981 the debt stood at $994 billion; by the time Reagan left office, it had jumped to almost $2.9 trillion. Third, the effects of mismanagement and outright fraud were beginning to show in certain industries, forcing the federal government to consider massive bailouts and threatening greater fiscal deficits. In 1989 Congress debated legislation to rescue insolvent savings-and-loan associations by paying the government's insurance obligations to depositors; the eventual cost was $153 billion.

When George Bush was inaugurated as the forty-first president of the United States on January 20, 1989, the American people prepared to greet not only a new presidency but also a new decade. It was clear that Americans and their leaders would have to make difficult economic, social, and political choices in the 1990s.

LEGACY FOR A PEOPLE AND A NATION
Ethnic America

The legacy of the new immigration of the 1970s and 1980s is evident in cities and towns across America. Mexican newcomers, for example, have opened restaurants, started Spanish-language newspapers and cable television channels, and flocked to the concerts of such Latino superstars as Selena and Ricky Martin. Meanwhile, Mexican culinary culture is being consumed by millions of Americans of all groups. Asian American immigrants constitute a diverse group, including Laotian and Vietnamese refugees drawn to Garden City, Kansas, to work in the world's largest meatpacking plant; Korean greengrocers opening shops on

Manhattan's Upper West Side; and Chinese workers assembling integrated circuits in California's Silicon Valley. Wherever they have settled, America's newcomers have established their own communities with their own distinctive cultures.

The legacy of America's new immigration resembles that of its predecessor one hundred years ago. With almost 9 million immigrants arriving in the 1980s, that decade surpassed the historic high mark set by the 8.7 million immigrants from Russia, Austria-Hungary, Italy, and other countries who had reached American shores between 1900 and 1909. In addition to the approximately 1 million people who move to the United States each year, an additional 300,000 come as undocumented, or illegal, aliens. Like the earlier immigration, the new influx has also provoked a nativist reaction. A *Newsweek* poll in 1993 reported that 60 percent of Americans believed that immigration was "bad for the country."

Immigrants have arrived from all over the world, bringing their cultures not merely from Latin America and Asia, but also from Europe, Africa, and the Middle East. Like the immigrants of a century before, these newcomers crave education and flock to public libraries to learn. The branch library in Flushing, New York, for example, has been inundated with Chinese, Korean, Indian, Russian, Colombian, and Afghan immigrants. "Watch Your Belongings" signs are displayed in several languages, and librarians are available who speak Russian, Hindi, Chinese, Korean, Gujarati, and Spanish. The legacy of the new immigration has permanently altered, and deeply enriched, the United States.

For Further Reading, see page A-40 of the Appendix. For Web resources, go to http://college.hmco.com.

Tuesday, April 20, 1999, began as it always did for some students at Columbine High School in Littleton, Colorado, with a popular early-morning bowling class. On this day, one of the bowlers, Dylan Klebold, wore a shirt that read "SERIAL KILLER." Classmates recalled that when he and his friend Eric Harris would hit strikes or spares, they would shout "Sieg Heil!" in celebration. And, in fact, April 20 was Adolf Hitler's birthday. Later that morning, after donning black trench coats, Harris and Klebold returned to the high school, armed with two shotguns, two semiautomatic rifles, and thirty pipe bombs filled with gunpowder, nails, and broken glass. Walking toward the school, one of the boys pointed a rifle at a seventeen-year-old student and fatally shot her in the head. It was a little after 11 A.M.

That morning, there were some five hundred people in the school cafeteria when Harris and Klebold opened fire and threw pipe bombs, filling the air with smoke. Teacher Dave Sanders ran from the cafeteria to warn students in the library, but Harris and Klebold, encountering him in the hallway, shot him in the chest. Sanders crawled to a nearby room, but bled to death. A teacher phoned 911: "Oh, God! Oh, God! Kids, just stay down. I'm in the library. . . . He's right outside of here." The gunmen then entered the library, laughing and taunting students, and shooting their victims at point-blank range. "All jocks stand up!" one gunman yelled. Isaiah Shoels, eighteen, was both an athlete and an African American. "Hey, I think we got a n——— here," one of the killers exclaimed, spotting Shoels. Then they shot him in the head and added two more bullets in the face. "Hey, I always wondered what n——— brains looked like," said one of the killers, laughing.

About 12:30 P.M., SWAT teams entered Columbine High School and began a room-by-room sweep of the building. At 4:30, police found Harris and Klebold in the library, both suicides, their bodies surrounded by the corpses of ten of their victims. In all, fifteen people were dead. And the nation was shocked and dumbfounded. What had motivated these two self-proclaimed members of the "Trenchcoat Mafia" to go on a hate-filled shooting spree? Did the massacre mean that guns were too readily available, or that there

On April 20, 1999, students evacuated Columbine High School in Littleton, Colorado, after two schoolmates went on a shooting rampage, killing twelve students and a teacher before killing themselves. (Wide World Photos, Inc.)

33

PROSPERITY, POWER, AND PERIL: AMERICA IN THE 1990s

947

was too much violence on television, or that America's children were troubled, or that American society was sick? The American people wanted answers, but each question only prompted more questions.

In the 1990s, violence of various kinds erupted in the United States. In addition to the Columbine shootings, students in Paducah, Kentucky; Jonesboro, Arkansas; Springfield, Oregon; and elsewhere opened fire on their schoolmates. Hate crimes against African Americans, homosexuals, and Jewish Americans produced gruesome deaths, and in the worst act of terrorism in U.S. history, 168 people were killed in 1995 in a bomb blast in Oklahoma City, Oklahoma.

The 1990s proved to be a decade of political volatility and cultural conflict, and it was not just the far right that was politically disaffected. People of far more moderate beliefs also abjured political participation, denouncing the government for being corrupt, arrogant, and downright stupid. In *Why Americans Hate Politics* (1991), E. J. Dionne, Jr., a columnist, ventured that voters were disgusted with the divisive debate that dominated politics in an era of negative attack advertisements. In the 1990s, moreover, many Americans did not know where to turn to make meaningful political choices in their lives. They rejected the Democratic Party for having lost touch with their cultural and moral values, and they rejected the Republicans for failing to represent their economic and social needs. Some Americans wanted new political parties.

America's president from 1989 to 1993 was George Bush. Victory in the Persian Gulf War in 1991 seemed to guarantee his reelection in 1992. But the economy had stagnated, and the president seemed without a plan to spur recovery. The Cold War was over, but the president seemed to lack vision for a new world order. And Ross Perot, a multibillionaire who vowed he could fix the fiscal deficit, waged a popular third-party campaign. But the winner and president-elect was the Democratic candidate, Governor Bill Clinton of Arkansas.

Politics grew even more volatile during Bill Clinton's two presidential terms in the 1990s, culminating in his impeachment in 1999. Clinton was the first baby boomer to become president, and his opponents argued that his character was severely flawed. In 1994, just two years after Clinton defeated Bush, the "Republican Revolution" led by Representative Newt Gingrich routed the Democrats in congressional elections, winning control of both houses of Congress. In 1996, however, Clinton revealed that he was a battler and still popular; and, running against the House Republicans, he won reelection. Aiding him, too, was

prosperity. The nation's economy began its recovery in 1991, and economic growth—marked by low inflation and a spectacular rise in stock prices—continued throughout the decade and into the new century.

But the president had a formidable enemy: himself, notably his history of philandering and lying. In 1999 Clinton was impeached by the House of Representatives, which alleged that he had committed perjury and obstructed justice. And while the Senate acquitted the president in a subsequent trial presided over by the chief justice of the United States, Clinton had permanently tarnished his historical reputation. Still, Clinton survived this grave crisis; his public approval rating remained high; and angry conservatives reproached the "immoral [American] majority" who supported the president and applauded his presidency. "Let's move on," said Bob Smith, a Republican senator who voted guilty. "He won. He always wins."

For both Bush and Clinton, the 1990s was a decade of power and perils in world affairs. The Bush administration witnessed the dramatic end of the Cold War, symbolized by the collapse of Communist regimes in eastern Europe, the reunification of Germany, and the dissolution of the Soviet Union. Disorder, however—created by ethnic wars, natural disasters, economic crises, and religious conflict—soon followed, disappointing Americans who wanted less overseas activism. The Clinton administration struggled to articulate new doctrines and to clarify U.S. interests in the absence of a Soviet threat. Moreover, some threats, long overshadowed by the Cold War, became more pressing: nuclear proliferation, chemical warfare, population explosion, drug trafficking, the spread of diseases, and pollution of the natural environment.

The decade of the 1990s concluded what some called the "American century." The nation, though basking in prosperity and power, was at the same time cautious about the future, very aware that perils at home and abroad could undermine its purpose and position. ■

Economic and Social Anxieties: The Presidency of George Bush

 As president from 1989 to 1993, George Bush had a rough ride. He and the Democratic Congress seemed unable to work together or agree on anything. Beginning in 1989 with his veto of an increase in the minimum wage, Bush vetoed thirty-seven bills during his presidency, only one of which was overridden by a two-thirds vote of both houses of Congress. Rarely in

IMPORTANT EVENTS

1989 Bush becomes president
Tiananmen Square massacre in China
Bush vetoes increase in minimum wage
World accord controls ozone-killing
   chemicals
Berlin Wall opens
U.S. troops invade Panama
Third World debt reaches $1.2 trillion

1990 Communist regimes in eastern Europe
   collapse
Sandinistas lose Nicaragua election
Recession begins; personal incomes fall
Americans with Disabilities Act passed
Iraq invades Kuwait
Reunification of Germany
Bush-Congress budget agreement raises
   taxes; Bush reneges on "no new taxes"
Clean Air Act reauthorization requires
   reduction in emission of pollutants
South Africa begins to dismantle apartheid

1991 Persian Gulf War
START I treaty reduces nuclear warheads
Ethnic wars flare in former Yugoslavia
Hill testifies at Thomas confirmation
   hearings; Thomas confirmed
USSR dissolves into independent states
U.N. mediation ends Salvadoran civil war

1992 Los Angeles riots erupt
U.S. in minority at Rio Earth Summit
Federal deficit hits $4 trillion
California pays employees with IOUs
Planned Parenthood v. Casey upholds the
   right to an abortion
Clinton elected president
Perot's third-party candidacy wins one-fifth
   of the vote
Bush pardons former government officials
   indicted in Iran-contra scandal
Twenty-seventh Amendment prohibits
   future midterm congressional pay raises
U.S. troops sent to Somalia
Canada, Mexico, and U.S. sign NAFTA

1993 Clinton becomes president
Clinton lifts restrictions on abortion
   counseling
START-II treaty reduces warheads and
   ICBMs
H. Clinton heads task force on healthcare
Branch Davidian compound burns in Waco
Clinton's proposal to lift ban on homo-
   sexuals in the military stirs controversy

Clinton appoints Ginsberg to Court
Congress approves NAFTA
Agreement for Palestinian self-rule
Motor-voter and family-leave acts passed
Gun control laws require waiting period for
   handguns and ban sale of assault weapons

1994 Republican candidates for Congress propose
   Contract with America
Clinton appoints Breyer to Supreme Court
Genocide in Rwanda
U.S. troops sent to Haiti
Clinton signs crime bill into law
Republicans win House and Senate

1995 Bombing in Oklahoma City kills 168 people
Nuclear nonproliferation treaty renewed
U.S. opens diplomatic relations with
   Vietnam
World Conference on Women
U.S. diplomats broker peace for Bosnia

1996 Telecommunications Act allows telephone
   and cable companies to compete
Helms-Burton Act tightens Cuba embargo
Freedom to Farm Act mandates phase-out
   of federal farm subsidies
Convictions in first Whitewater trials
Clinton signs welfare act eliminating Aid to
   Families with Dependent Children
Guatemalan civil war ends
Clinton reelected

1997 Albright is first woman secretary of state
Israeli withdrawal from Hebron
U.S. ratifies Chemical Weapons Convention

1998 Independent counsel investigates Clinton's
   relationship with Lewinsky
Independent counsel sends impeachment
   report to House
India and Pakistan explode nuclear devices
U.S. signs Global Warming Convention
Republicans lose seats in House
House votes to impeach Clinton

1999 Senate votes to acquit Clinton
NATO bombs Serbia over Kosovo crisis
Senate rejects Comprehensive Test Ban
   Treaty

2000 Y2K bug fails to precipitate computer collapse
Gore and Bush score major victories in spring
   primaries; Bradley and McCain end
   campaigns
Nation records longest economic expansion in
   its history

American history had the relationship between Congress and the president been as sour and the legislative results so meager. Among the major issues left unresolved were healthcare, the budget deficit, taxes, crime, and family leave.

Decisive presidential leadership might have broken the gridlock, but Bush was a political chameleon. Once a supporter of family planning and a woman's right to an abortion, he had switched his position and denounced abortion as murder. In the 1980 Republican primaries, he had dismissed Ronald Reagan's supply-side economic ideas as "voodoo economics," but he quickly endorsed these policies when he became Reagan's running mate in 1980. In loyally supporting all of Reagan's policies, even those that he formerly opposed, Bush seemed to lack firm convictions of his own. Still, when he was inaugurated in 1989, the future appeared bright. The Cold War was waning, and Americans looked forward to a "peace dividend" in the form of lower defense expenditures. The country had enjoyed six straight years of economic growth, and both unemployment and inflation were low. Bush hoped the good news would continue; and on inauguration day, when he called for a "kinder, gentler nation," it seemed that a compassionate president would be occupying the White House.

Soon, however, the economy took a nosedive. In late 1989 *Newsweek* detected a "peek-a-boo recession,"

Economic and Social Problems

pointing to slumping car and housing sales and declining orders for manufacturing products. By mid-1990, signs of recession were everywhere. Workers were laid off or furloughed, but Bush took no action, revealing the shallowness of his inaugural promise. The Bush administration, one columnist wrote, was "leading a retreat from social responsibility." He had vetoed an increase in the minimum wage and defended tax breaks for the rich while opposing extended relief payments to the long-term unemployed.

Yet the social ills that had plagued the United States in the 1980s—AIDS, homelessness, drug and alcohol addiction, racism and inequality, poverty among children, the day-to-day struggles of single-parent families—persisted unabated, and even the middle class experienced a decline in the standard of living. Scholars who tracked the "social health" of the nation diagnosed America's well-being as at its lowest level since 1970, when the data were first analyzed. Problems that reached their worst recorded levels in 1990 were child abuse, teen suicide, the gap between rich and poor, and lack of health insurance coverage. "If you look at it as a report card," observed the director of Fordham University's Institute for Innovation in Social Policy, "the country gets an F."

Healthcare, in particular, caused increasing anxiety. With few incentives to control healthcare costs and the spread of expensive technologies, medical expenses were rising rapidly. In 1992 healthcare costs absorbed 12 percent of the national income, appreciably more than in other industrialized nations. Health insurance also had become a leading labor issue in the country, as steeply rising insurance premiums ate into both profits and wages. In 1990, for example, disputes over health insurance sparked 55 percent of the strikes in the United States.

Still worse, some 33 million Americans, about 13 percent of the population, had no health insurance at all. Three-fourths of these people were employed but worked at minimum-wage jobs that did not provide health benefits. Additional tens of millions had such limited coverage that they constantly were at risk of financial devastation. The Price family of Mebane, North Carolina, already $1,000 in debt for medical expenses, was typical. Self-employed, William Price could not afford the family policy available at $350 per month; and at Paula Price's job, there was no group health insurance. As William said, "We just have to hope the family stays healthy."

Also fueling Americans' anxieties were the growing numbers of job layoffs, some temporary but many permanent. In a practice called "outsourcing," companies stopped making their components and began ordering them from factories in other states as well as other countries, where wages were far lower and benefit packages nonexistent. Other businesses replaced workers with computers and other machines to cut costs and increase productivity. Employment in the chemical industry, for example, had been declining for several years. "Companies in our industry," said the chief economist of the Chemical Manufacturers Association, "don't want to hire more people because people cost money." Numerous industries were deciding whether to reduce labor costs by opting for technology, outsourcing, or moving their plants to Mexico, South Korea, and other low-wage countries. Many businesses downsized, eliminating tens of thousands of jobs.

In the face of flat wages and job insecurity caused by downsizing, some Americans blamed their plight on job competition from the new immigrants who had arrived in increasing numbers in the 1970s and 1980s (see page 934). Politicians decried what they called the "flood" or the "invasion" of new immigrants. A *Newsweek* poll in 1993 reported that 60 percent of Americans believed that immigration was "bad for the country." And in 1994 voters in California approved Proposition 187, a ballot initiative to cut off social services to illegal aliens.

One group, however, made real progress in 1990. That year, President Bush signed the Americans with

Americans with Disabilities Act

Disabilities Act, which banned job discrimination, in companies with twenty-five or more employees, against the blind, deaf, mentally retarded, and physically impaired, as well as against those who are HIV-positive or have cancer. The act, which covered 87 percent of all wage earners, also required that "reasonable accommodations," such as wheelchair ramps, be made available to people with disabilities. Many businesses opposed the bill, but the U.S. Chamber of Commerce supported it. As a Chamber official explained, the bill "opens up a huge untapped resource of workers."

Bush's domestic problems were complicated by a pledge he had made at the 1988 Republican convention: "Read my lips: No new taxes."

Failed Promises

But during the 1990 budget summit with Congress, to keep the deficit from rising even higher, he agreed to a tax increase. Bush's press secretary was shocked: "That means we've broken the pledge."

Other campaign pledges were broken, too. As a candidate in 1988, Bush had promised that he would be the "education president" as well as the "environmental president"; but he failed in both areas. He was unable, and perhaps unwilling, to tackle the difficult problem of a nation with thousands of local school systems and much disagreement about education. Other than argue for government vouchers that parents could use to pay tuition at public or private schools of their choice, his administration did little to support educational reform despite his promise that by 2000 American students would lead the world in science and math. Bush got good marks from environmentalists for signing the 1990 reauthorization of the Clean Air Act, which limited emissions of sulfur dioxide and nitrogen oxides, but his Council on Competitiveness gutted enforcement. Headed by Vice President Dan Quayle, the council declared that environmental regulations were unnecessary and should be eliminated because they slowed economic growth and cost jobs. The council halted the enforcement of some regulations

The Americans with Disabilities Act of 1990 was the result of many people's efforts, including activists with disabilities. Daniel Wilkins became a paraplegic in an automobile accident at age twenty-three. An outdoorsman, he was determined not to be isolated from nature, even though he was confined to a wheelchair. Wilkins led efforts to devise trail-accessibility programs in Ohio and, with his mother, founded a chapter of the National Spinal Cord Injury Association. "Physical barriers are easily overcome," said Dan Wilkins, "once attitudinal barriers vanish." (© Junebug Clark)

and weakened others by rewriting them behind closed doors. In addition, the Justice Department overruled the Environmental Protection Agency's move to prosecute large corporate polluters.

Internationally, the Bush administration took the same cautious approach. In 1989 eighty-six nations, including the United States, agreed to phase out use of ozone-destroying chemicals by the year 2000. The following year the United States and twenty-five nations agreed to protect the fragile environment of Antarctica by banning oil exploration and mining there for fifty years. But at the 1992 Earth Summit in Rio de Janeiro, Brazil, Bush rejected key control agreements, including the Biodiversity Treaty designed to slow the loss of endangered species.

As the criticism of President Bush's performance grew, his credibility fell, especially during the confirmation hearings of Clarence Thomas, whom Bush nominated to

Clarence Thomas Nomination

the Supreme Court in fall 1991. Few believed this inexperienced federal judge was, as Bush put it, the "best man for the job." But Thomas, an African American, was highly conservative; and although he insisted that he had formulated no legal opinions on controversial issues, his writings and speeches made it clear that he opposed affirmative action in hiring, believed in returning prayer to the schools, and opposed abortion.

Bush's nomination of Thomas was clever but cynical. Eleanor Holmes Norton, the African American congressional delegate from Washington, D.C., denounced the choice as "calculated . . . to mute the expected reaction to yet another conservative nominee." Then, in October, the nation was electrified by the testimony of Anita Hill, an African American law professor at the University of Oklahoma, who charged that Thomas had sexually harassed her when she worked for him in the early 1980s. Republican senators on the Judiciary Committee sought to discredit Hill, but women around the country identified with her story. The Senate confirmed Thomas, but Hill's testimony—and the Senate's disregard of it—so angered women

that many thousands vowed to oppose the Republican Party in 1992.

The End of the Cold War and Global Disorder

When Bush became president, the Cold War was waning—the very Cold War that he had helped wage as ambassador to the United Nations, U.S. representative to China, CIA chief, and vice president. A cautious, reactive conservative, Bush seemed to set few long-range goals except to envision the United States as the supreme power in a unipolar world. "People say I'm indecisive," Bush once joked. "Well, I don't know about that."

In the mid-1980s, Communist Party chief Mikhail S. Gorbachev had set loose cascading changes in the

Collapse of Communist Regimes

Soviet Union (see page 914). He also had encouraged the people of East Germany and eastern Europe to go their own ways. No longer would a financially hobbled Moscow prop up unpopular Communist regimes. In October 1989 East Germans startled the world by repudiating their Communist government, and in November Germans scaled the Berlin Wall and then tore it down. On October 2, 1990, the two Germanys re-

"CONGRATULATIONS....YOU WON THE COLD WAR!"

The veteran cartoonist Jim Borgman captured the complexity of what many declared a simple matter: American triumph in the Cold War. Borgman reminded his readers that the Cold War had cost the United States itself a great deal—neglect of its domestic problems, deteriorating infrastructure, unemployment, and millions of people defined by the U.S. government as poor and homeless. (Jim Borgman for the *Cincinnati Enquirer*. Reprinted with special permission of King Features Syndicate) united. Veteran Communist oligarchs also fell in Poland, Hungary, Czechoslovakia, Romania, and Bulgaria.

The Union of Soviet Socialist Republics itself collapsed: in 1990 the Baltic states of Lithuania, Latvia, and Estonia declared independence; and in 1991 the Soviet Union disintegrated into independent successor states—Russia, Ukraine, Tajikistan, and many others (see Map 33.1). Muscled aside by Russian reformers who thought he was moving too slowly toward democracy and free-market economics, Gorbachev himself lost power. The breakup of the Soviet empire, dismantling of the Warsaw Pact, repudiation of communism by its own leaders, German reunification, and a significantly reduced risk of nuclear war signaled the end of the Cold War.

The Cold War ended because of the relative decline of the United States and the Soviet Union in the international system. Between the 1950s and the

Why the Cold War Ended

1980s, the contest had undermined the power of its two major protagonists. They moved gradually toward a cautious cooperation whose urgent goals were the restoration of their economic well-being and the preservation of their diminishing global positions.

Four influential trends explain this gradual decline and the resulting attractions of détente. First was the burgeoning economic cost of the Cold War—trillions of dollars spent on weapons and interventions such as that in Vietnam rather than on domestic improvements. As early as the 1950s President Eisenhower had pointed out that defense spending was undermining sound economic policy at home. In the 1960s Americans debated "guns versus butter." In the 1970s President Nixon, aware that Americans had grown weary of Cold War costs, appealed to allies for "burden-sharing." According to the historian Paul Kennedy's

Map 33.1   The End of the Cold War in Europe   When Mikhail Gorbachev came to power in the Soviet Union in 1985, he initiated reforms that ultimately undermined the communist regimes in eastern Europe and East Germany and led to the breakup of the Soviet Union itself, ensuring an end to the Cold War.

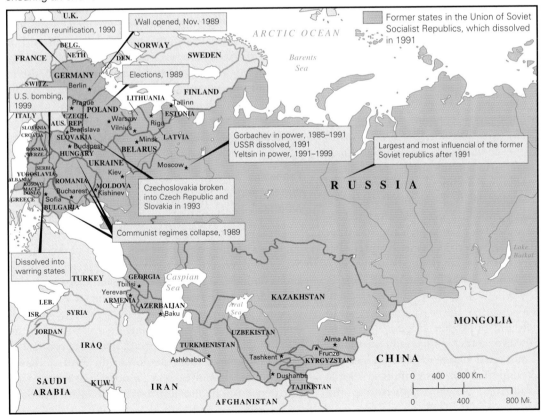

bestseller *The Rise and Fall of the Great Powers* (1987), the United States suffered from "imperial over-stretch." Kennedy argued that the United States, like Spain and Great Britain in earlier centuries, would continue to suffer the erosion of its power unless the nation restored its productive vitality and international marketplace competitiveness, reduced its huge federal debt, and improved its educational system. One way to stem economic decline, he claimed, was to curb America's costly global interventionism. Soviet reformers voiced similar arguments, urging foreign retrenchment from such places as Afghanistan to save money that could be spent to fix the USSR's domestic woes.

Challenges from within their own spheres of influence also help explain why the two major powers welcomed détente. Cuba's anti-American revolution and France's withdrawal from NATO in the 1960s are but two indications that the United States was losing power. The uprisings in Hungary and Czechoslovakia and the Sino-Soviet rift undercut the Soviet Union's hegemony within its network of allies. Détente seemed to offer a means to restore great-power management of unruly states.

Third, the Cold War ended because of the emergence of the Third World, which introduced new players into the international game, further diffused power, and challenged bipolarism. Soviet-American détente represented a means to apply leverage to volatile Third World nations. Finally, the worldwide antinuclear movement of the 1980s pressed leaders, especially in western Europe, to seek détente in order to stop the arms race.

These four elements—economic burden, challenges from sphere members, rise of the Third World, and antinuclearism—combined to weaken the standing of the two adversaries and ultimately to persuade them to halt their nations' declines by ending the Cold War. Gorbachev emerged as the primary agent for change, and Reagan and Bush eventually reacted favorably. Because the Soviet Union fell much harder than the United States, American leaders crowed that they had won the Cold War. But doubters calculated a high price in dollars and deaths for the United States, too.

As the Cold War closed, Bush struggled futilely to explain the dimensions or shape the agenda of a new world order. His administration sustained a large defense budget and continued to use military force abroad, denying Americans the

START Treaties

"peace dividend" they hoped would reduce taxes and free up funds to address domestic problems. Still, in mid-1991 the Soviet Union and the United States signed the START I treaty to reduce their long-range nuclear weapons (warheads and bombs) by one-third. In 1993 Bush signed the START II agreement with Russia's president Boris Yeltsin, who had ousted Gorbachev. This accord provided for a further 50 percent reduction of nuclear weapons and the elimination of all multiple warhead (MIRV) intercontinental missiles (ICBMs). In April 2000 Russia's parliament approved the agreement.

Bush also struggled to define America's policy toward the People's Republic of China. In June 1989 Chinese armed forces stormed into Beijing's Tiananmen Square, slaughtering hundreds—perhaps thousands—of unarmed students and other citizens who for weeks had been holding peaceful prodemocracy rallies. Bush officials initially expressed revulsion, but muted their response in the belief that America's global security and trade needs required friendly Sino-American ties. A symbol of improved relations and of changes within China was the opening in 1992, near Tiananmen Square, of the largest McDonald's restaurant in the world. Some Chinese citizens recoiled from the Golden Arches, charging cultural imperialism. But others embraced America's icon, not for its hamburgers, but for what McDonald's represented to them: modernization, good management, cleanliness, equality.

Tiananmen Square

Such U.S. symbols held appeal elsewhere in the world, too, especially in Latin America, a major source of immigrants who came to the United States searching for economic improvement in their lives. But immigration often disturbed U.S.–Latin American relations; by 1992 probably 2.5 to 4 million "illegal aliens" from around the world lived in the United States, and most of them came from Mexico. Political and economic refugees from Haiti and Cuba also generated anti-immigrant sentiment. When the Cold War ended, Latin America remained staggered by external debt ($431 billion by 1990), poverty (one-third of the region's people were afflicted), and environmental calamities such as deforestation of the Amazon River basin in Brazil and carbon monoxide emissions that threatened the public health of Mexico City and San-

Peace and War in Latin America

tiago de Chile. A positive note was the North American Free Trade Agreement (NAFTA) with Canada and Mexico. Signed in late 1992, the pact created the world's largest tariff-free trade bloc. Critics claimed that the agreement would cost many U.S. workers their jobs because corporations would move south to exploit less expensive Mexican labor and minimal environmental controls. The Clinton administration nonetheless lobbied NAFTA through Congress in 1993; the agreement became operative the following year.

In Central America, the Bush administration cooled the zeal with which Reagan had meddled because the interventions had largely failed and, with the Cold War over, anticommunism seemed irrelevant. The death-dealing, U.S.-financed contra war had not forced the Sandinistas from power in Nicaragua. Instead, in 1989 the Central American presidents devised a workable plan for free elections in Nicaragua (the Sandinista Front lost the 1990 elections) and the disbanding of the contras. In December 1991 U.N. diplomats mediated an agreement in El Salvador ending the civil war. In Guatemala in late 1996 Norwegian and U.N. representatives brokered a peace accord that terminated a civil war that had been raging since 1954. Three years later, after a truth commission in Guatemala issued a detailed report that blamed that country's military for the deaths of at least two hundred thousand people during the civil war, Clinton apologized for U.S. backing of the security forces that "engaged in violent and widespread repression" in that Central American nation.

As the Cold War receded, the drug war accelerated, and Washington attempted to use the U.S. military to quash drug producers and traffickers in Colombia, Bolivia, and Peru, sources of cocaine and crack, both processed from coca leaves. By 1990 the U.S. drug market was probably worth $100 billion. "This is more serious than the Vietnam War," declared Maryland's governor. U.S. officials concentrated on eradication programs and interrupting supply through interdiction. Many Latin Americans resented being blamed for the U.S. drug problem and stressed the need to halt consumer demand inside the United States itself. To this day the drug war has not been won.

Drugs became conspicuous in relations with Panama. Soon after General Manuel Antonio Noriega took power in 1983, he cut deals with Colombia's cocaine barons. Noriega also went on the CIA payroll and helped the United States aid the

Invasion of Panama

contras. Appreciative, Washington turned a blind eye to his drug trafficking. When exposés of Noriega's sordid record provoked protests in Panama, however, Bush decided to dump the dictator. Under Operation Just Cause, launched on December 20, 1989, 22,500 U.S. troops invaded Panama. More than three hundred Panamanians died; twenty-three American soldiers perished. Noriega was captured and taken to Miami, where, in 1992, he was convicted of drug trafficking and imprisoned. The chair of the Republican National Committee called the Panama invasion a "political jackpot" for Bush, whom some had been calling a "wimp." Devastated Panama, meanwhile, like war-torn Nicaragua, became all the more dependent on the United States, which offered little reconstruction aid.

Seeking to end apartheid in South Africa, the United States maintained sanctions against the segregated nation, costing South Africa billions of dollars. Fearing economic disaster and an ultimately successful black revolt, South African president F. W. de Klerk in 1990 lifted restrictions on dissent and legalized the militantly anti-apartheid African National Congress (ANC). De Klerk also released from prison his nation's most celebrated critic, ANC leader Nelson Mandela. In 1994 Mandela became his nation's first black president. When apartheid ended, the U.S. Congress repealed sanctions, and American companies invested once again in South Africa.

End of Apartheid in South Africa

The Middle East became the site of the Bush presidency's major foreign policy venture. When Iraq's dictator, Saddam Hussein, sent troops to invade his peaceful neighbor Kuwait in August 1990, oil-rich Saudi Arabia, long a U.S. ally, felt threatened. In Operation Desert Shield, Bush dispatched more than five hundred thousand U.S. forces to the region. Likening Saddam to Hitler and declaring the moment the first post–Cold War "test of our mettle," Bush rallied a deeply divided Congress to authorize "all necessary means" to oust Iraq from Kuwait (a vote of 250 to 183 in the House and 52 to 47 in the Senate). The United Nations helped organize a coalition of forces. Although many Americans believed that economic sanctions imposed on Iraq should be given more time to work, Bush would not wait. "This will not be another Vietnam," the president said. On the contrary, "Maybe I'll turn out to be a Teddy Roosevelt."

Persian Gulf War

In the Persian Gulf War of early 1991, Operation Desert Storm forced Iraqi troops out of Kuwait. Much of that nation's oil industry was destroyed by bombs and the retreating Iraqis, who torched oil facilities as they left. Oil wells burned for months, darkening the sky over these American forces and causing environmental damage.   (Bruno Barbey/Magnum Photos, Inc.)

Operation Desert Storm began on January 16, 1991, with the greatest air armada in history pummeling Iraqi targets. American missiles reinforced round-the-clock bombing raids on Baghdad, Iraq's capital. In late February, coalition forces launched a ground war that quickly routed the Iraqis from Kuwait. Critics called it "a war to make the world safe for gas-guzzlers," but the *Wall Street Journal* welcomed the Gulf War because it "lets America, and above all else its elite, recover a sense of self-confidence and self-worth." When the war ended on March 1, Bush's popularity in the polls soared to 89 percent, tied with the high set by Harry Truman in June 1945 after the surrender of Germany.

The war's toll: at least 40,000 Iraqis dead; 240 coalition soldiers dead, including 148 Americans. But Saddam Hussein remained in power. By 2000, although Saddam's chemical and nuclear weapons had been exposed by U.N. inspections and partially destroyed, U.N. restrictions had diminished Iraq's oil exports, and continued U.S. air attacks had punished violations of "no-fly zones," he remained defiant while his people suffered.

People suffered in Africa, too. In Somalia, strategically located on the Horn of Africa, famine joined political bickering to upend civil order. Jilting its Cold War ally the Soviet Union in the late 1970s, Somalia began to receive great amounts of U.S. foreign aid. That assistance stopped with the end of the Cold War. After Somalia's repressive dictator was driven from power in 1991, public authority broke down as rival clans vied for power. While gun-toting bandits stole international relief supplies, hundreds of thousands of Somalis died. Appalled by television pictures of starving children, President Bush ordered 28,150 American troops to Somalia in December 1992 to ensure the delivery of relief aid. A U.N. peacekeeping force, including 9,000 Americans, took over in mid-1993. After changing the mission from feeding to reforming Somalia, Washington soon admitted defeat and in early 1994 withdrew U.S. troops; U.N. peacekeepers left about a year later. The humanitarian mission had saved lives, but Somalia returned once again to violent politics and dire hunger.

Operation Restore Hope in Somalia

Economic Doldrums, American Voters, and the Election of 1992

 Success in the Persian Gulf obscured Bush's mixed success in foreign affairs, and Republicans were confident they would retain the White House in the 1992 presidential election. The Republican coalition was intact, uniting economic conservatives who had always voted Republican, cultural conservatives (the fundamentalist and evangelical Christians who advocated "family values"), "Reagan Democrats" (blue-collar workers and one-time Democrats who had supported Bush as Reagan's heir), white voters in the South, young Americans who had come of age politically during the Reagan years, and conservative voters in America's ever-growing suburbs, which in 1990 were home to almost half of the country's population. There was no denying the sheer size of the suburban vote, which tended to be antitax and antigovernment. In the 1980s what had held the Republican coalition together were economic growth, anticommunism, and Ronald Reagan. In 1992, however, these three factors were absent.

A Stagnant Economy

As the 1992 presidential election neared, the stagnant economy pushed the Gulf War into the background. Between 1989 and 1992, the economy had grown slowly or not at all; the gross domestic product averaged an increase of only 0.7 percent a year, the worst showing since the Great Depression of the 1930s. By 1992 several million Americans had joined the unemployment rolls, and factory employment was skidding to its lowest level since the recession of 1982. Even for Americans with jobs, personal income was stagnant. In fact, in 1991 median household incomes fell by 3.5 percent, the most severe decline since the 1973 recession. Mounting annual fiscal deficits and the $4.4 trillion federal debt meant the federal government could afford to do little to stimulate the economy and create jobs. And in 1992 the number of poor people in America reached the highest level since 1964.

Some city and state governments faced bankruptcy. California, out of money in mid-1992, paid its workers and bills in IOUs. A series of "tax revolts," beginning with Proposition 13 in 1978, had cut property taxes at just the time California's population was booming. But California was not alone; some thirty states were in serious financial difficulty in the 1990s. Businesses, too, were deeply burdened with debt; real-estate, home-building, and insurance companies were all overextended. And as companies tottered, the American people grew anxious about their jobs. "The recession that won't go away," *Newsweek* reported in November 1991, "has average Americans spooked and politicians running scared." And a poll that month showed that for the first time in Bush's presidency, less than a majority of the voters (47 percent) were inclined to reelect him in 1992.

Bush's greatest handicap as president was his inability to reassure Americans that he would take action on the economy. By January 1992 his approval rating had dropped to half of what it had been after the Persian Gulf War just ten months before. He seemed to be out of touch with the American people. He "lacks any fingertip feel," noted one political analyst, "for what it is to be a member of the wage-earning middle class in America."

Scandals in Congress

Bush's inaction gave the Democrats hope, but they had problems of their own, particularly in the 102nd Congress, which they controlled. The most blatant scandal involved the House bank, where members of Congress wrote thousands of bad checks, all of which the bank covered at no fee. In the Senate, several members did favors for Charles Keating, who had plundered a large California savings and loan association, causing many unsuspecting small investors to lose their savings. Many Americans also blamed Congress for the gridlock in Washington. Then, with few accomplishments to their credit, the members of Congress voted themselves a pay raise. Said Representative Leon Panetta, a Democrat from California, "When people look back on the 102nd Congress, they will say, 'Let's never repeat this experience again.'" Anti-incumbent sentiment was on the rise, along with calls for term limits.

Bill Clinton

Among the Democratic presidential hopefuls in 1992 was Bill Clinton, governor of Arkansas. Born in 1946, this baby boomer had wanted to be president most of his life. As a college student in the 1960s, he had opposed the Vietnam War and pulled strings to avoid being drafted (as had Vice President Dan Quayle, also of the Vietnam generation). After studying in England as a Rhodes scholar and graduating from Yale law school, Clinton returned to Arkansas and dived into politics, becoming governor in 1979 at the age of thirty-two. In the 1992 presidential primaries he slugged it out with Paul Tsongas, former senator from Massachusetts, and Jerry Brown, former governor of California. But by July, when the

Democrats met for their convention, Clinton emerged the clear victor.

Clinton's message to the voters was mixed. Calling himself a "New Democrat," Clinton sought to inch his party to the right to make it more attractive to white suburbanites, Reagan Democrats, and members of the business community. Clinton hoped, said an ally, "to modernize liberalism so it could sell again." He emphasized the need to move people off welfare, and he called for more police officers on the streets and for capital punishment. But he also advocated greater public investment in building roads, bridges, and communications infrastructure; universal access to apprenticeship programs and college educations; basic healthcare for all Americans; and a shift of funds from defense to civilian programs. Clinton's running mate, Tennessee senator Albert Gore, came from the same mold. He too was a baby boomer, a white southerner, a Baptist, and a moderate Democrat. Gore also appealed to environmentalists as the author of a best-selling book, *Earth in the Balance: Ecology and the Human Spirit* (1992).

Clinton was not Bush's only opponent in 1992. The case against the president was also being made by Patrick J. Buchanan, a conservative television talk-

Ross Perot

show regular and former Nixon speechwriter, who entered the New Hampshire primary to contest Bush for the Republican nomination. And in April 1992, H. Ross Perot, who had amassed a fortune in the computer industry, announced on a television call-in show that he would run for president if voters in all fifty states put his name on the ballot. Many people responded to Perot's candidacy, convinced that he had the answers and intrigued by the possibility of electing the first president since George Washington who belonged to no party. "He stands for a fresh start," explained one backer. "He doesn't have to answer to anybody but the people."

Still the chameleon, in 1992 Bush reverted to an earlier identity: "I care," he told the voters. He won the New Hampshire presidential primary, but just weeks later, during race riots in Los Angeles, he revealed his inability to respond to a domestic crisis. The violence erupted after a California jury had discounted videotaped evidence and acquitted four police officers charged with beating Rodney King, an African American motorist pulled over after a high-speed chase. In the bloodiest urban

Los Angeles Riots

The televised presidential debates took on an informal air in 1992. At this debate at the University of Richmond, President George Bush *(left)* talked with independent presidential candidate Ross Perot, while Democratic candidate Bill Clinton responded to a question from the audience.   (Wide World Photos, Inc.)

riot since the 1960s, forty-four people died and two thousand were injured. Entire blocks of houses and stores went up in flames, leaving $1 billion in charred ruins.

President Bush paid a two-day trip to Los Angeles and advocated emergency aid, but he missed an opportunity to take a bold step in addressing the nation's urban and racial problems. He gave no civil rights talks, and he avoided meeting with the nation's mayors. It seemed to increasing numbers of voters that President Bush did not really care after all.

In August, when the Republicans held their national convention, Bush promoted his identity as guardian of family values but had little new to offer. The "vision thing,"

Bush's Campaign

Bush once conceded, had eluded him. For a presidential candidate in changing times, this was a fatal flaw. The Bush-Quayle election strategy featured negative campaigning, particularly attacks on Clinton's character. He was caricatured as "Slick Willie," a draft-dodger, and a womanizer. Bush said the issue was trust, and he asked whether the American people could trust Clinton's international leadership.

But on November 3, with the highest voter turnout (55 percent) since 1976, the American people voted to make a change. The Clinton-

Clinton's Victory

Gore ticket swept all of New England and the West Coast and much of the industrial heartland of the Midwest (see Map 33.2). It also made the deepest Democratic inroads into the South since Jimmy Carter's 1976 near-sweep. The Republican coalition had not held. Clinton captured Democrats who earlier had fled to Ronald Reagan, and he ran well in the suburbs and among voters who labeled themselves independents and moderates. Although Perot won no electoral votes, he claimed almost one-fifth of the popular vote, demonstrating the public's dissatisfaction with both major parties. It was the most successful run for the presidency by a candidate unattached to the major parties in eighty years.

Voters also changed Congress. Though party distribution remained about the same, with the Democrats in control of both houses, four more women were sent to the Senate and nineteen more to the House. Voters also elected more African American and Hispanic American representatives. When the 103d Congress met in January 1993, it had 110 new representatives and eleven new senators. Many of the first-term members of Congress were—like Clinton—

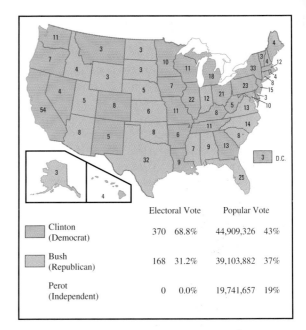

		Electoral Vote		Popular Vote	
	Clinton (Democrat)	370	68.8%	44,909,326	43%
	Bush (Republican)	168	31.2%	39,103,882	37%
	Perot (Independent)	0	0.0%	19,741,657	19%

Map 33.2 Presidential Election, 1992 Although a minority of voters cast ballots for Bill Clinton, he won handily in the electoral college. Clinton's share of the popular vote was the lowest for anyone elected president since Woodrow Wilson won with 42 percent of the popular vote in 1912. Exit polls revealed that the votes cast for Perot would have divided about evenly between Clinton and Bush had Perot not been in the race.

in their forties with advanced degrees, no military service, and considerable experience in politics at the state level. "The baby boomers' generation—or at least some of its most upwardly mobile members—is taking over," observed *Washington Post* columnist David Broder. "It will be different."

One of Bush's last decisions as president smacked of the discredited past. Just before leaving office, the president pardoned Reagan's secretary of defense Caspar Weinberger

Bush's Pardon of Iran-Contra Officials

and other Iran-contra figures who had been indicted on felony counts for lying to Congress and obstructing a congressional inquiry (see page 912). Had elected officials learned nothing from the Watergate scandal, asked David Broder, not even "their duty to obey the law"? The veteran journalist added a grim conclusion: "We have failed as a society to express our contempt and disgust for those who violate their oaths of office with such impunity."

..nton, Newt Gingrich, . Political Stalemate

President Bill Clinton was one of the most paradoxical presidents in American history. In a 1996 story for the *New York Times*, the journalist Todd S. Purdum observed that, "one of the biggest, most talented, articulate, intelligent, open, colorful characters ever to inhabit the White House [Clinton] can also be an undisciplined, fumbling, obtuse, defensive, self-justifying rogue. . . . He is essentially sunny, yet capable of black cloudbursts of thundering rage. He is a splendid salesman and tireless storyteller but confesses that he has failed to tell his Administration's story. . . . He is breathtakingly bright while capable of doing really dumb things."

Clinton's immediate goal as president was to mobilize the nation to pull itself out of its economic, social, and political doldrums. He named to his cabinet a mix of seasoned politicos, young politicians, intellectuals, women, and minorities. In his inaugural address, he called on Americans to "take more responsibility, not only for ourselves and our families, but for our communities and our country." One of Clinton's first acts was to overturn Bush's "gag rule," which had prohibited abortion counseling in clinics that received federal funds. And he appointed his wife, Hillary Rodham Clinton, to draft a plan for healthcare reform. He seemed to be off to a fast start but soon ran into trouble over a campaign pledge to lift the ban on homosexuals in the military. Finally accepting a "Don't ask, don't tell" compromise, he alienated both liberals and conservatives, both the gay community and the military. Clinton's honeymoon in office was brief.

In 1993 the unemployment rate stood at 7.2 percent, and IBM, General Motors, AT&T, and other corporations were laying off thousands of workers. The troubled economies of Europe and Japan portended lower U.S. exports and a bigger trade deficit; the trade deficit already had reached $84.3 billion in 1992, a 29 percent jump from 1991. Still reeling from losses on real-estate loans, banks were hesitant to lend to small businesses, although interest rates had begun to drop. Mounting healthcare costs threatened to drive up the federal deficit.

Economic Proposals

Clinton's economic plan, sent to Congress in early 1993, called for higher taxes for the middle class, a 10 percent surtax on individuals with taxable incomes over $250,000, an energy tax, and a higher corporate tax. Clinton promised to end business deductions for expense accounts, such as memberships in country clubs. He also proposed to cut government spending through a smaller defense budget and a downsized bureaucracy, and he offered an immediate stimulus to the economy through public works projects.

Interest-group lobbyists wasted no time in attacking Clinton's economic plan. Republicans protested that Clinton was not cutting back enough on spending, and other critics hammered him for going back on his campaign pledge to provide tax relief for middle-class Americans. The president fought back, arguing that federal indebtedness was graver than anticipated and that all Americans must pay to clean up the mess the deficit-spending Republicans had left them. Intent on avoiding the "trappings of Washington," he crisscrossed the nation to speak directly to people.

With reduced spending and higher taxes, the federal deficit declined by some $83 billion during Clinton's first fiscal year in office. The president touted the accomplishment but could not take credit alone. The economy rebounded in 1993, outperforming estimates, increasing tax revenues, and cutting interest on the federal debt. Spending for healthcare and for Social Security fell below estimates. The decline in the fiscal deficit begun in 1993 continued throughout the Clinton administration.

Clinton broke legislative gridlock. The so-called motor-voter act enabled people to register to vote when they applied for drivers' licenses, and the Family and Medical Leave Act required employers to grant workers unpaid family or medical leave of up to twelve weeks. Clinton also signed into law measures dealing with the sale of firearms. The Brady law (1993) required a short waiting period (to allow for a background check) before the sale of a handgun; a second law banned the sale of assault weapons. And in 1994 Clinton, with the help of three Republican senators who broke with their party, secured the enactment of a $30.2 billion crime bill that provided funds for building prisons and increasing the size of urban police forces. Finally, with considerable opposition from his own party and from organized labor, Clinton secured congressional approval of NAFTA (see page 955).

Legislative Successes

When Byron R. White, a conservative justice, retired in 1993, Clinton altered the outlook of the Supreme Court by appointing Ruth Bader Ginsburg, an experienced women's rights advocate and federal

Supreme Court Appointments

appeals court judge. The next year he named Stephen Breyer, a federal judge from Massachusetts, to succeed Justice Harry Blackmun. The Court would be less conservative, but it was deeply divided over cases involving gay rights, free speech, and voting rights. The right to an abortion had survived a Court challenge in 1992 by a 5-to-4 vote *(Planned Parenthood v. Casey)*, but the issue had not been laid to rest.

The 1994–1995 term produced conservative rulings that placed limits on affirmative action and school desegregation, but a year later the new justices began to speak up. In *U.S. v. Virginia*, the Court held that the Virginia Military Institute could not exclude women because to do so would violate the constitutional guarantee of "equal protection of the laws"; thus separate-but-equal was unconstitutional whether based on race or gender. Also in 1996, in a landmark gay rights case *(Romer v. Evans)*, the Court ruled unconstitutional a Colorado amendment that nullified civil rights protections for homosexuals.

Defeat of Healthcare Reform

Almost everyone—liberal and conservative, Democrat and Republican—agreed that the nation's healthcare system was in crisis and that its welfare system was a failure. Different constituencies, however, had vastly different "solutions" to offer. The result was continued gridlock between Democrats and Republicans, and between the White House and Congress, and eventual defeat for healthcare reforms, which were opposed by powerful business and insurance industry interests. The failure to deliver on healthcare was Clinton's major defeat, and it was one he shared with his wife, who cochaired the president's task force on healthcare reform.

A Controversial Couple

On the stump in 1992, Bill Clinton had praised his wife, Hillary Rodham Clinton, as a major asset, promising the voters, "Buy one, get one free." A Yale law school graduate, Hillary Clinton had her own career as a partner in a law firm in Little Rock and as a feminist and social activist. Both she and her husband were controversial. Bill Clinton conceded that he had smoked marijuana in the 1960s but insisted that he had not inhaled. Few people, conservative or liberal, believed him. As president, Clinton was the defendant in a civil lawsuit alleging sexual harassment, and he was the most frequent butt of jokes on the Jay Leno and David Letterman late-night television shows. Letterman cracked, for ex-

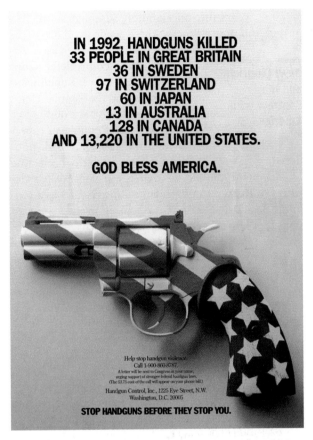

In 1993 Congress took action on gun control, passing the Brady Bill into law. Named for James Brady, paralyzed by a gunshot wound during an assassination attempt on President Ronald Reagan in 1981, the new law mandated a short waiting period before the purchase of a handgun. Brady and his wife Sarah founded Handgun Control, Inc., which sponsored this magazine advertisement.   (Handgun Control, Inc.)

ample, that Clinton had agreed to play a cameo role in an upcoming film, but "was disappointed that he didn't have to sleep with anybody to get the part." In addition, a scandal dating back to the mid-1980s began to embarrass the Clintons. It involved the Whitewater Development Company, and in 1994 Kenneth Starr was appointed special prosecutor to investigate the matter.

Hillary Clinton was also a magnet for criticism, having been in the middle of several of the defining controversies of the Clinton administration, including the firing of the White House travel office staff in 1993; the suicide later that year of her friend and former law partner, deputy White House counsel Vincent Foster; and the Whitewater land deal.

Two years into the Clinton administration, disgusted and angry voters vowed again to "throw the rascals out." This time the target was the Democratic-controlled Congress, and conservative Republicans stood ready to lead the assault. Meeting in 1989 and 1990, a group led by Newt Gingrich, a Republican representative from Georgia, had pondered ways to break America's habit of electing Democrats to the House even as it gave landslide victories to Republican presidents. The result was a ten-point legislative agenda, which, if events went as Gingrich hoped, would be tested in focus groups, endorsed by all Republican candidates, and enacted in the first one hundred days of the new Congress. Bush rejected the plan in 1992, and he went down to defeat. Gingrich resurrected the plan for the 1994 congressional elections and this time found many takers. Especially drawn to this Republican campaign was a group who felt that its needs and interests had been overlooked in recent political debates—the "angry white men."

Newt Gingrich and the Contract with America

Standing on the steps of the U.S. Capitol in September 1994, more than three hundred Republican candidates for the House of Representatives proclaimed their endorsement of the "Contract with America." The document called for a balanced-budget amendment to the Constitution; a presidential line-item veto; the prohibition of welfare payments to unmarried mothers under eighteen and a two-years-and-out limit on welfare benefits; more prisons and longer prison sentences; a $500-per-child tax credit; increased defense spending; a reduced capital gains tax; and congressional term limits. Lobbyists from conservative organizations, including the National Rifle Association, the Christian Coalition, and the National Federation of Independent Business, applauded the contract and gave money to Republican candidates.

In 1994 the Republican Party scored one of the most smashing victories in American political history, winning both houses of Congress for the first time since 1954 and making huge gains in statehouses and legislatures; thirty of fifty governors were Republicans. In the 104th Congress, the Republicans controlled the Senate by 52 seats to 48 and the House by 230 seats to 204, with one Independent. Not a single Republican incumbent lost, and many newcomers were elected, 73 in the House alone. Gingrich became Speaker of the

The "Republican Revolution"

House, and Bob Dole of Kansas became majority leader of the Senate.

Ideological passions ran high, and Republicans launched a counterrevolution to reverse more than sixty years of federal dominance and to dismantle the welfare state. "It's the Russian Revolution in reverse," gloated Bill Kristol, a Republican strategist. Confronted with the Contract with America, Democrats appeared helpless, and even President Clinton took time at a press conference to insist that he was still "relevant."

Anger, Apathy, and the Election of 1996

On April 19, 1995, 168 children, women, and men were killed in a powerful bomb blast that destroyed the nine-story Alfred P. Murrah Federal Building in downtown Oklahoma City. Americans were dazed, saddened, and incensed. In the aftermath of the tragedy, they called in to radio talk shows to denounce the bombers and express their sorrow for the victims and their families. At first, many thought the bomb had come from abroad, perhaps set off by Middle Eastern terrorists. But a charred piece of truck axle located two blocks from the explosion, with the vehicle identification number still legible, proved otherwise. Arrested and convicted of the crime in 1997 was Timothy McVeigh, a native-born white American and a veteran of the Persian Gulf War. He hated the federal government, which he condemned for betraying the American people and the Constitution.

McVeigh later said he was agitated by a tragedy in Waco, Texas, in 1993, when the FBI led an assault on the compound of a religious sect known as the Branch Davidians; a fire had broken out, and some eighty people died. He called the attack a deliberate slaughter by the FBI. In the months that followed, reporters and government investigators discovered networks of Militiamen, Patriots, tax resisters, and various Aryan-supremacist groups that thrived on the growing climate of fear and hatred. The Southern Poverty Law Center identified well over four hundred paramilitary groups operating across the country. Computer-literate "patriots" used the Internet to rally support for their view that the federal government was controlled by Zionists, corrupt politicians, cultural elitists, the Russians, the United Nations, and other "sinister" forces.

Hostility to Government and Political Alienation

Internet use skyrocketed in the 1990s, aided by the development of commercial Web "browsers" and by the Telecommunications Act of 1996, which stimulated mergers between telephone companies and cable companies. By 2000 there were two hundred million Internet users worldwide, including these patrons of a cybercafé.   (Markus Matzel/Das Fotoarchiv)

While terrorism was relatively new to the American experience, hostility to the government was not. In fact, the American Revolution was an antigovernment movement directed against George III and his rule in the colonies. The Civil War began as a revolt against the federal Union. In the twentieth century, antigovernment ideas ranged from McCarthyism in the 1950s, to the New Left a decade later, to the militias in the 1990s. As the historian Michael Kazin has noted, "Throughout American history groups on the right and the left have seen the Federal Government as an alien force, inimical to their interests." Some antigovernment movements have been bitter and resentful, lashing out at people of color, Jews, and Roman Catholics. Yet, no matter their form, these movements have believed that the government has betrayed the people; its leaders are corrupt; and the Constitution has been subverted. In the 1990s increasing numbers of Americans seemed to share this outlook.

For many Americans, the roots of hostility to government were planted during the Vietnam War. "What happened in the 1960s," stated Gerald Marwell, a sociologist at the University of Wisconsin, "was that the Government was successfully 'delegitimated.' We had a period from World War II through the 1950s," Marwell explained, "where the Government was seen as having rescued the nation from the Depression and successfully prosecuted the war, and then we were told in the 1960s that the emperor has no clothes and people shouldn't accept what they're told. And rather than going away, that sensibility has grown over the past 30 years."

In the 1960s, leftists had seen government as an instrument of the ruling classes, while libertarians called for freedom from government restraints. Student radicals opposed the draft and demanded the right to smoke marijuana. In the 1990s, conservatives railed against taxes and proclaimed the unfettered right to own handguns and assault weapons. The scandals— Watergate, Iran-contra—of the decades in between had only deepened Americans' distrust of the federal government. And in Clinton's era, scandal undermined the presidency once again.

In quite a different way, President Ronald Reagan had also fueled hostility to the government, in the process shifting American politics to the right. In his inaugural address in 1981, he had asserted that "government is not the solution to our problem; government *is* the problem." Reagan's continuing antigovernment rhetoric drew many devoted listeners. And his compounding of the federal debt (aided by a fiscally irresponsible Congress) from $1 trillion to $3 trillion set severe financial constraints on what the government could afford to do in the future. When George Bush left office in 1993, the federal debt was $4.4 trillion. No wonder many Americans believed government was more a burden than a benefit.

American voters felt deeply alienated. They had had their fill of political "dirty tricks" and negative attack advertisements on television. They were disgusted not only with the presidency and Congress but also with political parties, special-interest groups, and the press, and they found few politicians to admire or even trust. Journalists pointed to a "raw tomato-hurling fury that has characterized and transformed modern American politics."

Soon the Republicans in the 104th Congress, led by Newt Gingrich, proceeded to make the voters even angrier than Bush or Clinton had

Failures and Successes of the "Republican Revolution"

made them. It turned out that although Americans applauded economy in government, they were resistant to personal sacrifice. And under the Contract with America, most of those whose benefits would be cut were members of the middle class. People worried especially about Medicare and Medicaid, aid to education and college loans, highway construction and farm subsidies, Social Security, and veterans' benefits. When the Republicans attempted to turn over to the states responsibility for child nutrition programs, including school lunches, the Democrats resisted and the public rallied to their side. Republicans later repeated the mistake in pushing to cut spending for education and to repeal decades of environmental and occupational safety legislation. And the Republicans had underestimated Clinton, who frustrated the Republicans by positioning himself as the protector of the federal programs and policies under assault.

The Republicans also made a mistake when they used the threat of a federal government shutdown as a bargaining chip in their quest for a balanced budget by the year 2002. When the government temporarily closed its doors in 1995 and 1996, the public was inconvenienced and angry. Most Americans perceived Congress as ideologically inflexible but tended to see Clinton as moderate and reasonable. Speaker of the House Gingrich conceded that "our strategy failed" because Clinton and his allies, instead of surrendering and making a budget deal, "were tougher than I thought they would be."

Republicans in the 104th Congress were clearly frustrated. Their proposed constitutional amendments were defeated, and Clinton vetoed their tax cuts. Their domestic spending decreases were more than offset by defense spending increases. Congress did, however, pass several significant acts, including the line-item veto, which allowed the president to cut specific spending items from the federal budget. It also passed a measure to curb the federal government's practice of imposing programs on the states without paying for them—known as "unfunded mandates." Of far-reaching influence, the Telecommunications Act of 1996 made sweeping changes in federal law, allowing telephone companies and cable companies to compete, deregulating cable rates, and permitting media companies to own more television and radio stations. With the Freedom to Farm Act of 1996, Congress also made historic changes in farm policy, throwing out the 1938 law that established agricultural subsidies and mandating the seven-year phase-out of payments to farmers.

In 1996 Congress hiked the minimum wage and enacted legislation that made all health insurance portable from job to job and curtailed exclusions based on preexisting medical conditions. Most important, it passed a welfare reform act (The Personal Responsibility and Work Opportunity Act), which eliminated the provision in the Social Security Act of 1935 that guaranteed cash assistance for poor children (Aid to Families with Dependent Children). Instead, under the new law each state received a lump sum of federal money to design and run its own "welfare-to-work" programs. In addition to reducing food stamps and restricting welfare eligibility for legal immigrants, the law mandated that the head of every family on welfare must find work within two years, or the family loses benefits. And it decreed that no one can get more than five years of welfare benefits over a lifetime.

While the Republican 104th Congress elected in 1994 under Gingrich's leadership failed to secure most of its legislative goals, it did recast the American political debate. Many Democrats conceded that the government could not solve all problems and needed to be shrunk. Both Congress and the president urged returning power to the states. Sacred cows from the New Deal and the Great Society, such as Social Secu-

President Bill Clinton suffered political repudiation in the Republican sweep of Congress in 1994. But two years later his popularity was on the upswing. Here he and Hillary Clinton and Vice President Al Gore (with wife Tipper) celebrate their renomination at the 1996 Democratic National Convention in Chicago.   (Wide World Photos, Inc.)

rity and Medicare, were under scrutiny as never before. Civil rights issues seemed to be of secondary political importance to both major parties.

As the 1996 election neared, some political observers predicted that voters would send Clinton back to Arkansas and put a conservative Republican in the White House. But these pundits overlooked an essential segment of the electorate: women. Women tended to view the 104th Congress as hostile to measures essential to family welfare. For years, political scholars had identified a "gender gap" in voting behavior: women were more likely than men to vote Democratic. In the mid-1990s, that gap threatened to become a chasm.

The 1996 Election

"Women are still bigger believers in government," explained Andrew Kohut, a veteran pollster, in 1996. "Women are stronger environmentalists, more critical of business and less critical of government. This drives their party preferences." Issues like health insurance, daycare for children, and education were also of keen importance to women, who were more likely than men

to want an activist government. They also were more suspicious of attempts to downsize government, fearing for the future of safety-net programs and believing that the government should do more to help families. Looking to the 1996 elections, Democrats hoped that women could do for them what "angry white men" had done for the Republicans in 1994.

But Republicans remained confident that President Clinton was vulnerable. Among those running in the primaries was Bob Dole of Kansas, the Senate majority leader and an army veteran of the Second World War who had been badly wounded while fighting in Italy. Dole had served in Congress for thirty-five years, and many Republicans, believing that he had earned his party's presidential nomination, cast their votes for him. He chose Jack Kemp, a former congressman, cabinet officer, and professional football player, to be his running mate.

Both the Clinton-Gore and the Dole-Kemp tickets were amply funded by campaign contributors. Candidates running for federal offices spent a total of $2 billion. Businesses and labor unions alike used

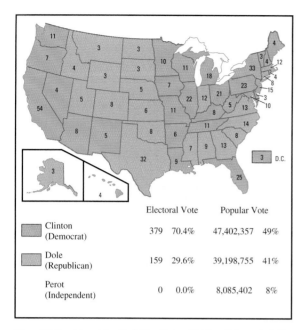

	Electoral Vote		Popular Vote	
Clinton (Democrat)	379	70.4%	47,402,357	49%
Dole (Republican)	159	29.6%	39,198,755	41%
Perot (Independent)	0	0.0%	8,085,402	8%

Map 33.3 Presidential Election, 1996 Although Bill Clinton did not win a majority of the vote, he came close at 49 percent, winning thirty-one states to nineteen for Bob Dole. Ross Perot, with 8 percent of the vote, was less of a factor than in 1992, when he had earned 19 percent of the vote. Despite Clinton's victory, the Republicans retained control of both houses of Congress.

loopholes in the campaign-financing laws to donate tens of millions of dollars, much of it used for costly attack advertisements on television. These negative ads offended many voters, and on election day turnout was a mere 49 percent, the lowest rate since before the Second World War.

On the eve of the voting, Clinton's approval rating stood at 56 percent, and in the election he carried thirty-one states. The public had responded to his promise that, if reelected, his administration would build "a bridge to the twenty-first century, wide enough and strong enough to take us to America's best days." But Clinton was reelected with only 49 percent of the popular vote, and he did not achieve his goal of winning a majority. Still, he easily defeated Dole (41 percent) and Ross Perot (8 percent), who ran again, this time as the Reform Party candidate (see Map 33.3). Although the Republicans lost the contest for the White House, they retained control of both houses of Congress.

Clinton had won, in part, because he stole some of the conservatives' thunder. He called for a balanced budget, declared "the era of big government" was over, and invoked family values such as "fighting for the family-leave law or the assault-weapons ban or the Brady Bill or the V-chip for parents or trying to keep tobacco out of the hands of kids." He had cooperated with Republicans in ending agricultural subsidies and ending "welfare as we know it." Bill Clinton, the first Democratic president to be reelected since Franklin D. Roosevelt in 1936, accomplished that feat partly by running against Roosevelt's New Deal. It was evident that the conservative revolution that had germinated in the 1970s, and that had come to fruition during the Reagan years of the 1980s, was very much alive as the United States entered the second half of the 1990s.

The Prospects and Perils of Hegemonic Power: Military Interventions, Peace Diplomacy, Trade, and Culture

 Clinton and his secretaries of state, the veteran diplomat Warren Christopher and Madeleine Albright, the first woman ever to hold that high post, championed domestic themes in their foreign policy agenda—especially the expansion of economic prosperity, democracy, and environmental controls. But the U.S. posture in world affairs seemed at times more reactive than promotional, especially as vicious ethnic rivalries erupted, making intrastate conflict more common than the interstate conflict of the Cold War era. Notwithstanding Clinton's reelection in 1996, moreover, Republicans in Congress derailed his ambassadorial appointments, cut foreign aid, refused to pay America's U.N. dues, and blocked major treaties. Clinton sustained a large military budget ($270 billion in 1999), in part because defense spending served as a federal jobs program, and like presidents before him, he repeatedly deployed U.S. armed forces abroad (see Table 33.1). He oversaw a changing CIA, which increasingly practiced economic espionage on the business activities and weapons contracts of other nations. Although some observers claimed that the United States, at the end of the twentieth century, had become the world's lone global policeman, foreign policy analyst Joseph S. Nye, Jr., identified America as the "sheriff of the posse, leading shifting coalitions of friends and allies."

One consequence of the end of the Cold War proved savage: ethnic wars in Yugoslavia, from which

Table 33.1   U.S. Military Personnel on Active Duty in Foreign Countries, 1996

Country	Personnel	Country	Personnel	Country	Personnel	Country	Personnel
In foreign countries*	**240,421**	Cote D'Ivoire	19	Japan	42,962	Qatar	43
		Croatia	4,007	Jordan	24	Romania	12
Ashore	213,467	Cuba (Guantánamo)	1,886	Kazakhstan	7	Russia	74
Afloat	26,954	Cyprus	50	Kenya	29	Saudi Arabia	1,587
Albania	3	Czech Republic	10	Korea, Rep. of	36,539	Senegal	11
Algeria	8	Denmark	38	Kuwait	5,531	Serbia	8
Angola	3	Diego Garcia	878	Kyrgyzstan	1	Sierra Leone	6
Antarctica	19	Djibouti	7	Laos	3	Singapore	158
Antigua	2	Dominican Republic	10	Latvia	1	Slovakia	4
Argentina	25	Ecuador	70	Lebanon	2	South Africa	23
Armenia	1	Egypt	1,066	Liberia	9	Spain	2,746
Australia	328	El Salvador	26	Lithuania	2	Sri Lanka	7
Austria	37	Eritrea	1	Luxembourg	9	St. Helena	3
Azerbaijan	1	Estonia	2	Macedonia	501	Suriname	2
Bahamas, The	53	Ethiopia	10	Madagascar	6	Sweden	13
Bahrain	598	Fiji	2	Malaysia	19	Switzerland	24
Bangladesh	10	Finland	17	Mali	6	Syria	11
Barbados	11	France	73	Malta	8	Tanzania, U. Rep. of	5
Belarus	2	Georgia	2	Mexico	35	Thailand	242
Belgium	1,646	Germany	48,878	Moldova	1	Togo	6
Belize	2	Ghana	7	Morocco	17	Trinidad and Tabago	32
Bolivia	24	Gibraltar	4	Mozambique	5	Tunisia	19
Bosnia and Herzegovina	15,003	Greece	507	Nepal	6	Turkey	2,922
		Greenland	141	Netherlands	747	Turkmenistan	1
Botswana	7	Guatemala	17	New Zealand	32	Uganda	9
Brazil	47	Guinea	6	Nicaragua	15	Ukraine	8
Bulgaria	14	Haiti	277	Niger	6	United Arab Emirates	23
Burma	11	Honduras	865	Nigeria	16	United Kingdom	11,662
Burundi	5	Hong Kong	29	Norway	104	Uruguay	9
Cambodia	5	Hungary	6,523	Oman	30	Uzbekistan	1
Cameroon	9	Iceland	1,893	Pakistan	26	Venezuela	30
Canada	208	India	24	Panama	6,435	Vietnam	6
Chad	9	Indonesia	43	Paraguay	10	Yemen	11
Chile	24	Ireland	8	Peru	26	Zaire	9
China	32	Israel	44	Philippines	138	Zambia	6
Colombia	34	Italy	12,401	Poland	20	Zimbabwe	8
Congo	5	Jamaica	10	Portugal	1,075		
Costa Rica	9						

*Includes areas not shown separately.

Source: U.S. Bureau of the Census, *Statistical Abstract of the United States: 1998* (Washington, D.C., 1998), p. 366.

Ethnic Wars in Former Yugoslavia

Slovenia, Croatia, and Macedonia seceded in 1991, followed the next year by Bosnia-Herzegovina. Yugoslavia (primarily Serbia but including Montenegro) fought these moves toward independence. Bosnian Muslims, Serbs, and Croats were soon killing one another by the hundreds of thousands. Noting Europe's reluctance to act in its own backyard, Clinton talked tough against Serbian aggression and atrocities in Bosnia-Herzegovina, especially the Serbs' cruel "ethnic cleansing" of Muslims through massacres and rape camps. On occasion he ordered U.S. airpower to strike Serb positions. In late 1995, after American diplomats brokered an agreement in Dayton, Ohio, among the belligerents for a new multiethnic state in Bosnia-Herzegovina, Clinton contributed thousands of U.S. troops to a NATO Implementation Force that continued to keep a fragile peace as the twentieth century closed.

American ideals, declared Clinton, had won the Cold War and were being tested in the Balkans. The president denounced an "isolationist backlash" and called the United States the world's "best peacemaker." "If we've got troops looking for somewhere to help," dissented a nurse in a high-crime district of St. Louis, "send them in here." In contrast, a Missouri trucker saw a moral duty: "You think of the pictures of those poor people, lying in the street, some of them kids, raped, tortured, murdered. That's pretty hard to turn away from." So it seemed in March 1999, when U.S. and NATO forces began to bomb Yugoslavia (Serbia) to stop the ethnic cleansing of its province of Kosovo, whose majority were ethnic Albanians. The bombing at first unleashed even more cruelties as the Serbs massacred, raped, and evicted ethnic Albanians from their homes; a huge refugee exodus burdened NATO, U.N., and international relief agencies in neighboring nations. Yugoslav president Slobodan

In spring 1999, as NATO bombing raids pounded Serbia (Yugoslavia) and Serb military positions in Kosovo to punish Serbia for killing and displacing ethnic Albanians, the number of Kosovar refugees dramatically increased. Desperate and hungry, they fled to neighboring nations. Here, in a NATO-run refugee camp outside Skopje, Macedonia, U.S. Marines distribute food to some of the 850,000 forced to leave their Kosovo homes.   (Wide World Photos, Inc.)

Milošević finally relented in June, withdrawing his brutal military from Kosovo, where U.S. troops joined a U.N. peacekeeping force. The International War Crimes Tribunal indicted Milošević and his top aides for atrocities. The Kosovo war revealed fissures in NATO as some allies, especially France, Greece, and Italy, opposed an aggressive bombing campaign.

Russia strongly protested the bombing of Yugoslavia. Economically hobbled, and led by an ailing and ineffective Boris Yeltsin, Russia found itself increasingly isolated. Just before the Kosovo crisis, Washington had expanded NATO to include Poland, Hungary, and the Czech Republic. Moscow read the expansion as an anti-Russian step. In 1997 Clinton and Yeltsin had negotiated a START-III agreement, cutting strategic nuclear weapons once again, but Moscow bristled against the U.S. decision to move ahead on an antiballistic missile system. When Russia would ratify START III remained a mystery. By 2000 a "Cold Peace" characterized U.S.-Russia relations over this issue as well as over Russia's inability to curb its rampant political and business corruption and refusal to launch effective reforms.

The Middle East also continued to draw intense U.S. interest. As Saudi Arabia punished the Palestine Liberation Organization for its sup-

Arab-Israeli Agreements

port of Iraq in the Persian Gulf War by trimming financial assistance, and as the *intifada* raised Israel's costs of maintaining control over occupied territories (see Map 31.2 on page 904), the PLO and Israel seemed more willing to settle their differences. U.S. diplomats once again took an active role in the peace process, encouraging Arab and Israeli leaders to attend a peace conference in Madrid in fall 1991. In September 1993 the PLO's Yasir Arafat and Israel's prime minister Yitzhak Rabin signed an agreement for Palestinian self-rule in the Gaza Strip and the West Bank's Jericho. In 1994 Israel signed a peace accord with Jordan, further reducing the chances of another full-scale Arab-Israeli war. Radical anti-Arafat Palestinians, however, continued to stage bloody terrorist attacks on Israelis, while extremist Israelis killed Palestinians and, in November 1995, even Rabin himself. Only after American-conducted negotiations and renewed violence in the West Bank did Israel agree in early 1997 to withdraw its forces from the Palestinian city of Hebron. Thereafter the peace process alternately sagged and spurted.

Ethnic rivalry also bewildered Africa. In mid-1994, in Rwanda, the majority Hutus butchered eight hundred thousand of the minority Tutsis. The United

Genocide in Rwanda

States and the United Nations responded too late, with Clinton resisting appeals for intervention to stop the killing. In 1998, while visiting Africa to promote trade and democracy, the president apologized for not "calling these crimes by their rightful name: genocide" and vowed never to let such a horror happen again.

Throughout Latin America, the Clinton administration continued to promote liberalized trade, private enterprise economies, orderly immigration, democratization, and the

Pressures Against Haiti and Cuba

war against drugs (spending some $3 billion a year). In the early 1990s in poverty-wracked and environmentally devastated Haiti, a military coup and political instability provoked U.S. economic sanctions. Tens of thousands of black Haitians fled in boats for U.S. territory, spawning an immigration crisis. After swinging between tough talk against the military junta and indecision, President Clinton sent Jimmy Carter to the Caribbean island nation in September 1994. The former president cut a deal granting amnesty to the generals, who stepped down. Clinton soon ordered U.S. troops to Haiti in Operation Uphold Democracy. In early 1996 American forces departed, their mission to revitalize Haiti unfulfilled.

As for Cuba, Clinton improved telecommunications and cultural linkages while maintaining the punishing economic embargo. In summer 1995 Cubans set to sea in all forms of craft for Florida, sparking dispute. Clinton decided to admit thousands of detained Cuban refugees while turning away new arrivals. In March 1996, after an airplane manned by a provocative anti-Castro group was shot down by Cuban fighter pilots near Cuba, Clinton, on the eve of the Florida primary, pandered to the politically influential Cuban-American community and signed the Helms-Burton Act. This legislation tightened the economic embargo by allowing American nationals and companies to sue in U.S. courts foreign companies that were using formerly American-owned properties in Cuba. The Castro government had seized these assets in the early days of the Cuban Revolution, and they were valued at $1.8 billion, or $5.5 billion with interest. Canada and the European Union, both of which traded with and invested in Cuba, condemned the measure. Alert to international protest, Clinton suspended the act's provision that permitted the suing of foreign companies. Meanwhile, eager U.S. companies scouted prospects in Cuba, where tourism was becoming big business.

Protesting that the World Trade Organization (WTO) possessed the dangerous power to challenge any nation's environmental laws if the WTO deemed them barriers to trade, chanting demonstrators marched in the streets of Seattle on November 30, 1999. Critics of the WTO have claimed that sea turtles and dolphins have already been victimized by the WTO. Demonstrators identified the WTO as an example of globalization gone wrong. The WTO meeting went on, but the results proved meager because nations could not agree on rules governing dumping, subsidies for farm goods, genetically altered foods, and lower tariffs on high-tech goods.   (Paul Joseph Brown/Seattle Post-Intelligencer)

Seeing flourishing foreign trade as essential to U.S. prosperity and to world economic and political stability, the Clinton administration strove to open foreign markets to American products and to close the U.S. trade gap (which in 1998 reached a record deficit of $233.4 billion). "If the past generation tended to produce soldier-statesmen," remarked one diplomat, "the next generation will have to produce economist-statesmen." Besides guiding NAFTA through Congress, Clinton announced in 1994, when granting China most-favored-nation trading status, that the United States was decoupling trade and human-rights issues. While Washington would not ignore human-rights violations in China, human-rights questions would not interfere with trade. In 1999 the United States supported China's membership in the World Trade Organization (WTO) in return for increased U.S. access to the Chinese domestic market.

Trade Expansion and Globalization

The WTO, which in 1994 replaced the General Agreement on Tariffs and Trade, became the main body regulating and settling disputes over international trade. As a symbol of globalization—the greater movement of goods, services, money, and people across national borders—the WTO became a target of environmental and labor groups, such as the Sierra Club and the AFL-CIO. They charged that the powerful organization of 135 nations served corporate interests and had the dangerous authority to overrule national laws protecting labor standards, human rights, and public health, if the WTO judged those laws barriers to trade. When the WTO held a summit meeting in Seattle in late 1999, antiglobalization protesters marched and nongovernmental organizations (NGOs) publicized their case against the WTO.

Economic and financial issues remained high on the administration's agenda. When politically corrupt Mexico's economy neared collapse in 1995, the United States bailed it out with large loans. Elsewhere, such as in Indonesia and Russia, the Clinton administration backed International Monetary Fund (IMF) efforts to rescue faltering economies and force banking and budget reforms that often undercut social welfare programs and stirred political crisis. In 1999, after the European Union banned hormone-treated American beef, the United States imposed 100 percent tariffs on some imported European goods, including Roquefort cheese and mustard. French protesters ransacked a McDonald's restaurant and one French town slapped a 100 percent tax on bottles of Coca-Cola because "it is a symbol of the American multinational that wants to uniformize taste all over the planet."

Trade issues also lay at the center of tense U.S.-Japanese relations. Most nettlesome was the huge trade deficit in Japan's favor (about $50 billion in the mid-1990s). American manufacturers protested that Japan's tariffs, cartels, and government subsidies blocked U.S. goods from Japanese markets. The Japanese countered that obsolete equipment, poor education, and inadequate spending on research and development undercut U.S. competitiveness. Trade talks with Japan proved divisive and produced small gains, but both nations knew that their economies were too interdependent for one to punish or isolate the other. By the late 1990s, as Japan's economy stagnated and America's galloped, "Japan bashing" declined, while McDonald's became Japan's largest restaurant chain.

The question of trade also influenced U.S. policy toward Vietnam. Military veterans and families of missing-in-action (MIA) soldiers berated Clinton's 1994 decision to lift the trade embargo against Vietnam and his 1995 opening of full diplomatic relations. American businesses such as Otis, General Electric, and Pepsico welcomed the new economic opportunities there. "English is the language of money, the language of our future," remarked a Vietnamese diplomat.

Weapons proliferation alarmed people everywhere. Arms sales, including surface-to-surface missiles, accelerated across the post–Cold War world and the United States continued as the world's largest arms merchant (see Figure 33.1). Nuclear proliferation continued to worry leaders, despite renewal of the nonproliferation treaty in 1995. Argentina, Brazil, and

Weapons of Mass Destruction

South Africa abandoned nuclear weapons programs, but India and Pakistan exploded nuclear devices in 1998. The United States spent more than a billion dollars to help Russia and other former Soviet republics dismantle their nuclear arsenals. The Comprehensive Nuclear-Test-Ban Treaty of 1996 earned 151 signatories, including the United States. But the Clinton administration seemed lackluster in its advocacy of U.S. ratification. In October 1999 the Republican-dominated Senate rejected the treaty by a vote of 51 to 48 (67 votes needed), causing an awakened Clinton to denounce "reckless partisanship." Secretary Albright soon announced that the United States would honor the treaty anyway. Still, the United States projected a negative image: indulging in narrow partisan politics at home while snubbing collective agreements for global security.

In 1997 the United States finally ratified the Chemical Weapons Convention, which required the destruction of chemical weapons, such as poison gas. Also that year, more than one hundred nations endorsed a treaty banning antipersonnel land mines, but Clinton refused to sign because U.S. troops in South Korea relied on mines along the border with North Korea. Terrorists with access to deadly explosives also threatened danger; in early 1993, for example, Islamic extremists bombed New York's World Trade Center. In 1998 Clinton ordered air attacks against suspected terrorist sites in Afghanistan and Sudan. The CIA paid increasing attention to the possibility that terrorists would use biological weapons, such as viruses, against the American people.

Environmental woes also continued to disturb world order and political stability. Acid rain, toxic

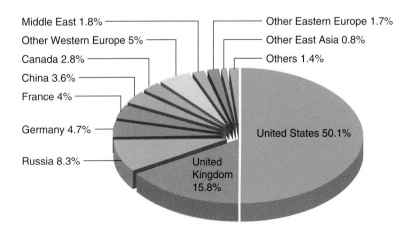

Middle East 1.8%
Other Western Europe 5%
Canada 2.8%
China 3.6%
France 4%
Germany 4.7%
Russia 8.3%
Other Eastern Europe 1.7%
Other East Asia 0.8%
Others 1.4%
United States 50.1%
United Kingdom 15.8%

Figure 33.1   Shares of World Arms Exports, 1992–1994   The United States led the world in the 1990s in the export of weapons. In 1992–1994 U.S. arms exports totaled more than $39 billion. Most went to the Middle East (especially Saudi Arabia, Egypt, and Israel), followed by western Europe and East Asia (especially Japan, South Korea, and Taiwan). Americans debated whether these weapons shipments helped keep the peace or helped fuel regional arms races that aggravated conflict.   (Source: Thomas G. Paterson, J. Garry Clifford, and Kenneth J. Hagan, *American Foreign Relations: A History,* vol. 2, 5th ed. Copyright © 2000 by Houghton Mifflin Company; Data from U.S. Arms Control and Disarmament Agency.)

Environmental and Population Crises

waste, deterioration of the protective ozone layer (which blocks the sun's carcinogenic ultraviolet rays), soil erosion, water pollution, and destruction of tropical forests spoiled the natural environment, killed wildlife, and poisoned land. Warming of the earth's climate due to the greenhouse effect—the buildup of carbon dioxide and other gases in the atmosphere—threatened a rise in ocean levels, flooding farmland and dislocating millions of people. As the world's population swelled to 6 billion in 1999 (increasing at a rate of some 80 million a year) and droughts unleashed killer famines and massive human migrations, ill-equipped governments struggled to provide welfare for the hungry. Still, analysts noted that women were having fewer babies; the global fertility rate declined from a high of 6 children per woman in the 1950s to 2.9 by 2000.

In contrast to the Bush administration, the Clinton administration, recalled Secretary Christopher, decided "to persuade the American people that a healthy environment is critical to national security." In 1993 Clinton signed the Biodiversity Treaty and sent it to the Senate, where it remains pending. The United States approved the Convention on Desertification (1994) to support land preservation and reclamation and signed the Global Warming Convention (1997) to reduce greenhouse gas emissions (not yet ratified). In fall 1997 Clinton transmitted the 1982 Convention on the Law of the Sea to the Senate. Although 129 nations and the European Union have ratified the accord and activated the International Seabed Authority, the Senate has so far refused to approve this convention.

Human Rights for Women

In the mid-1990s the State Department and the United Nations studied the treatment of women as a worldwide human rights issue. Their reports revealed that 70 percent of the world's poor people were women. Women faced not only job discrimination (women worldwide earned 30 to 40 percent less than their male counterparts for the same work) and political discrimination (women held only 10 percent of national legislative seats) but also forced sterilization and abortion, coerced prostitution, and genital mutilation. Half of the world's people were women, observed one U.S. official, "and until you improve their situation, you're not going to improve human rights around the world." The 1995 Fourth World Conference on Women, held in Beijing, called for the "empowerment of women" through "human rights and fundamental freedoms." Gender issues and international relations became intertwined. The United States soon made genital mutilation and other gender-based abuses grounds for asylum.

The U.N.'s specialized agency, the World Health Organization (WHO), continued its lifesaving work to combat diseases and promote medical research. The United States has traditionally supplied the largest share of WHO's regular budget and has also volunteered funds for WHO's Global Program on AIDS. The AIDS pandemic by the mid-1990s had taken the lives of millions, especially in sub-Saharan Africa. In 1997 WHO called cancer-causing smoking "a fire in the global village" and denounced the growing popularity in Asia of Western-style cigarettes marketed aggressively by U.S. firms that faced antitobacco sentiment at home.

Globalization of American Culture

The export of American popular culture became one of the 1990s' most prominent features. After the Cold War ended, American culture became particularly coveted in eastern Europe and the former Soviet republics. Featuring the "Beeg Mek," McDonald's in 1990 opened a fast-food restaurant in the very heart of Moscow; within five years it had served 80 million customers. Many residents of former Communist countries strove to learn the English language like their counterparts in western Europe, where 70 percent of people between the ages of eighteen and twenty-four spoke English. Interest in American basketball soared everywhere, especially after the American "Dream Team" (made up of National Basketball Association stars) triumphed at the televised 1992 Summer Olympics in Barcelona. Images of the slam-dunking Chicago Bulls hero Michael Jordan adorned T-shirts worldwide, and players from foreign lands, including eastern Europe, increasingly enrolled in U.S. colleges to play hoops.

American movies, TV programs, music, books, computer software, and other "intellectual property" dominated world markets in the 1990s. The TV soap opera *The Young and the Restless* became popular in New Delhi; people in Warsaw watched *Dr. Quinn, Medicine Woman*; even in Tehran, where anti-Americanism flourished and Muslim censorship prevailed, young people with VCRs watched the movie *Air Force One*. Time Warner, Inc., sold TV programs in 175 countries. *Reader's Digest* circulated in nineteen languages with sales of 28 million (compared to its U.S. circulation of 14.7 million). In thirty-six foreign editions, *Cosmopolitan* magazine touted the glamorous woman. An estimated 90 percent of all global Internet traffic was in English, and through e-mail people who lacked freedom abroad communicated with Americans who had it and wanted to promote it worldwide. The popularity of U.S. culture abroad stemmed in good part from the themes it presented: wealth, individuality, freedom, optimism, sex, violence, mobility, technological progress.

Some world affairs specialists predicted the growth of a single global culture, with the United States at its center. "It's inevitable," declared one Iranian. "I mean, it's happening in France. Do you know how many McDonald's are in France now? And the French are supposed to have the best cooking." The globalization of American culture, however, did not unfold conflict-free: some peoples protested the emasculation of their native ways by U.S. imports that seemed tawdry, unhealthy, and violent. Yet, with power in the world "no longer defined solely by territory or industrial capacity, but increasingly by the development of intellectual capital," the scholar Barry Fulton has suggested, the United States was well positioned to lead the so-called Information Age of the twenty-first century.

With its preeminent high-tech military, moreover, the United States could conduct information warfare, using "smart bombs" to target and destroy an enemy's information nerve center, as when in spring 1999 missiles destroyed Serbia's communications network and television system. At that time, too, U.S. defense officials considered but rejected hacking into Serbia's computer networks, conducting "cyberwarfare" to derail trains and disrupt electrical services. One reason for not doing so: American officials might be vulnerable to war crimes charges because civilians as much as military targets would be hurt.

Information Warfare

At the start of the twenty-first century, the United States held immense power, measured in so many ways. As "globocop" it intervened in other countries. As banker and trader, it pressed other nations to open their markets to U.S. commerce. Accelerated by the World Wide Web and the Internet, American culture spread everywhere. Yet, throughout history, hegemonic powers have had difficulty sustaining their supremacy. Would America, too, falter? By 2000 many nations and peoples had grown wary and critical of the United States. French foreign minister Hubert Vedrine declared, "we cannot accept either a politically unipolar world, not a culturally uniform world, nor the unilateralism of a single hyper-power" like the United States. Clinton's national security adviser Samuel R. Berger acknowledged America's reputation as a "hectoring hegemon." But he did not apologize.

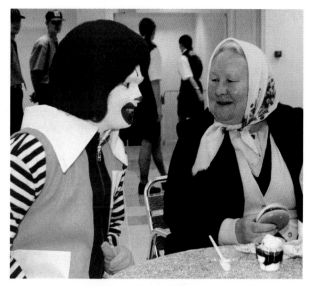

McDonald's restaurants circled the globe by the early twenty-first century, exemplifying the globalization of American culture. This Ukrainian woman in Kiev seems to enjoy both her hamburger and a conversation with the human symbol of the fast-food chain, Ronald McDonald. (Wide World Photos, Inc.)

Instead, in traditional American terms, Clinton's spokesman asserted that the United States put "the greater good" of other nations ahead of its selfish interests. Given such self-congratulatory utterances, the debate over America's global role did not abate.

Clinton's Second Term: Scandal, Impeachment, and Political Survival

Misconduct and scandals had tainted the Clinton White House from the beginning. Bill Clinton's character was often the issue, and allegations of his marital infidelity abounded. But, as one reporter noted, "If Ronald Reagan was the Teflon President, then Bill Clinton is the Timex President. He takes his lickings, keeps on ticking." Clinton's second term as president would test how durable he really was.

The scandal involving the Whitewater Development Company continued to dog the White House. In the mid-1980s, the Clintons had been partners in the company with James McDougal, who was later indicted for conspiracy and mail fraud, along with his wife Susan and Governor Jim

Whitewater Indictments and Investigation

Guy Tucker, Clinton's successor in Arkansas. In 1994 Kenneth Starr, the independent counsel investigating Whitewater, accepted a plea agreement with Webb Hubbell, former managing partner of the law firm in which Hillary Clinton had worked and a close friend whom President Clinton had appointed deputy attorney general. In return for his cooperation in the ongoing investigation, Hubbell was allowed to plead guilty to one count of tax evasion and one count of mail fraud.

During the 1996 elections, independent counsel Starr began to produce indictments and even convictions: the McDougals and Tucker were found guilty. Hillary Clinton, testifying before a Senate committee, could not explain how long-lost law-firm billing records from Little Rock, which had been subpoenaed, disappeared for two years before surfacing in the family quarters of the White House. At a later point, the Clinton administration said it was a mistake that in 1993 and 1994 the FBI had sent over to the White House the confidential records of some nine hundred Republicans. Others thought the manipulation of federal agencies smelled of an earlier scandal, Watergate.

Meanwhile, Starr expanded his investigation of Bill Clinton to matters unrelated to Whitewater, including allegations of illegal campaign contributions, sexual harassment, and lying to a grand jury about the nature of his relationship with a White House intern named Monica S. Lewinsky. In early 1998 Linda Tripp, a former White House employee, informed Starr's office that Clinton had had a sexual affair, and she had tapes of telephone conversations to prove it. A week later, in a sworn deposition to the grand jury investigating sexual harassment, Clinton denied the affair. But in late July, Starr granted Lewinsky and her mother full immunity in exchange for testimony, and the next day Clinton's lawyer announced that the president would also testify. Two weeks later Starr requested that the president provide a fresh sample of his DNA to test for a match with a semen stain on one of Lewinsky's dresses.

Monica Lewinsky

On the night of August 13, 1998, Bill Clinton confessed to his wife that he had had a sexual relationship with Monica Lewinsky. Four days later, Clinton testified, telling the grand jury that he recalled a half-dozen sexual encounters with Lewinsky, beginning in late 1995 and ending by 1997. That evening, he spoke from the Oval Office. "I have sinned," he told the American people, and he expressed "sorrow" for the "hurt" he had caused his family, his staff, Lewinsky and

her family, and the American people. "I have asked all for their forgiveness." But Clinton's testimony had been less than complete, and his tribulations were far from over; for at just that time, Starr was preparing a 445-page impeachment report for consideration by Congress.

Impeachment by the House

The Starr report described ten sexual encounters between Clinton and Lewinsky, as well as fifteen phone-sex conversations, and mapped out eleven possible grounds for impeachment of the president, accusing Clinton of lying under oath, obstruction of justice, witness tampering, and abuse of power. On December 19, the House voted on four articles of impeachment against Clinton; largely along party lines, the House passed two of the articles, one alleging that the president had committed perjury in his August 17 grand-jury testimony, the other that he had obstructed justice. With the House vote, Clinton became only the second president—and the first in 130 years—to face a trial in the Senate, which has the constitutional responsibility to decide (by a two-thirds vote) whether to remove a president from office.

But even as the House Republicans voted for Clinton's impeachment, poll after poll showed that the majority of Americans approved of the president's job performance and did not want him removed from office. In the 1998 congressional elections, voters expressed their opposition to the drive for impeachment by reducing the Republican majority in the House to ten seats (222 to 212, and one Independent). Republicans then turned on their leader, Newt Gingrich, blaming his confrontational leadership for the defeat; Gingrich resigned both the speakership and his seat in the House.

Acquittal by the Senate

The 1998 elections left the Republican majority in the Senate unchanged at 55 to 45, and everyone expected that the Senate vote would generally break along party lines. "It takes two-thirds to get rid of this fella," said Senator Strom Thurmond, a Republican from South Carolina. "We don't have it. Let's get it over." After a five-week trial, during which thirteen House Republicans acted as Clinton's prosecutors, the Senate, by a 55-to-45 vote, found the president not guilty of perjury. And voting 50 to 50, the Senate cleared him of obstructing justice. For his part, Clinton appeared contrite, saying that he was "profoundly sorry . . . for what I did and said to trigger these events and the great burden they have imposed on the Congress and the American people."

How do historians know...

that Bill Clinton lied to the American people when he denied having a sexual relationship with former White House intern Monica Lewinsky? The evidence is Clinton's DNA. For the first half of 1998, the president stuck by his adamant denial. But in July 1998, when Lewinsky agreed to cooperate with independent counsel Kenneth Starr, she also turned over to him a critical piece of evidence (see the photo): a navy blue dress stained with Clinton's semen. Two weeks later, the independent counsel requested that the president provide a DNA sample. Realizing that the FBI had analyzed the genetic material on Lewinsky's dress and that Starr was looking for a match, Clinton within days confessed the affair to his wife and later to the American people.

DNA evidence is crucial because each person's genetic makeup is unique. (DNA is the nucleic acid that carries genetic information in cells.) In recent years, DNA tests have helped not only to convict murderers, rapists, and other criminals, but also to establish the innocence of

people falsely accused, convicted, and/or imprisoned for violent crimes. Analysis of genetic material can also determine paternity; two hundred years after the fact, DNA evidence established with near certainty that Thomas Jefferson fathered at least one of the children born of his slave Sally Hemings in the 1790s. (Photo: Allan Tannebaum/Sygma)

Throughout 1999 bitter political partisanship impeded the passage of much-needed legislation. Rejected, vetoed, or left unacted upon were proposals to restructure Social Security and Medicare in preparation for the retirement of the baby-boom generation; to safeguard patients' rights in HMOs (health maintenance organizations); to cut taxes; and to reform campaign finance by regulating attack ads and banning unlimited "soft money" contributions to political parties. Even the shootings at Columbine High School could not propel through Congress legislation requiring criminal background checks of purchasers at gun shows. "This was not a session of great initiatives," lamented one senator. "This was a session that was post-impeachment and pre-[2000] election."

As America entered a new century, its people yearned for a president with character and leadership. Some Americans embraced Senator John McCain, a Republican from Arizona who championed campaign finance reform. McCain was also a war hero; as a navy pilot in 1967, he was shot down by a surface-to-air missile over Hanoi, captured by the Vietnamese, and

held as a prisoner of war under brutal conditions for the next five and a half years. The Democratic presidential race also featured a genuine hero; Bill Bradley had been an All-American basketball player at Princeton, a Rhodes scholar at Oxford University, a Hall of Fame basketball player for the New York Knicks, and a former U.S. senator from New Jersey. Bradley joined McCain in demanding campaign finance reform.

The race for the presidency accelerated in 2000 with primary elections, party caucuses, and state party conventions scheduled in thirty-two states during the first three months of the year, beginning in Iowa in January. The front runners were George W. Bush, the Republican governor of Texas, and Al Gore, Jr., Democratic vice president under Clinton. Bush's father, George H. W. Bush, had served as president; Gore's father had been an influential U.S. senator from Tennessee. Loyalists in both parties supported the younger Bush and Gore politically and financially. By 2000 Bush had amassed more than $67 million in political contributions, more than twice Gore's $28 million, but Gore would be receiving an additional $12

Just after midnight on January 1, 2000, these jubilant Americans welcomed the new year, century, and millennium in New York City's Times Square.   (Nicole Beniveno/The New York Times)

million in federal matching funds during the year. On Super Tuesday in March, Gore swept the presidential primaries, including California and New York, and Bush won all but a handful of states in New England. McCain and Bradley ended their campaigns, and Gore and Bush squared off for the November election.

Summary

In 2000 the United States was riding a wave of great prosperity. Prior to 2000, the longest economic expansion in American history had lasted for 106 months, from 1961 through 1969. But in February 2000 an expansion that had begun in 1991 eclipsed that record, and it did so without fueling inflation. In 1999 consumer confidence reached its highest level in three decades, and prices on the stock exchanges rose dramatically, establishing all-time highs by the end of the decade.

America at the turn of the twenty-first century was engaged in a technological and scientific revolution. A century earlier, electricity and the internal-combustion engine were transforming communica-

tions and transportation in the United States. And one hundred years before that, the steam engine was poised to initiate America's industrial revolution. But in 2000 it was a digitized revolution in communications and information that generated American prosperity and was transforming life in America and around the globe.

The United States was not only prosperous in 2000, it also was powerful. The 1990s began with challenges to the old world order. Like a retreating glacier, the Cold War left behind a scarred landscape and debris that complicated the shaping of a new world order. Localized conflicts and ethnic rivalries, such as those in the Balkans, Middle East, and Africa, crowded the international agenda, as did human rights, the natural environment, and the proliferation of deadly weapons. In the 1990s Bush and Clinton officials spoke of America's "world responsibilities" to spread democracy and free-market economics abroad and to intervene for humanitarian purposes. In the ensuing national debate, others argued that the United States lacked the cultural sensitivity, funds, or ability to build, reform, or police other societies. Reasserting traditional notions of U.S. world leadership, Clinton dismissed such thinking as a dangerous retreat to isolationism. His military interventions in a host of countries—especially against what Washington officials called "rogue states"—and trade and cultural expansion demonstrated a fervent traditional U.S. activism to make the world more American and to sustain U.S. hegemony against all challengers.

Envious of America's prosperity and power, nations everywhere struggled to adopt American economic and political institutions. But perils also confronted America and the world in the new century. Speaking just minutes before midnight on December 31, 1999, Bill Clinton called on the American people not to fear the future, but to "welcome it, embrace it and create it." Americans, however, were fearful about the future. For one thing, the State Department had warned of terrorist attacks to be launched on New Year's Eve. For another, the arrival of "Y2K" (year 2000) threatened to crash computer systems around the world. In the United States alone an estimated $100 billion was spent to prevent the collapse on January 1, 2000, of banks and automated teller machines, the Internet, financial markets, air traffic control, and the national defense system. But the Y2K catastrophe did not happen, and the few problems that did arise were more humorous than dangerous. In Albany, New York, for example, a customer returning a video was handed a $91,250 late fee after a computer showed the tape was a century overdue.

Just as no Y2K bug precipitated a computer collapse, so too no terrorist attacks marred the arrival of the new millennium. Ironically, however, at this time of apparent triumph, many Americans had lost faith in their own government. Confidence in government, which was expressed by 76 percent of Americans in 1964, plummeted to 19 percent by 1996. In 1996 a majority (51 percent) of voting-age Americans chose not to vote, and 64 percent did not vote in 1998. Americans were deeply skeptical about the political process, and they expressed disgust not only at Bill Clinton's behavior, but also at the Republicans' single-minded determination to destroy the president.

In his first newspaper column in 2000, David Broder observed a paradox in American democracy. In the preceding hundred years, thanks to persevering woman suffrage and civil rights movements, women and African Americans had gained the vote, thus enfranchising well over half the population. But the American voter in 2000 was cynical, having endured too many politicians who "find it easier to denigrate their opponents . . . than to describe their own views or defend their own records." "We begin the new century," Broder concluded, "with a paradox: Democracy is stronger than ever in the United States; representative government, weaker." The challenge of the new century would be to restore Americans' faith in their government.

LEGACY FOR A PEOPLE AND A NATION

The Internet

In the 1990s America—and the world—went online, forever changing the way people communicate (e-mail), do business (e-commerce), and experience life. Although a crude version of the Internet known as ARPANET went online in 1969, when two bulky computers were linked by a 15-foot cable, it was a series of developments in the late 1980s and 1990s that stimulated the Net revolution. First, Tim Berners-Lee, a British physicist, devised the three basic elements of the Web's operation: URL (uniform resource locator), HTML (hypertext markup language), and HTTP (hypertext transfer protocol). Then in 1993 the first commercial "browser" to aid navigation through the Web hit the market. Called Mosaic, it was soon followed by a much more successful product: Netscape. The prospect of millions of computers connected worldwide had become a reality.

By 2000 there were nearly 200 million Internet users worldwide, including 80 million Americans. By 2003 more than 500 million people will be surfing the World Wide Web. For their Christmas shopping in 1999, for example, millions of Americans avoided the malls and clicked through their gift lists. Some bought books from Amazon.com, while others bid on items being auctioned at eBay. Psychologists at Carnegie Mellon University, surveying the lives of Net users, found that people who spend even a few hours a week online suffer higher levels of loneliness and depression. Seemingly nothing, however, can slow down the digitized transformations in communications and information. Indeed, for the American people and nation in the new millennium, there could be no more fitting legacy than the Internet.

For Further Reading, see page A-41 of the Appendix. For Web resources, go to http://college.hmco.com.

APPENDIX

Suggestions for Further Reading

Chapter 16

National Policy, Politics, and Constitutional Law

Richard H. Abbott, *The Republican Party and the South, 1855–1877* (1986); Herman Belz, *Emancipation and Equal Rights* (1978); Herman Belz, *A New Birth of Freedom* (1976); Michael Les Benedict, *A Compromise of Principle: Congressional Republicans and Reconstruction, 1863–1869* (1974); Michael Les Benedict, *The Impeachment and Trial of Andrew Johnson* (1973); Charles S. Campbell, *The Transformation of American Foreign Relations, 1865–1900* (1976); Adrian Cook, *The Alabama Claims* (1975); Michael Kent Curtis, *No State Shall Abridge* (1987); David Donald, *Charles Sumner and the Rights of Man* (1970); Harold M. Hyman, *A More Perfect Union* (1973); Ronald J. Jensen, *The Alaska Purchase and Russian-American Relations* (1975); William S. McFeely, *Grant* (1981); William S. McFeely, *Yankee Stepfather: General O. O. Howard and the Freedmen* (1968); Eric L. McKitrick, *Andrew Johnson and Reconstruction* (1966); James M. McPherson, *The Abolitionist Legacy* (1975); Joel Silbey, *A Respectable Minority: The Democratic Party in the Civil War Era* (1977); Brooks D. Simpson, *Let Us Have Peace* (1991); Brooks D. Simpson, *The Reconstruction Presidents* (1998); Kenneth M. Stampp, *The Era of Reconstruction* (1965); Hans L. Trefousse, *Andrew Johnson* (1989).

The Freed Slaves

Roberta Sue Alexander, *North Carolina Faces the Freedmen* (1985); Ira Berlin, ed., *Freedom: A Documentary History of Emancipation, 1861–1867* (1984); Elizabeth R. Bethel, *Promiseland* (1981); Orville Vernon Burton, *In My Father's House Are Many Mansions* (1985); Edmund L. Drago, *Black Politicians and Reconstruction in Georgia* (1982); Paul D. Escott, *Slavery Remembered* (1979); Eric Foner, "Reconstruction and the Crisis of Free Labor," in *Politics and Ideology in the Age of the Civil War*, ed. Eric Foner (1980); Gerald Jaynes, *Branches Without Roots: The Genesis of the Black Working Class in the American South, 1862–1882* (1986); Leon Litwack, *Been in the Storm So Long* (1979); Edward Magdol, *A Right to the Land* (1977); Robert Morris, *Reading, 'Riting and Reconstruction* (1981); Howard Rabinowitz, ed., *Southern Black Leaders in Reconstruction* (1982); Emma Lou Thornbrough, ed., *Black Reconstructionists* (1972); Okon Uya, *From Slavery to Public Service* (1971); Clarence Walker, *A Rock in a Weary Land* (1982).

Politics and Reconstruction in the South

Robert W. Coakley, *The Role of Federal Military Forces in Domestic Disorders, 1789–1878* (1988); Richard N. Current, *Those Terrible Carpetbaggers* (1988); Jonathan Daniels, *Prince of Carpetbaggers* (1958); W. E. B. Du Bois, *Black Reconstruction* (1935); Paul D. Escott, *Many Excellent People: Power and Privilege in North Carolina, 1850–1900* (1985); W. McKee Evans, *Ballots and Fence Rails: Reconstruction on the Lower Cape Fear* (1966); Michael W. Fitzgerald, *The Union League Movement in the Deep South* (1989); Eric Foner, *Reconstruction: America's Unfinished Revolution, 1863–1877* (1988); Eric Foner, *Nothing but Freedom* (1983); William C. Harris, *The Day of the Carpetbagger* (1979); Thomas Holt, *Black over White: Negro Political Leadership in South Carolina During Reconstruction* (1977); J. Morgan Kousser and James M. McPherson, eds., *Region, Race and Reconstruction* (1982); Elizabeth Studley Nathans, *Losing the Peace* (1968); Michael Perman, *The Road to Redemption* (1984); Michael Perman, *Reunion Without Compromise* (1973); Lawrence N. Powell, *New Masters* (1980); George C. Rable, *But There Was No Peace* (1984); James Roark, *Masters Without Slaves* (1977); James Sefton, *The United States Army and Reconstruction, 1865–1877* (1967); Mark W. Summers, *Railroads, Reconstruction, and the Gospel of Prosperity* (1984); Allen Trelease, *White Terror* (1967); Ted Tunnell, *Carpetbagger from Vermont* (1989); Ted Tunnell, *Crucible of Reconstruction* (1984); Michael Wayne, *The Reshaping of Plantation Society* (1983); Sarah Woolfolk Wiggins, *The Scalawag in Alabama Politics, 1865–1881* (1977).

Women, Family, and Social History

Virginia I. Burr, ed., *The Secret Eye* (1990); Ellen Carol Dubois, *Feminism and Suffrage* (1978); Herbert G. Gutman, *The Black Family in Slavery and Freedom, 1750–1925* (1976); Elizabeth Jacoway, *Yankee Missionaries in the South* (1979); Jacqueline Jones, *Labor of Love, Labor of Sorrow* (1985); Jacqueline Jones, *Soldiers of Light and Love* (1980); Robert C. Kenzer, *Kinship and Neighborhood in a Southern Community* (1987); Mary P. Ryan, *Women in Public* (1990); Rebecca Scott, "The Battle over the Child," *Prologue* 10 (Summer 1978): 101–113.

The End of Reconstruction

Michael Les Benedict, "Southern Democrats in the Crisis of 1876–1877," *Journal of Southern History* 66 (November 1980): 489–524; William Gillette, *Retreat from Reconstruction, 1869–1879* (1980); William Gillette, *The Right to Vote* (1969); Keith Ian Polakoff, *The Politics of Inertia* (1973); John G. Sproat, *"The Best Men": Liberal Reformers in the Gilded Age* (1968); C. Vann Woodward, *Reunion and Reaction* (1951).

Reconstruction's Legacy for the South and the Nation

Robert G. Athearn, *In Search of Canaan* (1978); Edward L. Ayers, *The Promise of the New South* (1992); David W. Blight, *Race and Reunion: The Civil War in American Memory, 1863–1915* (2000); Norman L. Crockett, *The Black Towns* (1979); Stephen J. DeCanio, *Agriculture in the Postbellum South* (1974); Steven Hahn, *The Roots of Southern Populism* (1983); Jay R. Mandle, *The Roots of Black Poverty* (1978); Nell Irvin Painter, *Exodusters* (1976); Howard Rabinowitz, *Race Relations in the Urban South, 1865–1890* (1978); Roger L. Ransom and Richard Sutch, *One Kind of Freedom* (1977); Laurence Shore, *Southern Capitalists* (1986); Peter Wallenstein, *From Slave South to New South* (1987); Jonathan M. Wiener, *Social Origins of the New South* (1978); C. Vann Woodward, *Origins of the New South* (1951).

Chapter 17

Native Americans

Ralph K. Andrist, *The Long Death: The Last Days of the Plains Indians* (1964); Leonard A. Carlson, *Indians, Bureaucrats, and Land: The Dawes Act and the Decline of Indian Farming* (1981); David Courtwright, *Violent Land* (1996); Frederick E. Hoxie, *A Final Promise: The Campaign to Assimilate the Indians, 1880–1920* (1984); Janet A. McDonnell, *The Dispossession of the American Indian* (1991); Francis Paul Prucha, *The Great Father: The United States Government and the American Indians* (1984); Robert M. Utley, *The Lance and the Shield: The Life and Times of Sitting Bull* (1993); Robert M. Utley, *The Indian Frontier of the American West, 1846–1890* (1984); Philip Weeks, *Farewell, My Nation: The American Indian and the United States* (1990); Richard White, *The Roots of Dependency* (1983).

The Western Frontier

Ray A. Billington and Martin Ridge, *Westward Expansion*, 5th ed. (1982); Sara Deutsch, *No Separate Refuge: Culture, Class, and Gender on an Anglo-Hispanic Frontier in the American Southwest* (1987); James R. Grossman, ed., *The Frontier in American Culture* (1994); Robert V. Hine, *The American West*, 2d ed. (1984); Julie Roy Jeffrey, *Frontier Women* (1979); Patricia Limerick, *The Legacy of Conquest: The Unbroken Past of the American West* (1987); Timothy R. Mahoney, *River Towns in the Great West* (1990); Peggy Pascoe, *Relations of Rescue: The Search for Female Moral Authority in the American West* (1990); Rodman W. Paul, *The Far West and the Great Plains in Transition, 1859–1900* (1988); Robert J. Rosenbaum, *Mexican Resistance in the Southwest* (1981); Lillian Schlissel, *Women's Diaries of the Westward Journey* (1982); Richard White, *"It's Your Misfortune and None of My Own": A New History of the American West* (1991).

Water and the Environment

Roderick Nash, *American Environmentalism*, 3d ed. (1990); Joseph M. Petulla, *American Environmental History* (1977); Thurman Wilkins, *John Muir: Apostle of Nature* (1995); Donald Worster, *Rivers of Empire: Water, Aridity, and the Growth of the American West* (1985); Donald Worster, *An Unsettled Country: Changing Landscapes of the American West* (1994).

Railroads

Alfred D. Chandler, ed., *Railroads* (1965); Edward C. Kirkland, *Men, Cities, and Transportation* (1948); George R. Taylor and Irene Neu, *The American Railroad Network* (1956); Alan Trachtenberg, *The Incorporation of America* (1982); O. O. Winther, *The Transportation Frontier* (1964).

Ranching and Settlement of the Plains

Lewis Atherton, *The Cattle Kings* (1961); William Cronon, *Nature's Metropolis: Chicago and the Great West* (1991); Gilbert C. Fite, *The Farmer's Frontier* (1963); Robert V. Hine, *Community on the American Frontier* (1980); Richard W. Slatta, *Cowboys of the Americas* (1990); Walter Prescott Webb, *The Great Plains* (1931).

Chapter 18

General

Daniel J. Boorstin, *The Americans: The Democratic Experience* (1973); Alan Dawley, *Struggle for Justice: Social Responsibility and the Liberal State* (1991); Stephen Diner, *A Very Different Age* (1998); Ray Ginger, *The Age of Excess* (1965); Samuel P. Hays, *The Response to Industrialism* (1975); Thomas J. Schlereth, *Victorian America: Transformations in Everyday Life* (1991).

Technology and Invention

Robert W. Bruce, *Bell: Alexander Graham Bell and the Conquest of Solitude* (1973); Gary Cross and Rich Szostak, *Technology and American Society* (1995); David Hounshell, *From the American System to Mass Production* (1984); Thomas Parke Hughes, *American Genesis: A Century of Technological Enthusiasm* (1989); John P. Kasson, *Civilizing the Machine: Technology and Republican Values in America* (1976); Leo Marx, *The Machine in the Garden: Technology and the Pastoral Ideal* (1964); Andre Millard, *Edison and the Business of Innovation* (1990); David E. Nye, *Electrifying America* (1990).

Industrialism, Industrialists, and Corporate Growth

W. Eliot Brownlee, *Dynamics of Ascent: A History of the American Economy*, 2d ed. (1979); Stuart Bruchey, *Growth of the Modern Economy* (1973); Vincent P. Carosso, *The Morgans* (1987); Alfred D. Chandler, *The Visible Hand: The Managerial Revolution in American Business* (1977); Thomas C. Cochran, *Business in American Life* (1972); Francis L. Eames, *The New York Stock Exchange* (1968); David F. Hawkes, *John D.: The Founding Father of the Rockefellers* (1980); Robert Higgs, *The Transformation of the American Economy, 1865–1914* (1971); Harold C. Livesay, *Andrew Carnegie and the Rise of Big Business* (1975); Glen Porter, *The Rise of Big Business* (1973); Martin J. Sklar, *The Corporate Reconstruction of American Capitalism* (1988); Richard Tedlow, *The Rise of the American Business Corporation* (1991); Joseph Wall, *Alfred I. du Pont: The Man and His Family* (1990).

Work and Labor Organization

Alan Derickson, *Workers' Health, Workers' Democracy: The Western Miners' Struggle, 1891–1925* (1988); Melvin Dubofsky, *We Shall Be All: A History of the Industrial Workers of the World* (1969); Sarah Eisenstein, *Give Us Bread, Give Us Roses: Working Women's Consciousness in the United States* (1983); Leon Fink, *Workingmen's Democracy: The Knights of Labor and American Politics* (1982); Philip S. Foner, *The Great Labor Uprising of 1877* (1977); Herbert G. Gutman, *Work, Culture and Society in Industrializing America* (1976); Tamara K. Hareven, *Family Time and Industrial Time* (1982); Alice Kessler-Harris,

Out to Work: A History of Wage Earning Women in the United States (1982); Susan Lehrer, *Origins of Protective Labor Legislation for Women* (1987); Harold Livesay, *Samuel Gompers and Organized Labor in America* (1978); Milton Meltzer, *Bread and Roses: The Struggle of American Labor, 1865–1915* (1967); Ruth Milkman, ed., *Women, Work, and Protest* (1985); David Montgomery, *The Fall of the House of Labor: The Workplace, the State, and American Labor Activism, 1865–1925* (1987); Stephen H. Norwood, *Labor's Flaming Youth: Telephone Operators and Worker Militancy* (1990); Elizabeth Ann Payne, *Reform, Labor, and Feminism: Margaret Dreier Robins and the Women's Trade Union League* (1988); Leon J. Wolff, *Lockout: The Story of the Homestead Strike of 1892* (1965).

Living Standards and New Conveniences

Susan Porter Benson, *Counter Cultures: Saleswomen, Managers, and Customers in American Department Stores, 1890–1940* (1986); T. J. Jackson Lears and Richard W. Fox, eds., *The Culture of Consumption* (1983); Godfrey M. Lebhar, *Chain Stores in America* (1962); Harvey A. Levenstein, *Revolution at the Table: The Transformation of the American Diet* (1988); Kathy Peiss, *Hope in a Jar: The Making of America's Beauty Culture* (1998); Daniel Pope, *The Making of Modern Advertising* (1983); Peter R. Shergold, *Working Class Life* (1982); Susan Strasser, *Satisfaction Guaranteed: The Making of the American Mass Market* (1989); Gwendolyn Wright, *Building the Dream: A Social History of Housing in America* (1983).

Attitudes Toward Industrialism

Sidney Fine, *Laissez Faire and the General Welfare State* (1956); Louis Galambos and Barbara Barron Spence, *The Public Image of Big Business in America* (1975); Richard Hofstadter, *Social Darwinism in American Thought*, rev. ed. (1955); T. J. Jackson Lears, *No Place of Grace: Antimodernism and the Transformation of American Culture* (1981); Robert McCloskey, *American Conservatism in the Age of Enterprise* (1951); John L. Thomas, *Alternative America: Henry George, Edward Bellamy, Henry Demarest Lloyd, and the Adversary Tradition* (1983).

Southern Industrialism

Edward Ayers, *The Promise of the New South* (1992); James C. Cobb, *Industrialization and Southern Society, 1877–1984* (1984); Paul M. Gaston, *The New South Creed* (1970); C. Vann Woodward, *Origins of the New South* (1951); Gavin Wright, *Old South, New South* (1986).

Chapter 19

Urban Growth

Howard P. Chudacoff and Judith E. Smith, *The Evolution of American Urban Society*, 5th ed. (1999); David Goldfield, *Cotton Fields and Skyscrapers: Southern City and Region* (1982); Kenneth T. Jackson, *The Crabgrass Frontier: The Suburbanization of the United States* (1985); Harold Platt, *City Building in the New South* (1983); Jon Teaford, *The Unheralded Triumph: City Government in America, 1870–1900* (1984); Sam Bass Warner, Jr., *The Urban Wilderness* (1982).

Immigration, Ethnicity, and Religion

Aaron I. Abell, *American Catholicism and Social Action* (1960); John Bodnar, *The Transplanted* (1985); John Bodnar, Roger Simon, and Michael P. Weber, *Lives of Their Own: Blacks, Italians, and Poles in Pittsburgh, 1900–1960* (1982); Sucheng Chan, ed., *Entry Denied: Exclusion and the Chinese Community in America, 1882–1943* (1990); Elizabeth Ewen, *Immigrant Women in the Land of Dollars* (1985); Donna R. Gabaccia, *From the Other Side: Women, Gender, and Immigrant Life in the United States* (1994); Mario T. Garcia, *Desert Immigrants: The Mexicans of El Paso, 1880–1920* (1981); Oscar Handlin, *The Uprooted*, 2d ed. (1973); John Higham, *Strangers in the Land: Patterns of American Nativism* (1955); Yusi Ichioka, *The Issei: The World of the First Japanese Immigrants, 1885–1924* (1988); Matthew Frye Jacobson, *Whiteness of a Different Color: European Immigrants and the Alchemy of Race* (1998); Matt S. Maier and Felciano Rivera, *The Chicanos* (1972); Henry F. May, *Protestant Churches and Industrial America* (1949); Werner Sollors, *Beyond Ethnicity* (1986); Ron Takaki, *Iron Cages: Race and Culture in Nineteenth-Century America* (1979); Stephan Thernstrom, ed., *Harvard Encyclopedia of American Ethnic Groups* (1980).

Urban Services

Christine Boyer, *Dreaming the Rational City: The Myth of American City Planning* (1983); Charles W. Cheape, *Moving the Masses* (1980); Lawrence A. Cremin, *American Education: The Metropolitan Experience* (1988); David R. Johnson, *American Law Enforcement* (1981); Martin V. Melosi, *Garbage in the Cities* (1981); Eric Monkkonen, *America Becomes Urban* (1988); Mark Rose, *Cities of Light and Heat* (1995); Barbara Gutmann Rosencrantz, *Public Health and the State* (1972); Stanley K. Schultz, *Constructing Urban Culture: American Cities and City Planning* (1989).

Family and Individual Life Cycles

W. Andrew Achenbaum, *Old Age in the New Land* (1979); George Chauncey, *Gay New York* (1995); Howard P. Chudacoff, *The Age of the Bachelor* (1999); Howard P. Chudacoff, *How Old Are You? Age in American Culture* (1989); Carl N. Degler, *At Odds: Women and the Family in America* (1980); John D'Emilio and Estelle B. Freedman, *Intimate Matters: A History of Sexuality in America* (1988); Carole Haber, *Beyond Sixty-five: Dilemmas of Old Age in America's Past* (1983); Joseph Kett, *Rites of Passage: Adolescence in America* (1979); E. Anthony Rotundo, *American Manhood* (1994).

Mass Entertainment and Leisure

Gunther Barth, *City People* (1980); Jessica H. Foy and Thomas J. Schlereth, eds., *American Home Life, 1880–1930* (1992); Donna R. Gabaccia, *We Are What We Eat: Ethnic Food and the Making of Americans* (1998); Allen Guttmann, *A Whole New Ball Game: An Interpretation of American Sports* (1988); Katrina Hazzard-Gordon, *Lookin': The Rise of Social Dance Formulations in African-American Culture* (1990); George Juergens, *Joseph Pulitzer and the New York World* (1966); John F. Kasson, *Amusing the Million: Coney Island at the Turn of the Century* (1978); David Nasaw, *Going Out: The Rise and Fall of Popular Amusements* (1993); Kathy Peiss, *Cheap Amusements: Working Women and Leisure in Turn-of-the-Century New York* (1986); Benjamin G. Rader, *American Sports*, 4th ed. (1999); Steven A. Riess, *City Games* (1989); Roy Rosenzweig, *Eight Hours for What We Will! Workers and Leisure in an Industrial City, 1870–1920* (1983); Robert Sklar, *Movie-Made America* (1976); Ronald A. Smith, *Sports and Freedom: The Rise of Big-Time College Athletics* (1988); Robert V. Snyder, *The Voice of the City: Vaudeville and Popular Culture in New York City, 1880–1920* (1990); Robert C. Toll, *On with the Show: The First Century of Show Business in America* (1976).

Mobility and Race Relations

James Borchert, *Alley Life in Washington* (1980); Howard P. Chudacoff, *Mobile Americans* (1972); Clyde Griffen and Sally Griffen, *Natives and Newcomers* (1977); Jacqueline Jones, *Labor of Love, Labor of Sorrow: Black Women, Work and the Family from Slavery to the Present* (1985); David M. Katzman, *Before the Ghetto* (1973); Kenneth L. Kusmer, *A Ghetto Takes Shape* (1976); Gilbert Osofsky, *Harlem: The Making of a Ghetto* (1966); Elizabeth H. Pleck, *Black Migration and Poverty: Boston, 1865–1900* (1979); Howard N. Rabinowitz, *Race Relations in the Urban South* (1978); Allan H. Spear, *Black Chicago* (1967); Stephan Thernstrom, *The Other Bostonians: Poverty and Progress in the American Metropolis* (1973); Olivier Zunz, *The Changing Face of Inequality* (1982).

Boss Politics

Alexander B. Callow, Jr., ed., *The City Boss in America* (1976); Lyle Dorsett, *The Pendergast Machine* (1968); Leo Hershkowitz, *Tweed's New York: Another Look* (1977); Terrence J. McDonald, *The Parameters of Urban Fiscal Policy* (1986); Zane L. Miller, *Boss Cox's Cincinnati* (1968); Bruce M. Stave and Sondra Stave, eds., *Urban Bosses, Machines, and Progressive Reformers* (1984).

Urban Reform

John D. Buenker, *Urban Liberalism and Progressive Reform* (1973); James B. Crooks, *Politics and Progress* (1968); Doris Groshen Daniels, *Always a Sister: The Feminism of Lillian D. Wald* (1989); Allen F. Davis, *Spearheads for Reform* (1967);

Lori Ginzberg, *Women and the Work of Benevolence* (1991); Rivka Shpak Lissack, *Pluralism and Progressives: Hull House and the New Immigrants, 1890–1919* (1989); Roy M. Lubove, *The Progressives and the Slums* (1962); Clay McShane, *Technology and Reform* (1974); Robyn Muncy, *Creating a Female Dominion in American Reform* (1991); Martin J. Schiesl, *The Politics of Efficiency* (1977); Kathryn Kish Sklar, *Florence Kelley and the Nation's Work* (1995).

Chapter 20

General

Charles W. Calhoun, ed., *The Gilded Age: Essays on the Origins of Modern America* (1995); Sean Denis Cashman, *America in the Gilded Age* (1984); Steven J. Diner, *A Very Different Age* (1998); Ray Ginger, *The Age of Excess*, 2d ed. (1975); H. Wayne Morgan, ed., *The Gilded Age* (1970); Nell Irvin Painter, *Standing at Armageddon* (1987).

Parties and Political Issues

John M. Dobson, *Politics in the Gilded Age* (1972); Ari A. Hoogenboom, *Outlawing the Spoils: The Civil Service Movement* (1961); Morton Keller, *Affairs of State* (1977); Paul Kleppner, *The Third Electoral System, 1853–1892* (1979); Michael E. McGerr, *The Decline of Popular Politics* (1986); Walter T. K. Nugent, *Money and American Society* (1968); A. M. Paul, *Conservative Crisis and the Rule of Law: Attitudes of Bar and Bench, 1887–1895* (1969); John G. Sproat, *The Best Men: Liberal Reformers in the Gilded Age* (1968); Hal R. Williams, *Years of Decision: American Politics in the 1890s* (1978).

The Presidency

Kenneth E. Davison, *The Presidency of Rutherford B. Hayes* (1972); Justus D. Doenecke, *The Presidencies of James A. Garfield and Chester A. Arthur* (1981); Lewis L. Gould, *The Presidency of William McKinley* (1981); Homer E. Socolotsky and Allen B. Spetter, *The Presidency of Benjamin Harrison* (1987); Richard G. Welch, *The Presidency of Grover Cleveland* (1988).

Women's Rights and Disfranchisement of African Americans

Edward L. Ayers, *The Promise of the New South* (1992); Paula Baker, *The Moral Framework of Public Life* (1991); Beverly Beeton, *Women Vote in the West: The Suffrage Movement, 1869–1896* (1986); Fitzhugh Brundage, *Lynching in the New South* (1993); Glenda Elizabeth Gilmore, *Gender & Jim Crow* (1996); Elisabeth Griffith, *In Her Own Right: The Life of Elizabeth Cady Stanton* (1984); Joel Williamson, *The Crucible of Race* (1984); C. Vann Woodward, *The Strange Career of Jim Crow*, 3d rev. ed. (1974).

Protest and Socialism

William M. Dick, *Labor and Socialism in America* (1972); Ray Ginger, *Bending Cross: A Biography of Eugene Victor Debs* (1969); J. Anthony Lukas, *Big Trouble* (1997); Nick Salvatore, *Eugene V. Debs: Citizen and Socialist* (1982); Carlos A. Schwantes, *Coxey's Army* (1985); David Shannon, *The Socialist Party of America* (1955).

Populism and the Election of 1896

Donna A. Barnes, *Farmers in Rebellion: The Rise and Fall of the Southern Farmers Alliance and People's Party in Texas* (1984); Paolo Coletta, *William Jennings Bryan: Political Evangelist* (1964); Paul W. Glad, *McKinley, Bryan, and the People* (1964); Lawrence Goodwyn, *Democratic Promise: The Populist Movement in America* (1976); Steven Hahn, *The Roots of Southern Populism* (1983); J. Morgan Kousser, *The Shaping of Southern Politics* (1974); Robert C. McMath, Jr., *American Populism* (1993); Walter T. K. Nugent, *The Tolerant Populists* (1963); Jeffrey Ostler, *Prairie Populism* (1993); Norman Pollack, *The Populist Response to Industrial America* (1962); Barton C. Shaw, *The Wool-Hat Boys: Georgia's Populist Party* (1984); Allan Weinstein, *Prelude to Populism: Origins of the Silver Issue* (1970).

Chapter 21

General

Paul M. Boyer, *Urban Masses and Moral Order in America, 1820–1920* (1978); Walter M. Brasch, *Forerunners of Revolution: Muckrakers and the American Social Conscience* (1990); John M. Cooper, Jr., *The Pivotal Decades* (1990); Steven J. Diner, *A Very Different Age: Americans of the Progressive Era* (1998); Richard Hofstadter, *The Age of Reform* (1955); William R. Hutchinson, *The Modernist Impulse in American Protestantism* (1976); Morton Keller, *Regulating a New Economy* (1990); Gabriel Kolko, *The Triumph of Conservatism* (1963); Arthur Link and Richard L. McCormick, *Progressivism* (1983); Daniel T. Rodgers, *Atlantic Crossings: Social Politics in a Progressive Age* (1998); Robert Wiebe, *The Search for Order* (1968).

Regional Studies

Dewey Grantham, *Southern Progressivism* (1983); William A. Link, *The Paradox of Southern Progressivism* (1992); David P. Thelen, *Robert La Follette and the Insurgent Spirit* (1976); Richard White, *"It's Your Misfortune and None of My Own": A History of the American West* (1991); C. Vann Woodward, *Origins of the New South* (1951).

Legislative Issues and Reform Groups

Ruth H. Crocker, *Social Work and Social Order* (1992); Robert M. Crunden, *Ministers of Reform: The Progressives' Achieve-*ment in American Civilization* (1982); Allen F. Davis, *Spearheads for Reform: The Social Settlements and the Progressive Movement, 1890–1914* (1967); Ruth Rosen, *The Lost Sisterhood: Prostitution in America, 1900–1918* (1982); W. J. Rorabaugh, *The Alcoholic Republic* (1979); Kathryn Kish Sklar, *Florence Kelley and the Nation's Work* (1995); James H. Timberlake, *Prohibition and the Progressive Crusade* (1963); Walter I. Trattner, *Crusade for the Children* (1970); Irwin Yellowitz, *Labor and the Progressive Movement in New York State* (1965); James Harvey Young, *Pure Food* (1989). (For works on socialism, see the listings under "Protest and Socialism," Chapter 20.)

Education, Law, and the Social Sciences

Jerold S. Auerback, *Unequal Justice: Lawyers and Social Change in Modern America* (1976); Lawrence Cremin, *The Transformation of the School: Progressivism in American Education* (1961); Paula S. Fass, *Outside In: Minorities and the Transformation of American Education* (1989); Ellen Fitzpatrick, *Endless Crusade: Women Social Scientists and Progressive Reform* (1990); Lynn D. Gordon, *Gender and Higher Education in the Progressive Era* (1990); Thomas L. Haskell, *The Emergence of Professional Social Science* (1977); Helen Horowitz, *Alma Mater: Design and Experience in Women's Colleges* (1984); David W. Marcell, *Progress and Pragmatism: James, Dewey, Beard, and the American Idea of Progress* (1974); Lawrence Veysey, *The Emergence of the American University* (1970).

Women

Ruth Borden, *Women and Temperance* (1980); Ellen Chesler, *Woman of Valor: The Life of Margaret Sanger* (1992); Nancy F. Cott, *The Grounding of American Feminism* (1987); Carl N. Degler, *At Odds: Women and the Family in America* (1980); Linda Gordon, *Woman's Body, Woman's Right: A Social History of Birth Control in America* (1976); Evelyn Higginbotham, *Righteous Discontent: The Women's Movement in the Black Baptist Church, 1880–1920* (1993); Alice Kessler-Harris, *Out to Work: A History of Wage-Earning Women in the United States* (1982); Robyn Muncy, *Creating a Female Dominion in American Reform* (1991); Rosalind Rosenberg, *Beyond Separate Spheres: Intellectual Roots of Modern Feminism* (1982); Sheila M. Rothman, *Woman's Proper Place* (1978).

African Americans

John Dittmer, *Black Georgia in the Progressive Era* (1977); George Frederickson, *The Black Image in the White Mind* (1971); Glenda Elizabeth Gilmore, *Gender & Jim Crow* (1996); Louis R. Harlan, *Booker T. Washington*, 2 vols. (1972 and 1983); Jacqueline Jones, *Labor of Love, Labor of Sorrow: Black Women, Work and the Family from Slavery to the Present* (1985); David Levering Lewis, *W. E. B. Du Bois* (1993); August Meier, *Negro Thought in America, 1880–1915* (1963).

Roosevelt, Taft, and Wilson

Francis L. Broderick, *Progressivism at Risk: Electing a President in 1912* (1989); Paolo E. Coletta, *The Presidency of William Howard Taft* (1973); John M. Cooper, Jr., *The Warrior and the Priest: Woodrow Wilson and Theodore Roosevelt* (1983); Lewis Gould, *The Presidency of Theodore Roosevelt* (1991); August Hecksher, *Woodrow Wilson* (1991); Edmund Morris, *The Rise of Theodore Roosevelt* (1979); James Pednick, Jr., *Progressive Politics and Conservation: The Ballinger-Pinchot Affair* (1968).

Chapter 22

General

Robert L. Beisner, *From the Old Diplomacy to the New, 1865–1900*, 2d ed. (1986); Manfred F. Boemeke et al., eds., *Anticipating Total War: The German and American Experiences, 1871–1914* (1999); Daniel R. Headrick, *The Invisible Weapon: Telecommunications and International Politics, 1851–1945* (1991); Ronald J. Jensen, *The Alaska Purchase and Russian-American Relations* (1975); Paul Kennedy, *The Rise and Fall of the Great Powers* (1987); Paul A. C. Koistinen, *Mobilizing for Modern War: The Political Economy of American Warfare, 1865–1919* (1997); Walter LaFeber, *The American Search for Opportunity, 1865–1913* (1993); Walter LaFeber, *The New Empire*, anniv. ed. (1998); Ernest R. May, *American Imperialism* (1968); Emily Rosenberg, *Spreading the American Dream* (1982); William Appleman Williams, *The Tragedy of American Diplomacy*, new ed. (1988).

Imperial Promoters

Howard K. Beale, *Theodore Roosevelt and the Rise of America to World Power* (1956); H. W. Brands, *T.R.* (1997); John M. Cooper, Jr., *The Warrior and the Priest* (1983) (on Roosevelt and Wilson); Edward P. Crapol, *James G. Blaine* (1999); Lewis L. Gould, *The Presidency of Theodore Roosevelt* (1991); Lewis L. Gould, *The Presidency of William McKinley* (1981); Frederick Marks III, *Velvet on Iron: The Diplomacy of Theodore Roosevelt* (1979); Edmund Morris, *The Rise of Theodore Roosevelt* (1979); Ernest N. Paolino, *The Foundations of the American Empire: William Henry Seward and U.S. Foreign Policy* (1973); William C. Widenor, *Henry Cabot Lodge and the Search for an American Foreign Policy* (1980).

Economic and Financial Expansion

William H. Becker, *The Dynamics of Business-Government Relations* (1982); Robert B. Davies, *Peacefully Working to Conquer the World: Singer Sewing Machines in Foreign Markets, 1854–1920* (1976); David Pletcher, *The Diplomacy of Trade and Investment* (1998); Emily Rosenberg, *Financial Missionaries to the World: The Politics and Culture of Dollar Diplomacy, 1900–1930* (1999); Tom Terrill, *The Tariff, Politics, and American Foreign Policy, 1874–1901* (1973); Mira Wilkins, *The Emergence of the Multinational Enterprise* (1970); William Appleman Williams, *The Roots of the Modern American Empire* (1969).

Ideology and Culture

Gail Bederman, *Manliness & Civilization* (1995); Alexander DeConde, *Ethnicity, Race, and American Foreign Policy* (1992); Thomas G. Dyer, *Theodore Roosevelt and the Idea of Race* (1980); Willard B. Gatewood, Jr., *Black Americans and the White Man's Burden* (1975); Michael H. Hunt, *Ideology and U.S. Foreign Policy* (1987); Robert D. Johnson, ed., *On Cultural Ground* (1994); Amy Kaplan and Donald E. Pease, eds., *Cultures of United States Imperialism* (1993); Catherine A. Lutz and Jane L. Collins, *Reading National Geographic* (1993); Robert Rydell, *World of Fairs* (1993); Robert Rydell, *All the World's a Fair* (1985); David Spurr, *The Rhetoric of Empire* (1993).

Religious Missionaries

Nancy Boyd, *Emissaries: The Overseas Work of the American YWCA, 1895–1970* (1986); Wayne Flynt and Gerald W. Berkley, *Taking Christianity to China* (1997); John K. Fairbank, ed., *The Missionary Enterprise in China and America* (1974); Gael Graham, *Gender, Culture, and Christianity: American Protestant Mission Schools in China, 1880-1930* (1995); Patricia R. Hill, *The World Their Household* (1985); Jane Hunter, *The Gospel of Gentility: American Missionaries in Turn-of-the-Century China* (1984); Irwin T. Hyatt, Jr., *Our Ordered Lives Confess* (1976) (on China); Ian Tyrrell, *Woman's World, Woman's Empire: The Woman's Christian Temperance Union in International Perspective, 1880–1930* (1991).

Navalism and the Navy

Benjamin F. Cooling, *Gray Steel and Blue Water Navy* (1979); Frederick C. Drake, *The Empire of the Seas: A Biography of Rear Admiral Robert W. Shufelt* (1984); Kenneth J. Hagan, *This People's Navy* (1991); Peter Karsten, *The Naval Aristocracy* (1972); Mark R. Shulman, *Navalism and the Emergence of American Sea Power* (1995); Robert Seager II, *Alfred Thayer Mahan* (1977); Ronald Spector, *Admiral of the New Empire: The Life and Career of George Dewey* (1974).

The Spanish-American-Cuban-Filipino War

Graham A. Cosmas, *An Army for Empire* (1971); Kristin L. Hoganson, *Fighting for American Manhood* (1998); Gerald F. Linderman, *The Mirror of War* (1974); Joyce Milton, *The Yellow Kids* (1989); John Offner, *An Unwanted War* (1992); Louis A. Pérez, Jr., *The War of 1898* (1998); David F. Trask, *The War with Spain in 1898* (1981).

Anti-Imperialism and the Peace Movement

Robert L. Beisner, *Twelve Against Empire* (1968); Kendrick A. Clements, *William Jennings Bryan* (1983); Charles DeBenedetti, *Peace Reform in American History* (1980); C. Roland Marchand, *The American Peace Movement and Social Reform, 1898–1918* (1973); Thomas J. Osborne, *"Empire Can Wait": American Opposition to Hawaiian Annexation* (1981); David S. Patterson, *Toward a Warless World* (1976).

Cuba, Mexico, Panama, and Latin America

Arturo M. Carrión, *Puerto Rico* (1983); Richard H. Collin, *Theodore Roosevelt's Caribbean* (1990); Judith Ewell, *Venezuela and the United States* (1996); David Healy, *Drive to Hegemony: The United States in the Caribbean, 1898–1917* (1989); Walter LaFeber, *Inevitable Revolutions: The United States in Central America*, 2d rev. ed. (1993); Walter LaFeber, *The Panama Canal*, updated ed. (1990); Lester D. Langley, *Struggle for the American Mediterranean* (1980); Lester D. Langley, *The United States and the Caribbean, 1900–1970* (1980); John Major, *Prize Possession: The United States and the Panama Canal, 1903–1979* (1993); David McCullough, *The Path Between the Seas: The Creation of the Panama Canal, 1870–1914* (1977); Louis A. Pérez, Jr., *Cuba and the United States*, 2d ed. (1997); Louis A. Pérez, Jr., *Cuba Under the Platt Amendment, 1902–1934* (1986); Fredrick B. Pike, *The United States and Latin America* (1992); Brenda G. Plummer, *Haiti and the Great Powers, 1902–1915* (1988); Stephen J. Randall, *Colombia and the United States* (1992); Ramón E. Ruíz, *The People of Sonora and Yankee Capitalists* (1988); Lars Schoultz, *Beneath the United States* (1998); Josefina Vázquez and Lorenzo Meyer, *The United States and Mexico* (1985).

Hawai'i, China, Japan, and the Pacific

Warren I. Cohen, *America's Response to China*, 3d ed. (1989); Michael H. Hunt, *The Making of a Special Relationship* (1983) (on China); Akira Iriye, *Pacific Estrangement* (1972); Paul M. Kennedy, *The Samoan Tangle* (1974); Walter LaFeber, *The Clash: A History of U.S. Japanese Relations* (1997); Brian M. Linn, *Guardians of Empire* (1997); Charles J. McClain, *In Search of Equality: The Chinese Struggle Against Discrimination in Nineteenth-Century America* (1994); Thomas J. McCormick, *China Market* (1967); Craig Storti, *Incident at Bitter Creek: The Story of the Rock Springs Chinese Massacre* (1991); Merze Tate, *Hawaii: Reciprocity or Annexation* (1968); Merze Tate, *The United States and the Hawaiian Kingdom* (1965); Marilyn Blatt Young, *The Rhetoric of Empire* (1968).

The Philippines and the Insurrection

John M. Gates, *Schoolbooks and Krags* (1973) (on the U.S. Army); Stanley Karnow, *In Our Image* (1989); Brian M. Linn, *The Philippine War, 1899–1902* (2000); Brian M. Linn, *The U.S. Army and Counterinsurgency in the Philippine War* (1989); Glenn A. May, *Battle for Batangas* (1991); Glenn A. May, *Social Engineering in the Philippines* (1980); Stuart C. Miller, *"Benevolent Assimilation"* (1982); Peter Stanley, *A Nation in the Making* (1974); Richard E. Welch, *Response to Imperialism: American Resistance to the Philippine War* (1972).

Great Britain and Canada

Robert Bothwell, *Canada and the United States* (1992); Kenneth Bourne, *Britain and the Balance of Power in North America, 1815–1908* (1967); Charles S. Campbell, *From Revolution to Rapprochement* (1974); David Dimbleby and David Reynolds, *An Ocean Apart* (1988); Kurkpatrick Dorsey, *The Dawn of Conservation Diplomacy* (1999); Bradford Perkins, *The Great Rapprochement* (1968); William N. Tilchin, *Theodore Roosevelt and the British Empire* (1997).

Chapter 23

General

John W. Chambers, *The Tyranny of Change* (1992); Steven J. Diner, *A Very Different Age* (1998); Paul Fussell, *The Great War and Modern Memory* (1975); Otis L. Graham, Jr., *The Great Campaigns* (1971); Ellis W. Hawley, *The Great War and the Search for a Modern Order*, 2d ed. (1999); Clayton D. James and Anne S. Wells, *America and the Great War* (1998); Henry F. May, *The End of American Innocence* (1964); Stuart I. Rochester, *American Liberal Disillusionment in the Wake of World War I* (1977); Daniel T. Rodgers, *Atlantic Crossings: Social Politics in a Progressive Age* (1998); John A. Thompson, *Reformers and War* (1987).

Wilson, Wilsonianism, and World War I

Lloyd E. Ambrosius, *Wilsonian Statecraft* (1991); Thomas A. Bailey and Paul B. Ryan, *The Lusitania Disaster* (1975); Frederick S. Calhoun, *Power and Principle* (1986); Kendrick A. Clements, *The Presidency of Woodrow Wilson* (1992); John W. Coogan, *The End of Neutrality* (1981); John M. Cooper, Jr., *The Warrior and the Priest* (1983); Robert H. Ferrell, *Woodrow Wilson and World War I* (1985); Manfred Jonas, *The United States and Germany* (1984); Thomas J. Knock, *To End All Wars* (1992); N. Gordon Levin, Jr., *Woodrow Wilson and World Politics* (1968); Arthur S. Link, ed., *Woodrow Wilson and a Revolutionary World, 1913–1921* (1982); Arthur S. Link, *Woodrow Wilson: Revolution, War and Peace* (1979); Arthur S. Link, *Wilson* (1947–1965); Bert E. Park, *Ailing, Aging, Addicted* (1993) (on Wilson's health); Frank Ninkovich, *Wilsonian Century* (1999); J. W. Schulte Nordholt, *Woodrow Wilson* (1991); Tony Smith, *America's Mission: The United States and the Worldwide Struggle for Democracy in the Twentieth Century* (1994); Edwin A. Weinstein, *Woodrow Wilson: A Medical and Psychological Biography* (1981).

Fighting and Remembering the Great War in Europe

Allan M. Brandt, *No Magic Bullet: A Social History of Venereal Disease in the United States since 1880* (1985); John W. Chambers, *To Raise an Army* (1987); J. Garry Clifford, *The Citizen Soldiers* (1972); Edward M. Coffman, *The War to End All Wars* (1968); James J. Cooke, *The U.S. Air Service in the Great War: 1917–1919* (1996); Harvey A. DeWeerd, *President Wilson Fights His War* (1968); Byron Farwell, *Over There* (1999); Martin Gilbert, *The First World War* (1994); Paul G. Halpern, *A Naval History of World War I* (1994); G. Kurt Piehler, *Remembering War the American Way* (1995); Donald Smythe, *Pershing* (1986); Stephen R. Ward, ed., *The War Generation: Veterans of the First World War* (1975); Russell F. Weigley, *The American Way of War* (1973).

The Home Front

William J. Breen, *Labor Market Politics and the Great War* (1997); Thomas A. Britten, *American Indians in World War I* (1997); Craig W. Campbell, *Reel America and World War I* (1985); Valerie Jean Conner, *The National War Labor Board* (1983); Alfred W. Crosby, *America's Forgotten Pandemic: The Influenza of 1918* (1989); Robert D. Cuff, *The War Industries Board* (1973); Leslie M. DeBauche, *Reel Patriotism* (1997); David M. Kennedy, *Over Here* (1980); Paul A. C. Koistinen, *Mobilizing for Modern War* (1997); Seward W. Livermore, *Politics Is Adjourned* (1966); Frederick C. Luebke, *Bonds of Loyalty: German Americans and World War I* (1974); Joseph A. McCartin, *Labor's Great War* (1997); John F. McClymer, *War and Welfare* (1980); George H. Nash, *The Life of Herbert Hoover*, vol. 3 (1996); Ronald Schaffer, *America in the Great War: The Rise of the War Welfare State* (1991); Stephen L. Vaughn, *Holding Fast the Inner Lines: Democracy, Nationalism, and the Committee on Public Information* (1979); Neil A. Wynn, *From Progressivism to Prosperity* (1986).

Women and the War

Frances H. Early, *A World Without War: How U.S. Feminists and Pacifists Resisted World War I* (1997); Lettie Gavin, *American Women in World War I* (1997); Maurine W. Greenwald, *Women, War, and Work* (1980); Kathleen Kennedy, *Disloyal Mothers and Scurrilous Citizens: Women and Subversion During World War I* (1999); Erika A. Kuhlman, *Petticoats and White Feathers* (1997); Dorothy Schneider and Carl J. Schneider, *Into the Breach: American Women Overseas in World War I* (1991); Barbara J. Steinson, *American Women's Activism in World War I* (1982).

African Americans and Migration

Arthur E. Barbeau and Florette Henri, *The Unknown Soldiers* (1974); Marvin E. Fletcher, *The Black Soldier and Officer in the United States Army, 1891–1917* (1974); James B. Grossman, *Land of Hope: Chicago, Black Southerners, and the Great Migration* (1989); Robert V. Haynes, *A Night of Violence: The Houston Riot of 1917* (1976); Carole Marks, *Farewell—We're Good and Gone: The Great Black Migration* (1989); Elliot M. Rudwick, *Race Riot at East St. Louis, July 2, 1917* (1964); Joe William Trotter, Jr., ed., *The Great Migration in Historical Perspective* (1991); William M. Tuttle, Jr., *Race Riot: Chicago in the Red Summer of 1919*, rev. ed. (1996).

Dissenters, Wartime Civil Liberties, and the Red Scare

David Brody, *Labor in Crisis: The Steel Strike of 1919* (1965); Charles Chatfield, *The American Peace Movement* (1992); Stanley Coben, *A. Mitchell Palmer* (1963); Charles DeBenedetti, *Origins of the Modern Peace Movement* (1978); Sondra Herman, *Eleven Against War* (1969); C. Roland Marchand, *The American Peace Movement and Social Reform* (1973); Charles H. McCormick, *Seeing Reds* (1997); Elizabeth McKillen, *Chicago Labor and the Quest for a Democratic Diplomacy* (1995); Paul L. Murphy, *World War I and the Origin of Civil Liberties* (1979); Robert K. Murray, *Red Scare* (1955); William Pencak, *For God and Country: The American Legion, 1919–1941* (1989); H. C. Peterson and Gilbert C. Fite, *Opponents of War, 1917–1918* (1968); Richard Polenberg, *Fighting Faiths: The Abrams Case, the Supreme Court, and Free Speech* (1987); William Preston, *Aliens and Dissenters* (1995); Francis Russell, *A City in Terror: 1919, the Boston Police Strike* (1975).

The United States and the Bolshevik Revolution

Peter G. Filene, *Americans and the Soviet Experiment, 1917–1933* (1967); David S. Foglesong, *America's Secret War Against Bolshevism* (1995); John Lewis Gaddis, *Russia, the Soviet Union, and the United States*, 2d ed. (1990); Christopher Lasch, *The American Liberals and the Russian Revolution* (1962); David McFadden, *Alternative Paths* (1993); Betty M. Unterberger, *The United States, Revolutionary Russia, and the Rise of Czechoslovakia* (1989).

Paris Peace Conference, Treaty of Versailles, and League Fight

Manfred F. Boemeke et al., eds., *The Treaty of Versailles* (1998); Lloyd Ambrosius, *Woodrow Wilson and the American Diplomatic Tradition* (1987); Inga Floto, *Colonel House in Paris* (1973); Warren F. Kuehl, *Seeking World Order* (1969); Arno Mayer, *Politics and Diplomacy of Peacemaking* (1967); Keith Nelson, *Victors Divided* (1973); Ralph A. Stone, *The Irreconcilables* (1970); Arthur Walworth, *Wilson and the Peacemakers* (1986); William C. Widenor, *Henry Cabot Lodge and the Search for an American Foreign Policy* (1980).

Chapter 24

Overviews of the 1920s

William E. Akin, *Technocracy and the American Dream* (1977); Paul A. Carter, *Another Part of the Twenties* (1977); Lynn Dumenil, *Modern Temper* (1995); David J. Goldberg, *Discontented America: The United States in the 1920s* (1999); William E. Leuchtenburg, *The Perils of Prosperity* (1958); Robert Lynd and Helen Lynd, *Middletown* (1929); Geoffrey Perrett, *America in the Twenties* (1982).

Business and the Economy

William W. Barber, *Herbert Hoover, the Economists, and American Economic Policy, 1921–1933* (1986); Irving L. Bernstein, *The Lean Years: A History of the American Worker, 1920–1933* (1960); Morton Keller, *Regulating a New Economy* (1990); David Montgomery, *The Fall of the House of Labor* (1987); Allan Nevins, *Ford*, 2 vols. (1954–1957); Emily Rosenberg, *Spreading the American Dream* (1982).

Politics and Law

Christine Bolt, *American Indian Policy and American Reform* (1987); Paula Eldot, *Governor Alfred E. Smith: The Politician as Reformer* (1983); Allan J. Lichtman, *Prejudice and the Old Politics: The Presidential Election of 1928* (1979); Alpheus Mason, *The Supreme Court from Taft to Warren* (1958); Donald R. McCoy, *Calvin Coolidge* (1967); Robert K. Murray, *The Politics of Normalcy* (1973); George Tindall, *The Emergence of the New South* (1967); James Weinstein, *The Decline of Socialism in America, 1912–1925* (1967); Joan Hoff Wilson, *Herbert Hoover: The Forgotten Progressive* (1975).

African-Americans, Asians, and Hispanics

Rodolfo Acuna, *Occupied America: A History of Chicanos* (1980); Roger Daniels, *Asian America* (1988); James R. Grossman, *Land of Hope* (1989); Jacquelyn Jones, *Labor of Love, Labor of Sorrow* (1985); Gilbert Osofsky, *Harlem: The Making of a Ghetto* (1965); Ricardo Romo, *East Los Angeles: History of a Barrio* (1983); George Sanchez, *Becoming Mexican American* (1993); Judith Stein, *The World of Marcus Garvey* (1986); Ronald Takaki, *Strangers from a Different Shore* (1989).

Women, Family, and Lifestyles

W. Andrew Achenbaum, *Shades of Gray: Old Age, American Values, and Federal Policies Since 1920* (1983); Beth Bailey, *From Front Porch to Back Seat: Courtship in Twentieth Century America* (1988); Dorothy M. Brown, *Setting a Course: American Women in the 1920s* (1987); George Chauncey, *Gay New York* (1995); Howard P. Chudacoff, *How Old Are You? Age in American Culture* (1989); Nancy F. Cott, *The Grounding of Modern Feminism* (1987); John D'Emilio and Estelle B. Freedman, *Intimate Matters: A History of Sexuality in America* (1988); Elizabeth Ewen, *Immigrant Women in the Land of Dollars* (1985); Lillian Faderman, *Odd Girls and Twilight Lovers* (1991); Linda Gordon, *Woman's Body, Woman's Right: A Social History of Birth Control in America* (1976); J. Stanley Lemons, *The Woman Citizen: Social Feminism in the 1920s* (1973); Lois Scharf, *To Work and to Wed* (1980); Susan Strasser, *Never Done: A History of American Housework* (1982); Winifred D. Wandersee, *Women's Work and Family Values, 1920–1940* (1981).

Lines of Defense

Paul Avrich, *Sacco and Vanzetti* (1991); Edith L. Blumhofer, *Aimee Semple McPherson* (1993); Norman H. Clark, *Deliver Us From Evil: An Interpretation of American Prohibition* (1976); John Higham, *Strangers in the Land: Patterns of American Nativism* (1955); David A. Horowitz, ed., *Inside the Klavern* (1999); Kenneth T. Jackson, *The Ku Klux Klan and the City* (1967); Edward J. Larson, *Summer for the Gods* (1997); Nancy Maclean, *Behind the Mask of Chivalry: The Making of the Second Ku Klux Klan* (1994); George M. Marsden, *Fundamentalism and American Culture* (1980).

Mass Culture

Stanley Coben, *Rebellion Against Victorianism* (1991); Robert Creamer, *Babe* (1974); Kenneth S. Davis, *The Hero, Charles A. Lindbergh* (1959); Susan J. Douglas, *Inventing American Broadcasting* (1987); Paula Fass, *The Damned and the Beautiful: American Youth in the 1920s* (1977); James J. Flink, *The Car Culture* (1975); Richard Wightman Fox and T. Jackson Lears, eds., *The Culture of Consumption* (1983); William R. Leach, *Land of Desire* (1993); Harvey J. Levenstein, *Revolution at the Table: The Transformation of the American Diet* (1988); Roland Marchand, *Advertising the American Dream* (1985); Randy Roberts, *Jack Dempsey, the Manassa Mauler* (1979); Virgnina Scharff, *Taking the Wheel: Women and the Coming of the Motor Age* (1991); Robert Sklar, *Moviemade America* (1976); Ronald A. Smith, *Sports and Freedom: The Rise of Big-Time College Athletics* (1988); Susan Smulyan, *Selling Radio* (1994).

Literature and Thought

Mary Campbell, *Harlem Renaissance: Art of Black America* (1987); Robert Crunden, *From Self to Society: Transition in American Thought, 1919–1941* (1972); Nathan I. Huggins, *Harlem Renaissance* (1971); David L. Lewis, *When Harlem Was in Vogue* (1981); Cary D. Mintz, *Black Culture and the Harlem Renaissance* (1988); Roderick Nash, *The Nervous Generation: American Thought, 1917–1930* (1969); Kenneth M. Wheller and Virginia L. Lussier, eds., *Women and the Arts and the 1920s in Paris and New York* (1982).

Boom and Bust: The Crash

Peter Fearon, *War, Prosperity, and Depression* (1987); John Kenneth Galbraith, *The Great Crash: 1929* (1989); and Robert T. Patterson, *The Great Boom and Panic, 1921–1929* (1965).

Chapter 25

Hoover and the Worsening Depression

William J. Barber, *Herbert Hoover, the Economists, and American Economic Policy, 1921–1933* (1986); Michael A. Bernstein, *The Great Depression: Delayed Recovery and Economic Change in America, 1929–1939* (1988); David Burner, *Herbert Hoover* (1979); Martin L. Fausold, *The Presidency of Herbert C. Hoover* (1985); John A. Garraty, *The Great Depression* (1986); James S. Olson, *Herbert Hoover and the Reconstruction Finance Corporation, 1931–1933* (1977); Jordan A. Schwarz, *Interregnum of Despair* (1970).

The New Deal

Anthony J. Badger, *The New Deal: The Depression Years, 1933–1940* (1989); William J. Barber, *Designs Within Disorder: Franklin D. Roosevelt, the Economists, and the Shaping of American Economic Policy, 1933–1945* (1996); Alan Brinkley, *Liberalism and Its Discontents* (1998); Alan Brinkley, *The End of Reform: New Deal Liberalism in Recession and War* (1995); Steve Fraser and Gary Gerstle, eds., *The Rise and Fall of the New Deal Order, 1930–1980* (1989); Colin Gordon, *New Deals: Business, Labor, and Politics in America, 1920–1935* (1994); David M. Kennedy, *Freedom from Fear: The American People in Depression and War, 1929–1945* (1999); William E. Leuchtenburg, *Franklin D. Roosevelt and the New Deal* (1963); Albert U. Romasco, *The Politics of Recovery: Roosevelt's New Deal* (1983).

Franklin and Eleanor Roosevelt

James MacGregor Burns, *Roosevelt: The Lion and the Fox* (1956); Blanche Wiesen Cook, *Eleanor Roosevelt: Volume One, 1884–1933* (1992), and *Volume Two, 1933–1938* (1999); Kenneth S. Davis, *FDR: Into the Storm, 1937–1940* (1993); Kenneth S. Davis, *FDR: The New Deal Years, 1933–1937* (1986); Frank Freidel, *Franklin D. Roosevelt: A Rendezvous with Destiny* (1990); Joseph P. Lash, *Eleanor and Franklin* (1971); Arthur M. Schlesinger, Jr., *The Age of Roosevelt*, 3 vols. (1957–1960).

Voices from the Depression

James Agee, *Let Us Now Praise Famous Men* (1941); Federal Writers' Project, *These Are Our Lives* (1939); Robert S. McElvaine, ed., *Down and Out in the Great Depression* (1983); Studs Terkel, *Hard Times: An Oral History of the Great Depression* (1970); Tom E. Terrill and Jerrold Hirsch, eds., *Such as Us: Southern Voices of the Thirties* (1978).

Alternatives to the New Deal

Alan Brinkley, *Voices of Protest: Huey Long, Father Coughlin, and the Great Depression* (1982); William Ivy Hair, *The Kingfish and His Realm: The Life and Times of Huey P. Long* (1992); Robin D. G. Kelley, *Hammer and Hoe: Alabama Communists During the Great Depression* (1991); Fraser M. Ottanelli, *The Communist Party of the United States from the Depression to World War II* (1991); Leo Ribuffo, *The Old Christian Right: The Protestant Far Right from the Great Depression to the Cold War* (1983); Donald Warren, *Radio Priest: Charles Coughlin, the Father of Hate Radio* (1996); Frank A. Warren, *An Alternative Vision: The Socialist Party in the 1930s* (1976); Clyde P. Weed, *The Nemesis of Reform: The Republican Party During the New Deal* (1994).

Workers and Organized Labor

Irving Bernstein, *Turbulent Years: A History of the American Worker, 1933–1941* (1969); Lizabeth Cohen, *Making a New Deal: Industrial Workers in Chicago, 1919–1939* (1991); Melvin Dubofsky and Warren Van Tine, *John L. Lewis* (1977); Sidney Fine, *Sit-Down: The General Motors Strike of 1936–1937* (1969); Gary Gerstle, *Working-Class Americanism: The Politics of Labor in a Textile City, 1914–1960* (1989); Roger Horowitz, *Negro and White, Unite and Fight: A Social History of Unionism in Meatpacking, 1930-1990* (1997); Nelson Lichtenstein, *The Most Dangerous Man in Detroit: Walter Reuther and the Fate of American Labor* (1995); Robert H. Zieger, *The CIO, 1935–1955* (1995).

Agriculture and the Environment

William U. Chandler, *The Myth of TVA: Conservation and Development in the Tennessee Valley, 1933–1983* (1984); David E. Conrad, *The Forgotten Farmers: The Story of Sharecroppers in the New Deal* (1965); James N. Gregory, *American Exodus: The Dust Bowl Migration and Okie Culture in California* (1989); David E. Hamilton, *From New Day to New Deal: American Farm Policy from Hoover to Roosevelt, 1928–1933* (1991); Theodore M. Saloutos, *The American Farmer and the New Deal* (1982); John L. Shover, *Cornbelt Rebellion: The Farmers' Holiday Association* (1965); Donald Worster, *Dust Bowl: The Southern Plains in the 1930s* (1979).

People of Color

Dan T. Carter, *Scottsboro*, rev. ed. (1979); James Goodman, *Stories of Scottsboro* (1994); Camille Guerin-Gonzales, *Mexican Workers and American Dreams: Immigration, Repatriation, and California Farm Labor, 1900–1939* (1994); Laurence C. Kelly, *The Assault on Assimilation: John Collier and the Origins of Indian Policy Reform* (1983); George Lipsitz, *The Possessive Investment in Whiteness: How White People Profit from Identity*

Politics (1998); Donald J. Lisio, *Hoover, Blacks, and Lily-Whites* (1985); Kenneth R. Philp, *Termination Revisited: American Indians on the Trail to Self-Determination, 1933-1953* (1999); George J. Sanchez, *Becoming Mexican American: Ethnicity, Culture and Identity in Chicano Los Angeles, 1900–1945* (1993); Harvard Sitkoff, *A New Deal for Blacks* (1978); Patricia Sullivan, *Days of Hope: Race and Democracy in the New Deal Era* (1996); Mark V. Tushnet, *The NAACP's Legal Strategy against Segregated Education, 1925-1950* (1987); Nancy J. Weiss, *Farewell to the Party of Lincoln: Black Politics in the Age of FDR* (1983).

Women

Glen H. Elder, Jr., *Children of the Great Depression: Social Change in Life Experience* (1974); Linda Gordon, *Pitied but Not Entitled: Single Mothers and the History of Welfare, 1890–1935* (1994); Alice Kessler-Harris, "Designing Women and Old Fools: The Construction of the Social Security Amendments of 1939," pp. 87–106 in Linda K. Kerber et al., eds., *U.S. History as Women's History* (1995); Lois Scharf, *To Work and to Wed: Female Employment, Feminism, and the Great Depression* (1980); Winifred Wandersee, *Women's Work and Family Values, 1920–1940* (1981); Susan Ware, *Holding Their Own: American Women in the 1930s* (1982); Susan Ware, *Beyond Suffrage: Women in the New Deal* (1981).

Cultural and Intellectual History

Daniel Aaron, *Writers on the Left: Episodes in American Literary Communism* (1961); Michael Denning, *The Cultural Front: The Laboring of American Culture in the Twentieth Century* (1997); Jerre Mangione, *The Dream and the Deal: The Federal Writers' Project, 1935–1943* (1972); Barbara Melosh, *Engendering Culture: Manhood and Womanhood in New Deal Public Art and Theater* (1991); Richard H. Pells, *Radical Visions and American Dreams: Culture and Social Thought in the Depression Years* (1973); Warren I. Susman, "The Culture of the Thirties," pp. 150–183 in Warren I. Susman, ed., *Culture as History* (1984).

Chapter 26

General

Warren I. Cohen, *Empire Without Tears* (1987); Justus D. Doenecke and John E. Wilz, *From Isolation to War,* 2d ed. (1991); Karen A. J. Miller, *Populist Nationalism: Republican Insurgency and American Foreign Policy, 1918–1925* (1999); Elting E. Morison, *Turmoil and Tradition* (1964) (on Stimson); Brenda G. Plummer, *Rising Wind: Black Americans and U.S. Foreign Affairs, 1935–1960* (1996); Emily S. Rosenberg, *Spreading the American Dream* (1982); Joan Hoff Wilson, *Herbert Hoover* (1975).

Arms Control and the Military

Thomas H. Buckley, *The United States and the Washington Conference, 1921–1922* (1970); Emily O. Goldman, *Sunken Treaties* (1994); Paul A. C. Koistinen, *Planning War, Pursuing Peace: The Political Economy of American Warfare, 1920–1939* (1998); Brian M. Linn, *Guardians of Empire: The U.S. Army and the Pacific, 1902–1940* (1997); Michael S. Sherry, *The Rise of American Airpower* (1987); Mark A. Stoler, *George Marshall* (1989).

Peace Groups and Leaders

Harriet H. Alonso, *The Women's Peace Union and the Outlawry of War* (1989); Charles Chatfield, *For Peace and Justice* (1971); Charles DeBenedetti, *The Peace Reform in American History* (1980); Charles DeBenedetti, *Origins of the Modern American Peace Movement, 1915–1929* (1978); Carrie A. Foster, *The Women and the Warriors* (1995); Robert D. Johnson, *The Peace Progressives and American Foreign Relations* (1995); Warren F. Kuehl and Lynne K. Dunn, *Keeping the Covenant* (1997); Linda A. Schott, *Reconstructing Women's Thoughts: The Women's International League for Peace and Freedom Before World War II* (1997); Lawrence Wittner, *Rebels Against War* (1984).

Economic and Financial Relations

Frederick Adams, *Economic Diplomacy* (1976); Derek H. Aldcroft, *From Versailles to Wall Street, 1919–1929* (1977); Michael Butler, *Cautious Visionary: Cordell Hull and Trade Reform, 1933-1937* (1998); Michael J. Hogan, *Informal Entente: The Private Structure of Cooperation in Anglo-American Economic Diplomacy* (1977); Charles Kindleberger, *The World in Depression* (1973); Stephen J. Randall, *United States Foreign Oil Policy, 1919–1948* (1986); Emily S. Rosenberg, *Financial Missionaries: The Politics and Culture of Dollar Diplomacy, 1900–1930* (1999); Mira Wilkins, *The Maturing of Multinational Enterprise* (1974); Joan Hoff Wilson, *American Business and Foreign Policy, 1920–1933* (1971).

Cultural Expansion and Philanthropy

Frank Costigliola, *Awkward Dominion* (1984); Marcos Cueto, ed., *Missionaries of Science: The Rockefeller Foundation and Latin America* (1994); Mary Nolan, *Visions of Modernity: American Business and the Modernization of Germany* (1994); Thomas J. Saunders, *Hollywood in Berlin* (1994).

Latin America and the Good Neighbor Policy

G. Pope Atkins and Larman C. Wilson, *The Dominican Republic and the United States* (1998); John A. Britton, *Revolution and Ideology: Images of the Mexican Revolution in the United States* (1995); Bruce J. Calder, *The Impact of Intervention: The Dominican Republic During the U.S. Occupation of 1916–1924* (1984); Arturo Morales Carrión, *Puerto Rico* (1983); Paul J. Dosal, *Doing Business with the Dictators* (1993); Paul W.

Drake, *The Money Doctors in the Andes* (1989); Alton Frye, *Nazi Germany and the American Hemisphere, 1933–1941* (1967); Irwin F. Gellman, *Good Neighbor Diplomacy* (1979); Linda B. Hall, *Oil, Banks, and Politics: The United States and Postrevolutionary Mexico, 1917–1924* (1995); Walter LaFeber, *Inevitable Revolutions: The United States in Central America*, 2d and extended ed. (1993); Lester D. Langley, *The United States and the Caribbean, 1900–1970* (1980); Abraham F. Lowenthal, ed., *Exporting Democracy* (1991); John Major, *Prize Possession: The United States and the Panama Canal, 1903–1979* (1993); Louis A. Pérez, *Cuba and the United States*, 2d ed. (1997); Louis A. Pérez, *Cuba Under the Platt Amendment* (1986); Fredrick B. Pike, *FDR's Good Neighbor Policy* (1995); Brenda G. Plummer, *Haiti and the United States* (1992); W. Dirk Raat, *Mexico and the United States* (1997); Friedrich E. Schuler, *Mexico Between Hitler and Roosevelt* (1998); Bryce Wood, *The Making of the Good Neighbor Policy* (1961).

Isolationists and Isolationism

Wayne S. Cole, *Roosevelt and the Isolationists, 1932–1945* (1983); Manfred Jonas, *Isolationism in America, 1935–1941* (1966); Thomas C. Kennedy, *Charles A. Beard and American Foreign Policy* (1975); Richard C. Lower, *A Bloc of One: The Political Career of Hiram W. Johnson* (1993); Richard Lowitt, *George W. Norris* (1963–1978); John Wiltz, *In Search of Peace: The Senate Munitions Inquiry* (1963).

Europe, Roosevelt's Policies, and the Coming of World War II

J. Garry Clifford and Samuel R. Spencer, Jr., *The First Peacetime Draft* (1986); David H. Culbert, *News for Everyman* (1976) (on radio); Robert Dallek, *Franklin D. Roosevelt and American Foreign Policy* (1995); Robert A. Divine, *Roosevelt and World War II* (1969); Barbara R. Farnham, *Roosevelt and the Munich Crisis* (1997); Frank Freidel, *Franklin D. Roosevelt* (1990); Manfred Jonas, *The United States and Germany* (1984); Warren F. Kimball, *The Juggler* (1991); Warren F. Kimball, *The Most Unsordid Act: Lend-Lease, 1939-1941* (1969); Melvyn P. Leffler, *The Elusive Quest: America's Pursuit of European Stability and French Security, 1919–1933* (1979); Douglas Little, *Malevolent Neutrality: The United States, Great Britain, and the Origins of the Spanish Civil War* (1985); Thomas R. Maddux, *Years of Estrangement: American Relations with the Soviet Union, 1933–1941* (1980); Arnold A. Offner, *American Appeasement* (1969); David Reynolds, *The Creation of the Anglo-American Alliance* (1982); David F. Schmitz, *The United States and Fascist Italy* (1988); James C. Schneider, *Should America Go to War?* (1989); Richard Steele, *Propaganda in an Open Society* (1985); Donald C. Watt, *How War Came* (1989); Theodore A. Wilson, *The First Summit* (1991).

China, Japan, and the Coming of War in Asia

Dorothy Borg and Shumpei Okomoto, eds., *Pearl Harbor as History* (1973); R. J. C. Butow, *Tojo and the Coming of War* (1961); Warren I. Cohen, *America's Response to China*, 3d ed. (1990); Peter Conn, *Pearl S. Buck* (1996); Hilary Conroy and Harry Wray, eds., *Pearl Harbor Reexamined* (1990); Herbert Feis, *The Road to Pearl Harbor* (1950); Waldo H. Heinrichs, Jr., *Threshold of War* (1988); Akira Iriye, *The Origins of the Second World War in Asia and the Pacific* (1987); Akira Iriye, *Across the Pacific* (1967); Akira Iriye, *After Imperialism* (1965); T. Christopher Jespersen, *American Images of China* (1996); Walter LaFeber, *The Clash: A History of U.S.-Japan Relations* (1997); James Morley, ed., *The Final Confrontation* (1994); Jonathan Utley, *Going to War with Japan* (1985).

Attack on Pearl Harbor

David Kahn, *The Codebreakers* (1967); Robert W. Love, Jr., ed., *Pearl Harbor Revisited* (1995); Martin V. Melosi, *The Shadow of Pearl Harbor* (1977); Gordon W. Prange, *Pearl Harbor* (1986); Gordon W. Prange, *At Dawn We Slept* (1981); John Toland, *Infamy* (1982); Roberta Wohlstetter, *Pearl Harbor* (1962).

Chapter 27

The Second World War

John W. Dower, *War Without Mercy: Race and Power in the Pacific War* (1986); John Keegan, *The Second World War* (1989); David M. Kennedy, *Freedom from Fear: The American People in Depression and War, 1929–1945* (1999); Eric Larabee, *Commander in Chief* (1987); Samuel Eliot Morison, *The Two-Ocean War* (1963); Ronald Schaffer, *Wings of Judgment: American Bombing in World War II* (1985); Gordon W. Prange et al., *At Dawn We Slept: The Untold Story of Pearl Harbor* (1981); Ronald H. Spector, *Eagle Against the Sun: The American War with Japan* (1984); Gerhard L. Weinberg, *A World at Arms: A Global History of World War II* (1994).

Fighting the War: Americans in Combat

Robert H. Abzug, *Inside the Vicious Heart: Americans and the Liberation of Nazi Concentration Camps* (1985); Stephen E. Ambrose, *The Victors* (1998); Stephen E. Ambrose, *Citizen Soldiers* (1997); Stephen E. Ambrose, *D-Day, June 6, 1944* (1994); Allan Berube, *Coming Out Under Fire: The History of Gay Men and Women in World War II* (1990); Michael D. Doubler, *Closing with the Enemy: How GIs Fought the War in Europe, 1944–1945* (1994); Paul Fussell, *Wartime* (1989); Gerald F. Linderman, *The World Within the War: America's Combat Experience in World War II* (1997); David Reynolds, *Rich Relations: The American Occupation of Britain, 1942–1945* (1995); E. B. Sledge, *With the Old Breed at Peleliu and Okinawa* (1990).

Wartime Diplomacy

Russell Buhite, *Decisions at Yalta* (1986); Diane Clemens, *Yalta* (1970); Robert Dallek, *Franklin D. Roosevelt and Ameri-*

can Foreign Policy, 1932–1945 (1979); Henry L. Feingold, *Bearing Witness: How America and Its Jews Responded to the Holocaust* (1995); George C. Herring, *Aid to Russia, 1941–1946* (1973); Gary R. Hess, *The United States at War, 1941–1945* (1986); Robert C. Hilderbrand, *Dumbarton Oaks* (1990); Townsend Hoopes and Douglas Brinkley, *Franklin D. Roosevelt and the Creation of the United Nations* (1997); Akira Iriye, *Power and Culture: The Japanese-American War, 1941–1945* (1981); Warren Kimball, *Forged in War: Roosevelt, Churchill, and the Second World War* (1997); Gabriel Kolko, *The Politics of War: The World and United States Foreign Policy, 1943–1945*, rev. ed. (1990); Walter LaFeber, *The Clash: A History of U.S.-Japan Relations* (1997); Verne W. Newton, ed., *FDR and the Holocaust* (1996); Keith Sainsbury, *Churchill and Roosevelt at War* (1994); Mark Stoler, *The Politics of the Second Front* (1977); David S. Wyman, *The Abandonment of the Jews* (1984).

Mobilizing for War

Amy Bentley, *Eating for Victory: Food Rationing and the Politics of Domesticity* (1998); George Q. Flynn, *The Draft, 1940–1973* (1993); Gregory Hooks, *Forging the Military-Industrial Complex: World War II's Battle of the Potomac* (1991); Clayton R. Koppes and Gregory D. Black, *Hollywood Goes to War* (1987); Nelson Lichtenstein, *Labor's War at Home: The CIO in World War II* (1983); George H. Roeder, Jr., *The Censored War: American Visual Experience During World War II* (1993); Lawrence R. Samuel, *Pledging Allegiance: American Identity and the Bond Drive of World War II* (1997); Bartholomew H. Sparrow, *From the Outside In: World War II and the American State* (1996); Richard W. Steele, *Free Speech in America's Good War* (1999); Harold G. Vatter, *The U.S. Economy in World War II* (1985); Allen M. Winkler, *The Politics of Propaganda: The Office of War Information, 1942–1945* (1978).

The Home Front

John Morton Blum, *V Was for Victory: Politics and American Culture During World War II* (1976); John D'Emilio, *Sexual Politics, Sexual Communities: The Making of a Homosexual Minority in the United States, 1940–1970* (1983); Doris Kearns Goodwin, *No Ordinary Time: Franklin and Eleanor Roosevelt: The Home Front in World War II* (1994); Gerald D. Nash, *The American West Transformed* (1985); William L. O'Neill, *A Democracy at War: America's Fight at Home and Abroad in World War II* (1993); Studs Terkel, ed., *"The Good War": An Oral History of World War Two* (1984); William M. Tuttle, Jr., *"Daddy's Gone to War": The Second World War in the Lives of America's Children* (1993).

The Internment of Japanese-Americans and Enemy Aliens

Roger Daniels, *Prisoners Without Trial* (1993); Stephen Fox, *The Unknown Internment: An Oral History of the Relocation of Italian Americans During World War II* (1990); Peter Irons,

Justice at War (1983); Arnold Krammer, *Undue Process: The Untold Story of America's German Alien Internees* (1997); Gary Okihiro, *Cane Fires: The Anti-Japanese Movement in Hawaii, 1865–1945* (1991); Page Smith, *Democracy on Trial: The Japanese American Evacuation and Relocation in World War II* (1995).

African Americans and Wartime Violence

A. Russell Buchanan, *Black Americans in World War II* (1977); Dominic J. Capeci, Jr., *The Harlem Riot of 1943* (1977); Dominic J. Capeci, Jr., and Martha Wilkerson, *Layered Violence: The Detroit Rioters of 1943* (1991); Mauricio Mazon, *The Zoot-Suit Riots* (1984); Patrick S. Washburn, *A Question of Sedition: The Federal Government's Investigation of the Black Press During World War II* (1986); Neil A. Wynn, *The Afro-American and the Second World War*, rev. ed. (1993).

Women at War

Karen T. Anderson, *Wartime Women* (1981); D'Ann Campbell, *Women at War with America* (1984); Claudia Goldin, *Understanding the Gender Gap: An Economic History of American Women* (1990); Susan M. Hartmann, *The Home Front and Beyond* (1982); Leslie Haynsworth and David Toomey, *Amelia Earhart's Daughters* (1998) (about American women aviators in the war); Judy Barrett Litoff and David C. Smith, eds., *We're in This War, Too: World War II Letters from American Women in Uniform* (1994); Leisa D. Meyer, *Creating GI Jane: Sexuality and Power in the Women's Army Corps During World War II* (1996); Ruth Milkman, *Gender at Work: The Dynamics of Job Discrimination by Sex During World War II* (1987); Leila J. Rupp, *Mobilizing Women for War: German and American Propaganda, 1939–1945* (1978).

The Atomic Bomb and Japan's Surrender

Gar Alperovitz, *The Decision to Use the Atomic Bomb and the Architecture of an American Myth*, 2d ed. (1995); Michael Hogan, ed., *Hiroshima in History and Memory* (1995); Robert Jay Lifton and Greg Mitchell, *Hiroshima in America: Fifty Years of Denial* (1995); Richard Rhodes, *The Making of the Atomic Bomb* (1987); Stephen I. Schwartz, ed., *Atomic Audit: The Costs and Consequences of U.S. Nuclear Weapons since 1940* (1998); Martin J. Sherwin, *A World Destroyed: The Atomic Bomb and the Grand Alliance* (1975); Leon V. Sigal, *Fighting to a Finish* (1994); Ronald Takaki, *Hiroshima: Why America Dropped the Atomic Bomb* (1995); J. Samuel Walker, *Prompt and Utter Destruction: Truman and the Use of the Atomic Bombs Against Japan* (1997).

Chapter 28

An Age of Consensus

John Patrick Diggins, *The Proud Decades: America in War and Peace, 1941–1960* (1988); David Halberstam, *The Fifties*

(1993); Marty Jezer, *The Dark Ages: Life in the United States, 1945–1960* (1982); William L. O'Neill, *American High: The Years of Confidence, 1945–1960* (1986); James T. Patterson, *Grand Expectations: The United States, 1945–1974* (1996).

Cold War Culture

Paul Boyer, *By the Bomb's Early Light: American Thought and Culture at the Dawn of the Atomic Age* (1985); Tom Engel-hardt, *The End of Victory Culture: Cold War America and the Disillusioning of a Generation* (1995); William S. Graebner, *The Age of Doubt: American Thought and Culture in the 1940s* (1991); Margot A. Henriksen, *Dr. Strangelove's America: Society and Culture in the Atomic Age* (1997); Lary May, ed., *Recasting America: Culture and Politics in the Age of Cold War* (1989); Richard H. Pells, *The Liberal Mind in a Conservative Age* (1985); Lisle A. Rose, *The Cold War Comes to Main Street: America in 1950* (1999); Stephen J. Whitfield, *The Culture of the Cold War*, rev. ed. (1996).

The Truman Presidency

Robert J. Donovan, *Tumultuous Years: The Presidency of Harry S. Truman, 1949–1953* (1982); Robert J. Donovan, *Conflict and Crisis: The Presidency of Harry S. Truman, 1945–1948* (1977); Alonzo L. Hamby, *Man of the People: The Life of Harry S. Truman* (1995); Michael J. Hogan, *A Cross of Iron: Harry S. Truman and the Origins of the National Security State* (1998); David McCullough, *Truman* (1992); Paul G. Pierpaoli, Jr., *Truman and Korea: The Political Culture of the Cold War* (1999).

Eisenhower and the Politics of the 1950s

Stephen E. Ambrose, *Eisenhower: The President* (1984); Robert F. Burk, *Dwight D. Eisenhower* (1986); Donald L. Fixico, *Termination and Relocation: Federal Indian Policy, 1945–1960* (1986); Fred I. Greenstein, *The Hidden-Hand Presidency* (1982); Chester J. Pach, Jr., and Elmo Richardson, *The Presidency of Dwight D. Eisenhower*, rev. ed. (1991); Geoffrey Perret, *Eisenhower* (1999).

McCarthyism

Richard M. Fried, *Nightmare in Red* (1990); Robert Griffith, *The Politics of Fear: Joseph R. McCarthy and the Senate*, rev. ed. (1987); John Earl Haynes and Harvey Klehr, *Venona: Decoding Soviet Espionage in America* (1999); Harvey Klehr et al., *The Soviet World of American Communism* (1998); David M. Oshinsky, *A Conspiracy So Immense: The World of Joe McCarthy* (1983); Richard Gid Powers, *Not Without Honor: The History of American Anticommunism* (1995); Ellen W. Schrecker, *Many Are the Crimes: McCarthyism in America* (1998); Ellen W. Schrecker, *No Ivory Tower: McCarthyism in the Universities* (1986).

Race Relations and the Civil Rights Movement

Taylor Branch, *Parting the Waters: America in the King Years, 1954–1963* (1988); Robert F. Burk, *The Eisenhower Administration and Black Civil Rights* (1984); William H. Chafe, *Civilities and Civil Rights: Greensboro, North Carolina, and the Black Struggle for Freedom* (1980); David J. Garrow, *Bearing the Cross: Martin Luther King, Jr., and the Southern Christian Leadership Conference* (1986); Arnold R. Hirsch, *Making the Second Ghetto: Race and Housing in Chicago, 1940–1960* (1983); Richard Kluger, *Simple Justice: The History of Brown v. Board of Education and Black America's Struggle for Equality* (1975); Gail Williams O'Brien, *The Color of Law: Race, Violence, and Justice in the Post–World War II South* (1999); Thomas J. Sugrue, *The Origins of the Urban Crisis: Race and Inequality in Postwar Detroit* (1996); Jules Tygiel, *Baseball's Great Experiment: Jackie Robinson and His Legacy*, rev. ed. (1997); Juan Williams, *Thurgood Marshall: American Revolutionary* (1998).

The Baby Boom, Youth Culture, and Cold War Families

James Gilbert, *A Cycle of Outrage: America's Reaction to the Juvenile Delinquent* (1986); Landon Y. Jones, *Great Expectations: America and the Baby Boom Generation* (1980); James H. Jones, *Alfred C. Kinsey* (1997); Paul Leinberger and Bruce Tucker, *The New Individualists: The Generation After the Organization Man* (1991); Elaine Tyler May, *Homeward Bound: American Families in the Cold War Era* (1988); John Modell, *Into One's Own: From Youth to Adulthood in the United States, 1920–1975* (1989); Grace Palladino, *Teenagers* (1996).

Suburbia and the Spread of Education

Robert Fishman, *Bourgeois Utopias* (1987); Mark I. Gelfand, *A Nation of Cities* (1975); Dolores Hayden, *Redesigning the American Dream* (1984); Kenneth T. Jackson, *Crabgrass Frontier: The Suburbanization of the United States* (1985); Zane L. Miller, *Suburb* (1982); Diane Ravitch, *The Troubled Crusade: American Education, 1945–1980* (1983); Joel Spring, *The Sorting Machine: National Educational Policy Since 1945* (1976).

Women's Lives and Women's Rights

Wini Breines, *Young, White, and Miserable: Growing Up Female in the Fifties* (1992); Ruth Schwartz Cowan, *More Work for Mother* (1983); Myra Dinnerstein, *Women Between Two Worlds* (1992); Barbara Ehrenreich, *The Hearts of Men: American Dreams and the Flight from Commitment* (1983); Cynthia Harrison, *On Account of Sex: The Politics of Women's Issues, 1945–1968* (1988); Eugenia Kaledin, *Mothers and More: American Women in the 1950s* (1984); Susan Lynn, *Progressive Women in Conservative Times* (1992); Glenna Matthews, *"Just a Housewife"* (1987); Joanne J. Meyerowitz, ed., *Not June Cleaver: Women and Gender in Postwar America, 1945–1960* (1994); Leila J. Rupp and Verta Taylor, *Survival in the Dol-*

drums: The American Women's Rights Movement, 1945 to the 1960s (1987).

The Affluent Society

Loren Baritz, *The Good Life: The Meaning of Success for the American Middle Class* (1982); Kevin Fernlund, ed., *The Cold War American West* (1998); John Kenneth Galbraith, *The Affluent Society* (1958); Ann Markusen et al., *Rise of the Gunbelt: The Military Remapping of Industrial America* (1991); Kirkpatrick Sale, *Power Shift: The Rise of the Southern Rim and Its Challenge to the Eastern Establishment* (1975); Bruce J. Schulman, *From Cotton Belt to Sunbelt: Federal Policy, Economic Development, and the Transformation of the South, 1938–1980* (1991).

Farmers and Laborers

Gilbert C. Fite, *American Farmers* (1981); James R. Green, *The World of the Worker* (1980); Nelson Lichtenstein, *The Most Dangerous Man in Detroit: Walter Reuther and the Fate of American Labor* (1995); George Lipsitz, *Rainbow at Midnight: Labor and Culture in the 1940s* (1994); John L. Shover, *First Majority—Last Minority: The Transforming of Rural Life in America* (1976).

The Other America

Richard B. Craig, *The Bracero Program* (1971); J. Wayne Flint, *Dixie's Forgotten People: The South's Poor Whites* (1979); Mario T. Garcia, *Mexican Americans: Leadership, Ideology, and Identity, 1930–1960* (1990); Michael Harrington, *The Other America*, rev. ed. (1981); Dorothy K. Newman et al., *Politics and Prosperity: Black Americans and White Institutions, 1940–75* (1978); James T. Patterson, *America's Struggle Against Poverty, 1900–1994*, rev. ed. (1994).

Chapter 29

The Cold War: Overviews

Stephen Ambrose and Allen Brinkley, *Rise to Globalism*, 8th rev. ed. (1997); H. W. Brands, *The Devil We Knew* (1993); Warren Cohen, *America in the Age of Soviet Power, 1945–1991* (1993); Gordon A. Craig and Francis L. Loewenheim, eds., *The Diplomats, 1939–1979* (1994); John Lewis Gaddis, *We Now Know* (1997); John Lewis Gaddis, *The Long Peace* (1987); John Lewis Gaddis, *Strategies of Containment* (1982); Walter Isaacson and Evan Thomas, *The Wise Men* (1986); Robert H. Johnson, *Improbable Dangers: U.S. Perceptions of Threat in the Cold War and After* (1994); Paul Kennedy, *The Rise and Fall of the Great Powers* (1987); Walter LaFeber, *America, Russia, and the Cold War, 1945–1996*, 8th ed. (1996); Deborah Larson, *Anatomy of Distrust* (1997); Ralph Levering, *The Cold War*, 2d ed. (1994); Thomas McCormick, *America's Half-Century*, 2d ed. (1994); Thomas G. Paterson, *On Every Front: The Making and Unmaking of the*
Cold War, rev. ed. (1992); Thomas G. Paterson, *Meeting the Communist Threat* (1988); Michael S. Sherry, *In the Shadow of War* (1995).

Relations with the Third World: Overviews

Richard J. Barnet, *Intervention and Revolution* (1972); Edward H. Berman, *The Influence of the Carnegie, Ford, and Rockefeller Foundations on American Foreign Policy* (1983); Scott L. Bills, *Empire and Cold War* (1990); H. W. Brands, *The Specter of Neutralism* (1989); Gabriel Kolko, *Confronting the Third World* (1988); Michael L. Krenn, *Black Diplomacy: African Americans and the State Department, 1945–1969* (1998); Michael L. Krenn, ed., *Race and U.S. Foreign Policy during the Cold War* (1998); Brenda G. Plummer, *Rising Wind: Black Americans and U.S. Foreign Affairs, 1935–1960* (1996); David F. Schmitz, *Thank God They're on Our Side: The U.S. and Right-Wing Dictatorships, 1921–1965* (1999); Penny M. von Eschen, *Race Against Empire: Black Americans and Anticolonialism, 1937–1957* (1996).

Truman, Cold War Origins, Containment, and the National Security State

James Chace, *Acheson* (1998); Carolyn W. Eisenberg, *Drawing the Line: The American Decision to Divide Germany, 1944–1949* (1996); Bruce E. Field, *Harvest of Dissent: The National Farmers Union and the Early Cold War* (1998); Richard M. Fried, *The Russians Are Coming! The Russians Are Coming!* (1998); Frazer Harbutt, *The Iron Curtain* (1986); Walter Hixson, *George F. Kennan* (1990); Michael J. Hogan, *A Cross of Iron: Harry S. Truman and the Origins of the National Security State* (1998); Michael J. Hogan, *The Marshall Plan* (1987); Lawrence S. Kaplan, *The United States and NATO* (1984); Gabriel Kolko and Joyce Kolko, *The Limits of Power* (1972); Bruce R. Kuniholm, *The Origins of the Cold War in the Near East* (1980); Melvyn Leffler, *The Specter of Communism* (1994); Melvyn Leffler, *A Preponderance of Power: National Security, the Truman Administration, and the Cold War* (1992); Alan Milward, *The Reconstruction of Western Europe* (1984); Wilson D. Miscamble, *George F. Kennan and the Making of American Foreign Policy, 1947–1950* (1992); Ann Markusen et al., *The Rise of the Gunbelt* (1991); David Reynolds, ed., *The Origins of the Cold War in Europe* (1994); Thomas A. Schwartz, *America's Germany* (1991); Mark A. Stoler, *George C. Marshall* (1989); Marc Trachtenberg, *A Constructed Peace: The Making of the European Settlement, 1945–1963* (1999); Lawrence S. Wittner, *American Intervention in Greece, 1943–1949* (1982); Vladislav Zubok and Constantine Pleshakov, *Inside the Kremlin's Cold War* (1996); Randall B. Woods, *A Changing of the Guard: Anglo-American Relations, 1941–1946* (1990).

Eisenhower-Dulles Foreign Policy

Stephen E. Ambrose, *Eisenhower*, 2 vols. (1982, 1984); Stephen E. Ambrose, *Ike's Spies* (1981); Michael Beschloss,

MAYDAY: Eisenhower, Khrushchev, and the U-2 Affair (1986); Jeff Broadwater, *Eisenhower and the Anti-Communist Crusade* (1992); Robert A. Divine, *Eisenhower and the Cold War* (1981); Fred Greenstein, *The Hidden-Hand Presidency* (1982); Townsend Hoopes, *The Devil and John Foster Dulles* (1973); Richard Immerman, *John Foster Dulles* (1998); Richard Immerman, ed., *John Foster Dulles* (1990); Burton I. Kaufman, *Trade and Aid* (1982); Frederick W. Marks, *Power and Peace* (1993) (on Dulles); Jack M. Schick, *The Berlin Crisis* (1971).

The CIA and Counterinsurgency

Douglas S. Blaufarb, *The Counterinsurgency Era* (1977); Peter Grose, *Gentleman Spy: The Life of Allen Dulles* (1994); Rhodi Jeffreys-Jones, *The CIA and American Democracy* (1989); Loch K. Johnson, *America's Secret Power* (1989); Mark Lowenthal, *U.S. Intelligence* (1984); John Ranelagh, *The Agency* (1986); Jeffrey T. Richelson, *A Century of Spies* (1995); Jeffrey T. Richelson, *The U.S. Intelligence Community* (1999); Evan Thomas, *The Very Best Men* (1995).

Atomic Diplomacy, Nuclear Arms Race, and Public Attitudes

Howard Ball, *Justice Downwind: America's Atomic Testing Program in the 1950s* (1986); Paul Boyer, *Fallout* (1998); Paul Boyer, *By the Bomb's Early Light* (1986); McGeorge Bundy, *Danger and Survival* (1988); Campbell Craig, *Destroying the Village: Eisenhower and Thermonuclear War* (1998); Robert A. Divine, *The Sputnik Challenge* (1993); Robert A. Divine, *Blowing on the Wind: The Nuclear Test Ban Debate, 1954–1960* (1978); Margot Henriksen, *Dr. Strangelove's America* (1997); Gregg Herken, *Counsels of War* (1985); Gregg Herken, *The Winning Weapon* (1981); James G. Hershberg, *James B. Conant* (1993); Richard G. Hewlett and Jack M. Hall, *Atoms for Peace and War, 1953–1961* (1989); David Holloway, *Stalin and the Bomb* (1994); Robert Jervis, *The Meaning of the Nuclear Revolution* (1989); Fred Kaplan, *The Wizards of Armageddon* (1983); Milton Katz, *Ban the Bomb* (1986); Stuart W. Leslie, *The Cold War and American Science* (1994); John Newhouse, *War and Peace in the Nuclear Age* (1989); Richard Rhodes, *Dark Sun: The Making of the Hydrogen Bomb* (1995); David N. Schwartz, *NATO's Nuclear Dilemmas* (1983); Martin Sherwin, *A World Destroyed* (1975); Spencer Weart, *Nuclear Fear* (1988); Allan M. Winkler, *Life Under a Cloud* (1993); Lawrence S. Wittner, *The Struggle Against the Bomb* (1993, 1998).

Cultural Relations and Expansion

Robert H. Haddow, *Pavilions of Plenty* (1997); Walter L. Hixson, *Parting the Curtain: Propaganda, Culture, and the Cold War* (1997); Frank A. Ninkovich, *The Diplomacy of Ideas* (1981); Richard Pells, *Not Like Us: How Europeans Have Loved, Hated, and Transformed American Culture Since World War II* (1997); Reinhold Wagnleitner, *Coca-Colonization and the Cold War* (1994).

Japan, China, and Asian Issues

H. W. Brands, *India and the United States* (1989); Kenton J. Clymer, *Quest for Freedom: The United States and India's Independence* (1995); Gordon Chang, *Friends and Enemies* (1990); Thomas J. Christensen, *Useful Adversaries* (1996); Warren I. Cohen, *America's Response to China*, 3d ed. (1990); Nick Cullather, *Illusions of Influence: The Political Economy of United States–Philippines Relations, 1942–1960* (1994); Richard B. Finn, *Winners in Peace* (1995); Kyoko Hirano, *Mr. Smith Goes to Tokyo: Japanese Cinema Under the American Occupation, 1945–1952* (1992); E. J. Kahn, Jr., *The China Hands* (1975); Walter LaFeber, *The Clash: A History of U.S.-Japan Relations* (1997); Paul G. Lauren, ed., *The "China Hands" Legacy* (1987); Robert J. McMahon, *The Limits of Empire: The United States and Southeast Asia Since World War II* (1999); Robert J. McMahon, *Colonialism and Cold War: The United States and the Struggle for Indonesian Independence, 1945–49* (1981); Dennis Merrill, *Bread and the Ballot: The United States and India's Economic Development, 1947–1963* (1990); Robert P. Newman, *Owen Lattimore and the "Loss" of China* (1992); Michael Schaller, *Douglas MacArthur* (1989); Michael Schaller, *The American Occupation of Japan* (1985); William W. Stueck, Jr., *The Road to Confrontation* (1981); Nancy B. Tucker, *Taiwan, Hong Kong, and the United States* (1994); Nancy B. Tucker, *Patterns in the Dust: Chinese-American Relations and the Recognition Controversy, 1945–1950* (1983); Philip West et al., eds., *America's Wars in Asia* (1998).

The Korean War

Roy E. Appleman, *Disaster in Korea* (1992); Roy E. Appleman, *Escaping the Trap* (1990); Roy E. Appleman, *Ridgeway Duels for Korea* (1990); Conrad C. Crane, *American Airpower Strategy in Korea* (2000); Bruce Cumings, *Korea's Place in the Sun* (1997); Bruce Cumings, *The Origins of the Korean War* (1980, 1991); Rosemary Foot, *A Substitute for Victory* (1990); Rosemary Foot, *The Wrong War* (1985); Sergei Goncharov et al., *Uncertain Partners: Stalin, Mao, and the Korean War* (1993); John Halliday and Bruce Cumings, *Korea* (1989); Chen Jian, *China's Road to the Korean War* (1995); Burton I. Kaufman, *The Korean War*, 2d ed. (1997); Callum A. MacDonald, *Korea* (1987); John W. Spanier, *The Truman-MacArthur Controversy and the Korean War* (1959); William Stueck, *The Korean War* (1995); Shu Guang Zhang, *Mao's Military Romanticism* (1996).

Vietnam

David L. Anderson, ed., *Shadow on the White House* (1993); David L. Anderson, *Trapped by Success* (1991); Melanie Billings-Yun, *Decision Against War: Eisenhower and Dien Bien Phu, 1954* (1988); William J. Duiker, *U.S. Containment Policy and the Conflict in Indochina* (1994); Lloyd C. Gardner, *Approaching Vietnam* (1988); George C. Herring, *America's Longest War*, 3d ed. (1996); Gary R. Hess, *Vietnam and the United States*, rev. ed. (1998); Gary Hess, *The United States'*

Emergence as a Southeast Asian Power (1987); Lawrence S. Kaplan et al., eds., *Dien Bien Phu and the Crisis of Franco-American Relations* (1990); Gabriel Kolko, *Anatomy of a War* (1986); David G. Marr, *Vietnam 1945* (1995); Joseph G. Morgan, *The Vietnam Lobby: The American Friends of Vietnam, 1955–1975* (1997); Andrew Rotter, *The Path to Vietnam* (1987); Robert D. Schulzinger, *A Time for War* (1997); Anthony Short, *The Origins of the Vietnam War* (1989); Robert R. Tomes, *Apocalypse Then: American Intellectuals and the Vietnam War, 1954–1975* (1998); Stein Tonnesson, *The Vietnamese Revolution of 1945* (1991); Marilyn B. Young, *The Vietnam Wars* (1991).

Latin America

Cole Blasier, *Hovering Giant* (1974); John Coatsworth, *Central America and the United States* (1994); Michael Conniff, *Panama and the United States* (1992); Nick Cullather, *Secret History: The CIA's Classified Account of Its Operations in Guatemala, 1952–1954* (1999); Mark T. Gilderhus, *The Second Century* (2000); Piero Gleijeses, *Shattered Hope: The Guatemalan Revolution and the United States, 1944–1954* (1991); Richard Immerman, *The CIA in Guatemala* (1982); Walter LaFeber, *Inevitable Revolutions: The United States in Central America*, 2d and expanded ed. (1993); Walter LaFeber, *The Panama Canal*, updated ed. (1990); Lester Langley, *America and the Americas* (1989); Abraham F. Lowenthal, ed., *Exporting Democracy* (1991); A. W. Maldonado, *Teodoro Moscoso and Puerto Rico's Operation Bootstrap* (1997); Thomas G. Paterson, *Contesting Castro* (1994); Louis A. Pérez, Jr., *Cuba and the United States*, 2d ed. (1997); W. Dirk Raat, *Mexico and the United States*, 2d ed. (1997); Stephen G. Rabe, *Eisenhower and Latin America* (1988); Stephen G. Rabe, *The Road to OPEC: United States Relations with Venezuela* (1982); Lars Schoultz, *Beneath the United States* (1998); Gaddis Smith, *The Last Years of the Monroe Doctrine* (1994); Peter H. Smith, *Talons of the Eagle* (1996).

Middle East and Africa

Nigel J. Ashton, *Eisenhower, Macmillan, and the Problem of Nasser* (1996); James A. Bill, *The Eagle and the Lion: The Tragedy of American-Iranian Relations* (1988); Thomas Borstelmann, *Apartheid's Reluctant Uncle: The United States and Southern Africa in the Early Cold War* (1993); William J. Burns, *Economic Aid and American Policy Toward Egypt, 1955–1981* (1985); Michael J. Cohen, *Truman and Israel* (1990); Michael J. Cohen, *Palestine and the Great Powers, 1945–1948* (1983); Mark Gasiorowski, *U.S. Foreign Policy and the Shah* (1991); Peter L. Hahn, *The United States, Great Britain, and Egypt, 1945–1956* (1991); Mary Ann Heiss, *Empire and Nationhood: The United States, Great Britain, and Iranian Oil, 1950–1954* (1997); Burton I. Kaufman, *The Arab Middle East and the United States* (1996); Diane Kunz, *The Economic Diplomacy of the Suez Crisis* (1991); Zach Levy, *Israel and the Great Powers* (1998); William Roger Louis and Roger Owen, eds., *Suez 1956* (1989); Aaron D. Miller, *Search for Security* (1980); Donald Neff, *Warriors at Suez* (1981); Thomas J. Noer, *Cold War and Black Liberation* (1985); David Schoenbaum, *The United States and the State of Israel* (1993); Robert W. Stookey, *America and the Arab States* (1975); Daniel Yergin, *The Prize: The Epic Quest for Oil, Money, and Power* (1991).

Chapter 30

The 1960s

David Burner, *Making Peace with the 60s* (1996); Dominick Cavallo, *A Fiction of the Past: The Sixties in American History* (1999); David Chalmers, *And the Crooked Places Made Straight: The Struggle for Social Change in the 1960s* (1991); David Farber, *The Age of Great Dreams* (1994); David Farber, ed., *The Sixties* (1994); James J. Farrell, *The Spirit of the Sixties* (1997); Godfrey Hodgson, *America in Our Time* (1976); Michael Kazin and Maurice Isserman, *America Divided: The Civil War of the 1960s* (2000); Arthur Marwick, *The Sixties* (1998); Allen J. Matusow, *The Unraveling of America: A History of Liberalism in the 1960s* (1984); James T. Patterson, *Grand Expectations: The United States, 1945–1974* (1996).

The Kennedy Presidency

Irving Bernstein, *Promises Kept: John F. Kennedy's New Frontier* (1991); James Giglio, *The Presidency of John F. Kennedy* (1991); David Halberstam, *The Best and the Brightest* (1972); Christopher Matthews, *Kennedy and Nixon: The Rivalry That Shaped Postwar America* (1996); Herbert S. Parmet, *J.F.K.—The Presidency of John F. Kennedy* (1983); Thomas C. Reeves, *A Question of Character* (1991); Arthur M. Schlesinger, Jr., *Robert Kennedy and His Times* (1978); Arthur M. Schlesinger, Jr., *A Thousand Days: John F. Kennedy in the White House* (1965); Ronald Steel, *In Love with Night: The American Romance with Robert Kennedy* (1999); Garry Wills, *The Kennedy Imprisonment* (1982).

The Kennedy Assassination

Edward Jay Epstein, *Legend: The Secret World of Lee Harvey Oswald* (1978); Henry Hurt, *Reasonable Doubt* (1985); Gerald Posner, *Case Closed* (1993); Anthony Summers, *Conspiracy* (1980).

Lyndon B. Johnson and the Great Society

Irving Bernstein, *Guns or Butter: The Presidency of Lyndon Johnson* (1996); Robert Dallek, *Flawed Giant: Lyndon Johnson and His Times, 1961–1973* (1998); Doris Kearns, *Lyndon Johnson and the American Dream* (1976); Sar A. Levitan and Robert Taggart, *The Promise of Greatness* (1976); Charles Murray, *Losing Ground: American Social Policy, 1950–1980* (1983); James T. Patterson, *America's Struggle Against Poverty, 1900–1994*, rev. ed. (1994); John E. Schwarz, *Amer-*

ica's Hidden Success: A Reassessment of Twenty Years of Public Policy (1983); Irwin Unger, *The Best of Intentions: The Triumph and Failure of the Great Society Under Kennedy, Johnson, and Nixon* (1996).

Civil Rights, Black Power, and Urban Riots

Taylor Branch, *Pillar of Fire: America in the King Years, 1963-1965* (1998); Taylor Branch, *Parting the Waters: America in the King Years, 1954–1963* (1988); Clayborne Carson, *In Struggle: SNCC and the Black Awakening of the 1960s* (1981); John Dittmer, *Local People: The Struggle for Civil Rights in Mississippi* (1994); David J. Garrow, *Bearing the Cross: Martin Luther King, Jr., and the Southern Christian Leadership Conference* (1986); David Halberstam, *The Children* (1998); Gerald Horne, *Fire This Time: The Watts Uprising and the 1960s* (1996); Chana Kai Lee, *For Freedom's Sake: The Life of Fannie Lou Hamer* (1999); Malcolm X and Alex Haley, *The Autobiography of Malcolm X* (1965); August Meier and Elliott Rudwick, *CORE* (1973); Charles M. Payne, *I've Got the Light of Freedom: The Organizing Tradition and the Mississippi Freedom Struggle* (1995); David Remmick, *King of the World: Muhammad Ali and the Rise of An American Hero* (1999); Belinda Robnett, *How Long? How Long? African-American Women in the Struggle for Civil Rights* (1997).

The Warren Court

Gerald Dunne, *Hugo Black and the Judicial Revolution* (1977); Morton J. Horwitz, *The Warren Court and the Pursuit of Justice* (1998); Bernard Schwartz, *Super Chief: Earl Warren and His Supreme Court* (1983); G. Edward White, *Earl Warren* (1982).

The New Left and Protest for Peace and Justice

Terry H. Anderson, *The Movement and the Sixties* (1995); Wini Breines, *Community and Organization in the New Left, 1962–1968*, rev. ed. (1989); Dudley Clendinen and Adam Nagourney, *Out for Good: The Struggle to Build a Gay Rights Movement in America* (1998); Charles DeBenedetti, *An American Ordeal: The Antiwar Movement of the Vietnam Era* (1990); John D'Emilio, *Sexual Politics, Sexual Communities: The Making of a Homosexual Minority in the United States, 1940–1970* (1983); Todd Gitlin, *The Sixties* (1987); James Miller, *"Democracy Is in the Streets": From Port Huron to the Siege of Chicago* (1987); Doug Rossinow, *The Politics of Authenticity: Liberalism, Christianity, and the New Left in America* (1998); Kirkpatrick Sale, *The Green Revolution: The American Environmental Movement, 1962–1992* (1993); Tom Wells, *The War Within: America's Battle over Vietnam* (1994).

The Counterculture

Morris Dickstein, *Gates of Eden: American Culture in the Sixties* (1977); James Miller, *Flowers in the Dustbin: The Rise of Rock and Roll, 1947–1977* (1999); Tim Miller, *The Hippies and American Values* (1991); Charles Perry, *The Haight-Ashbury* (1984); Jay Stevens, *Storming Heaven: LSD and the American Dream* (1987); Jon Weiner, *Come Together: John Lennon in His Time* (1984); Tom Wolfe, *The Electric Kool-Aid Acid Test* (1968).

The Rebirth of Feminism

Flora Davis, *Moving the Mountain: The Women's Movement in America Since 1960* (1991); Alice Echols, *Daring to Be Bad: Radical Feminism in America, 1965–1975* (1989); Sara Evans, *Personal Politics* (1978); Jo Freeman, *The Politics of Women's Liberation* (1975); David J. Garrow, *Liberty and Sexuality: The Right to Privacy and the Making of* Roe v. Wade (1994); Cynthia Harrison, *On Account of Sex: The Politics of Women's Issues, 1945–1968* (1988); Judith Hole and Ellen Levine, *Rebirth of Feminism* (1971); Daniel Horowitz, *Betty Friedan and the Making of the "Feminine Mystique"* (1999); Ruth Rosen, *The World Split Open: How the Modern Women's Movement Changed America* (2000).

Year of Shocks: 1968

David Farber, *Chicago '68* (1988); Carole Fink et al., eds., *1968: The World Transformed* (1998); Ronald Fraser et al., *1968: A Student Generation in Revolt* (1988); Charles Kaiser, *1968 in America* (1988); Jules Witcover, *The Year the Dream Died: Revisiting 1968 in America* (1997) .

Richard M. Nixon and the Resurgence of Conservatism

Stephen E. Ambrose, *Nixon*, 3 vols. (1987–1991); William C. Berman, *Right Turn: From Nixon to Bush* (1994); Mary C. Brennan, *Turning Right in the Sixties: The Conservative Capture of the GOP* (1995); Dan T. Carter, *The Politics of Rage: George Wallace, the Origins of the New Conservatism, and the Transformation of American Politics* (1995); Robert Alan Goldberg, *Barry Goldwater* (1995); Allen J. Matusow, *Nixon's Economy: Booms, Busts, Dollars, and Votes* (1998); Herbert S. Parmet, *Richard Nixon and His America* (1990); James A. Reichley, *Conservatives in an Era of Change: The Nixon and Ford Administrations* (1981); Melvin Small, *The Presidency of Richard Nixon* (1999); Tom Wicker, *One of Us* (1991); Garry Wills, *Nixon Agonistes* (1970).

Watergate

Jim Hougan, *Secret Agenda: Watergate, Deep Throat and the CIA* (1984); Stanley I. Kutler, ed., *Abuse of Power: The New Nixon Tapes* (1997); Stanley I. Kutler, *The Wars of Watergate* (1990); J. Anthony Lukas, *Nightmare: The Underside of the Nixon Years* (1976); Kim McQuaid, *The Anxious Years: America in the Vietnam-Watergate Era* (1989); Michael Schudson, *Watergate in American Memory* (1992); Theodore H. White, *Breach of Faith* (1975); Bob Woodward, *Shadow: Five Presidents and the Legacy of Watergate* (1999); Bob Woodward and Carl Bernstein, *All the President's Men* (1974).

Chapter 31

General

See works listed under Chapter 29 and Richard J. Barnet, *Intervention and Revolution* (1972); Edward H. Berman, *The Influence of the Carnegie, Ford, and Rockefeller Foundations on American Foreign Policy* (1983); Alvin Z. Rubenstein and Donald E. Smith, eds., *Anti-Americanism in the Third World* (1985).

Foreign Policy in the 1960s: Kennedy and Johnson

LeRoy Ashby and Rod Gramer, *Fighting the Odds: The Life of Senator Frank Church* (1994); Michael Beschloss, *The Crisis Years* (1991); James A. Bill, *George Ball* (1997); Kai Bird, *The Color of Truth: McGeorge Bundy and William Bundy* (1998); H. W. Brands, ed., *The Foreign Policies of Lyndon Johnson* (1999); H. W. Brands, *The Wages of Globalism* (1995); Warren I. Cohen, *Dean Rusk* (1980); Warren I. Cohen and Nancy B. Tucker, eds., *Lyndon Johnson Confronts the World* (1995); Robert Dallek, *Flawed Giant: Lyndon Johnson and His Times, 1961–1973* (1998); Fritz Fisher, *Making Them Like Us: Peace Corps Volunteers in the 1960s* (1998); James N. Giglio, *The Presidency of John F. Kennedy* (1991); David Halberstam, *The Best and the Brightest* (1972); Seymour Hersh, *The Other Side of Camelot* (1997); Elizabeth Cobbs Hoffman, *All You Need Is Love: The Peace Corps and the Spirit of the 1960s* (1998); Robert D. Johnson, *Ernest Gruening and the American Dissenting Tradition* (1998); Doris Kearns, *Lyndon Johnson and the American Dream* (1976); Montague Kern et al., *The Kennedy Crises* (1984); Diane Kunz, ed., *The Diplomacy of the Crucial Decade* (1994); Herbert S. Parmet, *JFK* (1983); Thomas G. Paterson, ed., *Kennedy's Quest for Victory* (1989); Gerald T. Rice, *The Bold Experiment: JFK's Peace Corps* (1985); Arthur M. Schlesinger, Jr., *Robert Kennedy and His Times* (1978); Thomas J. Schoenbaum, *Waging Peace and War: Dean Rusk in the Truman, Kennedy, and Johnson Years* (1988); Deborah Shapley, *Promise and Power: The Life and Times of Robert McNamara* (1993); Mark J. White, *Kennedy* (1998); Randall Woods, *Fulbright* (1995); Thomas W. Zeiler, *Dean Rusk* (1999).

Cuba and the Missile Crisis

Graham Allison and Philip Zelikow, *Essence of Decision: Explaining the Cuban Missile Crisis*, 2d ed. (1999); James G. Blight, *The Shattered Crystal Ball* (1990); James G. Blight et al., *Cuba on the Brink* (1993); James G. Blight and Peter Kornbluh, eds., *Politics of Illusion: The Bay of Pigs Invasion Reexamined* (1998); James G. Blight and David A. Welch, *On the Brink* (1989); Raymond Garthoff, *Reflections on the Cuban Missile Crisis*, rev. ed. (1989); Trumbull Higgins, *The Perfect Failure: Kennedy, Eisenhower, and the CIA at the Bay of Pigs* (1987); Donna R. Kaplowitz, *Anatomy of a Failed Embargo: U.S. Sanctions Against Cuba* (1998); Richard Ned Lebow and Janice Gross Stein, *We All Lost the Cold War* (1993); Ernest R.

May and Philip Zelikow, eds., *The Kennedy Tapes* (1997); Morris Morley, *Imperial State and Revolution* (1987); James Nathan, ed., *The Cuban Missile Crisis Revisited* (1992); Thomas G. Paterson, *Contesting Castro* (1994); Louis A. Pérez, Jr., *Cuba and the United States*, 2d ed. (1997); Scott D. Sagan, *The Limits of Safety* (1993); Mark J. White, *The Cuban Missile Crisis* (1996).

The Vietnam War

See Duiker, Herring, Hess, Kolko, Morgan, Schulzinger, Tomes, and Young listed under Chapter 29 and David L. Anderson, *Facing My Lai* (1998); Loren Baritz, *Backfire* (1985); David M. Barrett, *Uncertain Warriors* (1993); Eric M. Bergerud, *The Dynamics of Defeat* (1991); Larry Berman, *Lyndon Johnson's War* (1989); Larry Berman, *Planning a Tragedy* (1982); Robert K. Brigham, *Guerilla Diplomacy: The NFL's Foreign Relations and the Viet Nam War* (1999); Robert Buzzanco, *Vietnam and the Transformation of American Life* (1999); Robert Buzzanco, *Masters of War: Military Dissent and Politics in the Vietnam Era* (1996); Larry Cable, *Unholy Grail* (1991); Mark Clodfelter, *The Limits of Power: The American Bombing of North Vietnam* (1989); Phillip B. Davidson, *Vietnam at War* (1988); Charles DeBenedetti and Charles Chatfield, *An American Ordeal: The Antiwar Movement of the Vietnam War* (1990); David L. DiLeo, *George Ball, Vietnam, and the Rethinking of Containment* (1991); Frances FitzGerald, *Fire in the Lake* (1972); Lloyd C. Gardner, *Pay Any Price* (1995); William C. Gibbons, *The U.S. Government and the Vietnam War* (1986–1994); Daniel C. Hallin, *The "Uncensored War"* (1986); George C. Herring, *LBJ and Vietnam* (1994); Michael H. Hunt, *Lyndon Johnson's War* (1996); Rhodri Jeffreys-Jones, *Peace Now!* (1999); Jeffrey Kimball, *Nixon's Vietnam War* (1998); Fredrik Logevall, *Choosing War* (1999); George McT. Kahin, *Intervention* (1986); Robert S. McNamara, James G. Blight, and Robert K. Brigham, *Argument Without End: In Search of Answers to the Vietnam Tragedy* (1999); Edwin E. Moïse, *Tonkin Gulf and the Escalation of the Vietnam War* (1996); William Prochnau, *Once upon a Distant War* (1995) (on journalists); William Shawcross, *Sideshow: Kissinger, Nixon, and the Destruction of Cambodia* (1979); Kevin Sim and Michael Bilton, *Four Hours in My Lai* (1992); Melvin Small, *Johnson, Nixon and the Doves* (1988); Ronald H. Spector, *After Tet: The Bloodiest Year in Vietnam* (1992); Ronald H. Spector, *United States Army in Vietnam* (1983); Brian VanDerMark, *Into the Quagmire* (1991).

Legacy and Lessons of the Vietnam War

Eric T. Dean, Jr., *Shook Over Hell: Post-Traumatic Stress, Vietnam, and the Civil War* (1998); John Hellman, *American Myth and the Legacy of Vietnam* (1986); Herbert Hendin and Ann P. Haas, *Wounds of War: The Psychological Aftermath of Combat in Vietnam* (1984); Ole R. Holsti and James Rosenau, *American Leadership in World Affairs: Vietnam and the Breakdown of Consensus* (1984); David Levy, *The Debate over Vietnam* (1991);

Myra MacPherson, *Long Time Passing* (1984); Norman Pod-horetz, *Why We Were in Vietnam* (1982); Earl C. Ravenal, *Never Again* (1978); Harrison E. Salisbury, ed., *Vietnam Reconsidered* (1984); Harry G. Summers, Jr., *On Strategy* (1982); Fred Turner, *Echoes of Combat: The Vietnam War in American Memory* (1996).

Nixon, Kissinger, and Détente

Stephen Ambrose, *Nixon*, 3 vols. (1987–1991); Michael B. Froman, *The Development of the Idea of Détente* (1992); Raymond L. Garthoff, *Détente and Confrontation* (1985); John R. Greene, *The Limits of Power* (1992); Seymour Hersh, *The Price of Power* (1983); Joan Hoff, *Nixon Reconsidered* (1994); Walter Isaacson, *Kissinger* (1992); Allen J. Matusow, *Nixon's Economy* (1998); Keith L. Nelson, *The Making of Détente* (1995); Herbert S. Parmet, *Richard Nixon and His America* (1990); Andrew J. Pierre, *The Global Politics of Arms Sales* (1982); Robert D. Schulzinger, *Henry Kissinger* (1989); Melvin Small, *The Presidency of Richard Nixon* (1999).

Carter Foreign Policy and Human Rights

Anne H. Cahn, *Killing Détente: The Right Attacks the CIA* (1998); Gary M. Fink and Hugh Davis Graham, eds., *The Carter Presidency* (1998); Erwin C. Hargrove, *Jimmy Carter as President* (1988); Charles O. Jones, *The Trusteeship Presidency* (1988); Burton I. Kaufman, *The Presidency of James Earl Carter, Jr.* (1993); David S. McLellan, *Cyrus Vance* (1985); Richard A. Melanson, *Reconstructing Consensus* (1990); A. Glenn Mower, Jr., *Human Rights and American Foreign Policy* (1987); John Newhouse, *Cold Dawn* (1973) (on SALT); Kenneth A. Oye et al., *Eagle Entangled* (1979); Herbert D. Rosenbaum and Alezej Ugrinsky, eds., *Jimmy Carter* (1994); Gaddis Smith, *Morality, Reason, and Power* (1986); Strobe Talbott, *Endgame: The Inside Story of SALT II* (1979); Sandy Vogelsang, *American Dream, Global Nightmare* (1980); Odd Arne Westad, ed., *The Fall of Détente* (1997).

Reagan's Foreign Policy and Military Buildup

Dana H. Allin, *Cold War Illusions* (1995); Michael R. Beschloss and Strobe Talbott, *At the Highest Levels* (1993); Archie Brown, *The Gorbachev Factor* (1996); Lou Cannon, *President Reagan* (1991); Theodore Draper, *A Very Thin Line: The Iran-Contra Affairs* (1991); John Ehrman, *The Rise of Neoconservatism* (1995); Beth A. Fischer, *The Reagan Reversal* (1997); Raymond L. Garthoff, *The Great Transition* (1994); Seymour Hersh, *"The Target Is Destroyed": What Really Happened to Flight 007 and What America Knew About It* (1986); Haynes Johnson, *Sleepwalking Through History* (1991); Robert G. Kaiser, *Why Gorbachev Happened* (1991); Peter Kornbluh and Malcolm Byrne, eds., *The Iran-Contra Scandal* (1993); Michael MccGwire, *Perestroika and Soviet National Security* (1991); Edmund Morris, *Dutch* (1999); Don Oberdorfer, *From the Cold War to a New Era* (1998); Kenneth A. Oye et al., eds., *Eagle Resurgent?* (1987); William E. Pember-ton, *Exit with Honor* (1997); Michael Schaller, *Reckoning with Reagan* (1992); Strobe Talbott, *The Master of the Game: Paul Nitze and the Nuclear Peace* (1988); Strobe Talbott, *Deadly Gambit* (1984); Daniel Wirls, *Buildup* (1992).

Latin America: General

Cole Blasier, *Hovering Giant* (1974); David W. Dent, ed., *U.S.–Latin American Policymaking* (1995); Guy Gugliotta and Jeff Leen, *Kings of Cocaine* (1989); Eldon Kenworthy, *America/Americas* (1995); Lester Langley, *America and the Americas* (1989); Abraham F. Lowenthal, ed., *Exporting Democracy* (1991); Abraham F. Lowenthal, *Partners in Conflict*, rev. ed. (1990); Donald J. Mabry, ed., *The Latin American Narcotics Trade and U.S. National Security* (1989); W. Dirk Raat, *Mexico and the United States*, 2d ed. (1997); Stephen G. Rabe, *The Most Dangerous Area in the World: John F. Kennedy Confronts Communist Revolution in Latin America* (1999); Stephen G. Rabe, *The Road to OPEC: United States Relations with Venezuela* (1982); William F. Sater, *Chile and the United States* (1990); Lars Schoultz, *Beneath the United States* (1998); Peter H. Smith, *Talons of the Eagle* (1996).

Central America and Panama

Cynthia J. Arnson, *Crossroads* (1989); Morris J. Blachman et al., eds., *Confronting Revolution* (1986); E. Bradford Burns, *At War in Nicaragua* (1987); John Coatsworth, *Central America and the United States* (1994); Kenneth M. Coleman and George C. Herring, eds., *Understanding the Central American Crisis* (1991); Michael L. Conniff, *Panama and the United States* (1992); Piero Gleijeses, Michael Klare and Peter Kornbluh, eds., *Low Intensity Warfare* (1988); Walter LaFeber, *Inevitable Revolutions*, 2d ed. (1993); Walter LaFeber, *The Panama Canal*, updated ed. (1989); William M. LeoGrande, *Our Own Backyard* (1998); John Major, *Prize Possession: The United States and the Panama Canal, 1903–1979* (1994); Robert A. Pastor, *Whirlpool: U.S. Foreign Policy Toward Latin America and the Caribbean* (1992); Robert A. Pastor, *Condemned to Repetition: The United States and Nicaragua* (1987); Peter Dale Scott and Jonathan Marshall, *Cocaine Politics* (1991); Christian Smith, *Resisting Reagan: The U.S.–Central America Peace Movement* (1996); Thomas W. Walker, ed., *Revolution and Counterrevolution in Nicaragua* (1991).

The Middle East and Iranian Hostage Crisis

James A. Bill, *The Eagle and the Lion: The Tragedy of American-Iranian Relations* (1988); William J. Burns and Richard W. Cottam, *Iran and the United States* (1988); Mark Gasiorowski, *U.S. Foreign Policy and the Shah* (1991); James E. Goode, *The United States and Iran* (1997); Burton I. Kaufman, *The Arab Middle East and the United States* (1996); William B. Quandt, *Peace Process* (1993); Cheryl A. Rubenberg, *Israel and the American National Interest* (1986); David Schoenbaum, *The United States and the State of Israel* (1993);

Gary Sick, *October Surprise: America's Hostages in Iran and the Election of Ronald Reagan* (1991); Steven L. Spiegel, *The Other Arab-Israeli Conflict* (1985); Robert W. Stookey, *America and the Arab States* (1975); Daniel Yergin, *The Prize: The Epic Quest for Oil, Money, and Power* (1991).

Africa

Pauline H. Baker, *The United States and South Africa: The Reagan Years* (1989); Christopher Coker, *The United States and South Africa, 1968–1985* (1986); David N. Gibbs, *The Political Economy of Third World Intervention : Mines, Money, and U.S. Policy in the Congo Crises* (1991); Richard D. Mahoney, *JFK: Ordeal in Africa* (1983); Robert K. Massie, *Loosing the Bonds: The United States and South Africa in the Apartheid Years* (1997); Thomas J. Noer, *Cold War and Black Liberation* (1985); Peter J. Schraeder, *United States Policy Toward Africa* (1994).

Asia

Walter LaFeber, *The Clash: A History of U.S.-Japan Relations* (1997); James Mann, *About Face: A History of America's Curious Relationship with China, From Nixon to Clinton* (1999); Robert McMahon, *The Limits of Empire: The United States and Southeast Asia Since World War II* (1999); Robert S. Ross, *Negotiating Cooperation: The United States and China, 1969–1989* (1995); Michael Schaller, *Altered States: The United States and Japan Since the Occupation* (1997); Nancy B. Tucker, *Taiwan, Hong Kong, and the United States* (1994). See above for Vietnam.

The World Economy and the Natural Environment

Richard J. Barnet, *The Lean Years* (1980); Richard J. Barnet and John Cavanaugh, *Global Dreams* (1994); Richard J. Barnet and Ronald Müller, *Global Reach* (1974); Richard E. Benedick, *Ozone Diplomacy* (1991); David P. Calleo, *The Imperious Economy* (1982); Alfred E. Eckes, *The United States and the Global Struggle for Minerals* (1979); David E. Fisher, *Fire & Ice: The Greenhouse Effect, Ozone Depletion, and Nuclear Winter* (1990); Edward M. Graham and Paul R. Krugman, *Foreign Direct Investment in the United States* (1989); Stephen D. Krasner, *Defending the National Interest* (1978); Diane B. Kunz, *Butter and Guns* (1997); John McCormick, *Reclaiming Paradise: The Global Environmental Movement* (1989); Joan E. Spero and Jeffrey A. Hart, *The Politics of International Economic Relations*, 5th ed. (1997); Herman Van Der Wee, *The Search for Prosperity: The World Economy, 1945–1980* (1986).

Chapter 32

Deficits, Deindustrialization, and Other Economic Woes

Barry Bluestone and Bennett Harrison, *The Deindustrialization of America* (1982); Richard Feldman and Michael Bet-

zold, *End of the Line: Autoworkers and the American Dream* (1988); Robert Heilbroner and Peter Bernstein, *The Debt and the Deficit* (1989); John P. Hoerr, *And the Wolf Finally Came: The Decline of the American Steel Industry* (1988); Gregory Pappas, *The Magic City: Unemployment in a Working-Class Community* (1989).

The Ford and Carter Administrations

Gary M. Fink and Hugh Davis Graham, eds., *The Carter Presidency* (1998); John Robert Greene, *The Presidency of Gerald R. Ford* (1995); Erwin C. Hargrove, *Jimmy Carter as President* (1989); Charles O. Jones, *The Trusteeship Presidency: Jimmy Carter and the United States Congress* (1988); Burton I. Kaufman, *The Presidency of James Earl Carter, Jr.* (1993).

Women and Children's Struggles

Marian Wright Edelman, *Families in Peril* (1987); Barbara Ehrenreich, *The Hearts of Men: American Dreams and the Flight from Commitment* (1983); David T. Ellwood, *Poor Support: Poverty in the American Family* (1988); Susan Faludi, *Backlash: The Undeclared War Against American Women* (1991); Sylvia Ann Hewlett, *When the Bough Breaks: The Cost of Neglecting Our Children* (1991); Arlie Russell Hochschild, *The Second Shift: Working Parents and the Revolution at Home* (1989); Rebecca E. Klatch, *Women of the New Right* (1987); Kristin Luker, *Abortion and the Politics of Motherhood* (1984); Winifred D. Wandersee, *On the Move: American Women in the 1970s* (1988).

People of Color and New Immigrants

Leslie W. Dunbar, ed., *Minority Report: What Has Happened to Blacks, Hispanics, American Indians, and Other Minorities in the Eighties* (1984); Reynolds Farley and Walter R. Allen, *The Color Line and the Quality of Life in America* (1987); Nancy Foner, ed., *New Immigrants in New York* (1987); Ronald P. Formisano, *Boston Against Busing* (1991); Joane Nagel, *American Indian Ethnic Revival: Red Power and the Resurgence of Identity and Culture* (1996); David M. Reimers, *Still the Golden Door: The Third World Comes to America* (1985); Paul Chaat Smith and Robert Allen Warrior, *Like a Hurricane: The Indian Movement from Alcatraz to Wounded Knee* (1996); Sanford J. Ungar, *Fresh Blood: The New Immigrants* (1995); William Julius Wilson, *The Truly Disadvantaged: The Inner City, the Underclass, and Public Policy* (1987).

The New Conservatism and the Election of 1980

William C. Berman, *America's Right Turn* (1994); Sara Diamond, *Not by Politics Alone: The Enduring Influence of the Christian Right* (1998); Thomas Byrne Edsall, *The New Politics of Inequality* (1984); Lee Edwards, *The Conservative Revolution* (1999); Jack W. Germond and Jules Witcover, *Blue Smoke and Mirrors: How Reagan Won and Why Carter Lost the Election of 1980* (1981); Godfrey Hodgson, *The World Turned*

Right Side Up: A History of the Conservative Ascendancy in America (1996).

Ronald Reagan and His Presidency

Lou Cannon, *President Reagan* (1991); Paul D. Erickson, *Reagan Speaks: The Making of an American Myth* (1985); Mark Hertsgaard, *On Bended Knee: The Press and the Reagan Presidency* (1988); Haynes Johnson, *Sleepwalking Through History: America in the Reagan Years* (1991); Nicholas Laham, *The Reagan Presidency and the Politics of Race* (1998); Jane Mayer and Doyle McManus, *Landslide: The Unmaking of the President, 1984–1988* (1988); William E. Pemberton, *Exit with Honor: The Life and Presidency of Ronald Reagan* (1997); John W. Sloan, *The Reagan Effect: Economics and Presidential Leadership* (1999); Garry Wills, *Reagan's America* (1987).

"Reaganomics"

Joan Claybrook, *Retreat from Safety: Reagan's Attack on America's Health* (1984); Benjamin Friedman, *Day of Reckoning: The Consequences of American Economic Policy Under Reagan and After* (1988); Jonathan Lash, *A Season of Spoils: The Story of the Reagan Administration's Attack on the Environment* (1984); Robert Lekachman, *Greed Is Not Enough: Reaganomics* (1982); William A. Niskanen, *Reaganomics* (1988); Charles Noble, *Liberalism at Work: The Rise and Fall of OSHA* (1986); Kevin Phillips, *The Politics of Rich and Poor* (1990); Kitty Calavita et al., *Big Money Crime: Fraud and Politics in the Savings and Loan Crisis* (1997).

A Polarized Society in the 1980s

Chandler Davidson, *Race and Class in Texas Politics* (1990); Michael Harrington, *The New American Poverty* (1984); Katherine S. Newman, *Declining Fortunes: The Withering of the American Dream* (1993); Randy Shilts, *And the Band Played On: Politics, People and the AIDS Epidemic* (1987); Studs Terkel, *The Great Divide* (1988); Edward N. Wolff, *Top Heavy: A Study of Increasing Inequality in America* (1995).

Presidential Politics: The Elections of 1984 and 1988

Sidney Blumenthal, *Pledging Allegiance: The Last Campaign of the Cold War* (1990); Richard Ben Cramer, *What It Takes* (1992); Thomas Byrne Edsall and Mary D. Edsall, *Chain Reaction: The Impact of Race, Rights, and Taxes on American Politics* (1991); Thomas Ferguson and Joel Rogers, *Right Turn: The Decline of the Democrats and the Future of American Politics* (1986); Marshall Frady, *Jesse: The Life and Pilgrimage of Jesse Jackson* (1996); Jack W. Germond and Jules Witcover, *Wake Us When It's Over: Presidential Politics of 1984* (1985); Peter Goldman and Tom Mathews, *The Quest for the Presidency: The 1988 Campaign* (1989).

Chapter 33

The Bush Administration

Donald L. Bartlett and James B. Steele, *America: What Went Wrong?* (1992); Michael Duffy and Don Goodgame, *Marching in Place: The Status Quo Presidency of George Bush* (1992); John Robert Greene, *The Presidency of George Bush* (2000); Dilys M. Hill and Phil Williams, eds., *The Bush Presidency* (1994); Herbert S. Parmet, *George Bush: The Life of a Lone Star Yankee* (1998).

Politics and the Election of 1992

Alan Ehrenhalt, *The United States of Ambition: Politicians, Power, and the Pursuit of Office* (1991); William Greider, *Who Will Tell the People: The Betrayal of American Democracy* (1992); Kathleen Hall Jamieson, *Dirty Politics* (1992); Kevin Phillips, *The Politics of Rich and Poor* (1990); Gerald Posner, *Citizen Perot* (1996); Ruy A. Teixeira, *The Disappearing American Voter* (1992); George F. Will, *Restoration: Congress, Term Limits and the Recovery of Deliberative Democracy* (1992).

American Society in the 1990s

Sheldon Danziger and Peter Gottschalk, *American Unequal* (1996); Robert H. Frank and Philip J. Cook, *The Winner-Take-All Society* (1995); Herbert J. Gans, *The War Against the Poor* (1995); Barry Glassner, *The Culture of Fear* (1999); David M. Gordon, *Fat and Mean: The Corporate Squeeze of Working Americans and the Myth of Managerial "Downsizing"* (1996); Jennifer L. Hochschild, *Facing Up to the American Dream: Race, Class, and the Soul of the Nation* (1995); Katherine S. Newman, *Declining Fortunes: The Withering of the American Dream* (1993); Robert J. Samuelson, *The Good Life and Its Discontents: The American Dream in an Age of Entitlements* (1995); Michael D. Yates, *Longer Hours, Fewer Jobs* (1994).

Disgruntled Americans: Political Apathy, Antigovernment Movements, and Culture Wars

Stephen Ansolabehere and Shanto Iyengar, *Going Negative: How Attack Ads Shrink and Polarize the Electorate* (1995); Sara Diamond, *Not by Politics Alone: The Enduring Influence of the Christian Right* (1998); E. J. Dionne, Jr., *Why Americans Hate Politics* (1991); James Fallows, *Breaking the News: How the Media Undermine American Democracy* (1996); Thomas Ferguson, *Golden Rule: The Investment Theory of Party Competition and the Logic of Money-Driven Political Systems* (1995); William Martin, *With God on Our Side: The Rise of the Religious Right in America* (1996); Larry J. Sabato and Glenn R. Simpson, *Dirty Little Secrets: The Persistence of Corruption in American Politics* (1996); Neil J. Smelser and Jeffrey C. Alexander, eds., *Diversity and Its Discontents: Cultural Conflict and Common Ground in Contemporary American Society* (1999);

Kenneth S. Stern, *A Force upon the Plain: The American Militia Movement and the Politics of Hate* (1996).

The Election of 1994: The "Republican Revolution"

Dan Balz and Ronald Brownstein, *Storming the Gates: Protest Politics and the Republican Revival* (1996); Elizabeth Drew, *Showdown: The Struggle Between the Gingrich Congress and the Clinton White House* (1996); David Frum, *Dead Right* (1994); Linda Killian, *The Freshmen: What Happened to the Republican Revolution?* (1998); David Maraniss and Michael Weisskopf, *"Tell Newt to Shut Up!"* (1996).

The 1996 Election and the Future of American Politics

E. J. Dionne, Jr., *They Only Look Dead: Why Progressives Will Dominate the Next Political Era* (1996); Martin Plissner, *The Control Room: How Television Calls the Shots in Presidential Elections* (1999); Jake H. Thompson, *Bob Dole* (1994); Ben J. Wattenberg, *Values Matter Most: How Republicans or Democrats or a Third Party Can Win and Renew the American Way of Life* (1995); Jacob Weisberg, *In Defense of Government: The Fall and Rise of Public Trust* (1996); Bob Woodward, *The Choice* (1996).

Clinton's Presidency, Impeachment, and Survival

Alan M. Dershowitz, *Sexual McCarthyism: Clinton, Starr and the Emerging Constitutional Crisis* (1998); Michael Isikoff, *Uncovering Clinton: A Reporter's Story* (1999); David Maraniss, *First in His Class: A Biography of Bill Clinton* (1995); Roger Morris, *Partners in Power: The Clintons and Their America* (1996); Richard A. Posner, *Affair of State: The Investigation, Impeachment, and Trial of President Clinton* (1999); Richard Reeves, *Running in Place: How Bill Clinton Disappointed America* (1996); Gail Sheehy, *Hillary's Choice* (1999); James B. Stewart, *Blood Sport: The President and His Adversaries* (1996); Jeffrey Toobin, *A Vast Conspiracy: The Real Story of the Sex Scandal That Nearly Brought Down a President* (2000); Bob Woodward, *The Agenda: Inside the Clinton White House* (1994).

The Foreign Policies and Wars of Bush and Clinton

See some works listed under Chapter 31 and Deborah Amos, *Lines in the Sand: Desert Storm and the Remaking of the Arab World* (1992); Michael R. Beschloss and Strobe Talbott, *At the Highest Levels: The Inside Story of the End of the Cold War* (1993); Douglas Brinkley, *The Unfinished Presidency: Jimmy Carter's Journey Beyond the White House* (1998); Archie Brown, *The Gorbachev Factor* (1996); Kevin Buckley, *Panama* (1991); John Coatsworth, *Central America and the United States* (1994); Michael Conniff, *Panama and the United States* (1992); Timothy J. Dunn, *The Militarization of the U.S.-Mexico Border* (1996); Lawrence Freedman and Efraim Karsh, *The Gulf Conflict, 1990–1991* (1993); John Lewis Gaddis, *The United States and the End of the Cold War* (1992); Raymond L. Garthoff, *The Great Transition* (1994); Stephen Graubard, *Mr. Bush's War* (1992); Avigdor Haselkorn, *The Continuing Storm: Iraq, Poisonous Weapons, and Deterrence* (1999); John L. Hirsch and Robert B. Oakley, *Somalia and Operation Restore Hope* (1995); Stanley Hoffmann, *World Disorders* (1999); Michael Hogan, ed., *The End of the Cold War* (1992); William G. Hyland, *Clinton's World* (1999); Burton I. Kaufman, *The Arab Middle East and the United States* (1996); Walter LaFeber, *The Clash: A History of U.S.-Japan Relations* (1997); Robert J. Lieber, ed., *Eagle Adrift* (1997); Robert K. Massie, *Loosing the Bonds: The United States and South Africa in the Apartheid Years* (1998); James Mayall, ed., *The New Interventionism* (1996); Larry Minear and Thomas G. Weiss, *Humanitarian Politics* (1995); John Mueller, *Policy and Opinion in the Gulf War* (1994); Don Oberdorfer, *From the Cold War to the New Era* (1998); Kenneth A. Oye et al., eds., *Eagle in a New World* (1992); W. Dirk Raat, *Mexico and the United States*, 2d ed. (1997); Jeffrey T. Richelson, *The U.S. Intelligence Community*, 4th ed. (1999); Jean Edward Smith, *George Bush's War* (1992); Peter H. Smith, *Talons of the Eagle* (1996) (on U.S.-Latin America); Stephen R. Weissman, *A Culture of Deference: Congress's Failure of Leadership in Foreign Policy* (1995); Susan Woodward, *Balkan Tragedy* (1995).

Global Economic and Cultural Issues

Richard J. Barnet and John Cavangh, *Global Dreams: Imperial Corporations and the New World Order* (1994); Ronald J. Bee, *Nuclear Proliferation* (1995); Thomas L. Friedman, *The Lexus and the Olive Tree* (1999) (on globalization); Laurie Garrett, *Microbes Versus Mankind: The Coming Plague* (1997); George W. Grayson, *The North American Free Trade Agreement* (1995); Frank Ninkovich, *Information Policy and Cultural Diplomacy* (1996); Richard Pells, *Not Like Us: How Europeans Have Loved, Hated, and Transformed American Culture Since World War II* (1997); Peter Dale Scott and Jonathan Marshall, *Cocaine Politics* (1991); Robert Soloman, *Money on the Move: The Revolution in International Finance Since 1980* (1999); Paul B. Stares, *Global Habit: The Drug Problem in a Borderless World* (1996); Jessica Stern, *The Ultimate Terrorists* (1999); James L. Watson, ed., *Golden Arches East: McDonald's in East Asia* (1997).

Historical Reference Books by Subject:
Encyclopedias, Dictionaries, Atlases, Chronologies, and Statistics

American History: General

Gorton Carruth, ed., *The Encyclopedia of American Facts and Dates* (1993); *Dictionary of American History* (1976) and Joan Hoff and Robert H. Ferrell, eds., *Supplement* (1996); John M. Farragher, ed., *The American Heritage Encyclopedia of American History* (1998); Eric Foner and John A. Garraty, eds., *The Reader's Companion to American History* (1991); Bernard Grun, *The Timetables of History* (1991); *International Encyclopedia of the Social Sciences* (1968–); Richard B. Morris and Jeffrey B. Morris, eds., *Encyclopedia of American History* (1996); Harry Ritter, *Dictionary of Concepts in History* (1986); Lawrence Urdang, ed., *The Timetables of American History* (1996); U.S. Bureau of the Census, *Historical Statistics of the United States* (1975).

American History: General, Twentieth Century

John D. Buenker and Edward R. Kantowicz, eds., *Historical Dictionary of the Progressive Era, 1890–1920* (1988); Robert H. Ferrell and John S. Bowman, eds., *The Twentieth Century: An Almanac* (1984); George H. Gallup, *The Gallup Poll: Public Opinion, 1935–1971* (1972), *1972–1977* (1978), and annual reports (1979–); Stanley Hochman, *The Penguin Dictionary of Contemporary American History* (1997); Stanley I. Kutler, ed., *Encyclopedia of the United States in the Twentieth Century* (1995); Peter B. Levy, *Encyclopedia of the Reagan-Bush Years* (1996); James S. Olson, *Historical Dictionary of the 1920s* (1988); Thomas Parker and Douglas Nelson, *Day by Day: The Sixties* (1983).

American History: General Atlases and Gazetteers

Geoffrey Barraclough, ed., *The Times Atlas of World History* (1994); Rodger Doyle, *Atlas of Contemporary America* (1994); Robert H. Ferrell and Richard Natkiel, *Atlas of American History* (1987); Edward W. Fox, *Atlas of American History* (1964); Archie Hobson, *The Cambridge Gazetteer of the United States and Canada* (1996); Eric Homberger, *The Penguin Historical Atlas of North America* (1995); Kenneth T. Jackson and James T. Adams, *Atlas of American History*

(1978); National Geographic Society, *Historical Atlas of the United States* (1994); U.S. Department of the Interior, *National Atlas of the United States* (1970). Other atlases are listed under specific categories.

American History: General Biographies

Lucian Boia, ed., *Great Historians of the Modern Age* (1991); John S. Bowman, *The Cambridge Dictionary of American Biography* (1995); *Current Biography* (1940–); *Dictionary of American Biography* (1928–); John A. Garraty and Mark C. Carnes, eds., *American National Biography* (1999); John Garraty and Jerome L. Sternstein, eds., *The Encyclopedia of American Biography* (1996); *National Cyclopedia of American Biography* (1898–). Other biographical works appear under specific categories.

African Americans

Molefi Asante and Mark T. Mattson, *Historical and Cultural Atlas of African-Americans* (1991); John N. Ingham, *African-American Business Leaders* (1993); Rayford W. Logan and Michael R. Winston, eds., *The Dictionary of American Negro Biography* (1983); Sharon Harley, *The Timetables of African-American History* (1995); Darlene C. Hine et al., eds., *Black Women in White America* (1994); Charles D. Lowery and John F. Marszalek, eds., *Encyclopedia of African-American Civil Rights* (1992); Larry G. Murphy et al., eds., *Encyclopedia of African American Religions* (1993); Jack Salzman et al., eds., *Encyclopedia of African-American Culture and History* (1996); Jessie Carney Smith, ed., *Notable Black American Women* (1992). See also "Slavery."

American Revolution and Colonies

Richard Blanco and Paul Sanborn, eds., *The American Revolution* (1993); Lester J. Cappon, ed., *Atlas of Early American History: The Revolutionary Era, 1760–1790* (1976); Jacob E. Cooke, ed., *Encyclopedia of the American Colonies* (1993); John M. Faragher, ed., *The Encyclopedia of Colonial and Revolutionary America* (1990); Jack P. Greene and J. R. Pole, eds., *The*

Blackwell Encyclopedia of the American Revolution (1991); Douglas W. Marshall and Howard H. Peckham, *Campaigns of the American Revolution* (1976); Gregory Palmer, ed., *Biographical Sketches of Loyalists of the American Revolution* (1984); John W. Raimo, ed., *Biographical Directory of American Colonial and Revolutionary Governors, 1607–1789* (1980); *Rand-McNally Atlas of the American Revolution* (1974); Seymour I. Schwartz, *The French and Indian War, 1754–1763* (1995).

Architecture

William D. Hunt, Jr., ed., *Encyclopedia of American Architecture* (1980).

Asian Americans

Hyung-Chan Kim, ed., *Dictionary of Asian American History* (1986); Brian Niiya, ed., *Japanese American History* (1993); Lynn Pan, ed., *The Encyclopedia of the Chinese Overseas* (1999). See also "Immigration and Ethnic Groups."

Business and the Economy

Christine Ammer and Dean S. Ammer, *Dictionary of Business and Economics* (1983); Douglas Auld and Graham Bannock, *The American Dictionary of Economics* (1983); Michael J. Freeman, *Atlas of World Economy* (1991); John N. Ingham, *Biographical Dictionary of American Business Leaders* (1983); John N. Ingham and Lynne B. Feldman, *Contemporary American Business Leaders* (1990); William H. Mulligan, Jr., ed., *A Historical Dictionary of American Industrial Language* (1988); Glenn G. Munn, *Encyclopedia of Banking and Finance* (1973); Paul Paskoff, ed., *Encyclopedia of American Business History and Biography* (1989); Glenn Porter, *Encyclopedia of American Economic History* (1980); Richard Robinson, *United States Business History, 1602–1988* (1990); Malcolm Warner, ed., *International Encyclopedia of Business and Management* (1996). See also "African Americans," "Native Americans and Indian Affairs," and "Transportation."

Cities and Towns

John L. Androit, ed., *Township Atlas of the United States* (1979); David J. Bodenhamer and Robert J. Barrows, eds., *The Encyclopedia of Indianapolis* (1994); Gary A. Goreham, ed., *Encyclopedia of Rural America* (1997); Melvin G. Holli and Peter d'A. Jones, eds., *Biographical Dictionary of American Mayors, 1820–1980: Big City Mayors* (1981); Kenneth T. Jackson, ed., *Encyclopedia of New York City* (1995); George T. Kurian, *World Encyclopedia of Cities* (1994); Ory M. Nergal, ed., *The Encyclopedia of American Cities* (1980); Neil Larry Shumsky, ed., *Encyclopedia of Urban America* (1998); David D. Van Tassel and John J. Grabowski, eds., *The Dictionary of Cleveland Biography* (1996); David D. Van Tassel and John J. Grabowski, eds., *The Encyclopedia of Cleveland History* (1987). See also "Politics and Government."

Civil War and Reconstruction

Mark M. Boatner III, *The Civil War Dictionary* (1988); Richard N. Current, ed., *Encyclopedia of the Confederacy* (1993); John T. Hubbell and James W. Geary, eds., *Biographical Dictionary of the Union* (1995); Kenneth C. Martis, *The Historical Atlas of the Congresses of the Confederate States of America: 1861–1865* (1994); James M. McPherson, ed., *The Atlas of the Civil War* (1994); Mark E. Neely, Jr., *The Abraham Lincoln Encyclopedia* (1982); Craig L. Symonds, *A Battlefield Atlas of the Civil War* (1983); Hans L. Trefousse, *Historical Dictionary of Reconstruction* (1991); U.S. War Department, *The Official Atlas of the Civil War* (1958); Jon L. Wakelyn, ed., *Biographical Dictionary of the Confederacy* (1977); Ezra J. Warner and W. Buck Yearns, *Biographical Register of the Confederate Congress* (1975); Steven E. Woodworth, ed., *The American Civil War* (1996). See also "South" and "Politics and Government."

The Cold War

Thomas S. Arms, *Encyclopedia of the Cold War* (1994); Michael Kort, *The Columbia Guide to the Cold War* (1998); Richard A. Schwartz, *Cold War Culture: The Media and the Arts* (1998). See also "Foreign Relations" and "Military and Wars."

Constitution, Supreme Court, and Judiciary

David Bradley and Shelly F. Fishkin, eds., *The Encyclopedia of Civil Rights* (1997); Congressional Quarterly, *The Supreme Court A to Z* (1994); Kermit L. Hall, ed., *The Oxford Companion to the Supreme Court of the United States* (1992); Kermit L. Hall, ed., *The Oxford Guide to United States Supreme Court Decisions* (1999); Richard F. Hixson, *Mass Media and the Constitution* (1989); Robert J. Janosik, ed., *Encyclopedia of the American Judicial System* (1987); John W. Johnson, ed., *Historic U.S. Court Cases, 1690–1990* (1992); Leonard W. Levy et al., eds., *Encyclopedia of the American Constitution* (1986); Fred R. Shapiro, *The Oxford Dictionary of American Legal Quotations* (1993); Melvin I. Urofsky, ed., *The Supreme Court Justices* (1994). See also "Politics and Government" and "Sexuality."

Crime, Violence, Police, and Prisons

William G. Bailey, *Encyclopedia of Police Science* (1994); Sanford H. Kadish, ed., *Encyclopedia of Crime and Justice* (1983); Marilyn D. McShane and Frank P. Williams III, eds., *Encyclopedia of American Prisons* (1995); Michael Newton and Judy Ann Newton, *Racial and Religious Violence in America* (1991); Michael Newton and Judy Newton, *The Ku Klux Klan* (1990); Carl Sifakis, *Encyclopedia of Assassinations* (1990); Carl Sifakis, *The Encyclopedia of American Crime* (1982).

Culture and Folklore

Hennig Cohen and Tristam Potter Coffin, eds., *The Folklore of American Holidays* (1987); Richard M. Dorson, ed., *Handbook of American Folklore* (1983); Robert L. Gale, *A Cultural Encyclopedia of the 1850s in America* (1993); Robert L. Gale, *The Gay Nineties in America* (1992); M. Thomas Inge, ed., *Handbook of American Popular Culture* (1979–1981); Wolfgang Mieder et al., eds., *A Dictionary of American Proverbs* (1992); J. F. Rooney, Jr., et al., eds., *This Remarkable Continent: An Atlas of United States and Canadian Society and Cultures* (1982); Jane Stern and Michael Stern, *Encyclopedia of Pop Culture* (1992); Justin Wintle, ed., *Makers of Nineteenth Century Culture, 1800–1914* (1982). See also "The Cold War," "Entertainment and the Arts," "Mass Media and Journalism," "Music," and "Sports."

Education and Libraries

Lee C. Deighton, ed., *The Encyclopedia of Education* (1971); Joseph C. Kiger, ed., *Research Institutions and Learned Societies* (1982); John F. Ohles, ed., *Biographical Dictionary of American Educators* (1978); Wayne A. Wiegard and Donald E. Davis, Jr., eds., *Encyclopedia of Library History* (1994).

Entertainment and the Arts

Tim Brooks and Earle Marsh, *The Complete Directory to Prime Time Network and Cable TV Shows, 1946–Present* (1995); Barbara N. Cohen-Stratyner, *Biographical Dictionary of Dance* (1982); John Dunning, *Tune in Yesterday* (radio) (1967); Larry Langman and Edgar Borg, *Encyclopedia of American War Films* (1989); Larry Langman and David Ebner, *Encyclopedia of American Spy Films* (1990); *Notable Names in the American Theater* (1976); Andrew Sarris, *The American Cinema: Directors and Directions, 1929–1968* (1968); Anthony Slide, *The American Film Industry* (1986); Anthony Slide, *The Encyclopedia of Vaudeville* (1994); Evelyn M. Truitt, *Who Was Who on Screen* (1977); Don B. Wilmeth and Tice L. Miller, eds., *The Cambridge Guide to American Theatre* (1993). See also "The Cold War," "Culture and Folklore," "Mass Media and Journalism," "Music," and "Sports."

Environment and Conservation

André R. Cooper, ed., *Cooper's Comprehensive Environmental Desk Reference* (1996); Forest History Society, *Encyclopedia of American Forest and Conservation History* (1983); Irene Franck and David Brownstone, *The Green Encyclopedia* (1992); Robert J. Mason and Mark T. Mattson, *Atlas of United States Environmental Issues* (1990); Robert Paehlke, ed., *Conservation and Environmentalism* (1995); World Resources Institute, *Environmental Almanac* (1992).

Exploration: From Columbus to Space

Silvio A. Bedini, ed., *The Christopher Columbus Encyclopedia* (1992); Michael Cassutt, *Who's Who in Space* (1987); W. P. Cumming et al., *The Discovery of North America* (1972); William Goetzmann and Glyndwr Williams, *The Atlas of North American Exploration* (1992); Clive Holland, *Arctic Exploration and Development* (1993); Adrian Johnson, *America Explored* (1974); Kenneth Nebenzahl, *Atlas of Columbus and the Great Discoveries* (1990). See also "Science and Technology."

Foreign Relations

Gerard Chaliand and Jean-Pierre Rageau, *Strategic Atlas* (1990); Alexander DeConde, ed., *Encyclopedia of American Foreign Policy* (1978); Margaret B. Denning and J. K. Sweeney, *Handbook of American Diplomacy* (1992); Graham Evans and Jeffrey Newnham, eds., *The Dictionary of World Politics* (1990); John E. Findling, *Dictionary of American Diplomatic History* (1989); Chas. W. Freeman, Jr., *The Diplomat's Dictionary* (1997); Michael Kidron and Ronald Segal, *The State of the World Atlas* (1995); Bruce W. Jentleson and Thomas G. Paterson, eds., *Encyclopedia of U.S. Foreign Relations* (1997); Warren F. Kuehl, ed., *Biographical Dictionary of Internationalists* (1983); Edward Lawson, *Encyclopedia of Human Rights* (1991); Jack C. Plano and Roy Olton, eds., *The International Relations Dictionary* (1988). See also "The Cold War," "Peace Movements and Pacifism," "Politics and Government," "Military and Wars," and specific wars.

Hispanics

Nicolás Kanellos, ed., *The Hispanic-American Almanac* (1993); Nicolás Kanellos, ed., *Reference Library of Hispanic America* (1993); Francisco Lomelí, ed., *Handbook of Hispanic Cultures in the United States* (1993); Matt S. Meier, *Mexican-American Biographies* (1988); Matt S. Meier, *Notable Latino Americans* (1997); Matt S. Meier and Feliciano Rivera, *Dictionary of Mexican American History* (1981); Joseph C. Tardiff and L. Mpho Mabunda, eds., *Dictionary of Hispanic Biography* (1996). See also "Immigration and Ethnic Groups."

Immigration and Ethnic Groups

James P. Allen and Eugene J. Turner, *We the People: An Atlas of America's Ethnic Diversity* (1988); Gerald Chaliand and Jean-Pierre Rageau, *The Penguin Atlas of Diasporas* (1995); Francesco Cordasco, ed., *Dictionary of American Immigration History* (1990); David Levinson and Melvin Ember, eds., *American Immigrant Cultures* (1997); Judy B. Litoff and Judith McDonnell, eds., *European Immigrant Women in the United States* (1994); Sally M. Miller, ed., *The Ethnic Press in the United States* (1987); Stephan Thernstrom, ed., *Harvard Encyclopedia of American Ethnic Groups* (1980); Rudolph J. Vecoli et al., eds., *Gale Encyclopedia of Multicultural America* (1995). See also "Asian Americans," "Jewish Americans," and "Hispanics."

Jewish Americans

American Jewish Yearbook (1899–); Jack Fischel and Sanford Pinsker, eds., *Jewish-American History and Culture* (1992); Geoffrey Wigoder, *Dictionary of Jewish Biography* (1991). See also "Immigration and Ethnic Groups."

Labor

Ronald L. Filippelli, *Labor Conflict in the United States* (1990); Gary M. Fink, ed., *Biographical Dictionary of American Labor* (1984); Gary M. Fink, ed., *Labor Unions* (1977); Philip S. Foner, *First Facts of American Labor* (1984).

Literature

James T. Callow and Robert J. Reilly, *Guide to American Literature* (1976–1977); *Dictionary of Literary Biography* (1978–); Eugene Ehrlich and Gorton Carruth, *The Oxford Illustrated Literary Guide to the United States* (1982); Jon Tuska and Vicki Piekarski, *Encyclopedia of Frontier and Western Fiction* (1983). See also "Culture and Folklore," "The South," and "Women."

Mass Media and Journalism

Robert V. Hudson, *Mass Media* (1987); Joseph P. McKerns, ed., *Biographical Dictionary of American Journalism* (1989); William H. Taft, ed., *Encyclopedia of Twentieth-Century Journalists* (1986). See also "The Cold War," "Constitution, Supreme Court, and Judiciary," "Entertainment and the Arts," and "Immigration and Ethnic Groups."

Medicine and Nursing

Rima D. Apple, ed., *Women, Health, and Medicine in America* (1990); Vern L. Bullough et al., eds., *American Nursing: A Biographical Dictionary* (1988); Martin Kaufman et al., eds., *Dictionary of American Nursing Biography* (1988); Martin Kaufman et al., eds., *Dictionary of American Medical Biography* (1984); George L. Maddox, ed., *The Encyclopedia of Aging* (1995).

Military and Wars

William M. Arkin et al., *Encyclopedia of the U.S. Military* (1990); Charles D. Bright, ed., *Historical Dictionary of the U.S. Air Force* (1992); John W. Chambers, ed., *Oxford Companion to United States Military History* (2000); Andre Corvisier, ed., *A Dictionary of Military History* (1994); R. Ernest Dupuy and Trevor N. Dupuy, *The Harper Encyclopedia of Military History* (1993); David S. Frazier, ed., *The United States and Mexico at War* (1998); John E. Jessup, ed., *Encyclopedia of the American Military* (1994); Kenneth Macksey and William Woodhouse, *The Penguin Encyclopedia of Modern Warfare* (1992); Franklin D. Margiotta, ed., *Brassey's Encyclopedia of Naval Forces and Warfare* (1996); David F. Marley, *Pirates and Privateers of the Americas* (1994); James I. Matray,

ed., *Historical Dictionary of the Korean War* (1991); Stanley Sandler, ed., *The Korean War* (1995); Roger J. Spiller and Joseph G. Dawson III, eds., *Dictionary of American Military Biography* (1984); Jerry K. Sweeney, ed., *A Handbook of American Military History* (1996); Peter G. Tsouras et al., *The United States Army* (1991); U.S. Military Academy, *The West Point Atlas of American Wars, 1689–1953* (1959); Bruce W. Watson et al., eds., *United States Intelligence* (1990); Bruce W. Watson and Susan M. Watson, *The United States Air Force* (1992); Bruce W. Watson and Susan M. Watson, *The United States Navy* (1991). See also "American Revolution and Colonies," "Civil War and Reconstruction," "The Cold War," "Vietnam War," and "World War II."

Music

John Chilton, *Who's Who of Jazz* (1972); Donald Clarke et al., eds., *The Penguin Encyclopedia of Popular Music* (1999); Edward Jablonski, *The Encyclopedia of American Music* (1981); Roger Lax and Frederick Smith, *The Great Song Thesaurus* (1984); Philip D. Morehead, *The New International Dictionary of Music* (1993); Austin Sonnier, Jr., *A Guide to the Blues* (1994). See also "Culture and Folklore" and "Entertainment and the Arts."

Native Americans and Indian Affairs

Gretchen M. Bataille, ed., *Native American Women* (1992); Michael Coe et al., *Atlas of Ancient America* (1986); Mary B. Davis, ed., *Native America in the Twentieth Century* (1994); Rayna Green, *The British Museum Encyclopedia of Native North America* (1999); *Handbook of North American Indians* (1978–); Sam D. Gill and Irene F. Sullivan, *Dictionary of Native American Mythology* (1992); J. Norman Heard et al., *Handbook of the American Frontier: Four Centuries of Indian–White Relationships* (1987–); Bruce E. Johansen, ed., *The Encyclopedia of Native American Economic History* (1999); Bruce E. Johansen, ed., *The Encyclopedia of Native American Legal Tradition* (1998); Bruce E. Johansen et al., eds., *The Encyclopedia of Native American Biography* (1997); Barry Klein, ed., *Reference Encyclopedia of the American Indian* (1993); Barry M. Plitzker, *Native Americans* (1998); Francis P. Prucha, *Atlas of American Indian Affairs* (1990); Paul Stuart, *Nation Within a Nation: Historical Statistics of American Indians* (1987); Helen H. Tanner, ed., *Atlas of Great Lakes Indian History* (1987); Carl Waldman, *Encyclopedia of Native American Tribes* (1988); Carl Waldman, *Atlas of the North American Indian* (1985).

The New Deal and Franklin D. Roosevelt

Otis L. Graham, Jr., and Meghan R. Wander, eds., *Franklin D. Roosevelt: His Life and Times* (1985); James S. Olson, ed., *Historical Dictionary of the New Deal* (1985). See also "Politics and Government."

Peace Movements and Pacifism

Harold Josephson et al., eds., *Biographical Dictionary of Modern Peace Leaders* (1985); Ervin Laszlo and Jong Y. Yoo, eds., *World Encyclopedia of Peace* (1986); Robert S. Meyer, *Peace Organizations Past and Present* (1988); Nancy L. Roberts, *American Peace Writers, Editors, and Periodicals* (1991). See also "Foreign Relations," "Military and Wars," and specific wars.

Politics and Government: General

Erik W. Austin and Jerome M. Clubb, *Political Facts of the United States Since 1789* (1986); *The Columbia Dictionary of Political Biography* (1991); Jack P. Greene, ed., *Encyclopedia of American Political History* (1984); Leon Hurwitz, *Historical Dictionary of Censorship in the United States* (1985); George T. Kurian, ed., *A Historical Guide to the U.S. Government* (1998); Philip Rees, *Biographical Dictionary of the Extreme Right Since 1890* (1991); Charles R. Ritter et al., *American Legislative Leaders, 1850–1910* (1989); William Safire, *Safire's Political Dictionary* (1993); Robert Scruton, *A Dictionary of Political Thought* (1982); Jay M. Shafritz, *The HarperCollins Dictionary of American Government and Politics* (1992). See also "Cities and Towns," "Constitution, Supreme Court, and Judiciary," "States," and the following sections.

Politics and Government: Congress

American Enterprise Institute, *Vital Statistics on Congress* (1980–); Donald C. Brown et al., eds., *The Encyclopedia of the United States Congress* (1995); Stephen G. Christianson, *Facts About the Congress* (1996); Congressional Quarterly, *Biographical Directory of the American Congress, 1774–1996* (1997); Congressional Quarterly, *Congress and the Nation* (1965–); Kenneth C. Martis, *Historical Atlas of Political Parties in the United States Congress, 1789–1989* (1989); Kenneth C. Martis, *Historical Atlas of United States Congressional Districts, 1789–1983* (1982); Joel H. Silbey, ed., *Encyclopedia of the American Legislative System* (1994).

Politics and Government: Election Statistics

Congressional Quarterly, *Guide to U.S. Elections* (1994); Congressional Quarterly, *Presidential Elections, 1789–1996* (1997); L. Sandy Maisel, ed., *Political Parties and Elections in the United States* (1991); Svend Petersen and Louis Filler, *A Statistical History of the American Presidential Elections* (1981); Richard M. Scammon et al., eds., *America Votes* (1956–); Harold W. Stanley and Richard G. Niemi, *Vital Statistics on American Politics* (1988–); Lyn Ragsdale, *Vital Statistics on the Presidency* (1998); G. Scott Thomas, *The Pursuit of the White House* (1987).

Politics and Government: Parties

Earl R. Kruschke, *Encyclopedia of Third Parties in the United States* (1991); George T. Kurian, ed., *The Encyclopedia of the Republican Party* and *The Encyclopedia of the Democratic Party* (1996); Edward L. Schapsmeier and Frederick H. Schapsmeier, eds., *Political Parties and Civic Action Groups* (1981). See also other listings for "Politics and Government."

Politics and Government: Presidency and Executive Branch

Alan Brinkley and Davis Dyer, eds., *The Reader's Companion to the Presidency* (2000); Henry F. Graff, *The Presidents* (1996); Bernard S. Katz and C. Daniel Vencill, eds., *Biographical Dictionary of the United States Secretaries of the Treasury, 1789–1995* (1996); Richard S. Kirkendall, ed., *The Harry S Truman Encyclopedia* (1989); Leonard W. Levy and Louis Fisher, eds., *Encyclopedia of the American Presidency* (1993); Merrill D. Peterson, ed., *Thomas Jefferson* (1986); Lyn Ragsdale, *Vital Statistics on the Presidency* (1998); Robert A. Rutland, ed., *James Madison and the American Nation* (1995); Robert Sobel, ed., *Biographical Directory of the United States Executive Branch, 1774–1977* (1977). See other categories for various presidents.

Politics and Government: Radicalism and the Left

Mari Jo Buhle et al., eds., *The American Radical* (1994); Mari Jo Buhle et al., eds., *Encyclopedia of the American Left* (1998); David DeLeon, ed., *Leaders of the 1960s* (1994); Bernard K. Johnpoll and Harvey Klehr, eds., *Biographical Dictionary of the American Left* (1986).

Religion and Cults

Henry Bowden, *Dictionary of American Religious Biography* (1993); S. Kent Brown et al., eds., *Historical Atlas of Mormonism* (1995); Edwin Gaustad and Philip L. Barlow, *New Historical Atlas of Religion in America* (1998); Michael Glazier and Thomas J. Shelley, eds., *The Encyclopedia of American Catholic History* (1997); Bill J. Leonard, *Dictionary of Baptists in America* (1994); Donald Lewis, ed., *A Dictionary of Evangelical Biography* (1995); Charles H. Lippy and Peter W. Williams, eds., *Encyclopedia of the American Religious Experience* (1988); J. Gordon Melton, *The Encyclopedia of American Religions* (1987); J. Gordon Melton, *The Encyclopedic Handbook of Cults in America* (1992); Mark A. Noll and Nathan O. Hatch, eds., *Eerdman's Handbook to Christianity in America* (1983); Stephen R. Prothero et al., *The Encyclopedia of American Religious History* (1996); Paul J. Weber and W. Landis Jones, *U.S. Religious Interest Groups* (1994). See also "African Americans."

Science and Technology

James W. Cortada, *Historical Dictionary of Data Processing* (1987); Clark A. Elliott, *Biographical Index to American Science: The Seventeenth Century to 1920* (1990); Charles C. Gillespie et al., eds., *Dictionary of Scientific Biography* (1970–); National Academy of Sciences, *Biographical Memoirs* (1877–);

Roy Porter, ed., *The Biographical Dictionary of Scientists* (1994). See also "Exploration."

Sexuality

Robert T. Francoeur, ed., *The International Encyclopedia of Sexuality* (1998); Wayne R. Dynes, ed., *Encyclopedia of Homosexuality* (1990); Steve Hogan and Lee Hudson, *Completely Queer: The Gay and Lesbian Encyclopedia* (1998); Arthur S. Leonard, ed., *Sexuality and the Law* (1993); Neil Schlager, ed., *Gay & Lesbian Almanac* (1998); Michael J. Tyrkus, ed., *Gay & Lesbian Biography* (1997); Bonnie Zimmerman and George Haggerty, eds., *Encyclopedia of Lesbian and Gay Histories and Cultures* (1999). See also "Social History and Reform."

Slavery

Seymour Drescher and Stanley L. Engerman, eds., *A Historical Guide to World Slavery* (1998); Paul Finkelman and Joseph C. Miller, eds., *Macmillan Encyclopedia of World Slavery* (1998); Randall M. Miller and John D. Smith, eds., *Dictionary of Afro-American Slavery* (1997); Junius P. Rodriguez, ed., *The Historical Encyclopedia of World Slavery* (1997). See also "African Americans."

Social History and Reform

Mary K. Cayton et al., eds., *Encyclopedia of American Social History* (1993); Louis Filler, *Dictionary of American Social Change* (1982); Robert S. Fogarty, *Dictionary of American Communal and Utopian History* (1980); Joseph M. Hawes and Elizabeth I. Nybakken, eds., *American Families* (1991); David Hey, ed., *The Oxford Companion to Local and Family History* (1996); Harold M. Keele and Joseph C. Kiger, eds., *Foundations* (1984); Mark E. Lender, *Dictionary of American Temperance Biography* (1984); Patricia M. Melvin, ed., *American Community Organizations* (1986); Randall M. Miller and Paul A. Cimbala, eds., *American Reform and Reformers* (1996); Roger S. Powers and William B. Vogele, eds., *Protest, Power, and Change* (1996); Alvin J. Schmidt, *Fraternal Organizations* (1980); Peter N. Stearns, ed., *Encyclopedia of Social History* (1993); Walter I. Trattner, *Biographical Dictionary of Social Welfare in America* (1986). See also "Crime, Violence, Police, and Prisons" and "Sexuality."

South

Edward L. Ayers and Brad Mittendorf, eds., *The Oxford Book of the American South* (1997); Robert Bain et al., eds., *Southern Writers* (1979); Kenneth Coleman and Charles S. Gurr, eds., *Dictionary of Georgia Biography* (1983); William S. Powell, ed., *Dictionary of North Carolina Biography* (1979–1996); David C. Roller and Robert W. Twyman, eds., *The Encyclopedia of Southern History* (1979); Walter P. Webb et al., eds., *The Handbook of Texas* (1952, 1976); Charles R. Wilson and William Ferris, eds., *Encyclopedia of Southern Culture* (1986).

See also "Civil War and Reconstruction," "Politics and Government," and "States."

Sports

Peter C. Bjarkman, ed., *Encyclopedia of Major League Baseball Team Histories* (1991); Ralph Hickok, *A Who's Who of Sports Champions* (1995); Ralph Hickok, *The Encyclopedia of North American Sports History* (1991); David Levinson and Karen Christensen, eds., *Encyclopedia of World Sport* (1996); Jonathan F. Light, *The Cultural Encyclopedia of Baseball* (1997); David L. Porter, *Biographical Dictionary of American Sports: Baseball* (2000), *Basketball and Other Indoor Sports* (1989), *Football* (1987), and *Outdoor Sports* (1988); Victoria Sherrow, *Encyclopedia of Women and Sports* (1996); David Wallechinsky, *The Complete Book of the Summer Olympics* (1996); David Wallechinsky, *The Complete Book of the Winter Olympics* (1993). See also "Culture and Folklore."

States

Gary Alampi, ed., *Gale State Rankings Reporter* (1994); Roy R. Glashan, comp., *American Governors and Gubernatorial Elections, 1775–1978* (1979); John Hoffmann, ed., *A Guide to the History of Illinois* (1991); Edith R. Hornor, *Almanac of the Fifty States* (1997); Joseph E. Kallenback and Jessamine S. Kallenback, *American State Governors, 1776–1976* (1977); Joseph N. Kane et al., eds., *Facts About the States* (1994); John E. Kleber et al., eds., *The Kentucky Encyclopedia* (1992); Thomas A. McMullin and Marie Mullaney, *Biographical Directory of the Governors of the United States, 1983–1987* (1988) and *1988–1993* (1994); Marie Mullaney, *Biographical Directory of the Governors of the United States, 1988–1994* (1994); Thomas J. Noel, *Historical Atlas of Colorado* (1994); John W. Raimo, ed., *Biographical Directory of the Governors of the United States, 1978–1983* (1985); James W. Scott and Ronald L. De Lorme, *Historical Atlas of Washington* (1988); Benjamin F. Shearer and Barbara S. Shearer, *State Names, Seals, Flags, and Symbols* (1994); Robert Sobel and John W. Raimo, eds., *Biographical Directory of the Governors of the United States, 1789–1978* (1978); Richard W. Wilkie and Jack Tager, eds., *Historical Atlas of Massachusetts* (1991). See also "Politics and Government," "South," and "West and Frontier."

Transportation

Keith L. Bryant, ed., *Railroads in the Age of Regulation, 1900–1980* (1988); Rene De La Pedraja, *A Historical Dictionary of the U.S. Merchant Marine and Shipping Industry* (1994); Robert L. Frey, ed., *Railroads in the Nineteenth Century* (1988). See also "Business and the Economy."

Vietnam War

John S. Bowman, ed., *The Vietnam War: An Almanac* (1986); Stanley I. Kutler, ed., *Encyclopedia of the Vietnam War* (1996); James S. Olson, ed., *Dictionary of the Vietnam War* (1988);

Harry G. Summers, Jr., *Vietnam War Almanac* (1985). Also see "Peace Movements and Pacifism" and "Military and Wars."

West and Frontier

William A. Beck and Ynez D. Haase, *Historical Atlas of the American West* (1989); Doris O. Dawdy, *Artists of the American West* (1974–1984); J. Norman Heard, *Handbook of the American Frontier* (1987); Howard R. Lamar, ed., *The New Encyclopedia of the American West* (1998); Clyde A. Milner III et al., eds., *The Oxford History of the American West* (1994); Jay Robert Nash, *Encyclopedia of Western Lawmen and Outlaws* (1992); Doyce B. Nunis, Jr., and Gloria R. Lothrop, eds., *A Guide to the History of California* (1989); Charles Phillips and Alan Axelrod, eds., *Encyclopedia of the American West* (1996); Dan L. Thrapp, *The Encyclopedia of Frontier Biography* (1988–1994); David Walker, *Biographical Directory of American Territorial Governors* (1984). See also "Cities and Towns," "Literature," and "Native Americans and Indian Affairs."

Women

Anne Gibson and Timothy Fast, *The Women's Atlas of the United States* (1986); Karen Greenspan, *The Timetables of Women's History* (1996); Maggie Humm, *The Dictionary of Feminist Theory* (1990); Edward T. James et al., *Notable American Women, 1607–1950* (1971); Lina Mainiero, ed., *American Women Writers* (1979–1982); Wilma Mankiller et al., *The Reader's Companion to U.S. Women's History* (1998); Kirstin Olsen, *Chronology of Women's History* (1994); Barbara G. Shortridge, *Atlas of American Women* (1987); Barbara Sicherman and Carol H. Green, eds., *Notable American Women, The Modern Period* (1980); Helen Tierney, ed., *Women's Studies Encyclopedia* (1991); James Trager, *The Women's Chronology* (1994); Angela H. Zophy and Frances M. Kavenik, eds., *Handbook of American Women's History* (1990). See also "African Americans," "Immigration and Ethnic Groups," "Medicine and Nursing," "Native Americans and Indian Affairs," and "Sports."

World War I

David F. Burg and L. Edward Purcell, *Almanac of World War I* (1998); Martin Gilbert, *Atlas of World War I* (1994); Holger H. Herwig and Neil M. Heyman, *Biographical Dictionary of World War I* (1982); George T. Kurian, *Encyclopedia of the First World War* (1990); Stephen Pope and Elizabeth-Anne Wheal, *The Dictionary of the First World War* (1995); Anne C. Venzon, *The United States in the First World War* (1995). See also "Military and Wars."

World War II

Marcel Baudot et al., eds., *The Historical Encyclopedia of World War II* (1980); David G. Chandler and James Lawton Collins, Jr., eds., *The D-Day Encyclopedia* (1993); I. C. B. Dear and M. R. D. Foot, eds., *The Oxford Companion to World War II* (1995); Simon Goodenough, *War Maps: Great Land Battles of World War II* (1988); Robert Goralski, *World War II Almanac* (1981); John Keegan, ed., *The Times Atlas of the Second World War* (1989); George T. Kurian, *Encyclopedia of the Second World War* (1991); Norman Polmer and Thomas B. Allen, *World War II: America at War* (1991); Louis L. Snyder, *Louis L. Snyder's Historical Guide to World War II* (1982); U.S. Military Academy, *Campaign Atlas to the Second World War: Europe and the Mediterranean* (1980); Peter Young, ed., *The World Almanac Book of World War II* (1981). See also "Military and Wars."

Documents

DECLARATION OF INDEPENDENCE IN CONGRESS, JULY 4, 1776

When, in the course of human events, it becomes necessary for one people to dissolve the political bonds which have connected them with another, and to assume, among the powers of the earth, the separate and equal station to which the laws of nature and of nature's God entitle them, a decent respect to the opinions of mankind requires that they should declare the causes which impel them to the separation.

We hold these truths to be self-evident: That all men are created equal; that they are endowed by their Creator with certain unalienable rights; that among these are life, liberty, and the pursuit of happiness; that, to secure these rights, governments are instituted among men, deriving their just powers from the consent of the governed; that whenever any form of government becomes destructive of these ends, it is the right of the people to alter or to abolish it, and to institute new government, laying its foundation on such principles, and organizing its powers in such form, as to them shall seem most likely to effect their safety and happiness. Prudence, indeed, will dictate that governments long established should not be changed for light and transient causes; and accordingly all experience hath shown that mankind are more disposed to suffer, while evils are sufferable, than to right themselves by abolishing the forms to which they are accustomed. But when a long train of abuses and usurpations, pursuing invariably the same object, evinces a design to reduce them under absolute despotism, it is their right, it is their duty, to throw off such government, and to provide new guards for their future security. Such has been the patient sufferance of these colonies; and such is now the necessity which constrains them to alter their former systems of government. The history of the present King of Great Britain is a history of repeated injuries and usurpations, all having in direct object the establishment of an absolute tyranny over these states. To prove this, let facts be submitted to a candid world.

He has refused his assent to laws, the most wholesome and necessary for the public good.

He has forbidden his governors to pass laws of immediate and pressing importance, unless suspended in their operation till his assent should be obtained; and, when so suspended, he has utterly neglected to attend to them.

He has refused to pass other laws for the accommodation of large districts of people, unless those people would relinquish the right of representation in the legislature, a right inestimable to them, and formidable to tyrants only.

He has called together legislative bodies at places unusual, uncomfortable, and distant from the depository of their public records, for the sole purpose of fatiguing them into compliance with his measures.

He has dissolved representative houses repeatedly, for opposing, with manly firmness, his invasions on the rights of the people.

He has refused for a long time, after such dissolutions, to cause others to be elected; whereby the legislative powers, incapable of annihilation, have returned to the people at large for their exercise; the state remaining, in the mean time, exposed to all the dangers of invasions from without and convulsions within.

He has endeavored to prevent the population of these states; for that purpose obstructing the laws for naturalization of foreigners; refusing to pass others to encourage their migration hither, and raising the conditions of new appropriations of lands.

He has obstructed the administration of justice, by refusing his assent to laws for establishing judiciary powers.

He has made judges dependent on his will alone, for the tenure of their offices, and the amount and payment of their salaries.

He has erected a multitude of new offices, and sent hither swarms of officers to harass our people and eat out their substance.

He has kept among us, in times of peace, standing armies, without the consent of our legislatures.

He has affected to render the military independent of, and superior to, the civil power.

He has combined with others to subject us to a jurisdiction foreign to our constitution, and unacknowledged by our laws, giving his assent to their acts of pretended legislation:

For quartering large bodies of armed troops among us;

For protecting them, by a mock trial, from punishment for any murders which they should commit on the inhabitants of these states;

For cutting off our trade with all parts of the world;

For imposing taxes on us without our consent;

For depriving us, in many cases, of the benefits of trial by jury;

For transporting us beyond seas, to be tried for pretended offenses;

For abolishing the free system of English laws in a

neighboring province, establishing therein an arbitrary government, and enlarging its boundaries, so as to render it at once an example and fit instrument for introducing the same absolute rule into these colonies;

For taking away our charters, abolishing our most valuable laws, and altering fundamentally the forms of our governments;

For suspending our own legislatures, and declaring themselves invested with power to legislate for us in all cases whatsoever.

He has abdicated government here, by declaring us out of his protection and waging war against us.

He has plundered our seas, ravaged our coasts, burned our towns, and destroyed the lives of our people.

He is at this time transporting large armies of foreign mercenaries to complete the works of death, desolation, and tyranny already begun with circumstances of cruelty and perfidy scarcely paralleled in the most barbarous ages, and totally unworthy the head of a civilized nation.

He has constrained our fellow-citizens, taken captive on the high seas, to bear arms against their country, to become the executioners of their friends and brethren, or to fall themselves by their hands.

He has excited domestic insurrection among us, and has endeavored to bring on the inhabitants of our frontiers the merciless Indian savages, whose known rule of warfare is an undistinguished destruction of all ages, sexes, and conditions.

In every stage of these oppressions we have petitioned for redress in the most humble terms; our repeated petitions have been answered only by repeated injury. A prince, whose character is thus marked by every act which may define a tyrant, is unfit to be the ruler of a free people.

Nor have we been wanting in our attentions to our British brethren. We have warned them, from time to time, of attempts by their legislature to extend an unwarrantable jurisdiction over us. We have reminded them of the circumstances of our emigration and settlement here. We have appealed to their native justice and magnanimity; and we have conjured them, by the ties of our common kindred, to disavow these usurpations, which would inevitably interrupt our connections and correspondence. They, too, have been deaf to the voice of justice and of consanguinity. We must, therefore, acquiesce in the necessity which denounces our separation, and hold them, as we hold the rest of mankind, enemies in war, in peace friends.

We, therefore, the representatives of the United States of America, in General Congress assembled, appealing to the Supreme Judge of the world for the rectitude of our intentions, do, in the name and by the authority of the good people of these colonies, solemnly publish and declare, that these United Colonies are, and of right ought to be, FREE AND INDEPENDENT STATES; that they are absolved from all allegiance to the British crown, and that all political connection between them and the state of Great Britain is,

and ought to be, totally dissolved; and that, as free and independent states, they have full power to levy war, conclude peace, contract alliances, establish commerce, and do all other acts and things which independent states may of right do. And for the support of this declaration, with a firm reliance on the protection of Divine Providence, we mutually pledge to each other our lives, our fortunes, and our sacred honor.

———

ARTICLES OF CONFEDERATION

(The text of the Articles of Confederation can be found at http://college.hmco.com.)

———

CONSTITUTION OF THE UNITED STATES OF AMERICA AND AMENDMENTS*

Preamble

We the people of the United States, in order to form a more perfect union, establish justice, insure domestic tranquillity, provide for the common defense, promote the general welfare, and secure the blessings of liberty to ourselves and our posterity, do ordain and establish this Constitution for the United States of America.

Article I

Section 1 All legislative powers herein granted shall be vested in a Congress of the United States, which shall consist of a Senate and a House of Representatives.

Section 2 The House of Representatives shall be composed of members chosen every second year by the people of the several States, and the electors in each State shall have the qualifications requisite for electors of the most numerous branch of the State Legislature.

No person shall be a Representative who shall not have attained to the age of twenty-five years, and been seven years a citizen of the United States, and who shall not, when elected, be an inhabitant of that State in which he shall be chosen.

Representatives and direct taxes shall be apportioned among the several States which may be included within this Union, according to their respective numbers, *which shall be determined by adding to the whole number of free persons, including those bound to service for a term of years and excluding Indians not taxed, three-fifths of all other persons.* The actual enumeration shall be made within three years after the first meeting of the Congress of the United States, and within

---

*Passages no longer in effect are printed in italic type.

every subsequent term of ten years, in such manner as they shall by law direct. The number of Representatives shall not exceed one for every thirty thousand, but each State shall have at least one Representative; *and until such enumeration shall be made, the State of New Hampshire shall be entitled to choose three, Massachusetts eight, Rhode Island and Providence Plantations one, Connecticut five, New York six, New Jersey four, Pennsylvania eight, Delaware one, Maryland six, Virginia ten, North Carolina five, South Carolina five, and Georgia three.*

When vacancies happen in the representation from any State, the Executive authority thereof shall issue writs of election to fill such vacancies.

The House of Representatives shall choose their Speaker and other officers; and shall have the sole power of impeachment.

Section 3   The Senate of the United States shall be composed of two Senators from each State, *chosen by the legislature thereof,* for six years; and each Senator shall have one vote.

Immediately after they shall be assembled in consequence of the first election, they shall be divided as equally as may be into three classes. The seats of the Senators of the first class shall be vacated at the expiration of the second year, of the second class at the expiration of the fourth year, and of the third class at the expiration of the sixth year, so that one-third may be chosen every second year; and if vacancies happen by resignation or otherwise, during the recess of the legislature of any State, the Executive thereof may make temporary appointments until the next meeting of the legislature, which shall then fill such vacancies.

No person shall be a Senator who shall not have attained to the age of thirty years, and been nine years a citizen of the United States, and who shall not, when elected, be an inhabitant of that State for which he shall be chosen.

The Vice-President of the United States shall be President of the Senate, but shall have no vote, unless they be equally divided.

The Senate shall choose their other officers, and also a President *pro tempore*, in the absence of the Vice-President, or when he shall exercise the office of President of the United States.

The Senate shall have the sole power to try all impeachments. When sitting for that purpose, they shall be on oath or affirmation. When the President of the United States is tried, the Chief Justice shall preside: and no person shall be convicted without the concurrence of two-thirds of the members present.

Judgment in cases of impeachment shall not extend further than to removal from the office, and disqualification to hold and enjoy any office of honor, trust or profit under the United States: but the party convicted shall nevertheless be liable and subject to indictment, trial, judgment and punishment, according to law.

Section 4   The times, places and manner of holding elections for Senators and Representatives shall be prescribed in each State by the legislature thereof; but the Congress may at any time by law make or alter such regulations, except as to the places of choosing Senators.

The Congress shall assemble at least once in every year, and such meeting *shall be on the first Monday in December, unless they shall by law appoint a different day.*

Section 5   Each house shall be the judge of the elections, returns and qualifications of its own members, and a majority of each shall constitute a quorum to do business; but a smaller number may adjourn from day to day, and may be authorized to compel the attendance of absent members, in such manner, and under such penalties, as each house may provide.

Each house may determine the rules of its proceedings, punish its members for disorderly behavior, and with the concurrence of two-thirds, expel a member.

Each house shall keep a journal of its proceedings, and from time to time publish the same, excepting such parts as may in their judgment require secrecy; and the yeas and nays of the members of either house on any question shall, at the desire of one-fifth of those present, be entered on the journal.

Neither house, during the session of Congress, shall, without the consent of the other, adjourn for more than three days, nor to any other place than that in which the two houses shall be sitting.

Section 6   The Senators and Representatives shall receive a compensation for their services, to be ascertained by law and paid out of the treasury of the United States. They shall in all cases except treason, felony and breach of the peace, be privileged from arrest during their attendance at the session of their respective houses, and in going to and returning from the same; and for any speech or debate in either house, they shall not be questioned in any other place.

No Senator or Representative shall, during the time for which he was elected, be appointed to any civil office under the authority of the United States, which shall have been created, or the emoluments whereof shall have been increased, during such time; and no person holding any office under the United States shall be a member of either house during his continuance in office.

Section 7   All bills for raising revenue shall originate in the House of Representatives; but the Senate may propose or concur with amendments as on other bills.

Every bill which shall have passed the House of Representatives and the Senate, shall, before it become a law, be presented to the President of the United States; if he approve he shall sign it, but if not he shall return it with objections to that house in which it originated, who shall enter the objections at large on their journal, and proceed to reconsider it. If after such reconsideration two-thirds of that house shall agree to pass the bill, it shall be sent, together with the objections, to the other house, by which it shall likewise be reconsidered, and, if approved by two-thirds of that house, it shall become a law. But in all such cases the votes of both houses shall be determined by yeas and nays, and the names of the persons voting for and against the bill shall be entered on the journal of each house respectively. If any bill shall not be returned by the President within ten days (Sundays excepted) after it shall have been presented to him, the same shall be a law, in like manner as if he had signed it, unless the Congress by their adjournment prevent its return, in which case it shall not be a law.

Every order, resolution, or vote to which the concurrence of the Senate and House of Representatives may be necessary (except on a question of adjournment) shall be presented to the President of the United States; and before the same shall take effect, shall be approved by him, or being disapproved by him, shall be repassed by two-thirds of the Senate and House of Representatives, according to the rules and limitations prescribed in the case of a bill.

Section 8   The Congress shall have power

To lay and collect taxes, duties, imposts, and excises, to pay the debts and provide for the common defense and general welfare of the United States; but all duties, imposts and excises shall be uniform throughout the United States;

To borrow money on the credit of the United States;

To regulate commerce with foreign nations, and among the several States, and with the Indian tribes;

To establish an uniform rule of naturalization, and uniform laws on the subject of bankruptcies throughout the United States;

To coin money, regulate the value thereof, and of foreign coin, and fix the standard of weights and measures;

To provide for the punishment of counterfeiting the securities and current coin of the United States;

To establish post offices and post roads;

To promote the progress of science and useful arts by securing for limited times to authors and inventors the exclusive right to their respective writings and discoveries;

To constitute tribunals inferior to the Supreme Court;

To define and punish piracies and felonies committed on the high seas and offenses against the law of nations;

To declare war, grant letters of marque and reprisal, and make rules concerning captures on land and water;

To raise and support armies, but no appropriation of money to that use shall be for a longer term than two years;

To provide and maintain a navy;

To make rules for the government and regulation of the land and naval forces;

To provide for calling forth the militia to execute the laws of the Union, suppress insurrections, and repel invasions;

To provide for organizing, arming, and disciplining the militia, and for governing such part of them as may be employed in the service of the United States, reserving to the States respectively the appointment of the officers, and the authority of training the militia according to the discipline prescribed by Congress;

To exercise exclusive legislation in all cases whatsoever, over such district (not exceeding ten miles square) as may, by cession of particular States, and the acceptance of Congress, become the seat of government of the United States, and to exercise like authority over all places purchased by the consent of the legislature of the State, in which the same shall be, for erection of forts, magazines, arsenals, dockyards, and other needful buildings; —and

To make all laws which shall be necessary and proper for carrying into execution the foregoing powers, and all other powers vested by this Constitution in the government of the United States, or in any department or officer thereof.

Section 9   *The migration or importation of such persons as any of the States now existing shall think proper to admit shall not be prohibited by the Congress prior to the year 1808; but a tax or duty may be imposed on such importation, not exceeding $10 for each person.*

The privilege of the writ of habeas corpus shall not be suspended, unless when in cases of rebellion or invasion the public safety may require it.

No bill of attainder or ex post facto law shall be passed.

No capitation, or other direct, tax shall be laid, unless in proportion to the census or enumeration herein before directed to be taken.

No tax or duty shall be laid on articles exported from any State.

No preference shall be given by any regulation of commerce or revenue to the ports of one State over those of another; nor shall vessels bound to, or from, one State, be obliged to enter, clear, or pay duties in another.

No money shall be drawn from the treasury, but in consequence of appropriations made by law; and a regular statement and account of the receipts and expenditures of all public money shall be published from time to time.

No title of nobility shall be granted by the United States: and no person holding any office of profit or trust under them, shall, without the consent of the Congress, accept of any present, emolument, office, or title, of any kind whatever, from any king, prince, or foreign state.

Section 10   No State shall enter into any treaty, alliance, or confederation; grant letters of marque and reprisal; coin money; emit bills of credit; make anything but gold and silver coin a tender in payment of debts; pass any bill of attainder, ex post facto law, or law impairing the obligation of contracts, or grant any title of nobility.

No State shall, without the consent of Congress, lay any imposts or duties on imports or exports, except what may be absolutely necessary for executing its inspection laws: and the net produce of all duties and imposts, laid by any State on imports or exports, shall be for the use of the treasury of the United States; and all such laws shall be subject to the revision and control of the Congress.

No State shall, without the consent of Congress, lay any duty of tonnage, keep troops or ships of war in time of peace, enter into any agreement or compact with another State, or with a foreign power, or engage in war, unless actually invaded, or in such imminent danger as will not admit of delay.

Article II

Section 1   The executive power shall be vested in a President of the United States of America. He shall hold his office during the term of four years, and, together with the Vice-President, chosen for the same term, be elected as follows:

Each State shall appoint, in such manner as the legislature thereof may direct, a number of electors, equal to the whole number of Senators and Representatives to which the State may be entitled in the Congress; but no Senator or Representative, or person holding an office of trust or profit under the United States, shall be appointed an elector.

The electors shall meet in their respective States, and vote by ballot for two persons, of whom one at least shall not be an inhabitant of the same State with themselves. And they shall make a list of all the persons voted for, and of the number of votes for each; which list they shall sign and certify, and transmit sealed to the seat of government of the United States, directed to the President of the Senate. The President of the Senate shall, in the presence of the Senate and House of Representatives, open all the certificates, and the votes shall then be counted. The person having the greatest number of votes shall be the President, if such number be a majority of the whole number of electors appointed; and if there be more than one who have such majority, and have an equal number of votes, then the House of Representatives shall immediately choose by ballot one of them for President; and if no person have a majority, then from the five highest on the list said house shall in like manner choose the President. But in choosing the President the votes shall be taken by States, the representation from each State having one vote; a quorum for this purpose shall consist of a member or members from two-thirds of the States, and a majority of all the States shall be necessary to a choice. In every case, after the choice of the President, the person having the greatest number of votes of the electors shall be the Vice-President. But if there should remain two or more who have equal votes, the Senate shall choose from them by ballot the Vice-President.

The Congress may determine the time of choosing the electors and the day on which they shall give their votes; which day shall be the same throughout the United States.

No person except a natural-born citizen, *or a citizen of the United States at the time of the adoption of this Constitution,* shall be eligible to the office of President; neither shall any person be eligible to that office who shall not have attained to the age of thirty-five years, and been fourteen years a resident within the United States.

In cases of the removal of the President from office or of his death, resignation, or inability to discharge the powers and duties of the said office, the same shall devolve on the Vice-President, and the Congress may by law provide for the case of removal, death, resignation, or inability, both of the President and Vice-President, declaring what officer shall then act as President, and such officer shall act accordingly, until the disability be removed, or a President shall be elected.

The President shall, at stated times, receive for his services a compensation, which shall neither be increased nor diminished during the period for which he shall have been elected, and he shall not receive within that period any other emolument from the United States, or any of them.

Before he enter on the execution of his office, he shall take the following oath or affirmation:—"I do solemnly swear (or affirm) that I will faithfully execute the office of the President of the United States, and will to the best of my ability preserve, protect and defend the Constitution of the United States."

Section 2   The President shall be commander in chief of the army and navy of the United States, and of the militia of the several States, when called into the actual service of the United States; he may require the opinion, in writing, of the principal officer in each of the executive departments, upon any subject relating to the duties of their respective offices, and he shall have power to grant reprieves and pardons for offenses against the United States, except in cases of impeachment.

He shall have power, by and with the advice and consent of the Senate, to make treaties, provided two-thirds of the Senators present concur; and he shall nominate, and by and with the advice and consent of the Senate, shall appoint ambassadors, other public ministers and consuls, judges of the Supreme Court, and all other officers of the United States, whose appointments are not herein otherwise provided for, and which shall be established by law: but Congress may by law vest the appointment of such inferior officers, as they think proper, in the President alone, in the courts of law, or in the heads of departments.

The President shall have power to fill up all vacancies that may happen during the recess of the Senate, by granting commissions which shall expire at the end of their next session.

Section 3   He shall from time to time give to the Congress information of the state of the Union, and recommend to their consideration such measures as he shall judge necessary and expedient; he may, on extraordinary occasions, convene both houses, or either of them, and in case of disagreement between them, with respect to the time of adjournment, he may adjourn them to such time as he shall think proper; he shall receive ambassadors and other public ministers; he shall take care that the laws be faithfully executed, and shall commission all the officers of the United States.

Section 4   The President, Vice-President and all civil officers of the United States shall be removed from office on impeachment for, and on conviction of, treason, bribery, or other high crimes and misdemeanors.

Article III

Section 1 The judicial power of the United States shall be vested in one Supreme Court, and in such inferior courts as the Congress may from time to time ordain and establish. The judges, both of the Supreme and inferior courts, shall hold their offices during good behavior, and shall, at stated times, receive for their services a compensation which shall not be diminished during their continuance in office.

Section 2 The judicial power shall extend to all cases, in law and equity, arising under this Constitution, the laws of the United States, and treaties made, or which shall be made, under their authority;—to all cases affecting ambassadors, other public ministers and consuls;—to all cases of admiralty and maritime jurisdiction;—to controversies to which the United States shall be a party;—to controversies between two or more States;—*between a State and citizens of another State;*—between citizens of different States;—between citizens of the same State claiming lands under grants of different States, and between a State, or the citizens thereof, and foreign states, citizens or subjects.

In all cases affecting ambassadors, other public ministers and consuls, and those in which a State shall be party, the Supreme Court shall have original jurisdiction. In all the other cases before mentioned, the Supreme Court shall have appellate jurisdiction, both as to law and fact, with such exceptions, and under such regulations, as the Congress shall make.

The trial of all crimes, except in cases of impeachment, shall be by jury; and such trial shall be held in the State where said crimes shall have been committed; but when not committed within any State, the trial shall be at such place or places as the Congress may by law have directed.

Section 3 Treason against the United States shall consist only in levying war against them, or in adhering to their enemies, giving them aid and comfort. No person shall be convicted of treason unless on the testimony of two witnesses to the same overt act, or on confession in open court.

The Congress shall have power to declare the punishment of treason, but no attainder of treason shall work corruption of blood, or forfeiture except during the life of the person attainted.

Article IV

Section 1 Full faith and credit shall be given in each State to the public acts, records, and judicial proceedings of every other State. And the Congress may by general laws prescribe the manner in which such acts, records, and proceedings shall be proved, and the effect thereof.

Section 2 The citizens of each State shall be entitled to all privileges and immunities of citizens in the several States.

A person charged in any State with treason, felony, or other crime, who shall flee from justice, and be found in another State, shall on demand of the executive authority of the State from which he fled, be delivered up, to be removed to the State having jurisdiction of the crime.

No person held to service or labor in one State, under the laws thereof, escaping into another, shall, in consequence of any law or regulation therein, be discharged from such service or labor, but shall be delivered up on claim of the party to whom such service or labor may be due.

Section 3 New States may be admitted by the Congress into this Union; but no new State shall be formed or erected within the jurisdiction of any other State; nor any State be formed by the junction of two or more States, or parts of States, without the consent of the legislatures of the States concerned as well as of the Congress.

The Congress shall have power to dispose of and make all needful rules and regulations respecting the territory or other property belonging to the United States; and nothing in this Constitution shall be so construed as to prejudice any claims of the United States, or of any particular State.

Section 4 The United States shall guarantee to every State in this Union a republican form of government, and shall protect each of them against invasion; and on application of the legislature, or of the executive (when the legislature cannot be convened), against domestic violence.

Article V

The Congress, whenever two-thirds of both houses shall deem it necessary, shall propose amendments to this Constitution, or, on the application of the legislatures of two-thirds of the several States, shall call a convention for proposing amendments, which, in either case, shall be valid to all intents and purposes, as part of this Constitution, when ratified by the legislatures of three-fourths of the several States, or by conventions in three-fourths thereof, as the one or the other mode of ratification may be proposed by the Congress; provided *that no amendments which may be made prior to the year one thousand eight hundred and eight shall in any manner affect the first and fourth clauses in the ninth section of the first article;* and that no State, without its consent, shall be deprived of its equal suffrage in the Senate.

Article VI

All debts contracted and engagements entered into, before the adoption of this Constitution, shall be as valid against the United States under this Constitution, as under the Confederation.

This Constitution, and the laws of the United States which shall be made in pursuance thereof; and all treaties made, or which shall be made, under the authority of the United States, shall be the supreme law of the land; and the judges in every State shall be bound thereby, anything in the Constitution or laws of any State to the contrary notwithstanding.

The Senators and Representatives before mentioned, and the members of the several State legislatures, and all executive and judicial officers, both of the United States and of the several States, shall be bound by oath or affirmation to support this Constitution; but no religious test shall ever be required as a qualification to any office or public trust under the United States.

Article VII

The ratification of the conventions of nine States shall be sufficient for the establishment of this Constitution between the States so ratifying the same.

Done in Convention by the unanimous consent of the States present, the seventeenth day of September in the year of our Lord one thousand seven hundred and eighty-seven and of the Independence of the United States of America the twelfth. In witness whereof we have hereunto subscribed our names.

AMENDMENTS TO THE CONSTITUTION*

Amendment I

Congress shall make no law respecting an establishment of religion, or prohibiting the free exercise thereof; or abridging the freedom of speech, or of the press; or the right of the people peaceably to assemble, and to petition the government for a redress of grievances.

Amendment II

A well-regulated militia being necessary to the security of a free State, the right of the people to keep and bear arms shall not be infringed.

Amendment III

No soldier shall, in time of peace, be quartered in any house without the consent of the owner, nor in time of war, but in a manner to be prescribed by law.

Amendment IV

The right of the people to be secure in their persons, houses, papers, and effects, against unreasonable searches and seizures, shall not be violated, and no warrants shall issue but upon probable cause, supported by oath or affirmation, and particularly describing the place to be searched, and the persons or things to be seized.

Amendment V

No person shall be held to answer for a capital, or otherwise infamous crime, unless on a presentment or indictment of a grand jury, except in cases arising in the land or naval forces, or in the militia, when in actual service in time of war or public danger; nor shall any person be subject for the same offense to be twice put in jeopardy of life or limb; nor shall be compelled in any criminal case to be a witness against himself, nor be deprived of life, liberty, or property, without due process of law; nor shall private property be taken for public use without just compensation.

Amendment VI

In all criminal prosecutions, the accused shall enjoy the right to a speedy and public trial, by an impartial jury of the State and district wherein the crime shall have been committed, which district shall have been previously ascertained by law, and to be informed of the nature and cause of the accusation; to be confronted with the witnesses against him; to have compulsory process for obtaining witnesses in his favor, and to have the assistance of counsel for his defense.

Amendment VII

In suits at common law, where the value in controversy shall exceed twenty dollars, the right of trial by jury shall be preserved, and no fact tried by a jury shall be otherwise reexamined in any court of the United States, than according to the rules of the common law.

Amendment VIII

Excessive bail shall not be required, nor excessive fines imposed, nor cruel and unusual punishments inflicted.

Amendment IX

The enumeration in the Constitution, of certain rights, shall not be construed to deny or disparage others retained by the people.

Amendment X

The powers not delegated to the United States by the Constitution, nor prohibited by it to the States, are reserved to the States respectively, or to the people.

Amendment XI

[Adopted 1798]
The judicial power of the United States shall not be construed to extend to any suit in law or equity, commenced or prosecuted against one of the United States by citizens of another State, or by citizens or subjects of any foreign state.

Amendment XII

[Adopted 1804]

The electors shall meet in their respective States, and vote by ballot for President and Vice-President, one of whom, at least, shall not be an inhabitant of the same State with themselves; they shall name in their ballots the person voted for as President, and in distinct ballots the person voted for as Vice-

---

*The first ten Amendments (the Bill of Rights) were adopted in 1791.

President, and they shall make distinct lists of all persons voted for as President, and of all persons voted for as Vice-President, and of the number of votes for each, which lists they shall sign and certify, and transmit sealed to the seat of government of the United States, directed to the President of the Senate;—the President of the Senate shall, in the presence of the Senate and House of Representatives, open all the certificates and the votes shall then be counted;—the person having the greatest number of votes for President shall be the President, if such number be a majority of the whole number of electors appointed; and if no person have such majority, then from the persons having the highest numbers not exceeding three on the list of those voted for as President, the House of Representatives shall choose immediately, by ballot, the President. But in choosing the President, the votes shall be taken by States, the representation from each State having one vote; a quorum for this purpose shall consist of a member or members from two-thirds of the States, and a majority of all the States shall be necessary to a choice. And if the House of Representatives shall not choose a President whenever the right of choice shall devolve upon them, before *the fourth day of March* next following, then the Vice-President shall act as President, as in the case of the death or other constitutional disability of the President.

The person having the greatest number of votes as Vice-President shall be the Vice-President, if such number be a majority of the whole number of electors appointed; and if no person have a majority, then from the two highest numbers on the list the Senate shall choose the Vice-President; a quorum for the purpose shall consist of two-thirds of the whole number of Senators, and a majority of the whole number shall be necessary to a choice. But no person constitutionally ineligible to the office of President shall be eligible to that of Vice-President of the United States.

Amendment XIII

[Adopted 1865]

Section 1   Neither slavery nor involuntary servitude, except as a punishment for crime whereof the party shall have been duly convicted, shall exist within the United States, or any place subject to their jurisdiction.

Section 2   Congress shall have power to enforce this article by appropriate legislation.

Amendment XIV

[Adopted 1868]

Section 1   All persons born or naturalized in the United States, and subject to the jurisdiction thereof, are citizens of the United States and of the State wherein they reside. No State shall make or enforce any law which shall abridge the privileges or immunities of citizens of the United States; nor shall any State deprive any person of life, liberty, or property, without due process of law; nor deny to any person within its jurisdiction the equal protection of the laws.

Section 2   Representatives shall be apportioned among the several States according to their respective numbers, counting the whole number of persons in each State, excluding Indians not taxed. But when the right to vote at any election for the choice of Electors for President and Vice-President of the United States, Representatives in Congress, the executive and judicial officers of a State, or the members of the legislature thereof, is denied to any of the male inhabitants of such State, being twenty-one years of age and citizens of the United States, or in any way abridged, except for participation in rebellion, or other crime, the basis of representation therein shall be reduced in the proportion which the number of such male citizens shall bear to the whole number of male citizens twenty-one years of age in such State.

Section 3   No person shall be a Senator or Representative in Congress, or Elector of President and Vice-President, or hold any office, civil or military, under the United States, or under any State, who, having previously taken an oath, as a member of Congress, or as an officer of the United States, or as a member of any State legislature, or as an executive or judicial officer of any State, to support the Constitution of the United States, shall have engaged in insurrection or rebellion against the same, or given aid or comfort to the enemies thereof. Congress may, by a vote of two-thirds of each house, remove such disability.

Section 4   The validity of the public debt of the United States, authorized by law, including debts incurred for payment of pensions and bounties for services in suppressing insurrection or rebellion, shall not be questioned. But neither the United States nor any State shall assume or pay any debt or obligation incurred in aid of insurrection or rebellion against the United States, or any claim for the loss of emancipation of any slave; but all such debts, obligations, and claims shall be held illegal and void.

Section 5   The Congress shall have power to enforce, by appropriate legislation, the provisions of this article.

Amendment XV

[Adopted 1870]

Section 1   The right of citizens of the United States to vote shall not be denied or abridged by the United States or by any State on account of race, color, or previous condition of servitude.

Section 2   The Congress shall have power to enforce this article by appropriate legislation.

Amendment XVI

[Adopted 1913]

The Congress shall have power to lay and collect taxes on incomes, from whatever source derived, without apportionment among the several States, and without regard to any census or enumeration.

Amendment XVII

[Adopted 1913]

Section 1 The Senate of the United States shall be composed of two Senators from each State, elected by the people thereof, for six years; and each Senator shall have one vote. The electors in each State shall have the qualifications requisite for electors of [voters for] the most numerous branch of the State legislatures.

Section 2 When vacancies happen in the representation of any State in the Senate, the executive authority of such State shall issue writs of election to fill such vacancies: Provided, that the Legislature of any State may empower the executive thereof to make temporary appointments until the people fill the vacancies by election as the Legislature may direct.

Section 3 This amendment shall not be so construed as to affect the election or term of any Senator chosen before it becomes valid as part of the Constitution.

Amendment XVIII

[Adopted 1919; Repealed 1933]

Section 1 After one year from the ratification of this article the manufacture, sale, or transportation of intoxicating liquors within, the importation thereof into, or the exportation thereof from the United States and all territory subject to the jurisdiction thereof, for beverage purposes, is hereby prohibited.

Section 2 The Congress and the several States shall have concurrent power to enforce this article by appropriate legislation.

Section 3 This article shall be inoperative unless it shall have been ratified as an amendment to the Constitution by the legislatures of the several States, as provided by the Constitution, within seven years from the date of the submission thereof to the States by the Congress.

Amendment XIX

[Adopted 1920]

Section 1 The right of citizens of the United States to vote shall not be denied or abridged by the United States or by any State on account of sex.

Section 2 The Congress shall have power to enforce this article by appropriate legislation.

Amendment XX

[Adopted 1933]

Section 1 The terms of the President and Vice-President shall end at noon on the 20th day of January, and the terms of Senators and Representatives at noon on the 3rd day of January, of the years in which such terms would have ended if this article had not been ratified; and the terms of their successors shall then begin.

Section 2 The Congress shall assemble at least once in every year, and such meeting shall begin at noon on the 3d day of January, unless they shall by law appoint a different day.

Section 3 If, at the time fixed for the beginning of the term of the President, the President-elect shall have died, the Vice-President–elect shall become President. If a President shall not have been chosen before the time fixed for the beginning of his term, or if the President-elect shall have failed to qualify, then the Vice-President–elect shall act as President until a President shall have qualified; and the Congress may by law provide for the case wherein neither a President-elect nor a Vice-President–elect shall have qualified, declaring who shall then act as President, or the manner in which one who is to act shall be selected, and such persons shall act accordingly until a President or Vice-President shall have qualified.

Section 4 The Congress may by law provide for the case of the death of any of the persons from whom the House of Representatives may choose a President whenever the right of choice shall have devolved upon them, and for the case of the death of any of the persons from whom the Senate may choose a Vice-President whenever the right of choice shall have devolved upon them.

Section 5 Sections 1 and 2 shall take effect on the 15th day of October following the ratification of this article.

Section 6 This article shall be inoperative unless it shall have been ratified as an amendment to the Constitution by the Legislatures of three-fourths of the several States within seven years from the date of its submission.

Amendment XXI

[Adopted 1933]

Section 1 The eighteenth article of amendment to the Constitution of the United States is hereby repealed.

Section 2 The transportation or importation into any State, Territory, or Possession of the United States for delivery or use therein of intoxicating liquors, in violation of the laws thereof, is hereby prohibited.

Section 3 This article shall be inoperative unless it shall have been ratified as an amendment to the Constitution by conventions in the several States, as provided in the Constitution, within seven years from the date of submission thereof to the States by the Congress.

Amendment XXII

[Adopted 1951]

Section 1 No person shall be elected to the office of President more than twice, and no person who has held the office of President, or acted as President, for more than two years of a term to which some other person was elected President shall be elected to the office of President more than once. But this article shall not apply to any person holding the office of President when this article was proposed by the Congress, and shall not prevent any person who may be holding the office of President, or acting as President, during the term within which this article becomes operative from holding the office of President or acting as President during the remainder of such term.

Section 2   This article shall be inoperative unless it shall have been ratified as an amendment to the Constitution by the legislatures of three-fourths of the several States within seven years from the date of its submission to the States by the Congress.

Amendment XXIII

[Adopted 1961]

Section 1   The District constituting the seat of Government of the United States shall appoint in such manner as the Congress may direct:

A number of electors of President and Vice-President equal to the whole number of Senators and Representatives in Congress to which the District would be entitled if it were a State, but in no event more than the least populous State; they shall be in addition to those appointed by the States, but they shall be considered for the purposes of the election of President and Vice-President, to be electors appointed by a State; and they shall meet in the District and perform such duties as provided by the twelfth article of amendment.

Section 2   The Congress shall have the power to enforce this article by appropriate legislation.

Amendment XXIV

[Adopted 1964]

Section 1   The right of citizens of the United States to vote in any primary or other election for President or Vice-President, for electors for President or Vice-President, or for Senator or Representative in Congress, shall not be denied or abridged by the United States or any State by reason of failure to pay any poll tax or other tax.

Section 2   The Congress shall have the power to enforce this article by appropriate legislation.

Amendment XXV

[Adopted 1967]

Section 1   In case of the removal of the President from office or of his death or resignation, the Vice-President shall become President.

Section 2   Whenever there is a vacancy in the office of the Vice-President, the President shall nominate a Vice-President who shall take office upon confirmation by a majority vote of both Houses of Congress.

Section 3   Whenever the President transmits to the President pro tempore of the Senate and the Speaker of the House of Representatives his written declaration that he is unable to discharge the powers and duties of his office, and until he transmits to them a written declaration to the contrary, such powers and duties shall be discharged by the Vice-President as Acting President.

Section 4   Whenever the Vice-President and a majority of either the principal officers of the executive departments or of such other body as Congress may by law provide, transmit to the President pro tempore of the Senate and the Speaker of the House of Representatives their written declaration that the President is unable to discharge the powers and duties of his office, the Vice-President shall immediately assume the powers and duties of the office as Acting President.

Thereafter, when the President transmits to the President pro tempore of the Senate and the Speaker of the House of Representatives his written declaration that no inability exists, he shall resume the powers and duties of his office unless the Vice-President and a majority of either the principal officers of the executive department[s] or of such other body as Congress may by law provide, transmit within four days to the President pro tempore of the Senate and the Speaker of the House of Representatives their written declaration that the President is unable to discharge the powers and duties of his office. Thereupon Congress shall decide the issue, assembling within forty-eight hours for that purpose if not in session. If the Congress, within twenty-one days after receipt of the latter written declaration, or, if Congress is not in session, within twenty-one days after Congress is required to assemble, determines by two-thirds vote of both Houses that the President is unable to discharge the powers and duties of his office, the Vice-President shall continue to discharge the same as Acting President; otherwise, the President shall resume the powers and duties of his office.

Amendment XXVI

[Adopted 1971]

Section 1   The right of citizens of the United States, who are eighteen years of age or older, to vote shall not be denied or abridged by the United States or by any State on account of age.

Section 2   The Congress shall have power to enforce this article by appropriate legislation.

Amendment XXVII

[Adopted 1992]

No law, varying the compensation for the services of the Senators and Representatives, shall take effect, until an election of Representatives shall have intervened.

The American People and Nation: A Statistical Profile

Population of the United States

Year	Number of States	Population	Percent Increase	Population Per Square Mile	Percent Urban/ Rural	Percent Male/ Female	Percent White/ Non-white	Persons Per House-hold	Median Age
1790	13	3,929,214		4.5	5.1/94.9	NA/NA	80.7/19.3	5.79	NA
1800	16	5,308,483	35.1	6.1	6.1/93.9	NA/NA	81.1/18.9	NA	NA
1810	17	7,239,881	36.4	4.3	7.3/92.7	NA/NA	81.0/19.0	NA	NA
1820	23	9,638,453	33.1	5.5	7.2/92.8	50.8/49.2	81.6/18.4	NA	16.7
1830	24	12,866,020	33.5	7.4	8.8/91.2	50.8/49.2	81.9/18.1	NA	17.2
1840	26	17,069,453	32.7	9.8	10.8/89.2	50.9/49.1	83.2/16.8	NA	17.8
1850	31	23,191,876	35.9	7.9	15.3/84.7	51.0/49.0	84.3/15.7	5.55	18.9
1860	33	31,443,321	35.6	10.6	19.8/80.2	51.2/48.8	85.6/14.4	5.28	19.4
1870	37	39,818,449	26.6	13.4	25.7/74.3	50.6/49.4	86.2/13.8	5.09	20.2
1880	38	50,155,783	26.0	16.9	28.2/71.8	50.9/49.1	86.5/13.5	5.04	20.9
1890	44	62,947,714	25.5	21.2	35.1/64.9	51.2/48.8	87.5/12.5	4.93	22.0
1900	45	75,994,575	20.7	25.6	39.6/60.4	51.1/48.9	87.9/12.1	4.76	22.9
1910	46	91,972,266	21.0	31.0	45.6/54.4	51.5/48.5	88.9/11.1	4.54	24.1
1920	48	105,710,620	14.9	35.6	51.2/48.8	51.0/49.0	89.7/10.3	4.34	25.3
1930	48	122,775,046	16.1	41.2	56.1/43.9	50.6/49.4	89.8/10.2	4.11	26.4
1940	48	131,669,275	7.2	44.2	56.5/43.5	50.2/49.8	89.8/10.2	3.67	29.0
1950	48	150,697,361	14.5	50.7	64.0/36.0	49.7/50.3	89.5/10.5	3.37	30.2
1960	50	179,323,175	18.5	50.6	69.9/30.1	49.3/50.7	88.6/11.4	3.33	29.5
1970	50	203,302,031	13.4	57.4	73.6/26.4	48.7/51.3	87.6/12.4	3.14	28.0
1980	50	226,542,199	11.4	64.1	73.7/26.3	48.6/51.4	85.9/14.1	2.75	30.0
1990	50	248,718,301	9.8	70.3	75.2/24.8	48.7/51.3	83.9/16.1	2.63	32.8
1998	50	270,299,000	8.0	76.4	NA	48.9/51.1	82.5/17.5	2.62	35.2

NA = Not available.

Vital Statistics

Year	Birth Rate*	Death Rate*	Life Expectancy in Years					Marriage Rate	Divorce Rate
			Total Population	White Females	Nonwhite Females	White Males	Nonwhite Males		
1790	NA	NA	NA	NA	NA	NA	NA	NA	NA
1800	55.0	NA	NA	NA	NA	NA	NA	NA	NA
1810	54.3	NA	NA	NA	NA	NA	NA	NA	NA
1820	55.2	NA	NA	NA	NA	NA	NA	NA	NA
1830	51.4	NA	NA	NA	NA	NA	NA	NA	NA
1840	51.8	NA	NA	NA	NA	NA	NA	NA	NA
1850	43.3	NA	NA	NA	NA	NA	NA	NA	NA
1860	44.3	NA	NA	NA	NA	NA	NA	NA	NA
1870	38.3	NA	NA	NA	NA	NA	NA	NA	NA
1880	39.8	NA	NA	NA	NA	NA	NA	NA	NA
1890	31.5	NA	NA	NA	NA	NA	NA	NA	NA
1900	32.3	17.2	47.3	48.7	33.5	46.6	32.5	NA	NA
1910	30.1	14.7	50.0	52.0	37.5	48.6	33.8	NA	NA
1920	27.7	13.0	54.1	55.6	45.2	54.4	45.5	12.0	1.6
1930	21.3	11.3	59.7	63.5	49.2	59.7	47.3	9.2	1.6
1940	19.4	10.8	62.9	66.6	54.9	62.1	51.5	12.1	2.0
1950	24.1	9.6	68.2	72.2	62.9	66.5	59.1	11.1	2.6
1960	23.7	9.5	69.7	74.1	66.3	67.4	61.1	8.5	2.2
1970	18.4	9.5	70.8	75.6	69.4	68.0	61.3	10.6	3.5
1980	15.9	8.8	73.7	78.1	73.6	70.7	65.3	10.6	5.2
1990	16.6	8.6	75.4	79.4	75.2	72.7	67.0	9.8	4.7
1998	14.4	8.5	76.5[†]	73.9[†]	76.1[°]	74.3[†]	68.9[°]	8.9[†]	4.3

Note: Data per one thousand for Birth, Death, Marriage, and Divorce Rates.

NA = Not available. *Data for 1800, 1810, 1830, 1850, 1870, and 1890 for whites only. [†]Data for 1997. [°]Data for 1996.

Immigrants to the United States

Immigration Totals by Decade			
Years	Number	Years	Number
1820–1830	151,824	1911–1920	5,735,811
1831–1840	599,125	1921–1930	4,107,209
1841–1850	1,713,251	1931–1940	528,431
1851–1860	2,598,214	1941–1950	1,035,039
1861–1870	2,314,824	1951–1960	2,515,479
1871–1880	2,812,191	1961–1970	3,321,677
1881–1890	5,246,613	1971–1980	4,493,314
1891–1900	3,687,546	1981–1990	7,338,062
1901–1910	8,795,386	1991–1997	6,944,591
		Total	63,938,605

Major Sources of Immigrants by Country or Region (in thousands)

Period	Asia[a]	Germany	Mexico	Italy	Great Britain (UK)[b]	Ireland	Canada	Austria and Hungary	Soviet Union (Russia)	Caribbean	Central America and South America	Norway and Sweden
1820–1830	—	8	5	—	27	54	2	—	—	4	—	—
1831–1840	—	152	7	2	76	207	14	—	—	12	—	1
1841–1850	—	435	3	2	267	781	42	—	—	14	4	14
1851–1860	42	952	3	9	424	914	59	—	—	11	2	21
1861–1870	65	787	2	12	607	436	154	8	3	9	1	109
1871–1880	124	718	5	56	548	437	384	73	39	14	1	211
1881–1890	70	1,453	2[c]	307	807	655	393	354	213	29	3	568
1891–1900	75	505	1[c]	652	272	388	3	593	505	33	2	321
1901–1910	324	341	50	2,046	526	339	179	2,145	1,597	108	25	440
1911–1920	247	144	219	1,110	341	146	742	896	921	123	59	161
1921–1930	112	412	459	455	340	211	925	64	62	75	58	166
1931–1940	17	114	22	68	32	11	109	11	1	16	14	9
1941–1950	37	227	61	58	139	20	172	28	—	50	43	21
1951–1960	153	478	300	185	203	48	378	104	—	123	136	45
1961–1970	428	191	454	214	214	33	413	26	2	470	359	33
1971–1980	1,588	74	640	129	137	11	170	16	39	741	430	10
1981–1990	2,738	92	2,336	67	160	32	157	25	58	872	930	15
1991–1997	2,134	66	1,801	56	118	54	143	20	357	750	786	13
Total	8,153	7,149	5,689	5,429	5,238	4,779	4,439	4,363	3,801	3,453	2,856	2,159

Notes: Numbers for periods are rounded. Dash indicates less than 1,000. [a]Includes Middle East. [b]Since 1925, includes England, Scotland, Wales, and Northern Ireland data. [c]No data available for 1886–1894.

The American Worker

Year	Total Number of Workers	Males as Percent of Total Workers	Females as Percent of Total Workers	Married Women as Percent of Female Workers	Female Workers as Percent of Female Population	Percent of Labor Force Unemployed	Percent of Workers in Labor Unions
1870	12,506,000	85	15	NA	NA	NA	NA
1880	17,392,000	85	15	NA	NA	NA	NA
1890	23,318,000	83	17	14	19	4 (1894 = 18)	NA
1900	29,073,000	82	18	15	21	5	3
1910	38,167,000	79	21	25	25	6	6
1920	41,614,000	79	21	23	24	5 (1921 = 12)	12
1930	48,830,000	78	22	29	25	9 (1933 = 25)	11.6
1940	53,011,000	76	24	36	27	15 (1944 = 1)	26.9
1950	62,208,000	72	28	52	31	5.3	31.5
1960	69,628,000	67	33	55	38	5.5	31.4
1970	82,771,000	62	38	59	43	4.9	27.3
1980	106,940,000	58	42	55	52	7.1	21.9
1990	125,840,000	55	45	54	58	5.6	16.1
2000	140,900,000	54*	46	53	60	4.0	13.9

NA = Not available.   *Data for 1999

The American Economy

Year	Gross National Product (GNP) and Gross Domestic Product (GDP)[a] (in $ billions)	Steel Production (in tons)	Corn Production (millions of bushels)	Automobiles Registered	New Housing Starts	Foreign Trade (in $ millions)	
						Exports	Imports
1790	NA	NA	NA	NA	NA	20	23
1800	NA	NA	NA	NA	NA	71	91
1810	NA	NA	NA	NA	NA	67	85
1820	NA	NA	NA	NA	NA	70	74
1830	NA	NA	NA	NA	NA	74	71
1840	NA	NA	NA	NA	NA	132	107
1850	NA	NA	592[d]	NA	NA	152	178
1860	NA	13,000	839[e]	NA	NA	400	362
1870	7.4[b]	77,000	1,125	NA	NA	451	462
1880	11.2[c]	1,397,000	1,707	NA	NA	853	761
1890	13.1	4,779,000	1,650	NA	328,000	910	823
1900	18.7	11,227,000	2,662	8,000	189,000	1,499	930
1910	35.3	28,330,000	2,853	458,300	387,000 (1918 = 118,000)	1,919	1,646
1920	91.5	46,183,000	3,071	8,131,500	247,000 (1925 = 937,000)	8,664	5,784
1930	90.7	44,591,000	2,080	23,034,700	330,000 (1933 = 93,000)	4,013	3,500
1940	100.0	66,983,000	2,457	27,465,800	603,000 (1944 = 142,000)	4,030	7,433
1950	286.5	96,836,000	3,075	40,339,000	1,952,000	9,997	8,954
1960	506.5	99,282,000	4,314	61,682,300	1,365,000	19,659	15,093
1970	1,016.0	131,514,000	4,200	89,279,800	1,434,000	42,681	40,356
1980	2,819.5	111,835,000	6,600	121,601,000	1,292,000	220,626	244,871
1990	5,764.9	98,906,000	7,933	143,550,000	1,193,000	394,030	485,453
1998	8,511.0	107,600,000	9,761	129,749,000[f]	1,617,000	682,100	911,900

[a]In December 1991 the Bureau of Economic Analysis of the U.S. government began featuring Gross Domestic Product rather than Gross National Product as the primary measure of U.S. production.

[b]Figure is average for 1869–1878.

[c]Figure is average for 1879–1888.

[d]Figure for 1849.

[e]Figure for 1859.

[f]Figure for 1997.

NA = Not available.

Federal Budget Outlays and Debt

Year	Defense[a]	Veterans Benefits[a]	Income Security[a]	Social Security[a]	Health and Medicare[a]	Education[a,d]	Net Interest Payments[a]	Federal Debt (dollars)
1790	14.9	4.1[b]	NA	NA	NA	NA	55.0	75,463,000[c]
1800	55.7	.6	NA	NA	NA	NA	31.3	82,976,000
1810	48.4 (1814: 79.7)	1.0	NA	NA	NA	NA	34.9	53,173,000
1820	38.4	17.6	NA	NA	NA	NA	28.1	91,016,000
1830	52.9	9.0	NA	NA	NA	NA	12.6	48,565,000
1840	54.3 (1847: 80.7)	10.7	NA	NA	NA	NA	.7	3,573,000
1850	43.8	4.7	NA	NA	NA	NA	1.0	63,453,000
1860	44.2 (1865: 88.9)	1.7	NA	NA	NA	NA	5.0	64,844,000
1870	25.7	9.2	NA	NA	NA	NA	41.7	2,436,453,000
1880	19.3	21.2	NA	NA	NA	NA	35.8	2,090,909,000
1890	20.9 (1899: 48.6)	33.6	NA	NA	NA	NA	11.4	1,222,397,000
1900	36.6	27.0	NA	NA	NA	NA	7.7	1,263,417,000
1910	45.1 (1919: 59.5)	23.2	NA	NA	NA	NA	3.1	1,146,940,000
1920	37.1	3.4	NA	NA	NA	NA	16.0	24,299,321,000
1930	25.3	6.6	NA	NA	NA	NA	19.9	16,185,310,000
1940	17.5 (1945: 89.4)	6.0	16.0	.3	.5	20.8	9.4	42,967,531,000
1950	32.2	20.3	9.6	1.8	.6	.6	11.3	256,853,000,000
1960	52.2	5.9	8.0	12.6	.9	1.0	7.5	290,525,000,000
1970	41.8	4.4	8.0	15.5	6.2	4.4	7.3	308,921,000,000
1980	22.7	3.6	14.6	20.1	9.4	5.4	8.9	909,050,000,000
1990	23.9	2.3	11.7	19.8	12.4	3.1	14.7	3,266,073,000,000
1998	16.2	2.5	14.1	22.9	19.6	3.3	14.7	5,555,565,000,000

[a]Figures represent percentage of total federal spending for each category. Not included are transportation, commerce, housing, and various other categories.

[b]1789–1791 figure.

[c]1791 figure.

[d]Includes training, employment, and social services.

NA = Not available.

The Fifty States, District of Columbia, and Puerto Rico

State	Date of Admission (with Rank)	Capital City	Population (1998) (with Rank)	Racial/Ethnic Distribution (1998)	Per Capita Personal Income (1998) (with Rank)	Total Area in Square Miles (with Rank)
Alabama (AL)	Dec. 14, 1819 (22)	Montgomery	4,352,000 (23)	White: 3,141,000; Black: 1,132,000; Hispanic: 36,000; Asian: 28,000; Native American: 15,000	$21,442 (40)	52,423 (30)
Alaska (AK)	Jan. 3, 1959 (49)	Juneau	614,000 (48)	White: 444,000; Black: 24,000; Hispanic: 19,000; Asian: 28,000; Native American: 100,000	$25,675 (20)	656,424 (1)
Arizona (AZ)	Feb. 14, 1912 (48)	Phoenix	4,669,000 (21)	White: 3,182,000; Black: 169,000; Hispanic: 963,000; Asian: 98,000; Native American: 256,000	$23,060 (35)	114,006 (6)
Arkansas (AR)	June 15, 1836 (25)	Little Rock	2,538,000 (33)	White: 2,055,000; Black: 408,000; Hispanic: 44,000; Asian: 19,000; Native American: 14,000	$20,346 (46)	53,182 (29)
California (CA)	Sept. 9, 1850 (31)	Sacramento	32,667,000 (1)	White: 16,511,000; Black: 2,456,000; Hispanic: 9,454,000; Asian: 3,938,000; Native American: 309,000	$27,503 (1)	163,707 (3)
Colorado (CO)	Aug. 1, 1876 (38)	Denver	3,971,000 (24)	White: 3,125,000; Black: 172,000; Hispanic: 541,000; Asian: 96,000; Native American: 37,000	$28,657 (18)	104,100 (8)
Connecticut (CT)	Jan. 9, 1788 (5)	Hartford	3,274,000 (29)	White: 3,125,000; Black: 172,000; Hispanic: 238,000; Asian: 96,000; Native American: 37,000	$37,598 (1)	5,544 (48)
Delaware (DE)	Dec. 7, 1787 (1)	Dover	744,000 (45)	White: 560,000; Black: 144,000; Hispanic: 22,000; Asian: 15,000; Native American: 2,000	$29,814 (6)	2,489 (49)
District of Columbia (DC)	U.S. Capital, Dec. 1, 1800	Washington (coextensive with DC)	523,000 (not ranked)	White: 149,000; Black: 326,000; Hispanic: 30,000; Asian: 16,000; Native American: 2,000	$33,433 (not ranked)	68 (not ranked)
Florida (FL)	Mar. 3, 1845 (27)	Tallahassee	14,916,000 (4)	White: 10,239,000; Black: 2,268,000; Hispanic: 2,080,000; Asian: 271,000; Native American: 58,000	$25,852 (19)	65,756 (22)
Georgia (GA)	Jan. 2, 1788 (4)	Atlanta	7,642,000 (10)	White: 5,100,000; Black: 2,181,000; Hispanic: 193,000; Asian: 149,000; Native American: 18,000	$25,020 (23)	59,441 (24)
Hawai'i (HI)	Aug. 21, 1959 (50)	Honolulu	1,193,000 (40)	White: 344,000; Black: 35,000; Hispanic: 51,000; Asian: 757,000; Native American: 7,000	$26,137 (17)	10,932 (43)
Idaho (ID)	July 3, 1890 (43)	Boise	1,229,000 (41)	White: 1,109,000; Black: 7,000; Hispanic: 82,000; Asian: 14,000; Native American: 17,000	$21,081 (43)	83,574 (14)
Illinois (IL)	Dec. 3, 1818 (21)	Springfield	12,045,000 (5)	White: 8,630,000; Black: 1,840,000; Hispanic: 1,145,000; Asian: 403,000; Native American: 27,000	$28,873 (8)	57,918 (25)
Indiana (IN)	Dec. 11, 1816 (19)	Indianapolis	5,899,000 (14)	White: 5,206,000; Black: 491,000; Hispanic: 132,000; Asian: 56,000; Native American: 15,000	$24,219 (29)	36,420 (38)

The Fifty States, District of Columbia, and Puerto Rico (continued)

State	Date of Admission (with Rank)	Capital City	Population (1998) (with Rank)	Racial/Ethnic Distribution (1998)	Per Capita Personal Income (1998) (with Rank)	Total Area in Square Miles (with Rank)
Iowa (IA)	Dec. 28, 1846 (29)	Des Moines	2,862,000 (30)	White: 2,709,000; Black: 57,000; Hispanic: 52,000; Asian: 36,000; Native American: 8,000	$23,925 (32)	56,276 (26)
Kansas (KS)	Jan. 29, 1861 (34)	Topeka	2,629,000 (32)	White: 2,278,000; Black: 155,000; Hispanic: 137,000; Asian: 46,000; Native American: 23,000	$24,981 (24)	82,282 (15)
Kentucky (KY)	June 1, 1792 (15)	Frankfort	3,936,000 (25)	White: 3,591,000; Black: 285,000; Hispanic: 28,000; Asian: 27,000; Native American: 6,000	$21,506 (39)	40,411 (37)
Louisiana (LA)	Apr. 30, 1812 (18)	Baton Rouge	4,369,000 (22)	White: 2,787,000; Black: 1,407,000; Hispanic: 100,000; Asian: 55,000; Native American: 19,000	$21,346 (41)	51,843 (31)
Maine (ME)	Mar. 15, 1820 (23)	Augusta	1,244,000 (39)	White: 1,215,000; Black: 6,000; Hispanic: 8,000; Asian: 9,000; Native American: 6,000	$22,952 (36)	35,387 (39)
Maryland (MD)	Apr. 28, 1788 (7)	Annapolis	5,135,000 (19)	White: 3,329,000; Black: 1,428,000; Hispanic: 158,000; Asian: 204,000; Native American: 16,000	$29,943 (5)	12,407 (42)
Massachusetts (MA)	Feb. 6, 1788 (6)	Boston	6,147,000 (13)	White: 5,217,000; Black: 395,000; Hispanic: 298,000; Asian: 223,000; Native American: 15,000	$32,797 (3)	10,555 (44)
Michigan (MI)	Jan. 26, 1837 (26)	Lansing	9,817,000 (8)	White: 7,961,000; Black: 1,405,000; Hispanic: 234,000; Asian: 158,000; Native American: 60,000	$25,857 (18)	96,705 (11)
Minnesota (MN)	May 11, 1858 (32)	Saint Paul	4,725,000 (20)	White: 4,328,000; Black: 141,000; Hispanic: 76,000; Asian: 124,000; Native American: 58,000	$27,510 (11)	86,943 (12)
Mississippi (MS)	Dec. 10, 1817 (20)	Jackson	2,752,000 (31)	White: 1,701,000; Black: 1,003,000; Hispanic: 18,000; Asian: 19,000; Native American: 10,000	$18,958 (50)	48,434 (32)
Missouri (MO)	Aug. 10, 1821 (24)	Jefferson City	5,439,000 (16)	White: 4,668,000; Black: 613,000; Hispanic: 77,000; Asian: 60,000; Native American: 21,000	$24,427 (28)	69,709 (21)
Montana (MT)	Nov. 8, 1889 (41)	Helena	880,000 (44)	White: 803,000; Black: 3,000; Hispanic: 13,000; Asian: 5,000; Native American: 56,000	$20,172 (47)	147,046 (4)
Nebraska (NE)	Mar. 1, 1867 (37)	Lincoln	1,663,000 (38)	White: 1,493,000; Black: 67,000; Hispanic: 66,000; Asian: 22,000; Native American: 15,000	$24,754 (27)	77,358 (16)
Nevada (NV)	Oct. 3, 1864 (36)	Carson City	1,747,000 (36)	White: 1,248,000; Black: 133,000; Hispanic: 253,000; Asian: 81,000; Native American: 31,000	$27,200 (14)	110,567 (7)
New Hampshire (NH)	June 21, 1788 (9)	Concord	1,185,000 (42)	White: 1,109,000; Black: 9,000; Hispanic: 16,000; Asian: 14,000; Native American: 2,000	$29,022 (7)	9,351 (46)
New Jersey (NJ)	Dec. 18, 1787 (3)	Trenton	8,115,000 (9)	White: 5,586,000; Black: 1,188,000; Hispanic: 866,000; Asian: 453,000; Native American: 22,000	$33,937 (2)	8,722 (47)
New Mexico (NM)	Jan. 6, 1912 (47)	Santa Fe	1,737,000 (37)	White: 834,000; Black: 45,000; Hispanic: 669,000; Asian: 26,000; Native American: 163,000	$19,936 (48)	121,598 (5)

The Fifty States, District of Columbia,
and Puerto Rico (continued)

State	Date of Admission (with Rank)	Capital City	Population (1998) (with Rank)	Racial/Ethnic Distribution (1998)	Per Capita Personal Income (1998) (with Rank)	Total Area in Square Miles (with Rank)
New York (NY)	July 26, 1788 (11)	Albany	18,175,000 (3)	White: 11,895,000; Black: 3,220,000; Hispanic: 1,990,000; Asian: 995,000; Native American: 76,000	$31,734 (4)	54,471 (27)
North Carolina (NC)	Nov. 21, 1789 (12)	Raleigh	7,546,000 (11)	White: 5,545,000; Black: 1,665,000 Hispanic: 139,000; Asian: 100,000; Native American: 98,000	$24,036 (31)	53,821 (28)
North Dakota (ND)	Nov. 2, 1889 (39)	Bismarck	638,000 (47)	White: 593,000; Black: 4,000; Hispanic: 6,000; Asian: 5,000; Native American: 30,000	$21,675 (38)	70,704 (19)
Ohio (OH)	Mar. 1, 1803 (17)	Columbus	11,209,000 (7)	White: 9,610,000; Black: 1,290,000; Hispanic: 158,000; Asian: 129,000; Native American: 23,000	$25,134 (21)	44,828 (34)
Oklahoma (OK)	Nov. 16, 1907 (46)	Oklahoma City	3,347,000 (27)	White: 2,668,000; Black: 262,000; Hispanic: 109,000; Asian: 45,000; Native American: 263,000	$21,072 (44)	69,903 (20)
Oregon (OR)	Feb. 14, 1859 (33)	Salem	3,282,000 (28)	White: 2,888,000; Black: 61,000; Hispanic: 182,000; Asian: 106,000; Native American: 45,000	$24,766 (26)	98,386 (9)
Pennsylvania (PA)	Dec. 12, 1787 (2)	Harrisburg	12,001,000 (6)	White: 10,354,000; Black: 1,166,000; Hispanic: 265,000; Asian: 198,000; Native American: 18,000	$26,792 (16)	46,058 (33)
Puerto Rico (PR)	Ascession 1898; Common-wealth Status 1952	San Juan	3,860,000 (not ranked)	White: <1,000; Black: <1,000; Hispanic: 3,856,000; Asian: <1,000	$7,882* (not ranked)	3,427*
Rhode Island (RI)	May 29, 1790 (13)	Providence	988,000 (43)	White: 859,000; Black: 49,000; Hispanic: 52,000; Asian: 23,000; Native American: 5,000	$26,797 (15)	1,545 (50)
South Carolina (SC)	May 23, 1788 (8)	Columbia	3,836,000 (26)	White: 2,603,000; Black: 1,147,000; Hispanic: 42,000; Asian: 34,000; Native American: 9,000	$21,309 (42)	32,008 (40)
South Dakota (SD)	Nov. 2, 1889 (40)	Pierre	738,000 (46)	White: 662,000; Black: 5,000; Hispanic: 7,000; Asian: 5,000; Native American: 59,000	$22,114 (37)	77,121 (17)
Tennessee (TN)	June 1, 1796 (16)	Nashville	5,431,000 (17)	White: 4,413,000; Black: 900,000; Hispanic: 54,000; Asian: 53,000; Native American: 12,000	$23,559 (33)	42,149 (36)
Texas (TX)	Dec. 29, 1845 (28)	Austin	18,760,000 (2)	White: 11,038,000; Black: 2,430,000; Hispanic: 5,640,000; Asian: 556,000; Native American: 96,000	$24,957 (25)	268,601 (2)
Utah (UT)	Jan. 4, 1896 (45)	Salt Lake City	2,100,000 (32)	White: 1,866,000; Black: 19,000; Hispanic: 132,000; Asian: 53,000; Native American: 30,000	$21,019 (45)	84,904 (13)
Vermont (VT)	Mar. 4, 1791 (14)	Montpelier	591,000 (49)	White: 577,000; Black: 3,000; Hispanic: 5,000; Asian: 5,000; Native American: 2,000	$24,175 (30)	9,615 (45)
Virginia (VA)	June 25, 1788 (10)	Richmond	6,791,000 (12)	White: 4,943,000; Black: 1,363,000 Hispanic: 220,000; Asian: 247,000; Native American: 19,000	$27,385 (13)	42,777 (35)

The Fifty States, District of Columbia, and Puerto Rico (continued)

State	Date of Admission (with Rank)	Capital City	Population (1998) (with Rank)	Racial/Ethnic Distribution (1998)	Per Capita Personal Income (1998) (with Rank)	Total Area in Square Miles (with Rank)
Washington (WA)	Nov. 11, 1889 (42)	Olympia	5,689,000 (15)	White: 4,743,000; Black: 198,000; Hispanic: 315,000; Asian: 330,000; Native American: 103,000	$27,961 (11)	71,302 (18)
West Virginia (WV)	June 20, 1863 (35)	Charleston	1,811,000 (35)	White: 1,732,000; Black: 58,000; Hispanic: 9,000; Asian: 9,000; Native American: 3,000	$19,362 (49)	24,231 (41)
Wisconsin (WI)	May 29, 1848 (30)	Madison	5,224,000 (18)	White: 4,687,000; Black: 291,000; Hispanic: 120,000; Asian: 80,000; Native American: 56,000	$25,079 (22)	65,499 (23)
Wyoming (WY)	July 10, 1890 (44)	Cheyenne	481,000 (50)	White: 435,000; Black: 4,000; Hispanic: 27,000; Asian: 4,000; Native American: 11,000	$23,167 (34)	97,818 (10)

*1996 figure.

Presidential Elections

Year	Number of States	Candidates	Parties	Popular Vote	% of Popular Vote	Electoral Vote	% Voter Participation[a]
1789	10	**George Washington**	No party			69	
		John Adams	designations			34	
		Other candidates				35	
1792	15	**George Washington**	No party			132	
		John Adams	designations			77	
		George Clinton				50	
		Other candidates				5	
1796	16	**John Adams**	Federalist			71	
		Thomas Jefferson	Democratic-Republican			68	
		Thomas Pinckney	Federalist			59	
		Aaron Burr	Democratic-Republican			30	
		Other candidates				48	
1800	16	**Thomas Jefferson**	Democratic-Republican			73	
		Aaron Burr	Democratic-Republican			73	
		John Adams	Federalist			65	
		Charles C. Pinckney	Federalist			64	
		John Jay	Federalist			1	
1804	17	**Thomas Jefferson**	Democratic-Republican			162	
		Charles C. Pinckney	Federalist			14	
1808	17	**James Madison**	Democratic-Republican			122	
		Charles C. Pinckney	Federalist			47	
		George Clinton	Democratic-Republican			6	
1812	18	**James Madison**	Democratic-Republican			128	
		DeWitt Clinton	Federalist			89	
1816	19	**James Monroe**	Democratic-Republican			183	
		Rufus King	Federalist			34	
1820	24	**James Monroe**	Democratic-Republican			231	
		John Quincy Adams	Independent Republican			1	

Presidential Elections (continued)

Year	Number of States	Candidates	Parties	Popular Vote	% of Popular Vote	Electoral Vote	% Voter Partici- pation[a]
1824	24	**John Quincy Adams**	Democratic-Republican	108,740	30.5	84	26.9
		Andrew Jackson	Democratic-Republican	153,544	43.1	99	
		Henry Clay	Democratic-Republican	47,136	13.2	37	
		William H. Crawford	Democratic-Republican	46,618	13.1	41	
1828	24	**Andrew Jackson**	Democratic	647,286	56.0	178	57.6
		John Quincy Adams	National Republican	508,064	44.0	83	
1832	24	**Andrew Jackson**	Democratic	701,780	54.2	219	55.4
		Henry Clay	National Republican	484,205	37.4	49	
		Other candidates		107,988	8.0	18	
1836	26	**Martin Van Buren**	Democratic	764,176	50.8	170	57.8
		William H. Harrison	Whig	550,816	36.6	73	
		Hugh L. White	Whig	146,107	9.7	26	
1840	26	**William H. Harrison**	Whig	1,274,624	53.1	234	80.2
		Martin Van Buren	Democratic	1,127,781	46.9	60	
1844	26	**James K. Polk**	Democratic	1,338,464	49.6	170	78.9
		Henry Clay	Whig	1,300,097	48.1	105	
		James G. Birney	Liberty	62,300	2.3		
1848	30	**Zachary Taylor**	Whig	1,360,967	47.4	163	72.7
		Lewis Cass	Democratic	1,222,342	42.5	127	
		Martin Van Buren	Free Soil	291,263	10.1		
1852	31	**Franklin Pierce**	Democratic	1,601,117	50.9	254	69.6
		Winfield Scott	Whig	1,385,453	44.1	42	
		John P. Hale	Free Soil	155,825	5.0		
1856	31	**James Buchanan**	Democratic	1,832,955	45.3	174	78.9
		John C. Frémont	Republican	1,339,932	33.1	114	
		Millard Fillmore	American	871,731	21.6	8	
1860	33	**Abraham Lincoln**	Republican	1,865,593	39.8	180	81.2
		Stephen A. Douglas	Democratic	1,382,713	29.5	12	
		John C. Breckinridge	Democratic	848,356	18.1	72	
		John Bell	Constitutional Union	592,906	12.6	39	
1864	36	**Abraham Lincoln**	Republican	2,206,938	55.0	212	73.8
		George B. McClellan	Democratic	1,803,787	45.0	21	
1868	37	**Ulysses S. Grant**	Republican	3,013,421	52.7	214	78.1
		Horatio Seymour	Democratic	2,706,829	47.3	80	

Presidential Elections (continued)

Year	Number of States	Candidates	Parties	Popular Vote	% of Popular Vote	Electoral Vote	% Voter Participation[a]
1872	37	**Ulysses S. Grant**	Republican	3,596,745	55.6	286	71.3
		Horace Greeley	Democratic	2,843,446	43.9	[b]	
1876	38	**Rutherford B. Hayes**	Republican	4,036,572	48.0	185	81.8
		Samuel J. Tilden	Democratic	4,284,020	51.0	184	
1880	38	**James A. Garfield**	Republican	4,453,295	48.5	214	79.4
		Winfield S. Hancock	Democratic	4,414,082	48.1	155	
		James B. Weaver	Greenback-Labor	308,578	3.4		
1884	38	**Grover Cleveland**	Democratic	4,879,507	48.5	219	77.5
		James G. Blaine	Republican	4,850,293	48.2	182	
		Benjamin F. Butler	Greenback-Labor	175,370	1.8		
		John P. St. John	Prohibition	150,369	1.5		
1888	38	**Benjamin Harrison**	Republican	5,447,129	47.9	233	79.3
		Grover Cleveland	Democratic	5,537,857	48.6	168	
		Clinton B. Fisk	Prohibition	249,506	2.2		
		Anson J. Streeter	Union Labor	146,935	1.3		
1892	44	**Grover Cleveland**	Democratic	5,555,426	46.1	277	74.7
		Benjamin Harrison	Republican	5,182,690	43.0	145	
		James B. Weaver	People's	1,029,846	8.5	22	
		John Bidwell	Prohibition	264,133	2.2		
1896	45	**William McKinley**	Republican	7,102,246	51.1	271	79.3
		William J. Bryan	Democratic	6,492,559	47.7	176	
1900	45	**William McKinley**	Republican	7,218,491	51.7	292	73.2
		William J. Bryan	Democratic; Populist	6,356,734	45.5	155	
		John C. Wooley	Prohibition	208,914	1.5		
1904	45	**Theodore Roosevelt**	Republican	7,628,461	57.4	336	65.2
		Alton B. Parker	Democratic	5,084,223	37.6	140	
		Eugene V. Debs	Socialist	402,283	3.0		
		Silas C. Swallow	Prohibition	258,536	1.9		
1908	46	**William H. Taft**	Republican	7,675,320	51.6	321	65.4
		William J. Bryan	Democratic	6,412,294	43.1	162	
		Eugene V. Debs	Socialist	420,793	2.8		
		Eugene W. Chafin	Prohibition	253,840	1.7		
1912	48	**Woodrow Wilson**	Democratic	6,296,547	41.9	435	58.8
		Theodore Roosevelt	Progressive	4,118,571	27.4	88	
		William H. Taft	Republican	3,486,720	23.2	8	
		Eugene V. Debs	Socialist	900,672	6.0		
		Eugene W. Chafin	Prohibition	206,275	1.4		
1916	48	**Woodrow Wilson**	Democratic	9,127,695	49.4	277	61.6
		Charles E. Hughes	Republican	8,533,507	46.2	254	

Presidential Elections (continued)

Year	Number of States	Candidates	Parties	Popular Vote	% of Popular Vote	Electoral Vote	% Voter Participation[a]
		A. L. Benson	Socialist	585,113	3.2		
		J. Frank Hanly	Prohibition	220,506	1.2		
1920	48	**Warren G. Harding**	Republican	16,143,407	60.4	404	49.2
		James M. Cox	Democratic	9,130,328	34.2	127	
		Eugene V. Debs	Socialist	919,799	3.4		
		P. P. Christensen	Farmer-Labor	265,411	1.0		
1924	48	**Calvin Coolidge**	Republican	15,718,211	54.0	382	48.9
		John W. Davis	Democratic	8,385,283	28.8	136	
		Robert M. La Follette	Progressive	4,831,289	16.6	13	
1928	48	**Herbert C. Hoover**	Republican	21,391,993	58.2	444	56.9
		Alfred E. Smith	Democratic	15,016,169	40.9	87	
1932	48	**Franklin D. Roosevelt**	Democratic	22,809,638	57.4	472	56.9
		Herbert C. Hoover	Republican	15,758,901	39.7	59	
		Norman Thomas	Socialist	881,951	2.2		
1936	48	**Franklin D. Roosevelt**	Democratic	27,752,869	60.8	523	61.0
		Alfred M. Landon	Republican	16,674,665	36.5	8	
		William Lemke	Union	882,479	1.9		
1940	48	**Franklin D. Roosevelt**	Democratic	27,307,819	54.8	449	62.5
		Wendell L. Wilkie	Republican	22,321,018	44.8	82	
1944	48	**Franklin D. Roosevelt**	Democratic	25,606,585	53.5	432	55.9
		Thomas E. Dewey	Republican	22,014,745	46.0	99	
1948	48	**Harry S Truman**	Democratic	24,179,345	49.6	303	53.0
		Thomas E. Dewey	Republican	21,991,291	45.1	189	
		J. Strom Thurmond	States' Rights	1,176,125	2.4	39	
		Henry A. Wallace	Progressive	1,157,326	2.4		
1952	48	**Dwight D. Eisenhower**	Republican	33,936,234	55.1	442	63.3
		Adlai E. Stevenson	Democratic	27,314,992	44.4	89	
1956	48	**Dwight D. Eisenhower**	Republican	35,590,472	57.6	457	60.6
		Adlai E. Stevenson	Democratic	26,022,752	42.1	73	
1960	50	**John F. Kennedy**	Democratic	34,226,731	49.7	303	62.8
		Richard M. Nixon	Republican	34,108,157	49.5	219	
1964	50	**Lyndon B. Johnson**	Democratic	43,129,566	61.1	486	61.7
		Barry M. Goldwater	Republican	27,178,188	38.5	52	
1968	50	**Richard M. Nixon**	Republican	31,785,480	43.4	301	60.6
		Hubert H. Humphrey	Democratic	31,275,166	42.7	191	
		George C. Wallace	American Independent	9,906,473	13.5	46	
1972	50	**Richard M. Nixon**	Republican	47,169,911	60.7	520	55.2

Presidential Elections (continued)

Year	Number of States	Candidates	Parties	Popular Vote	% of Popular Vote	Electoral Vote	% Voter Participation[a]
		George S. McGovern	Democratic	29,170,383	37.5	17	
		John G. Schmitz	American	1,099,482	1.4		
1976	50	**James E. Carter**	Democratic	40,830,763	50.1	297	53.5
		Gerald R. Ford	Republican	39,147,793	48.0	240	
1980	50	**Ronald W. Reagan**	Republican	43,904,153	50.7	489	52.6
		James E. Carter	Democratic	35,483,883	41.0	49	
		John B. Anderson	Independent	5,720,060	6.6	0	
		Ed Clark	Libertarian	921,299	1.1	0	
1984	50	**Ronald W. Reagan**	Republican	54,455,075	58.8	525	53.3
		Walter F. Mondale	Democratic	37,577,185	40.6	13	
1988	50	**George H. W. Bush**	Republican	48,886,097	53.4	426	50.1
		Michael S. Dukakis	Democratic	41,809,074	45.6	111[c]	
1992	50	**William J. Clinton**	Democratic	44,909,326	43.0	370	55.2
		George H. W. Bush	Republican	39,103,882	37.4	168	
		H. Ross Perot	Independent	19,741,048	18.9	0	
1996	50	**William J. Clinton**	Democratic	47,402,357	49.2	379	49.1
		Robert J. Dole	Republican	39,196,755	40.7	159	
		H. Ross Perot	Reform	8,085,402	8.4	0	
		Ralph Nader	Green	684,902	0.7	0	

Candidates receiving less than 1 percent of the popular vote have been omitted. Thus the percentage of popular vote given for any election year may not total 100 percent.

Before the passage of the Twelfth Amendment in 1804, the Electoral College voted for two presidential candidates; the runner-up became vice president.

Before 1824, most presidential electors were chosen by state legislatures, not by popular vote.

[a]Percent of voting-age population casting ballots.

[b]Greeley died shortly after the election; the electors supporting him then divided their votes among minor candidates.

[c]One elector from West Virginia cast her Electoral College presidential ballot for Lloyd Bentsen, the Democratic Party's vice-presidential candidate.

Presidents and Vice Presidents

1. President	**George Washington**	1789–1797	
Vice President	John Adams	1789–1797	
2. President	**John Adams**	1797–1801	
Vice President	Thomas Jefferson	1797–1801	
3. President	**Thomas Jefferson**	1801–1809	
Vice President	Aaron Burr	1801–1805	
Vice President	George Clinton	1805–1809	
4. President	**James Madison**	1809–1817	
Vice President	George Clinton	1809–1813	
Vice President	Elbridge Gerry	1813–1817	
5. President	**James Monroe**	1817–1825	
Vice President	Daniel Tompkins	1817–1825	
6. President	**John Quincy Adams**	1825–1829	
Vice President	John C. Calhoun	1825–1829	
7. President	**Andrew Jackson**	1829–1837	
Vice President	John C. Calhoun	1829–1833	
Vice President	Martin Van Buren	1833–1837	
8. President	**Martin Van Buren**	1837–1841	
Vice President	Richard M. Johnson	1837–1841	
9. President	**William H. Harrison**	1841	
Vice President	John Tyler	1841	
10. President	**John Tyler**	1841–1845	
Vice President	None		
11. President	**James K. Polk**	1845–1849	
Vice President	George M. Dallas	1845–1849	
12. President	**Zachary Taylor**	1849–1850	
Vice President	Millard Fillmore	1849–1850	
13. President	**Millard Fillmore**	1850–1853	
Vice President	None		
14. President	**Franklin Pierce**	1853–1857	
Vice President	William R. King	1853–1857	
15. President	**James Buchanan**	1857–1861	
Vice President	John C. Breckinridge	1857–1861	
16. President	**Abraham Lincoln**	1861–1865	
Vice President	Hannibal Hamlin	1861–1865	
Vice President	Andrew Johnson	1865	
17. President	**Andrew Johnson**	1865–1869	
Vice President	None		
18. President	**Ulysses S. Grant**	1869–1877	
Vice President	Schuyler Colfax	1869–1873	
Vice President	Henry Wilson	1873–1877	
19. President	**Rutherford B. Hayes**	1877–1881	
Vice President	William A. Wheeler	1877–1881	
20. President	**James A. Garfield**	1881	
Vice President	Chester A. Arthur	1881	
21. President	**Chester A. Arthur**	1881–1885	
Vice President	None		
22. President	**Grover Cleveland**	1885–1889	
Vice President	Thomas A. Hendricks	1885–1889	
23. President	**Benjamin Harrison**	1889–1893	
Vice President	Levi P. Morton	1889–1893	
24. President	**Grover Cleveland**	1893–1897	
Vice President	Adlai E. Stevenson	1893–1897	
25. President	**William McKinley**	1897–1901	
Vice President	Garret A. Hobart	1897–1901	
Vice President	Theodore Roosevelt	1901	
26. President	**Theodore Roosevelt**	1901–1909	
Vice President	Charles Fairbanks	1905–1909	
27. President	**William H. Taft**	1909–1913	
Vice President	James S. Sherman	1909–1913	
28. President	**Woodrow Wilson**	1913–1921	
Vice President	Thomas R. Marshall	1913–1921	
29. President	**Warren G. Harding**	1921–1923	
Vice President	Calvin Coolidge	1921–1923	
30. President	**Calvin Coolidge**	1923–1929	
Vice President	Charles G. Dawes	1925–1929	
31. President	**Herbert C. Hoover**	1929–1933	
Vice President	Charles Curtis	1929–1933	
32. President	**Franklin D. Roosevelt**	1933–1945	
Vice President	John N. Garner	1933–1941	
Vice President	Henry A. Wallace	1941–1945	
Vice President	Harry S Truman	1945	
33. President	**Harry S Truman**	1945–1953	
Vice President	Alben W. Barkley	1949–1953	
34. President	**Dwight D. Eisenhower**	1953–1961	
Vice President	Richard M. Nixon	1953–1961	
35. President	**John F. Kennedy**	1961–1963	
Vice President	Lyndon B. Johnson	1961–1963	

Presidents and Vice Presidents (continued)

36. President	**Lyndon B. Johnson**	1963–1969		Vice President	Walter F. Mondale	1977–1981
	Vice President	Hubert H. Humphrey	1965–1969	40. President	**Ronald W. Reagan**	1981–1989
37. President	**Richard M. Nixon**	1969–1974		Vice President	George H. W. Bush	1981–1989
	Vice President	Spiro T. Agnew	1969–1973	41. President	**George H. W. Bush**	1989–1993
	Vice President	Gerald R. Ford	1973–1974		Vice President	J. Danforth Quayle	1989–1993
38. President	**Gerald R. Ford**	1974–1977	42. President	**William J. Clinton**	1993–2001
	Vice President	Nelson A. Rockefeller	1974–1977		Vice President	Albert Gore	1993–2001
39. President	**James E. Carter**	1977–1981				

For a complete list of Presidents, Vice Presidents, and Cabinet Members, go to http://college.hmco.com.

Party Strength in Congress

Period	Congress	House			Senate			Party of President	
		Majority Party	Minority Party	Others	Majority Party	Minority Party	Others		
1789–91	1st	Ad 38	Op 26		Ad 17	Op 9		F	Washington
1791–93	2nd	F 37	DR 33		F 16	DR 13		F	Washington
1793–95	3rd	DR 57	F 48		F 17	DR 13		F	Washington
1795–97	4th	F 54	DR 52		F 19	DR 13		F	Washington
1797–99	5th	F 58	DR 48		F 20	DR 12		F	J. Adams
1799–1801	6th	F 64	DR 42		F 19	DR 13		F	J. Adams
1801–03	7th	DR 69	F 36		DR 18	F 13		DR	Jefferson
1803–05	8th	DR 102	F 39		DR 25	F 9		DR	Jefferson
1805–07	9th	DR 116	F 25		DR 27	F 7		DR	Jefferson
1807–09	10th	DR 118	F 24		DR 28	F 6		DR	Jefferson
1809–11	11th	DR 94	F 48		DR 28	F 6		DR	Madison
1811–13	12th	DR 108	F 36		DR 30	F 6		DR	Madison
1813–15	13th	DR 112	F 68		DR 27	F 9		DR	Madison
1815–17	14th	DR 117	F 65		DR 25	F 11		DR	Madison
1817–19	15th	DR 141	F 42		DR 34	F 10		DR	Monroe
1819–21	16th	DR 156	F 27		DR 35	F 7		DR	Monroe
1821–23	17th	DR 158	F 25		DR 44	F 4		DR	Monroe
1823–25	18th	DR 187	F 26		DR 44	F 4		DR	Monroe
1825–27	19th	Ad 105	J 97		Ad 26	J 20		C	J. Q. Adams
1827–29	20th	J 119	Ad 94		J 28	Ad 20		C	J. Q. Adams
1829–31	21st	D 139	NR 74		D 26	NR 22		D	Jackson
1831–33	22nd	D 141	NR 58	14	D 25	NR 21	2	D	Jackson
1833–35	23rd	D 147	AM 53	60	D 20	NR 20	8	D	Jackson
1835–37	24th	D 145	W 98		D 27	W 25		D	Jackson
1837–39	25th	D 108	W 107	24	D 30	W 18	4	D	Van Buren
1839–41	26th	D 124	W 118		D 28	W 22		D	Van Buren
1841–43	27th	W 133	D 102	6	W 28	D 22	2	W	W. Harrison
								W	Tyler
1843–45	28th	D 142	W 79	1	W 28	D 25	1	W	Tyler
1845–47	29th	D 143	W 77	6	D 31	W 25		D	Polk
1847–49	30th	W 115	D 108	4	D 36	W 21	1	D	Polk
1849–51	31st	D 112	W 109	9	D 35	W 25	2	W	Taylor
								W	Fillmore
1851–53	32nd	D 140	W 88	5	D 35	W 24	3	W	Fillmore
1853–55	33rd	D 159	W 71	4	D 38	W 22	2	D	Pierce
1855–57	34th	R 108	D 83	43	D 40	R 15	5	D	Pierce
1857–59	35th	D 118	R 92	26	D 36	R 20	8	D	Buchanan
1859–61	36th	R 114	D 92	31	D 36	R 26	4	D	Buchanan
1861–63	37th	R 105	D 43	30	R 31	D 10	8	R	Lincoln
1863–65	38th	R 102	D 75	9	R 36	D 9	5	R	Lincoln

Party Strength in Congress (continued)

Period	Congress	House Majority Party		House Minority Party		Others	Senate Majority Party		Senate Minority Party		Others	Party of President	
1865–67	39th	U	149	D	42		U	42	D	10		R	Lincoln
												R	A. Johnson
1867–69	40th	R	143	D	49		R	42	D	11		R	A. Johnson
1869–71	41st	R	149	D	63		R	56	D	11		R	Grant
1871–73	42nd	R	134	D	104	5	R	52	D	17	5	R	Grant
1873–75	43rd	R	194	D	92	14	R	49	D	19	5	R	Grant
1875–77	44th	D	169	R	109	14	R	45	D	29	2	R	Grant
1877–79	45th	D	153	R	140		R	39	D	36	1	R	Hayes
1879–81	46th	D	149	R	130	14	D	42	R	33	1	R	Hayes
1881–83	47th	D	147	R	135	11	R	37	D	37	1	R	Garfield
												R	Arthur
1883–85	48th	D	197	R	118	10	R	38	D	36	2	R	Arthur
1885–87	49th	D	183	R	140	2	R	43	D	34		D	Cleveland
1887–89	50th	D	169	R	152	4	R	39	D	37		D	Cleveland
1889–91	51st	R	166	D	159		R	39	D	37		R	B. Harrison
1891–93	52nd	D	235	R	88	9	R	47	D	39	2	R	B. Harrison
1893–95	53rd	D	218	R	127	11	D	44	R	38	3	D	Cleveland
1895–97	54th	R	244	D	105	7	R	43	D	39	6	D	Cleveland
1897–99	55th	R	204	D	113	40	R	47	D	34	7	R	McKinley
1899–1901	56th	R	185	D	163	9	R	53	D	26	8	R	McKinley
1901–03	57th	R	197	D	151	9	R	55	D	31	4	R	McKinley
												R	T. Roosevelt
1903–05	58th	R	208	D	178		R	57	D	33		R	T. Roosevelt
1905–07	59th	R	250	D	136		R	57	D	33		R	T. Roosevelt
1907–09	60th	R	222	D	164		R	61	D	31		R	T. Roosevelt
1909–11	61st	R	219	D	172		R	61	D	32		R	Taft
1911–13	62nd	D	228	R	161	1	R	51	D	41		R	Taft
1913–15	63rd	D	291	R	127	17	D	51	R	44	1	D	Wilson
1915–17	64th	D	230	R	196	9	D	56	R	40		D	Wilson
1917–19	65th	D	216	R	210	6	D	53	R	42		D	Wilson
1919–21	66th	R	240	D	190	3	R	49	D	47		D	Wilson
1921–23	67th	R	301	D	131	1	R	59	D	37		R	Harding
1923–25	68th	R	225	D	205	5	R	51	D	43	2	R	Coolidge
1925–27	69th	R	247	D	183	4	R	56	D	39	1	R	Coolidge
1927–29	70th	R	237	D	195	3	R	49	D	46	1	R	Coolidge
1929–31	71st	R	267	D	167	1	R	56	D	39	1	R	Hoover
1931–33	72nd	D	220	R	214	1	R	48	D	47	1	R	Hoover
1933–35	73rd	D	310	R	117	5	D	60	R	35	1	D	F. Roosevelt
1935–37	74th	D	319	R	103	10	D	69	R	25	2	D	F. Roosevelt
1937–39	75th	D	331	R	89	13	D	76	R	16	4	D	F. Roosevelt
1939–41	76th	D	261	R	164	4	D	69	R	23	4	D	F. Roosevelt
1941–43	77th	D	268	R	162	5	D	66	R	28	2	D	F. Roosevelt

Party Strength in Congress (continued)

Period	Congress	House Majority Party		House Minority Party		Others	Senate Majority Party		Senate Minority Party		Others	Party of President	
1943–45	78th	D	218	R	208	4	D	58	R	37	1	D	F. Roosevelt
1945–47	79th	D	242	R	190	2	D	56	R	38	1	D	Truman
1947–49	80th	R	245	D	188	1	R	51	D	45		D	Truman
1949–51	81st	D	263	R	171	1	D	54	R	42		D	Truman
1951–53	82nd	D	234	R	199	1	D	49	R	47		D	Truman
1953–55	83rd	R	221	D	211	1	R	48	D	47	1	R	Eisenhower
1955–57	84th	D	232	R	203		D	48	R	47	1	R	Eisenhower
1957–59	85th	D	233	R	200		D	49	R	47		R	Eisenhower
1959–61	86th	D	284	R	153		D	65	R	35		R	Eisenhower
1961–63	87th	D	263	R	174		D	65	R	35		D	Kennedy
1963–65	88th	D	258	R	117		D	67	R	33		D	Kennedy
												D	L. Johnson
1965–67	89th	D	295	R	140		D	68	R	32		D	L. Johnson
1967–69	90th	D	246	R	187		D	64	R	36		D	L. Johnson
1969–71	91st	D	245	R	189		D	57	R	43		R	Nixon
1971–73	92nd	D	254	R	180		D	54	R	44	2	R	Nixon
1973–75	93rd	D	239	R	192	1	D	56	R	42	2	R	Nixon
1975–77	94th	D	291	R	144		D	60	R	37	3	R	Ford
1977–79	95th	D	292	R	143		D	61	R	38	1	D	Carter
1979–81	96th	D	276	R	157		D	58	R	41	1	D	Carter
1981–83	97th	D	243	R	192		R	53	D	46	1	R	Reagan
1983–85	98th	D	269	R	166		R	54	D	46		R	Reagan
1985–87	99th	D	253	R	182		R	53	D	47		R	Reagan
1987–89	100th	D	258	R	177		D	55	R	45		R	Reagan
1989–91	101st	D	259	R	174		D	55	R	45		R	Bush
1991–93	102nd	D	267	R	167	1	D	56	R	44		R	Bush
1993–95	103rd	D	258	R	176	1	D	57	R	43		D	Clinton
1995–97	104th	R	230	D	204	1	R	52	D	48		D	Clinton
1997–99	105th	R	227	D	207	1	R	55	D	45		D	Clinton
1999–2001	106th	R	223	D	211	1	R	55	D	45		D	Clinton

AD = Administration; AM = Anti-Masonic; C = Coalition; D = Democratic; DR = Democratic-Republican; F = Federalist; J = Jacksonian; NR = National Republican; Op = Opposition; R = Republican; U = Unionist; W = Whig. Figures are for the beginning of the first session of each Congress, except the 93rd, which are for the beginning of the second session.

Justices of the
Supreme Court

	Term of Service	Years of Service	Life Span		Term of Service	Years of Service	Life Span
John Jay	1789–1795	5	1745–1829	Ward Hunt	1873–1882	9	1810–1886
John Rutledge	1789–1791	1	1739–1800	*Morrison R. Waite*	1874–1888	14	1816–1888
William Cushing	1789–1810	20	1732–1810	John M. Harlan	1877–1911	34	1833–1911
James Wilson	1789–1798	8	1742–1798	William B. Woods	1880–1887	7	1824–1887
John Blair	1789–1796	6	1732–1800	Stanley Mathews	1881–1889	7	1824–1889
Robert H. Harrison	1789–1790	—	1745–1790	Horace Gray	1882–1902	20	1828–1902
James Iredell	1790–1799	9	1951–1799	Samuel Blatchford	1882–1893	11	1820–1893
Thomas Johnson	1791–1793	1	1732–1819	Lucius Q. C. Lamar	1888–1893	5	1825–1893
William Paterson	1793–1806	13	1745–1806	*Melville W. Fuller*	1888–1910	21	1833–1910
*John Rutledge**	1795	—	1739–1800	David J. Brewer	1890–1910	20	1837–1910
Samuel Chase	1796–1811	15	1741–1811	Henry B. Brown	1890–1906	16	1836–1913
Oliver Ellsworth	1796–1800	4	1745–1807	George Shiras, Jr.	1892–1903	10	1832–1924
Bushrod Washington	1798–1829	31	1762–1829	Howell E. Jackson	1893–1895	2	1832–1895
Alfred Moore	1799–1804	4	1755–1810	Edward D. White	1894–1910	16	1845–1921
John Marshall	1801–1835	34	1755–1835	Rufus W. Peckham	1895–1909	14	1838–1909
William Johnson	1804–1834	30	1771–1834	Joseph McKenna	1898–1925	26	1843–1926
H. Brockholst Livingston	1806–1823	16	1757–1823	Oliver W. Holmes	1902–1932	30	1841–1935
Thomas Todd	1807–1826	18	1765–1826	William D. Day	1903–1922	19	1849–1923
Joseph Story	1811–1845	33	1779–1845	William H. Moody	1906–1910	3	1853–1917
Gabriel Duval	1811–1835	24	1752–1844	Horace H. Lurton	1910–1914	4	1844–1914
Smith Thompson	1823–1843	20	1768–1843	Charles E. Hughes	1910–1916	5	1862–1948
Robert Trimble	1826–1828	2	1777–1828	Willis Van Devanter	1911–1937	26	1859–1941
John McLean	1829–1861	32	1785–1861	Joseph R. Lamar	1911–1916	5	1857–1916
Henry Baldwin	1830–1844	14	1780–1844	*Edward D. White*	1910–1921	11	1845–1921
James M. Wayne	1835–1867	32	1790–1867	Mahlon Pitney	1912–1922	10	1858–1924
Roger B. Taney	1836–1864	28	1777–1864	James C. McReynolds	1914–1941	26	1862–1946
Philip P. Barbour	1836–1841	4	1783–1841	Louis D. Brandeis	1916–1939	22	1856–1941
John Catron	1837–1865	28	1786–1865	John H. Clarke	1916–1922	6	1857–1945
John McKinley	1837–1852	15	1780–1852	*William H. Taft*	1921–1930	8	1857–1930
Peter V. Daniel	1841–1860	19	1784–1860	George Sutherland	1922–1938	15	1862–1942
Samuel Nelson	1845–1872	27	1792–1873	Pierce Butler	1922–1939	16	1866–1939
Levi Woodbury	1845–1851	5	1789–1851	Edward T. Sanford	1923–1930	7	1865–1930
Robert C. Grier	1846–1870	23	1794–1870	Harlan F. Stone	1925–1941	16	1872–1946
Benjamin R. Curtis	1851–1857	6	1809–1874	*Charles E. Hughes*	1930–1941	11	1862–1948
John A. Campbell	1853–1861	8	1811–1889	Owen J. Roberts	1930–1945	15	1875–1955
Nathan Clifford	1858–1881	23	1803–1881	Benjamin N. Cardozo	1932–1938	6	1870–1938
Noah H. Swayne	1862–1881	18	1804–1884	Hugo L. Black	1937–1971	34	1886–1971
Samuel F. Miller	1862–1890	28	1816–1890	Stanley F. Reed	1938–1957	19	1884–1980
David Davis	1862–1877	14	1815–1886	Felix Frankfurter	1939–1962	23	1882–1965
Stephen J. Field	1863–1897	34	1816–1899	William O. Douglas	1939–1975	36	1898–1980
Salmon P. Chase	1864–1873	8	1808–1873	Frank Murphy	1940–1949	9	1890–1949
William Strong	1870–1880	10	1808–1895	*Harlan F. Stone*	1941–1946	5	1872–1946
Joseph P. Bradley	1870–1892	22	1813–1892	James F. Byrnes	1941–1942	1	1879–1972

Justices of the Supreme Court (continued)

	Term of Service	Years of Service	Life Span		Term of Service	Years of Service	Life Span
Robert H. Jackson	1941–1954	13	1892–1954	Thurgood Marshall	1967–1991	24	1908–1993
Wiley B. Rutledge	1943–1949	6	1894–1949	*Warren C. Burger*	1969–1986	17	1907–1995
Harold H. Burton	1945–1958	13	1888–1964	Harry A. Blackmun	1970–1994	24	1908–1998
Fred M. Vinson	1946–1953	7	1890–1953	Lewis F. Powell, Jr.	1972–1987	15	1907–1998
Tom C. Clark	1949–1967	18	1899–1977	*William H. Rehnquist*	1972–	—	1924–
Sherman Minton	1949–1956	7	1890–1965	John P. Stevens III	1975–	—	1920–
Earl Warren	1953–1969	16	1891–1974	Sandra Day O'Connor	1981–	—	1930–
John Marshall Harlan	1955–1971	16	1899–1971	Antonin Scalia	1986–	—	1936–
William J. Brennan, Jr.	1956–1990	34	1906–1977	Anthony M. Kennedy	1988–	—	1936–
Charles E. Whittaker	1957–1962	5	1901–1973	David H. Souter	1990–	—	1939–
Potter Stewart	1958–1981	23	1915–1985	Clarence Thomas	1991–	—	1948–
Byron R. White	1962–1993	31	1917–	Ruth Bader Ginsburg	1993–	—	1933–
Arthur J. Goldberg	1962–1965	3	1908–1990	Stephen Breyer	1994–	—	1938–
Abe Fortas	1965–1969	4	1910–1982				

Note: Chief justices are in italics.

*Appointed and served one term, but not confirmed by the Senate.

INDEX